Magill's
Cinema
Annual
2010

Magill's
Cinema
Annual
2010

29th Edition
A Survey of the films of 2009

Brian Tallerico, Editor

**With an Introduction by
Barry Keith Grant**

A VideoHound® Reference

GALE
CENGAGE Learning™

Detroit • New York • San Francisco • New Haven, Conn • Waterville, Maine • London

Magill's Cinema Annual 2010

Brian Tallerico, Editor

Project Editor: Michael J. Tyrkus

Editorial: Stephen Bridenstine, Margaret Mazurkiewicz, Jeff Muhr, Katherine H. Nemeh, Mary Ruby

Editorial Support Services: Wayne Fong

Composition and Electronic Prepress: Gary Leach, Evi Seoud

Manufacturing: Rita Wimberley

For product information and technology assistance, contact us at **Gale Customer Support, 1-800-877-4253.**
For permission to use material from this text or product, submit all requests online at **www.cengage.com/permissions.**
Further permissions questions can be emailed to **permissionrequest@cengage.com**

While every effort has been made to ensure the reliability of the information presented in this publication, Gale, a part of Cengage Learning, does not guarantee the accuracy of the data contained herein. Gale accepts no payment for listing; and inclusion in the publication of any organization, agency, institution, publication, service, or individual does not imply endorsement of the editors or publisher. Errors brought to the attention of the publisher and verified to the satisfaction of the publisher will be corrected in future editions.

EDITORIAL DATA PRIVACY POLICY: Does this product contain information about you as an individual? If so, for more information about our editorial data privacy policies, please see our Privacy Statement at www.gale.cengage.com.

Gale, Cengage Learning
27500 Drake Rd.
Farmington Hills, MI, 48331-3535

ISBN-13: 978-1-4144-4140-5
ISBN-10: 1-4144-4140-1

ISSN: 0739-2141

Printed in the United States of America
1 2 3 4 5 6 7 14 13 12 11 10 9

Contents

Preface

Magill's Cinema Annual 2010 continues the fine film reference tradition that defines the VideoHound® series of entertainment industry products published by Gale. The twenty-ninth annual volume in a series that developed from the twenty-one-volume core set, *Magill's Survey of Cinema,* the *Annual* was formerly published by Salem Press. Gale's fifteenth volume, as with the previous Salem volumes, contains essay-reviews of significant domestic and foreign films released in the United States during the preceding year.

The *Magill's* editorial staff at Gale, comprising the VideoHound® team and a host of *Magill's* contributors, continues to provide the enhancements that were added to the *Annual* when Gale acquired the line. These features include:

- More essay-length reviews of significant films released during the year
- Obituaries and book review sections
- Trivia and "un facts" about the reviewed movies, their stars, the crew, and production
- Quotes and dialogue "soundbites" from reviewed movies, or from stars and crew about the film
- More complete awards and nominations listings, including the American Academy Awards®, the Golden Globes, and others (see the User's Guide for more information on awards coverage)
- Box office grosses, including year-end and other significant totals
- Publicity taglines featured in film reviews and advertisements

In addition to these elements, *Magill's Cinema Annual 2010* still features:

- An obituaries section profiling major contributors to the film industry who died in 2009
- An annotated list of selected film books published in 2009
- Nine indexes: Director, Screenwriter, Cinematographer, Editor, Art Director, Music Director, Performer, Subject, and Title (now cumulative)

COMPILATION METHODS

The *Magill's* editorial staff reviews a variety of entertainment industry publications, including trade magazines and newspapers, as well as online sources, on a daily and

weekly basis to select significant films for review in *Magill's Cinema Annual*. *Magill's* staff and other contributing reviewers, including film scholars and university faculty, write the reviews included in the *Annual*.

MAGILL'S CINEMA ANNUAL: A VIDEOHOUND® REFERENCE

The *Magill's Survey of Cinema* series, now supplemented by the *Annual*, is the recipient of the Reference Book of the Year Award in Fine Arts by the American Library Association. Gale, an award-winning publisher of reference products, is proud to offer *Magill's Cinema Annual* as part of its popular VideoHound® product line, which includes *VideoHound®'s Golden Movie Retriever* and *The Video Source Book*. Other Gale film-related products include the four-volume *International Dictionary of Films and Filmmakers, Women Filmmakers & Their Films,* the *Contemporary Theatre, Film, and Television* series, and the four-volume *Schirmer Encyclopedia of Film*. Also, be sure to visit Video-Hound on the web at *www.MovieRetriever.com*.

ACKNOWLEDGMENTS

The editor would like to extend his gratitude to all of the talented contributors to *Magill's Cinema Annual* for their continuously impressive skill, expertise, and professionalism. This year's edition is honored to include a Guest Introduction by Barry Keith Grant, along with contributions from members of the Board of Directors of the Chicago Film Critics Association including President Dann Gire, Vice President Erik Childress, and Peter Sobcyzsnki. The staff at Gale Cengage—Mike Tyrkus, Jim Craddock, and Tom Burns—deserve thanks for their continued efforts on behalf of the book and the editor must finally note that he would accomplish nothing if not for the support of his loving wife Lauren and beautiful son Lucas.

We at *Magill's* look forward to another exciting year in film and preparing the next edition of *Magill's Cinema Annual*. As always, we invite your comments, questions, and suggestions. Please direct them to:

Editor

Magill's Cinema Annual

Gale, Cengage Learning

27500 Drake Road

Farmington Hills, MI 48331-3535

Phone: (248) 699-4253

Toll-Free: (800) 347-GALE (4253)

Fax: (248) 699-8865

The Year in Film: An Introduction

Without question, the dominant film event of 2009 was the mid-December release of James Cameron's long-awaited *Avatar* in digital 3-D. Budgeted at upwards of $250 million, it was the most expensive film ever produced and a gamble for 20th Century Fox. But even before year's end *Avatar* was in the black by $100 million, making it the second top-grossing film of 2009, not far behind Paramount's mind-numbing *Transformers: Revenge of the Fallen*. Early in 2010, *Avatar* would quickly become the top-grossing film in history, surpassing Cameron's own *Titanic* twelve years earlier, on its way to garnering nine Academy Award® nominations including Best Picture (which it lost to Kathryn Bigelow's Iraq War drama *The Hurt Locker*). The industry buzz was that *Avatar* would change the nature of cinema as we know it, like *The Jazz Singer* did in 1927. While this prediction remains to be seen, most of the year's other 3-D releases, including *My Bloody Valentine 3-D, The Final Destination, Jonas Brothers: The 3-D Concert Experience,* and *G-Force,* Disney's first venture into a mix of live action and animation, hardly held such promise.

Significantly, of the year's ten most successful films only two, Warner Bros.' raunchy comedy *The Hangover* and the inspirational drama *The Blind Side* with Sandra Bullock, did not make significant use of digital animation. Buena Vista's *Up* (also in 3-D) ranked fourth overall at the box-office, with Paramount's *Monsters vs. Aliens* and 20th Century Fox's *Ice Age: Dawn of the Dinosaurs* earning ninth and tenth spots, respectively. Although animated films still account for a relatively small number of the industry's total output, Hollywood released a noteworthy sixteen digitally animated and five stop-motion animated features in 2009, among them Robert Zemeckis' *A Christmas Carol, Astro Boy, Coraline,* and *Cloudy with a Chance of Meatballs.* While these films were aimed at the family market, Tim Burton's *9,* Wes Anderson's *Fantastic Mr. Fox,* Spike Jonze's *Where the Wild Things Are,* Terry Gilliam's *The Imaginarium of Dr. Parnassus,* and Peter Jackson's adaptation of Alice Sebold's best-selling novel *The Lovely Bones* showed talented filmmakers with distinctive visions using animation to explore more serious purposes.

Yet another successful mostly-animated feature, *Alvin and the Chipmunks: The Squeakquel,* was only one of 2009's numerous remakes and sequels. As in recent years, remakes tended to be in the horror genre, and this time around viewers were subjected to new versions of *The Last House on the Left, The Stepfather,* and *Friday the 13th.* There were also the sequels *Halloween II, Underworld 3,* and *Saw VI,* the latter vying to rival the Michael Meyers franchise for durability. The crime thriller *The Taking of Pelham One*

Two Three was updated for the recession, which dominated the news media throughout the year, but the horror film *Drag Me to Hell* will stand as the year's most memorable cinematic response to the current economic crisis. Other sequels included the disappointing *Terminator: Salvation, Night at the Museum: Battle of the Smithsonian, Pink Panther 2, Angels & Demons, Crank: High Voltage,* and the aforementioned *Transformers: Revenge of the Fallen,* but not Werner Hezog's deceptively titled *Bad Lieutenant: Port of Call New Orleans,* which has no relationship to Abel Ferrera's legendary *Bad Lieutenant* (1992). Warners' *Harry Potter and the Half-Blood Prince* was the third top earner of the year, and Paramount's prequel *Star Trek* bridged the generation gap by attracting both the youth market and baby boomer Trekkies, making it the fourth.

Another big summer hit was another science fiction tale, *District 9,* an extrapolative parable about racism involving alien ghettos in Johannesburg, South Africa. Made on a relatively small budget of $30 million, but preceded by a strong advertising blitz, it offered thematic depth with its visceral action and earned more than its cost on opening weekend alone. One of four science fiction films in the top ten earners of the year, it marked the continuing domination of the fantastic mode in domestic production and even landed an Oscar® nomination for Best Picture. While movies such as *Push, X-Men Origins: Wolverine, Gamer,* and *Surrogates* were predicable combinations of sci-fi premise and action narrative, *Moon, Pandorum,* and *Watchmen* were more intelligent entries in the genre. But as we moved a year closer to 2012, our collective anxieties were exploited in the apocalyptic films *The Road* and *2012,* the latter featuring lengthy set pieces of humanity's destruction.

More intimate horror continued unabated in 2009 with, among others, *Jennifer's Body, The Orphan, Sorority Row, The Haunting in Connecticut,* and *Paranormal Activity,* which on a reported budget of a mere $15,000 earned more than $100 million at the box office, making it one of the most profitable movies ever made. *The Twilight Saga: New Moon* drew the tween audience of its predecessor, lifting it to become the year's fifth top grosser with over $280 million, while *Cirque du Freak: The Vampire's Assistant* exploited the same demographic to lesser effect. *Zombieland,* billed as Hollywood's answer to the British horror parody *Shaun of the Dead* (2004), suggests that the current horror cycle may be wearing thin, but the Danish *Antichrist,* Norwegian *Dead Snow,* South Korean *Thirst,* and the Swedish *Let the Right One In* showed international filmmakers pushing the genre in interesting new directions and finding limited but devoted cult audiences in North America.

Hollywood continued to present radically opposite views on the male hero in 2009. On the one hand, the year saw the release of more than twenty romantic comedies, including *He's Just Not That Into You, Humpday, I Love You, Beth Cooper, Ghosts of Girlfriends Past, The Invention of Lying, The Proposal,* and *All About Steve,* the latter two starring Sandra Bullock, most of which sought to present a softer image of masculinity. On the other hand, indomitable macho machinations are the driving force of such action films as *Ninja Assassin, G.I. Joe: The Rise of Cobra, Public Enemies, Ong Bak 2,* and the new *Sherlock Holmes,* pumped up by director Guy Ritchie. In *Taken,* Liam Neeson takes out every Arab immigrant in France while searching for his kidnapped daughter, and in *Law Abiding Citizen,* the stoic Gerard Butler walks tall, is mad as hell, and states that he's not going to take it any more as he threatens to get "biblical" on the system. This split in the representation of masculine identity was literalized in the new-age hippie warrior played by Jeff Bridges in the black comedy *The Men Who Stare at Goats,* while Kathryn Bigelow's *The Hurt Locker* explored the attraction of action's adrenalin rush.

Costume biopics experienced something of a resurgence with *Julie & Julia, Amelia, The Young Victoria, Coco Before Chanel,* and Jane Campion's *Bright Star* about the English poet John Keats and his relationship with the young Fanny Brawn. By contrast, the musical seemed particularly moribund this year with *Bandslam, Hannah Montana: The Movie,* the remake of *Fame,* and the Wayans' parody *Dance Flick.* The fact that *Michael*

Jackson's This Is It, initially released with a reserve ticket strategy, was about the making of a spectacle that never happened due to the death of its star earlier in the year, seemed somehow indicative of the genre's current lowly state. This lack of energy was evident in the enervated *Nine,* the Weinstein Company's big budget musical version of Fellini's *8½* featuring Daniel Day-Lewis, a great actor who, alas, can neither sing nor dance.

Amid the wash of Hollywood's high and low concept movies, Michael Moore's personal documentary *Capitalism: A Love Story,* also produced through the Weinstein Company, managed to find limited distribution in mainstream multiplexes across the nation. Opening strong, Moore's subversive film generated $14 million at the box office, showing that it is still not entirely impossible to get truly alternative messages into mainstream theaters.

Barry Keith Grant
St. Catharines, Ontario

Contributing Reviewers

Michael Betzold
Author, Publishing Professional

David L. Boxerbaum
Freelance Reviewer

Tom Burns
Publishing Professional

Dave Canfield
Professional Film Critic

Erik Childress
Professional Film Critic

Dann Gire
Professional Film Critic

Joanna MacKenzie
Freelance Reviewer

Matt Pais
Professional Film Critic

Matthew Priest
Freelance Reviewer

Brent Simon
Professional Film Critic

Peter Sobczynski
Professional Film Critic

Collin Souter
Professional Film Critic

Michael J. Tyrkus
Publishing Professional

Nathan Vercauteren
Freelance Reviewer

User's Guide

ALPHABETIZATION

Film titles and reviews are arranged on a word-by-word basis, including articles and prepositions. English leading articles (A, An, The) are ignored, as are foreign leading articles (El, Il, La, Las, Le, Les, Los). Other considerations:

- Acronyms appear alphabetically as if regular words.

- Common abbreviations in titles file as if they are spelled out, so *Mr. Death* will be found as if it was spelled *Mister Death*.

- Proper names in titles are alphabetized beginning with the individual's first name, for instance, *Gloria* will be found under "G."

- Titles with numbers, for instance, *200 Cigarettes,* are alphabetized as if the numbers were spelled out, in this case, "Two-Hundred." When numeric titles gather in close proximity to each other, the titles will be arranged in a low-to-high numeric sequence.

SPECIAL SECTIONS

The following sections that are designed to enhance the reader's examination of film are arranged alphabetically, they include:

- *List of Awards.* An annual list of awards bestowed upon the year's films by the following: Academy of Motion Picture Arts and Sciences, British Academy of Film and Television Arts Awards, Directors Guild of America Awards, Golden Globe Awards, Golden Raspberry Awards, Independent Spirit Awards, the Screen Actors Guild Awards, and the Writer's Guild Awards.

- *Obituaries.* Profiles major contributors to the film industry who died in 2009.

- *Selected Film Books of 2009.* An annotated list of selected film books published in 2009.

INDEXES

Film titles and artists are separated into nine indexes, allowing the reader to effectively approach a film from any one of several directions, including not only its credits but its subject matter.

- *Director, Screenwriter, Cinematographer, Editor, Art Director, Music Director,* and *Performer* indexes are arranged alphabetically according to artists appearing in this volume, followed by a list of the films on which they worked. In the *Performer* index, a (V) beside a movie title indicates voice-only work and an (N) beside a movie title indicates work as narrator.

- *Subject Index.* Films may be categorized under several of the subject terms arranged alphabetically in this section.

- *Title Index.* The title index is a cumulative alphabetical list of films covered in the twenty-eight volumes of the *Magill's Cinema Annual,* including the films covered in this volume. Films reviewed in past volumes are cited with the year in which the film appeared in the *Annual;* films reviewed in this volume are cited with the film title in boldface with a bolded Arabic numeral indicating the page number on which the review begins. Original and alternate titles are cross-referenced to the American release title in the Title Index. Titles of retrospective films are followed by the year, in brackets, of their original release.

SAMPLE REVIEW

Each *Magill's* review contains up to sixteen items of information. A fictionalized composite sample review containing all the elements of information that may be included in a full-length review follows the outline on the facing page. The circled number following each element in the sample review designates an item of information that is explained in the outline.

1. **Title:** Film title as it was released in the United States.

2. **Foreign or alternate title(s):** The film's original title or titles as released outside the United States, or alternate film title or titles. Foreign and alternate titles also appear in the Title Index to facilitate user access.

3. **Taglines:** Up to ten publicity taglines for the film from advertisements or reviews.

4. **Box office information:** Year-end or other box office domestic revenues for the film.

5. **Film review:** A signed review of the film, including an analytic overview of the film and its critical reception.

6. **Reviewer byline:** The name of the reviewer who wrote the full-length review. A complete list of this volume's contributors appears in the "Contributing Reviewers" section which follows the Introduction.

7. **Principal characters:** Listings of the film's principal characters and the names of the actors who play them in the film.

8. **Country of origin:** The film's country or countries of origin and the languages featured in the film.

9. **Release date:** The year of the film's first general release.

10. **Production information:** This section typically includes the name(s) of the film's producer(s), production company, and distributor; director(s); screenwriter(s); cinematographer(s); editor(s); art director(s); production designer(s); music composer(s); and other credits such as visual effects, sound, costume design, and song(s) and songwriter(s).

11. **MPAA rating:** The film's rating by the Motion Picture Association of America. If there is no rating given, the line will read, "Unrated."

12. **Running time:** The film's running time in minutes.

13. **Reviews:** A list of brief citations of major newspaper and journal reviews of the film, including author, publication title, and date of review.

14. **Film quotes:** Memorable dialogue directly from the film, attributed to the character who spoke it, or comment from cast or crew members or reviewers about the film.

15. **Film trivia:** Interesting tidbits about the film, its cast, or production crew.

16. **Awards information:** Awards won by the film, followed by category and name of winning cast or crew member. Listings of the film's nominations follow the wins on a separate line for each award. Awards are arranged alphabetically. Information is listed for films that won or were nominated for the following awards: American Academy Awards®, British Academy of Film and Television Arts Awards, Directors Guild of America Awards, Golden Globe Awards, Golden Raspberry Awards, Independent Spirit Awards, the Screen Actors Guild Awards, and the Writers Guild of America Awards.

THE GUMP DIARIES ①
(Los Diarios del Gump) ②

Love means never having to say you're stupid.
—Movie tagline ③

Box Office: $10 million ④

In writer/director Robert Zemeckis' *Back to the Future* trilogy (1985, 1989, 1990), Marty McFly (Michael J. Fox) and his scientist sidekick Doc Brown (Christopher Lloyd) journey backward and forward in time, attempting to smooth over some rough spots in their personal histories in order to remain true to their individual destinies. Throughout their time-travel adventures, Doc Brown insists that neither he nor Marty influence any major historical events, believing that to do so would result in catastrophic changes in humankind's ultimate destiny. By the end of the trilogy, however, Doc Brown has revised his thinking and tells Marty that, "Your future hasn't been written yet. No one's has. Your future is whatever you make it. So make it a good one."

In *Forrest Gump*, Zemeckis once again explores the theme of personal destiny and how an individual's life affects and is affected by his historical time period. This time, however, Zemeckis and screenwriter Eric Roth chronicle the life of a character who does nothing but meddle in the historical events of his time without even trying to do so. By the film's conclusion, however, it has become apparent that Zemeckis' main concern is something more than merely having fun with four decades of American history. In the process of re-creating significant moments in time, he has captured on celluloid something eternal and timeless—the soul of humanity personified by a nondescript simpleton from the deep South.

The film begins following the flight of a seemingly insignificant feather as it floats down from the sky and brushes against various objects and people before finally coming to rest at the feet of Forrest Gump (Tom Hanks). Forrest, who is sitting on a bus-stop bench, reaches down and picks up the feather, smooths it out, then opens his traveling case and carefully places the feather between the pages of his favorite book, *Curious George*.

In this simple but hauntingly beautiful opening scene, the filmmakers illustrate the film's principal concern: Is life a series of random events over which a person has no control, or is there an underlying order to things that leads to the fulfillment of an individual's destiny? The rest of the film is a humorous and moving

attempt to prove that, underlying the random, chaotic events that make up a person's life, there exists a benign and simple order.

Forrest sits on the bench throughout most of the film, talking about various events of his life to others who happen to sit down next to him. It does not take long, however, for the audience to realize that Forrest's seemingly random chatter to a parade of strangers has a perfect chronological order to it. He tells his first story after looking down at the feet of his first bench partner and observing, "Mama always said that you can tell a lot about a person by the shoes they wear." Then, in a voice-over narration, Forrest begins the story of his life, first by telling about the first pair of shoes he can remember wearing.

The action shifts to the mid-1950s with Forrest as a young boy (Michael Humphreys) being fitted with leg braces to correct a curvature in his spine. Despite this traumatic handicap, Forrest remains unaffected, thanks to his mother (Sally Field) who reminds him on more than one occasion that he is no different from anyone else. Although this and most of Mrs. Gump's other words of advice are in the form of hackneyed cliches, Forrest, whose intelligence quotient is below normal, sincerely believes every one of them, namely because he instinctively knows they are sincere expressions of his mother's love and fierce devotion. ⑤

John Byline ⑥

CREDITS ⑦
Forrest Gump: Tom Hanks
Forrest's Mother: Sally Field
Young Forrest: Michael Humphreys
Origin: United States ⑧
Language: English, Spanish
Released: 1994 ⑨
Production: Liz Heller, John Manulis; New Line Cinema; released by Island Pictures ⑩
Directed by: Robert Zemeckis
Written by: Eric Roth
Cinematography by: David Phillips
Music by: Graeme Revell
Editing: Dana Congdon
Production Design: Danny Nowak
Sound: David Sarnoff
Costumes: David Robinson
MPAA rating: R ⑪
Running time: 102 minutes ⑫

REVIEWS (13)

Doe, Jane. *Los Angeles Times*. July 6, 1994.

Doe, John. *Entertainment Weekly*. July 15, 1994.

Reviewer, Paul. *Hollywood Reporter*. June 29, 1994.

Writer, Zach. *New York Times Online*. July 15, 1994.

QUOTES (14)

Forrest Gump (Tom Hanks): "The state of existence may be likened unto a receptacle containing cocoa-based confections, in that one may never predict that which one may receive."

TRIVIA (15)

Hanks was the first actor since Spencer Tracy to win back-to-back Oscars® for Best Actor. Hanks received the award in 1993 for his performance in *Philadelphia*. Tracy won Oscars® in 1937 for *Captains Courageous* and in 1938 for *Boys Town*.

AWARDS (16)

Academy Awards 1994: Film, Actor (Hanks), Special Effects, Cinematography

Nomination:

Golden Globes 1994: Film, Actor (Hanks), Supporting Actress (Field), Music.

A

ADAM

A story about two strangers. One a little stranger than the other.
—Movie tagline

Box Office: $2.3 million

Tropic Thunder (2008) had a blunt if less-than-politically correct assessment of movies' common presentation of people with disabilities, citing that if an actor wants to win an award for playing someone with a cognitive or physical handicap, the actor needs to go "full retard."

Sadly this is, crass or not, a fair evaluation of Hollywood's tendency to escalate stories of people with disabilities into melodramatic Oscar® bait anchored by big stars—rather than small, tender dramas about everyday challenges. That makes it particularly commendable that *Adam*, a romantic drama about a young man with Asperger's syndrome, not only casts lesser-known actors but mostly refuses grand, phony gestures. Hugh Dancy stars as the titular character, an electronic engineer for toys whose developmental disability is on the autism spectrum, and Rose Byrne plays Beth, Adam's neighbor who begins a relationship with him. What results is a refreshingly sincere look at what it is like to live with a disability, and what it is like to want to help someone who does.

When Adam and Beth meet, she is attracted to his sweetness, his energy and his passion for knowledge—he's particularly excited about things space-related. But she also notices that Adam is somewhat socially awkward and easily flustered, with a tendency to ramble. When he eventually tells her that he has Asperger's (which he describes as "mind blindness"), this leads to a necessary scene of Beth discussing Adam's condition. She explains that it is on the autism spectrum and results in Adam having trouble reading social cues. This is not subtle, but it is an important means to ensure audience members understand Adam's condition. Fortunately, even in this clarification writer-director Max Mayer does not pity Adam and does not let Beth pity him either. Learning about Adam's disability shakes her up slightly, but it does not stop her from wanting to get to know him. Or prevent her from dating him.

It does, however, generate skepticism from Beth's wealthy parents Marty (Peter Gallagher) and Rebecca (Amy Irving), who are turned off by Adam's social awkwardness and tell their daughter that her boyfriend is not suitable marriage material. Certainly, protective parents want the best for their child, and may have questions or concerns when learning that their child is dating someone with a disability. However, these scenes feel canned, as Marty's disapproval comes off as a generic example made by the film, rather than an authentic, expressive hitch in a father-daughter relationship. This is compounded by the larger weight put on Marty's pending indictment for improperly assisting a business partner's daughter with a job. Rather than emphasizing these scenes, the film should have examined how people adjust their perceptions of people with developmental disabilities after learning more about them.

Also disconcerting is Mayer's choice to amplify an otherwise subdued film with imposing music, as bursts of strings nearly ruin scenes that would play better as quiet rumination. This simply speaks to inexperience on Mayer's part, and an unwillingness to resist certain easy shortcuts. Similarly, while it is effective to begin Adam's story with the death of his widower father to present a new challenge that rocks Adam's already fragile need for stability, scenes involving Adam and his only friend, a wise, friendly old African American stereotype named Harlan (Frankie Faison), ring hollow.

For the most part, *Adam* feels lived-in and honest, largely because Dancy and Byrne play off each other so well and push neither their new-relationship emotions nor their personal concerns—both worried that Adam cannot be the man Beth wants him to be—too far.

With the exception of the film's patronizing opening, in which Beth's voiceover suggests *Adam* will be the kind of movie that wants a big round of applause for its character with disabilities, it does not condescend. It simply depicts, calmly and warmly, the circumstances of Adam's life and how he deals with them. (For example, he prefers a meticulous routine involving eating the exact the same food every day: All Bran and Amy's macaroni and cheese.) At one point, when he feels pitied by Beth apologizing with chocolates, Adam remarks, "I'm not Forrest Gump." This is but one time when *Adam* gives Adam his own voice, and shows the importance of treating a person with disabilities as an equal, not as someone different or a lesser member of society.

The ending of *Adam* would be more progressive were it less ambiguous about the long-term relationship potential of Adam and Beth. But the actors make the characters real, in spite of Mayer's occasional difficulties with the material. (Adam applying for 87 jobs in one day after being fired, for example, is presented as quirky, rather than a demonstration of Adam's extreme fear and determination.) Above all, the film works as a story about the need to love someone for who they are, without wishing they become someone they are not.

Matt Pais

CREDITS

Adam Raki: Hugh Dancy
Beth Buchwald: Rose Byrne
Harlin: Frankie Faison
Rebecca Buchwald: Amy Irving
Marty Buchwald: Peter Gallagher
Mr. Klieber: Mark Linn-Baker
Origin: USA
Language: English
Released: 2009
Production: Leslie Urdang, Miranda de Pencier, Dean Vanech; Serenade Films, Deer Path Films, VOX3 Films, Olympus Pictures; released by Fox Searchlight

Directed by: Max Mayer
Written by: Max Mayer
Cinematography by: Seamus Tierney
Music by: Christopher Lennertz
Sound: Philip Rosati
Music Supervisor: Robin Urdang
Editing: Grant Myers
Art Direction: Natalie Tyler
Costumes: Alysia Raycraft
Production Design: Tamar Gadish
MPAA rating: PG-13
Running time: 97 minutes

REVIEWS

Catsoulis, Jeanette. *New York Times.* July 29, 2009.
Chang, Justin. *Variety.* January 22, 2009.
Ebert, Roger. *Chicago Sun-Times.* August 6, 2009.
Honeycutt, Kirk. *Hollywood Reporter.* July 27, 2009.
Rea, Steven. *Philadelphia Inquirer.* August 6, 2009.
Smith, Anna. *Empire Magazine.* August 7, 2009.
Sobczynski, Peter. *eFilmCritic.* August 7, 2009.
Tallerico, Brian. *MovieRetriever.com.* August 7, 2009.
Taylor, Ella. *Village Voice.* July 30, 2009.
Thomas, Kevin. *Los Angeles Times.* July 29, 2009.

QUOTES

Beth Buchwald: "My favorite children's book is about a little prince who came to earth."

ADORATION

During the Nineties, enigmatic Canadian writer-director Atom Egoyan emerged from art-house obscurity to become one of the world's most celebrated filmmakers on the strength of such formally intriguing and emotionally powerful works as *Exotica* (1994) and *The Sweet Hereafter* (1997). In recent years, however, that reputation has been threatened by a series of creative misfires such as the ambitious-but-flawed *Ararat* (2002) and the deeply embarrassing *Where the Truth Lies* (2005), the latter being one of the most dubious films made by an internationally renowned director in this past decade. The good news about his latest film, *Adoration*, is that right from the start, he seems to have shaken the torpor that has plagued his recent work and presents us with the most skillful and intriguing filmmaking that he has done in years. The bad news is that this newfound sense of creative urgency only lasts for maybe the first half-hour or so before the whole thing devolves into yet another turgid and overly oblique melodrama that eventually becomes more frustrating than fascinating.

The film tells the story of Simon (Devon Bostick), a teenager who, as part of a classroom assignment, informs his classmates that his father was a terrorist who tried to use his late mother (Rachel Blanchard) as part of a plot to blow up an airplane while she was pregnant with him. Although his classmates accept his story as the truth, it is revealed early on that the entire thing is a fiction that he created with the encouragement of one of his teachers (Arsinee Khanjian). However, his story begins to grow a life of its own as it makes the leap onto the internet and inspires impassioned debates from a wide variety of people until the truth finally comes out and sparks outrage. As the fallout from the controversy intensifies, the film gradually begins to reveal why Simon would come up with such a tale in the first place and why his teacher both encourages it and attempts to insinuate herself into the lives of himself and his uncle (Scott Speedman).

During the initial half-hour or so, the film is a fairly fascinating meditation on the notions of family, loss, the cultural fascination with victimization in the post-9/11 era and the ways in which technology can both expose and muddy certain truths in equal measure (a conceit that Egoyan has been toying with as far back as *Speaking Parts* [1989]) and at this point, it feels as if Egoyan is firing on all cylinders for the first time in ages. Unfortunately, it is at precisely this point that the film begins to completely fall apart in a mess of muddled storytelling and implausible character behavior that feels more like someone trying and failing to approximate Egoyan's elliptical narrative style than an example of the real thing. By the time all of the mysteries and enigmas surrounding the characters and their respective pasts have been revealed, it is impossible to care either on an intellectual or an emotional level and matters are not helped much by a couple of exceptionally ill-timed bad laughs that appear at the exact moment when we should be completely wrapped up in the story proper.

While the end result may not be as irredeemably awful as *Where the Truth Lies*, the fact that *Adoration* comes apart after such a promising opening almost makes it a bigger disappointment in the long run. To be fair, the film does have its share of virtues—the performances by Bostick, Khanjian, and Speedman are strong and thoughtful, the contributions from such longtime Egoyan collaborators as cinematographer Paul Sarossy and composer Mychael Danna are striking and it shows that Egoyan can still create stretches of compelling cinema when he sets his mind to it. More importantly, it could inspire any number of fascinating post-screening discussions amongst audience members inspired by its provocations. Too bad, then, that *Adoration* turns out to be one of those films that itself is not nearly as interesting as any of the conversations that it may inspire.

Peter Sobczynski

CREDITS

Sabine: Arsinee Khanjian
Tom: Scott Speedman
Rachel: Rachel Blanchard
Sami: Noam Jenkins
Morris: Kenneth Welsh
Origin: Canada, France
Language: English, French
Released: 2008
Production: Atom Egoyan, Simone Urdl, Jennifer Weiss; Serendipity Point Films, ARP Selection, Ego Film Arts; released by Sony Pictures Classics
Directed by: Atom Egoyan
Written by: Atom Egoyan
Cinematography by: Paul Sarossy
Music by: Mychael Danna
Sound: Bissa Scekic
Editing: Susan Shipton
Art Direction: Barry Isenor
Costumes: Debra Hanson
Production Design: Phillip Barker
MPAA rating: R
Running time: 101 minutes

REVIEWS

Chang, Justin. *Variety.* October 18, 2008.
Demara, Bruce. *Toronto Star.* May 8, 2009.
Ebert, Roger. *Chicago Sun-Times.* May 21, 2009.
Foundas, Scott. *Village Voice.* May 5, 2009.
Holden, Stephen. *New York Times.* May 8, 2009.
Lacey, Liam. *Globe and Mail.* October 18, 2008.
Sarris, Andrew. *New York Observer.* May 6, 2009.
Sharkey, Betsy. *Los Angeles Times.* May 8, 2009.
Voynar, Kim. *Cinematical.* October 18, 2008.
Tallerico, Brian. *MovieRetriever.com.* May 22, 2009.

QUOTES

Morris: "When someone carries that kind of anger around all of the time, they can seem stupid. That's the thing about anger, it sucks up a lot of intelligence."

ADVENTURELAND

It was the worst job they ever imagined...and the best time of their lives.
—Movie tagline

> *Nothing brings people together like a crappy summer job.*
> —Movie tagline

Box Office: $16 million

Director Greg Mottola made his mark in the profane *Superbad*, but as a writer-director he takes an entirely different approach in the semiautobiographical coming-of-age pic *Adventureland*. Set in suburban Pennsylvania in the summer of 1987, Mottola's film is drenched in nostalgia for what now passes for the innocence of the writer's youthful days. James Brennan (Jesse Eisenberg) is a college graduate who's still a virgin, but instead of being the cause for crude jokes, his late-blooming sex life is here treated with respect and tenderness. Instead of the fashionable buffoonery so common in more contemporary flicks like *Superbad*, Mottola here creates a group of believable, down-to-earth characters and plays them off against each other in a gentle, surprisingly sympathetic fashion. Their suffering, though often funny and sometimes pitiable, is not played for laughs. Their foibles are not exploited.

James thought he was destined for New York City and the Ivy League, but his father has taken a pay cut, and his parents fail to come through on their promises to help him pay for grad school. Stuck at home, he ends up with a summer job at a local amusement park named Adventureland, a cheap joint run by a couple of hapless entrepreneurs who seem stuck, along with their business, in another era. The faded facades of outdated rides and cheap carnie games, made even cheaper by the owners' penny pinching, only serve to heighten James's disenchantment with a local life he is trying to escape. Adventureland, to him, is just an extension of "Boredomland."

In this unexpected milieu James gets an equally unexpected lesson in life. He falls hard for an achingly attractive coworker named Em (Kristen Stewart), who is sweet and kind to him but not as innocent as she seems. Her parents are wealthier than James's, but her mother is dead and her father has married a hateful woman whom Em cannot stand to live with. Em is also caught up in an extramarital relationship with Adventureland's heartthrob and slightly-older icon of hipness, Mike (Ryan Reynolds), who brags about stars who are his musical buddies but turns out to be a cad. The plot takes its time meandering in character studies but eventually hews to a predictable course as James falls in love with Em but finally discovers her dirty secrets and turns bitter and disillusioned.

People of a certain age will enjoy *Adventureland* more than others, because it is steeped in the pop culture of its era, especially musically. Some critics have even argued that it is the *American Graffiti* of a different era.

Certainly, the songs, dress, and language are authentic and emblematic. But it seems that in retrospect Mottola has colored 1987 with an aura of innocence that is a little out of step with the times. The young people in this film seem awfully naïve, or at least clueless. In fact, the characters in *Adventureland* seem more like high school graduates than college graduates; they all seem younger in their behavior and interactions than they are supposed to be.

What makes the film work so well are the deft characterizations of the cast. Martin Starr plays a latter-day beatnik who smokes a pipe and loves philosophy, but is actually shy and kind. Margarita Levieva plays a Madonna-esque bad girl who is trapped in her femme fatale role but also turns out to be not exactly what she seems. Mottola gives us real people behind the stereotyped fashions and behaviors of the day. What really makes *Adventureland* a ride worth taking, though, are the magnificent performances of Eisenberg and Stewart. He is clumsy and achingly awkward without ever being unsympathetic. She is sultry in an understated, appealing way, caught in her anger and rebelliousness. It is delightful to see how they dance around the social stumbling blocks that their age and situation throw up. At this age, everyone is desperately trying to look and act cool, but the performances are so easily betrayed by a slight slip of the tongue. Mottola seems quite at home with this adolescent angst. And thanks to the strong performances of his leads, his evocative ending is not disturbing in its contrivance. In fact, it is itself a new beginning of a path to adulthood, which is exactly what the climax of a coming-of-age story should be.

Michael Betzold

CREDITS

James Brennan: Jesse Eisenberg
Em: Kristen Stewart
Joel: Martin Starr
Bobby: Bill Hader
Paulette: Kristen Wiig
Connell: Ryan Reynolds
Origin: USA
Language: English
Released: 2009
Production: Anne Carey, Ted Hope, Sidney Kimmel; Sidney Kimmel Entertainment, This Is That Productions; released by Miramax Films
Directed by: Greg Mottola
Written by: Greg Mottola
Cinematography by: Terry Stacey
Editing: Anne McCabe

Art Direction: Matt Munn
Costumes: Melissa Toth
Production Design: Stephen Beatrice
MPAA rating: R
Running time: 107 minutes

REVIEWS

Ebert, Roger. *Chicago Sun-Times.* April 2, 2009.
Edelstein, David. *New York Magazine.* March 30, 2009.
Foundas, Scott. *Village Voice.* April 1, 2009.
Gleiberman, Owen. *Entertainment Weekly.* April 1, 2009.
McCarthy, Todd. *Variety.* January 21, 2009.
Phillips, Michael. *Chicago Tribune.* April 2, 2009.
Scott, A.O. *New York Times.* April 2, 2009.
Sobczynski, Peter. *EFilmCritic.* April 3, 2009.
Stevens, Dana. *Slate.* April 3, 2009.
Turan, Kenneth. *Los Angeles Times.* April 2, 2009.

QUOTES

James Brennan: "Yeah, Frigo was my best friend. Then, I
turned four."

TRIVIA

The real Adventureland park is really in Farmingdale, New
York on Long Island. The movie was originally set to be
showed the same day the real Adventureland park reopens
for business every year on March 27.

AWARDS

Nomination:
Ind. Spirit 2010: Screenplay.

ALIENS IN THE ATTIC

Be afraid. Be sort-of afraid.
—Movie tagline

They are home but they are not alone.
—Movie tagline

Box Office: $25.2 million

Aliens in the Attic is a rarity amongst films today
made for younger viewers—it does not utilize the
increasingly tiresome 3-D gimmick, it is not a slick
animated feature choked with big-name stars supplying
the voices and endless sequences of the characters sliding
down tunnels in scenes seemingly designed solely to
provide some action for the videogame tie-in, and it
does not come with a back story that is so dense and
convoluted with character and incident that it make the
Bible look like a Walter Hill creation by comparison.

Instead, it is a direct throwback to the live-action fantasy
adventures that Steven Spielberg used to crank out *en
masse* in the 1980s—stuff like *The Goonies* (1985), **bat-
teries not included* (1986) and *Harry and the Hendersons*—through his Amblin Entertainment production
company. Although the film as a whole may not be as
good as the best of those films, it does convey some of
their spirit and as a result, parents watching it with their
kids may find themselves experiencing a certain state of
Proustian recall as they watch it.

Carter Jenkins stars as Tom Pearson, a teen genius
who has been deliberately letting his grades go south so
that his classmates will stop looking at him as some
kind of freakish brainiac. In response, his dad (Kevin
Nealon) comes up with an exceptionally cruel punishment—a Fourth of July vacation with the entire family
in Michigan. Shortly after arriving, Tom, younger sister
Hannah (Ashley Boettcher) and cousins Jake (Austin
Butler), Art (Henri Young) and Lee (Regan Young)
discover that a quartet of aliens from the planet Zirko-
nia have landed on the roof of the house in search of a
transmitter that will allow them to signal their comrades
to begin a full-out invasion of the planet. To aid in their
quest, the creatures are carrying a mind-control device
that allows them to control anyone who gets zapped by
it but, in a fatal design flaw, it only works on adults.
Realizing that the future of the planet is at stake, the
kids band together and, with the help of one alien who
is befriended by Hannah, they try to defeat the intruders and stop the invasion without letting any adults
(who also include grandmother Doris Roberts, uncle
Andy Richter and lone cop Tim Meadows) suspect that
something is amiss.

The chief problem with *Aliens in the Attic* is that,
unlike the aforementioned Amblin productions, it is
aimed squarely at the littlest audience members and as a
result, it feels as if all the traces of danger and nastiness
that played such a big part of those films has been carefully sanded away so as not to upset anyone—at times,
it feels as if what *Gremlins* (1984) might have been like
if your mother had directed it. As a result, the whole
thing is kind of silly and innocuous and forgettable but
if you are able to look past all of that, it does contain a
few virtues worth noting. Although the adult actors are
pretty much wasted (why cast comic actors like Richter,
Nealon and Meadows and then have them play straight
men for the most part?), the kids are relatively appealing
and never grow too obnoxious. The special effects are
agreeably cartoony and never try to blow viewers away—
the right approach for a film of this type. While most of
the humor is silly slapstick aimed at kids, there are some
funny bits here and there—especially a line in which a
paintball gun is confiscated by a parent with the admonition that such a thing is a "gateway gun." Best of all, it

moves quickly enough (though not too quickly as to become incoherent) so that it never quite begins to wear out its welcome.

As family entertainment goes, *Aliens in the Attic* never comes close to hitting the heights of such 2009 fare as *Coraline Up* and *Harry Potter and the Half-Blood Prince*. That said, it does have its modest charms and it certainly did not deserve the treatment that 20th Century Fox gave it when they dumped it in theaters with little advertising and no press screenings. Maybe the best way to approach it is to look at it as sort of a gateway movie for kids—if they like it, perhaps it will inspire them to look up the movies that inspired it (and so on) and set them on the road to a more fully-formed cinematic education. If that happens, then it will have more than served its purpose.

Peter Sobczynski

CREDITS

Tom Pearson: Carter Jenkins
Bethany Pearson: Ashley Tisdale
Jake Pearson: Austin Butler
Hannah Pearson: Ashley Boettcher
Nana Rose Pearson: Doris Roberts
Ricky Dillman: Robert Hoffman III
Stuart Pearson: Kevin Nealon
Uncle Nathan Pearson: Andy Richter
Sheriff Doug Armstrong: Tim Meadows
Art Pearson: Henri Young
Lee Pearson: Regan Young
Julie: Malese Jow
Annie Filkins: Maggie VandenBerghe
Brooke: Megan Parker
Tazer: Thomas Haden Church (Voice)
Sparks: Josh Peck (Voice)
Skip: Ashley Peldon (Voice)
Razor: Kari Wahlgren (Voice)
Skip: J.K. Simmons (Voice)
Origin: USA
Language: English
Released: 2009
Production: Barry Josephson; Regency Enterprises, Josephson Entertainment; released by 20th Century Fox
Directed by: John Schultz
Written by: Mark Burton, Adam F. Goldberg
Cinematography by: Don Burgess
Music by: John Debney
Sound: Tony Johnson, Ken Saville
Music Supervisor: Billy Gottlieb
Editing: John Pace

Art Direction: Nigel Evans
Costumes: Mona May
Production Design: Barry Chusid
MPAA rating: PG
Running time: 86 minutes

REVIEWS

Burr, Ty. *Boston Globe*. August 3, 2009.
Berkshire, Geoff. *Metromix.com*. July 31, 2009.
Bradshaw, Peter. *Guardian*. August 14, 2009.
Clark, Shaula. *Boston Phoenix*. August 7, 2009.
Edwards, David. *Daily Mirror*. August 14, 2009.
Hale, Mike. *New York Times*. August 3, 2009.
Honeycutt, Kirk. *Hollywood Reporter*. July 31, 2009.
Leydon, Joe. *Variety*. July 31, 2009.
Sobczynski, Peter. *eFilmCritic*. August 7, 2009.
Whipp, Glenn. *Los Angeles Times*. July 31, 2009.

QUOTES

Stuart Pearson: "If you're smart enough to hack into the school's computer, you're smart enough to pass your classes."

ALL ABOUT STEVE

Box Office: $3.1 million

On the surface, *All About Steve* has a lot going for it. The movie stars Sandra Bullock, who, thanks to romantic comedy turns opposite everyone from Hugh Grant and Ryan Reynolds, is vying for the title of 'America's Sweetheart' left vacant by Meg Ryan; the love interest is played by Bradley Cooper, who won audiences over with his deadpan delivery and good looks in *The Hangover* (2009); and there are supporting comedic turns by Thomas Hayden Church and Ken Jeong. Yet despite all this, the movie falls flat on its pretty-on-the-surface face thanks to a non-existent plot, a lack of directorial vision and characters who try so hard to be wacky they end up embarrassing.

The loosely held together narrative follows Mary Horowitz (Bullock) a nerdy, crossword puzzle designer who lacks social and fashion skills. In reading between the oddball lines of writer Kim Barker's script, *All About Steve* is the tale of Mary embracing her eccentricities in a world demanding that she comply with a homogenous idea of normalcy. Her parents want Mary to move out and have babies, her newspaper boss wants her to get out more and everyone wants her to ditch the ugly red stripper boots she seems to wear with everything. So what does Mary do? She convinces herself she's in love with Steve (Cooper), a cute TV news cameraman with whom she's had one blind date, and follows him around parts of the U.S. trying to win his affection. En route, she meets other fellow, off-the-beaten-path weirdoes, gets trapped in an abandoned mine shaft and learns that friends are more important that attractive cameramen who find you annoying.

Paralleling Mary's personal quest for acceptance, Barker also tries to offer commentary on the news industry through Steve's job supporting a wannabe news anchor Hartman (Church) who will stop at nothing to sensationalize any and every news story, as well as propose that there are people in the country who travel around setting up sit-ins and vigils to accompany any issue du jour. The problems in Barker's set-up are two-fold: there is no balance in Mary's and Hartman's (and Steve's) storylines and the movie amounts to the cast of characters taking turns being schlocky inconsistent caricatures rather than anything resembling actual people. Though she has the wherewithal to present her editor with a model for a daily crossword puzzle program, we are also asked to believe that Mary will jeopardize her career by submitting for publication a crossword all about Steve, a man she just met. And while we are coming to terms with the fact that she just might be a crazy *Rain Man*-esque (she does know a lot of random facts that help her with work) stalker, Mary graces us with a trying hard to be insightful voice-over contemplating the ways in which life is just like a crossword puzzle. There is a grain of truth buried under these un-matching choices. For the movie to work Mary has to be loveable, vulnerable, funny and complex. She is, at times throughout the film, each one of these things, but the trouble is that she cannot pull off all traits at once and that none of them feel organic. In the same vein, Hartman is so very over the top in his comedy routine that he becomes completely unprofessional and it's hard to buy the fact that any news organization would even keep him on staff.

The only people who receive any audience sympathy are the actors who are stuck flailing around this sensational belly flop of a movie. The actors' hearts are in it—Bullock turns the cutesy charm on to "full-blast," Church milks Hartman's antics and Cooper goes topless. But it's director Phil Traill's decision to have the actors exploit every possible moment for full-throttle slapstick that's the final nail in the coffin. Instead of seeking out moments to pull Mary back, thereby taking her out of full-on physical comedy spiral, Traill layers on Mary's quirks. Bullock's flashy red boots (the only reminders that Mary is supposed to have a personality) end up buckling under the pressure of Mary's endless shenanigans and she gets buried.

The dim light at the end of the tunnel in this disastrous movie are Katy Mixon and DJ Qualls, who play Elizabeth and Howard a touring pair of bleeding hearts and also Mary's cohorts in weirdness. Although their characters are barely developed, they work because the actors have pretty much been left to do their thing. The result is a pair of cute, easy going social outcasts who are believable and are more fun to watch than the leads in the movie.

Joanna Topor MacKenzie

CREDITS

Mary Horowitz: Sandra Bullock
Steve: Bradley Cooper
Hartman Hughes: Thomas Haden Church
Angus: Ken Jeong
Howard: DJ Qualls
Elizabeth: Katy Mixon
Origin: USA
Language: English
Released: 2009
Production: Sandra Bullock, Mary McLaglen; Fortis Films, Fox 2000 Pictures, Radar Pictures; released by 20th Century Fox Films
Directed by: Phil Traill
Written by: Kim Barker
Cinematography by: Tim Suhrstedt
Music by: Christophe Beck
Sound: Jose Antonio Garcia, Tim Gomillion
Music Supervisor: John Houlihan
Editing: Ron Dean, Virginia Katz
Art Direction: Austin Gorg
Costumes: Gary Jones
Production Design: Maher Ahmad
MPAA rating: PG-13
Running time: 98 minutes

REVIEWS

Abele, Robert. *Los Angeles Times.* September 3, 2009.
Burr, Ty. *Boston Globe.* September 3, 2009.
Childress, Erik. *eFilmCritic.* September 4, 2009.
Dargis, Manohla. *New York Times.* September 4, 2009.
Ebert, Roger. *Chicago Sun-Times.* September 3, 2009.
Lowry, Brian. *Variety.* September 3, 2009.
Pais, Matt. *Metromix.com.* September 3, 2009.
Phillips, Michael. *Chicago Tribune.* September 4, 2009.
Sobczynski, Peter. *eFilmCritic.* September 3, 2009.
Tallerico, Brian. *MovieRetriever.com.* September 4, 2009.

QUOTES

Mary Horowitz: "I will eat you like a mountain lion."

ALVIN AND THE CHIPMUNKS: THE SQUEAKQUEL

Box Office: $219.1 million

For those looking for a film to take the entire family to that would enchant and entertain both younger and older viewers in equal measure, 2009 was a surprisingly strong year for such things. Sure, there were the occasional dregs like *Monsters Vs. Aliens* and *G-Force* but for every piece of junk along those lines that emerged, there would be either a solid piece of entertainment like *Cloudy with a Chance of Meatballs* or *The Princess and the Frog* or an instant classic like *Coraline, Up, Ponyo, Where the Wild Things Are,* and *Fantastic Mr. Fox.* It is therefore tragic to note that a year that had largely been an embarrassment of riches in this regard would end with a flat-out embarrassment like *Alvin and the Chipmunks: The Squeakquel,* the follow-up to *Alvin and the Chipmunks* (2007), the shockingly popular film that marked the big-screen debut of everyone's favorite trio of musically-inclined rodents. As bad as the original film was, and it was horrible beyond human comprehension, it could be argued that it at least made some token effort to entertain its target audience with a combination of silly humor, pat homilies and speeded-up renditions of popular tunes. This one, on the other hand, is nothing more than an ultra-cynical piece of junk put out by people who are so contemptuous of their audience that they clearly felt that they could slap together something as tacky, tasteless and ramshackle as this and get away with it because the success of the first one clearly demonstrated that families would flock to it regardless of its lack of any redeeming qualities, artistic or otherwise.

The film opens with Alvin (voiced by Justin Long) and brothers Simon (Matthew Grey Gubler) and Theodore (Jesse McCartney) as world-famous rock stars. Nevertheless, manager Dave Seville (Jason Lee in what has to be the most grudging contractually obligated cameo appearance in a sequel since Sarah Michelle Gel-

lar slouched through the opening scenes of *The Grudge 2* [2006]) inexplicably decides that they need to enroll in high school and, through a series of events too tedious to get into here, Alvin becomes the big vermin on campus thanks to his prowess on the football field and ignores his less-popular brothers. At the same time, the three are recruited by the principal (Wendie Malick) to represent the school in a talent contest with a $20,000 first prize that will save the music program. (After all, what better way to signify the importance of the program than by recruiting ringers instead of actual participants?) Meanwhile, disgraced record company weasel Ian Hawke (David Cross) is thirsting for a way to restore his reputation in the music industry and revenge himself upon Alvin and Co. and stumbles upon what may be the perfect solution when he cons his way into managing a trio of singing girl chipmunks—Brittany (Christina Applegate), Eleanor (Amy Poehler) and Jeanette (Anna Faris)—that he dubs the Chipettes. For this to happens, of course, he has to enroll them in school as well and pit them against the Chipmunks for the right to represent the school in the talent contest. It all ends happily with a finale that includes speeches about teamwork and friendship, a chase scene, a "spontaneous" musical collaboration that comes together perfectly without a single rehearsal or hiccup and, perhaps inevitably, a couple of shots to Ian's groin for good measure.

Obviously, there is only so much that can be done with material of this kind and to expect anything along the elevated lines of *Where the Wild Things Are* would be utterly foolish but even so, the film still utterly fails to come close to living up to those dramatically reduced expectations. The storyline is an incoherent mess that sounds less like a professional-grade screenplay and more like a Mad Lib composed by a hyperactive group of first-graders screaming things out at random. The human actors are all appallingly cartoonish while the cartoon characters are all appallingly unlikable and indistinct—it boggles the mind that the producers would go to the expense to hire talented actresses like Applegate, Faris, and Poehler to voice the Chipettes and then present their contributions in such a way that it is impossible to discern that it is actually them. The music is indescribably annoying even by Chipmunk standards—if there is one thing that tunes like Katy Perry's "Hot N Cold" and Beyonce's "Single Ladies (Put a Ring on It)" do not need, it is to be sped up to a helium-voiced consistency. A lot of the humor is also surprisingly inappropriate for a film aimed squarely at little kids—at one point, viewers are treated to the sight of Alvin quoting from *Taxi Driver* (1976) and *Silence of the Lambs* (1991) and at another, Theodore takes part in an on-screen depiction of the fetid glory that is a Dutch

Oven, even helpfully identifying it as such for an audience that by that point will no doubt sympathize with the plight of being trapped within something stinky with no apparent escape in sight.

Like the first film, *Alvin and the Chipmunks: The Squeakquel* turned out to be a huge hit at the box office, presumably because parents just assumed that it was safe to take their kids to it because it would not be filled with traditional bad elements like sex, graphic violence and dirty language. On the other hand, it also lacks such seemingly vital elements as humor, imagination and dignity and the absence of those elements can be far more damaging to young minds. Exposing kids to useless crap like this is, in a way, a form of genuine abuse from a cultural and artistic perspective. Remember, a terrible movie about animated chipmunks acting like idiots while squeaking out "You Really Got Me" at ear-piercing levels can hurt as much as a fist.

Peter Sobczynski

CREDITS

Dave Seville: Jason Lee
Toby Seville: Zachary Levi
Ian Hawke: David Cross
Becca: Bridgit Mendler
Alvin: Justin Long (Voice)
Simon: Matthew Grey Gubler (Voice)
Theodore: Jesse McCartney (Voice)
Brittany: Anna Faris (Voice)
Jeanette: Christina Applegate (Voice)
Eleanor: Amy Poehler (Voice)
Origin: USA
Language: English
Released: 2009
Production: Ross Bagdasarian Jr., Janice Karman; Bagdasarian Productions; released by 20th Century Fox
Directed by: Betty Thomas
Written by: Jonathan Aibel, Glenn Berger, Will McRobb, Chris Viscardi, Jon Vitti
Cinematography by: Anthony B. Richmond
Music by: Brian Bulman
Sound: Willis D. Burton
Music Supervisor: Julianne Jordan
Editing: Matthew Friedman
Art Direction: Bo Johnson
Costumes: Alexandra Welker
Production Design: Marcia Hinds
MPAA rating: PG
Running time: 88 minutes

REVIEWS

Adams, Derek. *Time Out.* December 18, 2009.
Burr, Ty. *Boston Globe.* December 22, 2009.

Leupp, Thomas. *Hollywood.com.* December 25, 2009.
Leydon, Joe. *Variety.* December 21, 2009.
Newman, Kim. *Empire Magazine.* January 5, 2010.
O'Sullivan, Michael. *Washington Post.* December 23, 2009.
Pais, Matt. *Metromix.com.* December 22, 2009.
Simon, Brent. *Screen International.* December 21, 2009.
Taylor, Ella. *Village Voice.* December 23, 2009.
Whipp, Glenn. *Associated Press.* December 22, 2009.

QUOTES

Alvin: "You taking to me? I don't see anyone else out here, so you must be talking to me."

TRIVIA

It was originally scheduled to be premiered on March 19, 2010, but it was moved up to be releases on Christmas 2009 instead.

AMELIA

Defying the impossible. Living the dream.
—Movie tagline

Box Office: $14 million

The presence of two-time Academy Award® winner Hilary Swank provides absolutely no sense of takeoff for *Amelia*, a tiresome biopic of American aviatrix Amelia Earhart, who rose to fame with a series of transatlantic flights in the 1930s before eventually disappearing over the Pacific Ocean, along with her navigator, in an attempt to circumnavigate the globe. Appropriately savaged by critics upon its stillborn theatrical release (the film earned a 20 percent rotten rating on RottenTomatoes.com), *Amelia* is in many ways a well-meaning movie, put together technically with a certain steady, economic reliability. Unfortunately, it is also entirely dramatically inert, distended to the point of collapse with its own swollen, deluded sense of uniqueness and self-importance.

Swank's status as an Oscar® darling, in addition to the plucky proto-feminism of the movie's subject, are the intertwined reasons for *Amelia*'s existence, but this blatant awards-bait formula failed to make inroads with autumnal audiences hungry for an adult drama—not particularly surprising given that, apart from *Insomnia* (2002), Swank has never had a film crack $12.5 million in its first week of wide release. Bowing to a semi-respectable if unspectacular $3.9 million in 820 theaters the week before Halloween, *Amelia* could never gain traction with older demographics required to confer success on this sort of big screen biography, and it consequently finished with a dismal $13.8 million theatrical haul. Critical reaction and public word-of-mouth was deadly, to be sure, but in retrospect one has to wonder whether, in an era of rampant, no-big-deal commercial air travel, the accomplishments at the core of the movie mattered at all to modern-day audiences.

After opening with footage from just prior to Earhart's departure on her fateful journey, and then a flashback to her childhood roots in rural Kansas that shamelessly apes some visual cues of *Gladiator* (2000) (what with fingers tracing stalks of wheat in an open field, and what not), *Amelia* mostly focuses on its subject's passion for flight as seen through the prism of the two men to whom she was closest. The first is her husband, promoter and publishing magnate George Putnam (Richard Gere); the second is pilot Gene Vidal (Ewan McGregor), a longtime friend and, though the movie scarcely acknowledges the specifics of it, part-time lover.

George is revealed as the architect of Earhart's image, lining her up for fashion spreads and speaking engagements, and raising enough capital to fund her expeditions by inking endorsement deals for luggage and cigarettes, even though she does not smoke. His work pays off biggest with an academic endowment at Purdue University, which allows for the custom-building of a Lockheed Electra airplane. Political riser Gene, meanwhile, excites more passion in Earhart, though the movie misguidedly consigns most of this revelation to a musty letter. Instead, priority ticketing is given to a beat-by-beat chronicling of Earhart's first transatlantic journey, her later solo trek and eventual doomed final flight with navigator Fred Noonan (Christopher Eccelston).

From *Kama Sutra: A Tale of Love* (1996) to *Vanity Fair* (2004), Indian-born director Mira Nair is known for films with strong female characters, so it is easy to see how and why she was approached to helm *Amelia*, which loosely slots in this mold—even if her selection is characteristic of the condescension often directed at female filmmakers, as if their talents and story qualifications cease at the outer edges of their gender. Nair cannot save a film, however, whose drama is so staid, predictable and safe and factoids so neatly bundled that its most comparable forebears are small screen, cable movies-of-the-week and PBS documentaries.

Based on the books *East To the Dawn* by Susan Butler and *The Sound of Wings* by Mary Lovell, *Amelia* feels exactingly work-shopped and designed not to offend or confuse any potential age group, to the point that it ends up saying absolutely nothing of consequence about its subject. Replete with newspaper headline montages that frequently explain the action that has just taken place, Ron Bass and Anna Hamilton Phelan's screenplay is a standard feminist tract, waterlogged by earnestness and vacuumed free of any psychological insight.

In short, the writing takes an extraordinary life of adventure and celebrity and drains it of excitement, makes it small. There is neither nuance nor any shades of grey to the character of Earhart, no hint that she might have been complicit in George's marketing schemes. The script sets up a potential rival, upstart Elinor Smith (Mia Wasikowska), and then has Earhart shrug off a loss to her in a barnstorming publicity race, all before kicking Elinor out of the narrative entirely. A meeting between Earhart and First Lady Eleanor Roosevelt (Cherry Jones), meanwhile, is so poorly set up and contextualized as to render it a *Forrest Gump*-style outtake—the "accidental," rib-nudging meeting of two figures of historical note.

Most chiefly problematic, though, is the film's obsessive preoccupation with attempting to impose a swooning, doomed love affair, a la *Titanic,* (1997), onto the narrative. In addition to creating one of the most tepid amorous triangles in recent big screen history, all the time spent dawdling on its subject's personal life could have been used to dig into Earhart's personality and ambitious drive in a much more substantive manner, or anchor the many fuzzy details that mar the doomed quest represented in the finale. Instead, bafflingly, as Earhart's last hours unfold, and naval trackers of the expedition try desperately to make radio contact with her and Noonan, it is casually explained that they did not take the Morse Code machine on the plane with them. Why? Viewers are left to supply their own answer.

From both of her Oscar®-winning performances, in *Boys Don't Cry* (1999) and *Million Dollar Baby* (2004), to the aforementioned *Insomnia* and ensemble fare like *The Core* (2003) and *The Black Dahlia* (2006), Swank's screen work has been mostly characterized, to be blunt, by a sexless intensity and physicality. This more or less matches Earhart's tomboy persona, but only further highlights the problems inherent in *Amelia*'s willful insistence on telling Earhart's story through two men, which is not at all at the crux of what she is defined by and known for in the present day. For her part, Swank's performance is committed, but the heartland accent is distractingly hit-and-miss and, combined with overly physical signifiers of emotion (toothy grins of gumption, furrowed brows of worry), it quickly starts to come across as distractingly one-note and cornpone.

Excepting composer Gabriel Yared's melodramatic score, technically the movie scores high marks almost across the board. Cinematographer Stuart Dryburgh crafts some striking from-the-cockpit horizons, abetted by a few visual effects tweaks. And despite its significant and inbuilt story problems, *Amelia*'s costumes and production design, crafted within the constraints of a $40 million budget, are attractive and engaging. Sadly, that is not nearly enough to give the gift of flight to this boring, imperceptive, two-dimensional biopic. Those interested in Earhart would do better simply reading the source material, or any other book about her.

Brent Simon

CREDITS

Amelia Earhart: Hilary Swank
George Putnam: Richard Gere
Gene Vidal: Ewan McGregor
Fred Noonan: Christopher Eccleston
Elinor Smith: Mia Wasikowska
Bill: Joe Anderson
Eleanor Roosevelt: Cherry Jones
Gore Vidal: William Cuddy
Origin: USA
Language: English
Released: 2009
Production: Lydia Dean Pilcher, Kevin Hyman, Ted Waitt; AE Electra Productions, Avalon Pictures; released by Fox Searchlight
Directed by: Mira Nair
Written by: Ronald Bass, Anna Hamilton Phelan
Cinematography by: Stuart Dryburgh
Music by: Gabriel Yared
Sound: Drew Kunin
Music Supervisor: Linda Cohen
Editing: Allyson C. Johnson, Lee Percy
Art Direction: Nigel Churcher
Costumes: Kasia Walicka-Maimone
Production Design: Stephanie Carroll
MPAA rating: PG
Running time: 111 minutes

REVIEWS

Bennett, Ray. *Hollywood Reporter.* October 18, 2009.
Chang, Justin. *Variety.* October 18, 2009.
Ebert, Roger. *Chicago Sun-Times.* October 22, 2009.
Germain, David. *Associated Press.* October 20, 2009.
Morgenstern, Joe. *Wall Street Journal.* October 22, 2009.
Phillips, Michael. *Chicago Tribune.* October, 22, 2009.
Pols, Mary F. *Time Magazine.* October 23, 2009.
Sharkey, Betsy. *Los Angeles Times.* October 22, 2009.
Tallerico, Brian. *MovieRetriever.com.* October 22, 2009.
Travers, Peter. *Rolling Stone.* October 23, 2009.

QUOTES

George Putman: "Come back to me."

TRIVIA

The movie shows Earhart finishing third in the first Santa Monica-to-Cleveland Women's Air Derby in 1929, but does not explain why. At the last stop before the final leg of the race to Cleveland, Earhart and her friend Ruth Nichols were tied for first. Nichols took off right before Earhart, but her aircraft clipped a tractor on the runway and flipped over. Instead of taking off, Earhart ran to Ruth's plane to drag her to safety. After Earhart was sure that Nichols was not seriously hurt, she took off for Cleveland but finished third largely due to her delayed takeoff.

AMREEKA

Life's best adventures are journeys of the heart.
—Movie tagline

The most surprising film title read on the morning of the Independent Spirit Awards nominations for the big category of the day was clearly the unheralded character piece *Amreeka,* a film that had built strong festival buzz and received a small arthouse release but nowhere near the attention of its fellow nominees *(500) Days of Summer, Precious: Based on the Novel 'Push' by Sapphire, Sin Nombre,* or *The Last Station.* After the fact, it seems a more natural culmination for a film that received applause at the Sundance Film Festival and won the coveted FIPRESCI prize at the Cannes Film Festival. Writer/director Cherien Debis (a writer on Showtime's *The L Word*) fashioned a human dramedy about an immigrant single mother and her teenage son and their experience in small town America. Without artifice or melodrama, Debis finds the humanity in her characters that so many Hollywood productions about the immigrant experience ignore entirely. With lead performances by Nisreen Faour and Melkar Muallem that feel so genuine that they almost come off as non-actors and wonderful supporting turns by Hiam Abbass (*The Visitor* [2008]) and Alia Shawkat (*Arrested Development, Whip It* [2009]), *Amreeka* is a touching slice of life rarely seen on film, independent or otherwise.

Muna (Faour) and her teenage son Fadi (Muallem) demand a better life than the one they have in war-torn Bethlehem, painted in dour, depressing browns and grays by Debis. The pair is granted green cards through a lottery system and move to a suburb of Chicago to live with her sister and two daughters. Of course, life in the Midwest for anyone from the Middle East was not easy in the 2000s and Muna and her son have the misfortune of coming to the windy city shortly after the start of the war in Iraq. With wounds form 9/11 still fresh, anti-Arab sentiment is a tragic part of the fabric of the life of a Palestinian immigrant in the U.S. from the very beginning. When Muna arrives, her life savings are taken from her by customs agents at O'Hare airport and she is forced to arrive on her sister's doorstep without a penny to their names.

Instead of continuing up the ladder to bank management that she was on in her home country, Muna is forced to take a job at White Castle. Meanwhile, Fadi and cousin Salma (Shawkat) form a bond and the latter works to make the former look and act more American. Fadi is demonized at school and his uncle (Yussef Abu Warda) watches his practice suffer due to anti-Arab sentiment. Prejudice and profiling are clearly elements of *Amreeka* but they are not the main focus. Dabis was a Jordanian growing up in Dayton, Ohio during the first Gulf War and discrimination in Middle America is clearly something she knows about but she wisely focuses on the humanity of her characters more than their racial situation. This is a heartwarming, human film, not a political one even though politics are so clearly a part of these people's everyday life.

There is a subtle, warm human quality to Debis' sense of humor in *Amreeka*. When Muna first arrives at customs and tells the agent that she is from the Palestinian territory, the officer's next question is if the woman has a job. "Occupation?" "Yes, it is occupied. For forty years." When Muna laments the fact that she needs to lose some weight, a relative notes that everyone in America is fat. These kind of quiet moments of humor weave together to form the fabric of a film about good people trying to keep their heads above water. Faour, Muallem, and the amazing Abbass shine in roles that never once feel forced or overdone. Sadly, the same cannot always be said for the portrayal of Americans in the film, often two-dimensionally drawn, particularly the sneering agents at O'Hare, the bank managers who will not hire Muna, and the bullies at school. An ironic twist involving the school principal displays an awareness that everything is not so cut and dry but it takes a bit too long for the rest of the world to catch up with the realism in Fadi and Muna's relationship and at the core of the film. Still, the film ends on a surprisingly touching note as cultures mix but also stay true to their history. Dabis ends the film with the words "For My Family." They will likely be happy to have received such a loving cinematic gift.

What most allows *Amreeka* to transcend the relatively predictable structure of immigrants moving to the United States is the love and care shown these characters by the film's creator. There is obvious affection for Muna and Fadi and, by extension, people in similar situations throughout America. It is far more difficult than it looks to replicate human, individual stories without artifice and that is clearly what drew awards groups to this gentle film throughout 2009. Through the remarkable performances of its leads—Faour gives one of the best performances of the year, herself an Independent Spirit nominee for Best Actress—and the talented work of its young writer/director,

Amreeka tells a common story in a uncommon way—believably.

Brian Tallerico

CREDITS

Muna Farah: Nisreen Faour
Fadi Farah: Melkar Muallem
Raghda Halaby: Hiam Abbass
Nabeel Halaby: Yussef Abu-Warda
Salma: Alia Shawkat
Mr. Novatski: Joseph Ziegler
Origin: USA, Canada
Language: English, Arabic
Released: 2009
Production: Christina Piovesan, Paul Barkin; Alcina Pictures, Buffalo Gal Pictures, Eagle Vision Media Group, First Generation Films; released by National Geographic Cinema Ventures
Directed by: Cherien Dabis
Written by: Cherien Dabis
Cinematography by: Tobias Datum
Music by: Kareem Roustom
Sound: Brock Capell
Music Supervisor: Doug Bernheim
Editing: Keith Reamer
Art Direction: Laura Souter
Costumes: Patricia Henderson
Production Design: Aidan Leroux
MPAA rating: PG-13
Running time: 96 minutes

REVIEWS

Ebert, Roger. *Chicago Sun-Times.* September 17, 2009.
Foundas, Scott. *L.A. Weekly.* June 25, 2009.
Holden, Stephen. *New York Times.* September 3, 2009.
Long, Tom. *Detroit News.* August 28, 2009.
Morris, Wesley. *Boston Globe.* September 24, 2009.
Nelson, Rob. *Variety.* February 13, 2009.
Rea, Steven. *Philadelphia Inquirer.* September 24, 2009.
Schwarzbaum, Lisa. *Entertainment Weekly.* September 2, 2009.
Taylor, Ella. *Village Voice.* September 1, 2009.
Turan, Kenneth. *Los Angeles Times.* September 3, 2009.

AWARDS

Nomination:
Ind. Spirit 2010: Actress (Faour), Film, First Screenplay.

ANGELS & DEMONS

The holiest event of our time. Perfect for their return.
—Movie tagline

Box Office: $130 million

Based on the Dan Brown novel of the same name, *Angels & Demons* is less controversial than its predecessor *The Da Vinci Code* (2006) and, all things considered, is, for that reason, even less interesting. This is not to say that there is nothing to enjoy in the film but that enjoyment of it is predicated on realizing what its creator's goals truly are in the making of it. Anyone following the marketing plan (or any of the signals the film itself sends) would have thought it must be an important film rather than a piece of throwaway popcorn fluff. It fails utterly as one and barely ekes out a claim on the other. But even that claim rests on the dubious present day notion that something less than the sum of its parts can still be regarded as a desirable whole. This conspiracy borne of consumerism is far more interesting than the films conspiracy borne of the Illuminati. Suffice to say, *Angels & Demons* contains everything a reasonably entertaining pot boiler should contain without actually being a reasonably entertaining pot boiler. It is, in fact, merely one more piece of bland product from the Ron Howard movie machine, probably most suited for those who will watch just about anything and say afterwards, "It was okay."

Like *The Da Vinci Code* (2006), *The Name of the Rose* (1986), and other films which deal in religion and history as a background for adventure, *Angels & Demons* plays fast and loose with history to tell a story. This is by no means a cinematic sin. *The Da Vinci Code* was actually fun to watch. *Angels & Demons* aims to provide the same basest form of escapism and if the cinematic result is a thinking man's rung below *National Treasure* (2004) that is far from its worst sin. That distinction emerges from the way the film dodges every opportunity to become anything relevant or memorable at all, revealing itself, ultimately, as an empty exercise in camera swooping, scene stealing musical crescendos, and bland characterization.

As the world mourns the death of Pope Pius XVI and the Vatican makes preparations for a papal election, the four most likely candidates for papal office are kidnapped and a vial of antimatter is stolen and set to explode over Vatican City at midnight. All signs point to the Church's arch rival, an ancient mysterious group known as the Illuminati, as the culprit. Every hour on the hour, a candidate will be killed, leading up to the destruction of Rome itself, unless Harvard University Symbologist Robert Langdon (Tom Hanks), scientist and creator of the antimatter device Vittoria Vetra (Ayelet Zurer), and temporary papal authority Camerlengo Patrick McKenna (Ewan MacGregor) can trace an ancient secret path through Rome through the hidden altars of the four elements in time to save each of the Cardinals and defuse the bomb. To do so they must work with a skeptical police force headed by Commander Richter (Stellan Skarsgard) and a church structure headed by Cardinal Strauss (Armin Mueller-Stahl), who is anxious to make it appear that everything is as usual in the election of the new pope.

Other subplots involving a paid assassin and the possibility of the pope having a secretly adopted child are shoehorned in to the already-crowded storyline and give the characters little time to do anything but exposit what the film should show in other ways. No human being could naturally come to any of the conclusions Langdon and his friends do when confronted with the "clues" of this mystery, so the film simply steps aside and has them spout whatever is necessary to get them hurtling in the direction the plot demands. It would be positively Holmesian if there was a character half as interesting as Sherlock Holmes here.

This is one of the film's biggest problems. If there were any more exposition in *Angels & Demons* the screenplay could have been published as an encyclopedia. The only problem is that the encyclopedia would contain spurious information on almost everything historical that the film touches on. This is hardly peripheral. *Angels & Demons* never shows us who the Illuminati are or why anyone who is not Catholic should care about them, and the Catholic Church itself is reduced to a lumbering clumsy giant, again mostly unconcerned with humanity outside its borders. Except for Langdon there is really nobody to root for or against and Langdon is given nothing to do and no one in particular to be.

It is pointless to comment on the performances here. They are solid in the main but this is like saying that the performances in a TV commercial are solid. Perhaps more important is a word regarding the vanilla cinema of Ron Howard, appropriate if only because, barring an act of divine intervention, he will likely continue making films. Audiences worldwide have spent over half a billion dollars alone on this Howard film. This follows the pattern of much of his work and it is fair to say that the blander his films are the more money and honors they tend to accrue. He has occasionally made good films. *Willow* (1988), *Parenthood* (1989) and *Apollo 13* (1995), are examples. But, for a long time, the better part of the last decade in fact, he has simply made profitable ones. Seldom has a director with less sense of what to do with his camera, or how to tell an interesting story, been rewarded so lavishly. *Frost/Nixon* (2008) was, in spite of a good cast and some nice moments, essentially reduced to whether or not David Frost was going to ruin the promising career that led him to eventually host all those Guinness World Record TV specials, *The Missing* (2003) offered an unneeded redux of *The Searchers* (1956) and the travesty of *How The Grinch Stole Christmas* (2000) (a film far more plastic than the cheapest Christmas decoration) speaks for itself. Perhaps his greatest sin, *A Beautiful Mind* (2001), dulled down the life of schizophrenic mathematician John Forbes Nash, Jr. into its least interesting details, ignoring the true story of the attack on his wife that caused her to leave him, his subsequent descent into complete madness and homelessness, and the great act of compassion in which she took him back.

"Religion is flawed because man is flawed" Cardinal Strauss, by way of apology, says at one point, as if this boring clichéd enterprise had anything at all to say about religion, agnosticism or history. Viewers end up with nothing except the memory of feeling pulled along on a journey that should have been far less complicated, more enlightening, and far more fun to get to where it ultimately takes them.

Dave Canfield

CREDITS

Robert Langdon: Tom Hanks
Vittoria Vetra: Ayelet Zurer
Carlo Ventresca: Ewan McGregor
Richter: Stellan Skarsgard
Straus: Armin Mueller-Stahl
Origin: USA
Language: English
Released: 2009
Production: John Calley, Brian Grazer, Ron Howard; Columbia Pictures, Imagine Entertainment; released by Columbia Pictures
Directed by: Ron Howard
Written by: Akiva Goldsman, David Koepp
Cinematography by: Salvatore Totino
Music by: Hans Zimmer
Costumes: Daniel Orlandi
Editing: Dan Hanley, Mike Hill
Sound: Anthony J. Ciccolini III
Production Design: Allan Cameron
MPAA rating: PG-13
Running time: 138 minutes

REVIEWS

Childress, Erik. *eFilmCritic.com.* May 14, 2009.
Edelstein, David. *New York Magazine.* May 11, 2009.
Knight, Richard. *Windy City Times.* May 15, 2009.
Lemire, Christy. *Associated Press.* May 12, 2009.
Parker, Patrick. *Premiere Magazine.* May 15, 2009.
Scott, A.O. *New York Times.* May 14, 2009.
Sharkey, Betsy. *Los Angeles Times.* May 14, 2009.
Tallerico, Brian. *HollywoodChicago.com.* May 15, 2009.
Young, Deborah. *Hollywood Reporter.* May 7, 2009.
White, Armond. *New York Press.* May 13, 2009.

QUOTES

Cardinal Strauss: "When you write about us, and you will, do so gently."

TRIVIA

The production had to build a scale replica of St. Peter's Square since Vatican officers banned the movie from being filmed in its grounds.

THE ANSWER MAN

He wrote the book on life's big questions. But the truth is he hasn't got a clue.
—Movie tagline

If you had an honest-to-goodness conversation with God, would you tell anybody? On one hand this is precisely the kind of can't-wait-to-share moment you would want to tell your friends, family or, at least, your priest about. But you would be viewed as am prophet or nut? Taken as Christ or David Koresh? It's the very definition of a no-win scenario in a cynical society where a newspaper can declare that God is dead and other media types report of a war on Christmas. Arlen Faber is a little of both though. Nut as defined by anti-social gestures rather than leading a mass suicide and prophet by means of a best-selling novel that purports to tell the tale of his conversation with the Almighty. It's an intriguing setup for a character study to explore man's spiritual connection to their beliefs. Sadly, the setup only leads to easily one of the most rambling, ill-defined films of the year.

Arlen Faber (Jeff Daniels) is "the man who redefined spirituality for a new generation" with his tome, *Me & God.* Twenty years later, he's the man who hates to have his daily meditation interrupted with delivery of more fan mail (placed in a labeled "Mail Room") and the ways his publishers can continue to milk his work for profit. Arlen does not do interviews, signs under an alias, and is generally an unpleasant human being. And then, a deus ex machina. His back goes out. It's so bad that he has to literally crawl to the local chiropractor, Elizabeth (Lauren Graham), who fixes him and is deemed "a miracle worker." When he gives his name, she has never heard of him, but her receptionist, Anne (Olivia Thirlby), has, leading to the eventual question, "Who is Arlen Faber?" We then cutaway only to rejoin the conversation at the point for Elizabeth to respond, "So THAT is Arlen Faber."

Much of *The Answer Man* is like that with questions posed and a reaction to the response with none of the theoretical life-changing answers everyone is praising its titular character for in between. Maybe *The Answer Man* sounds like a better title than *Arlen Faber*—as it was called when it premiered at Sundance—but one makes it the portrait of a man and the other is dealing in either truth or irony. What can we make of a man and a film that has no time for its audience and forces us to wish for the scenes between the scenes that don't really exist?

The Heaven which writer/director John Hindman would like to attain is within the traditional rom-com give and take between Arlen and Elizabeth, each apparently living by the quote, "give, and it shall be given to you." Their mutual attraction begins based on what the other can provide them—back therapy and spiritual guidance—leaving us with little to take away in the realm of romance. The film's true journey into limbo is paved by bookstore owner Kris Lucas (Lou Taylor Pucci), a former alcoholic struggling with his recovery. Arlen wants to sell back some of his books to him, but since the store has been closed for twenty-seven days thanks to his assistant (a thoroughly wasted Kat Dennings) losing the key, he can't afford it. After discovering his true identity, Kris offers to take his books off his hands for ten-second counseling sessions. Here we get to hear Arlen's takes on free will and why God does bad things, but with hardly enough insight to justify the cost of his book, let alone a movie ticket.

Having Arlen Faber adapt as a man who may have lost his faith over the last two decades while the public clings to his words would have made for a radically different film. Since Hindman's script is already light on the romance and the comedy, it wouldn't have been such a leap of faith to head in the other, more interesting course. Daniels and Graham are enormously appealing actors but neither are able to get a firm grasp on these characters who keep getting jerked apart at the slightest suggestion that their everyday groove is being disturbed. Jim Carrey experienced the pitfalls of unanswered prayers in *Bruce Almighty* (2003) and Ricky Gervais twice now has been plagued with the annoyance of being a spiritual guide in *Ghost Town* (2008) and as the guy who conceived "the man in the clouds" in *The Invention of Lying* (2009). That film, in particular, challenged through humor and not condescension about the power one can have over others through blind devotion. As Arlen makes his big revelation in the final minutes to a horrified crowd—just as he's doing a favor to save Kris' store—we have to wonder where in Hindman's world are the doubting Thomases?

Who knows if this was the same guy that had the Lord on speed dial when he wrote his book? Maybe he found a new messiah when he saw Jack Nicholson's Melvin Udall in *As Good As It Gets* (1997). There he

could find inspiration on how to be introduced to movie audiences by swearing towards the front door when interrupted or how to fall in love with a single mom and her kid or even helping a third party through his father issues after being at odds with him early on. It's funny that the only thing missing to make this journey into a pure rip-off is an actual road trip. The primary difference is that Udall discovered the universal adapter of love to make him want to be a better man while Faber's search for answers elsewhere turned him into a bitter pill that no one should want to take and is incapable of curing the ills brought on by bad writing.

Erik Childress

CREDITS

Arlen Faber: Jeff Daniels
Elizabeth: Lauren Graham
Kris Lucas: Lou Taylor Pucci
Anne: Olivia Thirlby
Dahlia: Kat Dennings
Terry Fraser: Nora Dunn
Mailman: Tony Hale
Origin: USA
Language: English
Released: 2009
Production: Kevin J. Messick, Jana Edelbaum; 120 db Films, iDeal Partners Film Fund; released by Magnolia Pictures
Directed by: John Hindman
Written by: John Hindman
Cinematography by: Oliver Bokelberg
Music by: Teddy Castellucci
Sound: Bruce Litecky
Music Supervisor: Linda Cohen
Editing: Jerry Greenberg
Art Direction: Dawn Masi
Costumes: Rebbeca Bentjen
Production Design: Alex DiGerlando
MPAA rating: R
Running time: 96 minutes

REVIEWS

Ebert, Roger. *Chicago Sun-Times.* August 6, 2009.
Gleiberman, Owen. *Entertainment Weekly.* July 22, 2009.
Lemire, Christy. *Associated Press.* July 22, 2009.
Rabin, Nathan. *AV Club.* July 23, 2009.
Rickey, Carrie. *Philadelphia Inquirer.* April 2, 2009.
Schager, Nick. *Slant Magazine.* July 19, 2009.
Scott, A.O. *New York Times.* July 24, 2009.
Tallerico, Brian. *MovieRetriever.com.* August 7, 2009.

Taylor, Ella. *Village Voice.* July 21, 2009.
Whipp, Glenn. *Los Angeles Times.* July 24, 2009.

QUOTES

Kris Lucas: "So you're just like the rest of us."

ANTICHRIST

When nature turns evil, true terror awaits.
—Movie tagline

Possessing a unique skill set that includes a technical proficiency as well as an unbridled agitator's soul, Danish director Lars von Trier is one of the more controversial filmmakers working today. As one of the founders of the avant-garde Dogma movement, he at one point early in his career embraced obstructions seemingly at odds with the spirit of modern moviemaking, like a strict adherence to source lighting and sound, and working with handheld cameras and no constructed sets. Yet he is no stuffy, didactical art school Luddite interested only in precious, shoe-gazing chamber dramas; with the award-winning *Dancer in the Dark* (2000), von Trier took up digital technology with the feverish intensity of a religious convert, and with the comedy *The Boss of It All* (2007) he implemented "Automavision," in which camera angles and movements are determined by a computer. In between, with first *Dogville* (2003) and then *Manderlay* (2006), von Trier lobbed incendiary, starkly executed, allegorical cinematic grenades at what he saw as American hypocrisy, despite the fact that a fear of air travel has prevented him from ever visiting the United States.

Von Trier's most recent film, the unrated *Antichrist*, is seemingly built for divisiveness, as its evenly split 50 percent rotten rating on RottenTomatoes.com attests. A thematically dense, disturbingly explicit drama that centers around an unnamed couple who grapple with grief after losing their young son in a tragic accident, *Antichrist* might best be described, broadly speaking, as a psychological horror film about the mysterious distance between a man and woman. The graphic nature of some of its material, though—including sexual penetration and genital mutilation—ensured limited theatrical bookings in the United States, where distributor IFC Films pulled in a little bit more than $325,000 in a release that never extended to more than six cities and 19 screens.

As always, von Trier is well served by a good, base-level instinct for what unnerves—a fact which often masks his dark but quite plentiful sense of humor, which is still fitfully at play here, believe it or not. The best amalgamation of his knack for marrying confrontational theses with hypnotically artistic execution does not evidence itself in *Antichrist*, however, and the result is a work whose intellectual hold cannot match the brio with which it is told. If the reach of many movies exceeds their grasp, *Antichrist* is the rare, somewhat disorienting example of a film whose scene-to-scene grasp outweighs the sum total of its uncommitted, winkingly insincere reach.

It opens with a gorgeous, emotionally evocative, black-and-white love scene that feels like an engagement ring commercial gone horribly wrong. As husband and wife kiss, clinch and then copulate in slow motion, their toddler climbs out of his crib and tumbles from an open window to his death in the snow below, seemingly at the very moment of his mother's orgasm. The man (Willem Dafoe), it turns out, is a psychoanalyst who is cerebral to the point of emotional coldness. The woman (Charlotte Gainsbourg) is a writer who viewers eventually come to learn is working in semi-secret on a book called *Gynocide*, an academic treatise about feminine pagan religious history. After the incident, and against the off-screen advice of a colleague, the husband starts to treat his wife, eschewing pharmacology and instead digging into what he characterizes as her swallowed, deepest fears. His probing clinician's tone is met at first with barbs ("You're indifferent to whether your child is alive or dead"), and then sexual acting out. To try to repair their relationship, and in particular, in the man's eyes, his wife's damaged psyche, the duo then retreat to an isolated cabin deep in the woods, where...well, bad things happen.

The performances from Dafoe and Gainsbourg are intense, full-throttle things, almost calculatedly designed to elicit dutiful critical praise of their "braveness." If that seems a backhanded compliment, it is not meant as such; the pair wholly submit to von Trier's macabre dance, and each convey, in their own way, a gaping emotional hollowness that informs what on the written page are some outrageous words and deeds. Still, despite all this, one never forgets for a moment that *Antichrist* is meant first and foremost to be experienced through the authorial prism of auteurism. Working for the third time with Oscar®-winning cinematographer Anthony Dod Mantle, who utilizes a slight camera unsteadiness to subliminally invoke apprehension, von Trier crafts a warped, claustrophobic two-character study that pulses, especially early on, with anguish and trepidation.

Despite the manifest ambition and visual distinction of many of his works, von Trier seems in many ways only incidentally a film director, and foremost an artist for whom belligerent affront, monastic challenge and perhaps even willful self-promotion are the main aims. (Born Lars Trier, he added the "von" to his name in film school, as an affected homage to Josef von Sternberg.) In a recent interview with *H Magazine* around the time of his latest film's release, von Trier even admitted to pondering naked provocations in shaping his movies, saying, "I have discovered that what I very often do is take a subject or opinion that my mother would have disagreed with very much, and then I defend it. So it's very immature, and I can understand that people get provoked."

Antichrist in many ways confirms this interpretation of his work. Its characters have no formal names, aiding in a strict reading of them as stand-ins for their respective genders. The laundry list of narrative occurrences—genital mutilation, talking animals, the ejaculation of blood—also comes across as more of a checklist assault on polite cinema than necessarily part of a cogent story.

The skill with which von Trier pushes and pulls the levers of cinema cannot be denied. In *Antichrist* there are fleeting moments of elementally unnerving dread and panic the sort of which are rarely captured on film. And yet, steeped in such intractable grimness and mournful despair, the movie is also constructed in a way that seems resolutely designed to help conceal a conceptual thinness, or at least a lack of plumbing thematic insight. The movie seems, alternately, a searing, scornful repudiation of the notion of a merciful God, as well as an attack on the fundamental unpleasantness of nature. (The sounds of acorns raining down on the getaway cabin's roof from a nearby oak tree grow everlouder, and interstitial shots show animals crawling with maggots and literally eating their own.) It is also a stripped-bare gender power struggle; it is not for nothing that the place the couple repairs to is called Eden.

The overarching problem is that *Antichrist* never deeply explores and binds together these themes in a satisfactory way, to match in a viewer's head the visceral horror of some of what unfolds on screen. It noodles, in other words, which is perfectly fine for dramatic ensembles or a plucky character study which depicts people grappling with issues of love, faith, sex and fear—putting one foot in front of the other, talking through their issues and reaching some sort of conclusion that feels if not necessarily like cathartic growth or self-actualization, then at least informed by their actual experiences. For a film that otherwise trades in extreme polarities, however, this tack feels like a shambling put-on, like shock divorced of greater contextual mooring.

In its home stretch, *Antichrist* particularly stumbles. As man and woman grapple with their despair, and a gulf widens between them, argumentative plot points—old photographs of the couple's son mysteriously show him with shoes on the wrong feet, and those falling acorns start to grate—come across as stillborn metaphor.

By the time the movie reaches its graphic climax, the subject of much of the movie's buzz at its Cannes Film Festival presentation, there is not a deep psychological investment in the horror unfolding on the screen, just the vague notion that it feels nipped from a Lucio Fulci fever dream, and a queasy acknowledgment of its effective staging.

In essence, one endures *Antichrist* more than one enjoys, appreciates or admires it, even if one's personal reaction leans more toward the positive. There are some gut-punching flashes of anxiety along the way, but they seem incidental, and remind one of the old adage that even a broken clock is right twice a day.

Brent Simon

CREDITS

She: Charlotte Gainsbourg
He: Willem Dafoe
Origin: Denmark, Germany, France, Sweden, Italy, Poland
Language: English
Released: 2009
Production: Meta Louise Foldanger; Zentropa Entertainment, Memfis Film Intl., Lucky Red, Zentropa Intl. Kohn, Slot Machine; released by IFC Films
Directed by: Lars von Trier
Written by: Lars von Trier
Cinematography by: Anthony Dod Mantle
Sound: Andre Rigaut
Editing: Anders Refn
Art Direction: Tim Pannen
Costumes: Frauke Firl
Production Design: Karl Juliusson
MPAA rating: Unrated
Running time: 105 minutes

REVIEWS

Brunette, Peter. *Hollywood Reporter.* May 18, 2009.
Ebert, Roger. *Chicago Sun-Times.* October 22, 2009.
Hoberman, J. *Village Voice.* May 27, 2009.
Lane, Anthony. *New Yorker.* October 19, 2009.
McCarthy, Todd. *Variety.* May 18, 2009.
Pais, Matt. *Metromix.com.* October 22, 2009.
Phillips, Michael. *Chicago Tribune.* October 22, 2009.
Stevens, Dana. *Slate.* October 22, 2009.
Tallerico, Brian. *MovieRetriever.com.* October 22, 2009.
Travers, Peter. *Rolling Stone.* October 15, 2009.

QUOTES

He: "Why did you give up? That's not like you."

TRIVIA

A video game based on the movie has been announced by the movie's production company Zentropa. The game "Eden" would supposedly be a continuation of the story.

ANVIL! THE STORY OF ANVIL

At fourteen, they made a pact to rock together forever. They meant it.
—Movie tagline

In the early 1980s, Canadian metal band Anvil was poised to make it big. They shared the stage at a Japanese Super Rock Festival with the likes of Whitesnake, Bon Jovi and Scorpions, and their single, "Metal on Metal," was the anthem for many young rockers. But nothing happened. Instead of rocketing to super stardom, Anvil pretty much vanished from the metal scene leaving many fans and colleagues scratching their heads. In "Where Are They Now?" fashion, the documentary, *Anvil! The Story Of Anvil*, reconnects with the two founding band members twenty-plus years after their almost success looking to uncover how and why a band with so much promise when nowhere. It turns out that the musicians have never stopped rocking-out—they have even released twelve studio albums, nor have they stopped wanting to become famous. Their drive to get their music heard—at times both inspiring and foolhardy—is the basis for this affecting and absorbing film destined to appeal to anyone who ever thought of trekking on the path less traveled.

When they were 14 years old, Steve "Lips" Kudlow and Rob Reiner started a band and wrote songs based on what they were studying in school. "Thumb Hang," for example, was inspired by lessons on the Spanish Inquisition. Now, at 50, Anvil's lead singer (Kudlow) and drummer (Reiner), look like other aging rockers parading around on VH1, clad in leather jackets and sporting long, albeit thinning, hair. The only difference is that instead of coming home to California mansions after arena tours, they play local halls in Toronto and hold down mundane day jobs between gigs, hoping to scrape together enough cash to pay for another recording session. Both Lips and Reiner are hard pressed to definitively answer the question "what went wrong?" citing everything from bad management to infighting as reasons for why Anvil never became a household name. The reason, if there is only one, becomes more difficult to discern the more time spent with the members of Anvil. When we see the band endure a shoddily organized European tour, it is easy to wonder if they did, in fact, settle for what they could get in terms of

record contracts and managers instead of striving for the best. When we hear from family members that span the spectrum from endlessly encouraging to completely doubtful, it's easy to think that maybe the boys felt too much pressure to live "normal" lives. And as we watch as Lips and Reiner exercise their creative and personal demons, it sparks the idea that they simply had too much baggage to carry along the road to fame.

Director Sacha Gervasi doesn't focus on assigning blame however, saving *Anvil* from becoming an elongated version of *I Love The 1980s*, full of eulogies to what might have been and bad hair photo montages. Instead *Anvil* reads like *Spinal Tap* meets *Metallica: Some Kind Of Monster*, a rock-heavy doc that concentrates on showcasing the complex lives of two driven and committed musicians holding on to their dreams despite increasingly insurmountable odds. And that is where the charm of this wonderful story lies. Gervasi sets up Anvil for viewers who may not be familiar with the band by interviewing known legends like Guns N' Roses Slash and Metallica's Lars Ulrich, each of whom give props to Anvil. Gervasi is obviously a fan; he approaches his subject matter with passion, making Lips' and Reiner's drive to succeed feel heroic at times. But despite his musical tastes, Gervasi keeps *Anvil* balanced. It is this measured insight into the lives of two guys holding on to their childhood dream for dear life that makes *Anvil* such a winning doc. Seeing Lips keep the faith while making deliveries for his subpar catering gig or grinning like the Cheshire cat whenever he receives positive feedback from an industry professional sucks the viewer in. And metal lover or not, it is impossible not to root for this underdog band as they line up for yet another 11am slot on a festival bill knowing that the crowd turnout will be minimal. Gervasi delivers the goods with photos and video from the 1980s, chronicling Lips' exhibitionism and Reiner's mad skills, but early into the film the camera melts away and the feels like the experience of just hanging out with the band—a band the viewer will want to see succeed. In as much as *Anvil* sets up a potential renaissance for Lips and Reiner, it also introduces Gervasi as a skilled director and storyteller, able to draw out a real time narrative structure that is not only surprisingly fulfilling, but as funny as it is touching.

Joanna Topor MacKenzie

CREDITS

Himself: Steve "Lips" Kudlow
Himself: Robb Reiner
Origin: USA
Language: English

Released: 2009

Production: Rebecca Yeldham; A Little Dean and Ahimsa Films; released by Abramorama Films

Directed by: Sacha Gervasi

Cinematography by: Christopher Soos

Sound: Mat Dennis

Music Supervisor: Dana Sano

Editing: Jeff Renfroe, Andrew Dickler

MPAA rating: Unrated

Running time: 90 minutes

REVIEWS

Ebert, Roger. *Chicago Sun-Times.* April 23, 2009.

Edelstein, David. *New York Magazine.* April 6, 2009.

Gleiberman, Owen. *Entertainment Weekly.* April 8, 2009.

Harvey, Dennis. *Variety.* January 28, 2008.

Lane, Anthony. *New Yorker.* April 13, 2009.

Pais, Matt. *Metromix.com.* April 9, 2009.

Scott, A.O. *New York Times.* April 10, 2009.

Stevens, Dana. *Slate.* April 10, 2009.

Tallerico, Brian. *MovieRetriever.com.* April 8, 2009.

Turan, Kenneth. *Los Angeles Times.* April 10, 2009.

QUOTES

Tiziana Arrigoni: "'S' like Sodom."

AWARDS

Ind. Spirit 2010: Feature Doc.

Nomination:

Directors Guild 2009: Doc. Director (Gervasi).

ARMORED

They have a plan that's going to catch everybody off-guard.
—Movie tagline

Armored opens with pulsing music and extreme close-ups of tight-lipped tough guys—a group of security guards who act like they are in the military special forces. Working for a fictionalized company named Eagle Shield, they meet at the crack of dawn for morning chalk talks led by their grizzled supervisor (the veteran Fred Ward). They trade legends about dangerous holdups. One man, Baines (Laurence Fishburne), shows off his big gun in the locker room. These men of few words are itching for action.

Despite the overwrought direction by Nimrod Antal (*Vacancy*), and a script by James V. Simpson that is not nearly as clever or as complicated as it needs to be to carry this genre thriller, *Armored* succeeds in casting a kind of noir-ish B-movie spell. It all takes place in a gritty world of graffiti-tagged streets, abandoned steel mills, and industrial ruins. Given how circumscribed their worlds are, and how little we know about their backgrounds or dreams, it is a little surprising how much these men are willing to risk to rob their own company and escape with some cool millions. Escape to where? What? These hard-bitten, going-nowhere guys do not look or act like they have be comfortable anywhere but in their trucks.

To be sure, there are loyalties and longstanding relationships involving some of the six men who plot the heist. Mike (Matt Dillon) has a sister who married Baines, a prankster with a tendency toward a short fuse. Mike also declares that Ty Hackett (Columbus Short) and his younger brother Jimmy (Andre Kinney) are "like family" to him. Mike was close friends with the brothers' parents, who have both recently died. Ty has just come back from Iraq with a Silver Star; he's a self-effacing war hero with a heroism that is clearly going to be tested. The first test comes when Mike lets him in on the group's plan to stage a holdup of their own trucks. At first, following standard script rules, Ty refuses; but then a state childhood welfare agent shows up and threatens to take Jimmy away from him because the teenage boy has been missing school. It's a clumsy and preposterous plot device—does any American state really mind its teenagers that closely—but it does the job, putting Ty in desperate straits.

When Ty tells Mike he'll go along with the scheme, he makes Mike promise no one will get hurt. If Mike is the mastermind of the scheme, he does not seem to have a very meticulously plotted plan. With the volatile Baines on board, plus a sullen Bible-reading quiet man (Amaury Nolasco), a jittery coward (Skeet Ulrich), and a cool but vaguely menacing veteran (Jean Reno), the film presents a standard cast of loose cannons.

It's no surprise when the plan goes awry, and it's not shocking how each of the men react. Dillon, who has come to specialize in parts like this, plays his character as a razor's-edge thinker, willing to do anything to make the plan work once it's set in motion—if for no other reason than sheer stubbornness. Part of the problem with *Armored* is that there is so little back story that it is never clear how these men have reached points of such extreme desperation.

Simpson's script follows the rules for awhile and then just abandons them. There's the mandatory ticking clock for action thrillers—provided by a fifty-five-minute window between times when the armored trucks have to check into dispatch. Once the plan goes awry, Mike begins counting down how much time is left, but our last update is at thirty-six minutes—and then the script just lets the clock go.

What does draw the audience in to this story is Antal's attentiveness to small details. There is a beautiful setup for the young cop (Milo Ventimiglia) who will be drawn into the heist scene when it unravels; he's at a hot dog stand talking to the owner about his late father, and then he's seen there again as he hears the siren that tips him off to something amiss at the abandoned steel mill where the guards are floundering. You see his babyish face against a dying-light backdrop of the lunch stand, and it's a sudden and powerful image of fate and destiny.

For the most part, this is a surprisingly quiet and thoughtful movie, given the action genre it's situated in. It is men against machine, as the plotters spend most of their time trying to break into their own armored truck, which leads to a lot of scenes of endless hammering at steel pins. It's not the most fantastic stuff, but the sense of hard work and frustration is somewhat evocative. There are a couple of armored car chase scenes, and some gunfire and bloody demises as the expected showdown looms between the protagonists, but that showdown is actually underplayed. Instead of the interminable violent, bloody confrontation you've come to expect in such movies, it's quick and fairly quiet and rather economical. Give credit to *Armored* for believing in this small story, even though it's not the most elegant or intricate or surprising one. Instead of going over the top to disguise its lack of new materials, the director sticks to the basics, and, for that, *Armored* earns some quiet and unexpected style points.

Michael Betzold

CREDITS

Ty Hackett: Columbus Short
Quinn: Jean Reno
Baines: Laurence Fishburne
Dobbs: Skeet Ulrich
Palmer: Amaury Nolasco
Ashcroft: Fred Ward
Mike Cochrane: Matt Dillon
Eckehart: Milo Ventimiglia
Jimmy Hackett: Andre Jamal Kinney
Origin: USA
Language: English
Released: 2009
Production: Josh Donen, Dan Farah; Stars Road Entertainment; released by Screen Gems
Directed by: Nimrod Antal
Written by: James V. Simpson
Cinematography by: Andrzej Sekula

Music by: John Murphy
Sound: Joseph Geisinger
Editing: Armen Minasian
Art Direction: Chris Cornwell
Costumes: Maya Leberman
Production Design: Jon Gary Steele
MPAA rating: PG-13
Running time: 88 minutes

REVIEWS

Collis, Clark. *Entertainment Weekly.* December 4, 2009.
Douglas, Edward. *ComingSoon.net.* December 4, 2009.
Gonzalez, Ed. *Slant Magazine.* December 4, 2009.
Moore, Roger. *Orlando Sentinel.* December 4, 2009.
Nelson, Rob. *Variety.* December 4, 2009.
Neumaier, Joe. *New York Daily News.* December 4, 2009.
Rechtshaffen, Michael. *Hollywood Reporter.* December 4, 2009.
Scott, A.O. *New York Times.* December 7, 2009.
Tobias, Scott. *AV Club.* December 4, 2009.
Whipp, Glenn. *Los Angeles Times.* December 7, 2009.

TRIVIA

There is only one woman who has a speaking role in the movie: the child protection agent, but her role is shorter than four minutes.

ASTRO BOY

Have a blast.
—Movie tagline

Box Office: $19 million

Astro Boy fails not because it Westernizes a beloved Japanese character but because it does so with such minimal effect for such minimal reasons. In fact, the film strips virtually all of the original character's seminal power away in a manner that suggests deliberate homogenization; as if someone said, "You know this anime stuff would be pretty neat if only it weren't so Japanese." Like the recent live action *Dragonball Evolution* (2009), and the Wachowski Brothers' sad adaptation of *Speed Racer* (2008), this film confection just barely qualifies as vanilla. But instead of vanilla ice cream this "treat" is more vanilla-tinged plain yogurt made to fool the kids into thinking they are eating something sweeter. How sad that in an age where stateside audiences are exposed to more world cinema than ever before that studios still dumb down the raw power of what has given these properties such long legs. Unlike the original *Astro Boy*, which was quintessentially Japanese in the way it handled the character's struggle with identity, this new incarnation is far from quintessentially American. It says nothing about American society and that struggle, ignoring it in favor of staging a series of predictable action sequences and even more predictable sentimentalist overtures designed to neatly tie up the emotional baggage the story flirts with.

Osama Tezuka's character Astro Boy started out as a manga in the early fifties and within ten years made its debut as what is now commonly understood as the first anime cartoon running on Japanese television from 1963 to 1966. To call both incarnations seminal is to grossly underestimate their cultural and social significance. *Astro Boy* introduced two primary things to the wide American audience. One was a style of art that has come to be intensely identified with Japanese culture in general and has had a huge influence on graphic art and popular culture stateside. The other was the theme of the robot and in particular the robot and the boy which has been ubiquitous in Japanese live action and anime series. Examples like *Johnny Sokko and His Flying Robot* (1967) and *Tetsujin 28-go* (1964, released as *Gigantor* in the U.S.), though English-dubbed, made it to the states culturally intact and accepted whole heartedly for what they were, making the changes to *Astro Boy* all the more wrong-headed.

The movie takes place in the future metropolis of Metro City where a brilliant scientist, Dr Tenma (Nicolas Cage) creates a high powered flying robot, Astro Boy, (Freddie Highmore) in his recently-deceased son's image only to reject him when he realizes that his son is truly gone forever. Left alone to find his true place in the world, Astro Boy embarks on a journey that carries him through rejection, triumph and self-discovery only to discover that he must return to his former home, Metro City, to put his amazing powers to the ultimate test and reconnect with his creator.

Former animator and storyboard artist David Bowers (the underrated *Flushed Away* [2006]) directs from a screenplay by Timothy Harris (*Trading Places* [1983], *Brewster's Millions* [1985], *Twins* [1988] *Kindergarten Cop* [1990], *Space Jam* [1996]) and is assisted by cinematographer Pepe Valencia, whose impressive animation credits (*The Polar Express* [2004], *Monster House* [2006], *Beowulf* [2007]) should have sealed the deal on an A-list production.

Likewise the experienced and talented leads including Freddie Highmore (*The Spiderwick Chronicles* [2007], *August Rush* [2007] *Arthur and The Invisibles* [2006], *Charlie and the Chocolate Factory* [2005]), who is fine as Astro Boy, exuding a dynamic enthusiasm and Nicolas Cage who sounds like he might actually be having fun here. Besides those listed above, *Astro Boy* boasts a plethora of great talents whose credits are so well-known that they scarcely bear mention; Samuel L. Jackson as Zog, fabulous character actor Bill Nighy as Dr. Elefun, Donald Sutherland as President Stone, Eugene Levy as Orrin, and Nathan Lane as Ham Egg.

What went wrong? Such a list could suggest overkill on the part of nervous producers who had already been through two directors, Eric Leighton (*Dinosaur* [2000]) and the renowned Genndy Tartakovsky (creator of *Dexter's Laboratory*, *Samurai Jack* and director of *Star Wars: Clone Wars* [2003-2005]). There were even rumors, as late as January of 2009, that production had been entirely shut down. The irony of a popular *Astro Boy* quote from the film is evident here, "I was made ready." On the contrary, all indications are that *Astro Boy* was simply readymade for a large opening weekend and decent DVD sales. *Astro Boy* will not be remembered for an influential animation style or for its cultural significance or even simple concerns about the individual search for meaning. It will not likely, in fact, be remembered any more than the cheap imitators of the original *Astro Boy* TV cartoon, which drew 40% of the TV viewing population of Japan at its height, will be.

In the 1950s, a wildly popular Japanese film was altered for American audiences with shots of Raymond Burr and other new American characters added to make the story more friendly to American audiences. That film, *Gojira* (1954), became *Godzilla; King of the Monsters* (1956). And, while it spread the character to a huge audience, the original film— with its highly developed themes of suffering under war, the dangers of technology, and man's responsibility to work for peace even at the risk of self sacrifice—was buried beneath what became an understanding of the film's main character as a kitsch icon. *Astro Boy* plays like someone saw that coming and decided to beat it to the punch.

Dave Canfield

CREDITS

Astro Boy/Toby: Freddie Highmore (Voice)
Dr. Tenma: Nicolas Cage (Voice)
President Stone: Donald Sutherland (Voice)
Cora: Kristen Bell (Voice)
Dr. Elefun/Robotsky: Bill Nighy (Voice)
Hamegg: Nathan Lane (Voice)
Orrin: Eugene Levy (Voice)
Sparx: Matt Lucas (Voice)
Zog: Samuel L. Jackson (Voice)
Narrator: Charlize Theron
Origin: USA, Hong Kong, Japan
Language: English
Released: 2009

Production: Maryann Garger; Imagi Animation Studios; released by Summit Entertainment
Directed by: David Bowers
Written by: Timothy Harris
Cinematography by: Pepe Valencia
Music by: John Ottman
Sound: James Bolt
Music Supervisor: Todd Homme
Editing: Robert Anich Cole
Art Direction: Jake Rowell
Costumes: Jane Poole
Production Design: Samuel Michlap
MPAA rating: PG
Running time: 94 minutes

REVIEWS

Barker, Andrew. *Variety.* October 15, 2009.
Corliss, Richard. *Time Magazine.* October 23, 2009.
Dargis, Manohla. *New York Times.* October 23, 2009.
Ebert, Roger. *Chicago Sun-Times.* October 22, 2009.
Gleiberman, Owen. *Entertainment Weekly.* October 21, 2009.
Lemire, Christy. *Associated Press.* October 21, 2009.
Long, Tom. *Detroit News.* October 23, 2009.
Pais, Matt. *Metromix.com.* October 22 2009.
Phillips, Michael. *Chicago Tribune.* October 22, 2009.
Snider, Eric D. *Film.com.* October 23, 2009.

QUOTES

Astro Boy: "I've got machine guns! In my butt!"

TRIVIA

Reports in late January 2009 stated that production had appeared, at the time, to have shut down, possibly due to the recession.

AVATAR

Enter the world.
    —Movie tagline

Box Office: $740.9 million

Based on various reports, the timeline for the development of *Avatar* changes. Some cite the twelve years since James Cameron's last epic, *Titanic* (1997); fifteen years since he thought of the idea; the movie he has been wanting to see since he was a wee little tyke. Mr. Cameron himself has used terms like "game changer" and "revolutionary"; the brand of science fiction spectacle that puts it on the groundbreaking visual effects level of *2001: A Space Odyssey* (1968), *Star Wars* (1977) and *Jurassic Park* (1993). When not being

trumped by Steven Spielberg, Robert Zemeckis or Peter Jackson, Cameron has been at the forefront of the next generation of filmmaking technology and his action spectaculars, one after the next, have produced new thrills that define the old adage of the money being on the screen. That is certainly true of *Avatar*, with every frame taking the depth of its 3-D motion-captured images to the maximum. But, like a fanciful dream without the meaning intact, Cameron's film suffers from a substandard screenplay that cannot escape its decidedly 1-D nature even when the film depends on it.

In the year 2154, the planet Earth is dying; a fact audiences do not hear too much about until it's explicitly spelled out late in the story. On the planet Pandora there is a precious mineral that holds the key to our survival, yet the indigenous species, the Na'vi, will not give it up. The humans have tried diplomacy, but cannot get an ounce. The corporate types like Parker Selfridge (Giovanni Ribisi) are desperate to get their hands on it and the military, led by Col. Miles Quaritch (Stephen Lang) is itching to scorch the woodland landscape to take it by force. Science is hoping to find another way. Under development by Dr. Grace Augustine (Sigourney Weaver) is a method by which the humans can interact with the Na'vi people while adapting to the atmosphere without their menacing gas masks. DNA of both species have been combined and grown into living, breathing ciphers known as avatars, beings that the humans can control via mind control in high-tech sun tanning beds. The bad news for them is that their prime subject has been killed in battle.

Lucky for them that he has a twin brother with a comparable life code. Jake Sully (Sam Worthington) is paralyzed, but that only helps sweeten the deal in getting him to volunteer. The avatar gives him the opportunity to walk, virtually, again and there is a promise on the table to get his real legs repaired if he does some reconnaissance work for Col. Quaritch. Perhaps a little overeager and ignorant to the indigenous creatures on the planet, Jake is nearly killed his first day out only to be rescued by the Na'vi Neyteri (Zoe Saldana). Aware that he is not of their kind, there is the usual uneasy symbiosis at first. When some flying dandelion angels decide to embrace this new being though, Neyteri takes it as a sign that she should to, thus showing Jake the ropes of bow hunting and how to make free creatures his personal transportation device. Back at the human compound, Jake's colleagues and supervisors begin to question his loyalty and the containment of Pandora may be reaching a fever pitch.

Structurally, the parts of *Avatar* reflect Cameron's epic *Titanic*. Establish a time and place not of their own to the viewers. Introduce a pair of would-be lovers from vastly different classes/cultures/species and watch as their relationship blossoms. Soon after consummation of their union, hit them with an iceberg or some kind of military hardware that disrupts their future plans and thrusts them into a final, sprawling battle for survival. Knowing where this journey is headed beat-by-beat, as anyone who has seen *Dances With Wolves* (1990), *The Last Samurai* (2003), *Joe Kidd* (1972) or even *The Ten Commandments* (1956) should attest, it gives us more time to appreciate the visual beauty dominating nearly every frame and to recognize that our involvement with the characters' journey is not nearly where it was with Jack and Rose.

Problems begin with our hero, Jake, who early on is not one who commands sympathy nor attention. As Grace is quick to point out, clearing his mind is likely not a difficult proposition for him and the audience is never invited into that empty space to get a clear grasp of his loyalty. Disrespected by his fellow grunts for his ability to do little, the desire to feel a want of purpose or just for his legs is never clear-cut since Worthington's performance is as much of a blank slate as his character and the screenplay never takes a moment for anyone to honestly address his role as a double-or-triple agent. Sure his fellow Avatarian scientist buddy (Joel David Moore) looks disapprovingly upon the Intel he is providing to the Colonel, but in the next scene they are all chummy again with the on-the-nose narration provided by Jake telling us that everything is cool between them again.

There is a fundamental miscalculation within the relationship between the humans and the Na'vi as well. They know what the humans want while they occupy their homeland. The humans know they won't give it to them no matter how many gifts are exchanged. The genetically-engineered avatars are more than just a breathing apparatus since the whole point is to either reason face-to-face in their own skin or infiltrate their ranks unknowingly. Best laid plans are rather pointless since Neytiri clearly sizes Jake up as an impostor right away and her people have clearly experienced enough of this to brand them with the name of "dream walkers." And if they are aware of the who and the what, then why do they accept Jake as just in it for the plant jumping and interspecies thrills? Because he was chosen by the dandelion angels? Certainly Jake's true belief system is a hazy, muted lot on par with the Na'vi's firm stance against killing—except in cases of defense and hunger pains.

All eyes will be rack focused squarely on the bright colors and dense palette of the characters' surroundings: Truly a sight to behold from a visual effects perspective, particularly in the case of the Na'vi themselves. With specially designed head-rig cameras invented by Cameron himself, he is able to film every nuance of the ac-

tors' facial expressions. They go into the camera human and Cameron can see them on the other side as their blue-skinned, ten-foot-tall counterparts. Ironically enough, in an effort to eliminate the criticized "dead-eyed" look of films *The Polar Express* (2004) and *Beowulf* (2007), the window into the soul still has not filled in the emptiness felt by watching characters, CG or not, whom the audience does not care about. The seduction of *Avatar* from a technical viewpoint will be greatly tempting, and few filmmakers can piece together an action sequence of depth, fury, and purpose better than Cameron.

During the interim of Cameron's absence, technological breakthroughs have been at the service of some of the very best and very worst blockbusters of the early 21st century. From the subtle robotics of *A.I.: Artificial Intelligence* (2001) to Peter Jackson's bravura retelling of *King Kong* (2005) and the *Lord of the Rings* (2001) trilogy to the hell hath fury of Michael Bay's more-(but really less)-than meets the eye films, special effects companies are not going to go out of business anytime soon. Look at *Avatar*'s pedigree though and consider how just 2009 alone produced films that took fully explored interesting new worlds. The continuation of the *Harry Potter* series, *Where The Wild Things Are* and *Up*, the latter also presented in 3-D. All three films were intelligent tales aimed at children with enough creative shrapnel to hit adults square in the heart all the while using their computer-generated images to service the richness of the writing and characters instead of the other way around.

That wincing effect some *Avatar* viewers felt came not from the occasional headache caused by the 3-D glasses but due to the poorly fleshed out motivations that pass as the evolution to the grand showdown. Folded into the mystery of why the benevolent Na'vi would not want to help the humans preserve their race is a spiritual connection that they maintain with the trees. Less an aspect of going "green" than not wanting their radio for speaking to God hitting dead air, the religious temperament does not follow the path to fanaticism that it might if this was a fully-fleshed Middle East parable. The audience is asked to put faith in their beliefs and elevate its importance over the cause of philanthropy. This could just be Pandora's punishment for humanity as prescribed in Greek mythology with hope resting firmly at the bottom of its box. Genocide-for-a-genocide may not be the best solution, but with such a one-note gung-ho at the command like Lang's Quaritch at the helm it is the only way to provide a rooting interest with the hypocritically selfish Blue Meanies. How the Colonel allows Rodriguez's pilot to abandon a mission midstream and not either court martial or shoot her upon return to base (giving her carte blanche to break her fellow civic-minded rank breakers from jail) is just one of the many lapses in consistency with *Avatar*'s primary antagonist and what all the fighting is about.

For some, the disconnect between the hypnosis with the groundbreaking aspects of *Avatar* and the familiarity that is too obtrusive to overcome will be vast. Forgiveness of the acting and the dialogue may be the play of the day just as it was when such elements were looked over in 1977 with *Star Wars*. Those same people grew up twenty-two years later to then criticize the same symbiosis with *Episode I*. Ten years later that same uneasy mix manifests in *Avatar* and one need look no further than a simple little gem such as Duncan Jones' *Moon* (2009) to find a low-tech sci-fi film that wonderfully interjects its mission against environmental extinction with the uneasy relationship between corporate bottom lines and the isolation of our need to act like human beings. If only the high-tech *Avatar* could have found the same human element to make the wait between Cameron films worth the hype.

Erik Childress

CREDITS

Jake Sully: Sam Worthington
Neytiri: Zoe Saldana
Trudy Chacon: Michelle Rodriguez
Dr. Grace Augustine: Sigourney Weaver
Parker Selfridge: Giovanni Ribisi
Tsu'Tey: Laz Alonso
Eytukan: Wes Studi
Col. Milo Quarich: Stephen Lang
Moha: CCH Pounder
Norm Spellman: Joel David Moore
Origin: USA
Language: English
Released: 2009
Production: James Cameron, Jon Landau; Lightstorm Entertainment, Giant Studios, Dune Entertainment, Ingenious Film Partners; released by 20th Century Fox
Directed by: James Cameron
Written by: James Cameron
Cinematography by: Mauro Fiore, Mauro Fiore
Music by: James Horner
Sound: James Tanenbaum, William B. Kaplan
Editing: James Cameron, John Refoua, Stephen E. Rivkin
Visual Effects: Joe Letteri, Stephen Rosenbaum, Richard Baneham, Andy Jones
Costumes: Mayes C. Rubeo, Deborah L. Scott
Production Design: Rick Carter, Robert Stromberg
MPAA rating: PG-13
Running time: 163 minutes

REVIEWS

Corliss, Richard. *Time Magazine*. December 14, 2009.
Ebert, Roger. *Chicago Sun-Times*. December 11, 2009.
Hoberman, J. *Village Voice*. December 15, 2009.
Honeycutt, Kirk. *Hollywood Reporter*. December 10, 2009.
Keough, Peter. *Boston Phoenix*. December 16, 2009.
McCarthy, Todd. *Variety*. December 10, 2009.
Phillips, Michael. *Chicago Tribune*. December 11, 2009.
Tallerico, Brian. *MovieRetriever.com*. December 16, 2009.
Tobias, Scott. *AV Club*. December 17, 2009.
Turan, Kenneth. *Los Angeles Times*. December 17, 2009.

QUOTES

Jake: "Everything is backwards now, like out there is the true world and in here is the dream."
Col. Quaritch: "A Marine in an Avatar body? Gives me the goosebumps!"

TRIVIA

The movie is 40% live action and 60% photo-realistic CGI. A lot of motion capture technology was used for the CGI scenes

AWARDS

Oscars 2009: Art Dir./Set Dec., Cinematog., Visual FX
British Acad. 2009: Visual FX, Prod. Des.
Golden Globes 2010: Director, Film—Drama
Nomination:
Oscars 2009: Director (Cameron), Film, Film Editing, Sound, Sound FX Editing, Orig. Score
British Acad. 2009: Cinematog., Director (Cameron), Film, Film Editing, Sound, Orig. Score
Directors Guild 2009: Director (Cameron)
Golden Globes 2010: Song ("I See You"), Orig. Score
Writers Guild 2009: Orig. Screenplay.

AWAY WE GO

Box Office: $9 million

Away We Go tells the story of an unmarried couple in their thirties who are about to have their first baby. The pregnancy itself is a bit of a shock to them, but they accept it. Inevitably, they ponder how they could possibly support this baby, since neither one of them is financially stable. But the bigger question in the film becomes "who should the child's secondary influence be?" The couple, completely untethered to any kind of responsibility at their current address (they both do freelance work), set out on a cross country quest for the perfect influence amongst their friends and relatives and to find themselves a new sense of "home." They get mixed results, ranging from the most ignorant of parental behavior to the flakiest.

The couple is Burt (John Krasinski) and Verona (Maya Rudolph). Burt's parents (Jeff Daniels and Catherine O'Hara) live nearby, but are on the verge of living one of their lifelong dreams (a new life in Antwerp), completely oblivious to the fact that their newfound sense of freedom has completely dashed Burt and Verona's hope for a stable family environment. After this bit of bad news, Burt and Verona set off to Arizona where they meet up with Verona's friends, Lily (Allison Janney) and Lowell (Jim Gaffigan), a married couple with two pre-teen children who may as well be mute. Lily talks endlessly without a filter and Lowell can only speak quietly with cynicism and apocalyptic notions.

Realizing this would not be a good enough "home," Burt and Verona make their way to Tucson to meet up with a slightly more well-adjusted sister Grace (Carmen Ejogo), but then retreat to Wisconsin to visit Burt's childhood friend Ellen (Maggie Gyllenhaal), now a mother who has gone off the new-age deep end and who goes by the more pretentious name of LN. The journey takes Burt and Verona to several different and dysfunctional scenarios, with a stop in Montreal offering them the only glimmer of hope.

The film is directed by Sam Mendes and came only six months after his hot-tempered tale of a marital breakdown, *Revolutionary Road* (2008). It could be argued that Mendes is forming something of a marital (or anti-marital) trilogy with *Revolutionary Road, Away We Go* and his Oscar®-winning *American Beauty* (1999). All three films, in their own way, thumb their noses at the notion of a perfect marriage being the end-all, be-all of true suburban happiness. But while *American Beauty* and *Revolutionary Road* take their stories to violent extremes, *Away We Go* keeps its tone gentle and hopeful, with the two leads opting to never, ever officially tie the knot, but instead make sweet promises to one another that, in their own special way, resemble the very marriage vows spoken regularly at the altar.

The film also displays a noticeable change in style from the director's past major studio efforts. *Away We Go* has the feel of a first or second-time indie director trying to make a name for themselves on the festival circuit. The movie inserts chapter marks every time Burt and Verona's journey takes a turn ("AWAY TO TUSCON," "AWAY TO MONTREAL," etc.). Scottish singer/songwriter Alexi Murdoch's music, which invites inevitable comparisons to Nick Drake, lends greatly to the film's gentle, easy-going nature. Overall, the film could also be the final chapter of another trilogy of sorts, that of the crowd-pleasing, surprise hit indies that started with *Little Miss Sunshine* (2006) (quirky roadtrip and dysfunctional families) and *Juno* (2007) (quirky pregnancy). It's a wonder the movie received an early summer release as opposed to the more traditional awards season (autumn and after).

Other than Mendes' change of pace, there's nothing particularly new on the surface of *Away We Go*, but the screenplay by cult favorite author Dave Eggers and his wife Vendela Vida and the charming cast make everything feel so fresh and vital, that it hardly matters. The movie has many original moments to make up for its pedestrian storyline. There is a scene late in the film in which one of Burt's friends confides in him that his wife had another in a series of miscarriages, all while she performs an alternately sad and sultry pole dance at an "amateur night" strip club to the tune of the Velvet Underground's devastating "Oh! Sweet Nuthin'." Even Verona's line (and others like it) "How can we take care of this baby? We can't even take care of ourselves. We have a cardboard window" has its own poetic touch. Krasinski and Rudolph seem perfectly at ease with the material, which is careful to make these two people sympathetic, but not always likable.

In the end, *Away We Go* is more about finding a sense of "home" within yourself and making peace with your past than about finding an agreeable, secondary source of happiness in one's surroundings. It comes to this conclusion in an unexpected way that could have easily come off as trite and disingenuous, but Mendes and his team play it out without a hint of cynicism or over-sincerity. It's "perfect," because to these people, something in this world has to be, so why not this?

Collin Souter

CREDITS

Burt: John Krasinski
Jerry Farlander: Jeff Daniels
LN Fisher-Herrin: Maggie Gyllenhaal
Munch Garnett: Melanie Lynskey
Verona: Maya Rudolph
Lily: Allison Janney
Gloria Farlander: Catherine O'Hara
Lowell: Jim Gaffigan
Grace: Carmen Ejogo
Roderick: Josh Hamilton
Tom: Chris Messina
Courtney: Paul Schneider
Origin: USA
Language: English
Released: 2009
Production: Edward Saxon, Marc Turtletaub, Peter Saraf; Big Beach, Neal Street Productions; released by Focus Features
Directed by: Sam Mendes
Written by: Dave Eggers, Vendela Vida
Cinematography by: Ellen Kuras

Music by: Alex Murdoch
Sound: Benjamin Patrick
Music Supervisor: Randall Poster
Editing: Sarah Flack
Art Direction: Henry Dunn
Costumes: John Dunn
Production Design: Jess Gonchor
MPAA rating: R
Running time: 97 minutes

REVIEWS

Denby, David. *New Yorker.* June 1, 2009.
Ebert, Roger. *Chicago Sun-Times.* June 11, 2009.
Gleiberman, Owen. *Entertainment Weekly.* June 3, 2009.
Lacey, Liam. *Globe and Mail.* June 12, 2009.

Lasalle, Mick. *San Francisco Chronicle.* June 12, 2009.
Long, Tom. *Detroit News.* June 12, 2009.
Phillips, Michael. *Chicago Tribune.* June 11, 2009.
Puig, Claudia. *USA Today.* June 5, 2009.
Scott, A.O. *New York Times.* June 5, 2009.
Turan, Kenneth. *Los Angeles Times.* June 5, 2009.

QUOTES

LN Fisher-Herrin: "I love my babies. Why would I want to push them away from me?"

TRIVIA

Melanie Lynskey, who plays Munch in the film, made her screen debut in *Heavenly Creatures* with Kate Winslet.

B

THE BAADER MEINHOF COMPLEX

The children of the Nazi generation vowed fascism would never rule their world again.
—Movie tagline

German-born director Uli Edel has spent most of his career in the television industry of his home country. His feature film's *Last Exit to Brooklyn* (1989) and *The Little Vampire* (2000) are not widely known and prepare the viewer not at all for this extraordinary and lengthy historical drama dealing with the formation and activities of the notorious 1970s German terrorist group the Red Army Faction.

By the 1970s, Germany had begun to deeply feel the generational divide. Haunted by the previous generation's Nazi past and spurred on by fears of a coming new fascism that would be led via American Imperialism and its influence over German society and government, any number of youth led protest movements made themselves felt. But the most famous and notorious of these, the Red Army Faction, was different in that it became deeply radicalized, planning and taking part in a variety of terrorist actions including but not limited to bombings, bank robberies and assassinations.

Germany's official submission to the Best Foreign Language Film Category of the 81st Annual Academy Awards® (2009) clocks in at 150-plus minutes and offers a stunning historical overview of the formation, activities and eventual self destruction of the group and is reportedly controversial due to its claim to fairly represent all sides in the conflict. Based on Stefan Aust's

book, *The Baader Meinhof Complex* is shot in a striking documentary style that emphasizes the human element of the history in question and succeeds in doing what few films of its type ever do—offering a gut level truth of the effects of violence on the perpetrators, be that violence politically motivated or a matter of simple vengeance. Viewers will watch a German society at war with itself as much as with any terrorist faction, and look on as those who demand a more human world become less and less human themselves.

The first half of the film acts almost as if it were a simple historical pastiche, offering a few well-developed characters. But this is where the film does its best trick by connecting the chaotic atmosphere of the German Counter Culture to the formation of the Red Army faction without demonizing either. Drugs, free love, and anarchy may have provided a social salon but the film is all about how the weak-willed in the room became subject to those who could shout the loudest.

In a humorous episode, the explosive, obnoxious Andreas Baader (Morris Bleibtreu) taunts the group's lawyer to steal the contents of a woman's handbag to prove that he is a man of courage who will truly follow through on the demands of the revolution. The lawyer reluctantly complies, throwing the wallet to Andreas who laughs until he realizes his own car is being stolen mere yards away. Watching him swearing and screaming, we get a picture of Andreas as the model for his own self-destruction, his own worst enemy, unable to take advice later on from the more mature and thoughtful Ulrike Meinhof (Martina Gedeck).

Early on, the suburban hippie Meinhof, a gifted journalist and social critic, slowly comes under the spell of Baader and the group, until she no longer has any ties to the human race she is supposedly trying to help. Estranged from her husband and children and finally arrested, she goes slowly mad in the manner of those who have had one too many dreams broken and who constantly retrace their steps trying to find out where they went wrong.

But by the time the second half of the epic film is underway and the Red Army Faction is on trial, the film splits into a large and very effective series of branches. There is the show trial that the Germans feel they must put on for the rest of the world with all of the expected counter culture disruption tactics and objections. There is the new, even less thought out and prepared, generation of young revolutionaries who having no personal ties to the original RAF members and are still convinced of the righteousness of the Red Army cause. They plan and botch operation after operation and the comparison to the disintegration of the counter culture in general is unmissable. An old guard German government struggles to understand the newly emerging terrorist mindset with its accompanying hunger strikes, and propaganda machine. Lastly, there is the heartbreaking story of Red Army Faction leaders who desperately hope for release or rescue as they endure hunger strikes, brutal beatings, and lengthy solitary confinement only to descend inexorably into madness and paranoid self-destruction, unable even to trust each other.

No one performance here stands out, almost all the major players are given a chance to shine brightly, but internationally acclaimed actress Martina Gedeck is certainly mesmerizing as Ulrike Meinhof. Gedeck is known best by American audiences for her turns in *Mostly Martha* (2001), the Oscar®-winning *The Lives of Others* (2006) and *The Good Shepherd* (2006). More recognizable is Moritz Bleibtreu as Andreas Baader whose role in the breakthrough hit *Run Lola Run* (1998) was just the first in a series of highly recognizable roles in films including *Das Experiment* (2001), *Munich* (2005), *The Walker* (2007), and *Speed Racer* (2008). Bruno Ganz (*Wings of Desire* [1987], *Downfall* [2004]) offers a masterful portrait of anti-terrorism expert Horst Herold who is fully aware that the Red Army Faction is only the beginning of such troubles for Germany.

Decades into the process that the Red Army Faction was fighting it is more than a little haunting to watch them die for their beliefs, even though their methods were despicable. If the counter culture was just a party gone sour and the RAF just a radicalized movement what is to be made of the broken American dream gone wild? *The Baader Meinhof Complex* seems to invite a deeper view, that never loses sight of people, husbands, parents, and children, in the struggle to combat a dehumanizing system.

Dave Canfield

CREDITS

Ulriche Meinhof: Martina Gedeck
Andreas Baader: Moritz Bleibtreu
Gudrun Ensslin: Johanna Wokalek
Horst Herold: Bruno Ganz
Brigitte Monhaupt: Nadja Uhl
Peter Homann: Jan Josef Liefers
Holger Meins: Stipe Erceg
Jan Carl Raspe: Niels Bruno Schmidt
Peter-Jurgen Boock: Vinzenz Kiefer
Horst Mahler: Simon Licht
Origin: Germany, France, Czech Republic
Language: English, Arabic, French, German
Released: 2008
Production: Bernd Eichinger; Constantin Film; released by Vitagraph
Directed by: Uli Edel
Written by: Uli Edel, Bernd Eichinger
Cinematography by: Rainer Klausmann
Music by: Peter Hindertuer, Florian Tesslof
Sound: Roland Winke
Editing: Alexander Berner
Costumes: Birgit Missal
Production Design: Bernd Lepel
MPAA rating: R
Running time: 150 minutes

REVIEWS

Dargis, Manohla. *New York Times*. August 21, 2009.
Ebert, Roger. *Chicago Sun-Times*. September 10, 2009.
Gordon, Bonnie J. *Hollywood Reporter*. October 3, 2008.
Hoberman, J. *Village Voice*. August 18, 2009.
Lane, Anthony. *New Yorker*. August 24, 2009.
Newman, Kim. *Empire Magazine*. November 14, 2008.
Stevens, Dana. *Slate*. August 21, 2009.
Tallerico, Brian. *MovieRetriever.com*. September 15, 2009.
Tookey, Christopher. *Daily Mail*. November 14, 2008.
Turan, Kenneth. *Los Angeles Times*. August 28, 2009.

TRIVIA

This was Germany's official submission to the Best Foreign Language Film Category of the 81st Annual Academy Awards®.

BAD LIEUTENANT: PORT OF CALL NEW ORLEANS

The only criminal he can't catch is himself.
—Movie tagline

Box Office: $1 million

Werner Herzog's *Bad Lieutenant: Port of Call New Orleans* was easily one of the most unexpected and surprisingly successful remakes of the first decade of the new millennium; a film with almost nothing to do with its predecessor outside of a title character with a penchant for what most would deem inappropriate behavior and a personality-filled auteur in the director's chair. By all standards, remaking a largely forgotten Abel Ferrara film from 1992 never should have worked but Herzog rarely operates under predictable standards and, through a career highlight performance from Nicolas Cage, the director of *Aguirre, Wrath of God* (1972), *Fitzcarraldo* (1982), *Grizzly Man* (2005), and *Rescue Dawn* (2006) turned his uniquely stylish take on the well-worn genre of "cop gone bad" into one of the most memorable films of 2009.

The plot of *Bad Lieutenant: Port of Call New Orleans* basically plays like an origin story for a corrupt cop. Said cop is named Terence McDonagh (Cage), a New Orleans officer introduced during Hurricane Katrina. McDonagh and fellow cop Stevie Pruit (Val Kilmer) come across a young man still trapped in a holding cell and, after ridiculing him, Terence jumps into a too-shallow pool of water and seriously damages his back. Even the choice to open the film with a Katrina-related event cleverly displays the fingerprint of a filmmaker who has worked the dramatic force of nature into many of his films.

Years later, McDonagh has become a Lieutenant and is trying his best to live the life of a Big Easy cop while managing incredible pain through medication. Both his back pain and the addiction to the painkillers that keep at bay are getting worse and he is slowly—and sometimes not so slowly—starting to crack. The spiral begins when McDonagh stumbles into a case involving the brutal murder of five Senegalese illegal immigrants. The hit clearly comes courtesy of the drug world and it sends Terence into the path of a turf war.

The case of *Port of Call New Orleans* is merely the backdrop for Cage and Herzog to paint a character study of a cop who does not traditionally push the envelope or cross the line to close the case. McDonagh barely seems concerned about solving any actual crimes. He is almost always acting on instinct; the one to ease his pain, get him laid, make him money, etc. Of course, he needs to keep his job, but actual law enforcement is a minor issue, only slightly enhanced by the brutal nature of the case he happens to be embroiled in.

While the case goes on, Terence also happens to be falling for a prostitute named Frankie (Eva Mendes), an enabler in McDonagh's increasingly erratic drug use who forces the anti-hero into the path of a violent mobster when he comes to her rescue after a brutal encounter with a john. As the film progresses, Terence slides deeper into insanity—shaking club goers down for drugs and cheap thrills, cutting off an elderly woman's oxygen, increased and more intense drug use— and literally becomes hunched over due to his back pain, beginning to resemble more of a creature than a man. Several familiar faces including Jennifer Coolidge, Fairuza Balk, Brad Dourif, and Michael Shannon pop up in small roles.

Werner Herzog could not possibly be accused of attempting to make any sort of grand statement about the police force or corruption with *Bad Lieutenant: Port of Call New Orleans*. From frame one, the film is clearly nothing more than a bizarre character study, one that gets more and more unusual as its lead character flies further off the rails. By the final act of the film, McDonagh is conversing with iguanas and hallucinating the dancing soul of a recently shot man and Herzog gleefully plays along with similarly unusual directorial decisions like the possibly landmark POV shot courtesy of a crocodile along the side of a highway.

Rarely has a director found an actor more willing to ride with him down a dark alley of film lunacy than Nicolas Cage. During most of his career, there have been two Cages: the movie star of films like *National Treasure* (2004) and the character actor of films like *Adaptation* (2002). Sadly, the latter Cage had not been seen for the better part of the last decade but Herzog found a way to tap the vein of unpredictable behavior that has marked many of the actor's best performances. Easily his most rewarding turn since *Adaptation*, Cage even earned citation in a few year-end pieces about the best performances of 2009 and arguably deserved more awards season attention for this fearless work.

So distinctly different from Ferrara's *Bad Lieutenant* in plot and tone that to compare the two is nearly useless, Werner Herzog's *Bad Lieutenant: Port of Call New Orleans* was as atypical a remake as its hero was atypical a police officer. Unlike so many attempts to rekindle the magic of an earlier film, it actually worked.

Brian Tallerico

CREDITS

Terence McDonagh: Nicolas Cage
Stevie Pruit: Val Kilmer
Frankie Donnenfeld: Eva Mendes
Heidi: Fairuza Balk
Genevieve: Jennifer Coolidge
Ned Schoenholtz: Brad Dourif
Mundt: Michael Shannon
Armand Benoit: Shawn Hatosy

Daryl: Denzel Whitaker
Justin: Shea Whigham
Big Fate: Xzibit
Pat McDonough: Tom Bower
Binnie Rogers: Irma P. Hall
James Brasser: Vondie Curtis-Hall
Yvonne: Brandi Coleman
Tina: Katie Chonacas
Jerimiah Goodhusband: Lance E. Nichols
Origin: USA
Language: English
Released: 2009
Production: Nicolas Cage, Randall Emmett, Edward R. Pressman, John Thompson, Stephen Belafonte, Alan Polsky, Gabe Polsky; Millennium Films, Nu Image Films, Osiris Films, Saturn Films; released by First Look Pictures
Directed by: Werner Herzog
Written by: William M. Finkelstein
Cinematography by: Peter Zeitlinger
Music by: Mark Isham
Editing: Joe Bini
Costumes: Jill Newell
Sound: Michael Baird
Production Design: Toby Corbett
MPAA rating: R
Running time: 121 minutes

REVIEWS

Coyle, Jake. *Associated Press.* November 18, 2009.
Ebert, Roger. *Chicago Sun-Times.* November 19, 2009.
Edelstein, David. *New York Magazine.* November 16, 2009.
Gleiberman, Owen. *Entertainment Weekly.* November 18, 2009.
Hoberman, J. *Village Voice.* November 17, 2009.
McCarthy, Todd. *Variety.* September 3, 2009.
Morgenstern, Joe. *Wall Street Journal.* November 20, 2009.
Phillips, Michael. *Chicago Tribune.* November 19, 2009.
Scott, A.O. *New York Times.* November 19, 2009.
Tallerico, Brian. *MovieRetriever.com.* November 20, 2009.

QUOTES

Big Fate: "You're interrupting my meal."

TRIVIA

This is veteran television writer William M. Finkelstein's first feature film screenwriting credit.

AWARDS

Nomination:
Ind. Spirit 2010: Cinematog.

BANDSLAM

Music has the power to rock your world.
—Movie tagline

Band together.
—Movie tagline

Box Office: $5 million

Phony musical adoration has a way of invalidating otherwise convincing characters. In *(500) Days of Summer* (2009), for example, Tom (Joseph Gordon-Levitt) and Summer (Zooey Deschanel) have their quirks, but it's their pat, joint love of The Smiths that makes it seem like the movie is using music as a shortcut to character development, rather than as a detail of the person as a whole. *Nick and Norah's Infinite Playlist* (2008), often succumbs to the same cop-out.

Similarly, there are musical moments in the high school dramedy *Bandslam* that do not ring true, such as when Will (Gaelan Connell) criticizes a bass player for trying to sound like "Flea from the Red Hot Chili Peppers." The film labors to present Will, an awkward teenager with little more than his musical knowledge, withdrawn disposition and caring mother (Lisa Kudrow) to ground him, as very savvy about music. So when he says "Flea from the Red Hot Chili Peppers," rather than just "Flea," it sounds like *Bandslam* is making sure viewers know who Flea is, rather than letting a character whose relationship with music define who he is.

Fortunately these moments are few and far between in the film, which at first threatens to become a clichéd coming-of-age tale but recovers to depict music as something that teenagers trust with feelings no one else gets to see. Will, a diehard David Bowie fan who often writes revealing letters to the legendary pop artist, is the new kid in school and glad to start over in New Jersey after being bullied and/or ignored in Cincinnati. At his new school, Will quickly bonds with Sa5m (Vanessa Hudgens), who informs him that "the 5 is silent." Before he can consider whether or not Sa5m is for real, Will befriends Charlotte (Alyson Michalka), a pretty ex-cheerleader and budding musician who quickly takes to Will, largely because of his musical smarts. (The two bond over a love of the Velvet Underground).

Soon Will and Sa5m are tip-toeing around being more than friends, and Will, no longer the wallflower he once was, is tasked with managing Charlotte's band and getting them ready to compete in Bandslam, a high school band competition in which the winner receives a recording contract. This mix of tame high school flirtation and musical preparation makes *Bandslam* a direct descendant of *School of Rock* (2003), and even the *High School Musical* (2006) franchise. Yet *Bandslam* resists clichés more than it succumbs to them, allowing its characters to behave, most of the time, like actual teenagers might behave, rather than how typically far-fetched movie characters frustratingly insist on acting.

Director/co-writer Todd Graff, who also helmed the musical-comedy *Camp* (2003), wisely resists developing a love triangle. He does, however, let Will become swept up in Charlotte's intoxicating energy, and lets Sa5m's insecurity play defense when she can tell her crush is at least a little smitten with another girl. In a similarly well-played scene, Charlotte's ex-boyfriend Ben (Scott Porter, who, at 30, is way too old to play an 18-year-old), jealous of the time Will is spending with his ex, attempts to instruct his bandmates to dig up dirt on Will—as the popular guy so often does in the usual, mediocre teen comedy. Yet Ben's pals resist immediately, informing him that they do not work for him and he can do his own reconnaissance.

Graff, however, seems less comfortable with bigger emotional gestures. A major scene between Will and Charlotte is the film's worst-acted, and overbearing strings accompany some of Kudrow's more significant scenes of maternal comforting. Issues involving Will and Charlotte's fathers also are diminished by heavy-handed direction.

The film's reliance on music also stumbles in trying to make timely references. By the time *Bandslam* hit theatres, included acts like Clap Your Hands Say Yeah, Peter Bjorn and John and The Arcade Fire were far from the phenomena they were a year or two prior. And the Bandslam event never feels legit, mostly because *Bandslam* presents the contest as the most important thing at Will's high school—and then glosses over the basics, such as who competes, how to enter, how to move onto regional finals and so forth.

The most rewarding and most surprising takeaway from this charming dramedy—which pulls off the tricky feat of depicting believable teenagers in a film that's appropriate for kids— is the constant teenage struggle of figuring out what's fake and what's real. Charlotte's motivations come into question at one point, but it's merely a factor of a teen girl's transient identity, not a black-and-white character who is all one thing. (Also refreshing is the film's refusal to overstate the presence of school cliques.) It is a rare movie about high school that realizes irony and sincerity often disguise themselves as one another, and that kids struggling with plenty of their own family, social and biological issues can hardly hope to always know the difference between a true friend and a temporary one, or a permanent quirk versus a brief phase. Awkward and funny, clumsy and true, *Bandslam* is a primer on the bonds of youth and the joy of playing, listening to, and discussing music with friends.

Matt Pais

CREDITS

Charlotte Barnes: Alyson Michalka
Ben Wheatly: Scott Porter
Sam: Vanessa Anne Hudgens
Karen Burton: Lisa Kudrow
Basher Martin: Ryan Donowho
Will Burton: Gaelen Connell
Bug: Charlie Saxton
Himself: David Bowie (Cameo)
Origin: USA
Language: English
Released: 2009
Production: Elaine Goldsmith-Thomas; Walden Media; released by Summit Entertainment
Directed by: Todd Graff
Written by: Todd Graff, Josh A. Cagan
Cinematography by: Eric Steelberg
Music by: Junkie XL
Sound: Ethan Andrus
Music Supervisor: Lindsay Fellows, Linda Cohen
Editing: John Gilbert
Art Direction: John Frick
Costumes: Ernesto Martinez
Production Design: Jeff Knipp
MPAA rating: PG
Running time: 111 minutes

REVIEWS

Bradshaw, Peter. *Guardian.* August 14, 2009.
Ebert, Roger. *Chicago Sun-Times.* August 13, 2009.
Nelson, Rob. *Variety.* August 10, 2009.
Phillips, Michael. *Chicago Tribune.* August 14, 2009.
Rabin, Nathan. *AV Club.* August 13, 2009.
Rechtshaffen, Michael. *Hollywood Reporter.* August 10, 2009.
Rodriguez, Rene. *Miami Herald.* August 13, 2009.
Smith, Anna. *Empire Magazine.* August 13, 2009.
Sobczynski, Peter. *eFilmCritic.* August 13, 2009.
Webster, Andy. *New York Times.* August 14, 2009.

QUOTES

Will Burton: "I think if you tried signaling, people would honk less."

TRIVIA

Originally the film was titled "Will," then the title was changed to "Rock On," and finally to "Bandslam."

BATTLE FOR TERRA

Their world is mankind's only hope for survival.
—Movie tagline

They are coming.
—Movie tagline

Box Office: $1 million

One of the great things about animation is the fact that it is a cinematic format in which entire worlds can be brought to life in the most unique and creative ways imaginable. Therefore, you would think that science-fiction, which thrives on just that, would be a natural for this type of filmmaking but, in America at least, the genre has more or less been a non-starter over the years (with the Pixar smash *WALL*E* (2008) being a rare exception). Bizarrely, it seems that when faced with the myriad possibilities of letting their imaginations run wild, most people charged with making an animated sci-fi film choose to avoid doing so and instead offer up listless variations of familiar formulas and the results have been so dire and unmemorable—just try to remember anything from the likes of *Titan A.E.* (2000), *Treasure Planet* (2002) or *Star Wars: The Clone Wars* (2008)—that you can't really blame audiences from staying away from them in droves. *Battle for Terra* is yet another failed attempt to fuse science-fiction and animation together in an attempt to tap into the insatiable market for fantasy filmmaking and not even the additional inducements of a top-name voice cast and the increasingly questionable miracle of 3-D are enough to generate any interest from even the most forgiving viewers.

The film takes place in the not-too-distant future when mankind has, through its own stupidity and wastefulness, finally exhausted Earth's remaining resources (and destroyed Mars and Venus in the process) and has sent patrols out in search of a hospitable planet that they can populate before all is lost forever. Eventually, they stumble upon the planet Terra, a bucolic hippie-like paradise in which the population of tadpole-like creatures live in a constant state of peace, love and understanding. Needless to say, the Earthlings begin an invasion of the planet in order to install a Terraformer machine that will make the atmosphere hospitable for them while simultaneously killing off all the natives. During this invasion, Terrian leader Roven (Dennis Quaid) is kidnapped and in trying to rescue him, his spunky daughter Mala (Evan Rachel Wood) comes across fallen Earth pilot Jim (Luke Wilson) and takes him back to her place to nurse him back to health. Naturally, these people from two different worlds realize that they have much in common and try to figure out a way for their two populations to co-exist peacefully. Of course, the Earthlings, led by the power-mad General Hemmer (Brian Cox) want nothing to do with that and launch a full-scale attack on the planet that will force both Mala and Jim to decide whether their friendship is more important than the survival of their respective species.

Although *Battle for Terra* may be slightly unusual by American animation standards—the story is told in a relatively straightforward manner without much in the way of comedy relief—it will come across as all too familiar to anyone with even a limited knowledge of the sci-fi genre. Outside of the notion of making the Earthlings the aggressive invaders, there is precious little originality or inspiration on display in the screenplay and it quickly degenerates into a treacle-y and overly obvious morality tale that quickly wears out its welcome thanks to its less-than-interesting characters and the obvious narrative padding employed by director Aristomenis Tsirbas to transform his 2003 short film into a full-length feature. Although a number of known actors contribute their voices—besides those already mentioned, it also features turns from the likes of Danny Glover, James Garner, Amanda Peet, David Cross, Ron Perlman and Rosanna Arquette—none of them make much of an impact and Wood and Wilson are so forgettable as the leads that they barely register at all. From a visual standpoint, the film is an even bigger disappointment; some of the early views of Terra are intriguing (especially the whale-like creatures that float through the skies) but beyond that, it only offers the usual compendium of quirky alien creatures and elaborate space battles that are indistinguishable from most other films of this type. The only truly unique aspect about the film is its finale and that is only because when you stop to analyze it, it seems to offer an implicit endorsement of suicide bombing as a manner of achieving one's goals—I for one would have loved to have seen a scene involving a debate over the construction of the memorial statue seen in all its glory during the epilogue.

As for the 3-D aspect, it is pretty much like the rest of *Battle for Terra* in that it is technically proficient without really adding anything to the proceedings. Although it shows restraint in not constantly throwing things into the laps of audience members in an effort to goose their interest, the format is utilized in such a half-hearted and uninvolving manner that, like with everything else about the film, most people will find themselves wondering why they bothered with it in the first place. Essentially, the only real thing achieved by utilizing the process is that the brightness of the picture has been inevitably reduced by about thirty percent. As a result, like most other entries in the current 3-D boom, *Battle for Terra* is a film that will look remarkably better at home than it does in the theater. Unfortunately, as anyone who does watch it at home will quickly discover, brighter does not mean better.

Peter Sobczynski

CREDITS

Mala: Evan Rachel Wood (Voice)

Jim Stanton: Luke Wilson (Voice)

General Hammer: Brian Cox (Voice)

Doron: James Garner (Voice)

Stewart Stanton: Chris Evans (Voice)

Roven: Dennis Quaid (Voice)

Giddy: David Cross (Voice)

Origin: USA

Language: English

Released: 2009

Production: Keith Calder, Jessica Wu, Dane Allan Smith, Ryan Colucci; Snoot Entertainment, MeniThings Entertainment; released by Roadside Attractions

Directed by: Aristomenis Tsirbas

Written by: Evan Spiliotopolos

Music by: Abel Korzeniowski

Sound: Nathan Smith

Music Supervisor: Bryan Elliott Lawson

Editing: J. Kathleen Gibson

MPAA rating: PG

Running time: 85 minutes

REVIEWS

Anderson, John. *Variety.* May 12, 2008.

Abele, Robert. *Los Angeles Times.* April 30, 2009.

Ebert, Roger. *Chicago Sun-Times.* April 30, 2009.

Genzlinger, Neil. *New York Times.* May 1, 2009.

Graham, Adam. *Detroit News.* May 1, 2009.

Honeycutt, Kirk. *Hollywood Reporter.* May 1, 2009.

Kennedy, Lisa. *Denver Post.* May 1, 2009.

Phillips, Michael. *Chicago Tribune.* April 30, 2009.

Puig, Claudia. *USA Today.* May 1, 2009.

Weinberg, Scott. *Cinematical.* May 7, 2008.

BIG FAN

As written and directed by former Editor-in-Chief of *The Onion*, Robert Siegel, *Big Fan* is a flawed but still compelling satire that offers a dark meditation on what it means to be a fan instead of a whole person, and whether or not that is enough to sustain the soul. Siegel's previous directing effort, *The Onion Movie* (2008) offers little hint of his ability to deal with serious character study. But he also wrote one of the best dramatic efforts of that same year, *The Wrestler* (2008). Like that film, *Big Fan* also tackles the life and dreams of a lovable loser who refuses to bend his principles to conform with other peoples idea of normal. Unlike *The Wrestler*, this film is directed by and stars a pair of relative newcomers and emerges as surprisingly light on

heart which is the last thing you'd expect from a movie called *Big Fan*.

Hardcore New York Giants football fan Paul Aufiero (Patton Oswalt), lives a simple life with his mother, working as a parking garage attendant by day and spending his nights prepping his speeches for call-in radio sports talk shows. On weekends, Paul heads to the stadium with his best friend Sal (Kevin Corrigan) and sits in his favorite seat—the parking lot, watching the game on a tiny TV hooked up to his car battery. This idyllic existence changes however, when Paul spots Quantrell Bishop (Jonathan Hamm), his favorite Giants player, on the street and decides to follow him in hopes of mustering up the courage to say hello. Arriving at a strip joint, he sits for hours, finally working up the courage to approach his now drunken hero who, thinking Paul is a stalker, beats him nearly to death.

Now Quantrell has been suspended pending an investigation, Police Detective Velarde (Matt Servitto) wants a statement, Paul's personal injury attorney brother Jeff (Gino Cafarelli) wants to sue, and his long suffering mother (Marcia Jean Kurtz) wants Paul to finally realize that he needs to move out the house, get a real job, and provide her some grandchildren, preferably by starting to date, find the right girl, and get married. All Paul wants is to go back to the way things were and to watch his beloved Giants play. Torn apart by the pressures of his situation Paul hatches a scheme that will let the Giants play, get everyone to leave him alone and finally silence his loudmouth trash-talking radio nemesis Philadelphia Phil. The question is to what length is Paul willing to go to prove his loyalty to the team?

The film is beautifully cast. Patton Oswalt (*Balls of Fury* [2007], *Observe and Report* [2009]), is a popular standup comedian best known for his film bit parts and appearances as a regular cast member of *The King of Queens*. But, here, Oswalt proves the oft-cited factoid that good comedians tend to make good dramatic actors by bringing a level of complexity to Paul. Beyond the issue of Paul's injury, which may have left him brain injured, is his general mental health. Why would an able bodied man choose the kind of life Paul has? Oswalt walks a fine line between realizing Paul's dysfunction and the simple acts of survival necessary to emotionally and psychologically survive the dysfunctions of those around him.

Oswalt does falter occasionally, bending under the weight of the role. Underacting can generally be a good choice for first time leads, but the character of Paul does not emerge as being as real world as those around him. In short, at times, he remains a writer's construction. In the same way, the script lacks the complexity to completely flesh Paul out, as if Siegel stopped writing and said to himself, "We'll handle that when we get in front of the camera."

But Siegel is an impressive director. While he cannot solve the problems in his script, he does make ample use of the tools at his disposal to communicate point of view, emotional state and establish an interesting tone. The look of *Big Fan* is down and dirty making it easy to imagine Paul's state of mind as he contemplates the futility of getting ahead in a world where cheaters prosper, heroes prove to be losers, and losers stay losers.

The supporting cast offers a sometimes heart-wrenching sense of the real. Kevin Corrigan (*The Last Winter* [2006], *Superbad* [2007], *Pineapple Express* [2008]) who plays Sal manages to be interesting precisely because he is uninvolved in the larger questions that bother Paul, while simultaneously proving loyal in even the worst circumstances. Michael Rappaport (*Bamboozled* [2000], *Special* [2006]) as Paul's arch-nemesis Philadelphia Phil brings trash talk to life in a way that is infuriating but also everyday. Special mention should be made of Marcia Jean Kurtz who plays Paul's mother with a special sense of desperation, able to convey motherly love, faded hopes and dreams, and wild lack of self-awareness. She comes close to stealing the show.

If, in the end, Oswalt prevails in his attempt to bring Paul's struggle to the fore perhaps it is because, unlike *The Wrestler*, *Big Fan* offers nothing truly noble or self-defining in Paul's love of the Giants. There are hints of it, such as in Paul's brief daydreams that show Quantrell Bishop suited up and ready to charge the field. But, on the whole, *Big Fan* haunts precisely because Paul lacks the pathos of someone who is on a path worth being on.

Dave Canfield

CREDITS

Paul Aufiero: Patton Oswalt
Sal: Kevin Corrigan
Quantrell Bishop: Jonathan Hamm
Jeff Aufiero: Gino Cafarelli
Det. Verlardi: Matt Servitto
Theresa Aufiero: Marcia Jean Kurtz
Philadelphia Phil: Michael Rapaport
Origin: USA
Language: English
Released: 2009
Production: Elan Bogarin, Jean Kouremetis; Big Fan Products; released by First Independent Pictures
Directed by: Robert Siegel
Written by: Robert Siegel
Cinematography by: Michael Simmonds

Music by: Philip Watts
Sound: Eric Walendzinski
Editing: Joshua Trank
Costumes: Vera Chow
Production Design: Sharoz Makarechi
MPAA rating: R
Running time: 86 minutes

REVIEWS

Byrge, Duane. *Hollywood Reporter.* August 25, 2009.
Dargis, Manohla. *New York Times.* August 27, 2009.
Gleiberman, Owen. *Entertainment Weekly.* September 2, 2009.
Hoffman, Jordan. *UGO.com.* August 25, 2009.
Lemire, Christy. *Associated Press.* September 3, 2009.
McCarthy, Todd. *Variety.* January 23, 2009.
Rea, Steven. *Philadelphia Inquirer.* August 27, 2009.
Schager, Nick. *Slant Magazine.* August 25, 2009.
Stevens, Dana. *Slate.* August 28, 2009.
Tallerico, Brian. *MovieRetriever.com.* October 2, 2009.

QUOTES

Paul Aufiero: "It's gonna be a great year!"

TRIVIA

Every football player referenced in the film by any of the characters or the radio host is a real NFL player other than Quantrell Bishop.

BLACK DYNAMITE

He's super bad. He's outta sight. He's...
—Movie tagline

Big screen satire is too frequently given a bad name by those who practice it witlessly and with a clamorous indelicacy. In all honestly, films like *Disaster Movie* (2008), *Superhero Movie* (2008) and *Meet the Spartans* (2008) barely qualify for the descriptive tag, because all they do is awkwardly recycle set-ups and snapshot moments of other popular movies and cultural signifiers; they are not satire so much as the cinematic equivalent of an elbow jammed repeatedly into an audience's ribs.

Black Dynamite, however, is spry and funny, and it never once pauses to wink at its audience. A lively, cocksure send-up of 1970s-era kung-fu cinema, urban action and blaxploitation films like *Shaft* (1971),*Sweet Sweetback's Baadasssss Song* (1971),*Three the Hard Way* (1974) and *Uptown Saturday Night* (1974), director Scott Sanders' movie is one of the most pure, unadulterated, adrenaline-hit pleasures of 2009 for in-the-know cinephiles. A referential, hyper-realistic action-comedy that also works perfectly well as an almost goofy, insanely capricious thrill ride for those less familiar with its source material, *Black Dynamite* regrettably flew under the radar of mainstream film audiences, never getting a release wider than 70 theaters, and grossing only $242,000 during its ultra-limited theatrical run.

As with many classic blaxploitation flicks, *Black Dynamite* centers its action around a streetwise African American stud butting heads with corrupt politicians and other white characters of ill repute, in this instance a same-named ex-CIA agent turned part-time pimp (Michael Jai White). The script—co-written by Sanders, White and Byron Minns, from a story by White and Minns—initially unfolds as a standard revenge tract. When his younger brother gets gunned down by drug runners, a flashback sequence's hilariously on-the-nose expository dialogue ("Jimmy, I am 18-year-old Black Dynamite, and you are my 16-year-old younger brother...") evokes the protagonist's deathbed promise to his mother to look after his sibling.

Tapping ex-soldier pal O'Leary (Kevin Chapman) for leads, Black Dynamite wades into the local seedy underworld. From there, ample opportunity is presented for skulls to get cracked, and various criminal-types to receive their comeuppance. Using his own personal brawn as well as a web of informants and recruited urban renewal volunteers, Black Dynamite finds out his brother's death is connected to a much wider scheme of racial blight than he could have ever imagined.

Rather characteristically, a little of this sort of over-the-top parody goes a long way, but *Black Dynamite* smartly mitigates any potential for drag. Pivoting like a tap dancer on an amphetamine high, the film sets up and cycles through more layers of conflict and nefarious corruption than several entire small screen serials. In this regard, *Black Dynamite* is like the seven-layer chip dip of homage movies, offering up such a disparate grouping of flavors that if one feels their level of engagement slipping they typically need only wait eight to ten minutes until a wild new plot twist is introduced. There is only one moment of true gear-grinding slip-up in the film's eighty-four minute runtime (a discursive sequence in which Black Dynamite and his pals verbally untangle a labyrinthine conspiracy), and even its bawdy payoff quickly eliminates any feelings of tedium.

White's physical bona fides have never been in question, whether audiences are familiar with him from *Spawn* (1997), the film in which he punched through into the larger mainstream consciousness, or a string of low-budget, straight-to-video action movies which showcased his martial arts acumen. *Black Dynamite*, though, vastly expands his range and profile. It represents a case of an actor creating his own opportunity, and

shining in said showcase. White is physically right for the role—rugged and thick-necked—but also brutishly charismatic and funny. It is the best role he has been given in his career, and thus not surprisingly his best performance as well.

White's engaging turn and the acting as a whole is appropriately pitched to register the sort of heightened-emotive vibe of many classic blaxploitation films, a credit to director Sanders since *Black Dynamite* also features a litany of cameos (from Arsenio Hall, Tommy Davidson and Mykelti Williamson to Nicole Sullivan, John Salley and singer Brian McKnight) that never come off as forced. The film also deftly works in almost all the expected story details (slang-laden language, sexual conquests featuring women with pendulous breasts, wild rooftop chase sequences) of the genre it is lampooning. Finally, Sanders deliberately seeds his movie with just the sort of mishaps—boom mic slippage, an obvious use of stunt doubles, etcetera—unintentionally present in so many low-grade productions of the 1970s.

Most importantly, though, all the corroborating filmic vocabulary is spot-on. From costume designer Ruth Carter's superlative work and Adrian Younge's appropriately funky music contributions to graded film stock, imperfectly framed camera push-ins and purpose-fully discombobulating editing choices, everything here is of a piece. In this regard, *Black Dynamite* is more authentically detailed and tonally faithful to its cinematic forebears than something like *Death Proof* (2007), Quentin Tarantino's half of the *Grindhouse* double-bill experiment he hatched in tandem with Robert Rodriguez. This detail, and the loving warmth of its keen presentation, marks the difference between true satire and the sort of lazy, mock-comedic assault that too frequently passes for modern-day genre spoofs.

Brent Simon

CREDITS

Black Dynamite: Michael Jai White
Bullhorn: Byron Keith Minns
Honey Bee: Kym E. Whitley
Osiris: Obba Babatunde
O'Leary: Kevin Chapman
Cream Corn: Tommy Davidson
Gloria: Salli Richardson-Whitfield
Tasty Freeze: Arsenio Hall
Chocolate Giddy Up: Cedric Yarbrough
Chicago Wind: Mykelti Williamson
Black Hand Jack: Bokeem Woodbine
Richard Nixon: James McManus
Patricia Nixon: Nicole Sullivan

Origin: USA

Language: English

Released: 2009

Production: Jon Steingart, Jenny Weiner Steingart; Ars Nova, Harbor Entertainment; released by Sony Pictures

Directed by: Scott Sanders

Written by: Michael Jai White, Byron Keith Minns, Scott Sanders

Cinematography by: Shawn Maurer

Sound: Sara Glaser

Music Supervisor: Adrian Younge, David Hollander

Editing: Adrian Younge

Costumes: Ruth E. Carter

Production Design: Denise Pizzini

MPAA rating: R

Running time: 90 minutes

REVIEWS

Abele, Robert. *Los Angeles Times.* October 16, 2009.

Anderson, Melissa. *Village Voice.* October 14, 2009.

Ebert, Roger. *Chicago Sun-Times.* October 15, 2009.

Gleiberman, Owen. *Entertainment Weekly.* October 14, 2009.

Morris, Wesley. *Boston Globe.* November 24, 2009.

Nelson, Rob. *Variety.* January 23, 2009.

Schager, Nick. *Slant Magazine.* May 3, 2009.

Thompson, Gary. *Philadelphia Daily News.* October 15, 2009.

Uhlich, Keith. *Time Out New York.* October 14, 2009.

Weinberg, Scott. *Cinematical.* February 2, 2009.

QUOTES

Gloria: "So you're one of those Tom Slick brothers that think they can get by on good looks, a wink and a smile, huh?"

TRIVIA

Roscoe's fictitious "Chili and Donuts" is a play on the real-life Roscoe's "House of Chicken and Waffles."

THE BLIND SIDE

Box Office: $250 million

John Lee Hancock's drama *The Blind Side* tells the fact-based story about a white, upper-middle class Memphis family who take in a homeless black teenager, feed him, clothe him, buy him a nice set of wheels and position him to become a high-school football star with excellent college prospects. The film is yet another classic example of Hollywood's infatuation with mainstream, crowd-pleasing movies built around beneficent white saviors who use their superior powers of wealth, education, position, experience and personal character to help downtrodden minority characters survive or preserve their dignity or achieve self-actualization. The popular genre has won Academy Awards® (*Dances With Wolves* [1990], *Glory* [1989]), met with critical approval and won box office applause. Many, like *Glory,* have been based, sometimes loosely, on real people and events. Others are works of fiction.

The Blind Side might well be just another commercial sports movie surfing along on this wave of inadvertently racist motion pictures, except for two elements: the sincerity and honesty of director Hancock and the career-reinventing performance by his star, romantic comedy commodity Sandra Bullock. Bullock plays tempered-steel magnolia Leigh Anne Tuohy (Sandra Bullock), a successful interior decorator married to the extremely patient Sean (Tim McGraw), a fast-food restaurant magnate in Memphis. They have two wonderfully behaved children in S.J. and Collins (played with cute and ample personality by Jae Head and Lily Collins).

One night during a driving rain, the Tuohys spot a large high school student called 'Big Mike' Oher walking along the road. On a hunch, Leigh Anne stops the car and asks Mike if he has a place to stay for the night. "Don't you lie to me!" she says, and there is fire in her eyes and flint in her voice that have never come out of a Bullock character before. Big Mike is played by Quinton Aaron as a gentle giant whose eyes are awash with profound sadness. Leigh Anne instantly makes an executive decision to take Mike in for a while, until he can get back on his feet.

Early on, Big Mike becomes just Michael after he tells Leigh Anne he hates being called 'Big.' During his first night at the Tuohy's palatial house, Mike comes across a coffee table picture book of Norman Rockwell paintings, and he opens the pages to see Rockwell's famous Thanksgiving Day feast, an idealized portrait of a happy, nuclear American family sitting around a table of plenty. Just a few brief scenes later, Hancock recreates this painting in the Tuohy's dining room on Thanksgiving Day, when the Tuohys are content to lounge around the family room watching football on a big-screen TV. Mike sits down at the formal dining table. Leigh Anne, taking his cue, cajoles the family into joining him. There they sit, Rockwell's happy, nuclear family around a table of plenty. Mike is also exerting an instant positive influence over the Tuohys, just as they are over him.

As he did in his fact-based baseball fantasy-fulfillment drama *The Rookie* (2002), Hancock (who also wrote the screenplay) takes a worn-out genre and reworks it into something fresh, funny and touching. *The Blind Side* turns a blind eye to all the clichés expected in this domestic drama. There are no paralyzing psychological barriers to overcome, no tacked-on criminal or romantic subplots, no silly sibling rivalries from the Tuohys' son and daughter gunking up the narrative as in most other films of this ilk. Amazingly, *The Blind Side* barely contains much traditional dramatic conflict, save for minor confrontations between Leigh Anne and some unsavory elements at Mike's home in the Memphis projects, and a college sports investigator who accuses the Tuohys of employing undue pressure to push Mike into accepting a scholarship at their own alma mater, Ole Miss, as payback for snatching him from the jowls of poverty and crime.

What *The Blind Side* projects is an honest, old-fashioned sense of idealism, a testimonial that the modern American family can be multi-racial, and still remain cohesive, happy and confident enough to think beyond its own needs, and be strong enough to withstand the glancing blows of bigotry and narrow minds. *The Blind Side* is an openly Rockwellian movie, detached from the gritty and harrowing abuses in *Precious: Based on the Novel 'Push' by Sapphire*.

The drama gives Bullock the best role of her 21st-century career as the headstrong Leigh Anne, an appealing balance of self-willed Southern grit and raw empathy. With her blonde tresses and total immersion into Leigh Anne, Bullock transforms herself into a dramatic dynamo resembling a 1970s-era Nancy Sinatra armed with a pitch-perfect accent. Aaron's performance as Mike is also the stuff of screen greatness. His laconic performance suggests intelligence and kindness hiding under his hulking, intimidating exterior. (Stick around at the film's end to see scenes featuring the real-life Oher, who sports fans know went on to play pro ball for the Baltimore Ravens.) Critical kudos should also go to Kathy Bates, who turns a small, supporting role into a humorous, stellar turn as Miss Sue, a high school tutor hired to help Mike navigate the Memphis educational system—despite the fact she's an admitted Democrat.

Dann Gire

CREDITS

Leigh Ann Touhy: Sandra Bullock
Sean Touhy: Tim McGraw
Michael Oher: Quinton Aaron
Miss Sue: Kathy Bates
Burt Cotton: Ray McKinnon
Origin: USA
Language: English
Released: 2009
Production: Gil Netter, Broderick Johnson, Andrew A. Kosove; Alcon Entertainment, Zucker Brothers Productions; released by Warner Bros.

Directed by: John Lee Hancock
Written by: John Lee Hancock
Cinematography by: Alar Kivilo
Music by: Carter Burwell
Sound: Jon Johnson
Music Supervisor: Julia Michels
Editing: Mark Livolsi
Art Direction: Thomas Minton
Costumes: Daniel Orlandi
Production Design: Michael Corenblith
MPAA rating: PG-13
Running time: 128 minutes

REVIEWS

Anderson, Melissa. *Village Voice.* November 17, 2009.
Hornaday, Ann. *Washington Post.* November 18, 2009.
Kennedy, Lisa. *Denver Post.* November 20, 2009.
Leydon, Joe. *Variety.* November 16, 2009.
Lumenick, Lou. *New York Post.* November 20, 2009.
Pais, Matt. *Metromix.com.* November 19, 2009.
Phillips, Michael. *Chicago Tribune.* November 19, 2009.
Sharkey, Betsy. *Los Angeles Times.* November 19, 2009.
Tallerico, Brian. *MovieRetriever.com.* November 23, 2009.
Whipp, Glenn. *Associated Press.* November 18, 2009.

QUOTES

Leigh Anne Touhy: "If you so much as set foot downtown you will be sorry. I'm in a prayer group with the D.A., I'm a member of the NRA and I'm always packing."

TRIVIA

The 35mm print sent to theatres was titled "Wonderbar."

AWARDS

Oscars 2009: Actress (Bullock)
Golden Globes 2010: Actress—Drama (Bullock)
Screen Actors Guild 2009: Actress (Bullock)
Nomination:
Oscars 2009: Film.

THE BOONDOCK SAINTS II: ALL SAINTS DAY

Box Office: $10 million

When it was initially released in theaters in 1999, *The Boondock Saints* could not have made less of a commercial or critical impact if it tried—it played in only a handful of theaters, grossed about $25,000 over a couple of weeks before being yanked from distribution and was largely slammed by the few critics who bothered to write about it. However, writer/director Troy Duffy's hyper-violent tale of a pair of Boston brothers who took it upon themselves to rid the city of its biggest criminals via a string of religiously inspired vigilante killings would prove to be a surprisingly popular hit on DVD—perhaps helped somewhat by the notoriety surrounding *Overnight* (2003), the fascinating behind-the-scenes documentary that showed newcomer Duffy behaving so badly to everyone he encountered that he single-handedly undid a fully-financed deal to make the film for Miramax Films. As a result, Duffy was released from the 'Director Jail' where he had been languishing for the last decade and given the money to make a sequel to the now-hot property. If the resulting film, *The Boondock Saints II: All Saints Day* was even a fraction as interesting as its back story, it might have been worth seeing but, if anything, it is even worse than the original—a smug, sadistic and overly slick Tarantino knockoff that will have all but the most dedicated *Boondock* devotees yearning for the days of such comparatively subtle and nuanced works as *Things to Do in Denver When You're Dead* (1995) or *Mad Dog Time* (1996).

Picking up the story a few years after the conclusion of the first, the film opens with the MacManus brothers, Connor (Sean Patrick Flannery) and Murphy (Norman Reedus), living in exile in a remote Irish village with their father (Billy Connolly). Their attempts to live quiet, normal lives are shattered when they get word that their former neighborhood priest back home has been murdered in the same manner that they used to dispatch their victims years earlier—two shots to the back of the head and pennies on the corpse's eyelids. Someone is obviously trying to set them up in order to draw them out of hiding and sure enough, the brothers immediately set sail for Boston to get to the bottom of who is responsible, picking up a wacky Mexican sidekick (Clifton Collins Jr.) along the way. After they arrive, our anti-heroes begin plowing their way through a new set of gangsters while trying to discover who is behind the plot to frame them. At the same time, their case is also being monitored by Special Agent Eunice Bloom (Julie Benz), a brilliant federal agent who knows that the brothers are not responsible for the killing of the priest and who may have her own reasons for catching up with them.

As noted earlier, *The Boondock Saints II* is the first film that Troy Duffy has made since the original but after only a few minutes, it becomes painfully evident that whatever he may have done to pass the time in the ensuing decade, going to remedial film school was not among his activities because it is really, really terrible in

every possible way. His screenplay is an overlong and overly convoluted collection of non-stop vulgarity, plenty of borderline racist/homophobic commentary and numerous self-conscious and self-congratulatory references alluding to the original film's cult following. His direction is equally bad in that he spends far more time trying to give viewers "cool" shots of guys leaping through the air or sliding along the floor with gun blazing than in trying to tell a coherent story. He also has no demonstrable facility in regards to working with actors—Flannery and Reedus are complete non-entities in the lead roles while the supporting players have apparently been told to either wildly overplay their roles (including Judd Nelson as a scenery-chewing mob boss) or wildly underplay them. (Peter Fonda pops up in the end in a performance so listless that he is almost completely unrecognizable.) Put all of these ingredients together and the end result is something that feels less like a movie and more like the world's longest, dullest and goriest light beer commercial.

The Boondock Saints II: All Saints Day is a dismal direct-to-video item that somehow lucked into a big-screen release in spite of its utter uselessness. Although fans of the original will no doubt seek it out, it is impossible to imagine many of them coming away from this tired rehash with any of the enthusiasm that they felt for the original. In fact, the only good thing to be said about this brutal and brutally boring bit of blarney is that it so relentlessly awful that, despite the laborious set-up that dominates the last few minutes, a third installment in 2019 looks highly unlikely. Of course, the same thing could have been said about a second film ten years ago and look how that turned out.

Peter Sobczynski

CREDITS

Connor MacManus: Sean Patrick Flanery
Murphy MacManus: Norman Reedus
Il Duce: Billy Connolly
Romeo: Clifton Collins Jr.
Eunice Bloom: Julie Benz
The Roman: Peter Fonda
Concezio Yakavetta: Judd Nelson
Origin: USA
Language: English
Released: 2009
Production: Don Carmody, Chris Binker; Stage Six Films; released by Apparition
Directed by: Troy Duffy
Written by: Troy Duffy, Taylor Duffy
Cinematography by: Miroslaw Baszak

Music by: Jeff Danna
Sound: John J. Thomson
Music Supervisor: Ross Elliot
Editing: Bill Deronde, Paul Kumpata
Art Direction: Dennis Davenport
Costumes: Georgina Yarhl
Production Design: Dan Yarhi
MPAA rating: R
Running time: 118 minutes

REVIEWS

Abele, Robert. *Los Angeles Times.* October 30, 2009.
Burr, Ty. *Boston Globe.* October 29, 2009.
Coyle, Jake. *Associated Press.* October 28, 2009.
Debruge, Peter. *Variety.* October 29, 2009.
Hillis, Aaron. *Village Voice.* October 27, 2009.
Loder, Kurt. *MTV.* October 30, 2009.
Rechtshaffen, Michael. *Hollywood Reporter.* October 29, 2009.
Schager, Nick. *Slant Magazine.* October 25, 2009.
Smith, Kyle. *New York Post.* October 30, 2009.
Uhlich, Keith. *Time Out New York.* October 28, 2009.

QUOTES

Concezio Yakavetta: "These saints put my father on his knees!"

TRIVIA

One of the newscasters is played by Joe Amorosino, a
sportscaster for WHDH channel 7 in Boston.

THE BOX

You are the experiment.
    —Movie tagline

Box Office: $15 million

"What would you do if you were offered a large sum of money, but told that in exchange, someone somewhere in the world, whom you do not know, would die?" This moral conundrum has become such a common part of American folklore, one might not realize that the question was actually whittled down from "Button, Button," a short story written just forty years ago by author Richard Matheson. Enter film director/mad scientist Richard Kelly, whose latest, *The Box*, suggests he is hell-bent on rescuing the concept from the realm of road-trip prattle and cocktail party ice breakers, in order to prove it worthy of a more thorough investigation.

The story is set in suburban Richmond Virginia in 1976, where Norma and Arthur Lewis (Cameron Diaz

and James Marsden) are awoken at the crack of dawn by the mysterious delivery of a plain, unmarked package to their doorstep. Upon opening it, they find a sleek wooden box that sports an ominous, red button and a note from a Mr. Steward, who claims he will return that evening with further instructions.

In the ensuing scenes, the couple attempts to go about their day normally; Norma attends the private school where she teaches and Arthur is seen at NASA, where he works in the development of technology destined for Mars. It is also revealed that Arthur is denied the promotion to astronaut on which he had been counting and Norma's school can no longer offer tuition discounts for the children of its faculty, including their son, Walter (Sam Oz Stone). But as their luck worsens and financial troubles increase, they are clearly drawn as an incredibly close, loving family. Accompanying this is a growing sense of dread that no one could be less deserving of the misfortune that is sure to soon befall them.

Later that evening, Mr. Steward (Frank Langella) returns and, though he is well-dressed and well-spoken, he is also horribly disfigured and appears to be missing an almost impossible chunk of his cheek and jaw. He proceeds to explain the aforementioned proposition (in this case, to the tune of $1 million) and asks that they simply push the red button if interested. He then promises to return in twenty-four hours and, should they choose to accept his offer, deliver their money.

It should be no surprise that after some deliberation, Norma and Arthur decide they can live with the guilt that comes with pushing the button and proceed to do just that. Though interestingly, this moment is not treated with the immense suspense one might expect. This is our first clue that Kelly has not made the movie anticipated by anyone familiar with the original story. Shortly thereafter, the Lewis family is revisited by Mr. Steward, who brings the money, reclaims the box and explains that it will now be "re-programmed" and delivered to someone else who, likewise, does not know *them*. It is at this point, the Lewis family comes to the frightening realization that they, themselves, are about to join the endangered masses. But whereas that moment served as the climactic ending to the half-hour, 1986 episode of TV's *The Twilight Zone* (which Matheson also penned), here, it is merely the end of the first of three acts and the impetus for a descent into a string of mind-bending consequences. And that is what is both intriguing and frustrating about Kelly's film. In many instances throughout, he refuses to spend time exploring the inherent moral drama that exists right in front of us and instead, eschews it for detours into much larger ramifications, some reaching as far as the universe, God and time, itself.

It is about halfway through the film when Kelly decides to dive head-first into weirdness. And before all is said and done, the audience is treated to images of nose-bleeding zombies, underground alien labs and watery, dimensional doorways. But Kelly is far too committed to his vision for it to be dismissed as mere pretension. And thankfully, his runaway imagination and lack of focus are anchored by expert filmmaking and solid performances. For starters, the film is sumptuous to look at. The juxtaposition of such bizarre imagery with Steven B. Poster's slow-creeping cinematography, Josiah Holmes Howison's gauzy lighting, and Priscilla Elliott's detailed, period art direction recalls Stanley Kubrick's *The Shining* (1980). And as strange as the film may be, at its heart, it is a suspense thriller. Kelly knows this and does not skimp on the honest-to-goodness scares nor the requisite, ongoing tension (thanks in no small part to the authentically Hitchockian-sounding score provided by Win Butler, Régine Chassagne, and Owen Pallett (members of indie rock acts Arcade Fire and Final Fantasy). Diaz and Marsden also do a nice job in roles that are obviously somewhat doomed from the start. Their concern for one another and their son comes across as truly heartfelt and although it falls by the wayside somewhere in the middle, by the film's end, it is back to the fore. Langella also deserves recognition, as the creepiness in his character is derived not so much from his ghastly appearance, but from the soft-spoken matter-of-factness with which he goes about his business.

The Box, which is Kelly's third film, is not in any position to threaten his remarkable debut, *Donnie Darko* (2001), as his undisputed masterpiece. And nor is it in danger of falling below *Southland Tales* (2006), his second film and one in which he indulged every impulse to the fullest, with confounding results. This film falls somewhere in between. But for every innovative concept in the film that has the viewer marveling at Kelly's unique approach, there is another left frustratingly unaddressed. And at a certain point, Kelly crosses the line and begins providing answers to questions that the story is not really asking. Fans of Kelly's other work should find plenty to love about *The Box*. He continues to be a whirlwind of ideas and displays no signs of a waning ambition. But everyone else should approach with caution. Still, it is Richard Kelly's movie and his alone. That is something to value. But viewers may find themselves wishing he were more keenly aware of the balance between their needs and his own desires.

Matt Priest

CREDITS

Norma Lewis: Cameron Diaz
Arthur Lewis: James Marsden
Arlington Steward: Frank Langella
Dana Steward: Gillian Jacobs
Norm Cahill: James Rebhorn
Dick Burns: Holmes Osborne
Walter Lewis: Sam Oz Stone
Origin: USA
Language: English
Released: 2009
Production: Richard Kelly, Dan Lin, Kelly McKittrick, Sean McKittrick; Darko Entertainment, Lin Pictures, Media Rights Capital, Radar Pictures; released by Warner Bros.
Directed by: Richard Kelly
Written by: Richard Kelly
Cinematography by: Steven Poster
Music by: Win Butler
Sound: Tom Williams
Music Supervisor: Christopher Mollere
Editing: Sam Bauer
Art Direction: Priscilla Elliott
Costumes: April Ferry
Production Design: Alec Hammond
MPAA rating: PG-13
Running time: 115 minutes

REVIEWS

Dargis, Manohla. *New York Times.* November 6, 2009.
Denby, David. *New Yorker.* November 9, 2009.
Ebert, Roger. *Chicago Sun-Times.* November 6, 2009.
Gleiberman, Owen. *Entertainment Weekly.* November 11, 2009.
McWeeny, Drew. *HitFlix.* November 5, 2009.
Mintzer, Jordan. *Variety.* October 28, 2009.
Orange, Michelle. *Movieline.* December 1, 2009.
Sobczynski, Peter. *eFilmCritic.com.* November 6, 2009.
Sorrento, Matthew. *Film Threat.* November 5, 2009.
Tallerico, Brian. *MovieRetriever.com.* November 6, 2009.

QUOTES

Arlington Steward: "I'm sorry, but I have a very busy day."

TRIVIA

This marks the first PG-13 film to be directed by Richard Kelly.

THE BOYS ARE BACK

Box Office: $81 million

In the Hallmark-Channel-for-the-big-screen drama *The Boys Are Back*, Clive Owen plays Joe Warr, a British-born sports writer based in Australia who becomes an overwhelmed, confused and bewildered single parent after his saintly wife Katy (Laura Fraser) passes away. Joe's life was all first-class travel, press boxes and front page by-lines until Katy's poignant death. It's only then that Joe realizes that he hasn't the first clue about how to be a parent to his young grieving son, Artie (Nicholas McAnulty). He left his first son from a previous marriage in the UK years ago and hasn't really been in the boy's life since. And he left the day-to-day responsibilities of raising Artie entirely to uncomplaining Katy. Propelled by a mix of guilt for his up-until-now-mediocre approach to fatherhood and grief over his loss, Joe opts for a casual and permissive brand of child rearing that he dubs "just say yes," where bedtimes are optional, dinner is take-out and no one ever has to clean up after themselves. Things seems to be going okay: Artie is having fun and Joe does not have to confront his son's feelings, and whenever he gets called on his lack of boundaries by any of the parents of Artie's classmates, Joe retaliates with a macho bravado. But Joe hits a road bump when his first son comes to stay. Harry (George MacKay) is old enough to know that Joe is messing up something awful, but young enough to still need some dad-enforced rules and the situation is more than Joe can handle. Luckily he's got Laura (Emma Booth), a pretty single mom who Joe selfishly takes advantage of by repeatedly playing his brokenhearted widower card. In the end Joe has an *About A Boy* wake-up call and realizes that he can't do it all alone. It will take a village—and a clean house—to raise his boys.

Based on the memoir by real life journalist and widower Simon Carr, *The Boys Are Back*, features elements of a heart-wrenching and at-times-charming drama about a father who has as much growing up to do as his two sons. And though it's hard not to get swept away in the tumultuous rollercoaster that is Joe's life, thanks to Owen's deep furrowed brow, as well as on the basis that no one should have to endure that much heartache, the film ultimately relies too much on predictable melodrama (sad kids and the sad parents that take care of them) as a placeholder for emotional gravitas, leaving *Boys* feeling more manipulative than organically touching.

Then there's the fact that Joe at times seems more clueless as an adult than a grieving parent should. Joe is perpetually battling bewilderment and confusion about how to talk to, comfort, and deal with his sons, but instead of driving home the idea that Joe is grieving and lost, he comes off more as an out of touch adult and it's hard not to wonder how one person can be so very clueless about kids and life in general. His biggest challenge seems to be balancing work and childcare, something that faces pretty much every parent the world over, yet for him it seems Herculean. Luckily, every time he's

about to hit a type of rock bottom, Katy pops up to tell him what to do. And while her ghostly apparitions are supposed to further illustrate Joe's grief, it's actually more frustrating to watch him not take his wife's from-beyond-the-grave advice in relation to Artie.

Still there is something about Joe's attitude that's intriguing and it's what keeps *Boys* from being chalked up as just another by-the-book father-and-son(s) drama. In as much as Joe's approach to his sons is frustrating, his selfishness is captivating because it comes from the place that would have any of us wondering why the world continues to operate as if nothing were off after the death of a loved one. Owen leads with this idea of tunnel vision brought on by shock and grief and his unapologetic take on Joe as a man who has really suffered a debilitating blow, more so than a man who is a crap parent, is captivating. Joe takes advantage of other people feeling bad for him, he doesn't want to confront his son's grief because he can barely get a handle of his own and all of this comes from a place of relatable frustration, anger, and betrayal. Joe fights with everyone who tries to help him, takes a my-way-or-the-highway attitude toward his life choices and his kids and it send him into a spiral of grief and selfishness that is powerful and captivating. It's the way we would want to be given the opportunity to act if faced with the same situation. Owen channels grief and frustration into a memorable performance, his portrayal of a bewildered Joe and his consequent bad decisions are what keep us hooked. Unfortunately there's not enough of this Joe on screen.

Joanna Topor MacKenzie

CREDITS

Joe Warr: Clive Owen
Harry Warr: George MacKay
Katy Warr: Laura Fraser
Laura: Emma Booth
Digby: Erik Thomson
Artie Warr: Nicholas McAnulty
Origin: Australian, Great Britain
Language: English
Released: 2009
Production: Greg Brenman, Timothy White; Australian Film Finance Corporation, BBC Films, Hopscotch Productions, Screen Australia, The South Australian Film Corporation, Southern Lights Films, Tiger Aspect Productions; released by Miramax Films
Directed by: Scott Hicks
Written by: Scott Hicks, Allan Cubitt
Cinematography by: Greig Fraser
Music by: Hal Lindes
Sound: Adrian Rhodes

Editing: Scott Gray
Costumes: Melinda Doring, Emily Seresin
Production Design: Melinda Doring
MPAA rating: PG-13
Running time: 104 minutes

REVIEWS

Chang, Justin. *Variety.* September 2009.
Ebert, Roger. *Chicago Sun-Times.* October 1, 2009.
Honeycutt, Kirk. *Hollywood Reporter.* September 15, 2009.
Pais, Matt. *Metromix.com.* October 1, 2009.
Phillips, Michael. *At the Movies.* September 28, 2009.
Rabin, Nathan. *AV Club.* September 25, 2009.
Rea, Steven. *Philadelphia Inquirer.* October 8, 2009.
Scott, A.O. *New York Times.* September 25, 2009.
Sharkey, Betsy. *Los Angeles Times.* September 25, 2009.
Simon, Brent. *Shared Darkness.* September 24, 2009.

TRIVIA

It took about eight weeks just to construct the Warr's house for
the film.

BRIDE WARS

*Even best friends can't share the same wedding
day.*
—Movie tagline

Box Office: $59 million

The title of *Bride Wars* suggests that the details of a
wedding—the date, location, DJ, etc.—are worth going
to battle for. While weddings do, of course, matter a
great deal to those involved, the fatal flaw of this shrill,
irritating and unfunny comedy is that it suggests the
perfect wedding is the *only* thing that does and should
matter to its dueling heroines.

Kate Hudson and Anne Hathaway star as Liv and
Emma, respectively, 20-something best friends who have
dreamed their whole lives of getting married in June at
New York's lush Plaza Hotel. When both women get
engaged at roughly the same time (to a pair of sidelined
dopes played by Steve Howey and Chris Pratt), they
meet with New York's foremost wedding planner, Marion
St. Claire (Candace Bergen, who also narrates), to lock
in their dream dates. An error—that St. Claire does
absolutely nothing to correct—causes Liv and Emma's
ceremonies to be booked on the same day, launching a
nasty, immature war between the two friends to own the
prospective day and undermine the other's nuptials.

At first, Liv and Emma try to play it cool, hoping
the other will cave and change her date—despite the

Plaza's next opening being a long three years away—and
agreeing not to move forward with any wedding plans
until they can sort out their conflict. It is understandable that they would not want to get married at the
same time; the girls are each other's maid of honor and
cannot be in two places at once. However, Liv and
Emma do nothing to help each other along or make the
best of a bad situation, as lifelong, adult best friends
should. Once Emma learns that Liv is shopping for
save-the-date invitations, Emma retaliates by sending a
rushed save-the-date e-mail, and all restraint and friendly
bonds are tossed aside.

Liv swipes Emma's DJ. Emma secretly sends
chocolate to Liv, who used to be overweight, hoping she
will gorge and no longer fit into her Vera Wang dress.
("You don't alter a Vera to fit you," the store clerk tells
Liv. "You alter yourself to fit Vera." This is clearly not
the best message to send to young girls about the value
of body image versus the value of an expensive gown.)
Liv sabotages Emma's dance lessons. Emma sabotages
Liv's hair treatment, causing Liv's hair to turn blue.

These actions, of course, sound like the doings of
spiteful 12-year-olds, not grown women employed as a
teacher (Emma) and lawyer (Liv). During *Bride Wars*,
these two seem like the last people in the world that
should play a role in guiding young minds and practicing law. Few, if any, actors could ground Emma or Liv
in anything that makes them seem more human or less
unlikable. But the performances by Hathaway and Hudson do little to endear the characters. Hathaway, who
received a Best Actress Oscar® nomination for *Rachel
Getting Married* (2008) less than two weeks after the
release of *Bride Wars*, spends much of the movie looking
like she knows that something better is out there. Hudson, on the other hand, shows none of the wounded
control she possessed in her Oscar®-nominated turn in
Almost Famous (2000). Rather, the actress delivers a shallow, impersonal performance during which Liv comes
off not as a formerly troubled child—aside from her
struggles with weight, Liv also lost both of her parents
years earlier—but a selfish woman with little sympathy
for others.

The movie is filled with contrivances that neither
generate laughs nor register as anything more than a lazy
story carelessly unraveling. One of the worst examples of
this is Emma, forced to find a new maid of honor after
her falling out with Liv, approaching her colleague Deb
(Kristen Johnston), whom she cannot stand, for the job.
Only a few scenes earlier Deb was manipulating Emma
and taking advantage of her pushover tendencies. Emma
is a pretty, previously stable girl who should have plenty
of potential friends and bridesmaids to promote to maid
of honor. Yet she resorts to asking Deb, a woman she

does not remotely like, to play a large role in her wedding.

This is but one example of a moment when *Bride Wars*, ostensibly a comedy, unintentionally plays out more like a drama or worse, a horror movie. The scene of Liv and Emma chasing down another bride at a department store, pointing registry guns at her and demanding that she change her wedding date, is pure, manic nonsense, overplayed in a way that, instead of lightening the tone, only presents the film's main characters as irrational and childish. Their behavior gets worse when Liv, after her hair has been turned blue, breaks down mid-meeting and nearly blows a big case for her firm. These scenes, coupled with dialogue that reinforces Liv and Emma's adolescent perceptions of marriage portrays women not as valuable members of society able to live and thrive independently, but lesser people who fail to achieve their purpose until they are part of a pair. To call that an unenlightened perspective in 2009 is an understatement, and the last message a supposed "chick flick" should offer to empower its target audience.

Matt Pais

CREDITS

Emma: Anne Hathaway
Liv: Kate Hudson
Deb: Kirsten Johnson
Nate: Bryan Greenberg
Daniel: Steve Howey
Fletcher: Chris Pratt
Marion St. Claire: Candice Bergen
John: John Pankow
Simmons: Bruce Altman
Kevin: Michael Arden
Origin: USA
Language: English
Released: 2009
Production: Julie Yorn, Alan Riche, Kate Hudson; New Regency, Fox 2000 Pictures, Regency Enterprises; released by 20th Century Fox
Directed by: Gary Winick
Written by: Casey Wilson, June Raphael
Cinematography by: Frederick Elmes
Music by: Ed Shearmur
Sound: William Sarokin
Music Supervisor: Linda Cohen
Editing: Susan Littenberg
Art Direction: James Donahue
Costumes: Karen Patch
Production Design: Dan Leigh

MPAA rating: PG
Running time: 90 minutes

REVIEWS

Dargis, Manohla. *New York Times.* January 9, 2009.
Ebert, Roger. *Chicago Sun-Times.* January 7, 2009.
Gleiberman, Owen. *Entertainment Weekly.* January 7, 2009.
Gronvall, Andrew. *Chicago Reader.* January 9, 2009.
McCarthy, Todd. *Variety.* January 8, 2009.
Pais, Matt. *Metromix.xom.* January 8, 2009.
Phillips, Michael. *Chicago Tributes.* January 8, 2009.
Puig, Claudia. *USA Today.* January 7, 2009.
Sobczynski, Peter. *EFilmCritic.* January 9, 2009.
Zacherek, Stephanie. *Salon.com.* January 9, 2009.

QUOTES

Liv: "If I were your wedding, I'd be sleeping with one eye open"

TRIVIA

During the reception, there is a shot involving a complicated series of dance steps in front of the camera. After many failed attempts, a dance instructor who happened to be an extra asked to teach the actors how to perform the maneuver correctly.

AWARDS

Nomination:

Golden Raspberries 2009: Worst Support. Actress (Bergen).

BRIGHT STAR

First love burns brightest.
—Movie tagline

Box Office: $4 million

Bright Star is as pretty as a poem. Writer/director Jane Campion's film about the love affair between 19th century Romantic poet John Keats (Ben Whishaw) and his young fashion-obsessed neighbor Fanny Brawne (Abbie Cornish) is the visual equivalent of the Keats' oeuvre, full of sensual imagery and possessing a quiet, earnest impact. Whether they are walking in the woods, sitting by a pond, or indulging in a forbidden kiss, everything that Keats and Brawne do on-screen is shrouded in a veil of meaningfulness. On the one hand, this has to do with their coming of age at a time when thoughts and feelings were given over to carefully chosen expression and social propriety was the order of the day, leaving the young lovers to sneak out in order to clock in some unsupervised quality time and to communicate effectively and efficiently when they were granted precious time alone. On the other hand, of course, the decision to bestow upon their relationship a shiny lyricism comes from Campion's internalizing what it must have meant to be John Keats and how the world must have looked to him—vitriolic, languid, expansive—in order to inspire his poetry. Campion composes a world full of crisp British mornings and foggy Dickensian forests which plant the viewer firmly in the moment of each scene so that we can fully understand what it must have been like to really be there. And it works. The English countryside is resplendent and so fresh and dewy that it is hard to imagine not being taken to writing poetry if one was lucky enough to call this place and time home. Against this backdrop, Fanny and her vibrant personality stand out like a shot that breaks the film's pensive silence; it would be impossible for Keats not to notice her. But *Bright Star* is not about initial infatuation, it's about the consuming love that causes one to think in rhyming couplets and as much as the actors try to create the burning fire of said fist love, the successful construction of their combustive relationship rests solely with Campion's fascination with Brawne.

In as much as *Bright Star* proposes to be a biopic about Keats, the movie really belongs to Fanny and more so to Campion's interest in the power (and melodrama) of Fanny's first love. Keats died believing that he was a subpar poet. What few positive reviews he did receive for his work were offset by lascivious slander of his poems. He made no money from his writing to the extent that his friends had to take up a collection to shuttle him to Italy when he became ill with consumption (where the air quality was reportedly better). His base caste in life made him a poor match for the well-to-do Fanny as far as society was concerned. So their love was all stolen moments, love letters, and across-the-room staring contests.

In the film, Whishaw's Keats comes off as a first generation emo rocker. He is lanky, perpetually glum, sarcastic and possessed of the type of shaggy hair that Edward Cullen would kill for. He is charming to be sure, but, more than that, he is handsome and that—as is typical—is what draws Fanny to him. And though some of Keats greatest writing is attributed to his love for her (his reading of his poems to Fanny and love letters pepper the film) it's hard to buy that this is so in Campion's take as Whishaw does not hold up his end of the relationship. On screen he is pursued, rather than doing the pursuing, he is reactive to Fanny's advances, rather than proactive, but the worst part is that the passion of first love doesn't burn as brightly in Whishaw's eyes as it does in Cornish's. Understandably, for Keats the character, his social status would make it difficult to

actively court a lady of higher stature, which Fanny was, but if we are being asked to believe theirs to be a consuming, poetry inspiring love, social propriety should take a back seat to romance—and Campion should take a page from Austen, who was always able to unlock the buried emotions in her characters, both male and female. Campion presents Fanny wonderfully, but in keeping a little too close to 19th century life, Campion reigns in Keats' character and consequently fails to extract the necessary chemistry from her male lead.

The era of chaperoned walks and balls with dance cards relied on rumor and missives to create tension. Talks of who was staying in the country and who was off to London were enough to break hearts, and letters were laced with secret desires—receiving them was akin to receiving a kiss. Campion achieves this sense with her screenplay. Keats' words are given the role of a supporting cast member and each delivery of a calligraphied note between him and Fanny holds promise. But for a period romance to work, no matter how intriguing the source material, this delicate and tangible tension of looks, gestures, and nuance relies on the chemistry of the actors on the screen and the chemistry between them. Every touch, every look, every letter has to be explosive, not only for the details to translate to a modern screen, but for the audience to be transported. Cornish rises to the occasion, but she is left holding it together for both her and Whishaw.

It is in the way that Brawne is swept away by love, consumed by Keats and made doe eyed by his words that *Bright Star* is transfixing. It is Fanny's obsessive pursuit of John that propels the viewer forward and her wrenching heartbreak that brings us to the verge of tears. Cornish plays Fanny with a lovely combination of vivacious flare, precious innocence and charm. Her desire to assimilate into John's life by trying to understand poetry reeks of teenagers changing their musical tastes to accommodate new partners, and her willingness to push the boundaries set by her mother is reminiscent of kids sneaking out to parties they've been prohibited from attending. She shows off to him with her knowledge of sewing, she intrudes in John's writing schedule, she is steadfast. She is in love. And her love is true, it is overwhelming, it sees past John's awkwardness, his sickness, his financial status and becomes all important the way first love should be. And she has the spark. When Cornish looks at Whishaw's Keats we can see her feelings for him, when they are apart, we can see her thinking of him. Cornish does this classic love justice and any talk of her being recognized come award time is duly deserved.

Luckily, Campion's interest in Fanny is front and center and Fanny's consumption with her relationship with John seems to translate to Campion's consumption with this material. In addition to creating a bucolic setting for Fanny to pursue Keats, she also creates a tranquil reality, mostly devoid of soundtrack. She opts instead to have the visuals take the dominant role in the film, relying on the images alone to be impactful and not interpreted with audio cues. The many gorgeous, ponderous moments of John and Fanny together in the wood, by a pond or in a sitting room in *Bright Star* therefore are reminiscent of the slow burn of Campion's previous films and she again shows her knack for composition here by playing with costumes and scenery. Fanny and her self-designed frocks and colorful, bustling hats pop against backdrops of stone grey houses, wood paneled sitting rooms and even Keats' dark blue velvet attire. She seems to exist in striking opposition to her surroundings and her very presence gives the film a subtle intensity and richness. In a way *Bright Star* is a filmic ode to Brawne as inspiration for Keats. In creating the stark setting to Fanny to stand out against, Campion plays her up as an obvious and transfixing muse, it's too bad then that she didn't spend as much time making sure that Keats was worthy of Brawne's advances.

Joanna Topor MacKenzie

CREDITS

Charles Armitage Brown: Paul Schneider
Samuel Brawne: Thomas Sangster
John Keats: Ben Whishaw
Fanny Brawne: Abbie Cornish
Mrs. Brawne: Kerry Fox
Toots Brawne: Edie Martin
Charles Dilke: Gerard Monaco
Abigail: Antonia Campbell-Hughes
Origin: Great Britain, Australia, France
Language: English
Released: 2009
Production: Jan Chapman, Caroline Hewitt; New South Wales Film & Television Office, U.K. Film Council, BBC Films, Hopscotch International, Screen Australia; released by Apparition
Directed by: Jane Campion
Written by: Jane Campion
Cinematography by: Greig Fraser
Music by: Mark Bradshaw
Sound: John Midgley
Editing: Alexandre De Francheschi
Art Direction: David Hindle
Costumes: Janet Patterson
Production Design: Janet Patterson
MPAA rating: PG
Running time: 119 minutes

REVIEWS

Burr, Ty. *Boston Globe*. September 24, 2009.
Denby, David. *New Yorker*. September 14, 2009.
Ebert, Roger. *Chicago Sun-Times*. September 24, 2009.
Edelstein, David. *New York Magazine*. September 14, 2009.
Hoberman, J. *Village Voice*. September 15, 2009.
Phillips, Michael. *Chicago Tribune*. September 25, 2009.
Scott, A.O. *New York Times*. September 16, 2009.
Stevens, Dana. *Slate*. September 25, 2009.
Tallerico, Brian. *MovieRetriever.com*. September 25, 2009.
Turan, Kenneth. *Los Angeles Times*. September 17, 2009.

QUOTES

Fanny Brawne: "You know I would do anything."

TRIVIA

The film shot for one day in Rome—Keats' funeral procession was the last scene to be filmed and was the only scene of the film not shot in the United Kingdom.

AWARDS

Nomination:

Oscars 2009: Costume Des.
British Acad. 2009: Costume Des.

BROKEN EMBRACES
(Los abrazos rotos)

Box Office: $4.1 million

Throughout a career that has seen him evolve from being the flamboyant bad boy of Spanish cinema to one of the most acclaimed directors in the world, Pedro Almodóvar has always been celebrated as a filmmaker who is truly in love with the possibilities of cinema and who knows how to create complex and well-written female characters and pull fine performances out of the actresses playing them. Even those observers who have otherwise never particularly sparked to his films (such creatures do exist, though they usually keep their feelings hidden so as not to seem non-au courant) are usually willing to concede these points. Therefore, it is perhaps not too surprising that he would one day make a film that is itself in part a celebration of the filmmaking world and which centers on the relationship between a director and his lead actress and he has finally done so with *Broken Embraces*, a mesmerizing meditation on the power of celluloid that is both one of the very best films of 2009 and one of his finest works to date.

The film tells the story of Mateo Blanco (Lluís Homar), a once-celebrated director whose career came to a sudden end fifteen years earlier when the production of his latest work, a frothy comedy with the wonderful title *Girls and Suitcases,* came to a tragic end after an auto accident that left him blind. Believing that his former life ended with that accident, he changed his name to Harry Caine, retired from filmmaking and now spends his time writing screenplays with the help of his loyal former production manager, Judit (Blanca Portillo), and sweet-talking beauties into his apartment for the occasional quickie. The low-key lifestyle that Mateo has constructed to escape his past existence comes crashing down with the arrival of two reminders of those days—the announcement of the death Ernesto Martel (José Luis Gómez), the sleazy millionaire who was the producer of *Girls and Suitcases* and the arrival of Ray X (Ruben Ochandiano), a creepy young man who wants Mateo to help him produce a screenplay that is a thinly veiled excoriation of Martel. Mateo quickly recognizes that Ray is actually Martel's son and while he refuses to be a part of the project, the two incidents cause him to begin to flash back on what happened all those years ago.

At this point, the story shifts to 1992 as Martel finds himself falling hopelessly in love with Lena (Penélope Cruz), a wannabe-actress/part-time hooker who is working as his secretary. She rebuffs his advances at first but when he uses his influence to help resolve a medical crisis involving her mother, she begins to relent and they become a couple. They seem happy enough but when she auditions for the lead in *Girls and Suitcases* a couple of years later and gets the role, she and Mateo find themselves instantly attracted to one another and embark on a passionate behind-the-scenes affair. Suspicious of what is going on between the two of them during the course of a project that he is funding, Martel appoints his flamboyant son to spy on them under the guise of directing a behind-the-scenes documentary on the making of *Girls and Suitcases*. Although the son makes himself a pest to virtually everyone involved with the film's production, the footage he captures does, according to the lip-reader Martel employs to translate what is going on between director and star from the footage, confirm his suspicions that Lena and Mateo are involved. After Martel and Lena go on a grim weekend trip to Ibiza (at one point, he pretends to be lying dead from a heart attack and she responds by casually sitting down and lighting a cigarette), they finally break up and he begins to plot a long, painful and costly revenge against Mateo and Lena that will end badly for them all.

In his previous film, the award-winning *Volver* (2006), Almodóvar took the risk of abandoning his typically self-conscious filmmaking approach in order to try to tell a direct and heartfelt manner without any of the irony or metaphorical quote marks around the scenes that often left a distance between audiences and the material that they were theoretically supposed to be car-

ing about. *Broken Embraces*, at first glance, would seem to be a deliberate return to the stylistic tics of earlier works—the narrative is wildly complicated (complete with a dual timeline structure that slips from one strand to the other with remarkable subtlety), the tone veers wildly between comedy and melodrama (often within the same scene), the visual style is of a candy-coated nature that practically screams *"Mireme!"* in every frame and it is filled with moments deliberately designed to call attention to themselves, right down to his cheeky decision to have the bits and pieces that we see of *Girls and Suitcases* specifically evoke the look and feel of his own breakthrough film, *Women on the Verge of a Nervous Breakdown* (1988)—but the end result is nowhere near as off-putting as it has been in the past. After only a few minutes, it becomes clear that, perhaps as the result of having worked in a more restrained manner in *Volver* he has finally figured out a way to deploy his more audacious stylistic flourishes in ways that accentuate the main story instead of overwhelming it completely as has been his tendency in the past. As for the story, it is true that the basic plot will come across as more than a little familiar to most viewers but instead of simply replaying genre conventions just for the sake of showing off his knowledge of screen history, he invests the material with enough genuine human emotion to make it resonate with viewers in ways that will remind them of what it was that got them hooked on the majesty and mystery of the moving picture in the first place. it completely. That said, the narrative does admittedly stumble a bit towards the very end when it deals with the question of what exactly happened to *Girls and Suitcases* after the accident—without getting into too much detail, it seems as though Judit, at the very least, should have known what occurred or at least suspected what happened—but to damn *Broken Embraces* for this comparatively minor flaw would be like dismissing *Psycho* (1960) solely on the basis of that concluding scene featuring the psychiatrist doing his needless monologue.

As fascinating as *Broken Embraces* is from a story-telling perspective—especially in the way that it transforms all of its complexities into a narrative that is endlessly twisty and yet always coherent—the real heart of the film and the thing that transforms it from the merely excellent to the utterly sublime is the extraordinary central performance from Penélope Cruz as Lena. This film marks the fourth collaboration between Almodóvar and Cruz and the relationship has proven to be highly beneficial for both sides—he has been able to get beyond her incredible beauty to see the talented actress underneath (which in turn has inspired other filmmakers to entrust her with roles with more depth than the spicy sexpot parts that she started out doing) and she has in turn inspired him to write real characters instead of mere caricatures. In many ways, what Cruz does here is similar to what Almodóvar does in that she plays a role that seems to be nothing more than a compendium of clichés at first (including the good girl trapped in a bad situation, the sultry seductress and the ambitious actress) and invests it with such humanity and emotion that she transforms Lena into a real person, a move that makes the film as a whole seem much more interesting and which makes the climax all the more devastating. Together, they have formed one of the great actor-filmmaker teams in recent memory and their efforts here makes *Broken Embraces* an alternately hilarious and haunting work for the ages.

Peter Sobczynski

CREDITS

Lena: Penélope Cruz
Mateo Blanco/Harry Caine: Lluís Homar
Judit Garcia: Blanca Portillo
Ernesto Martel: José Luis Gómez
Diego: Tamar Novas
Origin: Spain
Language: Spanish
Released: 2009
Production: Agustin Almodóvar, Esther Garcia; Canal + España, El Deseo S.A., Instituto de Crédito Oficial, Televisión Española, Universal International Pictures; released by Sony Pictures Classics
Directed by: Pedro Almodóvar
Written by: Pedro Almodóvar
Cinematography by: Rodrigo Prieto
Music by: Alberto Iglesias
Editing: José Salcedo
Production Design: Antxón Gómez
Sound: Miguel Rejas
Costumes: Sonia Grande
MPAA rating: R
Running time: 128 minutes

REVIEWS

Bradshaw, Peter. *Guardian.* August 29, 2009.
Ebert, Roger. *Chicago Sun-Times.* December 22, 2009.
Holland, Jonathan. *Variety.* March 18, 2009.
Morgenstern, Joe. *Wall Street Journal.* November 20, 2009.
Nelson, Rob. *Village Voice.* November 17, 2009.
Phipps, Keith. *AV Club.* November 19, 2009.
Puig, Claudia. *USA Today.* November 24, 2009.
Scott, A.O. *New York Times.* November 19, 2009.
Sharkey, Betsy. *Los Angeles Times.* December 11, 2009.
Tallerico, Brian. *MovieRetriever.com.* December 18, 2009.

TRIVIA

The car driven by Lena and Harry Caine/MateoBlanco in Lanzarote is the same red car that is used in *Volver* and in the final scenes of *¡Átame!* (1990).

AWARDS

Nomination:

British Acad. 2009: Foreign Film
Golden Globes 2010: Foreign Film.

BRONSON

The man. The myth. The celebrity.
—Movie tagline

Nicolas Winding Refn's viciously dark and violent *Bronson* is undeniably an exercise of style over substance. Even the subject of the film, the most notorious prison inmate in the history of the British prison system, would admit that there is not traditionally that much to his life story. A filmmaker could theoretically try and explain the actions of a lunatic like Michael Peterson through an examination of his likely disturbed past, but Refn is not interested in making his lead a relatable character. He offers no explanation as to why this man seemed determined to destroy all semblance of normalcy in his domesticity and presented few life goals outside of breaking as many prison guard bones as possible in the course of his existence. The man who would rename himself Bronson after his movie hero is portrayed as more of a force of nature than an average guy gone horribly awry. The purely visceral film about him is ultimately as shallow and single-minded as its insane protagonist, despite one of the most memorable lead performances of the year and style to spare. *Bronson* does not have much to say even if it is a notable exercise in how to tell a story without much to it with as much style as conceivably possible

Even the structure of *Bronson* is an audacious display of overabundant style. Michael Peterson aka Bronson (Tom Hardy) delivers his life story on a stage, in front of a live audience, in the format of an over-the-top one-man show. With makeup changes, exaggerated delivery, and even an applauding, well-dressed audience cheering him on, *Bronson* immediately takes on the nature of performance art. Refn is not striving for realism. He is telling the story of a ridiculous man in a ridiculous manner. Even Bronson himself looks nearly like a caricature of a British tough guy complete with borderline comical mustache. According to the film, Bronson is the kind of fellow who, when he knows guards are on the way to curb his rebellious behavior, likes to strip naked and oil himself up for the assault. It makes him harder to get a grip on in the heat of battle.

Michael Peterson was originally sentenced to only seven years in the U.K. penal system and it looked like he might get out in three. How did he go from a relatively short sentence to serving over three decades in prison, a large majority of which was spent in solitary confinement? The episodic film about him does not provide easy answers, merely the series of decisions that led him to becoming a legend in the British prison system. Bronson did a brief stint in an asylum, drugged to the point that he could barely move (a scene at a mental hospital soiree set to The Pet Shop Boys is a stylish highlight in a film filled with stylish moments), but even they could not handle a force of nature like this man.

Rarely has a film had less to it than a stylish production and a powerful lead performance. It is as if Refn realized that his lead was a hard-to-pin-down lunatic and made a companion piece that is both crazy and tough to put a finger on itself. The resulting mash-up of style can be both riveting and frustrating, sometimes in the same moment. Hardy is simply spectacular, delivering a fearless, mostly naked, unrelenting performance that cannot be slighted or criticized. He is powerful, riveting, and the kind of multi-talented performer that it is easy to believe could pull off a one-man show about a lunatic.

The fact is that *Bronson* is a one-note film (and that note is angry and loud). It is artistically daring to make a film that reflects its subject's personality more than tries to explain away his demons like a traditional biopic but it does not change the fact that all one-note films are, by their very nature, somewhat unsatisfying. *Bronson* is a rage-filled experience for roughly ninety minutes about someone who appears to feel no other emotion. It may be some of the most stylish anger ever put to celluloid, but it still results in a shallow film about a shallow man, distinguished only by ambitious directorial choices and a remarkable lead performance. Even if *Bronson* is arguably the best film that could have been made about the life of Michael Peterson, it does not mean that it is not more frustrating and forgettable than the stories likely told about this maniacal freak in prison yards around the world.

Brian Tallerico

CREDITS

Michael Peterson, Charles Bronson: Tom Hardy
Allison: Juliet Oldfield
Paul: Matt King
Uncle Jack: Hugh Ross
Prison Governor: Jonathan Phillips
Phil: James Lance

Origin: Great Britain
Language: English
Released: 2009
Production: Daniel Hansford, Rupert Preston; Vertigo Films, Aramid Entertainment Fund, Str8jacket Creations, EM Media, 4DH Films, Perfume Films; released by Magnet Releasing
Directed by: Nicolas Winding Refn
Written by: Brock Norman Brock, Nicolas Winding Refn
Cinematography by: Larry Smith
Sound: Tim Baker
Music Supervisor: Loi Hammond
Editing: Mat Newman
Art Direction: Janey Levick
Costumes: Sian Jenkins
Production Design: Adrian Smith
MPAA rating: R
Running time: 92 minutes

REVIEWS

Anderson, John. *Variety.* January 23, 2009.
Ebert, Roger. *Chicago Sun-Times.* October 29, 2009.
Goldstein, Gary. *Los Angeles Times.* October 16, 2009.
Hiltbrand, David. *Philadelphia Inquirer.* October 22, 2009.
Hoberman, J. *Village Voice.* October 6, 2009.
Musetto, V.A. *New York Post.* October 9, 2009.
O'Hehir, Andrew. *Salon.* October 8, 2009.
Phillips, Michael. *Chicago Tribune.* November 5, 2009.
Travers, Peter. *Rolling Stone.* October 8, 2009.
Weinberg, Scott. *Cinematical.* February 2, 2009.

QUOTES

Charles Bronson: "I gave you f**king magic in there!"

TRIVIA

Bronson was born under the name of Michael Gordon Peterson on the December 6, 1952, in Luton, England.

BROTHERS

There are two sides to every family.
—Movie tagline

Box Office: $28 million

Jim Sheridan's *Brothers* is an emotionally stagnant cover version of the superior original version of nearly the same note-for-note film by Danish director Susanne Bier. The original *Brothers* (2004) featured a spectacular trio of performances from Connie Nielsen, Ulrich Thomsen, and Nikolaj Lie Kaas in a shattering story of regret and the damaging force of suspicion on a family with already-tenuous ties. Bier's screenplay, co-written with regular collaborator Anders Thomas Jensen, was never the focus or main strength of a piece that was made exceptional by the performers who brought it realistically to life. Remaking a film in which the success is so reliant on the actors and actress at its center is an unusual decision from its very conception. Most remakes exist because they tell stories or bring concepts to life that simply must be told again. Remaking *Brothers* is akin to covering a song that is not all that well-written or catchy in the first place but beloved because of the original performer and what they do with it. It is not too far removed from a foreign remake of an American acting piece like *You Can Count On Me* (2000) or *The Squid and the Whale* (2005). Of course, it can be somewhat naïve of a critic to merely say, "watch the original," when so few film viewers are likely to seek out small foreign films but a work of art needs more than the desire to bring a subtitled movie to a wider audience to justify its existence. Despite strong work from Natalie Portman and Jake Gyllenhaal and a few notable technical elements, *Brothers* never does.

The title characters in *Brothers* are Sam Cahill (Tobey Maguire), a family man and accomplished soldier with a loving wife named Grace (Natalie Portman) and two sweet daughters (Bailee Madison, Taylor Geare), and his brother Tommy Cahill (Jake Gyllenhaal), the black sheep of a clan introduced coming home from a brief stint behind bars. The Cahills are led by gruff Hank (Sam Shepard) and peacemaker Elsie (Mare Winningham). As *Brothers* opens, the Cahills are at a crossroads with Tommy coming back to American society and Sam leaving it, heading off for another stint in the Middle East. Tommy has clearly always lived in the shadow of his more respected and beloved brother, a fact of life that his disapproving father has never even tried to keep too much of a secret.

Shortly after he arrives in country, Sam's helicopter is shot down and the soldier is presumed dead, news that travels back to the United States and rocks the Cahill family. Hank hides nothing from Tommy, making clear that he thinks the "good son" died. Sam's daughters struggle with the grief associated with losing their father. Grace does her best to move on and keep her family together. Interestingly, Grace seems the least racked with grief, expressing a bit of doubt that the center of her world has actually died because she does not "feel it."

As people do after tragedy, the Cahills try to continue living. Tommy naturally becomes a more vital part of the family of his brother's widow, reaching out to them not just as a gesture of support but also clearly to find some purpose and direction for his life as well. He becomes a father figure to Sam's daughters and does work around Grace's house, redesigning and doing major

construction work on their kitchen with a few of his friends. With very little melodrama, Grace and Tommy become shoulders of family comfort for one another. They share a brief kiss after an emotionally wrought evening, but nothing more and it is unclear if they would ever develop into lovers or merely be the support structure that each so clearly needs.

The audience will never find out if Tommy and Grace could develop into more than support because it turns out that Sam has not died in battle. He survived the crash and was taken as a prisoner of war along with a fellow soldier from his same hometown named Private Joe Willis (Patrick Flueger). Joe's wife Cassie (Carey Mulligan of *An Education*) is even friends with Grace and the girls back home. Sam and Joe are put through hell, kept in captivity, and forced to make unimaginable life-changing decisions while looking down the barrel of a gun. Joe does not come home and Sam barely does, returning a shattered, ghost of a man to a family that thought he was dead. He does not believe that Tommy and Grace were merely supportive and not lovers, he violently yells at his children, and it is clear that Tommy will be unable to move forward without a climactic confrontation and the revelation of what he experienced on the other side of the world.

In the original *Brothers,*, the soldier (named Michael in the original and played by Bier regular Ulrich Thomsen) was set up as a warm, powerful figure, a clear patriarch whose death would shatter everyone who knew him. Even when he was turned into a P.O.W., Michael radiated warmth for his fellow soldier in a way that made it clear that he had been supportive his entire life. For some reason, those character traits have been drained from Sheridan and writer David Benioff's version of Sam. In a bizarre decision that must have been jointly made by Maguire and Sheridan, Sam is played as a twitchy, wide-eyed victim of combat before he even heads overseas, almost as if he is a victim of previous trauma before the action of the film. Instead of the story of a good man pushed to the brink of insanity by a horrendous decision, the new version of *Brothers* tells the story of a man who seems like a fuse merely waiting to be lit. This drastic change in character tone is underlined by an argument between Tommy and Hank that implies that Sam was forced into life as a soldier by a demanding father. The removal of warmth and familial glow from Sam's character makes his fall from grace less effective and turns the entire piece into something more of an anti-war commentary than the character piece that drove the original film. Maguire seems miscast, but it was the decisions made after his casting (and partially in the writing by Benioff) that damage the overall film.

Significantly better are the performances from Gyllenhaal and Portman, rendered much more believably and three-dimensionally than Maguire's lead. In particular, Portman does very subtle work, refusing to allow her character to descend into the hand-wringing melodrama that many lesser actresses would have explored with the often-cliched role of the grieving widow. She is easily the best thing about the film. Jake Gyllenhaal tuned into Portman's wavelength and brought a similar sweet humanity to the one character/performance that is arguably an improvement on the original. The friendship and support between Grace and Tommy feels completely genuine and is easily the strongest element of the film.

And yet, even that is a flaw. The audience should not root for Tommy to steal Sam's wife. There needs to be an equal dimensionality to the brothers or the script falls apart. If Tommy feels more realistic than Sam, then the final act does not have the dramatic power of the original. Part of the problem is related to the fact that neither Maguire relationship—husband/wife with Portman, brother with Gyllenhaal—feels genuine. Neither pairing has the right chemistry or one as interesting as Portman and Gyllenhaal's. Like a chef trying to remake a recipe created by someone else but altering a few essential ingredients, the new *Brothers* just does not taste the same. It merely makes a viewer wonder why anyone thought to cook it again.

Brian Tallerico

CREDITS

Capt. Sam Cahill: Tobey Maguire
Tommy Cahill: Jake Gyllenhaal
Grace Cahill: Natalie Portman
Hank Cahill: Sam Shepard
Elsie Cahill: Mare Winningham
Joe Willis: Patrick Flueger
Cassie Willis: Carey Mulligan
Origin: USA
Language: English
Released: 2009
Production: Sigurjon Sighvatsson; Relativity Media; released by Lionsgate
Directed by: Jim Sheridan
Written by: David Benioff
Cinematography by: Frederick Elmes
Music by: Thomas Newman
Sound: Pud Cusack
Music Supervisor: Gina Amador
Editing: Jay Cassidy
Art Direction: Guy Barnes
Costumes: Durinda Wood
Production Design: Tony Fanning

MPAA rating: R
Running time: 110 minutes

REVIEWS

Chang, Justin. *Variety.* November 23, 2009.
Ebert, Roger. *Chicago Sun-Times.* December 3, 2009.
Edelstein, David. *New York Magazine.* November 30, 2009.
Honeycutt, Kirk. *Hollywood Reporter.* November 23, 2009.
Pais, Matt. *Metromix.com.* December 3, 2009.
Phillips, Michael. *Chicago Tribune.* December 3, 2009.
O'Sullivan, Michael. *Washington Post.* December 4, 2009.
Scott, A.O. *New York Times.* December 4, 2009.
Setoodeh, Ramin. *Newsweek.* December 4, 2009.
Tallerico, Brian. *MovieRetriever.com.* December 4, 2009.

QUOTES

Tommy Cahill: "Your nose is like the lunar eclipse. Come on let me touch it."

TRIVIA

Tobey Maguire nearly had to decline the lead role in *Spider-Man 2* due to back injuries and Jake Gyllenhaal was the top choice to replace him.

AWARDS

Nomination:

Golden Globes 2010: Actor—Drama (Maguire), Song ("Winter").

THE BROTHERS BLOOM

They'd never let the truth come between them.
—Movie tagline

Box Office: $3 million

Writer-director Rian Johnson made one of the more auspicious debuts of the decade with the release of his 2006 cult favorite *Brick*, a film that took a potentially indigestible conceit—resetting the elements of a classic film noir within the framework of a contemporary high school setting—and pulled it off with a lot of wit, style and intelligence. For his follow-up film, *The Brothers Bloom*, he is working on a much larger canvas and with a better-known cast but instead of tamping down the weirdness in exchange, he allows it to flower even more this time around. While the end result is nowhere near as satisfying as his first film, it contains so much charm and colorful energy that those viewers interested in something off the beaten path may be willing to overlook its excesses.

Adrien Brody and Mark Ruffalo star as the Bloom brothers, a duo that have devoted their lives to pulling one wildly elaborate con game after another on anyone who crosses their paths. As the film opens, the overly sensitive Bloom (Brody) wants out for good but the wildly ambitious Stephen (Ruffalo) convinces him to take part in one final fleecing with the target being Penelope (Rachel Weisz), a fabulously wealthy heiress who has plenty of money and hobbies but no real excitement in her life. At first, everything goes according to plan, but as the three, accompanied by the Blooms' ever-present and ever-silent ally Bang Bang (Rinko Kikuchi), hop around the world as part of the scam, some unexpected twists begin to emerge. Predictably, Bloom begins to fall for Penelope, which makes it a little hard to concentrate on conning her. Less predictably, there is the possibility that Penelope may not be the naïve innocent that she appears to be. To top things off, the dastardly Diamond Dog (Maximilian Schell), the brothers' former mentor and current rival, appears to be on their tail in order to get revenge on them for past inequities.

In creating *The Brothers Bloom*, Johnson seems to have taken his inspiration from the big-scale caper comedies that flourished during the Sixties—films like *How to Steal a Million* (1966), *Topkapi* (1964) and a good chunk of Blake Edwards' output during that period—that featured glamorous stars playing out ridiculously complicated plots amid lavish international settings. Unfortunately, the vast majority of these films were not actually that good and as the film goes on (and on) it succumbs to many of the same problems that befell them the first time around. For example, it spends so much time and energy pulling the rug out from under the audience with an endless array of double-crosses and unexpected reversals that it becomes a little wearying after a while—how can viewers be asked to make any kind of investment in the story if everything gets changed around every ten minutes or so? Another problem is the whimsically arch tone that Johnson goes for in every scene. He managed to keep things in check in *Brick* but he lets things get so overly quirky at times that it feels at times as if he has somehow compressed Wes Anderson's entire filmography into this one single film. Yes, the film has a lot of good ideas and entertaining moments but Johnson never figures out a way to pull them all together into the kind of cohesive whole that he did in his previous film.

That said, *The Brothers Bloom* contains a lot of elements worth admiring—the off-beat presence of Rinko Kikuchi in a role that suggests a gentle goof on her silent role in *Babel* (2006), a gorgeously gaudy visual style courtesy of cinematographer Steve Yedlin, and any number of jokes and sight gags that pop up unexpect-edly and score big laughs. More importantly, Rachel Weisz pretty much single-handedly keeps the entire thing afloat with her incredibly charming and engaging performance. Although primarily known for taking on serious roles, she lets her hair down and demonstrates such significant comedic chops that only an ogre with a heart of stone could possibly resist her here. And while *The Brothers Bloom* as a whole may not be a complete success, it does demonstrate that Rian Johnson is definitely a director worth paying attention to in the future—as he pretty much proves conclusively here, he may be capable of making bad movies but it seems impossible that he could ever make a boring one.

Peter Sobczynski

CREDITS

Bloom: Adrien Brody
Stephen Bloom: Mark Ruffalo
Penelope: Rachel Weisz
Diamond Dog: Maximilian Schell
Bang Bang: Rinko Kikuchi
Melville: Robbie Coltrane
Brody: Ricky Jay (Narrator)
Origin: USA
Language: English
Released: 2009
Production: Ram Bergman, James Stern; Endgame Entertainment; released by Summit Entertainment
Directed by: Rian Johnson
Written by: Rian Johnson
Cinematography by: Steve Yedlin
Music by: Nathan Johnson
Sound: Pavel Wdowczak
Music Supervisor: Brian Reitzell
Editing: Gabriel Wrye
Art Direction: Paul Kirby, Jasna Dragovic
Costumes: Beatrix Aruna Pasztor
Production Design: Jim Clay
MPAA rating: PG-13
Running time: 109 minutes

REVIEWS

Faraci, Devin. *CHUD.* September 5, 2008.
Childress, Erik. *EFilmCritic.* September 12, 2008.
Reaves, Jessica. *Chicago Tribune.* May 5, 2009.
Holden, Stephen. *New York Times.* May 12, 2009.
Lemire, Christy. *Associated Press.* May 14, 2009.
Abele, Robert. *Los Angeles Times.* May 15, 2009.
Stevens, Dana. *Slate.* May 15, 2009.
Ebert, Roger. *Chicago Sun-Times.* May 21, 2009.

O'Hehir, Andrew. *Salon.* May 21, 2009.

Tallerico, Brian. *MovieRetriever.com.* May 22, 2009.

QUOTES

Bloom: "Eat your waffles, fat man."

TRIVIA

Rachel Weisz was the first actor to sign on to the film.

BRÜNO

Borat was so 2006.
—Movie tagline

Box Office: $60 million

Brüno is not so much a movie as a full-frontal assault on both the comfort zone of mainstream moviegoing audiences and the American culture of celebrity. It's offensive, but not just because it's borderline pornographic. What should offend is not so much Sacha Baron Cohen's flame-throwing clown of a character, but his subjects and their willingness, representative of so many people, to do anything to get on camera. *Brüno* is a scurrilous, over-the-top, but devastatingly dead-on, critique of our widespread eagerness to be exploited.

While *Borat: Cultural Learnings of America for Make Benefit Glorious Nation of Kazakhstan* already established Cohen as willing to make fun of even the most taboo subjects (race, gender, sexuality), *Brüno* confirms the British-born comedian as a master of the ludicrous lampoon. Cohen established the character of Bruno on his television sketch show, *Da Ali G Show,* as the most flaming of all aggressively gay stereotypes, and on film he's a much more interesting and hilarious character than Borat. While Cohen as Borat feigned ignorance of American culture in order to expose its hate and stupidity—a sort of latter-day Tocqueville on steroids whose shtick quickly grew tiresome—Brüno is no yokel. Though superficially naïve, he is very much in the know about the culture he aspires to. He wants to be famous at all costs, and as such he represents not the outsider, but the epitome of the modern narcissistic poser, the acme of a culture of fame-seeking. Brüno is a much more believable character than Borat.

Brüno also has a much deeper and more coherent plot and purpose than *Borat,* and what audiences offended by all its anal sex may miss is that it's a wickedly serious enterprise. Exaggeration is its comic technique, taking what already exists to its preposterous conclusion is its preoccupation, and in this and other respects such as his unabashed egotism, Brüno resembles the character

Stephen Colbert plays on his *Colbert Report.* Brüno does not know shame; he defines himself, for no reason, as "amazing"—a narcissist with a self-ordained license to do whatever it takes to climb the ladder of instant celebrity.

No wonder what he does in pursuit of that goal is cringe-worthy. Cohen is willing to make his characters despicable to drive home his point. He makes fun of Brüno's own stupidity, shallowness and amorality. Critics who condemned Cohen as vapid missed the point completely. The overriding vapidity of the entertainment culture is Cohen's target, and Bruno is his vehicle for exposing it.

The hell with typical screenwriting protocol: *Brüno* jumps in with both feet immediately, with the title character introducing himself as the flamboyant host of an ultra-chic Austrian fashion show. Within the film's first ten minutes, audiences are treated to Brüno pronouncing Autism as "in" (Chlamydia is "out") on his TV show; practicing anal sex, using a variety of ingenious devices, including a dildo mounted on the end of an exercise bike, with his supposed true love (who quickly discards him once Brüno is on the outs as a celebrity); pronouncing himself the greatest Austrian since Hitler; and disrupting a fashion show after wearing an outfit made of Velcro. One of the quieter highlights of this introductory part of the movie is Brüno's interview with a fashion model, in which he agrees how hard her job is (Brüno pointing out how she has to keep remembering to put her right foot forward, then her left, and so on).

The boldness and inventiveness of the comic confidence of *Bruno* is unrelenting. Brüno moves to Los Angeles and decides to become famous by hosting a TV show that interviews celebrities. Perfect for the E! Network, which does nothing much but precisely that. But when he lures Paula Abdul for an interview, and uses Mexican laborers as chairs and tables during it, Abdul and her handler finally catch on and exit in a huff. It takes surprisingly long for her to do so.

The next person to fall into his trap is 2008 Republican presidential candidate Ron Paul, whom Brüno hilariously confuses with RuPaul. If, as with *Borat,* there is often a doubt about whether the victims in Cohen's "gotcha" skits are willing participants or actors in on the joke, that's not the case with Paul, who is caught on tape declaiming Brüno as a despicable "queer," surprisingly intolerant language for a libertarian-leaning politician. At this point, the film becomes distinctly pleasurable and subversive.

Brüno's pilot TV show falls flat with a test audience—it's insanely insipid, not to mention blatantly pornographic. Brüno's next brainstorm is to become a celebrity by doing what celebrities do, attaching themselves to a cause, and so he consults a pair of PR experts. He asks them what the next big hot issue will be ("We all know about Darfur, so what's Dar-five?") The issue of whether the subjects are accomplices in the comedy or dupes keeps recurring, but it is remarkable just how unclear the answer can be; they are plausible, but barely; outrageous, but no more so than what is seen regularly on reality TV. So, in the end, it does not really matter. Cohen's satire works in either event.

When Brüno decides to focus on bringing peace to the Middle East (calling it the Middle Earth), his self-appointed mission is ludicrously simpleminded, and his peacekeeping efforts consist of sitting down with leaders of opposed groups and (in a Groucho-Marx-worthy piece of brilliant doubletalk) confusing Hamas with hummus and then suggested that instead of killing each other, the Jews and the "Hindus" kill Christians instead. Brüno then decides the way to become famous is to get kidnapped, and meets with the head of a terrorist group and insults him to within an inch of his life. No one can accuse Cohen of cowardice.

But this is safe territory compared to where Brüno takes us next. Adopting an African baby in a blatant slap at Angelina Jolie's notoriety, he brings him home in a crate and presents him on a talk show to a stunned African American audience, dressing him in a "Gayby" shirt and named him O.J.. Since this is presented on *The Richard Bey Show*, it is an obvious stunt—especially the part where the child is taken away by protective service. But the studio audience is not in on the joke.

Brüno hilariously mourns the loss of his child by attempting to commit "carbicide"—chowing down on sweets at a diner—and then falls into the arms of his assistant's assistant, Lutz (Gustaf Hammarsten). Their version of a love nest (lots of bondage gear) is grossly upsetting to the hotel management.

The last third of the movie is devoted to Brüno's efforts to go straight after he decides that's the sure path to becoming a celebrity. He has several hilarious and disturbing encounters with ministers who try to convert gay people to heterosexuals, with military personnel, with hunters on a camping trip, and with a self-defense expert (who is called upon to explain how to fend off a gay man coming at him with dildos). This is Cohen's opportunity to depict again the depths of homophobia, and the extreme prejudices that are rampant in the culture.

The film triumphantly concludes in an illogical fake happy ending, the only really unsatisfying part of *Brüno*, but then Cohen brings down the house with a closing-credits music video that incorporates some of the targets of his prior jibes, including Bono. It's a fine end to a remarkable and utterly unique movie.

As Brüno, Cohen is consistently hilarious, a comic screen presence of devastating impact, and his film is a poke in the eye to the entertainment industry and our overgrown cult of celebrity. Cohen is a mostly unwelcome provocateur in the midst of this industry, exposing some of its smugness and a lot of its pretense by portraying a character even more shallow and pretentious, but barely so, than the members of the establishment he sends up. Cohen is an anarchist willing to explode and expose anyone he encounters, and part of the reason critics were not as kind to *Brüno* as to *Borat* is that *Brüno* is a viciously direct attack on uncomfortably close quarters.

For many audiences, *Brüno* will go way too far. But the real pornography in this film is the response of the parents of children whom Brüno interviews in his quest for stars in a photo shoot. If these are real parents of real children, they should be investigated for child abuse. If not, it diminishes Cohen's gambit a bit, but the fact that we suspect that they are real is itself a testament to the power of his satire. Cohen's tactics are nothing short of genius.

Michael Betzold

CREDITS

Brüno: Sacha Baron Cohen
Lutz: Gustaf Hammarsten
Diesel: Clifford Bañagale
Origin: USA
Language: English
Released: 2009
Production: Sacha Baron Cohen, Monica Levinson, Don Mazer, Jay Roach; Universal Pictures, Media Rights Capital, Four by Two, Everyman Pictures; released by Universal Pictures
Directed by: Larry Charles
Written by: Sacha Baron Cohen
Music by: Erran Baron Cohen
Cinematograpy by: Anthony Hardwick, Wolfgang Held
Editing by: Scott M. Davids, Eric Kissack, James Thomas
Production Design: Dan Butts, Denise Hudson, David Saenz de Maturana
Costumes: Jason Alper
Sound: Michael O'Farrell
MPAA rating: R
Running time: 83 minutes

REVIEWS

Anderson, Jason. *Toronto Star.* July 9, 2009.
Childress, Erik. *eFilmCritic.com.* July 9, 2009.

Ebert, Roger. *Chicago Sun-Times.* July 9, 2009.
Edelstein, David. *New York Magazine.* July 6, 2009.
Honeycutt, Kirk. *Hollywood Reporter.* June 30, 2009.
Lemire, Christy. *Associated Press.* July 9, 2009.
McCarthy, Todd. *Variety.* June 30, 2009.
Phillips, Michael. *Chicago Tribune.* July 9, 2009.
Scott, A.O. *New York Times.* July 9, 2009.
Sragow, Michael. *Baltimore Sun.* July 9, 2009.

QUOTES

Brüno: "I am going to be the biggest Austrian celebrity since Hitler."

TRIVIA

The "U" in Universal grows an umlaut—Ü, mimicking the film's title.

THE BURNING PLAIN

Love heals. Love absolves. Love burns.
 —Movie tagline

The writer of the highly-acclaimed *Amores Perros* (2000), *21 Grams* (2003), and *Babel* (2006) dipped his pen in his unusual anti-chronological narrative structure one too many times, turning his directorial debut into a dull dirge of a film that feels like nothing more than a well-made soap opera with its scenes set to shuffle. If the crisscrossing structures of Guillermo Arriaga's films with director Alejandro Gonzalez Inarritu were unraveled and the stories were forced to run chronologically, there would still be intriguing, interesting stories that unfolded with memorable characters. The structure of those films certainly added to the storytelling, most notably in *Babel,* where the subject of difficulties in communication made a narrative trick thematically pertinent, but they had emotional resonance that transcended the order of their scenes. Such is not the case with *The Burning Plain,* a film that has been chronologically put through a Cuisinart because it would be deadly dull without something to keep audiences awake. Arriaga's storytelling device has become so commonplace that most audiences and many critics are turned off by it so much that if a writer or director are considering using it they better have a more interesting reason to do so than merely to disguise a lack of interesting characters or a plot worth caring about.

The audience masochism masquerading as the plot of *The Burning Plain* opens with Sylvia (Charlize Theron), a deeply-damaged restaurant manager who finds time to sleep with a chef (John Corbett) at her work when she is not staring longingly into the sky.

(Almost everyone in *The Burning Plain* stares longingly to the horizon; so much so that there is even a montage of morose people doing exactly that which produces more laughter than the emotional punch that Arriaga was clearly intending.) The student level writing that uses an affair with a co-worker as proof of Sylvia's deeply damaged psyche is merely one of a cavalcade of clichés to follow. Sylvia mopes through her life, chain smokes, and scars herself, but her emotional pain never registers due to surface level writing that Theron does her best to make feel like more than a cliché. It is a testament to the actress' ability that she does sometimes break through the stereotypes to find a genuine moment here or there, but she is largely lost in the awful screenplay.

Through a flashback/flashforward structure, it is revealed that Sylvia's mother (Kim Basinger) died in a trailer explosion while mid-coitus with her lover (Joaquim de Almeida). Sylvia has more than enough reason to be scarred and the source of her depression and its link to sexuality and infidelity does explain a few of her actions. In another chronologically displaced arc, it is revealed that a young Sylvia, then known as Mariana (Jennifer Lawrence) as she would later change her name to escape her past, turned to the son of her dead mother's lover for comfort. The two shared the pain of losing cheating parents and formed a natural bond. In a final plot arc that is too clearly easy to connect to the rest of the film, a man tries to track down Sylvia with a young girl by his side after his friend, just injured in a disturbing plane accident, asks him to do so.

One of many problems with *The Burning Plain* is that nearly every dot of the intersecting plot is connected before the final act, removing any dramatic urgency from the piece. It is clear that Basinger and de Almeida's passionate affair will end in flames. It is transparent how Mariana/Sylvia and her young lover's plot are going to impact the rest of her life. After the first act, there are so few surprises in plot that all the audience has to focus on are the dull characters and the shockingly gray, predictable look of the film. When a screenplay reveals all of its twists and turns as early as *The Burning Plain,* it needs to provide characters worth caring about but everyone in Arriaga's film is so predictable and two-dimensional that they are impossible to invest in. Basinger does the most-layered work in the film and Lawrence is an intriguing young actress, but they are merely devices in the manipulative melodrama.

Brian Tallerico

CREDITS

Sylvia: Charlize Theron
Gina: Kim Basinger

Nick Martinez: Joaquim de Almeida
Santiago Martinez: Danny Pino
Carlos: Jose Maria Yazpik
Robert: Brett Cullen
Young Santiago: J.D. Pardo
John: John Corbett
Laura: Robin Tunney
Ana: Rachel Ticotin
Maria: Tessa la
Mariana: Jennifer Lawrence
Origin: USA
Language: English
Released: 2008
Production: Walter F. Parkes, Laurie MacDonald; 2929 Productions, Costa Films; released by Magnolia Pictures
Directed by: Guillermo Arriaga
Written by: Guillermo Arriaga
Cinematography by: Robert Elswit
Music by: Hans Zimmer, Omar Rodrguez Lopez
Sound: Lori Dovi, Jon Taylor, Christian Minkler

Music Supervisor: Dana Sano, Anette Fradera
Editing: Craig Wood
Art Direction: Naython Vance
Costumes: Cindy Evans
Production Design: Dan Leigh
MPAA rating: R
Running time: 111 minutes

REVIEWS

Childress, Erik. *eFilmCritic.com.* September 25, 2008.
Covert, Colin. *Minneapolis Star-Tribune.* September 25, 2009.
Ebert, Roger. *Chicago Sun-Times.* September 17, 2009.
Elley, Derek. *Variety.* August 29, 2008.
Hillis, Aaron. *Village Voice.* September 15, 2009.
Kaplan, Jeanne. *Kaplan vs. Kaplan.* September 23, 2009.
Pais, Matt. *Metromix.com.* September 23, 2009.
Scott, A.O. *New York Times.* September 18, 2009.
Tobias, Scott. *AV Club.* September 18, 2009.
Voynar, Kim. *Cinematical.* September 18, 2008.

C

CAPITALISM: A LOVE STORY

Box Office: $14 million

In 2004, documentary filmmaker Michael Moore had the distinction of directing and producing the first documentary film to gross over $100 million at the box office with his anti-President Bush tirade *Fahrenheit 9/11*, a film that went to great (and not always fair) lengths to discredit the Bush presidency, using the war in Iraq as its through-line. The film's success was an unprecedented event that many believed could have helped alter the outcome of the 2004 election. Today, the film comes off as a dated, overly manipulative and calculating rant unable to justify repeat viewings. But its success startled the industry and the pundits alike. Time will tell if a film is more than its moment, but at that moment, Moore's film was a rallying cry of outrage and a call for change that many wanted to hear. Moore soon became the object of adoration to college sophomore political science majors across the country.

The fallout from that moment was a curious one. If people did not know who Moore was after *Roger & Me* (1989), *The Big One* (1997) and *Bowling for Columbine* (2002), they definitely knew now. But *Fahrenheit 9/11* was Moore's ultimate golden ticket and earned him the ability to make whatever film he wanted next. He followed it up with *Sicko* (2007), an essay that called for change in the nation's health care system and a film that seemed almost bipartisan for a Moore project. After all, who can deny America needs a major healthcare overhaul? Yet, the problem with Moore's overexposure was that everyone knew who he was, knew his politics

and knew his deceptive and unbalanced methods of making a point. How would he get those who disagreed with him to talk before the cameras?

Therein lies one of the problems with *Capitalism: A Love Story*, a film that examines the downfall of America's financial institutions, the CEOs who reaped the rewards of the crash and the middle class who went broke and even homeless as a result of the greed that caused it. Moore's subject is typical, but certainly not unwarranted. The nation as a whole has felt outrage over the bailouts, CEO bonuses and the con artist loan sharks involved in the mortgage fraud that caused too many Americans to get evicted from homes they thought they could afford. It was only a matter of time before Moore turned on his cameras and went looking for answers that would suit his style of commentary and one-sided documentary filmmaking.

Capitalism: A Love Story begins with an old film of a man warning the audience that what they are about to see could make them incredibly upset and that if they have a weak stomach, they should just leave. This is done in good humor, of course, but Moore's audience presumably knows already what they are in for and that is why they keep coming back. His films take the side of the have-nots and works tirelessly to put the corporate bigwigs in their place in the grand moral scheme of things.

But he often does make some compelling cases. Take the airline pilots. Anyone who gets into the business of flying airplanes for a living clearly does it out of sheer passion for flying. The big airline companies know this and take advantage of it. As such, the average airline pilot lives paycheck to paycheck and has to take a second job just to make ends meet. We learn later on that an honestly, democratically run bread company pays its factory workers three times as much as an airline pilot, mainly because every single worker has a say in how the company is operated.

There is also the case against WalMart, which has supposedly been taking life insurance policies on 350,000 of its employees. The policies suggest that the younger a person is when they die, the more money they are worth to the company upon their death. One 26-year-old WalMart employee died and the company collected $86,000 as a result, a drop in the bucket for a corporation worth billions. Meanwhile, her widowed husband and children received nothing from the company to help pay for over $100,000 in medical bills or funeral expenses The policy also disturbingly refers to its workforce as "Dead Peasants." WalMart no longer practices these deeds, a point Moore buries as a random coda in the film's closing credits.

Still, Moore is at his best when pointing out the absurdities and outrageousness of such behavior and *Capitalism: A Love Story* could have used a bit more in this area. With *Sicko*, Moore kept a low profile throughout most of the film, a smart move and one that benefitted the movie considerably. Unfortunately, Moore's usual stunt of casually walking up to corporate headquarters to interview a CEO with his camera crew, only to be instantly turned away by the unamused security guards, has grown quite tiresome and pointless. What worked in the 1980s with *Roger & Me* as a bigger statement of "us vs. them" now just makes him look inept as a documentary filmmaker. Seeing Moore getting turned away carries no shock value or message. It has become a stunt for stunt's sake.

But that represents only one third of the Michael Moore aesthetic. The filmmaker consists of three parts. First, there is the aforementioned Moore, the Everyman. He walks the streets in his baseball cap, tries to score interviews with the head honchos and acts as the representative for America's downtrodden Middle Class. Then, there is Moore the Filmmaker who juxtaposes media clips to help make his point, often having a politician boasting grand notions of America while intercutting that footage with that of a family getting wrongfully evicted. Finally, there is Moore the Narrator, whose voice takes on a sarcastic tone with a sometimes childlike naïveté as he ponders the issues at hand, often ending the film with a blistering statement meant to rally the troops to the cause. *Capitalism: A Love Story* encompasses all of these traits, but the narration this time comes off as smug and condescending.

With the bailouts, AIG bonuses and the mortgage fraud rapidly becoming yesterday's headlines (though no less relevant), Moore's role in the media's playing field has become a huge question mark. While he will probably never have a hard time finding an audience for his films, it remains the same audience time and again. Conservatives know to stay away and to not give money to help fund what they see as lies and propaganda. Liberals, meanwhile, will continue to pay to hear the preaching to the choir. Moderates will likely see the films eventually and use them as a springboard for a good debate.

Moore is a satirist for the most part, yet he is beaten at his own game by the likes of *The Daily Show* and *The Colbert Report* on a nightly basis. *Capitalism: A Love Story* makes many worthwhile arguments and is very entertaining in spots, but Moore never takes the chance of interviewing anyone who will remotely disagree with his agenda. Instead, Moore invites his friend, actor Wallace Shawn, to participate in the discussion. Shawn is a respectable, talented and intelligent person who knows his subjects, certainly, but hardly a "get" for someone of Moore's stature.

Strangely enough, *Capitalism: A Love Story* arrived in the theaters not long after it was disclosed that Fox News commentator Glenn Beck had become the new media darling among hardcore Conservatives, perhaps becoming the Michael Moore of the GOP. One could argue that the playing field in the media between the left and the right has become a bit more evened out with these two titans. Both are extremists with substantial, loyal followings. But Moore has been around for a considerably longer period of time. How much more does he have to say and how many more ways can he repeat it? It is safe to say that the success of *Fahrenheit 9/11* was a fluke that could never be repeated. It is also safe to say that Moore could do himself and his audience huge favors by challenging them in a way they have never been challenged before.

Collin Souter

CREDITS

Himself: Michael Moore
Origin: USA
Language: English
Released: 2009
Production: Michael Moore, Anne Moore; Dog Eat Dog Productions, Paramount Vantage; released by Overture Films
Directed by: Michael Moore
Written by: Michael Moore
Cinematography by: Jayme Roy, Daniel Marracino
Music by: Jeff Gibbs
Sound: Francisco Latorre, Garry Rizzo

Editing: Jessica Brunetto, Conor O'Neill, Alex Meiller, Tanya Ager Meiller, T. Woody Richman, Pablo Proenza, John W. Walter

MPAA rating: R

Running time: 120 minutes

REVIEWS

Dargis, Manohla. *New York Times.* September 22, 2009.

Denby, David. *New Yorker.* September 28, 2009.

Ebert, Roger. *Chicago Sun-Times.* October 1, 2009.

Felperin, Leslie. *Variety.* September 9, 2009.

Scott, A.O. *At the Movies.* September 28, 2009.

Sobczynski, Peter. *EFilmCritic.* October 1, 2009.

Stevens, Dana. *Slate.* September 24, 2009.

Taylor, Ella. *Village Voice.* September 23, 2009.

Turan, Kenneth. *Los Angeles Times.* September 23, 2009.

Young, Deborah. *Hollywood Reporter.* September 9, 2009.

QUOTES

Michael Moore: "I refuse to live in a country like this, and I'm not leaving."

TRIVIA

Michael Moore presented his Detroit premiere of the film in the movie theater located in the same building as the General Motors Headquarters. He was denied entrance to his own premiere until he came in without cameramen and press a few hours later.

AWARDS

Nomination:

Writers Guild 2009: Feature Doc.

CHE

Steven Sodebergh's wildly ambitious and controversial *Che* would seem to be the kind of film that critics who decry a lack of original, daring voices in cinema would embrace with open arms. Very few directors have the raw nerve to make an artistic statement as unique as the four-hour-plus *Che,* an accomplishment on numerous levels—performance, technically, thematically, historically, etc. *Che* seems likely to be a film that history will be kinder to than audiences and even critics were at the turn of 2008 into 2009 (when the film opened in most markets). Sometimes screened as two films known as *The Argentine* and *Guerilla, Che* is better appreciated in one viewing and better dissected as one experience. Each half has its strengths and weaknesses and arguably different dramatic purposes but the two

work together to form one clear experience intended by their masterful director.

For years, Steven Soderbergh has been one of the most intriguing and important filmmakers in the world. There are very few directors at any level willing to take his creative risks but even fewer who have made so many box office hits as Soderbergh. It is clear that the man could make popcorn product like *Erin Brockovich* (2000) and *Ocean's Eleven* (2001) for the rest of his career and be successful at doing so. But Soderbergh demands more of himself. In the 2000s, he produced arguably the most diverse resume of any major American filmmaker, seamlessly segueing between small, low-budget films and high-profile, star-studded affairs. In 2009 alone, he released the historical epic *Che,* the modest drama *The Girlfriend Experience* (that runs less than a third of the running time of the first film), and the Matt Damon vehicle *The Informant!* There are directors who do not have that kind of diversity on their entire resume, much less within one year.

Clearly never designed as a piece that would set the box office on fire, *Che* is one of this master filmmaker's most divisive and unusual experiences. Many were turned off by the running time and the rambling nature of the second half of the film but it can be argued that Soderbergh is attempting something that challenges the viewer more than entertains him. His film is an effort to dare the viewer to look at the art form differently; to question what a biopic can be and what they should expect from it. Soderbergh attempts a nearly impossible approach to the historical biography, not merely hitting the highlights of a well-known life but trying to actually recreate for the viewer the experience of being in the vicinity of its subject matter. Both a subtle commentary on failed political ideals and a remarkably detailed character piece, *Che* is like no other film released in 2009.

Delivering one of the best performances of his acclaimed career, Benicio Del Toro stars as Ernesto 'Che' Guevara, the Marxist revolutionary who went from local hero to international icon to failed guerilla in a relatively short period of time. Soderbergh focuses on two of the most important periods of the icon's life with the two halves of *Che.* The first is a more traditional drama/action film, a piece that details the revolution led by Che and Fidel Castro (Demian Bichir) to topple the Cuban dictatorship of Fulgencio Batista starting in 1956 with Guevara's arrival in the country. Written by Peter Buchman, the action of the piece flashes back and forth between the revolution and a legendary speech that Che gave at the United Nations a few years later. By the time Che arrived in New York City, he was a counter-culture icon with hundreds of kids wearing T-shirts emblazoned with his image without being truly aware of who he was or what was happening in Cuba. Buchman and Soderbergh, working from Guevara's memoir *Reminiscences of the Cuban Revolutionary War* paint their subject as both a physical leader in Cuba and a controversial one around the rest of the world. It is a film about the emergence of an icon.

The second film presents the other side of the coin. It is the fall that eventually comes after the rise. Easily read as a commentary on the inevitable failure of Marxism, "Guerilla" is the mirror image of "The Argentine," as Che disappears into a failed revolution in Bolivia, where he would eventually die. Where the Che of the first half is a vibrant, popular leader, the Che of the second half is a rambling mess, a man who wanders the jungles of Bolivia and fails to inspire the people there in the way he did the first time. *Che* makes clear that revolution is a hard trick to pull off twice.

The sheer scope of *Che* is mesmerizing in its artistic ambition. It is not an easy film, particularly in the second half as Che meanders through the Bolivian jungles doing close to nothing and mumbling in a style familiar to fans of Del Toro. *Che* is undeniably slow and long but never boring or tedious. It is a mesmerizing work that tells the difficult life story of a complex man in a difficult, complex way. Ernesto Guevara's life does not have the typical beats of the standard biopic. He did not have a love story to write a Hollywood song about and he did not come to his end in a blaze of glory. He lit up the hearts and minds of Cubans and Americans but he slowly fizzled out in South America. The life story of such a complicated leader should be challenging and daring in a way that only someone as risk-taking as Soderbergh is willing to tell it. Sodebergh does not feed the audience lessons or highlights as much as present them with issues to discuss. And he draws from Del Toro one of the best performances of his career. These men are asking for discussion, disagreement, and debate much like the swirl of conversation that surrounded Che's arrival on the national scene. Very few filmmakers are willling to take a risk like this epic film that neither demonizes nor worships its subject matter, instead presenting him for audiences to come to their own conclusions.

Brian Tallerico

CREDITS

Ernest "Che" Guevara: Benicio Del Toro
Fidel Castro: Demian Bichir
Camillo Cienfuegos: Santiago Cabrera
Celia Sanchez: Elvira Minguez
Vilo: Jorge Perugorria
Ciro Redondo: Edgar Ramirez

Rogelio Acevedo: Victor Rasuk
Aleida Guevara: Catalina Sandino Moreno
Raul Castro: Rodrigo Santoro
Moises Guevara: Carlos Bardem
Rene Barrientos: Joaquim de Almeida
Captain Vargas: Jordi Molla
Lisa Howard: Julia Ormond
Mario Monje: Lou Diamond Phillips
Tania: Franka Potente
Benigno: Armando Riesco
Missionary: Matt Damon (Cameo)
Origin: USA
Language: English, Spanish
Released: 2008
Production: Laura Bickford, Benicio Del Toro; Wild Bunch, Morena Films, Telecino; released by IFC Films
Directed by: Steven Soderbergh
Written by: Peter Buchman
Cinematography by: Steven Soderbergh
Music by: Alberto Iglesias
Sound: Antonio Betancourt, Aitor Berenguer
Editing: Pablo Zumarraga
Art Direction: Clara Notari
Costumes: Bina Daigeler
Production Design: Antxon Gomez
MPAA rating: Unrated
Running time: 258 minutes

REVIEWS

Brunette, Peter. *Hollywood Reporter.* May 29, 2008.
Ebert, Roger. *Chicago Sun-Times.* January 15, 2009.
Gleiberman, Owen. *Entertainment Weekly.* January 7, 2009.
Loder, Kurt. *MTV.* January 26, 2009.
Morris, Wesley. *Boston Globe.* January 16, 2009.
Phillips, Michael. *Chicago Tribune.* January 16, 2009.
Phipps, Keith. *AV Club.* December 11, 2008.
Poland, David. *Movie City News.* September 16, 2008.
Puig, Claudia. *USA Today.* January 8, 2009.
Scott, A.O. *New York Times.* December 12, 2008.

QUOTES

Ernesto Che Guevara (to a Bolivian soldier about to execute him): "Shoot. Do it. Shoot me, you coward! You are only killing a man. You will never kill my spirit, or the spirit of the revolution!"

TRIVIA

Was the first feature-length movie to be shot with the Red One Camera

CHÉRI

In a game of seduction, never fall in love.
    —Movie tagline

Box Office: $2.1 million

Stephen Frears' *Chéri*, like the slick, dandy protagonist for whom it is named, is a beautiful thing to behold. With its exquisite costumes and gorgeous set designs, the film vividly captures the decadent environs of the idle rich in Paris in the first decade of the twentieth century. However, opulent *mise en scene* does not make a film and *Chéri*, like its protagonist, is ultimately gleaming eye candy with no substance or soul.

Based on Colette's 1920 novel, *Chéri* chronicles the passionate love affair of a wealthy, retired prostitute, Léa de Lonval (Michelle Pfeifer) and the spoiled, pampered son, Chéri (Rupert Friend), of Léa's old rival courtesan Charlotte Peloux (Kathy Bates). The film opens with Léa luxuriating in bed and telling her servant that the best bed is one with no partner, but this quickly changes when she is introduced to the dashing and handsome Chéri. Despite their age difference (he is twenty-five, she is forty-nine), the two quickly enter into a torrid romance. The film does not delve particularly deeply into what attracts the two to one another and this seems appropriate as there does not seem to be a lot of depth possessed by either character into which to delve. What seems to bind the two together is a dedication to hedonism, setting no plans for the future, and steadfastly avoiding any acknowledgment of a long term commitment to one another even while, ironically, their monogamous relationship sails along happily for six years.

The relationship ends abruptly when Charlotte arranges for a marriage between Chéri and the nineteen year-old virgin daughter of a retired courtesan acquaintance of hers. Despite being perfectly happy with Léa, Chéri mysteriously acquiesces to the marriage. Since the only distinguishing feature his character exhibits in the film is doing exactly what he wants all of the time without reference to what anyone else wants, his blind obedience in marrying is not convincing and seems the product of a straightforward plot device rather than an action consistent with his character. (If the issue is threatened disinheritance by Charlotte if he declines to marry, this is not made clear by the script).

Once Léa and Chéri are separated, each realizes that the relationship actually meant something to them, that they in fact love one another, and from that point on, each character pretends not to care about reestablishing their relationship while taking elaborate steps to secure exactly that outcome. Léa heads to the coast, purchases an expensive engagement ring for herself, and begins courting men, hoping that rumors will filter back to Chéri to make him jealous. Chéri meanwhile purchases a house close to Léa's house and interrogates Léa's servants about when she will return, while emotionally and physically punishing his unfortunate wife for not

being Léa. The film's otherwise light and comedic tone has difficulty accommodating the darker tone generated by Chéri's treatment of his wife. *Chéri* wants to be an Oscar Wilde like comedic romp (though its script proves woefully unequal to this task) but the comedy does not mesh particularly well with the abuse Chéri heaps on his wife.

All of this occurs against an exquisitely realized backdrop. *Chéri*'s production aesthetics are breathtaking. When Léa strolls along the beach, the color of her dress perfectly matches the color of the sea. A scene in which a top hat-wearing Chéri walks down a cobblestone Paris street, cane in hand, is like something out a Gustave Caillebotte painting. Production designer Alan MacDonald and costume designer Consolata Boyle do excellent, Oscar®-worthy work. Indeed, *Chéri* is almost worth seeing for its production elements alone.

Almost. Even the most gorgeous production cannot conceal the fact that the beautiful costumes and sets house shallow, selfish characters that the viewer does not care about or, in the case of Chéri himself, particularly like. Chéri is a spoiled, child of a man who has never had to work for anything in his life and has had his every whim indulged since birth. He feels entitled to rape his virgin wife on their wedding night and to punish her for his weakness in marrying her in the first place. Léa is a more sympathetic character, but, like Chéri, is an essentially shallow person whose idea of an ideal time is to head out to the country with Chéri so they can "look at each other." While it is sad for Léa that after a lifetime of lovers who, by her own admission, meant nothing to her, she has the misfortune of meeting her one true love too late in life, it is not a misfortune that has been made especially moving for the viewer. This is not the fault of the actors who do uniformly excellent work (particularly Michelle Pfiefer) but rather the shallow, unsympathetic characters the script has given them to play.

The film climaxes with Léa choosing to make a sacrifice that Chéri has not earned and does not deserve. Léa's sacrifice, and her explanation to Chéri that accompanies it, provides a welcome shift in the film to a more serious tone and greater depth of character. However, this shift is too little, too late. If the film had adopted this serious tone and character depth from its beginning, *Chéri* might have been the thought-provoking and affecting film it seeks to be in its final few minutes.

For a love story to be compelling, the viewer has to care about the people in love. Jane Campion's superb *Bright Star* (2009) demonstrated that a romantic film can be both visually exquisite and feature complex, compelling lovers the viewer cares about. *Chéri* succeeds memorably in the former area but fails utterly in the latter.

Nate Vercauteren

CREDITS

Léa de Lonval: Michelle Pfeiffer
Madame Peloux: Kathy Bates
Chéri: Rupert Friend
Edmee: Felicity Jones
Marie Laure: Iben Hjejle
Baronne: Bette Bourne
La Copine: Anita Pallenberg
Rose: Frances Tomelty
La Loupiote: Harriet Walter
Mme. Aldonza: Nichola McAuliffe
Narrator: Stephen Frears
Origin: Great Britain, France, Germany
Language: English
Released: 2009
Production: Bill Kenwright, Tiggy Films, Pathe Productions, MMC Independent; released by Miramax Films
Directed by: Stephen Frears
Written by: Christopher Hampton
Cinematography by: Darius Khondji
Music by: Alexandre Desplat
Editing: Lucia Zucchetti
Sound: Joakim Sundström
Art Direction: Mark Raggett
Costumes: Consolata Boyle
Production Design: Alan Macdonald
MPAA rating: R
Running time: 92 minutes

REVIEWS

Anderson, Melissa. *Village Voice.* June 24, 2009.
Bradshaw, Peter. *Guardian.* May 8, 2009.
Cole, Stephen. *Globe and Mail.* June 25, 2009.
Dargis, Manohla. *New York Times.* June 26, 2009.
Ebert, Roger. *Chicago Sun-Times.* June 25, 2009.
Edelstein, David. *New York Magazine.* June 22, 2009.
LaSalle, Mick. *Houston Chronicle.* June 26, 2009.
O'Sullivan, Michael. *Washington Post.* June 26, 2009.
Pols, Mary F. *Time Magazine.* June 26, 2009.
Travers, Peter. *Rolling Stone.* June 25, 2009.

QUOTES

Léa de Lonval: "I'm probably making a fool of myself…but then again, why not? Life is short!"

TRIVIA

When the project was in development during the 1990s, Jessica Lange planned to star as Léa de Lonval.

A CHRISTMAS CAROL
(Disney's A Christmas Carol)

Box Office: $137.9 million

Maybe there's a little Scrooge in all of us. As we grow older and experience more disappointment in our lives, how can a little part of us not identify with Ebenezer's anti-social, miserly ways—especially in the bad economy we keep hearing about? We have heard the story so many different times in so many different ways. If Charles Dickens' original text somehow escaped you, there are over twenty film adaptations, close to fifty takes on it from television and countless radio and theatre performances. Whatever your pleasure you could have Alistair Sim or Bill Murray, Mickey Mouse or Mr. Magoo, the Muppets or Matthew McConaughey. All have received the Scrooge treatment. So while the world may not need another retelling, the anticipation of one of the most innovative filmmakers of any generation blending the ghost of Dickensian language with that of the present and future of animation is worth one more spin of the old yarn, is it not? Somewhere along the way, unfortunately, the technology utilized by Robert Zemeckis to great effect in *The Polar Express* (2004) and *Beowulf* (2007) has finally caught up to its dead-eyed criticisms and exceeded even them by deadening the heart and soul of the story as well.

Jim Carrey—or the motion-captured version of him—stars as the stingy, heartless Scrooge first seen reimbursing himself of the burial rights of his deceased partner, Jacob Marley with the very coins used to pay the ferryman. Ol' Scrooge despises Christmas so. He humbugs the invitation by his nephew, Fred (Colin Firth), to holiday dinner and scoffs at Bob Cratchit (Gary Oldman) assuming he's to be given the full day off. Those coming for donations? Scrooge would rather support the prisons and the workhouses and those without shelter who are better off dying to "decrease the surplus population." Merry Christmas, everybody!

Crankiness doth never prosper in fiction though and on Christmas Eve Scrooge is visited by Marley's ghost (also played by Oldman), bound by the dangling chains of exploiting the everyman for his personal gain. Change your ways, Marley advises Scrooge, or suffer the same fate. To help bring him around, three ghosts will visit the grump and remind him of happier times, a present where he's equally scorned and toasted and the grim inevitability of his current path.

The story is known near and far, young and old, with differences only materializing in the modern twists of the adaptation. Zemeckis sticks with the very roots, maintaining the 19th century London setting and much of Dickens' original text. Akin to attempts at Shakespearean recreations like Baz Luhrmann's *Romeo and Juliet* (1996) and Michael Almereyda's *Hamlet* (2000) to manifest the anachronistic dialect into the present, Zemeckis' script in most instances goes verbatim with Dickens' dialogue. Unlike those other disastrous attempts, it's a fascinating choice particularly when highlighting an off-the-cuff performer like Carrey who poses the potential to riff and tweak on a moment's notice. With Carrey being noticeably devoted to the character's essence, the onus falls on Zemeckis to justify the methods he's used to bring this story to life once again. According to him, the more surreal elements of the story were limited in their presentation thanks to the antiquated processes filmmakers were hamstrung by. Others might argue that seeing Gary Oldman look like a botox-ed Alfred E. Neumann trumps any ghostly image of terror Dickens could have ever thought up.

Only Carrey comes off unscathed in both appearance and performance. The amount of detail put into every pore of Scrooge's face—right down to the hairs on his nose—swats away many of the arguments over the soulless representation of human actors in this face. Carrey is actually incredibly expressive, particularly in tone, leaving one to imagine how much more stunning it would have been to see the actual Carrey give what may be the best work as Scrooge since the vaunted portrayal by Alistair Sim. Having already recreated one small-hearted Christmas character in live action form for *How The Grinch Stole Christmas* (2000), Carrey doesn't just resort to the same bag of bombastic tricks to communicate his disdain for the manufactured happiness around a single day. Scrooge's putdowns are provoked and Carrey in these early scenes conveys the underlying disillusionment that's turned him into such a grump. With the chains unleashed for the actor to let it all out as the spirits, he balances a tight shift between creepiness and ethereal wisdom before the film betrays him into a reactionary passenger on an amusement ride.

The faithfulness that Zemeckis commits to Dickens' imagery extends to his recreation of the spirits themselves. The first spirit maintains its ageless, childlike appearance but is taken to a literal interpretation with its crown resembling a candle. Its head is no longer just a wick, it's an entire candle with an extinguisher cap. The spirit of the Present is the jolly giant Dickens thought up; a young Father Christmas-type that towers over Scrooge like a cross between Harry Potter's Hagrid

and the Burger King. And, of course, the final spirit is a mute shadow of the Grim Reaper that tries to chase Scrooge—literally—into his grave. It all begs one to wonder why the necessity for the animated approach. In *Beowulf* it made sense to blend the captured performers into a limitless world of creatures and superhuman feats. With *The Polar Express*, animation fit the storybook approach and likely saved millions of dollars in set recreations. Few would question Richard Linklater's use of rotoscoping his actors in the futuristic, drugged-out society of *A Scanner Darkly* (2006). As filmmaking challenges, few could compare to any of them. Precisely what was the challenge of *A Christmas Carol* other than a blind sense of obligation to explore the depths of the technology? Maybe no one would have cared to see the umpteenth version of the story had it been in live action, but was the gimmick so worth preserving until the human touch had been lost entirely?

In Hollywood the budgetary constraints between recreating in meticulous detail the 19th century setting versus the potential windfall of yet another 3-D holiday spectacular that can be blown up for IMAX theaters is probably a no-brainer. Robert Zemeckis is one of the smartest, most meticulous and well-respected directors in that town though and likely has the carte blanche to write his own ticket after a string of box office successes. (*Beowulf* was the first film of his not to break $100 million since *Death Becomes Her* [1992].) Yet he has never seemed bound to compromise for the sake of a few extra dollars on his resume. Think back to themes of potential incest, sex with "bad" drawings, and challenging the scientific and spiritual nature of the universe and you'll recognize the subversive streak that has permeated throughout his career. One of the best kept passages of Dickens' prose involves mankind's adherence to rules put in place by the Church; a flame normally worthy of Zemeckis' fanning. However, those folded-in explorations of the salacious never surmounted his grasp on the human heart and the greatest mystery may be how he was able to take a story which, when done half-right, inspires an instantaneous knot in one's throat, and drain it to the point where Tiny Tim's passing barely registers on an EKG.

With Scrooge's prickly personality well established in the first twenty minutes, there needs to be an equal formation of what caused this shift over time. Like the manner in which he is whisked like Superman across the skies of London, Zemeckis travels through one of his own wormholes and folds time into a muddled recreation of Scrooge's past. An estranged father is alluded to and a beloved sister that died giving birth to Fred, the first crack in Scrooge's armor is barely a footnote. Instead more time is devoted (not by much) to his boisterous first employer who adored Christmas and led to the meeting of Ebenezer's fiancé. We see their first dance and then a break-up, never to be referenced again. Only in the moment of a young Scrooge singing a Christmas song to his lonesome in an empty classroom do we feel the potential emotional weight of a character abandoned time and again until he began to embrace it. This expedited approach in adherence to Dickens' final paragraphs fails Zemeckis in the closing act as well. With Carrey's mannerisms still in check, Scrooge buys the big goose for the Cratchits, gives Bob a raise and has dinner at Fred's. Instead of padding the running time with another flying sequence or an extended chase by Future's dark carriage that's neither exciting nor frightening, why not embrace what's yet-to-come and earning the emotional payoff of Scrooge's overnight evolution? Would you rather see a genuine toast to Scrooge's graciousness or have 'Cratchit E. Neumann' break the fourth wall with his dead eyes and narrate the final passages of Dickens' epilogue to you verbatim?

That's a lot of tell for a normally showy director, especially when it comes to working for those unabashed moments that pull at your heartstrings. The coming together of Marty's parents or his attempts to save the Doc's life in *Back to the Future* (1985); the survival of Toontown in *Who Framed Roger Rabbit?* (1988); the reunion with Jenny at the Washington Monument in *Forrest Gump* (1994); Tom Hanks' realization that he's lost his true love for a second time in *Cast Away* (2000)—these moments are so perfectly calculated that they don't just flutter your heart, but are capable of piercing your soul. The instinctual opportunities that come with fables like this and *It's A Wonderful Life* (1941) should be that a viewer can just turn on the last fifteen minutes and watch the waterworks begin. There is no "Merry Christmas, moviehouse" without "God Bless Us, Everyone!" and the greater sadness in experiencing Zemeckis' *A Christmas Carol* is the Scrooge-like emptiness you leave with as you are reminded of better times.

Erik Childress

CREDITS

Ebeneezer Scrooge / Ghost of Christmas Past/Present/Yet to Come: Jim Carrey (Voice)
Bob Cratchit / Jacob Marley / Tiny Tim: Gary Oldman (Voice)
Fred: Colin Firth (Voice)
Mr. Fezziwig / Old Joe: Bob Hoskins (Voice)
Belle: Robin Wright Penn (Voice)
Mrs. Cratchit: Lesley Manville (Voice)
Origin: USA
Language: English

Released: 2009
Production: Jack Rapke, Steve Starkey, Robert Zemeckis; Imagemovers, Walt Disney Pictures
Directed by: Robert Zemeckis
Written by: Robert Zemeckis
Cinematography by: Robert Presley
Music by: Alan Silvestri
Sound: William B. Kaplan, James Tanenbaum
Editing: Jeremiah O'Driscoll
Art Direction: Marc Gabbana, Mike Stassi
Costumes: Anthony Almaraz
Production Design: Doug Chiang
MPAA rating: PG
Running time: 98 minutes

REVIEWS

Ebert, Roger. *Chicago Sun-Times*. November 5, 2009.
Honeycutt, Kirk. *Hollywood Reporter*. November 3, 2009.
McCarthy, Todd. *Variety*. November 3, 2009.
O'Sullivan, Michael. *Washington Post*. November 6, 2009.
Pais, Matt. *Metromix.com*. November 5, 2009.
Phillips, Michael. *Chicago Tribune*. November 5, 2009.
Rickey, Carrie. *Philadelphia Inquirer*. November 5, 2009.
Sharkey, Betsy. *Los Angeles Times*. November 5, 2009.
Sobczynski, Peter. *EFilmCritic*. November 5, 2009.
Tallerico, Brian. *MovieRetriever.com*. November 5, 2009.

QUOTES

Ebenezer Scrooge: "Haunt me no longer!"

TRIVIA

This was Jim Carrey's first project with Walt Disney Pictures.

CIRQUE DU FREAK: THE VAMPIRE'S ASSISTANT

Meet Darren. He's sixteen going on immortal.
—Movie tagline

Box Office: $13 million

Adapted from the best selling young adult book series by Darren Shan (the pen name of Darren O'Shaughnessy), *Cirque du Freak: The Vampire's Assistant*, a supernaturally-themed coming-of-age film is, sadly, like a circus side show that starts off strong and then ends with a weak blow-off. A knockout performance by John C. Reilly, and a very strong supporting cast cannot mask this cinematic cirque's weak points; a less-than-death-defying dynamic between two bland teen leads and a muddled, over-complicated narrative that does next to nothing with its far-more-interesting secondary characters.

Teenagers Darren (Chris Massoglia) and Steve (Josh Hutcherson) are best friends whose shared interest in strange stuff has kept them close. When they find out a traveling freak show is coming to town they attend only to discover that the Cirque du Freak is no ordinary circus. A host of supernatural creatures call it home, not the least of which is Larten Crepsley (John C. Reilly), a non-carnivorous vampire that Steve recognizes from his past researches into all things bloodsucker. Darren meanwhile finds himself drawn to Crepsley's beloved performing spider which he steals, drawing himself and Steve inextricably into the world of the Cirque du Freak. When Crepsley chooses Darren over Steve to be his next protégé and half-vampire manservant, the two friends are set on a collision course. Darren adapts to life in the cirque, mastering his new abilities and meeting new friends; the giant ringmaster Mr. Tall (Ken Watanabe), the beautiful, only-sometimes-bearded lady Madame Truska (Salma Hayek), and a would-be rocker roommate Evra the Snake Boy (Patrick Fugit).

But Darren also learns of supernatural beings that are decidedly unfriendly, beings that have taken the enraged Steve under their wing; the mysterious master manipulator Mr. Tiny (Michael Cerveris), who seems able to bend everyone to his slightest whim and the savage vampire race known as Vampaneze ,who, unlike Crepsley, hold to the old ways of slaughtering humans for their nourishment. Mr. Tiny, working hand-in-hand with the Vampaneze Murlaugh (Ray Stevenson), hopes to start a war for his own enjoyment, while Murlaugh hopes to eradicate Crepsley and his kind. Darren just wants to go back to the way things were and *that* is highly unlikely.

Director Paul Weitz (*About A Boy* [2002], *In Good Company* [2004] *American Dreamz* [2006]) and Co-Screenwriter Brian Helgeland (*A Nightmare on Elm Street 4: The Dream Master* [1988], *L.A. Confidential* [1997], *Mystic River* [2003], *Man on Fire* [2004]) fail to do more than amuse precisely because they themselves seem so in love with the world they are creating that they cannot be bothered to tell a simple story. Conflicts abound; Crepsley's conflict with Murlaugh and Mr Tiny, Darren's conflict with Steve, the Cirque's implied conflict with Darren, and of course Darren's conflict within himself. None of these coalesce into anything other than some inspired fantasy sequences involving the cirque performers and some surprisingly bland fight scenes that seem oddly at the metaphoric heart of why this film just is not compelling.

But the really sad thing here is the absolute waste of the freaks in the cirque who are brought to life in an amazing introductory sequence by a wonderful array of talent but barely given time to do anything at all before being whisked off-screen in favor of a constant barrage of unnecessary exposition, side-plotting and other broken down attractions.

Most of the lead performances are fair-to-middling. Newcomer Chris Massoglia is passable in a *Twilight* (2008) sort of way as Darren Shan, but he seems oddly uncomfortable in his role almost as if he were embarrassed to have a landed the lead. The very-experienced Josh Hutcherson (*Zathura: A Space Adventure* [2005], *Journey to the Center of the Earth* [2008]) brings nothing but tropes to his portrayal of Steve who is sadly reminiscent of, if far less interesting than, Evil Ed (Stephen Geoffreys) from *Fright Night* (1985). Michael Cerveris, known of late as The Observer on TVs *Fringe*, makes a marvelous villain in Mr. Tiny, though, as written, the character borders on self-parody.

The only real standout here, the only real reason to see this movie, is the magnificent John C. Reilly (*Magnolia* [1999], *Chicago* [2002]), who creates in Larten Crepsley a character that screams to be let loose into his own mythology. *Cirque du Freak: The Vampire's Assistant* is liable to join the ranks of films with a small cult following, much as many similar films from the eighties enjoy. It is colorful, often funny, and succeeds at being a light entertainment. But, as freak shows go, this is of the variety that promise much, only to distract and ultimately send customers out of the tent still wanting more.

Dave Canfield

CREDITS

Darren Shan: Chris Massoglia
Steve: Josh Hutcherson
Madame Truska: Salma Hayek
Larten Crepsley: John C. Reilly
Corma Limbs: Jane Krakowski
Murlaugh: Ray Stevenson
Evra the Snake Boy: Patrick Fugit
Mr. Tall: Ken Watanabe
Alexander Ribs: Orlando Jones
Rhamus Twobellies: Frankie Faison
Gavner Purl: Willem Dafoe
Mr. Tiny: Michael Cerveris
Rebecca the Monkey Girl: Jessica Carlson
Origin: USA
Language: English
Released: 2009
Production: Ewan Leslie, Lauren Shuler Donner, Paul Weitz; Relativity Media, Donners' Company, Depth of Field; released by Universal Pictures

Directed by: Paul Weitz
Written by: Paul Weitz, Brian Helgeland
Cinematography by: J. Michael Muro
Music by: Stephen Trask
Sound: David Wyman
Music Supervisor: Kathy Nelson
Editing: Leslie Jones
Art Direction: Seth Reed
Costumes: Judianna Makovsky
Production Design: William Arnold
MPAA rating: PG-13
Running time: 108 minutes

REVIEWS

Anderson, Jason. *Toronto Star.* October 23, 2009.
Burr, Ty. *Boston Globe.* October 22, 2009.
Coyle, Jake. *Associated Press.* October 21, 2009.
DeBruge, Peter. *Variety.* September 28, 2009.
Duralde, Alonso. *MSNBC.* October 21, 2009.
Ebert, Roger. *Chicago Sun-Times.* October 22, 2009.
Puig, Claudia. *USA Today.* October 23, 2009.
Scott, A.O. *New York Times.* October 23, 2009.
Stevens, Matt. *E! Online.* October 23, 2009.
Tallerico, Brian. *MovieRetriever.com.* October 22, 2009.

QUOTES

Larten Crepsley: "Your mouth says no, but your beard says yes."

TRIVIA

This is the first time Paul Weitz has made a film without help from his brother Chris Weitz

THE CLASS
(Entre les murs)

Box Office: $3.8 million

To describe *The Class* (*Entre les murs*) is to describe a tried and true Hollywood formula, that of the 'High School Teacher in a Troubled Neighborhood' drama. In this genre, the teacher works in a high school located in an urban area plagued with crime, an abundance of teen pregnancies and parents who have all but given up hope. One by one, the teacher slowly earns the respect of his students, usually by altering his/her lesson plans to their level of thinking. The tough, stoic student is the hardest nut to crack and the most talented student usually has the hardest home life. By the end, they have all graduated and a life lesson has been learned on both sides.

It is not so with *The Class*, a French drama told in a verité style that depicts a high school language teacher who is at odds on a daily basis with every class he teaches in a tough Parisian neighborhood. Two or three sentences into a lesson and a conflict erupts, usually a verbal one between him and one of his students who calls his logic into question as a way of antagonizing him and derailing him. Sometimes he falls for it and gives into their arguments. Other times, he throws the troublemakers out of class and sends them to the Dean's office. Making his job harder is his inherent desire to also be liked by his students.

The teacher is played by Francois Begaudeau, who also wrote the book on which this movie is based and who is (or was) also a high school Language teacher (the language, in this case, being French). The movie feels like a documentary even though all the students are being played by actors who are improvising the scenes in the film as they go along, a unique method employed by director Laurent Cantet as a way of getting as close to realism as possible. As a result, the movie's pace is almost like that of a thriller, as conflicts get more heated, the give-and-take between student and teacher more complex and the situations more delicate.

The movie follows Begaudeau through the entire school year. We get to know some of the students, but the movie carefully implies more about its characters more than it outright shows. Parent/teacher conferences, intended to be about parents and teachers coming together and being on the same page with how to go about teaching what is hard to understand, instead devolve into the parents blaming the teacher for their child's lack of progress, in spite of Begaudeau's best efforts. The teacher's lounge becomes a place of refuge and catharsis as educators blow off steam to no one in particular, a moment that every teacher recognizes and accepts as part of the job. The audience is put in the position of siding against Begaudeau in many instances, particularly when he accidentally lets the word "skank" slip out when describing how he feels about how his female students dress nowadays. His back peddling in the situation remains unconvincing.

The movie does not lay the groundwork for any platitudes or clichés about teaching and it does not lead to any great pay-off. The final moment is one of devastating realism, a harsh realty that every teacher must own up to, for better or worse. At the end of the day (or end of the year), what stays with a teacher are not the successes, but the failures. Whether or not Begaudeau carries that weight into the classroom at the start of the following school year is the part of the story *The Class* does not tell, nor does it necessarily need to.

This is not a film about how one teacher can make a world of difference, nor is it a subtly racist depiction of a white teacher trying to save the minorities from themselves. It is about the balancing act a teacher must walk on a daily basis. Begaudeau tries his damndest to be a teacher, friend, confidant and disciplinarian, sometimes in the same breath, while his students continue to stubbornly acknowledge the side of him that infuriates them the most. Begaudeau, meanwhile, has his own blind spot to deal with. The word "skank" does not just come about as a slip of the tongue. It is his secret perception of these students that has finally boiled to the surface. The movie ends with all the teachers playing a game of kickball as all the students at the school look on indifferently, perhaps a metaphor for every teacher really being at odds with themselves.

The Class was the surprise winner of the Palme d'Or at the 2008 Cannes Film Festival.

Collin Souter

CREDITS

Francois Marin: Francois Begaudeau
Esmeralda: Esmeralda Oeurtaini
Khoumba: Rachel Regulier
Souleymane: Franck Keita
Wei: Wei Huang
Origin: France
Language: French
Released: 2008
Production: Carole Scotta, Caroline Benjo, Simon Arnal, Barbara Letellier; Haut et Court, France 2 Cinema; released by Sony Pictures Classics
Directed by: Laurent Cantet
Written by: Laurent Cantet, Robin Campillo, Francois Begaudeau
Cinematography by: Pierre Milon, Catherine Pujol, Georgi Lazarevski
Sound: Olivier Mauvezin, Jean-Pierre Laforce, Agnes Ravez
Editing: Robin Campillo, Stephanie Leger
Costumes: Marie Le Garrec
MPAA rating: PG-13
Running time: 128 minutes

REVIEWS

Chang, Justin. *Variety.* October 18, 2008.
Dargis, Manohla. *New York Times.* September 26, 2008.
Denby, David. *New Yorker.* December 15, 2008.
Ebert, Roger. *Chicago Sun-Times.* February 5, 2009.
Edelstein, David. *New York Magazine.* September 22, 2008.
Honeycutt, Kirk. *Hollywood Reporter.* October 18, 2008.
Sarris, Andrew. *New York Observer.* September 24, 2008.
Stevens, Dana. *Slate.* December 18, 2008.
Tallerico, Brian. *MovieRetriever.com.* February 5, 2009.
Turan, Kenneth. *Los Angeles Times.* December 19, 2008.

TRIVIA

The French title *Entre les murs* translated into English means "Between the Walls" (as in a classroom).

AWARDS

Ind. Spirit 2009: Foreign Film
Nomination:
Oscars 2008: Foreign Film.

CLOUDY WITH A CHANCE OF MEATBALLS

Prepare to get served.
—Movie tagline

Box Office: $12 million

Judy and Ron Barrett's charming 1978 picture book *Cloudy with a Chance of Meatballs* tells a mostly plotless story of a grandfather telling his two grandchildren about the town of Chewandswallow, where food comes down from the sky three times a day—breakfast, lunch and dinner. But then one day the food became bigger and harder to manage, until the entire town was caught up in a storm that resembled a culinary Roland Emmerich disaster film. The townspeople had no choice but to abandon their otherwise idyllic home by making sailboats and rafts out of giant pieces of bread and pizza slices. The simple bedtime story ends with the people of Chewandswallow starting a new life in a more normal town where people have to go to the supermarket to buy their food.

The movie version jettisons the whole bedtime story concept entirely and reinvents the material for its own purpose. Instead of a grandfather serving as a narrator to a larger-than-life fantasy, the movie puts us straight into the fictional island town of Swallow Falls, located near one of the letter As on maps that include the Atlantic Ocean. The main protagonist is an aspiring scientist and inventor named Flint Lockwood (voice of Bill Hader), who lives with his sullen, widowed father (voice of James Caan), who never quite understood Flint's obsession with science. He owns a bait-and-tackle shop in this town, whose only means of edible delights comes from sardines.

This unfortunate circumstance inspires Flint to invent a machine that can rain different kinds of food from the sky. Why not? Naturally, everyone in the town treats Flint as an outsider and his inventions have been far from successful. But when the sky starts raining down cheeseburgers, he becomes the hero to all and a media darling. Of course, a love interest ensues with the Weather News Network intern/reporter Sam Sparks (voice of Anna Faris), who tries to hide her nerdy side until Flint proves to her that she actually looks more attractive with her hair tied back and with glasses than she does as a bombshell reporter (never mind that his nose is eight times the size of her nose). This probably marks the first time in cinema history that a love scene has taken place inside a jell-o mold.

Meanwhile, the town's mayor (voice of Bruce Campbell) becomes as big as the largest man in the world from *Monty Python's Meaning of Life* and as to be expected, things go horribly awry with the food/weather machine. A few wrong buttons get pushed and soon a storm brews much like the one illustrated in the book and it's up to Flint, Sam and Flint's pet monkey to save the day by trying to turn the machine against itself. The movie's second half depicts action scenes involving gummi bears, peanut brittle and an army of headless, cooked chickens.

The book's illustrations, which are similar in style to Maurice Sendak's colorful, detailed pencil sketches that accompanied "Where the Wild Things Are," clearly have an irresistibility to them that would entice producers to want to make an animated film out of it. The choice to go another direction with the story turned out to be a wise one. As has been demonstrated in the past by the beloved *The Polar Express*, the side effect of adapting a simple children's book almost word for word can produce a movie that has little in the way of message or substance. The movie version of *Cloudy with a Chance of Meatballs* encourages children to embrace their smart side, that to be a nerd can be the coolest thing of all. The film also works as a cautionary tale of overindulgence. The book, while working nicely as a fun little bedtime lullaby, simply makes one hungry before going to sleep.

Directors Phil Lord and Chris Miller, making their feature debut after working on the animated series *Clone High*, have as much fun with the sight gags, puns and background jokes as the book. The pacing never lags and the bizarre concept is executed with the same cheerful, go-for-broke enthusiasm of a Tex Avery cartoon. One smartly directed scene finds Flint having dinner with his father at a fancy steakhouse, where they try to talk about their differences and how they never saw eye to eye. In the background, we see big pieces of steak falling from the sky and onto people's plates. The background shenanigans are just funny enough without being too much of a distraction from the drama in the foreground.

The voice talent works just as well. Bill Hader and Anna Faris infuse nice personalities into their roles, giving Flint and Sam believable chemistry. Bruce Campbell has become a natural choice in animated films over the years and his town mayor is no exception. The only name in the cast that has an instantly recognizable vocal force is Mr. T, whose bellowing delivery fits perfectly with the freakishly disproportionate cop and loving father who is all to eager to give a ticket to anyone who is caught jaywalking.

Cloudy with a Chance of Meatballs was yet another computer animated film to be released in 3-D, but was the first of Sony's digital 3-D imaging software, giving the movie a brighter, cleaner look than most other films in the format. The storyline certainly lends itself to this gimmick, but it is to the directors' credit that the film works either way. One need not see a giant spaghetti tornado in 3-D to appreciate its appearance. One simply must accept the fantasy world that the creators have successfully brought to the screen, thanks mostly to a much-loved children's book that served as its catalyst. Even though Lord and Miller had started over from scratch, their love for the book remains evident. As Sam Sparks says, "There's a lot to be said for enthusiasm."

Collin Souter

CREDITS

Flint Lockwood: Bill Hader (Voice)
Sam: Anna Faris (Voice)
Brent: Andy Samberg (Voice)
Earl Devereaux: Mr. T (Voice)
Cal: Tracy Morgan (Voice)
Tim Lockwood: James Caan (Voice)
Mayor Shelbourne: Bruce Campbell (Voice)
Origin: USA
Language: English
Released: 2009
Production: Sony Pictures Animation; released by Columbia Pictures, Sony Pictures Entertainment
Directed by: Chris Miller, Phil Lord
Written by: Judi Barrett, Ron Barrett
Music by: Mark Mothersbaugh
Production Design: Justin Thompson
Sound: Jason George, Geoffrey G. Rubay
MPAA rating: PG
Running time: 81 minutes

REVIEWS

DeBruge, Peter. *Variety.* September 17, 2009.
Ebert, Roger. *Chicago Sun-Times.* September 17, 2009.

Farber, Stephen. *HollywoodReporter.* September 17, 2009.
Guzman, Rafer. *Newsday.* September 17, 2009.
Puig, Claudia. *USA Today.* September 17, 2009.
Busch, Jenna. *JoBlo's Movie Emporium.* September 18, 2009.
Demara, Bruce. *Toronto Star.* September 18, 2009.
Mondello, Bob. *NPR.* September 18, 2009.
Phillips, Michael. *Chicago Tribune.* September 18, 2009.
Tallerico, Brian. *MovieRetriever.com.* September 18, 2009.

QUOTES

Sam Sparks: "My forecast? Sunny side up."

TRIVIA

The door lock on Flint's laboratory is operated by a 1970s "Simon" game.

AWARDS

Nomination:

Golden Globes 2010: Animated Film.

COCO BEFORE CHANEL
(Coco avant Chanel)

Before she was France's famous mademoiselle.
—Movie tagline

Box Office: $6 million

Seeing as how there have been numerous biopics over the years about the life and work of Coco Chanel, it makes sense that the makers of *Coco Before Chanel* have chosen to set themselves apart from the pack by telling the story of what happened to her before she became the internationally renowned fashion icon. What this means, in other words, is that the film is asking viewers to spend two hours watching the stuff that they would normally skip over in a biography in order to get to the good stuff. The only trouble with this approach is the inescapable fact, based on the evidence presented here, that her pre-fame days simply were not very interesting and, if not for the fact that she would one day become incredibly famous and influential, there would be absolutely no reason why anyone would want to give the big-screen treatment to this portion of her life.

Determined to escape the poverty that she has known from an early age since the death of her mother and the departure of her father, the film opens with Coco (Audrey Tautou) eking out a meager living by working as a lowly seamstress by day and as a cabaret performer by night. It is in the latter capacity that she makes the acquaintance of the rich and powerful Etienne Balsan (Benoit Poelyoorde) and is soon ensconced in his lavish mansion as his mistress. Before long, she grows bored with simply serving as a kept woman and begins using her lover's clothes and curtains as materials in order to experiment with making clothing that will allow women to break free of the uncomfortable restraints that passed for feminine fashion at the time. At the same time, she also attracts the attention of a rich British industrial tycoon (Alessandro Nivola) and is eventually forced to decide whether she wants to ally herself to one of them or take the chance of striking out on her own as a fashion designer. (Viewers who want to remain unspoiled should try to avoid shopping at any high-end retail clothing store before going to see the film.)

The scenes involving Chanel's initial stabs at designing outfits have a certain kick to them and the first appearance of the legendary little black dress will surely have fashionistas swooning in the aisles. However, all of the stuff involving the romantic triangle that develops between the three key players and essentially dominates the film is as drab, lifeless and stultifying as the fashions that Chanel was trying to liberate women from in the first place. That said, Audrey Tautou is really quite good as Chanel as she gets to demonstrate the kind of steely-eyed determination that is completely removed from the sweetness and whimsical charm that helped make her an international star in *Amelie* (2001). Sadly, the same cannot be said of Anne Fontaine's direction—while technically fine and precise as one could hope for, it lacks any juice as it goes about its slow and far-too-respectable storytelling approach. As it plods along, it feels as if Fontaine was afraid to ruffle any feathers with the film, which is a strange approach to take when telling the story of a person who became famous for doing just that in her own work.

In the end, *Coco Before Chanel* suffers from the same basic problem as *Amelia* (2009), the Amelia Earhart biopic that hit theaters at roughly the same time—it is a film that seems to have been put into production not because of a burning desire to tell the life story of a complex and fascinating character but because such things have become popular in recent years with Oscar® voters. (It could also be noted that both tell the stories of fiercely independent women who nevertheless knew exactly who to sleep with in order to get ahead in the world—the difference being that Chanel could at least successfully stick a landing.) If it had demonstrated even a trace of the passion or inventiveness that the real Chanel demonstrated towards her own life and work, *Coco Before Chanel* might have turned out to be a fascinating look at the evolution of a true original. Alas, it does not and the end result is akin to a runway show consisting entirely of last year's fashions—it is pretty enough on the surface but there is nothing on display that has not already been seen before.

Peter Sobczynski

CREDITS

Gabrielle "CoCo" Chanel: Audrey Tautou
Etienne Balsan: Benoit Poelvoorde
Arthur "Boy" Capel: Alessandro Nivola
Adriennem Chanel: Marie Gillain
Emilienne d'Alencon: Emmanuelle Devos
Origin: France
Language: French
Released: 2009
Production: Simon Arnal, Caroline Benjo, Philippe Carcassonne, Carole Scotta; Haut et Court Ciné@, Warner Bros., France 2 Cinéma, Canal +, CinéCinéma, France 2; Films Distribution, Cofinova 5, Banque Populaire Images 9, Scope Pictures; released by Sony Pictures Classics
Directed by: Anne Fontaine
Written by: Anne Fontaine, Camille Fontaine, Christopher Gore
Cinematography by: Christophe Beaucarne
Music by: Alexandre Desplat
Sound: Nicolas Cantin, Jean-Claude Laureux
Editing: Luc Barnier
Art Direction: Olivier Radot
Costumes: Catherine Leterrier
Production Design: Olivier Radot
MPAA rating: PG-13
Running time: 105 minutes

REVIEWS

Ebert, Roger. *Chicago Sun-Times.* October 8, 2009.
Edelstein, David. *New York Magazine.* September 21, 2009.
Edwards, David. *Daily Mirror.* July, 31 2009.
Lane, Anthony. *New Yorker.* September 21, 2009.
LaSalle, Mick. *San Francisco Chronicle.* October 2, 2009.
Longworth, Karina. *Time Out New York.* September 23, 2009.
Mintzer, Jordan. *Variety.* April 24, 2009.
Morgenstein, Joe. *Wall Street Journal.* September 25, 2009.
Pols, Mary F. *Time Magazine.* September 24, 2009.
Puig, Claudia. *USA Today.* September 24, 2009.

TRIVIA

From 1934 to 1971 Coco Chanel made the Hotel Ritz in Paris, France her home. A suite, in honor of her memory, has been named after her.

AWARDS

Nomination:

Oscars 2009: Costume Des.

British Acad. 2009: Actress (Tautou), Costume Des., Foreign Film, Makeup.

COLD SOULS

A soul searching comedy.
—Movie tagline

If not outright impossible, it is probably at the very least irresponsible to review *Cold Souls* without referencing and comparing it to the films of screenwriter and director Charlie Kaufman, since the movie's conceit—in which souls can be extracted and traded as commodities—is so willfully outrageous and turned in on itself.

And yet no good can come of such comparisons, for regardless of what one individually thinks of *Being John Malkovich* (1999), *Confessions of a Dangerous Mind* (2002), *Adaptation* (2002) or *Synecdoche, New York* (2008), first-time French writer-director Sophie Barthes' film is an inexplicably tepid treatment of a heady concept—a movie that comes across as a wan, fifth-generation carbon copy of something that in other hands could have been far more inventive. *Cold Souls*, which premiered at the 2009 Sundance Film Festival, bills itself in its press notes as "a surreal comedy balancing on a tightrope between deadpan humor and pathos," but it is not terribly funny or tightly wound, and exhausts viewer patience long before any emotional poignancy is cultivated.

Paul Giamatti stars as an acutely concentrated version of himself, a same-named actor agonizing over his starring role in a stage version of *Uncle Vanya*. Paralyzed by anxiety and desperate to reclaim some inner peace, he stumbles upon a solution via a *New Yorker* article about an enigmatic high-tech company that promises to alleviate mental suffering by extracting and storing one's soul. After meeting with seemingly the only two employees of the company, Dr. Flintstein (David Strathairn) and receptionist Stephanie (Lauren Ambrose), Giamatti enlists their service, planning to reinstall his soul once he survives the production.

Suitably unburdened of apprehension, empathy and social awareness, Giamatti bewilders his director and fellow actors with a jazz-bop, William Shatner-esque interpretation of Vanya, and confounds his wife Claire (Emily Watson) with inappropriate social advice over dinner with friends. These behavioral problems in short order lead Giamatti to opt for the soul of a Russian poet. Further complications ensue, however, when a mysterious, soul-trafficking "mule" named Nina (Dina Korzun, looking like a Slavic Deborah Harry) steals Giamatti's stored soul for Sveta (Katheryn Winnick), the moll of a Russian gangster and an aspiring actress who is as insistent and demanding as she is talentless. (Sveta wants the soul of Al Pacino or another Oscar® winner, but Giamatti is the only American actor on file.) Panicked at his soullessness, Giamatti travels all the way to St. Petersburg, Russia, to try to sort things out and reclaim his "true self."

In films like *Sideways* (2004) and *American Splendor* (2003), Giamatti has shown himself to be a superb peddler of prickly, modern American masculine insecurity and ennui. Here, though, while there are enjoyably whimsical touches of angst to his performance, he is utterly handcuffed by the material. Giamatti's soul goes missing, but Barthes bafflingly does not give her lead actor the chance to blow up, or really seize control of the narrative. Supporting characters fare no better: Claire is woefully underutilized, an almost pointless addition to the story (especially disappointing considering the movie's writer-director is female), and Dr. Flintstein is sketched so thinly as to leave his motivations totally unapparent and his rich comedic potential untapped. It does not help that the entire subplot involving the Eastern European soul black market, and Nina's late-stage accumulation of trace amounts of soul residue from her work as a courier—two other sources of possible intrigue, either wild and crazy or dark and dangerous—feel leaden and lazy thought out.

There is no libidinal pulse to *Cold Souls*, no driving energy or clarity of thematic vision. By divorcing the soul from its traditional religious ineffability and trying to characterize it as more having to do with personality and affect, Barthes only nicks the surface of her concept. One yearns for the comedic grace notes and flourishes of roughhewn charm one can easily imagine Kaufman, or a likeminded writer, folding into the conceit—or, failing that, just an injection of some existential terror. But *Cold Souls* merely unwinds languidly. It is understated to the point of enervation. The most wit it can muster is when Giamatti snorts and impulsively spits out a dismissive "No!" when told that tax charges can be waived if he wants to store his soul in New Jersey. Even Giamatti's consternation at his discovery that his soul looks exactly like a chickpea is not adequately plumbed for more than surface laughs. It is never a good sign when one can, in the moment, come up with a half dozen or more interesting twists and turns for a given scene, and that happens repeatedly with Barthes' film.

If *Cold Souls* misfires on almost every narrative level, it can at least be said that the movie possesses a believably desolate production value, thanks in part to a location shoot that included time in St. Petersburg. Production designer Elizabeth Mickle and cinematographer Andrij Parekh assist Barthes in crafting a visual scheme that is in appropriate lockstep with the reserved, arms-length nature of the movie's emotional, intellectual and

philosophical engagement. If only *Cold Souls*' premise could be thawed out for a bit...

Brent Simon

CREDITS

Paul: Paul Giamatti
Nina: Dina Korzun
Sveta: Katheryn Winnick
Dr. Flintstein: David Strathrain
Claire: Emily Watson
Stephanie: Lauren Ambrose
Oleg: Boris Kievsky
Origin: USA
Language: English
Released: 2009
Production: Daniel Carey, Elizabeth Giamatti, Paul Mezey, Andrij Parekh; Journeyman Pictures, Touchy Feely Films; released by Samuel Goldwyn Films
Directed by: Sophie Barthes
Written by: Sophie Barthes
Cinematography by: Andrij Parekh
Music by: Dickon Hinchliffe
Sound: Judy Karp
Music Supervisor: Tracy McKnight
Editing: Andrew Mondshein
Art Direction: Michael Ahern
Costumes: Erin Benach
Production Design: Elizabeth Mickle
MPAA rating: PG-13
Running time: 101 minutes

REVIEWS

Abele, Robert. *Los Angeles Times.* August 7, 2009.
Chang, Justin. *Variety.* August 5, 2009.
D'Arcy, David. *Screen International.* April 8, 2009.
Dargis, Manohla. *New York Times.* August 7, 2009.
Ebert, Roger. *Chicago Sun-Times.* August 20, 2009.
Lane, Anthony. *New Yorker.* August 3, 2009.
Lowe, Justin. *Hollywood Reporter.* April 8, 2009.
Robinson, Tasha. *AV Club.* August 6, 2009.
Sragow, Michael. *Baltimore Sun,* September 4, 2009.
Tallerico, Brian. *MovieRetriever.com.* August 21, 2009.

TRIVIA

The film was inspired by a dream in which Woody Allen discovers that his soul looks just like a chickpea.

AWARDS

Nomination:

Ind. Spirit 2010: Cinematog., Support. Actress (Korzun), First Screenplay.

COLLAPSE

From the acclaimed director of "American Movie," this portrait of radical thinker Michael Ruppert explores his apocalyptic vision of the future, spanning the crises in economics, energy, environment and more.
—Movie tagline

It must be difficult to be the canary in the coal mine. And, of course, it is far more painful to go on when the powers that be refuse to listen to your chirping and run for safety. Such is the existence of Michael Ruppert, a man who claims to not have only predicted the current problems facing the United States but has a story to tell about what is just over the horizon. Fitting snugly in the thematic film landscape of 2009 that saw post-apocalyptic films like *Zombieland*, *The Road*, and *2012*, *Collapse* is the documentary of the year about the imminent downfall of humanity. Employing an interview style not unlike the master Errol Morris, director Chris Smith (*American Movie* [1999]) sat down for a conversation with a man that could arguably be called the prophet of death his viewpoints about the next few decades are so extreme. Not too far removed from a homeless man wearing a sandwich board proclaiming the arrival of the end of the world, Michael Ruppert does not have good news for the next few Presidents of the United States. The difference is that Ruppert has an interesting background and a dedicated following. Sadly, his theories start intriguing and eventually live up to the title of the film. He raises some interesting discussion points but Smith's documentary starts to become more about the collapse of an individual than a society. The canary may not always be right.

Ruppert is not an average talk show crackpot with a conspiracy theory. He was once a part of the system that he now points to as the main source of the collapse of our society. It started when Ruppert was an LAPD officer caught up in a wave of corruption and forced to turn on the institution that he loved to bring lawbreakers to justice. When he became aware of the corruption that was eating the system from within, Ruppert began to dig a little deeper and accused the CIA of drug running in the 1980s. When the façade fell and Michael Ruppert realized that the institution designed to protect us was doing the opposite, it was just the beginning of a life built around what most people would call conspiracy theories. Smith's film starts with a series of interviews about "Peak Oil," not a conspiracy theory but a concept that the world has reached the halfway point in its energy supply and are tragically headed down the other side of the bell curve, and what it means to society. Of course, the impact of an oil shortage cannot be undervalued and Ruppert uses it as a jumping off point to weave his way through the wars in the Middle East, the economy of the 1990s and 2000s, and eventually predictions about—and this is without exaggeration—the end of the world. His argument is that oil is even more fundamental and irreplaceable than people have been led to believe and that as it begins to run out, society will literally collapse. Most people would dismiss a lot of Ruppert's theories if not for the fact that he correctly predicted our current economic crisis back in 2005.

Smith has stated that he did not merely set out to give Ruppert a soap box but that he wanted to make a film that illustrates how a man's obsession with the collapse of the systems that rule our world led to the collapse of his own personal life. *Collapse* eventually gets to this concept but for too much of the film, Ruppert's arguments are presented not only with debate but as irrefutable fact. As his theories get more intense and debatable, he becomes a harder subject in which to maintain interest. The final act of the film, in which Smith starts to question Ruppert on subjects like his complete discounting of human ingenuity to stop the downfall of humanity, the man seems to simply ignore the concept and question, possibly because he is so single-minded but also possibly because he has been allowed free rein by Smith for so long that he does not accept now being confronted. Ruppert is clearly one of those writers and theorists who only use the statistics that support his argument and ignore all that do not lend credence to his view of life in 2030. By the time he is encouraging listeners to buy gold and seeds because they have actual value once our financial system collapses, he has lost so much credibility that the film becomes a bit uninteresting.

Despite the few flaws of Smith's film, Michael Ruppert is a fascinating figure, a bleak and relentlessly driven man whose obsessions have driven him at least to the brink of insanity if not well over it. Of course, if he is right about the future, he is merely in the mental state that anyone would be in with such awareness. If he has truly predicted the trajectory that will lead to proving true the idea that the boom in human population in the twentieth century must be matched by an equal fall in the twenty-first, perhaps everyone else is crazy for not paying attention.

Brian Tallerico

CREDITS

Himself: Michael Ruppert
Origin: USA
Language: English
Released: 2009

Production: Kate Noble, Chris Smith; Bluemark; released by Vitagraph Films

Directed by: Chris Smith

Cinematography by: Max Malkin, Edward Lachman

Music by: Didier Leplae, Joe Wong

Music Supervisor: Sara Matarazzo

Editing: Barry Poltermann

Art Direction: Andrew Reznik

MPAA rating: Unrated

Running time: 82 minutes

REVIEWS

Abele, Robert. *Los Angeles Times.* November 13, 2009.

Berkshire, Geoff. *Metromix.com.* November 5, 2009.

Catsoulis, Jeanette. *New York Times.* November 6, 2009.

Ebert, Roger. *Chicago Sun-Times.* December 10, 2009.

Fear, David. *Time Out New York.* November 4, 2009.

Gleiberman, Owen. *Entertainment Weekly.* November 4, 2009.

Musetto, V.A. *New York Post.* November 6, 2009.

Rapold, Nicolas. *Village Voice.* November 3, 2009.

Schager, Nick. *Slant Magazine.* November 1, 2009.

Tobias, Scott. *AV Club.* November 5, 2009.

THE COLLECTOR

He always takes one.
—Movie tagline

Box Office: $7 million

Without much fondness for the recent wave of so-called "torture porn" films—the horror subgenre that is singularly concerned with finding new ways of killing and maiming its characters in the most gruesome manner possible—it is difficult to go into *The Collector* (not, it should be noted right now, to be confused at all with either the celebrated John Fowles novel or its equally acclaimed 1965 screen adaptation) with much in the way of enthusiasm. Lowering expectations even further was the fact that its distributor, Freestyle Releasing, dumped it in theaters with no press screenings and an advertising campaign based solely on a couple of quotes from websites guaranteed to rave about anything in which gallons of gore is spilled. The fact that it came from the minds of the screenwriters responsible for *Saw IV* (2007), *Saw V* (2008) and *Saw VI* (2009) did not hint at a quality product. For the most part, those expectations were confirmed—the film is a nasty bit of work designed almost entirely to gross out viewers with one excessively gory bit of business after another—but at the same time, it does demonstrate a little more craft and artistry than most films of its particular type that have been released in recent years.

Josh Stewart stars as Arkin, an ex-con safecracker who is trying to make a new life for himself and his young daughter by working as a handyman. When his ex-wife runs up a huge gambling debt that is about to come due, he decides to break into the isolated home belonging to his latest client—a rich jeweler who is leaving on vacation with his family—and steal the precious gem stored in the house safe in order to set everything straight. Unfortunately for him, once he gets inside, he discovers that the house is not unoccupied after all and that the family has been taken prisoner by a brutal masked sadist who is slowly torturing them to death and who has rigged the entire house with lethal booby traps designed to fold, spindle and mutilate anyone attempting to escape. The rest of the film is essentially a long game of cat-and-mouse in which Arkin desperately tries to evade the killer and rescue the family's youngest daughter (Karley Scott Collins) from a fate worse than *Hostel* (2006) while the others are dispatched via increasingly nasty and elaborate methods.

The Collector has a lot of the same problems of most other films of this type—the bad guy is nothing more than a masked and motiveless cipher, the victims are so thinly sketched that their agonies have no real impact beyond the immediate shock effect of how they are dispatched, the screenplay is filled with holes that defy credulity (the entire thing would be over in a few minutes if Arkin just called the cops on his cell phone and the film could at least offer a reason as to why he does not have one) and even the most fanatical gorehounds may find themselves wondering exactly how the killer was able to rig up such elaborate traps in the space of only a few hours. However, the conceit of the film—a seemingly ordinary heist film that suddenly transforms into a horror enterprise—is interesting enough to make you wish that the producers had actually sold it as the former and let it wig out viewers as it shifted gears. The largely silent extended sequence in which Arkin breaks into the house and slowly and quietly (and painfully) discovers that something is very wrong with his surroundings is a nastily effective bit of work that has been staged by debut director Marcus Dunstan (who also co-wrote the screenplay with Patrick Melton) with a lot more style than one might expect. Unfortunately, once it shifts fully into horror mode, these concerns are tossed out the window in order to concentrate solely on the gross stuff and the whole thing falters as a result.

On the one hand, *The Collector* is not good enough to serve as either a buried treasure or a guilty pleasure because it never manages to live up to the promise of its opening scenes. At the same time, it is not bad enough to dismiss out of hand because it has been made with a certain degree of craft that cannot be denied, especially after seeing so many similar films of its type that have not. In other words, *The Collector* is not a very good movie, but on the bright side, such as it is, it does contain a few scenes that don't know that.

Peter Sobczynski

CREDITS

Arkin: Josh Stewart
Michael Chase: Michael Reilly Burke
Victoria Chase: Andrea Roth
Hannah Chase: Karley Scott Collins
Jill Chase: Madeline Zima
The Collector: Juan Fernandez
Origin: USA
Language: English
Released: 2009
Production: Brett Forbes, Julie Richardson, Patrick Rizzotti; Liddell Entertainment, Fortress Features; released by Freestyle Releasing
Directed by: Marcus Dunstan
Written by: Marcus Dunstan, Patrick Melton
Cinematography by: Brandon Cox
Music by: Jerome Dillon
Sound: Gary Day
Music Supervisor: Tricia Holloway
Editing: Alex Luna, James Mastracco
Art Direction: Michael Barton
Costumes: Ashlyn Angel
Production Design: Ermanno Di Febo-Orsini
MPAA rating: R
Running time: 88 minutes

REVIEWS

Anderson, John. *Variety.* July 31, 2009.
Catsoulis, Jeanette. *New York Times.* August 3, 2009.
Fear, David. *Time Out New York.* August 5, 2009.
Kennedy, Austin. *Sin Magazine.* August 16, 2009.
Loder, Kurt. *MTV.* August 3, 2009.
Morris, Wesley. *Boston Globe.* August 3, 2009.
Ordona, Michael. *Los Angeles Times.* July 31, 2009.
Rechtshaffen, Mark. *Hollywood Reporter.* July 31, 2009.
Sobczynski, Peter. *eFilmCritic.* August 7, 2009.
Tobias, Scott. *AV Club.* July 31, 2009.

CONFESSIONS OF A SHOPAHOLIC

All she ever wanted was a little credit.
—Movie tagline

Box Office: $44 million

Confessions of a Shopaholic is the latest attempt by Hollywood to see if an up-and-coming ingénue has what it takes to be a movie star by plucking them from a string of acclaimed supporting performances and putting them front-and-center in a vehicle that has been designed pretty much to live or die entirely on the strength of their charms—think Julia Roberts in *Pretty Woman* (1990) or Amy Adams in *Enchanted* (2007). This time around, the starlet on the spot is Isla Fisher, who turned many heads a couple of years ago as the only consistently amusing aspect on display in *Wedding Crashers* (2005) but this time around, the results aren't nearly as successful. Yes, Fisher is undeniably talented and charming and also displays a willingness to do the kind of physical shtick that most young actresses tend to shy away from so as not to risk looking less than salon-perfect at any given time. However, despite her best efforts, even she cannot quite overcome the fact that she is playing a somewhat disturbed and unlikable character in a film that is too innocuous to ever acknowledge that fact.

Fisher stars as Rebecca Bloomwood, an aspiring journalist whose uncontrollable urge to shop is so great that when she passes by store windows, she visualizes the mannequins coming to life to tell her that she will only find happiness and fulfillment by purchasing their pricey wares. One day, she goes to apply for her dream job as a columnist for a fashion magazine and when that falls through, she winds up, through circumstances too dodgy to get into here, being hired by a financial magazine to write a column offering advice to readers on how to save their money. Of course, she knows nothing about the subject but is able to fake it using insultingly simplistic metaphors (something about the economy being like a pair of shoes) and her column becomes an instant success. For a while, things go swimmingly for Rebecca—including a blossoming romance with her hunky young boss (Hugh Dancy)—but eventually, her secret life as a debt-ridden liar comes back to haunt her in the form of a relentless collector trying to get her to pay up the $16,000 she owes and for a while, it looks as though she will lose her job, her boyfriend, her best friend (Krysten Ritter) and her happiness in an avalanche of debt. However, in news that will presumably shock no one who has read this far, things pretty much work out for her in the end so that she gets everything that she wants without ever really having to pay much of a price for her transgressions or learn anything that might be considered a lesson.

The central problem with *Confessions of a Shopaholic* is not that it is bad as much as it is completely forgettable. The notion of a shopping addict being put in the unlikely position of advising people on money matters sounds like the launching pad for a spirited satire of the dark side of our contemporary consumerist culture (how can such a person hope to control such a habit when virtually every available surface nowadays contains an ad exhorting people to buy something or other) but it becomes very apparent early on that the filmmakers have no particular interest in this aspect of the storyline—after all, such an approach might disturb both potential audience members and potential promotional deals with companies looking to plug their own high-priced goods by having them be seen on screen. (At one point, there is a driving sequence in which a cab passes at least three billboards promoting upcoming projects from *Confessions* producer Jerry Bruckheimer.) Instead, the film follows the standard romantic comedy parameters with the kind of rigid formality that makes your typical passion play look like an evening at the Improv by comparison and what little life there is in these moments is almost entirely derived from the personal charms of a surprisingly strong supporting cast that also includes the likes of John Goodman, Joan Cusack, John Lithgow, Julie Haggerty and Lynn Redgrave. A much more interesting movie could have been made following director P.J. Hogan as he went about somehow convincing these people to all sign on for this particular project.

Although *Confessions of a Shopaholic* was based on a pair of popular books from chick-lit novelist Sophie Kinsella, the film itself found little favor with audiences when it came out despite its seemingly perfect Valentine's Day release date. At the time, many media experts speculated that it was because it had the unfortunate luck to be a comedy about reckless spending coming out at exactly the same point that talk about the cratering of the American economy was at its peak. Normally, I tend to resist the urge to link box-office performance to real-life concerns but in this particular case, I can understand how one could make such an argument. After all, if there is anything that the faltering financial situation has taught us, it is the importance of setting aside non-essential items and *Confessions of a Shopaholic* could not be more non-essential if it tried.

Peter Sobczynski

CREDITS

Rebecca Bloomwood: Isla Fisher
Luke Brandon: Hugh Dancy
Suze: Krysten Ritter
Jane Bloomwood: Joan Cusack
Graham Bloomwood: John Goodman
Alette Naylor: Kristin Scott Thomas
Alicia Billington: Leslie Bibb
Drunken lady at ball: Lynn Redgrave

Hayley: Julie Hagerty
Miss Korch: Wendie Malick
Miss Ptaszinski: Clea Lewis
TV Show Host: Christine Ebersole
Edgar West: John Lithgow
Ryan Koenig: Fred Armisen
Derek Smith: Robert Stanton
Origin: USA
Language: English
Released: 2009
Production: Jerry Bruckheimer; Touchstone Pictures; released by Walt Disney Pictures
Directed by: P.J. Hogan
Written by: Tim Firth, Tracey Jackson, Kayla Alpert
Cinematography by: Jo Willems
Music by: James Newton Howard
Sound: Robert Eber, T.J. O'Mara
Music Supervisor: Kathy Nelson
Editing: William Goldenberg
Art Direction: Paul D. Kelly
Costumes: Patricia Field
Production Design: Kristi Zea
MPAA rating: PG
Running time: 104 minutes

REVIEWS

Anderson, John. *Washington Post.* February 12, 2009.
Anderson, Melissa. *Village Voice.* February 10, 2009.
Ebert, Roger. *Chicago Sun-Times.* February 12, 2009.
Edelstein, David. *New York Magazine.* February 9, 2009.
Lemire, Christy. *Associated Press.* February 11, 2009.
Pais, Matt. *Metromix.com.* February 12, 2009.
Rabin, Nathan. *AV Club.* February 12, 2009.
Sarris, Andrew. *New York Observer.* February 11, 2009.
Simon, Brent. *Screen International.* February 12, 2009.
Stevens, Dana. *Slate.com.* February 12, 2009.

QUOTES

Rebecca Bloomwood: "You know that thing when you see someone cute and he smiles and your heart kind of goes like warm butter sliding down hot toast? Well that's what it's like when I see a store. Only it's better."

TRIVIA

Reese Witherspoon turned down the role of Rebecca Bloomwood because it was too much like Elle Woods, the role Witherspoon played in *Legally Blonde.*

CORALINE

Be careful what you wish for.
—Movie tagline

Box Office: $75 million

Adapted from the bestselling young adult novel by Neil Gaiman and directed by Henry Selick, *Coraline* offers multiple reasons to celebrate. This absolutely remarkable film is not only one of the best animated films in recent memory but among the very best 3-D films ever, utilizing the often gimmicky technique to advance both story and emotional resonance. It gives viewers the reason to hope that Gaiman's incredible body of work will continue to be adapted and adapted well by future filmmakers and it is an affirmation of the incredible talent of Henry Selick who has generally toiled in relative obscurity during a career that has generated three other feature efforts—*The Nightmare Before Christmas* (1993), *James and The Giant Peach* (1996) and *Monkeybone* (2001). Best known for the first, Selick labored under the shadow of Executive Producer Tim Burton who became so identified with the project that many assumed he directed it. Selick's next film, *James and the Giant Peach,* also a musical, also stop-motion animated, was subsequently assumed by many to be yet another Burton film and, though well-reviewed, did nothing in particular to enhance Selick's opportunities. This, followed by the disastrous box office failure of *Monkeybone* (2001), seemed to indicate that Selick might well never have the chance to see his potential realized and recognized. *Coraline* seems to signal that such fears were premature. *Coraline* is a film for the ages.

The movie opens as an old rag doll is taken apart and reassembled to look like a little girl, the hero of our story, eleven-year-old Coraline (Dakota Fanning) whom we meet as she and her overworked editor mother (Teri Hatcher) and writer father (John Hodgman) move into their new apartment. The 150-year-old pink Victorian is pretty rundown and so is the neighborhood. With no one to play with except a weird neighborhood boy named Wybie (Robert Bailey Jr.) and even weirder older neighbors like the acrobatic Sergei Alexander Bobinsky (Ian McShane) and the spinsters Miss April Spink (Jennifer Saunders) and Miss Miriam Forcible (Dawn French), it seems Coraline is doomed to a life of boredom.

But when she discovers a small hidden door in her house, she happens upon the weirdest most un-boring world of all; a duplicate universe that looks exactly the old one, but better. In it are 'Other Mother' and 'Other Father' who seem to want nothing more than to entertain her. At first, life with Other Mother and Other Father is grand. The food is better, the toys are better and, best of all, Coraline is never, ever bored. They even give her an Other Wybie to play with. But, slowly, Coraline, guided by a wise and mysterious feral cat (Keith David) realizes her new friends and family are not what they seem. Why does everyone have buttons for eyes?

Why does everything seem to center around her subtly controlling Other Mother?

When Other Mother offers Coraline the chance to stay forever she is sorely tempted. But, to stay, Coraline will have to let Other Mother replace her eyes with buttons too. Terrified she runs away, back to the real world only to discover the awful truth that there may be no way back to her real parents who have been imprisoned by Other Mother. To truly escape and rescue her real mother and father Coraline must win a game on Other Mother's own turf. Most of all, Coraline must face a world where everything is not fair, where the danger is all around, and where she must learn who she can trust and not to trust in mere appearances.

This film evokes the best and darkest of the fairy tale tradition from which it draws inspiration. Far from simply adapting Gaiman's story, Selick grasps the heart of it and wrings out on to the screen that sense of palpable danger that makes truly great children's films seem so vital and important. Like *The Wizard of Oz* (1939) and *Willy Wonka and the Charlie Factory* (1971) this film approaches a level of intensity that is the stuff nightmares are made of. One can easily see *Coraline* edging into that territory. But *Coraline*, like *The Wizard of Oz* is a film about facing fear, the importance of relationships and family in doing so, and the need to grow up, move on and see a little bit of wonder in the everyday world and the everyday people around us.

Voice performance in this film is truly notable. Teri Hatcher in particular is a revelation of sinister sweetness and maniacal matriarchy while John Hodgson sails through the very demanding role of father/Other Father, swooping through the demanding extremes of silliness and creepiness singing happy ditties one moment and sadly bowing to mother's evil will the next. Also a lot of fun is Ian McShane who lends the Russian acrobat Bobinsky just the right hint of crazed genius.

The role 3-D plays in *Coraline* makes it, sadly, unique in 3-D cinema these days. With the exception of *Avatar,* 3-D has continued to be used more or less as it has always been, as a gimmick, the main attraction of the film in question. In *Coraline,* however, the audience finds itself constantly confronted with the world in the way Coraline herself does thanks to a technique that can literally take us into the world she is trying to navigate. *Coraline* is a better film in 3-D because 3-D makes her journey an easier one with which to empathize.

So does the music. The film's diverse musicality is an example of film scoring at its best. French composer Bruno Coulais delights and terrifies with equal ease, making it seem as if the music flew literally from the character's hearts.

Films like *Coraline* only come along every so often; beautifully written, wonderfully realized, and technically groundbreaking. *Coraline* has the added virtue of being exactly the sort of film that can turn a young mind (perhaps even an old one) into a permanent lover of all that is best about cinema.

Dave Canfield

CREDITS

Coraline Jones: Dakota Fanning (Voice)
Mother/Other Mother: Teri Hatcher (Voice)
Mr. Bobinski: Ian McShane (Voice)
The Cat: Keith David (Voice)
Miss Forcible: Jennifer Saunders (Voice)
Miss Spink: Dawn French (Voice)
Father/Other Father: John Hodgman (Voice)
Wybie Lovat: Robert Bailey Jr. (Voice)
Origin: USA
Language: English
Released: 2009
Production: Bill Mechanic, Claire Jennings, C. Henry Selick, Mary Sandell; Laika Entertainment, Pandemonium; released by Focus Features
Directed by: Henry Selick
Written by: Henry Selick
Cinematography by: Pete Kozachik
Music by: Bruno Coulais
Sound: Ron Eng, David A. Cohen
Editing: Christopher Murrie, Ronald Sanders
Production Design: Henry Selick
MPAA rating: PG
Running time: 100 minutes

REVIEWS

Adams, Thelma. *Us Weekly.* February 5, 2009.
Biancolli, Amy. *Houston Chronicle.* February 6, 2009.
Chang, Justin. *Variety.* February 2, 2009.
Ebert, Roger. *Chicago Sun-Times.* February 5, 2009.
Larsen, Josh. *LarsenOnFilm.* February 5, 2009.
Rickey, Carrie. *Philadelphia Inquirer.* February 5, 2009.
Scott, A.O. *New York Times.* February 6, 2009.
Simon, Brent. *Shared Darkness.* February 4, 2009.
Sragow, Michael. *Baltimore Sun.* February 6, 2009.
Tallerico, Brian. *MovieRetriever.com.* February 5, 2009.

QUOTES

Coraline Jones: "You are not my mother."

TRIVIA

The "Detroit Zoo" snow globe featured in the film contains a model of the Horace Rackham Memorial Fountain, or the

"Bear Fountain," sculpted by Corrado Parducci in 1939 as the centerpiece of the Detroit Zoo's reflecting pool

AWARDS

Nomination:

Oscars 2009: Animated Film
British Acad. 2009: Animated Film
Golden Globes 2010: Animated Film.

COUPLES RETREAT

It may be paradise...but it's no vacation.
—Movie tagline

Box Office: $109 million

Some comedians can maintain their likeability even when stuck in a terrible movie. Paul Rudd, for example, has an uncanny charm that rises above even something as awful as *Over Her Dead Body* (2008). Vince Vaughn, on the other hand, is the life of the party in his best roles (like *Swingers* [1996]), but loses all appeal when he is the anchor of a real stinker.

That is certainly the case in *Couples Retreat*, a mean-spirited movie that continually embarrasses itself, and its cast, in service of half-hearted attempts to generate laughs or any non-obvious statements about modern relationships. The premise, for what it is worth, has potential for sufficient character-based comedy and insight: Jason (Jason Bateman) and Cynthia (Kristen Bell) tell their fellow suburban Chicago friends that they are contemplating divorce after an inability to conceive has fractured their marriage. However, they have a plan: Their social circle will take a trip to the luxurious Eden resort in Bora Bora, where Jason and Cynthia can rejuvenate their relationship and everyone else can enjoy some sun and sand.

Of course, things do not go as planned, and the couples discover that their stay at the uptight, couples-only Eden West—Eden East, on the other hand, is a highly desirable paradise of sexy, available singles—will center around therapy, not hedonism. This is particularly bad news for Dave (Vaughn) and Ronnie (Malin Akerman), who are convinced that their marriage is solid and have no interest in talking about their problems. Ditto for Joey (Jon Favreau) and Lucy (Kristin Davis), who have long since given up on their commitment—and fidelity—and prefer to spend their time looking to sleep with people who are not their spouse. Recently divorced Shane (Faizon Love), on the other hand, just hopes he can keep up with Trudy (Kali Hawk, a promising newcomer), the 20-year-old girlfriend he's only known for a few weeks.

Not only could *Couples Retreat* have shown the importance of ensuring that a marriage is continually polished to avoid becoming stale, but a talented cast is onboard to draw laughs from the uncomfortable position of combining tropical paradise with intense therapy. Yet the script, written by Vaughn and Favreau and the far less-credible Dana Fox (*What Happens In Vegas* [2008], *The Wedding Date*, [2005]), cannot figure out how to bring the comedy to life. As a result, the film is a slow, obnoxious series of one-liners and labored situations—at one point, a hotel employee walks in the room as Joey is about to pleasure himself—that suggest the writers spent more time on packing their bags for a Bora Bora vacation than on devising any inspired comic ideas.

As for the therapy, the couples never touch on anything other than surface-level observations about appreciating their partner, though a few chuckles are generated by therapists played by John Michael Higgins and Ken Jeong. Meanwhile, Bateman and Bell, playing two extremely neurotic people, emerge as the most welcome on-screen presences, but their bickering is so monotonous that it is difficult to see their strife as anything more than filler—until the film can get back to shenanigans like Dave being mildly bitten by a shark or imposing yoga instructor Salvadore (Carlos Ponce) thrusting in ways that make the men uncomfortable and some of the women, Lucy in particular, considerably happier.

The movie is full of cheap gags like this. Towards the beginning, it is revealed that Jason had a testicular cancer scare, and consequently the characters say the phrase "ball cancer"about nine times, seemingly believing that this will become funnier each time. This does not come close to working, nor does the pathetically trite attempt to be cute when Dave and Ronnie's son Kevin (Colin Baoicchi) urges them to go on the trip because he and his brother just want their parents to be happy. In a film that clearly considers itself edgy by presenting a lot of scantily clad beautiful people and firing off intentionally off-color one-liners, this sort of sentimentality not only lands with a thud but shakes the foundation of an already rocky movie.

Certainly, the chief problems here are Vaughn's smug performance and the overwritten script—for example, Jason can't just say a relationship has lasted two weeks; he has to feebly describe it as the length of an antibiotics cycle. Yet first-time feature director Peter Billingsley also deserves blame for the way that *Couples Retreat* drags just as it should be kicking into high gear. A good comedy should transmit energy that gets audiences on its wavelength. With no forward momentum or even anyone to root for, *Couples Retreat* becomes increasingly exhausting, to the point of feeling not elated from laughing but unhappy and frustrated from such an empty vacation with depressingly shallow people.

Couples Retreat, simply, is not any fun. Its characters are not likable and are not pleasant company on vacation. Fortunately, the sight of beautiful beaches reminds viewers of a place much, much more enjoyable than sitting in front of a screen showing this unpleasant excuse for Vaughn and Favreau to sit back on their comedic fame, rather than defend it.

Matt Pais

CREDITS

Dave: Vince Vaughn
Joey: Jon Favreau
Jason: Jason Bateman
Shane: Faizon Love
Lucy: Kristin Davis
Ronnie: Malin Akerman
Cynthia: Kristen Bell
Trudy: Kali Hawk
Marcel: Jean Reno
Therapist #2: Ken Jeong
Briggs: Temuera Morrison
Jennifer: Tasha Smith
Salvadore: Carlos Ponce
Therapist #1: John Michael Higgins
Therapist #4: Amy Hill
Therapist #3: Charlotte Cornwell
Origin: USA
Language: English
Released: 2009
Production: Scott Stuber, Vince Vaughn; Wild West Picture Show, Relativity Media; released by Universal Pictures
Directed by: Peter Billingsley
Written by: Vince Vaughn, Jon Favreau, Dana Fox
Cinematography by: Eric Alan Edwards
Music by: A.R. Rahman
Sound: Steve Cantamessa
Music Supervisor: John O'Brien
Editing: Dan Lebental
Art Direction: Curt Beech
Costumes: Susan Matheson
Production Design: Shepherd Frankel
MPAA rating: PG-13
Running time: 107 minutes

REVIEWS

Ebert, Roger. *Chicago Sun-Times*. October 8, 2009.
Gronvall, Andrea. *Chicago Reader*. October 8, 2009.
Harvey, Dennis. *Variety*. October 7, 2009.
Howell, Peter. *Toronto Star*. October 9, 2009.

Pais, Matt. *Metromix.com.* October 8, 2009.
Phillips, Michael. *Chicago Tribune.* October 8, 2009.
Pols, Mary F. *Time Magazine.* October 8, 2009.
Sobczynski, Peter. *EFilmCritic.* October 8, 2009.
Tallerico, Brian. *MovieRetriever.com.* October 9, 2009.
Zacharek, Stephanie. *Salon.com.* October 9, 2009.

QUOTES

Dave: "The Code? Asstastic…Yes, Asstastic. A-S-S-TASTIC did you get that? Are we good? Good."

TRIVIA

Vince Vaughn's character's father in this film, Grandpa Jim Jim, is played by his real life father, Vernon Vaughn.

THE COVE

Shallow water. Deep secret.
—Movie tagline

The winner of the Audience Award at the 2009 Sundance Film Festival, *The Cove* is a gripping, emotionally devastating documentary about a brutal and heretofore secret Japanese dolphin slaughter that takes place annually, each September. Powered by an ample reservoir of indignant sentiment, yet told as a bristling spy-versus-spy thriller, the movie plays and connects on multiple levels, and easily ranks as one of the best non-fiction films of the year.

Directed, in his feature debut, by *National Geographic* photographer Louie Psihoyos (rhymes with sequoias), *The Cove* tells the amazing story of how former *Flipper* trainer-turned-activist Richard O'Barry, Psihoyos and an elite team of eco-warriors, filmmakers, marine technicians and free-divers embark on a covert mission to penetrate a tightly guarded fishing cove in Taiji, Japan. There, while being harassed by both local government officials and fishermen none too happy with the prospect of negative publicity, the *Cove* team shines a light on a dark and deadly secret that involves the capture and lucrative sale of thousands of dolphins (sold to marine parks, they fetch up to $150,000) and the annual slaughter of twenty-three thousand more.

Smartly ripping a page from the playbook of similarly fervent social issue documentaries like *Who Killed the Electric Car?* (2006) and *An Inconvenient Truth* (2006), *The Cove* goes to great lengths to demonstrate not just one easy villain but the multiple root causes of the ill which it targets. O'Barry speaks with a great sense of guilt about the multi-billion dollar dolphin entertainment industry that he feels he helped create. His testimonial about one of the dolphins that played Flip-

per committing "suicide" by locking eyes with him before floating to the bottom of their tank (unlike humans, each breath dolphins take is voluntary), along with illustrative stories of dolphins coming to the rescue of humans, goes a long way toward muddying the ethical justification of dolphins in captivity, and solidifying an image of them as sentient, highly intelligent creatures that should be more respected.

It is not merely humans' insatiable desire for animals performing stupid tricks that is endangering dolphins, though. With some help from Greenpeace cofounder Paul Watson, Psihoyos also throws a spotlight on the bureaucratic intrigue of global vote-trading with respect to industrial whaling, and how certain members of the International Whaling Commission have banded together to deny protection to so-called "small cetaceans." Finally, Psihoyos reveals an underhanded market for mislabeled, mercury-spiked dolphin meat being packaged as part of compulsory Japanese elementary school lunches. While these investigatory strands—and in particular the latter thread, less well integrated than the whaling analysis—rob the movie of a bit of its forward-leaning momentum, they undeniably enhance its educational pedigree.

Still, while it blends heartfelt reminiscences from O'Barry with a handful of interviews of people who will actually speak on the record and on camera, *The Cove* is mostly structured and pieced together like one of Steven Soderbergh's slick *Ocean's* heist flicks, not some staid non-fiction film. Composer J. Ralph's score pulses with a funky, playful energy, and a big part of the film's cathartic thrill comes from seeing Psihoyos, O'Barry and their crew engage in cat-and-mouse games with the mayor's office and an antagonistic goon squad of local fishermen. "We're here to catch you at your worst," they seem to be saying. "Try to stop us." Proving that some good actually came out of the terrible *Evan Almighty* (2007), the filmmakers tap one of that movie's prop masters to help construct fake, hollowed-out rocks to house cameras. In clandestine fashion, the team then scurries out under the cover of night and hides the cameras, along with underwater microphones, to capture the brutal carnage.

In design, Psihoyos and editor Geoffrey Richman take a page from James Marsh's Academy Award®-winning *Man on Wire* (2008), wringing maximum drama from a foregrounded event whose outcome is already known. The film's finale is bloody, and definitely not for small children (it is rated PG-13, for "disturbing content"), but even though the audience knows what is coming, the sour fruits of Psihoyos' efforts pack more of a queasy punch than a dozen assembly line Hollywood horror thrillers.

Though very different from Michael Moore's spate of recent documentaries, *The Cove* is similar in at least one important respect—it is unapologetically subjective, a piece of social activist cinema all the way. It means to serve as a call to action (hence David Bowie's "Heroes" blasting over the end credits), and the fact that it had notable success in this regard—after much hullabaloo the film screened at the Tokyo Film Festival, which was instrumental in getting the word out to the Japanese press and public, and helping avert the slaughter in 2009—is a testament to the power of its construction. Yet the movie does not let its naked advocacy interfere with simple facts; it never feels lazy or false in its construction. One plainly sees police haranguing O'Barry, and fishermen engaging in tactics of intimidation.

Above all, *The Cove* is truly heartbreaking. A viewer will not necessarily feel good about feeling so wrapped up in the film, but they will *feel*. That much is certain.

Brent Simon

CREDITS

Herself: Hayden Panettiere
Himself: Richard O'Barry
Himself: Louie Psihoyos
Origin: USA
Language: English
Released: 2009
Production: Fisher Stevens, Olivia Ahnemann, Paula DuPre Pesman; Diamond DOcs, Oceanic Preservation Society, Quickfire Films, Fish Films; released by Roadside Attractions
Directed by: Louie Psihoyos
Written by: Mark Monroe
Cinematography by: Brook Aitken
Music by: J. Ralph
Sound: Glenfield Payne
Editing: Geoffrey Richman
MPAA rating: PG-13
Running time: 92 minutes

REVIEWS

Catsoulis, Jeanette. *New York Times.* July 31, 2009.
Chang, Justin. *Variety.* July 29, 2009.
Ebert, Roger. *Chicago Sun-Times.* August 7, 2009.
Edelstein, David. *New York Magazine.* July 27, 2009.
Gronvall, Andrea. *Chicago Reader.* August 7, 2009.
Kennicott, Phillip. *Washington Post.* August 7, 2009.
Pais, Matt. *Metromix.com.* August 7, 2009.
Rickey, Carrie. *Philadelphia Inquirer.* August 7, 2009.

Turan, Kenneth. *Los Angeles Times.* July 31, 2009.
Weinberg, Scott. *Cinematical.* March 3, 2009.

QUOTES

Richard O'Barry: "If you aren't an activist you're an inactivist."

TRIVIA

Kerner Optical, previously the Industrial Light and Magic model shop, created special camouflaged (rock-like) cameras that helped capture some of the footage in the cove.

AWARDS

Oscars 2009: Feature Doc.
Writers Guild 2009: Feature Doc.
Directors Guild 2009: Doc. Director (Psihoyos).

CRANK: HIGH VOLTAGE
(Crank 2: High Voltage)

He was dead...but he got better.
—Movie tagline

Box Office: $13 million

Crank High Voltage is a movie for people who like boobs, butts, guns, explicit onscreen violence and the look and feel of music videos. It is also a movie that, according to the writing and directing team of Mark Neveldine and Brian Taylor, is first and foremost about wish fulfillment. But more than anything else *Crank: High Voltage* is a leap into the hopeless abyss of sensory stimulation offered up to a society that is already drowning in it. Despite the often entertaining and thrilling visuals this film delivers little but shocks to the system, treating all images as if they were equal. Unless the common denominator for what is worth seeing is merely that which provokes, *Crank: High Voltage* fails to do more than take the viewer on seamy, hyperactive journey through a crime-ridden, ugly Los Angeles, playing like a cross between a visual dictionary of camera technique and a bloody geek burlesque.

Neveldine and Taylor, as they are usually credited, also wrote and directed *Crank* (2006), and the recent *Gamer* (2009), as well as penned the horror film *Pathology* (2008). While they show an astonishing ability to adapt to the advantages offered by increasingly compact and sophisticated camera equipment they make movies with an eye towards flash rather than story.

Chev Chelios (Jason Statham) the nearly indestructible hero from the first film, survives his free fall from a helicopter only to wake up as an artificial heart is being pushed into his chest to facilitate the harvesting of the rest of his organs. Fighting his way out of the facility, he escapes, only to be informed by Doc Miles (Dwight Yoakam), a disgraced doctor turned pimp, that his new heart is only designed to beat an hour at a time and Chev will need to regularly charge it to keep it going. His only hope is to have his old super-heart put back in, which Miles is "pretty sure" he can do. Chev needs to track down the thieves, avoid getting killed or arrested and electrocute himself every hour on the hour, all while gangs Spanish, Chinese, and Japanese do their best to stop him.

Along the way he finds help from other characters from the first film. Eve (Amy Smart) does not just stand by her man—she has rough public sex with him on a horse track during a race resulting in a repulsive closeup of the horse genitals during climax. Kaylo comes back in the form of his twin brother, played here by the same actor, Efren Ramirez. A new character named Ria (Bai Ling) is basically a hooker with a thong of gold looking to manipulate every situation she is in for a buck. These and other supporting characters are well played, but like everything else they basically exist to support the frenetic visual style, link the action sequences together, and setup the films never ending too oft repeated line, "F**k you Chelios."

As Chev Chelios, Jason Statham channels the same energy that made his character Bacon, in the breakout hit *Lock Stock and Two Smoking Barrels* (1998), crackle. Hollywood has been trying to exhaust him ever since but like Clive Owen (*Shoot 'Em Up* [2007]) he has found a way to parody his own image while still maintaining his box office appeal. The pity is that he shows promise as an actor of some depth when he is given anything to do that does not involve his fists, but, unlike Owen, Statham has stayed mainly in the action genre.

A number of fun cameos and smaller roles are dished out to the likes of David Carradine (here spoofing his *Kung Fu* TV show of the 1970s), Corey Haim, Geri "Ginger Spice" Halliwell, Troma Pictures president Lloyd Kaufman and the ubiquitous ex-porn actor Ron Jeremy.

The movie ends with a shot of a triumphant Chelios, head and face aflame, giving the audience the finger. Nothing could be more or less appropriate. More and more our culture seems to divide themselves into those who assume the shape of potatoes having just picked up the latest from Redbox, and those who simply ignore the box altogether. Thoughtful cinephiles, geeks and even casual viewers are left to ask, "Why would I want wishes like the ones appealed to in this movie to be fulfilled at all, much less by a loud, exhausting, collec-

tion of misogynistic, ultra-violent moments masquerading as a motion picture?"

Dave Canfield

CREDITS

Chev Chelios: Jason Statham
Randy: Corey Haim
Eve: Amy Smart
Ria: Bai Ling
Venus: Efren Ramirez
Doc Miles: Dwight Yoakam
El Huron: Clifton Collins Jr.
Origin: USA
Language: English
Released: 2009
Production: Gary Lucchesi, Tom Rosenberg, Skip Williamson, Richard S. Wright; Lionsgate, Lakeshore Entertainment, Radical Media; released by Lionsgate
Directed by: Mark Neveldine, Brian Taylor
Written by: Brian Taylor
Cinematography by: Brandon Trost
Editing: Fernando Villena, Marc Jakubowicz
Art Direction: Sebastian Schroder
Costumes: Dayna Pink
Music by: Mike Patton
Production Design: Jerry Fleming
Sound: Scott Martin Gershin
MPAA rating: R
Running time: 96 minutes

REVIEWS

Adams, Sam. *Los Angeles Times.* April 17, 2009.
Anderson, Jason. *Toronto Star.* April 20, 2009.
Bayer, Jeff. *Scorecard Review.* April 17, 2009.
Berkshire, Geoff. *Metromix.com.* April 17, 2009.
Catsoulis, Jeanette. *New York Times.* April 20, 2009.
Duralde, Alonso. *MSNBC.* April 17, 2009.
Gilchrist, Too. *Sci Fi Wire.* April 17, 2009.
Lacey, Liam. *Globe and Mail.* April 20, 2009.
Markovitz, Adam. *Entertainment Weekly.* April 17, 2009.
Sobczynski, Peter. *EFilmCritic.* April 17, 2009.

QUOTES

Chinese Doctor #2: "Maybe long time. He die hard with a vengeance."

TRIVIA

Mark Neveldine and Brian Taylor shot 300 hours of footage in 30 days of filming.

CRAZY HEART

The harder the life, the sweeter the song.
—Movie tagline

Box Office: $34 million

The career of a musician is a long, long road. Guys get old. Records stop selling. Beards turn gray. Yet for many, the booze never stops flowing.

In *Crazy Heart*, Bad Blake (Jeff Bridges) is that walking cliché, the forgotten star reduced to playing in bowling alleys and rundown bars. Gone are the big paydays and the widespread fame, though the diehard fans and occasional groupies remain. At fifty-seven, Bad (he refuses to reveal his real first name) is an overweight, alcoholic shadow of himself, playing nothing but old material whose words feel ever more profound as he sings, "I used to be somebody; now I am somebody else." Bad has been married four times, and he has mentored country music star Tommy Sweet (Colin Farrell) but does not want to talk about either issue. When Sante Fe newspaper reporter Jean Craddock (Maggie Gyllenhaal) requests an interview, Bad accepts, even though he has not done an interview in years. It is safe to assume this is not a result of turning them all down but that recently the offers have ceased.

As Jean ignores her gut instincts and falls for Bad, and as he confronts the bitterness and weariness that makes it nearly impossible for him to do right by himself or others, *Crazy Heart* begs comparison to other stories of fallen heroes—primarily, *The Wrestler* (2008) and *Tender Mercies* (1983). The latter is another story of an aging country singer that *Crazy Heart* references by casting that film's star, Robert Duvall, as one of Bad's old pals. Yet *Crazy Heart* is more grounded, detailed and convincing than its predecessor, whose Mac Sledge (Duvall) never comes into focus as strongly as Bad. *Crazy Heart* does not feel like a retread, partly because its story deals with the helpless sorrow of mistakes repeated, whether they are someone else's mistakes or one's own. Deep down, Bad seems to know he is lost, and his lyrics, such as "Funny how falling feels like flying, for a little while…," reveal a guy who sensed he was on the wrong track even when it still felt right.

The other reason the film never feels stale is the depth of the performances. Bridges has played worndown, responsibility-free characters before (in fact, the opening scene of Bad entering a bowling alley may bring back memories of *The Big Lebowski* [1998]). He has never been this locked into a life, though, where accomplishment turns into resentment and inspiration becomes detachment. Bad has not written a new song in three years, and it is clear this is because he has not experienced anything in that time worth writing about. Scenes between the veteran singer and Jean might feel dry had they involved a weaker actress. Instead, Bridges and Gyllenhaal achieve a marvelous push and pull between a guy who wants connection but does not know how to sustain it, and a woman who knows better but cannot help being taken by the entertainer's seasoned

charm. That he so easily plays with her 4-year-old son Buddy (Jack Nation) but does not know a thing about fatherhood makes it that much harder for her to know if this man can play a long-term part in her life.

The film even gets a great performance out of Farrell, whose casting is nothing less than fearless. In many roles the once-promising actor frequently brings with him his thick Irish accent, but as Tommy, Farrell not only comes off as a believable country star on the rise—simultaneously grateful for Bad's help and unsure how to deal with his struggling mentor—but he shows off a solid singing voice to boot. Ditto for Bridges. The music in *Crazy Heart* is beautifully bittersweet and revealing—country anthems of late, lonely nights and relentless uncertainty that appeal to even the most country music-averse listener.

The entire film works so well that it is too bad writer-director Scott Cooper—adapting Thomas Cobb's novel—included a final scene that seems to overcompensate for the poignantly heartbreaking scene that comes before. Otherwise, *Crazy Heart* is like watching a chip gradually fall off a shoulder. Nobody changes so much as evaluates the error of their ways and considers what to do about it—and if it is better to forgive or to simply adjust and move on.

That type of perspective appears far off towards the beginning of the film, when Bad promises to dedicate a song to a local couple only to leave the stage to vomit before even singing a word. (His temporary backing band picks up the slack.) This man plays the songs of a star but he is not the same guy that the fans knew and loved, and Bad eventually must realize that pride, ego and traditional celebrity vices have turned him into a masochist dangling dangerously close to rock bottom. It is a reminder that no one, even country singers, wants to live a life like a country song.

Matt Pais

CREDITS

Bad Blake: Jeff Bridges
Jean Craddock: Maggie Gyllenhaal
Wayne: Robert Duvall
Tommy Sweet: Colin Farrell
Bill Wilson: Tom Bower
Manager: James Keane
Doctor: William Marquez
Origin: USA
Language: English
Released: 2009
Production: Robert Duvall, Rob Carliner, Judy Cairo, T-Bone Burnett; Butchers Run Films, Informant Media; released by Fox Searchlight

Directed by: Scott Cooper
Written by: Scott Cooper
Cinematography by: Barry Markowitz
Music by: T-Bone Burnett, Stephen Bruton
Sound: Bayard Carey
Editing: John Axelrad
Art Direction: Ben Zeller
Costumes: Doug Hall
Production Design: Waldemar Kalinowski
MPAA rating: R
Running time: 112 minutes

REVIEWS

Ansen, David. *Newsweek.* December 4, 2009.
Denby, David. *New Yorker.* December 7, 2009.
Ebert, Roger. *Chicago Sun-Times.* December 24, 2009.
McCarthy, Todd. *Variety.* December 3, 2009.
Puig, Claudia. *USA Today.* December 16, 2009.
Scott, A.O. *New York Times.* December 16, 2009.
Stevens, Dana. *Slate.* December 17, 2009.
Tallerico, Brian. *MovieRetriever.com.* December 25, 2009.
Travers, Peter. *Rolling Stone.* December 11, 2009.
Turan, Kenneth. *Los Angeles Times.* December 17, 2009.

QUOTES

Bad Blake: "Ain't rememberin' wonderful?"

TRIVIA

Filmed in only 24 days.

AWARDS

Oscars 2009: Actor (Bridges), Song ("The Weary Kind")
Golden Globes 2010: Actor—Drama (Bridges), Song ("The Weary Kind")
Ind. Spirit 2010: Actor (Bridges), First Feature
Screen Actors Guild 2009: Actor (Bridges)
Nomination:
Oscars 2009: Support. Actress (Gyllenhaal)
British Acad. 2009: Actor (Bridges), Orig. Score
Ind. Spirit 2010: First Screenplay
Writers Guild 2009: Adapt. Screenplay.

CROSSING OVER

> *Every day thousands of people illegally cross our borders...only one thing stands in their way. America.*
> —Movie tagline

The best films about immigration to the United States (*El Norte* [1983], *Maria Full of Grace* [2003], *The Visitor* [2007], *Frozen River* [2008], *Sin Nombre* [2008]) convey the great complexity and humanity of the issue. These films are subtle, realistic and thought-provoking examinations of three-dimensional characters and the complicated intersection of dreams, desperation, bureaucracy, corruption, cynicism and heartbreak their journeys inevitably involve. Unfortunately, Wayne Kramer's *Crossing Over* is none of these things and is a case study of a film laid low by a substandard script.

With its large cast and seven overlapping narratives bound by the common theme of legal and illegal immigration, *Crossing Over* obviously wants to do for immigration what films like *Traffic* [2000] and *Crash* [2005] did for the drug trade and racism. Harrison Ford is Max Brogan, an immigration enforcement officer who cares too much about the illegal immigrants it is his job to pursue and deport. Brogan gets his suits cleaned at a dry cleaner owned by a Korean family nearing the end of the naturalization process. Brogan's partner, Hamid Baraheri (an excellent Cliff Curtis), is a naturalized U.S. citizen whose Iranian family has, superficially at least, successfully made the transition to America. Hamid's sister, Zahra, (Melody Khazae) works at print shop where she encounters Australian actress Claire (Alice Eve) who is pursuing a green card. Claire's friend Gavin (Jim Sturgess), a British musician, is also pursuing his green card. Ray Liotta is Cole Frankel, an unscrupulous immigration official who offers to grease the administrative wheels for Claire. Frankel's wife, Denise (Ashley Judd), is an immigration attorney defending a Muslim teenager (Summer Bishil) facing deportation following an unwise high school class presentation about 9/11. This interconnected narrative structure suits complicated, multifaceted societal issues such as immigration (or the drug trade or racism) in its ability to demonstrate the many different ways people are affected by the same issue. Once removed from an individual point of view, these issues reveal themselves to be not the black and white concepts they are often presented as but as various shades of grey, with meanings as diverse as the number of people who are affected by them.

The problem is *Crossing Over* has a black and white script which lacks the subtly, depth and realism its complex subject requires. Kramer's dialogue consists of exchanges between one-dimensional characters whose purpose is to voice the most extreme position available in the least subtle manner possible. The distinctly unsubtle tone of the film's dialogue is established from the first line of dialogue, spoken to Ford's Brogan as he asks a coworker about the welfare of an ailing immigrant he recently apprehended: "Jesus Christ Brogan! Everything is a humanitarian crisis with you!" This level of subtly is maintained throughout the rest of the film.

The unsubtle dialogue could have perhaps been overcome if it was issued by characters the viewer cared about in the service of a realistic, believable plot. However, the shallow script does not provide the actors with the opportunity to articulate their character's motivations and consequently the viewer does not understand why the characters do what they do or care about their fate. Harrison Ford obviously cares very deeply about the welfare of the people it is his job to capture and deport to almost certainly worse, perhaps fatal, conditions but this incongruity is not explored or explained. Claire and Gavin's burning desire for a green card causes them to go to desperate lengths (both comical and degrading) but since both come from first world countries and the motivations fueling their pursuit are not explained (other than straightforward careerism) it is hard to understand why they are willing to go to those lengths or care about whether they succeed or not. At its best, the script renders its characters' motives mysterious and, at its worst, cannot even maintain consistent behavior from its characters. Within seconds of Liotta's INS official meeting Claire he is blackmailing her into a sleazy quid pro quo (two months of sex on demand in return for an expedited green card). One minute he is an enslaving sociopath grabbing Claire by the hair—"I want you down on all fours at the edge of the bed!"—the next minute he is asking her to enter into a caring relationship—"I just want to start over again. I wouldn't say who I was. I wouldn't put a scare into you. I'd just ask you out for a cup of coffee." When Liotta turns away and closes his eyes in pain at her justifiably disbelieving and harsh response, the viewer is actually being invited to empathize with him and the result is unintentionally hilarious.

The viewer's engagement is further eroded by plot lines which range from the implausible (Ford calls in sick so he can drive to Mexico to check on a woman he has recently deported; a straightforwardly evil FBI agent deports a teenager for a high school class presentation; a rabbi lies so a complete stranger can get a green card) to the completely unbelievable (Cole and Claire's plot-line; the fate of Hamid's sister; an absurd climax in which multiple homicides coincide with an impassioned speech/civics lesson about the value and honor of American citizenship).

Ensemble films with overlapping plots in which the film's theme is the protagonist are by their very nature episodic and light on character development. However as the films of Robert Altman, Steven Soderbergh and P.T. Anderson, among others, have demonstrated, excellent writing, direction and performances can compensate for limited screen time. *Crossing Over* possesses an able

director and a large and talented cast who do their best with underwritten roles but the film simply cannot escape the profound limitations of its script. *Crossing Over* demonstrates the essential nature of the screenplay (ironically the least respected element of film production in mainstream Hollywood) to a film's artistic success. With a subtle, realistic script added to all of *Crossing Over*'s other elements one might have had an excellent film. Without it, none of those elements can save the film.

Nate Vercauteren

CREDITS

Max Brogan: Harrison Ford
Hamid Baraheri: Clifford Curtis
Denise Frankel: Ashley Judd
Chris Farrell: Sean Penn
Cole Frankel: Ray Liotta
Mireya: Alice Braga
Claire Shepard: Alice Eve
Gavin Kossef: Jim Sturgess
Taslima Jahangir: Summer Bishil
Yong Kim: Justin Chon
Cliff Curtis: Hamid Baraheri
Origin: USA
Language: English
Released: 2009
Production: Frank Marshall, Wayne Kramer; Kennedy/Marshall, Movie Prose; released by Weinstein Company
Directed by: Wayne Kramer
Written by: Wayne Kramer
Cinematography by: James Whitaker
Music by: John Murphy, Mark Isham
Sound: Lee Orloff
Music Supervisor: Brian Ross
Editing: Arthur Coburn
Art Direction: Peter Borck
Costumes: Kristen M. Burke
Production Design: Toby Corbett
MPAA rating: R
Running time: 140 minutes

REVIEWS

Childress, Erik. *eFilmCritic.com.* February 26, 2009.
Dargis, Manohla. *New York Times.* February 27, 2009.
Ebert, Roger. *Chicago Sun-Times.* March 12, 2009.
Edelstein, David. *New York Magazine.* February 23, 2009.
McCarthy, Todd. *Variety.* February 17, 2009.
Pais, Matt. *Metromix.com.* February 26, 2009.

Phillips, Michael. *Chicago Tribune.* March 12, 2009.

Stevens, Dana. *Slate.* February 26, 2009.

Tallerico, Brian. *MovieRetriever.com.* March 13, 2009.

Turan, Kenneth. *Los Angeles Times.* February 27, 2009.

QUOTES

Special Agent Ludwig: "Which is something the adjudicator who handled your case would have to have been aware of and yet he approved you for an EB-1. Miss Shepard we'd like you to tell us about your relationship with center adjudications officer Cole Frankel?"

TRIVIA

Director Wayne Kramer's original cut was 140 minutes long; but despite having the right to final cut, this films' producer agreed to be involved in editing the film down to two hours when Harvey Weinstein allegedly threatened to release the film straight to DVD, and bypass a theatrical release altogether. Kramer had nothing to do with the re-editing.

D

THE DAMNED UNITED

*They love me for what I'm not...they hate me
for what I am.*
—Movie tagline

Certain films offer up crisp characterizations, fault-less lead and supporting performances, and interesting, well delineated dramatic stakes, and yet still fail to make much of an impression. This is the unfortunate fate to which *The Damned United,* a perfectly acceptable and engaging little British sports drama adapted from an acclaimed, bestselling novel by David Peace, was consigned in the fall of 2009.

The movie was a critical darling—garnering a 94 percent positive rating on Rotten Tomatoes, with over 100 affirmative reviews to only seven negative notices, as well as a 96 percent rating among top critics—but unable to gain any Stateside commercial traction, where it grossed an anemic $438,000 in its 11-week run. This was due largely, one supposes, to a curious and/or off-putting title, and the shrugging disregard of its subject matter, where "that other football," or soccer, is relegated to second-class status among sports. A MPAA R rating, for language, certainly did not help matters, and may have cut into the movie's audience abroad as well, where it earned a curiously muted $3.6 million in theaters.

Set in 1960s and 1970s England, *The Damned United* recounts the confrontational and darkly humorous true story of wunderkind coach Brian Clough's doomed forty-four day tenure as manager of the reigning champions of English football, Leeds United. Previously managed by his bitter rival, Don Revie (Colm Meaney), and coming off their most successful period ever as a football club, Leeds was at the time perceived by many to represent a new, aggressive style of football—an anathema to the principled yet flamboyant star-on-the-rise Clough (Michael Sheen), who had achieved record-breaking success as manager of Hartlepool and Derby County, quickly building up smaller division teams in his own vision with trusty, older lieutenant Peter Taylor (Timothy Spall).

Flashing back and forward a bit in time, the film charts first Clough's rivalry with Leeds, after being hired by Derby Chairman Sam Longson (Jim Broadbent), and then his rocky transition after taking the Leeds job without Taylor by his side, and how things implode. With a locker room full of what in his mind are still "Revie's boys," Clough immediately butts heads with almost all of the Leeds players (including Stephen Graham and Peter McDonald), who bristle at his changes in style and decorum. As losses on the field mount and pressure for him to resign increases, Clough looks to reconnect with Taylor, professionally and personally, and try to remake his tattered career.

Sheen's big screen profile has increased ever since his lauded turn as British Prime Minister Tony Blair in *The Queen* (2006), and his portrayal of Clough is at the heart of the straightforward appeal of *The Damned United.* He captures both the coach's brilliance and obstinance, giving viewers a clear-eyed view of how ambition can corrode foresight and aptitude. Screenwriter Peter Morgan's adaptation of the source material is also smart, and powered by subtly revelatory dialogue. He seems to have a knack for capturing the easygoing, natural rhythms of Sheen's talent, this film marking their fourth collaboration together, including the aforementioned *The Queen* and *Frost/Nixon* (2008), both Academy Award®-nominated films.

Director Tom Hooper, whose work includes the Golden Globe®-winning *Longford* (2006), has a list of mostly small screen credits which nonetheless showcase his knack for digging into political biography, and while Clough's tale is not on the surface one of government affairs, there is no doubt that its narrative focus on clashing principles and juggled egos heavily evokes a feeling of political drama. This makes Hooper a solid choice for the material, and he delivers in streamlined fashion. The particulars of competition are communicated through title cards and standing charts, which underscore Clough's knack for turning underdogs into winners. The main concession that Hooper and Morgan make, in an attempt to curry favor with audiences who either do not know or care of soccer, is to shoot the movie's matches as mostly a series of reaction shots, with very little on-field action. This cuts both ways, though, as true soccer fans might feel gypped by the film in this regard.

Also aiding in *The Damned United* is a superlative group of cinematic technicians. Working in tandem with production designer Eve Stewart and costume designer Mike O'Neill, director of photography Ben Smithard crafts a beautifully dour and spare movie, filmed on locations throughout Yorkshire and Derbyshire. The dreariness of Leeds is a visual metaphor for how things go sour for Clough, and contrasted nicely with the sunny vistas of southern England when he and Taylor are offered a chance to reunite. Furthermore, while it may seem strange to single out hair and make-up design in what is a fairly contemporary and modest, naturalistic film, Jan Archibald's work on Sheen is noteworthy for what it conveys with no dialogue. Clough's tangle of swept-upward brown locks seems to almost lean forward, mirroring the brash confidence of his personality.

The Damned United is not a film that has innate wide appeal. Indeed, a description of its story might induce yawns of indifference from even fairly open-minded filmgoers, given the fact that it seems to tell such a niche story. Given a chance, however, even audiences with little interest in sports will find reward in this perceptive tale of talent brought low, and given a chance to shine again.

Brent Simon

CREDITS
Brian Clough: Michael Sheen
Peter Taylor: Timothy Spall

Don Revie: Colm Meaney
Manny Cussins: Henry Goodman
Jimmy Gordon: Maurice Roeves
Sam Longson: Jim Broadbent
Billy Bremner: Stephen Graham
Dave Mackay: Brian McCardie
Origin: Great Britain, USA
Language: English
Released: 2009
Production: Andy Harries, Grainne Marmion; BBC Films, Columbia Pictures Corporation, Left Bank Pictures, Screen Yorkshire; released by Sony Pictures Classics
Directed by: Tom Hooper
Written by: Peter Morgan
Cinematography by: Ben Smithard
Music by: Rob Lane
Sound: Martin Beresford, Paul Hamblin
Music Supervisor: Liz Gallacher
Editing: Melanie Oliver
Art Direction: Leon McCarthy
Costumes: Mike O'Neill
Production Design: Eve Stewart
MPAA rating: R
Running time: 97 minutes

REVIEWS

Bradshaw, Peter. *Guardian.* March 27, 2009.
Ebert, Roger. *Chicago Sun-Times.* October 15, 2009.
Edelstein, David. *New York Magazine.* October 5, 2009.
Edwards, David. *Daily Mirror.* March 27, 2009.
Felperin, Leslie. *Variety.* October 6, 2009.
Honeycutt, Kirk. *Hollywood Reporter.* September 10, 2009.
Morris, Wesley. *Boston Globe.* October 15, 2009.
Schwarzbaum, Lisa. *Entertainment Weekly.* October 7, 2009.
Thomas, William. *Empire Magazine.* March 27, 2009.
Wilson, Chuck. *Village Voice.* October 6, 2009.

QUOTES

Brian Clough: "You know he'll be making a file on us. A dossier."

TRIVIA

The scenes in the film set at the Derby County training ground were actually filmed in Leeds at a football pitch ironically overlooking the Leeds United stadium.

DANCE FLICK

Box Office: $26 million

Simply: *Dance Flick* stinks. Yet, as only the latest in a long line of onscreen insults from the Wayans family, this unimaginative and frequently tasteless spoof is, for what it is worth, far from the worst piece of rubbish the comedy crew has hurled into the laughter abyss.

Yes, *Dance Flick*, directed by Damien Dante Wayans, who wrote the script with Marlon, Shawn, Craig and Keenen Ivory Wayans, is not nearly as horrifying as *Little Man* (2006) or *White Chicks* (2004). Those two comedies seem to exist in an alternate reality where intelligent people do not exist or cannot, at least, recognize something as obvious as a black man posing as a white woman or a little person posing as a baby. The films take outrageous premises and not only fail to make them believable but merely use them as a set-up for horribly cheap and never funny humor. *Dance Flick*, on the other hand, is just a junky parody of already junky movies, which is pretty redundant considering the inherent, blatant cheesiness of targets like *Step Up* (2006) and *You Got Served* (2004).

Like the Keenen Ivory Wayans-directed *Scary Movie* (2000) and its sequel, *Scary Movie 2* (2001), *Dance Flick* recycles its plot from the source it is out to lampoon. Thus, cribbing from *Save the Last Dance* (2001), the film revolves around square white gal Megan (Shoshana Bush), who, after the tragic death of her mother, transfers from the suburbs to an inner-city high school. There she bonds and becomes dance partners with geeky African American Thomas (Damon Wayans Jr.), who, after his crew loses a dance battle, is in debt to gangster Sugar Bear (David Alan Grier, so big that his fat suit seems to have been piled onto another fat suit).

If *Dance Flick* stayed focused and lampooned the inauthentic look at urban life often provided by dancing-related teen films, the spoof could actually land some punches about the way these films sacrifice grit and truth for spiffy dance moves (which, arguably, is the only reason anyone sees these movies in the first place). It would also be interesting if *Dance Flick* gave Megan some credit and let her be savvy about hip-hop—only to have her black classmates continually try to teach her anyway. Instead, the film just sits on traditional stereotypes, in which Megan is totally oblivious and uncool and needs Thomas to school her in a less traditional type of dancing.

Without direction or inspiration, *Dance Flick* just pathetically searches for anything to mock, making references to unrelated films while rarely finding something even mildly funny. Perky Tracy (Chelsea Makela) is a nod to *Hairspray* (2007), Thomas chains Megan to a radiator as in *Black Snake Moan* (2006), and Megan performs a dance to Rick James' "Superfreak" a la *Little Miss Sunshine* (2006), a reference that is by now very

very dated. Other painful gags include the grossly overweight Sugar Bear singing a song about food to the tune of *Dreamgirls'* (2007) "And I Am Telling You I'm Not Going," a gay student (played by Brennan Hillard and modeled after Zac Efron's character in *High School Musical* [2006]) singing about being gay to the tune of "Fame," and, believe it or not, a teacher named Ms. Cameltoe (Amy Sedaris) beat-boxing with her vagina. (Even more inane, outdated references are also made to *Superbad* [2007], *Twilight* [2008], *Ray* [2004], and *Employee of the Month* [2006].) This is as desperate as comedy writing gets, and it is an indication that the Wayans clan assumes its audience seeks nothing but half-hearted references and cheap sexual humor. In perhaps the most egregious example of their distrust of the audience, they nod to Halle Berry's 2000 car accident when a car that runs over Megan's mom (Lauren Bowles) boasts a license plate with the name "Halle." Then, in case anyone struggles to identify which Halle the film is referencing, a woman in a catsuit from Berry's flop *Catwoman* (2004), gets out of the car, just to clarify that, yes, the joke is about Halle Berry.

To be fair: *Dance Flick* has a few laughs. At one point an undercover cop listens to a rapper freestyle about murder and then arrests him for murder, claiming that the rapper just confessed. Also earning a chuckle is when Thomas, trying to invite himself to a party, gets blown off but swiftly responds, "Cool, I'll bring the chips." That sort of quick wit is in very, very short supply in the film, so the rare occurrence of cleverness provides an oasis from stupidity that is all too brief. However, it should be noted and mildly appreciated that the movie at least comes up with a few actual jokes, as opposed to parodies such as *Disaster Movie* (2008), which literally get by on nothing but excruciating and crass references to other films.

Still, that *Dance Flick* can barely come up with enough jokes to sustain a feature length film (total running time sans credits is only slightly north of 70 minutes) is the ultimate sign of carelessness by the many Wayanses involved. Of course, when sight gags like Thomas urinating on a rival dancer or Megan's friend Charity (Essence Atkins) spinning on her pregnant belly make it into a film's very short final cut, perhaps it is better to be glad that the even-worse jokes left on the cutting floor stayed there.

Matt Pais

CREDITS

Mr. Moody: Marlon Wayans
Baby Daddy: Shawn Wayans
Mr. Stache: Keenen Ivory Wayans

Ms. Cameltoe: Amy Sedaris
Nora: Christina Murphy
Charity: Essence Atkins
Sugar Bear: David Alan Grier
Ron: Chris Elliott
Megan: Shoshana Bush
Thomas: Damon Wayans Jr.
Jack: Brennan Hillard
Truck: Craig Wayans
Origin: USA
Language: English
Released: 2009
Production: Keenen Ivory Wayans, Marlon Wayans, Shawn Wayans, Rick Alvarez; Wayans Bros. Entertainment, MTV Films; released by Paramount Pictures
Directed by: Damien Dante Wayans
Written by: Marlon Wayans, Shawn Wayans, Keenen Ivory Wayans, Damien Dante Wayans, Craig Wayans
Cinematography by: Mark Irwin
Sound: Richard Van Dyke
Music Supervisor: Lisa Brown
Editing: Scott Hill
Art Direction: Erin Cochran
Costumes: Judy Ruskin
Production Design: Aaron Osborne
MPAA rating: PG-13
Running time: 83 minutes

REVIEWS

Anderson, Jeffrey M. *Cinematical.* June 1, 2009.
Anderson, John. *Newsday.* May 21, 2009.
Debruge, Peter. *Variety.* May 21, 2009.
Moore, Roger. *Orlando Sentinel.* May 22, 2009
Puig, Claudia. *USA Today.* May 22, 2009.
Rabin, Nathan. *AV Club.* May 22, 2009.
Rickey, Carrie. *Philadelphia Inquirer.* May 22, 2009.
Sobczynski, Peter. *EFilmCritic.com.* May 22, 2009.
Smith, Kyle. *New York Post.* May 26, 2009.
Whipp, Glenn. *Los Angeles Times.* May 21, 2009.

QUOTES

A-Con: "All we need is D to do his signature move."

DEAD SNOW

When a movie trailer showcases a Nazi zombie charge across a winter field set to the tune of Beethoven's "Ode to Joy," a viewer has the right to expect something a little special. *Dead Snow* is certainly much more entertaining than most recent zombie films but it stops short of the grotesque glory that horror fans have long wanted from a Nazi zombie movie coming in more Guignol than grand. As the undead swell the ranks of cinema, especially *independent* horror cinema, so many truly awful zombie films have been getting made that it seems just a matter of time before the zombie as a character loses its cultural bite. Sadly, the question of where the metaphoric viability of the zombie movie stands in 2009 will not be definitively answered by *Dead Snow*'s energetic mix of horror, humor and gore but the Norwegian effort does make a good case that there is life in the walking dead yet.

Dead Snow opens on a snowy night in Norway as a woman is chased, caught and eaten by undead Nazi soldiers. This simple-but-promising beginning is then undercut by the introduction of the characters who will form the basis of the rest of the film and they are, sadly, just another bunch of horny, party-mad, young adults whose lack of common sense and mere presence here dooms them to be food for Der Fuhrer's festering fiends; an awkward alliterative description that is still less awkward than *Dead Snow* itself.

Seven medical students journey to a remote cabin to enjoy a weekend of skiing but, upon arrival, discover that Sara, the cabin owner, and victim from the opening scene, has not yet arrived. Deciding to wait until morning to look for her, they start to party. But their revelry is interrupted by the arrival of a mysterious hiker who chastises them for not learning more about the area into which they have hiked. During World War II, the area they are currently in was held by a group of especially ruthless *Einsatzgruppen* who tortured and murdered the locals over three long years. A village uprising near the end of the war only managed to kill some of the Nazis, who were surprised while looting the village during their retreat. Warning the students that the area is still considered an evil place, the hiker departs.

The next morning, while one of the students goes off to look for Sara, the rest discover an old wooden box hidden beneath the floorboards of the cabin containing gold coins and other objects hidden by the retreating Nazi soldiers. Not realizing their own fates are tied to that of the treasure they keep some of the items unleashing the wrath of the undead Nazi guardians.

Director Tommy Wirkola and his co-screenwriter Stig Frode Henriksen keep the emphasis on one-liners and gory set pieces, managing to generate some suspense and good laughs (and not a little bit of disgust), but the film feels somehow less inventive than it should. For example, *Dead Snow* is at its cleverest during moments of carnage. An outhouse becomes a den of unexpected iniquity, a snow mobile is equipped with a machine gun, and, at one point, a zombie's intestines are used to help someone climb over the side of a cliff. But the effect of the otherwise strong special effects throughout is undercut by the inexplicable use of CGI blood spattering.

The point here is that the zombies are nothing more than special effects themselves, monsters in the broadest sense. The fact that they are Nazis seems largely meaningless. Nazi zombie movies are actually fewer and farther between than many horror fans realize. In fact, depending on how the word zombie is defined there are as few as five (with the rest being *Zombie Lake* [1980], *Oasis of the Zombies* [1982], *Night of the Zombies* [1983], and *Outpost* [2007].)

It can well be argued that of the many zombie films in the last decade the best, *Shaun of the Dead* (2004), *Fido* (2006), *Dance of the Dead* (2008) and *Zombieland* (2009), are all comedies. Most discouragingly, the above are all better in almost every way than any of George Romero's recent more-serious zombie films (*Land of the Dead* [2005], *Diary of the Dead* [2007]) which is ironic considering Romero is often quoted as having said, "If you can't see the humor in dead people eating the living then I can't explain it to you." This riff on Louis Armstrong's famous quote about the nature of jazz is a good one to apply when evaluating *Dead Snow*, not just because it is a funny film that features the dead eating the living but because the overall effect of the film illustrates the fine line between horror and humor, a line that *Dead Snow* shambles back and forth over like a brain-dead zombie in the snow, thinking only about how to get to the next gag (a word that can be used to describe several elements of the film).

Dave Canfield

CREDITS

The Wanderer: Bjorn Sundquist
Martin: Vegar Hoel
Roy: Stig Frode Henriksen
Hanna: Charlotte Frogner
Chris: Jenny Skavlan
Erland: Jeppe Laursen
Vegard: Lasse Valdal
Liv: Evy Kasseth Rosten
Col. Herzog: Orjan Gamst
Sara: Ane Dahl Torp
Dying Zombie: Tommy Wirkola
Origin: Norway
Language: Norwegian
Released: 2009
Production: Terje Stromstad, Tomas Evjen; Yellow Bastard Productions, News on Request, Euforia Films; released by IFC Films

Directed by: Tommy Wirkola
Written by: Tommy Wirkola
Cinematography by: Matthew Weston
Music by: Christian Wibe
Sound: Kjetil Troan
Editing: Martin Stoltz
Costumes: Linn Henriksen
Production Design: Liv Ask
MPAA rating: Unrated
Running time: 91 minutes

REVIEWS

Dargis, Manohla. *New York Times.* June 19, 2009
Ebert, Roger. *Chicago Sun-Times.* July 16, 2009.
Farber, Stephen. *Hollywood Reporter.* June 11, 2009.
Goldstein, Gary. *Los Angeles Time.* July 1, 2009.
Pais, Matt. *Metromix.com.* June 18, 2009.
Reed, Rex. *New York Observer.* June 17, 2009.
Tobias, Scott. *AV Club.* June 18, 2009.
Weitzman, Elizabeth. *New York Daily News.* June 19, 2009.
Wilson, Chuck. *Village Voice.* June 16, 2009.
Wilson, Staci. *Layne Horror.com.* June 18, 2009.

QUOTES

Erland (quoting Indiana Jones): "Fortune and glory, kid...fortune and glory."

TRIVIA

Originally it was going to be called "Red Snow," as an homage to the Swedish/Norwegian mini-series with the same name.

DEPARTURES
(Okuribito)

Real life...real travel.
—Movie tagline

The 2009 Academy Award® winner for Best Foreign Language film as well as a huge commercial hit in its native Japan, director Yojiro Takita's *Departures* is a delicate, involving drama about emotional displacement, a pleasantly subdued rumination on the meaning and impact rituals have in our lives (whether we acknowledge it or not), and how they can ultimately help provide mooring and healing.

Departures's emphasis on formality and custom—a bigger part of Far Eastern culture, broadly speaking—no doubt played a big part in the movie's enormous financial success; it pulled in more than $61 million of its $68 million worldwide theatrical gross in its homeland, and also did exceedingly well in Hong Kong and Taiwan. And yet *Departures* is no empty bauble, praised Stateside merely for its exotic nature; the film's deceptively simple marvel is that it achieves emotional effect so quietly, without histrionics. While its cultural specificity and slightly malingering, 131-minute pace preclude widespread general audience embrace, this allowance for and emphasis upon the full spectrum of life's emotions—some scenes are imbued with lightly comedic flourishes, some marked with suppressed anger or depression—mark the film as undeniably universally relevant.

When his Tokyo symphony orchestra disbands, cellist Daigo Kobayashi (Masahiro Motoki) faces unemployment, and the adult-onset realization, or at least nagging feeling, that maybe his longtime dreams of pursuing music as a vocation exceeded the realities of his talent. With his wife Mika (Ryoko Hirosue), Daigo moves back into his late mother's house in his small rural hometown, a place which holds unsettled memories. Daigo answers an employment ad that leads to a meeting with funeral director Ikuei Sasaki (Tsutomu Yamazaki), who immediately offers him a job assisting in "encoffination," the ceremonial cleaning and preparation of bodies prior to their cremation.

Too embarrassed to tell Mika about his new job, Daigo dissembles, and lets her believe he helps plan parties and wedding ceremonies. Time passes, and the secret, casual at first, calcifies into something more sizable and telling—especially since Daigo also has unresolved issues regarding his father, who abandoned him and his mother when he was a child. Daigo reconnects with Tsuyako (Kazuko Yoshiyuki), an elderly woman who runs a local bathhouse, and the routine of his work begins to slowly dissipate a long-lingering, swallowed personal shame, even as it erects a wall between him and Mika.

There is a sense of well-ordered austerity, almost quiet nobility, to *Departures* that extends from the area of its natural narrative focus to its supporting characters, most robustly embodied by the operator of the local crematorium (Takashi Sasano), who movingly speaks about duty when an old friend passes away. Takita does not give this character a longwinded eulogy, as an American filmmaker might, but rather a simple and understated monologue, combined with dutiful action.

Montages are, of course, also part of the international vocabulary of cinema, but Takita artfully seeds a crucial part of his narrative with what might be described as a metaphorical tableau, interweaving sequences of Daigo's decorous work preparations with scenes of him practicing his recovered adolescent cello amidst windswept vistas. Combined with the aforementioned

penchant for restraint, this sort of wise directorial judgment gives the movie an elegiac underpinning without dragging it down into stifling lamentation. A couple plot-point particulars feel familiar and/or forced; an old friend going out of his way to ridicule and ostracize Daigo upon finding out about his occupation seems unduly harsh. But Takita connects all of these relatively unremarkable or at least relatively expected narrative turns with tenderness, and makes their relating just seem part of the grander inevitability of life. Just as we all die and lose loved ones, so too do we grapple with self-esteem and the (even willful) disappointment of friends and family—smaller, perhaps more difficult targets to dramatically illuminate in film, but certainly no less important.

Motoki deservingly won a number of acting awards for his performance, and his carefully modulated, uncommonly tender turn is at the heart of *Departures*'s appeal. What Daigo thought he had found in music—the ritualistic practice, playing and vocational pursuit of an instrument introduced to him by his absentee father—he eventually locates to a much more satisfying if seemingly initially unlikely degree in his new job. Without affectation, Motoki expertly captures his character's burgeoning sense of appreciation and honor for his duties, seeing as he does both his boss' unwavering professionalism and the intense emotional reactions the ceremonies elicit in the families of the deceased.

Aided by fine work from cinematographer Takeshi Hamada and composer Joe Hisaishi, who provides a stirring score, Takita crafts a quietly absorbing work—a fairly tranquil but uniquely honest film about inner turmoil and a raging sea within. In this respect, *Departures* is a reminder that fate seems far smoother once one finds their life's proper path.

Brent Simon

CREDITS

Daigo Kobayashi: Masahiro Motoki
Mika Kobayashi: Ryoko Hirosue
Ikuei Sasaki: Tsutomu Yamazaki
Origin: Japan
Language: Japanese
Released: 2008
Production: Toshiaki Nakazawa, Yasuhiro Mase, Toshihisa Watai; Tokyo Broadcasting System, Sedic; released by Shochiku Company
Directed by: Yojiro Takita
Written by: Kundo Koyama
Cinematography by: Takashi Hamada
Music by: Joe Hisaishi

Sound: Satoru Ozaki
Editing: Akimasa Kawashima
Costumes: Katsuhito Kitamura
Production Design: Fumio Ogawa
MPAA rating: Unrated
Running time: 130 minutes

REVIEWS

Cockrell, Eddie. *Variety.* February 18, 2009.
Ebert, Roger. *Chicago Sun-Times.* May 28, 2009.
Edelstein, David. *New York Magazine.* May 26, 2009.
Gleiberman, Owen. *Entertainment Weekly.* May 27, 2009.
Phillips, Michael. *Chicago Tribune.* May 29, 2009.
Phipps, Keith. *AV Club.* May 28, 2009.
Scott, A.O. *New York Times.* May 29, 2009.
Sharkey, Betsy. *Los Angeles Times.* May 29, 2009.
Tallerico, Brian. *MovieRetriever.com.* May 27, 2009.
Taylor, Ella. *Village Voice.* May 27, 2009.

AWARDS

Oscars 2008: Foreign Film.

DID YOU HEAR ABOUT THE MORGANS?

We're not in Manhattan anymore.
—Movie tagline

Box Office: $30 million

The inexplicably titled *Did You Hear About the Morgans?* is a chore of a romantic-comedy farce to sit through. With its labored, pedestrian plot and bored looking actors at the forefront, one has to wonder who were the poor souls who believed that Marc Lawrence's screenplay was so good that, come hell or high water, *this film must get made!?* That may be a frivolous and pointless question, seeing as how many of these types of films get produced in a year, many of which turn a profit for little cost. But the level of complacency from all talent involved with films such as these (as well as 2009's similarly themed *New In Town*) should cause everyone with a screen credit to ponder just what it is they are doing with their lives. What is the point of making movies if you have nothing interesting to say or do? Nobody really cares here and it has rarely been this obvious.

Hugh Grant has, in the past, at least feigned interest in a number of mediocre films in which he has appeared, but here he looks clueless and held at gunpoint. The same could be said for his unfortunate co-star Sarah

Jessica Parker, who looks as though she is clinging to the last hours of her run as a "Romantic Comedy Leading Lady" before entering phase three of her career playing moms and supporting lawyer characters in bad Joel Schumacher films. Both actors have been charming and appealing in the past and every romantic comedy, no matter how unlikely the story, can get by with the right script and the right actors to ooze the necessary amounts of charm and chemistry to help make it work. No such luck here.

The story finds New York couple Paul and Meryl Morgan (Grant and Parker, respectively) bickering and arguing about the state of their marriage and whether or not it might be worth saving. Paul, a lawyer, has cheated and is trying desperately to apologize and win back the heart of his wife, who works as a high-profile real-estate broker. Both have expressed interest in having kids, but cannot seem to make it work biologically or without getting into a fight or misunderstanding about it. The marriage might work, but Meryl cannot get over Paul's infidelity.

Then they witness a murder. Not just any murder, but the murder of a high-profile official. The feds know that the killer will hunt down the Morgans and, after he does, the couple gets shipped out to Wyoming where they must learn new laws of the land while getting to know the cantankerous small town simpletons. Meanwhile, their personal assistants Adam (Jesse Liebman) and Jackie (*Mad Men*'s Elizabeth Moss, who is completely wasted here) form a romantic bond of their own while their bosses are away in a top secret location.

The clichés pile up fast and frequent. Paul and Meryl have to spend their nights at a remote farmhouse with Clay and Emma Wheeler (Sam Elliot and Mary Steenburgen, respectively), an older married couple who often shelter government protected witnesses. Of course, them being small-town hayseeds, they do not understand the ways of vegetarianism, Democrats or people who do not like guns. And because Paul and Meryl are city slickers, they react with disdain at their surroundings, before predictably warming up to them.

While Paul and Meryl bicker incessantly throughout the movie's obligatory set pieces (surprise bears, horseback riding gone wrong and saying the wrong stupid thing in public), only Sam Elliot gets to express his frustration as the movie's lone voice of reason. During a town hall bingo game where Paul and Meryl find themselves in a state of pure bliss over winning fifty dollars, he states "There's never a fire when you need one." When asked if he actually read the immortal and simplistic *Men Are From Mars, Women Are From Venus*, he states that he only read the cover and that seemed to sum it up for him. He is correct in his assumption about the emptiness of that book, but unfortunately the same level of insight into relationships applies to this movie as well. Paul and Meryl are not characters that audiences have not met before. Grant and Parker serve as mere host bodies to plastic, unsympathetic dopes with cushy jobs and zero depth.

Likewise, with a typical condescending tone towards people who live in rural areas, the audience is meant to laugh at the stereotypes of small town life that have paraded through many a screenplay throughout the decades—the simple town Doctor, the simple town Mayor and the simple street that passes for a town, etc. As if the lack of imagination were not enough, the movie's final act involves a rodeo and the always upsetting image of rodeo clowns. None of this is directed with any flair or interest by Marc Lawrence, who is working with Grant for the third time after *Two Weeks Notice* (2002) and *Music and Lyrics* (2007), both of which had their moments of charm, but not enough to signal any kind of significant actor-director relationship.

Did You Hear About the Morgans? will certainly not signal the end of dopey, cliché-ridden romantic comedies. So long as people keep buying the tickets to see them (and history has shown that they will), the movies will keep getting made, with varying degrees of success. Grant will continue to play fops and Parker will still try to be the spokesperson for single women everywhere. Like thousands that have come before it, *Did You Hear About the Morgans?* will have been heard about by moviegoing audiences, but then quickly forgotten about as well.

Collin Souter

CREDITS

Paul: Hugh Grant
Meryl: Sarah Jessica Parker
Clay Wheeler: Sam Elliott
Emma Wheeler: Mary Steenburgen
Jackie Drake: Elisabeth Moss
Vincent: Michael Kelly
Marshall Lasky: Seth Gilliam
Origin: USA
Language: English
Released: 2009
Production: Liz Glotzer, Martin Shafer; Castle Rock Entertainment, Columbia Pictures; released by Sony Pictures
Directed by: Marc Lawrence
Written by: Marc Lawrence
Cinematography by: Florian Ballhaus
Music by: Thomas S. Drescher
Sound: Michael Barosky

Music Supervisor: Robert Schaper
Editing: Susan E. Morse
Art Direction: Stephen Carter
Costumes: Christopher Peterson
Production Design: Kevin Thompson
MPAA rating: PG-13
Running time: 103 minutes

REVIEWS

Anderson, John. *Variety.* December 15, 2009.
Holden, Stephen. *New York Times.* December 18, 2009.
Keough, Peter. *Boston Phoenix.* December 17, 2009.
O'Sullivan, Michael. *Washington Post.* December 17, 2009.
Pais, Matt. *Metromix.com.* December 17, 2009.
Phillips, Michael. *Chicago Tribune.* December 17, 2009.
Rickey, Carrie. *Philadelphia Inquirer.* December 17, 2009.
Rodriguez, Rene. *Miami Herald.* December 16, 2009.
Tobias, Scott. *AV Club.* December 17, 2009.
Whipp, Glenn. *Associated Press.* December 18, 2009.

QUOTES

Emma Wheeler (on horseback, pointing a gun at the killer who's about to shoot Paul Morgan): "Hey, I've got plenty of room on my wall for another head."

AWARDS

Nomination:

Golden Raspberries 2009: Worst Actress (Parker).

DISGRACE

He is what he calls himself, a monster.
    —Movie tagline
What is a mad heart?
    —Movie tagline

The term disgrace implies a willful separation from grace that one brings upon themselves. The film *Disgrace* offers a character study of same but hints at redemption in a bleak landscape where there is no way to change the past but to bravely take one step at a time through the world the way that it really is.

David Lurie (John Malkovich) is a middle-aged South African college professor who teaches the romantic poets but has learned all the wrong things from them. Divorced and blithely unaware of his tendency to quote Blake on desire when he should be examining his own amorality he starts an affair with the reluctant Melanie (Antoinette Engel), a student who is clearly too young to understand the ramifications of sleeping with her instructor. When the imbalance of power in their relationship comes to a head, David finds himself caught in the crosshairs of a disciplinary hearing but unwilling to budge. Admitting his guilt, but not his shame, he finds himself out of a job and a social pariah.

Deciding to visit his adult lesbian daughter Lucy (Jessica Haines) at her small farm he is surprised to find her living alone with only her business partner Petrus (Erig Ebouaney), a black tenant farmer, for protection from the increasing danger of break-in and attack from wandering thugs and disgruntled villagers crossing the post-Apartheid landscape. The inevitable attack comes as Petrus is away and just as David, who has begun to volunteer at the local animal shelter, has begun to soften towards rural life. Lucy is raped, David is beaten and set on fire.

Suspecting Petrus is in league with the young attackers, David is astonished to discover that Lucy will not press charges even when it is discovered that Petrus' wife is related to one of the boys. David fumes at Lucy's decision to stay and seek peace within the community. When Lucy reveals that she is pregnant from the attack and plans to keep the baby David is at first devastated, but soon has a revelation of his own. Returning to the city, he visits Melanie's family to ask for their forgiveness and then returns to the township where he accepts Lucy's decision to keep the baby and become Petrus' tenant in return for his protection.

Adapted from the Booker Prize-winning 1999 novel by J.M. Coetzee, *Disgrace* has been beautifully translated to the screen by an unlikely filmmaking team that had previously produced the obscure cult hit *La Spagnola* (2001). Director Steve Jacobs (*The Man You Know* [1984]) screenwriter Anna Maria Monticelli (*La Spagnoli* [2001]) and cinematographer Steve Arnold (*Feed* [2005]) make sure nothing is obscure, allowing the barren landscape and even more barren life of the central character to drive a story that is ultimately hopeful and full of metaphors for those with eyes to see and ears to hear.

Near the beginning of the film, we see David with a lover who turns to be merely a prostitute rebuffing his advances toward an actual relationship. Putting roughly four or five hundred rand on the table, David leaves. Later that same amount of money is mentioned as what Lucy makes in her village stall. The comparison is unavoidable. One relationship utterly embraces the economy of David's pretense, confusing sex with intimacy, while the other is communal even as it reflects commerce. One pretends a relationship is there and the other truly represents what a relationship is. One can offer growth and depth and one ends with David alone.

In another scene early in David's arrival to the township, a villager brings a goat to the clinic. As the animal struggles, David is asked to hold it by the horns, giving the clinician time to examine the problem, which proves to be an advanced case of blowflies in his testicles. When told that it is too late and that the animal should simply be given a quick peaceful death, the villager chooses to leave with it anyway as David watches mystified.

The animal and its condition could be a metaphor for South Africa from David's point of view because later he tells the story of a dog that is better off being shot than being punished for simply obeying its own nature. David's volunteer work at the clinic also points to this interpretation, as it consists mostly of helping euthanize and subsequently burn unwanted dogs and, later in the film, he confesses that he would rather be stood up against a wall and shot than admit to shame for what he has done.

Of course, this is the very character arc David himself travels through in the film. He is being asked, as it were by life, to grab the horns of a dilemma, to not make the grand Byronic gesture and instead come to an honest conclusion about whether hope is real and worth pursuing or whether he should simply give up on himself, his daughter, his unborn grandchild and by extension the township's situation. In the end, it is a choice, provided by two connecting scenes, between the burning dead dog and the unborn baby, a vibrant symbol of redemption, and metaphor for South Africa itself, that allows David the luxury of a broken-hearted, undefined faith that leaves everyone the room to be where they are and imagine where they might be able to go one faltering step at a time. In the end, the film seems to say, disgrace can be, like any other experience in a life, part of our movement forward if we only follow its true momentum.

Dave Canfield

CREDITS

David Lurie: John Malkovich
Petrus: Eriq Ebouaney
Lucy Lurie: Jessica Haines
Melanie Isaacs: Antoinette Engel
Origin: Australia, South Africa
Language: English
Released: 2008
Production: Emile Sherman, Anna-Maria Monticelli, Steve Jacobs; Fortissimo Films, Film Finance Corp; released by Paladin Productions
Directed by: Steve Jacobs
Written by: Anna Maria Monticelli
Cinematography by: Steve Arnold

Music by: Antony Partos, Greame Koehne
Sound: Sam Petty
Editing: Alexandre De Francheschi
Art Direction: Ann Marie Beauchamp
Production Design: Mike Berg
Costumes: Michelle Karavoussanos
MPAA rating: R
Running time: 119 minutes

REVIEWS

Burr, Ty. *Boston Globe*. September 24, 2009.
Cockrell, Eddie. *Variety*. April 23, 2009.
Ebert, Roger. *Chicago Sun-Times*. September 24, 2009.
Goldstein, Gary. *Los Angeles Times*. September 25, 2009.
Hall, Sandra. *Sydney Morning Herald*. June 21, 2009.
Holden, Stephen. *New York Times*. September 18, 2009.
Jones, J.R. *Chicago Reader*. October 2, 2009.
Mondello, Bob. *NPR*. September 18, 2009.
Phipps, Keith. *AV Club*. September 18, 2009.
Taylor, Ella. *Village Voice*. September 15, 2009.

DISTRICT 9

You are not welcome here.
—Movie tagline

Box Office: $116 million

With Neill Blomkamp's *District 9* and Duncan Jones's *Moon*, 2009 has been a banner year for that most endangered of film species: the intellectual science-fiction film. What was fairly plentiful in the 1960s and 1970s with films like *2001: A Space Odyssey* (1968), *Silent Running* (1971) and *Solaris* (1972) has largely given way in the modern age of computer generated imagery to the mindless spectacle of psychopathic aliens blowing up world famous landmarks. With *District 9*, Blomkamp returns the science fiction genre to the idea-driven stories of those classic films while using what those films did not have available to them, state of the art CGI, to do it. The result is a film which refreshingly uses its CGI to provoke thought on the part of the viewer as opposed to the CGI simply existing as an end unto itself.

Taking its cue from past race-based science fiction films such as the John Sayles's classic *The Brother From Another Planet* (1984) and the not-so-classic *Enemy Mine* (1985) and *Alien Nation* (1988), *District 9* uses refugee aliens to convey the horror and brutality of apartheid. Filmed in the style of a documentary, *District 9* opens with the viewer learning from talking heads ranging from history professors to people on the street of the aliens' arrival and subsequent treatment. Their massive

space ship, containing a million members of their species, appeared without warning over Johannesburg in 1982. For reasons that remain mysterious, the ship is no longer capable of movement and so, it seems, the aliens are here to stay. Initial acceptance on the part of humans quickly turns to intolerance and soon the aliens are being referred to by the derogatory slur "prawns," segregated into an alien only ghetto District 9 (an obvious reference to the real District 6, a Cape Town intercity residential area whose mostly black population of 60,000 was forcibly relocated by the South African apartheid regime in the 1970s) and humans are casually discussing ways in which to relocate or simply exterminate them (particularly chilling is one Johannesburg citizen's advocation for the creation and release of a selective, alien-specific virus, a reference to the real world apartheid regime's secret weapons program Project Coast which conducted research into race specific bacterial weapons). The decided upon solution is to forcibly relocate all one million aliens of District 9 to a supposedly superior tent city, several hundred miles from any human settlement. Glossy brochures display the camp invitingly but the reality, as one human character admits later in the film, is "more like a concentration camp."

The key to the film is the moral evolution of the unreflective, bureaucrat bumpkin, Wikus van der Merwe (Sharlto Copely), who has been assigned the task of managing the eviction and relocation of the aliens from District 9. Merwe is an employee of Multi-National United (MNU), a private company that has been given the contract of controlling the aliens. Wikus has been promoted to his position by his father in law and his bumbling, inspector Clouseau like efforts on eviction day indicate that nepotism has played a far greater role in his appointment than competence. Wikus is not an evil man so much as he is a man who has unthinkingly accepted the prevailing attitudes of his society and never questioned its perception and treatment of the aliens it is his job to relocate. All of this changes when Wikus, while inspecting the home of an alien scientist, Christopher Johnson, unwisely toys with a mysterious black canister. The canister releases a black fluid that results in life-changing events for Wikus and has profound implications for humanity and the aliens.

Copley does an excellent job with Wikus, convincingly portraying the transformation of a foolish, unthinking bigot to a being willing to sacrifice everything for the aliens he thought he despised. He is aided in his journey by the great empathy generated by the film's aliens (a seamless blending of CGI and the acting of Jason Cope playing all the alien roles). In Christopher Johnson and his son, Wikus discovers a humanity far greater than his own or any of the other human characters in the film and it is highly ironic that the most human characters in the entire film are CGI depictions of an alien race. It is deeply gratifying to see CGI used not to generate explosions and destruction but emotion and empathy on the part of the viewer and the effect of establishing this emotional connection is essential to the film's purpose. In applying apartheid to an imaginary race with whom the viewer has been enabled to identify, any pre-existing prejudices or baggage of a real world context are stripped away and apartheid, in all its stupidity and cruelty, stands naked before the viewer.

This is not to say that *District 9* is merely an apartheid allegory. It is also an exciting action film in its own right, skillfully edited by Julian Clarke and directed by Blomkamp and featuring some stunning special effects, particularly when Copely dons a robotic body suit, that is as good as anything in *Transformers: Revenge of the Fallen* (2009). Unlike *Transformers*, however, the CGI-driven action sequences in *District 9* have a purpose: furthering a story featuring characters, both human and alien, the audience cares about and, in doing so, provoking thought about how humans in the real world treat one another.

In 1968, Stanley Kubrick was able to create his epic, experimental three part meditation on man's relationship to the universe, *2001* , because he was one of the biggest directors in the world being bankrolled by a major studio that could pay for the film's revolutionary special effects. The invention of CGI and, most especially its steady decrease in cost, has expanded the tools available to Kubrick to virtually all filmmakers, even, as in the case of *District 9*, a first-time director with a tiny budget. This has greatly liberated film, allowing state of the art special effects to be wedded to innovative and inventive films where previously such effects were confined to conventional, commercial films due to their great expense. Now the potential for film, both science fiction and otherwise, is limited only by the director's imagination, not the film's budget. *District 9* is a mesmerizing and moving realization of that great potential.

Nate Vercauteren

CREDITS

Koobus: David James
Wikus van der Merwe: Sharlto Copley
Fundiswa: Mandla Gaduka
Tania: Vanessa Haywood
Christopher Johnson: Jason Cope (Voice)
Origin: New Zealand, USA
Language: English

Released: 2009
Production: Peter Jackson, Carolynne Cunningham; Wingnut Films, TriStar Pictures; released by Sony Pictures
Directed by: Neil Blomkamp
Written by: Neil Blomkamp, Terri Tatchell
Cinematography by: Trent Opaloch
Music by: Clinton Shorter
Sound: Ken Saville
Music Supervisor: Michelle Belcher
Editing: Julian Clarke
Art Direction: Emilia Roux
Costumes: Dianna Cilliers
Production Design: Philip Ivey, Mike Berg
MPAA rating: R
Running time: 111 minutes

REVIEWS

Burr, Ty. *Boston Globe.* August 13, 2009.
Chang, Justin. *Variety.* July 30, 2009.
Ebert, Roger. *Chicago Sun-Times.* August 13, 2009.
Franklin, Garth. *Dark Horizons.* August 13, 2009.
Hoffman, Jordan. *UGO.* August 13, 2009.
Larsen, Josh. *LarsenOnFilm.* August 13, 2009.
Pais, Matt. *Metromix.com.* August 13, 2009.
Sobczynski, Peter. *eFilmCritic.* August 13, 2009.
Tallerico, Brian. *MovieRetriever.com* August 13, 2009.
Tobias, Scott. *AV Club.* August 13, 2009.

QUOTES

Wikus van de Merwe: "Hello, little guy! It's the sweetie man coming!"

TRIVIA

Star Sharlto Copley had not acted before and had no intention of pursuing an acting career. He stumbled into the leading role as Neill Blomkamp placed him on-camera during the short film.

AWARDS

Nomination:

Oscars 2009: Adapt. Screenplay, Film, Film Editing, Visual FX
British Acad. 2009: Adapt. Screenplay, Cinematog., Director (Blomkamp), Film Editing, Sound, Visual FX, Prod. Des.
Golden Globes 2010: Screenplay.

IL DIVO

Paolo Sorrentino's *Il Divo* is both a terrifying character study of a corrupt and murderous politician and a dizzying highlight reel of some of the most explosive events in recent Italian political history. For the viewer unacquainted with the labyrinthine milieu of mafia-influenced Italian politics of the 1970s, 1980s and early 1990s, the film is almost impossible to follow. However, this does not operate to the film's detriment since Toni Servillo succeeds so thoroughly in portraying the film's enigmatic, sinister centerpiece and the film's light-speed pace, unconventional narrative structure, and electrifying direction renders the corrupt world in which he operates with such vivid panache.

The title of the film refers to Giulio Andreotti, a real-life, seven-time Italian Prime Minister and Senator for life. The film largely takes place in the early 1990s shortly after Andreotti has been elected prime minister for a seventh time. Servillo plays the politician as a cross between Nosferatu, Henry Kissinger and Machiavelli. With his humped back, pointy ears, limp arms and folded hands, Servillo's Andreotti greatly resembles Max Schreck's famous vampire. This physique is coupled with a penchant for dispensing ironic, real-politick one-liners and a seemingly serene demeanor bordering on sedation. Much of what makes Servillo's portrayal fascinating is the incongruity of this quiet, unassuming little man with the extreme cunning and absolute ruthlessness revealed in the murderous acts attributed to him. Indeed, Servillo's portrayal would be comical if what Andreotti was responsible for in his rise to power and the continued maintenance of that power weren't so horrific.

The viewer is treated to a sampler of Il Divo's transgressions. Text prior to the film implicates Andreotti in the 1979 kidnapping and murder of former Prime Minister Aldo Moro. The film's prologue is a montage of mafia hit men murdering various high level judges, bankers and journalists (including journalist Mino Pecorelli, responsible for articles critical of Andreotti). As the film progresses, the body count rises. The reasons for the murders are murky but their origins are unimportant. The murder victims were perceived as obstacles or threats by Andreotti and his mafia associates and therefore had to go.

Andreotti is never explicitly linked to these murders but the film persuasively implies that they are the result of his orders. In a brilliant scene that is a short film in itself, journalist Eugenio Scalfari (Giulio Bosetti) of *La Repubblica* delivers a devastating, three minute monologue to Andreotti cataloging decades of atrocities that have coincidentally benefitted Andreotti that plays like the closing argument to a jury: "You're either the most cunning criminal in the country because you never got caught or you're the most persecuted man in the history of Italy."

Scalfari might as well be addressing a brick wall and in *Il Divo*, as in real life, Andreotti denies everything.

However, Sorrentino goes a step further than the real Andreotti in providing him with a confession. In an unexpected and electrifying scene, the only scene in which Andreotti expresses emotion of any kind, he directly addresses the camera and provides the supposed justification for his deals with the mafia and murderous acts. It is the morally bankrupt answer that all corrupt leaders give: he did it all for the country: "We can't allow the end of the world in the name of what's right. We have a divine task. We must love God greatly to understand how necessary evil is for good. God knows it, and I know it too." And if Andreotti's "evil for good" acts on behalf of his country happen to result in him remaining in power for seven terms and the elimination of all his rivals this is just an incidental, unanticipated side development.

A dialogue-heavy film about Italian politics would seem a sleepy proposition, however few films possesses more energy and life than *Il Divo*. What distinguishes *Il Divo* from other political biographies or studies of power is its speed-of-light pace, non-linear narrative structure and its audacious, energetic direction. *Il Divo* refreshingly abandons the familiar, linear narrative structure (birth, early life, career, decline, death) that homogenizes most biographical films. *Il Divo* is not interested in telling the story of Andreotti's life from start to finish but rather capturing the essence of his character, the flavor and scope of his murderous reign and the nature of the corrupt world of Italian politics over which he rules. The film takes great advantage of its freedom, zooming backward and forward in time; flitting from one illuminating vignette to another to weave a multi-decade tapestry of corruption, mafia deals and murder. This free-form narrative structure is complemented by a daring and dynamic direction; indeed, *Il Divo* is one of the best directed and edited films of the year. Under Sorrentino, even the most mundane of situations is made engaging. For example, Sorrentino's stylish direction, replete with subtitles and freeze frames, manages to make the introduction of Andreotti's cabinet ministers an electrifying experience. Sorrentino also happily breaks narrative conventions as it suits him. Characters address the camera to explain themselves and realism shifts to surrealism at the drop of a hat. A breathtaking example of the latter occurs at a pivotal point in the film. When government prosecutor Giovanni Falcone is killed, a skate board shoots through the long marbled hallway outside parliament, smashes through a window and explodes.

The murder of Falcone, his flaming car sailing through the air following the detonation of a military strike level of C4 explosives beneath his car on a Palermo highway, is a recurrent and emblematic image in the film. Falcone's murder was a momentous and sad event in Italian history: the shocking death of a heroic foe of the mafia and an act of breathtaking brazenness even by the standards of the Italian mafia. His murder and the public outcry in response to it heralded the end for many corrupt government officials and mafioso. It is also what should have been an ending for Andreotti but was not an ending at all. For Il Divo, it is just a bump in the road. Following the public outrage over Falcone's death, Andreotti stands trial for the 1979 murder of journalist Mino Pecorelli. He is convicted and then, under most suspicious circumstances, acquitted on appeal. Today, Il Divo is still in power, a Senator for life at age 90, capable of viewing *Il Divo* and dryly commenting, "I would have happily lived without it."

Nate Vercauteren

CREDITS

Giulio Andreotti: Toni Servillo
Livia Andreotti: Anna Bonaiuto
Eugenio Scalfari: Guilio Bosetti
Franco Evangelisti: Flavio Bucci
Paolo Cirino Pomicino: Carlo Buccirosso
Salvo Lima: Giorgio Colangeli
Origin: Italy, France
Language: Italian
Released: 2008
Production: Francesca Cima, Nicola Giuliano, Andrea Occhipinti; Indigo Film, Lucky Red, Babe Film, Studio Canal, arte France Cinéma, MiBAC; released by Music Box Films
Directed by: Poalo Sorrentino
Written by: Poalo Sorrentino
Cinematography by: Luca Bigazzi
Music by: Teho Teardo
Editing: Cristiano Travaglioli
Sound: Emanuele Cecere
Costumes: Daniela Ciancio
Production Design: Lino Fiorito
MPAA rating: Unrated
Running time: 110 minutes

REVIEWS

Brunette, Peter. *Hollywood Reporter.* October 18, 2008.
Ebert, Roger. *Chicago Sun-Times.* July 9, 2009.
Holden, Stephen. *New York Times.* April 24, 2009.
Lacey, Liam. *Globe and Mail.* October 18, 2008.
Lane, Anthony. *New Yorker.* April 27, 2009.
Tallerico, Brian. *MovieRetriever.com.* July 10, 2009.
Taylor, Ella. *Village Voice.* April 22, 2009.
Tobias, Scott. *AV Club.* April 23, 2009.
Turan, Kenneth. *Los Angeles Times.* April 30, 2009.
Weissberg, Jay. *Variety.* October 18, 2008.

QUOTES

Giulio Andreotti: "A good man's meanness is always very dangerous."

AWARDS

Nomination:

Oscars 2009: Makeup.

DRAG ME TO HELL

Even nice people can go to hell.
—Movie tagline
Christine Brown has a good job, a great boyfriend, and a bright future. But in three days, she's going to hell.
—Movie tagline

Box Office: $42 million

Ever since he solidified his position as Hollywood's most unexpected A-list filmmaker with the enormously successful *Spider-Man* films, fans of Sam Raimi have been clamoring for him to return to his cheerfully schlocky B-movie roots to do something along the lines of his beloved *Evil Dead* trilogy. This approach may fly in the face of most normal directorial career trajectories—most filmmakers, as a rule, do not use the clout they have amassed as the director of some of the biggest movies ever made to make cheesy horror films at a fraction of the budgets they have grown accustomed to—but that is exactly what he has done with his latest, the gloriously gross *Drag Me to Hell*. It may not be *Evil Dead 4* but, in many ways, it serves as a continuation of those films—it takes a fairly standard genre tale and gooses it with a combination of silly humor, startling scares and gags (in every sense of the world) that are simultaneously so goofy and gruesome that the audience knows not whether to laugh or vomit. In a film of this type, that kind of comment is high praise indeed.

Alison Lohman stars as Christine Brown, a sweet-natured loan officer at a local bank under pressure to be a little more hard-nosed with her customers if she wants to be considered for a promotion. Unfortunately for her, her next applicant is Mrs. Ganush (Lorna Raver), an ancient Gypsy woman who needs a third extension on her mortgage so as not to be evicted from her home of thirty years. Even though the decision to give the woman the extension is hers, Christine decides to prove to her boss (David Paymer) that she has what it takes to make the "tough decisions" and turns her down. Not surprisingly, when Mrs. Ganush hears this news, she doesn't exactly take it with quiet grace—she elaborately begs Christine for help and when she doesn't get it, she attacks her later that night in a parking garage and in the midst of their epic struggle, she grabs a button off of Christine's coat, mutters some incantation and then hands it back to her with the promise that "Soon it will be you who comes begging to me." Christine is now under the spell of a good old-fashioned Gypsy curse, one that will torture her in myriad ways for the next three days before sending her straight to Hell. Her well-meaning but painfully square boyfriend (Justin Long) tries to convince her that it is all in her head but Christine knows better than that. Alas, when Christine goes to beg Mrs. Ganush for forgiveness, she finds that the old woman is in no condition to lift the curse (or anything else) and realizes that she is going to have to take matters into her own hands if she is to lift the curse and survive her seemingly inevitable fate.

As has been the case with most of his other self-generated genre efforts (which also include the somewhat underrated *Crimewave* [1985] and the mock superhero near-epic *Darkman* [1990]), the screenplay that Raimi has conjured up (this time in conjunction with brother Ivan) tells the kind of tale that almost seems too slight to serve as the basis for an average campfire story—little more than a paper-thin construct consisting of a bunch of big "Boo" moments and gross-out gags tenuously linked together and any subtext to be had (such as a commentary on the current economic crisis) coming across as more inadvertent than anything else. This might sound like a recipe for disaster—or at least the recipe for yet another crappy PG-13 horror film aimed squarely at slack-jawed kids who wouldn't recognize a good example of the genre if it slapped them in the face—but it works surprisingly well here because Raimi has not lost his touch for coming up with inspired versions of those necessary "Boo" moments and gross-out gags. Yes, Raimi unexpectedly springs visions of Mrs. Ganush upon us a lot throughout the film but he times most of them in such a way that they never quite happen exactly when we expect them to and as a result, he still manages to startle viewers with this particular trick even as the film enters the late innings. As for the grosser stuff, Raimi has focused almost entirely on the notion of one vile thing after another finding its way into Christine's mouth. Again, this sort of thing could get real old real quick but Raimi pulls these moments off with such cheerfully depraved aplomb that when he flat-out repeats one of the most memorable bits from *Evil Dead II* (1987), it works so well that you don't even resent the self-plagiarism.

While *Drag Me to Hell* may not be the high-water mark of Raimi's career, it is by far the liveliest and most energetic thing that he has done in a long time and fans of gooey horror nonsense will find a lot to love here. There is a spunky heroine who gradually becomes less of a "goody-two-shoes" as she begins to realize exactly what she is capable of doing in order to save herself. There is a villain who is gruesome and nasty as all get out who nevertheless evokes a certain amount of sympathy. There are a lot of in-joke references to Raimi's earlier films that will elicit knowing chuckles from certain audience members (such as the appearance of a certain car and a reference to an upcoming trip to a cabin in the woods) and a lot of perfectly done gags, figuratively and literally, that will have everyone else chuckling and chucking in equal measure. The film even manages to come up with an ending that manages to be both slightly surprising as well as eminently satisfying. *Drag Me to Hell* may be junk but it is junk of such a high degree that it is hard to imagine anyone failing to respond to its grubby charms.

Peter Sobczynski

CREDITS

Christine Brown: Alison Lohman
Clay: Justin Long
Mrs. Ganush: Lorna Raver
Mr. Jacks: David Paymer
Rham Jas: Dileep Rao
Shaun: Adriana Barraza
Leonard Dalton: Chelcie Ross
Stu Rubin: Reggie Lee
Origin: USA
Language: English
Released: 2009
Production: Robert Tapert, Grant Curtis; Ghost House Pictures; released by Universal Pictures
Directed by: Sam Raimi
Written by: Sam Raimi, Ivan Raimi
Cinematography by: Peter Deming
Music by: Christopher Young
Sound: Joseph Geisinger
Editing: Bob Murawski
Art Direction: James F. Truesdale
Costumes: Isis Mussenden
Production Design: Steve Saklad
MPAA rating: PG-13
Running time: 99 minutes

REVIEWS

Catsoulis, Jeanette. *New York Times.* May 29, 2009.
Childress, Erik. *EFilmCritic.* May 28, 2009.

Corliss, Richard. *Time Magazine.* May 29, 2009.
Debruge, Peter. *Variety.* May 20, 2009.
Miska, Brad. *Bloody Disgusting.* January 28, 2009.
Phillips, Michael. *Chicago Tribune.* May 29, 2009.
Rea, Steven. *Philadelphia Inquirer.* May 28, 2009.
Sharkey, Betsy. *Los Angeles Times.* May 29, 2009.
Tallerico, Brian. *HollywoodChicago.com.* May 29, 2009.
Tobias, Scott. *AV Club.* May 28, 2009.

QUOTES

Christine Brown: "I beat you, you old bitch!"

TRIVIA

The movie begins with the 1980s Universal logo, which refers to when director Sam Raimi got started in the horror genre with the first two "Evil Dead" movies. After the credits, there is also the title card that says to take a tour of Universal Studios. This was also used in the 1980s in other Universal movies, such as *An American Werewolf in London.*

DRAGONBALL: EVOLUTION

This Easter the legend comes to life.
—Movie tagline

Box Office: $9 million

Movies have always been a commodity. But the movie business has not always been run like a dollar store. To take the analogy further—even in a dollar store *Dragonball: Evolution* would be in the bargain bin. Based on one of the most popular manga series of all time *Dragonball* has previously been adapted into three separate anime series, a collectible trading card game and an extraordinary number of video games. A badly realized Mandarin Chinese live action film titled *Dragon Ball: The Magic Begins*, was released in Taiwan Province in Republic of China in 1989 but failed to win over fans or critics. This live action American version was not screened for critics, and was also rejected by fans, falling far short of box office expectations in the US and for good reason—it is indeed, as flat as a collectable trading card.

Odd then that *Dragonball: Evolution* lists as a producer the supremely talented Stephen Chow. Chow, a very big *Dragonball* fan, is best known for the dazzling kung fu fantasies *Shaolin Soccer* (2001) and *Kung Fu Hustle* (2004) and almost directed this film himself only to pass the torch in favor of continuing to helm only his own original projects.

A quick glance at director James Wong's credentials (*Final Destination* [2000], *The One* [2001]) shows him

to be in the habit of at least producing his better projects. That this is not the case here, and the fact that his last project is *Final Destination 3* (2006) suggests the strong possibility that his presence here is the result of work-for-hire. Nothing about the workman-like direction evinced here would contradict such an assumption especially when considering Wong's normally dynamic visual style and generally careful use of camera.

The film starts with an explanation of the origin of the Dragonballs, seven mystical crystal spheroids that offer unimaginable power to the one who possesses them. Scattered throughout history, they are eagerly sought after by Lord Piccolo (James Marsters) an evil supernatural being bent on world domination. Opposing Piccolo is young Goku (Jason Chatwin) who, in accordance with his grandfather's dying wishes, seeks out the great Master Roshi (Chow Yun-Fat) to find the spheres first and save the world. But as Goku discovers, the spheres are not the only key to keeping his promise, they are inextricably linked to his destiny.

Star Jason Chatwin makes admirable attempts to flesh out Goku but the material is so thin and shopworn there's very little to make a character out of. We see him training with his grandfather (a scene which offers a lame bit of wire work) and hassled at school because of his promise not to fight, but we never get any real back story to help us understand why he is such an important character. This Goku offers traits that would be interchangeable with any Disney Channel made-for-TV hero. Incredibly busy since his first film appearance in *Josie and the Pussycats* (2001), Chatwin has gone on to make a name for himself as a dependable talent appearing in a slew of high profile TV projects as well as Stephen Spielberg's *War of the Worlds* (2005), and the highly underrated *The Chumscrubber* (2005).

The well-known female *Dragonball* character of Bulma is mishandled as well. Instead of being in the search for a perfect boyfriend as in the original manga, Bulma simply wants to patent the Dragonballs. Replacing the romantic tension with crassly commercial motives seems to be the problem of this film all around and, as played by Emmy Rossum, the character plays like leftovers from the *Spy Kids* films. Rossum is best known for her Golden Globe-nominated performance as Christine in the film version of the Andrew Lloyd Webber musical *The Phantom of the Opera* (2004).

An unrecognizable James Marsters (Spike from TVs *Buffy The Vampire Slayer* [1997]) underplays Lord Piccolo perfectly and yet has so little screen time he seems hardly needed at all. When he is onscreen he is inevitably upstaged by whatever special effects come into play. Living legend Chow Yun-Fat (*A Better Tomorrow* [1986], *Hard Boiled* [1992], *Crouching Tiger Hidden Dragon*

[2000]), is embarrassingly over the top as Master Roshi and his presence again suggests the specter of mere work for hire. At the very least it calls into question whether director James Wong bothered directing Yun-Fat at all with his comedic choices and general level of intensity that are vastly out of step with the rest of the ensemble.

The saddest thing about all this excess is the way it clouds the contribution of Randall Duk Kim (*Anna and the King* [1999], *The Matrix Reloaded* [2003], *Memoirs of a Geisha* [2005]) as Grandpa Gohan. At his best, Kim is reminiscent of master Asian American character actors such as James Hong and Victor Wong, elevating the material by unabashedly humanizing what would otherwise be a mere stereotype.

In the history of live action anime, and video game films, *Dragonball: Evolution* is anything but evolutionary. Instead it stands as a virtual monument to the crassness of the current American trend in adapting and adulterating world culture for a quick buck. Stephen Chow is currently developing his own film based on the popular *Journey to the West* folk novel which served as the original inspiration for the *Dragonball* Manga. One can only hope that he will maintain control of the project and create a take on the material worth watching.

Dave Canfield

CREDITS

Goku: Justin Chatwin
Lord Piccolo: James Marsters
Master Roshi: Chow Yun-Fat
Bulma: Emmy Rossum
Master Mutaito: Ernie Hudson
Grandpa Gohan: Randall Duk Kim
Carey Fuller: Texas Battle
Origin: USA, Hong Kong
Language: English
Released: 2009
Production: Stephen Chow; 20th Century Fox, Star Overseas, Dune Entertainment; released by 20th Century Fox
Directed by: James Wong
Written by: James Wong
Cinematography by: Robert McLachlan
Music by: Brian Tyler
Editing: Matthew Friedman, Chris G. Willingham
Sound: Chuck Michael
Costumes: Mayes C. Rubes
Production Design: Bruton Jones
MPAA rating: PG
Running time: 84 minutes

REVIEWS

Berkshire, Geoff. *Metromix.com*. April 10, 2009.
Brown, Joel. *Boston Globe*. April 13, 2009.

Edwards, David. *Daily Mirror*. April 17, 2009.
Edwards, Russell. *Variety*. March 26, 2009.
Hillis, Aaron. *Village Voice*. April 13, 2009.
Orndorf, Brian. *BrianOrndorf.com*. April 9, 2009.
Punter, Jennie. *Globe and Mail*. April 13, 2009.
Robinson, Tasha. *AV Club*. April 13, 2009.
Snider, Eric D. *Cinematical*. April 12, 2009.
Sobczynski, Peter. *eFilmCritic*. April 10, 2009.

QUOTES

Goku: "Kamehameha!"

TRIVIA

According to the film's make-up expert Ed French, it took four hours to apply the prosthetics to James Marsters to change him into Piccolo. At first it took 17 hours, but Marsters had difficulty breathing and Piccolo's look also seemed overdone, so some prosthetics were removed, thus shortening the time to just four hours.

DUPLICITY

Outwit. Outspy. Outsmart. Outplay. Then get out.
—Movie tagline

Box Office: $40 million

After gaining fame as the screenwriter for the three *Bourne* films, Tony Gilroy used his considerable writing talents to make his directorial debut with the acclaimed *Michael Clayton* (2007), an intricate morality tale laced with his own impeccably written and gripping dialogue. The next step for Gilroy was to showcase—or perhaps show off—his virtuoso writing chops in *Duplicity*, a project high profile enough to gain the favors of Julia Roberts, who agreed to play the lead opposite Clive Owen.

In *Duplicity*, Gilroy displays his restless talent for making a movie plot into an intricate, fascinating puzzle. His touchstone in this film is a series of encounters between CIA agent Claire Stenwick (Roberts) and British intelligence agent Ray Koval (Owen). These meetings are spread over a series of times and exotic places and involve a set sequence of lines in which Claire claims not to remember Ray from a meeting in the past, and Ray insists they have not only been partners, but intimate ones. Not only are these conversations very clever and complex verbal dances that involve teasing and mutual deception, they serve as an innovative way to wrap the story line around a recurring central point, looping the plot around these encounters in non-chronological order.

The most obvious theme of the movie is trust; in particular, the considerable obstacles to trust between a man and a woman who are both masters of deception and who find themselves living in a world of paranoia and cunning. Perhaps there is mutual delusion and suspicion in many or most modern relationships, but in creating two characters who are expert at duplicity Gilroy raises both the tension and the stakes in this complex relationship of dueling peers, competitors, and sometimes comrades.

On the surface, *Duplicity* is a tall tale about two government spies who decide to go off the reservation and team up to game the much more lucrative world of corporate competition. It is a fantastic idea for a film, and one that is highly instructive in exposing audiences to what lengths competing businesses might go in a race to develop a game-changing new product. The corporate warfare is played as high satire between two bosses, Richard Garsick (Paul Giamatti), an agitated and paranoid nervous wreck, and his competitor, Howard Tully (Tom Wilkinson), a calmer and more cunning foe. In an opening scene, the two competitors wage a fist-fight on an airport tarmac as their management teams look on in horror. The scene, staged in slow motion, sets a tone of over-the-top business conflict, fear, and hatred—but also one of hilarious adventure. It's a clue to not take too seriously anything that follows, even though it's all played with a straight face.

Both men have set up elaborate squads of spies and infiltrators to ferret out the other company's plans, using methods both high-tech and remarkably clumsy. Gilroy has great fun pointing out the ruthlessness and frivolity of the business world. After considering some other easy targets, Claire and Ray decide to set up a plan to double-team the companies by placing Claire as a counter-intelligence operator in one company and Ray as a hired spy in the other. It's an elaborate con game, full of twists and turns, rife with danger and tension, and overflowing with comic and dramatic possibilities.

Laced through this plot is a continued and mounting uncertainty, which increases with each return to the central conversation, about whether Claire and Ray can actually trust each other—not only as partners in crime, but as lovers and friends. The prospect of each double-crossing the other is raised, setting up the possibility of Gilroy's beloved "reversals" or developments that turn the plot on its head. Watching the film is something like playing with a set of Russian nested dolls or a Rubik's Cube. Just when pieces start to cohere, something new is revealed. That's just the way Gilroy loves to write.

For audiences who like their plots straightforward, confusion and frustration will no doubt reign and overshadow all other pleasures that the film affords. For those who like to think hard and approach a movie as a series of complicated questions, *Duplicity* will be a delightful experience. It's quite similar to a David Mamet movie in that conning is the essence of the plot, and figuring out who's gaming whom is both an elaborate and enjoyable task.

Wilkinson invents yet another new twist on his stable of crazy, intelligent, unpredictable characters, in a performance that's brilliant even if not quite as engrossing as his amazing role as a bipolar corporate lawyer in *Michael Clayton*. For once, Giamatti has a part that suits his talents for over-the-top wackiness well. For his part, Owen is on somewhat familiar ground here; he has played a conniving, elusive figure many times before (including in the nearly contemporaneous film *The International*). His customary coolness as a character used to being in charge is perpetually flummoxed by the obviously superior cunning of Claire, and it's fun to watch his persona of calculating cockiness get continually unmasked by Claire, who repeatedly plunges him into desperate confusion.

Claire is emasculating and dominating in every sense. She is a figure of fantastic wit and resources who is ruthless about using her feminine wiles as part of an impressive arsenal of powerful weapons. There's only one big problem: her Claire seems so impregnable that it is out of character when she falls in love with Ray and displays a hidden vulnerability. With Ray that vulnerability is always just beneath the fragile surface of his machismo, which makes his comeuppances satisfying.

Roberts is very good at speaking the ultra-suave dialogue, but she's never completely convincing as the dangerously sophisticated femme fatale. In these glamorous settings in iconic cities, she is surprisingly unglamorous. Whereas Owen's rumpled scruffiness is barely in check but appropriate and attractive, Roberts looks too ordinary at times, like she's just gotten out of bed. Gilroy falls prey to relying on his star's natural beauty, but it isn't enough. For all her reputed status as an icon, Roberts simply can't carry her weight here. Naomi Watts, largely wasted in her pairing with Owen in *The International*, might have been a better choice. Roberts is cool as a cucumber all right, but perhaps a little too cool.

As Gilroy piles on the reversals, you can sense a director doing a dangerous high-wire act. *Duplicity* is definitely a risk-taking movie, with Gilroy refusing to settle for easy paths through his material, but his dialogue tricks mask a lack of depth in the material. Whereas *Michael Clayton* managed to probe a lot of extremely important issues while retaining its clever dialogue and plot tension, *Duplicity*—apart from its outrageous satire of corporate competitiveness—lacks sufficient gravitas. The main characters are so cunning that they become distant, and the audience is left grasping for a reason to care about their fate. They are likable as virtuoso players, but inherently unlikable for the same reason. They are selfish and smug and seemingly motivated by nothing but greed. They are scoundrels but Gilroy makes the fate of their relationship central to the movie, a huge gamble that fails utterly. Roberts and Owen are pretty, and they are endlessly clever, but they are nothing close to heroes, and the audience is not rooting for them, just waiting for one or the other to succumb to their little game.

Michael Betzold

CREDITS

Claire Stenwick: Julia Roberts
Ray Koval: Clive Owen
Howard Tully: Tom Wilkinson
Dick Garsik: Paul Giamatti
Barbara Boffered: Carrie Preston
Jeff Bauer: Thomas McCarthy
Duke Monahan: Denis O'Hare
Pam Frales: Kathleen Chalfant
Ned Guston: Wayne Duvall
Dale Raimes: Rick Worthy
Boris Detyov: Oleg Stefan
Origin: USA
Language: English
Released: 2009
Production: Jennifer Fox, Kerry Orent, Laura Bickford; Relativity Media; released by Universal Pictures
Directed by: Tony Golroy
Written by: Tony Golroy

Cinematography by: Robert Elswit
Music by: James Newton Howard
Sound: Michael Barosky
Music Supervisor: Brian Ross
Editing: John Gilroy
Art Direction: Stephen Carter, Tamara Marini
Costumes: Albert Wolsky
Production Design: Kevin Thompson
MPAA rating: PG-13
Running time: 125 minutes

REVIEWS

Ebert, Roger. *Chicago Sun-Times.* March 19, 2009.
Foundas, Scott. *LA Weekly.* March 19, 2009.
Honeycutt, Kirk. *Hollywood Reporter.* March 16, 2009.
McCarthy, Todd. *Variety.* March 16, 2009.
Phillips, Michael. *Chicago Tribune.* March 19, 2009.
Roeper, Richard. *RichardRoeper.com.* March 20, 2009.
Scott, A.O. *New York Times.* March 19, 2009.
Stevens, Dana. *Slate.* March 19, 2009.
Tallerico, Brian. *HollywoodChicago.com.* March 20, 2009.
Turan, Kenneth. *Los Angeles Times.* March 19, 2009.

QUOTES

Ray Koval: "You're gaming me?"

TRIVIA

The magazine that Claire is reading while she's waiting is the *Economist.*

AWARDS

Nomination:
Golden Globes 2010: Actress—Mus./Comedy (Roberts).

E

EARTH

The remarkable story of three families and their amazing journey across the planet we all call home.
—Movie tagline

Box Office: $32 million

Walt Disney's *Earth* arrived in theaters touted as the studio's big return to producing nature documentaries as it had so often done in the past (*The Living Desert* [1953] and *The Vanishing Prairie* [1954] being two examples). Its release date coincided with Earth Day (April 22) and promised three stories involving a diverse group of species' life on earth, while also hoping to cash in on the success of *March of the Penguins* (2005) and *Winged Migration* (2003).

Yet, as evidenced by the trailers, the Disney Studios had simply recycled footage from the highly ambitious BBC series (and DVD Blu-Ray favorite) *Planet Earth*. The images of the little black bird with the beautiful blue plumage hopping on a branch as a way of luring a female companion, the lone polar bear swimming desperately through melted icebergs, and thousands upon thousands of white birds migrating had all become iconic images of this wondrous series.

It's easy to be cynical about a major studio piggybacking on the success of another corporate entity's massive undertaking, but it's just as easy to set those issues aside and get swept up in the majesty of those wondrous moments. The *Planet Earth* series, by any name, remains a feast for the eyes and it only makes sense to blow the images up to theatrical proportions.

The only major change that Disney made to the product, aside from structure, is in the narration. For the U.S. version, actor James Earl Jones stepped into replace veteran documentary narrator Sir David Attenborough, while Patrick Stewart narrated the version shown in the UK. Jones' typically authoritative and charismatic narration sometimes veers off into mawkish territory, which, in a way, continues a Disney tradition of playing to a younger crowd. The slow motion images of the tree ducklings falling from a branch when taking their first flight is cute enough on its own without the cloying voice-over.

While the ads for the film suggested the audience would be following three storylines, the overall structure of *Earth* is not quite as simple as that. The film borrows bits and pieces from the entire BBC series and replays them almost as a 'Greatest Hits' package. The viewer gets taken to the Amazon rain forests, the deserts of Africa, the snow banks of Antarctica, the oceans and the jungles. We do follow the plight of the polar bear as it tries to find a habitable iceberg and a nourishing meal, but that is the closest thing the film has to an actual storyline. The rest of the film plays as you would expect a 90-minute Disney nature documentary to play out, with plenty of emphasis on the animals' behavior (simplified for the under-11 crowd) and less focus on anything scientific about the findings.

In fact, directors Alastair Fothergill and Mark Linfield keep the environmental message of their original series almost completely muted for this version, settling for a kinder, gentler "isn't our planet beautiful?" sentiment, while the original series devoted an entire chapter to the environmental devastation currently taking place around our globe and what we can all do to change it. Whether this change in agenda came at the insistence of studio officials or was a conscious choice not to overtly sermonize to the audience remains unclear. By the film's end, though, the message somehow resonates even without it being spoken to us. The image of the polar bear becomes a message in and of itself.

However many ways there are to nitpick the flaws in turning a 550-minute epic into a 90-minute bite-size sample, the overall impact of *Earth* (by any name) remains astonishing and serves as a true testament to the ambitions of the adventurous filmmakers. The sometimes painstaking and even life-threatening situations in which the filmmakers put themselves in order to obtain these natural wonders in the far corners of the globe is the reason why the *Planet Earth* series (and maybe this film) will endure. The behind-the-scenes glimpses of the documentarians at work (here seen during the film's closing credits) remain one of the great joys of the whole project.

As a way of further deterring the cynics for declaring this theatrical venture an obvious cash-grab, Disney pledged to plant a tree for every ticket purchased in the film's first five days of release. The studio partnered with The Nature Conservancy and ended up planting 2.7 million trees in Brazil's Atlantic Forest upon the film's release.

Collin Souter

CREDITS

Narrator: James Earl Jones
Origin: Great Britain, Germany, USA
Language: English
Released: 2007
Production: Alix Tidmarsh, Sophokles Tasioulis; BBC Natural History; released by Walt Disney Studios
Directed by: Alastair Fothergill, Mark Linfield
Written by: Alastair Fothergill, Mark Linfield, Leslie Megahey
Cinematography: Richard Brooks Burton, Mike Holding, Adam Ravetch, Andrew Shillabeer
Music by: George Fenton
Sound: Kate Hopkins, Tim Owens
Editing: Martin Elsbury
MPAA rating: G
Running time: 90 minutes

REVIEWS

Cole, Stephen. *Globe and Mail.* April 24, 2009.
Ebert, Roger. *Chicago Sun-Times.* April 23, 2009.
Gronvall, Andrew. *Chicago Reader.* April 24, 2009.
Howell, Peter. *Toronto Star.* April 24, 2009.
Kelly, Ann. *BBC.* November 24, 2007.
Pais, Matt. *Metromix.com.* April 20, 2009.
Puig, Claudia. *USA Today.* April 23, 2009.
Schwarzbaum, Lisa. *Entertainment Weekly.* April 15, 2009.
Tobias, Scott. *AV Club.* April 23, 2009.
Turan, Kenneth. *Los Angeles Times.* April 23, 2009.

TRIVIA

The Dutch audience awarded the film with the "TV Krant Filmposter Award" of 2007 for the poster featuring the swimming polar bear.

EASY VIRTUE

Let's misbehave!
—Movie tagline

Box Office: $2 million

For almost two decades, as they reliably racked up Oscar® nods and other award nominations, Merchant Ivory possessed a lock on the American imagination of what English-leaning, big historical dramas should and should not be. *Easy Virtue*, based on Noel Coward's 1925 stage play of the same name, upends many of those notions. A lively, engagingly acted, smartly scripted film, it is that rare period piece which refuses to yield to predictably stuffy interpretations of what constitutes familial screen conflict in times gone by. This is best illustrated through a scene in which Jessica Biel crushes a little dog to death with her ample derriere. Yes, seriously.

The film centers on John Whittaker (Ben Barnes), a young Englishman from a prim and proper family who falls madly in love with Larita (Biel), a sexy and glamorous American woman who, improbably enough, makes a living driving a motorcar. They marry impetuously, but when the couple returns to the sprawling, tradition-bound Whittaker family rural home, John's mother (Kristin Scott Thomas) has an instant allergic reaction to her new daughter-in-law. Sparks fly and a battle of wills and wits ensues, with the approval of John's sisters (Katherine Parkinson and Kimberley Nixon) serving as the swing-vote opinions on the nuptials and the couple's future.

Cast somewhat intriguingly against type as a bit of a cad and layabout, Colin Firth brings pleasantly shaded and subtle tones of swallowed sadness to his role as John's stubbled, war veteran father, even as he bickers and banters with relish. As the film unfolds we learn more about his outcast status, and the arm's-length disdain with which John's mother holds him. Biel, playing a bombshell, goes platinum blonde for her role and does a solid job. There is something inescapably modern about Biel, but in both *The Illusionist* (2006) and now here, she does the necessary work to make you believe her character fits within the times. Characters that were more demure wallflowers she might have trouble with, but slipping into corsets or flapper outfits and playing women a bit ahead of their respective times is well within Biel's grasp.

At its core, *Easy Virtue* is a light comedy of manners as well as a subversive attack on both the practice and practitioners of outmoded Victorian control, and those who try to live out their life (either vicariously or for material gain) through the lives of their children. It wears this subtext well, however. That it is a period piece is almost incidental, given the towel-snapping pleasure of much of the dialogue. (Where else does one get to hear one character slag another as "swinging around your wherewithal like a cat in heat"?) The cast accommodates the forthrightness of the material, trading collectively in wry line deliveries and knowing, askance glances.

Composer Marius de Vries provides a peppy score that serves the material quite well, but the grander portion of the film's vibrancy must be credited to Australian director Stephan Elliott. He stages scenes with a brisk, flirty touch while letting the dramatic stakes rise naturally to a slow boil, courtesy of a script, co-written with Sheridan Jobbins, that opens up the source material. Elliott also utilizes Cole Porter's "Let's Misbehave" (1927) as a sort of aural touchstone, utilizing the song a couple times and even letting Biel deliver a purring version over the soundtrack.

The only story strand that feels a bit off, or leaves one really wanting for some further connective tissue, concerns siblings Philip and Sarah Hurst (Christian Brassington and Charlotte Riley), longtime family friends of the Whittaker clan. John's casual shelving of Sarah as a potential mate—and her rather blithe acceptance of it—gets its own scene of explanation, but feels like it could have been milked for more effect, either dramatically or comedically. Similarly, the movie's ending may strike some as a bit pat; it is best if it is taken as a sort of tonal snapshot of the characters' minds at that particular moment rather than a fixed, end-point conclusion.

Finally, of course, there is that scene where Larita, quite accidentally, sits on the Whittaker's prized tiny pooch. In one sense, it feels like a put-on from a modern and much more conventionally raucous Farrelly brothers flick. But Elliott and his cast cleverly spin the incident forward, and let it be both silly and panicked, having actual consequences. *Easy Virtue* never stops having fun, but the fun its characters have comes at a tangible price.

A lot of comedies in general could learn something from that, regardless of the time period in which they are set.

Brent Simon

CREDITS

Larita: Jessica Biel
John Whittaker: Ben Barnes
Jim Whittaker: Colin Firth
Hilda: Kimberly Nixon
Furber: Kris Marshall
Lord Hurst: Pip Torrens
Sarah: Charlotte Riley
Veronica Whittaker: Kristin Scott Thomas
Marion: Katharine Parkinson
Origin: Great Britain, Canada
Language: English
Released: 2008
Production: Barnaby Thompson, James Stern, Joe Abrams; Ealing Studios, Endgame Entertainment, Odyssey Entertainment, Fragile Films; released by Sony Pictures Classics
Directed by: Stephan Elliot
Written by: Stephan Elliot, Sheridan Jobbins
Cinematography by: Martin Kenzie
Music by: Marius de Vries
Sound: John Midgley
Music Supervisor: Tris Pena, Michelle de Vries
Editing: Sue Blainey
Art Direction: Mark Scruton
Costumes: Charlotte Walter
Production Design: John Beard
MPAA rating: PG-13
Running time: 96 minutes

REVIEWS

Berkshire, Geoff. *Metromix.com.* May 21, 2009.
Ebert, Roger. *Chicago Sun-Times.* May 28, 2009.
Holden, Stephen. *New York Times.* May 22, 2009.
Honeycutt, Kirk. *Hollywood Reporter.* October 3, 2008.
Knight, Richard. *Windy City Times.* June 6, 2009.
McCarthy, Todd. *Variety.* October 18, 2008.
Mondello, Bob. *NPR.* May 28, 2009.
Phillips, Michael. *Chicago Tribune.* May 29, 2009.
Rosenbaum, Jonathan. *Chicago Reader.* May 29, 2009.
Tobias, Scott. *AV Club.* May 21, 2009.

QUOTES

Mr. Whittaker: "You're English dear, fake it."

TRIVIA

During the end credits all of the musicians who played in the orchestra featured on the soundtrack are introduced in voice-over simulating the introductions from the bandstand of a live performance, with each musician playing a brief sample.

AN EDUCATION

Box Office: $12 million

School girls do the silliest things: they sneak cigarettes during gym class, shirk their studies in favor of contraband music and if their parents really aren't paying attention, they get seduced and deflowered by charming older gentlemen, putting their futures at risk. Such is the fate of Jenny (Carey Mulligan), a precocious and clever girl growing up in 1960s London. The lone daughter of a regimented, school focused father (Alfred Molina) and passive mother (Cara Seymour), Jenny maintains her apple-of-their-eyes status by studying hard, playing the cello and by committing to their desired path for her: to study English at Oxford and find a suitable husband along the way. She, and her studies and her parents, get sidetracked by David (Peter Sarsgaard), a dashing older grifter who introduces Jenny to his more mature and sophisticated friends and whisks the 16-year-old away to nightclubs, art auctions and even a weekend in Paris all before sleeping with her on her 17th birthday and exhilaratingly proposing marriage. For Jenny, David is an answer to the monotony of her adolescent existence and an alternative to the few options afforded clever and precocious girls such as herself in the 1960s, namely it seems, being a schoolteacher. David is such a good scammer however, that even Jenny's parents fall for him, seduced by his worldly ways and made gullible by David's compliments, gifts and elaborate stories. But eventually David does slip up, and Jenny has to deal with heartbreak and saving face academically, which she does rather effortlessly as there is no permanent damage or fallout from this mark on her personal life. And therein lies the rub in this otherwise stellar film: it never really explores the creepy factor of Jenny and David's relationship, both while it's happening and after it unravels. *An Education* does a number of things well: it transports and roots the audience firmly in 1960s London, it features an array of fabulous performances by an astounding line-up of actors, and, for the most part, Nick Hornby's script provides said actors with witty dialogue and dimensional characters. So when the story fails to deliver the full impact surrounding the fallout of Jenny's relationship with David, instead wrapping up the narrative in a neat, but abrupt, box after so much skillful dramatic build-up, it's hard not to notice.

Without a doubt *An Education* is set to be a breakout vehicle for Mulligan, who is the perfect mix of girly, curious and wannabe mature as Jenny. She anchors the film with her charisma and is therefore the main reason why audiences don't trip over the fact that she's dating a man literally twice her age. She plays Jenny with a lovely mix of naïveté and the audacity of a child who is the sole focus of her parent's attention and therefore overly confident in herself (for example, Jenny initially doesn't even second guess her schoolgirl outfits in comparison to those of the older, more chic Helen (Rosamund Pike, David's partying companion). Mulligan is all awkward giggles and high school melodrama and a captivating presence on screen. It helps, of course, that the chemistry between her and Sarsgaard is electric. Jenny matches David witty quip for witty quip and between her outgoing personality and his infatuation with her, it is easy to get swept up in their inappropriate relationship. Sarsgaard himself delivers a layered, captivating turn as David. It's impossible not to be taken with him from the minute he appears on screen. On the surface, David is the epitome of calm, collected and dashing, but underneath there is a twinkle of something going horribly awry and Sarsgaard maintains this Jekyll and Hyde balance effortlessly, lulling both Jenny and the audience into a false sense of security.

In as much as the two leads shine, *An Education* also succeeds in that rare filmic event of selecting an all around amazing supporting cast that create not only a transporting atmosphere with their performances, but also reinforce the notion that there truly are no small parts. Each one of the actors, from Emma Thompson as Jenny's unforgiving headmistress to Olivia Williams as Jenny's more compassionate instructor, shine on screen. Molina as Jenny's torn father is also a standout. He is part overprotective, part self conscious, part hopeful, gullible and guilty—really all the traits that any parent who has tried but failed would possess. And all of it is communicated effectively and heartbreakingly in the short bursts we have with him. Cara Seymour, as Jenny's mom, is delightful in her worried eyes, and in the underhanded way she fights for her daughter by inviting boys her own age around. They gel as a family to the point where it's almost tempting to think "it's easy to see where Jenny gets her cleverness and spirit." Rosamund Pike and Dominic Cooper, who play David's friends and cohorts in business and pleasure, are also astounding. Cooper is mysterious and provocative and taps into the creepiness that is 30-year old men hanging out with high schoolers in a way that David doesn't and Pike plays the ditzy girl lost perfectly.

And Hornby gives them all solid material to work with. He captures the WASP-iness of the era in the things that Jack will and will not say to his daughter, as well as what he will and will not allow her to do. He creates a wonderfully pitched world that, compared to our modern one, was both a more innocent time as well as a more constricted one. He's helped here by director Lone Scherfig whose dark color palette for the film, such as Jenny's grey and navy school uniform and the brick grey streets of her neighborhood, only heighten the oppressive milieu. In Hornby's hands each character is also witty and wry and even their shortcomings are veiled with humorous one-liners—very much like the author's fiction. It's surprising then just how out of touch his script is with the eeriness of Jenny and David's relationship as well as with the ramifications such a coupling would have for so young a girl. Arguably the point is that Jenny grows up after meeting David. His ultimate betrayal of her is what makes her shed her naive school girl ways and grow up to be journalist Lynn Barber, on whose memoir the film is based. And also arguably it was part of Hornby, Barber and Scherfig's intention to plant audiences in a time where girls could get expelled for questionable virtue, where there was no such thing as safe sex, and where, simply put, women were not afforded the same opportunities as men. In this context, no doubt Jenny's pure survival of David in her life and the fact that she escaped unharmed is film worthy. But as a film, independent of whose life it's depicting, *An Education* doesn't feel whole with its out of the blue voice-over by Jenny claiming that she went off to Oxford and lied about ever having been to Paris. It is not a biting cautionary tale, nor is it a stay-with-you-after-the-credits zinger of a butterfly story. What *An Education* smells of is hindsight, which makes sense since it's based on a memoir. It's almost too easy to picture Barber and Hornby processing Jenny's story through their adult perspectives, discussing how funny, odd and weird the whole situation was and bypassing the in-the-moment teen experience of it. The scene where Jenny realizes that David wants to sleep with her is an example of this, the casualness with which she calculates that he will be the one to take her virginity feels more attributed to a seasoned adult rather than a 16-year old. Maybe it's too modern an idea to want the film to deliver more of a punch where Jenny's emotional state is concerned and maybe not going there is keeping in line with the 1960s era the film is depicting, but in the current context it leaves an otherwise unique and fascinating film feeling short-changed.

Joanna Topor MacKenzie

CREDITS

Jenny: Carey Mulligan
David: Peter Sarsgaard
Danny: Dominic Cooper
Helen: Rosamund Pike
Jack: Alfred Molina
Miss Stubbs: Olivia Williams
Headmistress: Emma Thompson
Marjorie: Cara Seymour
Graham: Matthew Beard
Sarah: Sally Hawkins
Origin: Great Britain
Language: English
Released: 2009
Production: Finola Dwyer, Amanda Posey; BBC Films, Endgame Entertainment; released by Sony Pictures Classics
Directed by: Lone Scherfig
Written by: Nick Hornby
Cinematography by: John de Borman
Music by: Paul Englishby
Sound: Simon Willis
Music Supervisor: Kle Savidge
Editing: Barney Pilling
Art Direction: Ben Smith
Costumes: Odile Dicks-Mireaux
Production Design: Andrew McAlpine
MPAA rating: PG-13
Running time: 100 minutes

REVIEWS

Childress, Erik. *EFilmCritic.* October 8, 2009.
Corliss, Richard. *Time Magazine.* October 9, 2009.
Ebert, Roger. *Chicago Sun-Times.* October 22, 2009.
Foundas, Scott. *Village Voice.* October 6, 2009.
McCarthy, Todd. *Variety.* October 6, 2009.
Pais, Matt. *Metromix.com.* October 8, 2009.
Phillips, Michael. *At the Movies.* October 12, 2009.
Stevens, Dana. *Slate.* October 8, 2009.
Tallerico, Brian. *MovieRetriever.com.* October 22, 2009.
Turan, Kenneth. *Los Angeles Times.* October 8, 2009.

QUOTES

Jenny (to her school headmistress): "It's not enough to educate us anymore. You have to tell us why you're doing it."
Jenny: "I feel old. But not very wise."

TRIVIA

Had previously made *Variety*'s 2007 list of best unproduced British screenplays.

AWARDS

British Acad. 2009: Actress (Mulligan)
Ind. Spirit 2010: Foreign Film
Nomination:
Oscars 2009: Actress (Mulligan), Adapt. Screenplay, Film

British Acad. 2009: Adapt. Screenplay, Costume Des.,
Director (Scherfig), Film, Makeup, Support. Actor (Molina)
Golden Globes 2010: Actress—Drama (Mulligan)
Screen Actors Guild 2009: Actress (Mulligan), Cast.

EVERY LITTLE STEP

The journey of "A Chorus Line."
—Movie tagline

Box Office: $1 million

In early 1974 in New York City, stage choreographer-director Michael Bennett gathered together almost two dozen dancers and, plying them with jugs of red wine, taped twelve hours of conversation about their creative passions, personal histories and occupational highs and lows. His goal was to craft a Broadway musical that placed the hardworking artisans at the center of its story, and the eventual result, *A Chorus Line*, became an international phenomenon that won multiple Tony Awards in 1976, as well as a Pulitzer Prize for Drama.

Exploring a bit of the history of this show but mostly chronicling the more than yearlong casting process leading up to a successful 2006 stage revival, the buoyant nonfiction film *Every Little Step* serves as a portrait of reach-for-the-stars aspiration, as well as a behind-the-scenes glimpse at the pre-rehearsal mounting of a Broadway show. Both its aims and achievement are modest, but for a country which regularly counts semi-celebrity dance-offs and other artistic competitions among its most popular TV series, this movie should satisfy a general audience's relatively uncomplicated interest in the specialized backdrop against which it unfolds.

A festival darling (the film played at the 2008 Toronto and Berlin festivals, as well as at 2009 New Directors/New Films), *Every Little Step* starts with footage from a massive open call audition, and tracks the process as potential cast members are whittled down from literally thousands to hundreds, and then only dozens. All of this is intercut with interview footage from some of those who have a hand in either this iteration of *A Chorus Line* or its original production, including Broadway legend Bob Avian, original cast members Baayork Lee and Donna McKechnie, and composer Marvin Hamlisch. Certain anecdotal tidbits prove fascinating. Hamlisch relates how audiences simply were not responding to what he felt was one of the best tunes he had ever written, a sardonic, woe-is-me tale of a dancer's body issues entitled "Tits and Ass." Figuring out that the program's song listing tipped off audiences to the punch line, he and Bennett changed the title to "Dance: 10, Looks: 3," and it received raucous reaction the very next evening.

Eschewing any florid stylistic touches, co-directors James D. Stern and Adam Del Deo tell the story in a fairly straightforward manner, hoping that the natural drama of watching actors being put through the paces of grueling song-and-dance routines will carry the day. In this manner, the documentary is not unlike the audition rounds of perennial small screen sensation *American Idol*, except for the fact that all the contenders have discernable talent.

In terms of overall tone, this approach mostly works, in that *Every Little Step* locates, engagingly if a bit fitfully, the sense of need in performers—their burning desire for expression, which is the very emotion that forms the spine of *A Chorus Line* itself. There is also pleasure to be found in simply bearing witness to the basic reaction of human joy attached to reward—of seeing someone become emotional after achieving a hard-fought dream, even if the dream is not your own. When one performer talks about dance being "the best part of me," her unsentimental, straightforward self-analysis is enough to give one a catch in his or her throat.

Unsurprisingly, there is something of a narrative imbalance, though. A couple of the actors speak articulately about their hopes, dreams and motivations, but others come across as ciphers merely set on a path to acting by a stage mother long ago. When, in the movie's most arresting unedited moment, Jason Tam brings tears to the eyes of Avian and several of the show's casting associates in an audition for what we are told is one of the more difficult and delicate parts to cast, a viewer wants to learn more about Tam, or at least his connection to the material. There is no follow-up with him, unfortunately—though he does ultimately win the role. A bit too much of the movie's 93-minute running time plays out in long-form takes; more judicious editing, and/or another ten to fifteen minutes focusing more forthrightly on both the off-screen personalities of those that win the parts and those that fall short, would fatten its emotional impact.

Where Stern and Del Deo further misstep is in not delving deeper into Bennett's groundbreaking concept of shaping both *A Chorus Line*'s music and book through a series of grueling workshops, for which all involved were paid only $100 per week. It also seems a bit strange that Bennett's death (he passed away from AIDS-related lymphoma in 1987), bisexuality and brief marriage to leading lady McKechnie are not mentioned. They are not necessarily matters to be doted on, but for either more casual followers of Broadway or those with no knowledge whatsoever of the show, they would augment and enhance a reading of the creation of the musical, so their absence seems a misguided choice erring on the side of personal privacy.

In the end, though, these are thinking criticisms that would offer a more fine-tuned product; *A Chorus Line* is ultimately about the depth of feelings of its subjects, and the price of consistently flaunted vulnerability—a brutal necessity in the acting trade. *Every Little Step* captures those difficulties, pitfalls, trade-offs and rewards, more than adequately.

Brent Simon

CREDITS

Herself: Donna McKechnie
Herself: Charlotte d'Amboise
Himself: Jacques D'Amboise
Himself: Marvin Hamlisch
Herself: Baayork Lee
Origin: USA
Language: English
Released: 2008
Production: James Stern, Adam Del Deo, Vienna Waits; Endgame Entertainment; released by Sony Pictures Classics
Directed by: James D. Stern, Adam Del Deo
Music by: Marvin Hamlisch, Jane Cornish
Editing: Fernando Villena, Brad Fuller
MPAA rating: PG-13
Running time: 96 minutes

REVIEWS

Ebert, Roger. *Chicago Sun-Times.* May 14, 2009.
Honeycutt, Kirk. *Hollywood Reporter.* April 23, 2009.
Jones, J.R. *Chicago Reader.* May 14, 2009.
Koehler, Robert. *Variety.* April 23, 2009.
Mondello, Bob. *NPR.* April 16, 2009.
Oxfeld, Jesse. *Village Voice.* April 14, 2009.
Rabin, Nathan. *AV Club.* April 16, 2009.
Rogers, Nathaniel. *Film Experience.* April 25, 2009.
Scott, A.O. *New York Times.* April 17, 2009.
Turan, Kenneth. *Los Angeles Times.* April 17, 2009.

QUOTES

Baayork Lee: "Eat nails!"

EVERYBODY'S FINE

*Frank wanted the holidays to be picture perfect.
What he got was family.*
—Movie tagline

Box Office: $9 million

"Everybody's Fine" is a most appropriate title for this particular family drama. The actors are all fine. The story is all right. The audience walks out pretty decently satisfied. Any medium road descriptive that you can think of to bridge your introductory small talk so as not to arouse worry or make the other party feel bad kind of works with this story. And the makers would probably be sort of fine with that. One could go the rest of his or her life without having someone tell them another yarn about estrangement and a family vacation. There is definitely a rest stop between the beginning and end of this anecdote and it only takes ninety-or-so minutes to tell.

Robert De Niro stars as Frank, a solitary, retired widower who contently spends his days perfecting his garden. This one day is special though as he is preparing for a visit by his four grown children. He buys the best steaks and the best grill only to come home to a string of messages that each of them have to cancel. Frank figures if they will not come to him, he will surprise them all and go to them. Against the advice of his doctor—never a good idea in movies—Frank hops a train, gleefully shows strangers pictures of his kids, and winds up waiting outside the New York apartment of his youngest son, David, who never shows.

Something has happened to him. Details are sketchy in the phone calls we hear from the kids, each advising the other to suppress what little they do know from dad, who they all of a sudden cannot get a hold of. Frank next surprises Amy (Kate Beckinsale), who is almost as quick to blow him off with travel plans. The grandson is happy to see him, but not so much his dad. Signs point to something amiss in Amy's home life. Next it is off to see Robert (Sam Rockwell), whom he thought was conducting an orchestra when he is actually just awaiting his cues on the drums. Finally it is off to Las Vegas when Rosie (Drew Barrymore) has a scenic apartment and reservations for a fancy restaurant. She seems very happy. Or is she also showing dad precisely what he wants for his kids?

Why keep referring to these grown adults as kids? Because that is how Frank sees them. Through all the years of being estranged from the home they grew up in after years of him pushing them to achieve the best in life, Frank still looks upon each of them as the little boys and girls whom he believed looked up to him. He was not a bad or abusive father, just strict in the old-fashioned way where hard work and criticism was used to help steer greatness. Sometimes it works. Sometimes it does not. One thing is for certain though, the successful tend not to hang regrets and animosity upon their greatest supporter.

This leads to scene after scene where each of his children have a disappointment to hide on top of the more troubling omissions about their absentee sibling. Because the audience is seeing events through the eyes of a quiet widower making every effort to reconnect, his children's reluctance to see him does little to endear our sympathies toward their issues. Writer/director Kirk Jones does a nice job of establishing the remoteness of Frank's first in-person encounter with Amy, whose Chicago home has a monochrome emptiness inside that makes it seem as cold as the approaching winter weather. Contrast the way Beckinsale keeps De Niro at a distance and how Barrymore is full of inviting Vegas cheeriness and the audience can easily surmise who has more to hide.

Harsh reality is stickered as the center of what *Everybody's Fine* purports to deliver in the middle of a seemingly harmless road movie. But neither do the revelations come off as rawly surprising nor disrupting enough to claim that only cinema can out-trump the faux grittiness of a nightly soap opera. Jones sets up the expected complications of Frank and his pills, perhaps even hinting at a pending tragedy with the sealed envelopes he leaves for each of his kin. At first the inevitable crisis is subverted only for an element to be introduced that is meant to convey Frank's stubbornness and frustration with his trip but plays more like an avoidable deus ex machina designed to set up the final act.

The true center of *Everybody's Fine* is not just the familiar cast but specifically De Niro trying to create an actual person again instead of just behaving like a movie character. Granted it is more in the vein of a *Falling In Love* (1984) or *Stanley & Iris* (1990), but that is a notable step up over the coasting he has done of late in dreck like *Hide and Seek* (2005) and *Righteous Kill* (2008). Metaphorizing constant shots of the telephone wire Frank made a career out of is a nice way of seeing the impersonal old school method of communication that connects and binds us all. Frank certainly would not be the e-mail or texting sort, but to completely avoid these even quicker, marginalized ways to stay in touch—particularly among the kids—keeps the audience at a greater distance of adapting to a metaphor that is not so profound to begin with. With Giuseppe Tornatore's *Stanno tutti bene* (1990) still unavailable on DVD, those who have not seen it will liken this version as more of a doppelganger to Alexander Payne's *About Schmidt* (2002). It too featured a larger-than-life actor (Jack Nicholson) dialing it down as a widower on a road trip to see his child while carrying on a penpal relationship with an African child he has never met. *Everybody's Fine* carries neither the emotional payoff of that film nor a standout performance from an actor with a career full

of standouts. The most common compliment to be heard about this film from its viewers will be that it is just about the most appropriate title for a movie to be released in 2009.

Erik Childress

CREDITS

Frank: Robert De Niro
Rosie: Drew Barrymore
Amy: Kate Beckinsale
Robert: Sam Rockwell
Jilly: Katherine Moenning
Tom: James Frain
Origin: USA
Language: English
Released: 2009
Production: Ted Field, Mario Cecchi Gori; Hollywood Pictures, Radar Pictures; released by Miramax Films
Directed by: Kirk Jones
Written by: Kirk Jones
Cinematography by: Henry Braham
Music by: Dario Marianelli
Sound: Thomas Gregory Varga
Editing: Andrew Mondshein
Art Direction: Drew Boughton
Costumes: Aude Bronson-Howard
Production Design: Andrew Jackness
MPAA rating: PG-13
Running time: 99 minutes

REVIEWS

Ebert, Roger. *Chicago Sun-Times.* December 3, 2009.
Grierson, Tim. *Screen International.* November 5, 2009.
Jones, J.R. *Chicago Reader.* December 4, 2009.
LaSalle, Mick. *San Francisco Chronicle.* December 4, 2009.
Pais, Matt. *Metromix.com.* December 3, 2009.
Phillips, Michael. *Chicago Tribune.* December 3, 2009.
Roeper, Richard. *RichardRoeper.com.* December 4, 2009.
Schwarzbaum, Lisa. *Entertainment Weekly.* December 2, 2009.
Stevens, Matt. *E! Online.* December 3, 2009.
Uhlich, Keith. *Time Out New York.* December 2, 2009.

QUOTES

Wine Man: "Well, we got wines from all over the world. We got, uh, English wines from France, we got Italian wines from all over Europe."

AWARDS

Nomination:

Golden Globes 2010: Song ("(I Want to) Come Home").

EXTRACT

Sticking it to the man has never looked so good.
—Movie tagline

A comedy with a flavor of its own.
  —Movie tagline

Box Office: $10.1 million

Easily one of the year's funniest movies, *Extract* is a career-best for writer-director Mike Judge. In the past, Judge zeroed in on the mundane operations of white-collar America in *Office Space* (1999) and the potential for the world to turn into a dimwitted dystopian nightmare in *Idiocracy* (2006). In *Extract*, though, Judge takes his closest look at the work that everyday people do or do not want to do to get by, and winds up with the rare film that delivers huge, loud laughs at a constant clip.

Though that success starts with the writing—Judge has long been a keen observer of behavior, particularly when dealing with the little things people might not want to admit about themselves—the cast is perfect all-around, and comes together the way an ensemble must for a comedy to truly go from good to great. That is part of the reason practically every scene in *Extract* crackles with wit, whether it is being anchored by a seasoned comedian like Jason Bateman or by someone like Ben Affleck, who has spent much of the last decade away from consistently lighthearted fare but proves to be anything but rusty.

The actors star as the sort of good friends who just barely make sense as friends, which makes their relationship that much funnier. Joel (Bateman), the owner of a California extract plant, is uptight and unhappy with his sexless marriage to Suzie (Kristen Wiig)—who, in one of the film's many hilarious running jokes, puts on sweatpants once the clock strikes eight to symbolically rule out any sexual possibilities for her husband. Dean (Affleck), on the other hand, is a laid-back bartender and casual drug user—he accidentally gives Joel horse tranquilizer instead of Xanax—who has a solution for Joel's sexual frustration, which fuels the temptation to chase his company's new temp Cindy (Mila Kunis). Dean will help hire attractive local guy Brad (Dustin Milligan) to seduce Suzie. If Brad succeeds Joel can pursue Cindy without feeling guilty, and if Brad fails Joel can feel better about his wife's level of commitment to him.

All of this is played with just the right amount of disbelief, as much of *Extract* deals with the intersection of opportunity and action. Joel can do something extreme about his wife and his crush, or he can do nothing. His employee Step (Clifton Collins Jr.), after being injured on the job, can either sue the company for all it is worth, or he can forgive and return to work. (Cindy, who is secretly stealing from the company and begins dating Step after she learns of the possible lawsuit, strongly encourages him to seek the maximum payout.)

Low-level employee Mary (Beth Grant) can work harder to set herself apart when seeing colleagues slacking off, but instead she insists, "If they're not going to do their job, I'm not going to do mine."

Ultimately, nearly everyone in the film is looking for a quick fix, or just a little something to make life more fun or manageable. (In a small, hilarious role, J.K. Simmons plays one of Joel's colleagues who does not know the names of his underlings so just sarcastically calls them all "Dinkus" or "boy genius.") That makes the setting of a plant specializing in extract—which Joel describes as spray-dried flavoring—a particularly good metaphor. Judge does not overdo this but lets it hang in the background, as context for people who just want a little more flavor in their routine.

More flavor would be useful in the way Judge writes his female characters. Cindy, while played with great agility and sexiness by Kunis, does not have a lot of depth, and Suzie is a caricature of a bored housewife. Yet much of the laugh-out-loud genius of *Extract* is in the details. This is seen in Joel's annoying neighbor (David Koechner), who always strikes up a conversation at the wrong time, and the way that Brad naively wants Joel to refer him to his friends so Brad can service unsatisfied wives as a full-time job. The pity Joel feels for Brad's stupidity shows Judge's sympathy—however twisted it may be—for those looking in from the outside of the functional working world.

Continuously, the film masterfully plays with the thin line between good and bad intentions; with people who either do not always understand the impact of their actions, or simply prefer to ignore them. This is an awfully good microcosm of the choices people face every day, and Judge, gifted at drawing out human weakness without condescending, has a terrific eye for folks who cannot see the silliness of their own behavior. Life, in many ways, is really funny, and *Extract* takes advantage.

Matt Pais

CREDITS

Joel: Jason Bateman
Cindy: Mila Kunis
Suzie: Kristen Wiig
Brad: Dustin Milligan
Dean: Ben Affleck
Step: Clifton Collins Jr.
Brian: J.K. Simmons
Nathan: David Koechner
Joe Adler: Gene Simmons
Origin: USA
Language: English

Extract

Released: 2009

Production: Michael Rotenberg, John Altschuler; Ternion Entertainment, 3 Arts Productions, F+A Productions; released by Miramax Films

Directed by: Mike Judge

Written by: Mike Judge

Cinematography by: Tim Suhrstedt

Music by: George C. Clinton

Editing: Julia Wong

Art Direction: Austin Gorg

Costumes: Alix Friedberg

Production Design: Maher Ahmad

MPAA rating: R

Running time: 91 minutes

REVIEWS

Chang, Justin. *Variety.* August 19, 2009.
Childress, Erik. *eFilmCritic.* September 3, 2009.

Dargis, Manohla. *New York Times.* September 3, 2009.
Ebert, Roger. *Chicago Sun-Times.* September 3, 2009.
Hoberman, J. *illage Voice.* September 1, 2009.
Hoffman, Jordan. *UGO.* September 4, 2009.
Honeycutt, Kirk. *Hollywood Reporter.* August 19, 2009.
Stevens, Dana. *Slate.* September 3, 2009.
Tallerico, Brian. *MovieRetriever.com.* September 4, 2009.
Tobias, Scott. *AV Club.* September 3, 2009.

QUOTES

Joel: "Just some criminal drifter."

TRIVIA

Director Mike Judge makes a brief appearance in the film as factory floor worker Jim.

F

FAME

Dream it. Earn it. Live it.
—Movie tagline

Box Office: $22 million

The original 1980 Alan Parker film *Fame* helped give rise to what would eventually become a ubiquitous subgenre of popular 1980s cinema: The Dance Movie. The year of its release came just as the disco movement started to die out, but before MTV debuted its first music video. Parker's film had the luxury of being simply a movie in and of itself and not a byproduct of marketing or trend-following. Although its stories took place in a New York high school for the performing arts, it was more about the characters' feelings of pressure and insecurity than about the art they created. In fact, the movie went so far as to suggest that these pompous, self-absorbed divas-to-be could peacefully coexist in a musical number without anyone trying to upstage everyone else.

Nearly thirty years later, Parker's movie has not quite stood the test of time, but that just might be the right reason to remake an average movie. Unfortunately, the 2009 version has little to say that can be relevant to today's hopeful up-and-comers and arrives ready to cash in on the popularity of TV's *Dancing With the Stars* and the *Step Up* films, complete with a wholesome and unexpected PG rating. Its characters are not interesting enough to be pompous. They simply exist to propel the story forward, one that seems to be in a big hurry to be told. Parker's *Fame* had a leisurely running time of 134 minutes, while this new version clocks in at 108 minutes, sacrificing the sense of a real journey from the audition

before freshman year to graduation at the end of senior year.

The remake follows the same structure as the original. Title cards indicate "The Audition," "Freshman Year," and so on. Likewise, it passively weaves in and out of its characters' lives and situations. Whereas the original felt almost Altman-esque, this one just seems confused and unfocused. It repeats many of the same scenes from the original, but using different characters. For example, a scene in the original when the wannabe actress finally cuts loose and joins the cast onstage at *The Rocky Horror Picture Show* is re-done here, only with a karaoke bar. Likewise, the scene in the 1980 film that finds Irene Cara's character Coco being asked to strip naked at what was supposedly a legit audition is replaced by a scene in which an aspiring actress gets taken advantage of in a television star's trailer.

These interchangeable story items are not the only problem with the newer *Fame*. The problem lies in the execution. For example, there is the troubled acting student Malik (Collins Pennie), who is probably this version's Leroy, the troubled dyslexic dance student from the original. His acting teacher (Charles S. Dutton) tries to get him to set aside his anger and let his acting come from another part of him, telling him that "there are no angry actors." The reluctant Malik does everything he can to hold back the source of his anger, only to come clean with "the age-old story" of his father leaving him at a young age. Such a belaboring build-up seems hardly worth the effort if all it leads to is a tale that has nothing fresh or remotely interesting.

These sorts of clichéd story devices are a symptom of remakes in general: the attempts to rework and update older material to say something relevant to a new generation often fails. *Fame*, like countless remakes before it, has nothing new to say, but rather old ways of saying the same old thing. This film could have made a statement against the rise of *American Idol*, media-driven socialites, and YouTube celebrities and could have been an interesting study of what it takes to truly earn one's fame. Instead, it gets bogged down in mundane drama, such as when the two lovestruck acting students have a tiff over one of them giving another person at a party a seemingly romantic look.

It should come as no surprise then that director Kevin Tancharoen is coming at this material as a director of Pussycat Dolls and Britney Spears videos. He clearly has more invested in the dance numbers, a couple of which are quite good, if highly unlikely and too sophisticated for high school kids. He has good ideas on where to put the camera for a solid dance number and will probably always have a steady career in that field. But drama is clearly not his forte. Too much of the new *Fame* is melodramatic, stilted and phony. The original film never seemed to need a conflict involving overbearing parents who would insist their kid take classical piano over singing, but this one does. Furthermore, since this is a school for the Performing Arts, it makes no sense to follow the pursuits of a character who is actually a filmmaker.

The argument could be made that musicals have never been known to truly explore the depths of their characters. This reasoning would stand had the movie possessed any conviction as a musical, but in order for it to work on that level, it would need actual songs. The original *Fame*, which was accompanied by a bestselling soundtrack, had a pulse all its own and had songs that, while they might appear dated today, could linger in one's head for hours. They had hooks that could catch a listener off guard. The new *Fame*, which seems hell-bent on updating its musical palette for the hip-hop crowd only, has nothing of the sort. In fact, it regurgitates "Out Here On My Own," one of the better songs from the original and used in the exact same context (aspiring singer sitting forlornly at the piano belting out her voice in hopes of being the next Jennifer Hudson).

The movie is filled with little nods to the original, giving the impression that it has reverence for its source material, but still has learned nothing from it. Only the actors playing the teachers give the film its dignity (Dutton, Bebe Neuwirth, Kelsey Grammer, Megan Mullally and Debbie Allen, who stared in the 1985 TV spin-off). They do the best they can with what they have been given. Mullally, in particular, has one of the film's better scenes in which she reluctantly talks to her students about her path that led to her becoming a teacher, a painful journey no doubt riddled with rejection and

self-doubt. The rest of the young actors in *Fame* have little to work with that the casts of the *High School Musical* franchise have not delved into already.

Collin Souter

CREDITS

Neil Baczynsky: Paul Iacono
Jenny Garrison: Kay Panabaker
Ms. Angela Simms: Debbie Allen
Mr. James Dowd: Charles S. Dutton
Rosie Martinez: Kristy Flores
Mr. Martin Cranston: Kelsey Grammer
Ms. Fran Rowan: Megan Mullally
Ms. Kraft: Bebe Neuwirth
Korean Boy: Tim Jo
Origin: USA
Language: English
Released: 2009
Production: Mark Canton, Gary Lucchesi, Tom Rosenberg, Richard S. Wright; Lakeshore Entertainment, Metro-Goldwyn-Mayer, United Artists; released by MGM
Directed by: Kevin Tancharoen
Written by: Allison Burnett, Christopher Gore
Cinematography by: Scott Kevan
Music by: Mark Isham
Sound: Michael Babcock
Music Supervisor: Eric Craig
Editing: Myron Kerstein
Art Direction: Scott A. Meehan
Costumes: Dayna Pink
Production Design: Paul Eads
MPAA rating: PG
Running time: 107 minutes

REVIEWS

Bradshaw, Peter. *Guardian.* September 25, 2009.
Ebert, Roger. *Chicago Sun-Times.* September 24, 2009.
Farber, Stephen. *Hollywood Reporter.* September 24, 2009.
LaSalle, Mick. *San Francisco Chronicle.* September 25, 2009.
Lowry, Brian. *Variety.* September 24, 2009.
Pais, Matt. *Metromix.com.* September 24, 2009.
Paras, Peter. *E! Online.* September 24, 2009.
Pols, Mary F. *Time Magazine.* September 25, 2009.
Sobczynski, Peter. *eFilmCritic.* September 24, 2009.
Webster, Andy. *New York Times.* September 25, 2009.

QUOTES

Joel Cranston: "You have talent. Now let's see what we can do with it."

TRIVIA

A photo is shown of Ms. Kraft (played by Bebe Neuwirth) with Broadway stage legend, Chita Rivera. Rivera notably played the role of Velma Kelly in the original 1975 Broadway production of "Chicago." Neuwirth also played Velma Kelly when "Chicago" was revived on Broadway in 1996. Both actresses received Tony Award nominations for their portrayals of the same character but only Neuwirth went on to win the honor.

FANBOYS

In 1998, five friends stole their way into history.
—Movie tagline

Never tell them the odds.
—Movie tagline

Fanboys tells the story of four male (and eventually one female) die-hard *Star Wars* fans who, in 1998, decide to take a road trip to Skywalker Ranch in the hopes of stealing a print of the highly anticipated *Star Wars Episode 1: The Phantom Menace* (1999). The impetus for this quest, other than fanboy adulation, was that one of the guys has cancer and wants to see the movie before he dies, no matter if it's a rough cut or the final cut. The original script of *Fanboys*, supposedly, kept this element of the storyline in the foreground while still having fun with the comedic aspects of fan-dom and road movies.

But then Bob and Harvey Weinstein got nervous. They had a different idea of what the movie should be. Their idea, in order to make it more commercially viable, was to jettison the cancer aspect of the storyline altogether and keep the comedy broad and the tone consistently upbeat. If there had to be a hospital scene, simply imply that the cancer character got hit on the head during a chase and had a concussion. Scenes were re-shot, an internet campaign was launched to try to make the Weinsteins listen to reason and the film ended up sitting on the shelf for a few years before finally hitting the screens without much fanfare to an indifferent audience.

The resulting movie appears to be a compromise on both ends. The character of Linus (Chris Marquette) still has cancer, but it only seems to be mentioned in passing during all the *Star Wars* inside jokes, broad slapstick sequences and endless cameos. The movie still tells the same story, but doesn't feel as though it comes from a personal place. To a viewer who does not know the full backstory of *Fanboys*, the cancer element feels like a forced and disingenuous afterthought. Whether this remains the fault of the filmmakers or the studio honchos who chose to meddle with something that otherwise might have had some true merit, we will never know.

The characters of *Fanboys* are typical misfits and geeks that have been seen in other movies. The portly

Hutch (Dan Folger) appears to be cut from the same mold as Jack Black's character in *High Fidelity* (2000). The nerdy character of Windows (Jay Baruchel) is on the quest to not only see *Star Wars*, but to meet a woman he met online, who naturally does not turn out to be what she seems. The straight-laced Eric (Sam Huntington) joins the boys as a way of avoiding responsibility and taking over his father's auto dealership. Finally, the lone female of the group Zoe (Kristen Bell), joins the boys mid-way through their journey after bailing them out of jail.

Along the way, the four take a detour to Iowa where *Star Trek* fans unveil a statue of Captain Kirk and the villain Kahn. A comedic rumble ensues between the two groups after the lead Trekkie (played by Seth Rogen, who has three roles in the film) makes a derogatory remark about the revered Han Solo. The boys also accidentally stumble upon a gay biker bar called The Mantina where they are forced to strip for the rowdy onlookers. Soon thereafter, they are rescued by shaman-like repairman (Danny Trejo) who takes them to the desert, feeds them peyote and sends them on their way. Also, it should be mentioned, the van in which they travel (decked out in true *Star Wars* glory) has hyperdrive, just like the Millennium Falcon. Real hyperdrive.

The filmmakers appear, in spots, to want to make a movie about the big role the *Star Wars* movies play in the lives of these people, but we never really learn what it is about these movies that resonates so deeply with them. The movie never explores the idea of super fan-dom and how it can either contribute to arrested adolescence or play a valuable role in one's means of getting through an otherwise dull existence (or both). All we ever learn about them is that they love *Star Wars* movies. Even in one of the film's final moments, where the new *Star Wars* film is watched for the very first time, we never get a sense of what it means in the grand scheme of things. It's not hard to guess, of course, since the scene is focused on only one character, but the sentiment is unearned and, more troubling, unclear.

Director Kyle Newman is clearly a die-hard *Star Wars* fan himself. The movie encompasses many of the familiar *Star Wars* sound effects from the Lucasfilm sound library and features cameos by Carrie Fisher, Billy Dee Williams and Ray Park (as well as a gag involving a movie poster of a certain 1998 Harrison Ford movie). Newman plays with as many *Star Wars* conventions as possible, from the opening title scroll to the transitional screen wipes, while also letting the true *Star Wars* fans in the audience know that they are not alone in their obsession. Unfortunately, the movie tries too hard. The score is overbearing and the roadtrip elements are pedestrian. Even cameos by Rogan, William Shatner, Will Forte, Craig Robinson, Danny McBride, Ethan Suplee (as Harry Knowels), Kevin Smith and Jason Mewes can't seem to rise above the material (it should be noted that McBride's scene was a re-shoot after it was originally shot with William Katt).

Fanboys might have had something to it in its original vision before being sent to the chopping block by the Weinsteins and their editors. The movie could have delved deeper in the lives of its five protagonists and even could have explored how the mysticism of the *Star Wars* saga helps Linus deal with his fate. Instead, *Fanboys* appears to accept the idea that fan-dom is skin deep and something to be used as a means to a gag rather than a means of introspection.

Collin Souter

CREDITS

Eric: Sam Huntington
Linus: Christopher Marquette
Hutch: Dan Fogler
Windows: Jay Baruchel
Zoe: Kristen Bell
THX Security Guard: Craig Robinson
Origin: USA
Language: English
Released: 2009
Production: Kevin Spacey, Matthew Perniciaro, Evan Astrowsky, Dana Brunetti; Trigger Street, Coalition Film; released by Weinstein Company
Directed by: Kyle Newman
Written by: Adam F. Goldberg, Ernest Cline
Cinematography by: Lukas Ettlin
Music by: Mark Mothersbaugh
Sound: Whit Norris
Music Supervisor: Michelle Silverman
Editing: Seth Flaum
Costumes: Johanna Argan
Production Design: Cory Lorenzen
MPAA rating: PG-13
Running time: 90 minutes

REVIEWS

Burr, Ty. *Boston Globe.* February 19, 2009.
DeBruge, Peter. *Variety.* July 28, 2008.
Ebert, Roger. *Chicago Sun-Times.* February 5, 2009.
Pais, Matt. *Metromix.com.* February 5, 2009.
Phillips, Michael. *Chicago Tribune.* February 5, 2009.
Roeper, Richard. *RichardRoeper.com.* February 7, 2009.
Schwarzbaumn, Lisa. *Entertainment Weekly.* February 4, 2009.
Sobczynski, Peter. *eFilmCritic.com.* February 5, 2009.

Tallerico, Brian. *MovieRetriever.com.* February 5, 2009.
White, Armond. *New York Press.* February 4, 2009.

QUOTES

Hutch: "You want to take your shirt off."

TRIVIA

Carrie Fisher, who played Princess Leia in the orignal *Star Wars* films, makes a brief cameo as Doctor.

FANTASTIC MR. FOX

Dig the life fantastic.
—Movie tagline

Box Office: $20.1 million

Curiously enough, Wes Anderson's animated adaptation of Roald Dahl's book *Fantastic Mr. Fox* opens much in the same way as his 2001 film *The Royal Tenenbaums*, with the film's title branded on a library book. This could be meant as a tip-off that this will be more of a Wes Anderson film than a Roald Dahl story (in this case, one of the simplest Dahl has ever written). Anderson's tales of familial angst (usually involving a matriarch) coupled with Dahl's straightforward story of a fox who outsmarts three evil farmers is a combination that seems rife with possibilities, both good and bad. On the plus side, Anderson's animated tale will lure in younger viewers who will be treated to a smarter-than-usual tale of plucky, furry animals. On the downside, however, is the notion of seeing a Wes Anderson movie that has already been made once or twice already.

This *Fantastic Mr. Fox* tells the story of a fox (voiced by George Clooney) who used to run wild stealing birds, but has since settled down as a newspaper journalist who wonders if anybody actually reads his stuff. His wife, Mrs. Fox (voiced by Meryl Streep), works as a landscape artist. They have a son, Ash (voiced by Jason Schwartzman), and a visiting cousin, Kristofferson (voiced by Eric Chase Anderson). Mr. Fox is currently suffering through a midlife crisis of sorts and spends his evenings stealing turkeys and cider as a way of staying young and avoiding responsibility. Settling down, holding a steady job and raising the kids just does not hold enough excitement for him. He has decided he does not want to live in a hole anymore.

Against the advice of his badger attorney Clive Badger (voiced by Bill Murray), Mr. Fox decides to buy a new tree not far from the three most evil farmers in the region: Boggis, Bunce and Bean (voiced by Robin Hurlstone, Hugo Guinness and Michael Gambon, respectively). Where Badger sees nothing but danger, Mr. Fox sees nothing but excitement because of the danger. Enlisting the help of his opossum friend Kylie (voiced Wallace Wolodarsky), Mr. Fox makes plans to steal chickens, cider and geese from the three respective farms. His plans involve dodging rat security guards, feeding sleep-inducing blueberries to guard dogs and wearing bandit masks. In true heist movie form, Mr. Fox insists that these will be his final jobs.

Mr. Fox eventually enlists the help of Kristofferson, who would prefer not to do anything dishonest. Mrs. Fox grows suspicious that her husband is returning to his old ways of thievery and the three framers, fully aware of their new fox problem, stake out their own houses waiting to fire their rifles at the critters. Mr. Fox and his family's problems increase when the farmers decide to plow under the tree and destroy the fox's home. The Fox's must dig their way to new underground homes before the tractors and plows reach them or the explosives blow them to smithereens. Soon, the entire underground village is forced out of their homes and it's up to Mr. Fox to set things right.

Meanwhile, Ash has to deal with feeling inferior to his cousin Kristofferson. Mr. Fox is clearly more impressed with Kristofferson's diving skills than his son's. Ash is different from other kids at school while Kristofferson nonchalantly brings home trophies on his first day of playing Whack Bat at school, a game for which Mr. Fox already holds world records. Ash aspires to be as good as his father at the game (and many other things), but has a ways to go.

The film runs eighty-seven minutes, which is about how long it takes to read the original source material. Anyone familiar with Roald Dahl's original story will notice a lot of add-ons in regard to the filmed adaptation. In Dahl's story, Mr. and Mrs. Fox have four children, none of whom have any of the hang-ups that Ash has. Mr. Fox regularly steals from the farmers, which Mrs. Fox accepts just fine (so long as he is careful). The farmers use their plows to dig the Foxes out, but they dig too fast to be caught. The Foxes run into the Badger family and devise a plan to tunnel under the farmers' houses to steal their food rather than come out of their foxholes. Boggis, Bunce and Bean wait by the hole knowing full well the foxes have to come out sooner or later. But Mr. Fox has already stolen enough food for his family and all the other families living below with them. The end.

Dahl wrote such a simple A-to-Z story for kids that one has to wonder why Anderson took such an interest in it. With Mr. Fox as the troubling matriarch too self-absorbed to notice his own flaws, which everyone else is quick to point out, he becomes much like the Gene Hackman or the Bill Murray characters in *The Royal Tenenbaums* (2001) and *The Life Aquatic With Steve Zis-*

sou (2004). Young Ash trying to win his father's acceptance while his cousin Kristofferson barely has to lift a finger to do just that reminds one of the sibling rivalry that exist in many of Anderson's films.

These additions do not necessarily hinder *Fantastic Mr. Fox*. The film could have easily been a labored affair with cliché-ridden filler. But Anderson is playing into conventions which, by now, have become clichés of his own. By now, it should be clear that any movie that bears Anderson's name will, in one way or another, be about dysfunctional families. Although he repeats himself, Anderson continues to explore this territory with wit, ease and insight, complete with his trademark visual style: Straight-to-camera declarations, large yellow captions and enough quick visual gags to warrant repeat viewings for new discoveries. Anderson does allude to Dahl's story with story songs and the poem about the farmers that opens Dahl's book.

For the animation, Anderson instructed his team to cross the stop-motion style of Rankin-Bass (creators of the holiday TV classics *Santa Claus is Comin' to Town* [1970] and *Rudolph, The Red-Nosed Reindeer* [1964]) with Anderson's own *The Royal Tenenbaums*. The result is an irresistibly charming visual feast that one hopes will be attempted more often. The tangible nature of the animals' appearance and their flawless facial expressions help make these characters truly come alive. Their movements might not be natural (a common trait of this type of animation), but there is considerable attention to detail in the areas where it counts most. When a character is supposed to feel a little melancholy or confused, it is triumphantly realized. Anderson and his team also have a lot of fun with the notion that, while these are meant to be three-dimensional characters, they are also animals that eat like slobs and fight like children.

Of course, credit should also go to the voice talent. Clooney is a natural choice to play the cocky and in-command Mr. Fox. Streep is incapable of phoning in a performance, even when she is not on screen. Anderson favorite Jason Schwartzman brings just the right amount of spitefulness and insecurity to Ash to make him sympathetic. Two of the lesser-known actors, Wallace Wolodarsky as Kylie and Eric Chase Anderson as Kristofferson, deliver their lines with the ease of laid back beachcombers and become the most engaging characters in the film. Anderson, like Pixar, knows how to cast the right actors for his roles without having to resort to familiar celebrity personalities.

As Ash states early on, "There's a lot of attitudes going on around here." This is true of all of Anderson's films, though. On one hand, they want the audience to connect with their troubled and idiosyncratic characters while at the same time, laugh at the visual gags of the world they inhabit. Anderson knows the complexities of his characters and has the decency not to ever look down on them. Yet at the same time, he manages to keep his audiences at an arm's length. Look, think and laugh, but do not touch. Still, with all its visual splendor, quick wit and musical detours, *Fantastic Mr. Fox* is truly a unique film even if it does not always feel that way.

Collin Souter

CREDITS

Mr. Fox: George Clooney (Voice)
Mrs. Fox: Meryl Streep (Voice)
Badger: Bill Murray (Voice)
Rat: Willem Dafoe (Voice)
Ash: Jason Schwartzman (Voice)
Franklin Bean: Michael Gambon (Voice)
Mrs. Bean: Helen McCrory (Voice)
Boggis: Brian Cox (Voice)
Rickity: Adrien Brody (Voice)
Coach Skip: Owen Wilson (Voice)
Weasel: Wes Anderson (Voice)
Linda Otter: Karen Duffy (Voice)
Origin: USA, Great Britain
Language: English
Released: 2009
Production: Allison Abbate, Wes Anderson, Jeremy Dawson, Scott Rudin; American Empirical Pictures, Regency Enterprises, 20th Century Fox, Indian Paintbrush; released by 20th Century Fox film corporation, Fox Searchlight Pictures
Directed by: Wes Anderson
Written by: Wes Anderson, Noah Baumbach
Cinematography by: Tristan Oliver
Music by: Alexandre Desplat
Sound: Noah Vivekanand Timan
Music Supervisor: Randall Poster
Editing: Andrew Weisblum
Art Direction: Tim Ledbury
Production Design: Nelson Lowry
MPAA rating: PG
Running time: 87 minutes

REVIEWS

Edelstein, David. *New York Magazine.* November 9, 2009.
Linden, Sherri. *Hollywood Reporter.* October 14, 2009.
McCarthy, Todd. *Variety.* October 14, 2009.
Pais, Matt. *Metromix.com.* November 12, 2009.
Pols, Mary F. *Time Magazine.* November 13, 2009.
Scott, A.O. *New York Times.* November 13, 2009.
Stevens, Dana. *Slate.* November 13, 2009.

Tallerico, Brian. *MovieRetriever.com.* November 25, 2009.
Travers, Peter. *Rolling Stone.* November 12, 2009.
Zacharek, Stephanie. *Salon.com.* November 12, 2009.

QUOTES

Mr. Fox: "Here we go. Mole! Talpa Europea! What d'you got?"

TRIVIA

The song "Looking For A Fox" by Clarence Carter was featured in the first trailer, though it doesn't appear in the film.

AWARDS

Nomination:

Oscars 2009: Animated Film, Orig. Score
British Acad. 2009: Animated Film, Orig. Score
Golden Globes 2010: Animated Film.

FAST & FURIOUS

New model. Original parts.
—Movie tagline

Box Office: $155 million

Fast & Furious is the fourth installment in a film series that is predicated on the race and the chase. Is it racing or chasing after anything new? No, but it does so with an awful lot of style. Directed by Justin Lin (*Better Luck Tomorrow* [2002], *Annapolis* [2006]) this lean, mean, stripped-down muscle-car of a movie takes full advantage of exotic locations, big budget and an experienced cast to create something part soap opera, part high-octane action film and part rump-thumping music video. But viewers are advised to keep brains in low gear. Other than an occasional flash of dramatic intensity, Lin keeps his camera, as expected, hanging out the window.

The resultant explosions, gun play and general lack of police presence during any of the major inner-city chases are far more fun than they are believable. Screenwriter Chris Morgan (*Cellular* [2004], *Wanted* [2008]) should be commended for staying out of the way with his characters, and their motivations as things made out of cardboard tend to get blown around a lot when placed next to a busy highway.

The film opens well enough with a breathtaking, high-speed robbery that quickly goes bad. Realizing he's put his gang and his girl, Letty (Michelle Rodriguez), at risk of discovery, group leader Dominic Toretto (Vin Diesel) becomes a loner fugitive. When he gets word that Letty has been killed on an assignment, Toretto returns to Los Angeles to settle the score. Standing in the way of his vengeance is former racer and police informant, now turned federal agent, Brian O'Conner (Paul Walker) who must find a way to work with Toretto to bring down the international drug lord for whom Letty was driving. Each man has his loyalties as well as his driving abilities tested through a series of precision tunnel crawls, races across international lines and big rig heists.

The cast here is top notch. Vin Diesel (*Pitch Black* [2000], *Boiler Room* [2000], *XXX* [2002]) oozes cool as Toretto, a man with nothing to lose and Paul Walker (*Joy Ride* [2001], *Flags of Our Fathers* [2006]) holds his own with Diesel, as a perfect counterpoint. O'Conner has everything to lose but might be willing to lose it if he can accomplish his goal. Unfortunately, the always dependable Michelle Rodriguez (*Resident Evil*, [2002]), *S.W.A.T.* [2003]), credited with a leading role, serves only in a supporting capacity here. The dynamic opening sequence uses her athleticism quite well but the plot quickly leaves her behind and the film gives the only other female lead, Jordana Brewster (*The Faculty* [1998], *The Texas Chainsaw Massacre: The Beginning* [2006], *Annapolis* [2006]) no way to take up the slack except to serve as a plot device. But, then again all the characters here are basically plot devices. The tagline "New Model Original Parts" is of course contradictory. There simply is not anything new here.

As a genre, or subgenre, car chase films tend to be at their best when they are their most stripped down. Justin Lin should be credited for not allowing a bloated budget to weigh down his movie's chassis. But a look under the hood does reveal a little too much tinkering goes on to give this movie the sort of street cred that would ring true outside of the suburbs. CGI is, as is the case with almost every film released these days, used in all the wrong places here, undercutting tension during climactic moments, revealing stunts to be shams. At a time when more and more people are experiencing the dynamism of world genre cinema, particularly the brutal stunt antics of Thai action films, this misuse of CGI makes it harder than ever to suspend disbelief when watching their American counterparts.

Also difficult to suspend disbelief in is the hope for the once promising career of Vin Diesel. Originally touted as a multi-threat talent, he broke out writing directing and starring in the feature *Strays* (1997) and the acclaimed short *Multi-Facial* (1999) which helped land him roles in, *Saving Private Ryan* (1998), the underappreciated animated feature *The Iron Giant* (1999), *Pitch Black* (2000) and the very good *Boiler Room* (2000). But since then, except for the occasional solid dramatic turn (*Find Me Guilty* [2006]), Diesel has appeared in forgettable genre films clearly designed to claim some sort of mantle from the last generation of action heroes. Whether taking a page from Stallone, Willis, or Schwarzenegger, the result is the same. Diesel is best when he breaks, rather than tries to fit into, the mold.

Too bad that a movie blessed with so much in the way of resources fails to generate more gravitas from, or at least sense the irony in Toretto's line, "We're all just along for the ride now." By adhering so closely to genre, Lin fails to elevate this material into much more than a forgettable, fun pastiche, and impossible to escape is the sense that it could have been something more, something a little ideologically racy.

Dave Canfield

CREDITS

Dominic Toretto: Vin Diesel
Brian O'Connor: Paul Walker
Letty Marciano: Michelle Rodriguez
Mia Toretto: Jordana Brewster
Fenix Rise: Laz Alonso
Origin: USA
Language: English
Released: 2009
Production: Vin Diesel, Michael Fottrell, Neal H. Moritz; Universal Pictures, Relativity Media, Original Film, One Race Productions, Neal H. Moritz Productions; released by Universal Pictures
Directed by: Justin Lin
Written by: Chris Morgan
Cinematography by: Amir M. Mokri
Music by: Brian Tyler
Sound: Peter Brown
Art Direction: David Lazan
Costumes: Sanja Milkovic Hays
Production Design: Ida Random
MPAA rating: PG-13
Running time: 107 minutes

REVIEWS

Childress, Erik. *eFilmCritic.* April 3, 2009.
Corliss, Richard. *Time Magazine.* April 3, 2009.
Ebert, Roger. *Chicago Sun-Times.* April 2, 2009.
Honeycutt, Kirk. *Hollywood Reporter.* April 2, 2009.
Lemire, Christy. *Associated Press.* March 31, 2009.
McCarthy, Todd. *Variety.* April 3, 2009.
Pais, Matt. *Metromix.com.* April 2, 2009.
Phipps, Keith. *AV Club.* April 2, 2009.
Sharkey, Betsy. *Los Angeles Times.* April 2, 2009.
Tallerico, Brian. *MovieRetriever.com.* April 3, 2009.

QUOTES

Brian O'Conner: "Ya know, I've been thinking, when you blew up your car, that means you blew up mine too."

TRIVIA

Vin Diesel originally wanted to make the fourth and fifth films back to back, but Universal decided to take some time to see how the current movie would work out before moving on to a fifth. Diesel was also allowed to direct an 18 minute short film set in the *Fast & Furious* world.

FIGHTING

Some dreams are worth the fight.
—Movie tagline

Box Office: $23 million

Dito Montiel's *Fighting* takes an unpromising subject, a secret world of underground fighting, and does little with it. Underwritten characters, undeveloped relationships and uninspired fight sequences result in a film that neither succeeds as a drama, nor an action film.

The film opens in New York City with a down-on-his-luck Shawn MacArthur (Channing Tatum) hawking black market items on the street. The minions of a nearby competitor, Harvey Boarden, (Terrence Howard) try to muscle Shawn off his spot and receive a concentrated beating in return. Boarden is impressed with MacArthur's fighting prowess and sees him as his meal ticket (literally, he dreams of owning an International House of Pancakes) out of the small time. Soon he is proposing that he and Shawn work together, as manager and fighter, competing in an underground fighting ring run by two men, Martinez (Luis Guzman) and Jack (Roger Guenveur Smith), with whom Harvey has a complicated past. Enticed by the prospect of a $5,000 payday, Shawn agrees and the fights begin.

The fights are bare-knuckle affairs with no apparent rules other than not killing the other fighter. There is no attempt to match the fighters by weight, height or age and the fights take place wherever someone will let them: a church, a yuppie's penthouse, an alley behind a convenience store. After Shawn embarks on his fighting career, two people come into his life: a waitress, Zulay Henao (Zulay Velez), he encounters in a club and, in an amazing coincidence, his high school wrestling nemesis, Evan Hailey (Brian J. White) who is now a professional fighter moonlighting on the underground circuit.

There are two routes a premise like this can take: a straightforward exploitation film like *Hard Times* (1975) or *BloodSport* (1986) or a nuanced character study like the *Hustler* (1961) or *Raging Bull* (1980). *Fighting* obviously wants to be something more than the former but lacks the chops to succeed at the latter. *Fighting* features characters, relationships and situations that have as much dramatic potential as any other film, but a lazy script fails to develop these elements into anything interesting or compelling.

Harvey is as much motivated by the desire to prove himself to Martinez and Jack as by the opportunity to make money, however the script does not make clear what occurred in the past to motivate Harvey's desire for vindication in the present. A rich, long back story between the three characters is hinted at but is not explained or explored. Harvey makes a vague reference to Martinez having had his leg broken for a few hundred dollars in the past but it is not clear why this occurred (was Harvey a fighter or did he owe Martinez money?) nor is it explained why Harvey is compelled to continue a relationship with two men who hate and belittle him at every opportunity or why securing their respect is important to him.

Similarly, Shawn's past and his present rivalry with Evan generated by that past is given the most threadbare of explanations (they were on the same wrestling team in high school and, when Shawn's father attempted to separate them during an out-of-ring altercation, Shawn savagely beat his father). Evan appears in the film because the film needs a villain for its climactic fight scene, not because he is the antagonist of a rivalry that has been convincingly developed. The relationship between Shawn and Zulay also feels scripted, resulting not from a demonstrated chemistry between the characters but rather because the film needs a love story at that point in the script. Among Shawn's first words to Zulay are that he "believes in fate." Since the two have never before met and know nothing of one another, it is not clear what is fueling his certainty (aside from having read the script) that they are fated to be together other than that she is a gorgeous waitress. Even the most fleshed out relationship in the film, between Shawn and Harvey, remains frustratingly ambiguous (though the script must be credited with mercifully sparing the viewer from the cliché of the manager betraying his protege). As a result of this ambiguity, the viewer does not understand why the characters do what they do or why they feel the way they do about one another and is given no incentive to care about the characters or what happens to them. *Fighting* wants the viewer to care about its characters but does not want to put in the hard work of earning that care by putting flesh to its bare-bones plot.

As a result of the film's failed emphasis on being a drama, it fails to succeed even on the visceral level of its title. The fights are brief, unoriginal and edited so quickly that it is often difficult to understand what is happening. Admittedly, coming up with a new variation on something that has been depicted in film since before film had sound is difficult, but *Fighting* does not even make the attempt because its commitment is to its characters not (as one might understandably expect from its title) the spectacle of its fights. This would be an acceptable approach if the film were successful on its intended level, but it is not.

Fighting's failures are particularly unfortunate because the cast features some excellent actors like Terence Howard, Luis Guzman and Roger Guenveur Smith, who are capable of excellent, memorable work when given dynamic, three dimensional characters to play. *Fighting* also has some nice, small touches that hint at what the film might have been: the "anywhere will do" fighting locales, Harvey's affinity for IHOP, a sequence in which Shawn and Zulay are continuously interrupted by Zulay's grandmother who was apparently, and hilariously, allowed to improvise 100% of her dialogue. But these tiny flourishes are not enough to save a film that feels in all other respects like merely an outline for a film. There is certainly something to be said for minimalism, and contemporary film could use a lot more of it. However, there is minimalist and there is incomplete. *Fighting* feels like a three-hour film that has been cut down to ninety minutes, leaving only broad plot points without the character development and depth to make those plot points compelling.

Nate Vercauteren

CREDITS

Shawn MacArthur: Channing Tatum
Harvey Boarden: Terrence Howard
Martinez: Luis Guzman
Evan Hailey: Brian White
Zulay Henao: Zulay Henao
Jack Dancing: Roger Guenveur Smith
Origin: USA
Language: English
Released: 2009
Production: Kevin Misher; Misher Films; released by Rogue Pictures
Directed by: Dito Montiel
Written by: Dito Montiel, Robert Munic
Cinematography by: Stefan Czapsky
Music by: Dave Wittman, Jonathan Elias
Sound: Danny Michael
Music Supervisor: Dave Jordan, JoJo Villanueva
Editing: Jake Pushinsky, Saar Klein
Art Direction: Randall Richards
Costumes: Kurt and Bart
Production Design: Therese DePrez
MPAA rating: PG-13
Running time: 105 minutes

REVIEWS

Adams, Mark. *Sunday Mirror.* May 15, 2009.
Anderson, John. *Variety.* April 23, 2009.
Ebert, Roger. *Chicago Sun-Times.* April 23, 2009.
Gronvall, Andrea. *Chicago Reader.* April 24, 2009.
Haar, Peter Vonder. *Film Threat.* May 8, 2009.
Honeycutt, Kirk. *Hollywood Reporter.* April 23, 2009.
Pais, Matt. *Metromix.com.* April 23, 2009.
Quill, Greg. *Toronto Star.* April 24, 2009.
Simon, Brent. *Screen International.* April 23, 2009.
Sobczynski, Peter. *eFilmCritic.* April 24, 2009.

QUOTES

Jack Dancing: "In the words of the late, great, Marvin Gaye. Let's... Get... It... On!"

TRIVIA

Channing Tatum broke his nose while filming one of the fight scenes.

THE FINAL DESTINATION
(Final Destination 4)
(Final Destination: Death Trip 3D)

The race of life can be so deadly.
—Movie tagline
Most people have dreams. For Alex, this is real.
—Movie tagline

Box Office: $66 million

Slapping an indefinite article on the title of the original 2000 film, and upping the gimmickry with a 3-D presentation, *The Final Destination* again pits a group of mostly teenage survivors of a traumatic accident against the faceless force of death. Yawningly stringing together a discrete series of gory dismemberments, the fourth entry in this once-intriguing teen horror franchise substitutes clamorous razzle-dazzle for tension-and-release suspense. It is a noisy slice of unsophisticated and unengaging pap given commercial punch solely by virtue of the novelty of its theatrical exhibition.

At a NASCAR race, Nick O'Bannon (Bobby Campo) envisions those surrounding him being torn to pieces by the flying debris of a violent automotive smash-up. He alerts his girlfriend Lori Milligan (Shantel VanSanten) and best friends Hunt Wynorski (Nick Zano) and Janet Cunningham (Haley Webb) to the danger, and they all escape death. As Nick's further intuitive visions involving those spared by the disaster start to come true (and Lori helpfully Googles "premonitions"), the aforementioned quartet, along with some other survivors (Justin Welborn, Krista Allen), try to make sense of the sequential order of cheated demise and stay alive.

Part of the success of *Final Destination* (2000) lay in its characterizations, as well as the Rube Goldberg-type scenarios by which its teen cast were felled, one by one, while trying to pick off clues and interrupt the chain of mortal comeuppance. The settings here (an escalator, a carwash, a swimming pool) are often novel on a surface level but feel thinly imagined, and the CGI special effects work (rendered chiefly by Hybride and KNB FX Group, and overseen by visual effects supervisor Erik Henry) is overly processed and unrealistic, especially during Nick's visions. Then there is the grander problem of lazy presentation. Once it becomes apparent that 3-D is being used so readily as a crutch to highlight only gore, the movie's intrigue slackens and the deaths themselves, already predetermined by the genre and narrative, become little more than boxes to indifferently check off on a not-particularly-interesting suburban safari.

The Final Destination reunites director David R. Ellis and screenwriter Eric Bress, who also collaborated on *Final Destination 2* (2003). Ellis presses down hard on all the stylistic buttons, marshaling kinetic camerawork (from cinematographer Glen MacPherson), pounding music (from composer Brian Tyler) and frenetic editing (from editor Mark Stevens), but the sum is far less than the whole of its parts, and those parts are already used and well-worn. Gone are attempts to substantively address or grapple with personally held notions of mortality; the plot is little more than a perfunctory set-up for a string of shrieking fatalities. While there is still some attempt to bring together surviving characters whose personalities and opinions chafe one another (an integral component of the first film), apart from a widowed security guard (Mykelti Williamson) there exists a pervasive sense that hardly anyone else in the movie is worth seeing saved.

Much else about *The Final Destination* feels prefabricated and test-marketed, from its bland casting and the setting of the movie's opening scene at a NASCAR event, an ascendant sport, to its music selection and a few seeming instances of product placement. None of the cast distinguishes themselves, though Van-Santen and Webb do get to exercise prodigious sets of lungs. Meanwhile, the movie's occasional stabs at humor—a racist (Justin Welborn) setting himself on fire while trying to burn a cross on a black man's yard, all while "Why Can't We Be Friends" blares from his car stereo—come across as strange and forced.

With a spate of horror films like *My Bloody Valentine* (2009) rushing to capitalize on the burgeoning trend, 3-D seems a way to good way to lure teenage audiences away from videogames or other activities, and out to theaters. How *The Final Destination* plays without 3-D is another matter, though. The gimmick of its exhibition (it also played in 2-D at less than half its 3,120 sites) surely helped deliver a huge, back-to-school opening weekend ($27.4 million) during its late August theatrical bow, and a worldwide gross north of $150 million, the highest of the series. At only 75 minutes minus credits, though, nothing about the story or execution seems developed or exceptional enough to merit another installation. Critical reaction, meanwhile, was appropriately sour and dismissive, with the *Hollywood Reporter*'s Kirk Honeycutt noting, "Death surely needs a holiday—he's tired and running out of ideas."

Brent Simon

CREDITS
Hunt: Nick Zano
Samantha: Krista Allen
Nick O'Bannon: Bobby Campo
Lori: Shantel VanSanten
Janet: Haley Webb
George: Mykelti Williamson
Carter: Justin Welborn
Origin: USA
Language: English
Released: 2009
Production: Craig Perry, Warren Zide; Practical Pictures, FlipZide Pictures; released by New Line Cinema
Directed by: David R. Ellis
Written by: Eric Bress
Cinematography by: Glen MacPherson
Music by: Brian Tyler
Sound: Jeffrey Haupt
Editing: Mark Stevens
Art Direction: Scott Plauche
Costumes: Claire Breaux
Production Design: Jaymes Hinkle
MPAA rating: R
Running time: 75 minutes

REVIEWS
Catsoulis, Jeanette. *New York Times.* September 1, 2009.
Duralde, Alonso. *MSNBC.* August 28, 2009.

Gilchrist, Todd. *Sci Fi Fire.* August 28, 2009.

Goldstein, Gary. *Los Angeles Times.* September 1, 2009.

Mintzer, Jordan. *Variety.* August 26, 2009.

Pais, Matt. *Metromix.com.* August 28, 2009.

Sobczynski, Peter. *EFilmCritic.com.* August 28, 2009.

Tallerico, Brian. *MovieRetriever.com.* August 28, 2009.

Weinberg, Scott. *FEARNet.* August 28, 2009.

Wilson, Staci Lynne. *Horror.com.* August 28, 2009.

QUOTES

Hare Krishna: "Death is not the end."

TRIVIA

The woman at the check-in desk at the airport tells Alex that the plane leaves at 9:25, which is the same as his birthday (September 25th). When he gets on the plane he sits in seat I (which is the ninth letter of the alphabet) and the seat is in row 25.

FIRED UP!

2 guys. 300 girls. You do the math.
—Movie tagline

Box Office: $17 million

There is nothing new or original about *Fired Up*, a teen movie about two high school studs who decide to sign up for summer cheerleader camp to get a wider choice of girls. The stereotypical gender attitudes in this film would have fit into a movie from the 1950s or 1960s. In that sense, but no other, you could say *Fired Up* is timeless. But it is hard to believe a script (written by Freedom Jones) that is this unoriginal and lacking in ideas could have gotten made in the twenty-first century.

First-time director Will Gluck was executive producer and co-creator of the television series *The Loop*, and he brought along a number of actors from that show for the movie, including Eric Christian Olsen as Nick Brady, a boastful high school football star who has dated and bedded down almost every willing girl at Gerald Ford High School. His best friend, also a football player, is Shawn Colfax (Nicholas D'Agosto), who at first reluctantly goes along with his idea to skip two weeks of football camp to enroll at cheerleader camp. He, too, is focused on girls, but he's a little less self-centered.

Because their school's squad has been a loser in previous years' cheerleading camp competitions, and because all the good cheerleading squads have males on their teams, Nick and Shawn are welcomed into camp by the faculty advisor (after Nick shamelessly flatters

her). They are not as welcomed by the head cheerleader, Carly (Sarah Roemer), but it is doubtful that anyone would be surprised that the initial tension is replaced by a budding romance between Shawn and Carly.

Of course, there's a rival for Carly's affection—a wealthy young med student stereotypically presented as being unworthy of her love. Gluck reveals the shocking truth by having Shawn and Nick hiding out in some bushes, where they overhear the gigolo talking about how he really does not love Carly and just keeps her around to please his family while he chases other skirts.

This obvious exchange displays the lack of inventiveness in Gluck's direction. Every plot development (and there are precious few of them) is nakedly displayed and telegraphed so that the most obtuse viewer can catch up. The level of humor is similarly dumbed down. Viewers are supposed to laugh, for instance, when the head cheerleader leads the camp in an acronym for "Fired Up!"

This is nothing but junk food aimed at adolescent males whose idea of relationships is leering, ogling, and preening. But even if one grades *Fired Up* on a curve, measuring it against other popular teen movies, it fails. It is not quite as raunchy, but neither is it halfway as clever, as a Judd Apatow film. The two protagonists have absolutely no depth or nuance; they really are just two egotistical guys on the make. And Gluck is not interested in the dynamics of how they get girls; most of the females are bimbos who simply fall into their arms. Relationships are not challenging or complicated; they are simply "boy meets girl and the chemistry takes over." Not that the movie gives us much about the romances or lustful liaisons; there is a little nudity but nothing beyond that. It's as if the coupling has already lost interest to the boys because it is merely the conquest itself that counts, not what follows.

Light, thin, and as superficial as a locally made TV commercial, *Fired Up* might be fun to ridicule if it did not take itself so seriously. There is a complete lack of irony or knowing humor, and that's where it most resembles a Frankie Avalon movie of the early 1960s. Gluck romps merrily along without seeing the need to create any problems for his characters; one day follows the next at camp, as if a film were merely a series of skits. Oh, of course there is a showdown with a snotty rival school's squad, but that expected plot twist plays out as predictably as the romance in the film.

Olsen's performance is the only thing that makes *Fired Up* even remotely interesting. Like the young Sean Penn character in *Fast Times at Ridgemont High*, Olsen's Nick is as true hedonist, and the actor occasionally makes his obnoxiousness funny. He plays Nick straight and over-the-top, even though the idea that a male could behave this way and not get reprimanded by most of the girls he courts is the most ludicrous thing in this silly movie.

Michael Betzold

CREDITS

Shawn Colfax: Nicholas D'Agosto
Nick Brady: Eric Christian Olsen
Carly: Sarah Roemer
Diora: Molly Sims
Biranca: Danneel Harris
Gwyneth: AnnaLynne McCord
Coach Byrnes: Philip Baker Hall
Coach Keith: John Michael Higgins
Poppy: Juliette Goglia
Dr. Rick: David Walton
Brewster: Adhir Kalyan
Origin: USA
Language: English
Released: 2009
Production: Charles Weinstock, Matthew Gross, Peter Jaysen; Screen Gems, Moving Pictures AMG, Gross Entertainment; released by Sony Pictures Entertainment
Directed by: Will Gluck
Written by: Freedom Jones
Cinematography by: Thomas Ackerman
Music by: Richard Gibbs
Sound: Douglas Axtell
Music Supervisor: Wende Crowley
Editing: Tracey Wadmore-Smith
Art Direction: Bo Johnson
Costumes: Mynka Draper
Production Design: Marcia Hinds
MPAA rating: PG-13
Running time: 89 minutes

REVIEWS

Berkshire, Geoff. *Metromix.com.* February 19, 2009.
Childress, Erik. *eFilmCritic.com.* February 19, 2009.
Dargis, Manohla. *New York Times.* February 19, 2009.
Ebert, Roger. *Chicago Sun-Times.* February 19, 2009.
Hillis, Aaron. *Village Voice.* February 18, 2009.
Koehler, Robert. *Variety.* February 11, 2009.
Long, Tom. *Detroit News.* February 20, 2009.
Olsen, Mark. *Los Angeles Times.* February 19, 2009.
Phillips, Michael. *Chicago Tribune.* February 20, 2009.
Rechtshaffen, Michael. *Hollywood Reporter.* February 12, 2009.

QUOTES

Shawn Colfax: "Screw football, let's go cheer!"

The film was written by four writers who were credited simply as "Freedom Jones."

(500) DAYS OF SUMMER

Boy meets girl. Boy falls in love. Girl doesn't.
—Movie tagline

Box Office: $32 million

At a time when new takes on the romantic comedy genre amount to farther-reaching liaison locations (Alaska!) and characters with increasingly ambiguous professions (a cruciverbalist!), *(500) Days of Summer* feels like a breath of fresh air. It does away with weighty minutia and goes back to the roots of the genre by exploring why and how we fall in—and out of—love. But in as much as this return to form is refreshing, *(500) Days of Summer* also suffers from cleverness-overload, possessing one too many too-hip-for-their-own-good narrative devices and a female lead who is more blah than breathtaking. Luckily, thanks to a charismatic male lead, a few sweep-you-off-your-feet montages and a desire to step outside the gift-wrapped romantic comedy package, the highlights outweigh the slip-ups in this charming piece of cinema.

(500) Days of Summer tells the story of Tom (Joseph Gordon-Levitt) and the object of his affection, Summer (Zooey Deschanel). Tom is in a quarter-life crisis, as a charming architect turned greeting card-writing hipster (read: accessorized with thin ties, Converse shoes, form-fitting pants and armed with a certifiable knowledge of all things vintage cool such as The Smiths and *Knight Rider*). Summer is a free-spirited, witty beauty who makes high-waisted jeans look natural and who can match Tom in 1980s trivia. But as the voice-over for the film mentions right off the bat, *(500) Days of Summer* is not a typical love story. The "500 Days" refers to the amount of time that Tom spends getting to know, falling in love with and obsessing about Summer. Though she features prominently in the narrative, this is really Tom's—and by extension Gordon-Levitt's—movie. It is through Tom that writers Scott Neustadter and Michael H. Weber dissect all aspects of the perilous journey to coupledom. And it is their no-holds-barred approach that makes *(500) Days of Summer* such a winning film.

As audiences watch Tom literally burst into song as a result of falling in love, the emotional high he is riding is palpable and relatable. We get so caught up in his drama that we root for him despite the fact that he has entered into a relationship with a girl who may just not be that into him. Tom's desire to make Summer into his perfect other half and to believe he can change her is what makes him such a watchable everyman. Neustadter and Weber get into Tom's head to the point of split-screen contrasts of how a scene is playing out in Tom's imagination versus real life. The result is both delightful and eerie because it's familiar. The added bonus is to have Gordon-Levitt as the guide on this journey. He navigates infatuation with wide-eyed puppy-dog awe and heartbreak with a pitch perfect mix of anger and depression. We watch him analyze conversations, looks and touches and we are right there with him because he captures the hope/devastation mix so well—and because we have all been there.

It's too bad then that Summer is, by contrast, a distant and unsympathetic character. She is the embodiment of the recently overly-pop-culturized manic pixie dream girl, a poster girl for the indie rock scene who is completely confident in her noncommittal-ness and just alluring enough to hide the fact that she's not sure who she is. Deschanel tries to breathe life into Summer and the actresses' inherent sparkle provides some pull, but it's not enough. Even though Summer exists primarily to propel Tom through his romantic coming-of-age odyssey, it would have helped if the audience could connect with her as well.

Unfortunately, Summer's scope of character is just one of the elements that attests to the overpowering over-hip vibe of the film. At times it feels like the combined wit and savvy of the team behind it makes the film too clever for its own good. Winks and nudges that allude more to the quirky yet hip pop-culture knowledge and film-school lexicon of the writing team, rather than attributed to the characters in the film, is a bit over the top. Can Tom really be both architect and artist as well as gifted karaoke-er and *Knight Rider* quiz master? It's almost as if the film is as interested in being a staple of pop culture as it is in being a solid film.

Director Marc Webb glosses over these little writing bumps however and gives us a spirited and visually delightful experience. He keeps the non-linear narrative focused and flowing with delightful animated cues and keeps Tom emotionally engaging and front and center. Ironically, the result seems to be a *Say Anything* for a new generation, which means that Tom will be going down in pop history after all.

Joanna Topor MacKenzie

CREDITS

Tom: Joseph Gordon-Levitt
Summer: Zooey Deschanel
McKenzie: Geoffrey Arend
Rachel: Chloe Grace Moretz

Paul: Matthew Grey Gubler
Vance: Clark Gregg
Alison: Rachel Boston
Origin: USA
Language: English
Released: 2009
Production: Mason Novick, Steven J. Wolfe, Jessica Tuchinsky, Mark Waters; Watermark; released by Fox Searchlight
Directed by: Marc Webb
Written by: Scott Neustadter, Michael H. Weber
Cinematography by: Eric Steelberg
Music by: Mychael Danna, Rob Simonsen
Sound: Lori Dovi
Editing: Alan Edward Bell
Art Direction: Charles Varga Jr.
Costumes: Hope Hannafin
Production Design: Laura Fox
MPAA rating: PG-13
Running time: 95 minutes

REVIEWS

Berkshire, Geoff. *Metromix.com.* July 15, 2009.
Burr, Ty. *Boston Globe.* July 16, 2009.
Childress, Erik. *eFilmCritic.* July 15, 2009.
Ebert, Roger. *Chicago Sun-Times.* July 16, 2009.
Fear, David. *Time Out New York.* July 15, 2009.
McCarthy, Todd. *Variety.* July 16, 2009.
Scott, A.O. *New York Times.* July 17, 2009.
Stevens, Dana. *Slate.* July 16, 2009.
Tallerico, Brian. *MovieRetriever.com.* July 17, 2009.
Tobias, Scott. *AV Club.* July 16, 2009.

QUOTES

Tom: "I love her smile. I love her hair. I love her knees. I love how she licks her lips before she talks. I love her heart-shaped birthmark on her neck. I love it when she sleeps."

TRIVIA

Paul says "humjob" instead of "blowjob" to avoid an "R" rating.

AWARDS

Ind. Spirit 2010: Screenplay
Nomination:
Golden Globes 2010: Actor—Mus./Comedy (Gordon-Levitt), Film—Mus./Comedy
Ind. Spirit 2010: Actor (Gordon-Levitt), Film
Writers Guild 2009: Orig. Screenplay.

FIVE MINUTES OF HEAVEN

To face the future, they must face the past.
—Movie tagline

The title *Five Minutes of Heaven* refers to the time it takes for a person to seize the opportunity for revenge by killing another person and basking in the heavenly relief once it's over. The man who craves those five minutes is Joe Griffin (James Nesbitt), who in Northern Ireland in 1975 witnessed his brother Jim getting killed when he was just a boy. The murderer was a teenage hired assassin committing his first kill. Now an adult, the lone gunmen-turned-retribution-guru Alistair Little (Liam Neeson) feels the full guilt-ridden affects his cold-blooded acts have had on his psyche and is more than willing to confront the brother of the first man he killed, knowing full well he might not be forgiven. Will Joe get his Five Minutes with Alistair? Will Alistair be granted forgiveness? Do either of them deserve what they want? Therein lies the compelling paradox that *Five Minutes of Heaven* does not solve easily.

The movie uses the real-life assassination as a springboard for this discussion. The real-life Alistair Little really did shoot Jim Griffin repeatedly, as Joe watched in horror. That part is true. The rest of the film is a fictionalized account of what might happen if the two were put in the same room today for a first-time, sit-down discussion before a television crew, whose sole purpose appears to be more sensationalism than pure journalism. The suspense of the film, however, is not what they would say, but if they could actually bring themselves to enter the same room knowing what deeply rooted emotions might come to surface and the consequences of uncontrollable urges, mainly Joe's. Even with a TV crew acting as a buffer between the two men, revenge remains a possibility and justice remains blind.

The story is told equally through the point of view of both men. Alistair is more introspective, with a zen-like calmness. Joe sees nothing genuine about Alistair's newfound sense of purpose of helping those who bear the guilt of committing wrongful acts. Joe only sees the killer and cannot fathom why Alistair only served twelve years in prison for the murder. A big portion of the film takes place in a large house where the filming of the TV show will take place. Joe sits in one room actively denouncing Alistair's good name every chance he gets while Alistair (in one beautiful single-take shot) films a seemingly rehearsed lamenting of the crime. Alistair's agenda consists of nothing more than listening to Joe, who has his own ulterior motives for the meeting.

But Joe's motives are not as shallow as an-eye-for-an-eye. Joe himself has borne the guilt of his own brother's murder, thanks in large part to his mother who never let Joe forget that he could have somehow stopped Alistair from pulling the trigger. As a child, Joe could only stand and watch with his jaw agape while Alistair's bullets flew through the living room window, completely oblivious he was being watched by young Joe. All he can

think about now is his mother laying blame on him for not stepping in.

It is this layer of the story that gives *Five Minutes of Heaven* its real weight. At the start of the film, Alistair's voiceover tells us that in order for us to know why he did what he did we have to look at who he was at the time and what role he wanted to play in the Troubles of Northern Ireland, circa 1975. The structure of *Five Minutes of Heaven* almost plays out as though Joe's reasons for wanting to kill Alistair will also have more meaning when the audience sees his own anger and guilt finally boil to the surface after seething for decades. The audience is meant to have some degree of sympathy for both men. Alistair's act of murder and later redemption is fully understood at the beginning of the film, but if Joe were to murder Alistair out of revenge, would the audience still sympathize? After all, both (potential) killers have been fully humanized.

Obviously, the performances by Neeson and Nesbitt are major components to the success in deconstructing these two men. Neeson exudes just enough remorse and shame while showing signs that he might be feigning all of it. It's as though Alistair might be putting up a false front for the public while searching for something deep within himself and knowing he has yet to come close to finding it. Nesbitt, while less subtle, still manages to keep us guessing about his character's motivations and willingness to follow through. He gives a fierce performance that gives the film its electricity.

The questions this movie poses are meant to be debated long after it ends, and it is to filmmaker Oliver Hirschbiegel's credit that he keeps the drama focused and the suspense heart-pounding so as not to lose the viewer to long-winded and heavy-handed diatribes. It's a refined, understated and mostly dialogue-driven work that plays like a thriller. One could easily make the assumption that these two men will eventually meet on this TV show, emotions will run high and at least one man will break down crying, but *Five Minutes of Heaven* has no interest in taking those kinds of cheap shots. Instead, Hirschbiegel and screenwriter Guy Hibbert take bold steps to eliminate any obvious sentiment, right down to the barely audible last line of dialogue.

Collin Souter

CREDITS

Alistair Little: Liam Neeson
Joe Griffen: James Nesbitt
Young Alistair Little: Mark David
Young Joe: Kevin O'Neill
Vika: Anamaria Marinca

Michael: Richard Dormer
Origin: Great Britain, Ireland
Language: English
Released: 2009
Production: Eoin O'Callaghan, Stephen Wright; Ruby Films, Big Fish Films, Element Films; released by IFC Films
Directed by: Oliver Hirschbiegel
Written by: Guy Hibbert
Cinematography by: Ruairi O'Brien
Music by: David Holmes, Leo Abrahams
Sound: Ronan Hill
Editing: Hans Funck
Art Direction: Mark Lowry, Gillian Devenney
Costumes: Maggie Donnelly
MPAA rating: Unrated
Running time: 89 minutes

REVIEWS

Adams, Sam. *AV Club.* August 20, 2009.
Dargis, Manohla. *New York Times.* August 21, 2009.
Fear, David. *Time Out New York.* August 19, 2009.
Goldstein, Gary. *Los Angeles Times.* August 28, 2009.
Harvey, Dennis. *Variety.* April 23, 2009.
Honeycutt, Kirk. *Hollywood Reporter.* August 18, 2009.
Pais, Matt. *Metromix.com.* September 10, 2009.
Rizov, Vadim. *Village Voice.* August 18, 2009.
Schwarzbaum, Lisa. *Entertainment Weekly.* August 26, 2009.
Weinberg, Scott. *Cinematical.* March 3, 2009.

QUOTES

Alistair Little: "They need their own people to say no."

FOOD, INC.

You'll never look at dinner the same way again.
—Movie tagline

Box Office: $4 million

Watching director Robert Kenner's powerhouse, revelatory *Food, Inc.*, justly short-listed for Academy Award® Best Documentary Feature consideration, one comes to realize just how much of our diet is outside our personal control, almost no matter how healthy we aim to be. Unless you grow and locally source all of your own food, we are each, to varying degrees, prisoners of a system in which giant corporations like McDonald's (to use but one example, since it is the world's largest purchaser of beef) can virtually dictate the terms by which cows are raised all across the United States. This means that even if you are not actually pulling into the drive-thru for a Big Mac®, you are apt to purchase

ground beef from cows fed with corn, something they were not biologically designed to eat.

The astounding ubiquity of corn and its many spin-off uses, chief among them high-fructose corn syrup, serves as the narrative leaping-off point for *Food, Inc.* Featuring interviews with experts such as *Fast Food Nation* author Eric Schlosser and *The Omnivore's Dilemma* scribe Michael Pollan, as well as forward-thinking social entrepreneurs like Polyface Farms' Joe Salatin and Stonyfield Farms' Gary Hirschberg, who serve as examples of businessmen trying to point their companies in directions that offer increased healthiness as well as transparency, *Food, Inc.* highlights how the governmental subsidization of corn massively affects food production and choice. By lifting the veil on our nation's food industry, Kenner exposes the highly mechanized underbelly that has been hidden from the sanitized, pastoral fantasy—big red barns, white picket fences, rolling green hills and happy farmers coexisting with animals that enjoy happy existences before being led placidly to slaughter—consumers have been, ahem, fed. It is an example of Americans willfully embracing blissful ignorance over informed consent with regard to the manufacturing and processing of items we utilize and consume.

In the wake of Michael Moore's numerous box office successes and Al Gore's Oscar®-winning *An Inconvenient Truth* (2006), politically active nonfiction films have a certain cachet they did not have a decade ago. Apart from its thought-provoking value in this arena, though, what helps truly distinguish *Food, Inc.* are three things. First is the polished sheen of the movie's production; there is just a pinch of animation and some of the same sort of wry, pop vibrancy that helped make *Super Size Me* (2004) a commercial hit with audiences disinclined to agree with what could be argued are its dietetic politics. Second, there is a counterbalancing optimism as to how to make positive changes, so that the movie does not come across as hopeless. And third, there is true heart. In fact, the inclusion of a story strand concentrating on a Colorado mother who lost her two-year-old son to E. coli from a hamburger gives *Food, Inc.* a tangible emotional punch that a lot of mainstream dramas, let alone like-minded documentaries, simply do not have.

In revealing surprising truths about what goes into the foods we eat and how they are produced, the film not only makes obvious links between our high-caloric modern diets and rising obesity, heart disease and adult-onset diabetes rates, but also the relative collective impotence of our government's main regulatory agencies, the USDA and FDA. In clear, concise terms, Kenner correlates how efficiencies achieved in food production and packaging are precariously built on a house of cards, since the trade-off comes via a food supply now controlled by an ever-dwindling handful of corporations that often put profit ahead of consumer health and the livelihood of the American farmer.

Perhaps most chillingly emblematic of this erosion in strict oversight and separation of business interests and those of the general collective well-being is found in Monsanto, whose genetic modification of a soybean resistant to the weed-killing chemical spray Roundup® has given them a patent on the seed. With skull-crushing efficiency, including lawsuits and private investigator enforcers, the company has driven small farmers who do not adopt their seed out of business, growing their market share from two to 90 percent in just over a decade. In a few years, as shocking as the prospect sounds to the normal consumer, it may be possible that regular, unaltered soybeans will not be domestically available at all.

No matter how much of a cinephile one is, it is reasonable to say that only a handful of films in any given year might actually impact your life. And it is a tough thing to be interesting and progressive, persuasive and affecting, all in almost equal measure. Yet Kenner pulls it off. *Food, Inc.* is definitely not the sort of film that puts a feel-good spring in your step, but it appeals to both the head and heart in such a clear-eyed fashion as to make you want to take better care of yourself—as well as those around you. And that is a powerful thing.

Brent Simon

CREDITS

Himself: Gary Hirshberg
Himself: Michael Pollan
Himself: Troy Roush
Himself: Joel Salatin
Himself: Eric Schlosser
Origin: USA
Language: English
Released: 2008
Production: Robbie Kenner, Elise Pearlstein; Participant Media, River Road Entertainment; released by Magnolia Pictures
Directed by: Robert Kenner
Written by: Robert Kenner, Elise Pearlstein, Kim Roberts
Cinematography by: Richard Pearce
Music by: Mark Adler
Sound: Steuart Pearce, Susumu Tokunow
Editing: Kim Roberts
MPAA rating: PG
Running time: 94 minutes

REVIEWS

Anderson, John. *Variety.* June 15, 2009.
Dargis, Manohla. *New York Times.* June 12, 2009.
Denby, David. *New Yorker.* June 22, 2009.
Ebert, Roger. *Chicago Sun-Times.* June 18, 2009.
Edelstein, David. *New York Magazine.* June 8, 2009.
Gleiberman, Owen. *Entertainment Weekly.* June 10, 2009.
Goldstein, Gary. *Los Angeles Times.* June 12, 2009.
Long, Tom. *Detroit News.* June 26, 2009.
Phillips, Michael. *Chicago Tribune.* June 18, 2009.
Travers, Peter. *Rolling Stone.* June 11, 2009.

QUOTES

Michael Pollan: "There are no seasons in the American supermarket. Now there are tomatoes all year round, grown halfway around the world, picked when it was green, and ripened with ethylene gas. Although it looks like a tomato, it's kind of a notional tomato. I mean, it's the idea of a tomato."

TRIVIA

Neither Eric Schlosser, Michael Pollan, or director Robert Kenner are vegetarians, despite the film's spotlight on meat cultivation and processing in the United States.

AWARDS

Nomination:

Oscars 2009: Feature Doc.
Ind. Spirit 2010: Feature Doc.
Directors Guild 2009: Doc. Director (Kenner).

THE FOURTH KIND

There are four kinds of alien encounters. The fourth kind is abduction.
—Movie tagline

Box Office: $25.5 million

Moviegoers of a certain age with a certain predilection for schlock cinema will no doubt recall with fondness the output of the late, great Sunn Classics studio. For those who were not around or not paying attention at the time, Sunn Classics was a Utah-based production company that specialized in low-budget pseudo-documentaries during the latter half of the 1970s backed by breathless ad campaigns that promised incontrovertible proof that there was indeed life after death, that Noah's Ark actually existed and that there really were aliens stashed away in Hanger 18. The only trouble is that when people actually went to these films at their local theater—which were rented out by Sunn themselves so that they could collect all the box-office receipts—the films turned out to be slipshod constructions composed mostly of nonsensical interviews with "experts" sitting in front of bookshelves heaped with books that appeared to have never been touched, "dramatic recreations" featuring no-name actors trying to keep straight faces and shocking evidence that never quite managed to conclusively prove much of anything. Whether the people behind the new alien abduction thriller *The Fourth Kind* ever saw any of the Sunn Classics epics is unknown but, for all intents and purposes, the film looks and feels like a full-scale homage to them, albeit with a higher caliber of acting talent than they could ever muster and with a slightly higher effects budget. However, the most significant element that it has in common with those earlier efforts is that it is one of the silliest and most preposterous things to appear on a movie screen in recent memory and that anyone foolish enough to pay money to go see it under the delusion that they will be encountering definitive proof that "We Are Not Alone" will pretty much get exactly what they deserve.

It kicks off with star Milla Jovovich introducing the film and telling the audience that everything that they are about to see has been corroborated by tapes, videos and sworn testimony in a speech that will remind some viewers of the way that the immortal Criswell kicked off the legendary *Plan 9 from Outer Space* (1959)—the only real difference is that it could be argued that Criswell had better writers. Jovovich plays Dr. Abigail Emily Tyler, a psychologist who, although still reeling from the unsolved murder of her husband two months earlier and the subsequent hysterical blindness of her young daughter, nevertheless is determined to return to her practice in Nome, Alaska. Before long, she begins to notice that many of her patients are showing similar symptoms: they claim to be awoken in the middle of the night by white owls perched outside their homes but when she puts them under hypnosis, they fall into hysterics at the memory of things that they cannot quite recall in detail and refuse to talk about anyway. Even though she tries to find rational explanations as to what is going on, she gradually becomes convinced that these patients have been abducted by aliens and that she herself was a victim as well. Naturally, the local sheriff (Will Patton) is highly skeptical of her claims, especially when those patients begin turning up dead or badly injured, but Abigail continues in her efforts until her own daughter is apparently abducted by the alien intruders as well.

Writer-director Olatunde Osunsanmi has inserted alleged corroborating evidence into the body of the film itself, albeit in the most incredibly awkward manner possible. He gives us audiotapes and videotapes that were reputedly rolling as key events in the story were unfolding and even frames the film with an on-camera interview that he conducts with the real and honest-to-goodness Dr. Abigail Emily Tyler herself under the

auspices of the renowned Chapman University. Not only does he present us with this material as a way of proving that everything is true, he often gives us a split-screen approach in which the recreation with Jovovich & Co. is playing on one half of the screen while the "authentic" footage is on the other. It all sounds utterly astounding but, without giving too much away, it should be noted that when it comes to the good parts that everyone is waiting for, the tapes that we see are about as revealing as a shower door in a PG-13 movie.

The whole gimmick of playing the "real" footage alongside the recreations may have sounded like an intriguing idea in theory, but it is a complete disaster in practice because it only serves to further muddle material that is not exactly clear to begin with. Since it is obvious right from the start that the whole thing is pretty much a fraud (as even the most cursory Googling will quickly reveal), it means that viewers are essentially being asked to watch a low-budget horror film and its glossier, though no less cheesy, remake at the same time. As things progress, it gets sillier and sillier because whatever sense of tension and paranoia that is being developed in the "real" footage is not being echoed in the recreations, which largely consist of generally reliable actors who seem to be channeling all of their talents to keep from bursting out into laughter at the nonsense that they are being asked to perform.

With its combination of embarrassingly bad performances, a bewildering and needlessly complicated stylistic gambit and scientific conclusions so goofy that they would give Peter Venkman of *Ghostbusters* (1984) pause, *The Fourth Kind* is brainless junk from start to finish that is so beyond the pale that the biggest mystery is why a putatively reputable movie studio like Universal would have anything to do with such a shoddy con job in the first place. Outside of the minor entertainment value derived from the various hoops that the film goes through in order to explain why you have never heard about these amazing events and why the surviving participants did not hit the talk show circuit in order to verify their claims, the best thing about the film is that if aliens from another world ever do come to Earth and get a look at it, they may decide that any species capable of creating anything this dumb is probably too stupid to probe and conquer in the first place.

Peter Sobczynski

CREDITS

Abbey: Milla Jovovich
Tommy: Corey Johnson
Scott Stracinsky: Enzo Cilenti
Cindy Stracinsky: Alisha Seaton

Abel Campos: Elias Koteas
Sheriff August: Will Patton
Origin: USA
Language: English
Released: 2009
Production: Paul Brooks, Joe Carnahan, Terry Robbins; Gold Circle Films, Dead Crow Productions, Focus Films; released by Universal Pictures
Directed by: Olatunde Osunsanmi
Written by: Olatunde Osunsanmi
Cinematography by: Lorenzo Senatore
Music by: Atli Orvarsson
Sound: Svetlosar Georgiev
Editing: Paul Covington
Art Direction: Axel Nicolet
Costumes: Johnetta Boone
Production Design: Carlos DaSilva
MPAA rating: PG-13
Running time: 98 minutes

REVIEWS

Biancolli, Amy. *Houston Chronicle.* November 6, 2009.
Corliss, Richard. *Time Magazine.* November 6, 2009.
Ebert, Roger. *Chicago Sun-Times.* November 5, 2009.
Foundas, Scott. *Village Voice.* November 3, 2009.
Nelson, Rob. *Variety.* November 4, 2009.
Pais, Matt. *Metromix.com.* November 5, 2009.
Rea, Steven. *Philadelphia Inquirer.* November 5, 2009.
Tobias, Scott. *AV Club.* November 5, 2009.
O'Sullivan, Michael. *Washington Post.* November 6, 2009.
Tallerico, Brian. *MovieRetriever.com.* November 6, 2009.

QUOTES

Abbey Tyler: "Please be advised, that some of what you're about to see is extremely disturbing."

TRIVIA

The real Nome is 51% Native American, but there are no indigenous characters in the film (at least none that are stated to be).

FRIDAY THE 13TH

Welcome to Crystal Lake.
    —Movie tagline

Box Office: $65 million

All you ever needed to know about Jason, you can learn from Marcus Nispel's *Friday The 13th.* This remake of the 1980s classic horror movie tries hard to be more than just a montage of promiscuous teens getting done-

in. Screenwriters Mark Swift and Damian Shannon also make the attempt to get into Jason's head. Jason's not just a kill-happy psycho, as all the other Jason movies would have you believe, they propose. He's really just a neglected backwoods boy with mommy issues taking his rage over her untimely demise out on anyone who comes near Crystal Lake, the summer camp where everything went wrong for a young Jason. Unfortunately, their attempt at an origin story falls flat at crucial moments and doesn't really work with what we've come to know about Jason. Still, Nispel knows gore and his skills at gross death scenes make up for a silly and tired plot.

This redux is really three movies in one. We start with a flashback to 1980 starring a young Jason and his vindictive mom. Then, even before the opening credits roll, Jason accumulates a significant body count courtesy of a group of co-eds who go looking for a secret cannabis crop at Crystal Lake and make a wrong turn onto Jason's turf. The present day storyline centers on yet another group of promiscuous party-hungry teens who come out to a lake house to enjoy a weekend of unsupervised debauchery. Their good times are spoiled by a disheveled yet handsome motorcyclist on the search for his sister who went missing around the area six weeks ago (yes, she was with the pot-hunting crowd). Taking a cue from Eli Roth, the screenwriters make sure to get the attractive cast high and naked as fast as possible before the blood starts to gush, ooze and spew. Too bad that their take never quite reaches the level of brash campiness with regard to plot and characters that Roth was able to attain.

The fun in watching morally questionable youths get terrorized onscreen comes from knowing something about them. Understandably, horror films are not the stuff of character studies, but the maximum fun comes from at least a little character development: we want to cheer when the jerk, cheating boyfriend finally gets it; feel a little bummed out that the cute sidekick had to die; and really hope that the hot, but straight-and-narrow heroine running for her life makes it out alive. This *Friday the 13th* focuses more on the gore rather than on any fragment of characterization and storyline. The characters don't even inhabit the land of cliché, which would at least make for a "so bad it's good" movie. They bypass predictable and head straight for blah. The guys are either jerks or completely dismissible, and the girls are pouty or angry, so much so that there is no resonance as we watch them get butchered. Even the sex lacks a level of fun because the characters on screen don't seem to be having a good time doing it.

Swift, Shannon and, to an extent, Nispel try to make up for these shortcomings by directing our attention toward Jason—as if exploring Jason's motivation would somehow make *Friday The 13th* a better horror movie. They propose that Jason not only watched his mother get murdered, but that he's been in search of someone who reminds him of her ever since. Yes, Jason is an underground-dwelling kidnapper holding on to his dead mother's locket for dear life. They also try to imbue Jason finding his famous goalie mask with meaning (it has none). None of this works because we don't want to understand Jason as a person; we just want to see him wreck havoc. Not only do these character traits not ring true with what we've come to know about Jason, all they succeed in doing is slowing down the pace of the movie.

Still, in the hands of Nispel, *Friday The 13th* is slick, and as ungrounded as it may be to superfans, Swift and Shannon transform Jason into a more inventive killer. Nispel maximizes the gross-out factor of each kill scene, drawing out the grizzliness of the weapons used and the carnage ravaged with high production value. And Swift and Shannon give Jason the opportunity to flex his psycho muscle by swapping his machete out for, well, anything within reach. Diehard Jason fans might not be impressed with this makeover, but those who are looking for a new take on an iconic antihero—and are willing to forgo plot and pacing for it—will find reason to squirm in their seats.

Joanna Topor MacKenzie

CREDITS

Clay: Jared Padalecki
Jenna: Danielle Panabaker
Whitney: Amanda Righetti
Trent: Travis Van Winkle
Jason Voorhees: Derek Mears
Chewie: Aaron Yoo
Chelsea: Willa Ford
Pamela Voorhees: Nana Visitor
Origin: USA
Language: English
Released: 2009
Production: Andrew Form, Brad Fuller, Michael Bay, Sean S. Cunningham; New Line Cinema, Platinum Dunes; released by Warner Bros.
Directed by: Marcus Nispel
Written by: Mark Swift, Damian Shannon
Cinematography by: Daniel Pearl
Music by: Steve Jablonsky
Sound: Stacy Brownrigg
Editing: Ken Blackwell
Art Direction: John Frick
Costumes: Mari-An Ceo
Production Design: Jeremy Conway

MPAA rating: R
Running time: 99 minutes

REVIEWS

Childress, Erik. *EFilmCritic.com.* February 12, 2009.
Ebert, Roger. *Chicago Sun-Times.* February 12, 2009.
Kennedy, Lisa. *Denver Post.* February 13, 2009.
Lane, Nathan. *New York Times.* February 13, 2009.
Nelson, Rob. *Variety.* February 13, 2009.
Olsen, Mark. *Los Angeles Times.* February 13, 2009.
Puig, Claudia. *USA Today.* February 13, 2009.
Rechtshaffen, Michael. *Hollywood Reporter.* February 13, 2009.
Ridley, Jim. *Village Voice.* February 12, 2009.
Tallerico, Brian. *HollywoodChicago.com.* February 12, 2009.

QUOTES

Richie: "Do you know how many lakes are probably called Crystal Lake? It's like Crystal Geyser, Crystal Water. Go to a supermarket. Every single bottled water is named 'Crystal' something."

TRIVIA

Warner Bros. (through its New Line Cinema label) distributed the film in North America while Paramount distributed it in most other territories. Ironically, and probably coincidentally, the 1980 original was distributed by Paramount in North America, with international distribution being handled by Warner Bros.

FUNNY PEOPLE

George Simmons was prepared to die, but then a funny thing happened.
—Movie tagline

Box Office: $52 million

Looking back at the end of the decade, it is hard to imagine a more influential or ubiquitous figure in the world of comedy than Writer/Producer/Director Judd Apatow. With several impressive television credits under his belt (*The Ben Stiller Show*, *The Larry Sanders Show* and *Freaks and Geeks* among them), his career in film seemed all but assured, in spite of a few misfires early in his résumé. In 2004, he co-produced the Will Ferrell comedy *Anchorman: The Legend of Ron Burgundy*, a movie that had lukewarm box office appeal but would become an almost instant cult classic upon its release on video. But it was his directorial debut, *The 40-Year-Old Virgin*, that helped cement his status as a director to watch. In the wake of the success of those two films, Apatow had twelve movies in production between 2005 and 2009, two of which he directed, and most of them keeping a regular stable of actors and directors in rotation, many of whom had their careers launched by this boom in productivity.

Apatow certainly knows his subjects, so it's only fitting that he would close out the decade with a film called *Funny People*. Less of a typical "raunch-mantic" comedy and more of a character examination in the tradition of James L. Brooks, *Funny People* stars Adam Sandler as George Simmons, an incredibly successful comedian and movie star who learns he has cancer. Without a friend to confide in, he enlists the help of amateur comedian Ira Wright (Apatow regular Seth Rogen) to write jokes for him for a special fundraising event, but eventually hires him to become his full-time aid. Soon he informs Ira of his condition and insists that he not tell anyone. Of course, Ira cannot help but tell his live-in housemates (Jason Schwartzman and Jonah Hill) and keeps the job of maintaining George's schedule, writing him jokes and trying to live the role of "new best friend."

George's present state of melancholia, even before the cancer, is rather transparent. He has found fame and fortune not through his own talent as a stand-up, but through lame-brained, high concept comedies such as *My Best Friend Is A Robot*. With this as his artistic legacy and without a soul to talk to, George has to find a way to make peace with himself and the choices he has made, which can be the kiss of death for any comic. After all, how can one be truly funny when they remain happy with life and themselves?

Naturally, George looks back on his life and realizes he needs to make amends with his family, himself and the "one that got away," Laura (Apatow's wife, Leslie Mann), who has long since departed George's life and who is now married with children. Nevertheless, George pursues and catches up with her, and they both realize that the flame has not died out yet.

That would be enough for one movie, but Apatow manages to stretch the proceedings out to a whopping 146 minutes. Seth Rogen's character has not only a love interest of his own, but a semi-famous housemate who fights for her. When Sandler learns he is no longer sick, he continues to pursue Laura, which results in a prolonged third act that has an unnecessary and clichéd climax in an airport. Combine that with several montage sequences in the first two acts, and *Funny People* ends up showing signs of strain more than strength of character.

This should not be surprising for an Apatow film, considering his tendency to improvise on the set and the wealth of deleted footage and outtakes that accompany every DVD release. After all, he is partly responsible for creating a whole new film out of deleted scenes (*Anchor-man*'s direct-to-video sequel/remake, *Wake Up, Ron Burgundy*). But *Funny People* does not know where to cut and where to explore more fully. Simmons' quest to patch things up with his supposedly domineering father and estranged sister seems to wrap itself up a little too nicely and quickly, while a scene in which Laura's kids needlessly recite Cantonese with their father (Eric Bana) exists just so Seth Rogen can make a funny *Deer Hunter* joke.

Funny People also never quite justifies Apatow's own self-indulgence. The movie marks the second time he has cast his two young daughters in major roles, one of whom we see in a video of a recital where she sings "Memories," which we are supposed to find unquestionably adorable, so much so he repeats it over the end credits. We are also meant to marvel at just how many celebrities he can get into one setting, evidenced by a scene in which Sandler's character throws a no-more-cancer party for himself, with Ray Romano and Eminem (among others) in attendance. Apatow also wants us to know just how attractive his wife looks in tight jeans.

Yet in spite of its obvious flaws, *Funny People* manages to be highly watchable, thanks largely to its incredibly talented cast and the choice of having George go back to his old ways after the cancer ordeal. Sandler, who has already proven himself in dramatic roles, excels as Simmons, preferring to keep the audience and those around him at arms length as he closely ponders and reexamines his career choices and life experiences. Rogen also tries his best to create a new character for himself, that of a wide-eyed learner trying to do the right thing by George's will, instead of playing the lovable, pot-smoking shlub that has become his persona. Unfortunately, one scene in a restaurant where Rogen breaks down crying, fails to do anything but call Rogen's range into question (he does show more promise in 2009's *Observe and Report*).

Apatow tries to continue his winning streak of accurately depicting the behavior of men who seem to revel in their insecurities before reluctantly rising above them. Humor has always been defined as (among other things) a defense mechanism for self-aware outsiders, and his characters reflect that mindset perfectly. Where most romantic comedies give us perfectly quaffed alpha-males to root for, Apatow's films prefer to give us more down-to-earth, vulnerable and pop-culture-savvy protagonists that seem more like a cross between Albert Brooks and characters out of a Nick Hornby novel. This trait has become Apatow's specialty, but here that role (typically filled by Rogen) takes a backseat to Sandler's darker, more reserved George Simmons.

Like George, Sandler himself has a résumé filled with comedies much like the ones depicted and invented for this film—and he knows it. It goes to explain why he veers off to attempt more dramatic roles in films such as *Punch-Drunk Love, Reign Over Me* or James L. Brooks' equally muddled and similarly toned *Spanglish*. Here, Sandler has a tough balancing act. On one hand, he appears to be accepting critics at their word, that his comedies have been juvenile at best and not worth remembering. Yet the audience—presumably made up of people who have paid money to see those films and who have shown their appreciation for them when meeting Sandler—must still find a way to like George Simmons and have sympathy for him. George is nice and appreciative to the strangers he meets in airports, as is Sandler in real life. Unfortunately, the movie fails to fully explore how George really feels about the quality of his work and whether his audience should have demanded better from him. Sandler himself basically has to say to the paying audience of *Funny People*, "Thanks for my success...but why did you do it?"

Pushed as one of the bigger titles to be released in the summer of 2009, *Funny People* failed to truly connect with mass audiences. It was produced with a bloated budget of $75 million, unusually high for an Apatow production, which is normally shot in L.A. and with modest backdrops, this being no exception. It opened at number one, as expected, but quickly dropped out of the top ten within a month of its release, marking Apatow's second major disappointment of 2009 (the first being *Year One*, which he co-produced). Whether it was the unjustified length of the film, the dark subject matter, the ubiquity of the Apatow factory over the years or a combination of the three that kept audiences from being enthusiastic, it nevertheless depicted a director unafraid of taking a risk with his subject matter. The biggest risk of all for *Funny People*, however, proved to be a director spending a little too much time in his comfort zone.

Collin Souter

CREDITS

George Simmons: Adam Sandler
Ira Wright: Seth Rogen
Laura: Leslie Mann
Clarke: Eric Bana
Leo Koenig: Jonah Hill

Mark Taylor Jackson: Jason Schwartzman
Daisy Danby: Aubrey Plaza
Ingrid: Iris Apatow
Mabel: Maude Apatow
Chuck: RZA
Origin: USA
Language: English
Released: 2009
Production: Judd Apatow, Clayton Townsend, Barry Mendel; Relativity Media, Madison 23; released by Universal Pictures
Directed by: Judd Apatow
Written by: Judd Apatow
Cinematography by: Janusz Kaminski
Music by: Michael Andrews
Sound: John Pritchett
Music Supervisor: Jonathan Karp
Editing: Brent White, Craig Alpert
Art Direction: James F. Truesdale
Costumes: Nancy Steiner, Betsy Heimann
Production Design: Jefferson Sage
MPAA rating: R
Running time: 146 minutes

REVIEWS

Dargis, Manohla. *New York Times.* July 30, 2009.
Denby, David. *New Yorker.* July 27, 2009.
Ebert, Roger. *Chicago Sun-Times.* July 30, 2009.
Edelstein, David. *New York Magazine.* July 27, 2009.
Honeycutt, Kirk. *Hollywood Reporter.* July 25, 2009.
McCarthy, Todd. *Variety.* July 25, 2009.
Pais, Matt. *Metromix.com.* July 30, 2009.
Roeper, Richard. *RichardRoeper.com.* July 30, 2009.
Stevens, Dana. *Slate.* July 30, 2009.
Tallerico, Brian. *HollywoodChicago.com.* July 31, 2009.

QUOTES

Mark: "When my grandfather died, there was one candle next to his bed. And the candle started flickering. We all thought it was him going to Heaven, you know?"

TRIVIA

In *Knocked Up*, there is a scene where the guys are sitting around talking about that, if they "got laid," it was because of Eric Bana in *Munich*. Bana also stars in this film, and coincidentally the director of photography on both *Munich* and this film is Janusz Kaminski. Barry Mendel, one of the producers of *Munich*, is also a producer on this film as well.

G

GAMER

In the near future, you don't live to play...you'll play to live.
—Movie tagline

Box Office: $21 million

In the heyday of the 1980s video game revolution, there were two movies that were able to capture the zeitgeist of the moment and still exist within their own originality, unlike today when the words "based on the video game" are a sure sign of a project that is dead on arrival. The first of these films was *Tron* (1982), which also tapped into areas of computer animation never seen before. The other was *The Last Starfighter* (1984), also envisioning the obsessed gamer as hero for another world beyond ours. These were the days of *Pac-Man* and *Space Invaders* though, and as one character says in Mark Neveldine and Brian Taylor's latest, "the game must evolve." The gaming world of our 21st century is a markedly different beast with extreme violence and close-to-life scenarios of crime and war. The writing/directing duo have molded the landscape from light cycles to full-armored combat, but their ideas have only advanced a few years beyond those for which we now celebrate the 25th Anniversary. It would be simple enough to say that these auteurs of Ritalin cinema had just seen *The Running Man* (1987) a few too many times, but the truth is that Gamer can't even compare to the Emilio Estevez segment of *Nightmares* (1983).

Gamer depicts a future society in which gaming technology has reached beyond the limits of interactive play. Now players at home can control actual human beings from the comfort of their encompassing game rooms. At first it was "Society," which took the concept of *The Sims* to the worst ideas imagined by *Leisure Suit Larry* fetishists. Then came "Slayers," which, evidenced by its exact copy of the Spike TV logo, is a game for men but controlled by boys. The creator of both games is Ken Castle (Michael C. Hall), who helped develop the microchips that make the human volunteers susceptible to every whim, thought and spoken word controlled by us at home. Since Slayers is a no-holds-barred, shoot-em-up with real bullets and real death, who better than convicts and the dregs of society to participate?

The current champion of the game is Kable (Gerard Butler), just three battles away from receiving the full pardon promised for survival. While the details of his incarceration are never revealed, he has a family on the outside waiting for him, including a young daughter put into foster care and his wife, Angie (Amber Valletta), using herself as one of the surrogates in Society to make ends meet. Someone is trying to orchestrate Kable's demise though in the form of a brutish thug (Terry Crews) with "no strings attached." Kable is "played" by Simon (Logan Lerman), a 17-year-old all-star gamer who is about to get some help by a group of revolutionaries led by Chris 'Ludacris' Bridges and Alison Lohman, who want to see the human race left to its own devices.

Two-thousand nine already had its fill of attempting to resurrect the currently defunct big screen adaptation of Halo with the vastly superior *District 9* (2009). Where director Neill Blomkamp created a possible jumping off point for such a film, Neveldine & Taylor want to bring the battleground chaos front and center and show where

Doom (2005) went so dreadfully wrong. The problem with *Gamer* is that outside of the loosely presented social commentary that keeps invading the action's space, it has some of the poorest excuses for big screen action yet seen. Fashioned around a third person's perspective of Kable in action, there is not an ounce of satisfactory adrenaline even if you can decipher who's who and what's what. There are some head shots and torn limbs but no inclination as to objective. As gamers will tell you, simulations from *Halo* to *Rainbow Six* to *Call Of Duty* are as much about geography and strategy as they are about pulling the trigger. Neveldine and Taylor bring the same ADD-style of their *Grand Theft Auto*-inspired *Crank* films to the game-framed sequences of the first half, and it is an incalculable failure in judgment.

Working from their own story-challenged script, the directors never seem to take off running with the potential insanity of being controlled in wartime by another human being—either literally or philosophically. They actually simplify things by having Simon only control Kable's body movements and hand-to-hand encounters. The gun is left solely in Kable's capable fingers. At one point as this crucial detail is explained: the concept of a "ping" is introduced, involving the rumored delay time between a player and his commands to their battle-scarred avatar when in full control. This element is never explored. All we know is that the convict must make it to the safe zone (i.e. the next level when game play can be saved without starting over). What about the other at-home players, though? There have to be some, right? All of these convicts are being shipped in and out of the game zone, but the only one we follow is Kable? (Zoe Bell gets barely enough time to introduce herself before her head is exploded three minutes later.) Are the other gamers restricted from teaming up with the dead-eyed Kable? It seems the one place where alliances might be a good idea. The Slayers game cannot be bothered to flesh itself out, so why should we care about all the charred flesh left within it?

Stephen King's original vision for *The Running Man* had its hero play the game in order to feed his wife and sick child in a decrepit, game-show-obsessed culture. It is unclear whether Neveldine & Taylor could tear themselves away from their own attention disorders long enough to read it, but they certainly grabbed whatever bits and pieces they could remember from the movie, including a corrupt game host, viewing parties across the land, the name Slayers as variation on that film's stalkers, and a revolutionary group that has evolved in leaders from Mick Fleetwood to Ludacris.

Gamer fumbles through its bid for making whatever statement about the media, society or video games they were going for. It is hard to combat Big Brother when the good guys use a similar visual technique. It is barely able to sneak its cinematic lifts from Schwarzenegger, *Strange Days* (1995), and *Blade Runner* (1982). Castle's domain may have the greatest security lapse since Eldon Tyrell, and as Kable enters the home it is basked in the same shadows and light familiar to anyone who remembers Deckard's trek into the dangers of J.F. Sebastian's apartment. The film even ends like Ridley Scott's theatrical cut with a wistful drive through the country-side and an aerial shot to take us into darkness.

Gerard Butler may be getting achingly close to the period where he needs to trade in the macho bravado and begin doing family films. He already has *Nim's Island* (2008) under his belt, but this is precisely the kind of rock bottom material that forces one into projects like *The Pacifier* (2005) and *The Game Plan* (2007). As for Neveldine and Taylor, these guys cannot even film a game of air hockey without trying to induce an epileptic seizure in the audience. A rave sequence may have more individual edits than Eisenstein's Odessa Steps, but only one will ever be studied in film classes. With the imagination-challenged *Gamer*, they have succeeded only in bringing about the equivalent of a diabetic coma.

Erik Childress

CREDITS

Kable: Gerard Butler
Ken Castle: Michael C. Hall
Ric Rape: Milo Ventimiglia
Trace: Alison Lohman
Angie: Amber Valletta
Simon: Logan Lerman
Gina Parker Smith: Kyra Sedgwick
Freek: John Leguizamo
Hackman: Terry Crews
Sandra: Zoe Bell
Origin: USA
Language: English
Released: 2009
Production: Gary Lucchesi, Tom Rosenberg, Skip Williamson, Richard S. Wright; Lionsgate, Lakeshore Entertainment; released by Lionsgate
Directed by: Mark Neveldine, Brian Taylor
Written by: Mark Neveldine, Brian Taylor
Cinematography by: Ekkehart Pollack
Music by: Robert Williamson, Geoff Zanelli
Sound: Scott Martin Gershin
Editing: Fernando Villena, Peter Amundson, Doobie White
Art Direction: Peter Borck
Costumes: Alix Friedberg
Production Design: Jerry Fleming
MPAA rating: R
Running time: 95 minutes

REVIEWS

Duralde, Alonso. *MSNBC.* September 4, 2009.

Gilchrist, Todd. *Sci Fi Wire.* September 4, 2009.

Hoffman, Jordan. *UGO.com.* September 4, 2009.

McWeeny, Drew. *HitFix.* September 4, 2009.

Modell, Josh. *AV Club.* September 4, 2009.

Nelson, Rob. *Variety.* September 4, 2009.

Neumaier, Joe. *New York Daily News.* September 4, 2009.

Pais, Matt. *Metromix.com.* September 4, 2009.

Schager, Nick. *Slant Magazine.* September 4, 2009.

Sobczynski, Peter. *eFilmCritic.com.* September 4, 2009.

QUOTES

Ken Castle: "I hope one day to have the opportunity to breach your firewall, Miss Parker Smith."

TRIVIA

The motorcycle driven by Trace is a Buell Firebolt.

GENTLEMEN BRONCOS

Napoleon Dynamite (2004) was the love-it-or-hate-it affair of its year that burst from January's Sundance film festival to become a little indie sensation that summer. Its filmmakers Jared and Jerusha Hess had a quirky style all their own that translated into cinema's equivalent of a live-action cartoon. If it wasn't for the when-is-this-taking-place rock tunes and the instrumental two-step of D-Qwon, you could easily hear Vince Guaraldi's theme for Charlie Brown on the soundtrack casually moving the characters to its melody. The characters in the Hess' third feature, *Gentlemen Broncos*, don't move as smoothly. They hardly appear to be alive at all. And for those who never understood why others couldn't see what they did in the bizarro world of *Napoleon Dynamite*, well, welcome to their field of vision.

Michael Angarano stars as Benjamin, a teenager who has spent a good portion of his time working on his science-fiction stories. Perhaps it was to escape from his mundane life with his mom (Jennifer Coolidge), who sells over-priced homemade nightgowns, although she seems to love him so. She even allows him to attend the weekend Cletus Fest for young authors. On the bus over he meets wannabe romance novelist Tabatha (Halley Feiffer), who takes advantage of him. She's joined at the hip by Lonnie (Hector Jimenez), who has made dozens of low-budget films and is always on the lookout for his next project.

The keynote speaker at this year's conference is Dr. Ronald Chevalier (Jemaine Clement), a longtime idol of

Benjamin's, who will be judging submissions. Benjamin's magnum opus is named *Yeast Lords: The Bronco Years*, a goofy pastiche of *Dune* (1984) and *Flesh Gordon* (1974) (yes, "Flesh" not "Flash"), which materializes in his head with Sam Rockwell taking on the role of its long-haired hero, modeled after his father. Lonnie and Tabatha are so inspired by it that they want to do an adaptation. Chevalier, whose latest work has been rejected by his editor, also sees the potential in Benjamin's work. Using his specialty for changing names into sci-fi mainstays, the ostentatious author passes off *Yeast Lords* as his own.

The theft of a novel would normally be the impetus for conflict in a typical plot about a struggling writer. The Hess' plotting is anything but typical, although beneath the self-conscious quirk is the potential for a fresh statement on the practice of adaptation. Precisely what is the acceptable price to give a writer peace of mind over the relinquishment of control over his vision? Is Lonnie's $500 enough for a first paycheck if the production value is barely up to the quality of Ed Wood? The finished film might be considered a greater crime against art than Chevalier's method of updating the work for the masses. Robert A. Heinlein once sued Roger Corman over *The Brain Eaters* (1958) for being a not-too-thinly veiled adaptation of his seminal sci-fi tale *The Puppet Masters* (1951), but what could he say about Jack Finney's *The Body Snatchers* (1955) which inspired more than a few film versions? Was Heinlein happy just to have comparisons bring people back to his original work, and would he have been any more satisfied when a direct adaptation of his novel was met with disdain by critics and viewers in 1994? Is Hess revisiting Isaac Asimov's *Mirror Image* (1972) where two scientists have their robot counterparts interrogated over an issue of authorship?

These are lofty notions for a film that is more content to deliver python diarrhea and projectile vomit resulting from bad yeast. To expect this from a gross-out humorist in Adam Sandler's repertoire or National Lampoon post-1990 would be par for the course, except Jared Hess has not built a reputation on this kind of material. His humor has been gentler, almost kid-friendly, with previous features—*Nacho Libre* (2006) was his successful follow-up to *Napoleon*—being rated "PG." Distracting us with cheap laughs from a greater dissertation on selling out could be a method to make the medicine go down more smoothly, but the trouble with *Gentlemen Broncos* extends beyond the more overt attempts at humor.

None of Hess' characters are remotely likable or worth rooting for. Benjamin appears to be in a constant state of apathy and Coolidge instantly exceeds her usual level of kook as his mom. Feiffer's Tabatha never generates interest as a romantic foil for Benjamin, and Nelson

Jimenez's wide-jawed performance as the asexual Lonnie is most annoying of all, as his sole purpose materializes as an attempt to out-circumference Steven Tyler's mouthpiece. If it wasn't for Jemaine Clement's early scenes as Chevalier, *Gentlemen Broncos* would be a laugh-free phantom zone. Not even the always reliable Sam Rockwell can wring laughs in the dual role of competing fusions of Benjamin and Chevalier's fictional hero.

Celebrated science-fiction writer Harlan Ellison said that "It's the amateurs that make it tough for the professionals," referring to up-and-comers substituting mere exposure over monetary gain. Considering Hess' clear fondness for the genre—represented in the film's best inspiration with fake sci-fi paperback covers introducing the opening credits—it's a tad disingenuous not to include a little more affection with all the mocking its fans and creators are treated to. Between Lonnie's short films and the sudden shifts towards the repugnant, Hess appears to be channeling a cross between the early work of John Waters and the entire filmography of the Kuchar Brothers, only lacking the necessary insanity to keep us looking at this particular wreck. The counterpoint to Ellison's statement would be the natural assumption of selling out. Jared Hess certainly shouldn't be accused of any such thing. But with *Gentlemen Broncos* he should feel a bit like this own protagonist, Benjamin, who has to sit back and watch while someone desperately tries to do a version of his unique storytelling.

Erik Childress

CREDITS

Benjamin Purvis: Michael Angarano
Ronald Chevalier: Jemaine Clement
Bronco/Brutus: Sam Rockwell
Dusty: Mike White
Judith: Jennifer Coolidge
Lonnie Donaho: Héctor Jiménez
Todd Keefe: Josh Pais
Tabitha Jenkins: Halley Feiffer
Origin: USA
Language: English
Released: 2009
Production: John J. Kelly, Mike White; Rip Cord Productions; released by Fox Searchlight Pictures
Directed by: Jared Hess
Written by: Mike White, Jared Hess, Jerusha Hess
Cinematography by: Munn Powell
Music by: David Wingo
Editing: Yuka Ruell
Sound: David Kitchens
Costumes: Jerusha Hess, April Napier

Production Design: Richard Wright
MPAA rating: PG-13
Running time: 90 minutes

REVIEWS

Berkshire, Geoff. *Metromix.com.* October 29, 2009.
Dargis, Manohla. *New York Times.* October 30, 2009.
DeBruge, Peter. *Variety.* September 28, 2009.
Edelstein, David. *New York Magazine.* October 26, 2009.
Foundas, Scott. *Village Voice.* October 27, 2009.
Goldstein, Gary. *Los Angeles Times.* October 30, 2009.
Howell, Peter. *Toronto Star.* November 6, 2009.
LaSalle, Mick. *San Francisco Chronicle.* November 5, 2009.
Phillips, Michael. *At the Movies.* November 2, 2009.
Scheck, Frank. *Hollywood Reporter.* October 26, 2009.

TRIVIA

The artwork in the opening credits is by acclaimed fantasy and science fiction artist David Lee Anderson.

AWARDS

Nomination:

Ind. Spirit 2010: Support. Actor (Clement).

G-FORCE

Gadgets, gizmos, guinea pigs. In 3-D.
—Movie tagline
The world needs bigger heroes.
—Movie tagline

Box Office: $119 million

G-Force is the first 3-D live action film (not counting *Hannah Montana/Miley Cyrus: Best of Both Worlds Concert Tour* [2008] and *Jonas Brothers: The 3D Concert Experience* [2009]— both concert films) to be produced by Walt Disney Studios and joins a flood of other 3-D kiddie flicks that, truth be told, have little going for them other than the gimmick of 3-D. Watching *G-Force* evokes a sad-eyed nostalgia for other, far-better live action flicks that the studio has produced in its long and illustrious history. No critic in their right mind would expect to be able to draw a comparison between *G-Force* and A-list fare like *20,000 Leagues Under The Sea* (1954) or *Treasure Island* (1950). It even seems unfair somehow to expect Disney's first 3-D effort to be as magical as stuff like *The Absent Minded Professor* (1961), *The Love Bug* (1968), or *Escape To Witch Mountain* (1975) (especially since those films have all been badly remade in recent years). But a viewer does have the right to expect something. In the seventies, many of Disney's live action movies intended to be mere throwaway popcorn fluff were inventive and enjoyable. No one would say that *The Computer Wore Tennis Shoes* (1969), *Now You See Him Now You Don't* (1972), *The Strongest Man in the World* (1975), *The Boatniks* (1970), or even *The Shaggy DA* (1976) were exactly good films, but they are fondly remembered by many who saw them. Will anyone look back on *G-Force* with the same fond memories? There is something sad about the way that so much of today's children's cinema comes and goes without leaving a trace. Often it seems that the more colorful and action-packed the trailer, the more forgettable the final film.

G-Force tells the story of a group of animals specially trained and equipped to run spy missions for the United States government. Team leader Darwin (Sam Rockwell), the alluring Juarez (Penélope Cruz), and the street smart Blaster (Tracy Morgan) are guinea pigs aided by ace mole hacker Speckles (Nicolas Cage) and Mooch, a fly who does surveillance. Together with their human trainers Ben (Zach Galifianakis) and Marcie (Kelli Garner) they are forced underground when their program is shut down by CIA pinhead Kip Killian (Will Arnett) just as they are closing in on a dangerous plot headed by the baddie billionaire Leonard Saber (Bill Nighy). But hostile government agents and Saber may be the least of their worries when Saber's web-connected network of home appliances becomes self-aware and goes rogue.

Hoyt Yeatman makes his feature directorial debut here after an extensive visual effects career that dates back all the way back to *Close Encounters of the Third Kind* (1977), but the unimaginative screenplay by Cormac and Marianne Wibberley seems interested mainly in plugging in enough clichés to get their project greenlit. On the whole, this is anything but surprising. With the exception of *The 6th Day* (2000), their résumé is as follows: the tepid *I Spy* (2002), the plastic *Charlie's Angel's: Full Throttle* (2003), the downright offensive *Bad Boys II* (2003), the creaky *National Treasure* (2004) and its sequel *National Treasure: Book of Secrets* (2007), and the simply horrible *The Shaggy Dog* (2006). This is not a writing team that needs to make more movies. Word has it the Wibberleys are currently developing both *Moby Dick* and *Fantastic Voyage*. One can hardly imagine either of those films contextually accommodating fart jokes but, if there is a way, the Wibberleys' track record attests to their ability to find it.

The 3-D effects are spectacular, offering very little ghosting or color desaturation, and during the film's many action sequences they offer ample evidence that the technique is indeed coming of age technically. But sadly the 3-D here is used as little more than a gimmick in a movie that is itself already a gimmick. There is nothing to distinguish *G-Force* and its endless series of action sequences, fart jokes and CGI creations from the 1001 kiddie films that have come before it.

The human cast in this film is capable given what they have to do, which is basically sell type. But nobody really rises above that level or even looks like they are having much fun. The usually dynamic and scene stealing Bill Nighy normally makes for a great villain, but here he merely ends up looking flat in a role that not only plays to type but ends up playing second fiddle to one of the CGI characters.

G-Force is produced by Jerry Bruckheimer, whose action films basically ruled the North American box office during the nineties and who has used his influence mainly to help launch and maintain the careers of the Wibberleys and Michael Bay while also occasionally producing good films. Now that Bruckheimer is getting into kiddie movies and Michael Bay has the *Transformers* franchise, one can only imagine them getting together to make some much needed R-rated culturally insensitive children's fare. Heavens knows a kiddie version of *Bad Boys II* (2003) is long overdue in a culture that embraces the forgettable.

Dave Canfield

CREDITS

Bucky: Steve Buscemi
Leonard Saber: Bill Nighy
Agent Kip Killian: Will Arnett
Dr. Ben Kendall: Zach Galifianakis
Marcie: Kelli Garner
Connor: Tyler Patrick Jones
Penny: Piper Mackenzie Harris
Darwin: Sam Rockwell (Voice)
Blaster: Tracy Morgan (Voice)
Juarez: Penélope Cruz (Voice)
Speckles: Nicolas Cage (Voice)
Hurley: Jon Favreau (Voice)
Origin: USA
Language: English
Released: 2009
Production: Jerry Bruckheimer; Jerry Bruckheimer Films, Walt Disney Pictures, Whamaphram Productions; released by Walt Disney Pictures
Directed by: Hoyt Yeatman
Written by: Cormac Wibberley, Marianne S. Wibberley, Tim Firth
Cinematography by: Bojan Bazelli
Music by: Trevor Rabin
Sound: Lee Orloff

Music Supervisor: Kathy Nelson
Editing: Mark Goldblatt, Jason Hellmann
Art Direction: Ramsey Avery
Costumes: Ellen Mirojnick
Production Design: Deborah Evans
MPAA rating: PG
Running time: 86 minutes

REVIEWS

Burr, Ty. *Boston Globe.* July 23, 2009.
Cane, Clay. *BET.com.* July 24, 2009.
Ebert, Roger. *Chicago Sun-Times.* July 23, 2009.
Kois, Dan. *Washington Post.* July 23, 2009.
Lowenstein, Lael. *Variety.* July 23, 2009.
Pais, Matt. *Metromix.com.* July 23, 2009.
Puig, Claudia. *USA Today.* July 24, 2009.
Rea, Steven. *Philadelphia Inquirer.* July 23, 2009.
Scott, A.O. *New York Times.* July 24, 2009.
Snider, Snider D. *Cinematical.* July 24, 2009.

QUOTES

Darwin: "Yippie-ki-yay, coffeemaker!"
Blaster: "I'm pretty sure this is animal cruelty."

TRIVIA

Harry Gregson-Williams, the film's original composer, dropped out to work on *Prince of Persia: The Sands of Time.*

GHOSTS OF GIRLFRIENDS PAST

You can't always run from your past.
—Movie tagline

Box Office: $55 million

This reworking of Charles Dickens' time-honored classic *A Christmas Carol* starts out novel enough by marrying Dickens' treatment of soul-searching redemption to the romantic comedy genre. If only *Ghosts of Girlfriends Past* had a soul, the film might emerge as more than just a throwaway bit of occasionally outright annoying fluff. But director Mark Waters, whose previously good-to-excellent work (*Freaky Friday* [2003], *Mean Girls* [2004], *The Spiderwick Chronicles* [2008]), would normally give a viewer ample reason to hope, proves limited by the screenwriting team of Jon Lucas and Scott Moore, who seem far more interested in satisfying tired rom-com conventions than in offering up anything as subversive or outrageous as their recent riff on the perils of matrimonial rituals (*The Hangover* [2009]).

Originally slated to begin shooting in 2003 with Ben Affleck in the lead, the project was held up after the highly publicized box office failure of *Gigli* (2003). This is instructive because it may explain why the film seems so flat and watered down. What once was a film on the fast-track with a lot of resources was kept in limbo only to emerge later as a stripped-down shadow—a ghost, if you will, of what could have been a very good film. Sadly under-developed, *Ghosts of Girlfriends Past* is almost saved by a decent cast and solid director, but, like many romantic comedies, the film commits the unpardonable move of being merely adequate, and thus boring. Everybody here seems like they're trying to make the best of the situation, thus the presence of Affleck's wife, Jennifer Garner, in the lead seems like an afterthought—a favor or a studio stipulation, rather than a reasoned choice made by a director or casting person in search of the right person for the right role. Further proof of this is the special effects, which are unimaginative to the point of being unnecessary. The final nail in the coffin is the ending of the film, which settles the characters into places dictated by the genre the movie is in instead of a more interesting story the movie could have told.

Connor Mead (Matthew McConaughey) is a hugely successful fashion photographer whose idea of honesty in relationships is dumping three women simultaneously via conference call. He travels to his brother Paul's (Breckin Meyer [*Garfield* (2004), *Stag Night* (2009)]) wedding to convince him that love is an illusion for suckers, only to run into Jenny Perotti (Jennifer Garner [*13 Going on 30* (2004), *Elektra* (2005), *Juno* (2007)]) the only woman who ever managed to truly capture his heart. As if that didn't make for conflict enough he then, literally, runs into the ghost of his Uncle Wayne (Michael Douglas) who has come back from the grave to apologize for leading him into his philandering ways. To help Connor see the light, three spirits will visit him, allowing him to gain a new perspective on his romantic past, present and future.

McConaughey isn't given much to do here but mug and follow the script to a foregone conclusion. But he does more than phone it in, trying gamely to act surprised, embarrassed, confused, horny and sad on cue, even though an actor of his ability is certainly aware he can't save this film alone. Supporting players fare a little better. Paul's fiancé Sandra is played by Lacey Chabert (*Mean Girls* [2004], *Black Christmas* [2006]) who has always been an expert at playing a shrieking, freak-out queen. Father of the bride Sergeant Volkrom is brought sternly to life by Robert Forster (*Mulholland Drive* [2001], *Charlie's Angels; Full Throttle* [2003]), who fans may recognize as Arthur Petrelli from TV's *Heroes.*

The adept way these two character actors handle the more kinetic comedic elements of this script should have triggered a rethink. This should never have been a romantic comedy but a dark-edged satire that used the genre as a leaping off point about why we crave Hollywood's bland idea of love at all. The truth, of course, is somewhere beyond Connor Mead's selfish indulgence, but it also goes far beyond the sort of cinematic Hallmark card that reads like the ones viewers have repeatedly gotten from a Hollywood desperate to mine gold rather than tell stories through cinema. This is where Connor Mead gets it right. If real love is this shallow, offers this much closure, then who needs more than a warm form to snuggle up next to now and then? Commitment is for suckers is Mead's maxim, and one can almost imagine him solemnly nodding his way through the spirit's admonitory adventure even as he plots his next sexual conquest.

Dave Canfield

CREDITS

Connor Mead: Matthew McConaughey
Uncle Wayne: Michael Douglas
Paul: Breckin Meyer
Jenny Perotti: Jennifer Garner
Sandra: Lacey Chabert
Sergeant Volkom: Robert Forster
Vonda Volkom: Anne Archer
Allison: Emma Stone
Brad: Daniel Sunjata
Young Connor: Devin Brochu
Origin: USA
Language: English
Released: 2009
Production: Jonathan Shestack, Brad Epstein; Panther Entertainment; released by New Line Cinema
Directed by: Mark S. Waters
Written by: Jon Lucas, Scott Moore
Cinematography by: Daryn Okada
Music by: Rolfe Kent
Sound: Danny Michael
Editing: Bruce Green
Art Direction: Maria Baker
Costumes: Denise Wingate
Production Design: Cary White
MPAA rating: PG-13
Running time: 115 minutes

REVIEWS

Berkshire, Geoff. *Metromix.com.* April 30, 2009.
Dargis, Manohla. *New York Times.* May 1, 2009.
Ebert, Roger. *Chicago Sun-Times.* April 30, 2009.
Howell, Peter. *Toronto Star.* May 1, 2009.
Lumenick, Lou. *New York Post.* May 1, 2009.
McCarthy, Todd. *Variety.* April 27, 2009.
Phillips, Michael. *Chicago Tribune.* April 30, 2009.
Rickey, Carrie. *Philadelphia Inquirer.* May 1, 2009.
Sobczynski, Peter. *eFilmCritic.com.* April 30, 2009.
Tobias, Scott. *AV Club.* April 30, 2009.

QUOTES

Connor Mead: "Someone once told me that the power in all relationships lies with whoever cares less, and he was right. But power isn't happiness, and I think that maybe happiness comes from caring more about people rather than less."

TRIVIA

Christa B. Allen, who plays teenage Jenny, the younger version of Jennifer Garner's character in the movie, also starred in *13 Going on 30*, in which she played a teenage version of Jennifer Garner's character as well.

G.I. JOE: THE RISE OF COBRA

When all else fails, they don't.
—Movie tagline

Box Office: $150.2 million

What criteria should one use to judge a bad movie? Should it be dissected with the same seasoned, weary critical eye that assesses the strengths and weakness of Martin Scorsese or Lars Von Trier films? Should it be automatically shunned for its lack of cohesion or artistic merit? Should it be given a free pass as a lark, a commercial exercise, or a guilty pleasure? All of these questions come to mind when considering a movie like Stephen Sommers' *G.I. Joe: The Rise of Cobra*, a film—unquestionably a "bad" film—that does such a good job at being bland and inoffensive that it is hard to hold a grudge against the final product. One reason that it is so difficult to stay angry at *G.I. Joe* is that the majority of the world is familiar with the property's origin as a merchandising-driven cartoon and toy line from the 1980s, so, as a result, almost no one was expecting a *G.I. Joe* live-action film to rewrite the visual language of the cinema. (Though one could argue that other corporate-manufactured film properties—like Disney's theme park-based *Pirates of the Caribbean: The Curse of the Black Pearl*—have done much better jobs at existing as clever, well-conceived films in their own rights.)

In fact, *G.I. Joe*'s origins as an offshoot of the Hasbro toy company stands as one of its greatest strengths, since it is almost impossible to discuss *G.I. Joe: The Rise of Cobra* critically without considering the recent film versions of another 1980s Hasbro toy line, *The Transformers*, and, let it be said, that the cheesy melodrama in Sommers' *Rise of Cobra* is infinitely more watchable and forgivable than the soulless narcissism of Michael Bay's *Transformer* films. While Bay's *Transformers* have mined box office gold by pandering to the worst tendencies of his audience—reducing everything into ugly, intangible buzzwords and transforming his visuals and actors into simply "violence!" and "sex!"—Sommers, to his credit, actually attempts to develop some drama, giving his characters motivation to do things and feel emotions. The director obviously wants to deliver an old-fashioned, rollicking adventure, the kind of movie that Steven Spielberg used to do so well, and, though he fails (and he does fail), the fact that he avoided the dead-eyed machismo of Bay's *Transformer* films makes *G.I. Joe: The Rise of Cobra* all the more palatable in comparison.

But is that enough to redeem *G.I. Joe*? It has to be said, one does have to give a director some points for opening a film about modern hi-tech warfare in medieval Scotland, solely to explain why one of the characters will be wearing a steel mask at the end of the story. The opening does nothing except tell the audience that Sommers is devoted to trying to make the cartoonish antics of the *G.I. Joe* legacy as plausible on-screen as possible, a fact that audiences will either find endearing or eye-rolling. The story quickly shifts to modern times, where James McCullen (Christopher Eccleston), head of the weapons manufacturer M.A.R.S, has developed a new nano-based missile warhead that can release a swarm of nanites capable of devouring almost anything—tanks, military bases, even whole cities. The warheads are stolen from their NATO convoy, led by all-American Duke (Channing Tatum) and Ripcord (Marlon Wayans), by a group of well-armed bad guys. Duke recognizes the leader of the raiding party, The Baroness (Sienna Miller), as his ex-lover Ana and, before he can figure out what's happened to her, the thieves are repelled by the members of G.I. Joe, an international military task force aimed at doing good all over the world.

The strangely Anglo "international" super-squad takes Duke, Ripcord, and the saved warheads back to their secret base near the Egyptian Pyramids, where General Hawk (Dennis Quaid) hesitantly allows Duke and Ripcord join his team, based on their knowledge of the Baroness and the convoy's assailants. (Duke had been engaged to Ana, but, after he failed to save her brother Rex, a military analyst, in the line of duty, he decided that he could never face her again.) Cut to a training montage where the new recruits are initiated into the world of G.I. Joe, where they marvel at the ninja skills of Snake Eyes (Ray Park), strain under the

tutelage of drill sergeant Heavy Duty (Adewale Akinnuoye-Agbaje), and Ripcord lusts after the Amazonian redhead Scarlett (Rachel Nichols). Not surprisingly, it turns out that McCullen was behind the attempted theft of his own warheads, acting as an agent of the terrorist group Cobra, which wants to use the warheads to blackmail the planet into a new world order—pretty standard super-villain boiler-plate demands.

McCullen and the villainous Doctor (an underused Joseph Gordon-Levitt) locate the G.I. Joe base and send in a team to re-steal the nano-warheads, led by the Baroness, Storm Shadow (Byung Hun-Lee), Snake Eyes' ninja arch-rival, and the shape-shifting Zartan (Arnold Vosloo). When two out of three of the members of the bad guys' raiding party have difficult personal pasts with our heroes, it definitely brings to mind the words "soap opera" and that is a pretty accurate way to describe Sommers' *G.I. Joe*. It exists in a world where all of the heroes and villains went to high school with each other, where their petty personal gripes are now being acted out against a violent global backdrop, which might be ideal wish-fulfillment fodder for a thirteen-year-old boy, but anyone more sophisticated than an eighth-grader will have a hard time holding back their moans.

As anyone who has seen a movie before can see from a mile off, Cobra steals back the warheads and starts a complicated series of events as they attempt to weaponize the missiles, leading to an explosive free-for-fall through the streets of Paris, ending in the Eiffel Tower being eaten by a swarm of hungry nanites. (Forget innocent bystanders. National landmarks are the true casualties when it comes to big-budget summer movies.) The Paris sequences are probably the strongest in the entire movie, largely due to the beyond-goofy thrills of the G.I. Joe's accelerator suits, bizarre robot exo-skeletons that allow the Joes to defy all laws of physics and probability. The accelerator scenes are patently ridiculous, but they are directed with such giddy, wish-fulfillment abandon that they end up being strangely infectious. After the Paris debacle, the Joes race to stop Cobra from using the other three warheads, while Duke keeps searching for a good reason why his ex-girlfriend has uncharacteristically transformed into a cleavage-obsessed super-villainess. It all leads to a confrontation in Cobra's secret sub-Artic base, where Ripcord gets to prove himself, Snake Eyes and Storm Shadow finally have it out, the audience witnesses the rise of Destro and the Cobra Commander, and the Baroness' veiled past is revealed.

If this all sounds corny, if it sounds like a cartoon, that's because it is. And, while, yes, Sommers' take on *G.I. Joe* as a giant high-school soap opera is more engaging that Bay's empty *Transformers* films, that does not mean that all of *Rise of Cobra*'s sins should be forgiven. For starters, Sommers, a filmmaker who seemingly lives on bombast and excess, fails to make *G.I. Joe* as fun and forgivable as his previous guilty pleasures, *The Mummy* and *Deep Rising*. (The less that is said about *Van Helsing* and *Mummy Returns*, the better.) Throughout the film, Sommers appears so constricted by his role as a franchise creator, as the director who needs to set up later and better *G.I. Joe* films, that the vast majority of the film feels perfunctory and lifeless. (Arnold Vosloo's character, Zartan, seems to exist solely to set up a potential *G.I. Joe 2*.) This is a film that should have felt cartoony in a good way—a fun, escapist military fantasy for pre-teens where every plane that explodes is accompanied by a parachuting pilot that tells us that everyone is OK—but the demands of franchise building, pleasing *G.I. Joe*'s rabid fanbase (Did every major character really need to appear in the first film?), and balancing the story's light and dark tone proved to be too much for Sommers, and the resulting film just collapses under its own weight.

Yes, *G.I. Joe: The Rise of Cobra* is better than *Transformers*, but, yes, it is still a bad movie, a film, despite its few strengths, that never gets beyond setting up a sequel that it probably does not deserve.

Tom Burns

CREDITS

Gung Ho: Brendan Fraser
Duke: Channing Tatum
Cobra Commander: Joseph Gordon-Levitt
The Baroness: Sienna Miller
Gen. Hawk: Dennis Quaid
Shana "Scarlett" O'Hara: Rachel Nichols
Snake Eyes: Ray Park
Ripcord: Marlon Wayans
Destro: Christopher Eccleston
Zartan: Arnold Vosloo
President: Jonathan Pryce
Breaker: Said Taghmaoui
Origin: USA
Language: English
Released: 2009
Production: Lorenzo di Bonaventura, Bob Ducsay, Stephen Sommers; Paramount Pictures, Spyglass Entertainment, Hasbro, Di Bonaventura Pictures; released by Paramount Pictures
Directed by: Stephen Sommers
Written by: Stuart Beattie, Skip Woods
Cinematography by: Mitchell Amundsen
Music by: Alan Silvestri
Editing: Bob Ducsay, Jim May
Sound: Karen M. Baker, Per Hallberg
Costumes: Ellen Mirojnick

Production Design: Ed Verreaux
MPAA rating: PG-13
Running time: 117 minutes

REVIEWS

Berkshire, Geoff. *Metromix.com*. August 7, 2009.
Corliss, Richard. *Time Magazine*. August 7, 2009.
Duralde, Alonso. *MSNBC*. August 7, 2009.
Ebert, Roger. *Chicago Sun-Times*. August 9, 2009.
Howell, Peter. *Toronto Star*. August 7, 2009.
Kuipers, Richard. *Variety*. August 6, 2009.
Scheck, Frank. *Hollywood Reporter*. August 7, 2009.
Setoodeh, Ramin. *Newsweek*. August 7, 2009.
Sharkey, Betsy. *Los Angeles Times*. August 7, 2009.
Sobczynski, Peter. *eFilmCritic.com*. August 7, 2009.

QUOTES

The Baroness: "That redhead is really starting to piss me off."

TRIVIA

Actor Sam Worthington was originally considered for the role of Duke, but had to turn it down due scheduling conflicts with *Avatar*.

AWARDS

Golden Raspberries 2009: Worst Support. Actress (Miller)

Nomination:

Golden Raspberries 2009: Worst Picture, Worst Support. Actor (Wayans), Worst Director (Sommers), Worst Screenplay, Worst Remake, Rip-Off or Sequel.

THE GIRLFRIEND EXPERIENCE

See it with someone you ****.
—Movie tagline

A number of films have taken on the lifestyle of prostitution—some for comedic effect like Ron Howard's *Night Shift* (1982), others more bluntly like Ken Russell's *Whore* (1991), but most involve the ones with hearts of gold that find romance like *Pretty Woman* (1990) or at least temporary solace in a loveless profession as in *Leaving Las Vegas* (1995). The word itself, prostitute, has taken on larger meaning though both as a verb describing the loosening of morals or principles or an altogether twist on the job description that softens the blow. Put call girl or escort on the W-2 and everyone still knows what it means. Or do they? In the audacious new film from Steven Soderbergh, he tackles many of the unanswered curiosities of the industry while back-dropping the current financial crisis and slyly skewering the politics of Hollywood.

To play the entry point into this world, Soderbergh has cast real-life adult film actress Sasha Grey, ironically the most experienced of all the actors on camera. Grey plays Chelsea, a $2,000-an-hour escort who caters more to the distinguished gentleman looking to spend a full evening of company instead of just the wham-bang-thank-you-ma'am. She lives with her boyfriend, Chris (Chris Santos), who also specializes in cleansing bodies as a personal trainer. Clearly she is the breadwinner of the household but both are feeling the pinch of a strug-gling economy in their own ways. Set in the waning weeks before the 2008 Obama/McCain election, each are looking to pick up more clients but the needs of the people are being prioritized, including Chelsea's.

There is little to suggest that Chelsea and Chris are of a happy union in their upper Manhattan loft. Through the course of a film she speaks with a journal-ist (Mark Jacobson) that feels more like a therapist as he tries to break through the guarded persona Chelsea has built for herself. Despite being relegated to the role of the listener on her "dates," Chelsea is never less than the dominating presence, even in her soft-spoken demeanor, and has a policy to only take clients with previous escort experience, thus increasing the chances they are equally of a professional nature. Get in, get out and never fall in love. When she breaks that rule and accepts a married man's invitation though, Chelsea finds herself on the other end of her own rules and sucked into the very fantasy she's been providing. Soderbergh never imposes any sort of moral judgment on Chelsea and isn't inviting us to subscribe to anything so simplistic. If anything, we're more likely to look down upon the rich male clientele dropping a large chunk of money for just a few hours of companionship.

Chris and Christine (Chelsea's real name) become two sides of the same coin; each becoming corrupted by the empty promises of the better life. As Chris' own real girlfriend experience with Christine goes south while his clientele dwindles, he accepts a Vegas invitation to become one of the guys in an exclusive flight of strangers. Chelsea continues to seek avenues to improve her status in the world's oldest profession by taking up the offer of the new media. An escort reviewer, played by film critic Glenn Kenny, pursues her for a free preview in exchange for positive press on his website. Going so far as to create his own overseas junket to convince the Arabs to "buy American," Soderbergh exposes another type of whore in this character. An all-too-common practice to utilize "easy" reviewers to help sell their product, the marketers of the film industry spend countless dollars on these people (flights, food, hotels) with the knowledge of having as close to a sure thing as Chelsea's customers.

Leaving all this behind is the temptation Chelsea faces in becoming Christine for good. Soderbergh maximizes the technique of double-backing upon the various spans of time, creating an intellectual puzzle rather than one of mere twists in the plot. There's a calculation in hearing one character say, "If I hear the word Maverick one more time I'm going to throw up" followed up by another pontificating that the "real you" could mean a lot of money for a very short time. In such a way, Soderbergh is riffing, almost autobiographi-cally, on the plight of artists everywhere. Everyone from the screenwriter to the personal trainer are seduced into the compromise of ignoring their true selves and remain-ing true to his nature at the expense of another's career and feelings—in a business where everything is supposed to be fake. But real enough for a couple hours of escape.

Erik Childress

CREDITS

Chelsea: Sasha Grey
Chris: Chris Santos
Wealthy Client: Peter Zizzo
Erotic Connoisseur: Glenn Kenny
Origin: USA
Language: English
Released: 2009
Production: Gregory Jacobs; 2929 Entertainment, Extension 765; released by Magnolia Pictures
Directed by: Steven Soderbergh
Written by: Brian Koppelman, David Levien
Cinematography by: Steven Soderbergh
Music by: Ross Godfrey
Sound: Larry Blake
Editing: Steven Soderbergh
Art Direction: Carlos Moore
Costumes: Christopher Peterson
MPAA rating: R
Running time: 78 minutes

REVIEWS

Abele, Robert. *Los Angeles Times.* May 22, 2009.
Burr, Ty. Boston. *Globe.* May 21, 2009.
Ebert, Roger. *Chicago Sun-Times.* May 21, 2009.
Edelstein, David. *New York Magazine.* May 18, 2009.
Honeycutt, Kirk. *Hollywood Reporter.* April 28, 2009.
Jones, J.R. *Chicago Reader.* May 21, 2009.
Scheib, Ronnie. *Variety.* April 28, 2009.
Stevens, Dana. *Slate.* May 22, 2009.

Tallerico, Brian. *MovieRetriever.com.* May 22, 2009.
Tobias, Scott. *AV Club.* May 21, 2009.

QUOTES

Chelsea: "This David and I clicked. There was something there. And I told him that."

TRIVIA

Steven Soderbergh first heard about Sasha Grey when he read an article in *Los Angeles* magazine about her.

GOMORRAH

Box Office: $1.6 million

Critics loved *Gomorrah*, a devastatingly unsparing examination of life in the Naples region of Italy, where much of daily activity is controlled by the multi-tentacled mob called the Camorra. The film does not lack for grit and authenticity, and is full of frank, arresting images and well-drawn, complex characters. For American audiences unfamiliar with the subject matter, however, the cold, documentary-style treatment and lack of narrative connection make the story awfully difficult to follow.

Despite that, the film has plenty of reach and power. Its refusal to indulge in easy sentiment or spurious humor sets it apart from a lot of highly stylized gangster flicks. Director Matteo Garrone is clearly not interested in making his film into mass entertainment, though he does fall prey occasionally to the genre conventions of spectacular killings. The movie opens with a bang, bathed in blue light, as a group of knuckleheads is gunned down in a tanning salon. It is a fantastic start, but soon things get murky.

Garrone, who risked reprisal by making a movie (based on a book by Robert Saviano) so close to the truth about life in the Camorra-controlled provinces, does not shy away from stark images or disturbing scenes. In one arresting sequence, a group of young boys is lined up awaiting a mob firing squad—they are shot one by one, but while wearing a bulletproof vest, and it turns out to be a rite of passage (later they compare burn scars on their chests).

One of the boys is Toto (Salvatore Abruzzese), an errand boy who brings groceries to neighbors and later guns and other contraband to gangsters once he is under the control of the mob. His are innocent eyes corrupted gradually by the world he inhabits and the killings he witnesses. In this world, the police are watched for but never intervene; they are all seemingly paid off and leave all enterprise to the control of the crime bosses.

Toto is but one among many protagonists for Garrone. The others include two young hotheads who steal guns from the mob bosses, shoot up a beach, rob a video store, rip off drugs from dealers, break rules in a strip club, and generally become such a nuisance that the mob bosses must eliminate them. There is also a semi-legitimate garment maker who nonetheless must ride in a car trunk for protection, a hapless mob bag man who pays off people whose relatives are in prison, and a mob boss whose business is waste disposal, by any means necessary, including hiring young kids to drive his dump trucks around a quarry.

Unlike the interlocking-tale structure so popular in Hollywood movies and on TV shows, Garrone barely makes any connections between his scenes, much less his story lines. Without prior knowledge of the place and culture being depicted, it is very difficult to follow what's going on. Garrone's movie is a like a pile of sticks rather than a structure; there is no glue holding the stories together. For much of the movie, one wonders who is living where, what relationship the characters have to other characters, and what really is going on and why. It is easy to grasp that this world is controlled by mobsters and that some of the dealings are shady and violent, but Garrone leaves audiences without a road map to navigate their way through his nightmarish world.

This refusal to follow basic narrative rules leaves the viewer with an unrelenting feeling of disorientation, which perhaps is Garrone's intent. In this unfamiliar landscape, shot mostly in medium or long shots, with rarely a close-up, it is unclear what reality to count on. Garrone has been compared by some critics to the 1960s New Wave auteur Michelangelo Antonioni, and indeed *Gomorrah* has the same kind of bleak industrial landscapes and arm's-length detachment as Antonioni's *Red Desert* (1964).

The film is like a documentary in some ways, but it is one in which essential information is withheld. Only before the closing credits does Garrone provide helpful titles explaining what Camorra is, what it controls, and how many people die under its rule. If those facts had been imparted at the beginning of the movie, or even sprinkled throughout by a narrator, the movie would make more sense. It is as if Garrone is being deliberately opaque to heighten our sense of disorientation. The viewer has to piece together what is happening scene by scene but, even with rapt attention, it is difficult to find clues to unlock the overriding structure of the film. *Gomorrah* is not just a foreign-language film, it is a movie without the customary language of cinema at all, and with no guideposts, so that watching it one feels like a tourist who not only does not speak the language, but is completely disoriented. Still, the chilling and sometimes bracing images linger on. Garrone is clearly a cunning and talented filmmaker, but perhaps he needs to understand that you can be artsy and still give your audience the help it needs to decode your art.

Michael Betzold

CREDITS

Toto: Salvatore Abruzzese
Don Ciro: Gianfelice Imparato
Maria: Maria Nazionale
Franco: Toni Servillo
Roberto: Carmine Paternoster
Pasquale: Salvatore Cantalupo
Iavarone: Gigio Morra
Marco: Marco Macor
Piselli: Ciro Petrone
Piselli: Ciro Petrone
Origin: Italy
Language: Italian
Released: 2008
Production: Domenico Procacci; Fandango, RAI Cinema; released by IFC Films
Directed by: Matteo Garrone
Written by: Matteo Garrone, Ugo Chiti, Massimo Gaudioso, Roberto Saviano, Maurizio Braucci
Cinematography by: Marco Onorato
Music by: Neil Davidge, Robert Del Naja, Euan Dickinson
Sound: Leslie Shatz, Maricetta Lombardo, Daniela Cassani
Editing: Marco Spoletini
Costumes: Alessandra Cardini
Production Design: Paulo Bonfini
MPAA rating: Unrated
Running time: 137 minutes

REVIEWS

Berkshire, Geoff. *Metromix.com.* December 18, 2008.
Dargis, Manohla. *New York Times.* February 13, 2009.
Ebert, Roger. *Chicago Sun-Times.* February 26, 2009.
Edelstein, David. *New York Magazine.* February 9, 2009.
Hoberman, J. *Village Voice.* February 10, 2009.
Phillips, Michael. *Chicago Tribune.* February 26, 2009.
Tallerico, Brian. *MovieRetriever.com.* February 27, 2009.
Tobias, Scott. *AV Club.* February 12, 2009.
Turan, Kenneth. *Los Angeles Times.* December 19, 2008.
Weissberg, Jay. *Variety.* February 9, 2009.

TRIVIA

The film won the Grand Prix at the 61st Annual Cannes Film Festival, 2008.

GOOD HAIR

Sit back and relax.
—Movie tagline

Box Office: $4 million

Mid-budget, high-yield comedies such as *Barbershop* (2002), *Barbershop 2: Back in Business* (2004) and *Beauty Shop* (2005) shined a collective light on African American salons as unique social centers. Comedian Chris Rock's *Good Hair*, a documentary exposé about the manner in which hairstyles—particularly the high demands of female hair care—impact the activities, pocketbooks, sexual relationships and self-esteem of the black community, one-ups the aforementioned lightweight diversionary entertainments by serving up both laughs and material that invites some pensive reflection. Like the best of Rock's stand-up material, *Good Hair* blends ribald observational humor with pointed social commentary, and the result—which was the winner of a Special Jury Prize at the 2009 Sundance Film Festival—is a winning movie with spryness that may surprise general audiences.

Rock's inspiration for the film was personal, prompted by his five-year-old daughter approaching him and asking, "Daddy, how come I don't have good hair?" Curious as to where her ingrained feelings of inadequacy sprang from, Rock did some research, and was surprised to find that African Americans make up around 12 percent of the population and yet account for approximately 80 percent of the sales in the hair products business, which rakes in more than $9 billion annually. *Good Hair* aims to get to the bottom of this gaping disparity. A diverse roster of celebrities such as Ice-T, Nia Long, Raven Symoné, Maya Angelou, Cheryl "Salt" James, Sandra "Pepa" Denton, Eve and Reverend Al Sharpton all candidly offer up stories and their own observations to Rock, while he struggles with the task of figuring out how to ultimately respond to his daughter's question.

With Rock's help as the movie's on-camera guide and occasional narrator, director Jeff Stilson smartly frames *Good Hair* as a probative sociological tract, scoring points for astutely interweaving thoughtful questioning and concrete factoids, all while never losing grasp of a humorous, slightly self-scolding pulse. (Rapper and actor Ice-T gets off a couple of the movie's best lines, including relating a pimp's advice to him when he was young: "The best way to have the upper hand on a woman is to be flyer than her.") Broadly speaking, there is an element of personal vanity in how African Americans value the presentation of their hair, the movie seems to acknowledge, but a large part of this is also rooted in a mass media that continually and sometimes insidiously reinforces the virtues of more traditionally European hairstyles. As the film assays the highly potent chemical relaxers and other products meant to tame "nappiness" and give African Americans more straightened locks, it is certainly hard to fathom those in the cultural majority putting themselves through the sort of personal aggravation that comes with this pursuit.

The fact that *Good Hair* concerns such a niche subject may on the surface seem to limit its audience, but natural curiosity about the vivacity of this subculture easily elicits attention and pulls viewers along, no matter their ethnicity. Rock's charismatic, inquisitive noodling is juxtaposed with footage from the Bronner Brothers Hair Show, an annual convention in Atlanta which draws 120,000 visitors to its 1,800-plus proprietor booths, which sell everything from relaxers and gels to curlers, coloring and wigs. The centerpiece of the Bronner show, however, is a wild styling competition with a $20,000 prize. A colorful quartet of contestants—which include a young Caucasian hairdresser, a woman who insists on cutting hair upside down, and a stocky, flamboyant returning champion who skirts around the edges of the rules by incorporating a full-fledged marching band into his routine—nicely serve as the movie's window into this outlandish world, with the competitive stakes giving the proceedings a fixed end point.

As it moves into the final third of its 95-minute running time, *Good Hair* posits, somewhat provocatively and absolutely dishearteningly, that minority women of lesser economic means often have to make tough and/or bad choices to pay for weaves whose initial cost and maintenance can run into the thousands of dollars. (And yes, layaway plans are alive and well in urban salons, it seems.) Rock also talks with young African American men, who relate some surprising stories about how female hair care impacts their lives. These anecdotes range from amusing (a woman becoming violent at the touching of her hair during sex) to sort of rather sad (a teenager admitting that he looks at certain women as out of his league simply because he knows he is not in a position to pay for their hair care), and in turn prompts the movie's most surreal passage, in which Rock visits Indian temples where hair is harvested for weaves and wigs sold overwhelmingly to African Americans. The mere existence of this weirdly symbiotic if hardly entirely necessary trans-global relationship—human hair is a valuable export in India, where 85 percent of the adult population has shaved their head at least twice, most in an annual Hindu tonsure religious ceremony—is fascinating to ponder, and definitely not something addressed in any other current news program, magazine or book.

It is this sort of capacity to continually surprise, intrigue and shock—in modulated, pleasant ways relating to both individual interviewees and overarching thematic examinations—that most marks *Good Hair* as such an engaging offering. One need not be high-

maintenance at all to find fascinating this examination of the huge effects of social pressure.

Brent Simon

CREDITS

Himself: Chris Rock
Origin: USA
Language: English
Released: 2009
Production: Jenny Hunter, Kevin O'Donnell, Jeff Stilson; Chris Rock Entertainment, HBO Films; released by Roadside Attractions
Directed by: Jeff Stilson
Written by: Chris Rock, Jeff Stilson, Lance Crouther, Chuck Sklar
Cinematography by: Cliff Charles
Music by: Marcus Miller
Sound: Robert Jackson
Music Supervisor: P.J. Bloom
Editing: Paul Marchand, Greg Nash
MPAA rating: PG-13
Running time: 95 minutes

REVIEWS

Catsoulis, Jeanette. *New York Times.* October 9, 2009.
Chang, Justin. *Variety.* October 6, 2009.
Ebert, Roger. *Chicago Sun-Times.* October 8, 2009.
Gleiberman, Owen. *Entertainment Weekly.* October 7, 2009.
Pais, Matt. *Metromix.com.* October 8, 2009.
Phillips, Michael. *Chicago Tribune.* October 8, 2009.
Sharkey, Betsy. *Los Angeles Times.* October 8, 2009.
Stevens, Dana. *Slate.* October 9, 2009.
Weinberg, Scott. *Cinematical.* March 3, 2009.
Weitzman, Elizabeth. *New York Daily News.* October 9, 2009.

AWARDS

Nomination:
Writers Guild 2009: Feature Doc.

GOODBYE SOLO

An unusually quiet and low-key drama, *Goodbye Solo* is not your standard buddy movie. For one thing, Ramin Bahrani's pairing of a gregarious Senegalese cab driver, Solo (Souleymane Sy Savane), and a prickly old loner, William (Red West), never gets cute or predictable. Neither actor plays to a mainstream audience's need for emotional payoff, because the script by Bahrani (*Chop Shop, Man Push Cart*) and his screenwriting partner Bahareh Azimi avoids the usual easy hooks—even those involving the familiar character of a precocious child. It's a dignified, down-to-earth, bracingly human film that travels a difficult emotional landscape without embellishments.

The film's opening scene lays out the plot in a few minutes. Winston-Salem, North Carolina cabbie Solo is ferrying William, an elderly curmudgeon, to a movie. William gives him a $100 bill as a down payment on a $1,000 offer that involves driving him, ten days hence, to a place in the Great Smoky Mountains National Park called Blowing Rock (where it's said things thrown off the mountain blow back upwards). William makes clear it's a one-way trip, and Solo immediately starts quizzing the old man about its purpose, quickly surmising that he intends to jump off and commit suicide, though William refuses to confirm this, telling him in no uncertain terms to stay out of his business.

Solo accepts the money—he needs it to pay rent to his ex-wife, with whom he is on tenuous terms. He is stepfather to her daughter, Alex (Diana Franco Galindo), who serves as the knowledgeable cultural insider of the film. Quiera (Carmen Levya) is pregnant with their own child, but she disapproves of Solo's plans to become a flight attendant; she would rather he stay closer to home. Solo seems oddly distanced from Quiera; he is much closer to Alex. It is clear he is also ambitious; it's a trait that comes naturally to a man who is clearly friendly and open-hearted, even though some of his friends are drug dealers and low-lifes.

William's unstated plans to end his life puzzle and disturb Solo, who embraces his existence, paltry as it might seem to others. For most of the movie, he tries to befriend William and earn his confidence. It is clear that Solo thinks that he can dissuade the old man by proving to him there are people worth living for. William, who brings a whole new meaning to the word "taciturn," just wants to be left alone.

But for all Solo's rather pushy efforts, giving William a couch to spend the night on (and then later moving in with William in a seedy motel), connecting Alex to William in a quiet way, trying to give the man a substitute family for the one he claims he does not have, Solo fails to crack William's iron armor, and it is only when Solo realizes he cannot change other people that he gains the satisfaction of being William's truest friend.

In a setup that is ripe for melodrama, Bahrani provides nothing of the sort. He does not milk the story for laughs or tears, and though Solo is a winningly warm character that audiences would want to root for, the director and the script do not provide a satisfying payoff, at least in conventional terms. This quiet movie eschews most cinematic conventions, in fact. It employs a dogged

realism, and there is not one scene in the movie that seems forced or overwritten.

The danger is that some audiences will find *Goodbye Solo* underwritten, instead. There is little or no action, and some shots drag on deliberately a moment too long, confident in their contemplative reach. It is a slow and thoughtful movie but somewhat unsatisfying because it does not provide standard explanations. Like Solo, we have to piece together William's murky back story from a few thin threads of information, and by the movie's climax we are as frustrated as he is.

West, a longtime character actor and second banana whose TV and film career dates back to 1959, plays William as an iconic character, a sort of last cowboy. His face is chiseled and rocky, but in a disturbingly broken rather than handsome fashion, West has soulful, cloudy eyes concealing a world of pain that will remain buried. John Wayne would seem talkative and gushy next to West's William. He's not just prickly, he's emotionally unassailable.

Solo, on the other hand, wears his heart on his sleeve. Savane plays him as a proud, noble, but nonetheless everyday man, heroic in his optimism but clueless about how to make his dreams come true. As a cabbie, he can only facilitate other people's progress, and even his own great ambition, to be a flight attendant, puts him in the same position. He wants only to make other people happy.

Shot on location, *Goodbye Solo* prowls a bleak urban landscape of a city that seems wretchedly old and worn out. In fact, the settings mirror the two protagonists' spirits. William is a part of this old South, an American dream gone to seed, living a life that hasn't a hope of touching beauty or glamour. To Solo, however, this is something like the Promised Land. The climactic scenes in the Smokies provide a breathtaking, quiet contrast, a beauty that speaks for itself, almost heavenly just in its existence, a more worthy Promised Land.

This is a thoughtful, spookily quiet, and determinedly unembellished movie, revealing Bahrani as a new old master of sorts. Rejecting gimmickry and easy palliatives, this promising director displays a wonderful confidence in his simple story and in his two ordinary characters. *Goodbye Solo* is a movie that soars in its own way, and it's a welcome change of wind.

Michael Betzold

CREDITS

Solo: Souleymane Sy Savane
William: Red West
Alex: Diana Franco-Galindo

Quiera: Carmen Leyva
Origin: USA
Language: English, French, Wolof, Spanish
Released: 2008
Production: Ramin Bahrani, Jason Orans; Gigantic Pictures, ITVS, Lucky Hat Entertainment, Noruz Films; released by Roadside Attractions
Directed by: Ramin Bahrani
Written by: Ramin Bahrani, Bahareh Azimi
Cinematography by: Michael Simmonds
Sound: Tom Efinger
Editing: Ramin Bahrani
Music by: M. Lo
Art Direction: Adam Willis
Production Design: Chad Keith
MPAA rating: R
Running time: 91 minutes

REVIEWS

Denby, David. *New Yorker*. April 6, 2009.
Ebert, Roger. *Chicago Sun-Times*. March 26, 2009.
Edelstein, David. *New York Magazine*. March 23, 2009.
Foundas, Scott. *Village Voice*. March 24, 2009.
Pais, Matt. *Metromix.com*. March 26, 2009.
Phillips, Michael. *Chicago Tribune*. March 26, 2009.
Scott, A.O. *New York Times*. March 26, 2009.
Stevens, Dana. *Slate*. March 26, 2009.
Tallerico, Brian. *MovieRetriever.com*. March 26, 2009.
Turan, Kenneth. *Los Angeles Times*. April 9, 2009.

AWARDS

Nomination:
Ind. Spirit 2010: Actor (Savane).

THE GOODS: LIVE HARD, SELL HARD
(The Goods: The Don Ready Story)

Box Office: $15.1 million

The Goods: Live Hard, Sell Hard. is more like an impression of what is thought to be a funny comedy these days than an actual example of one. Sure, it has laughs, including several big ones. But a good comedy moves smoothly and lightly, and *The Goods*, which is set at a sleazy California used-car lot, is a big, wheezing, clunker.

The simple set-up: the bank will foreclose Selleck Motors, long-operated by Ben Selleck (James Brolin) in

Temecula, California, unless the staff of slackers (which includes Tony Hale as Wade Zooha, Ken Jeong as Teddy Dang and Charles Napier as intensely bigoted Dick Lewiston) can sell more than 200 cars. They are not even close to up to the task, so Selleck recruits hotshot salesman Don "The Goods" Ready (Jeremy Piven) to come in and get the job done. Don's crew includes tough guy Jibby Newsome (Ving Rhames), Brent Gage (David Koechner), who's made very uncomfortable by sexual advances from Ben, and fearless Babs Merrick (Kathryn Hahn), who develops a crush on Selleck's son Peter (Rob Riggle), a 10-year-old with a genetic condition that makes him look about 20 years older than he really is.

Produced by Adam McKay and Will Ferrell—the team behind *Anchorman: The Legend of Ron Burgundy* (2004) and *Talladega Nights: The Ballad of Ricky Bobby* (2006)—*The Goods* is pretty much a carbon copy of the formula that typically casts Ferrell as an ultra-competitive and ultimately lovable dope. However, Piven does not possess the comedic fearlessness or endearing presence that allows Ferrell to play obnoxious morons with such charm. Instead, Don, whose business card simply boasts "I move cars, motherf***er," often comes off as angry and unlikable.

Plot-wise the film mostly goes through the motions, as Don falls for Ben's daughter Ivy (Jordana Spiro), who is engaged to Paxton Harding (Ed Helms), an arrogant salesman at a rival dealership. Nothing is said about how Ivy came to date a direct competitor of her father's, or why she sticks by Paxton even as she demonstrates to Don that she thinks her fiancée is beneath her. (Though the joke is as fresh as a 1998 Accord, Helms scores some laughs as Paxton rehearses with a grown-up version of a boy band, dubbed a "man band.") Actually, *The Goods* pays little mind to the mechanics of its story, both rushing through a quick and dirty 90 minutes and clearly laboring to fill the screen with anything that will move things along.

Of course, in comedies, the best moments can be the throwaway gags, and *The Goods* has enough ridiculous asides to keep laughs from totally disappearing for too long. Jibby tells Babs that he has never made love to a woman but when she asks if he is a virgin, he explains that he has been with tons of women—performing unprintable acts that may or may not actually exist—but simply has never "made love" to one. Coupled with Rhames' strong presence and Jibby's love for actor James Van Der Beek's work on *Dawson's Creek*, this presentation of a lovelorn, sensitive sexual dynamo helps make Jibby a far more memorable character than Don, the focus of the movie, ever is. The same goes for a cameo by Ferrell as Don's friend McDermott, who has a tattoo of the Hawaiian Punch mascot on his back and is killed after a botched skydiving jump—while wearing an Abraham Lincoln costume.

Hahn is also very funny as Babs, who knows she should not be attracted to Peter but indulges in amusing come-ons nonetheless. Unfortunately, writers Andy Stock and Rick Stempson—who also scripted the straight-to-DVD tennis comedy *Balls Out: Gary the Tennis Coach* (2009), which says a lot about their adherence to formula—do not give Hahn enough material to work with. During an improvised speech to her co-workers, Babs informs them, "When you die, poop leaves your butt." Even an actress as appealing as Hahn cannot make a line like this better than it is on the page.

Mostly, *The Goods* is just out to mix together a lot of bad taste and hope that people will chuckle at the mess. For example, Don motivates Dick to beat up Teddy as payback for the Japanese's role in the attack on Pearl Harbor, despite the fact that Teddy is actually Korean. Don also claims that all exotic dancers are students, single mothers or cocaine addicts. (Needless to say, he explains this in less polite language). Aside from the periodic highlights—Craig Robinson has fun with the role of DJ Request, a DJ who refuses to take any requests—*The Goods* is just pushing buttons for the sake of pushing them, and filling in the gaps with jokes about MC Hammer that come about 15 years too late. That kind of timing is the exact opposite of good comedy.

Matt Pais

CREDITS

Don Ready: Jeremy Piven
Jibby Newsome: Ving Rhames
Wade Zooha: Tony Hale
Brent Gage: David Koechner
Babs Merrick: Kathryn Hahn
Ivy Selleck: Jordana Spiro
Teddy Dang: Ken Jeong
Paxton Harding: Ed Helms
Ben Selleck: James Brolin
Stu Harding: Alan Thicke
Peter Selleck: Rob Riggle
Dick Lewiston: Charles Napier
Origin: USA
Language: English
Released: 2009
Production: Kevin J. Messick, Adam McKay, Will Ferrell, Chris Hency; Gary Sanchez Prods.; released by Paramount Vantage
Directed by: Neal Brennan
Written by: Andy Stock, Rick Stempson
Cinematography by: Daryn Okada

Music by: Lyle Workman
Sound: Marc Weingarten
Music Supervisor: Dave Jordan, JoJo Villanueva
Editing: Michael Jablow, Kevin Tent
Costumes: Mary Jane Fort
Production Design: Stefania Cella
MPAA rating: R
Running time: 89 minutes

REVIEWS

Abele, Robert. *Los Angeles Times.* August 14, 2009.
Childress, Erik. *eFilmCritic.* August 14, 2009.
Dargis, Manohla. *New York Times.* August 14, 2009.
Ebert, Roger. *Chicago Sun-Times.* August 13, 2009.
Hornaday, Ann. *Washington Post.* August 14, 2009.
Lemire, Christy. *Associated Press.* August 13, 2009.
Lowry, Brian. *Variety.* August 13, 2009.
Phillips, Michael. *Chicago Tribune.* August 14, 2009.
Phipps, Keith. *AV Club.* August 13, 2009.
Rechtshaffen, Michael. *Hollywood Reporter.* August 13, 2009.

QUOTES

Jibby Newsome: "Listen man, I haven't been home in a year and a half...and I'm about 90% sure I left the front door open."

THE GREAT BUCK HOWARD

Get ready for the comeback of a lifetime.
—Movie tagline

As executed by writer-director Sean McGinly, a former road manager for The Amazing Kreskin, *The Great Buck Howard* is a strange hybrid, a tribute to a performer who apparently did not allow his name to be used in the title, or wasn't asked. The film basically recapitulates McGinly's experience, as a young man in show business barely wet behind the years, with Kreskin, a fading celebrity mentalist. Colin Hanks plays the McGinly surrogate character, Troy Banks, as a clueless gee-whiz kid who stumbles into entertainment promotion simply for lack of knowing what else he wants to do (he just knows he does not want to finish law school, as his father expects him to). He meets Buck Howard (John Malkovich), a faded legend who is apparently unaware that he has passed his prime.

Malkovich is the main reason to see this movie, as is true of many movies that Malkovich has been in. His portrayal of a man used to being treated as a star, and trying to pretend he still is, is almost painfully spot-on.

Howard throws temper tantrums, dreams of a huge comeback, and oozes phony sentiment for the small towns—and their fawning residents—that he is now stuck playing, while secretly despising them. Malkovich plays Buck Howard as exceedingly vain, self-absorbed, and clueless, if not addled. He mimics Kreskin's personality ticks, including the exaggerated handshakes—a routine that is not even funny the first time and grows gruesomely tiring in quick order. His stage act is creaky and worn but somehow seems to touch something genuine in his audiences. The film fails to convey a clue as to what.

Banks develops an ambivalent fascination with the man whose needs he is supposed to anticipate and meet, even when they are impossible to satisfy and even when his boss is contradictory and peevish. Banks is in awe of one bit of Howard's act, a closing trick in which his night's pay in cash is hidden somewhere in the audience, and he always finds it. Is he employing a plant? Or is there something genuine about his mentalist powers despite the corniness and staginess of the rest of his act?

Malkovich has fun with his role, but after a while there is nothing new to gape at. It is too easy to grow tired of this tiresome old man. Banks keeps tagging along, and McGinly must develop some plot twist, so why not a girlfriend? Luckily, he has Emily Blunt to fill the role, and Blunt makes her character, a TV publicist named Valerie, into a spunky helpmate for Troy. There is a predictable romance, an even more predictable tiff, and Troy has to choose between Emily and Buck Howard. Given that this is a movie about how the show must go on, his choice is obvious.

There's also a scene in which Troy's father— played by Colin's real father, Tom Hanks—has a heart-to-heart with his son. In a scene that plays like obvious padding, the elder Hanks looks uncomfortable scolding his real son. For his part, Colin Hanks is remarkably depthless; his Troy seems to be operating in the same time warp as Buck Howard, that magical land of show business where the act never changes. There is no logic to why Troy is hooked up with the mentalist in the first place, no reason why he takes a liking to him, and no reason why we should care very much how the relationship pans out.

In the end, of course, since this is a movie about show business, Buck Howard engineers an unlikely comeback and then manages an exit with extreme grace. That this exit is inconsistent with the selfish, deluded character we have seen is inconsequential to the film. By all rights, the film should end with Buck Howard going off the deep end, breaking down on-stage, or doing something completely nuts. He seems ready to burst the seams of his character at many points, but is held in check, sadly. The result is a mediocre film about mediocrity draped in the entertainment myth that there is some special depth in this sort of performance. Alas, there is absolutely no magic in *The Great Buck Howard*— only cheap tricks and a stab at gushing sentiment that is hardly earned.

Michael Betzold

CREDITS

Troy Gabel: Colin Hanks
Mr. Gable: Tom Hanks
Buck Howard: John Malkovich
Valerie Brennan: Emily Blunt
Johnathan Finerman: Griffin Dunne
Michael Perry: Patrick Fischler
Dan Green: Wallace Langham
Cindy Crown: Stacey Travis
Kenny: Steve Zahn
Gil Bellamy: Ricky Jay
Tonight Show producer: Donny Most
Sheila Haller: Jacquie Barnbrook
Charley: Matt Hoey
Himself: Conan O'Brien (Cameo)
Himself: George Takei (Cameo)
Himself: Tom Arnold (Cameo)
Origin: USA
Language: English
Released: 2009
Production: Gary Goetzman, Tom Hanks; Playtone Pictures, Bristol Bay Prods.; released by Magnolia Pictures
Directed by: Sean McGinly
Written by: Sean McGinly
Cinematography by: Tak Fujimoto
Music by: Blake Neely
Editing: Myron Kerstein
Art Direction: Tristan Paris Bourne
Sound: Alan Robert Murray
Costumes: Johnetta Boone
Production Design: Gary Frutkoff
MPAA rating: PG
Running time: 87 minutes

REVIEWS

Chang, Justin. *Variety.* January 22, 2008.
Childress, Erik. *EFilmCritic.com.* July 16, 2008.
Ebert, Roger. *Chicago Sun-Times.* March 19, 2009.
Gleiberman, Owen. *Entertainment Weekly.* March 19, 2009.
Holden, Stephen. *New York Times.* March 20, 2009.
Kennedy, Lisa. *Denver Post.* March 20, 2009.
Lane, Anthony. *New Yorker.* March 16, 2009.
Long, Tom. *Detroit News.* March 20, 2009.
Puig, Claudia. *USA Today.* March 19, 2009.
Tallerico, Brian. *MovieRetriever.com.* March 19, 2009.

QUOTES

Buck Howard: "That's distilled water. I'm not an iron."

TRIVIA

The Las Vegas scene was filmed in Hollywood on the same set that was used for the Palace Hotel Ballroom scene in *The Blues Brothers*.

H

HALLOWEEN II
(H2: Halloween 2)

Family is forever.
—Movie tagline

Box Office: $33 million

John Carpenter's classic *Halloween* (1978) at once invented and transcended the slasher genre. Its own sequels and innumerable imitators all failed (if indeed they even tried) to capture its unsurpassed terror and suspense. Such was the case with Rob Zombie's disappointing 2007 remake and now his sequel to that film, *Halloween II*.

Carpenter's masterpiece made its terrifying impact through excellent direction, one of the best scores in film history, a superb use of darkness and light, and the masterstroke of the William Shatner mask, its corpse white color interplaying perfectly with the darkness of Halloween night (culminating in the justly famous scene where Michael Myers' mask slowly comes into view from the darkness behind Jamie Lee Curtis). As that chilling scene demonstrates, Carpenter's commitment was to creating suspense and fear. Key to his success was the film's measured, dread-inducing pacing. Like Steven Spielberg's *Jaws* (1975), Carpenter's film built its tension and suspense slowly by giving the viewer only shadowy, half-glimpses of its agent of death, allowing his mystery and murderous potential to slowly permeate the viewer before his killing begins.

Few of these elements were present in the slasher films that followed, movies which were only capable of duplicating and exaggerating the superficial elements of Carpenter's film: the un-killable mute psychopath, a female protagonist whose teenage friends are picked off one by one, sexual activity punished by death and, of course, gore. That these elements have gone on to become iconic genre conventions, ends unto themselves, is highly ironic in that they were essentially incidental features of a film whose primary purpose was to frighten.

Nowhere was this deficiency more apparent than in the sequel to the original *Halloween*. The original *Halloween 2* (1981) lacked the first film's director, suspense and tension-building pacing, and shared only Curtis' heroine, the excellent Donald Pleasance as the indomitable Dr. Loomis, and Carpenter's haunting score. *Halloween 2* was, though released just three years after the original, already a routine slasher film, possessing only the superficial elements of the original film and an agenda concerned not with generating suspense but generating gore and lots of it.

This was, unfortunately, the agenda of Rob Zombie's 2007 *Halloween* remake and now his *Halloween II*, a remake of a sequel which itself was a resounding disappointment compared to its brilliant predecessor. Zombie's *Halloween II* fares much better compared to its 2007 predecessor because it has less distance to fall than the original sequel from its predecessor. Indeed, Zombie's *Halloween II* feels like hours three and four of his 2007 film and measured by the standards of that film is a success. However, it is highly disappointing as compared to the Carpenter original for the same reasons Zombie's 2007 film was a disappointment compared to that film.

As with the original sequel, Zombie's sequel begins minutes after the events of the first film. The apparently dead Michael Myers (Tyler Mane) reveals himself to be anything but and resumes his deadly killing spree, once again relentlessly pursuing his little sister (Scout Taylor Compton) and dispatching colorfully (if briefly) drawn victims along the way. (Zombie has a flair for creating memorable snapshot portraits of his mostly scumbag victims, which makes one wish he would try his hand at a non horror film). As with the 2007 film, there is little attempt to generate suspense, and the tension-building pacing of the Carpenter original is long gone. In its place is the standard genre emphasis on intense gore, body count and inventing novel ways to eliminate the cast. Indeed, the sequel ratchets up the intensity of the carnage even higher than the first film, and the viewer can look forward to being treated to seeing a strip club employee's head graphically crushed under Myer's repeated foot stomps; a sleazy coroner's assistant's head sawed off, in pornographic slowness, by Myers with a piece of glass; a hillbilly impaled on deer horns mounted on the grill of his pickup truck; and a naked stripper's face slammed into a strip club mirror at least half a dozen times.

Halloween II also continues (albeit in mercifully shorter form) Zombie's unwise decision to analyze Michael Myers. Approximately forty percent of Zombie's 2007 film was consumed with the biography and psychological development of Myers. In the sequel, the viewer must endure Myers' hallucinatory visions which come to him in pretentious "film school 101" imagery featuring his dead mother (Sheri Moon Zombie) clad in a white dress, leading a white horse, and accompanied by Michael's younger self in a clown suit all surrounded by a shimmering white glow. Explaining Myers is an admirable attempt on Zombie's part to do something new, but it misunderstands the character's role in the films. Myers' purpose is to be an enigmatic murder machine and to psychologize him is to eliminate the mysteriousness which makes him so terrifying. Carpenter understood this and rendered Myers far more terrifying with two sentences of dialogue from Dr. Loomis than Zombie does in two films worth of psychological analysis—"I met this six-year-old child, with this blank, pale, emotionless face and, the blackest eyes...the devil's eyes. I spent eight years trying to reach him, and then another seven trying to keep him locked up because I realized what was living behind that boy's eyes was purely and simply...evil."

Furthermore, *Halloween II* succeeds in undoing the character of Dr. Loomis (Malcolm McDowell), the one thing the 2007 film managed to get right. In the original *Halloween* films and the 2007 remake, Dr. Loomis was the only empowered adversary of Michael Myers, the only character who was running towards Myers instead of away from him. Loomis' goodness was the counterpoint to Myers' evil, and he was as committed to stop-

ping Myers from killing as Myers was committed to that killing. In Zombie's *Halloween II* Loomis' screen time has been reduced to an extended cameo and his character has undergone a thoroughly unconvincing and emasculating transformation that has more to do with plot requirements than consistency with his character. In so doing, Zombie deprives the series of its moral center and only interesting character.

How much the viewer will enjoy *Halloween II* will depend on his or her appetite for stomach-churning violence and gore, the intensity of which is all that distinguishes it from the hundreds of unimaginative slasher films spawned by Carpenter's film. As with the slasher genre as a whole, *Halloween II* shares little of what made the original genre-establishing film so unique and terrifying and is a tired exercise in an exhausted genre.

Nate Vercauteren

CREDITS

Laurie Strode: Scout Taylor-Compton
Michael Myers: Tyler Mane
Dr. Samuel Loomis: Malcolm McDowell
Deborah Myers: Sheri Moon Zombie
Sheriff Lee Brackett: Brad Dourif
Annie Brackett: Danielle Harris
Uncle Meat: Howard Hesseman
Barbara Collier: Margot Kidder
Mya Rockwell: Brea Grant
Nancy McDonald: Mary Birdsong
Origin: USA
Language: English
Released: 2009
Production: Malek Akkad, Rob Zombie, Andy Gould; released by Dimension Films
Directed by: Rob Zombie
Written by: Rob Zombie
Cinematography by: Brandon Trost
Music by: Tyler Bates
Sound: Buck Robinson
Music Supervisor: Rob Zombie
Editing: Glenn Garland
Art Direction: Timothy "TK" Kirkpatrick
Costumes: Mary McLeod
Production Design: Garreth Stover
MPAA rating: R
Running time: 101 minutes

REVIEWS

Berkshire Geoff. *Metromix.com* August 28, 2009.
Doerksen, Cliff. *Chicago Reader.* September 1, 2009

Edelstein, David. *New York Magazine.* August 31, 2009.

Faraci, Devin. *CHUD.* August 29, 2009.

Miska, Brad. *Bloody Disgusting.* August 28, 2009.

Nelson, Rob. *Variety.* August 28, 2009.

Phipps, Keith. *AV Club.* September 1, 2009

Russo, Tom. *Boston Globe.* September 1, 2009.

Sobczynski, Peter. *eFilmCritic.com.* August 28, 2009.

Weinberg, Scott. *FEARNet.* August 28, 2009.

QUOTES

Deputy Webb: "Hey, Annie, I just do what the boss tells me."

TRIVIA

Laurie has a picture of Charles Manson over her bed. Later, after Lynda's father tries to kill Loomis, it is revealed that the gun was not loaded—just like the gun Manson follower Squeaky Fromme pointed at President Gerald Ford.

THE HANGOVER

Some guys just can't handle Vegas.
—Movie tagline

Box Office: $277.3 million

The crazy-Vegas-bachelor-party-goes-awry movie, to some extent, provides a filmmaker with a simple opportunity to give the people what they want—major drinking, wild debauchery, a little skin, a little violence and everyone learns a valuable lesson. There's nothing too smart, nothing too stupid. The crowd goes home happy.

Thus, it is particularly surprising that director Todd Phillips' *The Hangover* so blatantly fails to deliver even the basest bits of pleasure for the hedonistically inclined viewer. Theoretically, the premise is directly geared towards generating vicarious thrills: Three idiotic dudes (Bradley Cooper, Ed Helms, Zach Galifianakis) retrace their steps in Vegas the day after an out-of-control bachelor party that results in the groom, Doug (Justin Bartha), going missing, the straight-edge pal Stu (Helms) losing a tooth, and the guys' Caesars Palace suite totally trashed—not to mention the unexplainable presence of a chicken, a baby and a big, live tiger in the bathroom.

Unfortunately, *The Hangover* goes through the motions to explain the story behind all this outrageousness in a methodical manner that does not let viewers experience any carefree entertainment along with the characters. Rather, the gang encounters a variety of friends and foes who just explain their actions the night before. This disappointing storytelling decision deprives viewers of any enjoyment and consistently affirms that

living the event in real time—not just hearing about it later—is the only true way to appreciate the scenes' supposedly legendary, unforgettable absurdity. No one wants to just hear about the theft of a cop car or a marriage to a stripper; they want to see it unfold in all its drunken glory.

Complicating things further is that the guys do not work as a balanced onscreen trio. As Doug's loose cannon and brother-in-law-to-be Alan, Galifianakis is playing "the funny one," except he is not funny, just unsettling. The charismatic Cooper plays Phil, the big, type-A personality who takes the lead in the guys' search, but he doesn't have enough domineering attitude to register. And Helms, so amusingly foolish on *The Office*, (2005), is the worrywart—he is constantly concerned about how he looks to his longtime girlfriend Melissa (Rachael Harris), whom he told he was going to Napa Valley—without much room to showcase his chops. Throughout the movie, supporting characters drop hints that last night he unleashed some sort of inner animal, but this is just another idea that *The Hangover* mentions and does not represent visually.

That said, the movie is not free of laughs. They come, usually, not from knockout one-liners but just the ridiculousness of situations. And that is where writers Jon Lucas and Scott Moore (the even less-inspired *Four Christmases*, [2008]) frequently miscalculate. Yes, a naked man leaping groin-first out of a car's trunk onto Galifianakis' shoulders earns a laugh. As does a surprisingly effective cameo by Mike Tyson who, among other things, is featured performing a mini-rendition of Phil Collins' "In the Air Tonight" (1981). The same cannot be said for scenes of the guys throwing around a used condom or an extended sequence in which Officer Franklin (Rob Riggle) demonstrates how to use a Taser. This gag merely registers as a lack of imagination—how many viewers really have never seen a version of this joke before? Ditto for Phillips falling back on a cheap doctor's office gag (Phillips' *Road Trip*, [2000], pulled a similar stunt at a sperm donor clinic), with a brief scene of an elderly man showing his butt. This seems to happen for no reason other than because someone behind the scenes thought the sight of an old man's rear end was funny/gross. Gross? Eh, kinda. Funny? No.

What has never interested Phllips as much as men being examined sans pants is what the fairer sex has to say about things—unless one counts the general female interest in giving better oral sex in *Old School*, (2003)—and *The Hangover* does nothing to turn that around. The only women visible are oblivious fiancées, evil girlfriends, invisible wives or airhead strippers, and no one is around for more than a scene or two. (Heather Graham turns up as a stripper who does not strip on camera but does whip out a boob to breastfeed. Chances are most audiences will not consider this a sufficient helping of nudity.) This male-focused standpoint is no big shock in a guy-oriented movie like this—Judd Apatow's movies do not emphasize female perspectives either—but *The Hangover* demonstrates a misogyny both latent and direct.

Simply, none of the guys seems to value any woman very much. This ranges from Cooper's constant anti-marriage commentary to Helms' denial over how unhappy his shrew-like significant other makes him. Together, these perspectives seem to position men and women as natural enemies, asking the audience to bond with the main male characters and, implicitly, take a stand against the women that complicate their lives. And that's saying nothing of the film generally relegating minority characters into antagonistic roles, presenting the white protagonists as heroes, and their minority obstacles as villains they must defeat or evade.

These messages make the immense box office success of *The Hangover* particularly distressing. If it were simply a meaningless comedy of debatable appeal, fans and detractors could agree to disagree and it would not matter. However, when a film deals in as much negativity and lazy, lowbrow humor as *The Hangover* does, its widespread popularity only becomes that much more distressing of a commentary on what the general public finds funny, and what it wants in a comedy.

Warner Bros., the studio behind *The Hangover*, seems to have predicted this, however. The studio reportedly greenlit a sequel for the film before its release, despite its lack of high-profile stars or a director with a flawless track record. (Phillips' previous film, *School for Scoundrels*, [2006], was far from a critical or box office hit.) Yet Warner Bros. apparently knew audiences would flock to *The Hangover*. What does that say about the way that studios craft films they expect to connect with audiences—and, in turn, what does that then say about how the average moviegoer is perceived by the people making the movies?

Worth noting is that the leaden, mean-spirited storytelling in *The Hangover* never rises to dark satire; it merely buries the energy of a movie most audiences will expect to be a raunchy good time. This problem is not new for Phillips. Even his biggest hits, *Road Trip* and *Old School,* suffer from buzz-killing lags, like Barry's (Tom Green) snake-feeding shenanigans in the former and Mitch's (Luke Wilson) flirtation with Nicole (Ellen Pompeo) in the latter. But Phillips has never put a damper on fun the way he does in *The Hangover,* which could have been a blast if it would just let the adrenaline pump through its veins, instead of merely letting the alcohol seep through its pores. (Even a few more minutes

of the deliciously bad behavior found in *Very Bad Things*, [1998] would have helped greatly.)

The added dulling effect of *The Hangover* comes from the fact that the main characters simply do not do enough on screen. They recap, they discover and they observe. But they do not want anything in the present—other than to find their friend and make it back for his wedding—and their supposedly indulgent past is something they can't remember. (No discernible lessons are taken from this, and the movie does nothing to suggest that it is, as some have commented, a statement about Vegas partygoers' subconscious intent to forget everything that happens there.) Thanks to a movie that's not remotely as enjoyable as an actual Vegas bachelor party, the guys never really relive their bash. What good is the best night ever if no one—neither the characters nor the viewers—feels the lingering satisfaction of what actually happened?

Matt Pais

CREDITS

Phil: Bradley Cooper
Stu: Ed Helms
Alan: Zach Galifianakis
Doug: Justin Bartha
Jade: Heather Graham
Mr. Chow: Ken Jeong
Sid: Jeffrey Tambor
Melissa: Rachael Harris
Black Doug: Mike Epps
Himself: Mike Tyson
Tracy: Sasha Barrese
Origin: USA
Language: English
Released: 2009
Production: Todd Phillips, Dan Goldberg; Legendary Pictures, Green Hat Films; released by Warner Bros.
Directed by: Todd Phillips
Written by: Jon Lucas, Scott Moore
Cinematography by: Lawrence Sher
Music by: Christophe Beck
Sound: Lee Orloff
Music Supervisor: George Drakoulias, Randall Psster
Editing: Debra Neil-Fisher
Art Direction: Andrew Max Cahn
Costumes: Louise Mingenbach
Production Design: Bill Brzeski
MPAA rating: R
Running time: 100 minutes

REVIEWS

Childress, Erik. *eFilmCritic.com.* June 5, 2009.
Corliss, Richard. *Time Magazine.* June 5, 2009.
Ebert, Roger. *Chicago Sun-Times.* June 4, 2009.

Kennedy, Lisa. *Denver Post.* June 5, 2009.

Leydon, Joe. *Variety.* May 26, 2009.

Pais, Matt. *Metromix.com.* June, 4, 2009.

Phillips, Michael. *Chicago Tribune.* June 5, 2009.

Scott, A.O. *New York Times.* June 5, 2009.

Stevens, Dana. *Slate.* June 5, 2009.

Tallerico, Brian. *MovieRetriver.com.* June 5, 2009.

QUOTES

Phil Wenneck: "Would you please put some pants on? I feel weird having to ask you twice."

TRIVIA

During filming in Las Vegas, one of the Mercedes (a very beat up and distinctive one) was stolen from the lot where the vehicles were being kept. The next day the production was filming driving sequences and traffic was being held up by the local police. A production person noticed that a very distinctive Mercedes was part of the cars being held, the police were told, the driver was arrested and the car was recovered.

AWARDS

Golden Globes 2010: Film—Musical or Comedy

Nomination:

British Acad. 2009: Orig. Screenplay

Writers Guild 2009: Orig. Screenplay.

HANNAH MONTANA: THE MOVIE

She has the best of both worlds...now, she has to pick just one.
—Movie tagline

Box Office: $80 million

A more appropriate title would be *Hannah Montana: The 90-Minute Advertisement.* That is because *Hannah Montana: The Movie* has no positive messages to relate to young viewers. It has no laughs and no story that makes even the slightest bit of sense. The only purpose of the film is to perpetuate the popularity of the Disney franchise and its star, whose fame is baffling on many levels.

Miley Cyrus, who plays Miley Stewart and her blonde wig-wearing pop star alter ego Hannah Montana, has no comic timing. She has a completely impersonal singing voice and immensely generic songs. And in the *Hannah Montana* TV series and film, she has no identifiable characteristics that would establish her character as a role model for her fans.

The only thing there is to know about Miley Stewart and Hannah Montana is that Miley, as most teen girls probably would, likes the fame and attention that comes with being Hannah. However, her dad Robby Ray (Cyrus' real-life father, country singer Billy Ray Cyrus) is constantly afraid that success will go to his daughter's head and she will neglect her family, friends and roots as a small-town Tennessee gal—reasonable concerns for a pop star's dad to have. Thus, Miley spends all of her time and energy trying to prevent the world from finding out that she is Hannah Montana.

It is a ruse that brings her not privacy and comfort but endless frustration and a detachment from fans. If she would just stop pretending, her life would be less confusing and would tell kids that pop stars are real people too. Considering fans do not realize Miley is Hannah without the wig, Miley could probably admit she's Hannah and still fool people when she wanted to just by putting on sunglasses. Yet if Miley did that there would be no franchise, so she constantly puts on and takes off her wig to go in and out of being Hannah. It is exhausting for her to do, and it is exhausting to watch her do it.

This foundation leaves little room for a feature film, and consequently *Hannah Montana: The Movie* is just an incoherent reiteration of Hannah's stardom. Fittingly, the movie opens with a huge crowd of young fans screaming "Hannah! Hannah!" and eagerly awaiting a performance from the singer. Yet as the fans cheer, Miley Stewart and her best friend Lilly (Emily Osment) are attempting to enter the stadium through the ticket counter. It is ridiculous to think a pop star would need to enter her own concert along with the fans. And even if she did, would supposedly diehard fans not recognize their favorite singer just because her hair color has changed? Miley's attempt to remain anonymous offstage makes Clark Kent look like a master of disguise.

Soon Miley's refusal to let people know she's Hannah ruins Lilly's "Sweet 16" party, so Robby Ray brings his daughter back to Tennessee for her grandma Ruby's (Margo Martindale) birthday to ensure Miley has her priorities straight. In Tennessee, Miley reconnects and flirts with young farmhand Travis (Lucas Till) and is pursued by British tabloid reporter Oswald Granger (Peter Gunn), who hopes to dig up juicy information about Hannah Montana for a big story. Meanwhile, the small town strives to raise money to drive away a developer (Barry Bostwick) who wants to cover the part of the town's land with a mall, which is pretty much the laziest, most obvious small-town-values-versus-big-city-expansion subplot imaginable.

A summary of the comedy that results: Miley switches bowls of hot and mild salsa to trick Oswald into burning his tongue. Robby Ray knocks grandma's collector plates off the shelf. When Hannah agrees to perform a concert to raise money, Miley winds up dashing back and forth between being Hannah at a dinner with community leaders and being Miley at dinner with Travis. And every so often Miley's brother Jackson (Jason Earles) gets bit by an alligator or falls off a ladder or makes some other big, manic and terribly unfunny gesture.

In one of the film's early scenes, Hannah goes shoe shopping and winds up in a loud wrestling match with Tyra Banks as the two stars fight over shoes. Clearly just an excuse to drop another celebrity into the movie, the scene accidentally winds up asserting that, yes, Hannah Montana just might be as shrill and obnoxious as Tyra Banks.

The Banks' fight is a tough sequence to top in terms of how painful it is to watch. Yet *Hannah Montana: The Movie* pulls it off later as Miley, performing as herself, teaches the townspeople "Hoedown Throwdown," a hip-hop-influenced country line dance that should revolt any fans of hip-hop or country music. The song is not only alarmingly terrible—lyrics include "Pop it, lock it, polka-dot it"—but contradicts the idea that Miley, when she is not pretending to be Hannah, is just an innocent country girl with no connection to the world outside Tennessee, which the film presents as so detached from Hollywood that it may as well be another country. (Tennessee-based rock stars Kings of Leon, among countless others, would beg to differ.)

Throughout, Cyrus embarrassingly mugs for the camera while Miley faces no problems outside of the complications resulting from trying to be two people at once. (Still, she finds remarkable profundity in Travis' statement that "Life's a climb, but the view's great," which sounds like the world's lamest greeting card.) When she both comes clean and maintains the lie, viewers receive not lessons about self-image or the perils of fame, just some new, bland songs to purchase after the movie.

Of course, *Hannah Montana: The Movie* is not trying to deliver a message, only a product. It is an excuse to expand a brand and sell tickets, CDs, lunchboxes and stickers. In fact, that's the one thing that makes sense about Hannah Montana and her movie: the business strategy behind them.

Matt Pais

CREDITS

Miley Stewart/Hannah Montana: Miley Cyrus
Lilly Truscott/Lola Luftnagle: Emily Osment
Robby Stewart: Billy Ray Cyrus
Heather Truscott: Heather Locklear
Jackson Stewart: Jason Earles
Aunt Dolly Stewart: Dolly Parton
Rico: Moises Arias
Travis Brody: Lucas Till
Origin: USA
Language: English
Released: 2009
Production: Billy Ray Cyrus, Alfred Gough, Miles Millar; It's a Laugh Productions, Millar Gough Ink, Walt Disney Pictures; released by Walt Disney Pictures
Directed by: Peter Chelsom
Written by: Daniel Berendsen
Cinematography by: David Hennings
Music by: Alan Silvestri
Editing: Virginia Katz
Sound: Todd Toon
Art Direction: Elliott Glick
Costumes: Christopher Lawrence
Production Design: Caroline Hanania
MPAA rating: G
Running time: 102 minutes

REVIEWS

Anderson, John. *Newsday.* April 9, 2009.
Barnard, Linda. *Toronto Star.* April 10, 2009.
Kaltenbach, Chris. *Baltimore Sun.* April 10, 2009.
Lowenstein, Lael. *Variety.* April 7, 2009.
MacDonald, Moira. *Seattle Times.* April 9, 2009.
McNamara, Mary. *Los Angeles Times.* April 9, 2009.
Morris, Wesley. *Boston Globe.* April 9, 2009.
Rabin, Nathan. *AV Club.* April 9, 2009.
Sobczynski, Peter. *eFilmCritic.* April 9, 2009.
Zacharek, Stephanie. *Salon.com.* April 10, 2009.

QUOTES

Hannah Montana: "The last time I was on this stage I was 6, I was…Miley. And I still am."

TRIVIA

One day on set, the winds were very high, and blew a piece of lighting equipment onto a ferris wheel full of extras, injuring several of them. Miley Cyrus had just finished shooting a scene next to the ferris wheel when the accident occurred.

AWARDS

Golden Raspberries 2009: Worst Support. Actor (Cyrus)
Nomination:
Golden Raspberries 2009: Worst Actress (Cyrus).

HARRY POTTER AND THE HALF-BLOOD PRINCE

Dark secrets revealed.
—Movie tagline

Once again I must ask too much of you, Harry.
  —Movie tagline

Box Office: $302 million

What is the purpose of the Harry Potter films at this point? On the surface, that may seem like an easy-to-answer question—people enjoy J.K. Rowling's Harry Potter books and the box-office tallies suggest that they enjoy the movie versions as well—but it speaks to many of the issues surrounding the complicated science of adapting popular written works for the silver screen. What is Warner Brothers trying to accomplish with their Harry Potter series? The first two Potter films, directed by the saccharine, literal Chris Columbus, were rote exercises in reproducing text on film, capturing moment after moment of Rowling's earliest and shortest works on screen with the detached efficiency of a stenographer. The third movie, *Prisoner of Azkaban*, directed by Alfonso Cuarón, was a watershed for the series, a definite move in the right direction, because it marked the first time a director, due to his own virtuosity and the physical need to compress the storyline to fit a film's running time, was able to truly make the movie his own. Because, unlike Columbus' films, *Prisoner of Azkaban* could not, for time's sake, recount beat-for-beat the entirety of Rowling's text, Cuarón created a movie adaptation that focused more on capturing the emotions and tone of the original text rather than the storyline itself. While this approach was undeniably successful—*Prisoner of Azkaban* remains the best Potter film to date—it did have a profound effect on the future of the Harry Potter film series, an effect with both positive and negative consequences.

David Yates has directed two of the three Potter films that followed Cuarón's *Prisoner of Azkaban*, and he will also be helming the seventh and final chapter in the Potter series, making him the most direct descendant of Cuarón's cinematic legacy, in terms of Harry Potter films. And what is Cuarón's legacy? Unfortunately, following *Azkaban*, it seems like the filmmakers decided, since it would be impossible to capture every beat of Rowling's beloved text on film, that narrative itself would become a secondary priority, a policy that is firmly in effect in Yates' *Harry Potter and the Half-Blood Prince*. The sixth chapter of the Potter franchise unquestionably has a high pedigree—amazing visuals, a fantastic cast, and mood dripping out of its ears—and yet it has apparently abandoned one of the most basic filmmaking elements of all: storytelling. While Yates' *Half-Blood Prince* seems to acknowledge the most superficial lessons learned from Cuarón's *Azkaban*, in terms of atmosphere and creative editing, it completely fails to find *Azkaban*'s difficult balance between story and mood, instead offering up a

skeleton narrative that no one except an already-committed Potter fan could ever be expected to follow.

Half-Blood Prince opens in the immediate aftermath of the previous *Harry Potter and the Order of the Phoenix*, a reality in which the wizarding community is now forced to recognize that the evil Lord Voldemort has returned to power and the Dark Lord and his dastardly Death Eaters have begun a campaign of terror against the mundane and magical worlds. (Forget any "Previously on Harry Potter" recap. If you have not seen or read *Order of the Phoenix*, there is little reason to see *Half-Blood Prince*.) As the Dark forces rally against Headmaster Albus Dumbledore (Michael Gambon) and the students of Hogwarts, Professor Severus Snape (Alan Rickman) is strong-armed into making an Unbreakable Vow to help Voldemort-controlled student Draco Malfoy (Tom Felton), under pains of death, complete some secret, dark task. Meanwhile, Dumbledore enlists Harry Potter (Daniel Radcliffe) to help him lure an influence-hungry ex-professor, Horace Slughorn (Jim Broadbent), back to Hogwarts. Slughorn, apparently, holds in his head a pivotal memory related to Lord Voldemort's rise to power, and Dumbledore makes it Harry's semester-long mission to cozy up to Slughorn in order to obtain the details of said memory. In his first class with Slughorn, his new Magic Potions professor, Harry is given an aging copy of a Potions textbook with hand-annotated notes by someone called "the Half-Blood Prince," notes that allow Potter to suddenly and unexpectedly excel at his Potions work.

While Harry slowly works at becoming Slughorn's new favorite student, other tensions are on the rise at Hogwarts. Draco Malfoy becomes obsessed with his secretive task, Harry's friends become concerned about the origins of the "Half-Blood Prince," and the romantic friction continues to build between Harry's pals Ron Weasley (Rupert Grint) and Hermione Granger (Emma Watson). Since the pair continues to refuse to admit their mutual attraction, their escalating arguing sends them into the arms of other suitors, leaving Ron stuck in the clingy, petulant hands of fellow student Lavender Brown. Making matters worse, Harry is quickly realizing his increasing attraction to Ron's younger sister, Ginny (Bonnie Wright).

While the romantic entanglements unfold, Harry is finally able to obtain Slughorn's forbidden memory and discovers that Voldemort, as a student, split his soul into seven different pieces, trapping each piece into physical objects known as Horcruxes. Dumbledore realizes that two of the Horcruxes have already been destroyed, so he and Harry search for the remaining five, in hopes of destroying Voldemort once and for all. After an intense magical showdown in an enchanted cave that holds one of the Horcruxes, Harry is forced to drag a horribly wounded Dumbledore back to Hogwarts, only to discover that Malfoy has succeeded in his plan, altering a magic Vanishing Cabinet to allow a strike-team of Death Eaters to sneak into the school in order to murder Dumbledore. However, in the final moments of the siege, Malfoy is unable to bring himself to finish off the aging headmaster, and, in accordance with his vow, Professor Snape kills Dumbledore in front of Harry, leaving the young wizard with a quest to find and destroy the other Horcruxes and avenge his fallen mentor.

With all that said, is it fair to criticize *Harry Potter and the Half-Blood Prince* for its abbreviated story-telling? It is definitely fair to say that other classic films, adapted from other long-form works of literature, have made similar cuts without jeopardizing the quality of their final product. And certainly one would have a hard time making heads or tails of Peter Jackson's *Return of the King* if they had not seen the previous Lord of the Rings movies. So what does *Harry Potter and the Half-Blood Prince* really do wrong? In the end, it's not the fact that the movie cuts and abbreviates, it's with *what* they cut and abbreviate. The number one storytelling fatality in the later Potter films is character (and, as a result, character motivation) and that's a terrible place to skimp when it comes to narrative. Yates is so concerned with hitting the biggest beats—showing the action sequences, the mood moments, the kisses, the murders, the betrayals—that he barely pays any attention to how those beats are set up, how they're earned or paid off. And, as such, when those moments happen, the audience feels nothing because Yates has not done his due diligence.

The two biggest moments in *Half-Blood Prince* are Snape killing Dumbledore and Harry realizing that Ginny Weasley is the love of his life, and neither moment has an ounce of impact because neither Snape nor Ginny has been established as characters viewers should care about in the Potter cinematic universe. Both characters have had barely four lines apiece over the past three Potter films, and yet audiences are suddenly expected to feel something when they participate in huge, life-changing events in the story? That's impossible. (The pay-off on the mystery of "who is the Half-Blood Prince?" is particularly pathetic on film.) And the only reason that audiences have been forgiving such lazy storytelling in, particularly, Yates' Potter movies is that J.K. Rowling created such a ubiquitous, world-recognized pop culture universe that audience members have been filling in the blanks of the movies' anemic narrative. Yates doesn't spend thirty minutes setting up the Ginny-Harry romance because, knowing that his audience will be primarily comprised of people who have read the original book, he'd rather just give glimpses and use that extra time to have a Quidditch match or monster attack or two. It is an interesting technique, but it begs the

question—is this really storytelling? Could anyone who hadn't already read J.K. Rowling's original book actually follow, understand, or enjoy *Harry Potter and the Half-Blood Prince*? Is it enough to lay out an outline and let the audience fill in the rest or is there any responsibility placed on the filmmaker to create a self-sustained story with a beginning, middle, and end?

This all leads back to the question of "What is the purpose of the Harry Potter films?" Are they supposed to be movies that exist on their merit as works of art? Or are they merely visual representations of a popular storyline that the world already knows by heart? The answer probably lies in the grey realm of personal preference, but it is hard to imagine anyone being satisfied with Yates' *Harry Potter and the Half-Blood Prince* without the help of J.K. Rowling silently supplementing the film in the background. Such is the power of a true storyteller.

Tom Burns

CREDITS

Harry Potter: Daniel Radcliffe
Hermione Granger: Emma Watson
Ron Weasley: Rupert Grint
Albus Dumbledore: Michael Gambon
Severus Snape: Alan Rickman
Horace Slughorn: Jim Broadbent
Bellatrix Lestrange: Helena Bonham Carter
Rubeus Hagrid: Robbie Coltrane
Minerva McGonagall: Maggie Smith
Remus Lupin: David Thewlis
Draco Malfoy: Tom Felton
Ginny Weasley: Bonnie Wright
Molly Weasley: Julie Walters
Arthur Weasley: Mark Williams
Narcissa Malfoy: Helen McCrory
Petunia Dursley: Fiona Shaw
Lavender Brown: Jessie Cave
Vernon Dursley: Richard Griffiths
Wormtail: Timothy Spall
Argus Filch: David Bradley
Filius Flitwick: Warwick Davis
Origin: USA, Great Britain
Language: English
Released: 2009
Production: David Heyman, David Barron; Heyday Films; released by Warner Bros.
Directed by: David Yates
Written by: Steve Kloves
Cinematography by: Bruno Delbonnel

Music by: Nicholas Hooper
Sound: Stuart Wilson
Editing: Mark Day
Art Direction: Neil Lamont
Costumes: Jany Temime
Production Design: Stuart Craig
MPAA rating: PG
Running time: 153 minutes

REVIEWS

Busch, Jenna. *JoBlo's Movie Emporium.* July 7, 2009.
Childress, Erik. *eFilmCritic.com.* July 13, 2009.
Corliss, Richard. *Time Magazine.* July 13, 2009.
Ebert, Roger. *Chicago Sun-Times.* July 13, 2009.
Edelstein, David. *New York Magazine.* July 13, 2009.
Kois, Dan. *Washington Post.* July 14, 2009.
Long, Tom. *Detroit News.* July 14, 2009.
McCarthy, Todd. *Variety.* July 6, 2009.
Phillips, Michael. *Chicago Tribune.* July 13, 2009.
Turan, Kenneth. *Los Angeles Times.* July 14, 2009.

QUOTES

Arthur Weasley: "Times like these, dark times, they do funny things to people. They can tear them apart."

TRIVIA

Director Guillermo del Toro reportedly turned down directing this film so he could instead make *Hellboy II: The Golden Army.*

AWARDS

Nomination:

Oscars 2009: Cinematog.
British Acad. 2009: Visual FX, Prod. Des.

THE HAUNTING IN CONNECTICUT

Some things cannot be explained.
—Movie tagline

Box Office: $55 million

The Haunting in Connecticut is a haunted house thriller that comes billed not just as being "based on a true story" but "based on *the* true story." Of course, wiser moviegoers will instinctively understand that this admonition is virtually a guarantee that everything about to be shown is just as completely made up as any ordinary horror movie. Just for a moment, though, let us give it the benefit of the doubt and assume that

everything seen and heard in the film really happened to the unfortunate family at its center. Do you suppose that, while on a brief respite from fighting off all varieties of supernatural terrors, any of them ever remarked on how closely their lives and the events they were experiencing matched up with virtually every other haunted-house movie ever made? After all, the family consists of a stalwart mom who will do anything to protect her family (save moving out at the first sign of trouble), a father with a long-buried personal problem that rears its ugly head at the first sign of trouble, an isolated teen who proves to be the ideal conduit for evil spirits, a couple of little kids who exist only to be occasionally spooked, and a nubile niece who exists primarily to supply a shower scene when needed. Face it, from a paranormal perspective, this family is pretty much asking for everything that they get right from the get-go.

The family in question is the Campbell clan—mom Sara (Virginia Madsen), dad Peter (Martin Donovan), teen son Matt (Kyle Gallner), moppets Mary (Sophi Knight) and Billy (Ty Wood) and niece Wendy (Amanda Crew)—and as things kick off, they are already at the end of their mental and financial ropes thanks to special medical treatments for cancer-stricken Matt that require extensive and extended car trips to a faraway clinic. Finally, Sara decides that it would be easier to simply rent a home nearer to the clinic and move there for the duration of the treatment, and she finds a rambling Victorian home in upstate Connecticut that includes a huge lawn, plenty of bedrooms, a rock-bottom rent and, as the real estate agent eventually admits, "a bit of a history." This turns out to be real-estate talk for "a house that was once a funeral parlor in which the owner routinely held séances conducted by his young assistant (Erik Berg) and defiled many of the corpses as a way of boosting his protégé's abilities even further." Nevertheless, the yard is really impressive, the family moves in and you can pretty much fill in the blanks from that point on: Matt begins seeing hideous visions of that assistant, along with the usual array of bugs, blood and long-ago atrocities, the family slowly but surely begins to experience odd things as well, ancient secrets are uncovered—via rotten floorboards and the local library—and a dying priest (Elias Koteas) shambles in during the final act in the hopes of setting everything right.

The trouble with *The Haunting in Connecticut* is not that it is just another haunted house thriller but that it is pretty much *every* haunted house thriller ever made rolled into one. There is not one element on display that even a casual fan of the genre will not find to be anything other than utterly familiar. And while the idea of an old-school story of this type sounds kind of appealing as a rejoinder to all the horror movies of late featuring mad slashers and glittery vampires, the material is handled in such a pedestrian and lethargic manner that the only time most viewers will be on the edge of their seats is when they are getting up to hit the concession stand, content in the knowledge that they will not be missing much of anything. It is useless to criticize the screenplay since it is so obviously a load of malarkey consisting almost entirely of material that worked in other movies. No, the film's biggest sin is that it is not frightening or unnerving for even a second—instead of trying to build any real sense of tension or fear, director Peter Cornwell instead fills the screen with "BOO!" moments when something suddenly appears in the background, usually accompanied by a loud musical blast, to startle viewers. This is an approach that can be effective when used sparingly but when it is deployed over and over, it quickly becomes annoying. The sole exception is a moment in which we allegedly see ectoplasm emerging from someone's mouth as some kind of paranormal puke, but even though the producers were proud enough to make it the central image of the promotional campaign, the effect is not as much terrifying as it is inadvertently hilarious.

There are plenty of questions that anyone watching *The Haunting in Connecticut* might be ready to ask as the end credits roll, and the one at the top of my list was "For God's sake, what is Virginia Madsen doing in this?" Madsen is one of those actresses who, despite her obvious beauty and talent, never quite made it as a star in Hollywood until her career received a much-deserved second act with her Oscar®-nominated performance in *Sideways* (2004). On the strength of that film and the heat that it generated for her career, one might have expected that she would be working on more prestigious projects, but, instead, she is appearing in a film like this, something that she sensibly might have turned down even back in the days when her career was on the fallow side. One can only conclude that she took the part for one of two reasons—she was offered a ton of money or it was literally the best thing that she was offered at the time. If it is the former, the impulse is understandable, and one can only hope that whatever she used the money for was worth it. If it is the latter, then that is a far scarier notion than anything on display here.

Peter Sobczynski

CREDITS

Sara Campbell: Virginia Madsen
Matt Campbell: Kyle Gallner
Reverend Popescu: Elias Koteas
Wendy: Amanda Crew
Peter Campbell: Martin Donovan

Billy Campbell: Ty Wood
Mary: Sophi Knight
Jonah: Erik J. Berg
Ramsey Aickman: John Bluethner
Origin: USA, Canada
Language: English
Released: 2009
Production: Paul Brooks, Daniel Farrands, Wendy Rhoads, Andrew Trapani; Gold Circle Films, Integrated Film & Management; released by Lionsgate
Directed by: Peter Cornwell
Written by: Adam Simon, Tim Metcalfe
Cinematography by: Adam Swica
Music by: Robert Kral
Sound: Anke Bakker
Editing: Tom Elkins
Art Direction: Edward S. Bonutto
Costumes: Meg McMillan
Production Design: Alicia Keywan
MPAA rating: PG-13
Running time: 102 minutes

REVIEWS

Catsoulis, Jeanette. *New York Times.* March 27, 2009.
DeFore, John. *Hollywood Reporter.* March 18, 2009.
Ebert, Roger. *Chicago Sun-Times.* March 26, 2009.
Foundas, Scott. *Village Voice.* March 24, 2009.
Leydon, Joe. *Variety.* March 18, 2009.
Long, Tom. *Detroit News.* March 27, 2009.
Morris, Wesley. *Boston Globe.* March 26, 2009.
Olsen, Mark. *Los Angeles Times.* March 27, 2009.
Pais, Matt. *Metromix.com.* March 26, 2009.
Phillips, Michael. *Chicago Tribune.* March 26, 2009.

QUOTES

Matt Campbell: "Doctor says to patient, 'You have cancer and you have Alzheimer's.' Patient says to doctor, 'Wooo! At least I don't have cancer.'"

TRIVIA

In the original story, the one trapped in the bathroom curtain is Sara and not Wendy.

HE'S JUST NOT THAT INTO YOU

Are you the exception...or the rule?
—Movie tagline

Box Office: $94 million

He's Just Not That Into You attempts to break down relationships into black-and-white, hard-and-firm rules. In theory, this is a good idea: Anyone struggling with relationship woes—according to the movie, this appears to be practically all good-looking people in their 20s and 30s—would surely be thrilled to have a straightforward guide to love, with surefire tips on when to call, when not to call, and so forth.

In practice, however, *He's Just Not That Into You*, adapted by writers Abby Kohn and Marc Silverstein from the self-help book by Greg Behrendt and Liz Tuccillo (2004), is anything but helpful. Too often it depicts women as needy and neurotic, and men as sex-obsessed and commitment-phobic. For a romantic comedy that attempts to survey the challenges involved in modern dating, these presentations are far from modern.

The movie is an unfunny, over-stuffed ensemble piece in which few of the relationships receive much depth. Jennifer Aniston stars as Beth, who wants to marry Neil (Ben Affleck), her boyfriend of seven years. Neil does not believe in marriage. That is their story, and all there is to it. Then there is Ben (Bradley Cooper), who feels that he rushed into marriage with Janine (Jennifer Connelly) and consequently begins a fling with Anna (Scarlett Johansson), a young, sexually aggressive yoga instructor who asks Ben, "Why are you married, again?" The film's most emotionally unstable character is Gigi (Ginnifer Goodwin), a single girl who commits social faux pas after faux pas in blunt, desperate attempts to make guys tell her exactly what they mean all the time.

In fact, much of *He's Just Not That Into You* revolves around the notion that relationships—and life in general—would be much easier if everyone was always direct and honest, all the time. This, of course, is both a minor truth and a major oversimplification. Humans, by nature, can be dishonest and confused and flawed. Instead of understanding and interpreting this, the film merely seems to dream about things being different, to no dramatic avail or benefit to lovelorn viewers.

Some of the worst scenes involve workplace discussions among Beth, Janine and Gigi. The women work together at an ad agency but spend practically all of their time gossiping about their romantic problems. Not only does this reflect negatively on women in the workplace, but it becomes particularly absurd when Janine is in the midst of a breakdown about her marriage yet still becomes immensely excited by the opportunity to hear about Gigi's latest dating exploits. This makes already immature discussions sound all the more detached from reality.

At the heart of the movie is the truth that when people lie to each other, it often causes people to lie to

themselves. (Several female characters concoct far-fetched explanations for why a guy hasn't called, such as suspecting he was hit by a cab or his grandmother died.) This could be an intriguing point about the nature of relationships, but, like so many of the thought-provoking ideas floating around in *He's Just Not That Into You*, this is not explored, but instead beaten down by forced dialogue—Anna notes that Ben has "an ass that makes me want to dry hump"— and even more forced comedic antics.

The movie's better moments come from discussions about uniquely 21st century dating challenges. At one point, Mary (Drew Barrymore) complains about how complicated it can be when people simultaneously try to make contact through phone, email, text, MySpace, Blackberry and more. However, scenes like this are few and far between and, while amusing, typically feel more like recognition than analysis. A more compelling, bold—and, perhaps, funnier—movie might look at the popularity of Internet dating compared to, say, meeting people in bars, and why some people may or may not thrive meeting in person versus on a computer.

Periodically, the story stops and title cards present a situation, such as "If he's not marrying you." Then, actors (playing average people on the street) offer anecdotal advice about what it means if (in this case) a man will not propose. While sporadically entertaining and useful in breaking up the plot's onslaught of relationship-focused conversations, these scenes merely deliver concrete generalizations that seem flimsy and naïve. Worse, these scenes further reinforce gender stereotypes, as women are exclusively used to comment on emotionally related issues, and the only subject that men are asked to comment on is "If she's not sleeping with you." This again reduces men and women to single-minded concepts, not equally intelligent people with complex, varied needs and desires. Consequently, it is unlikely that *He's Just Not That Into You* would make a very pleasant date movie, nor much of an enjoyable outing for a group of men or women. Neither men nor women should be happy with how they are portrayed in the movie, and both singles and couples are given much more to fight about than to laugh about or really discuss.

It is also debatable if general audiences want to hear so much relationship chatter from a cast of exclusively attractive and familiar celebrities. Perhaps the implicit message could be that, yes, even beautiful people have problems with love. However, the all-star cast proves to be a curse rather than a blessing, as the largely insincere performances render many conversations as more like rehearsal for a play, not a productive commentary on universal romantic concerns. The irony is that, as anyone who reads publications like *People Magazine* knows, the issues covered in the movie—insecurity, communication problems, commitment fears, etc.—are indeed perfectly relevant to the wealthy, beautiful celebrities being paid to discuss them.

Actually, the rote conversational stream found in *He's Just Not That Into You* might work better on stage, where live, one-note reflections might seem more urgent and less shallow. On the big screen, it's like a term paper that needs a lot of rewrites.

Matt Pais

CREDITS

Mary: Drew Barrymore
Beth: Jennifer Aniston
Connor: Kevin Connolly
Janine: Jennifer Connelly
Ben: Bradley Cooper
Gigi: Ginnifer Goodwin
Alex: Justin Long
Anna: Scarlett Johansson
Neil: Ben Affleck
Nathan: Wilson Cruz
Ken Murphy: Kris Kristofferson
Tyrone: Cory Hardrict
Joshua: Leonardo Nam
Origin: USA
Language: English
Released: 2009
Production: Nancy Juvonen; New Line Cinema, Flower Films; released by Warner Bros.
Directed by: Ken Kwapis
Written by: Abby Kohn, Marc Silverstein
Cinematography by: John Bailey
Music by: Cliff Eidelman
Sound: Richard Goodman
Music Supervisor: Danny Bramson
Editing: Cara Silverman
Art Direction: Andrew Max Cahn
Costumes: Shay Cunliffe
Production Design: Gae Buckley
MPAA rating: PG-13
Running time: 129 minutes

REVIEWS

Anderson, John. *Variety.* February 2, 2009.
Bradshaw, Peter. *Guardian.* February 6, 2009.
Burr, Ty. *Boston Globe.* February 5, 2009.
Dargis, Manohla. *New York Times.* February 6, 2009.
Ebert, Roger. *Chicago Sun-Times.* February 5, 2009.
Honeycutt, Kirk. *Hollywood Reporter.* February 2, 2009.
Rickey, Carrie. *Philadelphia Inquirer.* February 5, 2009.
Sharkey, Betsy. *Los Angeles Times.* February 6, 2009.
Sobczynski, Peter. *eFilmCritic.com.* February 5, 2009.
Tallerico, Brian. *HollywoodChicago.com.* February 5, 2009.

QUOTES

Alex: "You're my exception."

TRIVIA

This film is set in Baltimore, Maryland. In the film Beth's cousin says that it's too bad that cousins can't marry. However, in the state of Maryland, first cousins can get married.

HOTEL FOR DOGS

No stray gets turned away.
—Movie tagline

Box Office: $73 million

The direct, animal-focused title of this film does not do justice to this surprisingly charming, people-centered family movie that results. Charismatic canines abound and provide much comic relief, to be sure, but they are mostly background (and heavy-handed allegory) for the story of two orphaned kids looking for a home. Andi (Emma Roberts) and Bruce (Jake T. Austin) have been shuffling their way from uncaring foster parents to even more uncaring foster parents for the last couple of years, and have now found themselves at the mercy of two self-centered, over-aged wannabe rockers, Lois and Carl Scudder (hilariously coiffed Lisa Kudrow and Matt Dillon), who have a "no animals allowed" policy for their tiny apartment/recording studio. The problem is that the kids want to hold on to Friday, their cutie-pie of a dog and the only connection they have left to their parents. Luckily, Bruce is an MIT-worthy inventor and the duo moonlight as quick-witted petty thieves. Bruce's machines, assembled from "borrowed" household goods allow Friday to get in and out of the apartment unnoticed and their double-dealing provides cash for Friday's food.

When the kids get caught scamming a local pawn shop, even their sympathetic and even-tempered child services counselor Bernie (Don Cheadle) is at a loss. He tells them that if they mess up again he will not be able to keep placing them in foster homes together. Andi is ready to give up Friday in the hopes that she and her brother could lead a more steady life away from one another, but Bruce will not hear of it. He is determined to keep his family together, no matter what. Amazingly, but not surprisingly, it is Friday who stumbles on to the answer. He runs away into an abandoned downtown hotel, leading Bruce and Andi to chase after him. The hotel, it turns out, has already been claimed by a couple of strays who take to Friday immediately. What starts as a temporary solution to Andi and Bruce's dog troubles provides the kids with a makeshift family when the duo join forces with the teen staff of a nearby pet store—handsome Dave (Johnny Simmons) and catty but harmless Heather (Kyla Pratt)—and start rescuing other strays in town. Bruce's quick thinking transforms the hotel into doggie camp heaven and the kids finally start to feel wanted and accepted. Still the balance is precarious at best: lying to Bernie about the hotel and sneaking out of the Scudder's apartment to manage the hotel is one thing, but Andi's refusal to tell the truth about her family life to any of her new friends ultimately lands her and Bruce in some deep emotional doo-doo. Obviously, the inherent bubbly nature of this kid and his/her dog story necessitates a happy ending, but surprisingly much genuine nail-biting and heart-tugging ensues before these resourceful and determined kids land on their feet.

Hotel for Dogs marks German director Thor Freudenthal's Hollywood debut, and while some directors might balk at entering the game with a kid's flick, Freudenthal approaches the material with genre savvy and it pays off. The visual elements move at a tight pace and none of the emotional pull of the story is sacrificed—which is good for any adults who will be chaperoning a screening. Though a discerning adult viewer might have questions about some narrative details that could use more explanation (such as how exactly the Scudders managed to become foster parents, and when Bernie became so invested in Andi and Bruce's life, and why exactly Andi feels the need to lie about her real family situation) and may find themselves questioning how Andi and Bruce can be so well-adjusted given the loss of their parents, any concerns are quickly forgotten as the story plows ahead with more heart-tugging high jinks. Attention-grabbing action for kids, mom-friendly emotion and grammar-school level comedy (gross poop jokes and yucky kissing puppies) are all kept in check, and Freudenthal weaves all elements expertly and effectively. In a sea of talking animal films, it is refreshing to have dog characters that charm because of their dog attributes (big ears, too much drool)—even if some of them are a bit cheesy. The Friday POV cam Freudenthal interjects throughout the film also adds charm and feels seamless. Freudenthal gives equal weight to Friday, Andi, and Bruce's stories, so one cannot help but fall for both types of cast members. Stars Roberts and Austin imbue their lost but delightful characters with heart and provide the movie with relatable, engaging heroes that are full of life and full of screen presence.

Joanna Topor MacKenzie

CREDITS

Andi: Emma Roberts
Bruce: Jake T. Austin
Lois: Lisa Kudrow
Bernie: Don Cheadle
Carl: Kevin Dillon
Heather: Kyla Pratt
Mark: Troy Gentile
Dave: Johnny Simmons
Carol: Robine Lee
Origin: USA
Language: English
Released: 2009
Production: Lauren Schuler Donner, Jonathan Gordon, Ewan Leslie, Jason Clark; Nickelodeon Movies, Cold Spring Pictures, Montecito Picture Co.; released by Dreamworks Pictures
Directed by: Thor Freudenthal
Written by: Jeff Lowell, Robert Schooley, Mark McCorkle
Cinematography by: Michael Grady
Music by: John Debney
Sound: Steve Nelson
Editing: Sheldon Kahn
Art Direction: Bradford Ricker
Costumes: Beth Pasternak
Production Design: William Sandell
MPAA rating: PG
Running time: 100 minutes

REVIEWS

Burr, Ty. *Boston Globe*. January 16, 2009.
Ebert, Roger. *Chicago Sun-Times*. January 15, 2009.
Holden, Stephen. *New York Times*. January 16, 2009.
Honeycutt, Kirk. *Hollywood Reporter*. January 12, 2009.
Pais, Matt. *Metromix.com*. January 15, 2009.
Phillips, Michael. *Chicago Tribune*. January 16, 2009.
Phipps, Keith. *Onion AV Club*. January 15, 2009.
Rickey, Carrie. *Philadelphia Inquirer*. January 15, 2009.
Sharkey, Betsy. *Los Angeles Times*. January 22, 2009.
Tookey, Christopher. *Daily Mail*. February 13, 2009.

QUOTES

Bruce: "If you look at it, dogs have three basic needs. That's...that's eatting, sleeping, peeing and pooping."
Andi: "That's four."
Bruce: "No, I think peeing and pooping is one."
Heather: "Uh, I've stepped in both and I have to disagree."

TRIVIA

Many different types of dogs can be seen in the film: Lenny is a Bullmastiff, Georgia is a Boston Terrier, Cooper is a

English Bulldog, Shep is a Border Collie, Romeo is a Chinese Crested Dog, Juliet is a Poodle, and Henry is a Beauceron.

THE HOUSE OF THE DEVIL

Talk on the phone. Finish your homework. Watch T.V. DIE!
—Movie tagline

"*During the 1980s over 70% of American adults believed in the existence of abusive Satanic Cults…Another 30% rationalized the lack of evidence due to government cover ups…The following is based on true unexplained events….*"

So opens this unusually effective horror film, which trades on the foolishness of the past to provide present-day chills. The sad, true history of what came to be called "Satanic Panic" is well documented. As American society became more and more invested in the spiritual awakening of the 1970s, urban myths regarding the occult flourished, specifically belief in a widespread underground cult of Satanism which supposedly accounted for the disappearance of (and one assumes sacrifice of) tens of thousands of children per year. Buttressed by the false print and broadcast testimony of fake former Satanists and occultists on programs as mainstream as ABC's *20/20*, this belief was reinforced to such a degree that family counselors, many of whom can charitably be described as unqualified and lacking accountability, "discovered" that various patients had repressed memories of Satanic Ritual Abuse. Said "memories" would typically be recovered via hypnosis and/or the asking of leading questions and, more often than not, those accused—most often family members, teachers or daycare workers—suffered public disgrace, sometimes even prison sentences. By the time the urban myth of SRA was unpacked and thoroughly discredited the damage was done.

By dragging out the old based-on-a-true-story chestnut and linking it to dubious statistics and a historical context that has taken on the patina of kitsch, director/writer Ti West (*The Roost* [2005], *Trigger Man* [2007]) is signaling something about societal willingness to believe, even when confronted with cliché. But he is also saying something about the power of film. As cinematic clichés go, the virgin sacrificed to Satan and the babysitter in danger seem far riper for the creation of parody than peril. But West's almost pitch-perfect manipulation of viewer paranoia goes a long way towards proving that there is something powerful and universal in the fears and anxieties viewers harbor about such

things. Though his underdeveloped but seemingly instinctual grasp of film technique shows him to be a better visual conductor than writer, his clichéd storyline works precisely because he is able to exploit that simplicity for an unnerving, almost unpleasantly intense, slow burn. The film's many jump scares and walks down dark hallways and staircases may culminate in a sadly unsatisfying bloodbath but not until the viewer is shaken to the core and laughing at themselves a little for having been taken in so easily. This is an homage not to the eighties devices of rubber monster gags and over the top bloodletting but to the visceral suspense and unpleasant realism of films like William Lustig's *Maniac* (1980) that, while violent, are, in the end, about not just spectacle but about the landscape of fear itself.

Desperate to pay her rent on a new apartment and anxious to get away from her slob roommate, college student Samantha Hughes (Jocelin Donahue) answers a babysitting ad on campus. After getting the runaround initially, she gets the job and persuades her reluctant friend Megan (Greta Gerwig) to drive her out to the house on the edge of town on the condition they leave if anything seems amiss. Sure enough, they arrive only to discover that Mr. and Mrs. Ullman (Tom Noonan, Mary Woronov) are anything but normal, and that the job does not exactly involve babysitting but listening out for Mrs. Ullman's aged mother, asleep upstairs. Urged by Megan to leave, Samantha agrees to stay when she is offered an exorbitant amount of money. Megan leaves and Samantha discovers the worst after a nerve-wracking night of exploring the house and feeling sure that someone is watching her; her employers mean to use her in a demonic ritual that has something to do with that evening's eclipse.

West takes plenty of time setting up his situation and introducing the viewer to his characters, but he does so carefully using all the things viewers associate with eighties horror cinema to provoke that winsome hint of nostalgia. The score by Jeff Grace and Graham Reznick is surely one of the best horror had to offer in 2009; a nerve-jangling series of well-placed stabs and building whines complimented by the careful use of bouncy eighties period new wave and rock hits. Throughout, the viewer is carried back and forth across the threshold of belief and disbelief, alternately enjoying the ride and then getting sucked in.

Effective too is the films judicious, if graphic, use of gore, which is fairly disturbing and shocking precisely because it is, in the main, well-timed and well-executed. The exception is the film's ending in which Samantha tries to escape the coven, which results in several shots that seemed almost shoehorned in to satisfy horror fans.

Both Jocelin Donahue (*The Burrowers* [2008], *He's Just Not That Into You* [2009]) and Greta Gerwig (*Baghead* [2008] *Nights and Weekends* [2008]) are excellent as Samantha and Megan. And enough cannot be said about veteran performers Tom Noonan and Mary Woronov. Noonan is best known as the original villain Frances Dollarhyde in *Manhunter* (1986), but has risen into one of the most dependable and creative characters actors working today. The criminally underused Mary Woronov has had a fascinating career ranging from early and extensive work with Andy Warhol to roles in many much-beloved B-movies including *Death Race 2000* (1975), *Rock 'n' Roll High School* (1979), *Eating Raoul* (1982) and *Chopping Mall* (1986). In addition to her prolific film career, Woronov is an accomplished artist, writer and teacher and effortlessly transcribes Renaissance sensibilities into the types of characters she often plays.

The House of the Devil does suffer from an ending that feels a little lost, as if West ultimately knew where he wanted to go but felt pressured to get there in a hurry. This hardly ruins the film. If anything it lets the viewer down a little gently after a nerve-wracking ride through an enduring urban myth.

Dave Canfield

CREDITS

Samantha: Jocelin Donahue
Victor Ulman: AJ Bowen
Landlady: Dee Wallace
Mr. Ulman: Tom Noonan
Mrs. Ullman: Mary Woronov
Megan: Greta Gerwig
Origin: USA
Language: English
Released: 2009
Production: Josh Braun, Roger Kass, Peter Phok; MPI Media Group, Constructovision, Glass Eye Pix, RingTheJing Entertainment; released by Magnet Releasing
Directed by: Ti West, Tom Noonan
Written by: Ti West, Tom Noonan
Cinematography by: Eliot Rockett
Music by: Tom Noonan, Jeff Grace
Editing: Ti West
Sound: Tom Efinger
Costumes: Robin Fitzgerald
Production Design: Jade Healy
MPAA rating: R
Running time: 95 minutes

REVIEWS

Berkshire, Geoff. *Metromix.com*. October 21, 2009.
Collura, Scott. *IGN Movies*. October 26, 2009.
Dargis, Manohla. *New York Times*. October 29, 2009.
Debruge, Peter. *Variety*. October 8, 2009.
Douglas, Edward. *ComingSoon.net*. October 27, 2009.
Germain, David. *Associated Press*. October 27, 2009.
Honeycutt, Kirk. *Hollywood Reporter*. October 26, 2009.
Pinkerton, Nick. *Village Voice*. October 27, 2009.
Snider, Eric D. *Cinematical*. October 26, 2009.
Tallerico, Brian. *MovieRetriever.com*. November 13, 2009.

TRIVIA

Promotionally released on VHS in a clamshell box. The last major motion picture released in that format was *A History of Violence*.

HUMPDAY

Sometimes male bonding can be taken a little too far.
—Movie tagline

If there are any signs of hope that our culture is finally loosening up a little bit in regards to sexual taboos, the last few years have seen an upsurge in films about "average Joes" dabbling in the porn industry. Granted, few people were fortunate enough to see *The Amateurs* (2005) with Jeff Bridges thanks to some legal entanglements with its financiers. And Kevin Smith's film was not quite the success it probably should have been in 2008, but he had "porno" right there in the title—at least until some twitchy TV execs started advertising it simply as "Zack and Miri." People need opportunities to laugh at the expense of an industry they may detest. *Humpday* may not work within the parameters of actual porn, but Lynn Shelton and her cast have tapped into something even more outrageous, and instead of using it for mere shock or gross-out value, they explore the deepest rooted fears of every red-blooded American male.

Ben (Mark Duplass) is a happily married guy and homeowner, living in Seattle with an attractive wife, Anna (Alycia Delmore). They are at the stage of wanting their first child, but even she is understanding enough to recognize when they are both too tired to conceive. Ovulation be damned, they want to be in the mood and not just go through the mechanics. Their tired eyes are nevertheless awoken that night when Ben's college buddy, Andrew (Joshua Leonard), excitedly knocks on their door looking for a place to crash. Not the most convenient of favors, but Anna appears to accept the code of male bonding (including all the rapid punching between the pals) and raises not a finger of protest while the backpacking Andrew gets a spot in the basement.

Anna even agrees to make the trio her famous pork chops for dinner the next night. But Andrew comes along other plans when he meets another free-spirited bohemian (played by director Lynn Shelton) and invites Ben to stop by her pad. A casual drink turns into a few more, and a night of music and pot and a lot of talk ensues. Andrew has been introduced to a Seattle film festival known as "Humpfest" and discusses his interest in participating in it amongst his newfound friends. Ben hits upon the potential for the "ultimate art project": what if two completely heterosexual male buddies were to have sex on camera? It is thrown out there in the spirit of libation initially, but even after Ben has sobered up, he pledges his sincerity on following through on his pitch.

Who in their right mind would go along with such an idea? It is a question that the film leaves on the surface for us to figure out for ourselves and chooses for the most part to never offer a definitive answer. Even as Ben recounts a story from his past that might suggest some untapped curiosity, the screenplay never quite gets around to accepting why he might be the aggressor in this situation. It is a chink in *Humpday*'s armor that some might found difficult to get around. And maybe if the film went down the route of some pretentious statement about homophobia in our culture, we would have washed our hands of it and not anticipated the climactic act and how our boys would handle it. But *Humpday* uses its absurd premise for maximum comic discomfort, and it is this approach that should have audiences unable to look away unless they are doubled over in laughter.

Anyone can just write sitcom punchlines or try to copy the reference humor of Kevin Smith or the Apatow oeuvre. To develop situations that corner its characters in a trap of their own mistruths and then force them to confront those moments—instead of delaying inevitable unmaskings until the last possible moment—is not just tricky; it is almost a lost art. Comedies of manners even in the golden age had a dependence on slapstick that always kept us at ease as if we were watching a cartoon rather than flesh-and-blood humans. The characters in *Humpday* bleed a fear of normality and take refuge in wanting to prove to just one other person that they have not conformed to societal pressure for good. Watching Ben try to talk his way around his impending experimentation to his wife is somehow more hilariously cringe-inducing than the moment of truth, which itself is a classic stretch of comic acting perfectly realized by Duplass and Leonard.

Duplass is most known for his work in the labeled Mumblecore indie features, particularly another wonderful relationship journey called *The Puffy Chair* (2005) which he also co-wrote. With his work on *Humpday*, he is poised to become not just one of the indie staples around the festivals but the reliable Everyman character

actor that may soon be seen in wide releases. Joshua Leonard also breaks free from the decade-long funk of being just one of those *Blair Witch* guys, and he knows just how far to stretch Andrew's care-free attitude and where to pull back so the audience does not unfairly label him as just another antagonistic influence or hippie without a cause. Both actors are great and Lynn Shelton shows a tremendous flair for staging comic dialogue and knowing just when to deliver the punch that sends it into overdrive—and eventually from shock into awwwww.

Erik Childress

CREDITS

Ben: Mark Duplass
Andrew: Joshua Leonard
Anna: Alycia Delmore
Lily: Trina Willard
Monica: Lynn Shelton
Origin: USA
Language: English
Released: 2009
Production: Lynn Shelton; Seashel Pictures; released by Magnolia Pictures
Directed by: Lynn Shelton
Written by: Lynn Shelton
Cinematography by: Benjamin Kasulke
Music by: Vinny Smith
Sound: Vinny Smith
Editing: Nat Sanders
Production Design: Jasminka Vukcevic
MPAA rating: R
Running time: 94 minutes

REVIEWS

Bayer, Jeff. *Scorecard Review.* August 3, 2009.
Douglas, Edward. *ComingSoon.net.* July 7, 2009.
Holden, Stephen. *New York Times.* July 10, 2009.
Lewis, Don R. *Film Threat.* March 17, 2009.
Michel, Brett. *Boston Phoenix.* July 31, 2009.
Mondello, Bob. *NPR.* July 10, 2009.
Pols, Mary F. *Time Magazine.* July 10, 2009.
Rodriguez, Rene. *Miami Herald.* July 24, 2009.
Weber, Bill. *Slant Magazine.* July 6, 2009.
White, Armond. *New York Press.* July 8, 2009.

QUOTES

Ben: "Not yet, but we're on the path. We've officially removed the goalie, and now we're just doing free kicks."

TRIVIA

As he walks to the hotel room for the final scene, Andrew walks in front of the home of Edith Macefield. Macefield was famous for stubbornly resisting the offers of developers and remaining in her tiny 108-year-old farmhouse while the surrounding properties were turned into a five-story commercial development.

THE HURT LOCKER

You'll know when you're in it.
—Movie tagline

You don't have to be a hero to do this job. But it helps.
—Movie tagline

Box Office: $16.4 million

For reasons that are unfortunate yet understandable, audiences have mostly avoided films dealing with the war in Iraq. Perhaps they would rather not be reminded of the questionable decisions that sent military members into the region. Or they may not want to hear the liberal politics and thematics that go into condemning this military action. It could also be they have already seen the forty-plus documentaries on the subject from every point of view. Or maybe, just maybe, the films themselves have not been very much to speak about. With the exception of Paul Haggis' *In The Valley of Elah* (2007), the list of mediocre to downright embarrassing films includes *Home of the Brave* (2006), *Grace Is Gone* (2007), *Stop-Loss* (2008) and *The Lucky Ones* (2008). Those were all films that dealt with the after-effect though—about the fatigue of battle more than the actual battle. Kathryn Bigelow's *The Hurt Locker* is about both. Some may believe that creating an action film out of an ongoing situation demeans the efforts and memories of those facing the real bullets, but it is likely that most soldiers would identify this film as the most honest and intense portrayal of their experiences to date.

The film opens a little more than a month before Bravo Company is finishing its tour of duty in Iraq. We meet Sergeant JT Sanborn (Anthony Mackie), Specialist Owen Eldridge (Brian Geraghty) and Staff Sergeant William James (Jeremy Renner); each part of the company's bomb defusing unit. James is a new addition to the team, replacing their previous leader. Eldridge blames himself for this loss and, in-between missions, is seeing an Army psychiatrist (Christian Camargo) who is unfortunately saddled with being "that guy" in a war film who has never seen combat. Sanborn gets a little taste of what he's in for with James, who likes to isolate himself by listening to metal music and smoke by his lonesome. Or is he merely just pumping himself up for the next dispatch?

Reckless is an understatement of James' behavior: in his first mission he disorients his team members from

seeing the battle field, and he is ready to take on a runaway cab driver with just a pistol. The image of him standing like a spaceman with a pointed gun couldn't be a more perfect visual representation of this guy. The usual bomb defuser he is certainly not, and if the opening scene is any indication, all the safety equipment in the world is just for show. If James wants to blow himself up that's his business, but Sanborn is concerned about their fellow soldiers and wonders out loud if Bravo would be better off if an accident were to come James' way.

There is little time for such didactic ruminations though, since *The Hurt Locker* is first and foremost an action thriller. Of the film's 125 minutes, around 90 of them are dedicated to the seven (or eight) set pieces that Bigelow and screenwriter Mark Boal have devised. Any critical reaction to their work can be based solely around the strength and potential repetition of these calls to duty. Once you've dismantled one bomb and cut the right-colored wire where else is there to go, right? In terms of pure adrenaline, the 100% promised in Bigelow's *Point Break* (1991) gets more than its share of competition here. From the getcha-going opening sequence right through an excruciatingly tense and brilliantly executed desert gunfight, there's barely an opportunity in between breaths—and gasps—during the first hour alone. If Bigelow presumably shoves the best sequences to the film's front half, it doesn't mean the latter confrontations carry any less tension or are any less complex.

As James and Sanborn begin to trust, if not fully understand, each other, whatever lack of politics or perspective viewers may feel the film is lacking come to the forefront as we appreciate this is a film for the soldier, of the soldier, and by the soldier. Scripter Mark Boal spent time with a bomb squad in Iraq and has acclimated more than just the exhaustion and stress of being in the hurt. The comaradarie even amidst conflicting personalities is more than just a wartime cliché. The film's literal centerpiece sequence in the middle of the desert is equally exceptional for its quiet moments of waiting and reassurance. James' handling of his brothers is this scene has an unexpectedly calming effect on us as well as them, and it is moving in a way that exemplifies the code about fighting not for a cause or a country, but for the man right next to you.

Everyone is certain to come away talking about the relentless action of *The Hurt Locker*, either as a positive or something that simply just wore them into submission. Hopefully this focus doesn't shed aside the film's two chief components. This is not to forget about the strong work turned in by Mackie and Geraghty, nor the notable supporting turns by Guy Pierce, David Morse and Ralph Fiennes. But when the bombs don't have our full attention, it's on Jeremy Renner who could easily have become just another wild man caricature, juiced up to the hilt and purposefully ignoring authority. The film's opener about war being a drug sets us in motion for an upfront and personal reflection in the character of William James—and is unnecessarily bookended by a too on-the-nose piece of dialogue towards the end—but Renner does not resort to playing him like just another Martin Riggs. Instead he puts on a game face that becomes a mesmerizing blend of bravado and disintegration. As he becomes just one man against a world that could end in a second, his obsession in saving—or avenging—one man at a time is a riveting tumult that Renner perfectly portrays in a slow melt of disquietude. Director Kathryn Bigelow, who has cut her teeth at being one of the most dependable action filmmakers around in films like the aforementioned *Point Break* (1991), *Near Dark* (1987), and the underappreciated *Strange Days* (1995), more than earned her stripes with action aficionados. *The Hurt Locker* earns its place on that list as a pure example of directorial fortitude, multiplying virtuoso suspense sequences with the human connection and disorientation of the people in the battlefield.

One might have to go back to *The Wages of Fear* (1953)—or, at least, William Friedkin's exceptional remake, *Sorcerer* (1977)—to find a film designed around one intimately dangerous, and voluntary, scrape after another. Where the truckers of those films were just in it for the money, *The Hurt Locker*'s characters are in harm's way for what is meant to be a greater purpose. Politics and morality aside, these are guys thanklessly protecting the faceless, and it's in their search to find any sense of humanity in their task that they begin to feel the futility of their efforts. The symbolic deadbolts that make up the final set piece are proof positive that one man and one country are not enough to defuse all the bombs in the world. That, ultimately, might be more profound than all the films, documentaries and media coverage yet produced about the war in Iraq.

Erik Childress

CREDITS

Staff Sgt. William James: Jeremy Renner
Sgt. J.T. Sanborn: Anthony Mackie
Spec. Owen Eldridge: Brian Geraghty
Sgt. Matt Thompson: Guy Pearce
Contractor Team Leader: Ralph Fiennes
Col. Reed: David Morse
Connie James: Evangeline Lilly
Col. John Cambridge: Christian Camargo
Beckham: Christopher Sayegh

Prof. Nabil: Nabil Koni
Origin: USA
Language: English
Released: 2008
Production: Kathryn Bigelow, Greg Shapiro, Mark Boal, Nicolas Chartier; Voltage Pictures, First Light, Grosvenor Park, Kingsgate Films; released by Summit Entertainment
Directed by: Kathryn Bigelow
Written by: Mark Boal
Cinematography by: Barry Ackroyd
Music by: Marco Beltrami, Buck Sanders
Sound: Ray Beckett
Music Supervisor: John Bissell
Editing: Bob Murawski, Chris Innis
Art Direction: David Bryan
Costumes: George L. Little
Production Design: Karl Juliusson
MPAA rating: R
Running time: 131 minutes

REVIEWS

Corliss, Richard. *Time Magazine.* April 3, 2009.
Denby, David. *New Yorker.* June 22, 2009.
Ebert, Roger. *Chicago Sun-Times.* July 9, 2009.
Edelstein, David. *New York Magazine.* June 22, 2009.
Foundas, Scott. *Village Voice.* June 24, 2009.
Howell, Peter. *Toronto Star.* July 10, 2009.
Jones, J.R. *Chicago Reader.* July 10, 2009.
Phillips, Michael. *Chicago Tribune.* July 9, 2009.
Tallerico, Brian. *HollywoodChicago.com* July 9, 2009.
Turan, Kenneth. *Los Angeles Times.* June 26, 2009.

QUOTES

Eldridge to James: "Not very good with people, are you, but you're a good warrior."
Staff Sergeant William James: "There's enough bang in there to blow us all to Jesus. If I'm gonna die, I want to die comfortable."

TRIVIA

The film was shot on location in Jordan. Part of the shoot (one week) was to take place in Kuwait on a US Military Base. Access was denied.

AWARDS

Oscars 2009: Director (Bigelow), Film, Film Editing, Orig. Screenplay, Sound, Sound FX Editing
British Acad. 2009: Cinematog., Director (Bigelow), Film, Orig. Screenplay, Sound, Fim Editing
Directors Guild 2009: Director (Bigelow)
Writers Guild 2009: Orig. Screenplay

Nomination:

Oscars 2009: Actor (Renner), Cinematog., Orig. Score

British Acad. 2009: Actor (Renner), Visual FX

Golden Globes 2010: Director (Bigelow), Film—Drama, Screenplay

Ind. Spirit 2009: Actor (Renner), Support. Actor (Mackie)

Screen Actors Guild 2009: Actor (Renner), Cast.

I

I CAN DO BAD ALL BY MYSELF

(Tyler Perry's I Can Do Bad All By Myself)

Hope is closer than you think.
—Movie tagline

Box Office: $52 million

The funny thing about the fact that most critics have completely written off the work of Tyler Perry, to the point that his films rarely if ever screen for them anymore, is that he has actually improved with nearly every film (the horrendous *Madea Goes to Jail* [2009] excepted), culminating with his best work to date, the confident, joyful *I Can Do Bad All By Myself*. There are still bizarrely broad tone changes from wacky comedy to character-driven melodrama, but the shifts are not nearly as off-putting as relative junk like *Diary of a Mad Black Woman* (2005), *Madea's Family Reunion* (2006), and *Daddy's Little Girls* (2007). In fact, the relative accomplishments of *I Can Do Bad All By Myself*, mostly strengthened by a great lead performance from Oscar® nominee Taraji P. Henson (*The Curious Case of Benjamin Button* [2008]) and far more confident director from Perry, led to the best reviews of his career and the first film of his to garner a fresh rating on Rotten Tomatoes (meaning that more than 60% of critics who did see the film granted it a positive review). As with all Perry films, the dramedy took off with its target audience, resulting in the fourth highest domestic gross of his remarkably successful career. There is still a bit of work to be done, and the film is far from perfect, but one wonders if they should not start showing Perry films to critics again. They are arguably good enough.

I Can Do Bad All By Myself comes from a classic morality tale archetype in that it features a nasty, bitter heroine who learns a lesson about the importance of family only when she really has no choice not to do so. Based on his own 1999 play, the film stars Henson as April, a borderline alcoholic nightclub singer who sleeps all days and seemingly cares about no one but herself and possibly her married boyfriend Randy (Brian J. White). The streetwise urchins who change April's worldview are Jennifer (Hope Olaide Wilson), Manny (Kwesi Boakye), and Byron (Frederick Siglar), the singer's niece and nephews. They are introduced breaking into the home of beloved Perry character Madea (the writer/director himself), who does not just discard the would-be robbers but tries to help them put their lives back together. Madea brings the kids to April's house, the only relative who could conceivably care for them, and Jennifer and the lead butt heads on the way to her inevitable about face.

Meanwhile, the local church, led by Pastor Brian (Marvin Winans), sends over a Columbian immigrant named Sandino (Adam Rodriguez) to help around the house and, of course, serve as a much better male role model than the truly disgusting Randy, who takes the first chance to ridicule everyone and sexually threaten young Jennifer. Randy is drawn way too broadly, but the parallel is clear from his first scene with the majority of the cast—this is the kind of scumbag that April used to date and her family will show her the error of her ways. And the comeuppance of Randy has a cathartic power that cannot be denied. Perry recognizes well the strength of seeing a scumbag reduced to a sniveling, bloody mess. Singers Mary J. Blige and Gladys Knight appear in small roles in a film in which music plays a strong, entertaining role. Naturally, both get a moment behind the mic and rock it, proving why they are still reigning queens of soul. And if there was a local pastor with the voice of Marvin Winans, it would be difficult to think of anything better to do on a Sunday morning than head to church.

The morals of *I Can Do Bad All By Myself* are typically surface level and predictable, but there is an assured pacing and tonal consistency to this film that has been missing from a lot of Perry's work. It still sags in the middle (there is no reason for it to run nearly 120 minutes) but the love for the characters shines through more than the overwritten dialogue that has so hampered Perry's work in the past. Henson delivers the best work in any of Perry's films, turning what could have been a caricature into something genuine. Perry still injects way too much of his Madea character into the film, but Henson and Rodriguez add emotional gravity to the center of the film and mostly hold it together.

A little less Madea, dialogue that did not feel so underlined in its moral message, one or two shorter motivational songs in the second half, and an actual subtle moment or two and *I Can Do Bad All By Myself* would have worked a little better, but the film is a notable improvement for a filmmaker who is clearly growing with each work—even when he has already reached a level of success where he could easily coast to the box-office bank.

Brian Tallerico

CREDITS

Madea/Joe: Tyler Perry
Aunt April: Taraji P. Henson
Wilma: Gladys Knight
Randy: Brian White
Sandino: Adam Rodriguez
Jennifer: Hope Olaide Wilson
Tanya: Mary J. Blige
Pastor Brian: Marvin Winans
Manny: Kwesi Boakye
Byron: Frederick Siglar
Origin: USA
Language: English
Released: 2009
Production: Tyler Perry, Reuben Cannon; Tyler Perry Co.; released by Lionsgate
Directed by: Tyler Perry
Written by: Tyler Perry

Cinematography by: Alexander Grusynski
Music by: Aaron Zigman
Sound: Michael D. Wilhoit
Editing: Maysie Hoy
Art Direction: Mayne Berke
Costumes: Keith Lewis
Production Design: Ina Mayhew
MPAA rating: PG-13
Running time: 113 minutes

REVIEWS

Abele, Robert. *Los Angeles Times.* September 14, 2009.
Burr, Ty. *Boston Globe.* September 14, 2009.
Clark, Shaula. *Boston Phoenix.* September 17, 2009.
Cordova, Randy. *Arizona Republic.* September 15, 2009.
Debruge, Peter. *Variety.* September 11, 2009.
Genzlinger, Neil. *New York Times.* September 14, 2009.
Humanick, Rob. *Slant Magazine.* September 12, 2009.
Rabin, Nathan. *AV Club.* September 11, 2009.
Rickey, Carrie. *Philadelphia Inquirer.* September 14, 2009.
Schwarzbaum, Lisa. *Entertainment Weekly.* September 14, 2009.

QUOTES

Jennifer: "You brought his insulin. I was gonna do it."

I HOPE THEY SERVE BEER IN HELL

Box Office: $1.4 million

Boozy, testosterone-fueled excess proved a successful narrative backdrop for the summer hit *The Hangover* (2009), which opened big and rode superb word-of-mouth to become the highest-grossing R-rated comedy of all-time with over $275 million in domestic theatrical receipts. Much further down the sliding scale of successfully peddled big screen crassness, but definitely of the same genus, is *I Hope They Serve Beer in Hell*, the first cinematic entry from screenwriter-producer Tucker Max.

The movie is based on his bestselling book and button-pushing blog of the same name, each of which details in blunt language (if somewhat hazy veracity) his collegiate and post-collegiate party-hearty lifestyle. But Max is a polarizing figure: in his endless and seemingly successful quests for as much sex with as many different partners as possible, twenty-something guys (and plenty of girls, too) see a straight-talking hero, while some others view his behavior as misogynistic. Purportedly turning down a $2 million offer for the script from Fox Searchlight, and instead choosing to independently produce the film himself, May's *I Hope They Serve Beer in Hell* represents his play at becoming a self-branded, Internet-era multimedia mogul for college-age kids looking to live vicariously through his exploits.

Sprinkling in just the smallest pinch of lesson-learning and interpersonal growth amidst its heaping helpings of abusive language, nudity, diarrhea-focused set pieces and otherwise unremitting tonal crudeness, *I Hope They Serve Beer in Hell* revolves around college student Tucker (Matt Czuchry), an id-driven narcissist who relates to women in a manner seemingly informed solely by hardcore mid-1990s hip-hop—which is to say that to him that they are all "bitches, hoes or tricks." With his best friend Dan (Geoff Stults) set to soon be married, Tucker whisks him away from his fiancée Kristy (Keri Lynn Pratt) for a combination bachelor party and out-of-town road trip, along with their friend Drew (Jesse Bradford). Both Tucker and Drew use standoffish humor as a way to mask an inability to relate to people on a personal level, but whereas Tucker's cutting remarks are leavened somewhat by his jocular demeanor, a recent breakup has rendered Drew a seemingly sociopathic misanthrope.

After an early encounter with a bridal party at a bar, the guys eventually alight upon a strip club, and more alcohol flows freely. In what feels like a bit of a contrivance, a drunken Dan ends up by himself in prison after Tucker pursues his personal holy grail of having sex with a midget, and Drew ends up going home and playing videogames with a single mother/stripper, Lara (Marika Dominczyk). When they reunite, Dan is beaten and bruised, and understandably upset. With Tucker able to muster only the barest shrug of an apology (he had a chance at having sex with a midget, he rationalizes), Dan makes the decision to cut him out of the wedding, forcing Tucker to think a bit more than he is accustomed to about the effects of his actions upon others.

The filmmaking prowess on display in *I Hope They Serve Beer in Hell* is not quite up to snuff, as the edits frequently work against the quick pacing of the dialogue. Director Bob Gosse never figures out a way to impress a correlatively brisk, fun visual scheme upon the movie, in the fashion that Doug Liman's bristling camerawork on *Swingers* (1996) complemented Jon Favreau and Vince Vaughn's loose, warm rapport, and the spirited rhythms of that movie's patter. The result is a choppily shot and edited low-budget movie that too frequently wears its production limitations front and center, rather than artfully obscuring them. Furthermore, a couple hyper-stylized sequences, most notably a segment in which Drew aggressively defends the merits of a pancake sandwich, seem over-the-top and out of step with the rest of the film, and interrupt the flow of what is otherwise very much a naturalistic narrative.

Not much of what unfolds narratively is particularly original, but it is delivered with conviction. What *I Hope They Serve Beer in Hell* most has going for it is lively dialogue and a cocksure sense of self, as powered by Czuchry's huge smirks. Whereas the vast majority of Hollywood studio comedies to some degree equivocate or worry about offending different slivers of their potential audience, Max's film exhibits a devil-may-care vibe from frame one, and benefits from it. Some jokes doubtlessly will sail over the heads of some its audience ("You had so much surrender in your eyes I thought I was walking into Vichy France," says Tucker at one point), and some will certainly offend, but Max and co-writer Nils Parker never play it safe. The script is also seeded with visual references and other inside jokes from the book and his blog, and at one point even uses Max's real cell phone number.

While the movie—said to be the first in a quartet of films Max wants to do charting the slow development of his screen alter ego—did not do extremely well in theaters, if there is anything that 2009's sequel to *The Boondock Saints* (2000) taught us, it is that the DVD format is a great equalizer, sometimes allowing for franchises to survive and thrive in the unlikeliest of places. If that happens with *I Hope They Serve Beer in Hell*, maybe Max will have the last laugh after all, and succeed in becoming a Tyler Perry for the frat-house set.

Brent Simon

CREDITS

Tucker Max: Matt Czuchry
Lara: Marika Dominczyk
Dan: Geoff Stults
Drew: Jesse Bradford
Kristy: Keri Lynn Pratt
Origin: USA
Language: English
Released: 2009
Production: Karen Firestone, Ted Hamm, Richard Kelly, Tucker Max, Sean McKittrick, Nils Parker, Aaron Ray, Max Wong; Rudius Films, The Collective Studios, Darko Entertainment, Pink Slip Pictures; released by Freestyle Releasing
Directed by: Bob Grosse
Written by: Tucker Max, Nils Parker
Cinematography by: Suki Medencevic
Music by: James L. Venable
Sound: Jeff Kushner
Editing: Jeff Kusher
Costumes: Alison Parker
Production Design: Eve Cauley

MPAA rating: R
Running time: 105 minutes

REVIEWS

Berton, Justin. *San Francisco Chronicle.* September 25, 2009.
Childress, Erik E. *FilmCritic.* September 24, 2009.
Gleiberman, Owen. *Entertainment Weekly.* September 23, 2009.
Holden, Stephen. *New York Times.* September 25, 2009.
Meek, Tom. *Boston Phoenix.* September 24, 2009.
Phillips, Michael. *Chicago Tribune.* September 25, 2009.
Schager, Nick. *Slant Magazine.* September 21, 2009.
Scheck, Frank. *Hollywood Reporter.* September 25, 2009.
Scheib, Ronnie. *Variety.* September 24, 2009.
Thomas, Kevin. *Los Angeles Times.* September 25, 2009.

QUOTES

Tucker Nax: "I'm gonna hit that so hard, the person that pulls it out will become the next king of England."

TRIVIA

The best man at the wedding is the real life Tucker Max.

I LOVE YOU, BETH COOPER

Five little words can change your life.
—Movie tagline

Box Office: $15 million

In the spirit of *Superbad* (2007) and *The Girl Next Door* (2004), *I Love You, Beth Cooper* is a movie about a dorky teen who finally gets to have the night of his life (said night to include drinking, fighting and hooking up). The teen in question is Denis Cooverman (Paul Rust), a nerdy, humorless valedictorian bound for an accelerated med school program at Stanford. Denis has always had a crush on bombshell head cheerleader Beth Cooper (Hayden Panettiere) and he uses the time allocated during his speech at graduation to tell her—and the entire auditorium audience, including all fellow classmates and Beth's military boyfriend—that he loves her. Because she is part mean girl, Beth, with friends in tow, crashes Denis' parent-sponsored, kindergarten-caliber, single best friend in attendance (Rich Munsch played by Jack Carpenter), graduation party. But because she is also part golden girl, she takes Denis and Rich with her when her boyfriend shows up looking to prove his claim on Beth. Together, the quintet embark on a night of fast driving, underage drinking, breaking and entering and kissing—along with the obligatory

emotionally based self-revelation. But unlike *Superbad* and *The Girl Next Door*, which compel with a charismatic cast and engage with spot-on humor, *I Love You, Beth Cooper* is absolutely devoid of teen spirit, lacking in all manner of comedic timing and generally more cringeworthy than earnestly funny.

So many factors, it seems, contributed to the failure of this film, it's almost difficult to know where to start. Though he has a knack with children's adventure movies, there is a reason that director Chris Columbus was replaced once the subject matter in the *Harry Potter* movies moved toward darker, emotionally complex material. His approach to this teen comedy is too brightly lit and too cartoonish. And while it seems wrong to pick on the cast, it's impossible not to note that the initial glaring problem with the movie stems from the casting choices made. Rust as Denis is awkward—and not in a good way—in part due to the fact that he is obviously not teenaged (arguably actors cast to play high schoolers never are, but here it seems astonishingly obvious), but also because he lacks the charisma necessary to inhabit the everyman dork for which the film calls. His delivery feels calculated (too much shrieking and exaggerated falling), his timing is off, and, worst of all, there does not seem to be any heart involved in his performance. His dorkiness is not earnest, but neither is his emotional reaction to Beth, and that is more frustrating. He does not get flustered when she flirts with him, he does not become overwhelmed and exhilarated when she pours her heart out to him. Panettiere as Beth is also generally disappointing. For the most part she calls in her turn as head cheerleader (understandably she is well versed in the territory thanks to her role on TV's *Heroes*), but then, remarkably, she also provides the few honest and engaging moments the movie has to offer. Beth Cooper knows she will peak in high school, and part way through the film, after breaking into the school gym, she realizes this fact. Those moments with Beth, when it dawns are her that this might be as good as it gets, anchor the film and keeps the audience watching. Unfortunately, there are not enough of those moments to sustain interest.

What is worse than the pitch-poor acting is the complete lack of chemistry between everyone on screen. Denis and Beth do not spark, apart or together. Beth's best friends also fail to come off as the tight-knit circle of queen bees they purport to be. Most disappointing, Denis does not even feel compatible with his best friend, Rich. Instead of sharing inside jokes and understanding each other's witty banter, they seem to exchange forced dialogue and regard each other as weirdoes that have been paired up against their will.

Of course, the poor script the actors are given to work with does not help matters. Larry Doyle, who adapted his own novel for the screen, succeeds in turning his book's characters into schlocky screen stereotypes who just bump into one another for the duration: nerdy boys are useful because they possess heaps of information disposable at a moments notice; cheerleaders are vapid, like to drink and will pretty much make out with anyone; and meatheads settle matters with their fists and like their recreational drugs a little too much. The weird thing is that, as a novel, Doyle's absurdist teen reality works. But there is a disconnect that obviously does not translate to the screen. Doyle's Denis is not a hip, techno-savvy dork who exists at the fringes of popular culture. He is a coddled, awkward mommy's boy, but we like him when we read about him because we can get into his head. That Doyle chooses to make cocaine snorting, college-aged military thugs the bad guys in his narrative as opposed to the usual jocks or popular kids can be swallowed on paper, but on-screen it just feels off and ultimately unrelatable.

Joanna Topor MacKenzie

CREDITS

Beth Cooper: Hayden Panettiere
Kevin: Shawn Roberts
Treece: Lauren Storm
Cammy: Lauren London
Denis Cooverman: Paul Rust
Rich: Jack Carpenter
Mr. Cooverman: Alan Ruck
Mrs. Cooverman: Cynthia Stevenson
Origin: USA
Language: English
Released: 2009
Production: Chris Columbus, Mark Radcliffe, Michael Barnathan; 1492 Pictures; released by Fox Atomic
Directed by: Chris Columbus
Written by: Larry Doyle
Cinematography by: Phil Abraham
Music by: Christophe Beck
Sound: Michael Williamson
Music Supervisor: Patrick Houlihan
Editing: Peter Honess
Art Direction: Sandra Tanaka
Costumes: Karen Matthews
Production Design: Howard Cummings
MPAA rating: PG-13
Running time: 102 minutes

REVIEWS

Anderson, Jason. *Toronto Star.* July 10, 2009.
Burr, Ty. *Boston Globe* July 9, 2009.

Childress. Erik. *EFilmCritic.* July 9, 2009.
Ebert, Roger. *Chicago Sun-Times.* July 9, 2009.
Lowry, Brian. *Variety.* July 10, 2009.
Pais, Matt. *Metromix.com.* July 9, 2009.
Phillips, Michael. *Chicago Tribune.* July 9, 2009.
Russell, Mike. *Oregonian.* July 10, 2009.
Scott, A.O. *New York Times.* July 10, 2009.
Tobias, Scott. *AV Club.* July 9, 2009.

QUOTES

Denis Cooverman: "Thanks. You hit me with your car. That was pretty cool."

TRIVIA

In the afterword to the book the film was based on, author Larry Doyle admitted he initially conceived this story as a movie. When he was unable to generate interest, he published the story as a novel. It subsequently generated enough popularity to spark interest in adapting it to film, and Doyle was invited to write the screenplay.

I LOVE YOU, MAN
(Let's Make Friends)

Are you man enough to say it?
—Movie tagline

Box Office: $71 million

Classifying *I Love You, Man* as a "bromantic comedy" cheapens the deceptively challenging task writer-director John Hamburg pulls off: This is a romantic comedy about the love between friends—and, more specifically, dudes. There have been, of course, many films celebrating friendship between women—if the word "sisterhood" is in the title, count on that story revolving around female bonding and involving plenty of shamelessly emotional conflicts and reunions. Yet Hamburg knows male bonds typically are not developed or challenged by such dramatic circumstances, and consequently *I Love You, Man* excels in finding the affection that can form over a concert, a discussion about women or just a round of beers.

The anchor of this story is Peter (Paul Rudd), a sensitive realtor who has always been a "girlfriend guy" and never had any close male friends. That finally becomes a problem when Peter proposes to Zooey (Rashida Jones) and realizes he does not have anyone to fill out his wedding party. So Peter sets out on "man-dates" to find some buddies and, perhaps, a best man. Peter's brother Robby (Andy Samberg), a gay gym employee who enjoys the challenge of hitting on straight men, advises Peter on the rules of these encounters: No movies. No dinners. Keep it casual. Peter discovers that these rules do, in fact, hold weight after he goes to dinner with Doug (Thomas Lennon), who thinks Peter is gay and kisses him at the end of the evening. That pretty much crosses Doug off the list of potential best men.

Later, at an open house for *The Incredible Hulk* TV star Lou Ferrigno, Peter strikes up a conversation with Sydney Fife (Jason Segel), an easygoing investor who can tell Peter is a good guy and, after the two exchange business cards, eventually invites him out for some beers and what he calls the world's best fish tacos, over which the two talk about life and women and booze and, in a night, go from acquaintances to friends. Though Sydney is underwritten—little is ever learned about his background or why he is so determined to avoid commitment and seduce divorcees—the believability of his progressing connection with Peter comes from the rapport between Rudd and Segel, who previously worked together on *Forgetting Sarah Marshall* (2008) and *Knocked Up* (2007) and are friends off-screen. That does not always translate to the camera, yet the actors play off each other in a way that suggests two guys gradually getting know each other, opening up and growing comfortable with having the other in his life.

Fortunately, this progression is also very funny and perceptive about the dynamic between bros. With no idea about an appropriate conversational style when hanging with a guy, Peter is easily flustered, nicknaming Sydney, for no reason at all, "Jobin" and saying awkward things like "Totes magotes," "See you in a jiff" and "We will talk when I talk to you." He often treats his interactions with Sydney like a date—at first he even prepares what he is going to say in a phone call—because, despite the lack of open emotion typically present between guys, they still care how they come off, and a faux pas is as easy as saying something totally uncool.

Peter does that often in *I Love You, Man,* as well as accidentally winning a hand of poker and throwing up in Barry's (Jon Favreau) face in his attempt to win friends. This behavior could come off as pathetic, but Rudd's vulnerable charm makes Peter totally endearing. He is just a nice guy who is not inclined to binge drinking but is secure enough in his manhood to admit that his favorite night with Zooey involved a bottle of wine, a summer salad and watching *Chocolat* (2000), a point which results in a hilarious back-and-forth between Peter and Sydney about the proper pronunciation of the film's title.

Every so often Hamburg kills the good vibes, such as when Peter hangs out with a guy (Joe Lo Truglio) whose defining characteristic is that he has a squeaky voice or when Doug reappears to call Peter a whore.

Doug is little more than a gay stereotype, and Lo Truglio is nothing but a strained attempt at comedy, when in reality Peter would probably appreciate the guy's friendly demeanor rather than run from his unusual voice.

For most of *I Love You, Man*, though, the characters are simply great company, to the point that most viewers will probably want to hang out with Peter and Sydney after the movie is over. The two demonstrate the different bond that a guy gets from his bud than from his fiancée, and that friendship cannot be forced. The conflict Hamburg throws in to briefly push the two apart, on the other hand, does feel forced, but it is a small problem in a movie that mines such amusing dialogue and detail from the weird process of establishing a friendship. And as Peter and Sydney rock out on the bass and guitar, respectively, while playing Rush songs—and later seeing the band in concert—these guys show that sometimes men need to act like boys, and it is good to have a dude to do it with.

Matt Pais

CREDITS

Peter Klaven: Paul Rudd
Sydney Fife: Jason Segel
Barry: Jon Favreau
Zooey: Rashida Jones
Robbie: Adam Samberg
Denise: Jaime Pressly
Oz: J.K. Simmons
Joyce: Jane Curtin
Origin: USA
Language: English
Released: 2009
Production: Donald De Line, John Hamburg; Dreamworks Pictures, Montecito Picture Co., Bernard Gayle Prods.; released by Paramount
Directed by: John Hamburg
Written by: John Hamburg, Larry Levin
Cinematography by: Lawrence Sher
Music by: Theodore Shapiro
Sound: Ken Segal
Music Supervisor: Jennifer Hawks
Editing: William Kerr
Art Direction: Eric Sundahl
Costumes: Leesa Evans
Production Design: Andrew Laws
MPAA rating: R
Running time: 105 minutes

REVIEWS

Burr, Ty. *Boston Globe.* March 19, 2009.
Dargis, Manohla. *New York Times.* March 20, 2009.

Ebert, Roger. *Chicago Sun-Times.* March 19, 2009.
Edelstein, David. *New York Magazine.* March 16, 2009.
Graham, Adam. *Detroit News.* March 20, 2009.
McCarthy, Todd. *Variety.* March 16, 2009.
Phillips, Michael. *Chicago Tribune.* March 19, 2009.
Rickey, Carrie. *Philadelphia Inquirer.* March 19, 2009.
Sharkey, Betsy. *Los Angeles Times.* March 19, 2009.
Tobias, Scott. *AV Club.* March 19, 2009.

QUOTES

Oswald Klaven: "Also, you got to understand, Zooey, Peter matured sexually at a very early age. I remember taking him swimming when he was twelve-years-old, kid had a bush like a forty-year-old Serbian."

TRIVIA

The bass that Peter plays "Tom Sawyer" on during his first jam with Sydney is a Fender Geddy Lee Jazz Bass, from Fender's Artist Series of electric basses, and is a near-perfect replica of the instrument that Geddy Lee usually plays onstage with Rush. Geddy can be seen playing the original instrument during the Rush show later in the movie.

ICE AGE: DAWN OF THE DINOSAURS

The sub-zero heroes are back, on an incredible adventure...for the ages.
—Movie tagline

Box Office: $196 million

There was a time not so long ago when animation seemed to lack the capacity to be forgettable. We are already two decades removed from the revitalization of the Disney animated feature with *The Little Mermaid* (1989), where year-by-year such a release was hailed as an event to behold. Then along came Pixar in 1995, almost constantly reestablishing the bar for the art form. An animated feature category was added to the Oscars® in 2001, just in time for Disney/Pixar to lose the first award to one of the many other players getting into the game. As technology has improved and made it easier to produce these colorful spectacles, the onus has been taken off their writers to craft a story worthy of the painstaking effort from start-to-finish. Enter *Ice Age* (2002), a reasonably entertaining film during one of the weakest years for animation this century and successful enough to spawn a sequel, *Ice Age: The Meltdown* (2006), with a plot too forgettable for most over the age of six. Watching the third entry in the series, you might wish you had someone of that age to remind you what's going on and hope that they were not actually retaining it for their history classes.

The original heroes of the franchise consisted of woolly mastodon Manny (voiced by Ray Romano), sabertooth tiger Diego (Denis Leary) and wacky motor-mouth sloth Sid (John Leguizamo). Their first adventure together was to return a human baby to its tribe while facing the perils of seeking a warmer climate in a glacier-filled landscape. For their second escapade, the trio had to leave the valley they call home and trek to the other side to avoid the titular meltdown. Manny found a potential mate in Ellie (Queen Latifah), just when he thought he was the last of his kind. For their third journey, Manny and Ellie are headed to Mordor to drop a magical ring. Wait, that's wrong. Actually they are looking to up the mastodon quotient by one and are having their first baby.

Manny settling down once and for all has his friends thinking about their own futures. The always reluctant outsider, Diego, misses the thrill of the hunt and is losing his touch, while Sid would like a little piece of Manny's happiness and become a papa. Luck would have it that Sid comes upon three dinosaur eggs, which he assumes have been abandoned. Taking them for himself, the eggs hatch and three little dinos assume Sid to be their parent. Of course, the tyke-rexes have not been abandoned and when mama Rex finds them, she scoops them up—along with Sid—to an underground utopia underneath the ice. Despite the constant troublemaking ear-sore that Sid is, Manny, Diego and Ellie head out with opossums Crash (Seann William Scott) and Eddie (Josh Peck) to save Sid while facing the perils of marauding dinosaurs with the help of a new friend. If it seems like the plot of the first two movies, that's because it pretty much is.

The only thing worth remembering from the first two films is the appearance of Scrat (voiced by the film's original director, Chris Wedge), the squirrel-ish creature whose only care in the world is his precious acorn. Since the original's teaser trailer that made a sensation out of the character—who was only supposed to appear in the film's opening minutes—his role has been bulked up considerably for our enjoyment. Like the clowns of a Cirque du Soleil show entertaining the audience while the primary cast does costume changes and sets up the next stunt, Scrat breaks up the monotony of *Ice Age*'s usual shtick and provides the film with its momentary bursts of inspiration. Provided a foil this time with a rascally female after the same nut, the desperate creature becomes our Wile E. Coyote and our attention is piqued whenever he's on screen.

On the flip side, the aforementioned new friend is a weasel named Buck (Simon Pegg), doing his best Dread Pirate Robert routine, as he plays guide through the dangerous dino landscape. Significant lifts from *The Princess Bride* (1987) abound here, right down to the aftermath of a life spent seeking revenge. Buck is cut from the same type of cloth, but from more like the leftover edges. So while anything new is certainly welcome, the character is never quite unique and can't even live up to the moxie of The Mole from *South Park: Bigger, Longer and Uncut* (1999). In one scene, Buck recalls his battle with the biggest and baddest of the dinosaurs which we see as a flashback. It ends with the lament how he "may have lost an eye that day" but gained the dino's tooth as a trusty weapon. However, during the visualization of the mêlée, Buck is always seen wearing his leafy eye patch. For writers sticking to formula consistency, it's amazing that this little bit of continuity would escape them.

The *Ice Age* series may be for the kiddies, but tries to work in such adult themes as settling into the big fade of domestication over everyday thrill-seeking. Kids might not pick up on the "never gonna yabba-dabba-doo that again" ride down a brontosaurus' neck or the "coming out" of a caterpillar. But better that than using the film as a basis for their book report on dinosaurs. If they were extinct before the actual ice age and now rediscovered as living beneath the ice, how precisely is this a "Dawn" again? Maybe they will be too busy singing "Walk the Dinosaur" to notice. Alas, a couple hundred of million dollars later, the studio gets a summer blockbuster with minimal creativity plus a direct tie-in joke to their next holiday sequel involving singing chipmunks, and parents can distract their children for 85 minutes until they finally grow up and discover the pleasures of Jurassic Park and Skull Island.

Erik Childress

CREDITS

Sid: John Leguizamo (Voice)
Manny: Ray Romano (Voice)
Ellie: Queen Latifah (Voice)
Diego: Denis Leary (Voice)
Scrat: Chris Wedge (Voice)
Buck: Simon Pegg (Voice)
Crash: Seann William Scott (Voice)
Eddie: Josh Peck (Voice)
Gazelle: Bill Hader (Voice)
Origin: USA
Language: English
Released: 2009
Production: Lori Forte, John C. Donkin; Blue Sky Studios; released by 20th Century Fox
Directed by: Carlos Saldanha

Written by: Michael Berg, Peter Ackerman, Mike Reiss, Yoni Brenner
Music by: John Powell
Sound: Randy Thom
Editing: Harry Hitner
Art Direction: Michael Knapp
MPAA rating: PG
Running time: 94 minutes

REVIEWS

Ebert, Roger. *Chicago Sun-Times.* June 30, 2009.
Gleiberman, Owen. *Entertainment Weekly.* July 1, 2009.
Howell, Peter. *Toronto Star.* July 1, 2009.
Leydon, Joe. *Variety.* June 22, 2009.
Pais, Matt. *Metromix.com.* June 30, 2009.
Phillips, Michael. *Chicago Tribune.* July 1, 2009.
Scott, A.O. *New York Times.* June 30, 2009.
Sharkey, Betsy. *Los Angeles Times.* June 30, 2009.
Sobczynski, Peter. *eFilmCritic.* June 30, 2009.
Tallerico, Brian. *MovieRetriever.com.* July 1, 2009.

QUOTES

Manny: "Guys don't talk to guys about guy problems. We just punch each other on the shoulders."
Diego: "Look, who are we kidding, Manny, I'm-I'm-I'm not a kitty-cat, I'm a sabre. I'm not really built for chaperoning play-dates."

TRIVIA

The largest dinosaur, Rudy, is based on the dinosaur Baryonyx. The animators chose this dinosaur because of it's crocodile-like appearance, which differentiated him from the Tyrannosaurs. His white color and bloodshot eyes were added to make him even more menacing.

THE IMAGINARIUM OF DOCTOR PARNASSUS

Box Office: $7.6 million

It is inevitable that when most people sit down to see the Terry Gilliam film *The Imaginarium of Doctor Parnassus* it will not be primarily to experience the latest work from the director of such cult classics as *Brazil* (1985), *12 Monkeys* (1995) and *Fear & Loathing in Las Vegas* (1998). Instead, they will be coming primarily to experience the last performance from Heath Ledger, who passed away partway through its filming before completing his role, and to see how successfully Gilliam managed to overcome this seemingly insurmountable hurdle with his decision to finish the film with no less than three top stars—Johnny Depp, Jude Law and Colin Farrell—filling in for the late actor at various points. However, it stands as a testament to the strength of this dark and dazzling fantasy that when Ledger's character makes his initial appearance maybe twenty minutes or so into the film, many viewers will be so captivated by the seductive spell that Gilliam has cast on them that any thoughts of Ledger's passing and the effort needed to keep the film going in the light of such a tragedy will be quickly forgotten.

The film stars Christopher Plummer as the aging Dr. Parnassus, who haunts the parking lots and back alleys of modern-day London with his Imaginarium, a traveling show that he runs with his lovely young daughter Valentina (Lily Cole) and assistants Anton (Andrew Garfield) and Percy (Verne Troyer) that allows patrons to magically enter the vast landscapes of their imaginations and make fateful decisions about their lives under the guidance of his mysterious powers. It turns out that these powers are only the tip of the iceberg with Parnassus. A thousand years earlier, he made a bet with Mr. Nick (Tom Waits)—better known to most people as the Devil—and won the gift of immortality as a result. Centuries later, Parnassus met the woman who would become the love of his life and made a new deal with Mr. Nick in which he would trade in his immortality for the gift of youth—the condition being that if there was a child, the offspring would belong to Mr. Nick upon turning sixteen. Now Valentina is about to celebrate that fateful birthday and Mr. Nick has turned up to collect his unsuspecting prize, though Parnassus is nowhere near ready to let go or even to inform Valentina about what is really going on.

Mr. Nick is a sporting type, however, and offers Parnassus yet another wager—whoever manages to convince five unsuspecting people to voluntarily give away their souls by the time Valentina turns sixteen wins her for good. At first, Parnassus despairs of being able to pull this off but salvation of a sort arrives in the form of Tony Sheppard (Ledger), a man who has no memory of who he is or what he has done in the past, though the fact that he is rescued by the Imaginarium troupe when they find him dangling from a bridge by the neck suggests a certain shadiness. Nevertheless, Tony proves to be an enormous asset in luring people to the Imaginarium and easily wins the heart of Valentina as well, pushing aside the jealous Anton in both departments. However, there are many different sides to Tony, as is revealed each time he enters the Imaginarium himself—there is the slick charmer (Depp), the starry-eyed dreamer (Law) and the corrupt sleaze (Farrell)—and as things progress, it is entirely possible that he may be more dangerous to Parnassus in the long run than even the Devil himself. It all climaxes, naturally, within the confines of the Imagi-narium, where one of the characters is forced to make their own choice at last.

The Imaginarium of Doctor Parnassus is an elaborate and densely packed fantasy dealing with such heady concepts as fate, the eternal struggle between good and evil, the importance of storytelling and of maintaining a sense of true imagination in a world that looks askance upon such things, parent-child conflicts and the struggle to maintain a certain sense of nobility and dignity in increasingly amoral times. In other words, it is a Terry Gilliam film through and through. Of course, that may seem more like a warning than anything else to some in the wake of such recent efforts as the admittedly scatter-shot *The Brothers Grimm* (2005) (which nonetheless demonstrated that a sub-par Gilliam was still more interesting than the top-shelf work of most other current filmmakers) and the admittedly abrasive *Tideland* (2006). In those regards, this film is a return to form as Gilliam, along with longtime collaborator Charles McKeown, has created a tale that is more straightforward and lighter in tone than anything he has done since *The Adventures of Baron Munchausen* (1989); (a film that this one resembles in many ways), although it is still off-kilter enough to require a couple a viewings to fully understand what is going on at certain points and even then, some parts (such as the exact nature of Parnassus' powers in regards to the Imaginarium) are still a bit of a muddle. However, Gilliam directs the material in such a confident and headlong manner that even though some of the details may not completely add up, the story as a whole rings clear and true throughout.

Besides, one does not necessarily go to a Terry Gilliam film for the prose. One goes to see the surreal and eye-popping sights that he has in store for audiences, and along those lines, *The Imaginarium of Doctor Parnassus* is an unqualified success. From the initial view of the Imaginarium sitting in the middle of a forlorn London street to the flashback showing the first meeting of Parnassus and Mr. Nick in a remote monastery to the final chase through the hallucinatory confines of the Imaginarium, this is a film that is a feast of visual astonishments from start to finish that will leave even Gilliam's most devoted fans knocked out.

The film also serves to highlight an aspect of Gilliam's skill as a filmmaker that often gets overlooked in the rush to discuss his visual flights of fancy, and that is his facility for handling actors. Over the years, his movies have included a number of wonderful performances—Jonathan Pryce in *Brazil*, Robin Williams and Jeff Bridges in *The Fisher King* (1991), Bruce Willis and Brad Pitt in *12 Monkeys*, Johnny Depp and Benicio del Toro in *Fear & Loathing in Las Vegas* and Jodelle Ferland in *Tideland* immediately leap to mind—and this one has a few more to add to his personal pantheon. Christopher

Plummer does some of the best work of his career as Parnassus, a man who comes across as part Faust, part Lear, part Dr. Lao and entirely, achingly human. Tom Waits supplies a lot of offbeat charm with his oddball turn as Mr. Nick, an interpretation of the Devil that will certain go down as one of the more interesting takes on the role that you will ever see. British model Lily Cole, in her first major role as Valentina, may not have a lot to do but she is such a compelling presence that she more than manages to hold her own against her better-known co-stars. The contributions from Depp, Law and Farrell may be brief but they are memorable—Depp may have the least screen time of the three but makes the most of it with a charming and captivating turn topped off by a lovely speech that almost serves as a eulogy for the actor whom he is replacing.

As for Heath Ledger, it is unlikely that his performance here will receive the same acclaim as his work in such films as *Brokeback Mountain* (2005) and *The Dark Knight* (2008), if only because those were lead roles while his character here is clearly a supporting player in the service of the central part of Parnassus. And yet, one still gets the sense of what a gifted and ambitious actor he truly was from his appearance here—the performance itself shows him finding a nice balance between sweetness and sleaziness, and his willingness to take on a quirky character part like this at a point when he clearly could have hired on to something far more lucrative and high-profile based on the advanced word of his work as the Joker demonstrates that he was one of those increasingly rare birds whose interest really was in the work. Thanks to his performance, not to mention Gilliam's determination to make sure that it would be seen, *The Imaginarium of Doctor Parnassus* works both as one of the best fantasy films of recent years and as a fitting final tribute to an actor whose career ended much too soon.

Peter Sobczynski

CREDITS

Dr. Parnassus: Christopher Plummer
Tony: Heath Ledger
Imaginarium Tony 1: Johnny Depp
Imaginarium Tony 2: Jude Law
Imaginarium Tony 3: Colin Farrell
Mr. Nick: Tom Waits
Valentina: Lily Cole
Percy: Verne Troyer
Anton: Andrew Garfield
Origin: Great Britain, Canada, France
Language: English
Released: 2009

Production: William Vince, Amy Gilliam, Samuel Hadida, Terry Gilliam; Infinity Features Entertainment, Poo Poo Pictures, Davis Films, Telefilm Canada; released by Sony Pictures Classics
Directed by: Terry Gilliam
Written by: Terry Gilliam, Charles McKeown
Cinematography by: Nicola Pecorini
Music by: Mychael Danna, Jeff Danna
Sound: Tim Fraser, Eric J. Batut
Editing: Mick Audsley
Art Direction: Terry Gilliam, Dave Warren
Costumes: Monique Prudhomme
Production Design: Anastasia Massaro
MPAA rating: PG-13
Running time: 122 minutes

REVIEWS

Bradshaw, Peter. *Guardian.* May 22, 2009.
Burr, Ty. *Boston Globe.* January 7, 2010.
Childress, Erik. *eFilmCritic.com.* December 25, 2009.
Dargis, Manohla. *New York Times.* December 25, 2009.
Ebert, Roger. *Chicago Sun-Times.* January 7, 2010.
McCarthy, Todd. *Variety.* May 22, 2009.
Pais, Matt. *Metromix.com.* December 23, 2009.
Travers, Peter. *Rolling Stone.* December 22, 2009.
Uhlich, Keith. *Time Out New York.* December 16, 2009.
Weinberg, Scott. *Cinematical.* September 21, 2009.

QUOTES

Dr. Parnassus: "Your mother and I went away together, grew old, and one day she came to me and told me she was pregnant! Can you believe it, at sixty and pregnant. A miracle."

TRIVIA

Heath Ledger improvised half of his comedic dialogue on set.

AWARDS

Nomination:

Oscars 2009: Art Dir./Set Dec., Costume Des.
British Acad. 2009: Makeup, Prod. Des.

IMAGINE THAT
(Nowhereland)

What if your daughter's imagination…was the secret to your success?
—Movie tagline

Box Office: $16 million

Back when Eddie Murphy was a dominant presence on the 1980s movie scene and helping set new records for the amount of times the F-bomb was dropped, who could have ever imagined that a decade would come where he would practically become the new Dean Jones? That may be over-accentuating it a bit, but thanks to films like *Dr. Dolittle* (1998) *Shrek* (2001) as well as further kiddie efforts including *Daddy Day Care* (2003) and *The Haunted Mansion* (2003), Eddie Murphy has certainly changed the "F" in "F-bomb" to "family" The once-edgy actor has not appeared in an R-rated feature since *Life* (1999). That is ten years of projects ranging from the quality of *Bowfinger* to the depths of *Norbit* (2007). When his sci-fi family comedy, *Meet Dave* (2008), opened to little fanfare and even less positive notices, some thought he had reached a new low. Imagine that they spoke too soon though because just a year later Murphy somehow found himself involved in a film that seems to neglect every fan he has ever had, regardless of the rating.

Murphy plays Evan Danielson, a hard-working investment banker, who has already failed a marriage and has little time for his 7-year-old daughter, Olivia (Yari Shahidi). He is in the middle of competing for a big promotion against his rival, Johnny Whitefeather (Thomas Haden Church), who uses spiritual mumbo jumbo to convince clients he is one with the stock trends. It is not a good time for his week with Olivia, who just wants her daddy to play with her at times when Evan just needs her to be quiet. Olivia has her own friends, though, in the form of some imaginary princesses, and though they must see how Evan ignores his daughter, they nevertheless supply a couple of tips that might help daddy advise Wall Street.

Evan naturally does not recognize this at first and has an in-office breakdown when Olivia uses his porfolio for a coloring canvas. In desperation he uses the advice of the fairy princesses and, much to everyone's surprise, it turns out to be right on. Now with a step-up in the office, Evan wants to take part in his daughter's fantasies and meet these buying-and-selling fairies despite not being able to see or hear them. They never disappoint and, soon enough, neither does Evan who begins to play with Olivia regularly and make the pancakes she's always wanted.

If your children have a fascination with the business world and would prefer to see absentee dads get stock tips rather than flying houses, magical lost worlds or historical museum figures coming to life, than by all means put *Imagine That* at the top of of their moviegoing list. Maybe their imaginations are strong enough to conjure up the same visions that Olivia receives with the magic blanket she cannot function without. Realistically though, even the most precocious of children are liable to turn to their own daddy to ask why they cannot see the fairy princesses and then receive their answer 45 minutes later when daddy wakes up.

Watching *Imagine That* is like seeing a big movie star vehicle that was put into turnaround when the cameras were literally still rolling. After a half-hour of establishing Evan's struggles at work and with Olivia, at some point you expect the magical aspects to start rolling in and transport kids into a world of fairy dust and dragons. Once the plot does finally kick in, Murphy's scenes with Shahidi appear as if the budget had just run out and director Karey Kirkpatrick is off-screen ordering them to stretch. No more actors. No costumes. No sets. No special effects. Just Eddie Murphy running around with a blanket pretending to see what none of us can. During one crucial scene, we suspect they were unable to fly Martin Sheen in to do his scenes in person and instead performs them via teleconferencing where we see, what we imagine, is a copy of the script handed to him. When Adam Sandler played a similar relative using his sister's kids for life success in the unimaginative *Bedtime Stories* (2008), there was also a cheat aspect to its magical reality—but at least we had a chance to see raining gumballs and heroic fantasies.

The summer of 2009 had already suffered through the misguided take on television's *Land of the Lost*, which blurred the line between the obvious kiddie origins with a decidedly more adult sense of humor. *Imagine That* takes the cake though in fashioning a story that any age should be baffled by even if they have "greed is good" crocheted on their bedroom pillow. No attempts at satire are made for the adults who might envision this as an ironic take on the current financial crisis. Kids are liable to be savvy enough to wonder why they spent money on this instead of staying home with the hours of live-action entertainment they could get on Nickelodeon or the Disney channel. That's just good economic sense.

No matter what anyone thought about *Meet Dave* (2008), no one can argue that changing its title from *Starship Dave* made little sense as it turned a recognizable sci-fi term into something out of an AA meeting. Changing *Imagine That* from its original title of *Nowhereland* proves to be just the opposite—an effort to actually hide what audiences would be walking into.

Erik Childress

CREDITS

Evan: Eddie Murphy
Tricia Danielson: Nicole Ari Parker
Whitefeather: Thomas Haden Church
Lori Struthers: Vanessa Williams

Tom Stevens: Ronny Cox
Olivia Danielson: Yara Shahidi
Dante D'Enzo: Martin Sheen
Origin: USA
Language: English
Released: 2009
Production: Lorenzo di Bonaventura, Ed Solomon;
    Nickelodeon Movies; released by Paramount Pictures
Directed by: Karey Kirkpatrick
Written by: Edward Solomon, Chris M. Theson
Cinematography by: John Lindley
Music by: Mark Mancina
Sound: Willis D. Burton
Editing: David Moritz
Art Direction: Sue Chan
Costumes: Ruth E. Carter
Production Design: William Arnold
MPAA rating: PG
Running time: 107 minutes

REVIEWS

Ebert, Roger. *Chicago Sun-Times.* June 11, 2009.
Gleiberman, Owen. *Entertainment Weekly.* June 10, 2009.
Goldstein, Gary. *Los Angeles Times.* June 12, 2009.
Honeycutt, Kirk. *Hollywood Reporter.* June 8, 2009.
Leydon, Joe. *Variety.* June 8, 2009.
Morgenstern, Joe. *Wall Street Journal.* June 12, 2009.
Morris, Wesley. *Boston Globe.* June 11, 2009.
Pais, Matt. *Metromix.com.* June 11, 2009.
Pinkerton, Nick. *Village Voice.* June 10, 2009.
Puig, Claudia. *USA Today.* June 11, 2009.

AWARDS

Nomination:

Golden Raspberries 2009: Worst Actor (Murphy).

IN THE LOOP

> *The fate of the world is on the line.*
> —Movie tagline

Box Office: $2 million

The scathing political comedy *In the Loop* took the arthouse circuit by storm in 2009, earnings several awards season nominations, ending up on dozens of top ten lists, while grossing just over $2 million in US theaters with a remarkable 94% of critics granting the film a "Fresh" rating on Rotten Tomatoes. Very loosely based on the BBC TV series *The Thick of It, In the Loop* is an often-brilliant, scathing stab at international politics

in which characters spew witty repartee the way an action movie hero sprays bullets. A perfect antidote to the summer bloat that infected the multiplex in 2009, *In the Loop* had dozens of critics grinning with glee. Featuring a wonderful blend of actors and actresses from around the world, the joint production between BBC Films and the UK Film Council was heralded and beloved by those paid to watch movies for a living on both shores. It did not quite connect at the box office in the way most critics would hope that it would, but time will almost certainly be kind to the film.

As the film opens, Simon Foster (Tom Hollander), the U.K.'s Minister for International Development, has put his foot in his mouth. The awkward government employee went on BBC Radio 4's "PM" program and stated that he thought a proposed war in the Middle East was "unforeseeable," just the kind of confusing choice of words that could start an international political battle. The off-the-cuff remark sends the Prime Minister's Director of Communications, Malcolm Tucker (Peter Capaldi), into an absolute, profanity-laced tirade. Both sides of the pond are trying to downplay the possibility of an invasion of Iraq, and the new-found publicity has led to more than a few problems. Without much warning, the awkward Foster is thrust on to the national stage, as everyone in his office rushes to do damage control. With every word analyzed, the team behind Simon, including communications director Judy (Gina McKee) and political advisor Toby (Chris Addison) rush to clean up the political mess.

Eventually, the action moves to Washington, D.C. and becomes even more of a tug of war between government officials planning for battle, those trying to stop it, and everyone else who just wants to keep the discussion out of the public discourse. While in D.C., State Department big wig Linton Barwick (David Rasche), Pentagon leader General Miller (James Gandolfini), and a former flame of Toby named Liza (Anna Chlumsky) join in the lunacy. Zach Woods, Mimi Kennedy, Paul Higgins, and Scott Coogan also appear in small roles.

Written by Jesse Armstrong, Simon Blackwell, Armando Iannucci, and Tony Roche, the screenplay for *In the Loop* (nominated for several awards from critic's groups) is both its strongest and weakest asset. Whip-smart dialogue from characters with vocabularies much larger than the average multiplex moviegoer is refreshing, but the script for *In the Loop* can often feel a bit too aware of its own cleverness, as if the writers are winking at the audience and pointing out just how smart they are with each new turn of a phrase. Certain cast members are better at selling the dry, razor-sharp dialogue, most notably the movie-stealing Peter Capaldi, who earned enough awards-season buzz that some considered him a viable candidate for an Oscar®

nomination (he was nominated for Best Supporting Actor by the Chicago Film Critics Association). Capaldi spits profanity with the best of them and actually sells the deeply intellectual repartee as if his character is thinking of it off the cuff. Some of the supporting characters, however, do not fare as well in this department. The problem with scripts that contain as much clever dialogue as *In the Loop* is making it believable that even the minor supporting characters would know exactly what to say at just the right time. Like a David Mamet film, everyone in *In the Loop,* Stateside and in the U.K., seems to have the exact same vocabulary and a nearly superhuman way with words.

It is unsurprising that a comedy that does not rely on gross-out humor or human stupidity to produce laughs found a loyal, devoted following among critics and audiences. Expertly acted and conceived, *In the Loop* is the rare quotable satire that does not fall back on traditional clichés of its genre. Despite its flaws, intelligent political comedy is unbelievably rare. It is somewhat disheartening that the film generated as small a box office gross as it did (although the minute budget made it a financial success) but it is the kind of work that will almost certainly develop a fan base on DVD. Screenplays this smart typically do.

Brian Tallerico

CREDITS

Simon Foster: Tom Hollander
Malcolm Tucker: Peter Capaldi
Judy: Gina McKee
Gen. George Miller: James Gandolfini
Toby: Chris Addison
Liza Weld: Anna Chlumsky
Jamie MacDonald: Paul Higgins
Karen Clarke: Mimi Kennedy
Linton Barwick: David Rasche
Paul: Steve Coogan
Sir Jonathan Tutt: Alex MacQueen
Origin: Great Britain
Released: 2009
Production: Kevin Loader, Adam Tandy; BBC Films, Aramid Entertainment Fund, UK Film Council; released by IFC Films
Directed by: Armando Iannucci
Written by: Armando Iannucci, Jesse Armstrong, Simon Blackwell, Tony Roche
Cinematography by: Jaimie Cairney
Music by: Adem Ilhan
Sound: Bob Newton
Editing: Billy Sneddon
Art Direction: Nick Dent
Costumes: Ros Little
Production Design: Cristina Casali
MPAA rating: Unrated
Running time: 105 minutes

REVIEWS

Bradshaw, Peter. *Guardian.* April 17, 2009.
LaSalle, Mick. *San Francisco Chronicle.* July 24, 2009.
Long, Tom. *Detroit News.* July 31, 2009.
MacDonald, Moira. *Seattle Times.* July 30, 2009.
Mondello, Bob. *NPR.* July 24, 2009.
Pais, Matt. *Metromix.com.* July 23, 2009.
Scott, A.O. *New York Times.* July 24, 2009.
Stevens, Dana. *Slate.* July 23, 2009.
Travers, Peter. *Rolling Stone.* July 16, 2009.
Weitzman, Elizabeth. *New York Daily News.* July 24, 2009.

QUOTES

Jamie MacDonald: "You think that's his real name? Iceman? To Mr. and Mrs. Man, a son…Ice?"

TRIVIA

The shooting script after thirty days of filming was 237 pages long. The first cut of the film was 4.5 hours long. The final edit ultimately took four months to complete.

AWARDS

Nomination:

Oscars 2009: Adapt. Screenplay
British Acad. 2009: Adapt. Screenplay.

THE INFORMANT!

Based on a tattle-tale.
—Movie tagline

Box Office: $33 million

Who can you trust in today's society? Our sports heroes have all been tainted with steroids. Advertisers are all trying to sell you a bigger, better product destined for repairs—one that you didn't get an extended warranty for anyway. Even a certain faction of film critics have been seduced by the dark side of junkets and celebrity hand-holding, subconsciously corrupted into giving soft opinions. These are just on consumer pastimes too. Do you even want to get started on politicians or the news media lost on the integrity of Edward Murrow and the first rule of objective journalism? Make no mistake we are living in an unjust and imbalanced time. A time when we need to go back in time to be reminded of those like Jeffrey Wigand and Erin Brockovich in the movies where every frame is truth. Thankfully we have people like Mark Whitacre out there; guys who recognize when something is not right and are willing to put their career and family on the line to expose the filth and corruption aimed at hard-working Americans.

In the early 1990s Whitacre was the Vice President at Archer Daniels Midland, the agribusiness firm from Decatur, Illinois known for its promotion of food additives. It is not exactly the company that Clark Griswold worked for and today, at least, Whitacre is not exactly interested in keeping cereal crunchy. Mark believes he has discovered a mole in the company that is feeding info to a Japanese competitor. FBI agent Brian Shepard (Scott Bakula) is called in, but is met with resistance when it comes to tapping phones of the high-level executives. Mark is fine with it though and doesn't waste time in letting Shepard know of why his bosses are squeamish about recorded conversations. Seems they are all in cahoots in an international price fixing scheme that is defrauding Americans out of precious nickels and dimes.

Aware he is now onto a groundbreaking case, Shepard gets the support of his superiors to use Whitacre as their own inside man and get the goods on these corporate wise guys once and for all. Mark could not be more excited, getting a chance to be a real-life hero like in all those Michael Crichton novels he reads. Plus it's an opportunity to do the right thing. Reminding us how he was orphaned as a child and worked his way up the success ladder, Mark now has a chance to give something back to a world that has given him so much. He's the good guy in all of this. Right?

The less one knows about Mark Whitacre the more comically fascinating his journey over this period becomes and a greater appreciation forms in what Soderbergh and screenwriter Scott Z. Burns are doing with his story in *The Informant!* As played by Damon, Whitacre is a bit of a schlub; spare tire in tow and always talking to himself (within his head, heard in voiceover) about a myriad of everyday thoughts. Having gained a reported thirty pounds for the role, Damon's physique is more of a commentary on actors changing their physical appearance to inhabit someone they are clearly not. Whether it be Russell Crowe going from beefy to bulky for *The Insider* (1999) or Julia Roberts using special bras to add weight to her chest for *Erin Brockovich* (2000), *The Informant!* is having fun with this particular convention and slowly makes it clear that movies and truth go together like business and philanthropy.

Damon's performance is key to blurring these lines and it is one of his best. Having already played Linus Caldwell for Soderbergh three times, the young progeny of the Danny Ocean gang is always looking for a bigger role to play, Damon is already perfectly at home at accentuating the goofier traits of a wannabe outsider. As Whitacre he now gets to live out that fantasy of being a secret agent. Mark is already a VIP, respected if just another cog in the company wheel. But now he is getting his big break to jump from supporting player to the lead. No longer "M," he is now James Bond out in the field; double-O 14 "because he's twice as smart." Except he's still well below the level of a Jason Bourne or even Matt Helm, Derek Flint or Austin Powers.

Soderbergh's career has been marked with a complicity in alternating between big star vehicles like the *Ocean's Eleven* (2001) series and small-scale indie experiments such as *Bubble* (2005) and *The Girlfriend Experience* (2009). Sometimes the line is even blurred between the two as evidenced in *The Good German* (2006) and his remake of *Solaris* (2002). *The Informant!* blurs all the lines, playfully goofing on his own *Erin Brockovich* (2000) but also in crafting the type of film that Whitacre might pitch to a studio executive with himself as hero. Only Mark would not get the sexy, hunky Matt Damon to play him. He gets the one who let himself go. Guys like Ed Harris and Tommy Lee Jones pass on the role of his FBI contact, so Scott Bakula steps in. The rest of the *Ocean's* gang is busy? No problem. Call in the hosts and commentators of E!'s *The Soup* and VH-1's *Best Week Ever*, Joel McHale, Patton Oswalt and Paul F. Tompkins. What are The Smothers Brothers up to? Call them in. This is no knock on their performances or talent, all of whom only accentuate Whitacre's grandeur delusion and Soderbergh's eye for inspired casting. His ear for music doesn't go unnoticed either as Marvin Hamlisch's score—his first narrative-based since, ironically, *The Mirror Has Two Faces* (1996)—itself mirrors a kind of breezy, Ramada-room-like feel as Whitacre strolls through his double life not with the suave swagger of a spook with brandy glass in tow but like a guy who wants a soundtrack you can hop and skip to work with.

The Informant! never misses a beat in wringing laughs out of Whitacre's unpredictability and the reactions of his various handlers in discovering new layers to his intentions. Alternately though it brings to light the sad actuality of our theoretical heroes having more than just surface flaws or the irregular vice. Accepting the preordained stereotype of industry being the enemy and the motion of lips signaling a lie, we consciously hold their combatants to a higher standard and feel betrayed when dirt turns up on them. Does it make the real bad guys less guilty? No, but there's a bigger story in tearing down the white hat. Naturally no one will admit to wearing the black one and in the case of another high-up Illinois official, ousted Governor Rod Blagojevich, he's on the offensive as to prove he's been wronged and has the goods to shame the real villains of his story. What's real? What's delusion? The parallels between his story and Whitacre's are chillingly comical in the way they play out.

Viewers do not need to trouble themselves with understanding the bottom line of the corn industry or the purpose of lysine. Yet this is more outrageous than science fiction. We may have Dr. Sam Beckett and Biff Tannen in the same film, but we do not need to travel back in time to see *The Informant!* as much of a story of today as the period in which it takes place. With *The Girlfriend Experience* (2009) and this, Soderbergh has paralleled his award-winning double-dip of *Erin Brockovich* (2000) and *Traffic* (2000). Nearly some ten years later, by returning to what some might label a sell-out year (both films doubled the box office take of his first eight films), Soderbergh has brought the dangers of unchecked capitalism and the government's inability to stabilize it full circle. Michael Moore may believe that's what he was doing with his latest documentary, *Capitalism: A Love Story* (2009), but maybe he's just the Mark Whitacre of his own story while Soderbergh is the true whistle blower we can believe in.

Erik Childress

CREDITS

Mark Whitacre: Matt Damon
Brian Shepard: Scott Bakula
Ginger Whitacre: Melanie Lynskey
Ed Herbst: Patton Oswalt
Robert Herndon: Joel McHale
Origin: USA
Language: English, French
Released: 2009
Production: Howard Braunstein, Kurt Eichenwald, Jennifer Fox, Gregory Jacobs, Michael Jaffe; Warner Bros. Pictures, Participant Media, Groundswell Productions; released by Warner Bros.
Directed by: Steven Soderbergh
Written by: Scott Burns
Music by: Marvin Hamlisch
Editing: Stephen Mirrione
Costumes: Shoshana Rubin
Production Design: Doug Meerdink
MPAA rating: R
Running time: 108 minutes

REVIEWS

Corliss, Richard. *Time Magazine.* September 15, 2009.
Dargis, Manohla. *New York Times.* September 17, 2009.

Denby, David. *New Yorker.* September 14, 2009.
Ebert, Roger. *Chicago Sun-Times.* September 17, 2009.
Edelstein, David. *New York Magazine.* September 14, 2009.
Honeycutt, Kirk. *Hollywood Reporter.* September 9, 2009.
Howell, Peter. *Toronto Star.* September 18, 2009.
McCarthy, Todd. *Variety.* September 9, 2009.
Tallerico, Brian. *MovieRetriever.com.* September 18, 2009.
Turan, Kenneth. *Los Angeles Times.* September 17, 2009.

QUOTES

Terry Wilson: "Well, there you have it, from Mark Whitacre, Ph.D. You know what the Ph.D. stands for, don't you? Piled higher and deeper."

TRIVIA

This story was the subject of the September 15, 2000 episode (#168) of *This American Life* entitled "The Fix is In."

AWARDS

Nomination:

Golden Globes 2010: Actor—Mus./Comedy (Damon), Orig. Score.

THE INFORMERS

Greed is good. Sex is easy. Youth is forever.
—Movie tagline

"I need someone to tell me what is good," says Graham (Jon Foster) to his friend Martin (Austin Nichols). "I need someone to tell me what's bad."

That, in a nutshell, is the point of *The Informers*, a cold yet intriguing adaptation of author (and co-screenwriter) Bret Easton Ellis' 1994 book of short stories. The film is largely populated with spoiled, disaffected wealthy people like Graham, who deals drugs, engages in a casual relationship with frequently topless beauty Christie (Amber Heard) and sneers over his parents' (Billy Bob Thornton, Kim Basinger) failed relationship. Yet Graham does not absorb much of anything; he is a privileged kid who, on the surface, has everything, but has little sense of what is supposed to matter or how to get whatever it is that makes him happy.

Martin and Christie are similarly desensitized, including when mysterious spots begin to appear on Christie's body. (The film takes place in 1983 Los Angeles with increased awareness of HIV lingering in the background, though its only direct mention is when a nameless character turns off a news report about HIV to watch the music video for Men Without Hats' "The

Safety Dance"). This is clear early on after their friend Bruce (Fernando Consagra) is fatally struck by a car; neither Christie nor Graham wants to go to his funeral, and Martin has nothing nice to say about the deceased. In response to Raymond (Aaron Himmelstein), who is deeply distraught over the death, Graham says, "There's nothing we can do. It happened. It's over. It's time to move on." In *The Informers* death is casual, since people who feel so little barely recognize the significance when that feeling comes to an end.

While this may sound monotonous and grim, the film works on a much broader canvas and becomes, at times, somewhat of a dark comedy. When kind desk clerk Jack (the late Brad Renfro) discovers a sick-looking girl in his sleazy uncle Peter's (Mickey Rourke) van and asks if the girl is OK, Peter replies, "She's sort of taking it all in. She saw some stuff." Elsewhere, Graham's movie executive dad William (Thornton) tells his daughter Susan (Cameron Goodman) about a film in development that he thinks she will like. The plot: a 12-year-old boy becomes president. This sort of absurdity calls out the insulated world of these privileged people, identifying, in this case, William's inability to tell the difference between quality and garbage.

Of course, that is far from his primary concern. William's wife Laura (Basinger) wants him back, but he is still fixated on his former lover, a TV reporter named Cheryl (Winona Ryder) who is frequently recognized but seems to get little pleasure from her fame. That parallels with perhaps the film's most hopeless and tragic character, rock star Bryan Metro (Mel Raido). He is the mega-popular lead singer of The Informers and is in such a careless daze that he sleeps with underage kids and wakes up the next morning and thoughtlessly orders his underlings to get rid of them. (Another hilariously dry moment comes later, when one of William's employees offers Bryan the starring role in "Your typical rock-star-in-outer-space-type-thing.") Bryan is so detached from himself that when he slips on a bathroom floor and cuts his hand on a broken liquor bottle, he sits there smoking and staring at the blood without causing much of a stir. He does ask for help, but it is safe to assume that without seeing the blood, this guy would not even realize he had a problem.

Clearly *The Informers* is nothing if not episodic, a result of its short-story source material that does not always gel into a consistent film. In Hawaii one of Graham's friends (or is he more of a client?), Tim (Lou Taylor Pucci) becomes frustrated by his estranged father's (Chris Isaak) attempts to bond and pick up women, but the storyline goes nowhere. And while there is at least a hint of humanity in the segment involving Jack and his horrified discovery of the boy in his bathtub that Peter kidnapped, its connection to the rest of the film is fragile at best. (At one point Jack, an aspiring actor, tries to befriend Graham in hopes that he'll connect him with Martin, a music video director, but Graham offers no assistance.)

Even when it feels fractured, though, *The Informers* maintains a thought-provoking command of the tension that results when someone who does not care talks to someone who does. The narcissism within is typical of Ellis, who has made a career (in other novels like *American Psycho* [1991]) exploring the chilly decisions of ruthless characters. While the film does not represent Ellis's most potent work, it is nonetheless fascinating to watch people, more connected to the emptiness of success than to the thrill, dangling on the edge without much sense of what to do about it. They live in a bubble, and it is always ready to burst.

Matt Pais

CREDITS

William Sloan: Billy Bob Thornton
Laura Sloan: Kim Basinger
Peter: Mickey Rourke
Cheryl Moore: Winona Ryder
Graham Sloan: Jon Foster
Christine: Amber Heard
Martin: Austin Nichols
Brad Renfro: Lou Taylor Pucci
Les Price: Chris Isaak
Roger: Rhys Ifans
Mel Raido: Bryan Metro
Origin: USA
Language: English
Released: 2009
Production: Marco Weber; released by Senator Film Entertainment
Directed by: Gregor Jordan
Written by: Bret Easton Ellis, Nicholas Jarecki
Cinematography by: Petra Korner
Music by: Christopher Young
Sound: David O. Daniel
Music Supervisor: Justin Meldal-Johnsen
Editing: Robert Brakey
Art Direction: Nick Ralbovsky, Ines Olmedo
Costumes: Sophie de Rakoff
Production Design: Cecilia Montiel
MPAA rating: R
Running time: 100 minutes

REVIEWS

Abele, Robert. *Los Angeles Times.* April 23, 2009.
Burr, Ty. *Boston Globe.* April 23, 2009.

Ebert, Roger. *Chicago Sun-Times.* April 23, 2009.

Hoberman, J. *Village Voice.* April 22, 2009.

Long, Tom. *Detroit News.* April 24, 2009.

Lumenick, Lou. *New York Post.* April 24, 2009.

Murray, Noel. *AV Club.* April 23, 2009.

Phillips, Michael. *Chicago Tribune.* April 24, 2009.

Puig, Claudia. *USA Today.* April 23, 2009.

Scott, A.O. *New York Times.* April 24, 2009.

QUOTES

Susan Sloan (dryly, to a topless Christie): "Nice Shirt."

TRIVIA

Brad Renfro's final film.

INGLOURIOUS BASTERDS

A basterd's work is never done.
—Movie tagline

Box Office: $121 million

Quentin Tarantino's World War II epic *Inglourious Basterds* has been in the planning stages for more than a decade—more than twice as long as America's participation in that conflict, one might note—and when most viewers see it, it is likely that the wait, not to mention the various rumors that have developed about it over the year, will cause them to have certain expectations about what they are about to see, mostly that Tarantino was going to give people an action-packed guys-on-a-mission spectacular along the lines of *The Dirty Dozen* (1967) or *Where Eagles Dare* (1968). Instead, he has shifted gears and presented us with a film comprised of maybe a dozen or so scenes, broken up over five chapters, in which epic battle sequences have been replaced with epic-length conversations in which language is the weapon of choice and the tiniest slip of an accent can be as deadly as a bullet to the head. The result may be the first WWII epic that, save for the grand *Grand Guignol* finale, could be produced as a stage presentation without losing anything in the translation. More significantly, it demonstrates that a film consisting of nearly two-and-a-half hours of conversation can be just as gripping and exciting as an endless array of pyrotechnics and stunts in the hands of the right filmmaker.

The film stars Brad Pitt as Lt. Aldo Raine, a snuff-snorting hillbilly charged with leading a special platoon of all-Jewish soldiers on a special mission to kill as many Nazi soldiers as possible in the nastiest ways possible (complete with post-mortem scalpings) as a way of throwing fear into the heart of the Third Reich. As the war progresses, so does their infamy, and in the days after D-Day, they are given their biggest mission to date when they are assigned to assist a British spy (Michael Fassbender) and a glamorous German actress-turned-double-agent (Diane Kruger) in infiltrating a Parisian cinema during the premiere of a new German propaganda epic and kill the members of the Nazi high command who will be in attendance, including Hitler himself. What they don't realize is that the owner of the theater, the brave and beautiful Shosanna Dreyfus (Melanie Laurent) is planning something similar—with the help of the hundreds of unstable nitrate film prints that she has on hand—in order to avenge her family, all of whom were slaughtered a few years earlier under the floorboards of the French farmhouse where they were hiding on the orders of Col. Landa (Christoph Waltz in what may be the single best performance in any Tarantino film), the cruelly efficient Nazi who just happens to be in charge of security for the premiere.

Although *Inglourious Basterds* may appear on the surface to be the ultimate World War II film in the way that *Kill Bill* (2003) was the ultimate martial arts revenge extravaganza, those going into it looking for a traditional war film are likely to come out of it somewhat confused and disoriented by the way that it subverts those expectations at every turn. Instead of intricately choreographed battle sequences punctuated by, at most, a pithy line of dialogue here or a gung-ho speech there, Tarantino instead gives us a series of intricately choreographed dialogue sequences that are often punctuated by brief and brutal bursts of violence. Instead of offering up the standard narrative approach of following a bunch of guys as they go about pulling off their seemingly impossible mission, he gives us several different and disparate storylines and narrative tones and then figures out a way to logically tie them all together in the final scenes as he did to a certain degree in *Pulp Fiction* (1994). If you had to compare this to another WWII movie, the closest one would be Paul Verhoeven's *Black Book* (2006), another slyly subversive work that delighted in confounding genre expectations at every turn. Actually, if you have to compare it to anything, you would be better off comparing it to the spaghetti-western epics of Sergio Leone—like *Basterds* those films told long tales filled with violence and revenge that nevertheless subverted their conventions by stretching them to the breaking point and adding in bits of satire and weirdo humor amidst the carnage.

The difference between the Leone films and *Inglourious Basterds* is that while Leone used as little dialogue as possible to tell his stories (the better to redub them for the international market), Tarantino's film is a multilingual talkfest from beginning to end. This is not to say that Tarantino is not a cinematic storyteller by any means—from a visual standpoint, this may be his most accomplished work to date. However, while his past films have always been filled with characters who have gloried in their long flights of verbal fancy, the extended dialogue sequences here also take on a second dramatic level in the ways that they show just how important language can be and how the tiniest turn of the phrase or slip of the tongue can have lasting repercussions. The opening scene between Landa and the dairy farmer has already been labeled an instant classic and while it is definitely the high-point of the show, there are plenty of other impressive moments along those lines as well that do an incredible job of simultaneously moving the narrative forward, allowing the characters to come across as unique individuals instead of just as pawns being driven by the plot and slowly but surely ratcheting up the tension in ways that would have done even Hitchcock proud. The best of the bunch is the inadvertent meeting between Landa and Shosanna in which we are never quite sure if the former realizes that this isn't his first encounter with her and the extended set-piece in a remote barroom meeting between some ersatz Nazis and some real ones that goes to pieces with just the wave of a finger.

At the same time, all the elements that have made Tarantino such a distinctive cinematic voice are fully on display here. There are many bits of sly comedy, one of the best being the seemingly superfluous bit in which a British commander (played by a cameoing Mike Myers) explains the parameters of an upcoming mission in a way that serves as a straight-faced parody of such scenes—so much so that some have cited it as the weakest and most inessential scene in the entire film—while quietly setting up some important details that will pay off in the next sequence. (Even if you don't buy this scene as parody, it is still worth it just for the appearance of Rod Taylor as none other than Winston Churchill himself.) Although the film may not be the wall-to-wall gorefest promised by the ads, the violence on display is done in such a way that even the most bloodthirsty audiences will find themselves affected by it, mostly because, like much of the brutality that he has displayed over the years, Tarantino never quite shows us everything that we think we are seeing and allows our minds to fill in the gory details. And once again, he stuffs in enough film references throughout the proceedings so that the film could almost serve as a screen adaptation of *The Filmgoer's Companion*—this time around, they range from the fairly obvious (Emil Jannings is one of the invitees at the film premiere) to the fairly obscure (Myers' character is named Ed Fenech, an obvious nod to famed Eurosleaze sexpot Edwige Fenech) to the wildly unexpected. Who else, after all, would give

us a climactic attack scene in a World War II movie that somehow manages to work in exact visual quotes from not one, but two Brian DePalma movies?

Inglourious Basterds is a great movie, but many of Tarantino's detractors seem to have taken umbrage over its very existence. One reason is the alleged tastelessness of having Jewish characters in a WWII film gleefully doing the things that we would normally associate with the Nazis (apparently this is only allowed if such behavior is presented in an appropriately mournful/dull manner a la *Defiance* [2008] or *Valkyrie* [2008]). Another is the extreme liberties played with the historical record (forgetting that there were a number of movies made during the war period, many of them outright comedies, that dealt with hunting down Hitler and eradicating him for good). And even little things like having an allegedly anachronistic song like David Bowie's *Cat People* playing on the soundtrack at a key point in the narrative—a glorious bit that I defend on the grounds that a.) the song perfectly encapsulates the mood of that particular moment and b.) the fact that Strauss wrote *Also Sprach Zarathustra* well after the Dawn of Man didn't hurt the opening of *2001* [1968] a bit) seems to rankle critics. In a typically cheeky bit, Tarantino actually goes so far as to conclude his film with a character remarking "I think this just might be my masterpiece." While that might not be precisely the case in regards to the film as a whole, it is enough of a masterful example of contemporary popular entertainment to at least warrant such thinking.

Peter Sobczynski

CREDITS

Lt. Aldo Raine: Brad Pitt
Bridget Von Hammersmark: Diane Kruger
Soshana Dreyfus: Melanie Laurent
Col. Hans Landa: Christoph Waltz
Pvt. Hirschberg: Samm Levine
Pvt. Utivich: B.J. Novak
Sgt. Donnie Donowitz: Eli Roth
Frederick Zoller: Daniel Bruhl
Sgt. Hugo Stiglitz: Til Schweiger
Gen. Ed Fenech: Mike Myers
Mrs. Himmelman: Cloris Leachman
Lt. Archie Hicox: Michael Fassbender
Madame Mimieux: Maggie Cheung
Winston Churchill: Rod Taylor
Cpl. Wilhelm Wicki: Gedeon Burkhard
Pfc. Ulmer: Omar Doom
Maj. Dieter Hellstrom: August Diehl
Francesca Mondino: Julie Dreyfus
Adolph Hitler: Martin Wuttke

Pfc. Zimmerman: Michael Bacall
American Colonel: Bo Svenson
Marcel: Jacky Ido
Perrier LaPadite: Denis Menochet
Joseph Goebbels: Sylvester Groth
Mathilda: Anne-Sophie Franck
Narrator: Samuel L. Jackson
Origin: USA
Language: English
Released: 2009
Production: Lawrence Bender; Universal, Weinstein Co., A Band Apart; released by Universal Pictures
Directed by: Quentin Tarantino
Written by: Quentin Tarantino
Cinematography by: Robert Richardson
Editing: Sally Menke
Sound: Wylie Stateman
Costumes: Anna Sheppard
Production Design: David Wasco
MPAA rating: R
Running time: 153 minutes

REVIEWS

Corliss, Richard. *Time Magazine.* August 20, 2009.
Denby, David. *New Yorker.* August 17, 2009.
Ebert, Roger. *Chicago Sun-Times.* August 20, 2009.
Edelstein, David. *New York Magazine.* August 17, 2009.
Honeycutt, Kirk. *Hollywood Reporter.* May 20, 2009.
Jones, J.R. *Chicago Reader.* August 20, 2009.
McCarthy, Todd. *Variety.* May 20, 2009.
Pais, Matt. *Metromix.xom.* August 20, 2009.
Phillips, Michael. *Chicago Tribune.* August 21, 2009.
Tallerico, Brian. *MovieRetriever.com.* August 21, 2009.

QUOTES

Lt. Aldo Raine: "That's what I like to hear. But I got a word of warning for all you would-be warriors. When you join my command, you take on debit. A debit you owe me personally. Each and every man under my command owes me one hundred Nazi scalps. And I want my scalps. And all y'all will git me one hundred Nazi scalps, taken from the heads of one hundred dead Nazis. Or you will die tryin'."

TRIVIA

Despite this being Brad Pitt and Quentin Tarantino's first time working together, Brad had co-starred in *True Romance* (which was written by Tarantino).

AWARDS

Oscars 2009: Support. Actor (Waltz)
British Acad. 2009: Support. Actor (Waltz)
Golden Globes 2010: Support. Actor (Waltz)

Screen Actors Guild 2009: Support. Actor (Waltz), Cast
Nomination:
Oscars 2009: Cinematog., Director (Tarantino), Film, Film Editing, Orig. Screenplay, Sound, Sound FX Editing
British Acad. 2009: Cinematog., Director (Tarantino), Film Editing, Orig. Screenplay, Prod. Des.
Directors Guild 2009: Director (Tarantino)
Golden Globes 2010: Director (Tarantino), Film—Drama, Screenplay
Screen Actors Guild 2009: Support. Actress (Kruger).

INKHEART

Every story ever written is just waiting to become real.
—Movie tagline

Box Office: $17 million

Ever since the Harry Potter series proved to be as immensely popular on the big screen as it was on the page, movie producers have been snapping up every piece of vaguely well-known children's fantasy literature featuring similar ingredients (little kids, magical creatures, additional stories that can form the basis of sequels) that they can get their hands on in the hopes of inspiring their own money-spinning franchises by filling in the sometimes agonizing gaps between Potter films. A couple of these attempts have resulted in pretty good films (one of the best being the surprisingly effective *The Spiderwick Chronicles* (2008)) but for the most part, these films have spent more time trying to follow in the footsteps of the Potter films than in trying to inspire or entertain viewers on their own terms and the results have include such deadly dull and largely forgettable behemoths as *The Seeker* (2007), *The Golden Compass* (2007) and *City of Ember* (2008). The latest entry into the fray is *Inkheart*, based on the book by author Cornelia Funke, and while it contains many of the elements that will seem familiar to Potter fans, such as elaborate special effects sequences, well-scrubbed kids and appearances by several of England's top ranked actors in supporting roles, it lacks the very things that have made the Potter stories so popular—a compelling narrative and interesting characters.

The film stars Brendan Fraser as Mo Folchart, a seemingly ordinary antique bookbinder who, it is soon revealed, is a "silvertongue"—a person with the ability to bring characters and items from books into our world (and vice-versa) simply by reading from them out loud. Under normal circumstances, most people with this ability would lock themselves away with copies of *The Story of O, Fear and Loathing in Las Vegas* and Klaus Kinski's autobiography, but when Mo discovers that he has this talent, he has the bad luck to do so while reading to his wife (Sienna Guillory) and young daughter Maggie (Eliza Bennett) from what appears to be the dullest fantasy novel ever written. By doing this, he inadvertently sets free Capricorn (Andy Serkis), the book's villain, a few of his henchmen and a fire juggler by the name of Dustfinger (Paul Bettany) while plunging his wife into the book. Horrified by what he has done, Mo tells his daughter and kooky great aunt Elinor (Helen Mirren) that Mom has just taken off while beginning a search for another copy of the book in the hopes that he can use it to bring back his wife. Nine years later, he and Maggie finally come across one, but it turns out to be a trap laid by Capricorn to lure Mo into becoming his personal reader and bringing over a demonic creature from the book that will allow him to either conquer or destroy the world. Mo, Maggie and Dustfinger, who wants to be returned to the book and will ally with whomever seems more likely to achieve that goal, escape Capricorn's clutches and go in search of the book's author (Jim Broadbent) in the hopes that he might have a copy they can use in order to save the day, defeat Capricorn and rescue Mom, who, as it turns out, has been a captive of Capricorn's in our world for quite a long time now.

There are a lot of problems with *Inkheart*—the characters are not very interesting, the special effects are loud and expensive without ever being especially memorable, and the story has so many gaping plot holes that even the youngest viewers may turn to their parents and ask "Why did it take the guy nine years to think of contacting the author and asking if he had a copy of the book?" However, the biggest problem with the film goes back to the heart of why the Harry Potter books and films have worked so beautifully and why this one does not. Yes, both deal with kids and magic and whatnot, but the difference is that while the Potter tales offer up fully developed stories and characters, *Inkheart* gives us a premise—not the most original premise in the world, but a premise nevertheless—and then does absolutely nothing to develop it at all. For example, when a character gets zapped out of the book and into our world, what happens to them in the rest of the book—when Toto from *The Wizard of Oz* pops up in our world, are third-graders the world over confused and traumatized by his sudden and inexplicable disappearance? There are lots of similar lapses of logic on display and while a smarter or more ambitious film would have either dealt with them or at least had some fun with them, *Inkheart* just ignores them completely, presumably under the impression that audiences would be so blown away by the noisy effects-heavy finale and the blatant sequel setup (one that appears to be unlikely given the

film's woeful box-office performance) that they would fail to notice.

The only thing about *Inkheart* that comes close to providing something resembling fun is the performance by Helen Mirren as the wacky great-aunt. Granted, this is not the sort of performance that will loom heavily in any potential lifetime achievement tribute reels—you get the sense that she took the role mostly because she appears to be the only major British actor not to be asked to appear in a Harry Potter movie—but her cheerfully goofball turn does breathe some life into the otherwise turgid proceedings. That said, my guess is that as things progressed and it became evident that this was not going to be the next big film franchise, she spent most of her downtime in her dressing room praying fervently for a silvertongue to read her the hell out of that script and into a better one.

Peter Sobczynski

CREDITS

Mo Folchart: Brendan Fraser
Meggie Folchart: Eliza Bennett
Dustfinger: Paul Bettany
Capricorn: Andy Serkis
Elinor Loredan: Helen Mirren
Theresa: Sienna Guillory
Farid: Rafi Gavron
Fenoglio: Jim Broadbent
Origin: USA
Language: English
Released: 2009
Production: Iain Softley, Diana Pokorny, Cornelia Funke; New Line Cinema; released by Warner Bros.
Directed by: Iain Softley
Written by: David Lindsay-Abaire
Cinematography by: Roger Pratt
Music by: Javier Navarrete
Sound: David Stephenson
Music Supervisor: Sara Lord
Editing: Martin Walsh
Art Direction: Rod McLean, Stuart Rose
Costumes: Verity Hawkes
Production Design: John Beard
MPAA rating: PG
Running time: 105 minutes

REVIEWS

Chang, Justin. *Variety.* December 11, 2008.
Ebert, Roger. *Chicago Sun-Times.* January 22, 2009.
Honeycutt, Kirk. *Hollywood Reporter.* December 22, 2008.
Lemire, Christy. *Associated Press.* January 21, 2009.

Linden, Sheri. *Los Angeles Times.* January 22, 2009.

Morgenstern, Joe. *Wall Street Journal.* January 22, 2009.

Pais, Matt. *Metromix.com.* January 22, 2009.

Phillips, Michael. *Chicago Tribune.* January 23, 2009.

Puig, Claudia. *USA Today.* January 22, 2009.

Scott, A.O. *New York Times.* January 23, 2009.

QUOTES

Mo "Silvertongue" Folchart: "Hey, don't take this the wrong way, but don't come back, ok?"

TRIVIA

Brendan Fraser was Cornelia Funke's personal choice for the role of Silvertongue, as he was her inspiration for the character. She even dedicated the second novel of the trilogy to him and sent him a signed copy. The producers originally wanted a bigger Hollywood star but on the insistence of Funke they gave in and accepted him in the role.

THE INTERNATIONAL

They control your money. They control your government. They control your life. And everybody pays.
—Movie tagline

Box Office: $25.5 million

The timing of the release of *The International* was certainly fortuitous. Released during the global recession of early 2009, this movie with a sinister bank as the enemy had the kind of villains audiences love to hate, and a hero everyone could root for, an Interpol agent (Clive Owen) dedicated to bringing the malevolent bankers to justice. The fictionalized bank launders money for arms traffickers, destabilizes governments for profit, and is on a ruthless quest for world domination. There is nothing subtle about this foe, but then there is little subtlety at all in *The International.* The film opens with Owen's Louis Salinger witnessing the assassination of one of his colleagues in broad daylight by inexplicable means. The mayhem and violence continue to spread on a worldwide stage.

Salinger is partnered with a Manhattan district attorney, Eleanor Whitman (Naomi Watts), who has a history of working with Salinger. It is no surprise that Salinger has a checkered past; he fits a favorite Hollywood profile of the compromised agent operating barely within the law—used by the authorities when it is convenient, discarded if he blows his cover. Salinger is a very loose cannon, and Owen plays him with a kind of barely controlled madness. He's used to risking his

life and dedicated to saving the world from obvious evil, but whether it's for reasons of pride or a loyalty to justice is hard to say. He is something of a cipher, his background murky, an impatient man of action.

If this description sounds familiar, something that would fit dozens of modern action-thriller movie heroes, it's because *The International* often seems like a film we have seen before. Director Tom Tykwer splashes his film's violent encounters across several exotic locations peopled with slick and nasty bad guys. It has familiar plot twists in which some bad guys prove to be good and some good guys prove bad. Its pace is hyperactive, its musical score overdrawn, and its action hyperkinetic.

The talented Watts plays off Owen in familiarly written scenes of verbal jousting filled with clever repartee. The two characters have an uneasy history with a dollop of sexual tension that is never realized. She is married and has children, he is a disconnected soul too tough for personal compassion, but they have an obvious affection for each other, based on a mutual admiration. Yet that is never allowed to blossom.

Unfortunately, screenwriter Eric Singer and German director Tykwer do not know quite what to do with Watts' character. Movie trailers had a scene with her children in peril, but in the final cut that has been excised, and Eleanor is simply dismissed from the movie when the going gets really dangerous, at Louis's request. Watts, a talented actress, is not given a strong role, but one in which she recedes into the background.

All the twists and turns are clever enough at the moment, but the film leaves you feeling increasingly empty. In the end, the villains become caricatures and the movie itself becomes nearly a parody of its overstuffed genre.

There is one memorable scene though: a shootout in New York's Guggenheim Museum of Art. It is an extended sequence in which Salinger and a bad-guy-turned-good-guy are pinned down by ruthless shooters, and it features screaming and distraught patrons, a hall-of-mirrors-type game of hide-and-seek among the exhibits, plenty of shattered glass, and a spectacular falling chandelier. The shootout goes beyond the usual movie time allotted to such mayhem, is both outrageous and realistic-looking, and is a much better extended action scene than the customary car chases (though there is one of those too). It's a big, loud, chaotic, and very satisfying set piece in an otherwise merely adequate film.

Owen's Salinger gets banged up, betrayed, and abandoned so many times that by the movie's end it's no big surprise that he takes the law into his own hands. We are supposed to cheer him on, but the motif of the vigilante bringing justice to the world secretly and off the record has become such an overused and tired cliché that *The International* fails to distinguish itself in tone, plot, or execution. It is one cliché after another, one violent confrontation after another, one over-the-top villain after another. It all adds up to a tiresome mess.

Still, Owen and Watts make a marvelous couple, and it's too bad the script doesn't give them more with which to work. The supporting cast is merely a bunch of cartoonish characters, which doesn't help either. When Watts' character is written out of the movie, we're left with a standard macho thriller of one man against a worldwide conspiracy so ruthless that it stretches credibility beyond the breaking point.

Michael Betzold

CREDITS

Louis Salinger: Clive Owen
Eleanor Whitman: Naomi Watts
Wilhelm Wexler: Armin Mueller-Stahl
The Consultant: Brian F. O'Byrne
Jonas Skarssen: Ulrich Thomsen
Det. Bernie Ward: Jack McGee
Arnie Goodwin: James Rebhorn
Origin: USA, Germany, Great Britain
Language: English
Released: 2009
Production: Charles Roven, Richard Suckle, Lloyd Phillips; Relativity Media, Atlas Entertainment, Rose Line Prods., Siebente Babelsberg Film; released by Columbia Pictures
Directed by: Tom Tykwer
Written by: Eric Singer
Cinematography by: Frank Griebe
Music by: Tom Tykwer, Reinhold Heil, Johnny Klimek
Sound: Ed Cantu
Editing: Mathilde Bonnefoy
Art Direction: Kai Koch
Costumes: Ngila Dickson
Production Design: Uli Hanisch
MPAA rating: R
Running time: 118 minutes

REVIEWS

Denby, David. *New Yorker.* February 23, 2009.
Ebert, Roger. *Chicago Sun-Times.* February 12, 2009.
Edelstein, David. *New York Magazine.* February 17, 2009.
Foundas, Scott. *LA Weekly.* February 12, 2009.
McCarthy, Todd. *Variety.* February 6, 2009.
Phillips, Michael. *Chicago Tribune.* February 13, 2009.
Puig, Claudia. *USA Today.* February 12, 2009.
Scott, A.O. *New York Times.* February 13, 2009.
Tallerico, Brian. *HollywoodChicago.com.* February 12, 2009.
Turan, Kenneth. *Los Angeles Times.* February 12, 2009.

QUOTES

Wilhelm Wexler: "Character is easier kept than recovered."

TRIVIA

Inspired by the BCCI (Bank of Credit and Commerce International) banking scandal, which took place in the 1980s and early 1990s.

THE INVENTION OF LYING
(This Side of the Truth)

In a world where everyone can only tell the truth...he's just invented the lie!
—Movie tagline

Box Office: $18.4 million

The world of movie comedies is so often dominated by such a tried-and-true menagerie of clichéd and boilerplate premises—ranging from the all-too-familiar tropes of the romantic comedy, the gross-out comedy, etc.—that, when a film comes along as self-consciously high concept as Ricky Gervais and Matthew Robinson's *The Invention of Lying*, it is hard to not automatically give the film, at least, some benefit of the doubt. Here, at last, is a comedy that actually seems like it is trying to do something different, something atypical, and the sheer ambition behind the premise of *Invention of Lying* makes one willing to forgive a lot of sins. (The on- and off-screen presence of Ricky Gervais, who has so dominated British comedy over the past five years with *The Office, Extras*, his stand-up comedy, and his series of podcasts, also lends a hand.) Unfortunately, the film ultimately needs that handicap to stay afloat, and one's final opinion of *The Invention of Lying* will depend largely on how predisposed they are to allow Gervais and his humorous premise to overshadow other aspects like pacing, editing, production design, and overall narrative flow.

The Invention of Lying is a comedy of ideas, albeit half-formed ideas, which seems tailor-made to fit Gervais' sensibilities. The concept is golden—in an alternate world, humans never developed the ability to lie and thus their lives are filled with brutal honestly and are devoid of such intangibles as fiction and religion. (One complaint some had with the film is that Gervais' characters not only fail to lie, but also seem completely incapable of internal monologue, spouting out any rude comment or odd aside without any sense of self-control.)

Gervais plays Mark Bellison, an unsuccessful screenwriter for the lecture-film industry. The closest analog to entertainment in the lie-free world, the lecture-films essentially consist of a single narrator sitting in front of a camera, reading out loud the dry facts of historical events from a binder. The appeal of these films depend totally on the events they are based on, since the screenwriters are physically unable to embellish details, and so Bellison finds himself struggling to write an audience-friendly screenplay about his assigned time period, the fourteenth century, home of the Black Death. As such, Bellison is constantly on the verge of being fired by his boss (Jeffrey Tambor), is reminded daily of how much his secretary (Tina Fey) despises him, and is forced to live in the shadow of his callow colleague, Brad Kessler (Rob Lowe), the world's most successful screenwriter. Things do not get better for Bellison when he is set up on a blind date with the beautiful Anna McDoogles (Jennifer Garner), seemingly the woman of his dreams, who openly tells Bellison that the two of them make a bad genetic match.

After losing his job, getting evicted, and overall hitting rock bottom, Bellison has an epiphany while closing out his bank account. Even though he only has $300 in his bank account, he tells the bank teller that he, in fact, has $800 in the account—in his own words, he tells her something that "wasn't." The bank teller happily hands over the $800, having no experience with verbal deception, and, thus, the first lie ever is born.

The resulting scenes are strongly reminiscent of Jim Carrey's *Bruce Almighty* as Gervais' Bellison quickly tests his newfound ability to lie, convincing attractive women to sleep with him (he's too nice to go through with it), getting his best friend Greg (Louis C.K.) out of a drunk driving arrest (he simply tells the police officer that Greg is not drunk), and using his new skills at embellishment to rapidly replace Brad Kessler as the world's most sought-after screenwriter (which is relatively easy now that he can claim that robots and aliens existed in the fourteenth century). He also talks Anna into a follow-up date, where he is stymied to discovered that, although Anna believes everything he tells her and does seem to enjoy being with him, she still admits that she is not particularly attracted to Bellison and is worried that, if they had children, they might be overweight and unattractive.

The movie takes a thematic turn when their date is suddenly interrupted—Bellison learns that his mother Martha (Fionnula Flanagan) is dying at a hospital and he rushes to her side. Bellison's mother is terrified at the thought of the finality of death, so, to comfort her, Bellison begins to spin an elaborate lie about an afterlife filled with riches, love, and mansions for everyone. His mother is instantly calmed, believing her son totally, and

everyone within earshot—doctors, nurses, and patients—begs Bellison for more details about what happens after death. Bellison rushes back to his apartment and finds himself cast as a prophet figure for the whole world, with thousands of curious spectators camped outside of his apartment to learn more of his privileged knowledge of the workings of the universe. Bellison eventually invents the concept of a "man in the sky" who controls the universe to his new followers, which only leaves the beleaguered Bellison on the hook to explain such vagaries of the universe as "why do bad things happen to good people."

This turn in the narrative is both one of the most intriguing and most problematic aspects of *The Invention of Lying*. It turns the film into a hybrid of the aforementioned *Bruce Almighty*—another high-concept romantic comedy about a man turned loose with near-omniscient powers—and Monty Python's *Life of Brian*, a satire that lampoons the single-mindedness of religious fundamentalism, and the two styles do not particularly mesh well. As soon as Gervais grows a Jesus-esque beard and writes his own Ten Commandments on pizza boxes, one can not deny that he's attempting to take aim at certain religious taboos, and yet the film keeps coming back to the fairly staid romantic comedy subplot of "will Jennifer Garner and Ricky Gervais ever get together?" The boiler-plate romance sections completely undercut the bite of Gervais' more satirical moments, and the satire sticks out like a sore thumb, reading more like off-topic asides rather than crucial parts of the narrative, as the romance heats up.

This all points to the one major weakness of *The Invention of Lying*—Gervais is a significantly better writer and performer than he is a film director. Yes, the film is full of tangents and cross-purposes, but the disparate elements of Gervais and Matthew Robinson's script are so inherently strong that they could have worked in the hands of a more skilled director, a craftsman who could've brought together the narrative strands and given the plot the real sense of drive and urgency that it needed. Robinson and Gervais, as directors, display a few sparks of ingenuity, but they are unquestionably amateurs and, as such, delivered a shaggy-dog of a final product that is simply too ponderous and vague to make much of an impact. (Technically, the duo is not particularly talented either. Few major releases in recent memory have had such cheap-looking production design.)

In the end, *The Invention of Lying* is a fantastic idea with a strong cast that was simply brought to the big screen by the wrong production team. If anyone ever debates the importance of the director in the filmmaking process, this film will stand as an excellent example of how one person can stand as the lynchpin figure between a movie being a great on paper and being great on the big screen.

Tom Burns

CREDITS

Mark Bellison: Ricky Gervais
Anna McDoogles: Jennifer Garner
Martha Bellison: Fionnula Flanagan
Brad Kessler: Rob Lowe
Frank: Jonah Hill
Shelley: Tina Fey
Nathan Goldfrappe: Christopher Guest
Doctor: Jason Bateman
Anthony: Jeffrey Tambor
Greg: Louis CK
Blonde: Stephanie March
Bartender: Philip Seymour Hoffman
News Reporter: Nathan Corddry
Son: Conner Rayburn
Cop: Edward Norton
Narrator: Patrick Stewart
Origin: USA
Language: English
Released: 2009
Production: Ricky Gervais, Dan Lin, Lynda Obst, Oly Obst; Focus Features International, Radar Pictures, Media Rights Capital, Lynda Obst Productions, Lin Pictures; released by Warner Bros.
Directed by: Ricky Gervais, Matt Robinson
Written by: Ricky Gervais, Matt Robinson
Cinematography by: Tim Suhrstedt
Music by: Tim Atack
Editing: Chris Gill
Art Direction: Priscilla Elliott
Sound: Glenn Freemantle
Costumes: Suzie DeSanto
Production Design: Alec Hammond
MPAA rating: PG-13
Running time: 99 minutes

REVIEWS

Chang, Justin. *Variety.* September 30, 2009.
Childress, Erik. *eFilmCritic.com.* September 22, 2009.
Dargis, Manohla. *New York Times.* October 2, 2009.
Ebert, Roger. *Chicago Sun-Times.* October 1, 2009.
Edelstein, David. *New York Magazine.* September 21, 2009.
Phipps, Keith. *AV Club.* October 1, 2009.
Pinkerton, Nick. *Village Voice.* September 29, 2009.
Puig, Claudia. *USA Today.* October 2, 2009.
Rechtshaffen, Michael. *Hollywood Reporter.* September 30, 2009.
Tallerico, Brian. *MovieRetriever.com.* October 2, 2009.

QUOTES

Anna's Mother: "Just because he's talking to the man in the sky doesn't mean he's good enough to be your friend."

TRIVIA

When Philip Seymour Hoffman's agent claimed he was too busy to film a cameo for the film, Ricky Gervais requested Hoffman's email address and sent him the following: "Dear Philip, will you please appear in my new film? There is very little money involved as I spent the budget on testicular implants, but don't look upon them as my testicles, look at them as our testicles."

INVICTUS

His people needed a leader. He gave them a champion.
—Movie tagline

Box Office: $37 million

Invictus tells an inherently inspiring story. When Nelson Mandela was elected president of South Africa in 1990 after twenty-seven years of imprisonment and forty years of apartheid, a desire for retribution against the nation's white minority would have been understandable. Instead, Mandela chose to attempt to unify his racially divided country and the vehicle he selected to both symbolize and effectuate that unity was the Springboks, South Africa's national rugby team, popular with white South Africans and despised by black South Africans. Just as Mandela has beat incredible odds to become president of South Africa, can the underdog Springboks overcome incredible odds to win the World Cup and unify their countrymen? Director Eastwood and screenwriter Anthony Peckham provide a competent rending of these historical events, but only that. To the limited extent the film is moving and inspirational, it is the product of the historical events being depicted, not something generated by the film's simplistic and inadequate script.

In Mandela (Morgan Freeman) and the Springboks' captain Francois Pienaar (Matt Damon), *Invictus* tries to tell two parallel stories of leadership: one of a leader trying to inspire his nation to overcome its racist past and unify as a country, and one of a leader of a sports team trying to bring that unity about by inspiring his team to win games. The film tells the first story well enough, recounting the political maneuverings on Mandela's part to preserve and promote the Springboks in the face of understandable opposition on the part of the black majority that elected him to the presidency. The hated gold and green Springbok jerseys symbolize for many black Africans the oppression of apartheid (a clumsy scene in which a white missionary woman tries to give a donated jersey to an impoverished black child who refuses to accept it clubs this home to the viewer) and the film amusingly reveals that black South Africans have historically rooted for the Springboks opponents, whoever those opponents happened to be. Although Mandela confesses that in the past he too rooted against the Springboks, when the new government votes to eliminate the jerseys emblematic of the apartheid regime he movingly addresses the government members, persuading them with his eloquence to retain the jerseys in the interest of the unity of the country.

The second story is hardly told at all. Mandela invites Pienaar to tea and shares with him the poem, "Invictus," that helped him get through his long confinement and, he hopes, can help inspire Francois and his team to win games. Francois takes the poem to heart and the Springboks start training for the World Cup for which they have only been granted admission due to their status as a host nation, not their skill (a point pointed out by a mustachio twirling sportscaster with a personal vendetta against the team). Once they enter the tournament they, of course, against all odds, start winning and start unifying their black and white countrymen who line up together to cheer for them. However, how Pienaar's leadership inspires his woefully outmatched team is not made clear by the patchy script. After Francois meets with Mandela and the importance of the rugby game to the nation is communicated to him, he is inspired to win games but it is never made clear how that inspiration translates into his team winning games against tremendously long odds. It's not clear what the team did differently, other than really wanting to achieve those wins.

If the team's victories materialize out of thin air, so too does the unity created by those victories. The unity Mandela and the team bring about is too simplistic to be convincing and comes across as a Walt Disney version of racial division. At its outset, the film establishes a very obvious, simplistic metaphor for the nation in Mandela's merging of his pre-election all-black security team with De Klerk's all-white security team. Mandela has purposefully retained De Klerk's detail for this purpose to symbolize the unity he wants for the country as a whole. As might be expected, there is a lot of distrust on the part of both security teams. By the end of the film, however, the white and black security teams are playing rugby with one another! If the importance of rugby in unifying the nation still is not apparent to the viewer, Mandela, viewing the security teams playing together, clears it up by turning to a subordinate and

saying, "still think I'm wasting my time with this rugby stuff?" The unsubtle script fails to treat its subject with the complexity it requires and deserves and delivers racial unity out of thin air via eye-rolling clichés. Following an important goal by the Springboks at the climactic game, a black and white security team duo almost hug each other in excited celebration and then have a sitcom worthy moment where they stop and stare at each other in shocked surprise. Prior to the big game Francois asks his team to sing the new national anthem. His team refuses, calling the song a terrorist anthem and crumpling the lyrics into balls and throwing them away. Of course, at the big game they rise to the occasion and sing the anthem. Francois's mother, who has brought the family's black maid to the final match, experiences a meaningful moment as she stares at her black maid beside her enjoying the game and appreciates how she has been a racist.

The real-life events chronicled in *Invictus* are inherently stirring and certainly have the potential to provide the racial unity the film alleges it does. Mandela really went from political prisoner to the presidency and the Springboks really went from world-class chumps to World Cup champions. When Mandela tells a subordinate doubtful of the Springboks chances that "if we were to rely on the odds, both of us would be sitting in prison cells right now" he is stating a clear, compelling fact. There is no reason to coat everything in the thick layer of cheese Peckham does, and doing so simply detracts from the inspiration inherent in the material.

The single superb element of the film is Morgan Freeman's Nelson Mandela. (Damon does well enough with his bare bones character—with his bulked up frame and bleached blond hair strangely resembling an athletic Phillip Seymour Hoffman—but his part is so woefully underwritten that his character possesses not a single memorable characteristic.) Freeman was born to play Mandela and was Mandela's own choice to play him. Freeman captures Mandela's physical mannerisms, speech pattern and, to the extent the script allows him, his eloquence, generosity and wiliness as a politician. On Mandela's first day in office, he gathers De Klerk's staff, most of who assume they will be fired, and in a stirring speech invites them to remain in his administration. In this scene, as in the earlier scene persuading his countrymen to retain the Springbok jerseys, Freeman conveys Mandela's Lincolnesque capacity for forgiveness that made him such a great leader. Freeman's Mandela is the embodiment of forgiveness: If he can forgive, anyone can, and for South Africa to move on, this forgiveness must take place. However these moments are few and far between as the film's pedestrian script otherwise fails to supply Mandela with his real world eloquence. The problem is not solely a script that is not up to providing Freeman with Mandela's articulateness but also that confines him, for the most part, to discussing rugby. Reportedly, for years Freeman explored making the film about Mandela that makes him a compelling subject for a film in the first place—his incredible journey from political prisoner to president and the destruction of apartheid—but concluded that the scope of that story was simply too great. This is an unfortunate decision (and a questionable one given the success of rich biographical films from Gandhi *Gandhi* [1982] to Genghis Kahn *Mongol* [2007] that were successful despite the massive scope of their subject's lives). Freeman is so electrifying in a very brief flashback to his days as a prisoner that the viewer cannot help but wish that the film had made that its subject. Mandela is such a fascinating person and has led such an incredible life that it is frankly a waste to confine him to the context of rugby. Imagine having the opportunity to speak with Abraham Lincoln for two-and-a-half hours and having the conversation confined to baseball.

A reasonable question to ask when viewing a fictional film based on historical fact is whether or not the dramatization justifies itself. Does the drama provide a dimension to the subject that a documentary could not have? *Invictus* not only fails to provide any additional illumination but it detracts from the inspiring story inherent to the material with its hammy and inadequate script. The only element that justifies viewing the film is Freeman, and the viewer is left with a magnificent performance in search of film that is telling a story worthy of its magnificence.

Nate Vercauteren

CREDITS

Nelson Mandela: Morgan Freeman
Francois Pienaar: Matt Damon
Willem: Robert Hobbs
George: Langley Kirkwood
Ruben Kruger: Grant Roberts
Origin: USA
Language: English
Released: 2009
Production: Clint Eastwood, Robert Lorenz; Spyglass Entertainment, Revelations Entertainment; released by Warner Bros.
Directed by: Clint Eastwood
Written by: Anthony Peckham
Cinematography by: Tom Stern
Music by: Steve Juliani
Sound: Walt Martin
Music Supervisor: Chris McGeary
Editing: Joel Cox

Art Direction: Tom Hannam
Costumes: Deborah Hopper
Production Design: James Murakami
MPAA rating: PG-13
Running time: 134 minutes

REVIEWS

Ansen, David. *Newsweek.* December 4, 2009.
Childress, Erik. *eFilmCritic.com.* December 11, 2009.
Corliss, Richard. *Time Magazine.* December 7, 2009.
Gleiberman, Owen. *Entertainment Weekly.* December 9, 2009.
McCarthy, Todd. *Variety.* November 29, 2009.
Phillips, Michael. *Chicago Tribune.* December 10, 2009.
Poland, David. *Movie City News.* December 4, 2009.
Reed, Rex. *New York Observer.* December 10, 2009.
Rickey, Carrie. *Philadelphia Inquirer.* December 10, 2009.
Turan, Kenneth. *Los Angeles Times.* December 11, 2009.

QUOTES

Nelson Mandela: "I thank whatever gods may be / For my unconquerable soul. / I am the master of my fate / I am the captain of my soul."

TRIVIA

Nelson Mandela himself has said that only Morgan Freeman could portray him. And so Freeman was the first actor cast.

AWARDS

Nomination:

Oscars 2009: Actor (Freeman), Support. Actor (Damon)
Golden Globes 2010: Actor—Drama (Freeman), Director (Eastwood), Support. Actor (Damon)
Screen Actors Guild 2009: Actor (Freeman), Support. Actor (Damon).

IS ANYBODY THERE?

Box Office: $2 million

Shortly into the film *Is Anybody There?*, the mother of a boy growing up in a senior citizens home she runs tells him that he is fortunate to be living among all these fascinating old people with their amazing life stories. That might be true if this movie actually had any old people with great stories, but it does not. Instead, the home, in seaside England in the 1980s, has what is supposed to be an endearingly quirky collection of doddering imbeciles, senile loonies, and childishly gullible sweet old ladies. There is not a good story to be had among them—not even in the tale of Clarence

(Michael Caine), a retired magician who fills the familiar slot of the crotchety, misogynistic crank. The audience learns surprisingly little about him, considering his central role in the film.

In short, this is another collection of movie old people, laughably inept and inarticulate, stereotypically senile down to the last character, none of them in any way believable or intriguing. Writer Peter Harness and director John Crowley seem disinterested in using them as anything but props for this story of Edward (Bill Milner), a boy obsessed with death who has grown up in the middle of death. Expectedly, the old folks die off, one by one, in variously pedestrian ways. Edward, with nothing better to do, makes video recordings of their deaths, hoping to find out something about ghosts. He is fascinated with tales he has read and seen of ghost hunters, but even this central element of the plot fails to ever make much sense. Most ghost hunters look for spirits long after death, not at the moments that they leave the body.

The movie seems to start in midstream. It is a clanging, cluttered mess of disconnected images without much narrative identification of the characters. Harness and Crowley could not think of, or could not be bothered with, an explanation of how Edward came to live in this place, or even why his father (David Morrissey) is at odds with his mother (Anne-Marie Duff), and certainly not why his dad seems to be catching early-stage Alzheimer's in his thirties (maybe it is contagious?). Crowley grasps the way that some movies can be presented as grotesque juxtapositions of weird images, but his images are not that interesting to stand on their own, and a little narrative underpinning would not have hurt.

Instead, the audience is treated to Clarence's poorly explained arrival. He is a physical mess of a man, not at all approachable, and Caine gives him a brave go as a sort of aged antihero, some sort of rebel with some sort of undefined cause, but it is never clear what. Similarly, we see that Edward is interested in mortality, which makes sense the way he has grown up, but it is never clear why. He does not seem scared of dying, and his actions seem emotionally disconnected to his isolation as a child in an old folk's home and to his feelings about his parents.

The film is a jumble, a frenzied mess that settles into a slogging, ill-defined story about the growing friendship between Clarence and Edward, which also seems under-explained. Clarence does not have any reason to turn into a sweet, soft-hearted fool who falls for the affections of a boy, but of course he does, just because Edward persists in using him as something of a prop for his experiments in pseudoscientific inquiry.

Critics had praise for Caine's performance, but then veteran actors who play cranks at an advanced age always seem to get kudos. Caine gives Clarence a pleasingly unusual off-putting personality for awhile, but soon he too seems to succumb to the tendency of the film to treat old people as goofy curiosities rather than real individuals. Milner does nicely as the morbid young boy, keeping a keen balance between precocious and too cute. The British accents are thick enough, and the dialogue so mumbled and chancy, that subtitles might have helped. But *Is Anybody There?* does not seem to have anything much new to say about growing up, growing old, or dying, as it fails to answer the question posed by its title. The short answer is yes, probably, there is somebody there, somewhere, but the drama never makes it as black comedy (it is too dull) and falls flat as an existential examination. It is a fairly pedestrian movie that expects us to delight in it simply because it has a young kid coupled with a grumpy old man.

Michael Betzold

CREDITS

Clarence Parkinson: Michael Caine
Edward: Bill Milner
Mum: Anne-Marie Duff
Dad: David Morrissey
Elsie: Rosemary Harris
Bob: Peter Vaughan
Prudence: Elizabeth Spriggs
Origin: Great Britain
Released: 2008
Production: David Heyman, Peter Saraf, Marc Turtletaub; BBC Films, Big Beach Films, Heyday Films; released by Stony Island Entertainment
Directed by: John Crowley
Written by: Peter Harness
Cinematography by: Rob Hardy
Music by: Joby Talbot
Editing: Trevor Waite
Sound: Julian Slater
Costumes: Jane Petrie
Production Design: Kave Quinn
MPAA rating: PG-13
Running time: 94 minutes

REVIEWS

Berkshire, Geoff. *Metromix.com.* April 16, 2009.
Childress, Erik. *EFilmCritic.* April 16, 2009.
Fear, David. *Time Out New York.* April 15, 2009.
Holden, Stephen. *New York Times.* April 17, 2009.
Jones, J.R. *Chicago Reader.* May 15, 2009.

Long, Tom. *Detroit News*. May 8, 2009.

Robinson, Tasha. *AV Club*. April 16, 2009.

Sharkey, Betsy. *Los Angeles Times*. April 17, 2009.

Thompson, Gary. *Philadelphia Daily News*. May 1, 2009.

Travers, Peter. *Rolling Stone*. April 16, 2009.

QUOTES

Clarence: "Huh. He's gonna be pissed off when he wakes up."

TRIVIA

The last film of Elizabeth Spriggs. She died during post production.

IT MIGHT GET LOUD

Box Office: $1.6 million

Forget the popular videogame series; it is a real-life version of *Guitar Hero* when Jimmy Page, The Edge, and Jack White get together for the music documentary *It Might Get Loud*, an exploration of the electric guitar that spans roughly three different musical generations, and encompasses several different modes of expression. Director Davis Guggenheim's non-fiction follow-up to the Oscar®-winning *An Inconvenient Truth* (2006), *It Might Get Loud* works as a sort of three-for-one biography, with just a handful of glancing, macro-analytical musical insights scattered and tossed in for good measure.

Starting with his subjects' formative years, Guggenheim structures his movie in discrete narrative strands. He does not waste time with critics or other talking heads trying to frame or debate the importance of his subjects' bands, or their respective places in music history. In fact, even band mates, managers or other intimates are not granted any screen time; the only interviewees are the three men themselves, which helps give *It Might Get Loud* a sense of well-groomed intimacy.

Jimmy Page, of both Led Zeppelin and the Yardbirds, has probably the deepest reservoir of stories, and therefore the most fascinating back story, having started out as a for-hire session guitarist who also laid down licks for commercial jingles. For all the ribbing that U2's perpetually-skullcapped The Edge takes for his seemingly manufactured zen-guitarist persona, it is Jack White—of The White Stripes, The Raconteurs, The Dead Weather and whatever new side project he is putting together this week—who is clearly the most interested and invested in artificial persona. He taps a miniaturized version of himself for his biographical segment, and stages scenes where he teaches this younger

"mini-Jack" how to play the blues, and even kick down a piano stool for added effect. He also cops to the art-house conceit of The White Stripes, and the fact that the group's red-and-white costuming was all misdirection and window-dressing, so that they (or he, really, since band mate Meg White comes across as doing little more than what Jack tells her) could play earthy blues and folk music as white musicians without facing a harsh, skeptical vox populi.

Because of these types of quick glimpses behind the curtain that it affords, *It Might Get Loud* is in sum never less than engaging, most notably for fans of these bands. Still, there is a lingering feeling that the conversational roundtable gathering between the three men which forms the film's spine—what Guggenheim called "The Summit" in the movie's press notes, a meandering exploration of a couple of the gentleman's big tunes and adolescent breakthroughs—could perhaps have used a bit more structure or inquisitive prodding, to get at the marrow of exactly why and how sometimes (or even especially) trite musical expressions achieve significant emotional lift-off. Godhead jam session footage is great, and introspective first-person narration placed over footage of subjects gazing out car windows makes for evocative scenes, but neither approach is particularly intellectually deep. More focused conversation and pointed self-questioning between the men would have likely yielded insights that no regular interviewer could have mined.

Guggenheim is not afraid of embracing ambiguity, however. In many ways, that is the lesson of the movie—that there is no one true recipe for creative invention. *It Might Get Loud* quietly serves up contradictions (White talks about technology being "a big destroyer of emotion and truth," even as he mounts a microphone into the carved-out body of a guitar, allowing for greater feedback and distortion) in a fashion that underscores how a lot of music, and indeed maybe art in general, is about learning and knowing the rules, and then consciously breaking or tearing them down. There are some great song stories illustrative of this fact along the way, whether it is Page recounting the drum set-up for "When the Levee Breaks" or The Edge stumbling across an early cassette recording of a work-shopped version of "Where the Streets Have No Name," with Bono calling out time shifts in the background.

What most pokes through, though, is the depth of emotion—the sheer joy and even anger—attached to artistic expression. "There was a thrill in doing, even if we were doing it badly," says the Edge at one point, discussing U2's teenage years. Later, White (resembling a ghostly, slightly pudgy Johnny Depp) talks about the aggressive quality of music, and seemingly channels the spirit of a bullied-too-long sensitive soul who has finally screwed his courage to the sticking place, saying, "It's our chance to push you down now." In its bluntness, this statement is a reminder that music matters so much precisely because it has the capacity to make us feel differently than we perhaps are, and feelings of course so often can and do trump dispassionate rationality.

Brent Simon

CREDITS

Himself: Jimmy Page
Himself: The Edge
Himself: Jack White
Origin: USA
Language: English
Released: 2009
Production: Davis Guggenheim, Peter Afterman, Thomas Tull, Leslie Chilicott; released by Sony Pictures Classics
Directed by: Davis Guggenheim
Cinematography by: Erich Roland, Guillermo Navarro
Sound: Skip Livesay
Music Supervisor: Margaret Yen
Editing: Greg Finton
MPAA rating: PG
Running time: 97 minutes

REVIEWS

Adams, Sam. *AV Club.* August 13, 2009.
Anderson, John. *Variety.* October 18, 2008.
Lowe, Justin. *Hollywood Reporter.* July 2, 2009.
Pais, Matt. *Metromix.com.* August 27, 2009.
Phillips, Michael. *Chicago Tribune.* August 28, 2009.
Puig, Claudia. *USA Today.* August 14, 2009.
Scott, A.O. *New York Times.* August 14, 2009.
Sharkey, Betsy. *Los Angeles Times.* August 14, 2009.
Weitzman, Elizabeth. *New York Daily News.* August 14, 2009.
Wilonsky, Robert. *Village Voice.* August 11, 2009.

QUOTES

The Edge: "Those 20 minutes in that shop defined our sound as a band."

IT'S COMPLICATED

First comes marriage. Then comes divorce. And then...
—Movie tagline

Box Office: $112 million

Perhaps writer-director Nancy Meyers has a deeply ironic sense of humor. Maybe she wants to assist her critics. Or maybe she is just oblivious to her own faults. How else to explain that a filmmaker so uninterested in complexity would title her latest romantic comedy *It's Complicated* only to turn drama into farce and favor superficiality over substance at nearly all times. Even in the context of former spouses considering reconnection, Meyers is not going for complicated. The effect she is after may as well come from a film titled "It's Adorable." A commitment to excruciating cuteness was one of the major faults of Meyers' *The Holiday* (2006), a film considerably more irritating than *It's Complicated*. The latter does not, for example, lean on the gooey sweetness of young children to generate the preferred audience review of "It was cute." The movie also at least rests on the shoulders of actors who add shine to a script that would not do much glowing without them.

The amazingly reliable Meryl Streep plays professional chef Jane, whose divorce ten years earlier happened after Jake (Alec Baldwin) cheated with the much-younger Agness (Lake Bell), whom he later married. (This came after Agness briefly left him and mothered a child with another man.) Jane is uncomfortable around Jake and Agness at an anniversary party; it is clear Jane's wounds have not fully healed. Yet as her daughter Gabby (Zoe Kazan) moves out and her son Luke (Hunter Parrish) graduates college, Jane, for the first time in years, has time to put her focus back on her own happiness. She can finally renovate the house she bought after her divorce and get the kitchen of her dreams. She can date, too, something her friends strongly support. One, played by Alexandra Wentworth, claims to have heard a story about a woman whose vagina closed up from lack of sex. But Jane quickly finds herself in familiar territory.

While in New York for Luke's graduation, Jane and Jake bump into each other at the hotel bar. Soon, wine flows; memories are recalled; feet hit the dance floor. And Jane and Jake lay in bed exhausted from sex that now comes charged with carefree electricity like never before. Jane is no longer the cuckolded wife. She is the other woman. It is a situation that, in theory, should be very complicated.

The movie pretty much takes it nowhere, though. Jake is not at all conflicted about this tryst; he is no longer happy with Agness and is sure that sleeping with Jane is the right thing to do. Jane laments the predicament—"Turns out I'm a bit of a slut," she says to her friends with a laugh—and consults a therapist. Yet she never really confronts the way her actions fall into the overall timeline of her relationship with Jake. Certainly, over time, resentment fades and people forgive. *It's Complicated*, however, minimizes any truly sticky feelings—and, of course, pays no mind to the effect on Agness, who is presented only as an unappealing villain—in order to keep the tone peppy and fun.

This is too bad. Streep and Baldwin have a wonderful rapport, and Steve Martin, as Jane's architect Adam, winningly plays a man who is endearing and good but not in an overly sentimental way. (Though Meyers does go a little far in making him lovable: Adam's ex ran off with his best friend. The wench!) He is a nice guy who is interested in Jane, but the love triangle that results is less a product of an indecisive woman than a main character who makes impulsive decisions and talks about thinking, but rarely thinks before acting.

Not that a complex portrait of divorce would have much of a place in the sort of comedy Meyers creates. Her humor does occasionally come from a line spiked with truth, such as when one of Jane's friends (Rita Wilson) asks, "Do you want to meet a guy on Match.com that I didn't like?" More often the jokes come from Jake falling into the bushes as he peers into Jane's window while she dines with Adam. Or Jane and Adam smoking pot for the first time in twenty-seven years and giggling at Luke's graduation party. For what it is worth, Streep and Martin make this more fun than it should be on paper.

The most revealing lines come when Meyers ditches the wacky stuff and expands her characters' relationships. When the phone rings and Jake tells Jane not to answer, she responds, with the firm sensibility of a caring mother, "I always get it. I have three kids." When Jane, out of concern for Jake's health, stops him from putting salt on his food, he tells her, "You have no idea. Not everyone's like that." Here, thanks to the way Streep and Baldwin handle these exchanges, these two really seem like people whose spark is still alive. Jake has not forgotten what is special about his ex-wife, whom he has known since she was twenty-three.

That specificity frequently disappears behind otherwise conventional proceedings, during which the people in *It's Complicated* feel only like movie characters and not a real family with depth, personality, anger and connection. Luke, Gabby and their older sister Lauren (Caitlin Fitzgerald) do not have a relationship that real siblings have. They are merely perky, perfect children, used only to give Jane and Jake places to go and people to talk about and, eventually, kids to comfort as they all huddle in bed while trying to figure out what is going on between their parents. Meanwhile, Lauren's husband Harley (John Krasinski) is strained comic relief as he labors to keep his knowledge of Jane and Jake's affair from the rest of the family. This allows Krasinski to do nothing but replicate the charming sheepishness of his Jim Halpert on *The Office*.

It's Complicated nevertheless represents the rare opportunity to see a film semi-confront the sex lives and romantic entanglements of people in their late 50s—far from the prime demographic studios usually want to depict and serve. That provides a chance for Jane to feel insecure about her body—she does not want Jake to see her naked while standing up, since he has not seen her since her 40s. She even, at the beginning of the film, considers cosmetic surgery to elevate a saggy eyelid. These scenes are simple but deal with a time in life when physical beauty is frequently fading, a process that is far from favorable for people still looking for a fulfilling romantic life with a new partner.

Throughout the superficial film, the characters' age brings juvenile situations instead of adult laughs. Meyers spends much of the movie suggesting that Jane and Jake may be ready to get back together but cannot, in the end, figure out how they should feel about the prospect of actually doing it. The film backs away from the details and focuses on generalities to the point that it is not clear that Jane and Jake have really considered their situation at all. Clearly *It's Complicated* is only meant to be light and breezy and, yes, it qualifies as watchable holiday fluff. But a premise does not get off the ground when the writer does not seem interested in letting her characters work through that premise in an interesting way. Consequently the main pleasures in *It's Complicated* only derive from watching seasoned actors have fun. That is not a movie, it is a Hollywood cocktail party.

Matt Pais

CREDITS

Jane Alder: Meryl Streep
Jake Alder: Alec Baldwin
Adam: Steve Martin
Harley: John Krasinski
Gabby Adler: Zoe Kazan
Luke Adler: Hunter Parrish
Agness: Lake Bell
Trisha: Rita Wilson
Joanne: Mary Kay Place
Sally: Nora Dunn
Diane: Alexandra Wentworth
Lauren Adler: Caitlin Fitzgerald
Origin: USA
Language: English
Released: 2009
Production: Nancy Meyers, Scott Rudin; Relativity Media, Waverly Films; released by Universal Pictures
Directed by: Nancy Meyers
Written by: Nancy Meyers
Cinematography by: John Toll

Music by: Hans Zimmer, Hector Pereira
Editing: Joe Hutshing
Sound: Xavier Horan
Art Direction: W. Steven Graham
Costumes: Sonia Grande
Production Design: Jon Hutman
MPAA rating: R
Running time: 118 minutes

REVIEWS

Ebert, Roger. *Chicago Sun-Times.* December 24, 2009.
Foundas, Scott. *Village Voice.* December 23, 2009.
McCarthy, Todd. *Variety.* December 10, 2009.
O'Sullivan, Michael. *Washington Post.* December 25, 2009.
Phillips, Michael. *Chicago Tribune.* December 23, 2009.
Pols, Mary F. *Time Magazine.* December 24, 2009.
Scott, A.O. *At the Movies.* December 21, 2009.
Stevens, Dana. *Slate.* December 23, 2009.

Tallerico, Brian. *MovieRetriever.com.* December 25, 2009.
Travers, Peter. *Rolling Stone.* December 22, 2009.

QUOTES

Jake: "And what's with the "big guy"? Is it because I'm fat?"

TRIVIA

Meryl Streep had asked her alma mater, Vassar College, if they could film the college graduation scenes on their campus. They refused even though Streep serves on their Board of Trustees and two of her children are enrolled there.

AWARDS

Nomination:

British Acad. 2009: Support. Actor (Baldwin)
Golden Globes 2010: Actress—Mus./Comedy (Streep), Film—Mus./Comedy, Screenplay.

J–K

JENNIFER'S BODY

She's evil...and not just high school evil.
—Movie tagline

Box Office: $16.2 million

Jennifer's Body is a disastrously dismal horror-comedy that marks screenwriter/cultural icon Diablo Cody's follow-up to the Oscar®-winning triumph of her previous effort, *Juno* (2007). Granted, it would be hard for anyone to replicate the acclaim that she received for that debut but it is difficult to imagine even the most forgiving of her fans being willing to accept this mess, a bag of goods that is so shabby that if it had been written by anyone else in the Writer's Guild, it probably would have landed squarely in the direct-to-video trenches and even there, it would have suffered in comparison to its less-than-stellar competition.

The film stars Megan Fox as Jennifer, a high school sexpot who fills out her tight outfits with equal parts brazen bravado and a desire to escape her small-town existence, and Amanda Seyfried as Needy, a sweet-but-nerdy girl who has been Jennifer's best friend (and occasional doormat) since they were little. The relationship has presumably lasted so long because it provides Jennifer with someone to boss around in order to mask her own insecurities and Needy someone to subliminally crush on despite the presence of her nice-guy boyfriend, Chip (Johnny Simmons). One fateful night, Jennifer drags Needy out to a local roadhouse to see an appearance by a struggling indie rock band led by the slightly sinister Nikolai (Adam Brody), and, after a series of strange events, Jennifer accepts a ride from the band in their van and leaves Needy behind. Later that night at

home, Needy is visited by a blood-soaked Jennifer who proceeds to vomit a bizarre tar-like substance all over the floor before staggering out into the darkness. The next day, however, Jennifer shows up at school, snarkier and more salon-perfect than ever. Of course, no mere foundation garment alone could trigger such a change (which isn't really much of a change when you think about it) and before long, we discover that she has been transformed into a demon who soon begins eviscerating her male classmates one by one. In moves that will surprise no one, Jennifer sets her sights on Chip (mostly because she can), Needy vows to stop her at all costs (mostly because the movie will end thirty minutes earlier if she doesn't), and the whole thing comes to a head at prom (mostly because it makes a little more sense than trying to figure out a way to end things with a courtroom scene).

Successfully blending horror and comedy is an extraordinarily difficult thing for any film to accomplish—too much comedy can destroy the suspense and too much blood and violence can do equal damage to the humor—and only a few have really managed to pull it off with any degree of success. Fans of *Juno* went into *Jennifer's Body* hoping that Cody had figured out a way of achieving the combination using the distinctive voice that she cultivated in that earlier film. Not only has she failed to pull that trick off here, but her screenplay is actually the worst thing about the entire enterprise. As a horror film, it stinks because it is utterly devoid of scares, tension or creative gruesomeness. As a comedy, it is equally bad because the broad jokes aren't very funny, the attempts to satirize mean girl behavior and the conventions of dumb horror movies fall flat because she offers no new or interesting insights, and the arch dialogue, which worked so well in *Juno* because Cody created characters that could be believed actually spoke like that, comes across so badly this time around (instead of calling someone jealous, they are referred to as being "lime-green Jell-O") that they feel like the efforts of someone trying and failing to sound like Diablo Cody. There are a couple of flashes of genuine wit here and there, but for the most part, the screenplay feels like someone channel-hopping between *Heathers* (1989) and *Species* (1995) and transcribing the experience without ever managing to hit upon any of the good parts.

While Cody deserves the hardest hits for the failures of *Jennifer's Body*, there is plenty of blame to spread around. The film was directed by Karyn Kusama, who made a Cody-like splash with her debut film *Girlfight* (2000) and then squandered nearly all the good will that she accumulated by following it up with the disastrous sci-fi fantasy *Aeon Flux* (2005). *Jennifer's Body* is flat and graceless from start to finish, and she demonstrates absolutely no flair for comic timing (all the dialogue-driven scenes feel like rehearsal footage), for building suspense and tension, or even for the simple act of startling viewers by having things suddenly jump out at them. Likewise, the performances are pretty ineffectual, although it says a lot about the lack of quality of the film as a whole when the increasingly intolerable Megan Fox is *not* the worst thing about it. She has the swaggering bitchiness and the surface-level sexuality of her character down pat—unfortunately, whenever she opens her mouth, it becomes painfully clear that she lacks any trace of the kind of comedic timing and sensibility that is usually a requirement for anyone signing on for a comedy. Amanda Seyfried is a little better but her character is such a bore that it is hard to work up much of a rooting interest for her either. As for the others, the only performer who makes any sort of impression is the increasingly invaluable J.K. Simmons as apparently the only member of the high school faculty—he scores actual laughs every time he appears, but that is more because he is one of those people who can sell even the weakest screenplays. *Jennifer's Body* is something that, unfortunately, allows him ample room to demonstrate that particular talent.

Peter Sobczynski

CREDITS

Jennifer Check: Megan Fox
Needy Lesnicky: Amanda Seyfried
Chip Dove: Johnny Simmons
Nikolai Wolf: Adam Brody
Mr. Wroblewski: J.K. Simmons

Toni Lesnicky: Amy Sedaris
Officer Roman Duda: Chris Pratt
Colin Gray: Kyle Gallner
Mrs. Dove: Allison Janney
Origin: USA
Language: English
Released: 2009
Production: Daniel Dubiecki, Mason Novick, Jason Reitman; Dune Entertainment, Hard C, Fox Atomic; released by 20th Century Fox
Directed by: Karyn Kusama
Written by: Diablo Cody
Cinematography by: M. David Mullen
Music by: Theodore Shapiro
Editing: Plummy Tucker
Sound: Jorge Montijo
Costumes: Katia Stano
Production Design: Arvinder Grewal
MPAA rating: R
Running time: 102 minutes

REVIEWS

Chang, Justin. *Variety.* September 10, 2009.
Ebert, Roger. *Chicago Sun-Times.* September 17, 2009.
Fendelman, Adam. *HollywoodChicago.com.* September 17, 2009.
Honeycutt, Kirk. *Hollywood Reporter.* September 10, 2009.
Phillips, Michael. *Chicago Tribune.* September 17, 2009.
Pols, Mary F. *Time Magazine.* September 18, 2009.
Roeper, Richard. *RichardRoeper.com.* September 18, 2009.
Scott, A.O. *New York Times.* September 18, 2009.
Stevens, Dana. *Slate.* September 17, 2009.
Zacharek, Stephanie. *Salon.com.* September 18, 2009.

QUOTES

Needy Lesnicky: "I will finish you if I have to."

TRIVIA

Diablo Cody wrote the screenplay for the film in 2006, the same year she wrote *Juno*.

AWARDS

Nomination:

Golden Raspberries 2009: Worst Actress (Fox).

JONAS BROTHERS: THE 3D CONCERT EXPERIENCE

Box Office: $19 million

Even by the loosest artistic standards imaginable, it is hard for anyone to consider *Jonas Brothers: The 3D Concert Experience* an actual movie. Pure and simple, it is a product—one that was no doubt launched into existence approximately ten seconds after Walt Disney Studios received word of the record-breaking opening weekend grosses of the similar *Hannah Montana/Miley Cyrus: Best of Both Worlds Concert Tour* (2008). From the standpoint of a critic, this makes for an intriguing conundrum—how does one go about discussing the artistic qualities of a film seemingly designed to collect allowance money from pre-teen girls eager to see their latest pop-culture obsession up on the screen?

The Jonas Brothers—Kevin, Joe and Nick—are a fraternal trio that has managed to parlay their non-threatening good looks and passable musical skills into becoming this generation's equivalent of Ricky Nelson, Shaun Cassidy and/or Hanson. For most of the film, we see them on stage grinding out their hits—a group of largely forgettable tunes that rank somewhere between Rick Astley and the Banana Splits on the grand scale of bubblegum pop—before a crowd of relentless screeching fans. Between the songs (which also include guest appearances from Disney stablemate Demi Lovato, with whom they appeared on the hit Disney Channel TV movie *Camp Rock* [2008] and country starlet Taylor Swift, whom one of them was dating at the time of the filming), we are treated to numerous behind-the-scenes glimpses of their lives as superstars—many of which are clearly designed to evoke *A Hard Day's Night* (1964), perhaps as a nod to older viewers in the audience chaperoning younger charges. It hardly seems worth saying but as the Jonas Brothers are to the Beatles, so this film is to *A Hard Day's Night*.

In the old days, most self-respecting teen idols at least had the temerity to come up with a catchy tune or two; the songs on display here are so formulaic that they all pretty much blend into one another—you can tell that they are doing "edgier" material only when the guitars are mixed a little louder than usual. As for the guys themselves, they seem nice enough in the background segments, but they are so bereft of individual personalities that when a trio of fake Jonas Brothers makes an appearance, they seem far more lively and interesting than the real ones. This extends to their on-stage performances as well. They jump around the stage and cannily play to the crowd, but the moves are so ritualized and devoid of genuine passion that the whole things seems about as rocking and spontaneous as a Disney shareholder's meeting. (Actually, when you consider the amount of Disney-related product placement on display—everything from *Good Morning America* plugs to the sight of one of the brothers actually wearing a shirt plugging his own concert tour while on stage—it could pretty well serve as the visual minutes for such a meeting.)

As the title indicates, *Jonas Brothers: The 3D Concert Experience* was originally released in theaters in the miracle of 3D, a move that concerned many movie fans because it was released a couple of weeks after the glorious *Coraline* (2009) and wound up taking many of the screens equipped to show such things. (As it turns out, the film wound up underperforming at the box-office and *Coraline* was soon restored to many of the screens from which it had been dumped.) I should probably admit that I never actually saw it in its 3D iteration—it did not pre-screen for critics and there was no way that I was going to pay the outrageously jacked-up $15 ticket price—but after watching the standard 2D version, I don't feel as if I missed much of anything outside of a couple of gimmicky effects involving tossing guitar picks and drumsticks into the crowd. To sum up, even if you look at it from the level of disposable pop music, *Jonas Brothers: The 3D Concert Experience* comes up short.

Peter Sobczynski

CREDITS

Himself: Joe Jonas
Himself: Kevin Jonas
Himself: Nick Jonas
Origin: USA
Language: English
Released: 2009
Production: Phil McIntyre, Art Repola, Johnny Wright, Kevin Jonas Sr.; Jonas Films; released by Walt Disney Pictures
Directed by: Bruce Hendricks
Cinematography by: Mitchell Amundsen, Reed Smoot
Sound: Robert Scott, Eric Pierce
Editing: Michael Tronick
MPAA rating: G
Running time: 76 minutes

REVIEWS

Adams, Mark. *Sunday Mirror.* May 29, 2009.
Anderson, Jason. *Toronto Star.* February 27, 2009.
Burr, Ty. *Boston Globe.* March 2, 2009.
Debruge, Peter. *Variety.* February 25, 2009.
Honeycutt, Kirk. *Hollywood Reporter.* February 25, 2009.
Lee, Nathan. *New York Times.* February 27, 2009.
Olsen, Mark. *Los Angeles Times.* February 27, 2009.
Pinkerton, Nick. *Village Voice.* February 24, 2009.

Rickey, Carrie. *Philadelphia Inquirer.* March 2, 2009.
Schwarzbaum, Liza. *Entertainment Weekly.* February 25, 2009.

QUOTES

Joe Jonas: "3-4, Kevin gets himself a new set of pajamas. Ohhh!"

AWARDS

Golden Raspberries 2009: Worst Actor (Jonas Brothers).

JULIA

Dealing with someone as he/she descends into full-blown alcoholism is a harrowing experience. Perhaps the most frustrating part is the alcoholic's incessant use of self-pity as an excuse to justify his/her irrational and often dangerous behavior. *Julia*, starring Tilda Swinton in the title role, is a daring, but ultimately frustrating film which takes that to an extreme, thrusting the addict at its center into grave situations that force her to reckon with the consequences of her actions, as the drunken haze begins to clear. But what begins as an extremely promising character study—centered on a brave performance—eventually loses its way when it attempts to master multiple genres as a road movie/suspense thriller, leaving the audience in a fog of its own.

When the viewer first meets Julia, she is already well on her way hitting to rock-bottom. Just minutes into the film, the single, aging drunk is fired from her job at an L.A. real estate agency, and after a series of blackouts, one night stands, and failed A.A. meetings, she is desperate to turn her luck around. She soon finds herself entertaining two offers: one, from Mitch (Saul Rubinek), a caring, ex-lover and a second, from Elena (Kate del Castillo), an unstable, but kind, Mexican neighbor she meets in A.A. Mitch, himself a recovering alcoholic who lost his family as a result of his addiction, offers Julia a promise of support in cleaning herself up. Elena, on the other hand, offers Julia $50,000 in exchange for assistance in kidnapping her son, Tom (Aidan Gould), from his wealthy grandfather, so she can return with him to Mexico, where she insists they belong. Unfortunately, Julia decides that the latter is the more direct route to reaching the life she thinks she deserves and agrees to take part in the crime. But unsatisfied with the amount Elena is willing to pay, Julia sees an opportunity to turn the kidnapping into something larger and opts to seize it, despite the numerous dangers that she will likely face as a result.

After a recent series of memorable turns in supporting roles, in films such as *The Curious Case of Benjamin Button* (2008), *Michael Clayton* (2007) and *Broken Flowers* (2005), it is exciting to see Swinton rewarded with a rich, central character such as this one. She tears into the role with aplomb and the results are often stunning. As Julia tells a potential suitor in the film's opening sequence, she is good at selling people whatever it is they want (usually, in order to get something she thinks she needs in return). This set-up allows Swinton to play a wide range of personae: unjustly maligned victim, sexed-up tramp, street-wise criminal, loving maternal figure and so on. Add in the fact that Julia is never too far from her next/last drink—which distorts her judgment at every turn—and it becomes impossible to predict which side of herself she will present next. Swinton also fearlessly embodies the unsightly, physical side of alcoholism; she spends a good portion of the movie hung over, her lanky frame staggering about with squinted eyes, frazzled hair and smeared mascara. Her performance is award-worthy throughout and goes a long way towards carrying this often confused film.

This is the first feature for which writer/director Erick Zonca took on both positions since 1999's *Le petit voleur*. And though that long break does not seem to have dulled his talent for carving out characters, her ability to distill a story down to its key ingredients here is questionable. She displays moments of brilliance in both writing and directing, but had she chosen a single focus, the film would have likely been streamlined into something more effective. From very early on, the film makes it clear that Julia's true struggle will revolve around coming to grips with her addiction and taking responsibility for own happiness. So it is disappointing when the film becomes, instead, preoccupied with the kidnapping storyline, relying on clichéd props like a briefcase full of money and a locker at the airport. To Zonca's credit, while it is certainly a common film convention to have the captive child eventually win the affections of his/her kidnapper, any such moments in this film feel well-earned. Some of the best scenes involve an inebriated Julia conversing with Tom as though he were some sort of bartender at the local pub, working through her inner conflicts aloud. In this respect, the film feels unlike others with similar storylines.

Julia should be respected for the chances it takes. As a protagonist, Julia's relationships to those around her are complicated, as is her moral compass, which shifts from moment to moment, to suit her needs. She does some unforgivable things that make it a real challenge for viewers to stay invested in her story. But that process—one in which initial concern becomes pity, but eventually gives way to anger and a desire to shake her from her stupor—accurately reflects the real-life obstacles one faces when dealing with any alcoholic. But the film eventually requires more patience than most are willing to give. As this 144-minute story enters its third act and moves the action south of the border for one tired double-crossing on top of another, Julia gets further away from, not closer to, some sort of personal resolution. And the viewer feels previously strong emotions deteriorating into apathy, at which point, Julia is pretty much on her own.

Matt Priest

CREDITS

Julia: Tilda Swinton
Mitch: Saul Rubinek
Elena: Kate del Castillo
Nick: Jude Ciccolella
Diego: Bruno Bichir
Johnny: Kevin Kilner
Tom: Aidan Gould
Santos: Horacio Garcia Rojas
Origin: USA
Language: English, Spanish
Released: 2008
Production: Bertrand Faivre, Francois Marquis; Studio Canal; released by Magnolia Pictures
Directed by: Erick Zonca
Written by: Erick Zonca, Aude Py
Cinematography by: Yorick Le Saux
Music by: Pollard Berrier, Darius Keeter
Editing: Philippe Kotlarski
Production Design: Francois-Renaud Labarthe
Sound: Pierre Mertens
MPAA rating: R
Running time: 144 minutes

REVIEWS

Berkshire, Geoff. *Metromix.com.* May 7, 2009.
Cockrell, Eddie. *Variety.* February 13, 2008.
Dargis, Manohla. *New York Times.* May 8, 2009.
Ebert, Roger. *Chicago Sun-Times.* July 3, 2009.
Foundas, Scott. *Village Voice.* May 5, 2009.
Keough, Peter. *Boston Phoenix.* December 3, 2009.
Rodriguez, Rene. *Miami Herald.* August 27, 2009.
Schwarzbaum, Lisa. *Entertainment Weekly.* May 6, 2009.
Sharkey, Betsy. *Los Angeles Times.* May 8, 2009.
Thomas, William. *Empire Magazine.* May 28, 2009.

QUOTES

Julia: "Well, I'm not really down with the good neighbor sh*t."

TRIVIA

On the cover of the DVD, Tilda Swinton is incorrectly referred to as Tilda Swanton.

JULIE & JULIA

Passion. Ambition. Butter. Do you have what it takes?
—Movie tagline

Box Office: $94.1 million

Writer-director Nora Ephron gets degree-of-difficulty points for *Julie & Julia*, a hybridized, somewhat herky-jerky dramedy that most effectively serves as a showcase for its two Oscar®-nominated actresses, Meryl Streep and Amy Adams. A much more lighthearted collaboration than their previous joint offering, the Academy Award®-nominated *Doubt* (2008), *Julie & Julia* is derived from a nonfiction book about a lapsed writer's quest to reenergize herself by diving into the recipes of author and television personality Julia Child. The film ambitiously marries that story to a separate biographical strand about Child, creating a cinematic casserole that is sometimes unwieldy but still full of flavorful charms.

The movie's more emotionally resonant storyline begins in France in 1949, where the vivacious, Pasadena-born Child (Streep) and her doting husband Paul (Stanley Tucci), an ex-Office of Strategic Services employee turned diplomat, live a charmed life. Unabashedly in love, they dine in style and soak up the local culture. Not satisfied with "proper" feminine diversions of the era like bridge and hat-making lessons, Child enrolls in cooking school, where she proves a quick study.

After a whirlwind visit from her sister Dorothy (Jane Lynch), Child then hooks up with two Frenchwomen (Linda Emond and Helen Carey) to form "The Three Gourmands," teaching cooking to American ex-pats. When her new friends' book deal falls through, Child takes the reins of a tome much grander in design, targeted at "servantless" American housewives nonetheless interested in expanding the palates of their families.

In 2002 Queens, meanwhile, Julie Powell (Adams) finds herself worn down by the emotional toll of her job with the Lower Manhattan Development Corporation, where she deals day in and day out with angry and shattered people looking for bureaucratic assistance in the wake of the September 11th terrorist attack on the World Trade Center. With the encouragement of her husband Eric (Chris Messina), Julie decides to jump start her dormant creative inclinations by undertaking a special project—cooking her way in one year through all 524 recipes in Child's book, all while blogging about it. She starts out with simpler recipes, but soon works her way deeper into unfamiliar territory, and her posts about the bewilderment, stresses and delights of her unique endeavor soon capture an appreciative audience.

Perhaps somewhat surprisingly, *Julie & Julia* gets into the sex lives of its respective subjects (Julia and Paul enjoy afternoon trysts, Eric makes a play to trade food for sex), though not always convincingly. Given both the artistic license involved in adaptation and the split of source material (the film is based on two books, Powell's *Julie & Julia* and Julia Child and Alex Prudhomme's *My Life in France*), it's hard to pin down how much of this is truly pertinent and how much is fanciful invention. Regardless, it feels like a bit of a generational sop—an unnatural play at cheekiness to make hip a film whose appeal would otherwise naturally skew older. Ephron seeds portion of her dialogue with some facts (that Child was a virgin until her marriage late in her 30s, for instance), but never really pulls off anything illuminating concerning the connection between food and sensuality in the way that *Eat Drink Man Woman* (1994), Tucci's own *Big Night* (1996), *Chocolat* (2000), *Woman on Top* (2000) and other films have.

The performances, ergo, are what hold *Julie & Julia* together. Streep is characteristically wonderful, and the movie's main attraction. Communicating Child's joy of life with both chirpy tones and the manner in which she physically carries herself, Streep again shows why she is the most Oscar®-nominated actress in history. Tucci, meanwhile, turns in deceptively subtle work as the mannered, encouraging Paul. When he says, "You're the butter to my bread, the breath of my life..." to Julia in a dinner toast, one sees and feels the regard in which he holds her, and their relationship. Given a bit less with which to work, Adams still captures Julie's plaintiveness and creative yearning. The only weak link among the four main players is Messina, who seemingly makes the obvious, theatrical choice for every scene, whether it be mouthy, exaggerated chewing to convey delight with a particular dish, or merely overemphasized line readings.

To be fair, Messina is not aided by a script that, late in the film, stokes artificial conflict by making him pointlessly start an argument he cannot win. While the arc of Child's struggle to get her book published provides for some natural dramatic tension, Ephron never strikes upon a way to flesh out Julie's story as anything more than a modern-day framing device for the film. Every element of conflict they foist upon this portion of the story to putatively establish angst and stress for Julie (from Julie's too-busy, self-involved white collar friends to rather inexplicable snipes from a boss and her husband) feels empty and contrived.

A bit overlong at 123 minutes, *Julie & Julia* is also curious in where it chooses to end, not delving substantively into the stateside TV career that would make Child a rich target of lampoon for *Saturday Night Live*'s Dan Aykroyd. With no disrespect to Adams, most

viewers would likely gladly trade some of the time spent with Julie's recipes for some of that dessert.

Brent Simon

CREDITS

Julie Powell: Amy Adams
Julia Child: Meryl Streep
Paul Child: Stanley Tucci
Dorothy McWilliams: Jane Lynch
Eric Powell: Chris Messina
Sarah: Mary Lynn Rajskub
Cassie: Vanessa Ferlito
Madame Brassart: Joan Juliet Buck
Simone Beck: Linda Emond
Louisette Bertholle: Helen Carey
Irma Rombauer: Frances Sternhagen
Origin: USA
Language: English
Released: 2009
Production: Amy Robinson, Nora Ephron, Laurence Mark, Eric Steel; Easy There Tiger, Columbia Pictures; released by Sony Pictures
Directed by: Nora Ephron
Written by: Nora Ephron
Cinematography by: Stephen Goldblatt
Music by: Alexandre Desplat
Sound: Tod A. Maitland
Editing: Richard Marks
Art Direction: Ben Barraud
Costumes: Ann Roth
Production Design: Mark Ricker
MPAA rating: PG-13
Running time: 123 minutes

REVIEWS

Berkshire, Geoff *Metromix.com.* August 6, 2009.
Chang, Justin. *Variety.* July 25, 2009.
Ebert, Roger. *Chicago Sun-Times.* August 6, 2009.
Edelstein, David. *New York Magazine.* August 3, 2009.
Honeycutt, Kirk. *Hollywood Reporter.* July 25, 2009.
Scott, A.O. *New York Times.* August 6, 2009.
Stevens, Dana. *Slate.* August 6, 2009.
Tallerico, Brian. *HollywoodChicago.com.* August 7, 2009.
Turan, Kenneth. *Los Angeles Times.* August 7, 2009.
Wilonsky, Robert. *Village Voice.* August 4, 2009.
Washington Post Online. August 7, 2009.

QUOTES

Julia Child: "If no one's in the kitchen, who's to see?"

TRIVIA

This is the second film that Meryl Streep has appeared in that has the name "Julia" in the title. The first was her film debut, *Julia* in 1977.

AWARDS

Golden Globes 2010: Actress—Mus./Comedy (Streep)

Nomination:

Oscars 2009: Actress (Streep)
British Acad. 2009: Actress (Streep)
Golden Globes 2010: Film—Mus./Comedy
Screen Actors Guild 2009: Actress (Streep)
Writers Guild 2009: Adapt. Screenplay.

KILLSHOT

> *Yesterday she was a witness. Today she's a target.*
> —Movie tagline

Michigan-based writer Elmore Leonard has written several novels and stories that have been turned into movies, including *Get Shorty* (1995), *Jackie Brown* (1997), *Out of Sight* (1998), and *3:10 to Yuma* (2007). His novel *Killshot*, set mostly in Michigan, was adapted for the screen by Hossein Amini and directed by John Madden. Best known for the more gauzy *Shakespeare in Love* (1998) and *Captain Corelli's Mandolin* (2001), Madden seems an odd choice to direct a shoot-'em-up.

The plot seems thinner than other Leonard works. It features an aging hit man with a Native American background, Blackbird (Mickey Rourke), who is working for the Toronto Mafia (who knew Toronto even had a Mafia?). At the opening of the film, he takes a job for a gang upstart, rubbing out the longtime head of the crime family (Hal Holbrook, in a frustratingly brief role). Blackbird, whose given name, strangely, is Armand Degas, has a lifelong habit of killing anyone who sees him killing, so he shoots the mob boss's girlfriend too, which does not endear him to his employers.

The uber-cool, calculating Blackbird then returns to Michigan to visit his grandmother, a medicine woman, but it turns out she's died. He meets up with a crazy young hothead crook, Richie Nix (Jason Gordon-Levitt), who tries to steal his blue Cadillac and his money. For some reason, they become partners, though they could not be more opposite in temperament. The implausible explanation for this is that Blackbird has lost his young brother in a previous gun battle, and he sees Richie as some sort of replacement. Nix is doing ridiculous jobs, including blackmailing a real estate agent, demanding money to keep him from destroying model homes.

Nix brings Blackbird to the real estate office for his attempted shakedown. Carmen Colson (Diane Lane)

works there. Her estranged husband, Wayne (Thomas Jane), just happens to be there looking for a job and manages to throttle the hyperbolic Nix, wound him, and send him fleeing away.

This first part of the movie is stylishly done but confusingly directed. Lots of people are getting killed, for reasons that are not immediately clear (an old friend of Blackbird's is offed in a marsh, gratuitously). It's also unclear why the police are suspicious of the Colsons, especially Wayne, when he fends off the attack, or why Blackbird is hanging around Algonac, Michigan, at all. He's targeting the Colsons because Carmen has seen his face, and he never leaves a job unfinished.

Leonard's novel may have been elegant, but this movie falters at finding a mood and style. The plot seems clunky. Suddenly, the Colsons are put into a federal witness protection program, given new identities, and sent to Missouri, where they must impersonate a happily married couple. Carmen has filed for divorce for reasons neither Wayne nor we can fully fathom—apparently because they could not have a child. The movie settles into a slow hunt by Blackbird and Nix to find their targets, with the couple as bait.

To pass the time, there's Nix's Elvis-obsessed girlfriend, Donna (Rosario Dawson), who seems to be there just as ornamentation and for a quick romantic pairing with Blackbird, which is as implausible as the scene in which Nix gives Carmen's mother a back rub while seeking information about her daughter's whereabouts. Wayne is also trying to win back Carmen, but she is resolute.

Spurts of cold violence interrupt these threads and scenes, and it's all more than a little incoherent. Rourke, in a performance that is quiet and compelling, pulls off his reserved but tortured hit man role well, even though he's a bit of a Tarantino-style stereotype. But why we should care about his character is a good question.

It's almost as if each of the main actors is performing in a different movie. Rourke is a barely bemused cold-blooded killer who seems to be auditioning for a potential *Godfather* remake. Gordon-Levitt has walked in out of some hyperkinetic video-game-style punk slasher flick; his character is way over the top, completely out of kilter with the rest of the film, and never believable in the least. Lane is plodding in all-too-familiar territory as the attractive woman in peril of being stalked, raped, and murdered—and you wonder why such a fine actress keeps taking these same B-movie sorts of roles. Jane is starring in a chick flick as the sensitive man, wrongly dumped by his cruel wife for something he didn't do, begging for her to give him a second chance for the entire movie. And Dawson is sort of a walk-on tease from some steamy cheap soft-porn flick.

Put them all together, and you've got a jumpy mess. Rourke, in a long braid with muddled dignity and confusion, gives the film an emotional center, but the other characters keep pulling it apart. This is not so much a movie as a ball of yarn played with by a bunch of cats. Leonard had a quirky story, but in Madden's ham-handed directorial treatment, it's splattered all over the place.

Michael Betzold

CREDITS

Carmen Colson: Diane Lane
Armand "The Blackbird" Degas: Mickey Rourke
Wayne Colson: Thomas Jane
Richie Nix: Joseph Gordon-Levitt
Donna: Rosario Dawson
Papa: Hal Holbrook
Origin: USA
Language: Killshot
Released: 2009
Production: Lawrence Bender, Richard N. Gladstein; Film Colony, Lawrence Bender Productions, Road Rebel, Weinstein Company; released by Third Rail Releasing
Directed by: John Madden
Written by: Hossein Amini
Cinematography by: Caleb Deschanel
Music by: Klaus Badelt
Sound: Glen Gauthier
Editing: Mick Audsley, Lisa Gunning
Art Direction: Brandt Gordon
Costumes: Beth Pasternak
Production Design: Andrew Jackness
MPAA rating: R
Running time: 95 minutes

REVIEWS

Anderson, Jeffrey M. *Combustible Celluloid.* June 1, 2009.
Goodykoontz, Bill. *Arizona Republic.* January 22, 2009.
Hunter, Rob. *Film School Rejects.* May 15, 2009.
Johans, Jen. *Film Intuition.* January 23, 2009.
Laforest, Kevin N. *Montreal Film Journal.* June 16, 2009.
Legan, Mark Jordan. *National Public Radio.* January 23, 2009.
Nusair, David. *Reel Film Reviews.* May 28, 2009.
Orndorf, Brian. *BrianOrdorf.com.* May 7, 2009.
Proimakis, Joseph. *Movies For the Masses.* May 10, 2009.
Wilmott, Don. *Filmcritic.com.* June 12, 2009.

QUOTES

Richie Nix: "Well, my name's Richie Nix, in case you've ever heard of me. That's N- i-x; it's not the way Stevie Nicks spells hers."

TRIVIA

Viggo Mortensen and Justin Timberlake were considered for the roles of Wayne Colson and Richie Nix, respectively.

KNOWING

Knowing is everything.
—Movie tagline

Box Office: $80 million

The premise of *Knowing* promises yet another dopey thriller in which Nicolas Cage rushes from one locale to the next, solving puzzles and saving the day in the service of another easy paycheck gig—in other words, the same basic film that he has been cranking out with depressing regularity over the last decade or so. Even though it did fairly well at the box-office, many people probably wound up staying away from because they feared it was going to be another piece of junk along the lines of such other recent Cage efforts as *Next* (2007), *Ghost Rider* (2007) and *Bangkok Dangerous* (2008). For their sakes, they should eventually catch up with the film at some point because not only is it decidedly not the next *Next*, it is actually a thrilling and mind-blowing blend of apocalyptic imagery and metaphysical discussion that is easily the best film of its type since *Southland Tales* (2007).

The film opens in 1959 as a group of schoolchildren hurry to finish their drawing of what they imagine the future will look like for a time capsule that will be opened in fifty years. Instead of the expected scribblings of rocket cars, soylent green factories and African American presidents, one girl hands in a piece of paper covered with thousands of seemingly random numbers. Naturally, the kid, Caleb Koestler (Chandler Canterbury), who gets this particular picture in 2009 is not exactly thrilled with it, but when dad John (Nicolas Cage)—an astrophysics professor at MIT who is still in the dumps over the recent passing of his wife and struggling to bond with his equally depressed child—begins to look at the numbers one night, he discovers that they reference the dates and body counts of major disasters that have occurred over the last half century right down to the latitude and longitude. Of course, when he tries to demonstrate this to his colleagues, they don't believe him. When one of the three remaining number groups indicating future disasters, the last of a truly apocalyptic nature, comes horrifyingly true, he enlists the help of the grown daughter (Rose Byrne) of that little girl to try to help him make sense of it all and, more importantly, figure out what to do with his knowledge, since it appears that there is nothing he can do to actually stop the events from occurring.

Yes, the premise of *Knowing* seems borderline insane—it sounds like what *The Da Vinci Code* might have turned out like in the hands of Irwin Allen—but it manages to transcend its ridiculously pulpy roots to become the kind of smart and genuinely interesting thriller that has become increasingly rare these days. The secret to its success is that director Alex Proyas, the man behind the cult classic *Dark City* (2008) and someone deserving of the appellation "visionary filmmaker," takes the truly audacious premise presented to him in the screenplay by Ryne Douglas Pearson, Juliet Snowden & Stiles White and has the nerve to see it all the way through to its ultimate implications, without pulling any punches or creating loopholes that will allow Cage to indulge in run-of-the-mill heroics. Instead of cheap theatrics, he is more interested in creating something a little more thought-provoking than is normally seen in mass-market entertainment these days. (When was the last time that you saw a film of this type that paused to allow its characters to contemplate notions of fate and thoughtfully debate whether the universe as we know it is merely the result of billions of coincidences or part of some pre-determined plan that we are all unwittingly following?) That is not to say that Proyas has skimped on the visual splendors—the various disaster set-pieces are some of the most sensational to hit the screen in a long time, and the plane crash that marks the first of them is worth the price of several admissions alone.

Knowing does have a few hiccups here and there—a couple of the subplots, specifically John's estrangement from his pastor father, are not developed as fully as they could have been, and there is one aspect to the story that smacks a little too closely to one of the key elements of *Dark City* for its own good. And yet, there is so much about the film that does work—an intelligent screenplay that does not succumb to silliness, top-notch direction from Proyas (after the stumble of *I Robot* [2004], this single-handedly reinstates him as one of the great genre filmmakers working today) and even a nice low-key performance from Cage—that it is easy to set those relatively minor missteps aside. This is a wildly ambitious piece of filmmaking, from both a narrative and visual standpoint, and it proves that a contemporary genre film of this kind can indeed dazzle both the eye and the mind.

Peter Sobczynski

CREDITS

John Koestler: Nicolas Cage
Diana Whelan: Rose Byrne
Phil Bergman: Ben Mendelsohn
Caleb Koestler: Chandler Canterbury
Abby/Lucinda: Lara Robinson
Grace: Nadia Townsend
Origin: USA
Language: English
Released: 2009
Production: Todd Black, Jason Blumenthal, Steve Tisch, Alex Proyas; Mystery Clock Cinema, Escape Artists; released by Summit Entertainment
Directed by: Alex Proyas
Written by: Juliet Snowden, Stiles White, Ryne Pearson
Cinematography by: Simon Duggan
Music by: Marco Beltrami
Sound: Peter Grace
Editing: Richard Learoyd
Art Direction: Andrew Walpole
Costumes: Terry Ryan
Production Design: Steven Jones-Evans
MPAA rating: PG-13
Running time: 121 minutes

REVIEWS

Adams, M. *Sunday Mirror.* March 27, 2009.
Ebert, Roger. *Chicago Sun-Times.* March 19, 2009.
Honeycutt, Kirk. *Hollywood Reporter.* March 19, 2009.
McCarthy, Todd. *Variety.* March 19, 2009.
O'Sullivan, Michael. *Washington Post.* March 20, 2009.
Pais, Matt. *Metromix.com.* March 19, 2009.
Sartin, Hank. *Time Out New York.* March 18, 2009.
Scott, A.O. *New York Times.* March 20, 2009.
Sharkey, Betsy. *Los Angeles Times.* March 20, 2009.
Zacharek, Stephanie. *Salon.com.* March 23, 2009.

QUOTES

John Koestler: "Stay with me. I know how this sounds, but I've mapped these numbers to the dates of every major global disaster from the last 50 years in perfect sequence. Earthquakes, fires, tsunamis...the next number on the chain predicts that tomorrow, somewhere on the planet, 81 people are going to die, in some kind of tragedy."

TRIVIA

The perceptual phenomenon of people looking for patterns in randomness (number strings, faces in trees, shapes in clouds etc.) is called Apophenia.

L

LAND OF THE LOST

Right place. Wrong time.
—Movie tagline

Box Office: $49 million

Long before the scene in which countless baby Pterodactyls emerge through cracking shells, *Land of the Lost* had convinced most viewers that a sizeable egg had been laid with the film itself. Many in the audience were there due to fond childhood memories of the 1970s Saturday morning television series upon which the film is rather tenuously based. Such moviegoers recalled how they had curled up with a bowl of brightly-colored cereal in front of a black-and-white set for each episode, their imaginations piqued by the adventures of a father, son and daughter who have been suddenly transported to another dimension and must somehow find their way home. The strange world in which the Marshall family found themselves was inhabited by rampaging, ravenous T-rexes, zombie-like lizard-men called Sleestaks (who trudged along creepily at a pace that molasses would mock), and a cave boy named Chaka, who was almost as friendly as he was furry. While the settings, costumes and not-especially-special effects of the Sid and Marty Krofft show often looked acutely fake, the enjoyment the program was able to create was nonetheless real. Unfortunately, the same cannot be said for the woefully misguided big-budget big-screen adaptation. In addition, nostalgia-seeking parents looking to enjoy a family-friendly film with their kids may be more than a little uncomfortable due to repeated injection of humor as lascivious and lowbrow as the film's all-too-fresh version of Chaka (Jorma Taccone).

Shortly into the film, a palpably disdainful Matt Lauer (playing himself) interviews quantum paleontologist Rick Marshall (Will Ferrell) on NBC's *Today Show*, clearly deeming the man's newly-published, taxpayer-funded research into time warps and parallel dimensions to be sheer far-out nonsense. As the segment progresses (or, more accurately, degenerates), the host visibly chafes at people's time and money being wasted on such drivel (a sentiment those watching *Land of the Lost* will shortly share about the film itself). Rick's apparent self-assurance cracks on live television to reveal a volcanic insecurity below, erupting like a petulant child as he stalks off and then crazily lunges at Lauer. Rick is a laughing stock after this high-profile hissy-fit, reduced to half-heartedly fielding the less-than-profound questions of children, feeling unjustly stifled all the while, and sniffling forlornly in the restroom.

The sulking scientist gets a much-needed morale boost with the arrival of idolatrous Holly (Anna Friel, worthy of better), who studied at lofty Cambridge University and declares the butt of everyone's jokes to be abundantly brilliant. Now reassuringly bolstered, Rick is able to finish an invention he theorizes will unlock the door to where elements of the past, present and future exist simultaneously. He and Holly arrive with the Tachyon Amplifier at the tacky desert tourist attraction they suspect to be a portal, and soon find themselves conveyed along with its coarse, redneck proprietor and tour guide, Will (Danny McBride), to a place in which lame, often belabored comedy segments and CGI-laden *Jurassic Park* (1993)-retread adventure sequences come together to disappoint moviegoers.

Listening to Rick's repeated assertions about dinosaur cognitive deficiencies, one begins to wonder if some might have had a hand in crafting *Land of the Lost*. Little has successfully evolved from an apparent initial idea to create an affectionate send-up with a mischievous wink and a nod toward the original. Adult fans of the show will feel that, like those unwise enough to purchase "Mexican vasectomy" fireworks from Will's Desert Canyon Mystery Cave gift shop, what remains has been made decidedly impotent. The film merely drifts along shooting blank after comedic blank in what often seems like uninspired improvisation. The characters endlessly dash to and fro, but they cannot escape the fact that scenes are simply being strung together rather than purposefully building upon each other in the creation of an increasingly-engaging whole. Rick and Co. must retrieve the now-missing Tachyon Meter to not only return home but also save the universe itself from a cold-blooded reptilian schemer (John Boylan), and yet finding viewers who were actually caught up in it all was at least as challenging a task. (One thing that does succeed in garnering interest is the desert expanse surreally littered with an eclectic assortment of odds and ends like a Bob's Big Boy statue, an expanse of the Golden Gate Bridge and what appears to be a Viking ship, making for a rather Daliesque dump.)

The original television series surmounted its paltry production values with absorbing stories scripted by highly regarded science fiction writers like Ben Bova and Larry Niven, intent on intriguing their young audience. However, it is exceedingly tough to ascertain what target audience was in mind while making the cinematic adaptation. Adults who wished to preserve untarnished memories of G-rated fun from a more innocent time should certainly have stayed home. Having a little fun with the original is fine, but since Rick and Holly were father and daughter in the original, their having a little fun in each other's arms here added an unpleasant ick-factor. What was particularly squirm-inducing when sitting next to one's own offspring, however, is the film's repeated insertion of startlingly-adult references, a *Land of the Lost* that would have had 1970s mothers and fathers absolutely lunging for the television off-switch before furiously dashing off letters to those responsible. Watching the film, today's parents likely echoed Ferrell's line of "I gotta say, I did not see that coming!" as an enchanted Chaka gropes Holly's breast yet again, even hornier Sleestaks engage in French-kissing foreplay, or Rick finds comfort with a hand shoved down the front of his pants. That does not even touch upon jokes pertaining to ejaculation or female sexual response. (There is also a fair amount of swearing, including one F-bomb hurled by a peevish Rick when he deems Chaka insufficiently cooperative and subservient.) Whatever

may have gone over younger heads, things like Rick pouring a jug full of dinosaur urine over his own head and then drinking some of it will likely connect with young boys just fine. They are also apt to be appreciative of the spewing of Tyrannosaurus rex mucus and proceedings which are generally and lazily grouted together with gross-out excrement jokes, such as a temporarily-gobbled-up Rick acting as a laxative within a sorely-constipated creature's colon.

Although Rick returns triumphantly vindicated to the present along with Holly at the end of *Land of the Lost*, Will feels no desire whatsoever to leave, an emotion to which few watching the film will be able to relate. Ferrell can be enjoyable playing imperfectly-matured fools with ridiculously-incorrect assessments of their own capabilities, proceeding as if things are under control until becoming utterly—and wholly predictably—overwhelmed, but the script here was in even greater need of fixing than Chaka's unfortunate teeth. Made on a budget that rose just above $100 million, the film failed to gross even half of that before slinking out of theaters. The vast majority of reviews were negative, with more than a few potently scathing. Paying good money to see such a negligible misfire truly stings, perhaps not as badly as dinosaur urine in the eyes apparently does, but stings, nonetheless.

David L. Boxerbaum

CREDITS

Rick Marshall: Will Ferrell
Holly Cantrell: Anna Friel
Will Stanton: Danny McBride
Chaka: Jorma Taccone
Enik: John Boylan
Himself: Matt Laurer
Origin: USA
Language: English
Released: 2009
Production: Jimmy Miller, Sid Krofft, Marty Krofft; Relativity Media, Mosiac; released by Universal Pictures
Directed by: Brad Silberling
Written by: Dennis McNicholas, Chris Henchy
Cinematography by: Dion Beebe
Music by: Michael Giacchino
Sound: Pud Cusack
Editing: Peter Teschner
Art Direction: John Dexter
Costumes: Mark Bridges
Production Design: Bo Welch
MPAA rating: PG-13
Running time: 93 minutes

REVIEWS

Childress, Erik. *eFilmCritic.* June 5, 2009.
Dargis, Manohla. *New York Times.* June 5, 2009.

Ebert, Roger. *Chicago Sun-Times.* June 4, 2009.

Honeycutt, Kirk. *Hollywood Reporter.* June 4, 2009.

Knight, Richard. *Windy City Times.* June 6, 2009.

Lemire, Christy. *Associated Press.* June 3, 2009.

Lowry, Brian. *Variety.* June 3, 2009.

Pais, Matt. *Metromix.com.* June 4, 2009.

Stevens, Dana. *Slate.* June 5, 2009.

Tallerico, Brian. *HollywoodChicago.com.* June 6, 2009.

QUOTES

Dr. Rick Marshall: "Matt Lauer can suck it!"

TRIVIA

The original *Land of the Lost* series was remade in the 1990s, with Timothy Bottoms as the father, although in this version his name was Tom Porter, not Will Marshall. Bottoms and Will Ferrell are both well known for their impersonations of George W. Bush.

AWARDS

Golden Raspberries 2009: Worst Remake, Rip-Off or Sequel

Nomination:

Golden Raspberries 2009: Worst Picture, Worst Actor (Ferrell), Worst Support. Actor (Taccone), Worst Director (Silberling), Worst Screenplay.

LAST CHANCE HARVEY

It's about first loves, last chances and everything in between.
—Movie tagline

Box Office: $15 million

The male menopause film has a long and not so distinguished history, ranging from the rarely seen truly original (William Holden in *Network* (1976), Albert Brooks in *Lost In America* (1985), Jack Nicholson in *About Schmidt* (2002)) to the far more frequently encountered execrable (*City Slickers* (1991), *Wild Hogs* (2007), *The Bucket List* (2007)). Joel Hopkins' *Last Chance Harvey* falls somewhere between these two extremes, not up to the task of bringing something new to the table but rescued from mediocrity by two bravura performances from Dustin Hoffman and Emma Thompson.

The film follows 48 hours of the lives of American Harvey and British Kate. Harvey is a songwriter for TV commercials who has reached the end of the line both personally and professionally. 70ish, divorced, estranged from his adult daughter and in danger of losing his job to his younger co-workers, the film opens with Harvey facing two significant late life events: giving his daughter away at her wedding in London and closing a deal in New York the day after that his boss (Richard Schiff) wants to entrust to his younger colleagues. ("This is your last chance Harvey!"he helpfully informs Harvey and the viewer.) Kate, middle-aged, lacking much in the way of a social life, and working in an unexciting job as a airline survey taker, fields daily phone calls from her mother about her perpetually single status and, while occasionally making token efforts towards changing that status, is uncomfortable with most people and afraid of serious relationships.

Harvey and Kate have one of those false starts common to romances when Harvey arrives at Heathrow and, in a hurry to get his hotel and his daughter, brushes Kate and her survey questions rudely aside. However, after arriving at his hotel, Harvey finds that he didn't pay enough attention to his daughter's plans and that she and the rest of the wedding party are staying at a house outside the city. This "out of step" quality characterizes Harvey's appearance at the rehearsal dinner later that evening. The narrative purpose of the dinner is to demonstrate that Harvey's past priority on his career has justifiably estranged him from his ex-wife and daughter. The problem is that the screenplay over does it with Harvey all but slipping on a banana peel in his ineptitude. An anti-theft device the size of a TV remote control (that Harvey somehow failed to notice while trying the suit on in his hotel room) dangles from his sleeve. His cell phone chirps at precisely the wrong moments interrupting his unimaginative speech to his daughter, and he nearly falls, slipping on decorative rocks as he scurries away from the dinner table to answer it. To cap the evening off, his daughter informs him that she is going to let her stepfather give her away at the wedding because he has been a bigger part of her life than Harvey has.

Fortunately for Harvey and Kate (and the viewer as well) they meet again the next day in an airport bar. Harvey has just missed his flight to New York and lost his job as a result ("It's over Harvey," his boss declares, continuing his role as a straightforward plot device). Harvey apologizes for being rude the previous day and, after trading some insults, the two begin to enjoy one another. His persistence amuses her, and he finds her honesty refreshing. "I have to tell you that it's a relief to find someone who actually says what they're feeling and what they're thinking." This is where the film begins to both relax and come alive, and the viewer laments that the film did not start in the bar. A man picking a woman up in a bar is a cliché, a stock acting exercise done in film a thousand times before, but Hoffman and Thompson remind the viewer that excellent acting, coupled with good dialogue, enlivens the most familiar of situations.

The viewer also laments that the film does not remain in the bar. For a promising while, the film is a middle-aged *Before Sunrise* (1995) as Harvey and Kate walk the streets of London together, discovering one another and falling in love. Unfortunately, Hopkins's film is not as bold as Richard Linklater's film and is very much a lost opportunity in that respect. Linklater's film had the confidence to assume that its characters alone were interesting enough to sustain the film. His characters were the film. Hopkins's film lacks this audacity and, attempting to play it safe, dilutes its potential by shackling his characters to a disappointingly conventional and predicable plot. Kate insists that they attend his daughter's wedding reception and, once there, Harvey unsurprisingly redeems himself with a heartfelt speech. After spending a whirlwind day together, Harvey tells Kate to meet him the next day at a specified time and place, a meeting which Harvey then misses due to a predicable health emergency. And when Harvey has finally located Kate after missing their meeting, his boss is again on the phone with a plot-necessitated dramatic change of heart ("We need you back Harvey!"). Will Harvey race to New York and save his job at the expense of his personal life (as has always been the case in the past) or pursue his last chance at romance?

The real reason to see *Last Chance Harvey* is not the false suspense of whether Harvey and Kate will end up together but for the way Dustin Hoffman pauses and closes his eyes when asked if he was good enough to be the jazz piano player he dreamed of being in his youth ("No, not good enough," he says, the opportunity to verbalize this truth both painful and cathartic) and the way Emma Thompson manages to make Kate both sexy and vulnerable at the same time. In a film telling a story this familiar, the pleasure comes not in the outcome but in the execution, and in *Last Chance Harvey* that execution is just good enough to make it worthy of viewing.

Nathan Vercauteren

CREDITS

Harvey Shine: Dustin Hoffman
Kate: Emma Thompson
Jean: Kathy Baker
Brian: James Brolin
Maggie Walker: Eileen Atkins
Marvin: Richard Schiff
Susan: Liane Balaban
Pete: Michael Landes
Origin: USA

Language: English
Released: 2008
Production: Nicola Usborne, Tim Perrell; Process Prods.; released by Overture Films
Directed by: Joel Hopkins
Written by: Joel Hopkins
Cinematography by: John de Borman
Music by: Dickon Hinchliffe
Sound: Mark Holding
Music Supervisor: Michael Hill
Editing: Robin Sales
Art Direction: Patrick Rolfe, Suzanne Austin
Costumes: Natalie Ward
Production Design: Jon Henson
MPAA rating: PG-13
Running time: 92 minutes

REVIEWS

Anderson, John. *Variety.* November 19, 2008.
Burr, Ty. *Boston Globe.* January 16, 2009.
Dargis, Manohla. *New York Times.* December 29, 2008.
Ebert, Roger. *Chicago Sun-Times.* January 15, 2009.
Gleiberman, Owen. *Entertainment Weekly.* January 7, 2009.
Honeycutt, Kirk. *Hollywood Reporter.* November 19, 2008.
Morgenstern, Joe. *Wall Street Journal.* December 29, 2008.
Phillips, Michael. *Chicago Tribune.* January 16, 2009.
Sarris, Andrew. *New York Observer.* December 31, 2008.
Tallerico, Brian. *MovieRetriever.com.* January 16, 2009.

QUOTES

Kate Walker: "I'm not gonna do it, because it'll hurt! Sometime or other there'll be, you know 'It's not working.' or 'I need my space.' or whatever it is and it will end and it will hurt, and I won't do it."

TRIVIA

Emma Thompson and Dustin Hoffman worked so well together in *Stranger Than Fiction,* they wanted to do another project together and got involved in *Last Chance Harvey.*

AWARDS

Nomination:

Golden Globes 2009: Actor—Mus./Comedy (Hoffman), Actress—Mus./Comedy (Thompson).

THE LAST HOUSE ON THE LEFT

If bad people hurt someone you love, how far would you go to hurt them back?
—Movie tagline

Box Office: $33 million

In both versions of *The Last House on the Left* (1973, 2009), two teenage girls in search of a little weed, find themselves at the mercy of fugitives who brutally torture, rape and then kill them. The fugitives, in need of a place to stay, unknowingly knock on the door of the parents of one of the murdered girls. The parents, fine upstanding suburban types, discover the crime, the identity of the fugitives, and then, essentially, repeat the same brutal crimes in revenge. It sounds loosely like the plot of any number of revenge shockers, which is a base testimony to the idea that imitation is a form of flattery, even if all a filmmaker is trying to imitate is the box-office take.

But few would argue that Wes Craven's seminal 1973 reworking of Ingmar Bergman's *The Virgin Spring* (1960) wasn't at least a little more clever than its cinematic spawn. Indeed the film has achieved a sort of mythic status as much for a dynamic ad campaign as for the undeniable visceral impact that it had on movie goers of the time. The phrase "Just keep telling yourself, it's only a movie, only a movie, only a movie...." was a masterful bit of marketing but less than honest advertising. The truth is the original *Last House on the Left* was as much a movie made for countercultural intellectual insiders as it was a movie made to shock outsiders. Though it was certainly subversive, it was indeed only a movie, and those who didn't get the in-joke took it way more seriously than even Craven intended.

Craven's original is highly experimental in almost every regard, melding raw unpolished performances with an unusual approach to score and almost documentary-like take on violence that shook more than a few viewers to their core. Craven's exploration of how quickly people abandon societal norms of morality and civility when threatened comes across as pretty ham-fisted, but perhaps not that much more so than the same object lessons that can be gleaned from reading the evening paper. *The Last House on the Left* was not anti-religious or anti-family as much as it questioned religion and family as infallible institutions. By the time the father takes his revenge in the film, we have been given plenty of reminders that modern man seems lost inside a number of casually held assumptions that have little to do with his survival. Pressed, any man will revert to bestial self-righteous rage.

Bergman's *The Virgin Spring* (1960) is, in comparison, almost wholly a religious film and makes the same basic point while offering a clarification. Man and his social and religious customs may be fallible but God is not. Where Craven's film ends with the reverberations of a chainsaw, Bergman's ends with a prayer and babbling brook, a symbol of hope and forgiveness—a redirection.

The new version on this oft-told tale is far and away a better film than almost all the horror classic remakes of recent years (*The Texas Chainsaw Massacre* [2003], *Black Christmas* [2006], *Halloween* [2007]) but ultimately, it too, fails to be more than a movie offering a problematic screenplay by Adam Alleca and Carl Ellsworth (*Red Eye* [2005], *Disturbia* [2007]) that ultimately settles for dishing out the old ultra-violence when it could have searched the tension between Craven and Bergman. The screenplay also makes significant, and wholly unnecessary, changes in plot that accomplish nothing except the softening of what should have been a hard-as-nails look at human nature. Director Dennis Iliadis (*Hardcore* [2004]) is also to blame here, choosing to employ unconvincing, merely entertaining, CGI just when the audience should be forced to consider the difference between demanding justice and sadistically wielding your own perverted version of it.

The film starts with more than a few ideas for what should be solidly motivated characters but is not able to escape caricature, even through the solid-to-great performances. Paige, as played by Martha MacIsaac, and the daughter Sara Paxton, as played by Mari Collingwood (*Aquamarine* [2006]), are representative less of girlish innocence and naiveté than of the mini-adulthood that has replaced adolescence with jaded experimentation. Never are we given the idea that going off alone with the strange new kid in town to score some weed should have been a problem. By comparison, Sara's parents, John Collingwood, played by Tony Goldwyn (*The Last Samurai* [2003], *The Sisters* [2005]), and Emma Collingwood, played by Monica Potter, are simply there. The closeted class consciousness and middle-class morality of the original parents are nowhere to be seen here. These parents do not seem to be guilty of anything except being in the wrong place at the wrong time, and we certainly never see them being the worse off for the horrific vengeance they subject Krug's gang to.

The gang themselves are finely drawn. Spencer Treat Clark (*Unbreakable* [2000], *Mystic River* [2003]), is positively haunting as Justin, the teenage son of the sadistic Krug. Struggling with the desire to please his father without losing his own soul. In contrast, Garrett Dillahunt (*No Country for Old Men* [2007], *The Assassination of Jesse James by the Coward Robert Ford* [2007]) is able to effectively hint at Krug being as much a creature of survival as cruelty, and at certain moments we think we might actually see him cross over into a wounded but open humanity. The script does not give Aaron Paul (*Daydreamer* [2007]) much to do besides play the weaselly cutthroat, but he channels his character type almost as memorably as Ben Foster channeled the similar stranger in *30 Days of Night*. And Riki Lindhome makes Sadie the worst of female psycho criminals, conveying an instinctual selfish bitchy glee that seems born out of constant misuse and abuse.

The Last House on the Left ends on a particularly savage yet ridiculous note (involving a microwave) that neither shocks nor surprises. And that is perhaps the biggest problem of all with the film. It updates the original into a simple thriller, becoming utterly just another movie.

Dave Canfield

CREDITS

Krug: Garret Dillahunt
Morton: Michael Bowen
Sadie: Riki Lindhome
Mari Collingwood: Sara Paxton
Emma Collingwood: Monica Potter
John Collingwood: Tony Goldwyn
Francis: Aaron Paul
Paige: Martha MacIsaac
Justin: Spencer Clark
Giles: Joshua Cox
Origin: USA
Language: English
Released: 2009
Production: Wes Craven, Sean S. Cunningham, Marianne Maddalena; released by Rogue Pictures
Directed by: Dennis Iliadis
Written by: Carl Ellsworth, Adam Alleca
Cinematography by: Sharon Meir
Music by: John Murphy
Editing: Peter McNulty
Sound: Ben Wilkins
Art Direction: Cecilia van Staaren, Shira Hockman
Costumes: Katherine Jane Bryant
Production Design: Johnny Breedt
MPAA rating: R
Running time: 109 minutes

REVIEWS

Berkshire, Geoff. *Metromix.com.* March 12, 2009.
Catsoulis, Jeanette. *New York Times.* March 13, 2009.
Childress, Erik. *EFilmCritic.* March 12, 2009.
Ebert, Roger. *Chicago Sun-Times.* March 12, 2009.
Harvey, Dennis. *Variety.* March 11, 2009.
Phillips, Michael. *Chicago Tribune.* March 12, 2009.
Pinkerton, Nick. *Village Voice.* March 10, 2009.
Simon, Brent. *Screen International.* March 13, 2009.
Tallerico, Brian. *HollywoodChicago.com.* March 13, 2009.
Tobias, Scott. *AV Club.* March 12, 2009.

QUOTES

John Collingwood: "By land. Six miles by land. Okay, we are going to do this. We'll get through it. We are going to do it."

TRIVIA

Bruises are visible on both Paige and Mari's legs during the scenes in the hotel room. According to interviews, the bruises were a result of filming the scenes in the forest, which were filmed before the motel room scene. The makeup crew tried to cover up the bruises, but since the actors did their own stunts, the marks were too severe to be covered up by any makeup.

THE LAST STATION

Intoxicating. Infuriating. Impossible. Love.
—Movie tagline

Box Office: $6 million

The manner in which Hollywood studio films most commonly deal with themes of love and the convention of marriage is of great disservice to men and women alike. When they do deign to focus on something other than love's bloom, as frequently filtered through some ridiculous comedic set-up, they rarely do so in multidimensional fashion. Rather, love in middle-agedness or old age is shown refracted through the prism of family, or perhaps in a jokey manner with regards to libidinal pulses either waning or still going strong. It is extraordinarily atypical when a film gets into the weight of the emotional investment in a relationship that spans time, and the hard, decades-long, subtle tugs-of-war of which marriages must be comprised.

In some ways that opportunity again missed colors the disappointment surrounding *The Last Station,* an earnest and intermittently engaging but ultimately forgettable drama that cannot decide whether it wants to be a straight-on historical period piece or a heady, psychologically insightful investigation of love's flickering flame in the twilight of two intertwined lives. Director Michael Hoffman's film has an awards-season pedigree (and hence the Golden Globe and Screen Actors Guild nominations for its headlining performers), but there is unfortunately not enough cathartic dramatic punch here to mark the movie as something of recommendation outside its core demographic of mostly white-haired history buffs and biography cinephiles.

After almost fifty years of marriage, Countess Sofya Andreevna Bers (Helen Mirren) finds herself increasingly at odds with husband Leo Tolstoy (Christopher Plummer), Russia's most celebrated novelist. In the name of a newly created, quasi-separatist, Christian "Tolstoyan" movement that has cropped up around his provocative essay writing, the 82-year-old writer has renounced his noble title, and a good bit of his property, in favor of poverty, vegetarianism and celibacy. In the dusk of their time together—years after the publication of *War and Peace* and *Anna Karenina*, and with the eight of their thirteen children together that survived childhood all adults—the devoted Sofya now finds her well-ordered world turned upside down.

Chiefly at issue at the time of the movie's setting, in 1910, is the issue of Tolstoy's still-considerable estate, and whether the rights to his writings will remain owned by his widow-to-be (Sofya is sixteen years younger) or revert to the public domain. Eying to make the latter scenario a reality, a leader of the Tolstoyan movement with perhaps conflicting motives, Vladimir Chertkov (Paul Giamatti), dispatches young writer Valentin Bulgakov (James McAvoy) to Tolstoy's estate as his new personal secretary, with orders to report back on Sofya's statements and actions. Valentin's work, and sincere belief in an ascetic set of principles that Tolstoy himself seems to regard with bemusement, is complicated by burgeoning feelings for Masha (Kerry Condon), another Tolstoyan disciple who lives in a nearby commune.

Hoffman has hopscotched between comedy and drama for most of his directing career, but with *The Last Station* he seems uncertain of his fundamental area of concentration. In his first produced screenplay in a decade, Hoffman, working from a novel by Jay Parini, veers unsteadily between thematically-interlinked ensemble drama and a more tightly focused examination of the Tolstoy's complex relationship. Eschewing any attempts at linguistic realism, Hoffman more or less lets his players speak in their normal accents. This occasionally produces moments of pause or incongruous hiccup, chiefly courtesy of a burst of fluttery laughter from Mirren or a muttered aside by Giamatti—behaviors much more associated with Western conversational mores, and thus films, than anything in the Slavic tradition.

Obviously working under budgetary constraints that would not be imposed in a studio-funded film, production designer Patrizia Von Brandenstein and costume designer Monica Jacobs create a suitably austere backdrop; if one never really feels the wind chill of a cloudy Russian day, they at least get a proper sense of time and place. Other technical credits are solid and economical as well, giving the movie a low-key, modest and straightforward feel—the exact opposite of the sweeping epic scope for which so many period pieces aim, in knee-jerk fashion.

On a very basic level, though, certain story beats do not match up; at one point Tolstoy, certain that he and Sofya cannot reconcile their diverging beliefs, absconds in secret, but his doctor literally climbs up on a soapbox and gives a detailed account of his health to the gathered press. Some of the movie's edits in simple dialogue exchanges are also counterintuitive and against the weight of an inveighing character's passionate argument. This helps feed the notion that *The Last Station* is not so much a well-stitched together drama as a listless exercise in historical dramatic reenactment, full of the type of scenes that literal-minded high school or college students would dream up for a performance, sketch, or oral presentation assignment.

To be fair, not the entire film plays like this. There are flashes of magic, mainly courtesy of Plummer and Mirren's graceful, wonderfully understated performances, which manage to locate a full-bodied complexity in the Tolstoy's relationship—passionate, playful and genuine, yet marked by a mutually acknowledged chasm that has grown over the years, and shows no signs of shrinking—that the script does not fully plumb. Composer Sergei Yevtushenko's delicate score also abets this examination of whether such a shared history outweighs fundamentally opposed worldviews, which is by the most interesting part of the movie. If only Hoffman had the courage to jettison Valentin and Masha's treacly, misguided parallel tract, and instead focus solely on Sofya and Leo. Then *The Last Station* might be something different, and of note. As is, it is just another period-piece drama which trades on the notion of a celebrated subject, but does not offer much more than a thumbnail's depth of actual human analysis.

Brent Simon

CREDITS

Leo Tolstoy: Christopher Plummer
Countess Sofya: Helen Mirren
Vladimir Chertov: Paul Giamatti
Valentin Bulgakov: James McAvoy
Sasha: Anne-Marie Duff
Masha: Kerry Condon
Dushan: John Sessions
Sergeyenko: Patrick Kennedy
Origin: Great Britain, Germany, Russia
Language: English
Released: 2009
Production: Chris Curling, Jens Meurer, Bonnie Arnold; Zephyr Films, Egoli Tossell Film, Andrei Konchalovsky Production Center; released by Sony Pictures Classics
Directed by: Michael Hoffman

Written by: Michael Hoffman
Cinematography by: Sebastian Edscmid
Music by: Sergey Yevtushenko
Sound: Martin Trevis
Editing: Patricia Rommel
Art Direction: Erwin W. Prib
Costumes: Monika Jacobs
Production Design: Patrizia Von Brandenstein
MPAA rating: R
Running time: 112 minutes

REVIEWS

Ansen, David. *Newsweek.* December 4, 2009.
Clifford, Laura. *Reeling Reviews.* December 13, 2009.
Denby, David. *New Yorker.* December 7, 2009.
Douglas, Edward. *ComingSoon.Net.* January 12, 2009.
Morgenstern, Joe. *Wall Street Journal.* January 14, 2010.
Puig, Claudia. *USA Today.* December 3, 2009.
Taylor, Ella. *Village Voice.* December 2, 2009.
Travers, Peter. *Rolling Stone.* December 3, 2009.
Turan, Kenneth. *Los Angeles Times.* December 3, 2009.
White, Armond. *New York Press.* January 13, 2010.

QUOTES

Vladimir Chertkov (to Countess Sofya): "If I had a wife like you, I would have blown my brains out. Or gone to America."

TRIVIA

There still is a real Tolstoy family, who live in Yasnaya Polyana in Russia. This film was made with their support and they like the film, although they were surprised that one could laugh about Lev. (If you look closely, you can catch Anastasia Tolstoya, an Oxford graduate, in a short scene at the end of the film.)

AWARDS

Nomination:

Oscars 2009: Actress (Mirren), Support. Actor (Plummer)
Golden Globes 2010: Actress—Drama (Mirren), Support. Actor (Plummer)
Ind. Spirit 2010: Actress (Mirren), Director (Hoffman), Film, Screenplay, Support. Actor (Plummer)
Screen Actors Guild 2009: Actress (Mirren), Support. Actor (Plummer).

LAW ABIDING CITIZEN

The system must pay.
—Movie tagline

Box Office: $73 million

Thrillers, by definition, do not necessarily have to make a lot of sense. Yet if a film is going to become as completely inane as *Law Abiding Citizen* becomes, it should not be so ridiculously humorless.

The subject matter is, obviously, no laughing matter. The film begins with Clyde (Gerard Butler) enjoying a night at home with his wife (Brooke Stacy Mills) and daughter (Ksenia Hulayev). Clyde answers the door, robbers bash him in the head with a bat, and soon this average dad's family has been killed and he's left for dead.

For reasons the film completely obscures, Nick Rice (Jamie Foxx), an attorney committed to maintaining his 96 percent conviction rate, makes a deal with Darby (Christian Stolte), the more vicious of the murderers, to flip on his partner Ames (Josh Stewart). Why does Nick not make the deal with the more timid Ames, who surely would have been glad to testify against the immensely cruel Darby? *Law Abiding Citizen* does not address this. Instead, Darby is out of prison in a few years and, ten years after the murders, Ames is executed.

This is approximately where the film really starts to lose it, which is awfully early on in the story for that to happen. Somehow Clyde, who apparently has sustained himself for a decade since his family's murder yet remains hungry for violent revenge, switches the chemicals involved in Ames' lethal injection to make his death much more painful. He also helps Darby escape from the police—in an absurd sequence that suggests Clyde's entire plan hinges on a convicted killer's ability to scamper across rooftops—only to kidnap and chop him up in a grisly fashion that would make the Jigsaw killer in the *Saw* franchise (2004-2009) proud.

Through all of this, Butler portrays Clyde as far too methodical to be so far off the deep end. This formerly stable, loving family fan has been turned into a merciless killer, yet still seems awfully in control. This continues as Clyde is arrested but proceeds to orchestrate a series of murders (which appears to revolve around Nick and his staff) from inside prison. At this point, there is a bit of curiosity that comes from wondering how Clyde pulls this off, be it with an accomplice or just a lot of advance planning in the decade he had to prepare (which would be another very Jigsaw-esque strategy). Yet the explanation for his actions, which is as far-fetched as anything onscreen in 2009, comes with the same dose of straight-faced earnestness that suggests *Law Abiding Citizen* expects to be taken seriously.

Foxx's one-note performance also suggests he does not, deep-down, take any of this seriously or understand what is going on. His character accomplishes very little as an attorney, yet his one sensible statement, "It's not what you know; it's what you can prove in court," is something that Clyde takes exception to and the film implies is a compromise that deprives victims of justice. It is understandable that Clyde wants proper punishment for the men that murdered his wife and daughter; however, it is a losing argument to complain that the American legal system's need to confirm information in court is inherently unjust.

With a moral discussion so off-center, *Law Abiding Citizen* pretty much just turns into an increasingly far-fetched excuse to kill a lot of people. This is not a film about legal compromises and the victims that get the short end of the stick. It is a case of screenwriter Kurt Wimmer trying to up the stakes and the body count at every turn, regardless of the impact on the story or what the movie, with several major tweaks, could have been about: A father pushed over the edge by unthinkable loss and who no longer feels connected to the system he once supported.

Instead, Clyde turns out to be an expert technician and former special ops agent. (As an indication of his less-than-admirable research skills, Nick learns this late in the game after a secret meeting with a source, who insists, "If Clyde wants you dead, you're dead." That removes the sense that Clyde is just a regular guy who becomes a victim of a horrible crime. Nope, he's a diabolical genius who, when circumstances call for it, can easily and expertly present Nick with deadly challenges on short timelines, from which the movie generates only casualties, not suspense.

Yet perhaps the most stunning choice by director F. Gary Gray comes early on as he continually cuts back and forth between Ames' execution and Nick's daughter Denise's (Emerald-Angel Young) music recital (which Nick skips to attend the execution). As the curtains opening both on a young girl performing and a man about to die, Gray finds no parallel between the two scenarios. If he is merely establishing the priorities of a father who foregoes his only child's big moment for a work event, certainly Gray does not need to tie the locations together in such a strangely similar way—which may lead some viewers to wonder if Gray is comparing a school music performance to a lethal injection. Watching kids perform is, of course, not even close to as harrowing as watching a person put to death. Nor is the experience of watching a movie, but sitting through *Law Abiding Citizen* is pretty brutal all the same.

Matt Pais

CREDITS

Clyde Shelton: Gerard Butler
Nick Rice: Jamie Foxx

Sarah Lowell: Leslie Bibb
Det. Dunnigan: Colm Meaney
Mayor: Viola Davis
Jonas Cantrell: Bruce McGill
Kelly Rice: Regina Hall
Rupert Ames: Josh Stewart
Det. Garza: Michael Irby
Origin: USA
Language: English
Released: 2009
Production: Gerard Butler, Lucas Foster; Film Department, The; released by Overture Films
Directed by: F. Gary Gray
Written by: Kurt Wimmer
Cinematography by: Jonathan Sela
Music by: Brian Tyler
Sound: Bruce Litecky
Music Supervisor: Jim Black
Editing: Tariq Anwar
Art Direction: Jesse Rosenthal
Costumes: Jeffrey Kurland
Production Design: Alex Hajdu
MPAA rating: R
Running time: 109 minutes

REVIEWS

Chang, Justin. *Variety.* October 15, 2009.
Ebert, Roger. *Chicago Sun-Times.* October 15, 2009.
Honeycutt, Kirk. *Hollywood Reporter.* October 15, 2009.
Pais, Matt. *Metromix.com.* October 15, 2009.
Rea, Stephan. *Philadelphia Inquirer.* October 15, 2009.
Roeper, Richard. *RichardRoeper.com.* October 16, 2009.
Scott, A.O. *New York Times.* October 16, 2009.
Sobczynski, Peter. *EFilmCritic.* October 15, 2009.
Tallerico, Brian. *MovieRetriever.com.* October 16, 2009.
Tobias, Scott. *AV Club.* October 15, 2009.

QUOTES

Clyde Shelton: "I'm gonna pull the whole thing down. I'm gonna bring the whole fuckin' diseased, corrupt temple down on your head. It's gonna be biblical."

TRIVIA

Director F. Gary Gray decided to use Del Frisco's Double Eagle Steakhouse as the restaurant that caters Clyde's lunch after dining there several times during filming. The restaurant was also the location of the film's after-party following its screening at the Philadelphia Film Festival.

LET THE RIGHT ONE IN
(Låt den rätte komma in)

Eli is 12 years old. She's been 12 for over 200 years and, she just moved in next door.
—Movie tagline

Box Office: $2 million

The vampire genre pre-dates the medium of film, and for as long as world cinema has existed, it has been making vampire films. With a century's worth of predecessors to contend with, a modern filmmaker is hard pressed to put a new spin on such a well-established genre. However Tomas Alfredson's *Let the Right One In* does exactly that and is unlike any vampire film the viewer has encountered before.

The innovations of *Let the Right One In* are immediately apparent in the film's unconventional setting (a dispiriting apartment complex and elementary school), its decidedly unromantic view of vampirism and, most especially, its prepubescent human and vampire protagonists. The film opens with twelve-year-old Oskar (Kare Hedebrant) observing the arrival, in the dead of night, of two strange new residents to his apartment complex: Eli (Lina Leandersson), to all outward appearances a twelve-year-old girl, and her creepy middle-aged male escort Hakan (Per Ragnar), who promptly boards up the apartment's windows with cardboard. Hakan, as revealed in a chilling and clinically shot sequence set in a nearby park and enhanced by Hoyte Van Hoytema's beautiful and atmospheric cinematography, is Renfield to her Dracula.

Eli, however, is hardly the stereotypical vampire aristocrat charismatically seducing her victims at gatherings of high society. She instead lives the lonely and nomadic existence on the margins of society that one might expect for a being who subsists on human blood. Blood collection is a grubby and gruesome affair and, in the hands of Eli's assistant, a darkly comic one, as a typical example of his subtlety in victim acquisition is standing in full view of a gymnasium full of teenagers staring at them ominously and hungrily through enormous, well-lit windows. When Eli draws blood from her victims, it's hardly the traditional erotic experience depicted in countless previous vampire films. Rather, it is an animalistic attack which Alfredson vividly amplifies by cross cutting an image of Eli's "true self"—a grotesque adult woman—against the twelve-year-old Eli as she greedily drains the blood of her victims. Eli's apartment, devoid of furniture and containing only a few easily transportable possessions, is that of a permanent fugitive. In Alfredson's film, vampirism is denied its usual exoticism and romanticism and is instead depicted as a disease-like condition to be contended with. Yes, the film admits, as a vampire you get to live forever, but do you want to? At least one of Eli's victims is confronted with exactly that choice.

Shortly after Eli's arrival, she and Oskar meet in the apartment complex's courtyard and a tentative friendship is formed. The film's key innovation is desexualizing that friendship by making both human and vampire prepubescent. As Eli drily puts it, "I'm twelve but I've been twelve for a really long time." What might seem initially to be a gimmick, child protagonists, is in fact the film's strongest, most original element. This narrative choice allows Oskar and Eli's relationship to be unburdened by the clichéd sexual sub-text which weighs down nearly all vampire films. This, in turn, allows the script to focus on what the film is really about: Oskar and Eli's shared status as outsiders, each uniquely equipped to help the other against forces which seek to destroy them. Eli is being hunted by a fellow apartment complex resident (Peter Carlberg) whose suspicion turns towards Eli as her need to feed inevitably racks up a string of grisly homicides in the area. That the viewer is not particularly disturbed by these killings—other than to be concerned that they will lead to Eli's discovery—demonstrates the great power of narrative perspective and is a testament to the empathy generated by John Ajvide Lindqvist's excellent screen adaptation of his novel, as well as Hedebrant's and Leandersson's compelling performances. As Eli is being stalked, Oskar is being mercilessly bullied by three sociopathic classmates at his school. Each character plays a key role in the resolution of the other's dilemma: Oskar because he can operate in the daylight, and Eli because of her vampire-enhanced strength and speed. Each plot line produces a culminating sequence of great suspense and, in Oskar's case, an electrifying climax of breathtaking directorial ingenuity.

As important as what Eli and Oskar to do to help one another is why they choose to help one another. They do not help one another simply because they are each in a jam and in a unique position to help the other. They help one another in the face of their own justifiable reservations because their affection for one another will not allow them to do otherwise. Oskar is not attracted to Eli because of her vampirism—which repels him—but in spite of it. He is horrified by her killing but, when presented with the opportunity to ensure that she never kills again, he chooses to attempt to save her. Elie, though she initially says that they cannot be friends, understanding the great vulnerability such a friendship will cause her, nonetheless chooses to help Oskar, at great risk to herself. Far from the cheap horror movie thrills and suave, seductive vampires of most of its predecessors, *Let the Right One In* is a sophisticated and surprisingly touching examination of the sacrifices people are willing to make for those who they love.

The end of 2008 and beginning of 2009 gave us two films featuring adolescent vampires, *Let the Right One In* and *Twilight*. Of the two films, *Let the Right One In* is the film with ambitions beyond satisfying an adolescent audience. Indeed, *Let the Right One In* reinvents the vampire genre and imbues it with an unexpectedly touching aspect in its relationship between its two main characters. It is the most original, haunting and visually arresting vampire film since Werner Herzog's *Nosferatu* (1979).

Nathan Vercauteren

CREDITS

Oskar: Kare Hedebrant
Eli: Lina Leandersson
Hakan: Per Ragnar
Erik: Henrik Dahl
Yvonne: Karen Berquist
Lacke: Peter Carlberg
Origin: Sweden
Language: Swedish
Released: 2008
Production: Carl Molinder, John Nording; EFTI, Sandrew Metronome Distribution Sverige AB, Sveriges Television, Ljudligan; released by Magnet Releasing
Directed by: Thomas Alfredson
Written by: John Ajvide Lindqvist
Cinematography by: Hoyte van Hoytema
Music by: Johan Soderqvist
Sound: Per Sundstrom
Editing: Thomas Alfredson, Dino Jonsalter
Costumes: Maria Strid
Production Design: Eva Noren
MPAA rating: R
Running time: 114 minutes

REVIEWS

Anderson, John. *Washington Post.* November 7, 2008.
Ansen, David. *Newsweek.* October 23, 2008.
Chocano, Carina. *Los Angeles Times.* October 24, 2008.
Dargis, Manohla. *New York Times.* October 24, 2008.
Ebert, Roger. *Chicago Sun-Times.* November 14, 2008.
Howell, Peter. *Toronto Star.* October 31, 2008.
Long, Tom. *Detroit News.* January 23, 2009.
Oumano, Elena. *Village Voice.* October 22, 2008.
Phillips, Michael. *Chicago Tribune.* November 13, 2008.
Tallerico, Brian. *MovieRetriever.com.* November 14, 2008.

QUOTES

Oskar: "Twelve years, eight months and nine days. What do you mean, 'more or less?'"

TRIVIA

The title of the film (as well as the novel upon which it was based) refers to the Morrissey song "Let the Right One Slip In." In addition, it also refers to the fact that, according to vampire myths, vampires must be invited in before they can enter someone's home (this is shown in the film when Eli asks Oskar to invite her into his apartment).

AWARDS

Nomination:
British Acad. 2009: Foreign Film.

THE LIMITS OF CONTROL

For every way in, there is another way out.
 —Movie tagline

Box Office: $ million

Compared unfavorably to watching paint dry by some critics, *The Limits of Control* is another Jim Jarmusch experiment in minimalism. The veteran indie director, known for playing with the conventions of cinema in films like *Broken Flowers* (2005), is reunited here with several of his regulars, including Tilda Swinton, John Hurt, and Bill Murray in bit parts, and a starring role for Isaach De Bankole (*Ghost Dog: Way of the Samurai* [1999]). Gael Garcia Bernal also lends his star power to the cast, so Jarmusch has plenty of acting chops at his disposal.

Unfortunately, he makes little use of them. De Bankole, despite being on screen for most of the movie's 100 minutes, rarely speaks. Instead, he simply waits for other strangers he meets to talk to him. The film is set in Spain, and all the conversations begin with "You don't speak Spanish, right?" De Bankole's character, known only as the Lone Man, hardly registers a response.

The conventions of the genre Jarmusch is playing with lead you to believe the Lone Man is a hit man. At the beginning, he meets a couple characters in sunglasses at an airport terminal, and they give him a mysterious assignment and instructions: go to a hotel, wait a couple days, and look for the violin. The Lone Man travels to Madrid, checks into a hotel, sits in a café, and watches and waits. We see him every morning, lying in his bed with his eyes open (he seemingly never sleeps) as the darkness turns to dawn. Occasionally, he visits the art museum and stares, mesmerized, at certain paintings, which have some connection to his experiences. In the café, he always orders two cups of espresso, often sees a helicopter hover overhead, and notices a flock of birds noisily settle on the roof.

All the other characters in the story come to him, usually with a grand entrance in slow motion announcing their arrival. They give set speeches and the Lone Man hardly responds to them. Tilda Swinton, dressed all in white and with a blonde wig, remarks on how she enjoys old movies, because they provide detailed observations of how life was lived in the time they were made. John Hurt notices a pack of passing punkers and opines that they really do not deserve to be called bohemians because they are not as serious about art as the bohemians of his youth. All of the man's visitors give him a matchbox in exchange for the one he has, and in each new matchbox is a paper with a new set of numbers. Presumably, these numbers contain a clue as to where he will go next, as he moves from Madrid to Seville to another town and then further to a rural compound.

A nude woman (Paz de la Huerta) appears in his bed in Madrid. She has another matchbox and carries a gun. Despite her beauty, she cannot entice him because, he says, he is busy working, even though all he seems to be doing is waiting. "No guns? No sex? Mmm," the naked woman remarks, practically writhing on the bed. "How can you stand it?" (It is a question that Jarmusch is really asking of his audience.) When she later refers to their "beautiful love story," it is one of the film's few clever, satirical moments. It's clear Jarmusch is making fun of the conventions of the hired-gun thriller, in which the protagonist is always almost led astray by a gangster's moll.

But the Lone Man is single-minded. The trouble is that his mission or his motivation are always unclear. He is a blank, a protagonist who is a cipher, and the images of De Bankole are so still and chiseled that they, too, could be paintings. Perhaps he is not really a hired gun, but simply a man moving through the world by chance, encountering what fate deals out to him, meeting others who direct him to places not of his choosing. Or maybe it is all a dream. After all, Jarmusch tells us, in the voice of his characters, that "reality is arbitrary" and that perception is what determines experience. Some of them lecture him, and us, with snippets of existentialist philosophy.

Something deep certainly must be going on here. The spacey, cool soundtrack; the striking images; the flouting of conventions; the repetition of images and phrases and speeches, especially one in which the audience is told that those who think they are better than others end up in the cemetery and discover the true meaning of life; namely, that life is a "handful of dirt"—surely these all mean that Jarmusch is saying something very profound. Or maybe he is doing nothing more than just toying with the expectations of his audience. *The Limits of Control* tests the viewer's limits of tolerance for tedium for an undefined and unclear purpose. Swinton's character muses: "Sometimes, I just like to see films where people just sit there not saying anything."

Viewers who agree with her will enjoy the *The Limits of Control*.

Michael Betzold

CREDITS

Lone Man: Isaach de Bankole
Nude: Paz de la Huerta
Creole: Alex Descas
Violin: Luis Tosar
Guitar: John Hurt
Blonde: Tilda Swinton
French: Jean-Francois Stevenin
Mexican: Gael Garcia Bernal
American: Bill Murray
Origin: USA
Language: English
Released: 2009
Production: Stacey Smith, Gretchen McGowan; Entertainment Farm, Tom Bastounes; released by Focus Features
Directed by: Jim Jarmusch
Written by: Jim Jarmusch
Cinematography by: Christopher Doyle
Music by: Boris
Sound: Drew Kunin
Editing: Jay Rabinowitz
Costumes: Bina Daigeler
Production Design: Eugenio Caballero
MPAA rating: R
Running time: 116 minutes

REVIEWS

Dargis, Manohla. *New York Times.* May 1, 2009.
Hoberman, J. *Village Voice.* April 28, 2009.
Lane, Anthony. *New Yorker.* April 27, 2009.
McCarthy, Todd. *Variety.* April 23, 2009.
Puig, Claudia. *USA Today.* April 30, 2009.
Reed, Rex. *New York Observer.* April 29, 2009.
Sharkey, Betsy. *Chicago Tribune.* April 30, 2009.
Tobias, Scott. *AV Club.* May 1, 2009.
Travers, Peter. *Rolling Stone.* April 30, 2009.
Uhlich, Keith. *Time Out New York.* April 30, 2009.

QUOTES

Blonde: "Are you interested in films, by any chance? I like really old films. You can really see what the world looked like, thirty, fifty, a hundred years ago. You know the clothes, the telephones, the trains, the way people smoked cigarettes, the little details of life. The best films are like dreams you're never sure you've really had. I have this image in my head of a room full of sand. And a bird flies towards me, and dips its wing into the sand. And I honestly have no idea whether this image came from a dream, or a film. Sometimes I like it in films when people just sit there, not saying anything."

TRIVIA

When Tilda Swinton talks about a swooping bird in a room full of sand she is referring to a scene in the Andrei Tarkovsky film *Stalker.*

THE LOSS OF A
TEARDROP DIAMOND

Tennessee Williams: An American legend is back.
—Movie tagline

Once a scribe achieves a certain level of success or celebrity, whatever unproduced manuscripts were lining the bottom of their desk drawers suddenly have new cachet. The same is doubly true once a writer passes away, as something like the adaptation of Hunter S. Thompson's *The Rum Diary* (2010) proves, having sat around unpublished as a novel for over three decades, and then another half-dozen years in book form until his self-inflicted death in 2005 kick-started plans for a film version. Sometimes, though, there is a good reason said material had been either rejected by publishers, or shelved by its creator.

Such is the case with *The Loss of a Teardrop Diamond,* based on a recently rediscovered original screenplay penned by legendary writer Tennessee Williams at the height of his late-1950s heyday. The feature directorial debut of actress Jodie Markell, the film is a dispiritingly literal-minded, class-based relationship drama (even its title is derisorily straightforward, as its commotion hinges chiefly an expensive, vanished clasp earring) in which any and all subtext is dragged up to a textual level, and delivered with a pinched gusto that is at first curious and then eventually embarrassing.

Set in the early 1920s in Williams' hometown of Memphis, the film tells the story of Fisher Willow (Bryce Dallas Howard), a debutante partially ostracized and looked down upon owing to her father's unintentional destruction of a Mississippi River levee the year prior. A headstrong only child who chafes under the constraints of proper Southern society, Fisher is the heiress to two fortunes, including that of her controlling aunt, Cornelia (Ann-Margret). Fisher is also practical-minded too, mindful of the need (or perhaps just married to the ritual) of keeping up appearances on the party circuit. She rebels in kind by asking the impoverished but handsome Jimmy Dobyne (Chris Evans) to escort her to a handful of the major social events of the season. Though he is the namesake grandson of a former governor, Jim-

my's father (Will Patton) is a hopeless drunk and his mother (Barbara Garrick) institutionalized and near-catatonic, which marks him as decidedly from the wrong sides of the tracks. Their relationship is purely a business arrangement at the outset, with Fisher paying for Jimmy's clothes and time, but she soon discovers she might have deeper feelings for him.

After this set-up, the bulk of the movie unfolds at a tony Halloween party thrown by Fisher's friend Julie (Mamie Gummer), whose cousin Vinnie (Jessica Collins) has designs on Jimmy. It is here that Fisher loses one of her aunt's expensive earrings, and here that she stumbles across Addie (Ellen Burstyn), a bedridden morphine addict, in an upstairs bedroom. After misinterpreting a comment from Fisher about where her earring could have gone, Jimmy has a conniption, and insists on being strip-searched. The rest of the evening is a pas de deux with recrimination, generalized misunderstanding and misplaced feelings of hormonal connection coloring the proceedings.

Williams is widely considered the most important American playwright of the post-World War II era, and he adapted many of his best-known stage works for the big screen. *The Loss of a Teardrop Diamond,* however, is a lesser work through and through. There is unembellished and then there is the story here, in which everything resides on the surface. The movie's dialogue is ridiculously on-the-nose, and characters speak in stilted self-analyzing bromides that sometimes work in print but not on screen. "A girl who works at the cosmetics counter of Leggett's Drug Store on the side street in Memphis does not think about pride and honesty standing between her and release," says a character at one point, when confronted over the prospect of telling the truth or profiting from a found valuable. Williams also has two characters engage in a weird post-coital chat ("Like back in the car there… it took my breath away," says the girl. "Didn't you hear me gasping for breath?") as they dress, and stand directly next to the vehicle they are actually referencing. Stupid staging thus makes a poorly written scene even more awkwardly realized.

The accents, especially from Howard and Evans, are molasses-thick, and initially jarring. In an apparent nod to the project's theatrical lineage, the acting is pitched at a slightly exaggerated or heightened style; lines are frequently not so much delivered with weighted intention as much as just volume. Everyone in this movie seems agitated from the get-go, and almost every interaction seems to be a big deal. With the dramatic stakes so leveled, one quickly loses interest in the characters and their problems or feelings, and while the earrings are expensive ($10,000 for the pair), it is never the cost that drives Fisher's mania at recovering the lost one.

To match all this overt theatricality, Markell employs several low-fidelity directorial stage tricks, most notably in a sequence between Fisher and Addie in which the lights dim and ellipsoidal spotlights illuminate the characters. It is a nice moment, but illustrative of how the material would likely benefit from a stage production in lieu of the more expansive palettes that film affords. That said, cinematographer Giles Nuttgens does capture some beautiful, orange-kissed, "magic hour" landscapes in a few outdoor sequences, as well as glimpses of the sort of iconic plantation architecture (columned porticoes, trees beset with hanging moss) one associates with much of Williams' work. It is just a shame that everything else going on in *The Loss of a Teardrop Diamond* is so utterly rote and tedious. It distracts from this beauty of nature.

Brent Simon

CREDITS

Fisher Willow: Bryce Dallas Howard
Jimmy Dobyne: Chris Evans
Miss Addie: Ellen Burstyn
Julie: Mamie Gummer
Cornelia: Ann-Margret
Mr. Dobyne: Will Patton
Mr. Van Hooven: Peter Gerety
Vinnie: Jessica Collins
Origin: USA
Language: English
Released: 2008
Production: Brad M. Gilbert; Constellation Films; released by Paladin Productions
Directed by: Jodie Markell
Written by: Tennessee Williams
Cinematography by: Giles Nuttgens
Music by: Mark Orton
Sound: Robert Fernandez
Music Supervisor: Joe Mulherin
Editing: Susan E. Morse
Art Direction: David Stein
Costumes: Chris Karvonides-Dushenko
Production Design: Richard Hoover
MPAA rating: PG-13
Running time: 102 minutes

REVIEWS

Anderson, Melissa. *Village Voice*. December 30, 2009.
Duralde, Alonso. *IFC.com*. December 30, 2009.
Ebert, Roger. *Chicago Sun-Times*. January 7, 2010.
LaSalle, Mick. *San Francisco Chronicle*. January 7, 2010.
Lumenick, Lou. *New York Post*. December 30, 2009.
Reed, Rex. *New York Observer*. December 22, 2009.
Schwarzbaum, Lisa. *Entertainment Weekly*. December 31, 2009.
Smithey, Cole. *ColeSmithey.com*. December 27, 2009.
Tallerico, Brian. *MovieRetriever.com*. January 8, 2010.
Weber, Bill. *Slant Magazine*. December 27, 2009.

LOVE HAPPENS
(Brand New Day)

Sometimes when you least expect it...
—Movie tagline

Box Office: $23 million

The title of Brandon Camp's directorial debut was changed from *Brand New Day* to *Love Happens* in order to help sell it as a "romantic drama," a marketing move that involved about as much candor as the production's pretender of a protagonist. While it is not hard to accept the trailer's assertion that "Sometimes when you least expect it, love happens," it is exceedingly difficult to detect that it ever happens in this film. The type of movie this was intended to be should have the power to make hearts flutter and race, but *Love Happens* is itself devoid of a pulse. The same amount of chemistry occurs between the leads as takes place in a laboratory with non-functioning Bunsen burners. Made on an estimated budget of $18 million, the film was able to gross over $22 million. It was widely panned by critics.

Love Happens is actually about a self-help guru who writes books about being "A-Okay!" but is far from it himself. A fetching florist—only on the scene as a rather cursory catalyst—imparts life-altering wisdom like "Give yourself a break." One might say that both the film and the characters' connection are decidedly-dull affairs, except that the latter never develops into anything one can rightfully call an "affair." The truth is that the proceedings are leadenly dreary rather than dreamy, perhaps calling for hankies but devoid of anything close to amorous hanky-panky.

Widowed Dr. Burke Ryan (Aaron Eckhart) may be selling thousands of psychobabbling books about proceeding with life after immobilizing loss, but it is made clear from the outset that the audience should not buy his act. The first shots of the film show the preparation of Vodka with a lemon twist, yet soon after Burke claims to abstain. He urges people to confront their crippling fears, even though he takes the stairs to avoid elevators. Before making a beaming, energetic entrance into the hotel conference room packed with fanatical fans counting on him to cure their woes, he appears downcast, tense and tentative out in the hallway. Still,

Burke does not come off as just another slick hypocrite, soullessly capitalizing on his wife's death three years prior in a car accident in order to build a lucrative media empire. The divergence between what he advocates and what he does himself is not the result of deviousness: this huckster is hurting. Burke seems genuine in his desire to bolster others so they can succeed where he has so far failed, helping them to rise above what continues to weigh him down.

Burke's sincerity is particularly established in his persistent, patient, empathetically gentle handling of grudging seminar attendee Walter (John Carroll Lynch), who has been steeped in and stopped by a bitter blend of rage, grief and guilt since the death of his young son. (Lynch's potent, affecting performance is unquestionably the film's most memorable.) Also, when agent and friend Lane (Dan Fogler) speaks of the Lear Jet and other tony benefits that will result from an impending deal making the motivational author a multi-millionaire megastar, Burke's grounded response is telling: "You know that's not why I wrote it." Finally, when a calorie-reduction plan is pitched as a merchandizing tie-in to the potentially lucrative contract, featuring the appallingly-callous slogan of "Finally—a loss you can feel good about," Burke honorably sees red instead of envisioning all the green that he could rake in. As the overall deal gets closer to being finalized, it is clear that Burke is gnawed at by a sense of unworthiness, understandably feeling like a fraud.

Psychotherapist heal thyself, or, in this case, be sure to bump into a woman who, like Burke himself, is somehow able to mend others despite being messed-up herself. Unfortunately, Eloise Chandler (Jennifer Aniston) is an insubstantial, sketchily-defined character; all the audience learns about her are through briefly-rendered tidbits. Viewers are cursorily clued into the fact that this woman who "finally got up the courage" to open her own flower shop has had a knack for choosing the loveliest of blooms and the most two-timing of boyfriends. Eloise also scrawls obscure words behind the hotel's hallway paintings, a penchant that is supposed to be intriguingly quirky but is simply inexplicable and thoroughly odd. (Should she have been arrested for this vandalism, the film would probably have had her plead not guilty by reason of whimsy.) Then there is the brief, wholly-extraneous interlude that introduces her mother (Frances Conroy) and mentions the woman's alcoholism, a scene that is surely a surviving snippet of something more extensive that landed on the cutting-room floor. That is about it for nebulous Eloise, unfortunately surpassed in terms of vibrancy by her own bouquets.

Despite publicity photos that showed Burke and Eloise in a sunlit, smiling embrace, she is simply trotted in to give the man a nudge toward his eventual, predict-able recovery, a fairly muted facilitator to help him get back on his feet rather than a vivacious love partner who palpably knocks him off of them. There is supposedly love in the air, but even when the two rise high up into it within the cozy confines of a telephone truck's repair bucket, one may detect appreciation but never burgeoning passion. There is not even a first kiss until just before the final credits, after which Burke and Eloise are "interested in getting to know" one another. Good for them, but viewers were far more likely to yawn than sigh contentedly.

The climactic, watershed scene of *Love Happens* is profoundly lachrymose and schmaltzy amidst soaring music, featuring Walter and the others supportively standing up one-by-one after Burke breaks down. The author unites in a mutually healing hug with his previously estranged father-in-law (Martin Sheen), who had earlier shown up at the seminar to forlornly and resentfully spit out the word hypocrite. Resentment is certainly a good word for what more than a few moviegoers felt toward the deceptive ad campaign for this film. Perhaps those responsible for it should have first been forced to hold some of those truth candles from Burke's seminar.

David L. Boxerbaum

CREDITS

Eloise: Jennifer Aniston
Burke Ryan: Aaron Eckhart
Burke's Father-in-Law: Martin Sheen
Marty: Judy Greer
Jessica: Sasha Alexander
Walter: John Carroll Lynch
Origin: USA
Language: English
Released: 2009
Production: Mary Parent, Scott Stuber, Mike Thompson; Universal Pictures, Relativity Media, Stuber Productions, Scion Films; released by Universal Pictures
Directed by: Brandon Camp
Written by: Brandon Camp, Mike Thompson
Cinematography by: Eric Alan Edwards
Music by: Christopher Young
Editing: Dana E. Glauberman
Sound: Richard Dwan, Jr.
Costumes: Trish Keating
Production Design: Sharon Seymour
MPAA rating: PG-13
Running time: 109 minutes

REVIEWS

Abele, Robert. *Los Angeles Times.* September 17, 2009.
Farber, Stephen. *Hollywood Reporter.* September 17, 2009.

Holden, Stephen. *New York Times.* September 18, 2009.
Lemire, Christy. *Associated Press.* September 17, 2009.
Lowry, Brian. *Variety.* September 17, 2009.
Moore, Roger. *Orlando Sentinel.* September 16, 2009.
Pols, Mary F. *Time Magazine.* September 18, 2009.
Puig, Claudia. *USA Today.* September 17, 2009.
Rickey, Carrie. *Philadelphia Inquirer.* September 18, 2009.
Simon, Brent. *Screen International.* September 17, 2009.

QUOTES

Burke: "I happen to know a thing or two about people. You get approached a lot. Probably have since the day you strapped on your first training bra. But you're smart, and you're creative, and you're caring and big…but, how come the guys only see the package it comes in, sure…you're flattered. But ultimately, ultimately it's tiresome because it has nothing to do with you. You were born that way, you can't take credit for it. Your insides though, that's yours. That's what you want someone to truly see. Even a stranger. Ergo…you fake a handicap. Rather than to have a conversation with a fellow human being. You prefer sign language? Fine. (shows middle finger)"

THE LOVELY BONES

The story of a life and everything that came after.
—Movie tagline

Box Office: $44 million

Peter Jackson's highly anticipated adaptation of Alice Sebold's *The Lovely Bones* features such an array of styles and complex themes that the ambition of the piece can make some awkward and ill-advised filmmaking decisions easier to overlook. When Jackson (and co-writers Fran Walsh & Phillipa Boyens) stay thematically focused, their talented cast and skilled technical team work together to produce moments of emotional power, but the story too often gets cluttered with varying styles and divergent tones that undermine the narrative thrust of the overall piece. For every element of *The Lovely Bones* that clicks beautifully into place, the film also strikes a note that seems out of tune. Successful elements like excellent lead work, a memorable visual, an emotionally powerful sequence, and an amazing score are undercut by a weak supporting performance, a few ill-conceived concepts, abrupt tone changes, and underdeveloped subplots. *The Lovely Bones* has too many moments that work to dismiss it entirely, but it equally has too many moments that do not connect to be considered the artistic triumph that many hoped it would be.

Set in Norristown, Pennsylvania, in 1973, the film opens with 14-year-old narrator Susie Salmon (Saoirse Ronan) talking about her murder. There is no question about her death or her killer. Sebold's tale is not a mystery or a thriller as much as a piece about the emotional devastation that surrounds one of the most painful things in the world—the loss of a child. Susie is a beautiful, confident, intelligent young girl right on the cusp of becoming a woman, falling in love with a fellow student and gaining independence as teenagers do. Before she can follow the path that millions of teenagers take, Susie is murdered by George Harvey (Stanley Tucci), a neighbor who is eventually revealed as a serial killer. The film makes clear to the audience that Susie has been murdered, but to the world around her, she simply does not come home from school one day, her hat found in a pile of debris in a cornfield with too much blood nearby to make anyone comfortable.

Susie leaves behind a younger brother named Buckley (Christian Thomas Ashdale), an older sister named Lindsay (Rose McIver), and two grieving parents, Abigail (Rachel Weisz) and Jack (Mark Wahlberg). Abigail becomes emotionally distant, leaving Susie's room untouched as a shrine in the middle of their house. On the other hand, Jack turns borderline obsessive, trying to solve the disappearance himself while he slowly develops Susie's recently shot photographs, in an attempt to keep his daughter's memory alive. The disconnect between Abigail and Jack's response is never fully developed, even though it leads to the couple splitting up. Susie's mother leaves their home for a large portion of the film, forcing Grandma Lyn (Susan Sarandon) to move in and drunkenly assist in the child-rearing. As one would imagine the murder of a child would do, Susie's death tears the Salmon family to pieces.

But Susie is not traditionally dead. She exists in what her brother refers to as "the in-between," a place that is not quite heaven and not quite hell. In this fantasy world, Susie makes a friend named Holly (Nikki SooHoo) and tries to reach out to her father from the great beyond, all while her murderer continues to go about his daily life, far from the clutches of law enforcement. Eventually, Susie figures out how to move on to the next step of the afterlife, and her family comes to terms with their grief, as much as one can after such a horrible loss.

The first act of *The Lovely Bones* is a strikingly moving coming-of-age piece with spectacular work from Ronan, tinged with the awareness that her happy family life will be short-lived. When Susie passes away and Jackson is forced to balance mystery, melodrama, fantasy, and thriller elements at the same time—while also juggling multiple emotional arcs in a story that spans years—the piece gets away from him. The small moments of the film, like an incredibly powerful scene between Tucci and Wahlberg as the father becomes suspicious and the killer becomes a bit aware of said suspicion, or nearly every emotional beat that Ronan is asked to hit, are easily the most effective. Tucci is spectacular throughout and earned the most acclaim for the film—a performance buoyed by the exact tonal opposite from the actor earlier in the year in *Julie & Julia*. Rather than turn his serial killer into a cliché, Tucci finds realism in the creepiness, resulting in a character who feels more believable than most of his co-stars. It is his smaller decisions and many similar ones made by Ronan, proving as she did in *Atonement* (2007) that she is a young performer to watch, that carry the film over its many bumpy patches.

It is the larger beats of the film that Jackson and his team either mismanage, ignore entirely, or tragically overplay. Wahlberg and Weisz's relationship is woefully underdeveloped, resulting in an emotionally stagnant resolution to their arcs. Sarandon's Lyn seems to be comic relief in a film that would have been stronger without it. Even the in-between feels minimally conceived as if Jackson did not want to go "too fantasy" and instead ended up with something that looks a bit too much like a Brian Eno music video (the legendary rock producer composed the memorable score).

A film that was suffering from a surfeit of awkward tone changes rendering it emotionally ineffective goes completely haywire during a third act sequence in a corn field, in which the power of the storytelling—what the characters are actually doing—is undermined by one too many poor style decisions. From here, the film loses any emotional urgency it had left, producing very little concern as to if Susie's murder will be solved, when she will move on from the great unknown, how/if her family's wounds will be healed, etc. While the movie has its ups and downs in the first two acts, the final act is filled with so many moments that ring false that it collapses. A disturbing sequence that reveals that Mr. Harvey had killed before Susie is too stylish to have emotional strength, a scene involving a piece of evidence that would point to Susie's killer is woefully mishandled, and the resolution of Susie's arc is dragged out to the point of exhaustion. Only the capper to the story of George Harvey provides any sort of emotional catharsis.

Sebold's book clearly struck a nerve with readers who found strength and emotional weight in its themes of loss, family, and the life-changing effect of grief. So many ideas and plots in such an emotionally dense story clearly would have presented a challenge to any filmmaker, but one has to wonder if Jackson was the right choice in the first place. He has proven himself to be such a technically proficient director and everyone around him surely had such high expectations for his first film since his Best Picture winner, that the pressure to produce a worthy follow-up that had so much pre-release baggage and thematic depth resulted in a work with surprisingly little to remember after the credits roll.

Brian Tallerico

CREDITS

Susie Salmon: Saoirse Ronan
Jack Salmon: Mark Wahlberg
Abigail Salmon: Rachel Weisz
George Harvey: Stanley Tucci
Grandma Lynn: Susan Sarandon
Len Feneman: Michael Imperioli
Lindsay Salmon: Rose McIver
Ruth: Carolyn Dando
Origin: USA
Language: English
Released: 2009
Production: Carolynne Cunningham, Peter Jackson, Aímée Peyronnet, Fran Walsh; Wing Nut Films, DreamWorks SKG, Fim4, Key Creatives; released by DreamWorks SKG and Paramount
Directed by: Peter Jackson
Written by: Peter Jackson, Fran Walsh, Philippa Boyens
Cinematography by: Andrew Lesnie
Editing: Jabez Olssen
Sound: Brent Burge, Chris Ward
Costumes: Nancy Steiner
Production Design: Naomi Shohan
MPAA rating: PG-13
Running time: 139 minutes

REVIEWS

Adams, Thelma. *Us Weekly.* December 9, 2009.
Ansen, David. *Newsweek.* December 4, 2009.
Corliss, Richard. *Time Magazine.* November 24, 2009.
Denby, David. *New Yorker.* December 7, 2009.
Germain, David. *Associated Press.* December 9, 2009.
Hoberman, J. *Village Voice.* December 8, 2009.
Honeycutt, Kirk. *Hollywood Reporter.* November 24, 2009.
McCarthy, Todd. *Variety.* November 24, 2009.
Stevens, Dana. *Slate.* December 10, 2009.
Turan, Kenneth. *Los Angeles Times.* December 11, 2009.

QUOTES

Susie Salmon (from the trailer): "My name is Salmon, like the fish. First name, Susie. I was fourteen years old when I was murdered on December 6, 1973. I wasn't gone. I was alive in my own perfect world. But in my heart, I knew it wasn't perfect. My murderer still haunted me. My father had the pieces but he couldn't make them fit. I waited for justice but justice did not come."

TRIVIA

Mark Wahlberg replaced Ryan Gosling just days before shooting began. In preparation for the role, Gosling had gained 20 pounds and grew out a beard. However, he vacated the role due to creative differences. Wahlberg, who had just completed shooting *The Happening,* another production in Pennsylvania, became available just in time to accept Gosling's role.

AWARDS

Nomination:

Oscars 2009: Support. Actor (Tucci)
British Acad. 2009: Actress (Ronan), Support. Actor (Tucci)
Golden Globes 2010: Support. Actor (Tucci)
Screen Actors Guild 2009: Support. Actor (Tucci).

LYMELIFE

> *The American dream sucks.*
> —Movie tagline

Lymelife is a pleasant surprise: a low-budget, coming-of-age-in-suburbia story that seems at first glance to be derivative of many other films, but in fact is uniquely perceptive, poignant, and punchy. Directed by first-timer Derick Martini from a script he wrote with his brother Steven, it's an unsparing-yet-sympathetic look at growing up on Long Island in the late 1970s, at a time when Lyme disease provided the scare of the moment. Despite the unfortunate title, it's really not about Lyme disease, but about other destructive forces that assault the fictional Bartlett and Bragg families.

Derick Martini was not even born until 1975, so if there's autobiographical material here, as there's said to be, he's transported it to another era. (That might account for the occasional anachronistic songs in the otherwise canny soundtrack.) The themes are universal, swirling around teenager Scott Bartlett's uneasy confrontations about unpleasant truths. (It's also not clear why Scott [Rory Culkin] is supposedly fifteen in the movie, yet he's only now undergoing Catholic Confirmation, which usually happens at age thirteen.)

When the movie opens, Scott admires his father Mickey (Alec Baldwin), an ambitious real estate developer, and thinks his mother Brenda (Jill Hennessy) is crazy; she drinks too much and has lost his respect. He's shocked when he discovers that his dad is a cad; he's been sleeping with his employee, Melissa Bragg (Cynthia Nixon). Both of them are taking advantage of the debilitation that has beset her husband Charlie (Timothy Hutton, in an outstanding performance worthy of an Oscar® nomination), who does have Lyme disease. The free-floating danger of the disease looms as something of an existential threat; when a tick is found on Scott's neck, you suspect he may develop the illness as well, but the movie does not go in that direction. In a

fantastic later scene, when Charlie obliquely confronts Mickey in a barroom, he asks him if he's ever thought how his life would have changed had the tick bit him instead while they were side by side, hunting together. It's a thoughtful question in a thoughtful but never moralistic movie.

Lymelife is a completely believable account of adolescent disillusionment, unflinchingly told. When Scott's older brother, Jimmy (Kieran Culkin), comes roaring home on a short leave from the service, the first thing he does is exact revenge on a bully who beat up Scott, and there's a raw brutality to his sudden spurt of violence. Both Culkins do an admirable job of summoning up adolescent misery; Rory has a perpetual depressed grimace and stooped walk, as if he's carrying the weight of the world on his shoulders (as his character must feel he is). Kieran's bitterness and hard-earned wisdom have barely covered up his zest for life; when he confronts his father, it's a scene of barely repressed rage that rings true.

Lymelife is a treasure trove of wonderful little scenes and telling observations, even though they are sometimes clumsily connected and not always smoothly executed. One of the best is when Scott is practically dragged into bed by his longtime best friend, Adrianna (Emma Roberts), the daughter of the Braggs. Scott's awkwardness is emphasized by his reluctant wonder at what is about to happen; they fumble with clothes, and the scene is real in a way Hollywood love scenes rarely are. The brothers have several awkward moments with their mother, as well, particularly a Thanksgiving dinner gone badly awry. Perhaps the best scene is one between Baldwin and Rory Culkin, when, after being kicked out of the house, Mickey begs his son to come down from his bedroom window and spend some time with him; it's a sad and moving depiction of a father who's lost the respect of his son.

There are smaller moments as well: Scott, who rehearses lines to woo Adrianna in front of a mirror, is holding a skin magazine, and the image of the scantily clad model appears on the bed behind him, a fantasy wish-fulfillment. Martini's direction, though not always masterful, can be occasionally quite deft; several scenes play out in mirrors or car windows. He skillfully frames many shots and intriguingly mixes close-ups and longer shots to create a sort of claustrophobic world in the middle of a larger natural landscape: the perfect depiction of suburbia.

Like many other notable dramas of disintegrating families in suburbia, from *Ordinary People* (1980) to *Rachel Getting Married* (2008), *Lymelife* offers up great ensemble acting. In this film, only Nixon's character gets short shrift. Hutton is barely recognizable as a man trying to hold onto a semblance of health. He's been robbed and he's lost, but not bitter. He's compelling. Baldwin's Mickey, meanwhile, is a bully barely concealed beneath the veneer of respectability, and the movie offers two visions of flawed manhood, leaving the young Scott to find his own way among the debris of ruined lives. What really redeems *Lymelife* is its unfailing, sometimes begrudging, humor. These characters may be down, but they are gritty. And never does the film wallow in unjustified sentimentality. It is one of the best small movies of 2009.

Michael Betzold

CREDITS

Scott Bartlett: Rory Culkin
Mickey Bartlett: Alec Baldwin
Brenda Bartlett: Jill Hennessy
Jimmy Bartlett: Kieran Culkin
Adrianne Bragg: Emma Roberts
Charlie Bragg: Timothy Hutton
Melissa Bragg: Cynthia Nixon
Origin: USA
Language: English
Released: 2008
Production: Alec Baldwin, Barbara De Fina, Steven Martini, Joe Cornick, Angela Somerville, Michele Tayler; Bartlett Films, Cappa De Fina Productions, El Dorado Pictures; released by Screen Media
Directed by: Derick Martini
Written by: Derick Martini, Steven Martini
Cinematography by: Frank Goodwin
Music by: Derick Martini, Steven Martini
Sound: Richard Murphy, Lukasz Singh
Editing: Derick Martini, Steven Martini, Mark Yoshikawa
Art Direction: Matt Munn
Costumes: Erika Munro
Production Design: Kelly McGehee
MPAA rating: R
Running time: 95 minutes

REVIEWS

Anderson, John. *Newsday.* April 9, 2009.
Berkshire, Geoff. *Metromix.com.* April 9, 2009.
Dargis, Manohla. *New York Times.* April 8, 2009.
Ebert, Roger. *Chicago Sun-Times.* April 30, 2009.
Foundas, Scott. *Village Voice.* April 8, 2009.
Nelson, Rob. *Variety.* April 6, 2009.
Ordona, Michael. *Las Angeles Times.* April 17, 2009.
Sarris, Andrew. *New York Observer.* April 8, 2009.
Tallerico, Brian. *MovieRetriever.com.* May 1, 2009.
Travers, Peter. *Rolling Stone.* April 2, 2009.

QUOTES

Mickey Bartlett: "So you're telling me you weren't happy on your wedding day either?"

TRIVIA

While the film was being developed at the Sundance filmmaker's lab, Kieran Culkin played the role of Scott in all of the experimental scenes the Martinis shot. When it came time to make the film for real, Kieran's younger brother, Rory Culkin was offered the role because Kieran had become too old to play it. After reading the script and watching the experimental scenes from the lab, Rory said yes.

M

MADEA GOES TO JAIL
(Tyler Perry's Madea Goes
to Jail)

Mother. Sister. Grandma. Gangster.
    —Movie tagline

Box Office: $90.5 million

Since 2006, Tyler Perry has written, produced, directed and occasionally acted in an average of two feature films a year—not to mention the fact that he also fills many of the same capacities on two syndicated television shows that he currently has running as well—and to judge by his IMDB listing, it does not appear that he will be slowing down anytime soon. This is an astonishing workload—he almost makes Steven Soderbergh seem like Terrence Malick by comparison in terms of productivity—and so one would think that the sheer amount of on-the-job training that Perry has been getting as a result would have led to improvements in his skills as a filmmaker. Alas, based on the evidence of *Madea Goes to Jail*, his latest work and the first to feature his inexplicably popular Madea character (a tough-talking, gun-toting old lady that he plays in painfully unconvincing drag) since *Madea's Family Reunion* (2006), those skills have not only *not* improved over time, they seem to have actually atrophied to the artistic level of a film student during his very first day of class.

In Perry's latest comedy, up-and-coming assistant District Attorney Joshua Hardaway (Derek Luke) is revisited by a guilt-inducing ghost from his past when he is asked to defend former friend and current crack whore Candy (Keisha Knight Pulliam) in court. Because

he feels responsible for the sad turn that her life has taken, he asks his colleague/fiancee (Ion Overman) to handle Candy's legal case while he does what he can to help her turn her life around. Alas, the fiancée is a jealous and conniving woman and instead arranges to land Candy in the slammer for 17 years on a variety of trumped-up charges. Meanwhile, in what feels like another movie (although not necessarily a better one), Madea (Perry) is in legal hot water of her own after a high-speed police pursuit. While she manages to stay out of the stir thanks to the cops forgetting to read her the Miranda Rights, she is ordered to undergo anger management therapy. Of course, this does not work—possibly because her therapist is none other than Dr. Phil (in a scene that plays like what a middling Marx Brothers routine might have been like if all the parts had been played by Zeppo)—and, after trashing a car in a K-Mart parking lot when the driver (naturally a nasty white woman) steals her space, she winds up in jail as well. There, she befriends Candy and defends her from attacks from the bull dyke in charge (naturally a nasty white woman who sounds like a man) while Joshua tries to find a way to free her from both prison and her current life for good.

Like Perry's previous efforts, *Madea Goes to Jail* offers viewers an unruly combination of over-the-top melodrama and over-the-top broad comedy topped off with remarkably unsubtle moments of Christian proselytizing. Such rapid shifts in tone would challenge even the most gifted filmmakers and Perry is once again unable to successfully reconcile them—the two storylines do not so much intertwine as they smash into each other head-on leaving no survivors. In fact, the connection between the two narratives is so tenuous that while the Madea portion of the film was the one to get most of the promotional hype (it is the only aspect that is discussed on the DVD box), the entire thing could have been excised without causing a single story hiccup. (Despite the promise of the title and the advertising, Madea doesn't even wind up in prison until the movie is more than half over.) Unfortunately, even if this had been done, it would have only made the film shorter instead of better because the dramatic stuff is just as badly written, staged, and executed as everything else. Like Perry's other projects, this was originally a stage production and in many ways, it still feels like one. Most of the actors are still overplaying to the people in the cheap seats and many scenes are allowed to ramble on and on, a move that can work when the actors are playing off of the response of a live audience but not so within a cinematic context. The only things about the film that actually don't hurt too much when you think about them are the performances from Pulliam and Viola Davis as a social worker trying to get Candy and her ilk off the streets. Both are quite good in what are fairly hackneyed roles but that only suggests that not even someone as all thumbs as Perry could screw up their work.

If Tyler Perry were just another cheap huckster trying to make a quick buck by exploiting a criminally underserved audience with a bag of shoddy goods, a film like *Madea Goes to Jail* would not be so aggravating. The thing is, Perry seems completely sincere in regards to the messages that he is trying to convey to his viewers (especially in comparison to the cynical copycat films that have sprung up in his wake) and in his desire to please his viewers by giving them a formula that he knows will please them. The problem is that by refusing to even attempt to step up his game by either trying to do something new or to do the old stuff better, he is doing a grave disservice to himself and his audience.

Madea Goes to Jail is an embarrassment but it is difficult to determine who should be more embarrassed—Perry for foisting something so lazy onto an audience that will cheerfully watch anything he offers at this point or the audience for blindly accepting it instead of demanding something better.

Peter Sobczynski

CREDITS

Candace Washington: Keisha Knight Pulliam
Madea/Joel/Brian: Tyler Perry
Joshua Hardaway: Derek Luke
Donna: Vanessa Ferlito
Chuck: RonReaco Lee

Linda Holmes: Ion Overman
Ellen: Viola Davis
Brown: David Mann
Cora: Tamela Mann
Origin: USA
Language: English
Released: 2009
Production: Tyler Perry, Reuben Cannon; Tyler Perry Studios; released by Lionsgate
Directed by: Tyler Perry
Written by: Tyler Perry
Cinematography by: Alexander Grusynski
Music by: Aaron Zigman
Sound: Shirley Libby
Music Supervisor: Joel High
Editing: Maysie Hoy
Art Direction: Mark Erbaugh, Roswell Hamrick
Costumes: Keith Lewis
Production Design: Ina Mayhew
MPAA rating: PG-13
Running time: 103 minutes

REVIEWS

Adams, Sam. *Los Angeles Times.* February 23, 2009.
Anderson, Melissa. *Village Voice.* February 25, 2009.
Berkshire, Geoff. *Metromix.com.* February 20, 2009.
Gleiberman, Owen. *Entertainment Weekly.* February 23, 2009.
Honeycutt, Kirk. *Hollywood Reporter.* February 23, 2009.
Jones, J.R. *Chicago Reader.* February 23, 2009.
Leydon, Joe. *Variety.* February 23, 2009.
Morris, Wesley. *Boston Globe.* February 23, 2009.
Scott, A.O. *New York Times.* February 23, 2009.
Zacharek, Stephanie. *Salon.com.* February 23, 2009.

QUOTES

Madea: "Put the shut, to the up. Okay? Shut to the up."

THE MAID
(La nana)

She's more or less family.
—Movie tagline

The cultural conflict of the comedy *The Maid* could easily be remade into an absolutely horrible American vehicle. The plot reads like a September release that would star a Jessica (Alba, Biel, Simpson) and probably feature Jason Biggs in a supporting role, but the wacky remake would almost certainly miss the humanity that makes the first film so effective (as they usually do). The set-up and synopsis of *The Maid* could easily play like a quirky sitcom, but writer/director Sebastian Silva wisely focuses on character instead of caricature, resulting in a semi-comedy that is ultimately moving but the time it reaches its bittersweet final act. Garnering rave reviews, critic's awards, and further nominations, the success of *The Maid* makes it inevitable that a potential remake will be brought up at a production meeting in the near future if it has not happened already (with character-based foreign film remakes *Everybody's Fine* and *Brothers* in theaters near the end of 2009 as examples, a foreign film this acclaimed seems unlikely to avoid becoming part of the machine). This version of *The Maid* is slightly overrated and falls short of perfection but Silva avoids so many of the pitfalls of his concept that a remake is simply too risky an idea.

A large reason that Silva's film works and the element most likely to be derailed during an American remake is the emotional tightrope walked in the performance by Catalina Saavedra as the title character, Raquel. *The Maid* opens on her birthday, as she sits in what looks like common solitude, even as the family for which she has been working most of her life tries to drag her into something of a celebration. Silva and Saavedra immediately convey the odd mix of sadness and pride that comes with a lifetime of servitude accompanied by the fact that this woman may not even have the conscious awareness that she may have lost something by giving everything to a family other than her own. But Raquel considers this family her own. They may not be blood, but they are hers. And nothing, not health nor a potential replacement, is going to take them away from her. She has watched the children grown up and managed her employer's flights of shopping fancy for more than two decades, but as the children have gone from cute to pubescent, her job has become increasingly difficult. Raquel is starting to snap under the pressure, managing migraine headaches, exhaustion, and the occasional miscommunication with children who have started to taking her for granted (if they have not always done so). The family brings in some help in the form of another maid and Raquel sees this as an advance on her territory, a potential replacement more than merely a helping hand. Raquel reacts. She sabotages each new employee—locking them out of the house, letting the cat out so the new girl will be blamed, etc. Raquel is losing it, both mentally and physically, until the hiring of Camila (Andrea Garcia-Huidobro) really changes her life by reminding her what she's been missing.

For two acts, *The Maid* often plays as a broad comedy. Saavedra is compelling and consistent, but the film verges on the edge of being a bit too slight and simple for more than half of its running time. Silva's script also walks a very fine line with Raquel's behavior.

If Raquel had driven one more maid to quit without repercussion, *The Maid* would have lost its heroine by turning her into too much of an anti-hero. The film progresses from something of a diary of a madwoman to the one that earned nominations and rave reviews around the world with the arrival of Camila in the final act. Silva makes a left turn by hiring a real friend for Raquel, exposing a sad truth of life that is basically live in servitude. Raquel does not know her mother, has no idea about love or sex, and looks like she can barely breathe outside of her little room in the back of the house. She works through exhaustion and sabotages those who move in on her turf because, as the final act reveals, she seems almost to fear survival outside of the world she knows. She might not survive in the real world. Can anyone blame her for fighting to keep her own from falling apart?

The final twenty minutes of *The Maid* is some of the most interesting and confident of the year and the film would have been stronger overall with more of it and less of the wacky comedy of the first half. Locking out a maid while she has something in the oven is borderline sociopathic and it is hard to root for a character who behaves so erratically. But, ultimately, Silva is not necessarily asking viewers to root for Raquel. He is asking them to take a second look and realize the choices people like her make every day—to give so much while taking so little.

Brian Tallerico

CREDITS

Raquel: Catalina Saavedra
Pilar: Cladia Celedon
Lucy: Mariana Loyola
Mundo Valdes: Alejandro Goic
Sonia: Delfina Guzman
Camila: Andrea Garcia-Huidobro
Lucas: Augustin Silva
Origin: Chile, Mexico
Language: Spanish
Released: 2009
Production: Gregorio González; Forastero, Tiburón Filmes, Punto Guion Punto Producciones; released by Elephant Eye Films
Directed by: Sebastian Silva
Written by: Sebastian Silva, Pedro Peirano
Cinematography by: Sergio Armstrong
Sound: Raul Sotomayor
Music supervisor: Ruy Garcia
Costumes: Francisca Román
Editing: Danielle Fillios

Art Direction: Pablo González
MPAA rating: Unrated
Running time: 96 minutes

REVIEWS

Berkshire, Geoff. *Metromix.com.* October 15, 2009.

Dargis, Manohla. *New York Times.* October 15, 2009.

Edelstein, David. *New York Magazine.* October 12, 2009.

Murray, Noel. *AV Club.* October 15, 2009.

Musetto, V.A. *New York Post.* October 16, 2009.

Phillips, Michael. *Chicago Tribune.* December 3, 2009.

Schager, Nick. *Slant Magazine.* March 30, 2009.

Schwarzbaum, Lisa. *Entertainment Weekly.* October 14, 2009.

Stevens, Dana. *Slate.* October 16, 2009.

Turan, Kenneth. *Los Angeles Times.* October 23, 2009.

AWARDS

Nomination:

Golden Globes 2010: Foreign Film
Ind. Spirit 2010: Foreign Film.

MAMMOTH

Mammoth is the latest example of one of the most tiresome cinematic subgenres to emerge in the last decade or so—the sprawling multi-storyline narrative that introduces viewers to a number of seemingly disparate characters from wildly different social, economic, racial and geographical backgrounds and then illustrates the myriad ways in which they affect each other's lives in unexpected ways, usually through the advent of one unlikely screenplay development after another. While it may not be as flat-out awful as such similar films as *Crash* (2005), *Babel* (2006) or *The Burning Plain* (2009), it is arguably the most disappointing of the bunch simply because of its pedigree. This is the first English-language film from Swedish writer-director Lukas Moodysson, who made one of the stronger debuts in recent years with his electrifying coming-of-age comedy-drama *Show Me Love* (1998) and whose subsequent career, ranging from straightforward dramas like *Together* (2000)and *Lilya 4-Ever* (2002) to edgy experimental work like *A Hole in My Heart* (2004) have shown him to be a filmmaker willing to take chances even if they do not always pay off in the end. Unfortunately, that willingness to take chance is nowhere on display here as Moodysson has instead chosen to present a muddled, cloying, and obvious melodrama.

Moodysson's conceit is to show us three different sets of parents, all of whom wind up connecting with each other, who are so consumed with making enough money through their work to provide for their families that they barely get to see their children as a result. First up is well-to-do New York City couple Leo (Gael Garcia Bernal) and Ellen (Michelle Williams). He is a hugely successful website designer who is off to Thailand to sign a deal that will make him immensely wealthy and she is a surgeon who spends long hours in the hospital saving the lives of strangers. As a result, the care and raising of their young daughter has been placed in the hands of Filipino nanny Gloria (Marife Necesito) and she does such a good job of it that even when Ellen is around to spend time with her child, she resentfully notices that the kid would rather be with Gloria. Gloria has two sons of her own back in the Philippines that she is unable to see and during her phone calls home to them, they inevitably lay guilt trips on her in the hopes that she will eventually come home. When their grandmother tries to explain that she is off making money to make their lives better, the older boy takes it upon himself to find a job that will allow her to come home for good and through a tragic turn of events, he manages to do just that.

Meanwhile, Leo's negotiations in Thailand have mysteriously bogged down and he takes off to a remote village where he makes the acquaintance of Cookie (Natthamonkarn Srinikornchot), an incredibly friendly local prostitute who, naturally, is hooking in order to provide for her own child who is being cared for by her family. At first, Leo does not sleep with her—he even makes the grand gesture of paying her not to sleep with anyone for the night—but eventually he succumbs to her charms and begins idly speculating about leaving the rat race behind and starting a new life before eventually coming to his senses and returning to his normal life none the worse for wear.

The notion of exploring globalism through the impact that it has on varying family units is an interesting one but it quickly becomes evident that Moodysson does not really have much of anything to say about it that goes beyond what one might find in an entry-level magazine article on the subject. As soon as he sets up the characters and their varying circumstances, he simply refuses to explore them in depth in the way that one might if they actually had a genuine interest in the subject. Instead, he is far more content to jam in as many melodramatic contrivances as possible and all that this does is highlight just how hollow and artificial everything is. (The most profound life lesson on display is the reminder that if you are a young boy in need of an explanation regarding the intricacies of the flesh trade in the Philippines, be sure not to get it from your grandmother.) Another strange mistake on Moodysson's part is his decision to put most of his focus on the travails of the American couple and most viewers are unlikely to work up that much sympathy for the comparatively minor travails of those characters. About the only smart thing that Moodysson has done here has been to resist the urge to play with the timeline in the manner of other films of this type—in this case, however, the end result is that most viewers will now be able to see exactly where the whole thing is headed much quicker than they might have with a more fractured narrative approach.

The only thing that really works in *Mammoth* is the performance by Michelle Williams as Ellen. In the last few years, she has unexpectedly developed from the *Dawson's Creek* cutie into one of the more interesting and inventive young American actresses working today thanks to her superlative work in such films as *Me and You* (2001), *Land of Plenty* (2004), *Brokeback Mountain* (2005) and *Wendy & Lucy* (2008). What is especially impressive about her work here is that she manages to take a character that is arguably the least interesting person on the page (and that says a lot) and somehow manages to transform her from a shallow portrait of walking white liberal guilt into a convincing human being—when her character sadly observes her daughter forming a closer bond with the nanny than with her, she somehow manages to make the moment feel real without getting bogged down in soap-opera shamelessness. It is a very impressive performance from a very impressive actress and it is a shame that it is not in the service of a film worthy of it.

Peter Sobczynski

CREDITS

Leo: Gael Garcia Bernal
Ellen: Michelle Williams
Bob: Thomas McCarthy
Grandmother: Maria del Carmen
Gloria: Marife Necesito
Jackie: Sophie Nyweide
Cookie: Run Srinikornchot
Salvador: Jan Nicdao
Manuel: Martin Delos Santos
Origin: Denmark, Germany, Sweden
Language: English
Released: 2009
Production: Lars Jonsson; ApS, Zentropa Entertainment; released by IFC Films
Directed by: Lukas Moodysson
Written by: Lukas Moodysson
Cinematography by: Marcel Zyskind
Music by: Jesper Kurlandsky, Linus Gierta, Erik Holmquist

Sound: Hans Moller
Editing: Michael Leszcylowski
Costumes: Denise Osthom
Production Design: Josephin Asberg
MPAA rating: Unrated
Running time: 125 minutes

REVIEWS

Anderson, Melissa. *Village Voice.* November 17, 2009.
Berkshire, Geoff. *Metromix.com.* November 20, 2009.
Dargis, Manohla. *New York Times.* November 20, 2009.
Edelstein, David. *New York Magazine.* November 23, 2009.
Lumenick, Lou. *New York Post.* November 20, 2009.
Morgenstern, Joe. *Wall Street Journal.* November 20, 2009.
Murray, Noel. *AV Club.* November 19, 2009.
Rothkopf, Joshua. *Time Out New York.* November 18, 2009.
Simon, Alissa. *Variety.* February 13, 2009.
Tallerico, Brian. *MovieRetriever.com.* November 20, 2009.

MANAGEMENT

A touching comedy.
—Movie tagline

No film in which a character's romantic pursuit reaches the level of stalking could be considered sweet, right? Indeed, *Management* could have been a forced, potentially disturbing love story with an overdose of quirk. Yet there is a very delicate sensitivity fueling the engine of this blissful film, which finds credibility in the offbeat because its characters just do not know what beat they should march to in the first place.

Like many inferior indie comedies, *Management* begins as the story of two unhappy people who make sense together but do not initially agree on that. Mike (Steve Zahn), the lonely night manager of his parents' Arizona motel, has minimal social skills and no real goals or prospects. His life perks up suddenly, however, when Sue (Jennifer Aniston), an uptight, uninspired saleswoman from Maryland, spends a couple nights in Mike's family's motel. They do not hit it off, exactly. Mike awkwardly presents her with a complimentary bottle of wine and then, the next night, a complimentary bottle of champagne, hoping to share a drink with Sue and get to know a woman he is at first too shy to talk to in the motel lobby. Sue easily detects Mike's inexperience and desperation—he pretty much wears it like a tattoo on his forehead—but she sees in him all-important good intentions, turning Mike into not a creep but a nice guy without an internal compass.

Sue's patience becomes crucial very soon. After she sleeps with Mike in the motel laundry room, she leaves without giving him her phone number or email address. Yet Mike, very worked up over his sexual encounter— this is certainly a big step up from the night before, when Sue pities him enough to let him touch her butt on the condition that he will leave her alone—buys a one-way ticket to Maryland, where he shows up at Sue's office to his delight and her horror. She wants him gone. He wants to go with her to her weekly soccer game and to distribute Burger King food vouchers to homeless people. She seems frustrated by his intrusion. He is just happy to be with her and pretty much refuses to give up until she agrees to be with him.

Clearly, Mike's behavior is enough to scare off a potential partner. The key to this relationship, and to *Management*, is Zahn's vulnerable, endearing performance that always asserts that Mike may not have a complex soul, but he has a good one. He has genuine interest in Sue and her work, and Sue, who recently got out of a relationship with an "ex-punk" named Jango (Woody Harrelson), is smart enough to recognize a decent guy when she sees one. Even if the guy is a little awkward and overeager, he has a romantic spirit and a belief in persistent, irrational love, which can be hard to turn down for anyone who believes in it too.

That balance, and the ensuing humor—which, to the film's benefit, always seems a half-second late on purpose—are a credit to writer and first-time director Stephen Belber. His script for the 2001 drama *Tape* (based on Belber's play about high school friends discussing painful memories) demonstrated a knack for writing characters who always speak from experience, even if that experience has only confused them further. In *Management* he identifies a man who needs a woman to teach him about life (Mike's parents, played by Margo Martindale and Fred Ward, are kind but not much for guidance), and a woman who needs a man to make her embrace the kind of life she deserves. Casting Aniston was risky; she has nothing if not a spotty big-screen career, with performances that have ranged from well-drawn (as in *The Good Girl* [2002]) to flat (*Marley and Me* [2008]). Aniston is very good here. Sue is more committed to her causes (such as recycling) than her work or her romantic life—when she returns to Jango midway through the film, she makes it clear her feelings for him largely rest on the security that this wealthy yogurt magnate can provide—. But Aniston offers glimpses of what Sue really wants and the notion that, deep down, she sees that Mike may supply the type of shaggy, energized happiness she is missing.

At times the film does, unfortunately, stroll lazily into overwritten silliness, such as when Jango and a fellow ex-punk cartoonishly assault Mike and demand that he leave Sue alone. Worse is when, a few scenes earlier, Mike skydives into the Sue and Jango's pool and Jango

shoots him with a BB gun. (All of this played for cuteness and laughs it does not deserve.) As for the contrived presence of Al (James Liao), a stranger who offers Mike work, a place to stay and immediate, devoted friendship, well, that pretty much speaks for itself.

Still, *Management* offers a welcome change of pace from the usual comedy, and a better grasp of love and human idiosyncrasy than most indie romances. (See *Gigantic* [2009] for an example of the opposite style, in which weirdness is used as a substitute for personality and feeling.) Sue is ready to shake up her life; she just does not know it yet. And Mike, totally unaware (or in denial) of the reasons Sue may not want to be with him, only cares about staying with the woman he loves. That is what is great about this guy: He has no idea what he is doing, but his heart makes him do it anyway.

Matt Pais

CREDITS

Sue Claussen: Jennifer Aniston
Mike Cranshaw: Steve Zahn
Jango: Woody Harrelson
Jerry Cranshaw: Fred Ward
Trish Cranshaw: Margo Martindale
Al: James Hiroyuki Liao
Origin: USA
Language: English
Released: 2009
Production: Sidney Kimmel, Wyck Godfrey, Marty Bowen; Temple Hill; released by Samuel Goldwyn Films
Directed by: Stephen Belber
Written by: Stephen Belber
Cinematography by: Eric Alan Edwards
Music by: Mychael Danna, Rob Simonsen
Sound: Glenn Micallef
Editing: Kate Sanford
Art Direction: Simon Dobbin
Costumes: Christopher Lawrence
Production Design: Judy Becker
MPAA rating: R
Running time: 93 minutes

REVIEWS

Brunette, Peter. *Hollywood Reporter.* May 12, 2009.
Ebert, Roger. *Chicago Sun-Times.* May 14, 2009.
Gronvall, Andrea. *Chicago Reader.* May 14, 2009.
Holden, Stephen. *Los Angeles Times.* May 15, 2009.
Leydon, Joe. *Variety.* May 12, 2009.
Phillips, Michael. *Chicago Tribune.* May 29, 2009.

Puig, Claudia. *USA Today.* May 14, 2009.
Sarris, Andrew. *New York Observer.* May 13, 2009.
Sharkey, Betsy. *Los Angeles Times.* May 15, 2009.
Tallerico, Brian. *MovieRetriever.com.* May 15, 2009.

QUOTES

Mike: "Take care of yourself a little...so that the people who love you don't feel like they're annoying you!"

THE MARC PEASE EXPERIENCE

Marc Pease (Jason Schwartzman) is annoying, like an itch. Eight years after running out of New Ashby High School crying before singing his big song as the Tin Man in a production of *The Wiz*, Marc is still living in the past. Despite dressing like he just played a softball game and sporting unappealing long hair, Marc, now a part-time limo driver, dates high school senior Meg (Anna Kendrick), who does not seem to like him very much. Marc also still sings with high school friends in the a cappella group Meridian 8, which has shrunk from eight people to four as Marc's bandmates have grown up and moved on. Marc is sure that he is destined for great things, and opportunity has arrived: He is going to sell his condo and finance the recording of Meridian 8's demo, which, he believes, is only the first step towards a long successful music career.

These delusions of grandeur stem from support Marc received in high school from his music teacher and theater director Jon Gribble (Ben Stiller). Then, Gribble (as Marc calls him) told Marc that Meridian 8 was one of the hottest high school a cappella groups ever and would love the opportunity to produce their demo. This, of course, was merely a teacher doing his job and trying to boost his student's confidence. The concept of a kid who cannot tell the difference between encouragement and truth could be a sweet story about the way so many teens eventually must give up their dreams and adjust to the realities of the adult world.

That is not something anyone will get out of *The Marc Pease Experience*, however. In fact, it does not seem like director Todd Louiso—who wrote the script with Jacob Koskoff—knows what he wants out of the film either. Marc learns that there has been some degree of a romantic relationship between Meg and Gribble, but Louiso underplays this to the point of incoherence. Plus, Meg's apparent frustration with and distaste for both Marc and Gribble make it hard to believe she has ever had affection for either. This love triangle seems like a mangled retread of *Rushmore* (1998) without any understanding of how anyone involved feels and why.

Many other elements fail to convince, no matter how many times Louiso tries to hammer them home. It might be reasonable to think that, in high school, an a cappella group would be overjoyed at the opportunity to record a demo and have a shot at stardom. That Marc's fellow singers, who seem to be far more well-adjusted and mature than Marc, are still deluded enough to think that in their mid 20s that this is still a life-changing opportunity is simply too far-fetched. It all plays out like group denial, which is why Gribble gets fed up when Marc finally confronts him about producing the demo. Gribble cannot believe that Marc still revolves his life around Gribble's encouragement from eight years ago, and he feels not compassion but irritation for him.

That is because Schwartzman plays Marc as a character whose delusions do not make him sympathetic, just pathetic. He is a pest, and his personality is obnoxious—while leaving a message for Gribble hinting at his impending condo sale and demo recording, Marc identifies himself as Marc "the man with the big news" Pease. If Marc were a real person, most people would not want to hang out with him or even console him. They would swat him away like a fly.

Maybe if *The Marc Pease Experience* had more detailed characters Marc, Gribble and Meg would not seem so unlikable. Yet there is little chance to get to know much about them other than their very superficial feelings about each other and singing. (The only discernible reason Meg is with Marc is that he frequently compliments her singing voice.) Thus, it is impossible to care when Meg laments that Marc does not really know who she is because viewers barely know who she is either. She merely appears to be a high school girl dating an obnoxious older man, cheating on him with an even older and not much more appealing man and not really being clear with anyone, including herself, about her feelings.

Most of the film takes place on the day leading up to Gribble's first staging in eight years of *The Wiz*, in which Meg sings in the chorus. As this, of course, reminds Marc of his own experience in the play, he sings the Tin Man's big song during Meridian 8's performance that same afternoon. Marc tries to gain closure to his legacy of failure, even as Gribble advises his cast not to repeat the actions of his departed Tin Man eight years prior. Marc is a cautionary tale who thinks he is a hero, but Louiso simultaneously suggests Marc is kidding himself while asserting that Marc does have the talent and determination to be a star. When a filmmaker is as confused as his protagonist, their movie, all seventy-nine irritating minutes of it, does not stand a chance.

Matt Pais

CREDITS

Marc Pease: Jason Schwartzman
Jon Gribble: Ben Stiller
Meg Brickman: Anna Kendrick
Gavin: Ebon Moss-Bachrach
Tracey: Gabrielle Dennis
Gerry: Jay Paulson
Origin: USA
Language: English
Released: 2009
Production: Michael London, Bruna Papandrea, David Rubin; Firefly Pictures, Groundswell Productions, Paramount Vantage; released by Paramount Vantage
Directed by: Todd Louiso
Written by: Todd Louiso, Jacob Koskoff
Cinematography by: Tim Suhrstedt
Music by: Christophe Beck
Sound: Whit Norris
Music Supervisor: Matt Sullivan, Kimberly Oliver
Editing: Julie Monroe, Peter Teschner
Costumes: Daniel Orlandi
Production Design: Maher Ahmad
MPAA rating: PG-13
Running time: 84 minutes

REVIEWS

Covert, Colin. *Minneapolis Star Tribune.* August 21, 2009.
Ebert, Roger. *Chicago Sun-Times.* August 20, 2009.
Gibron, Bill. *FilmCritic.com.* August 20, 2009.
Hiltbrand, David. *Philadelphia Inquirer.* August 20, 2009.
Hewitt, Chris. *St. Paul Pioneer Press.* August 21, 2009.
Kennedy, Austin. *Sin Magazine.* August 29, 2009.
MacDonald, Moira. *Seattle Times.* August 21, 2009.
Nelson, Rob. *Variety.* August 24, 2009.
Rabin. Nathan. *AV Club.* August 27, 2009.
Rodriguez, Rene. *Miami Herald.* August 21, 2009.

TRIVIA

Ben Stiller filmed all of his scenes during the first two weeks of shooting as he was busy working on other projects.

MARY AND MAX

Two-thousand nine was a landmark year for animation, headlined by acclaimed works like *Coraline, Up,* *Cloudy with a Chance of Meatballs, Fantastic Mr. Fox, Princess and the Frog,* and *Ponyo.* Even with that remarkable slate of animation quality, it is possible that the best film in the medium was the least seen, Adam Eilliot's shockingly moving and accomplished *Mary and Max.* Another notable trend of 2009 was using traditionally family-oriented films to tell stories that arguably appealed more to adults than children (examples include *Where the Wild Things Are, Coraline,* and *9.*) Elliot's film uses the form of stop-motion animation to craft a modern fable that is undeniably more targeted at parents than their children. This is bittersweet, serious, moving screenwriting with title characters that are more well-rounded and interesting than the flesh and bones ones from most major Hollywood films. With pitch-perfect voice work, a great screenplay, and some of the most interesting visuals of the year, the most disheartening thing about *Mary and Max* is how few people saw it in theaters. With a very limited release, nearly everyone who saw the film did so at a festival or On Demand through Sundance Selects, but that does not keep a work this accomplished from being one of the most notable ones of 2009.

Mary Dinkle (later voiced by Toni Collette) is an insecure, chubby, lonely, eight-year-old Australian girl with an embarrassing birthmark on her forehead and an acute case of boredom. Mary's parents are laughably awful at raising her with a mother who seems fueled by cooking sherry and a distant father. The poor girl was recently told that babies come into the world after being found at the bottom of a glass of beer but was also informed that she was an accident—two statements that the poor girl is having trouble reconciling. To discover how she could accidentally be found at the bottom of a pint glass, Mary randomly plucks a name and address from a New York phone book and writes an inquisitive letter. Her correspondence lands on the desk of Max Horowitz (voiced by Philip Seymour Hoffman), an obese, 44-year-old Jewish man with Asperger's Syndrome who suffers with similar bouts of loneliness and confusion with the rest of the world. Mary and Max form a remarkable bond over thousands of miles, helping each other to deal with a species that does not seem to welcome them with open arms and one that they do not really understand—Mary due to her age and bad parenting and Max due to his mental handicap. From her adolescence through her adulthood, Mary counts on letters from Max, and vice versa. They are possibly each other's only friends.

The whole piece is almost consistently narrated (by the great Barry Humphries), in the style of a modern fairy tale but a dark one. Elliott never shies away from the more serious notes of this semi-true story, including representations of severe depression and social fear. *Mary and Max* is a saga of life that includes many dark chapters but finds beats that are ultimately inspirational and moving without ever once feeling manipulative. At one point, Max is handed a candy heart that reads "Love Yourself First." Elliot's film is about how sometimes it can take someone else, even one incredibly far away, to make that a possibility.

Like a lot of the great animation of 2009, *Mary and Max* is a visual stunner as well, although it is a much more spare one than vibrantly colorful films like *Coraline*. The scarcity of design elements allows the viewer to focus on what he should—the two title characters, a pair of perfectly rendered, unique creations. Elliott and his team also design effective color motifs for the two main settings of the film. Mary's Australia is washed out in brown and sepia colors, adding to the dirty feel of her home life, while Max's New York is a gray, cold place, mirroring the way he feels alone in a city of millions.

On a performance level, *Mary and Max* features one of the best vocal accomplishments in the history of animation from the marvelous Hoffman. He turns this tricky character into so much more than the simple caricature that he would have been in another actor's hands. Of course, Collette is typically fantastic (and Eric Bana also pops up in a small role), but this is Hoffman's film. It helps that all of the actors have been given such interesting, well-rounded characters to play in a truly witty screenplay. *Mary and Max* sags a little bit as it approaches its final act and it starts to feel a bit like an extended animated short (Elliott did win the Oscar® in that category for *Harvey Krumpet*), but the final act has an impact and a dramatic weight nearly unmatched in the medium in not just 2009 but the history of animation. Hopefully, Elliott's film will find a wider audience and this one will become the beloved work that anyone who saw it knows it deserves to eventually be.

Brian Tallerico

CREDITS

Mary Daisy Dinkle: Toni Collette (Voice)
Max Jerry Horovitz: Philip Seymour Hoffman (Voice)
Damien: Eric Bana (Voice)
Narrator: Barry Humphries
Origin: Australia
Released: 2009
Production: Melanie Coombs; Melodrama Pictures; released by Sundance Selects
Directed by: Adam Elliot
Written by: Adam Elliot

Cinematography by: Gerald Thompson
Sound: Andrew McGrath
Music Supervisor: Leanne Smith
Music by: Dale Cornelius
Production Design: Adam Elliot
Editing: Bill Murphy
Art Direction: Craig Fison
MPAA rating: Unrated
Running time: 92 minutes

REVIEWS

Byrnes, Paul. *Sydney Morning Herald.* April 10, 2009.
Childress, Erik. *eFilmCritic.com.* October 8, 2009.
Goodridge, Mike. *Screen International.* January 16, 2009.
Howell, peter. *Toronto Star.* November 20, 2009.
Keller, Louise. *Urban Cinefile.* March 31, 2009.
Lacey, Liam. *Globe and Mail.* November 20, 2009.
Mohan, Marc. *Oregonian.* October 30, 2009.
Pais, Matt. *Metromix.com.* October 13, 2009.
Smithey, Cole. *ColeSmithey.com.* October 11, 2009.
Thomas, Kevin. *Los Angeles Times.* September 25, 2009.

QUOTES

Max Jerry Horovitz: "Do you have a favourite-sounding word? My top 5 are ointment, bumblebee, Vladivostok, banana, and testicle."

TRIVIA

All of the scenes featuring water in the film were created using lubricant.

ME AND ORSON WELLES

All's fair in love and theater.
—Movie tagline

Box Office: $1.2 million

In a holiday season of loud and in-your-face movies, Richard Linklater's *Me and Orson Welles* arrived as a warm, gentle alternative—a loving, highly observant, and meticulously crafted paean to the performing arts. Intelligent but never too high-minded, Linklater's film is a unique, clever combination of historical near-fiction, biography, coming-of-age story, and celebration of the theater.

Set in 1937, the story is based on Welles' radical production of Shakespeare's *Julius Caesar* at the Mercury Theater on Broadway. At the age of twenty-two, Welles was already being hailed as a theatrical genius, but the movie accurately portrays him as a complex, grandiose, manipulative egocentric. With his producer partner, the actor John Houseman, frequently feuding with him as well, Welles was a sort of holy terror, revered for his genius and feared for his arbitrary decisions.

As originally conceived in a novel by Robert Kaplow, adapted into a screenplay by Holly Gent Palmo and Vince Palmo, *Me and Orson Welles* imagines the experience of a seventeen-year-old high school student, Richard Samuels (Zac Efron), who talks his way into Welles' orbit a week before the opening and lands the small but key role of Lucius. He joins a cast that includes other actors who would become part of Welles' stable as he soon expanded his genius from theater and radio into Hollywood—including Joseph Cotton (James Tupper) and George Coulouris (Ben Chaplin).

Linklater tracks the freewheeling atmosphere of a play coming together under the unpredictable grasp of Welles, an unreliable taskmaster who might disappear for hours on end to bed down a new female conquest or scoot off for the performance of a radio play. Upon joining the cast, Richard is quickly clued in by the other actors that Welles is capricious and frustrating to work for, but that just being in the orbit of such a genius is intoxicating enough to endure his foibles. Richard will be working for nothing except the chance to be bathed in Welles's spit, he is told. And indeed, later in the film, as Welles (who is playing Brutus) is performing a key scene, Linklater shows the spittle of the genius spraying from his mouth as he recites Shakespeare's lines.

Richard meets Sonja (Clair Danes), Welles' administrative assistant, a sweet yet ambitious social climber who sees her connection with the acclaimed genius as her ticket to fame. But as played by Danes in an utterly disarming and winsome fashion, Sonja does not have a trace of a cruel edge—she is just a practical girl who knows the score and how to get ahead in the entertainment world. Desired by all the other men in the cast, she zeroes in on Richard, charmed by his romanticism and naiveté.

Linklater does not view his troupe with cynicism, and his movie is more romp than farce. Yet, whenever Linklater's material pulls dangerously close to cutesy romanticism, it is sprinkled with a hard dose of reality. His viewpoint mirrors that of his protagonist: Richard arrives with a starry-eyed love of theater, but no practical experience in it. He soon realizes that it is a mix of B.S., mayhem, chance, bravado, and occasional magic. There is disillusionment for Richard, both in his hero worship and in romance, but as the instrumental version of the song "You Can't Take That Away from Me" testifies during a scene where Richard goes through his press clippings and souvenirs, he has learned a lesson but not been crushed. (Linklater makes good use of mid-1930s jazz standards throughout the film.)

The irony of Efron, the teen heartthrob who starred in Disney's *High School Musical* (2006), being cast in this role as a theater newcomer whose part includes singing a lullaby on stage, is apparent. There is a little more bluster and less subtlety in Efron's performance than would make his character totally lovable, but the combination of his charm and bravado works reasonably well. He is overshadowed by both his co-stars, by Danes's wonderful evocation of a girl who has learned how to get ahead yet still is entirely likeable, but especially by Christian McKay as Welles.

McKay, a British actor in his thirties who has never had a major role, is a little old to play the twenty-two-year-old Welles, except for the fact that Welles was a wunderkind wielding the power of a man twice his age. McKay inhabits his character thoroughly, blustering and scattering bombast, yet he somehow manages not to make the man hateful because, like Welles himself, he exudes an aura of humanity and occasionally reveals the wounded child pouting behind the air of mastery. The movie brilliantly keeps pulling us into Welles' orbit and then dousing cold water on our affections, and in this way, too, makes the audience's experiences exactly parallel Richard's journey.

This is a smart movie that has just the right mix of romanticism and cynicism. The film is about what happens when we participate in performance art, either as performer or audience: we agree to tolerate human foibles in search of a larger, elusive truth. That enterprise sometimes works masterfully, sometimes not. Linklater himself embodies the spirit of this ethos he invokes in this warmhearted tribute to theater. In every movie he makes, he tackles a wildly different subject and uses a vastly different yet appropriate style: from *Before Sunrise* (1995) to *Waking Life* (2001) to *School of Rock* (2003) to *Fast Food Nation* (2006) and *A Scanner Darkly* (2006), Linklater delves into his subject matter and artfully and creatively exploits all the connections between form and substance, just as good actors do. Linklater is unafraid to make a movie that is old-fashioned and even a little corny; he is a romantic at heart but never settles for less than a full examination of his characters and story. *Me and Orson Welles* is a gentle, loving, but perceptive addition to his work.

Michael Betzold

CREDITS

Orson Welles: Christian McKay
Richard Samuels: Zac Efron
Sonja Jones: Claire Danes
Gretta Adler: Zoe Kazan
Joseph Cotten: James Tupper

Norman Lloyd: Leo Bill

John Houseman: Eddie Marsan

George Coulouris: Ben Chaplin

Muriel Brassler: Kelly Reilly

Grover Burgess: Patrick Kennedy

Origin: Great Britain, USA

Language: English

Released: 2009

Production: Richard Linklater, Marc Samuelson, Ann Carli; Detour Filmproduction, Framestore Features, CinemaNX; released by Freestyle Releasing

Directed by: Richard Linklater

Written by: Holly Gent Palmo, Vince Palmo

Cinematography by: Richard Pope

Music by: Michael J. McEvoy

Sound: Colin Nicholson

Music Supervisor: Marc Marot

Editing: Sandra Adair

Art Direction: Bill Crutcher

Costumes: Nic Ede

Production Design: Laurence Dorman

MPAA rating: PG-13

Running time: 114 minutes

REVIEWS

Childress, Erik. *eFilmCritic.com.* September 16, 2008.

Denby, David. *New Yorker.* November 23, 2009.

Ebert, Roger. *Chicago Sun-Times.* December 10, 2009.

MacDonald, Moira. *Seattle Times.* December 10, 2009.

McCarter, Jeremy. *Newsweek.* December 4, 2009.

McCarthy, Todd. *Variety.* September 9, 2008.

Morgenstern, Joe. *Wall Street Journal.* November 29, 2009.

Puig, Claudia. *USA Today.* November 24, 2009.

Scott, A.O. *New York Times.* November 25, 2009.

Tallerico, Brian. *MovieRetriever.com.* December 11, 2009.

TRIVIA

Christian McKay previously portrayed Orson Welles onstage in *Rosebud: The Lives of Orson Welles.*

AWARDS

Nomination:

British Acad. 2009: Support. Actor (McKay)

Ind. Spirit 2010: Support. Actor (McKay).

THE MEN WHO STARE AT GOATS

No goats. No glory.
    —Movie tagline

Box Office: $32 million

In the late 1970s and early 1980s, the United States military experimented with training some soldiers in us-ing psychic powers to conduct warfare. Based on the work of Lt. Col. Jim Channon in the human potential movement, the Army formed something called the First Earth Battalion and explored the idea of being able to kill goats with mental thoughts and of walking through walls. The experiments have enjoyed something of a revival during the Iraq War. At least, that's what British Gonzo journalist Jon Ronson reported in his book, *The Men Who Stare at Goats.*

The movie version of the book has the formidable task of convincing audiences that such activities really could have taken place in the U.S. Army. Veteran actor and first-time director Grant Heslov begins by inserting a title that playfully warns audiences that more of what they are about to see is actually true than they could possibly believe. That's supposed to lend an air of authenticity to the supreme silliness that's about to unfold—and for awhile it works.

With a high-powered dream cast to work with— George Clooney (who co-produced the film), Ewan McGregor, Jeff Bridges, and Kevin Spacey—Heslov has veteran comic potential and seemingly a rich subject to mine. But with Peter Straughan and Ronson's rambling screenplay, the material meanders over a series of sketch-like scenes and ends up going nowhere. Part of the problem is that the film treats the program as pure farce, when in fact there is no doubt the military was deadly serious.

Despite the talents on display and the intriguing nature of its subject matter, the film is practically weightless. McGregor plays Bob Wilton, the Ronson character in the guise of an American small-town newspaper reporter, and he's not believable for a minute as a journalist. He's rather naïve and gullible. First, there's some pathos as Wilton is left by his wife and goes to Iraq in search of some credibility, hoping to win her back. As Wilton unnecessarily tells us later, he's gone to war to find meaning in his empty life. By movie's end, he's been invested with the task of telling the world about what he's learned about the Army's psychic operations program, but in fact all that's reported from his book is that the military played a Barney the Dinosaur song over and over to torture Iraqi prisoners. But if the film is Ronson's revenge for the poor coverage of the book, letting the world know he should not have been ignored, it is a paltry one.

The potentially hilarious performance by Bridges, who seems well suited for this role, based on his classic performance as The Dude in *The Big Lebowski*, goes as stale as the in-joke of having *Star Wars* star Ewan McGregor in a film that frequently characterizes the psychic soldiers as "Jedis." While The Dude found comfort in being the ultimate slacker, Bridges' Bill Django, who plays the Channon character, must prance ridiculously around, leading a dance class for soldiers, presenting them with flowers, and rubbing elbows in hot-tub encounter groups. These scenes are amusing but tiresome, because they are a bunch of worn-out clichés and familiar tropes about the 1960s counter-culture and its aftermath, the New Age movement. The soldierly peace-and-love routine is not in the least bit credible, even if it is based on a true story. So divorced from reality is this film that the characters spend most of their time in a supposed war zone, yet, despite guns being brandished and fired, no one is ever killed.

A semblance of a plot seems to unfold when Wilton means Lyn Cassady (Clooney) in Kuwait and goes with him on a mission into Iraq. While practicing his cloud-bursting technique, Cassady crashes their car in the desert, they are kidnapped, and the group has a series of middling adventures. So little actually occurs—as the supposed mission dissolves into nothing—that Wilton's narrative retelling of the Earth First Battalion's history comes to dominate the film. It's a bad sign in a movie when the back story eclipses the action. The screenplay becomes nothing more than a series of mildly-humorous-yet-pointless vignettes. The filmmakers try to wring some tension out of the efforts by a disgruntled competitor of Cassady, Larry Hooper (Kevin Spacey, playing his typical conniving villain), to disrupt the unit, which succeed. There's a nonsensical and poorly explained reunion to close the movie—but then, in a movie about psychic phenomena, there's hardly a need to apply the rules of logic.

Clooney's performance carries most of the comic load, and the veteran proves up to the task. Except for the latter part of the movie, when Cassady has become a pitiable figure, Clooney's wacky Jedi warrior is a perfect balance of preposterous and sincere. Clooney makes us believe that Cassady believes in his powers, even when (as they frequently do) they fail.

The Men Who Stare at Goats is all lightweight farce that quickly grows tiresome despite the chops of its cast. In its moments of crushingly inane dialogue, the movie veers dangerously close to *Ishtar* (1987) territory. Luckily, the formidable actors here are almost able to conceal the fact that the emperor that has no clothes—for this is a film that asks us to believe in something that it does not take seriously in the least.

Michael Betzold

CREDITS

Lyn Cassady: George Clooney
Bob Wilton: Ewan McGregor
Bill Django: Jeff Bridges
Larry Hooper: Kevin Spacey
Helen: Rebecca Mader
Todd Nixon: Robert Patrick
Gen. Hopgood: Stephen Lang
Gus Lacey: Stephen Root
Origin: USA
Language: English
Released: 2009
Production: George Clooney, Grant Heslov, Paul Lister; BBC Films, Smokehouse Pictures; released by Overture Films
Directed by: Grant Heslov
Written by: Peter Straughan
Cinematography by: Robert Elswit
Music by: Rolfe Kent
Sound: Jared Marshack
Music Supervisor: Linda Cohen
Editing: Tatiana S. Riegel
Art Direction: Peter Borck
Costumes: Louise Frogley
Production Design: Sharon Seymour
MPAA rating: R
Running time: 94 minutes

REVIEWS

Ebert, Roger. *Chicago Sun-Times.* November 5, 2009.
Elley, Derek. *Variety.* September 9, 2009.
Germain, David. *Associated Press.* November 3, 2009.
Hoffman, Jordan. *UGO.* November 5, 2009.
Lane, Anthony. *New Yorker.* November 2, 2009.
Pais, Matt. *Metromix.com.* November 5, 2009.
Roeper, Richard. *RichardRoeper.com.* November 5, 2009.
Travers, Peter. *Rolling Stone.* November 5, 2009.
Turan, Kenneth. *Los Angeles Times.* November 5, 2009.
Young, Deborah. *Hollywood Reporter.* September 9, 2009.

QUOTES

Lyn Cassady: "I think I just ran him over. Oh crap."

TRIVIA

The one-sheet (advertising poster) for this movie is a spoof of a frequently used style for movie posters in which, instead of trying to communicate anything about the plot or content of the film, the poster just contains multiple stacked faces of the stars. On this poster, the last face visible in the row is a goat's, and the billing line above their photos reads, "George Clooney, Jeff Bridges, Ewan McGregor, Kevin Spacey, and Goat."

THE MESSENGER

Box Office: $1.1 million

Oren Moverman's powerful debut *The Messenger* transcends what could have been a straightforward melodrama to bring the humanity of men and women at devastating life crossroads into sharp focus. Highly acclaimed to the point that many were predicting multiple Oscar® nominations, Moverman's film struck a nerve with critics due to its refusal to play the cliché over the truth. On paper, the subject matter of *The Messenger* could have easily turned into nothing more than TV movie pablum, but rarely has an entire team of performers and behind-the-scenes collaborators so clearly worked against melodrama in favor of honest emotion. Effective, expertly made, and spectacularly performed, *The Messenger* is a film about something everyone will likely have to come to terms with at some point in their life—the way we deal with unique, unpredictable tragedy and how no two reactions are the same. Incredibly authentic, *The Messenger* is not a film for the dramatically faint of heart but it says more about honest, relatable humanity more than nearly any drama of the year. Moverman's cowritten script handles an unpopular subject matter that has dominated the headlines for the last decade—the human cost of war—but does so by staying true to its characters through every believable twist and turn. Dramas this human are rare and must be seen even if the subject matter is not that easy to swallow.

After a few interesting scene-stealing turns in films like *Alpha Dog* (2006) and *3:10 to Yuma* (2007), Ben Foster was handed the role of his young career as Staff Sergeant Will Montgomery, a young soldier just returned home from his tour with a few months left in service. Montgomery has been sent back early due to an injury suffered during an incident that has clearly left the young man even more emotionally shattered than most returning soldiers. He reaches out for support from old girlfriend Kelly (Jena Malone), but she has moved on to a new life and a new man. To finish out his time of duty, Will is handed an assignment that would be tough for anyone, much less someone so emotionally bottled up—stationed in the Casualty Notification Office, where the men and women work who knock on the door of the next of kin when their loved one has been killed in the line of duty.

Montgomery is partnered with the stern-but-supportive Captain Tony Stone (Woody Harrelson, giving an award-winning performance almost certain to be nominated for a Best Supporting Actor Oscar®). The more experienced but equally out of touch with his emotions older officer occasionally butts heads with his new protégé, but they develop an organic camaraderie that never feels forced like a traditional buddy movie. Harrelson and Foster have an easy-going, perfectly balanced chemistry that never feels anything less than completely genuine.

The structure of Alessandro Camon & Oren Moverman's screenplay is an episodic one that allows for character development through a series of assignments from the CNO. As Will and Tony do their gut-wrenching job, Moverman often shoots them with unbroken takes from a handheld camera and the actors were often allowed to improvise their scenes and reactions. Foster and Harrelson rarely knew how their notifications would unfold or how their fellow actors would respond, resulting in dramatic moments that feel genuine and never manipulative. Each visit is a bit different, but Will seems most struck by the relatively placid response of a newly widowed mother played by Samantha Morton. He begins to follow her and work his way into her life but never in a predictable fashion. Will merely seems fascinated by how well this woman appears to be dealing with grief not dissimilar to what he has brought back with him from his time overseas.

Foster, Harrelson, and Morton are all spectacular in *The Messenger,* giving the film its beating heart, but a lot of credit for its overall success must be placed at the feet of director Moverman. He has a remarkably genuine style, shooting most of the film merely as if he (and, by extension, the audience) were merely a third member of the CNO, dealing with grief along with Officers Montgomery and Stone. It seems like every time an artistic decision was placed in front of this promising young filmmaker, he made the right choice. He takes a script with many plot points that could have descended into melodrama and refuses to do so. Only a late script trip to a wedding feels forced. Overall, *The Messenger* never feels false. It is easily one of the most memorable dramas of the year.

Brian Tallerico

CREDITS

Staff Sgt. Will Montgomery: Ben Foster
Capt. Anthony Stone: Woody Harrelson
Olivia Pitterson: Samantha Morton
Col. Stuart Dorsett: Eamonn Walker
Kelly: Jena Malone
Dale Martin: Steve Buscemi
Origin: USA
Language: English
Released: 2009
Production: Mark Gordon, Lawrence Inglee, Zach Miller, Benjamin Goldhirsh; Sherazade Film Development, BZ Entertainment, Good Worldwide, Omnilab Media, Mark Gordon Company; released by Oscilloscope Laboratories
Directed by: Oren Moverman
Written by: Oren Moverman, Alessandro Camon
Cinematography by: Bobby Bukowski
Music by: Nathan Larson

Sound: Javier Bennassar
Music Supervisor: Tracy McKnight
Editing: Alex Hall
Art Direction: Scott Anderson
Costumes: Catherine George
Production Design: Stephen Beatrice
MPAA rating: R
Running time: 112 minutes

REVIEWS

Denby, David. *New Yorker.* November 9, 2009.
Ebert, Roger. *Chicago Sun-Times.* November 19, 2009.
Gleiberman, Owen. *Entertainment Weekly.* November 11, 2009.
LaSalle, Mick. *San Francisco Chronicle.* November 19, 2009.
Long, Tom. *Detroit News.* November 25, 2009.
Lowe, Justin. *Hollywood Reporter.* October 26, 2009.
Pais, Matt. *Metromix.com.* November 12, 2009.
Phillips, Michael. *Chicago Tribune.* November 20, 2009.
Scott, A.O. *New York Times.* November 13, 2009.
Travers, Peter. *Rolling Stone.* November 12, 2009.

TRIVIA

Sgt. Brian Scott, who served as a technical advisor to the film, was training to deploy to Iraq at Ft. Dix in New Jersey and was subsequently injured in an IED attack in Baghdad.

AWARDS

Ind. Spirit 2010: Support. Actor (Harrelson)

Nomination:

Oscars 2009: Orig. Screenplay, Support. Actor (Harrelson)
Golden Globes 2010: Support. Actor (Harrelson)
Ind. Spirit 2010: First Feature, Screenplay, Support. Actress (Morton)
Screen Actors Guild 2009: Support. Actor (Harrelson).

MICHAEL JACKSON'S THIS IS IT

(This Is It)

Like you've never seen him before.
—Movie tagline

Box Office: $72.1 million

Only a few days after Michael Jackson's sudden and unexpected death last June while rehearsing for a series of comeback concerts in London, it was announced that Sony Pictures had acquired the rights to over 100 hours of behind-the-scenes footage with plans to whittle it down into a feature film of some kind less than four months later. This announcement split many observers right down the line—loyal fans hoped that it would serve as a final artistic triumph that would solidify his position as one of the all-time great performers while more cynical types assumed that it would simply be a tacky attempt by its producers to make a few more bucks off of his name and notoriety. (There were even rumors floating around at one point that the film would end with footage shot at his funeral.) As it turns out, the resulting film, *Michael Jackson's This Is It*, lands somewhere in the middle of those two extremes—it is not quite the ghoulish exploitation that it could have been (although there is no way that a perfectionist like Jackson would have allowed it to be released if he had any say in the matter) but from a cinematic standpoint, it feels more like an exceptionally lengthy and elaborate DVD supplement than an actual movie.

The film is not a standard-issue Jackson documentary and makes no mention of his passing outside of a brief reference in one of the opening title cards. Instead, it consists almost entirely of footage shot during the intense rehearsal process for the shows that was originally intended for Jackson to watch in order to better gauge his own performances. Under the watchful eye of show director/choreographer Kenny Ortega, we see Jackson and the small army of background dancers, musicians and technicians struggling to bring Jackson's increasingly immense visions to life on the stage through elaborate choreography, lavish special effects and even filmed sequences as dramatically detailed as any full-scale Hollywood production—an intro to "Smooth Criminal" finds him interacting with clips from *film noir* classics like *Gilda* (1946) and *In a Lonely Place* (1950) while a reconceptualization of the famous "Thriller" video offers up zombies set to leap into the laps of viewers via 3-D.

Behind the scenes, the film details such sights as dancers rehearsing Jackson's infamous crotch grab, a slightly testy Jackson explaining to his musical director exactly how he wants the opening of "The Way You Make Me Feel" to sound and a wardrobe designer saying with a straight face that his efforts are so cutting-edge that he has been "working with scientists in the Netherlands." Most significant, of course, is the footage of Jackson throwing himself full-out into the rehearsals with the determination of someone who knows that he has something to prove—although he sloughs off the singing at some points in order to save his voice, he hits his marks with such intense energy that some viewers may get exhausted just watching him.

As a behind-the-scenes look at how a concert of this size and scope actually comes together, *This Is It* is undeniably intriguing but as a testament to the artistic talents of Michael Jackson, it comes up a little short. For starters, most of the performances are cobbled together from bits and pieces of different rehearsals and as a result, there are not many chances to see him develop any real performance rhythms. It also appears as if Jackson decided early on that he was going to play it somewhat safe and not do anything that would possibly challenge his fans in any way. The musical arrangements are virtually indistinguishable from the ones heard in the original recordings and the stage choreography has been designed to hew as closely to what was seen in his ground-breaking music videos. Other flaws are extensions of the same hurdles that helped send his career into a nosedive in the first place—namely the weakness of much of the music he recorded after "Thriller" and a grisly physical appearance that is painfully accentuated by the unforgiving video cameras.

The central problem with *This Is It*, both the film and the concept behind the concerts, is that Jackson tries so hard to dazzle the audience with all of its gimmicks and elaborate choreography that the most spectacular special effect of all—namely his stunning gifts as a performer—winds up getting lost amidst the surrounding sound and fury. (Remember, this is a guy who once captivated the world by performing "Billie Jean" on television with no special accoutrements other than a spangled glove and some electrifying dance moves.) Perhaps Jackson was afraid that either he did not have the chops to simply perform his songs unadorned anymore or that his fans would not stand for such an approach and so he decided to throw in stuff like aerialists, giant robot spiders and a bulldozer to distract them. Unfortunately, based on the evidence seen here, it seems as though the show may have turned out to be an overproduced mess that spent so much time trying to dazzle people that it wound up exhausting them instead.

The irony of all this is that the single most effective sequence in the entire film is the one that is the inevitable medley of Jackson Five hits that he performs without the lavish trappings of the other selections. When we see him beginning to rehearse this particular number, he is in an uncharacteristically testy mood—possibly because the no-frills staging leaves him with nowhere to hide and possibly because of the memories evoked by the material—but as it goes on, he invests it with more and more emotion and by the time he gets to the soaring climax of *I'll Be There* even the most cynical viewers will be blown away by how deeply he has gotten into what could have been just another tossed-away chestnut. If it had contained more moments like that, *Michael Jackson's This Is It* might have been a truly memorable and penetrating look at a true artist practicing and perfecting his craft. Instead, it is more or less the cinematic equivalent of a T-shirt that might have been purchased at the show—a flashy but ultimately flimsy souvenir that will inevitably fade and shrink away even as the memories of the man and his music continue to linger on.

Peter Sobczynski

CREDITS

Himself: Michael Jackson
Origin: USA
Language: English
Released: 2009
Production: Randy Phillips, Kenny Ortega, Paul Gongaware; Columbia Pictures, AEG Live, Michael Jackson Co.; released by Sony Pictures
Directed by: Kenny Ortega
Cinematography by: Sandrine Orabona
Music by: Michael Bearden
Sound: Tim Hays
Editing: Don Brochu, Kevin Stitt
Production Design: Bernt Capra
MPAA rating: PG
Running time: 112 minutes

REVIEWS

Barker, Andrew. *Variety.* October 28, 2009.
Corliss, Richard. *Time Magazine.* October 28, 2009.
Ebert, Roger. *Chicago Sun-Times.* October 28, 2009.
Fendelman, Adam. *HollywoodChicago.com.* October 28, 2009.
Gardner, Elysa. *USA Today.* October 28, 2009.
Honeycutt, Kirk. *Hollywood Reporter.* October 28, 2009.
Long, Tom. *Detroit News.* October 28, 2009.
Pais, Matt. *Metromix.com.* October 28, 2009.
Phillips, Michael. *Chicago Tribune.* October 28, 2009.
Richards, Chris. *Washington Post.* October 28, 2009.

QUOTES

Michael Jackson: "It's an adventure. It's a great adventure. We want to take them places that they've never been before. We want to show them talent like they've never seen before."

TRIVIA

The footage was originally intended for the private library of Michael Jackson. It was also to be used to help the concert's creative team analyze, review, and alter aspects of the show before it was performed live before an audience.

MISS MARCH

After four years in a coma, Eugene Bell is going to be reunited with his high school sweetheart...on pages 95-97.
—Movie tagline

Box Office: $5 million

In the long history of low-brow sex comedies, you have to reach down far into the bottomless pit to find one as pathetically unfunny and unpleasant as *Miss March*. This is a film that has traveled from another dimension where comedy is outlawed and punishable by having to watch *Miss March*. Worse than the most distasteful and graphic horror films that find new orifices to slice with a razor or pierce with an axe, it would be a welcome appearance to find a new slasher icon to do his business on the lead characters.

After discovering their first Playboy at a young age, best friends Eugene and Tucker have taken different paths in their views of the opposite sex. Eugene (Zach Cregger) preaches abstinence to horrified grade schoolers while Tucker (Trevor Moore) sees women only for the sum of their best, most objectified parts. Eugene's partner in virginity is the comely Cindi Whitehall (Raquel Alessi) who is just about ready to explore her womanhood. On prom night, she and Eugene make a pledge to experience their first time with each other. In an effort to loosen him up and make him a longer-lasting lover, Tucker gets Eugene drunk and a wrong door sends him tumbling down the stairs into a four-year coma.

When he awakes, thanks in part to Tucker hitting him in the face with a baseball bat, Eugene realizes he has missed his opportunity and, thanks to atrophy, is left with a body more flaccid than ever. There is promise on the horizon though when Tucker discovers that Cindi has posed for Playboy—in a centerfold without nudity, the next step in the devolution of women having sex with their bras on in the movies. "The girl next door is now one of the Girls Next Door," says Tucker in one of his classier witticisms. After busting out of the hospital, the pair hit the road on a journey to Hugh Hefner's mansion with no real plan. Luckily for them they know a successful rapper from their high school days (Craig Robinson) who goes by a moniker combining a horse appendage and a computer file and he promises to get them in so Eugene can find his beloved Cindi.

Few long distance love stories involve characters named after equine members. They also tend to avoid creating an atmosphere of misogyny so thick that most men in the audience would consider a sex change before admitting their male parts make them think this way. Where *The Sure Thing* (1985) carries its potentially offensive title right up front or *Superbad* (2007) plots its heroes into getting girls drunk to have sex, those were at least films that presented their characters as human beings. Horny, occasionally alcohol-impaired ones, but nothing like Trevor and Eugene who would normally be mocked one-scene characters—Rosencrantz and Guildenstern to *Superbad*'s Seth and Evan; characters we hope will be tricked into delivering their own execution.

Getting past whatever lessons Cusack's Walter Gibson may have learned on his journey or the ones Ben Stiller's Ted already knew deep down in *There's Something About Mary* (1998), at least they were funny. The list of supposedly planned laugh moments in *Miss March* would not pass in a first grade improvisation class. Tucker's suggestive family photography is a gag taken straight from Adrian Zmed of all people in *Bachelor Party* (1984). There are no less than four bowel gags, three by sound, one by sight as Eugene suffers one of the side effects of a multi-year coma. One playmate unknowingly enjoys drinking dog urine. Said dog being tossed and a close-up view of abnormal male genitalia are two more lifts straight from the Farrelly Brothers. After buying a stripper pole for his girlfriend (Molly Stanton) on their "13-month boning anniversary," Tucker discovers that oral sex, strobe lights and epilepsy do not mix and is forced to stab her multiple times in the face with a fork. And if a writer is going to make a joke out of the rapper's lyrics being forced into radio-friendly lyrics, it is a mistake to have the DJ then announce his decidedly un-friendly name immediately after. Just one of many areas where George Carlin would cry foul on these supposed sketch comedy masters.

Cregger and Moore are responsible for the comedy troupe known as *The Whitest Kids U Know* (2007). They say you never get a second chance to make a first impression and based on their performances and ideas in *Miss March*, it should have been a red flag to have their show canceled immediately. While Cregger is basically playing the straight man here and endearing himself to us by calling Cindi a whore in the first conversation of their reunion, Moore mugs his way through every scene with a bug-eyed "who me?" approach that is aggravating to the max. Guys looking to combine their fantasy of vicariously getting inside the Playboy mansion and ogling gorgeous girls who also happen to have a head for comedy should enjoy Anna Faris and company in *The House Bunny* (2008). For women being portrayed as bubbleheads, vengeful shrews or lesbians who enjoy public and backseat displays of affection, just call the cable company and order up a subscription to Cinemax. Even their late-night selections are much funnier than anything in *Miss March*.

Erik Childress

CREDITS

Eugene Bell: Zach Cregger
Tucker Cleigh: Trevor Moore
Cindi Whitehall: Raquel Alessi
Phil: Craig Robinson
Candace: Molly Stanton

Fireman Rick: Geoff Meed
Himself: Hugh Hefner (Cameo)
Origin: USA
Language: English
Released: 2009
Production: Tom Jacobson, Steven J. Wolfe, Tobie Haggerty, Vincent Cirrincione; Jacobson Co., Alta Loma Entertainment; released by Fox Atomic
Directed by: Zach Cregger, Trevor Moore
Written by: Zach Cregger, Trevor Moore
Cinematography by: Anthony B. Richmond
Music by: Jeff Cardoni
Sound: Matthew Nicolay
Music Supervisor: Dave Jordan, JoJo Villanueva
Editing: Tim Mirkovich
Art Direction: Dins W.W. Danielsen
Costumes: Alexis Scott, Sarah de Sa Rego
Production Design: Cabot McMullen
MPAA rating: R
Running time: 89 minutes

REVIEWS

Anderson, John. *Variety.* March 13, 2009.
Anderson, Melissa. *L.A. Weekly.* March 19, 2009.
Burr, Ty. *Boston Globe.* March 16, 2009.
Honeycutt, Kirk. *Hollywood Reporter.* March 16, 2009.
Jones, J.R. *Chicago Reader.* March 13, 2009.
Pais, Matt. *Metromix.com.* March 12, 2009.
Rabin, Nathan. *AV Club.* March 12, 2009.
Villarreal, Phil. *Arizona Daily Star.* March 13, 2009.
Whipp, Glenn. *Chicago Tribune.* March 13, 2009.
Zacharek, Stephanie. *Salon.com.* March 13, 2009.

QUOTES

Tucker Cleigh: "Well the country is like, what, 10 states wide? And each state is roughly 100 miles across. So that's like 1,000 miles. We're going about 60 miles an hour, so we should be there in like 600 minutes."

TRIVIA

In the early scene at the "Abstinence Now" seminar, some of Raquel Alessi's (Cindi Whitehall's) lines were dubbed over for the movie's final release. Originally, the story she told on stage prominently featured the word "retard," referring to a baby that was born to an illegitimate mother who smoked. Due to concerns over bad press, the word was changed to "crackhead."

AWARDS

Nomination:
Golden Raspberries 2009: Worst Support. Actor (Hefner).

MONSTERS VS. ALIENS

Oooze gonna save us?
—Movie tagline

Box Office: $198 million

One of the monsters in *Monsters vs. Aliens* finds himself attracted to a lime-green Jell-O mold that is temptingly studded with chunks of pineapple. Few humans would finds themselves drawn to the dessert in a similarly-romantic way, but most would nonetheless describe the creation as appealing to the eye and at least passably enjoyable, even if the satisfaction it provides does not linger long. That description also applies to *Monsters vs. Aliens* itself, DreamWorks' tremendously-touted first computer-animated feature "totally authored in 3-D." CEO of DreamWorks Animation Jeffrey Katzenberg breathlessly asserted that the rise of this new generation of 3-D will enable the film industry to "almost reinvent itself," magnetically drawing audiences by changing "the movie experience in a way that literally has not happened since we went from black and white to color." The film that aims to launch audiences forward in A-1 style harks back to B-movie sci-fi fare of the 1950s and 1960s. For example, in a nod to *Attack of the 50 Foot Woman* (1958), this lighthearted, fond homage flick features a heroine that suddenly sprouts to 49 feet 11½ inches. While her height is unquestionably far above average, the film she inhabits is unfortunately not.

If "Here Comes the Bride" is heard during a wedding in the form of a horrified, hollered heads-up, a warning that makes shrieking guests lurch from the church and tear off in the opposite direction, then a monumentally unusual and unexpected kind of hitch has occurred. Such is what happens in *Monsters vs. Aliens,* when wife-to-be Susan Murphy (well-voiced by Reese Witherspoon) gets walloped by a meteor that then alters her at the altar to a profoundly-startling statuesqueness. As if this space junk smackdown and resultant shocking nuptials interruptus were not jolting enough, poor Susan's lesser-half, groom Derek Dietl (Paul Rudd), had self-centeredly altered the destination of their honeymoon plans from rapturously-romantic Paris to much-less-so Fresno, where he will interview for a new television weatherman position. After briefly balking, she tries to be happy for his gain rather than sad about her loss, resignedly convincing herself that togetherness is more important than the town.

Unfortunately, Susan ends up suffering a fate worse than Fresno, as special government forces drag the beautiful behemoth off to an austere, ultra-secret facility where monstrous creatures are permanently hidden away for the good of a skittish public. Though an eye-popping oddity now herself, Susan is initially horrified by the singularly-strange beings that soon become the dismayed, discombobulated, and thoroughly-homesick woman's friends. Like Susan's character, all of the other monsters have clearly-identifiable cinematic ancestors. Dr. Cockroach, PhD (Hugh Laurie), an erudite mad scientist whose self-experimentation has turned him into a brilliant, maniacally-laughing bug, is a tip of the hat to *The Fly* (1958). The macho Missing Link (Will Arnett), the thawed-out evolutionary connection between land and sea, especially reminds one of *The Creature from the Black Lagoon* (1954). Insectosaurus (co-director Conrad Vernon), a gargantuan grub due to radiation exposure, can clearly be traced back to *Mothra* (1962). Finally, with a blue, gelatinous body that is fairly clear but thinking that definitely is not, there is B.O.B. (Seth Rogan), the previously-mentioned Jell-O lover who is an obvious descendent of *The Blob* (1958). He is the most entertaining, endearing and memorable (by far) of the monsters Susan encounters. As for her, she is dubbed "Ginormica" by the government, which is probably not a descriptive moniker Susan had ever fantasized about garnering on the day she donned her wedding dress.

Monsters vs. Aliens then moves on from Earth's oddities to otherworldly ones. When hopefully-peaceful first contact is rebuffed by a colossal and seemingly-indestructible alien probe decidedly uninterested in playing nice, further film references are let fly along with the explosives. President Hathaway, who looks like the love child of his portrayer, Stephen Colbert, and rock legend Buddy Holly, plays the unmistakable initial notes from *Close Encounters of the Third Kind* (1977). (He then launches into a rendition of "Axel F" from 1984's *Beverly Hills Cop*.) Hathaway flashes the Vulcan salute from the *Star Trek* television series and films. Harking back to the 1982 Spielberg classic, a rocket is emblazoned with the words "E.T. GO HOME!" Afterward, when Hathaway and his advisors consult in the cavernous Pentagon War Room with gruff, gravelly-voiced monster-keeper Gen. W.R. Monger (a surprisingly-versatile Kiefer Sutherland), one cannot help but think of *Dr. Strangelove* (1964). It is in that scene that Monger asserts the only way to repel the alien invaders is to unleash the monsters. Most people would not consider an alien onslaught to be good news, but Susan and Co. are resultantly given their freedom in exchange for the kind of assistance that only they can provide.

During the course of *Monsters vs. Aliens*, the film's five screenwriters also affectionately refer to many other films, including *King Kong* (multiple versions), *Gulliver's Travels* (ditto), *The Wizard of Oz* (1939), *Jaws* (1975), and *Independence Day* (1996). Such an homage collage will, of course, go over the heads of the younger set the way Gen. Monger appears to hover out over the audience thanks to a jet pack and 3-D. Those not old enough to remember such films will, however, likely enjoy the duck-inducing manner in which the meteor, a paddleball, or various outstretched arms travel towards them both startlingly and rather impressively. Most striking to all is the scene in which the title's promised showdown

begins on the streets of San Francisco and its Golden Gate Bridge. (The inspiration for this scene was 1955's *It Came From Beneath the Sea,* in which a giant octopus gave the full tentacle treatment to the city by the bay.) The action sequence is the centerpiece set piece of *Monsters vs. Aliens,* the show of visual prowess that made the chests of those responsible for the film understandably puff up the most with pride. The look of the sequence is certainly laudable, the studio's new InTru3D technology creating a spectacular sort of 3-D photorealistic animation.

Now that the males in the audience have been satisfied with some dazzling, destructive mayhem, *Monsters vs. Aliens* aims for the distaff half of the audience with a purposeful and pervasive pushing of female empowerment. Derek had wanted to be the next big thing in TV news and Susan was going to be sitting in the passenger seat on his ride onwards and upwards. However, it is Susan who both figuratively and literally becomes a big deal in her own right, walking tall and being delightedly surprised by her own strengths and accomplishments. Where Susan once looked with wide-eyed adoration at the man at the center of her world (even then possessing quite prodigious peepers), as Ginormica she squints determinedly as she confidently saves the planet. She not only cannot but will not stand in the shadow of any man again, especially one like jerky Derek who will not stand by her through thick and thin—or short and tall. With the help of her new, mutually-loyal companions, Ginormica defeats the evil alien leader Gallaxhar (Rainn Wilson), a thoroughly unpleasant being that appears to be part-squid and part-Dr. Seuss' Grinch. He had wanted to extract the highly-potent Quantonium from her that was imparted by the meteor strike. She will retain the power within herself, thank you very much.

"Ginormically showy but super average" is the way Entertainment Weekly's Lisa Schwarzbaum described *Monsters vs. Aliens,* and it is an apt description. If one sets aside the innovative special effects, what remains is genial, good for some chuckles, and has positive things to say, but is not especially memorable. Made on a budget of $175 million, the film grossed over $193 million domestically and approached $400 million worldwide. Critical reaction was mixed. While DreamWorks had spoken the word "franchise" in reference to *Monsters vs. Aliens,* Katzenberg announced late in 2009 that its underperformance in certain key markets overseas had cancelled such plans. "At DreamWorks, it all starts with a great story," he asserted. However, *Monsters vs. Aliens* proves once again that such a declaration can be more credibly made by the folks at Pixar.

David L. Boxerbaum

CREDITS

Ginormica/Susan Murphy: Reese Witherspoon (Voice)

B.O.B.: Seth Rogen (Voice)

General W.R. Monger: Kiefer Sutherland (Voice)

Derek: Paul Rudd (Voice)

Dr. Cockroach: Hugh Laurie (Voice)

Gallaxhar: Rainn Wilson (Voice)

The Missing Link: Will Arnett (Voice)

The President: Stephen Colbert (Voice)

Cuthbert: John Krasinski (Voice)

Katie: Renee Zellweger (Voice)

Carl Murphy: Jeffrey Tambor (Voice)

News Reporter: Ed Helms (Voice)

Computer: Amy Poehler (Voice)

Wendy Murphy: Julie White (Voice)

Origin: USA

Language: English

Released: 2009

Production: Lisa Stewart; DreamWorks; released by Paramount

Directed by: Rob Letterman, Conrad Vernon

Written by: Rob Letterman, Maya Forbes, Wally Wolodarsky, Jonathan Aibel, Glenn Berger

Music by: Henry Jackman

Sound: Erik Aadahl

Editing: Joyce Arrastia, Eric Dapkewicz

Art Direction: Scott Wills, Michael Isaak

Production Design: David A.S. James

MPAA rating: PG

Running time: 94 minutes

REVIEWS

Burr, Ty. *Boston Globe.* March 26, 2009.

Ebert, Roger. *Chicago Sun-Times.* March 26, 2009.

Honeycutt, Kirk. *Hollywood Reporter.* March 23, 2009.

Lemire, Christy. *Associated Press.* March 24, 2009.

McCarthy, Todd. *Variety.* March 23, 2009.

Pais, Matt. *Metromix.com.* March 26, 2009.

Scott, A.O. *New York Times.* March 26, 2009.

Sharkey, Betsy. *Los Angeles Times.* March 26, 2009.

Tallerico, Brian. *HollywoodChicago.com.* March 27, 2009.

Wilonsky, Robert. *Village Voice.* March 24, 2009.

QUOTES

B.O.B.: "SUUUUSSAAANN! Ooh, I just scared myself! That is scary!"

TRIVIA

The multi-colored pads that Dr. Cockroach dances on use the same sound effects as the light-up memorization game "Simon." The dancing in sync with the lighted pads is a reference to the arcade game Dance Dance Revolution, in which you do the same thing, only in sync with the on-screen prompts.

MOON

The last place you'd ever expect to find yourself.
—Movie tagline

Box Office: $5 million

Released to coincide with the fortieth anniversary of the first human step on the moon, Duncan Jones's *Moon* spends its entire time on the dark side—literally and figuratively. It's an odd, cold, (but not chilling), look at the near future, when a lone astronaut, Sam Bell (Sam Rockwell), is in charge of a lunar mining operation.

The set-up for the story is cleverly explained at the film's opening in a commercial for the Japanese-owned company that provides seventy percent of the Earth's energy needs by shipping something called "helium 3" from the dark side of the moon back to Earth. (It may not make sense why the part of the moon that never gets sunlight would have helium energy, but that does not matter—it is still an intriguing idea.)

When we first meet Sam, he is two weeks away from finishing his contracted three-year stint running the automated mining operation. He is all by himself—unless you count the companionship of GERTY (voiced by Kevin Spacey), an intelligent computer that takes care of all Sam's needs, cooking him dinner, cutting his hair, and even providing wise counsel. Having been alone so long, Sam may be talking to himself, his plants, and his machines, as well as GERTY, but he seems only borderline stir-crazy, at first. He is overjoyed to receive a videotaped message from his wife, Tess (Dominique McElligott), who shows him their daughter, Eve, who he left when she was just a baby. Tess tells Sam she thinks he is a hero, cannot wait for his return, and still loves him.

Sam is haunted by dreams about Tess, and things start to go awry when Sam sees a hallucination of another woman aboard the mining operations center where he lives and works. Traveling outside in a land rover to investigate a malfunctioning digging machine, he sees another hallucination and then mysteriously crashes. He seemingly awakens in the infirmary, being tended to by GERTY, who tells him he has suffered a head injury and may have partial amnesia.

Orders from company headquarters on Earth are for Sam to stay inside the spaceship until he recovers and a rescue crew is sent, but Sam ventures out to the crash scene despite GERTY's efforts to keep him locked up, and there he finds himself, injured and trapped in the land rover. He brings this other Sam back to the ship, where he is placed in the infirmary.

For awhile there is absurdist interplay between the two Sams, and there is a delicious tension about what has really taken place. Is Sam out of his mind and hallucinating that he has been split into two people? Too soon, we learn, from a surprisingly open GERTY, that the new, vigorous Sam is a clone of the old, injured, and increasingly feeble Sam.

The rest of the film depicts the two Sams trying to discover the bigger truths about the mission and their role in it, and the story turns into an implausible but satisfying rebellion against their corporate overlords. Since GERTY is programmed to help Sam and keep him safe, he can even be enlisted in the cause, though he is really part of the company's control apparatus.

Director Jones, who conceived the story (though Nathan Parker wrote the screenplay), has fashioned a simple but effective tale that combines some standard elements of science fiction without too many weird plot twists. It's really a tale of worker exploitation, and it cleverly uses the technology of cloning to explore what this practice could lead to in the future.

It's filmed without frills, but with an appropriate claustrophobia, which makes one wonder from the start how a man could survive on this mission and not go crazy. Rockwell, in what amounts to a performance in a one-man show, displays a wide range of acting talent, playing on the edge of mania and creating two distinct characters that are plausible as closely related beings. Despite his efforts, though, it is a little hard to continue to be empathetic when it is revealed that the emotional energies invested have been in a clone. Clones are real people, Bell reminds us late in the film, but still the revelations tend to distance the audience from the multidimensional protagonist.

Moon has a brave story concept and is a rather unique and neat little sci-fi tale. The lone astronaut and the talking computer take us back to *2001: A Space Odyssey* and HAL, but this is a quieter and, in many ways, a more coherent movie and not nearly as grandiose. Rockwell's performance and some sparse but quite believable dialogue carry the tale into something both plausible and thought-provoking. While *Moon* avoids the grandiosity typical of sci-fi and dystopian movies, it rewards the viewer with a restrained, effective experience.

Michael Betzold

CREDITS

Sam Bell: Sam Rockwell
Eve Bell: Kaya Scodelario

Overmeyers: Matt Berry
Sam: Robin Chalk
Thompson: Benedict Wong
Tess Bell: Dominique McElligott
Gerty: Kevin Spacey (Voice)
Origin: Great Britain
Language: English
Released: 2009
Production: Trudie Styler, Stuart Fenegan; Liberty Films, Stage Six Films; released by Sony Pictures Classics
Directed by: Duncan Jones
Written by: Nathan Parker
Cinematography by: Gary Shaw
Music by: Clint Mansell
Sound: Patrick Owen
Editing: Nicolas Gastor
Art Direction: Hideki Arichi
Costumes: Jane Petrie
Production Design: Tony Noble
MPAA rating: R
Running time: 97 minutes

REVIEWS

Ebert, Roger. *Chicago Sun-Times.* June 18, 2009.
Howell, Peter. *Toronto Star.* July 3, 2009.
Jones, J.R. *Chicago Reader.* July 10, 2009.
LaSalle, Mick. *San Francisco Chronicle.* June 19, 2009.
Morgenstern, Joe. *Wall Street Journal.* June 12, 2009.
Puig, Claudia. *USA Today.* June 11, 2009.
Rogers, Nathaniel. *Film Experience.* July 2, 2009.
Scott, A.O. *New Yorker.* June 12, 2009.
Sharkey, Betsy. *Los Angeles Times.* June 12, 2009.
Tallerico, Brian. *MovieRetriever.com.* June 19, 2009.

QUOTES

Sam Bell: "You look like a radioactive tampon."

TRIVIA

According to director Duncan Jones, the film was shown to some NASA scientists who questioned why harvesting of He3 would not take place on the near side of the moon, where He3 is in more abundance. The explanation given was that the choice was made to harvest the far side so as not to affect wildlife.

AWARDS

British Acad. 2009: Outstanding Debut (Jones).

MORE THAN A GAME

The incredible true story of LeBron James and the Akron Fab Five.
—Movie tagline

More than a team—more than a coach.
  —Movie tagline

The skills of high school basketball phenom turned NBA icon LeBron James may have always set him apart from the rest, but the player anointed at seventeen by *Sports Illustrated* as "The Chosen One" readily points out that his road to singular accomplishments was not a solitary one. Born to a loving mother whose troubles were not limited to getting pregnant at sixteen and then constantly uprooted during his youth from one crime-corroded part of Akron, Ohio, to another, James found some much-needed security and stability when he tightly bonded with three fellow B-ballers who permanently became the perpetually-displaced only child's brothers. Dru Joyce III, Willie McGee and Sian Cotton, all of whom had their own challenges to overcome, coalesced with James into what was initially the "Fab Four," fueling their Amateur Athletic Union team to an impressive near-miss at the National Championship Tournament in 1999. Steadfastly vowing to maintain their cohesiveness as their high school years began, they went on to form the core of a nearly-invincible St. Vincent-St. Mary's squad and, along with initially-problematic transfer student Romeo Travis, achieved their collective dream of a No. 1 ranking and a National Championship trophy in 2003. *More Than A Game*, an expansion of the ten-minute documentary Kristopher Belman made as a student at Loyola Marymount University, tells their story, an absorbing, earnestly inspiring, and often quite affecting one that is neither limited to standout James nor the sport of basketball.

As he has in the lives of the "Fab Five," St. Vincent-St. Mary's Head Coach Dru Joyce II looms large in *More Than a Game*. Indeed, the film begins with Joyce speaking in a manner reminiscent of UCLA's legendary John Wooden, exhibiting a sincere interest in imparting the fundamentals of a worthwhile life and not just those that will bring success within the confines of the court. Rather than solely stressing the scoring of points he became determined to make them, devotedly mentoring boys into men who would value cooperation, loyalty, trustworthiness, and the resolute pursuit of worthwhile dreams. One piece of advice was especially crucial for the vast majority who aimed for a shot at the pros but fell short of the net: participation in a sport is not an end-all and be-all but a useful, enriching "vehicle." Joyce has been a father figure to all the members of the familial "Fab Five," not just his point guard son: James grew up without a dad, the film's production notes only mention Travis' mother, and McGee was rescued from a troubled home in Chicago by a brother who raised him as his own. Joyce found the corporate world empty but coaching fulfilling, teaching himself about basketball so that he could share in his son's passionate pursuits. Without

a doubt, he comes off in the film as a meritorious role model. The film that begins with him also ends with him, noting that he "continues to work with kids." One feels confident that he is also still teaching them about more than just a game.

More Than a Game is composed of Belman's footage, poorer-quality home videos, and photographs, as well as recent and often quite candidly-illuminating interviews, all of which are edited together for maximum effect. It is book-ended by the players' defining moment, down at the half and taking in Coach Joyce's heartfelt locker room motivation with their last chance to win a National Championship together on the line. Before the stirring climactic scene of the team's 2003 triumph, heavily underlined by crescendo-reaching musical accompaniment, the film includes an engrossing seesawing of fortunes reminiscent of a well-played game. Along the way, mere boys from Akron who practiced at a decrepit Salvation Army gym, sold duck tape to afford uniforms, and squeezed into a minivan to be driven to games would eventually become arena-packing, autograph-hounded celebrities jetting cross country and, in LeBron's case, tooling around in a $55,000 Hummer. They had come back from that devastating loss at the final buzzer of the AAU National Championship Tournament in 1999. Joyce had fortuitously stepped in when SV-SM Coach Keith Dambrot broke a promise to the young men and used their second state championship to catapult himself up and away to coach at The University of Akron. The tumultuous circus, withering scrutiny and pedestal-tipping backlash resulting from James' ascension to teenaged superstardom had become a poise-testing distraction for all. He had crushingly been declared ineligible to complete his senior season for accepting a gift, but was then reinstated through the legal system just in time to proceed to the National Championship Game and victory. Through it all, what is even more striking than the compelling play is the camaraderie—and how lucky the Fighting Irish were to have Joyce as their coach.

Another James is responsible for perhaps the most powerful and thought-provoking film of this genre, director Steve James' award-winning *Hoop Dreams* (1994), which multiple members of the "Fab Five" have pointed to as a highly-relatable favorite. (Film critic Roger Ebert has declared *Hoop Dreams* the best motion picture of the 1990s.) There are obvious parallels between the two documentaries. Both follow talented, inner-city African American basketball players over a span of years, and particularly focus on their high-school careers. The two films deal not only with big hopes but also big hurdles, speaking of the basketball court as a sort of sanctuary, one with a possible exit door from travails that could lead toward a more promising future. Both *Hoop Dreams* and *More Than a Game* speak of growing up in neighborhoods rife with strife, and delve into the stresses and strains of the players' family lives. Like LeBron and his comrades, *Hoop Dreams'* William Gates and Arthur Agee also enrolled in a predominantly-white high school where a more favorable basketball program awaited. (Belman's film notes the resulting criticism from within the black community.) Still, despite the films' similarities, *More Than a Game*, which received favorable reviews, is unquestionably outmatched in terms of complexity, depth, and vividness by its superior, indelible predecessor.

David L. Boxerbaum

CREDITS

Himself: LeBron James
Himself: Dru Joyce
Himself: Romeo Travis
Himself: Sian Cotton
Himself: Willie McGee
Origin: USA
Language: English
Released: 2008
Production: Harvey Mason, Kristopher Belman, Matthew Perniciaro, Kevin Mann; released by Lionsgate
Directed by: Kristopher Belman
Written by: Kristopher Belman, Brad Hogan
Cinematography by: Kristopher Belman
Music by: Harvey W. Mason
Sound: Chauncey Taylor
Editing: V. Scott Balcerek
MPAA rating: PG
Running time: 105 minutes

REVIEWS

Gleiberman, Owen. *Entertainment Weekly.* September 30, 2009.
Honeycutt, Kirk. *Hollywood Reporter.* October 2, 2009.
Lemire, Christy. *Associated Press.* September 29, 2009.
Morgenstern, Joe. *Wall Street Journal.* October 2, 2009.
Pinkerton, Nick. *Village Voice.* September 29, 2009.
Puig, Claudia. *USA Today.* October 1, 2009.
Scott, A.O. *New York Times.* October 2, 2009.
Smith, Kyle. *New York Post.* October 2, 2009.
Tobias, Scott. *AV Club.* October 1, 2009.
Turan, Kenneth. *Los Angeles Times.* October 2, 2009.

QUOTES

Dru Joyce II (to his team): "Basketball is a vehicle, not a be-all and end-all. Use basketball; don't let it use you."

AWARDS

Nomination:
Ind. Spirit 2010: Feature Doc.

MOTHERHOOD

There are no time-outs in...motherhood.
—Movie tagline

Katherine Dieckmann's awful *Motherhood* purports to turn the harried life of an intellectual, social, stressed, loving mother in New York City into the stuff of hilarious comedy and touching drama. Neither funny nor moving, *Motherhood* serves more as an offense to the institution which it hopes to humanize. Star Uma Thurman said in interviews supporting the film that she was attracted to the role because there had not been enough films made about the day-to-day life of the modern matriarch. There is no arguing with this statement. The problem, however, is that this film does not serve her reported motivation. There should be more films about how uniquely challenging and rewarding, sometimes in the same moment, that it can be to be a mother. Sadly, *Motherhood* is not one of those films. It is manipulative dreck of the highest order, a film that justifies the producers who have not made too many films about modern mothers. It is a misguided, cluttered, annoying mess of a dramedy only mildly redeemed by the still-great and tragically underused Thurman, but even she cannot overcome a truly horrendous screenplay.

Motherhood unfolds over the course of one crazy day in the life of a Manhattan mother. Thurman is in every scene of this maternal *24*, trying to balance life as a wannabe blogger with also being a supportive wife and loving mother. Eliza Welsh has to stage a birthday party for her toddler daughter and the poor woman has apparently done no planning whatsoever. The film is framed by Eliza getting the party together while working on an essay for web submission entitled "What Does Motherhood Mean to Me?" The fatal flaw in a film with many of them is that Dieckmann never comes close to answering that crucial question, arguably the driving force of the film (or at least it should have been). This is a day in the life of a West Village mother that hardly ever feels organic, genuine, or like actual motherhood.

While working on the party that will clearly end the film, Eliza also has to manage a distant husband (Anthony Edwards), a friend (Minnie Driver) who feels betrayed after Eliza writes about her on her blog, and the general difficulties of living life in New York City, including things like parking restrictions and movies shoots that interrupt daily life. It is unclear if this is just a rough day or if Eliza is perpetually harried, running from the party store to a special sale to her kid's school and so on. Of course, as any parent can attest, some days are simply ridiculous in their requirements but not all are quite as nuts as the one portrayed in *Motherhood* and, even worse, Eliza's cramming comes off more flighty than maternal. Why she did apparently no planning at all before the day of the party is never answered and she has time to go to clothes shopping with her friends (although it is noted that this is for a sale that cannot be missed—although Eliza's financial situation, one that allows for two Manhattan apartments in the same building, certainly does not seem to demand sale shopping at the most inconvenient times) and to flirt/dance with a cute messenger who stops by her house and makes her feel young again. Eliza comes across as whiny and unfocused, something which most average mothers would not identify. There are rough days as a parent, but on those days most people do not dance with the cute messenger or go shopping with their friends no matter the sale. And the timing of lamenting career decisions not made could not be worse. True motherhood is often in the timing; sacrificing the little things, not cramming them into an overcrowded, meandering semi-comedy.

Despite the significant problems with the screenplay, Uma Thurman remains one of the most interesting actresses of her generation and nearly finds a way to life *Motherhood* out of its TV-movie structure and sense of falseness by doing everything in her power to make this character three-dimensional. Far more than most actresses, she balances being strong, sexy, and smart, often in the same moment. Sadly, her casting was the only smart choice when it came to *Motherhood* . Actual motherhood is not one bad day. It is a life of ups and downs. By cramming so many elements of it into one day, Dieckmann deflates her own good intentions by draining the piece of any trace of realism. Mothers have it tough in both the world of cinema and the real one. *Motherhood* does not help the cause.

Brian Tallerico

CREDITS

Eliza Welch: Uma Thurman
Sheila: Minnie Driver
Avery: Anthony Edwards
Sandrine Dumas: Stephanie Szostak
Herself: Jodie Foster (Cameo)
Origin: USA
Language: English
Released: 2009
Production: Rachel Cohen, Jana Edelbaum, Pamela Koffler, Christine Vachon; John Wells Prods., Killer Films; released by Freestyle Releasing

Directed by: Katherine Dieckmann
Written by: Katherine Dieckmann
Cinematography by: Nancy Schreiber
Music by: Joe Henry
Sound: Brian Miksis
Music Supervisor: Jim Dunbar
Editing: Michael R. Miller
Art Direction: Charles Kulsziski
Costumes: Susan Lyall
Production Design: Debbie DeVilla
MPAA rating: PG-13
Running time: 90 minutes

REVIEWS

Dujsik, Mark. *Mark Reviews Movies.* October 22, 2009.
Duralde, Alonso. *MSNBC.* October 20, 2009.
Lumenick, Lou. *New York Post.* October 23, 2009.
Nelson, Rob. *Variety.* September 1, 2009.
Orange, Michelle. *Village Voice.* October 20, 2009.
Pais, Matt. *Metromix.com.* October 22, 2009.
Phipps, Keith. *AV Club.* October 22, 2009.
Schager, Nick. *Time Out New York.* October 21, 2009.
Scott, A.O. *New York Times.* October 23, 2009.
Weber, Bill. *Slant Magazine.* October 20, 2009.

MY BLOODY VALENTINE 3D

Nothing says date movie like a 3D ride to hell!
    —Movie tagline
Are you ready for your heart to be broken? He's going to do it.
    —Movie tagline

Box Office: $51.5 million

The 3D process and the modern horror film should go together like blood and guts but *My Bloody Valentine 3D* goes straight for the eyes only to pass through the mind like a ghost. If it did not employ the gimmick of 3D it would barely rate mention at all. The original *My Bloody Valentine* is a film older horror fans remember with a certain fondness. Like other slashers of the eighties period it maintains a sense of humor that puts it on the shelf next to *When A Stranger Calls*, *Prom Night* and *Black Christmas*. It may not be a traditionally good film but it is an enjoyable one that many slasher movie fans would not part with in their collection.

As has always been the case with 3D and horror, the good film is a true rarity. The 3D horror classics like *Creature From The Black Lagoon* and *House of Wax* are far outweighed by the number of flicks that simply use the 3D process to get butts in seats. *My Bloody Valentine 3D* is, sadly, a simple case of gimmick marketing. The effects work well, and fans of 3D in general are unlikely to be disappointed, but critics looking for anything to hang their hat on but narrative clichés and dubious subtexts should revisit the original.

Young Tom Hanniger (Jensen Ackles of TV's *Supernatural*) returns home to the small town of Harmony ten years after causing an accident at his father's mine. Intent on selling the mine, he is faced with open hostility by survivors families, townsfolk, and suspicion from the town sheriff Axel. who has married Tom's old flame, Sarah, and questions his real motives for coming back.

Complicating matters is their shared history of having lived through the Valentine's Day Massacre perpetrated by Harry Warden, the lone survivor of the accident. Having pick-axed the other trapped miners to conserve oxygen, Harry Warden was discovered in a coma, only to reawaken, escape the hospital and massacre 22 townsfolk on Valentine's Day. When a trail of new victims, their hearts ripped out and placed in candy boxes all over town, coincides with Tom's sudden arrival, suspicion threatens to erupt into vigilante justice. Soon, dark secrets are uncovered and confessions make everyone a suspect. Unless of course Harry Warden has returned from the grave.

It should be noted that serious fans of slasher cinema or 3D movies will find something to latch on to in *My Bloody Valentine 3D* to make it worth watching once. The kills are imaginative, and the cast is clearly having fun under the direction of Patrick Lussier, previously best known for the highly imaginative*Dracula 2000*. Unlike many 3D horror efforts *My Bloody Valentine 3D* even flirts with the idea of using the effect to tell the story. But, ultimately, Lussier and company stick to throwing things at, and poking the audience with, whatever is at hand. You can almost hear the cast and crew chuckle.

But just as an actor's job isn't to provide giggly fodder for the outtake reel Lussier lets things go too far right at the point that it matters most. Much was made during the films marketing of a record-breaking four-minute-plus sequence in which the totally nude actress Betsy Rue is bedded, shoots a man, and then is chased and brutally killed. There is no reason for the actress to be naked other than the obvious. But the plain truth is, this is, at the risk of a bad pun, serious overkill. Nudity was a very small part of what made the slasher genre so fun for so many. Many of the greatest slashers did not use nudity at all. It's sad to see Lussier settle for that sort of ignominy, especially considering the efforts to ratchet up the tension through the film's intense and

sometimes surprisingly effective violence, and a plot which at least nods toward character development.

While speaking at a 2009 Fangoria Weekend of Horrors convention noted Italian Giallo director Lamberto Bava said that in his opinion it was impossible to remake the great Giallo films because they are far too identified with their time. The remark also seems applicable to eighties slasher films which, thus far, as the indirect spawn of Giallo, have been remade one-by-one with a humorless lack of skill and ignorance of what made fans embrace slashers in the first place. *My Bloody Valentine 3D* fails to break that pattern, 3D or not.

Dave Canfield

CREDITS

Tom Hanniger: Jensen Ackles
Sarah Palmer: Jaime King
Axel Palmer: Kerr Smith
Deputy Martin: Edi Gathegi
Mayor Ben Foley: Kevin Tighe
Harry Warden: Rich Walters
Irene: Betsy Rue
Burke: Tom Atkins
Megan: Megan Boone
Deputy Ferris: Karen Baum
Origin: USA
Language: English
Released: 2009
Production: Jack Murray; Lionsgate; released by Lionsgate
Directed by: Patrick Lussier
Written by: Todd Farmer, Zane Smith
Cinematography by: Brian Pearson
Music by: Michael Wandmacher
Sound: James Emswiller
Editing: Cynthia Ludwig
Art Direction: Andrew E. W. Murdock
Costumes: Leeann Radeka
Production Design: Zack Grobler
MPAA rating: R
Running time: 101 minutes

REVIEWS

Anderson, Jason. *Toronto Star.* January 20, 2009.
Catsoulis, Jeanette. *New York Times.* January 20, 2009.
Leydon, Joe. *Variety.* January 16, 2009.
Loder, Kurt. *MTV.* January 26, 2009.
McDonough, Maitland. *Time Out New York.* January 21, 2009.
Olsen, Mark. *Los Angeles Times.* January 20, 2009.
O'Neil, Phelim. *Guardian.* January 16, 2009.
Sobczynski, Peter. *EFilmCritic.com.* January 16, 2009.

Tobias, Scott. *AV Club.* January 20, 2009.

Weinberg, Scott. *FEARNet.* December 15, 2008.

QUOTES

Ben Foley: "Eloquent, Sheriff. You make us look like an inbred mining community."

TRIVIA

The first two characters killed onscreen are named Jason and Michael—an homage to characters from *Friday the 13th* and *Halloween.*

MY LIFE IN RUINS

The most fun you can have without a passport.
—Movie tagline

Box Office: $8.7 million

Writer/actress Nia Vardalos' *My Big Fat Greek Wedding* (2002) was "The Little Film That Could," an ethnically-specific romantic comedy that mainstream audiences discovered and celebrated as their own. Shocking professional box office analysts every bit as much as it delighted paying customers, the movie played in theaters for a full year, en route to a $240 million domestic gross and a cumulative $370 million haul. The question surrounding Vardalos' Greece-set *My Life in Ruins*, then, is whether one can ever really go home again.

The answer, it turns out, is not really. A stale, awkwardly staged and utterly banal comedy that lumbers gracelessly from one wince-inducing set-up to another, *My Life in Ruins* unfolds, in terms of pure story or plot, as if designed by some computer algorithm to appeal to the same audience who just again wants to see that nice professional girl finally find someone worthy of her charms. It is not for nothing that the film's poster trumpeted "The star of *My Big Fat Greek Wedding* is finally going to Greece."

The problem is that *My Life in Ruins* is both flatly imagined and entirely unaware of its harebrained jocularity. The level of mirthless tedium on display wears one down with dispiriting quickness, which makes its ninety-five minute running time feel far longer. The film is the equivalent of the extended family member who corners you and tells the same lame jokes at every holiday gathering, and then looks at you with wide, expectant eyes and an inane, self-satisfied grin—waiting for your response, unfazed by the weakness of your polite smile.

Mostly just a gun-for-hire here (though she does rate a producer credit as the result of a quick production

rewrite), Vardalos stars as Georgia, a thirtysomething singleton who has lost her job as a history professor, and works in disgruntled fashion as a travel guide at Pangloss Tours in Athens. On the precipice of considering another big life change, Georgia struggles with leading around a motley crew of tourists (a group that includes Richard Dreyfuss, Harland Williams and Rachel Dratch), trying to show them the beauty of her native country even as they seem more concerned with air conditioning, ice cream, and shopping time. Worn down by their collective disinterest in cultural antiquity, as well as a snooty rival colleague (Alistair McGowan) out to show her up, Georgia eventually begins to let go and see things in a new light. After some mistaken identity shenanigans involving a secret admirer, the lovelorn Georgia even comes around to the possibility of a relationship with carefree, crush-worthy bus driver Poupi Kakas (Alexis Georgoulis), whose mullet magically becomes acceptable once he simply shaves off his bushy beard.

Directed by Donald Petrie, *My Life in Ruins* plays as relatively sweet and well-meaning when Vardalos is on-screen and given a chance to exercise her unvarnished charm, but it is nonetheless done in by fusty execution and tonal unevenness. A mirthless opening fifteen or twenty minutes, full of painfully telegraphed shtick, finally gives way to some passably funny if very small, discrete moments, including Dratch coining the collapsed slang "sh-load," possibly the result of a moment of improvisation. In its third act, though, the film awkwardly tries to segue into emotionally substantive territory, without success.

My Life in Ruins is written by veteran sitcom scribe Mike Reiss (*The Simpsons*), which one could intuit without looking at the credits based simply on the episodic, choppy feeling of the movie's set pieces, its preoccupation with trite, juvenile wordplay jokes (see: Poupi Kakas), and the otherwise tired stereotypes of its over-the-top characterizations. The supporting characters are by turns wacky, rude, sullen or spiritedly helpful (whatever the moment's situation whimsically dictates) as to become downright wearying. Most problematically, the film does not arrive at its emotional moments honestly.

The film's basic premise or set-up is not in and of itself inherently false. Any sort of group travel, after all, frequently brings together disparate groups of people, nudging them a bit out of their normal comfort zones and forcing them to consider life from a slightly adjusted point-of-view. *My Life in Ruins*, though, just throws together two-dimensionally dissimilar characters, and asks that viewers accept that change eventually flows from that. There is a lot of talk about "kefi" (Greek for passion, spirit or mojo, depending on the character doing the defining), and certainly enough beautiful scenery to qualify the movie as an exotic travelogue bauble, but Vardalos' character is not strongly sketched enough to make it all work as a sort of "How Georgia Got Her Groove Back." She feels like a bystander in her own life.

Essentially, *My Life in Ruins* is just a series of moments aping other film moments we have all seen before. That it tries to piggyback so blatantly on the nostalgia for and success of *My Big Fat Greek Wedding* is perhaps not surprising, but it certainly proves that cinematic leftovers do not always keep well.

Brent Simon

CREDITS

Georgia: Nia Vardalos
Irv: Richard Dreyfuss
Kim: Rachel Dratch
Dorcas: Maria Botto
Big Al: Harland Williams
Poupi: Alexis Georgoulis
Dorcas: Sheila Bernette
Barnaby: Ralph Nossek
Maria: Bernice Stegers
Lena: Maria Adanez
Origin: USA
Language: English
Released: 2009
Production: Michelle Chydzik Sowa, Nathalie Marciano; Twenty Six Films, Kanzaman Prods.; released by Fox Searchlight
Directed by: Donald Petrie
Written by: Mike Reiss
Cinematography by: Jose Luis Alcaine
Music by: David Newman
Sound: Kelly Oxford, Victor Ray Ennis
Music Supervisor: Deva Anderson, Delphine Robertson
Editing: Patrick J. Don Vito
Art Direction: Jonathan McKinstry
Costumes: Lala Huete, Lena Mossum
Production Design: David Chapman
MPAA rating: PG-13
Running time: 95 minutes

REVIEWS

Berkshire, Geoff. *Metromix.com.* June 4, 2009.
Biancolli, Amy. *Houston Chronicle.* June 5, 2009.
Ebert, Roger. *Chicago Sun-Times.* June 4, 2009.
Foundas, Scott. *Village Voice.* June 3, 2009.
Holden, Stephen. *New York Times.* June 5, 2009.
Moore, Roger. *Orlando Sentinel.* June 3, 2009.

Ogle, Connie. *Miami Herald.* June 5, 2009.
Rabin, Nathan. *AV Club.* June 4, 2009.
Rickey, Carrie. *Philadelphia Inquirer.* June 5, 2009.
Stuart, Jan. *Washington Post.* June 5, 2009.

TRIVIA

This is the first Hollywood movie to be given permission to film at the Acropolis since *Boy on a Dolphin.*

MY ONE AND ONLY

An almost perfect portrait of a family comedy.
—Movie tagline

Box Office: $2.5 million

My One and Only is an unusual sort of biopic. It tells the story of actor George Hamilton, but only up to the point where Hamilton discovers acting and decides to try and make it his career. It uses his teenage years spent with his flighty and domineering mother as a way of explaining the rest of his personal and professional choices. Many people who watch this film might not be familiar with Hamilton's life or persona, but that does not seem to matter much. It remains a funny, smart and moving road picture with few clichés and many rewards. A movie about Hamilton becoming famous would have been pointless. This movie knows the wisdom that one year can decode an entire life and that the journey is far more interesting than the arrival.

The movie opens with one of the most inventive opening credits sequences of recent memory. It puts the audience right into 1953 with a collage of Americana postcards, nuclear tests and drive-in theaters, all while the music shifts repeatedly from rockabilly to advertisements to everything else in between, much like the central character who is incapable of staying in one place too long. The story is told at first in flashback-within-flashback form, as teenager George Devereaux (Logan Lerman) explains to some auto dealers why he has a huge wad of cash in his pocket and is ready to buy a car with it. His mother Anne (Renee Zellweger) has just left her cheating husband, bandleader Dan Hamilton (Kevin Bacon), has taken all of his savings and is ready to take her two sons on a roadtrip to Boston.

Within one night in their new surroundings, Anne has one disastrous date with an old acquaintance and meets her first of many prospective husbands, Harlan (Chris Noth), a soldier who does not take kindly to any mockery from her sons about his pursuit to help wipe out communism. George and his brother Robbie (Mark Rendall) do not take kindly to him either. When that relationship fails, they leave for Pittsburgh where Anne makes a few more wrong turns in her hunt for a suitable husband and father. George decides he wants to head back to New York and live with his father, who states at the beginning of film that he loves his kids, but is a horrible father. George visits him backstage after a show in Pittsburgh and learns the cold, hard truth about him.

Naturally, nothing goes according to Anne's half-baked plans. The story then takes them through St, Louis, Albuquerque, and Hollywood, where the plan is to help make George's brother Robbie become a famous actor. The journey finds the Devereaux's meeting their relatives, Anne briefly taking a job as a waitress and meeting up with Bill Massey (David Koechner), a troubled, but friendly hardware store owner, who vows to name his next color of paint after Anne's hair color ("Heavenly gold!"). When that relationship fails, the story makes its most significant turn. George has had enough of moving from town to town with the frequency of a salesman. He refuses to keep going with her.

My One and Only may sound like a meandering, pointless affair, but one of the miracles about the movie is how grounded and purposeful it remains even as its backdrop seemingly alters every fifteen minutes. The locations change frequently, but the story about a flighty mother, a hopeless father and two teenage sons stays in the foreground. Anne keeps telling her boys that everything will eventually work out in the end. The outcome, of course, is that George Hamilton will become a movie star, but that seems irrelevant. This foregone conclusion surprisingly does not rob the film of any real suspense.

The complexities amongst these characters are rich. *My One and Only* does not set out to paint some sort of oedipal portrait of a boy and his mother. It is as much about George's relationship with his father. Even though Dan fooled around with other women, Anne does not want George to curse his father's name for the rest of his life. Anne puts on a hardened front when it comes to Dan Devereaux (whose stage name is Dan Hamilton), but Zellweger is careful to give the viewer enough sense that there exists a lingering ache in her pursuit to fill a void left by her ex-husband. When Dan confronts her towards the end and asks how her experiment is going, she tells him that all of this travelling from town to town in search of a husband and father is not an experiment. It is a gut reaction.

George, however, takes it personally. As Anne drives further and further away from their home in New York, George, who often has his nose buried in a copy of *Catcher in the Rye*, feels more and more on the sidelines of her life than in the forefront. As a test to see how well his mother knows him, George asks her to name either his favorite color, his shoe size, or his favorite

book. If she can name any of those things, he will continue to go with her. With every guess, their divide grows bigger and more heartbreaking.

But the heartbreaking thing about *My One and Only* is how little attention it received upon its release. With little in the way of backing from a major studio (or even a modest indie), the film all but disappeared from critics' and audience's radars, despite good reviews. Zellweger gave the best performance of her career with this film and the gorgeous cinematography by Marco Pontecorvo went completely unnoticed. Perhaps on paper, nobody really cares about the life story of George Hamilton. Too bad, because *My One and Only* understands more about its subject than most biopics about major historical figures that many people do care about.

Collin Souter

CREDITS

Ann Devereaux: Renee Zellweger
George Devereaux: Logan Lerman
Dan Devereaux: Kevin Bacon
Becker: Troy Garity
Robbie Devereaux: Mark Rendall
Bill Massey: David Koechner
Charlie: Eric McCormack
Dr. Harlan Williams: Christopher Noth
Bud: Nick Stahl
Wallace McAllister: Steven Weber
Hope: Robin Weigert
Paula: Molly C. Quinn
Origin: USA
Language: English
Released: 2009
Production: Aaron Ryder, Norton Herrick; Raygun Productions, Merv Griffin Entertainment, George Hamilton Entertainment; released by Freestyle Releasing
Directed by: Richard Loncraine
Written by: Charlie Peters
Cinematography by: Marco Pontecorvo
Music by: Mark Isham
Sound: Bruce Litecky
Music Supervisor: Steve Lindsey
Editing: Humphrey Dixon
Art Direction: Guy Barnes, Halina Gebarowicz
Costumes: Doug Hall
Production Design: Brian Morris
MPAA rating: PG-13
Running time: 108 minutes

REVIEWS

Anderson, Melissa. *Village Voice.* August 18, 2009.
Ebert, Roger. *Chicago Sun-Times.* Septemebr 3, 2009.
Felperin, Leslie. *Variety.* February 13, 2009.

Kaufman, Joanne. *Wall Street Journal.* August 21, 2009.
LaSalle, Mick. *San Francisco Chronicle.* September 4, 2009.
Phillips, Michael. *Chicago Tribune.* September 4, 2009.
Puig, Claudia. *USA Today.* August 20, 2009.
Rickey, Carrie. *Philadelphia Inquirer.* September 3, 2009.
Sharkey, Betsy. *Los Angeles Times.* August 21, 2009.
Smith, Kyle. *New York Post.* August 21, 2009.

TRIVIA

The story is based on the life of George Hamilton's mother.

MY SISTER'S KEEPER

Box Office: $49.2 million

Most of Jodi Picoult's novels already read like movies of the week, featuring children embroiled in ripped-from-the-headlines distress (school shootings, for example). The author has earned a reputation for heading a new genre: "children in peril lit." Despite this obvious theme to her body of work, it is hard to deny that Picoult does what she does very well. Her stories are layered, her characters complicated, and her themes full of discussion-worthy gray areas. (Would you take the blame for your kid's car accident? Discuss). *My Sister's Keeper*, the book, is no exception. It is an emotionally-driven, fast-paced, and gut-wrenching story featuring a complex and intriguing cast of characters—the stuff that great, issue-driven Sunday night made-for-TV movies are made of. It could also be the stuff that great, issue-driven feature films are made of if given the right treatment. However, in the hands of Nick Cassavetes, the film version of *My Sister's Keeper* loses touch with the moral issues that are the backbone of the narrative, instead grabbing a choke-hold on viewers' heartstrings. The result is a manipulative cry fest that might have had a chance on the Hallmark Channel, but which flops on the big screen.

Anna Fitzgerald (Abigail Breslin) is the younger sister to Kate (Sofia Vassilieva) and Jesse (Evan Ellingson), and daughter to Sara (Cameron Diaz) and Brian (Jason Patric). Anna's having a profound existential crisis. She conveys to the audience that her family has been slowly unraveling since Kate was diagnosed with a rare form of leukemia. After finding out that neither parent or brother were a genetic match for the bone marrow transplants that Kate needed, Sara, who quit her lawyer job to care for Kate fulltime, and Brian, a pensive fireman, took matters into their own hands and genetically engineered a baby girl who would act as Kate's organ and tissue back-up. That baby was Anna. Now their plan is backfiring. Kate's health is failing and she needs a

kidney from Anna. However, Anna has had enough and plans to sue her parents for medical emancipation.

But this isn't just Anna's story. In fact, everyone from Kate to Anna's schlocky-but-effective lawyer has a side to share and they do it in distracting voiceover, offering sentimental insight and repetitive observations. Their points of view are welcome and even necessary, since the substance of an "issue movie" boils down to the people who sit on either side of the divide, but all these spoken asides take away from the filmic aspect of the story. Instead of getting to know characters by how they interact with others and seeing their emotional conflicts unfold, we're told about them. This telling takes away from the dimensionality of the characters on screen and consequently lessens the audience's in-the-moment connection to their experiences. To truly experience how the Fitzgerald family is being tormented by their daughter's illness and their other daughter's decision, we have to care for them as people. The problem is that we never get to know them as such. In choosing to give so many characters a say, Cassavetes is now forced to give them all attention. Maintaining the balance is too much and for the most part they come off like caricatures. Mom yells a lot and cries; dad internalizes and doesn't cry enough; Jesse is tortured and rebellious. To maintain the connection to the characters, Cassavetes opts for a mellow, time-of-your-life soundtrack to back montages of family bonding. It works—only the completely heartless would fail to well-up watching a dying kid enjoy her last day at the beach—but its effects are only temporary. The issues introduced in the film: genetic engineering, control over a child's decision making process, aren't explored thoroughly enough to elevate *My Sister's Keeper* past the well known and well received TV genre of "sick child melodrama."

Cassavetes is as his best when he focuses on the little things in the film. Kate's sweet relationship with a fellow cancer patient is touching and shows the real life effects of the disease in a way that the rest of the film glosses over. Joan Cusack has a wonderful turn as the conflicted and grieving judge assigned to Anna's case. But her weighing of the court case isn't enough to give substance to the film as a whole. Cassavetes also deserves credit for embracing Kate's disease head-on in full, stomach-turning detail. These moments are genuine and intriguing, but there aren't enough of them. *My Sister's Keeper's* tear jerker approach would have been better digested with commercial breaks.

Joanna Topor MacKenzie

CREDITS

Sara Fitzgerald: Cameron Diaz
Anna Fitzgerald: Abigail Breslin

Kate Fitzgerald: Sofia Vassilieva

Brian Fitzgerald: Jason Patrick

Campbell Alexander: Alec Baldwin

Jesse Fitzgerald: Nick Cassavetes

Jesse Fitzgerald: Evan Ellingson

Origin: USA

Language: English

Released: 2009

Production: Stephen Furst, Scott Goldman, Mark Johnson, Chuck Pacheco, Mendel Tropper; Curmudgeon Films, Gran Via Productions, Mark Johnson Productions; released by New Line Cinema

Directed by: Jeremy Leven

Written by: Jeremy Leven

Cinematography by: Caleb Deschanel

Music by: Aaron Zigman

Editing: Jim Flynn, Alan Heim

Sound: Kelly Cabral

Costumes: Shay Cunliffe

Production Design: Jon Hutman

MPAA rating: PG-13

Running time: 109 minutes

REVIEWS

Burr, Ty. *Boston Globe.* June 25, 2009.

Chang, Justin. *Variety.* June 22, 2009.

Ebert, Roger. *Chicago Sun-Times.* June 25, 2009.

Honeycutt, Kirk. *Hollywood Reporter.* June 22, 2009.

Phillips, Michael. *Chicago Tribune.* June 25, 2009.

Pinkerton, Nick. *Village Voice.* June 24, 2009.

Puig, Claudia. *USA Today.* June 26, 2009.

Scott, A.O. *New York Times.* June 26, 2009.

Smith, Neil. *Total Film.* July 3, 2009.

Sobczynski, Peter. *EFilmCritic.com.* June 25, 2009.

QUOTES

Anna Fitzgerald: "Most babies are accidents. Not me. I was engineered. Born to save my sister's life."

TRIVIA

Real-life sisters Elle and Dakota Fanning were originally set to play Anna and Kate Fitzgerald, but when Dakota reportedly refused to shave her head, the parts were recast.

N

NEW IN TOWN
(Chilled in Miami)

She's an executive on the move. But her career is taking her a little farther than she expected.
—Movie tagline

Box Office: $16.7 million

New In Town carries about as much freshness and intrigue as its title. It tells the story of an ambitious, Miami-based, unmarried and untethered career girl named Lucy Hill (Renee Zellweger) who must relocate to small town New Ulm, Minnesota, where she must oversee the production in one of her company's factories. She's straight-laced and uptight. The locals are kind and colorful. She goes jogging. They go ice fishing. She doesn't understand the ways of Midwestern hospitality. They don't understand how she is qualified to tell them how to do business. Of course, this being the fish-out-of-water romantic comedy that it is, the town just so happens to be the home to one sexy, charming, and rugged single dad named Ted Mitchell (Harry Connick Jr.).

Lucy's journey from Miami to New Ulm takes place within the first ten minutes of the film, giving the feeling that screenwriters Ken Rance and C. Jay Cox adhered strictly to every rule in the old and dated Syd Field screenwriters' guide book. After the obligatory ten minute set-up, Lucy's story goes exactly according to plan. She arrives at the airport unprepared for the harsh blizzards and deep snow banks of Minnesota. She is taken in by good-natured and hospitable Blanche (Siobahn Fallon Hogan) and her two friends, all of whom have deep and exaggerated Minnesota accents

and all of whom form a Scrapper's Club, where they gossip while putting together scrapbooks.

Soon after Lucy's arrival, Ted (Connick) arrives for dinner with her and the rest of the women. Blanche has secretly assumed the role of matchmaker for Lucy and Ted. The two have a war with words about city vs. small town life. He also works in the plant with most of the rest of the townfolk, who need the plant to stay open in order for the town to truly survive. But Lucy's job is to try and downsize the plant and change the way it operates. She attempts this, of course, with little conscience and with little regard for these people's families and livelihood. Leading the workers is the scruffy looking Stu (J.K. Simmons), who seems to have final say on whether everyone follows Lucy's orders or refuse her demands by playing pranks on her as a way of putting her back in her place on the social latter.

Over the course of several months as a resident in this town, Lucy grows to like everyone and they grow to like her. Lucy and Ted keep ending up in situations together that force them to let down their guard. Lucy helps Ted's teenage daughter out on her first school dance and a date with a boy. Blanche's tapioca pudding makes reoccurring appearances throughout the film, signaling a big plan for the third act, when a major plant shutdown seems inevitable and alliances between Lucy, the townfolk and the big, bad corporation begin to shift.

New In Town came out at a time when the country felt the effects of the worst economic meltdown since the Great Depression. A frothy romantic comedy isn't necessarily obligated to accurately or bleakly depict the inner struggles of the working class in these tough situations (the movie was in production while the crash was taking shape), but if it had, at least there would have been a trace of ambition here. Even if the film had failed, at the very least it might have sparked some discussion about the state of corporate America and how these plant shutdowns have become a sad fact of life. Even under the guise of forced pratfalls and romantic delusions, that could have worked.

The actors seem to be trying, although there's little in the way of fresh material to work with. Zellweger and Connick probably had it in mind that this could be a throwback to Hepburn and Tracy films; a battle of the sexes with traces of a social conscience laced with fast one-liners where the two leads have chemistry to spare. Yet, the film just seems to sit there and go about its daily routine. The supporting cast all seem to be filling in their roles not as colorful, quirky locals, but as tired stereotypes. The comedic situations (Lucy getting trapped in her car during a blizzard until you-know-who shows up, Lucy and Ted going bird hunting, Lucy drinking with the boys) feel stale and obligatory. There doesn't seem to be a single scene that can function without the aide of an overbearing score.

There are ways to take unoriginal storylines and still turn them into smart, entertaining films. Judd Apatow has made a nice career for himself in that realm. *New In Town*, unfortunately, cannot pull off such a feat. It is a movie that people can describe to their friends as "a romantic comedy about a big city girl who moves to a small town" without leaving much detail out of the picture.

Collin Souter

CREDITS

Lucy Hill: Renee Zellweger
Ted Mitchell: Harry Connick Jr.
Blanche: Siobhan Fallon Hogan
Stu Kopenhafer: J.K. Simmons
Natalie: Rashida Jones
Trudy: Frances Conroy
Origin: USA
Language: English
Released: 2009
Production: Paul Brooks, Daryl Taja, Peter Safran, Tracey Edwards; Gold Circle Films, Epidemic Pictures; released by Lionsgate
Directed by: Jonas Elmer
Written by: C. Jay Cox, Kenneth Rance
Cinematography by: Chris Seager
Music by: John Swihart
Sound: Leon Johnson

Music Supervisor: Alexandra Patsavas
Editing: Troy Takaki
Art Direction: Edward S. Bonutto
Costumes: Darena Snowe
Production Design: Daniel Davis
MPAA rating: PG-13
Running time: 96 minutes

REVIEWS

Anderson, John. *Newsday.* January 29, 2009.
Bradshaw, Peter. *Guardian.* February 27, 2009.
Burr, Ty. *Boston Globe.* January 29, 2009.
Ebert, Roger. *Chicago Sun-Times.* January 29, 2009.
Holden, Stephen. *New York Times.* January 30, 2009.
Leydon, Joe. *Variety.* January 23, 2009.
Miller, Brian. *Village Voice.* January 27, 2009.
Mondello, Bob. *NPR.* January 30, 2009.
Rickey, Carrie. *Philadelphia Inquirer.* January 30, 2009.
Stevens, Dana. *Slate.* January 29, 2009.

QUOTES

Ted Mitchell: "No, robber barons built this country, and they did it from the blood of working folks. Hell, you steal somebody's car, you get thrown in jail, you steal somebody's life savings, you get to be a CEO."

TRIVIA

Actor J.K. Simmons actually gained over 40 pounds for his role and did not wear a fat suit.

NEW YORK, I LOVE YOU

Every moment another story begins.
—Movie tagline

Box Office: $1.6 million

Experiencing *New York, I Love You* roughly equates to sitting through a mini-festival of film shorts all set in the Big Apple and centered around its cosmopolitan denizens. Most of the shorts are stand-alones, although a couple of characters pop up in more than one segment. A video artist (Emilie Ohana) wandering the New York streets while armed with a consumer-grade handicam serves as a link for a few stories, each one clocking in at around the eight-minute mark.

Ten directors from around the world agreed to abide by two basic rules: They could shoot no more than two days and had to edit their films within one week. That noted, the intriguing concept of *New York, I Love You* exceeds its actual execution. Some of the segments make the weakest of Woody Allen's Apple-centric efforts look masterful. A few rank as nice tries, given the tough time limits. Only a couple rises to the level of memorable.

At the top would be Joshua Marston's unfussy, actors' showcase starring venerable veterans Cloris Leachman and Eli Wallach, who pump feisty life into their stock characters of an elderly couple bickering all the way to a nostalgic Coney Island visit. Lesser actors would merely be irritating in these familiar roles. Yet, each critical comment and sharp rebuke by Leachman and Wallach masks an endearing sense of underlying affection.

More sensational is the sexy short from Brett Ratner, whose un-PC pharmacist (James Caan) suggests that a recently spurned high school student (Anton Yelchin) attend the prom with his lovely daughter (Olivia Thirlby). What Dad does not mention is that his daughter comes with a wheelchair. Then there are the other things the characters don't mention, either.

Jiang Wen's segment starts the anthology on a promising note. Hayden Christensen stars as a slick pickpocket who makes the mistake of lifting tough guy Andy Garcia's billfold, then doubles his error by inadvertently pilfering the cell phone of his young mistress, Rachel Bilson. The two men meet, and each instantly gets the other's number in a confrontation where subtle conflict rages between their words. The sterling element in the following short, Shunji Iwai's, turns out to be Christina Ricci's beaming, moon-like countenance, the subject of on-going, passionate curiosity by Orlando Bloom's movie soundtrack composer, driven crazy by only hearing her seductive voice on the phone for days.

Mercifully, O. Henry-esque twist endings are kept to a minimum. And yet the one in Yvan Attal's New York strangers-in-the-night segment, featuring Chris Cooper and Robin Wright Penn as a couple meeting on a street corner, will seem a bit obvious to savvy viewers. Sharper and more fun is the stinger conclusion to Attal's earlier story in which Ethan Hawke's sleazy hustler throws his best pitches to Maggie Q's resistant beautiful woman, figuratively and literally smoking outside of a restaurant.

The strangest entry comes from Shekhar Kapur, directing a story initially intended for the late Anthony Minghella. Julie Christie stars as a famous opera singer who checks into a posh hotel, apparently planning to kill herself among billowing white curtains bathed in celestial light. A meeting with Shia LaBeouf's odd, physically challenged bellhop alters her destiny.

Less compelling is a wistful, subtle passion play from Mira Nair in which Natalie Portman's betrothed Hasidic diamond buyer shares a special moment with Ir-

fan Khan's Arabic jeweler and both daydream of a romance that can never happen.

Portman double-dips as the director (her debut) of a sad segment about the defacto father-and-daughter bond that develops between Taylor Geare's sweet little girl and Carlos Acosta's hunky male nanny, a muscular performance artist more tuned into her needs than her own parents are.

Another tale of quiet yearning is told by Fatih Akin. Ugur Yucel's lonely, poverty-row painter becomes obsessed with the face of a young Asian woman (Shu Qui) he spots at a Chinatown store, and sets out to capture it in whatever medium he has at his disposal.

The weakest segment, outside of some visually candid skin-on-skin contact, comes from Allen Hughes directing Bradley Cooper and Drea de Matteo as one-night standers nervously on their way to tell each other not to expect their relationship to progress beyond the one night.

Randall Balsmeyer directs several transitional scenes, mostly with Ohana's videographer, intended to smooth the jump from one story to the next, but the differing subjects and directorial styles still bounce viewers around like narrative bumper cars.

New York, I Love You is a sequel of sorts to the 2006 anthology release, *Paris, Je T'aime* in which thirteen directors, among them the Coen brothers, Gus Van Sant, Wes Craven, Tom Tykwer and Alexander Payne, mounted a much more imaginative and broader kaleidoscopic view of the City of Light.

Dann Gire

CREDITS

Rifka: Natalie Portman
Jacob: Shia LaBeouf
Mitzie: Cloris Leachman
Girlfriend: Blake Lively
Ben: Hayden Christensen
Camille: Christina Ricci
Boy in the park: Anton Yelchin
David: Orlando Bloom
Molly: Rachel Bilson
Anna: Robin Wright Penn
Writer: Ethan Hawke
Lydia: Drea De Matteo
Mr. Riccoli: James Caan
Isabella: Julie Christie
Gus: Bradley Cooper
Waiter: John Hurt
Call Girl: Maggie Q
Actress: Olivia Thirlby

Gary: Andy Garcia
Alex: Chris Cooper
Abe: Eli Wallach
Origin: USA
Language: English
Released: 2009
Production: Emmanuel Benbihy, Marina Grasic; Grand Army Entertainment, Visitor Pictures; released by Palm Pictures
Directed by: Natalie Portman, Fatih Akin, Yvan Attal, Shunji Iwai, Joshua Marston, Allen Hughes, Shekhar Kapur, Mira Nair, Brett Ratner, Wen Jiang
Written by: Natalie Portman, Fatih Akin, Yvan Attal, Shunji Iwai, Joshua Marston, Anthony Minghella, Alexandra Cassavetes, Jeff Nathanson
Cinematography by: Benoit Debie, Pawel Edelman, Declan Quinn, Mauricio Rubinstein
Sound: Ken Ishii
Music Supervisor: Ed Gerrard
Editing: Jacob Craycroft
Art Direction: Katya Debear
Costumes: Victoria Farrell
Production Design: Teresa Mastropierro
MPAA rating: R
Running time: 103 minutes

REVIEWS

Abeel, Erica. *Hollywood Reporter.* October 6, 2009.
Ebert, Roger. *Chicago Sun-Times.* October 15, 2009.
Howell, Peter. *Toronto Star.* November 29, 2009.
Lemire, Christy. *Associated Press.* October 16, 2009.
Orange, Michelle. *Village Voice.* October 14, 2009.
Scott, A.O. *New York Times.* October 16, 2009.
Sharkey, Betsy. *Los Angeles Times.* October 16, 2009.
Sobczynski, Peter. *EFilmCritic.* October 15, 2009.
Tallerico, Brian. *MovieRetriever.com.* October 16, 2009.
Weissberg, Jay. *Variety.* September 30, 2009.

TRIVIA

The runtime of the film is 1 hour 43 minutes—"143" is a common numerical representation for the phrase "I love you."

NEXT DAY AIR

It's all in the delivery.
—Movie tagline

Box Office: $10 million

Of the many laws that should be imposed upon the modern screenplay, perhaps the foremost should be that no film is allowed to climax with all of the main characters in the same room together shouting and pointing guns at each other. Fewer things are more indicative of a lazy screenplay than "resolving" multiple disparate plotlines by collecting all of the film's major characters together in a room and killing ninety percent of them in a big shootout. Such is unfortunately the case with Benny Boom's *Next Day Air*, a film that wants to be a wild, wacky screwball comedy about murderous criminals and the innocent schlubs caught in their crossfire like *A Rage In Harlem* (1991), *Get Shorty* (1995), *The Pineapple Express* (2008) and the films of Guy Ritchie, but whose weak script renders it more akin to a stale episode of *Sanford and Son*.

The less than hilarious hijinks are set in motion when a stoned delivery man, Leo Jackson (Donald Faison), delivers ten bricks of cocaine to the wrong address. It is delivered to three idiot bank robbers Brody (Mike Epps), Hassie (Malik Barnhardt), and Guch (the excellent Wood Harris, absolutely wasted here) who are so dumb that the previous day they held up a bank but only stole the bank's surveillance tapes because when Guch said "get to the safe" Brody thought he said "get the tapes" (A flashback reveals that this isn't the first time the two have had communication errors. In a previous heist "knock him out" was somehow interpreted as "cut his tongue out"). The third member of the gang, Hassie, lies asleep on the couch in the apartment throughout the entirety of the film, waking up occasionally to utter a confused line of dialogue and then falling back asleep. This was funny the first time it was a joke with Brad Pitt in *True Romance* (1993), sort of funny the second time with Suzy Ratner in *Lock Stock and Two Smoking Barrels* (1998), and vaguely funny the third time with Steven Wright in *Half Baked* (1998) but by this point its comedic gold has been fully mined.

Brody and Guch view the mistaken delivery as a gift from God and Brody contacts his drug dealer cousin, Shavoo (Omari Hardwick), to see if he wants to purchase the bricks. Brody and Shavoo have an unfunny coded phone conversation (with *Annie Hall* like subtitles revealing what they're actually talking about to the viewer) in which "bitches" stands in for "cocaine" and the degree of "hotness" of the bitches stands in for "purity" that seems to go on forever. Intrigued, Shavoo soon shows up in the apartment with his henchman (Darius McRary), a character given no name (he is simply listed as "buddy" in the credits) and there is much verbal sparring between Guch and the henchman as Guch tries to trick the henchman into revealing his name and the henchmen tries to avoid revealing it. Shavoo likes what he sees and promises to purchase the bricks for $150,000 in two hours. However when he arrives at the commercial storage facility where he has unwisely chosen to store his money, he discovers that his money has been stolen and he and his henchmen have to delay their purchasing rendezvous to solve the mystery.

Meanwhile, the couple who the drugs should have been delivered to, Jesús (Cisco Reyes), a low level drug dealer, and his assertive girlfriend Chita (Yasmin Deliz) are desperately trying to determine what happened to the drugs before the Mexican drug lord who sent the drugs, Bodego Diablo (Emelio Rivera), comes calling. (Sadly Jesús has been given his name solely for a string of feeble jokes involving his name and the savior's, such as an instance in which he is beating a character who, in pain, exclaims, "Jesus!" and is then more severely beaten by Jesús for "taking his name in vain.").

Jesús and Chita hit the streets and apprehend a delivery man who they think is Leo but who is actually Leo's best friend, Eric (Mos Def). The film's sole laughs (weak though they may be) are generated by Eric's comic attempts to persuade the couple that they've got the wrong man. Eventually persuaded, Jesús and Chita return home to find Diablo and his sociopathic henchman, Rhino (Lobo Sebastion), waiting for them. Soon the quartet tracks down Leo, who is eventually able to cut through his weed-clogged memory to remember where he delivered the package and lead them to the bank robber's apartment. By coincidence, Shavoo and his henchman, having recouped their stolen money, have also just arrived at the apartment and the aforementioned comedic collision of shouting and sidearms between all of the film's main characters is set in motion.

For material like this to work, a script needs sharp, funny dialogue, a clever plot, and a tone that is capable of balancing violence with comedy. *Next Day Air* is unable to satisfy any of these requirements. Miscommunication between characters can form the basis for comedy but isn't, by itself, sufficient to produce it. Not knowing someone's name and trying to guess it isn't funny. Jokes regarding a character's name aren't amusing but desperate. The film's comically intended dialogue falls flat in scene after scene and feels as though it was improvised by the actors with only an outline, at best, acting as the script. As for the plot, rather than a set of cleverly connected plot-lines that feel as though they inevitably lead to a climax involving all of the main characters, the various sub plots feel like they're killing time (Shavoo's storage facility mystery, Mos Def's wrong delivery man) until the commercially acceptable film length of 84 minutes is reached and then everyone can go to the bank robber's apartment for the big shootout. Most fatally of all, the film features wild, unsustainable shifts in tone as it tries to alternate between beatings, stabbings, shootings, slapstick comedy, and, most unwisely of all, poignancy. The result is an uneven and unfunny combination of failed comedy, graphic violence, and misplaced, unintentionally hilarious, attempts at

pathos. *Next Day Air* is a waste of a talented group of actors and the viewer's time.

Nate Vercauteren

CREDITS

Brody: Mike Epps
Guch: Wood Harris
Bodega Diablo: Elilio Rivera
Leo: Donald Adeosun Faison
Shavo: Omari Hardwick
Buddy: Darius McCrary
Eric: Mos Def
Ms. Jackson: Debbie Allen
Jesus: Cisco Reyes
Chita: Yasmin Deliz
Origin: USA
Language: English
Released: 2009
Production: Scott Aronson, Inny Clemons; A-Mark Entertainment, Melee Entertainment, Next Day Air Productions, Secret Society Films; released by Summit Entertainment
Directed by: Beeny Boom
Written by: Blair Cobbs
Cinematography by: David Armstrong
Music by: The Elements
Editing: David Checel
Sound: Chris Reynolds
Costumes: Rita S. McGhee
Production Design: Bruton Jones
MPAA rating: R
Running time: 90 minutes

REVIEWS

Adams, Sam. *Los Angeles Times.* May 8, 2009.
Chang, Justin. *Variety.* May 7, 2009.
Ebert, Roger. *Chicago Sun-Times.* May 7, 2009.
Hartlaub, Peter. *San Francisco Chronicle.* May 8, 2009.
Kennedy, Lisa. *Denver Post.* May 8, 2009.
Lee, Nathan. *New York Times.* May 8, 2009.
Long, Tom. *Detroit News.* May 8, 2009.
Pais, Matt. *Metromix.com.* May 7, 2009.
Rabin, Nathan. *AV Club.* May 7, 2009.
Rodriguez, Rene. *Miami Herald.* May 7, 2009.

TRIVIA

The film was shipped to theaters under the code name "Express."

NIGHT AT THE MUSEUM: BATTLE OF THE SMITHSONIAN

When the lights go off the battle is on.
—Movie tagline

Box Office: $177.2 million

In concept, the *Night at the Museum* films have all the makings of a perfectly realized family film. For the kids, they provide a goofy adventure tale with a lot of colorful characters to spark their imaginations as to how historical figures might interact with one another. The adults who take them get to see some very talented comic actors in those roles riff off the next and perhaps improvise some ironic footnotes about their real-life counterparts that may fly over the kiddies' heads. And by the end, maybe the young ones will be inspired enough to go deeper into the history books to learn more. Perhaps they will even recognize all of the opportunities this series lost thanks to a director and writers lacking in their own inspiration. The first *Night at the Museum* (2006) was passable enough thanks mostly to the all-star casting. Its follow-up has added to the cast, promises a beat-the-clock scenario with more excitement and features the funniest scene in either of the films, and yet still somehow comes up shorter than its blockbuster predecessor.

The hero from the first film, Larry Daley (Ben Stiller), has left his job as night guard at the Museum of National History to pursue his dream as an inventor. He has struck gold with a glow-in-the-dark flashlight but is disappointed to learn that many of the exhibits he used to watch are being shipped into storage to make room for more high-tech virtual displays for museum patrons. One night he gets an emergency call from miniature cowboy Jedediah (Owen Wilson) that havoc has broken out at the Washington Smithsonian where they have been sent and they need their old friend to help set things straight. It seems like Egyptian ruler Kahmunrah (Hank Azaria) is bent on reclaiming his rightful place as ruler and he's enlisted the likes of Ivan the Terrible (Christopher Guest), Napoleon (Alain Chabat) and Al Capone (Jon Bernthal) to assist.

With the help of his son back home, Larry finds his way into a uniform and connects with a pair of new allies. The first is General Custer (Bill Hader), whose preoccupation with single-minded attack methods will take up much of his time. The other is Amelia Earhart (Amy Adams), a thunderbolt up for any good adventure that comes her way. Flying cross-Atlantic this may not be, but a challenge nevertheless for her and Larry to discover the secret combination of the magical tablet that breathes life into all the inanimate objects. Kahmunrah hopes to raise some bird army from the dead and is giving Larry just one hour to find the code or Jedediah will perish within the hour glass raining the sands of time over his head.

It all seems like a can't-miss-scenario with so very many directions to play with the material. The first film was confined to a single location over several days while this battle is set over a single night over a chain of build-

ings that would give Danny Ocean's crew pause over hitting up. As a child I know I would have been up for an adventure story of this type. The difference between then and now is not that I have grown up but that this type of film would have been directed by the likes of Joe Dante and there's a big difference between the man who made *Gremlins* (1984) and *Explorers* (1985) and the filmmaker responsible for the remakes of *Cheaper by the Dozen* (2003) and *The Pink Panther* (2006). Shawn Levy, besides having no visual flair outside of a close-up, simply has no clue how to manufacture excitement or find creative ways for his eclectic cast of characters to interact. A good portion of them spend most of their time locked in a box with Custer having a variation on the same conversation. And Levy's best innovation—a black-and-white sequence where the characters jump in and out of paintings—is not only a direct lift from Dante's *Looney Tunes: Back In Action* (2003), but he does not have the know-how to bring it back and explore it further.

Levy certainly isn't helped by the pedestrian script by *Reno 911*'s Thomas Lennon & Robert Ben Garant, who may have considered giving the painting gimmick a little play in the lackluster climax. All of their ideas are of the one-and-done variety including ther very rules established from the first film. Nobody bothers to bring up the caveat of the statues —wax, stone or otherwise— turning to dust if caught in the dawn sunlight. How does the Lincoln Memorial get around that one? Digging into precisely how much knowledge these statues have of their own history is almost picking at straws in a film like this. A more adult film may have added the idea that history is indeed written by the winners and one or more of these figures end up searching for the blanks not supplied by museum tour guides. Of course, Lennon & Garant completely miss the irony of their message that doing what you love brings you the greatest happiness. Considering Custer spent a lot of time killing Indians, should Sacajawea really support him finding his inner attack monger?

Chuckles pop up here and there throughout *The Battle of the Smithsonian*, but no scene really delivers as much as Jonah Hill's verbal sparring match with Stiller over how close he gets to the exhibits. Compare this scene with a later one where Stiller talks logic with Azaria's Kahmunrah and you will see the noticable difference between two pros having a natural improv and a director letting the camera roll on and on with no clue how painfully forced the latter conversation looks on film. Amy Adams may be channeling the stylings of Katharine Hepburn —or, at least, someone else channeling her like Cate Blanchett in The Aviator (2004) or Jennifer Jason Leigh in *The Hudsucker Proxy* (1994)— but there's a life to her performance that is severely lacking in virtually every other aspect on screen. If nothing else, perhaps kids will learn a little something about irony.

Erik Childress

CREDITS

Larry Daley: Ben Stiller
Jedediah: Owen Wilson
Octavius: Steve Coogan
Amelia Earhart: Amy Adams
Gen. George Armstrong Custer: Bill Hader
Dr. McPhee: Ricky Gervais
Cecil: Dick Van Dyke
Kahmunrah: Hank Azaria
Ivan the Terrible: Christopher Guest
Einstein: Eugene Levy
Nick Daley: Jake Cherry
Al Capone: Jon Bernthal
Teddy Roosevelt: Robin Williams
Smithsonian security guard: Jonah Hill
Napoleon: Alain Chabat
Origin: USA
Language: English
Released: 2009
Production: Shawn Levy, Chris Columbus, Michael Barnathan; 21 Laps, 1492 Pictures; released by 20th Century Fox
Directed by: Shawn Levy
Written by: Robert Ben Garant, Thomas Lennon, Scott Frank
Cinematography by: John Schwartzman
Music by: Alan Silvestri
Sound: Paul Massey, David Giammarco
Editing: Dan Zimmerman, Dean Zimmerman
Art Direction: Helen Jarvis
Costumes: Marlene Stewart
Production Design: Claude Pare
MPAA rating: PG
Running time: 105 minutes

REVIEWS

Burr, Ty. *Boston Globe.* May 21, 2009.
Ebert, Roger. *Chicago Sun-Times.* May 21, 2009.
Gleiberman, Owen. *Entertainment Weekly.* May 20, 2009.
Lowenstein, Lael. *Variety.* May 20, 2009.
Luscombe, Belinda. *Time Magazine.* May 22, 2009.
Orange, Michelle. *Village Voice.* May 19, 2009.
Pais, Matt. *Metromix.com.* May 21, 2009.
Puig, Claudia. *USA Today.* May 20, 2009.
Scott, A.O. *New York Times.* May 22, 2009.
Tallerico, Brian. *MovieRetriever.com.* May 22, 2009.

QUOTES

Kah Mun Rah: "Who ever you are Archie Bunker, you have a very comfortable throne."

TRIVIA

This is the first movie to be filmed in the Smithsonian Institution.

9

When our world ended their mission began.
—Movie tagline

Box Office: $31.7 million

Watching *9*, Shane Acker's feature-length adaptation of his 2005 Academy Award®-nominated short, is like getting better acquainted with a mysterious stunner who had riveted one's attention with a quick-but-memorable glance, only to be let down because the person fails to measure up. Sometimes that wordless communication turns out to have been the high point, with what one eventually comes to know unable to trump what the imagination had conjured up. With unfortunate irony, this latest version that provides more information is less intriguing by comparison.

In just eleven minutes and without a single line of dialogue, Acker's computer-animated student project at UCLA created a sense of wonder in viewers who glimpsed his distinctive depiction of a steampunk-inspired, post-apocalyptic dystopia. Amidst the mangled odds and ends of civilization's remains, a pint-sized burlap being with the number nine enigmatically printed upon his back uses his wits to triumph over a massive, mechanized hodgepodge of a monster. One could not help but be drawn in by the arresting, innovative visuals and a story that amounted to David and Goliath amongst the detritus. Peering into the murky, mysterious mise-en-scène and pondering an existence that is in every way unsettlingly dark, viewers were enticed to come up with their own speculative horror stories to explain how what is at least assumed to be our Earth came to be laid so low.

As in the 2005 telling of the tale, the titular character in the full-length version is reminiscent of a goggle-eyed, elongated gingerbread man whose recipe called for fabric instead of flour. Unlike before, however, *9* is only silent at the outset here, temporarily unable to speak after coming to life. The film would certainly have lived up to the audacity of its plucky protagonist if viewers had once again been called upon to decipher the action sans dialogue. When 9 throws open shutters and gets his first astonishing glimpse of vast, sooty bleakness, the spectacle's stunning impact upon him is conveyed through the repeated blinking of astonished eyes. Rubble and jagged, twisted metal are everywhere under smoky skies, disturbing images that recall the most horrific instances of urban obliteration during World War II. Had 9 been able to talk at that moment, it would have surprised no one if the sight had rendered him speechless on the spot.

The enjoyment previously had in hypothesizing about the catastrophe's cause is not to be had here, as the specifics of what triggered a war between people and machines are made clear fairly early on. It seems that the dictatorial head of a Reich-like regime had commandeered an invention that could have been used peaceably for the populace's welfare, choosing instead to proceed headlong down a slippery slope toward the finish line of the human race. Sophisticated new machines developed to possess a mind of their own quickly developed terrifying plans of their own, and have since crushed the foolhardy life form that created it. The concept of technology made too smart for our own good is unquestionably not a novel one, but still chills. Thus, *9* is something like a textile *Terminator: Salvation* (2009), with underdogs who are humanity's last hope in a daunting struggle for survival against imposing, relentless killing machines. Rampaging upon Acker's fascinating and forbidding landscape, which is simultaneously both a chaotic jumble and eerie void, are thoroughly-contrary contraptions made from bits of bone and mechanical remnants. They are hell-bent on seizing the group of fabricated little cloth beings and sucking out their essence, something akin to what this explanatory expansion of 9's saga has done to Acker's effective short.

The beginning of *9* is reminiscent of Henry Selick's *Coraline* (2009), similarly featuring a doll being sewn together. (A fan of Acker's aesthetic coined the apt term "stitchpunk.") As a voice intones during the endeavor that "our world is ending, but life must go on," most viewers, unlike 1 through 9 themselves, will likely understand the creatures' vital reason for being from the start. Later on, things are made clearer to all: the well-intentioned inventor whose innovation had been used for ill by the state had aimed to atone for his part in mankind's downfall, endeavoring to parcel-out his own life force into nine survivable vessels of hope. (Can it be mere coincidence that the remorseful scientist whose creativity led to such singularly sobering repercussions is voiced by an actor named Oppenheimer?)

Even after the story's diminutive hero saved the souls of his eight similarly-constructed brethren at the conclusion of Acker's short, viewers were not at all sure whether rejoicing was quite in order as 9 plodded off alone into bombed-out emptiness. What was decidedly dreary throughout is brightened at least to some degree this time around, the perilous proceedings infused with a reassuringly upbeat and constructive message. Setting things right may be a tall order for an eight-inch sentient doll, but 9 is set forth here as the moxie-filled, chivalrous, and humane savior of nearly-extinguished humanity. He has an inextinguishable can-do attitude and selfless, heroic nature meant here to inspire. Soon after meeting 1 through 8, 9 stresses the necessity for cooperation, the gathering of knowledge, and the girding of loins if the tiny troop is to survive against their considerable foes. In contrast and opposition to his tenaciously-held conviction not to cower is the group's imperious, glowering leader, 1 (Christopher Plummer), who is all-too-sure that they should stay cautiously hidden and as intact as events will allow. To him, daring equals dying. However, 9 is determined to not only best The Beast but also The Machine, the colossal, thundering, metallic arachnid that is the source of all these malevolent machines of mass destruction. No matter how dark things get, 9, who is significantly depicted carrying a makeshift, luminous staff on the film's posters, steadfastly shows the way toward a light at the end of an exceedingly dark tunnel.

Especially in juxtaposition with the wealth of tantalizing uniqueness here upon which the eyes can feast, the story devised for the adaptation cannot help but seem rather paltry, bland, and stale. It amounts to little more than repetitive cycles of attacks, message imparting, and rescue missions, not to mention dialogue that was apparently thought to be deeper than it actually is. Two of the most haunting moments are actually in between the mayhem: 9's mournful first look at the world's lost lushness as depicted upon a mural, and the single (and painfully brief) soothing interlude in which mute 3 and 4 dance upon an old Victrola playing "Somewhere Over the Rainbow" amidst relief-induced laughter by all. The blue skies and rainbows spoken of in the old-time comforting lyrics are in sharp contrast to the muted grays and rusts of their current harrowing environment.

9 displays the influence of stop-motion works by the Quay brothers and Jan Svankmajer. There are also echoes of Tim Burton and Timur Bekmambetov, 9's producers, with the pen-fingers of 6 (Crispin Glover) reminding one of the former's *Edward Scissorhands* (1990) and kick-ass 7 (Jennifer Connelly) recalling Angelina Jolie's character in the latter's *Wanted* (2008). Made on a budget of $33 million, it grossed just short of that at the box office. Most critics were enthralled with the look of the film but found the script wanting. Things had simply lurked and loomed more fascinatingly and disconcertingly when left in the enigmatic unknown, making Acker's short stay with one longer. In the words of wise old 2 (Martin Landau), "Some things in this world are better left where they lie."

David L. Boxerbaum

CREDITS

9: Elijah Wood (Voice)
7: Jennifer Connelly (Voice)
6: Crispin Glover (Voice)
2: Martin Landau (Voice)
1: Christopher Plummer (Voice)
5: John C. Reilly (Voice)
Origin: USA
Language: English
Released: 2009
Production: Tim Burton, Jim Lemley, Timur Bekamambetov; Relativity Media, Starz Animation; released by Focus Features
Directed by: Shane Acker
Written by: Pamela Pettler, Shane Acker
Music by: Deborah Lurie
Sound: Will Files
Editing: Nick Kenway
Art Direction: Fred Warter, Christophe Vacher
Production Design: Robert St. Pierre
MPAA rating: PG-13
Running time: 79 minutes

REVIEWS

Edelstein, David. *New York Magazine.* September 7, 2009.
Foundas, Scott. *Village Voice.* September 8, 2009.
Lane, Anthony. *New Yorker.* September 7, 2009.
Long, Tom. *Detroit News.* September 9, 2009.
McCarthy, Todd. *Variety.* August 18, 2009.
Pais, Matt. *Metromix.com.* September 8, 2009.
Phillips, Michael. *Chicago Tribune.* September 8, 2009.
Scott, A.O. *New York Times.* September 8, 2009.
Sobczynski, Peter. *EFilmCritic.com.* September 8, 2009.
Tallerico, Brian. *MovieRetriever.com.* September 9, 2009.

QUOTES

Scientist: "We had such potential. Such promise. But we squandered our gifts. And so, 9, I am creating you. Our world is ending. Life must go on."

TRIVIA

The "sanctuary" where 1 and 9 a hiding is the famed Notre Dame Cathedral, which was referred to as "sanctuary" in the classic film *The Hunchback of Notre Dame.*

NINE

This holiday season, be Italian.
—Movie tagline

Box Office: $19.7 million

Nine, based on the 1980 stage musical, which is based on Federico Fellini's film *8½* (1963), tells the story of a filmmaker with a creative block, which is interesting, considering this film is the work of a director going back to his comfort zone. The film is directed by Rob Marshall, who made one of the most confident and career-propelling debuts of the decade with the Oscar®-winning musical *Chicago*. Though Marshall did not win the Best Director Academy Award®, *Chicago* did win Best Picture, a feat which put him in the upper echelon of Hollywood directors. Marshall followed up his success with the beautifully produced, but emotionally distant *Memoirs of a Geisha* (2005). For his third film, Marshall went back to a formula that proved to be his strong suit, a big-screen adaptation of a big Broadway musical. With *Nine*, Marshall proved he had his stylistic niche and was unbeatable at it.

The story of *Nine* centers on Guido Contini (Daniel Day-Lewis), a filmmaker who is about to embark on a new project. He has everyone in his stable of crew members lined up to accept direction from him and the press cannot wait to hear what the film will be about. Guido's problem, however, is that he has no film, no story and no direction to give. Within the film's first act, Guido's costume designer Lilli (Judi Dench) tells him that directing is one of the most overrated jobs there is. All one has to do is make a series of yes/no decisions. Guido's problem, with regards to his personal life, is that he cannot say no where it is important to do so. He is not only blocked creatively, but in life as well.

Predictably, the problem is women. Guido has a wife, a mistress, a mother, a journalist, his costume designer, a muse, and memories of discovering the beauty of women at an early age, all vying for his attention. First and foremost on his mind is the seductive Carla (Penélope Cruz), his mistress. He books her in a remote hotel, far from all the cameras and attention of the movie set and its surrounding residencies. The two have a playful and difficult relationship. True to the original Fellini film, they do role playing games in bed where Guido wants her to pretend she has entered the wrong room, perhaps subtly suggesting that she keeps making wrong turns with her life by choosing him as her lover.

Guido's other angels and demons come in the form of his long suffering wife Louisa (Marion Cotillard), who understands she has married a philanderer and is close enough to rejecting it once and for all, and his mother (Sophia Loren), who makes appearances mostly in the musical numbers, but is significant enough to warrant many psychological maternal complexes. Naturally, Guido being a public figure, a journalist from

Vogue (Kate Hudson) takes a sizable interest in him, mainly out of a fetishistic attraction to all things Italian than anything else (and Guido, supposedly, represents the pinnacle of all things Italian). Guido's long-time muse, Claudia (Nicole Kidman), no longer seems to carry the inspiration necessary for Guido to come through with a viable project. Finally, there is Guido's impenetrable memory of Saraghina (Stacey Ferguson, a.k.a. Fergie), a prostitute whom Guido and his friends paid to perform a sexy dance on a beach when he was just a boy.

Of course, every woman has a musical number all her own, none more alluring than Cruz's, whose Carla is an even more sexually expressive hellcat than Fellini's original incarnation played by Sandra Milo. But the song that resonates more as a showstopper is inarguably Fergie's take on the play's centerpiece, "Be Italian." The sequence goes back and forth from the black-and-white memory of Saraghina on the beach doing her dance to the stage where she is joined by a strong chorus of singers who incorporate sand and tambourines into the choreography. In fact, almost every musical number takes place on an empty stage, which is where most of these characters exist psychologically anyway.

Everyone in the cast appears to be comfortable in these surroundings. The tunes are carried nicely and the choreography is mostly fun to watch. The songs, unlike those in *Chicago*, do not resonate fully, with few exceptions. But Marshall knows exactly where to put the camera and when to cut so as to keep anything from becoming truly dull. Day-Lewis is a natural choice for Guido, throwing himself into the role with typical abandon and conviction. Hudson and Kidman's roles could have been played by anybody, really. The screenplay by Michael Tolkin and the late Anthony Minghella keeps everything moving at a satisfactory pace during the non-musical sequences.

Nine's aesthetic is similar to that of *Chicago*'s. The musical numbers happen outside, or parallel to, the drama taking place. Nobody suddenly decides they will sing their way through a conversation. It appears as though the musical numbers take place in the character's heads. This choice seems to free the director of having to cover obligatory reaction shots of the characters so that the musical numbers can come alive as pure spectacle. It works quite well and the story of *Nine* (such as it is) lends itself to that sort of loose storytelling structure.

But *Nine* has the disadvantage of arriving in the shadow of two far superior films: Fellini's *8½*, of course, and Marshall's *Chicago*. It almost seems pointless to list the many obvious flaws *Nine* has when compared to Fellini's masterpiece, especially a film that is still

referenced frequently in film schools. It would be more suitable for viewers to pretend Fellini's film does not exist when watching Marshall's film of the same material. One is the deeply personal, dreamlike work of an established auteur; the other is a crafty little bit of entertaining fluff concocted by a studio hungry for an awards slam-dunk and a director settling into his niche. Perhaps the fact that Marshall is going back to old territory signals a bit of a director's block within himself, but that remains to be seen, judging by whatever project(s) come next.

It should come as no surprise how much attention *Nine* garnered during awards season in late 2009. It contains all the elements to become a favorite, particularly for the Hollywood Foreign Press Association, a.k.a. the Golden Globes. How can the Hollywood Foreign Press resist a musical about a Hollywood Foreign director that features their old favorites Penélope Cruz, Nicole Kidman, and Sophia Loren in her most prominent role in over a decade? Furthermore, the film is the product of the tyrannical Bob and Harvey Weinstein, who have always been notorious for their Oscar® campaigns. This might be why *Nine* seems like such a calculated affair. The Weinsteins have not tasted true Oscar® glory since Marshall's *Chicago* took home the grand prize in 2002.

Still, in spite of its inferiority and the baggage that comes with its release, *Nine* manages to be an entertaining and energetic bit of fun, especially for those who have a weakness for films about the creative process (or lack thereof). It comes to life when it needs to and tells its story efficiently. There may not be much here to reference in historical essays about specific film movements in the 2000s and it may not deserve whatever awards attention it might have received, but musicals in general still remain one of the hardest genres to pull off in such a cynical culture that seems prone to reject them. For every big screen success like *Chicago*, there is a *Rent* or *Mamma Mia!* in its wake. *Nine* falls somewhere in between, which is good enough. More like a seven than a nine.

Collin Souter

CREDITS

Guido Contini: Daniel Day-Lewis
Claudia Nardi: Nicole Kidman
Stephanie Necrophores: Kate Hudson
Carla Albanese: Penélope Cruz
Liliane La Fleur: Judi Dench
Luisa Contini: Marion Cotillard
Mamma: Sophia Loren
Saraghina: Stacy "Fergie" Ferguson

Origin: USA, Italy

Language: English

Released: 2009

Production: Marc Platt, Harvey Weinstein, John DeLuca, Rob Marshall; Relativity Media, Marc Platt Productions, Cattleya (Italy), Lucamar Productions; released by Weinstein Co.

Directed by: Rob Marshall

Written by: Anthony Minghella, Michael Tolkin

Cinematography by: Dion Beebe

Music by: Andrea Guerra

Sound: Wylie Stateman, Renee Tondelli

Music Supervisor: Paul Bogaev

Editing: Claire Simpson, Wyatt Smith

Art Direction: Simon Lamont

Costumes: Colleen Atwood

Production Design: John Myhre

MPAA rating: PG-13

Running time: 110 minutes

REVIEWS

Foundas, Scott. *Village Voice.* December 15, 2009.

Germain, David. *Associated Press.* December 15, 2009.

Lane, Anthony. *New Yorker.* December 14, 2009.

McCarthy, Todd. *Variety.* December 4, 2009.

Scott, A.O. *New York Times.* December 18, 2009.

Sharkey, Betsy. *Los Angeles Times.* December 17, 2009.

Sobczynski, Peter. *EFilmCritic.* December 25, 2009.

Tallerico, Brian. *MovieRetriever.com.* December 25, 2009.

Travers, Peter. *Rolling Stone.* December 16, 2009.

QUOTES

Liliane La Fleur: "Directing a movie is a very overrated job, we all know it. You just have to say yes or no. What else do you do? Nothing."

TRIVIA

Javier Bardem was originally cast as Guido Contini. When he dropped out due to exhaustion, the role eventually went to Daniel Day-Lewis.

AWARDS

Nomination:

Oscars 2009: Art Dir./Set Dec., Costume Des., Song ("Take It All"), Support. Actress (Cruz)

British Acad. 2009: Makeup

Golden Globes 2010: Actor—Mus./Comedy (Day-Lewis), Actress—Mus./Comedy (Cotillard), Film—Mus./Comedy, Song ("Cinema Italiano"), Support. Actress (Cruz)

Screen Actors Guild 2009: Support. Actress (Cruz), Cast.

NINJA ASSASSIN

Box Office: $38.1 million

Ninja Assassin could have been a tongue-in-cheek meta movie, a throwback to those ridiculous Cannon ninja films of the 1980s produced by Menahem Golan and Yorum Globus (*Enter the Ninja* [1981], *Nine Deaths of the Ninja* [1985], and *American Ninja* [1985]). With no video game product attached to it, the movie comes free of expectation and, unfortunately, free of irony. What could have been a fun look back at mullet haircuts, cheesy synth scores and low-budget set pieces is instead a self-serious, uninspired, and ultimately generic action film not worthy of the likes of Shô Kosugi, Michael Dudikoff, or even Lucinda Dickey.

The movie comes off immediately as a no-joke, no-fun exercise in splatter, multiple flashbacks, and fortune cookie-isms masquerading as depth. The first fight scene demonstrates the movie's zeal for gore, but displays it in an unconvincing fashion, utilizing too much CGI to give it its splattering effect. The audience for this kind of film knows CGI gore when hey see it and are rarely impressed by it. One convention *Ninja Assassin* thankfully avoids is shifting to slo-mo during the action, which helps make the movie considerably shorter.

It opens with a gang of young yakuza suddenly under attack by the titular assassin, which prompts a serious investigation by Europol forensic researcher Mika (Naomie Harris), who has been following the ninja attacks with great interest (the story takes place in Berlin). Her partner, Agent Maslow (Ben Miles) reluctantly joins in on the hunt, knowing full well their case might also be investigated by a higher-up who would rather have the case be kept closed. Mika and Maslow keep their moves and findings under wrap until Maslow comes under suspicion by Zabranski (Thorston Manderlay).

On the other side of the story, there is the ninja assassin himself, Raizo (played by pop star Rain), a loner who trains in his empty apartment and who has since left the clan of the Black Sand, where he was trained as a young boy to become an emotionless assassin. Flashback upon flashback reveals how Raizo is told by his unmerciful master Ozunu (Shô Kosugi) to not feel any sympathy or remorse for anybody, that pain breeds weakness and that a cut across the face is not nearly as painful as what his master can and does to him. All of this training makes for an affective assassin, but the root of Raizo's current cause—to get revenge on Ozunu before his henchmen ninjas can capture Raizo and return him to Ozunu's clan—stems from the fact that Raizo's childhood sweetheart was killed by the clan after attempting an escape.

All of this culminates to a third act, which brings Raizo and Mika together to fight for the same cause. She wants to solve the mysterious murders of the yakuza and other such nasty people who might be associated with the ninja assassin. He wants to find the person responsible for turning him into this assassin. Here, the movie forces a slightly romantic bonding between the two, but comes up short. The screenplay has failed to make either of these characters remotely interesting or three-dimensional. They are together because the pedestrian screenplay demands it. Why is Mika in Europol? What makes her do what she does? The audience never learns. While the movie shows signs of progression by putting a female in such a place and with respect to that character, it never goes that extra mile or two necessary to flesh her (or any of the other characters for that matter) out.

Of course, nobody watches a film titled *Ninja Assassin* for its character development, but these considerable setbacks might have been forgivable had the action sequences adequately showcased some of the talent involved. Rain (the actor) moves ferociously through his self-training sequences, clearly the right person for the part. But director James McTeigue cuts his action scenes too quickly so that the audience has no idea what is going on. The fact that the majority of the action takes place in the dark does not help matters. The stunt people's supposedly carefully orchestrated and choreographed work goes completely unnoticed and unrewarded. The CGI splatter takes center stage every time and the result is just plain numbing when it should have been exciting and even wince-inducing.

These bloody and fast-paced action sequences—which feature many severed limbs, decapitations, and bodies split in half—call into question the MPAA ratings system and why, in 2003, Quentin Tarantino was forced to change his equally gory display of mayhem in *Kill Bill Vol. 1* from color to black-and-white in order to keep from earning an NC-17 rating. If he had used more CGI gore, would it have been an issue? Perhaps audiences have grown accustomed in the past few years since Tarantino's film to such sequences that the effect hardly registers anymore. *Ninja Assassin*, minus the gore, might have actually earned itself a PG-13, but at the end of it all, the gore exists in extreme amounts because the rest of the movie has so little else going for it to begin with.

Collin Souter

CREDITS

Raizo: Rain
Mika Coretti: Naomie Harris
Takeshi: Rick Yune
Ryan Maslow: Ben Miles
Lord Ozunu: Sho Kosugi
Raizo: Sung Kang

Agent Zabranski: Thorston Manderlay
Origin: USA, Germany
Language: English
Released: 2009
Production: Grant Hill, Joel Silver, Larry Wachowski, Andy Wachowski; Legendary Pictures, Dark Castle Entertainment, Silver Pictures, Anarchos Prods., Studio Babelsberg; released by Warner Bros.
Directed by: James McTeigue
Written by: Matthew Sand, J. Michael Straczynski
Cinematography by: Karl Walter Lindenlaub
Music by: Ilan Eshkeri
Sound: Eric Lindemann
Editing: Gian Ganziano, Joseph Jett Sally
Art Direction: Sebastian Krawinkel
Costumes: Carlo Poggioli
Production Design: Graham Walker
MPAA rating: R
Running time: 99 minutes

REVIEWS

Anderson, Jason. *Toronto Star.* November 25, 2009.
Berkshire, Geoff. *Metromix.com.* November 24, 2009.
Catsoulis, Jeanette. *New York Times.* November 25, 2009.
Nelson, Rob. *Variety.* October 22, 2009.
Simon, Brent. *Screen International.* November 23, 2009.
Morris, Wesley. *Boston Globe.* November 24, 2009.
Phillips, Michael. *Chicago Tribune.* November 24, 2009.
Tallerico, Brian. *MovieRetriever.com.* November 25, 2009.
Whipp, Glenn. *Associated Press.* November 24, 2009.
Zacharek, Stephanie. *Salon.com.* November 24, 2009.

NOT EASILY BROKEN

Life tries to break you. Love holds you together.
—Movie tagline

Box Office: $10.6 million

He is a proud African American male whose feelings of emotional emasculation are putting him on the verge of giving up on his marriage and falling into the arms of a white she-devil. She is an abrasive workaholic who loves living beyond her means, refuses to have a child because it would take away from her career and has allowed her embittered mother to drive a wedge between her and her husband that may very well send him into the arms of a white she-devil. Can this marriage be saved? That is the chief question on hand in *Not Easily Broken*, an adaptation of the novel from the well-known clergyman Bishop T.D. Jakes that is an exceptionally blatant attempt to replicate the mélange of soapiness, soupiness, and salvation that Tyler Perry has made a fortune from over the last few years. Unfortunately, on an artistic level, the film succeeds in doing just that and the end result is just as shrill, condescending and badly made as anything Perry has ever done.

When we first see Dave and Clarice Johnson (Morris Chestnut and Taraji P. Henson), it is on their wedding day as their pastor (Albert Hall) advises them that marriage is filled with struggles that can be overcome as long as they stick together and put their faith in God. When we pick up with them a few years later, we discover that their original hopes and dreams have gone somewhat astray over the passing of time. Dave's dreams of glory as a pro baseball player where shattered by injury and he earns a modest living doing something or other in a beat-up truck while indulging his former dream by coaching a Little League team despite not having a child of his own. On the other hand, Clarice has become the main breadwinner as a high-powered real estate agent, leaving her no time to give Dave either the loving or the baby that he so desperately wants.

Things come to a head when a car crash leaves Clarice seriously injured, an incident that heralds the arrival of her abrasive mom (Jennifer Lewis), an embittered crone who has made it her lot in life to project all the resentments of her own failed marriage onto her daughter's, and a comely physical therapist (Maeve Quinlan) with a son and no apparent outside ambition other than to find a good man to love. Although Clarice's physical recovery process is surprisingly quick (so quick, in fact, that it seems to have existed only to bring the cranky mother-in-law and the white she-devil into the narrative), the various emotional and financial pressures that she and Dave are now facing begin to drive them to the breaking point. Luckily for them, there is a peripheral character who is perfectly willing to make the ultimate sacrifice in a twist that serves no other purpose than to help inspire them to work things out.

To be fair, *Not Easily Broken* is a film that has been made with all sorts of good intentions and the theme running through it about using spiritual beliefs as a way of helping to guide yourself through rough emotional times is one that few people could immediately object to on the surface. The trouble is that pretty much every other aspect of the film is handled so ineptly that even those who agree with its message will find themselves at odds with it after a while. For one thing, the other implicit message on display—that any form of female empowerment is a bad thing because it threatens the males who are supposed to be in charge of everything—is fairly appalling. And the way that the film shows just how monstrous women can become when given any sort of power or say-so over their lives (such as Clarice's refusal to have a baby or her mother's constant attempts to split her and Dave apart) is borderline offensive,

though eventually too boring to make it across the border. The performances are universally terrible and range the gamut from shrill overplaying (Lewis and Kevin Hart as the wacky best pal) to near somnambulism (Chestnut and Quinlan)—even the usually reliable Henson, who transcended potential clichés in her performances in *Hustle & Flow* (2005) and *The Curious Case of Benjamin Button* (2008), is stuck with a character that is so resolutely one-note that even she fails to make anything out of it. From a directorial standpoint, the film is pretty much useless—everything is directed on the level of a second-rate soap opera and the whole thing plods along without any energy—and what is especially surprising about that is the fact that it was directed by Bill Duke, a man who became one of the leaders of the renaissance of African American filmmakers in the early 1990s with the one-two punch of *A Rage in Harlem* (1991) and the astonishing *Deep Cover* (1992); to judge by his work here, you would be hard-pressed to believe that he ever saw those movies, let alone made them.

Peter Sobczynski

CREDITS

Dave Johnson: Morris Chestnut
Clarice Johnson: Taraji P. Henson
Julie Sawyer: Maeve Quinlan
Bryson Sawyer: Cannon Jay
Mary Clark: Jenifer Lewis
Tree: Kevin Hart
Darnell: Wood Harris
Brock: Eddie Cibrian
Michelle: Niecy Nash
Bishop Wilkes: Albert Hall
Origin: USA
Language: English
Released: 2009
Production: T. D. Jakes, Curtis Wallace, Bill Duke, Aaron Norris; TriStar Pictures, Duke Media; released by Sony Pictures
Directed by: Bill Duke
Written by: Brian Bird
Cinematography by: Geary McLeod
Music by: Kurt Farquhar
Sound: Mark Steinbeck
Music Supervisor: Alison Ball, David Lombardo
Editing: Josh Rifkin
Art Direction: Craig Pavilionis
Costumes: Diane Charles
Production Design: Cecil Gentry
MPAA rating: PG-13
Running time: 100 minutes

REVIEWS

Foundas, Scott. *L.A. Weekly.* January 15, 2009.

Honeycutt, Kirk. *Hollywood Reporter.* January 9, 2009.

Koehler, Robert. *Variety.* January 9, 2009.

Pais, Matt. *Metromix.* January 8, 2009.

Phillips, Michael. *Chicago Tribune.* January 8, 2009.

Puig, Claudia. *USA Today.* January 9, 2009.

Sartin, Hank. *Time Out New York.* January 7, 2009.

Scott, A.O. *New York Times.* January 9, 2009.

Tallerico, Brian. *MovieRetriever.com.* January 9, 2009.

Whipp, Glenn. *Los Angeles Times.* January 9, 2009.

QUOTES

Dave Johnson: "But whatever the cause, the world took away a man's reason for being a man. It told him he wasn't important anymore and when that happened, it turned the whole world upside down."

NOTORIOUS

No dream is too big.
—Movie tagline

Box Office: $36.8 million

In the spirit of rap biopics like *8 Mile* (2002) and *Get Rich Or Die Tryin'* (2005), comes *Notorious*, the life story of Christopher Wallace, better know to the masses as East Coast rapper Biggie Smalls or The Notorious B.I.G (played here by Jamal Woolard). While Eminem and 50 Cent's movies span the spectrum of "making it" narratives—with *8 Mile* going for broke with rap battle scenes and raunchy sex and *Get Rich Or Die Tryin'* shallowly proposing that drug dealing leads to successful a rap career—*Notorious* plops itself squarely in the middle, embracing Biggie's drug-dealing lifestyle and violent tendencies (and offering some R-rated bedroom shots), but ultimately relying on viewers' familiarity with the larger than life star to fill in the blanks of a rushed, though at times entertaining, narrative.

In any biopic the hope is to get a peek behind the curtain. For a character as, well, notorious as Biggie Smalls, fans would be yearning for an engrossing and honest account of his family life as well as an exploration the many relationships that defined his career—not only was Biggie discovered by/affiliated with Sean "Puffy" Combs, involved with and responsible for the career of Lil' Kim, married to Faith Evans, and frenemies with Tupac, he was the focus of an East Coast vs. West Coast rap rivalry that ultimately claimed his life. Unfortunately, in trying to check all the milestones and connections of Biggie's life off of the list, screenwriters Cheo Hodari Coker and Reggie Rock Bythewood sacrifice dimension. As a character, Biggie is flat and his

relationships mere after-thoughts. For a man who was gunned down when he was only twenty-four, the story of his life could be dwindled down to a coming-of-age tale, wrought with teen angst and drama, more about guns and drugs than the quest for meaning behind it all. But, Biggie was no ordinary teenager. He was a storyteller, known for his dark autobiographical lyrics, his ability to observe and talk about life on both the street and in the spotlight. And he became famous for it. So that the film fails to do the legend justice is disappointing.

Instead of a man trying to balance love and fame, driven by his talent and hindered by industry politics, Biggie, the character, comes off as a money-hungry womanizer bent on rap world domination. The writers try for depth by having Biggie provide a voice-over narration where he claims to be looking for a clean slate in life, and by having him repeat the film's mantra—before you can change the world, you first have to change yourself—repeatedly. The result is textbook tension between showing and telling. As much as Biggie tells us about his emotional struggles and quest to change himself, we never see (and feel) this playing itself out on screen.

Instead of an insider's view, we get a simplified version of Biggie's rise to fame. As a kid he makes the decision to leave his mom's stoop in Brooklyn and go sell drugs, drawn by the blinding white sneakers and bling the established dealers are sporting. Soon he is ditching his baby-mama for Kim and drawing a crowd on the street corner with his rhymes. In *Notorious*, Biggie's rise to stardom just happens. He deals drugs, gets a gun, meets the right people, records a demo, and the rest is, seemingly, history. The problem is that the legend of The Notorious B.I.G. has become bigger than the man himself. So much is known about him—so much that is glossed over in this film. The biggest disappointment is the handling of his bittersweet relationship with Tupac Shakur (Anthony Mackie), who was gunned down a few months before Biggie. Their relationship is boiled down to a few pool games.

And then there is the music. The killer soundtrack that should have accompanied this film is nowhere to be found. The hits make an appearance, but the walk down rap history memory lane is absent. In his twenty-four years, Biggie Smalls turned himself into an icon. What would have been an opportunity to get to know the man behind the legend and maybe comment on the tension between talent and industry and on the media and record biz's role in creating and fuelling the East Coast vs. West Coast rivalry that lead to so much tragedy is wasted on a lacklustre rags-to-riches story.

Joanna Topor MacKenzie

CREDITS

Sean Combs: Derek Luke
Tupac Shakur: Anthony Mackie
Voletta Wallace: Angela Bassett
Lil Cease: Marc John Jefferies
Notorious B.I.G./Chirstopher "Biggie Smalls" Wallace: Jamal Woodard
Lil Kim: Naturi Naughton
Faith Evans: Antonique Smith
Suge Knight: Sean Ringgold
Origin: USA
Language: English
Released: 2009
Production: Robert Teitel, Voletta Wallace, Wayne Barrow, Mark Pitts, Trish Hoffman; By Storm Films, State Street Pictures, Bad Boy Films; released by Fox Searchlight Pictures
Directed by: George Tillman Jr.
Written by: Reggie Rock Bythewood, Cheo Hodari Coker
Cinematography by: Michael Grady
Music by: Danny Elfman
Sound: Matthew Price
Music Supervisor: Barry Cole, Francesca Spero
Editing: Dirk Westervelt, Steven Rosenblum
Art Direction: Laura Ballinger Gardner
Costumes: Paul Simmons
Production Design: Jane Musky
MPAA rating: R
Running time: 122 minutes

REVIEWS

Anderson, John. *Variety.* January 12, 2009.
Denby, David. *New Yorker.* January 20, 2009.
Ebert, Roger. *Chicago Sun-Times.* January 15, 2009.
Gleiberman, Owen. *Entertainment Weekly.* January 14, 2009.
Honeycutt, Kirk. *Hollywood Reporter.* January 12, 2009.
Puig, Claudia. *USA Today.* January 16, 2009.
Samuels, Allison. *Newsweek.* January 5, 2009.
Scott, A.O. *New York Times.* January 16, 2009.
Sobczynski, Peter. *EFilmCritic.* January 16, 2009.
Stevens, Dana. *Slate.* January 15, 2009.

QUOTES

Voletta Wallace: "What kind of grown-ass man calls himself 'Puffy'?"

TRIVIA

At one point, Sylvester Stallone was rumored to be attached to the project as director.

O

OBSERVE AND REPORT

Box Office: $24 million

Jody Hill's *Observe and Report* is Martin Scorsese's *Taxi Driver* (1976) re-imagined as a slapstick comedy. Unsurprisingly, this makes a poor premise for comedy and whatever slim potential there is for amusement is completely overwhelmed by the protagonist's stupidity and nihilism.

Observe and Report's Travis Bickle is Ronnie Barnhardt (Seth Rogan), a thirty-ish loser mall security guard who lives at home with his alcoholic mother, takes medication for his homicidal rage, fantasizes about losing his virginity to a vacuous perfume counter girl, and entertains dangerous delusions of grandeur that he's both a brilliant detective and all-around cool guy. Ronnie is the latest version of the overdone character who thinks he's clever and witty but who is in reality a total idiot and completely unaware of the fact that everyone around him thinks he is an idiot and is incapable of learning that fact no matter how many people tell him or how much real world evidence there is available to inform him of that fact. Imagine Steve Carell's Michael Scott from *the Office* if Scott was a sociopath.

Ronnie's delusions extend to every aspect of his life: his work, his romantic longings, his dreams for the future. Where the police officer's credo is to "protect and serve," a rent-a-cop's job is to simply "observe and report" to the police officer. Ronnie does not understand these limitations and plays the clichéd part of the overly officious blowhard with limited authority and zero intelligence. He strides around the mall as if he is patrolling a military outpost, dispensing tough guy advice to eye rolling mall employees. He fires thousands of rounds of ammunition at the firing range with his fellow security guards John and Matt Yuen (played by twin actors John and Matt Yuan, neither of whom can act worth a lick) and the excessively agreeable Dennis (a beyond over the top Michael Pena) when he's not conducting overly serious meetings with them. Ronnie does everything except actually apprehend the mysterious thief who has been breaking into the mall at night or the flasher who has been terrorizing mall patrons.

Predictably, Ronnie dreams of becoming a real cop, a desire put into overdrive when an actual police officer, Detective Harrison (Ray Liotta), comes to investigate the mall thefts. Harrison patiently listens while Ronnie insults him and provides his own ludicrous theories behind the robberies until he finally explodes, screaming at Ronnie that he's a total idiot. Unable to allow anything resembling outside reality to impinge on his fantasy life, Ronnie embarks on a quest to become a real cop to prove Harrison wrong. When this quest inevitably fails due to his mental health issues, Ronnie takes on half the police department, including Harrison, in hand-to-hand combat.

Ronnie's other great project in life is stalking the gorgeous and totally vacuous perfume saleswoman, Brandi (Anna Faris), who works in one of the department stores on "his beat." No matter how strongly she makes it clear to Ronnie that she is not interested in him, he is not capable of understanding this either because he is stupid or because her disliking him is not consistent with his fantasy world or both. Ronnie forces her into going out on a date with him (he refuses to release her from his mall golf cart until she agrees) and then essentially rapes her when she enters a coma level of intoxication following the date. After she passes out in his arms on her own front lawn, Ronnie takes her inside and the next scene shows him pumping away on her as she lies unconscious on the bed, vomit stains on the pillow. The film tries to rescue the scene from rape at the last minute by having Brandi wake up, when Ronnie pauses for a second, and ask, "why the f**k did you stop?" but this last-minute addition is unconvincing.

The comedy of obliviousness is certainly fertile ground for humor and no more so than with detectives who live (and die) by their wits. Some of the great, classic comedy characters of the cinema have been clueless detectives (Inspector Clouseau from the *Pink Panther* series, Lt. Frank Drebin from the *Naked Gun* series, Michael Caine's hapless Sherlock Holmes in *Without a Clue* [1988]). However, unlike those characters, Ronnie is not a well meaning but bumbling detective but a vicious, violent, mentally ill person who hurts others in the narcissistic pursuit of imposing his fantastical self image upon the world. The films above show that it is certainly possible to make a successful comedy with a totally delusional, idiotic main character but it is not possible with a character as psychotic and unaware as Ronnie. Inspector Clouseau's obliviousness causes him to step on rake that hits him in the face. Ronnie's obliviousness causes him to rape a woman.

The danger with black, misanthropic comedy films is that the darkness will overwhelm the light. This is what happened with *Happiness* (1998) and *Bad Santa* (2003) and is the fate that befalls *Observe and Report*. All three films get credit for how far they're willing to go but their commitment to darkness doesn't translate into laughs. Ronnie Barnhardt makes for a very poor vehicle for comedy and is instead a stupid, suffocating character who the viewer is relieved to escape after enduring the film's 86 minute running time.

Nate Vercauteren

CREDITS

Ronnie Barnhardt: Seth Rogen
Det. Harrison: Ray Liotta
Brandi: Anna Faris
Cinnabon Man: Patton Oswalt
Dennis: Michael Pena
Charles: Jesse Plemons
Origin: USA
Language: English
Released: 2009
Production: Donald De Line; De Line Pictures, Legendary Pictures; released by Warner Bros.

Directed by: Jody Hill
Written by: Jody Hill
Cinematography by: Tim Orr
Music by: Joey Stephens
Editing: Zene Baker
Sound: Terry Rodman
Art Direction: Masako Masuda
Costumes: Gary Jones
Production Design: Chris Spellman
MPAA rating: R
Running time: 86 minutes

REVIEWS

Childress, Erik. *EFilmCritic,*. April 9, 2009.
Corliss, Richard. *Time Magazine.* April 9, 2009.
Dargis, Manohla. *New York Times.* April 10, 2009.
Edelstein, David. *Slate Magazine.* April 6, 2009.
Leydon, Joe. *Variety.* March 18, 2009.
Phillips, Michael. *Chicago Tribune.* April 9, 2009.
Sharkey, Betsy. *Los Angeles Times.* April 9, 2009.
Stevens, Dana. *Slate.* April 9, 2009.
Tallerico, Brian. *HollywoodChicago.com.* April 10, 2009.
Tobias, Scott. *AV Club.* April 9, 2009.

QUOTES

Brandi: "It's like my mom always said: you can polish a turd, but it's still a piece of s**t."

TRIVIA

The role of Detective Harrison was originally written with Danny McBride in mind. When he was unavailable, the part went to Ray Liotta instead.

OBSESSED

Sharon and Derek have all they've ever wanted...but someone else wants it more.
—Movie tagline
How far would you go to protect what's yours?
—Movie tagline

Box Office: $68.3 million

Obsessed is a film inspired by any countless number of *Fatal Attraction* (1987) ripoffs which automatically makes it anything less than inspired. Stories like these are intrinsically designed to either scare men into being faithful or to scare women into being even more distrustful of their brethren than ever before—domestic horror disguised as a morality tale. There is no disguising what *Obsessed* actually is though. Aside from being what could have been just another dismissable stalker flick, *Obsessed* has been marketed to fill the void left within the community demanding more interracial battle royales amongst the fairer sex. Make no mistake, this is the lowest of common denominator films whose poster title even divides its letters into black and white—and not for the purposes of justifying right and wrong.

Derek Charles (Idris Elba) has the proverbial perfect life—a top job in a good company, a beautiful wife named Sharon (Beyonce Knowles), a little baby, and a brand new house. He's all smiles, bobbing his head to any musical beat in the area, but even he admits to not everything being perfect. At least that is what he tells his new temp secretary Lisa (Ali Larter) to placate this leggy blonde about her own perceived imperfections. Not a great idea considering she has been making goo-goo eyes at him the second they shared an elevator. And he has noticed her as well. First it is a glance at her calves, then an exposed knee.

Lisa is about as subtle as a suicide bomber too. After jumping Derek in the restroom at the office Christmas party, she apologizes in his car by flashing her lingerie at him. Derek does not fall for it though, resisting her advances at every opportunity and trying to protect his interests at the company where he has already had a fling with one of his secretaries. It is cool though because he married that one, clearly following company policy that states if you like it then you "shoulda put a ring on it." Lisa needs no permission to follow Derek to his work retreat and engage in actions that get a detective (Christine Lahti) involved and instantly leads his wife to blame him for everything despite her once being in Lisa's less crazy shoes herself.

Normally, the equations for these films usually involve boring white people having their apple cart upset by crazy white people. With the added element of a mixed race, we see not a casual integration of loony behavior being color blind but some pseudo-revenge fantasy being perpetrated for those individuals out there sexually threatened by their exact opposites. Penned by David Loughery, who also used a brush fire as a metaphor for suburban race relations in *Lakeview Terrace* (2008) and was credited with *Passenger 57*'s (1992) money line of "always bet on black" against a psychotic white terrorist, *Obsessed* does not shove the racial angle to the forefront. Loughery is just keeping the plotting to the bare minimum possible until the coup de grace that the film can market—a drag-down catfight between an angry black woman and the crazy white one trying to steal her man. If you think too much is being made of this one element, consider that the DVD's only advertised special feature is "an inside look at the climactic fight sequence" and it is entitled "Girl Fight!"

Fetishware for the masses, considering it is the only thing that can be labeled "special" about the movie entire. As just your standard trashy thriller fare, Obsessed is far below the standard of even the dumbest of the Alex Forrest clones like *Swimfan* (2002) or the more closely resembled *The Temp* (1993). Dumb is the password *Obsessed* continually tries to get across to the audience though since most of what passes for thrills combine poor direction with the dumbest stock characters imaginable. Lisa is portrayed as just a delusional nut and nothing more, concocting a fictional relationship out of Derek's resistance. None of Derek's work colleagues notice he has been sent a drink by a woman on their work retreat while he is sitting right across from them. Nor that the woman is Lisa in a burning red dress from just across the pool by the bar. So much for that alibi. And he certainly needs one with Lahti's Lifetime Channel detective on the case who asks a lot of questions but never thinks that maybe something a little more scientific like a genital swab could determine if Derek and Lisa actually had sex. She is a genius though compared to the babysitter (Scout Taylor-Compton) who allows Lisa into the home and up the stairs to where baby is all alone.

Steve Shill, making his feature film debut after a decade-and-a-half of television, does not even bother to set up enticing suspense sequences nor develop tension by stacking the deck against Derek's will. *Obsessed*'s big twist is having him be the perfect husband. This only makes Sharon come off as more of a clueless, reactionary shrew when she becomes privy to hubby's situation. "How far would you go to protect what's yours?" reads the film's tagline, ironically suggesting that Elba's Derek is the piece of meat being fought over by a pair of bitchy secretaries. "I knew it would come to this," "You want crazy? I'll show you crazy," and "I'm gonna wipe the floor with your skinny ass," are all part of the ra-ra rallying cry that passes for Beyonce's performance.

Closing shots that end in a freeze frame normally signal that all is right with the world of the characters or something ominous is on the horizon as we fade to black. *Obsessed*'s final image puts Beyonce front and center while the closing song she sings begins to play. Poor Idris Elba's face isn't even fully on screen for this fade out. This is all about Beyonce. It is her moment. She has vanquished the evil and this character who has basically been third fiddle to Elba and Larter the whole film is now the focal point. Who precisely is the Obsessed one in this whole scenario?

Erik Childress

CREDITS
Derek Charles: Idris Elba
Sharon Charles: Beyonce Knowles

Lisa Sheridan: Ali Larter
Detective Reyes: Christine Lahti
Joe Gage: Bruce McGill
Samantha: Scout Taylor-Compton
Ben: Jerry O'Connell
Patrick: Matthew Humphreys
Origin: USA
Language: English
Released: 2009
Production: Will Parker; Screen Gems, Rainforest Films; released by Sony Pictures
Directed by: Steve Shill
Written by: David Loughery
Cinematography by: Ken Seng
Music by: James Dooley
Sound: Tateum Kohut, Greg Orloff
Editing: Paul Seydor
Art Direction: Chris Cornwell
Costumes: Maya Lieberman
Production Design: Jon Gary Steele
MPAA rating: PG-13
Running time: 101 minutes

REVIEWS

Anderson, John. *Variety.* April 27, 2009.
Berkshire, Geoff. *Metromix.com.* April 24, 2009.
Holden, Stephen. *New York Times.* April 27, 2009.
Honeycutt, Kirk. *Hollywood Reporter.* April 27, 2009.
Meek, Tom. *Boston Phoenix.* May 1, 2009.
Puig, Claudia. *USA Today.* April 27, 2009.
Rickey, Carrie. *Philadelphia Inquirer.* April 27, 2009.
Sobczynski, Peter. *eFilmCritic.* April 30, 2009.
Tobias, Scott. *AV Club.* April 27, 2009.
White, Armond. *New York Press.* April 29, 2009.

QUOTES

Sharon Charles: "You better do something about this woman, or I will!"

TRIVIA

The backless red dress that Lisa wears in the film's poster was sewn from scratch, using design elements that actress Ali Larter liked from a variety of dresses considered for the sequence.

AWARDS

Nomination:

Golden Raspberries 2009: Worst Actress (Knowles), Worst Support. Actress (Larter).

OLD DOGS

Sit. Stay. Play Dad.
—Movie tagline

Box Office: $48.8 million

Consider only a recent sampling of films like *License to Wed* (2007) and *Wild Hogs* (2007) and remember that comedy veterans Robin Williams and John Travolta are also veterans of bad movies. Yet *Old Dogs*, a family comedy starring the actors as lifelong friends feebly taking care of two kids, is a particular strain of terrible that approaches the most shameless work these actors have ever delivered.

In the film, helmed by *Wild Hogs* director Walt Becker, Dan (Williams) looks after Zach (Conner Rayburn) and Emily (Travolta's daughter Ella Bleu Travolta), 7-year-old twins Dan never knew he had, when their mother Vicki (Kelly Preston) returns to Dan's life just before a two-week jail sentence for trespassing. Dan and Vicki's marriage lasted only as long as their one-night stand, but despite his complete lack of parenting skills, Dan is eager to bond with the children (who, conveniently, are excited and not at all apprehensive to meet the father they never knew). So Dan recruits his pal and business partner Charlie (Travolta)—a playboy with no interest in a family of his own—to help watch the youngsters. Just think of the hilarity that could result when two old dogs have to learn a new trick as wacky and unpredictable as child care!

What results is not laughter but a film whose creators obviously have a remarkably low opinion of their audience. As Disney's *Old Dogs* is a studio family comedy released the day before Thanksgiving, it is no big surprise that the film would aim for broad, simple humor in an attempt to appeal to the largest possible audience during a holiday when families frequently go to the movies. Surely, though, parents are reluctant to take kids to films featuring many instances of casual prejudice (treating gays and multiple minorities as both walking stereotypes and general inconveniences). And surely kids are interested in seeing comedies (like Pixar's *Up* [2009]) with jokes about something other than feces or farting. Or just scenes offering more than just once-great comedians over-acting, followed by multiple shots of Charlie's dog giving a goofy look about how oh-so outrageous all this behavior is.

Writers David Diamond and David Weissman obviously do not think such feelings exist in their audience, packing the movie with nothing but an onslaught of exaggerated facial expressions and uninspired antics. Examples include Dan overdoing it during a session in a tanning booth and Charlie, after the guys' pills are mixed up and both take the wrong ones, carelessly devouring the pot-luck lunch put together by the bereavement group of a woman (Lori Loughlin) he's interested in. (Charlie then, as a result of the medication snafu, wears a giant smile throughout the group's meeting.) Yet this inappropriate behavior still wins him Amanda's (Loughlin) heart, since *Old Dogs* has much more interest in letting its featured clowns get their way than allowing the women on hand to expect better.

The movie is a constant barrage of ideas that are either absurdly unfunny, cheap, idiotic, or all of the above. Vicki's best friend Jenna (Rita Wilson) is a hand model, so naturally Dan slams a car trunk on Jenna's hands. Charlie, apparently not knowing any better, asks Zach and Emily if they have ever been to a casino or seen the movie *Casino* (1995). Vicki is serving a very brief sentence for a mild offense, yet she comes out of prison having made license plates, as if she has spent months (or years) in a high-security facility.

In scene after scene of *Old Dogs*, nothing is entertaining and even less is consistent. At times the kids are well-behaved, and at other times, for no particular reason, they scamper around like wild animals. One minute Charlie disregards Dan's interests completely (during Dan's tanning ordeal Charlie is hitting on the salon employee) and the next he claims to always be there for Dan. First, the guys can barely move without having knee or back problems, and later they are playing a physical game of ultimate Frisbee.

Such shoddy filmmaking makes it that much more alarming that the film is filled with familiar faces. Matt Dillon and Justin Long appear in a brief, agonizing sequence involving Zach and Emily's camping troop. Ann-Margaret plays the horrified leader of the bereavement group. Seth Green plays Dan and Charlie's inept colleague Craig. Paolo Costanzo turns up for a quick appearance as a zoo employee. And the late Bernie Mac, who died in August 2008, plays "master puppeteer" Jimmy Lunchbox who, in another brutally unfunny scene, fits Dan with a body suit that allows his behavior to be controlled by Charlie and Jimmy from another room. Their goal is to help Dan competently play with his daughter. This is not only reminiscent of similarly strained scenes of the Eddie Murphy vehicle *Imagine That* (2009), but it is yet another moment in *Old Dogs* where the actors flail wildly, less interested in creating characters than cartoons.

As proven by recent films like *Four Christmases* (2008), family comedies around the holidays have hit an awfully low point in the style of humor they provide and the superficial emotions they peddle. Even audiences who want more than that can no longer expect it. Based on the worthless *Old Dogs*, which teaches nothing about being a parent or being a kid or even just the importance of family, perhaps expectations are not even as low as they should be.

Matt Pais

CREDITS

Dan: Robin Williams
Charlie: John Travolta
Zach: Conner Rayburn
Marley Greer: Ella Bleu Travolta
Vicki: Kelly Preston
Jimmy Lunchbox: Bernie Mac
Ralph White: Seth Green
Amanda: Lori Loughlin
Yancy Devlin: Matt Dillon
Gloria Lawrence: Rita Wilson
Kelly: Laura Allen
Martha: Ann-Margret
Condo Woman: Amy Sedaris
Origin: USA
Language: English
Released: 2009
Production: Peter Abrams, Robert Levy, Andrew Panay, Brian Robbins; Tapestry Films; released by Walt Disney Pictures
Directed by: Walt Becker
Written by: David Diamond, David Weissman
Cinematography by: Jeffrey L. Kimball
Music by: John Debney
Sound: James Sabat
Music Supervisor: Dave Jordan
Editing: Tom Lewis, Ryan Folsey
Art Direction: Peter Rogness
Costumes: Joseph G. Aulisi
Production Design: David Gropman
MPAA rating: PG
Running time: 88 minutes

REVIEWS

Burr, Ty. *Boston Globe.* November 24, 2009.
Ebert, Roger. *Chicago Sun-Times.* November 25, 2009.
Gronvall, Andrea. *Chicago Reader.* November 25, 2009.
Harvey, Dennis. *Variety.* November 24, 2009.
Holden, Stephen. *New York Times.* November 25, 2009.
Honeycutt, Kirk. *Hollywood Reporter.* November 24, 2009.
McWeeny, Drew. *HitFlix.* November 24, 2009.
Phillips, Michael. *Chicago Tribune.* November 24, 2009.
Phipps, Keith. *AV Club.* November 24, 2009.
Stevens, Matt. *E! Online.* November 29, 2009.

QUOTES

Dan: "If I'm gonna be an old dad, you're gonna be Uncle Charlie."

TRIVIA

The film's release date was postponed three times. First, due to the death of Bernie Mac. Then because of the death of John

Travolta's son. Finally, when Robin Williams had a health scare that required surgery. This resulted in the film being released more than a year after its original release date.

AWARDS

Nomination:

Golden Raspberries 2009: Worst Picture, Worst Actor (Travolta), Worst Support. Actress (Preston), Worst Director (Becker).

ONG BAK 2

(Ong Bak: The Beginning)

Warrior. Conqueror. Legend.
—Movie tagline

Calling *Ong Bak 2* a good action film is dangerous. *Ong Bak 2* is a good action film. But it is also a good *film*, at least in the sense that it faithfully uses cinema as an art form towards ends that resonate within the viewer. There is a lot more going on here besides action and it would be very easy to see someone reading up on the folklore and legends of Thailand after a viewing.

The history of the martial arts film indicates the same pattern of rise and fall in stateside popularity that most genres do but with a key difference. Most film genres have emerged from within the United States and grown outward with various countries making significant, sometimes even resuscitative contributions. But the production of martial arts cinema not only started outside the boundaries of the U.S. but has, largely, remained there, due to a variety of factors that, some would argue, have kept the U.S. from making even a single serious contribution toward the growth and development of the form. A great deal of this is no doubt socio-historical in nature. While the widespread appeal of martial arts cinema for American audiences has always been rooted in the connection that Americans make between martial arts and American action cinema in general, the reality is that the genre has flourished and remained largely overseas due to the complex rooting of the various fighting forms to national identity, shared cultural and folkloric traditions, and even religious traditions.

Thai action cinema has made a name for itself in the usual manner stateside. Spectacular fights, involving a distinctive martial arts style have been combined with brutal action sequences that are constructed as much if not more from real human sweat and blood as they are from any cinematic trickery to create a dynamic presentation of the Muay Thai fighting form as part Jackie Chan do-it-yourself-no-stuntman-here-heroics and part Bruce Lee pushing-the-human-body-to-its-limits-bravado. Films like *Ong Bak* (2003), *Born to Fight* (2004) and *The Protector* (2008) have become the new standard by which virtually all martial arts/fighting films are now judged among aficionados.

And, though a huge early portion of this Thai cinema form has long been missing in action, it is hardly hyperbole to point to producer-director-writer-performer Panit Rittikrai (*Spirited Killer* [1994], *The BodyGuard* [2004]) as the driving force behind its development, recent upsurge in popularity and strong focus on national pride. His protégés Tony Jaa and Chupong Changprung (aka Dan Chupong) have become world-renowned action stars and Rittikrai himself has starred in and directed more than fifty low-budget Thai action films as well as become a highly-in-demand fight choreographer (*Mercury Man* [2006], *Chocolate* [2008]). Initially, the screenwriter here, Rittikrai was brought in to co-direct after Jaa reportedly walked off the set of this highly-publicized sequel to *Ong Bak*. Riitikrai quickly re-established the balance needed for the filming to resume.

Tien (Natdanai Kongthong) is a ten-year-old born into nobility under the reign of King Narresuan in ancient times. But his peaceful life is shattered when his parents are viciously attacked and killed, leaving him homeless until a band of thieves take pity on him and teach him to steal. As the years pass, Tien (Tony Jaa) becomes head thief, his skill at stealing and fighting surpassed by none, but the memory of his parent's unjust death eats away at him and he hungers for revenge. When a competition is held to choose a second in command for his parent's killer, Tien jumps at the chance, easily overcoming all the others. But, just as revenge would be easy, Tien realizes that he must embark on the most dangerous fight of all—a fight within himself for the courage to do more than seek vengeance. As he seeks to rid the land of a tyrant his own life and the future of his people hang in the balance.

Told in a style that incorporates supernatural elements from Thai legend and folklore, *Ong Bak 2* is absolutely spectacular to look at even when it stretches the suspension of disbelief. The film is decidedly melodramatic. Evil characters mug at the camera, lead villains swagger, and impossible creatures come to test Tien's skills. But the overall impact is of a strong fantasy film with fighting elements. Part Indiana Jones, part Braveheart, part all out martial arts massacre, *Ong Bak 2* is fun even when the fighting stops. A dance sequence near the end, preceding the final battle, is one of the most hypnotic sequences from any Thai action film ever.

The obvious strong points here are the presence of Jaa and the action sequences which are often breathtaking. In one, Jaa wrestles alligators in a brutal death match. In another lengthy sequence, Jaa defends himself against an endless series of fighters amidst an elephant herd leaping on and off the animals, even using their tusks for balance and support to launch himself at his enemies. Jaa's mastery of Muay Thai martial arts, Tae Kwon Do, swordplay and gymnastics is in full effect throughout and no stunt performers are used to supplement the very obvious danger Jaa was in during the filming.

At its best, martial arts cinema has always found a way to transcend the borders of geography and culture, entrancing audiences who likely have little or no stock in the traditions that have shaped it. *Ong Bak 2* is a marvelous example, offering spectacle without leaving the wonder behind.

Dave Canfield

CREDITS

Tien: Tony Jaa
Chernang: Sorapong Chatree
Rajasena Lord: Sarunyu Wongkrachang
Master Bua: Nirut Sirichanya
Crow Ghost: Dan Chupong
Nobleman Siha Decho: Santisuk Promsiri
Pim: Primorata Dejudom
Origin: Thailand
Language: English, Thai
Released: 2008
Production: Panna Rittikrai; Sahamongkol Film International, Iyara Films; released by Magnet Releasing
Directed by: Tony Jaa, Panna Rittikrai
Written by: Panna Rittikrai
Cinematography by: Nattawhut Khittikhun
Music by: Terdsak Janpan
MPAA rating: R
Running time: 115 minutes

REVIEWS

Berkshire, Geoff. *Metromix.com.* October 22, 2009.
Bradshaw, Peter. *Guardian.* October 16, 2009.
Crook, Simon. *Empire Magazine.* October 16, 2009.
Hendrix, Grady. *Slate.* October 22, 2009.
Murray, Noel. *AV Club.* October 22, 2009.
Punter, Jennie. *Globe and Mail.* September 14, 2009.
Rapold, Nicholas. *Village Voice.* October 20, 2009.
Savlov, Marc. *Austin Chronicle.* November 6, 2009.
Tallerico, Brian. *MovieRetriever.com.* October 22, 2009.
Turan, Kenneth. *Los Angeles Times.* October 22, 2009.

Many scenes shot in Cambodia were cut from the film because of clashes between Cambodia and Thailand regarding the Preah Vihear temple.

ORPHAN

There's something wrong with Esther.
    —Movie tagline
Can you keep a secret?
    —Movie tagline

Box Office: $41.6 million

Orphan offers good performances, is beautifully photographed, and has a twist haunting enough to survive the fact that first time screenwriter David Johnson (working from a story by Alex Mace) has written what amounts to a rather standard mainstream suspense thriller. This is no faint praise. At its best, *Orphan* is a very entertaining film. But there is the whiff of warmed-over Hitchcock about it—a connection back to far better films like *Psycho* (1960) and even the deeply-flawed *Frenzy* (1972), films that had many of the above advantages while also managing to deeply explore the character and motivations of the psychopaths at their respective centers. *Orphan* chooses a less introspective approach, emerging as a rather well-made, entertaining film with a jarring finale good enough to get people buzzing around the water cooler, but one senses that it could have been much more, especially in the capable hands of director Jaume Collet-Serra. Collet-Serra is previously known for his monstrously fun *House of Wax* (2005), one of the best of the recent spate of remakes of classic horror films managing to mix laughs, gross-out chills, and considerable suspense without taking itself too seriously. *Orphan* puts him in decidedly more serious territory, telling the story of a broken marriage, deeply wounded people, and a very scary identity crisis.

The marriage of John (Peter Sarsgaard) and Kate Coleman (Vera Farmiga) has snowballed out of control; John's decade old affair may or may not have led to Kate's drinking problem, which decidedly led to the loss of her prestigious job, and the near drowning of their young daughter, who is deaf as a result of her injuries. When a miscarriage robs them of a much-needed symbol of hope and healing they decide to adopt even though it's clear that Kate has not yet overcome all her demons.

At the orphanage, they meet Esther (Isabelle Fuhrman), a Russian whose prodigious art skills, and stunning sensitivity and intelligence captivates them. Encouraged by Sister Abigail (CCH Pounder), they formalize the adoption and bring Esther home to meet the rest of the family; daughter Max (Aryana Engineer) and pre-teen son Daniel (Jimmy Bennett). But, as Esther and Max bond, Kate and Daniel suspect something is, as the tagline says, "…wrong with Esther." Soon, a trail of wreckage, human and otherwise, prove that the remarkably precocious Esther is indeed "wrong." The question now is, what is she and what does she really want?

The movie goes about unraveling this mystery rather laconically, instead of developing more interesting or believable characters for us to empathize with. Kate becomes isolated and paranoid, John becomes less engaged and leery of his wife, and Esther terrorizes and masterfully manipulates those who get in her way. But these could almost be called mere genre mechanics, rather than characters, so expected are they in a film such as this one.

Vera Farmiga (*The Departed* [2006]) played a virtually identical role in *Joshua* (2007]) and, though she has shown she can deliver stunning performances, there simply fails to be anything in *Orphan* for her to use to her advantage. The equally brilliant Peter Saarsgard (*Boys Don't Cry* [1999], *Elegy* [2008]) is stuck with John, a character who seems motivated primarily by what the script, rather than his heart or mind, would require. Jimmy Bennett (*The Amityville Horror* [2005], *Star Trek* [2009]), who plays Danny, and first-timer Aryana Engineer, who plays Max, barely rate mention not because they are bad but because they are present only as reflection of the other characters. The story gives them nothing to do but be terrorized. Likewise, the venerable CCH Pounder (*Face/Off* [1997], *End of Days* [1999], *Avatar* [2009]), whose portrayal as the doomed Sister Abigail would be far more compelling if the viewer had any reason to expect she might live past the first half of the film.

Esther herself, played with a creepy determination by Isabelle Fuhrman (*Hounddog* [2007]), is a fine movie psycho but this really could have been a character for the ages if approached more deeply. In short, none of these characters generate much real empathy and thus the revelation about Esther's true nature has enough power to provoke gasps but not near enough to generate honest feelings. Without anything else original to offer, *Orphan* plays more like William Castle by way of the art house. This is adequately-written, well-acted, very well-made fluff that manages to offer some haunting imagery as it plays off of metaphors lost in the 'durm and strang' of pure B-movie genre thrills.

Dave Canfield

CREDITS

Kate Coleman: Vera Farmiga
John Coleman: Peter Sarsgaard

Daniel: Jimmy Bennett
Esther: Isabelle Fuhrman
Max Coleman: Aryana Engineer
Sister Abigail: CCH Pounder
Dr. Browning: Margo Martindale
Dr. Varava: Karel Roden
Grandma Barbara: Rosemary Dunsmore
Origin: USA
Language: English
Released: 2009
Production: Joel Silver, Steve Richards, Susan Downey, Leonardo DiCaprio, Jennifer Davisson Killoran; Dark Castle Entertainment, Appian Way; released by Warner Bros.
Directed by: Jaume Collet-Serra
Written by: David Leslie Johnson
Cinematography by: Jeff Cutter
Music by: John Ottman
Sound: Patrick Rousseau
Editing: Tim Alverson
Art Direction: Pierre Perrault, Patrick Banister
Costumes: Antoinette Messam
Production Design: Tom Meyer
MPAA rating: R
Running time: 101 minutes

REVIEWS

Burr, Ty. *Boston Globe.* July 23, 2009.
Dargis, Manohla. *New York Times.* July 24, 2009.
Ebert, Roger. *Chicago Sun-Times.* July 23, 2009.
Honeycutt, Kirk. *Hollywood Reporter.* July 22, 2009.
Lemire, Christy. *Associated Press.* July 22, 2009.
McCarthy, Todd. *Variety.* July 22, 2009.
Simon, Brent. *Screen International.* July 23, 2009.
Smith, Kyle. *New York Post.* July 24, 2009.
Sobczynski, Peter. *EFilmCritic.* July 24, 2009.
Tallerico, Brian. *MovieRetriever.com.* July 24, 2009.

QUOTES

Esther: "If I find out that you're lying, I'll cut your hairless little prick off before you even figure out what it's for. Do you understand me?"

TRIVIA

The character of Esther was originally intended to have fair skin, delicate features, and platinum blonde hair. However, the filmmakers were so impressed with Isabelle Fuhrman that they cast her anyway and changed the character's appearance accordingly.

OUTRAGE

Do ask. Do tell.
—Movie tagline

Representative Barney Frank (Democrat-MA) provides the statement that serves as the thematic foundation of Kirby Dick's controversial documentary *Outrage* when he says, "The only reason people hate gay people is because their leaders tell them to." Unless one assume that homophobia is instinctual for some people, it is a statement that is impossible to argue with. Religious leaders, community leaders, political leaders—they all shape and form opinions like the ones that have made equal rights for gay people so hard to come to pass. Even teachers and the media industry—other forms of the word "leaders"— shape and define the battle for gay rights in America. Dick's controversial documentary tries to outline the twisted, masochistic, self-loathing dynamic at play when closeted, gay politicians vote against gay rights. Some argued that Dick had no right outing politicians who were not ready to come forward with their sexuality and *Outrage* was dismissed from the public conversation much more swiftly than it should have been. This is a complex issue deftly handled by a talented documentarian who recognizes that the long battle for equal rights for homosexuals stands at a turning point and shines a light on an important aspect of this war that has gone underreported.

The backlash against *Outrage*—that it was merely a slice of sensationalism outing people who refuse to come out on their own—painted the film in far too broad a brush. The arguments about invasion of privacy missed a crucial talking point of the film: Dick only targets reportedly gay politicians who are spewing vitriolic, anti-gay sentiment on Capitol Hill, voting against gay rights, and striving to keep America in the last century on this important issue and he argues that many of their actions are because they have chosen to stay in the closet. Privacy is no longer a viable argument when that privacy is impacting so many lives. Dick's argument, supported by interviews with former politicians who have now come out of the closet, is that the shame these people feel by having to keep their personal live relegated to back alleys and airport bathrooms has forced them into feeling shameful about their own sexuality. Because of that shame, they have masochistically pushed forward laws against gay rights in a convoluted perspective regarding what is right and wrong. They turn their followers against their very way of life, resulting in a never-ending spiral of self-loathing that has an impact on the entire country.

Kirby Dick is careful to aim his camera at politicians who have been a part of the national debate over gay rights. He is careful to match up and display voting records with each of his targets, all of whom have been carefully sourced. This is not a tabloid film, using rumors and innuendo about powerful men. Dick often interviews former lovers of politicians and clearly vetted each

of his subjects. *Outrage* is filled with the stories of secret trysts and, disturbingly, of people who died in the shadows, never able to admit the source of their happiness when they were alive, often dramatically impacted by the legal decisions of the men they loved. Their stories should be heard. Of course, the film starts with the public, controversial outing of Larry Craig but moves on to such diverse figures as Florida Governor Charlie Crist and former New York City Mayor Ed Koch.

The smartest move that Dick makes with *Outrage* is to not make the film "Anger." There is a subtle but important difference. The latter is often unfocused and would have turned this documentary into the tabloid journalism that its detractors too successfully painted it as being. On the other hand, outrage results from recognizing that something is wrong and trying to do something about it. Some argued that Dick was overly aggressive in his approach but the anti-gay rights movement has certainly been anything but passive. These are issues that need to be a much bigger part of the national discussion (and Dick is unafraid to point a finger at the journalism industry in their failure to do so) and documentaries like *Outrage* are an important part of bringing them to the surface. It is far from the first film to argue for more discussion regarding the gay rights debate but it could ultimately be one of the most important.

Brian Tallerico

CREDITS

Origin: USA

Language: English

Released: 2009

Production: Amy Ziering Kofman; Chain Camera Pictures, Red Envelope Entertainment, The Sundance Institute, Tectonic Theater Project, Tic Tonic; released by Magnolia Pictures

Directed by: Kirby Dick

Written by: Kirby Dick

Cinematography by: Thaddeus Wadleigh

Music by: Peter Golub

Sound: Michael Boyle, Sean O'Neil

Editing: Doug Blush, Matthew Clarke

MPAA rating: R

Running time: 98 minutes

REVIEWS

Anderson, John. *Variety.* May 1, 2009.

Foundas, Scott. *Village Voice.* May 5, 2009.

Gleiberman, Owen. *Entertainment Weekly.* May 6, 2009.

Levy, Emanuel. *EmanuelLevy.com.* May 2, 2009.

MacDonald, Moira. *Seattle Times.* May 14, 2009.
Rabin, Nathan. *AV Club.* May 7, 2009.
Scheck, Frank. *Hollywood Reporter.* May 7, 2009.

Scott, A.O. *New York Times.* May 8, 2009.
Turan, Kenneth. *Los Angeles Times.* May 8, 2009.
Zak, Dan. *Washington Post.* May 7, 2009.

P

PANDORUM

Don't fear the end of the world. Fear what happens next.
—Movie tagline

Box Office: $10.3 million

Even those who never went to see *Pandorum* could honestly say that they had already seen it. This sci-fi horror film is a patchwork quilt of a production, borrowing obviously and unabashedly from a host of cinematic predecessors. While *Pandorum*'s amnesia-hampered space travelers cannot quite put their finger on much of anything, those who merely heard about the film's plot were quickly able to point out numerous similarities to other motion pictures. Yet those responsible for this one touted it as "fresh" and "original," with a "completely unique vision." (One thing they did not do, however, was make their creation available to critics before its release to the public, a telltale sign of recognized inferiority.) The Earth could very well end up running out of resources and be uninhabitable by the 22nd Century as in *Pandorum*, but it seems clear that fresh ideas for this genre were apparently already in short supply during the making of the film.

Suddenly being awakened from a deep sleep is a jolting experience for anyone, but it is even more profoundly discombobulating for two crewmembers who had been hibernating in pods for years on end aboard the faltering Elysium. Corporal Bower (a fiercely-determined Ben Foster) is wrested out of hypersleep in his sealed containment chamber, and agonizingly frees himself. Soon after, Lieutenant Payton (a grumpy Dennis Quaid) also plops out onto the floor with little

clothes but a lot of questions. He asks where they are, where the rest of the crew is, and where the ship is headed, but Bower is in no way able to enlighten him. Payton tries to radio for help, but there is only desolate, dead silence on the other end. As the Elysium's flickering lights signal that its power source is petering out, these men who are figuratively in the dark may soon also find themselves literally in the dark, stranded and hurtling uncontrollably through the mysterious, infinite inkiness of outer space. It is a promising premise, both intriguing and rather unsettling.

Particularly as Bower blindly crawls through the dark confines of the ship's ventilation ducts, there is success in making viewers share the man's feelings of claustrophobia and disorientation. Indeed, atmosphere is what *Pandorum* excels at most, creating an unnerving sense of being dauntingly trapped amidst the disquietingly-dim, eerily-echoing unknown. Director Christian Alvert and production designer Richard Bridgland deserve praise for creating *Pandorum*'s futuristic, tight-quartered and creepy ambience. As Bower begins to see terrifying things in the Elysium's corridors, he ponders whether he might be afflicted with pandorum, a kind of spacecraft cabin fever with symptoms ranging widely from nosebleeds, tremors, and hallucinations to psychotic, amoral savagery. Actually pandorum is not setting in, which unfortunately means that the horrors he is encountering are all too real. As the danger begins to reveal itself in earnest, so does the film's derivativeness. Already, talk of the mind-bending toll of being cooped-up in space will remind one of films like *Solaris* (2002). The ominous absence of crewmembers that is later found to be the result of a shocking degeneration into twisted chaos was recently found in *Event Horizon* (1997). When roaring, relentless, and ravenous creatures that are nightmarishly part human and part hell come on the scene, they are extremely reminiscent of the eminently-eager flesh-munchers in *The Descent* (2005). A spaceship within which a battle ensues against a voracious, seemingly-unstoppable, and unearthly menace, one apt to joltingly jump out at any time with grisly results, cannot help but remind one of *Alien* (1979) and its sequels. Many people also had no trouble noting elements seemingly cherry-picked from *Pitch Black* (2000), *Resident Evil* (2002), *Serenity* (2005), and a host of other such productions, as well as the video game *Dead Space*. (It is not surprising, therefore, when one notes that *Pandorum* producer Paul W.S. Anderson directed both *Event Horizon* and *Resident Evil*.) Extended space flight may lead to pandorum, but *Pandorum* will undoubtedly cause 108 minutes of chronic déjà vu.

It is revealed that the Elysium is like a Noah's Ark launched into the heavens, filled with human settlers and desperately aimed at a potentially-viable, far-off planet as our own—and all who inhabit it—are taking their last gasp. When the passengers learned that home and help were no longer possibilities, the shock was too great for one of the crew, who had proceeded to make the word mankind sound like a monumental oxymoron. As a result of his unhinged depravity, most of those lucky enough to be carrying their one-way tickets to Tanis became horrendously unlucky, either mutating into the aforementioned appalling beings or becoming their sustenance. Anyone who has taken a long car trip with kids knows how they can turn into decidedly-cranky, snack-demanding little beasts, but nothing compares to being around irritable, insatiable mutants confined to a spacecraft during a mission lasting more than a century.

Bower must press on to save the Elysium's nuclear reactor even after he can no longer pick up Payton's guiding radio transmissions, which is meant, of course, to heighten the audience's concern for the corporal's welfare. From then on, *Pandorum*'s plot basically splits to proceed along two separate tracks during its running time, hurriedly merging again in the end with revelations that fail to make jaws drop in awe. "Running time" is actually an apt description of much of *Pandorum*, as Bower is constantly dashing here and there about the ship in an effort to both restore power and remain out of the mutants' clawed clutches. The repeated encounters with these powerful and agile monstrosities become quite tedious, and the effectiveness of fight scenes is significantly reduced by exceedingly low-key lighting and an overfondness for rapid-fire editing. (Foster kindly referred to the latter as the composition of a "mosaic of flash images.") Antje Traue, as surviving scientist Nadia,

is merely remembered best for her breasts, and the most notable scene featuring Mixed Martial arts World Champion Cung Le's agricultural specialist Manh is a spooky one in which the character is done in by a less-than-cherubic fledgling fiend.

Back where everything began, Payton finds it challenging to deal with the sudden, nearly-out-of-thin-air appearance of a Corporal Gallo (Cam Gigandet), who may be having a pandorum-induced nervous breakdown. Viewers who noted the way the camera had spun around Payton just as Gallo arrived were not surprised to learn that the lieutenant is actually in every sense beside himself, loopy from pandorum and arguing with a hallucination without while struggling mightily within. By the time confirmation comes that it was his perverse, horrific actions that brought the Elysium to this dreadfully-low point, things have gone laughably over the top. (When Gallo's maniacally-contorted mouth bleeds, it is surely due in part to Gigandet's chewing of the scenery.) It turns out in the end that the Elysium has been on Tanis for quite some time, and Bower and Nadia reach the surface along with other pod-encased survivors in anticipation of a planned sequel and prequel. Sadly for them but fortuitously for moviegoers, both of those have likely been put on hold indefinitely.

Made on a budget of $40 million, *Pandorum* was only able to gross just over $10 million. It received unfavorable reviews, with some critics savaging it like a mutant tearing into its prey. Like the psychological disorder referred to by its title, the justly-panned, derivative dud *Pandorum* is something one would hope to avoid.

David L. Boxerbaum

CREDITS

Payton: Dennis Quaid
Bower: Ben Foster
Shepard: Norman Reedus
Gallo: Cam Gigandet
Manh: Cung Le
Leland: Eddie Rouse
Nadia: Antje Traue
Origin: USA
Language: English
Released: 2009
Production: Paul W.S. Anderson, Jeremy Bolt, Robert Kulzer, Martin Moszkowicz; Constantin Film Produktion, Impact Pictures; released by Overture Films
Directed by: Christian Alvart
Written by: Christian Alvart, Travis Milloy
Cinematography by: Wendigo von Schultzendorff

Music by: Michi Britsch
Editing: Phillip Stahl
Sound: Adrian Baumeister
Costumes: Ivana Milos
Production Design: Richard Bridgland
MPAA rating: R
Running time: 108 minutes

REVIEWS

Catsoulis, Jeanette. *New York Times.* September 27, 2009.
Cole, Stephen. *Globe and Mail.* September 25, 2009.
Creepy, Uncle. *Dread Central.* September 28, 2009.
Doerksen, Cliff. *Chicago Reader.* September 27, 2009.
Elias, Justine. *Boston Globe.* September 25, 2009.
Floyd, Nigel. *Time Out.* October 4, 2009.
Howell, Peter. *Toronto Star.* September 25, 2009.
Nelson, Rob. *Variety.* September 25, 2009.
Newman, Kim. *Empire Magazine.* October 4, 2009.
Rabin, Nathan. *AV Club.* September 27, 2009.

QUOTES

Payton: "I can't remember any of my life before this flight began."

TRIVIA

Actor Ben Foster insisted on eating live insects instead of fake or dead ones in the film when required to do so.

PAPER HEART

A story about love that's taking on a life of its own.
—Movie tagline

Box Office: $1.3 million

For a "Romantic Comedy," arguably one of the more safe genres in film, *Paper Heart* takes many chances. Instead of just going through the motions of its simple premise and taking it into familiar territory with a predictable ending, it tries to make sense of its own premise as we watch it unfold. Part documentary, part fiction, *Paper Heart* is about one young woman's quest for what love actually means and if it is actually worth believing in, while also being a perfectly charming Romantic Comedy in the truest sense of the genre.

Most of the movie is fictional. Its director, Nicholas Jasenovec, hired actor Jake Johnson to play the documentary filmmaker who happens to be named Nicholas Jasenovec in the film. Nicholas (the character) wants to make a movie following around comedienne Charlyne

Yi (playing herself), who has decided in her young life that she does not believe in love. It simply does not exist and she does not feel she is capable of feeling it for herself. The documentary will follow Yi as she travels across the country interviewing regular people as well as experts on the merits and possibilities of true love and to see if this journey will change her mind or have any affect on her.

Since Yi plays herself and since she was featured most prominently in the Judd Apatow comedy *Knocked Up* (two brief scenes in which she had two memorable lines), it only makes sense that regular members of the Apatow clan make brief appearances, also as themselves (Seth Rogen and Martin Starr, for starters). But one night at a party, she meets actor Michael Cera (*Superbad, Juno*), who has never met Yi, but is intrigued by her. She mentions to Nicholas that he would like to know more about her and, wisely, Nicholas sees this interest as a major turning point for the film. Yi is naturally reluctant to take the film down that path, but finds Michael Cera charming enough to spend some time with him. Mutual interest between the two slowly develops and soon they start dating, but with a camera crew constantly in their presence.

The documentary half of the film consists of Yi stopping in between dates with Cera to interview random strangers, including an Elvis impersonator who also happens to be a priest in a Las Vegas wedding chapel, a group of bikers who claim they are a tight family and that is the love in their life, and even elementary school students who turn the tables on Yi by getting her to confess that she may well be in love, whether she wants to admit it or not. These are not staged or scripted interviews, but the subjects themselves are surprisingly frank and open about their lives and what makes them capable of feeling true love. Some of them have funny stories to tell, which are accentuated by animated reenactments created by Yi.

Paper Heart is the brainchild of Yi and filmmaker Jasenovec and while its premise might seem to err on the side of whimsy and quirkiness for quirkiness' sake, its questions are relevant for its time and Yi, who will never be accused of taking herself too seriously, is just the right person to be asking these questions. She made the film at the age of 21 and is of the generation who often measure love by how many "friends" they have on their Facebook or Myspace pages and where the checklist mentality of finding a mate (via Match.com or eHarmony) has become more commonplace. *Paper Heart's* half documentary/half fictional set-up seems like an idea that should have been done by now, but its timing could not be better.

The film also moves at a brisk pace and has the good nature to not look down on its documentary subjects or to make fun of them. Yi is a perfectly likable and funny person, someone worth rooting for in a Romantic Comedy. With her and Michael Cera in the leads, *Paper Heart* demonstrates that two people who have no business gracing the covers of GQ or Cosmopolitan magazine can carry a film of this type better than anyone on Hollywood's A-list. Their chemistry does not feel forced or contrived, but realistically awkward, uncertain and with a sense of hope that it will last.

When the filmmakers' presence in the love lives of Cera and Yi begin to wear out their welcome, *Paper Heart* wisely keeps the film about its three central characters without trying to engage the audience in a pseudo intellectual dissection on the role a filmmaker plays in the lives of his/her subject and whether or not the film is "real" if the director tries to alter the events for the sake of the final product. Such problems occur and are dealt with in the latter half of the film, but *Paper Heart* stops just short of losing its audience to such diatribes. In the end, it remains a movie about these three people: one who needs a story to tell (Jasenovic, the character) and the two people who have to let the story unfold while staying true to themselves, for better or for worse.

Collin Souter

CREDITS

Himself: Michael Cera
Herself: Charlyne Yi
Nicholas Jasenovec: Jake M. Johnson
Origin: USA
Language: English
Released: 2009
Production: Elise Salomon, Sandra Murillo; Paper Heart; released by Overture Films
Directed by: Nicholas Jasenovec
Written by: Charlyne Yi, Nicholas Jasenovec
Cinematography by: Jay Hunter
Music by: Michael Cera, Charlyne Yi
Sound: Devendra Cleary, Jacob Riehle
Editing: Ryan Brown
MPAA rating: PG-13
Running time: 88 minutes

REVIEWS

Anderson, Jason. *Toronto Star.* August 7, 2009.
Baxter, Jessica. *Film Threat.* June 1, 2009.
Berkshire, Geoff. *Metromix.com.* August 6, 2009.
Ebert, Roger. *Chicago Sun-Times.* August 6, 2009.
Harvey, Dennis. *Variety.* August 5, 2009.
LaSalle, Mick. *San Francisco Chronicle.* August 7, 2009.
Lemire, Christy. *Associated Press.* August 5, 2009.
Long, Tom. *Detroit News.* August 7, 2009.
Lowe, Justin. *Hollywood Reporter.* August 5, 2009.
Sharkey, Betsy. *Los Angeles Times.* August 7, 2009.

TRIVIA

Although Charlyne Yi claimed while promoting the movie that she and Michael Cera never dated, they actually dated for three years before the relationship ended in July 2009.

PARANORMAL ACTIVITY

Don't see it alone.
    —Movie tagline
What happens when you sleep?
    —Movie tagline

Box Office: $108 million

Directed by first-timer Oren Peli and hyped as one of the scariest films in recent years, *Paranormal Activity* is unnerving indeed. But what makes it truly extraordinary as a film is the way in which it achieves powerful resonance with so many viewers while using what are essentially cinematic gimmicks that viewers have become all too familiar with in recent years. Indeed what viewers experience through found footage, or faux documentary/true story cinema has been around almost as long as film itself; from the earliest days of Nickelodeons when trains roared at the screen and guns fired directly at the camera with little or no narrative context offered to viewers to help separate fact from fiction. These techniques, however implicit in cinema itself, have bred anything but contempt when put to good use. As audiences grew more savvy so did filmmakers understanding of how to manipulate them.

Probably the best found footage film ever, Gillo Pontecorvos *The Battle of Algiers* (1967) showcased a countries fight for independence and human rights while a few years later the entirely fictional *Texas Chainsaw Massacre* (1974), though it lacked a found footage element, offered a decidedly documentary-like feel preceded by a long prologue linking itself to a completely false "real-life" series of murders. It is worth noting that, more often than not, the found footage, faux documentary/true story card is played by filmmakers working in the horror or thriller genre, but whether romanticizing mans struggle for basic human dignity or being used for exploitation purposes these techniques, like any other, seem to have lost none of their persuasiveness in an era dominated by YouTube and reality television. When one considers the intense viewer saturation of *The Blair Witch Project* (1999), *Cloverfield* (2008) and *Quarantine* (2008) a remake of the Spanish film *[REC]* (2007) the continued effectiveness of such films would seem written in stone. Especially if the film in question is as carefully constructed as *Paranormal Activity*.

Micah (Micah Sloat) and Katie (Katie Featherston) are boyfriend and girlfriend who become concerned enough about the spooky goings on in their home to set a video camera up in their bedroom. But once the camera is up and running the unsettling occurrences accelerate, becoming more frequent and hostile. They try everything to rid their home of the unwelcome presence even going so far as to bring in a psychic (Mark Fredrichs). Secrets from Katie's past lead the psychic to caution them about playing games with the entity, which he believes is demonic in nature. Soon Katie begins to act strangely and they plot to leave, unsure of whether or not escape is still possible.

Shot entirely with a handheld video camera for a reported $15,000 over the course of one week, *Paranormal Activity* does an awful lot with a little. Both Micah Sloat and Katie Featherstone excel as the couple, generating solid chemistry and, early on, a believable sense of confusion about how seriously they should take these initially creepy but rather minor inconveniences. Performances aside, the real strength of *Paranormal Activity* lies in an inexorable movement away from near normalcy toward a horrifying chaos where basic concepts of evil reassert their dominance over suburban daydreams.

The chatty build is slow, too slow for some no doubt, but it is pleasant and "real" enough to reflect the sort of stupefied enjoyment of life that our possessions and relationships with others bring us outside of any moral context. When the evil comes it is a wake-up call to a life beyond comfort, challenging the very idea of survival not just in a physical sense but in one of personhood. The film presses home that emotionally charged touch point by setting the camera in the couple's bedroom where a series of scenes offer stripped down special effects in place of the sort of effects overkill found in far lesser big-budget cinema ghost stories like *The Haunting* (1999) or *Gothika* (2003). In contrast to full bodied monstrous apparitions and living statues, *Paranormal Activity* offers self-slamming doors, ghostly footprints, wails, and unnatural body motions which are far more effective simply because they are within the realm of how we really think of ghosts and demons manifesting themselves. Peli understands these are the things that frighten us when we are alone in bed at night.

Producer Stephen Spielberg reportedly brought his copy of *Paranormal Activity* back to the studio in a garbage bag, convinced it was haunted, and incidents of audience walkouts, due to the frightening nature of the film, are widespread. Whether true or not the precocity of such tales point to a deep desire—we want them to be true. In the blandly believable world of *Paranormal Activity* we sense a verisimilitude, a deeper truth presented, hinted at, through a falsity. Our lives really are a struggle against evil. We can win the struggle with the tax man, the health care provider, the job, the bank, even win at romance. But the real struggle is not against flesh and blood but against that which can claim the soul. Horror cinema at its most powerful is our collective emotional witness.

Dave Canfield

CREDITS

Katie: Katie Featherston
Micah: Micah Sloat
Amber: Amber Armstrong
The Psychic: Mark Fredrichs
Diane: Ashley Palmer
Lt. Randy Hudson: Randy McDowell
Richard: James Piper
Exorcism Nanny: Crystal Cartwright
Origin: USA
Language: English
Released: 2009
Production: Jason Blum, Oren Peli; Blumhouse Productions; released by Paramount Pictures, DreamWorks
Directed by: Oren Peli
Written by: Oren Peli
Cinematography by: Oren Peli
Editing: Oren Peli
MPAA rating: R
Running time: 99 minutes

REVIEWS

Bayer, Jeff. *Scorecard Review.* October 18, 2009.
Edelstein, David. *New York Magazine.* October 12, 2009.
Gleiberman, Owen. *Entertainment Weekly.* September 30, 2009.
Harvey, Dennis. *Variety.* January 22, 2008.
Howell, Peter. *Toronto Star.* October 12, 2009.
Phillips, Michael. *At the Movies.* October 12, 2009.
Scott, A.O. *New York Times.* October 9, 2009.
Sharkey, Betsy. *Los Angeles Times.* October 8, 2009.
Sobczynski, Peter. *EFilmCritic.* October 8, 2009.
Tallerico, Brian. *MovieRetriever.com.* October 12, 2009.

QUOTES

Micah: "So you'd think a psychic would, uh, be on time. You know, like he could foretell if the traffic was going to be bad?"

TRIVIA

The film's original ending was changed when Steven Spielberg suggested a different route.

AWARDS

Nomination:

Ind. Spirit 2010: First Feature.

PAUL BLART: MALL COP

Safety never takes a holiday.
—Movie tagline
Don't mess with his mall!
—Movie tagline

Box Office: $146.3 million

In the first four months of 2009, audiences got their taste of a pair of mall cop comedies. The first in January went on to be one of the biggest success stories of the year, a PG-rated pseudo-*Die Hard* (1988) parody that struck a chord with family audiences. The more adult *Observe and Report* (2009) would open in April to more favorable reviews yet little fanfare. Were moviegoers truly burnt out on stories about mall cops? Was Jody Hill's film perceived as a blatant copy job trying to latch off of *Paul Blart*'s success? Or was it simply too dark for crowds who just wanted to laugh at a fat man who constantly needs food for energy? The darker discomfort of Hill's film was certainly understandable, but that still fails to explain why *Paul Blart* was so embraced. Harmless to everyone except the gods of comedy, *Paul Blart: Mall Cop*'s greatest compliment amongst many viewers was that it was "not so bad." Maybe not. That just means it's not really good either.

Kevin James is Paul Blart, the portly head of security at a New Jersey shopping mall. Don't let his weight fool you. He can make his way through the police academy's obstacle course better than most skinnies. If it was not for that darned hypoglycemia, he might make it through the whole thing without collapsing like a narcoleptic. Back to the indoor Segway for him. Poor Blart. He lives at home with his doting mom (Shirley Knight) and daughter (Raini Rodriguez) from a green card marriage. On the job, despite being in charge, he is not respected by his fellow rent-a-cops nor the shoppers none-too-pleased to get a ticket for not sticking to Blart's perceived

handicap lane. Blart loves the job nevertheless and coming to work has recently become more pleasant with the addition of the doe-eyed Amy (Jayma Mays) whom he's sweet on.

On Black Friday though, the busiest shopping day of the year, Blart's mall is taken over by some bad guys. Their leader—to everyone's surprise but the audience—is Blart's new trainee, Veck (Keir O'Donnell), whose crew plans to grab millions in credit card transactions by means of the machine codes. Blart's preoccupation with a video game—a gag done to greater effect in *Grosse Pointe Blank*— causes him to miss the initial ruckus. Once he's wise to the takeover Blart is nearly evacuated thanks to the cops on the scene, but when he realizes that Amy is one of the hostages, he Segways back in with a vow to protect the mall he swore to defend. Even if there's no such vow.

About halfway through the film's 90 minutes at this point in the plot recap and so far the film has relied on the most basic of fat guy humor to get its yuks. Blart's quiet proclamation of using peanut butter to spread over the holes inside is pretty funny, but after that it's fat guy out of breath, fat guy unable to jump, fat guy crashing through stuff, and fat guy being dragged by a motorized wheelchair. To pepper things up, it resorts to fat guy not being able to hold his liquor in a scene that reeks of padding out the running time more than its intention of driving some momentary—and unnecessary—wedge between Blart and Amy.

The film occasionally does come out of its one-joke funk in the second half and it does so by almost ditching its labeling as a comedy and becoming a full-blown action film. The martial arts movement known as parkour must be mortified that its gone from its coming out party in *District B-13* (2006) to helping kickstart Daniel Craig as James Bond in *Casino Royale* (2006) to being used to rob a mall. Audiences have not seen mass shopping gymnastics like this since Schwarzenegger's balloon swing in *Commando* (1985). It is unclear if the filmmakers intended for any of these action beats to be taken seriously, although it does come off like the one element they put some pride into. Blart's subsequent dispatching of Veck's team goes beyond mere accidental knockouts. He is happy to use full hockey gear or to repeatedly pummel one guy out of commission and these moments do provide a little charge not just because Blart is a likable enough guy—if only a one-dimensional fella—but because we are surprised these acts of retribution are taken seriously.

No one is going to confuse *Paul Blart: Mall Cop* with *Taken* (2009) and certainly not *Die Hard* (1988)— even if the film borrows a late-act twist right out of *Die Hard 2* (1990). The comparisons to *Observe and Report*

(2009) though are too great to ignore. Coincidental to a fault, but a clear example of Godard's theory that "to criticize a movie is to make another movie." Both films are about mall cops with aspirations to be a real one; each with a condition proving detrimental to their pursuit. Both Paul Blart and *Observe*'s Ronnie Barnhardt (played by Seth Rogen) live with their mother. They each have a thing for a cute blonde working at a specialty counter; Blart's is played by Jayma Mays—the poor man's Anna Faris—while Ronnie's is actually played by Anna Faris. Blart uses a Segway. Ronnie enjoys his lot cart. They both have some weight issues and butt heads with a top cop. Ronnie's was Ray Liotta, Blart's is Bobby Cannavale. And each is forced to react violently when intruders invade their proud domain. There is even a sign in Blart's security room that reminds his staff that the final two rules of their job is to observe and report.

No matter which film is viewed first, the second one is going to have that been-there/done-that quality to it. The difference obviously is in tone and this is where the game of opposites begin. Paul Blart is the kind of a lovable underdog hindered by a glucose deficiency that can be cured with something as easily as sugar. Ronnie Barnhardt is a bipolar ball of grandeur delusions that needs pills to keep himself in check. Blart's mom will fix him whatever he wants to eat and Amy is forgiving enough to accept the advances of this overweight man a decade-plus her senior. Ronnie's mom cares but is a barely functional drunk. *Observe* uses a trio of Queen songs on its soundtrack. Blart's anthem comes from Survivor. When enforcing mall authority, Blart allows himself to be dragged across the floor by someone who doesn't respect him. Ronnie Barnhardt uses a tazer at close range, beats up a gaggle of skateboarders with their own equipment and shoots someone point blank in the chest. George Carlin, God rest him, could have had an entire follow-up to his baseball vs. football bit, but you can begin to understand maybe why the public may have chosen to avoid *Observe and Report*.

What it does not explain is how *Paul Blart: Mall Cop* was able to rake in over $146 million in tickets. Kevin James has a certain amiable charm about him and probably evokes that John Candy sensibility more than anyone since his untimely passing. Since when has being a good sport though translated into instant word-of-mouth success? The film was directed by Steve Carr, whose previous baggage consists of two Eddie Murphy family comedies (*Dr. Dolittle 2* [2001] & *Daddy Day Care* [2003]), a Martin Lawrence kids basketball film (*Rebound* [2005]) and may have helped Ice Cube lose the rest of his street cred after going from *Next Friday* (2000) to *Are We Done Yet?* (2007). *Paul Blart* may have been Carr's first foray into dopey white man comedy but laughter is color blind and his directorial skills are

far more seriously impaired. James, who is a credited co-writer along with Nick Bakay, never finds what's funny about this lovable loser and surrounds him with equally uninteresting and unfunny characters. It is not yuk-yuk playful enough to be considered a true kid's comedy just because it contains a minimal amount of swearing and innuendo. Unless those same kids were lucky enough to have seen the original *Die Hard* (1988) already, they may not recognize some of the gags in the second half. Of course, if they are sophisticated enough for John McClane they might be ready to move on to a more challenging mall cop like Ronnie Barnhardt.

Erik Childress

CREDITS

Paul Blart: Kevin James
Veck Sims: Keir O'Donnell
Amy: Jayma Mays
Vijay: Erik Avari
Mom: Shirley Knight
Chief Brooks: Peter Gerety
Commander Kent: Bobby Cannavale
Sgt. Howard: Adam Ferrara
Maya Blart: Raini Rodriguez
Stuart: Stephen Rannazzisi
Origin: USA
Language: English
Released: 2009
Production: Todd Garner, Barry Bernardi, Adam Sandler, Jack Giarraputo, Kevin James; Happy Madison Productions, Relativity Media; released by Columbia Pictures
Directed by: Steve Carr
Written by: Kevin James, Nicky Bakay
Cinematography by: Russ T. Alsobrook
Music by: Waddy Wachtel
Sound: Deborah Adair, William Freesh
Music Supervisor: Michael Dilbeck
Editing: Jeff Freeman
Art Direction: Alan Au
Costumes: Ellen Lutter
Production Design: Perry Andelin Blake
MPAA rating: PG
Running time: 91 minutes

REVIEWS

Ebert, Roger. *Chicago Sun-Times*. January 15, 2009.
Hartlaub, Peter. *San Francisco Chronicle*. January 16, 2009.
Honeycutt, Kirk. *Hollywood Reporter*. January 14, 2009.
Kennedy, Lisa. *Denver Post*. January 16, 2009.
Long, Tom. *Detroit News*. January 16, 2009.

Lowry, Brian. *Variety.* January 14, 2009.
Morris, Wesley. *Boston Globe.* January 16, 2009.
Pais, Matt. *Metromix.com.* January 15, 2009.
Rabin, Nathan. *Onion AV Club.* January 15, 2009.
Whipp, Glenn. *Los Angeles Times.* January 16, 2009.

QUOTES

Veck Sims: "It's like my mother always said, if you want something done right, waste them yourself. I'm paraphrasing, but you get the idea."

A PERFECT GETAWAY

Let the games begin.
—Movie tagline

Everyone needs a place to escape.
—Movie tagline

Box Office: $15.5 million

A Perfect Getaway is basically a B-movie thriller through and through and in the hands of lesser people, it might have just turned out to be the kind of dull programmer that seems to exist only to pop up on obscure cable channels in the dead of night in order to fill time. Luckily, the film was written and directed by David Twohy, whose previous films (including *The Arrival* (1996), *Pitch Black* (2000) and *Below* (2002)) have all demonstrated what can happen when unabashedly pulpy material is put in the hands of someone talented enough to make something interesting out of it instead of merely following the usual clichés. In the case of *A Perfect Getaway*, he has taking a premise that might have otherwise fueled a Lifetime Original Movie and juiced it up in enough clever ways to transform it into a highly entertaining pulp thriller that delivers the goods in such a stylish and effective manner that beats most other recent films of its ilk like a gong.

Milla Jovovich and Steve Zahn star as Cydney and Cliff, a sweet-faced newlywed couple who have chosen to spend their honeymoon hiking through a remote area of one of the Hawaiian Islands. On the way to the trail that they are going to be hiking on, they stop for a pair of sinister-looking hitchhikers (Marley Shelton and Chris Hemsworth) but tensions between them quickly flare up and they wind up not giving them a ride after all. While beginning their hike, Cydney and Cliff make the acquaintance of Nick (Timothy Olyphant), a strange guy packing a huge knife, plenty of survival skills and any number of too-good-to-be-true tales about his adventures that he believes that screenwriter Cliff can turn into a blockbuster film. While making their way along the trail, they run into a bunch of fellow hikers who have just learned that a honeymooning couple was found brutally murdered in Oahu and that the suspects—a man and a woman—are now believed to be somewhere on their island. Things get tense for Cydney and Cliff when they decide to continue on with Nick and discover that he is not alone but has his girlfriend Gina (Kiele Sanchez) in tow and get even tenser when it turns out that the creepy hitchhikers have caught up with them and are lurking about the scene. Nevertheless, Cydney and Cliff decide to press on with Nick and Gina but as they progress further along the trail, they begin to suspect that they may indeed be in over their heads with no easy way out.

As with many films of this type, there are a number of narrative twists and turns ahead but one of the fun things about *A Perfect Getaway* is how Twohy anticipates our anticipation of those twists and plays with expectations. Throughout the film, for example, he has screenwriter Cliff and unabashed movie fan Nick discussing various screenplay conventions in ways that offer viewers a not-so-subtle condemnation of the lazy hackwork that they too often settle for in Hollywood thrillers. This is all pretty funny, though those without a working knowledge of screenplay construction may find it a bit irritating after a while, but what makes it work is that while Twohy is distracting us with all that stuff, he is quietly setting up the real story and any number of payoff moments right under our noses up until the point where he reveals all in an exceptionally audacious manner. And for viewers who may complain that the first hour involves little more than people talking and hiking, be assured that once the action kicks in during the last third, Twohy proves to be equally adept in that area as well with a bloody and brutal final act that is equal parts breathlessly exciting and darkly funny.

Although *A Perfect Getaway* did not break any records at the box-office, it did get slightly stronger reviews than expected and some critics even went so far as to describe it as being Hitchcockian in its approach. While that may be overstating the case just a tad—if it is to be compared to anything made by Hitchcock, it would be to either one of the better episodes of *Alfred Hitchcock Presents* or one of the second-tier films like *Dial 'M' For Murder* (1953) that he occasionally did simply to keep busy or to reestablish himself commercially after a couple of failures—the film does offer viewers a clever screenplay that ratchets up the tension for the first two-thirds before going cheerfully nuts in the last, sure-footed direction and strong performances from all four of the leads. The result is a low-key, solidly made and enormously entertaining thriller that comes at a time when such things are at an absolute premium and which is likely to finally score the audience that it deserves when it hits home video in much the same way that Twohy's *Pitch Black* did a decade earlier.

Peter Sobczynski

CREDITS

Cydney Anderson: Milla Jovovich
Cliff Anderson: Steve Zahn
Nick: Timothy Olyphant
Gina: Kiele Sanchez
Cleo: Marley Shelton
Kale: Chris Hemsworth
Origin: USA
Language: English
Released: 2009
Production: Mark Canton, Tucker Tooley, Robbie Brenner, Ryan Kavanaugh; Relativity Media, QED International; released by Rogue Pictures
Directed by: David N. Twohy
Written by: David N. Twohy
Cinematography by: Mark Plummer
Music by: Boris Elkis
Sound: Steven D. Grothe
Music Supervisor: Gina Amador
Editing: Tracy Adams
Costumes: Laura Goldsmith
Production Design: Joseph C. Nemec III
MPAA rating: R
Running time: 98 minutes

REVIEWS

Anderson, Jason. *Toronto Star.* August 7, 2009.
Burr, Ty. *Boston Globe.* August 6, 2009.
Dargis, Manohla. *New York Times.* August 7, 2009.
Ebert, Roger. *Chicago Sun-Times.* August 6, 2009.
Honeycutt, Kirk. *Hollywood Reporter.* August 7, 2009.
Pais, Matt. *Metromix.com.* August 6, 2009.
Sobczynski, Peter. *eFilmCritic.* August 6, 2009.
Tallerico, Brian. *HollywoodChicago.com.* August 7, 2009.
Tobias, Scott. *AV Club.* August 6, 2009.
Whipp, Glenn. *Los Angeles Times.* August 7, 2009.

QUOTES

Cliff: "Remember, nothing exists until we get there!"

TRIVIA

Director David Twohy purportedly fought with the studio to retain the film's R-rating rather than editing it to achieve a PG-13 rating.

THE PINK PANTHER 2

Inspect the unexpected.
—Movie tagline

Box Office: $35.9 million

The Pink Panther diamond is in peril again. The French national treasure has been stolen by a mysterious world-traveling thief known only as "The Tornado." In addition to the Pink Panther, The Tornado has helped himself to various priceless artifacts from across the globe, including the Magna Carta and the Shroud of Turin. Naturally, the burgled countries are outraged. So they get together and devise a plan to capture the bandit and retrieve their artifacts. They compile a Dream Team of investigators comprised of a tech-savvy Japanese agent (Yuki Matsuzaki), a Casanova Italian cop (Andy Garcia), a brisk British investigator (Alfred Molina), a sultry crime expert (Aishwarya Rai) and Inspector Jacques Clouseau (Steve Martin), the clumsy, awkward, but surprisingly effective investigator from France, to solve the crime. The Dream Team travels from France to Italy in search of The Tornado, making headlines over their screw-ups rather than their crime-solving skills. It also doesn't help that Inspector Clouseau has more on his mind than just the missing jewel. He is battling his feelings for his assistant, the brainy, but beautiful beneath her glasses, Nicole (Emily Mortimer). The two-sided plot opens the door for much malarkey as Clouseau tries to navigate the obstacle course that is being part of an international task force and deal with his attraction to Nicole, but it's hard to care for either angle when the slap-stick routine feels as old and overdone as this one does.

At first glance, it's hard to pinpoint exactly where *The Pink Panther 2* goes awry. On paper, the cast is formidable. It would be quite hard to assemble the likes of Martin, Mortimer, John Cleese, and Lily Tomlin and have them all fail at being even remotely funny. The set up for the film is also clever enough. It allows for the introduction of new secondary characters and a change of scenery for Clouseau. And the physical comedy is exploited to the max throughout the movie. Martin is perpetually falling and stumbling with his accent. But as a whole, *The Pink Panther 2* just doesn't come together. The scenarios succeed only in feeling tired (*Eurotrip* (2004) did a better and more believable job at having their characters wreak havoc at the Vatican), the characters disappointingly misused (Tomlin as a political correctness coach feels trite) and the slapstick relies too heavily on characters hurting themselves rather than on the situational comedy of being their oddball selves in the real world (Martin burns down the same restaurant twice and Cleese bangs his head against walls in frustration).

It is also apparent that the movie never settled on an audience. In trying to cast a wide net for its potential viewership, *The Pink Panther 2* succeeds in appealing primarily to kids who don't mind repetitive physical comedy and find men in tights a hilarious concept. But the leads here are adults, dealing with and working in the adult world. They should be about more than just tripping over one another. Between solving the crime and trying to win Nicole's heart there seem to be many opportunities for double entendres, situational comedy and dramatic irony for Clouseau to find himself in. The fact that the jokes amount to nothing more than a lot of falling and almost-falling and the dialogue between characters seems to exist only as a means for Clouseau to practice his accent is disappointing—especially when the cast includes so many comedy veterans. What makes Clouseau a loveable Mr. Bean-esque character is that he has an uncanny ability to get the job done even though he is extremely socially inept. Its Clouseau's stumbling through the real world that audiences come to watch. This Clouseau however, is more idiot than savant. It doesn't help that his fellow cast members are caricatures as well. So instead of Clouseau being the funny one on screen, we get a bunch of loosely drawn stereotypes bumping into one another. Though Martin commits to Clouseau wholeheartedly—and deserves credit for doing so—he has little substantive material to work with. This is surprising considering how over-stuffed the plot of this 92-minute movie feels. The screenwriters have layered storylines in an attempt to create jokes, hoping that an over-cluttered narrative would make up for lack of timing and nuance. The result is a showcase of one-liners whose only function seem to be to drag the narrative from one Clouseau wipe-out to the next.

Unfortunately, the first Martin-led *Pink Panther* remake didn't fare much better. Even starring Beyonce Knowles, it also lacked the spirit, timing, and originality of the Peter Sellers films. One lack-luster movie could have been labeled a failed attempt at an homage of sorts. The sequel to the failed remake not only feels unnecessary, but also deeply misguided.

Joanna Topor MacKenzie

CREDITS

Inspector Jacques Clouseau: Steve Martin
Ponton: Jean Reno
Nicole: Emily Mortimer
Chief Inspector Dreyfus: John Cleese
Vincenzo: Andy Garcia
Pepperidge: Alfred Molina
Sonia: Aishwarya Rai
Kenji: Yuki Matsuzaki
Mrs. Berenger: Lily Tomlin
Joubert: Geoffrey Palmer
Avellaneda: Jeremy Irons
Milliken: Johnny Hallyday

Origin: USA
Language: English
Released: 2009
Production: Robert Simonds; MGM; released by Columbia Pictures
Directed by: Harald Zwart
Written by: Steve Martin, Scott Neustadter, Michael H. Weber
Cinematography by: Denis Crossan, Rick Butler
Music by: Christophe Beck
Sound: David Obermeyer
Editing: Julia Wong
Costumes: Joseph G. Aulisi
Production Design: Rusty Smith
MPAA rating: PG
Running time: 92 minutes

REVIEWS

Bradshaw, Peter. *Guardian.* February 13, 2009.
Ebert, Roger. *Chicago Sun-Times.* February 5, 2009.
Holden, Stephen. *New York Times.* February 6, 2009.
McCarthy, Todd. *Variety.* February 6, 2009.
Morris, Wesley. *Boston Globe.* February 5, 2009.
Pais, Matt. *Metromix.com.* February 5, 2009.
Phillips, Michael. *Chicago Tribune.* February 5, 2009.
Puig, Claudia. *USA Today.* February 6, 2009.
Sobczynski, Peter. *EFilmCritic.com.* February 5, 2009.
Tookey, Christopher. *Daily Mail.* February 13, 2009.

QUOTES

Inspector Jacques Clouseau: "Let me bring you up to speed. We know nothing. You are now up to speed."

TRIVIA

The Boston area serves as Paris, France in some scenes.

AWARDS

Nomination:

Golden Raspberries 2009: Worst Actor (Martin), Worst Remake, Rip-Off or Sequel.

PIRATE RADIO
(The Boat That Rocked)

They rocked. They rolled. Then they sank.
—Movie tagline
On air. Off shore. Out of control.
—Movie tagline

Box Office: $8 million

Rock 'n' roll will always be somewhat of an interesting beast. The definition may have changed over the years, but whether you consider it hard, soft, metal, or alternative, by designation it's going to upset somebody. Offended or merely scared by the freedom represented in its passion, parents, the government and general old fuddy duddys who dread change have tried to discourage the younger generations from being polluted with these chords of evil. And where there is opposition, there is the rebellion. Director Richard Curtis is no stranger in drawing out the various fantasies we have when it comes to what we love. Famously for him it's been the central idea of love itself. With his latest film he is playing with an actual reality; a true story ruffled into a male fantasy of reliving the youthful urges of music, sex, and being a pirate. While not without its charms, there's an irony that the result has been edited down in the manner of a good record, all scratched up and skipping.

Based in part on the story of the infamous Radio Caroline that broadcasted signals from miles off the coast of England, *Pirate Radio* focuses on one boat crew satisfying the needs of a culture hampered by less than 45 minutes of rock a day on the BBC. The year is 1966, right at the outset of the British Invasion. Kicked out of school, young Carl (Tom Sturridge) has been sent to Radio Rock where his godfather, Quentin (Bill Nighy) is the Captain. Amongst the DJs performing round-the-clock are the "beefy" but smooth, Dave (Nick Frost), the even smoother and almost mute, Midnight Mark (Tom Wisdom), the less-than-smooth, but amiable Simon (Chris O'Dowd), and the one American known as The Count (Philip Seymour Hoffman).

With obviously less pressing matters on the docket, Parliament is interested in shutting down pirate radio. Specifically, Sir Alistair Dormandy (Kenneth Branagh), who along with ambitious right-hand man, Twatt (Jack Davenport), explore cutting off their advertising and other methods. ("You see that's the whole point of being the government. If you don't like something you simply make up a new law that makes it illegal.") Radio Rock's latest answer to the government's interference is to beef up their talent roster with the return of Gavin Cavanaugh (Rhys Ifans), a move that rubs their current star, The Count, the wrong way.

Dormandy's crusade against the anchored broadcast is the closest thing to a driving force the film has and for films like *Pump Up The Volume* (1990) and *Private Parts* (1997), such a subplot has been enough to keep the moments in-between transmissions afloat. Except Curtis never conveys the true force of Dormandy's objections to Quentin's crew. Is he looking out for the local economy? A problem with the actual music or foul language perpetrated in, at least, one instance? Or is he

just another fuddy duddy influenced by some misplaced sense of duty to the law? With his rolling R's and occasional bridge in-between the chorus of boat antics, Branagh's appearance merely recalls his Nazi commander role in *Swing Kids* (1993); a film no one ever wants to be reminded of.

Curtis showed such a knack for mixing the lovelorn with politics in the HBO telefilm, *The Girl In The Cafe* (2005), that it's a wonder how the little details eluded him here. Back on the boat, there's always something going on that leaves too much in the dark. The Count's initial animosity to Gavin is more mysterious than John C. Reilly's to the last minute addition of William Fichtner to *The Perfect Storm* (2000). How the chunky Dave expects to fool a visiting babe that the far thinner Carl is really him in bed—even in pitch black conditions—is beyond understanding, resulting in something more creepy than funny. One of the recurring ideas that Curtis focuses on, but never fully fleshes out, is the perception of these isolated outsiders using what their listeners cannot see to make them more desirable. Dave and The Count may not inspire gals to drop their knickers on sight, but on the air they are gods to them; their own fantasy. Midnight Mark admits to saying as little as possible, but he's got the rugged looks to back it up. Guys like Carl, Simon, and the unpopular Angus (Rhys Darby) searching for true love are ruined by what has been built up in their listeners minds as the ultimate rebellion against the norm.

That's a fascinating approach to the subject if Curtis could have pulled it off, but even in the international version—originally titled *The Boat That Rocked*—the fifteen minutes that were trimmed for the U.S. release amount to very little. A scene where Twatt sneaks aboard and an extended stag sequence with the DJ's indulging bar-to-bar on shore turn out to be good cuts. But even at just under two hours, there's a stagnate feel to it all especially when Carl is in play. As the model for the audience's introduction to everything, he's fine. As a more-or-less lead character throughout, Curtis makes the same mistake that Richard Linklater's *Me and Orson Welles* (2009) does in taking the least interesting person amongst a collection of colorful personalities and putting him center stage. It doesn't help that Sturridge plays him as such a drip that we can't imagine what he could have done to get expelled—even if it was just smoking. He's not even THAT cool. Therefore the in-and-out search for his mystery father on the boat rings hollow compared to the randy exploits, the war of chicken between Gavin and The Count, and Nighy's welcomely droll commentary on the state of each moment. Carl isn't even smart enough to consider that one of the paternal suspects may have tried to set him up with his own cousin. And Kevin (Tom Brooke) is supposed to be the "Thick" one?

Pirate Radio works when it brings its ensemble together as a collective, much as the multiple we-get-it montages of the UK's society dancing in unison to their airwaves suggest how music is more than just an individual experience. And for all that, until its closing credits reminding us of "40 good years" of rock through album covers (Duffy, really?), the film never has a single conversation about why it would endure. Maybe there's something to be said for the music speaking for itself on the fabulous soundtrack, but with Hoffman in a sort of pre-Lester Bangs mode, it's impractical not to remember the passion for what makes music tick that leapt from the screen in Cameron Crowe's *Almost Famous* (2000)—in both its truncated and director's cut. In either form, Pirate Radio is a bit of a mess, though an occasionally funny one that owes a deep credit to its cast since even as their dreams of rock-and-roll are going "the full Titanic," we wish for them not to go down with the ship.

Erik Childress

CREDITS

The Count: Philip Seymour Hoffman
Quentin: Bill Nighy
Gavin: Rhys Ifans
Dave: Nick Frost
Minister Dormandy: Kenneth Branagh
Angus: Rhys Darby
Felicity: Katharine Parkinson
Mark: Tom Wisdom
Carl: Thomas Sturridge
Twatt: Jack Davenport
Charlotte: Emma Thompson
Thick Kevin: Tom Brooke
Simon: Chris O'Dowd
Origin: USA, Great Britain, Germany, France
Language: English
Released: 2009
Production: Tim Bevan, Eric Fellner; StudioCanal; released by Universal Pictures
Directed by: Richard Curtis
Written by: Richard Curtis
Cinematography by: Danny Cohen
Sound: Simon Gershon
Music Supervisor: Nick Angel
Editing: Emma E. Hickox
Art Direction: Thomas Brown
Costumes: Joanna Johnston
Production Design: Mark Tildesley

MPAA rating: R
Running time: 134 minutes

REVIEWS

Berkshire, Geoff. *Metromix.com*. November 12, 2009.
Burr, Ty. *Boston Globe*. November 12, 2009.
Dargis, Manohla. *New York Times*. November 13, 2009.
Ebert, Roger. *Chicago Sun-Times*. November 12, 2009.
Germain, David. *Associated Press*. November 12, 2009.
LaSalle, Mick. *San Francisco Chronicle*. November 12, 2009.
Scott, A.O. *At the Movies*. November 16, 2009.
Sharkey, Betsy. *Los Angeles Times*. November 13, 2009.
Sobczynski, Peter. *EFilmCritic*. November 13, 2009.
Tallerico, Brian. *MovieRetriever.com*. November 13, 2009.

QUOTES

The Count: "To all our listeners, this is what I have to say—God bless you all. And as for you bastards in charge, don't dream it's over. Years will come, years will go, and politicians will do f**k all to make the world a better place. But all over the world, young men and young women will always dream dreams and put those dreams into song."

TRIVIA

Kenneth Branagh's character Alistair Dormandy, is based on Tony Benn, the United Kingdom's Post Master General during the time period in which the film is set.

PLANET 51

Something strange is coming to their planet...Us!
    —Movie tagline
Right stuff. Wrong planet.
    —Movie tagline

Box Office: $42 million

A piece of advice to anyone making a movie: First come up with a few good ideas. It sounds like an obvious statement that no filmmakers would need to be told. That is not the case, and a prime example is the painfully uninvolving *Planet 51*, whose writer Joe Stillman (an alum of *Shrek* [2001] and *Shrek 2* [2004]) seems to have spent zero minutes working to craft an original story or even a mildly clever joke. Visually, *Planet 51* is a perfectly fine animated film, but everything else about it is so dry that enduring the 90-minute movie feels like a grueling, five-hour marathon.

The plot is essentially an inversion of *E.T.: The Extra Terrestrial* (1982). In Planet 51's city of Glipforg—which resembles the United States, circa 1950—the extraterrestrials' calm lives are rocked with the arrival of human astronaut Charles Baker (voiced by Dwayne Johnson), who, of course, is an alien to them. Even though the planet's beings speak English and behave like humans, they are terribly afraid of Charles, whose sole local ally is Lem (Justin Long), a shy guy with the hots for next-door neighbor Neera (Jessica Biel).

Perhaps this set-up would provide an opportunity to send-up sci-fi conventions, where governments are cynical and untrustworthy and a pair of loners must fight to survive. Or maybe the film will explore the fear of the unknown in a new way. (The message that kids should not believe everything they hear is always valuable.) Or maybe it can just be a fun kids' movie with some appealing creatures—the characters look like rubbery toys that would be fun to play with, likely a deliberate merchandising tie-in—and a few laughs. Yet *Planet 51* never takes a fresh look at its sci-fi foundations; instead, the film constantly reverts to juvenile humor—Lem's pal Skiff (Seann William Scott) says a properly placed cork will prevent humans from performing anal probes he presumes they do—and cliché, including repetitive instances in which Lem and Neera almost get together but then, at the last minute, something gets in the way.

Obviously originality is not *Planet 51*'s forte, a point reiterated by the film's conceptual similarity to *Battle for Terra* (2009), in which an alien species is unsettled by the arrival of humans. That film, while visually inferior, at least attempted to address environmental issues. *Planet 51* only calls to mind the importance of grounding animated movies in engaging stories and memorable characters, neither of which this comedy comes close to delivering. Part of that void comes from the presence of actors who are decent when on-screen but contribute nothing as voice actors. Knowing that Dwayne Johnson is doing a voice for an animated movie should not make a large number of people want to see it. Rather, believing that an animated movie is going to capture viewers' imagination should be what brings in audiences, and characters should be cast based on what voice actor can best play the part. Sure, it is easier to finance a movie when a big star like Johnson or Biel is involved, but it is to the detriment of the viewer, who not only feels nothing for Lem or Neera or Charles because they have bland personalities but because the actors portraying them do nothing to make these characters any funnier or unique.

These flaws would be forgivable if a laugh appeared every few minutes. Instead, Stillman's idea of cleverness is naming an alien dog, who looks like it was born on the set of *Alien* (1979), Ripley (which of course, is the name of Sigourney Weaver's character in that film). Another gag involves a comment about Skiff feeding his puppy candy just so it will poop jelly beans. (Only viewers who crack up from hearing the word "poop" will find

this amusing.) Later, when Charles is naked, a Planet 51 resident stupidly remarks, "That's a funny place for his antenna." And when someone drops an MP3 player, Los Del Rio's once-popular song *Macarena* plays, causing everyone around to cover their ears. This is not funny. This is barely a joke. It is just a random reference to something the filmmakers assume the audience thinks is funny, hoping to get a chuckle. (More appropriate references are made to *The Right Stuff* [1983], to no greater effect.)

All of this inoffensive mediocrity prevents *Planet 51* from becoming anything truly noxious or objectionable. Still, ceaseless boredom and lack of inspiration in a film can be awfully taxing as well. There is no intelligent life on Planet 51, but smart moviegoers will know to avoid the trip.

Matt Pais

CREDITS

Captain Charles T. Baker: Dwayne "The Rock" Johnson (Voice)
Neera: Jessica Biel (Voice)
Lem: Justin Long (Voice)
Skiff: Seann William Scott (Voice)
General Grawl: Gary Oldman (Voice)
Professor Kipple: John Cleese (Voice)
Origin: USA
Language: English
Released: 2009
Production: Guy Collins, Ignacio Perez Dolset; Ilion Animation, Handmade Films, Antena 3; released by TriStar Pictures
Directed by: Jorge Blanco, Javier Abad, Marcos Martinez
Written by: Joe Stillman
Music by: James Seymour Brett
Sound: Martin Cantwell
Music Supervisor: Liz Schrek
Editing: Alex Rodriguez
Art Direction: Fernando Juarez
Costumes: Carine Gillet
Production Design: Julian Munoz Romero
MPAA rating: PG
Running time: 91 minutes

REVIEWS

Burr, Ty. *Boston Globe.* November 24, 2009.
Doerksen, Cliff. *Chicago Reader.* November 20, 2009.
Ebert, Roger. *Chicago Sun-Times.* November 19, 2009.
Holden, Stephen. *New York Times.* November 20, 2009.
Honeycutt, Kirk. *Hollywood Reporter.* November 16, 2009.
McCarthy, Todd. *Variety.* November 16, 2009.

O'Sullivan, Michael. *Washington Post.* November 20, 2009.
Tallerico, Brian. *MovieRetriever.com.* November 20, 2009.
Thompson, Gary. *New York Daily News.* November 19, 2009.
Whipp, Glenn. *Los Angeles Times.* November 19, 2009.

QUOTES

Skiff: "I love fake alien-poop-day."

TRIVIA

Even though much on the alien planet is round in its design, no wheels are present.

POLICE, ADJECTIVE
(Politist, Adj.)

The highly acclaimed *Police, Adjective* is a procedural film for people who find traditional procedurals too fast paced. The film does not remotely glamorous police work, featuring long, unbroken shots of one man following another, a cop smoking a cigarette as he stakes out a subject, and other daily minutia. To say *Police, Adjective* is a slow film is an understatement of more drastic proportions than anything that happens in the film. And yet, *Police, Adjective* starts to weave a hypnotic spell. It is not as if the audience is a fly on the wall—the camera is often at a distance from its lead as he follows his subject— but there is an honest realism to the piece that lends it an ultimately mesmerizing sense of drama. For many viewers, watching a man stake out a house, smoke nearly an entire cigarette, watch someone leave, watch someone come, and then light another cigarette could be something akin to arthouse torture and *Police, Adjective* is surely the kind of film that should only be viewed by ticket buyers firmly aware of what they are in for, but those foreign film fans are likely to find one of the more intriguing films of 2009.

Written and directed by Romanian Corneliu Porumboiu (the award-winning *12:08 East of Bucharest* [2006]) tells the relatively mundane story of Cristi (Dragos Bucur), an unassuming young man who happens to be a police officer. Porumboiu spares nothing in the details of his day, including filming him walking to and from work, putting away his coat, dropping his keys on his desk, smoking, etc. Like an incredibly detailed police report, there is barely any detail of the few days of Cristi's life on display deemed too inconsequential to highlight. Those days feature an unusual case. Cristi has been tasked with following a sixteen-year-old kid who has been suspected of smoking marijuana. Like a lot of kids, the kid does smoke pot. But the suspicion that he also deals it (perhaps with his girlfriend) forces Cristi to follow him ceaselessly in an attempt to catch him in the act. Cristi knows this is a waste of time. This kid is no dealer. But he has a job to do. When he realizes that this job could lead him to send a relatively innocent kid to jail for eight to fifteen years, Cristi begins to question his daily routine. As he mentions to his captain, in Prague you can smoke weed in the street, but in Romania it is still illegal. But Cristi clearly comes from a society and worldview where a cop is not supposed to have a personal adjective. They do not have feelings; merely enforce the law.

The procedural nature of *Police, Adjective* adds weight to the inner turmoil of its lead. This is not merely the story of a man who lives life by-the-numbers, it counts out those numbers for you, sometimes effectively but also sometimes to the film's detriment, as the unbroken, dull takes can be a challenge even for the most daring movie watcher. Helping alleviate the boredom is Bucur, who is in nearly every frame and gives a genuine, believable performance with almost no dialogue. There is an amazingly long shot of Cristi eating dinner while his wife listens to music in the other room. The shot is through a doorway, distant from Cristi's expression, and yet it is clear this man has quite a bit on his mind. He is going about the mundane task of a daily meal that he seems to enjoy but he is also listening to the lyrics and, presumably, thinking about his job and the current case. He eventually retires to the company of his wife but there is no revelation about the clear internal conflict he feels about his case and no heartbreaking conversation. He merely discusses the song. All of these elements are conveyed not merely without melodrama but without any actual real drama or traditional filmmaking tools. The final act of the film features more conflict—mostly between cop and captain—but far from in the traditional way of a police procedural.

The fact that *Police, Adjective* is a Romanian film cannot be divorced from its appraisal. The country only recently emerged from the shadow of the Ceausescu regime, one that repressed a society under the guise of law enforcement. The young men of that regime, one that Porumboiu grew up during, probably had similar doubts and questions to those of Cristi. And they probably kept them as secret from their wives and office mates as this young police officer daring enough to ask why enforce seemingly random laws instead of merely doing so. The artistic statements coming out of the country twenty years after the end of that regime include both Porumboiu's films and the highly acclaimed *4 Months, 3 Weeks, 2 Days.* As is often the case, the wounds of a country are being reflected in the works of their most talented filmmakers.

Brian Tallerico

CREDITS

Anghelache: Vlad Ivanov
Cristi: Dragos Bucur
Nelu: Ion Stoica
Anca: Irina Saulescu
Costi: Cosmin Selesi
Vali: George Remes
Vic: Dan Cogalniceanu
Victor: Radu Costin
Origin: Romania
Released: 2009
Production: Corneliu Porumboiu; 42 KM Film, Racova, Raza Studio; released by IFC Films
Directed by: Corneliu Porumboiu
Written by: Corneliu Porumboiu
Cinematography by: Marius Panduru
Music by: Mirabela Dauer, Yan Raiburg
Sound: Alexandru Dragomir, Sebastian Zsemlye
Editing: Roxana Szel
Costumes: Giorgiana Bostan
Production Design: Mihaela Poenaru
MPAA rating: Unrated
Running time: 113 minutes

REVIEWS

Ebert, Roger. *Chicago Sun-Times.* December 23, 2009.
Goss, William. *Cinematical.* December 28, 2009.
Morgenstern, Joe. *Wall Street Journal.* December 18, 2009.
Phillips, Michael. *Chicago Tribune.* December 22, 2009.
Punter, Jennie. *Globe and Mail.* September 11, 2009.
Rothkopf, Joshua. *Time Out New York.* December 16, 2009.
Scott, A.O. *New York Times.* December 22, 2009.
Tobias, Scott. *AV Club.* December 23, 2009.
Weissberg, Jay. *Variety.* May 13, 2009.
Young, Deborah. *Hollywood Reporter.* May 16, 2009.

TRIVIA

The film was Romania's official submission in the Best Foreign Language Film category for the 82nd Academy Awards®.

PONYO
(Gake no ue no Ponyo)
(Ponyo on the Cliff by the Sea)

Welcome to a world where anything is possible.
—Movie tagline

Box Office: $15.1 million

Loosely inspired by Hans Christian Andersen's *The Little Mermaid*, *Ponyo*, the latest epic from Japanese animation legend Hayao Miyazaki, tells the story of an adorable little fish (voiced by Noah Cyrus), albeit one sporting a human-like face and a kicky red dress, who lives beneath the sea with her father (Liam Neeson), a human who has rejected his own kind because of their destructive tendencies towards the oceans while trying to develop a magical elixir that will restore them once and for all, and hundreds of tiny look-alike sisters. Curious about the surface world that her father is always ranting about, she hitches a ride upon a jellyfish and floats up to the surface just in time to be caught up in a dredging net collecting the junk that has carelessly been tossed into the water over the year. Ponyo escapes but finds herself trapped inside a glass jar that washes ashore. There, she is rescued by Sosuke (Frankie Jonas), a little boy who lives in a remote house high above the ocean with his frazzled mom (Tina Fey) and largely absent sailor father (Matt Damon) and the two become fast friends. Ponyo loves the human world—especially when she discovers the joys of ham—but before long, her father manages to retrieve her and bring her back to her home beneath the sea.

Of course, Ponyo is heartbroken and immediately makes plans to escape in order to be reunited with Sosuke. In attempting to do this, she accidentally unleashes the elixir and it transforms her into a real girl and her sisters into enormous fish that take her to the surface and speed her through the ocean in search of Sosuke. Unfortunately, by being able to move between the two worlds, Ponyo unwittingly upsets the balance of nature and, unless she chooses one or the other, the entire planet is in danger of being destroyed. Ponyo doesn't notice any of this—she is too excited about being reunited with her friend and delicious ham—but after Sosuke's mom goes off to check on the residents of the nursing home she works at in the aftermath of the tsunami that she and her sisters inadvertently caused, the two kids set sail on a journey themselves that is ostensibly about finding Mom but which leaves the possible fate of the world hanging in the balance.

Over the years, Miyazaki has given us some of the greatest animated films ever made—*Princess Mononoke* (1999), *Spirited Away* (2002) and *Howl's Moving Castle* (2005) among them—but while they have been perfectly suitable for families interested in exposing their kids to movies that aren't merely extended toy commercials, they have never really been kid films per se with their advanced themes, reasonably complex narratives and decidedly non-cutesy visual styles. With *Ponyo*, Miyazaki has shifted his cinematic approach by making a film that is deliberately aimed at younger viewers—the storytelling is simple and the visual design is bright, colorful, and reminiscent of simple children's drawings throughout. At first, the shift from the more literal and realistic visual style of much of his previous work may seem a bit jarring for longtime fans, that feeling quickly disappears when it becomes obvious that, while the animated style may look simpler, it is actually just as formally complex and aesthetically dazzling as anything he has done before. Some of the scenes here, such as the first look at Ponyo's undersea world and the jaw-dropping sequence in which she cheerfully hops from fish to fish in search of Sosuke while blithely leaving untold destruction in her wake, are breathtaking to behold. The character design is also extraordinary, especially when you consider that a creature that resembles a giant goldfish with a human face in a red dress should theoretically be more appalling than appealing. Nevertheless, all of the characters in the film are beautifully rendered, none more so than Ponyo's mother, Gran Mamare (Cate Blanchett), a creature so ravishing that she makes Jessica Rabbit seem practically dowdy by comparison.

When people write about Miyazaki and his extraordinary gifts as a filmmaker, they tend to focus almost exclusively on the visual aspects of his films and you can hardly blame them for that. However, what sometimes gets lost in the rush to praise those visuals is the fact that he is also a pretty extraordinary storyteller as well. As mentioned earlier, *Ponyo* is a story that is clearly aimed at a younger audience than usual and as a result, the narrative isn't quite as complex as those found in most of his other projects. That said, the themes that emerge—the struggle to maintain a harmonious balance between mankind and nature, the natural conflicts that arise between parents and children and the like—are far deeper and more profound than the ones normally found in kid-oriented films. At the same time, Miyazaki has figured out how to deploy these themes in such a way so that children can easily grasp what they are trying to say without doing it in such a ham-handed way that older viewers get bored or irritated. Beyond that, the storyline is genuinely compelling in that even if you suspect that everything is going to turn out more or less okay, he still finds a way of letting things develop in such a way that there are still some surprises in store. Another plus is the relaxed pacing that Miyazaki employs here—at a time when most films seem to steamroll their way from one big set piece to the next, this is one that has the wisdom to take the time to slow down and let viewers get caught up in the gentle rhythms of the story.

At one point during *Ponyo*, a character remarks that "you can't be human and magic at the same time." In the context of this particular film, that seems like an odd sentiment to espouse since every single frame on display seems to definitively prove the fact that hu-

mans—or Miyazaki, at the very least—possess those very powers. This is a gorgeously realized fairy tale for audiences of all ages that enraptures them not with elaborate special effects, obnoxious pop-culture references and noise but with a gently soothing approach, a story that will capture the imaginations of kids and adults alike and some of the most beautiful animation ever seen on a movie screen. Whether you are a small child awaiting his or her first trip to the movies, a jaded teenager looking for something new and different, or a parent trying to find something to see that will not only be suitable for the entire family but entertaining as well, *Ponyo* is the kind of dazzling cinematic experience that will resonate in the hearts and minds of viewers for a long time to come.

Peter Sobczynski

CREDITS

Gran Mamare: Cate Blanchett (Voice)
Lisa: Tina Fey (Voice)
Fujimoto: Liam Neeson (Voice)
Yoshie: Betty White (Voice)
Toki: Lily Tomlin (Voice)
Noriko: Cloris Leachman (Voice)
Ponyo: Noah Lindsey Cyrus (Voice)
Koichi: Matt Damon (Voice)
Sosuke: Frankie Jonas (Voice)
Origin: Japan
Language: English
Released: 2008
Production: Toshio Suzuki; Studio Ghibli; released by Walt Disney Pictures
Directed by: Hayao Miyazaki
Written by: Hayao Miyazaki
Music by: Joe Hisaishi
Cinematography by: Atsushi Okui
Sound: Shuji Inoue
Editing: Hayao Miyazaki, Takeshi Seyama
MPAA rating: G
Running time: 100 minutes

REVIEWS

Dargis, Manohla. *New York Times.* August 14, 2009.
Ebert, Roger. *Chicago Sun-Times.* August 13, 2009.
Edelstein, David. *New York Magazine.* August 3, 2009.
Kois, Dan. *Washington Post.* August 14, 2009.
Lemire, Christy. *Associated Press.* August 12, 2009.
Morris, Wesley. *Boston Globe.* August 13, 2009.
Quill, Greg. *Toronto Star.* August 14, 2009.
Rickey, Carrie. *Philadelphia Inquirer.* August 14, 2009.

Stevens, Dana. *Slate.* August 12, 2009.
Turan, Kenneth. *Los Angeles Times.* August 14, 2009.

QUOTES

Noriko: "I'd let a fish lick me if it'd get me out of this wheelchair."

TRIVIA

The writer of the English translation for the film, Melissa Matheson, also penned *E.T.: The Extra-Terrestrial.*

POST GRAD

(Ticket to Ride)

(The Post Grad Survival Guide)

Now what?
—Movie tagline

Box Office: $6.4 million

Fans of television's *Gilmore Girls* will, undoubtedly, have trouble separating the delightful Alexis Bledel from her role of Rory Gilmore. So sunny, smart, and well-played, the only thing that drove viewers nuts was her penchant for dating jerkbag guys that were not worthy of her charms. Try as Bledel might have to take a one-eighty turn by playing a tempting, backstabbing prostitute in *Sin City* (2005), it was still a character that had her talking to her mom on a cell phone. The show ended its seven-year run not so long ago and like her character in *Post Grad*, Bledel has now been thrust into the big world of movies looking for a job suited for her talents. She has found one in Ryden Malby, another smart and sunny college graduate making the wrong choice in boys in a rather aimless film that, nevertheless, is momentarily saved by a hysterical supporting cast.

Ryden (Bledel) is ready to take on the world right out of school. The publishing world that is, as she has an interview all lined up at her dream firm where she hopes to discover the next great American novel. If the hit-and-run accident inflicted on her car wasn't enough, how could she predict that there would be other people up for the same position, including her Valedictorian rival, Jessica Bard (Catherine Reitman, daughter of producer Ivan)? Without the means to secure that fancy apartment she had her eye on, Ryden is forced into moving back home with, gasp, her family. While her mom Carmella (Jane Lynch) deals with a precocious younger brother, Hunter (Bobby Coleman) and sassy grandma, Maureen (Carol Burnett), her dad, Walter

(Michael Keaton), naturally suggests alternatives to her dream job.

After a first act of interviews and rejection, Ryden finds another avenue to fill her post-grad days—boys or, more specifically, a man, her 34-year-old neighbor, David Santiago (Rodrigo Santoro). Ryden has a conflicting suitor—that she basically ignores—in the crush by her childhood friend, Adam (Zach Gilford). He's an aspiring musician whose indecisiveness about his acceptance letter to Columbia University is so troubling that his father (J.K. Simmons) leaves the movie after two scenes. Adam's focus is on Ryden though. He's loved her since whenever and is not exactly shy in facetiously proclaiming that love through song, massaging her calves or flat-out pointing out how blind she is to his feelings. What is a college graduate to do with all these choices?

If you are a character in *Post Grad* you more or less string them out as long as you can or forget about them entirely until screenwriter Kelly Fremon can get around to making the decisions for you. Moms may not really want Miss Fremon in their daughters' corners. Seemingly more concerned with the people shaping Ryden's life around her, the independent streak she's built upon in the early scenes gives way to giving in, flaking out and, ultimately, dropping everything in favor of a boy who is just starting law school and may wind up being the bread winner in her new family. Perhaps less egregious than the recent insulting trend of female screenwriters crafting tales where successful, single women need a man to complete them (see: *The Proposal* [2009] and *The Ugly Truth* [2009]), but hardly the right message to send to young women. Quit the job you have always wanted and find yourself a lawyer.

Much of this will becomes clear during the final act and upon reflection on the film as a whole. During it though there is a welcome streak of oddball characters and skilled comic actors to serve as a distraction through the film's questionable ethics and ironic lack of direction. Carol Burnett takes the standard issued grandmother-of-contempt and turns it into a reminder of why her talent needs to be shared with the world more often. Keaton, who has unfortunately been going through the comically concerned dad portion of his career in films like *First Daughter* (2004) and *Herbie Fully Loaded* (2005), provides a welcome reminder of the ace delivery we came to love about him. Walter is still written as the overtly earnest dad—and shockingly clueless when it comes to the bizarre belt buckle sales subplot he has been given—but no one buries a cat in a pizza box quite like Michael Keaton. Scenes like that and other throwaways like Craig Robinson's brief role as a funeral director, what becomes of that casket—along with a roadside tribute to its purchase—and a guacamole mascot fruitlessly trying to get out of a boxing ring in the background almost make *Post Grad* worth recommending.

It has been just over twenty-five years since *Risky Business* (1983) applied Reagan-era economics to the corruption of suburban youth. This year also marks the 15th anniversary of *Reality Bites* (1994) providing its own vision of Generation X's post graduation blues. *Post Grad* hardly speaks for any generation or singular age for that matter. It is hard to feel bad for a spunky white girl from a reasonably well-off middle-class suburban family who does not realize that you have to likely pay your dues as an assistant before hitting the big time. That is actually a bigger fitting monetary reference than anything in *Post Grad*. There is no breakdown of college costs or detail of the struggles of moving into a big city to pursue one's dream. Ryden doesn't even blink writing up a $3500 check to secure an apartment. By the time the Malby family is done plunking down for car repairs, busted caskets and bail money it is no wonder that dad cannot bother to drive her to the airport and give his blessing to pursue a male suitor with a lucrative job in waiting. It is not clear that Walter would approve of the pitiful clichés resorted to in these final moments. Then again, most *Gilmore Girls* fans did not care for the direction its final season took either. But most do wish Rory well, no matter what name she is going under these days.

Erik Childress

CREDITS

Ryden Malby: Alexis Bledel
Walter Malby: Michael Keaton
Carmella Malby: Jane Lynch
David Santiago: Rodrigo Santoro
Adam Davies: Zach Gilford
Funeral Director: Craig Robinson
Maureen Malby: Carol Burnett
Guacanator Pitchman: Fred Armisen
Lloyd Hastings: Andrew Daly
Jessica Bard: Catherine Reitman
Hunter Malby: Bobby Coleman
Origin: USA
Language: English
Released: 2009
Production: Ivan Reitman, Joe Medjuck, Jeffrey Clifford; Cold Spring Pictures, Montecito Picture Co., Dune Entertainment, Fox Atomic; released by 20th Century Fox
Directed by: Victoria Jenson
Written by: Kelly Fremon
Cinematography by: Charles Minsky
Music by: Christophe Beck

Sound: Willie Burton
Music Supervisor: Patrick Houlihan
Editing: Dana Congdon
Production Design: Mark Hutman
Art Direction: Michael Rizzo
Costumes: Alexandra Welker
MPAA rating: PG-13
Running time: 88 minutes

REVIEWS

Catsoulis, Jeanette. *New York Times.* August 21, 2009.
Debruge, Peter. *Variety.* August 19, 2009.
Ebert, Roger. *Chicago Sun-Times.* August 20, 2009.
Honeycutt, Kirk. *Hollywood Reporter.* August 19, 2009.
Lemire, Christy. *Associated Press.* August 19, 2009.
Pais, Matt. *Metromix.com.* August 20, 2009.
Phillips, Michael. *Chicago Tribune.* August 21, 2009.
Phipps, Keith. *AV Club.* August 20, 2009.
Puig, Claudia. *USA Today.* August 20, 2009.
Rea, Steven. *Philadelphia Inquirer.* August 20, 2009.

QUOTES

David Santiago: "What you do with your life is just one-half of the equation more importantly it's who you're with when you're doing it."

TRIVIA

Amanda Bynes was the original choice to play Ryden Malby.

PRECIOUS: BASED ON THE NOVEL 'PUSH' BY SAPPHIRE

Life is hard. Life is short. Life is painful. Life is rich. Life is...Precious.
—Movie tagline

Box Office: $47.4 million

The producers of *Precious: Based on the Novel 'Push' by Sapphire* want to make sure you connect their movie with the best-selling 1996 novel that Oprah Winfrey took under her powerful wing. So they—including executive producers Winfrey and filmmaker Tyler Perry—gave the film perhaps the most pretentious title in movie history. The in-your-face marketing is appropriate for a movie that gives a whole new dimension to that phrase.

Heavy-handed? Or just shrewd? Hard to say. But certainly the phenomenon of this book-turned-movie is fascinating. Some of the biggest African American stars of the entertainment world —Winfrey, Perry, Mariah Carey, Lenny Kravitz, and Mo'Nique—threw their enormous collective influence behind a movie that features a villain who is problematic. The mother of Precious, the name of the film's title character, goes beyond a white racist's most virulent stereotype of a welfare queen, and Precious herself is a young heroine who is obese, abused, and semi-literate, and dreams of being white and blonde. Politically incorrect? If the story had been penned or filmed by someone not black, it would have resulted in a firestorm.

The villain is Mary (Mo'Nique), a mother so vile that she constantly berates her daughter for her feeblest attempts to maintain her dignity by getting an education. Mary is so cruel that she employs her daughter as a household slave, so vacuous that she spends her days watching television game shows, so deceitful that she puts on a wig and a cynical show of being a caring mother and grandmother when the welfare case worker visits, and so utterly amoral that she allows her boyfriend to rape and impregnate his own daughter. Watching Monique's portrayal of Mary is jaw-dropping; it's a journey into a hall of domestic horrors.

Precious indulges in such bottom-feeding because it is a morality lesson with a capital "L." It is also a redemption story with a capital "R." The moral, practically an Oprah trademarked idea, is that you can triumph over anything, even the worst upbringing imaginable, if only you believe in yourself. Somehow, Precious (Gabourey Sidibe) has hung onto a shred of her dignity. It is unclear how, as most days in school she does not even bother to open her book, but instead dreams of becoming the wife of the handsome white teacher. She is barely present in the classroom, and she's a zombie at home, but inside her is a beautiful person just waiting for someone to care about her. We are waiting for that to happen too, because she is obviously scripted to be the ultimate underdog. Precious dreams of being in the arms of a Handsome Prince, on a BET network show, even as she is being harassed and pushed into the mud by neighborhood bullies. It's an amazingly powerful scene, despite its utter shamelessness. And such shoddy dreams do ring true for girls like Precious.

It turns out that she is rescued instead by a Lovely Princess (and, as Precious narrates, a "straight-up lesbian" to boot), an impossibly patient, dedicated, beautiful, and well-dressed teacher implausibly named Blu Rain (Paula Patton). Ms. Rain welcomes her into her class in an alternative school program after Precious is suspended from school for getting pregnant again (why this is grounds for suspension, or how anyone even knows she is pregnant, is left unexplained). With the encouragement of her fairy-tale teacher, Precious soon finds her voice amid a class of sassy, sullen, seemingly dangerous

girls who all turn out, beneath their bluster, to have hearts of gold. Well, it is a fairy tale, after all.

There's also a male nurse's aide (Kravitz) who takes an unlikely shining to Precious, for reasons also unexplained. But even as Precious finds something to believe in after giving birth to her second bastard child at home, there's just a nasty showdown awaiting with the witch queen mom when Precious brings home her new baby. From then on, it's teenage mom and her babies against the world, but the fight turns out to be one-sided, since everyone in authority seems remarkably ready to help Precious regain her footing.

It's a fairy tale all covered in grit, and the direction by Lee Daniels is something like amateur Disney. Gauzy golden light surrounds Ms. Rain and infuses all the moments when Precious begins to glimpse her potential. (The horror scenes at home are mostly shot through a dirty window, or some kind of haze.) In Technicolor fantasy sequences, Precious indulges her escapist fantasies of being a television sex goddess, a fashion model, or a sought-after celebrity. But paltry as those dreams are, they are light years beyond her hopeless life.

Yet, there is hope, because of the strong women who intervene. One of them is a welfare case worker, Mrs. Weiss (an unrecognizable Mariah Carey), who insists on getting at the truth. Carey's transformation from the kind of celebrity Precious dreams of being to a quiet, sympathetic actress is something to behold. Oozing tough love, Mrs. Weiss insists that Precious tell her story in all its gruesome details, even though the girl is reluctant to pull the curtain aside on her family drama, presumably because she feels guilty about her victimization. Eventually, Mrs. Weiss leads Mary to choke out one of the more wrenching confessions you're ever likely to witness and then beg for sympathy because she feels unloved. It's hard to know what to make of this—is the audience supposed to feel sorry for Mary, angry at her, or just sad that they have to hear her horrid story? Most certainly they feel lucky not to have been raised like Precious and smug about how wonderful it would be to rescue her and all the other Precious girls of the world—and that seems to be the effects this shameless movie is aimed at.

The film opens with a measure of its own audacity, giving the titles and dedication of the film in Precious's broken, misspelled English and then providing standard English translations for them. This suggests that the heroine of the film is a stranger in our midst whose limitations are some sort of badge of honor. And that's exactly how she's treated. Despite strong portrayals by Sidibe and Mo'Nique, the characters have a strong whiff of unreality. They seem to have been constructed by people who want to honor the pain of real victims of poverty by making their characters as extremely victimized or gruesome or saintly as possible. But the book's author, Sapphire, and the movie's writers and producers do not live in the actual worlds of pain they are trying to summon up. They have created compelling but hopelessly unreal caricatures, and Precious' entire story is an elaborate set-up, a morality tale rescued from a long-forgotten, suddenly celebrated novel. *Precious: Based on the Novel 'Push' by Sapphire* seems to be based on good intentions, but it makes the audience feel slapped in the face for not being one of the rescue squad. The movie wallows in the muck it swears can be overcome with good deeds and believe-in-yourself intentions. It is strong medicine and hard to swallow. As wake-up calls go, this one lacks the force of believability.

Michael Betzold

CREDITS

Clareece "Precious" Jones: Gabourney "Gabby" Sidibe
Mary: Mo'Nique
Ms. Rain: Paula Patton
Mrs. Weiss: Mariah Carey
John: Lenny Kravitz
Cornrows: Sherri Shepherd
Origin: USA
Language: English
Released: 2009
Production: Lee Daniels, Sarah Siegel-Magness, Gary Magness; Smokewood Entertainment; released by Lionsgate
Directed by: Lee Daniels
Written by: Geoffrey "Damien Paul" Fletcher
Cinematography by: Andrew Dunn
Music by: Mario Grigorov
Sound: Ken Ishii
Music Supervisor: Lynn Fainchtein
Editing: Joe Klotz
Art Direction: Matteo De Cosmo
Costumes: Marina Draghici
Production Design: Roshelle Berliner
MPAA rating: R
Running time: 109 minutes

REVIEWS

Anderson, John. *Variety.* May 15, 2009.
Ebert, Roger. *Chicago Sun-Times.* November 5, 2009.
Edelstein, David. *New York Magazine.* November 2, 2009.
Fine, Marshall. *Hollywood & Fine.* November 5, 2009.
Foundas, Scott. *Village Voice.* November 3, 2009.
Lane, Anthony. *New Yorker.* November 2, 2009.
Pais, Matt. *Metromix.com.* November 5, 2009.
Phillips, Michael. *Chicago Tribune.* November 5, 2009.
Stevens, Dana. *Slate.* November 5, 2009.
Tallerico, Brian. *HollywoodChicago.com.* November 6, 2009.

QUOTES

Clareece "Precious" Jones: "Some folks has a lot of things around them that shines for other peoples. I think that maybe some of them was in tunnels. And in that tunnel, the only light they had, was inside of them. And then long after they escape that tunnel, they still be shining for everybody else."

TRIVIA

This was the first film with an African American director to be nominated for a Best Picture Oscar®.

AWARDS

Oscars 2009: Adapt. Screenplay, Support. Actress (Mo'Nique)
British Acad. 2009: Support. Actress (Mo'Nique)
Golden Globes 2010: Support. Actress (Mo'Nique)
Ind. Spirit 2010: Actress (Sidibe), Director (Daniels), Film, Support. Actress (Mo'Nique), First Screenplay
Screen Actors Guild 2009: Support. Actress (Mo'Nique)

Nomination:

Oscars 2009: Actress (Sidibe), Director (Daniels), Film, Film Editing
British Acad. 2009: Actress (Sidibe), Adapt. Screenplay, Film
Directors Guild 2009: Director (Daniels)
Golden Globes 2010: Actress—Drama (Sidibe), Film—Drama
Screen Actors Guild 2009: Actress (Sidibe), Cast
Writers Guild 2009: Adapt. Screenplay.

THE PRINCESS AND THE FROG

Box Office: $103.4 million

When 2-D Disney animated films revolve around a female protagonist, the heroine's objective frequently involves being rescued by a man. This is often a literal or figurative Prince Charming. Recall *Cinderella* (1950), *Sleeping Beauty* (1959), and *The Little Mermaid* (1989), to name a few.

That is part of what makes *The Princess and the Frog* a pleasant surprise. In the film, the studio's first 2-D animated picture since *Home on the Range* (2004), Tiana (voiced by Anika Noni Rose) does not believe in wishing on a star, and she is not concerned with finding true love. Her goal is to fulfill her deceased father's (Terrence Howard) goal of opening a restaurant called Tiana's Place, where she will serve gumbo, jambalaya, and other cuisine native to their hometown of New Orleans. That the film winds up pushing her toward love is less significant than Tiana's constant commitment to hard work and, as her dad advised, not expecting wishes to take care of all her needs. She is brought up to value elbow grease and *The Princess and the Frog* allows her to maintain that priority even as it, like so many Disney movies past, turns an ordinary girl into a princess.

Not that such a development is a surprise. (It is, after all, in the title of the film, which is inspired by the fairy tale *The Frog Princess*.) In fact, a good amount of *The Princess and the Frog* is relatively conventional. Tiana thinks she is about to realize her dream until she is outbid for her desired venue. Then she kisses a frog, thinking she will turn him back into Prince Naveen of Maldonia (Bruno Campos), who was cut off by his parents and turned into a frog as part of a deal made with the voodoo-practicing Dr. Facilier (Keith David). Instead, Tiana also turns into a frog, pushing her farther from her goals of entrepreneurship and closer to goofy supporting characters like Louis (Michael-Leon Wooley), an alligator who plays the trumpet, and Raymond (Jim Cummings), a firefly in love with Evangeline, not knowing that his object of affection is actually just a star in the distance.

It is during these characters' interactions that *The Princess and the Frog* feels most familiar and, to an extent, dry. Disney has exhausted the potential from the big personalities of sideline characters like Iago (Gilbert Godfried) in *Aladdin* (1992) and the manic behavior of Louis and Raymond add little entertainment value. The same goes for the shenanigans of Lawrence (Peter Bartlett), Naveen's assistant who, with the help of Dr. Facilier, becomes a Naveen look-alike in hopes of winning the heart of Charlotte (Jennifer Cody), a spoiled princess eager to marry her own Prince Charming.

However, there is also sweetness to the story that, in some ways, is a product of what the film is not. It is not a painful onslaught of pop culture references found in animated films like *Over the Hedge* (2006). It is not as irritating and unimaginative as Disney's *Bolt* (2008). And it sure looks a lot more polished than recent 2-D animated films like *Happily N'Ever After* (2006). Rather, *The Princess and the Frog* is a return to Disney family films of old, with pure heroes, straightforward stories, and a handful of songs to carry the plot along a pleasant tune.

While the New Orleans jazz music is joyful, the songs, written by Randy Newman, are not as memorable as those found in earlier Disney animated films. Rose, best known for her role in *Dreamgirls* (2006), belts the heck out of "I'm Almost There," a hopeful song about Tiana feeling close to her lifelong dream. More often,

though, the magic is lacking in other featured songs like "When We're Human" and "Friends on the Other Side." Perhaps this is because Newman has written better melodies in the past, such as "You've Got a Friend In Me" from *Toy Story* (1995). Perhaps it is because the characters singing the songs in *The Princess and the Frog* do not make as strong an impression as those in films past. (Dr. Facilier is a particularly unrewarding villain, whose evil associates from "the other side" just look like the shadows of Frank the Bunny from *Donnie Darko* [2001].) Or maybe the concept of characters wishing they had access to something outside their reach—for example, Louis wants to be human so he will be accepted as a trumpet player—seems stale after years of brilliantly written Pixar films (like *Ratatouille* [2006]) have tackled this from a more unique angle.

In spite of frequently failing to stand out from its predecessors, *The Princess and the Frog* thrives on a positive vibe and a handful of nice moments that show directors Ron Clements and John Musker (*Aladdin* [1992], *Treasure Planet* [2002]) have their hearts in the right place. At one point, Tiana and Naveen dance (as frogs) on a lily pad while Raymond sings and Louis plays trumpet. This scene has a gentle, romantic spirit, something that is not often found genuinely in family comedies anymore. (It is almost needless to say that Disney's other late 2009 family comedy, *Old Dogs*, offers neither romance nor laughs and is totally reprehensible for both kids and adults.) The same goes for when Raymond, while talking about his love for Evangeline, flies behind a heart-shaped leaf, brightening the heart with his flickering taillight. Sweet, maybe a little sappy, but just nice.

Certainly, it is worth noting that Tiana is Disney's first African American heroine, and that it comes during the first full year of America's first African American president surely is no coincidence. This is noteworthy as history and also because the film, appropriately, does not do anything to suggest that this story is any different from previous stories as a result of its main character's race. Sure, Prince Naveen's indeterminate race does not appear to be white (he certainly is not as pale as Charlotte), preventing his relationship with Tiana from being seen as a white-black relationship—which would be even more progressive for the studio. It could also be argued that by not really presenting the story with a racial perspective and by reducing New Orleans to a lively setting filled with stereotypical sounds and personalities, the movie confronts an updated context for its story only to retreat from it. Still: It is good to see a Disney princess who is not the typical pasty white woman.

On that note, it would really be something if Disney continued to expand its mind and stop suggesting that all young girls want to be princesses. Yes, Tiana's primary goal is opening her restaurant, but she eventually gives into wishing on a star and, of course, falls for a prince. It is likely that young viewers (and young girls in particular) will consequently pull less from Tiana's work ethic and instead lump her love story in with the countless other family films that find a young woman looking for happiness in a man.

Those issues aside, there is fun to be had in *The Princess and the Frog*, a light diversion that may be remembered less for its content than for what it represents: a new face of a Disney heroine and a return to a style of animation that has been mostly ignored in favor of busier CGI and 3-D films (or the vastly superior and better-looking Pixar movies). The progress of animation in the last ten to fifteen years may be why the images in *The Princess and the Frog* sometimes lack that old magic, or why it feels distracting when the sugar on Tiana's beignets looks blurry, as if there is a glare from the sun on the movie. Yet with this animation also comes comfort and nostalgia for simpler days and simpler movies, like the pleasure of a good meal among loved ones. In the context of a story about a woman who just wants to do her family proud and make something of herself, that feels old-fashioned and modern, and just plain right.

Matt Pais

CREDITS

Princess Tiana: Anika Noni Rose (Voice)
Prince Naveen: Bruno Campos (Voice)
James: Terrence Howard (Voice)
Eli "Big Daddy" LaBouff: John Goodman (Voice)
Dr. Facilier: Keith David (Voice)
Ray: Jim Cummings (Voice)
Mama Odie: Jenifer Lewis (Voice)
Eudora: Oprah Winfrey (Voice)
Charlotte LaBouff: Jennifer Cody (Voice)
Origin: USA
Language: English
Released: 2009
Production: Peter Del Vecho; Walt Disney Animation Studios; released by Walt Disney Pictures
Directed by: Ron Clements, John Musker
Written by: Ron Clements, John Musker
Music by: Randy Newman
Sound: Odin Benitez
Editing: Jeff Draheim
Art Direction: Ian Gooding
Production Design: James Aaron Finch
MPAA rating: G
Running time: 97 minutes

REVIEWS

Bell, Josh. *Las Vegas Weekly.* December 9, 2009.
Biancolli, Amy. *Houston Chronicle.* December 11, 2009.

Chang, Justin. *Variety.* November 24, 2009.
Corliss, Richard. *Time Magazine.* December 7, 2009.
Dargis, Manohla. *New York Times.* November 25, 2009.
Ebert, Roger. *Chicago Sun-Times.* December 10, 2009.
Honeycutt, Kirk. *Hollywood Reporter.* November 24, 2009.
Samuels, Allison. *Newsweek.* November 24, 2009.
Sharkey, Betsy. *Los Angeles Times.* November 24, 2009.
Tallerico, Brian. *MovieRetriever.com.* December 11, 2009.

QUOTES

Princess Tiana: "Look, I'm sorry. I'd really like to help you, but I do not kiss frogs."

TRIVIA

This is the first hand-drawn animated Disney film since *Home on the Range.*

AWARDS

Nomination:

Oscars 2009: Animated Film, Song ("Down in New Orleans," "Almost There")
Golden Globes 2010: Animated Film.

THE PRIVATE LIVES OF PIPPA LEE

The life you love may be your own.
—Movie tagline

There is a fascinating, close-ended, and emotionally satisfying movie yet to be made about the particular ennui, born of personal sacrifice, of a modern-day second wife, neither quite curvaceous trophy prize nor life companion version 2.0. Working from an adaptation of her own novel, writer/director Rebecca Miller gets a lot right in that vein, but does not quite fully deliver said film with the split-era *The Private Lives of Pippa Lee,* an ensemble drama starring Robin Wright Penn as the title character, a reformed party girl who starts to panic about mortality when her older husband (Alan Arkin) finally retires. A wry, rather shrewdly observed and colorfully decorated character study goes awry when, after about seventy minutes, some forced drama kick-starts a parade of increasingly dubious narrative twists and turns. An uncaged Pippa takes flight and prepares for new chapters in her life, but not in a way that feels especially convincing.

Despite the presence of a well known, star-studded cast (and Brad Pitt as an executive producer), *The Private Lives of Pippa Lee* could not attract studio financing, or even a wide-scale independent release. This is in many ways a shame, given the excellent showcase it provides for the criminally underrated Penn, who over the course of the film's 98-minute running time demonstrates a voyage self-discovery dancing across her eyes. Boutique distributor Screen Media picked up the movie off of a festival screening, but never expanded the film past the top 10 markets, and it disappeared quietly after five weeks and only $261,000 at the box office.

From all outward appearances, Pippa (Penn) leads a charmed existence. She is the devoted wife of an accomplished New York City publisher, Herb Lee (Arkin), nearly three decades years her senior, as well as the proud mother of two grown children, Ben (Ryan McDonald) and Grace (Zoe Kazan). Quiet, well mannered and a trusted friend to even those new in her life, Pippa seemingly settles into the staid Connecticut community residence she has chosen for retirement life with Herb.

The idyllic nature of Pippa's current situation belies more than her fair share of youthful turmoil, however, including a Dexedrine junkie mother (Maria Bello). Flashing back on her volatile past (Blake Lively costars as the young Pippa) in a manner that informs some of the hidden resentments she now harbors, Pippa begins struggling with mysterious bouts of sleepwalking, and makes a strange new acquaintance in the form of Chris (Keanu Reeves, trading in the sort of stock soulfulness he employs in untold studio romances), the divorced son of a neighbor. Her own interpersonal fumbling, along with Herb's agitation at withdrawing from the professional world he has known for so long, help bring into focus for Pippa a truer sense of self. Winona Ryder, as a manic friend; Monica Belluci, as Herb's first wife; and Julianne Moore, as the lesbian girlfriend of young Pippa's aunt, also costar.

Films like *The Ice Storm* (1997), *American Beauty* (1999), *Far From Heaven* (2002) and *Revolutionary Road* (2008) have all, to varying degrees, explored unhappy housewives, but typically through the prism of either a period piece, or a more skewed sensibility. *The Private Lives of Pippa Lee* unfolds in more or less naturalistic fashion, and while it does flashback to Pippa's adolescence, it remains emotionally rooted in the present day. Miller seeds her movie with one or two outrageous tidbits (Pippa was born with vestigial hair, we find out in a jarring flashback), but is otherwise interested and wholly invested in the way in which characters talk and relate to one another.

It is a great and largely unexplored truth that we typically do not regard our parents as actual people throughout our teenage years and into our self-centered twenties, and it frequently remains a struggle to do so even after that. They gave us life, but (if we're lucky) we know them primarily as caregivers—not for their own sins, sacrificed dreams, outside interests or personal happiness. *The Private Lives of Pippa Lee* explores a specific type of this ugly truth unmasked too soon, showing Pippa's mother as a woman who, if present physically, was very much not there—as well as a minister father, and siblings, who blankly looked past the family's problems. In the slow untangling of some of this back story, the film smartly reveals how Pippa's adult choices have become a series of reactionary chess moves, and plays for security. A bit of rather unnecessary voiceover narration drives home this point with inelegant obviousness, but Miller for the most part artfully presents a past that informs the action unfolding in the present. Only in its final act does the movie seem to tip headlong into more boring and conventional territory, evincing narrative choices we have seen before in all sorts of "divorcée cinema," and certainly the films of Nancy Meyers.

Miller is the daughter of playwright Arthur Miller and photographer Inge Morath (as well as the wife of Daniel Day-Lewis), and *The Private Lives of Pippa Lee* again showcases both her eye for winning composition and especially deft touch with actors. Lively is a young actress of incredible charm, but frequently rather one-note energy and delivery. Her work in the two *Sisterhood of the Traveling Pants* films (2005/08), and on the small screen in the hit series *Gossip Girl*, have not required her to stretch outside of her comfort zone, and show much range. Here, Miller draws something entirely new out of Lively—a stillness and quiet reflection, a sense of reserve, and swallowed discovery and acknowledgment rather than expressly articulated lesson-learning. It is a good performance, one that certainly augurs well for Lively's career path. But it is also, more importantly, a reflection of Miller's skill at capturing honest depictions of the most elusive, faintest pulses of genuine human interaction.

Brent Simon

CREDITS
Pippa Lee: Robin Wright Penn
Herb Lee: Alan Arkin
Chris Nadeau: Keanu Reeves
Dot Nadeau: Shirley Knight
Trish Sarkissian: Robin Weigert
Kat: Julianne Moore
Young Pippa: Blake Lively
Suky Sarkissian: Maria Bello
Des Sarkissian: Tim Guinee
Sandra Dulles: Winona Ryder
Gigi Lee: Monica Bellucci
Grace Lee: Zoe Kazan

Ben Lee: Ryan McDonald
Origin: USA
Language: English
Released: 2009
Production: Lemore Syvan, Dede Gardner, Jeremy Kleiner; Elevation Filmworks, Plan B Entertainment; released by Screen Media
Directed by: Rebecca Miller
Written by: Rebecca Miller
Cinematography by: Declan Quinn
Music by: Michael Rohatyn
Sound: Jeff Pullman
Music Supervisor: Linda Cohen
Editing: Sabine Hoffman
Art Direction: Melissa B. Miller
Costumes: Jennifer von Mayrhauser
Production Design: Michael Shaw
MPAA rating: R
Running time: 93 minutes

REVIEWS

Abele, Robert. *Los Angeles Times.* November 29, 2009.
Anderson, Noel. *Village Voice.* November 25, 2009.
Beardsworth, Liz. *Empire Magazine.* July 10, 2009.
Lumenick, Robert. *New York Post.* November 29, 2009.
Murray, Noel. *AV Club.* November 24, 2009.
Pols, Mary F. *Time Magazine.* November 29, 2009.
Puig, Claudia. *USA Today.* November 29, 2009.
Quinn, Anthony. *Independent.* July 10, 2009.
Weber, Bill. *Slant Magazine.* November 22, 2009.
Whitty, Stephen. *Newark Star-Ledger.* November 29, 2009.

TRIVIA

Julianne Moore spent only two days on set filming her part in the film.

THE PROPOSAL

> *Here comes the bribe...*
> —Movie tagline

Box Office: $164 million

Sandra Bullock starred in two pretty bad romantic comedies in 2009. *The Proposal* is not nearly as bad as *All About Steve*, which featured Bullock as a woman with several behaviors that suggest an undiagnosed disability that goes totally unrecognized in the film. Calling *The Proposal* the less-awful Sandra Bullock movie of 2009, though, is really all the praise it deserves.

The film is a quintessential example of why the term "studio comedy" frequently comes with a negative connotation. Rather than slick and entertaining, *The Proposal* is just painfully formulaic and condescending, as if audiences do not expect or require their breezy entertainment to come with a brain. Bullock stars as workaholic grouch Margaret Tate, a Canadian-born New York book editor too busy to bother with renewing her visa. When faced with deportation, Margaret convinces her long-suffering assistant Andrew Paxton (Ryan Reynolds) to pose as her fiancée and then marry her, promising him a quick divorce and a promotion in return.

Before long, the pretend couple is in Alaska for the 90th birthday party of Andrew's grandmother (Betty White). There, Margaret and Andrew attempt to maintain their ruse while his family tries to get to know a woman about which Andrew has spent years complaining. During this time Margaret and Andrew never once make a believable couple, interacting with each other as if their supposed spouse-to-be is covered in poison ivy. Andrew's family never suspects anything, though, other than initial skepticism from Andrew's stubborn father, played by Craig T. Nelson. So the film just plods along while Margaret and Andrew behave awkwardly and the family comes off not as a real, supportive family but a bunch of oblivious fools.

Some quick examples: A bird steals Margaret's cell phone, so Margaret runs around holding up the family dog as an offer for the bird to exchange with the phone. (Andrew's grandmother and mom, played by Mary Steenburgen, simply think it is cute that Margaret is playing with the dog.) At a family party, everyone pushes the couple to kiss—this weird, pushy scene likely will not be familiar to viewers with even mildly well-adjusted families—but when they do, after much resistance, it is as if they are being asked to make out with their cousin. Regardless: Big, satisfied cheers from the crowd.

This might be somewhat forgivable if, by the time Margaret and Andrew develop the inevitable spark between them, Bullock and Reynolds had any degree of sexual chemistry between them. The two, who do have plenty of comic timing with the right material and earn a few laughs throughout, have been off-screen friends for years and certainly have an onscreen rapport. But Margaret and Andrew never seem to want more than close friendship from each other. Actually, it would not be unthinkable for strangers to think that they may be brother and sister. This sucks all the desire and romance out of a love story that just feels forced and false.

Also forced are the comedic detours that do not move along the plot so much as throw it into the lake. Margaret stumbles upon grandma dancing in the woods, and the two join together in a wild dance to the tune of Lil' Jon's "Get Low," an idea that may sound funny on paper but disintegrates on screen. Margaret also is subjected to a horrible performance by Ramone (Oscar Nunez), who would be the worst exotic dancer in most cities but, as he is the only one in small Sitka, Alaska, is the best in town. This scene, written by first-time screenwriter Pete Chiarelli, has no direction or thought put into it other than hoping that Nunez's outrageously bad, unsexy behavior will generate some laughs. That the scene feels so fluffy and unnecessary is not the fault of Nunez, who is as funny as he can be in the role. It is simply a factor of a film that cannot glide along the romantic potential of its leads and thus searches for anything it can find to generate a spark.

Meanwhile, immigration officer Mr. Gilbertson (Denis O'Hare), thinking fraud is afoot, pursues Margaret and Andrew in hopes of finding proof that they are not getting married for the right reasons. Yes, this film is a diverting romantic comedy, and it is reasonable for a few logical liberties to be taken. But Gilbertson focuses attention on these two with nearly as much determination as Ed Rooney (Jeffrey Jones) pursuing Ferris Bueller (Matthew Broderick) in *Ferris Bueller's Day Off* (1986). If all immigration officials spent this much time and energy on each case, one can just imagine the backlog of work to be done.

Underneath all of this nonsense Margaret gradually thaws from an icy boss into a more kind-hearted, multi-faceted woman with room in her life for romance. This might be rewarding if it felt like a person expanding her priorities, not just another big-screen judgment of high-powered working women. Rarely are male movie characters too busy for romantic or sexual satisfaction. Yet Margaret begins as a cold, cruel corporate leader and spends the rest of the movie being embarrassed and softened into a more approachable but far less professional person. As women continually work to be seen as equal in the workplace and, particularly, on a company's letterhead, this manner of undermining Margaret—similar to presentations in other 2009 films like *Bride Wars* and *The Ugly Truth*—is far from enlightened. And, like most of *The Proposal*, it is not funny.

Matt Pais

CREDITS

Margaret Tate: Sandra Bullock
Andrew Paxton: Ryan Reynolds
Joe Paxton: Craig T. Nelson
Grace Paxton: Mary Steenburgen
Grandma Annie: Betty White
Mr. Gilbertson: Denis O'Hare
Gertrude: Malin Akerman
Ramon: Osmar Nunez

Bergen: Michael Nouri
Bob Spaulding: Aasif Mandvi
Origin: USA
Language: English
Released: 2009
Production: David Hoberman, Todd Lieberman; Mandeville Films, Touchstone Pictures; released by Walt Disney Studios
Directed by: Anne Fletcher
Written by: Peter Chiarelli
Cinematography by: Oliver Stapleton
Music by: Aaron Zigman
Sound: David MacMillan
Music Supervisor: Buck Damon
Editing: Priscilla Nedd Friendly
Art Direction: Scott A. Meehan
Costumes: Catherine Thomas
Production Design: Nelson Coates
MPAA rating: PG-13
Running time: 107 minutes

REVIEWS

Berkshire, Geoff. *Metromix.com.* June 18, 2009.
Childress, Carrie. *EFilmCritic.* June 19, 2009.
Dargis, Manohla. *New York Times.* June 19, 2009.
Ebert, Roger. *Chicago Sun-Times.* June 18, 2009.
Gronvall, Andrea. *Chicago Reader.* June 19, 2009.
Long, Tom. *Detroit News.* June 19, 2009.
Phillips, Michael. *Chicago Tribune.* June 18, 2009.
Phipps, Keith. *AV Club.* June 18, 2009.
Rickey, Carrie. *Philadelphia Inquirer.* June 18, 2009.
Sharkey, Betsy. *Los Angeles Times.* June 19, 2009.

QUOTES

Andrew Paxton: "Three days ago, I loathed you. I used to dream about you getting hit by a cab. Then we had our little adventure up in Alaska and things started to changed. Things changed when we kissed. And when you told me about your tattoo. Even when you checked me out when we were naked. But I didn't realize any of this, until I was standing alone...in a barn...wifeless. Now, you could imagine my disappointment when it suddenly dawned on me that the woman I love is about to be kicked out of the country. So Margaret, marry me, because I'd like to date you."

TRIVIA

When Julia Roberts refused to take a pay cut to appear in the film, Sandra Bullock took over the role.

AWARDS

Nomination:

Golden Globes 2010: Actress—Mus./Comedy (Bullock).

PUBLIC ENEMIES

America's most wanted.
—Movie tagline

Box Office: $97.1 million

At a time when American filmmaking has seemingly become divided into two distinct camps—empty-headed popcorn entertainment and solemn Oscar® bait—Michael Mann has been effortlessly straddling the line in order to provide audiences with films that are both intelligently crafted and enormously entertaining. Never has that been more evident than in his latest work, *Public Enemies,* an endlessly fascinating examination of one of the key events in America's history of criminal behavior—the crime spree committed by bank robber John Dillinger in the early 1930s until he was finally brought down by Melvin Purvis, an agent from the newly-formed Federal Bureau of Investigation—that tells its tale in a sumptuously designed and minutely detailed fashion that manages to remain compelling despite its essential familiarity and features top-notch contributions from everyone on both sides of the camera. Anyone walking into the film expecting just another gangster movie is going to come away shocked and surprised at what Mann has in store for them for this is a pop-art American epic that works equally well as a gripping action extravaganza and as a gorgeous art-house ravishment.

The film opens in 1933, a time described in a title card as "The Golden Age of the Bank Robbery," and kicks off with Dillinger (Johnny Depp) engineering the spectacular escape of a number of his cohorts from the Indiana State Penitentiary, a facility from which he had been released from only a few weeks earlier after doing a nine-year stretch. He begins a string of dazzling and intricately planned bank robberies that earn him thousands of dollars and which make him a hero to much of the Depression-era populace, who look at him as a sort of Robin Hood sticking it to the banks that they blame for their current financial hardships. Dillinger embraces that man-of-the-people pose—he refuses to take part in a kidnapping plot because "the public don't like kidnappers" and believes that part of his success is because he is able to hide in plain sight amidst a public that would not dream of turning him in. He is so confident about this, in fact, that when he first meets Billie Frechette (Marion Cotillard), the hat-check girl who would become the love of his life, he flat-out tells her exactly who he is and exactly what he does for a living.

Meanwhile, back in Washington D.C., J. Edgar Hoover (Billy Crudup) is trying to convince the government to expand the budget and powers for the newly formed Federal Bureau of Investigation that he runs.

Hoover designates Dillinger as Public Enemy #1 and assigns top field agent Melvin Purvis (Christian Bale) to head the Chicago branch of the FBI with the top priority being the capture of Dillinger utilizing the new-fangled scientific methods of investigation that he is putting into place. After one blown stakeout, Purvis realizes that the sophisticated means by which he is supposed to capture his quarry simply won't do against the ferocious and determined likes of Dillinger's men. It is only when he brings in a few exceptionally hard-boiled gunmen from down south to lend assistance is he able to finally apprehend Dillinger in Arizona and extradite him to Indiana to stand trial, though his imprisonment there doesn't last very long.

It is at this point that things begin to go wrong for both the pursued and the pursuer alike. Because they perceive him as a loose cannon who answers to nobody and whose exploits are bringing undue heat upon their own endeavors, organized crime leaders such as Frank Nitti no longer allow Dillinger to utilize any of their safe houses or assets while hiding out. As a result, Dillinger begins to grow desperate and allows himself to take part in poorly planned criminal acts that result in high body counts and low dollar amounts. At the same time, Purvis is under increasing pressure from Hoover to apprehend Dillinger at all costs and this drives him to make mistakes as well. Eventually, Dillinger's whereabouts are uncovered not by technological means but by a longtime associate who sells him out in order to prevent her deportation. This all leads to the inevitable final scene in which Dillinger is gunned down by Purvis' men outside Chicago's Biograph Theatre after taking in a screening of *Manhattan Melodrama* (1934), a gangster film that, ironically enough, was at least partially inspired by public interest in criminals such as him.

Over the years, Mann has developed an interesting narrative approach for his films that involves selecting stories that audiences already have some degree of familiarity with due to historical knowledge (*The Insider* [1999], *Ali* [2001]), popular culture (*Manhunter* [1986], *Last of the Mohicans* [1992], *Miami Vice* [2005]) or generic conventions (*Thief* [1981], *Heat* [1995], *Collateral* [2004]) and then focusing less on the broad narrative strokes and more on the exquisite details that he clearly finds more fascinating—the sound of a gunshot, the look of a coat, and the revelation that the infamous Lady in Red did not quite come as advertised. Although this particular approach may seem a little too cold and analytical to someone in the mood for a simpler effort along the lines of previous Dillinger biopics, it is in the end far more riveting than a standard take on the material might have been. He also refreshingly resists the urge to burden the film and its characters with long expository scenes in which they reveal their histories as a way of explaining what motivates them. Dillinger sums up his early life in a couple of terse sentences and nothing more needs to be said on the subject. Instead, Mann prefers to let his characters express themselves purely through their actions—both Dillinger and Purvis are bold, strong and efficient when they are in control, less so when they are not and both are undone in the end by their inability to fully understand the forces surrounding them.

While most filmmakers probably would have done everything in their power to accentuate the period nature of the story by accentuating a self-consciously retro visual style, Mann has gone in the exact opposite direction by shooting the entire film using the same digital process that he has utilized since *Collateral*. When the first trailers for the film emerged, some felt that the combination of the period subject matter and the cutting-edge visual style was a bit disconcerting but seen in context, it makes a lot more sense. Essentially, Mann is trying to remove the distance between the audience and the subject matter by choosing a visual style that brings the two closer together and it works beautifully—the camerawork allows us to get right into the middle of the chaotic action scenes while also giving us gorgeous period recreations as lush and lustrous as any that have been captured on DV.

Another method of bringing the audience and the subject together is the casting of Johnny Depp, one of the biggest movie stars of our time and one of the few who still maintains a certain rebellious public persona, as Dillinger. Some have criticized Depp's performance for being more of a series of poses than anything else but that is to seriously undervalue his work here. Yes, he is all brash movie-star charisma in the first half of the film but that is how Dillinger is supposed to be during that period—brash, bold, and in love with his own growing legend. As the second half progresses and things begin to go downhill for him, he suggests that in any number of small but telling ways—he is a little more slumped over, a little sweatier and he develops the kind of half-hearted mustache that you normally only seen on the lips of the loser characters in B-movies. In fact, this is probably the best and least-mannered performance that he has done in a long time and it serves as a reminder that he does not need to play a totally outsized character in order to hold the attention of viewers.

Public Enemies is prime Michael Mann material from start to finish and he does not let viewers down for a second. Having already created some of the great action scenes of modern cinema in his previous films, he all but tops himself here with the extended sequence chronicling Purvis' botched assault on the Little Bohemia lodge to capture a hiding Dillinger, a stunning chunk of pure cinema that stands in blessed relief to

most similar scenes seen these days. The action has been choreographed in such a way so that we always have a firm grasp on where the various participants are at any given time despite the chaos and it has been captured by cinematographer Dante Spinotti in such striking tableau of midnight-black backgrounds punctuated by brief bursts of gunfire that you almost want to frame individual shots and hang them on your wall in order to better study their terrible beauty.

Although this is the action highlight of *Public Enemies* the other key set-pieces are nothing to sneeze at either—the bust-out from the Indiana prison at the midway point is another stunning bit of choreography and the finale outside the Biograph actually builds a considerable amount of tension despite its foregone conclusion—and there are plenty of other things to love as well. Mann does a wonderful job of wrangling together an enormous cast and giving each one a moment or two to shine. Although the romance between Dillinger and Billie Frechette does not dominate the proceedings in the way that it might have in another film, Marion Cotillard brings a lot of fire to the role and Christian Bale does a good job of conveying the outwardly cool, inwardly tormented mindset of Purvis. There are even nice bits of dark humor strewn throughout the screenplay that comes as a surprise from someone normally as dead-serious as Mann. At one point, one of the investigators learns that Dillinger will be at one of two movie theaters, looks up what is playing at both and confidently concludes "John Dillinger ain't going to see Shirley Temple." Truer words were never spoken.

Peter Sobczynski

CREDITS

Melvin Purvis: Christian Bale
John Dillinger: Johnny Depp
Baby Face Nelson: Stephen Graham
Pretty Boy Floyd: Channing Tatum
J. Edgar Hoover: Billy Crudup
Polly Hamilton: Leelee Sobieski
Homer Van Meter: Stephen Dorff
Alvin Karpis: Giovanni Ribisi
Peter Pierpont: David Wenham
Billie Frechette: Marion Cotillard
Anna Patzke: Emilie de Ravin
Carter Baum: Rory Cochrane
John Madala: Shawn Hatosy
Red Hamilton: Jason Clarke
Charles Winstead: Stephen Lang
Frank Nitti: Bill Camp
Louis Piquett: Peter Gerety

Anna Sage: Branka Katic
Walter Dietrich: James Russo
Origin: USA
Language: English
Released: 2009
Production: Kevin Misher, Michael Mann; Relativity Media, Forward Pass Productions, Tribeca Productions, Appian Way; released by Universal Pictures
Directed by: Michael Mann
Written by: Ronan Bennett, Ann Biderman
Cinematography by: Dante Spinotti
Music by: Elliot Goldenthal
Sound: Edward Novick
Music Supervisor: Bob Badami, Kathy Nelson
Editing: Paul Rubell, Jeffrey Ford
Art Direction: Patrick Lumb
Costumes: Colleen Atwood
Production Design: Nathan Crowley
MPAA rating: R
Running time: 140 minutes

REVIEWS

Dargis, Manohla. *New York Times.* June 30, 2009.
Ebert, Roger. *Chicago Sun-Times.* June 30, 2009.
Foundas, Scott. *Village Voice.* July 1, 2009.
LaSalle, Mick. *San Francisco Chronicle.* July 1, 2009.
Lemire, Christy. *Associated Press.* June 29, 2009.
Long, Tom. *Detroit News.* July 1, 2009.
Phillips, Michael. *Chicago Tribune.* June 30, 2009.
Tallerico, Brian. *MovieRetriever.com.* July 1, 2009.
Travers, Peter. *Rolling Stone.* June 30, 2009.
Turan, Kenneth. *Los Angeles Times.* July 1, 2009.

QUOTES

John Dillinger: "We're having too good a time today. We ain't thinking about tomorrow."

TRIVIA

When the film was initially put into development in 2004, Leonardo DiCaprio was attached to star as John Dillinger.

AWARDS

Nomination:

Screen Actors Guild 2009: Stunt Ensemble.

PUSH

One push can change everything.
—Movie tagline

Box Office: $31.8 million

There is a scene in the dismal sci-fi thriller *Push* in which the heroes, all of whom possess some form of psychic ability, have to come up with a brilliant plan to defeat the villains, all of whom also possess some form of psychic ability, and save the day or the world or some damn thing. Their big idea is to come up with a final solution to the problem and then approach it in a wild and deliberately incoherent manner as a way of completely confusing the pursuers who are psychically following their moves. The trouble with the film is that it feels as if the screenplay was written utilizing those same guidelines—it is clear pretty much right from the start how it is going to end up but the path its takes to get there is so completely convoluted that it is unlikely that anyone involved with its production could offer up a logical explanation for what transpires at any given moment.

Stealing elements from the likes of *Heroes, Alias,* and the *X-Men* films (along with the more obscure likes of *Firestarter* (1984) and *The Fury* (1978) for good measure), the film stars Chris Evans as Nick Gant, a young man with telekinetic abilities that he inherited from his father. In an opening flashback, we learn that people with such abilities have been rounded up over the years by a government agency known as "The Division" that has been trying to develop a drug that will increase their powers and transform them into supersoldiers. Alas, the drug has steadily killed every single test subject over the years until Kira (Camilla Belle), who can control someone's thoughts with her mind, survives the procedure and immediately goes on the lam with a syringe containing the drug. Loafing about in Hong Kong while on the run from Division, Nick is visited by Cassie (Dakota Fanning), a 13-year-old girl who can sort of see into the future and draw the results on her handy sketch pad, who tells him that they have to find Kira before she is captured by either Division leader Carver (Djimon Hounsou) or an Asian gang family or they will die. That is about as far as the film goes in terms of plot development—the rest of it is pretty much solely dedicated to one endless scene after another in which the characters deploy their powers in elaborate yet deeply unconvincing ways.

Watching *Push* is a lot like reading the 17th issue of a cheap comic book produced by people who are more interested in ripping off other, better properties than in coming up with a decent one of their own. Because it never bothers to explain itself in a manner that even approaches coherence, it is virtually impossible to get enough of a fix on the story or the characters to be able to care about either one in the slightest. (If ever there was a film in need of one of those commentary tracks where the participants merely explain what is going on in every shot, this is that film.) Of course, the film might have gotten away with this if it had been placed in the hands of a director with the kind of keen visual sense to be able to properly embrace the wackiness of the material in cinematic terms, especially during the scenes in which our heroes begin acting crazier and crazier. Unfortunately, Paul McGuigan, the auteur behind such lemons as *Wicker Park* (2004) and *Lucky Number Slevin* (2006) is simply not that director—he has little idea of how to shoot an effects-heavy action scene and even when the screenplay hits upon a burst of inspiration, such as the moment when two psychics engaged in a gun battle decide to hide behind corners and send their guns floating through the air to do their dirty work for them, he handles it in such a pedestrian manner that it serves as a textbook example of a potentially great idea destroyed by faulty execution. As for the performances, they are pretty bad and unmemorable across the board but you can hardly blame the actors—they clearly realized early on that no one was going to be paying attention to them and just decided to plod ahead in order to continue with their working holiday in Hong Kong.

There is one memorable performance in *Push*, albeit for all the wrong reasons, and that is the one turned in by the talented child actress Dakota Fanning. Throughout the film, she runs about in a miniskirt and knee-high boots, curses like a stevedore, has a gun pointed at her head and, in the oddest moment of all, downs an entire bottle of rotgut liquor and gets completely blitzed as a result. Clearly, she is trying to demonstrate that she can handle more mature roles in the same way that Jodie Foster and Brooke Shields did when they appeared in such grown-up fare as *Taxi Driver* and *Pretty Baby* (1978). The difference, of course, is that those films were thought-provoking dramas that earned the right to have their young actresses performing such potentially questionable material while *Push* merely exploits Fanning for the sake of a few cheap jokes/thrills in such a way that it makes her appearance in the equally sleazy *Hounddog* (2007) seem dignified by comparison. Fanning does have the talent to make the transition from child star to adult actress but she apparently doesn't have the ability to pick the right scripts to help make that transition—either she or her advisors need to take a long time-out and think about what they have done and make adjustments before it is too late.

Peter Sobczynski

CREDITS

Nick Gant: Chris Evans
Cassie Holmes: Dakota Fanning

Kira Hudson: Camilla Belle
Agent Henry Carver: Djimon Hounsou
Hook: Clifford Curtis
Victor Budarin: Neil Jackson
Teresa Stowe: Maggie Siff
Emily Wu: Ming Na
Pinkey Stein: Nate Mooney
Origin: USA
Language: English
Released: 2009
Production: Bruce Davey, William Vince, Glenn Williamson; Icon Productions, Infinity Features Entertainment; released by Summit Entertainment
Directed by: Paul McGuigan
Written by: David Bourla
Cinematography by: Peter Sova
Music by: Neil Davidge
Sound: Pavel Wdowczak
Music Supervisor: Liza Richardson
Editing: Nicolas Trembasiewicz
Art Direction: Michael Norman Wong
Costumes: Laura Goldsmith, Nina Proctor
Production Design: Francois Seguin
MPAA rating: PG-13
Running time: 111 minutes

REVIEWS

Catsoulis, Jeanette. *New York Times.* February 6, 2009.
Ebert, Roger. *Chicago Sun-Times.* February 6, 2009.
Koehler, Robert. *Variety.* February 2, 2009.
Lacey, Liam. *Globe and Mail.* February 6, 2009.
Long, Tom. *Detroit News.* February 6, 2009.
Morris, Wesley. *Boston Globe.* February 5, 2009.
Rechtshaffen, Michael. *Hollywood Reporter.* February 2, 2009.
Rodriguez, Rene. *Miami Herald.* February 5, 2009.
Simon, Brent. *Screen International.* February 2, 2009.
Whipp, Glenn. *Los Angeles Times.* February 6, 2009.

QUOTES

Cassie Holmes: "I think I just saved your life. No need to thank me, you should just start listening to me."

TRIVIA

A prequel comic book mini-series to the film was written by Marc Bernardin and Adam Freeman with art by Bruno Redondo and published by WildStorm, an imprint of DC Comics.

R

RACE TO WITCH MOUNTAIN

The race is on.
—Movie tagline

Box Office: $67.2 million

Disney has been to Witch Mountain before, only this time they forgot to bring back the magic. Their first trip, which took place in 1975, was by way of literary adaptation and managed to distill a sense of danger and high adventure from Alexander Keys' 1968 novel. It offered a great cast, state-of-the-art special effects and has aged, as have many of the Disney live action films from this period, with an awkward grace becoming instantly identifiable with when it was made, as part of a single studio's body of work, full of the type of b-movie heart that breeds nostalgia even among grumpy film critics. This remake has an even better cast, much better special effects, and is also likely to become strongly identified by the period in which it was made, but in no way is that intended to pay it a compliment.

Sara (AnnaSophia Robb) and Seth (Alexander Ludwig) are alien brother and sister who crash land on earth during a crucial mission to recover a device that will save their home planet from sure destruction. Pursued by stock Department of Defense bad guys and an alien bounty hunter, the siblings find an unwilling helper in the person of ex-con cab driver Jack Bruno (Dwayne Johnson) who wants nothing more than to stay out of trouble and thus stay out of jail. Together with astrophysicist Dr. Alex Friedman (Carla Gugino) they

race towards Witch Mountain, back to their ship and make their final race towards home.

If the plot sounds thin it should be remembered that the story really has not changed. What worked before worked because it made room for heartfelt sentiment, an occasionally compelling sense of child endangerment and everyman heroics. But director Andy Fickman (*She's The Man* [2006], *The Game Plan* [2007]) signals early on that this new incarnation of those plot elements will be offered up as an action film, and his car chase driven, CGI light show jumps from highway to fist fight in a vain attempt to amaze or at least amuse a generation that has been raised on the credo "shoot first." It may briefly amuse a few, and it does stop short of being outright boring but not because it causes the viewer to care about any of the characters or wish they could step into the frame and be part of the action. This is video game cinema without the video game. Actually, this is video game cinema precisely because it was made so that Disney could make a video game, a lunchbox, etc. Too bad their director nearly forgot to make a movie.

Fans of the old film are offered some nice cameos by the original *Witch Mountain* kids, Kim Richards and Ike Eisenmann, and another by science fiction author and supposed alien abductee Whitley Strieber. But even these niceties signal a primary problem. Such moments in other movies are like icing on the cake. But here such moments *are* the cake. Nothing substantial really works in this film. A major problem is the flat dialogue and failed attempts at humor by scriptwriters Matt Lopez (*The Wild* [2006], *Bedtime Stories* [2008]) and Mark Bomback (*The Night Caller* [1998], *Godsend* [2004],

Live Free Die Hard [2007]). Whenever there's a lull in the action and sometimes during the action, *Race* unexplainably stops dead in path so that some character can mangle a one-liner.

Though most of the cast clearly tries, nobody is able to connect very effectively. Repeated viewings will certainly cause viewers to blame the script but the cast cannot be completely let off the hook here. Nothing is keeping an outstanding force like Ciaran Hinds (*Munich* [2005], *There Will Be Blood* [2007], *In Bruges* [2008]) from breathing threatening life into Henry Burke, the head government baddie. But, as played, his character is almost completely unnecessary. Dwayne 'the Rock' Johnson (*The Scorpion King* [2002], *Southland Tales* [2006]) is a comic natural with action chops to boot who has saved more than one film (*Be Cool* [2005] *Get Smart* [2008]) from complete unwatchability. But here he simply is not able to elevate the material into that kind of airy fun. Carla Gugino, who made no fewer than three *Spy Kids* films, seems to get what she should be doing here, but is ultimately just as lost in the action as everyone else.

Per performance this is true over and over again. No one in this film, despite the wide array of experience and talent they have shown elsewhere seems to know where the heart of *Race To Witch Mountain* is. This is a film that should be remembered and referenced regarding exactly what was wrong with the movies of this time period. *Race To Witch Mountain* is not an awful film, but it makes an awful lot of noise, to very little effect and contains very little of the human element that made the original so memorable. All people are liable to remember about this *Race To Witch Mountain* is that it was yet another missed opportunity on the part of Disney to stop robbing their own heritage.

Dave Canfield

CREDITS

Sarah: AnnaSophia Robb
Seth: Alexander Ludwig
Dr. Friedman: Carla Gugino
Henry Burke: Ciaran Hinds
Jack Bruno: Dwayne "The Rock" Johnson
Matheson: Tom Everett Scott
Eddie: Richard "Cheech" Marin
Dr. Donald Harlan: Garry Marshall
Origin: USA
Language: English
Released: 2009
Production: Andrew Gunn; GUNNFilms; released by Walt Disney Pictures

Directed by: Andy Fickman
Written by: Matt Lopez, Mark Bomback
Cinematography by: Greg Gardiner
Music by: Trevor Rabin
Sound: Nelson Stoll
Music Supervisor: Lisa Brown
Editing: David Rennie
Art Direction: John R. Jensen
Costumes: Genevieve Tyrrell
Production Design: David J. Bomba
MPAA rating: PG
Running time: 98 minutes

REVIEWS

Berton, Justin. *San Francisco Chronicle.* March 13, 2009.
Ebert, Roger. *Chicago Sun-Times.* March 12, 2009.
Honeycutt, Kirk. *Hollywood Reporter.* March 11, 2009.
Leydon, Joe. *Variety.* March 11, 2009.
Pais, Matt. *Metromix.com.* March 12, 2009.
Phillips, Michael. *Chicago Tribune.* March 12, 2009.
Scott, A.O. *New York Times.* March 13, 2009.
Sharkey, Betsy. *Los Angeles Times.* March 13, 2009.
Smith, Kyle. *New York Post.* March 13, 2009.
Sobczynski, Peter. *eFilmCritic.* March 12, 2009.

QUOTES

Sara: "Well, what does an alien look like, Jack Bruno?"
Jack Bruno: "You know what aliens look like. They look like, like little green people with antennas and, and laser guns and, 'Take me to your leader, Earthlings.'"

TRIVIA

Jack's cab number is the year of release for the original *Escape from Witch Mountain*.

RED CLIFF
(Chi bi)

The future will be decided.
—Movie tagline
Destiny lies in the wind.
—Movie tagline

John Woo's *Red Cliff* boasts several things which will recommend it across a wide variety of film interests, but its spectacular visuals and sophisticated narrative treatment, make it easy to overlook that this historical epic also marks the rebirth of one of the twentieth century's most famous and influential filmmakers.

John Woo is best known stateside among two fairly distinct camps of viewers. The first discovered his work during the late eighties and early nineties when he was producing action films overseas. Beloved among action aficionados for their tightly choreographed gun play and highly charged stunt work, *A Better Tomorrow* (1986), *The Killers* (1989) and *Hard Boiled* (1992) are indeed films every action lover should see. Besides Woo's distinctive style they also introduced a little-known actor named Chow Yun-Fat to the American and International audiences and helped broaden the audience that eventually made American stars out of Jet Li, Jackie Chan and other martial arts stars just beginning to see their films distributed stateside.

The second group was exposed to Woo's American mainstream work with a variety of top action talent during a decade beginning roughly in 1993 in which he was wooed to Hollywood. Woo's move from China to the United States was seen as a sign by his fans as a cinematic sure thing that could only result in superstardom. Sadly, this was not to be. His films during this period, which include, *Hard Target* (1993), *Broken Arrow* (1996), *Face/Off* (1997), *Mission Impossible II* (2000), and *Windtalkers* (2002) were not successful enough to establish Woo as more than a niche director and after a period of deep personal contemplation he opted to return to China where he has remained ever since. *Red Cliff* is his first feature film since then.

To call Woo a director of action films is to miss the point of his work, which is often suffused with complex symbolism and a deep respect for life. A self-described Christian he often makes use of religious symbols in his films—his favorites being doves, fire and the cross. These are not thoughtless stylistic flourishes and it is impossible for any discerning viewer to follow Woo's oeuvre without seeing the intent. Major themes in his work include the redemptive power of love, self-sacrifice and the purifying nature of earthly trial. It would be a gross overstatement to call Woo a director primarily interested in religion but a gross understatement to ignore the role it plays in his continued fascination with onscreen violence and spectacle. As one of the most studied non-American film directors he has remained incredibly influential both in terms of style and way he integrates the concerns that drive him as a storyteller.

The Battle of the Red Cliffs is one of most important military conflicts in Chinese history occurring at the end of the Han Dynasty in the third century and immediately preceding the formation of what have been called The Three Kingdoms. Much romanticized, the conflict has provided endless grist for storytellers who have typically used it as a springboard for larger than life mythmaking. With *Red Cliff*, Woo sets out to stay as true to history as he can and works hard throughout the film to portray everyone in the most honorable light possible.

The plot of *Red Cliff* centers on leader Cao Cao (Fengyi Zhang) guiding an army of one million soldiers to invade the land of Wu to quell what he sees as rebellion but then being opposed not only by Wu ruler Sun Quan (Chen Chang) but Wu's rival Liu Bei (Yong You). A series of breathtaking battles ensues which leads to the dramatic defeat of the much larger army and the fast creation of the Three Kingdoms.

The battle scenes in this film offer virtually everything a genre fan could want but they seldom stretch the suspension of disbelief to the breaking point. A problem with large scale battle films is they often lend themselves to scenes of frenetic obscurity. A few close-up heroic flourishes cutting to a wide shot of a teeming mass of humanity can work well in the right hands. But Woo operates at a level far above this. *Red Cliff*'s staged battles feature believable numbers of fighters and techniques, while slow motion and the use of CGI blood spatter, typically utilized in a look-what-I-can-do manner are offered in an almost documentary style. The overall effect is a far more believable and engrossing sense of action, especially when wire work, stylized swordplay and martial arts come into play. The wide shots are impressive. But, in the main, Woo and his accomplished action director Cory Yuen are geniuses in showcasing his individual character's bravery and military acumen and it is these moments that make his battle scenes more than just mano-a-mano cliché.

At times, the special effects in *Red Cliff* set a new standard. CGI is used frequently but almost always effectively. Woo and his crew rarely sacrifices art to spectacle. In one naval sequence, a fleet of CGI warships shoot thousands upon thousands of arrows into the fog at the opposing fleet. The whimsical aim of the scene is not the spectacle but the collection of arrows into the ships, which prove not to be warships but decoys. In another naval battle, fire plays a key role. In both instances the human element remains supreme, CGI spectacle works hand in hand with narrative to tell the story of a key moment rather than deliver a series of money shots.

The score, credited to no one musician but conducted by Taro Iwashiro (*Shinobi* [2005], *To the Ends of the Earth and Sea* [2007]) is at once grand and intimate, rarely reaching past the emotions that the images themselves have earned. Lastly, the cast soars through the operatic highs and lows with a steadied hand and a dynamic presence. The internationally acclaimed Tony Leung (*Lust Caution* [2007], *2046* [2004], *Infernal Affairs* [2004]) brings a bemused sense of authority to his scenes as Zhou Yu, Wu's Chief Military strategist and invader Cao Cao makes for an elegant but powerfully motivated and sympathetic villain in the hands of Fengyi

Zhang (*Farewell My Concubine* [1993], *The Emperor and the Assassin* [1998]).

A full listing of credits for those involved in this production would form a small book. Cast and crew are among some of the most distinguished in their craft in the world and space simply fails to allow for an adequate accounting. But in *Red Cliff* they have come together to make a film for the ages. *Red Cliff* is not an action film to be watched once, and put away on a shelf to merely be part of a collection. It will stand up to many viewings, inspiring a variety of emotions and thoughts about one of the most complex military engagements in human history. And for true cineastes it will bring a warm smile attaching itself to the notion that John Woo continues to establish himself as a director of noble intent, immaculate craft and thrilling skill.

Dave Canfield

CREDITS

Yu Zhou: Tony Leung Chiu-Wai
Liang Zhuge: Takeshi Kaneshiro
Cao Coa: Fengyi Zhang
Quan Sun: Chang Chen
Bei Liu: You Yong
Shanxiang Sun: Vicki Zhao
Yun Zhao: Jun Hu
Xing Gan: Shido Nakamura
Emperor Xian: Ning Wang
Qiao Xiao: Chiling Lin
Origin: China
Language: Mandarin
Released: 2008
Production: Terence Chang, John Woo; China Film Group, Chengtian Entertainment, Avex Entertainment; released by Magnet Releasing
Directed by: John Woo
Written by: John Woo, Khan Chan, Cheng Kuo, Heyu Sheng
Cinematography by: Lu Yue, Li Zhang
Music by: Taro Iwashiro
Sound: Roger Savage
Editing: Angie Lam, Hongyu Yang, Robert A. Ferretti
Costumes: Tim Yip
Production Design: Tim Yip
MPAA rating: R
Running time: 131 minutes

REVIEWS

Anderson, Jason. *Toronto Star.* December 4, 2009.
Edelstein, David. *New York Magazine.* November 9, 2009.
Elley, Derek. *Variety.* July 21, 2008.
Foundas, Scott. *Village Voice.* November 17, 2009.
Germain, David. *Associated Press.* November 18, 2009.
Hale, Mike. *New York Times.* November 19, 2009.
Morgenstern, Joe. *Wall Street Journal.* November 20, 2009.
Noble, Elliott. *Sky Movies.* June 12, 2009.
Tallerico, Brian. *MovieRetriever.com.* November 25, 2009.
Turan, Kenneth. *Los Angeles Times.* November 24, 2009.

QUOTES

Liu Bei: "Truth and illusion are often disguised as each other."

TRIVIA

Yun-Fat Chow was originally supposed to play Zhou Yu but dropped out the day principal photography began.

THE ROAD

In a moment the world changed forever.
—Movie tagline

Box Office: $8.1 million

Writer Cormac McCarthy had a big year in 2007. While a film adaptation of his novel, *No Country For Old Men* (2007), was about to go onto major critical acclaim and win four Academy Awards®, his latest work received even greater hype. None other than Oprah Winfrey recommended his apocalyptic survival tale, *The Road* (2006), to her minions. A few weeks later, it won the Pulitzer Prize for Fiction. With the movie rights already snatched up, filming began in the middle of *No Country*'s awards season, with a late 2008 release date, suggesting that The Weinstein Company was going to ride the McCarthy statuette train. Alas, they went with Oprah's 1999 book club selection, *The Reader* (2008), to chase accolades and shelved *The Road* for a full year; rarely a good sign amongst industry analysts. Was the film too uncommercial? How could it be with Oprah behind it? Recommendations of books, *The Deep End of the Ocean* (1999), *Where The Heart Is* (2000) and *White Oleander* (2002) went over swimmingly with moviegoers, right? Everyone is quick to point out how the nuances of the page are frequently lost in the slimmed down cinema translations, but rarely do they admit to the shortcomings of the original text as a contributing factor to a lackluster film.

McCarthy's grim tale picks up some time after a cataclysmic event has scorched the Earth entire. At the time of the big flash of light, a man (Viggo Mortensen) and his wife (Charlize Theron) were about to bear a child together. After the baby's birth and hope for survival seemingly lost, the wife gave up and left the man alone with his son. Ten years later, the father and his boy (Kodi Smit-McPhee) have also left their home and now scour what remains of the land in search of food and, hopefully, a warmer climate. With all modes of power all but wiped out, the duo travel on foot with a shopping cart and a pistol carrying two bullets— protection first, suicide when the road gets too rough.

Survivors of this future have taken on many forms. Some are loners like the father and son while others have become scavengers and are not to be trusted. With nary an animal in sight, suggestions of cannibalism are abound. We have become the animals. Unless you are as fortunate as the man and his boy who luck into such treats as a can of Coca-Cola or a full pantry of canned food at a home whose evident preparation for the end of the world didn't exactly benefit the previous owners. Dad can't afford to trust anyone or stay in any one place too long. His mission is to protect his son at all costs for as long as he is still breathing. The boy, on the other hand, is longing for further companionship and may be too naive to know the difference between compassion and deception.

Fans of McCarthy (and Oprah) may share some of the boy's sensibilities in that respect. Reclusive for years, until Oprah's recommendation prompted him to agree to an interview with her, McCarthy often found his work appreciated years after the fact. His western, *Blood Meridian* (1985), has been cited in numerous circles as one of the best works of the 20th century, but was deemed as "unfilmable" by Roger Ebert. That was until he saw *The Proposition* (2006), a brutally violent western by director John Hillcoat who just happens to now find himself at the helm of McCarthy's most directly celebrated work.

Whatever may or may not have happened in the editing room in the year since *The Road*'s delay is between the director and Harvey Weinstein's reputation for tinkering with everyone from Martin Scorsese to adaptations of Elmore Leonard. Hillcoat didn't shy away from the aftermath of violence in his last film so it's a mystery why some of McCarthy's more graphic passages of discovery have been toned down or eliminated entirely. The cinematography by Javier Aguirresarobe is bleak enough with its constant overcast of grays and every speckle of world-weary grime on the faces of its survivors. But the lifeblood of the story appears buried under the ash of moments rather than what it's supposed to be about.

Some may have taken the simple prose of the source material to greater meaning; poetry in long form akin to Yeats' Second Coming. That's all surface though. McCarthy's ambivalence to declare the ultimate reasoning behind the sealing of man's fate suggests he was well

beyond metaphors of nuclear or environmental terror. Life was his metaphor. Survival passed on to the next generation in not just heartbeats and brainwaves but of the moral conscience and humanity that previous ones may have lost in a cynically divided world of politics and keeping up with the Joneses. This is not the world where paradise can be found if you look hard enough and it's not a far leap to empathize with the one person who gave up.

The wife character has been considerably beefed up for the film, providing for more extensive time with Theron. These scenes, like the book, are played in flashback but, unlike the book, portray the sadness of a dying relationship rather than the depiction of an impatient shrew. Mortensen and Theron have a believably fractured chemistry in the aftermath while his scenes with the obliviously stiff Kodi Smit-McPhee project the weight of a pro having to act for two. It's not just the boy's gratefulness when Robert Duvall shows up for a dignified single scene as an old man they share a campfire with. There's also momentary amusement when it's discovered that Michael K. Williams (aka the practically indestructible Omar from TV's *The Wire*) has survived the apocalypse.

The film, like its source material, is as cold as Anton Chigurh only without the personality. To take such a widely celebrated novel and then pitch it to the unfamiliar as some Romero-esque horror adventure should be clue one that those behind it didn't exactly know what they were buying. Frights did not exactly leap from the page as what was supposed to be a general terror of every step becoming one closer to a natural death. Dad's insistence on traveling the road instead of settling down in one place and take a stand could have become an agreeable metaphor about paving the future for the next generation. Don't be content with the damage that's already been done. Instead save the planet through love for itself and its people. Since that never registers, viewers are more likely to wonder whether Dad really has his son's best interest at heart when he chooses to abandon at least two homes with running water, a stockpile of food and all the other trimmings for domestic survival. Isn't the search for something greater beyond our means the very warped definition of the post-Gordon Gekko American dream?

Whatever happened to defending the island, the beaches, the fields and the streets whatever the cost may be? Maybe if McCarthy set his fiction in the United Kingdom, Churchill's words might have carried more meaning. Pacifism hasn't exactly been a motif within the author's works and it's hard to empathize with a central humanity that would be quicker on the draw to himself and his son rather than the next bad guy that comes along, an aspect that Frank Darabont's *The Mist* (2007) handled with vicious irony. Apocalyptic calamity has had its share of burnable celluloid dedicated to it over the years and it's no surprise that it's more memorable presentations have involved some form of action-packed conflict or thought-inflammation. No one forgets the chases of *The Road Warrior* (1982), although its simple plot about a man with limited ammunition and a dirty, grunting child trying to salvage oil from a group of intruding marauders has evolved into any number of prescient discussions over time. In-between the twisty sci-fi logic of Terry Gilliam's *12 Monkeys* (1995) and Alfonso Cuaron's *Children of Men* (2006), its reluctant heroes rediscovered the virtues that made the human race worthy of preservation. Even something as silly and seemingly non-significant as *Zombieland* (2009) managed to touch upon the central theme of maintaining one's child-like demeanor in the face of everlasting peril; something *The Road* never approaches. It wasn't literal enough to end *Terminator 2* (1991) or *Dazed and Confused* (1993) with shots of an unknown road traveling into uncertainty? We had to craft an entire book and movie out of that overused metaphor and walk it off the flat Earth the early believers once put their faith in.

Erik Childress

CREDITS

The Man: Viggo Mortensen
The Boy: Kodi Smit-McPhee
The Wife: Charlize Theron
The Veteran: Guy Pearce
Old Man: Robert Duvall
The Gang Member: Garret Dillahunt
The Thief: Michael K. Williams
Origin: USA
Language: English
Released: 2009
Production: Steve Schwartz, Nick Wechsler; Dimension Films, 2929 Productions, Nick Wechsler Productions, Chockstone Pictures, Road Rebel; released by Dimension Films
Directed by: John Hillcoat
Written by: Joe Penhall
Cinematography by: Javier Aguirresarobe
Music by: Nick Cave
Editing: Jon Gregory
Art Direction: Gershon Ginsburg
Costumes: Margot Wilson
Production Design: Chris Kennedy
MPAA rating: R
Running time: 119 minutes

REVIEWS

Ebert, Roger. *Chicago Sun-Times*. October 15, 2009.
Edelstein, David. *New York Magazine*. November 16, 2009.
Hoberman, J. *Village Voice*. November 25, 2009.
Long, Tom. *Detroit News*. November 25, 2009.
McCarthy, Todd. *Variety*. September 3, 2009.
Pais, Matt. *Metromix.com*. November 24, 2009.
Phillips, Michael. *Chicago Tribune*. November 24, 2009.
Stevens, Dana. *Slate*. November 25, 2009.
Tallerico, Brian. *MovieRetriever.com*. November 25, 2009.
Turan, Kenneth. *Los Angeles Times*. November 24, 2009.

QUOTES

The Man: "I told the boy when you dream about bad things happening, it means you're still fighting and you're still alive. It's when you start to dream about good things that you should start to worry."

TRIVIA

Actor Kodi Smit-McPhee's actual father makes an appearance as one of the cannibals on the back of the loffy.

AWARDS

Nomination:
British Acad. 2009: Cinematog.

RUDO Y CURSI

La vida es un volado.
—Movie tagline
Life is a coin toss.
—Movie tagline

Box Office: $1.8 million

Gael García Bernal and Diego Luna were only in their early twenties when they costarred in *Y Tu Mamá También* (2002), a raunchy road movie in which two sex-crazed best friends get caught up in a love triangle with an older woman. The low budget, subtitled film went on to gross an astonishing $13.9 million in the United States and garner a Best Original Screenplay Oscar® nomination, catapulting the pair into high profile projects and, along with *Amores Perros* (2001), helping to establish an American arthouse beachhead in the early millennial resurgence of Mexican cinema that would further the careers of a number of performers, writers and directors. Re-teaming the personable actors with the co-writer of that movie, Carlos Cuarón, *Rudo y Cursi* unfolds as a shaggy, intermittently entertaining parable of fraternal strife, again exploiting to the hilt for full comedic effect the off-screen rapport of Bernal and Luna.

Bickering Mexican half brothers Beto (Luna) and Tato Verdusco (Bernal) work at a rural banana plantation and spend their free time on a dusty pitch at the edge of town, playing for their village soccer team. Nicknamed "Tough" because of his coarse personality and athletic style, Beto dreams of becoming a famous goalkeeper, which hardly seems practical given that he is married to Toña (Adriana Paz) and already has two small children. An amiable, unattached "himbo," Tato's secret dream is to be a famous singer-accordionist.

Both young men, however, share the aspiration of building a house for their mother Elvira (Dolores Heredia), even though their meager earnings do not seem to indicate that is likely anytime in the near future. Their luck appears to change when a traveling soccer talent scout, Batuta (Guillermo Francella), accidentally discovers them. Explaining, though, in a bit of pure movie contrivance, that he only has the ability to recommend one of them to his superiors, Batuta suggests they decide for him with a penalty kick. This fateful if misunderstood kick (Beto suggests kicking to the right, which Tato misunderstands as his right) earns Tato the chance to move to the big city, where he becomes a star for the prestigious Deportivo Amaranto club. There, his flamboyant and goofy style of play earns him the nickname "Corny."

Although Beto feels betrayed and left behind, he soon wins an opportunity to become the goalkeeper for Atlético Nopaleros, a second division team in Mexico City. Success ensues for each brother. Animosity wanes for a while, then resurfaces as their rivalry gets played up in the media. While his independent-minded wife pursues a sales career, Beto allows a gambling addiction to drag him down. Unable to recognize his innate talents and unwilling to exercise the work ethic necessary to hone them, Tato trips into crossover celebrity and strikes up a tawdry tabloid relationship, which leads to the movie's eccentric high point—a bizarre music video for Tato's accordion-infused cover version of Cheap Trick's "I Want You To Want Me." Things come full circle when the brothers' individual destinies cross during a highly touted grudge match, and, yes, come down to one final penalty kick.

Perhaps because *Rudo Y Cursi* is the feature directorial debut of Cuarón, the younger brother of Alfonso Cuarón, and perhaps because it is so specifically tailored to its stars' real-life friendship, a thick lacquer of slapdash feeling encompasses the movie. Luna and Bernal oblige the director's breakneck pace by throwing themselves into dialogue with abandon, whether it is merely the gleeful relish behind a zonked-out simile ("This beer is as cold as a nun's tit!") or more emotionally substantive familial angst. The entire film, in fact, exhibits a loose-limbed, fraternal energy befitting a project made by friends.

But while Cuarón nicely sets up jostling masculine conflict and gives his movie a solid parallel structure, he seems uninterested or unconcerned with many of the second and third act specifics of its plot. The looming threat of Beto's gambling debt is only serious when a given scene calls for it, never longer, while other gambits—sister Nadia (Tania Esmeralda Aguilar) marries a drug kingpin (Alfredo Alfonso), scotching the guys' shared dream/duel of building their mother a house—come across as underdeveloped and/or extraneous narrative escape clauses. Also curious is voiceover narration by scout Batuta. This choice is obviously meant to impress upon the proceedings the bird's eye view of an impartial parabolist, but Batuta is a marginal character, and not functional enough to the unfolding story to give his musings any real psychological or emotional heft.

Instead, Cuarón seems more preoccupied with contrasting tone, and the ways in which melancholy, vivacity, anger and humor all abut one another in a life lived fully, and at full speed. The movie's cheerfully absurd atmosphere feels informed by some of the same sense of magical realism that has more darkly informed the native language work of Guillermo del Toro (a close friend of the Cuaróns, and a producer on *Rudo y Cursi*), but the first-time director is not yet technically skilled enough to marry that style intellectually with the transportive sweep of visually rich and idiosyncratic filmmaking.

In the end, *Rudo y Cursi* is a modest work whose charms are minutely targeted. This is not a dour or self-serious foreign film, but rather a modern pop valentine for those already converted to the charms of south-of-the-border cinema. Fans of Bernal and Luna will swoon accordingly; others will enjoy varying degrees of fitful bemusement.

Brent Simon

CREDITS

Tato: Gael Garcia Bernal
Beto: Diego Luna
Elvira: Dolores Heredia
Batuta: Guillermo Francella
Toma: Adriana Paz
Maya: Jessica Mas
Origin: Mexico, USA
Language: Spanish
Released: 2009
Production: Alfonson Cuaron, Guillermo del Toro, Alejandro Gonzalez Inarritu, Frida Torresblanco; Cha Cha Cha Films; released by Sony Pictures Classics
Directed by: Carlos Cuaron

Written by: Carlos Cuaron
Cinematography by: Adam Kimmel
Music by: Felipe Perez Santiago
Sound: Martin Hernandez
Music Supervisor: Anette Fradera
Editing: Alex Rodriguez
Costumes: Annai Ramos, Ana Terrazas
Production Design: Eugenio Caballero
MPAA rating: R
Running time: 103 minutes

REVIEWS

Abele, Robert. *Los Angeles Times.* May 8, 2009.
Ebert, Roger. *Chicago Sun-Times.* May 14, 2009.
Edelstein, David. *New York Magazine.* May 4, 2009.
Pais, Matt. *Metromix.com.* May 8, 2009.
Rabin, Nathan. *AV Club.* May 7, 2009.
Rea, Steven. *Philadelphia Inquirer.* May 29, 2009.
Scott, A.O. *New York Times.* May 8, 2009.
Stevens, Dana. *Slate.* May 8, 2009.
Tallerico, Brian. *MovieRetriever.com.* May 15, 2009.
Zak, Dan. *Washington Post.* May 15, 2009.

QUOTES

Jorge W.: "Catch me up Rudo, it's not me, I'm just the executive, I lead the operation, it's just that they want their money, that's obvious."
Beto: "Well, tell them to rise my credit."
Jorge W.: "I swear you man, I'm really ashamed but that's impossible. You got a Tsunami like debt, dude."

TRIVIA

All of the soccer teams and players featured in the film are completely fictional.

S

SAW VI

The game comes full circle.
—Movie tagline

Box Office: $27.7 million

The film *Saw* (2004) was a reasonably interesting variation on the serial-killer genre that featured a creepy and unique visual style, a couple of interesting plot twists, and a number of memorably gruesome set-pieces involving the fiendishly elaborate torture devices designed by its villain, the mysterious and creepy Jigsaw, to ensnare and educate those people that he felt were wasting the precious gift of life. The film became a cult hit and soon spawned a cottage industry that would see to the yearly production of a new installment of the franchise in time to flood multiplexes in the days leading up to Halloween. Of course, to keep up with such a killer pace, some things needed to be discarded. So, while the subsequent installments made sure to include plenty of nasty and graphic scenes of torture and bloodletting, they chose to eschew the creepy look and intriguing plot twists—the elements that require a certain degree of time, talent and finesse to achieve—in exchange for a murky visual style and a murkier narrative approach that would grow more and more befuddling with each subsequent film. Jigsaw would continue to be the central character despite being killed off decisively at the end of *Saw III* (2006) while barely remembered plot details and incidents from the earlier chapters would wind up appearing front-and-center in the later ones in ways that ensured that you not only needed to see all the previous entries before watching the newest one, you had to watch all of them maybe five minutes beforehand if you wanted to have even a shot at understanding what the hell was going on. *Saw VI* continues to follow this increasingly convoluted formula to a T and the nicest thing that one can say about it is that it is not quite as contemptuous of its audience as the incredibly lazy and unnecessary *Saw V* (2008). In other words, it is clear that the filmmakers put a little more effort into this one than normal—the story is a little less insular and the final twist is a little more clever than usual—but the overall film is just as stupid and repellent as the previous installments.

Set in the immediate aftermath of *Saw V*, Jigsaw (Tobin Bell) is still dead and his secret accomplice, mush-mouthed cop Lt. Hoffman (Costas Mandylor), is still carrying on his absurdly complex work of teaching hapless individuals morality lessons via the deployment of torture devices that are so elaborately contrived that Rube Goldberg himself would have pushed for simplification. This time around, the target of Jigsaw's posthumous wrath is William (Peter Outerbridge), a sleazy insurance agency bigwig who, with the aid of his crack staff of heartless Yuppie scum, has saved his company millions of dollars over the years by figuring out a way of denying claims whenever the policy holders have the audacity to take ill. While William is running through the various hoops set up for him, all of which involve him saving or sacrificing his underlings in gruesome ways, Hoffman is trying to clear up the loose ends regarding his involvement with the case, which include Jigsaw's widow (Betsy Russell), an ambitious reporter (Samantha Lemole) and at least one character previously assumed to have shuffled off this mortal coil in a previous installment.

Unless you are a student of all things *Saw*-related, it is likely that the previous paragraph reads as utter gibberish. Of course, no one goes to a movie like this for the plotting, except possibly to see how Cubist the narrative structure has become over the years in the effort to continue to include a popular central character who definitively died three sequels ago. No, the reason that people flock to it (though in surprisingly smaller number than in the past, as it turns out) is to see what grisly and elaborately violent set-pieces the filmmakers have dreamed up this time around. Unfortunately, while the red stuff flows as freely as ever, the grisly gruesomeness on display in the original has devolved into the blandest bloodshed imaginable. Two predatory lenders are forced to cut off portions of their own bodies in order to avoid getting their skulls crushed with screws. Another pair of unlucky types is hooked up to oxygen machines that crush their chests with every breath that they take. Another is forced to run through a maze in which she is hit with painful bursts of steam until her skull is eventually smashed open for her troubles while someone else is messily dissolved by acid. Outside of a murder-go-round in which William is allowed to save only two of his six sleaziest underlings, the kill scenes are so rote and repetitive that when it finally gets to the big climax, the film winds up simply reusing one of the more memorable devices from the first one. Considering the fact that the entire point of this series is to come up with wildly original kill scenes, the lack of any real ingenuity in this regard is likely to annoy whatever fans the series has managed to retain over the years.

The one interesting aspect of *Saw VI*, to use the term promiscuously, is the way that it cravenly uses the current economic and health care crises as story fodder. Having rejected seeing these problems depicted on screen in documentaries like *Sicko* (2007) and *Capitalism: A Love Story* (2009), perhaps the only way to get the movie-going public to accept them as compelling cinematic fare is to place them in the context of a bone-headed horror film along these lines. If nothing else, it suggests that if Tobin Bell ever decided to leave the series behind for good, the producers could potentially replace him with the likes of Keith Olbermann or Michael Moore—a notion infinitely more terrifying than anything else on display here.

Peter Sobczynski

CREDITS

Mark Hoffman: Costas Mandylor
Dan Erickson: Mark Rolston
Jill Tuck: Betsy Russell
Jigsaw/John Kramer: Tobin Bell

Amanda Young: Shawnee Smith
William Easton: Peter Outerbridge
Agent Perez: Athena Karkanis
Harold: George Newbern
Origin: USA
Language: English
Released: 2009
Production: Mark Burg, Oren Koules; Twisted Pictures; released by Lionsgate
Directed by: Kevin Greutert
Written by: Marcus Dunstan, Patrick Melton
Cinematography by: David Armstrong
Music by: Charlie Clouser
Sound: Keith Elliott
Editing: Andrew Coutts
Art Direction: Elis Lam
Costumes: Alex Kavanagh
Production Design: Anthony Ianni
MPAA rating: R
Running time: 90 minutes

REVIEWS

Abele, Robert. *New York Times.* October 26, 2009.
Gleiberman, Owen. *Entertainment Weekly.* October 23, 2009.
Graham, Adam. *Detroit News.* October 23, 2009.
Hale, Mike. *New York Times.* October 23, 2009.
Miska, Brad. *Bloody Disgusting.* October 23, 2009.
Nelson, Rob. *Variety.* October 25, 2009.
Pais, Matt. *Metromix.com.* October 23, 2009.
Scheck, Frank. *Hollywood Reporter.* October 23, 2009.
Tobias, Scott. *AV Club.* October 23, 2009.
Weinberg, Scott. *FEARNet.* October 23, 2009.

QUOTES

Jigsaw: "You think it's the living who have ultimate judgment over you, because the dead will have no claim over your soul. But you may be mistaken."

TRIVIA

Copies of the script that were given to the cast were titled "Evolution III" to discourage the script being leaked to the world at large.

THE SEPTEMBER ISSUE

Fashion is a religion. This is the bible.
   —Movie tagline

Box Office: $3.8 million

Anna Wintour, the legendary Editor-in-Chief of *Vogue* for the past 21 years, sits at the center of *The*

September Issue, a mostly engaging documentary which details a production cycle of the magazine's annual, trend-setting, behemoth, autumnal issue. The inspiration for Meryl Streep's imperious character in *The Devil Wears Prada* (2006), the British-born Wintour is arguably the most powerful and polarizing figure in fashion. It is not for nothing that early in the movie an interview subject characterizes the fashion community as a church, and Wintour as the pope; her whims can make or break a new designer or emergent trend.

R.J. Cutler's film only slightly succeeds in its effort to melt the façade of its famously icy subject. There is an affecting moment of quiet human frailty in Wintour's shrugging admission that her siblings are, in her words, "amused" by what she does, and the film opens with a knowing, effective rebuttal of those that look down on fashion and assert it does not matter or have an impact on most people's lives. Whether it is helping Fashion Fund scholarship recipient Thakoon Panichgul land his own line at The Gap, or fielding entreaties from high-end department store owners to get designers to deliver their clothes in a more expeditious manner since the latter will not return their phone calls, Wintour's industry bona fides and influence are never in doubt, communicated as they are here clearly and in telling details that give a sense of the larger undying passion for her industry which her withdrawn personality frequently masks.

Yet despite all these glimpses behind-the-scenes as well as a good number of accumulated small personal moments (including some screen time with her college-age daughter, who comes off as charming and perhaps surprisingly well adjusted), there is little sense of stark definition of the actual guiding principles that inform Wintour's dictatorial snap-judgments about what matters for *Vogue*. It basically seems to just boil down to whatever she feels at the moment, and that may change with the wind. This means that for those for whom fashion is a tertiary consideration at best, Wintour as a person remains at worst entirely unsympathetic, and at best distant and desperately unknowable on even a professional level—just another snooty, smart-talking boss above any rational dissection or accountability.

Thankfully, the movie has many other things going for it other than just an examination of Wintour's workplace decision-making. A superb political documentary which Cutler produced, *The War Room* (1993), made the frenetic particulars of a campaign for the American presidency seem invigorating and relatable on a personal level, and *The September Issue* similarly locates a humanistic pulse that renders its high-powered, ultra-specific setting irrelevant in the grand scheme of things. While nicely complemented with direct address interviews, Cutler's fly-on-the-wall observational tack otherwise smartly trusts viewers to track small non-verbal details themselves. The captured reward involves the sort of carping and back-biting that almost any office employee will recognize in their own corporate culture.

There is a good deal of hullabaloo kicked up over a Rome cover photo shoot with Sienna Miller meant to evoke some of the iconic works of Italian cinema, particularly when photographer Mario Testino shoots one less set-up than was planned. Later, there is discussion of Photoshopping the actress' head onto a different picture of her body, a decision which kicked up some notable public controversy after the movie's premiere at the 2009 Sundance Film Festival, where director of photography Robert Richman's work also won the Cinematography Award.

But *The September Issue*'s main drama, its bass line of swallowed conflict, is wrapped up in the two-decade relationship between "frenemies" Wintour and Grace Coddington, *Vogue*'s creative director. It is a case of the pretty and pedigreed versus a life tragically altered. Icy and possessing a stylish yet severe bob haircut, Wintour has an impassive, queen-bee countenance that does not invite much discussion in the way of alternate opinion. Meanwhile, Coddington's often seemingly low-held ground in arguments is not made easier by her frazzled, slightly frumpy demeanor, or the fact that the one-time model is scarred by an auto accident that has left her vaguely resembling a cross between Cathy Guisewite's eponymous comic strip character and a theoretical imaginary sister of Eric Stoltz's character from *Mask* (1985).

It is this stark contrast, though, that helps *The September Issue* succeed and connect with general audiences as a portrait of teeth-grinding workplace friction. "You have to find a way to make *Vogue* work for you," says a frustrated Coddington at one point. In this moment, and others like it, a viewer feels Coddington's sense of aggrieved angst, and has some emotional stake in the proceedings, even if they do not know Manolo Blahniks from Skechers, or Christian Louboutins from Keds.

Brent Simon

CREDITS
Herself: Sienna Miller
Herself: Anna Wintour
Origin: USA
Language: English
Released: 2009
Production: R.J. Cutler, Eliza Hindmarch, Sadia Shepard; A&E Indiefilms, Actual Reality Pictures; released by Roadside Attractions

Directed by: R.J. Cutler
Cinematography by: Bob Richman
Music by: Craig Richey
Sound: Edward L. O'Connor
Music Supervisor: Margaret Yen
Editing: Azin Samari
MPAA rating: PG-13
Running time: 90 minutes

REVIEWS

Anderson, Melissa. *Village Voice.* August 25, 2009.
Dargis, Manohla. *New York Times.* August 28, 2009.
Ebert, Roger. *Chicago Sun-Times.* September 10, 2009.
Kaufman, Joanne. *Wall Street Journal.* August 28, 2009.
Lemire, Christy. *Associated Press.* August 26, 2009.
Morris, Wesley. *Boston Globe.* September 10, 2009.
Pols, Mary F. *Time Magazine.* August 28, 2009.
Rabin, Nathan. *AV Club.* August 27, 2009.
Smith, Kyle. *New York Post.* August 27, 2009.
Smith, Neil. *Total Film.* September 11, 2009.

QUOTES

Anna Wintour: "There is something about fashion that can make people really nervous."

A SERIOUS MAN

Box Office: $9.2 million

If there is one thing about the career arc of Joel & Ethan Coen, it is that they certainly respond to success and acclaim in decidedly offbeat ways. When their debut film, *Blood Simple* (1985), put them on the map as neo-noir stylists of the highest order, they followed it up with the broad slapstick silliness of *Raising Arizona* (1987). When their small, dark and highly metaphorical art film *Barton Fink* (1991) scored the Palme d'Or at Cannes a couple of years later and secured their positions as artistes of the highest rank, they returned with the fairly expensive and cheerfully silly fable *The Hudsucker Proxy* (1994). When *Fargo* (1996) became one of the most unexpected award-winning hits of the decade, they responded with *The Big Lebowski* (1998), a movie which has since become a huge cult hit but which was largely written off at the time by many people as nothing more than a weird bit of hazy-headed fluff. Therefore, when *No Country for Old Men* (2007), their uncharacteristically straightforward adaptation of the Cormac McCarthy novel, became their biggest critical and commercial hit to date, their fans probably assumed that they would once again respond to that unexpected suc-

cess with something decidedly offbeat and wholly unexpected. (Their actual follow-up, *Burn After Reading* (2008), doesn't count because it was already in the works before the *No Country* juggernaut began.) Even so, it is unlikely that any of them pictured the brothers coming up with something along the lines of *A Serious Man*, a brilliant and bracingly original work that is funny and thought provoking in equal measure and which is one of the finest and most fascinating works of their entire careers.

Set in 1967 in a Minnesota suburb in which the cultural changes of the era have yet to arrive, save for the exception of the sounds of Jefferson Airplane's "Somebody to Love" emerging from the occasional teen-wielded transistor radio, *A Serious Man* gives us a glimpse at a couple of weeks in the life of Larry Gopnick (Michael Stuhlbarg), a Jewish academic who teaches physics at a local college and whose life, as the story opens, is about to take a series of grim and unexpected turns both personally and professionally. At home, his brilliant-but-lazy brother Arthur (Richard Kind) is sleeping on the couch without any evident intention of finding a job and moving out. His son, Danny (Aaron Wolff) is supposed to be studying for his upcoming Bar Mitzvah but would rather get stoned and listen to rock music, his older daughter (Jessica McManus) is complaining that she wants a nose job. His wife, Judith (Sari Lennick), poleaxes him one morning with the unexpected news that she wants a divorce, that she has begun a friendship with the gruesomely unctuous widower Sy Abeleman (Fred Melamed), and that it would be better off for everyone if Larry left the house and moved into a nearby motel called the Jolly Roger.

At work, things are not much better. While sweating out the wait to learn if he made tenure, he is confronted with a Korean student who insists that he change an "unjust" failing grade and even offers a bribe as encouragement. After Larry refuses it, the kid's father threatens to sue him on grounds that are never quite made clear. To top things off, the tenure committee has been receiving a series of letters denigrating Larry and while the committee head keeps blandly assuring him that the letters will not influence the decision in any way, the mere fact that he repeatedly mentions that fact is proof positive that they will.

This is not merely a bad patch that Larry is experiencing—this is a string of bad luck to rival the trials of Job—and for someone whose entire life is based upon the notion that actions have consequences, he is dumbfounded as to why all of this is befalling him. After all, he is a good and decent man who has tried to live a life of strong moral and ethical standards and he simply does not understand why God would make someone who follows all the rules of decency suffer so much while others seem to get away with anything they want. Needing answers, Larry seeks out advice for his spiritual and secular problems from a variety of rabbis, lawyers, colleagues and other allegedly learned people but in every case, all he gets in return is either long-winded parables that have nothing to do with his situation or revelations that will either get him into more trouble, cost him more money or, worst of all, dangle a brief bit of hope before cruelly snatching it away from him.

Because the Coen brothers grew up in a neighborhood not unlike the one seen here at the same time that it is set and because they were from an academic family, there has been much speculation that *A Serious Man* is a far more autobiographical work than their previous efforts—at the very least, it has the look and feel of the kind of small-scale and highly symbolic personal project that a filmmaker is generally expected after coming up with an award-winning hit along the lines of *No Country for Old Men*. While the sequence involving young Danny trying to make it through his Bar Mitzvah while stoned has a verisimilitude to it that suggests that it wasn't invented entirely out of whole cloth, it seems absurd to think, after building an entire career on films, save for *No Country for Old Men*, that are arch and irony-drenched commentaries on various film genres (even the beloved *Fargo* was a bit of a put-on of the true-crime docudrama genre) that they would suddenly open up and let viewers into their lives by celluloid proxy. Instead, it feels like it is an arch and irony-drenched commentary on the kind of small-scale and highly symbolic personal project that filmmakers are expected to make after a massive commercial and critical hit.

If there is an autobiographical aspect to *A Serious Man*, it comes in the way that the film serves as a way for the Coens to respond to their critics who complain that their films are cynical constructions in which they jerk their characters around from one bizarre situation to another with the detachment of cruel and dispassionate gods who let their creations suffer for no particular reason and with no satisfactory explanations for either the characters or the audience members observing their plights. Read in this light, the film stands as a fascinating meditation on the responsibility that artists have towards their creations and their audiences—by not explaining things in detail and wrapping everything up in the end, are they encouraging viewers to engage with the story that they are telling or are they just being smirky assholes? How this question is answered is best left for viewers to discover for themselves except to note that the denouement is especially brilliant in the way that it seemingly wraps things up tidily while still coming across in such a fascinatingly oblique manner that it

makes the controversial end of *No Country for Old Men* seem like a studio-demanded reshoot by comparison.

Even without this particular interpretation of *A Serious Man*, there are plenty of other reason to admire the film. Although it may not contain the most straightforward of narratives, the screenplay has the charm of a rambling shaggy dog story containing plenty of oddball divergences that don't really add much to the story proper but which are nevertheless absolutely essential to its feel—one standout is the sequence in which one of the rabbis (George Wyner) recounts the parable of "The Goy's Teeth." The direction is pitch-perfect in the way that it transforms material that could have been painful to behold in the hands of others into the kind of hilariously discomforting and mordant comedy that is rarely seen these days. All of the performances from the relatively unknown cast are spot-on as well in capturing the deadpan attitude that the Coens are truly striving for here. As Larry, stage actor Michael Stuhlbarg turns in one of the best pieces of acting seen this year and Fred Melamed is absolutely hysterical as the man who cuckolds Larry and then insists on making it up to him with a bottle of wine that he then uses as a ham-fisted metaphor for justifying his behavior. Most amazingly, there are even a few moments that cut through the dark humor and hit upon simple emotional truths in an affecting manner without making a big deal out of it—after spending most of the film offering the rabbi characters as people who are out-of-touch with those they are supposed to be helping, the chief rabbi gets a moment with Danny in one of the closing scenes in which he finally and unexpectedly offers advice that is direct, to the point and helpful to boot.

A Serious Man is one of the very best films of 2009 and it reconfirms that the Coen Brothers are among the most daring and audacious filmmakers working today. Of course, the lack of stars and the somewhat outré subject manner suggests that it probably will not reach as many viewers as some of their broader-based entertainments. That said, it is as funny, thought-provoking, off-beat and fiercely original as anything that they have done in the past and viewers willing to simply sit back and, to quote the proverb that opens the film, accept everything that happens with simplicity are likely be struck by just how deeply felt and deeply hilarious it really is.

Peter Sobczynski

CREDITS

Larry Gropnik: Michael Stuhlbarg
Arthur Gropnik: Richard Kind
Judith Gropnik: Sari Lennick

Sy Ableman: Fred Melamed
Don Milgram: Adam Arkin
Groshkover: Fyvush Finkel
Danny Gropnik: Aaron Wolff
Sarah Gropnik: Jessica McManus
Origin: USA
Language: English
Released: 2009
Production: Ethan Coen, Joel Coen; Relativity Media, Studio Canal; released by Focus Features
Directed by: Joel Coen, Ethan Coen
Written by: Joel Coen, Ethan Coen
Cinematography by: Roger Deakins
Music by: Carter Burwell
Sound: Peter Kurland
Music Supervisor: Todd Kasow
Editing: Joel Coen, Ethan Coen
Art Direction: Deborah Jensen
Costumes: Mary Zophres
Production Design: Jess Gonchor
MPAA rating: R
Running time: 105 minutes

REVIEWS

Corliss, Richard. *Time Magazine.* October 2, 2009.
Denby, David. *New Yorker.* September 28, 2009.
Ebert, Roger. *Chicago Sun-Times.* October 8, 2009.
Edelstein, David. *New York Magazine.* September 28, 2009.
Lemire, Christy. *Associated Press.* September 30, 2009.
Phillips, Michael. *Chicago Tribune.* October 8, 2009.
Scott, A.O. *New York Times.* October 2, 2009.
Stevens, Dana. *Slate.* October 1, 2009.
Tallerico, Brian. *MovieRetriever.com.* October 9, 2009.
Turan, Kenneth. *Los Angeles Times.* October 2, 2009.

QUOTES

Larry Gopnik: "I've tried to be a serious man, you know? Tried to do right, be a member of the community."

TRIVIA

The film runs for nearly nine minutes before the first English is spoken.

AWARDS

Ind. Spirit 2010: Cinematog
Nomination:
Oscars 2009: Film, Orig. Screenplay
British Acad. 2009: Orig. Screenplay
Golden Globes 2010: Actor—Mus./Comedy (Stuhlbarg)

Ind. Spirit 2010: Director (Coen Brothers)
Writers Guild 2009: Orig. Screenplay.

17 AGAIN

Who says you're only young once?
—Movie tagline

Box Office: $64.2 million

Having managed to largely avoid the mistakes that have crippled the careers of many a hunky heartthrob over the years by alternating his appearances in the enormously popular *High School Musical* franchise with relatively ambitious projects like *Hairspray* (2007) and Richard Linklater's *Me and Orson Welles* (2009) instead of squandering his talents on low-grade exploitation trash aimed solely at the slumber party circuit, it is more than a little surprising to see the talented Zac Efron wasting his time on something so trashy and devoid of purpose as *17 Again.* Lacking any trace of intelligence, ingenuity or energy, this painfully derivative knock-off of all those body-switching movies that clogged multiplexes in the late eighties is one of the laziest things to appear in a movie theater in 2009. In fact, the only people who could possibly come out of this movie not feeling simultaneously bummed out and ripped off are undiscriminating tween girls willing to sit through anything in order to get a glimpse of their collective crush object and New Line Pictures executives thrilled with the amount of money that those tween girls contributed to their bottom line by being willing to sit through anything in order to get a glimpse of their collective crush object.

The film opens in 1989 as high school basketball star Mike O'Donnell (Efron) is about to score the college scholarship that will make all his dreams come true when he discovers that his girlfriend, Scarlett, is pregnant. As a result, Mike throws away the scholarship to marry Scarlett and when we pick up with him twenty years later (now in the form of Matthew Perry), he is separated from Scarlett (Leslie Mann), alienated from teenaged kids Maggie (Michelle Trachtenberg) and Alex (Sterling Knight), and stuck in a dead-end job. While visiting his old high school, he begins to reminisce about how great things were back then and if he had a chance to do it all again, he would do everything right this time and become the success that he feels he was destined to be. Because the time-space continuum primarily exists to help whiny and self-absorbed white guys solve their petty personal problems, Mike wakes up the next morning transformed back into his teenage self and, with the help of his geeky millionaire best pal (Thomas Lennon), he decides to return to his old high school and redo his life. Although this ruse allows him to get to know his own kids better by befriending them—he teaches his daughter not to run around with bad boys and his son that there are few problems in life that cannot be solved on the basketball court—it also leads to any number of awkward moments with Scarlett in which he tries to reconnect with her and she tries to figure out why this teenager with an eerie resemblance to her ex-husband in his youth is apparently trying to woo her.

17 Again is a piece of product that is so utterly lackluster in every single area that one wonders how it is able to muster up the strength to actually make it from the projector to the screen without crumbling—it even climaxes with a courtroom scene that all but screams "We couldn't think of any other way of wrapping up this story and, frankly, we don't care." The screenplay is little more than a string of incidents copied from other films of this type that are so badly handled that it feels as if screenwriter Jason Filardi did not even bother to actually watch the movies he was ripping off and instead relied on second-hand recollections to help fuel his "original" screenplay. (The only unexpected moment comes during one of the basketball sequences in which audiences are treated to the highly unusual sight of a referee actually calling someone for traveling.) The comedic elements fall flat, the dramatic elements are unintentionally hilarious and the tone weirdly shifts from the moralistic to the creepy without rhyme or reason. At one point, while trying to prevent his daughter from being seduced by her thuggish boyfriend, our hero interrupts a safe sex discussion in class by arguing so forcefully for abstinence that all the girls in the class pledge purity forever. Maybe twenty minutes later, however, those exact same girls start coming on to him. On the other hand, that is nothing compared to the moment when Maggie unknowingly attempts to seduce her own father in a long and painful sequence that is meant to be funny but which is almost Cronenbergian in its creepiness. As for the cast, they seem to have resigned themselves to the fact that no one is going to be paying attention to their efforts and go through the motions with little more than the energy required to keep their eyes open during the takes.

The only person who actually makes any sort of effort during *17 Again* is Efron himself and while he is by far the best thing about the film, the sight of him stumbling through the kind of third-rate material that he has already long outgrown is a grim one indeed. While a film like this certainly will not sink his career by any means—indeed, its box-office success amply demonstrated that he could open a film entirely on his name—the absolute lousiness of the whole enterprise should hopefully remind him that he should avoid similar endeavors in the immediate future if he wants to

be taking seriously as an actor. If not, he runs the risk of one day standing outside of a multiplex thinking back on his bad decisions while wishing he could go back and make the right choices. Based on the evidence that is *17 Again*, we all know how grimly unpleasant that could be.

Peter Sobczynski

CREDITS

Mike O'Donnell: Matthew Perry
Teenaged Mike: Zac Efron
Scarlett O'Donnell: Leslie Mann
Ned Freedman: Thomas Lennon
Maggie O'Donnell: Michelle Trachtenberg
Alex O'Donnell: Sterling Knight
Origin: USA
Language: English
Released: 2009
Production: Jennifer Gibgot, Adam Shankman; Offspring Entertainment; released by New Line Cinema
Directed by: Burr Steers
Written by: Jason Filardi
Cinematography by: Tim Suhrstedt
Music by: Rolfe Kent
Editing: Padraic McKinley
Sound: Hugh Waddell, Perry Robertson
Costumes: Pamela Withers-Chilton
Production Design: Garreth Stover
MPAA rating: PG-13
Running time: 102 minutes

REVIEWS

Burr, Ty. *Boston Globe.* April 16, 2009.
Chang, Justin. *Variety.* April 10, 2009.
Dargis, Manohla. *New York Times.* April 17, 2009.
Ebert, Roger. *Chicago Sun-Times.* April 16, 2009.
Edelstein, David. *New York Magazine.* April 13, 2009.
Gronvall, Andrea. *Chicago Reader.* April 16, 2009.
Pais, Matt. *Metromix.com.* April 16, 2009.
Phillips, Michael. *Chicago Tribune.* April 17, 2009.
Rickey, Carrie. *Philadelphia Inquirer.* April 16, 2009.
Tobias, Scott. *AV Club.* April 16, 2009.

QUOTES

Mike O'Donnell: "Come on, man! Don't you ever wanna go back and do high school again?"
Ned Freedman: "No. I'm rich and no one has shoved my head in a toilet today!"

TRIVIA

The film was shipped to theaters using the title "Remind."

SHERLOCK HOLMES

Nothing escapes him.
—Movie tagline

Box Office: $206.6 million

Guy Ritchie's *Sherlock Holmes* faces a dilemma common to long running franchises: how to render the material appealing for a modern, mass audience while not changing it so much that it destroys the original qualities that made the subject appealing in the first place. Rebooting a franchise as old and storied as Sherlock Holmes comes with its upsides and downsides. On the one hand, there is an enormous, century plus back catalogue to live up to (stretching all the way back to J. Stuart Blackton's *Adventures of Sherlock Holmes* [1905]). On the other hand, it is a back catalogue that has accommodated quite a varied range of interpretations (from Basil Rathbone's "modern" Holmes films of the 1930s and 1940s—Sherlock Holmes vs. Nazis!—to Billy Wilder and Nicholas Meyer's revisionist Holmes films of the 1970s to Jeremy Brett's faithful BBC series of the 1980s and 1990s). Ironically, what causes *Sherlock Holmes* to fail is not taking too many liberties with the source material but failing to get the most basic element down that has been a requirement all the way back to the original Conan Doyle stories of the late nineteenth century: providing a mystery clever enough to engage its master detective protagonist and the viewer.

The film's pulpy premise is appropriate enough, opening mid-adventure in 1891 London as Holmes (Robert Downey Jr.) and Watson (Jude Law) race to stop the latest human sacrifice in a string of ritual murders perpetrated by the sinister Lord Blackwood (Mark Strong). The first inkling the viewer receives of Ritchie and screenwriter Anthony Peckham's approach to the material is the introduction of Holmes in which the great detective uses his deductive powers not to solve a clever puzzle but to determine how best to incapacitate an approaching thug. Holmes crouches in the darkness, mentally calculating via voiceover the precise series of attacks necessary to take out his victim and then executes them, Bruce Lee style. It is disconcerting to see the world's greatest detective's deductive abilities harnessed to a kung fu fight and is emblematic of a film that places too much emphasis on action and not enough on detection.

Once apprehended, Blackwood hints that his impending execution will not be the end of him or London's troubles. He informs Holmes through his jail cell window that following his execution three more people will die and that these deaths are merely a prelude to much worse and much larger events to come. Sure enough, although executed by hanging (confirmed dead by none other than Dr. Watson himself,) Blackwood soon reappears, apparently very much alive. Sinister machinations are at work. Meanwhile, an old acquaintance of Holmes, Irene Adler (Rachel McAdams), re-enters Holmes's life, hiring him to locate a ginger haired midget named Reardon on behalf of her secret employer, a mysterious professor. Adler is presented as Holmes's intellectual equal, if not superior (the film hints that she has outwitted him twice in the past) and the verbal banter between the two should crackle as the two great minds lock wits. However, the scenes between Holmes and Adler fall flat as the script fails to provide them with witty dialogue equal to their characters' intellect.

And that intellect ebbs and flows for both characters throughout the rest of the film, their detective abilities varying according to plot requirements. Although McAdams is supposed to be at least as wily as Holmes, when the plot requires it she falls into the stock damsel in distress role (a more ambitious script would have put their detective abilities in competition with one another). And while Holmes, in one scene, is able to deduce from a few personal items belonging to Watson's new fiancé, whom he has just met, that she was engaged to another man before meeting Watson, in a following scene he is unable to figure out that his wine has been drugged by a person he has known intimately and for years because the plot requires it. This is not to suggest that Holmes and Adler should not be capable of being outsmarted, only that characters as allegedly clever as they are have to be provided with mysteries equal to their intellect for them to be convincingly fooled.

The midget Reardon unsurprisingly turns up murdered and Holmes and Watson's investigation of the dead midget's flat reveals that he was at work on a most mysterious device. Before they can discover more, they are interrupted by three thugs. Fisticuffs ensue and lead to a major set piece battle in a shipyard in which one of the thugs, in trying to hammer Holmes to death, knocks a ship under construction loose which then dramatically slides loose into the Thames. Soon, as promised, two more people are dead, killed off by Blackwood in a seemingly supernatural manner. Blackwood then sets a trap for Holmes and Watson in a slaughter house, kidnapping Adler and chaining her to an assembly line advancing towards buzz-saws (railroad tracks evidently being already passé in 1891). The trio narrowly escapes, only to fall victim to multiple, massive explosions (rendered in extended slow motion) outside of the warehouse. With Watson in the hospital, Holmes engineers his own capture by a member of Blackwood's secret society from whom he learns of sinister plans for parliament (and later the world) involving Reardon's device. Apprised of the nefarious plot, Holmes escapes his captor by diving out a window twenty stories into the Thames and races to intercept Blackwood atop the latticework of the under-construction Tower Bridge.

These events describe not a meticulously crafted mystery but rather a generic tent pole summer action film masquerading as a Sherlock Holmes film. For Ritchie's *Holmes*, the mystery is an afterthought. There is no step-by-step, linear solving of a mystery that the viewer can participate in, no series of clever, interlocking clues teased out by Holmes that inevitably lead to one plot development and then another. Instead what the viewer receives is two hours of seemingly inexplicable things occurring that are then unconvincingly "explained" by Holmes at a hundred miles an hour at the film's climax. How much the viewer enjoys *Sherlock Holmes* will depend on how much the lack of an intriguing mystery for the detective to solve bothers them.

Sherlock Holmes's failings are certainly not the fault of Downey who does the best he can with a script that is not clever enough to allow him be a great detective or funny enough to let him cut loose as comedy hero. His strengths as an actor make him a natural Holmes, his intelligence conveying the detective's brilliance more than the weak mystery the script gives him to solve and his quick wit supplying more humor than the weak dialogue is capable of carrying on its own. Similarly, Jude Law plays an able straight man and Rachel McAdams does well enough with her inconsistent role (though adding a romantic element to Sherlock Holmes is a dodgy business) but like Downey, their talent and charisma can only compensate so much for a flat script that fails to live up to their characters' intelligence. Nor is the problem Richie's direction, which, with its speed and trademark edits, refreshingly enlivens the typically staid direction of past Holmes adaptations like a welcome shot of the famous detective's cocaine.

The bottom line is that for all the nefarious villains, fog enshrouded foot chases and pistol duels, Holmes is a cerebral hero whose appeal lies in his deductive abilities and he needs a story that allows him to demonstrate those abilities. Holmes is hardly an armchair detective, all detection and no action (that certainly was not the case in the original films or fiction) but the action has to flow from the detection. Otherwise, Holmes is just another generic action hero: James Bond 1891. And with Ritchie's *Sherlock Holmes* that is exactly what you get: a generic Victorian action film possessing all the superficial elements of Sherlock Holmes but none of its substance or subtly.

What is wrong with a Victorian action film? Nothing if there were not such a rich back catalogue of Holmes films and television shows to draw on instead of it. Any new entry into such a long running franchise needs to give the viewer a reason not to simply draw on

the old stuff. Richie's film fails to do so. The game is not afoot.

Nate Vercauteren

CREDITS

Sherlock Holmes: Robert Downey Jr.
Dr. John Watson: Jude Law
Irene Adler: Rachel McAdams
Lord Blackwood: Mark Strong
Mary Morstan: Kelly Reilly
Inspector Lestrade: Eddie Marsan
Sir Thomas Rotheram: James Fox
Lord Coward: Hans Matheson
Mrs. Hudson: Geraldine James
Origin: USA
Language: English
Released: 2009
Production: Susan Downey, Joel Silver, Lionel Wigram, Dan Lin; Village Roadshow Pictures, Silver Pictures; released by Warner Bros.
Directed by: Guy Ritchie
Written by: Guy Ritchie, Michael R. Johnson, Anthony Peckham, Simon Kinberg
Cinematography by: Philippe Rousselot
Music by: Hans Zimmer
Sound: Chris Munro
Editing: James Herbert
Art Direction: Niall Moroney
Costumes: Jenny Beavan
Production Design: Sarah Greenwood
MPAA rating: PG-13
Running time: 128 minutes

REVIEWS

Bradshaw, Peter. *Guardian.* December 18, 2009.
Denby, David. *New Yorker.* December 16, 2009.
Ebert, Roger. *Chicago Sun-Times.* December 24, 2009.
Germain, David. *Associated Press.* December 21, 2009.
Graham, Adam. *Detroit News.* December 24, 2009.
McCarthy, Todd. *Variety.* December 16, 2009.
Reed, Rex. *New York Observer.* December 22, 2009.
Robey, Tim. *Daily Telegraph.* December 15, 2009.
Tallerico, Brian. *MovieRetriever.com.* December 25, 2009.
White, Armond. *New York Press.* December 22, 2009.

QUOTES

Sherlock Holmes: "You've never complained about my methods before."
Dr. John Watson: "I'm not complaining. How am I complaining? When have do I ever complain about you

practicing the violin at three in the morning, or your mess, your general lack of hygiene, or the fact that you steal my clothes?"

TRIVIA

The set for Sherlock Holmes's residence previously doubled as Sirius Black's home in *Harry Potter and the Order of the Phoenix*.

AWARDS

Golden Globes 2010: Actor—Mus./Comedy (Downey)

Nomination:

Oscars 2009: Art Dir./Set Dec., Orig. Score.

SHORTS: THE ADVENTURES OF THE WISHING ROCK

Not so tall tales from the director of "Spy Kids."
—Movie tagline

Box Office: $21 million

Director Robert Rodriguez has distinguished himself as both a proponent of digital cinema, and as a high-powered creative entity able to move effortlessly between genres and the world of adult and kiddie fare. His most accomplished adult film, *Sin City* (2005) and his most accomplished kids film, *Spy Kids* (2001), have in common a maverick free spirit that lifts them a little above the genres of which they grow out. More often than not, Rodriguez' do-it-yourself sensibility has been a stumbling block to making truly great films. While his more problematic adult films remain fun and watchable despite their flaws, his problematic kiddie films are resolutely awful.

This is what most directors do, of course. They bounce from strength to weakness, leaving behind a body of work that offers highs and lows. But with his last three films *The Adventures of Shark Boy and Lava Girl 3-D* (2005), *Planet Terror aka Grindhouse* (2007), and *Shorts* (2009) Rodriguez threatens to devolve into stock-in-trade parody of his own maverick style, offering precious little substance to go with the spectacle. These films are simply forgettable and anyone who has watched enough of Rodriguez' movies knows how much better he can be. *El Mariachi* (1992) showed a solid grasp on genre mechanics and low to the ground bare bones film-making technique, and *The Faculty* (1998) offered a gripping, often witty take on *Invasion of the Body Snatchers* (1956) and *Invaders from Mars* (1953). Even the entertaining excess of *Once Upon A Time In Mexico*

(2003), and *Spy Kids 2: Island of Lost Dreams* could be excused as the efforts of a wunderkind working out the kinks of, and having fun with, his craft. But the above former films, especially *Shorts*, fail to be fun enough to beg viewer forgiveness. *Shorts* itself plays like a hyperactive fruit chews commercial splashing color all over the screen without the authority of 3-D to lend any oomph for the viewers trouble. The end result is a unmemorable blur.

Eleven-year-old Toe Thompson (Jimmy Bennett) has it rough. His parents have moved him into the ho-hum homogeny of Black Falls, a suburb owned by their employer, Black Box Unlimited Worldwide Industries Incorporated. Mr. Black (James Spader), the company owner, is bent on taking over the world with their latest product, the Black Box communication device that transforms into whatever the user needs. But what Toe needs are parents, not corporate drones in fear of losing their careers as they try to work the kinks out of the unreliable product the company has staked a massive fortune on. And it isn't enough that Toe is parentless, weighed down by his obnoxiously self-centered sister and saddled with the title of the friendless new-guy-in-town. He also has to contend with Mr. Black's children, Helvetica (Jolie Vanier) and her older brother Cole (Devon Gearhart), who, along with their gang of cronies, have decided to make him the village punching bag.

All is not well until a rainbow-colored rock drops from the sky after an unusually severe storm. Unlike the Black Box, the rock works perfectly, granting any wish of the owner. The end result is of course a mess. Soon the entire town is overrun with weird creatures and other disastrous results of human greed and good intentions gone awry and all the kids must band together to save the world.

Rodriguez offers an unusual narrative structure for a family film choosing to tell a rather straightforward story by tying together several short films. So, like an anthology, it is visually split up. But, unlike most film anthologies, the stories of *Shorts* fit tightly together to little effect, failing to help the film do any more than present a cohesive bland plot made up of stock family film elements.

The film is blessed with a truly great cast even if the material they gamely try to bring to life is constantly overshadowed by lame jokes that seem to exist only because they give Rodriguez the chance to fiddle with pixels. Jimmy Bennett is clearly having a blast as Toe Thompson and he has the chops to make something fun of the role. His list of credits are very impressive for a performer of his age and include *Orphan* (2009), the role of the young James T. Kirk in *Star Trek* (2009), *Evan Almighty* (2007), *Poseidon* (2006), the breakout hit*Firewall* (2006), *The Amityville Horror* (2005) and the role of the lonely boy in *The Polar Express* (2004). Not all of these were big hits or good films but they were well promoted major studio efforts and they represent only a small fraction of his resume.

Newcomer Jolie Vanier also deserves special mention as Toe Thompson's nemesis and possible love-interest Helvetica Black. Made up to look like a slightly less creepy version of Wednesday from *The Addams Family*, she might have fallen into the obvious trap of under-performing, but here she makes a great foil, able to ooze disdain one minute and blush when appropriate.

The rest of the cast is so experienced that they all look relieved to be in a family film where they can simply mug if they don't feel like acting. Jon Cryer and Leslie Mann are fine as the parents who wind up literally joined at the hip when the wife wishes they could be closer. William H. Macy seems to be having a great time as the germ-a-phobic father scientist and James Spader makes a decent "evil corporate boss." But the material they gamely try to bring to life is constantly overshadowed by lame jokes that seem to exist only because they give Rodriguez the chance to fiddle with pixels. Booger monsters, alligator armies, and giant robots might be ingredients for a family film, but it is ironic that the wittiest moment in the *Shorts* occurs during the first short and involves an impossibly long staring contest between two of the kids. If only watching movies like this were that easy they could be enjoyed via willpower alone. Sadly that is not the case here. *Shorts* is short on all the things that would make it not seem way too long.

Dave Canfield

CREDITS

Toby "Toe" Thompson: Jimmy Bennett
Stacey Thompson: Kat Dennings
Loogie Short: Trevor Gagnon
Nose Noseworthy: Jake Short
Helvetica Black: Jolie Vanier
Laser Short: Leo Howard
Cole Black: Devon Gearhart
Lug Short: Rebel Rodriguez
Mom Thompson: Leslie Mann
Dad Thompson: Jon Cryer
Dr. Noseworthy: William H. Macy
Carbon Black: James Spader
Origin: USA
Language: English
Released: 2009
Production: Robert Rodriguez, Elizabeth Avellan; Troublemaker Studios; released by Warner Bros.

Directed by: Robert Rodriguez
Written by: Robert Rodriguez
Cinematography by: Robert Rodriguez
Music by: Carl Thiel, George Oldziey
Sound: Ethan Andrus
Editing: Robert Rodriguez, Ethan Maniquis
Art Direction: Suzanne Stover
Costumes: Nina Proctor
Production Design: Steve Joyner
MPAA rating: PG
Running time: 89 minutes

REVIEWS

Berkshire, Geoff. *Metromix.com.* August 21, 2009.
Catsoulis, Jeanette. *New York Times.* August 21, 2009.
Chang, Justin. *Variety.* August 10, 2009.
Gronvall, Andrea. *Chicago Reader.* August 21, 2009.
Honeycutt, Kirk. *Hollywood Reporter.* August 10, 2009.
Puig, Claudia. *USA Today.* August 20, 2009.
Sharkey, Betsy. *Los Angeles Times.* August 21, 2009.
Simon, Brent. *Screen International.* August 12, 2009.
Tallerico, Brian. *MovieRetriever.com.* August 21, 2009.
Weitzman, Elizabeth. *New York Daily News.* August 21, 2009.

QUOTES

Cole Black: "Hey metalmouth! Got another date with the trashcan."

TRIVIA

Black Falls Community is constructed in the shape of the Wishing Rock.

SIN NOMBRE

The greatest sin of all is risking nothing.
—Movie tagline

Box Office: $2.5 million

Their journey is a dangerous one. Illegal immigrants hoping to enter the United States from Mexico risk robbery, rape and death for a share of the American Dream. Still, most are not dissuaded. The promise of a safer and more plentiful tomorrow keeps them coming north. Writer-Director Cary Fukunaga tracks this perilous journey in vivid detail through the eyes of an unlikely teen duo in his visually captivating debut, *Sin Nombre*.

A festival darling, *Sin Nombre* is intriguing because it reads like a documentary thanks to transporting cinematography and minimalist, but focused directing. But stripped of its absorbing visuals, the skeleton of the film feels more like a by-the-books thriller. Casper (Édgar Flores) is a mid-level member of the super violent Mara Salvatrucha gang in a southern Mexico town. There he spends his days shirking his gangland responsibilities and instead meeting up with his wrong-side-of-the-tracks girlfriend. It is clear he is not cut out for the thug life. He's a gangster with a good heart and from the moment we meet him, it's easy to see that things will not go his way. Far away in Honduras, Sayra (Paulina Gaitan) is a rule-abiding teen who's being taken to the US by her estranged father to start fresh with his new, expanded family. Though they are worlds apart, Casper and Sayra meet atop a Texas-bound train where Casper and his fellow goons have come to rob Sayra and her fellow travelers. The former has a change of heart and finds himself on the lam from his gang brothers with a bounty on his head, the latter clings to Casper after he saves her life, putting herself in the path of the Mara Salvatrucha, who seem to possess a tangible evil that makes their very presence on screen daunting. As does the US-bound trains that Sarya and her family run to climb and perch upon. In addition to these ever-present dangers, there's a countdown that dominates the story: the Mara Salvaturcha moving ever closer on Casper's tail and Sarya's father pushing her on to the next leg of their travels. As Fukunaga juxtaposes the rail journey through Mexico with gang members tracking Casper, the result is a movie full of shootouts, chases, plotting and edge-of-your-seat action.

But despite these narrative cues, *Sin Nombre* transcends being type-cast as an action movie. Guns and gangs aside, the film forces audiences to ponder this particular immigrant experience in all its heart wrenching detail. Etching the turbulent ride firmly into the viewer's minds is Adriano Goldman's cinematography. Every aspect of Sayra and Casper's journey, from the mad scramble to get on the train, to the crowds on the train roofs dodging trees, overpasses and border patrols and from the locals who toss fruit to the riders giving them hope to those who lie in wait to pelt them with rocks, is rendered in rich, instant and enthralling detail. Fukunaga has the camera create a tangible immediacy with everyone and everything in its path—so much so that it feels like we are watching real lives unfold onscreen. Everyone from the scary, tattooed members of Casper's gang to Sarya's driven and guilt-ridden father are given a wide breadth and at times it feels like we are witnessing things we should not in the brutal gang initiations and desperation of the travelers. There are no film-school angles and layered mise-en-scenes here directing viewers to the film's intended effect, instead the camera is simply documenting the action as it unfolds. Fukunaga is confident in his story, his actors and his direction, relying on the emotion conveyed by Flores and

Gaitan and the accessible photography to draw audiences in. The naturalistic feel imbues every scene with purpose, so that the predictability of the thriller-esque narrative gives way to an effecting story of survival that's poignant without being pointed. Every time Sayra becomes discouraged her father pulls out a map of Mexico that dead-ends into Texas, with the United States demarcated by a quarter-inch of graying Texan land, and runs his finger across the intended path of the train. His gesture is supposed to be reassuring, seemingly compressing the journey into a digestible diagram while also keeping the focus on the path ahead, but instead it renders Mexico insurmountable and the US an empty, unknown void. It's these subtle, fleeting moments that stay with the viewer long after the credits roll, attesting to a directorial vision that is balanced and purposely understated and to a director worth noticing.

Joanna Topor MacKenzie

CREDITS

Sayra: Paulina Gaitan
Horacio: Gerardo Taracena
Willy/El Casper: Edgar Flores
Martha Marlene: Diane Garcia
Tia Tona: Catalina Lopez
Origin: Mexico, USA
Language: Spanish
Released: 2009
Production: Amy J. Kaufman, Creando Films; Creando Films, Canana Films, Primary Productions; released by Focus Features
Directed by: Cary Fukunaga
Written by: Cary Fukunaga
Cinematography by: Adriano Goldman
Music by: Marcelo Zarvos
Editing: Craig McKay
Art Direction: Carlos Benassini
Sound: Elma Bello
Costumes: Leticia Palacios
Production Design: Claudio Contreras
MPAA rating: R
Running time: 96 minutes

REVIEWS

Dargis, Manohla. *New York Times.* March 20, 2009.
Ebert, Roger. *Chicago Sun-Times.* April 2, 2009.
Gronvall, Andrea. *Chicago Reader.* April 3, 2009.
Howell, Peter. *Toronto Star.* April 3, 2009.
LaSalle, Mick. *San Francisco Chronicle.* March 20, 2009.
McCarthy, Todd. *Variety.* March 18, 2009.

Morgenstern, Joe. *Wall Street Journal.* March 19, 2009.

Pais, Matt. *Metromix.com.* March 19, 2009.

Sharkey, Betsy. *Los Angeles Times.* March 19, 2009.

Tallerico, Brian. *MovieRetriever.com.* April 3, 2009.

TRIVIA

Director Cary Fukunagra spent around two years researching the film. He spent time with train people and gang members in Central America to make the language as up to date and believable as possible.

AWARDS

Nomination:

Ind. Spirit 2010: Cinematog., Director (Fukunaga), Film.

A SINGLE MAN

Box Office: $8.6 million

Christopher Isherwood's semi-autobiographical novel of love and loss in Los Angeles forms the basis of *A Single Man,* American fashion designer and Gucci impresario Tom Ford's directorial debut. An exactingly constructed, mostly well-acted period piece drama about a broken man who, in the wake of his longtime companion's death, can scarcely see any sort of future on the horizon, this movie virtually defines the category of narrow-stream metropolitan appeal. This stems partially from its homosexual protagonist, certainly, but mostly from the fact that it is a fairly spare and ponderous work—an elegiac, triple-dipped bon-bon of melancholic despair, and the upward-angle view that ultimately only a spot on the bottom of the floor can provide.

A Single Man unfolds over the course of two days in 1962, set in the well-off portions of Hollywood, Santa Monica, Beverly Hills and the Westside, and hermetically sealed off from any of the social unrest or tension bubbling up elsewhere around the country. The film centers on George Falconer (Colin Firth), a 52-year-old, English-born college literature professor struggling to find meaning after the sudden death of his boyfriend of sixteen years, Jim (Matthew Goode), who is glimpsed in several flashback sequences. George is consoled, if often rather brusquely and at times downright offensively, by his closest friend and neighbor, Charley (Julianne Moore), a boozy, brassy Tanqueray depository irritated with the lack of her own romantic prospects, and wrestling with questions about her future.

Having quietly come to a decision to commit suicide, George heads to class, convinced to go about his day and settle some affairs before tidily shuffling off this mortal coil. His plans hit a speed bump, however, when a young student coming to terms with his own true nature, Kenny Potter (Nicholas Hoult), senses in George a kindred spirit, and makes it a point to reach out to him. Over a chat on a walk to the campus bookstore, then drinks at a local bar, and then back at the home he has shared for years with Jim, George weighs Kenny's advances, and ponders the future of his life in such a radically changed world.

In adapting Isherwood's beautifully descriptive novel (David Scearce also receives a screenplay credit, for penning a draft that the writer-director ultimately decided not to use), Ford jettisons the interior monologue-heavy style of the source text, instead inventing a variety of personal encounters for George throughout the day, as well as the plan to kill himself. While purists may decry them, such changes to the book are necessary and for the most part positive. If there is a problem, though, it is that these inclusions further highlight the movie's compressed timeline, which at times comes off as contrived.

Plenty of movies are deemed too "depressing" for general audiences in knee-jerk critical fashion, maybe because a character dies, or the nerdy writer does not get the girl, or an ending does not feature a song by Smashmouth. But *A Single Man* seems to further posit that isolation and loneliness are an inescapable and inherent part of the human condition, and perhaps even our default setting—a mildly provocative (and not especially comforting) notion. There is a reason why Harold Kushner's *When Bad Things Happen To Good People* is a perennial bestseller, and it is not because people want to be told that there is a grey cloud that comes with all of life's silver linings. People know bad things happen, and grief and depression intrude on lives, but the unblinking acceptance of a "new normal"—and that sixteen years with a lover who was such a perfect match was actually a great run, no matter how it ended—is a story many folks will just not have an interest in sitting through.

All of this—the weightiness of such a conclusion, and how George must be pushed in that direction not by more awful things befalling him, but rather the enticement of pleasure—points to what is certainly one of if not the single biggest problem with the film: namely, the performance of Hoult. A lanky, hollow-cheeked youngster heretofore best known as the kid opposite Hugh Grant in *About a Boy* (2002), Hoult has a pleasantly crooked smile and striking, pale blue eyes that could serve as miniature reflecting pools; with just a squint, he could easily pass as James Marsden's younger brother.

In *A Single Man*, though, Hoult communicates mainly in batted eyelashes, and seems a little too cutesy-pinup to pull off the necessary emotional maturity required in the series of increasingly suggestive flirtations with his teacher. The look is vaguely right—windswept bangs falling delicately across his forehead—but the confident, undemonstrative brazenness of someone who makes a play at an older partner does not credibly register. Ergo, Kenny comes across as an idealized angel ripped from the pages of some Calvin Klein ad and not someone that George would be interested in, particularly given what we see of his relationship with Jim. The film tries to mitigate this problem by having George hit on by another hunky young man, Carlos (Jon Kortajarena), outside a liquor store, thereby ratifying his piqued curiosity in Kenny. In reality, though, the single scene with Carlos—a smoldering sequence partly set in front of a billboard Alfred Hitchcock's *Psycho* (1960), in which even the purchase of beer is ripe with subtext—is much more interesting than the sum of George's interactions with Kenny.

Visually, *A Single Man* is a treat. Ford is aided by a talented behind-the-camera team, including production designer Dan Bishop, costume designer Arianne Phillips and director of photography Eduard Grau, who works in slightly saturated tones, and lets the film's color palettes occasionally pulse, sweat and darken, to match its libidinal waxing, and George's changes in mood. There is also a bit of corresponding fussiness in some of the admittedly gorgeous art direction, credited to Ian Phillips. Given his golden touch with respect to fashion and photography, it is not surprising that Ford excels at constructing frames that sometimes feel nipped from a coffee table tome or art gallery. Clean lines dominate the backdrops of settings, from the steel, glass and dark wood colors of George and Charley's modernist abodes to the angled pitch of George's university classroom, all subliminally communicating, in contrast, the shattered nature of George's world. A little of Ford's design and artistic instinct goes a long way, though. *A Single Man* at times feels fetishistic simply for the sake of being fetishistic; by the time the third symbolic underwater sequence comes along, it feels a bit much.

Most directly put, *A Single Man* is most worth seeing because of Firth. A longtime working actor who in the past decade has ridden roles in *Bridget Jones's Diary* (2001), its 2004 sequel, the musical *Mamma Mia!* (2008) and a whole string of literary adaptations, such as *The Importance of Being Earnest* (2002), into the rarefied territory of thinking woman's sex symbol, the 49-year-old Firth knows how to ease back on the throttle and simply let tremors of anguish and resignation play across his face. In his portrayal, Firth captures the ineffable sadness of a life lived outside the boundaries of public sanction. Part of this is foisted upon George by those not in his life (a relative who advises him not to attend Jim's funeral), but it is also ugly and up close, as when Charley gracelessly but quite apparently genuinely asserts that George did not have a "real relationship" with Jim.

When Firth delivers a superb, powerfully metaphorical lecture about how society fears what it is not, the universality and specificity within *A Single Man*'s portrait of grief collide. Momentarily trading in George's clipped tones and slightly hunched, defeated posture for one of strident disregard, an audience recognizes the battle fought again and again: to remain upright and honest to oneself, facing outward, ready to be seen.

Brent Simon

CREDITS

George Falconer: Colin Firth
Charley: Julianne Moore
Kenny: Nicholas Hoult
Jim: Matthew Goode
Carlos: Jon Kortajarena
Grant: Lee Pace
Alva: Paulette Lamori
Jennifer Strunk: Ryan Simpkins
Mrs. Strunk: Ginnifer Goodwin
Mr. Strunk: Paul Butler
Christopher Strunk: Aaron Sanders
Hank: Jon Hamm (Voice)
Origin: USA
Language: English
Released: 2009
Production: Tom Ford, Chris Weitz, Andrew Miano, Robert Salerno; Depth of Field, Artina Films; released by Weinstein Co.
Directed by: Tom Ford
Written by: Tom Ford, David Scearce
Cinematography by: Eduard Grau
Music by: Abel Korzeniowski
Sound: Lori Dovi
Music Supervisor: Julie Michaels
Editing: Joan Sobel
Art Direction: Ian Phillips
Costumes: Tom Ford, Arianne Phillips
Production Design: Dan Bishop
MPAA rating: R
Running time: 99 minutes

REVIEWS

Adams, Thelma. *Us Weekly.* December 9, 2009.
Ansen, David. *Newsweek.* December 4, 2009.

Berkshire, Geoff. *Metromix.com*. December 10, 2009.
Dargis, Manohla. *New York Times*. December 11, 2009.
Ebert, Roger. *Chicago Sun-Times*. December 24, 2009.
Felperin, Leslie. *Variety*. December 11, 2009.
Gleiberman, Owen. *Entertainment Weekly*. December 9, 2009.
LaSalle, Mick. *San Francisco Chronicle*. December 11, 2009.
Sharkey, Betsy. *Los Angeles Times*. December 11, 2009.
Travers, Peter. *Rolling Stone*. December 8, 2009.

QUOTES

George: "Looking in the mirror staring back at me isn't so much a face as the expression of a predicament."

TRIVIA

Jon Hamm (*Mad Men*) makes a brief voice cameo near the beginning of the film as Hank Ackerley.

AWARDS

British Acad. 2009: Actor (Firth)

Nomination:

Oscars 2009: Actor (Firth)
British Acad. 2009: Costume Des.
Golden Globes 2010: Actor—Drama (Firth), Support. Actress (Moore), Orig. Score
Ind. Spirit 2010: Actor (Firth), First Feature, First Screenplay
Screen Actors Guild 2009: Actor (Firth).

THE SOLOIST

Life has a mind of its own.
    —Movie tagline
No one changes anything by playing it safe.
    —Movie tagline

Box Office: $31.7 million

In *The Soloist*, veteran star Jamie Foxx takes on an entirely different sort of role. He plays Nathaniel Ayers, a homeless, emotionally disturbed classical music virtuoso: a genius lost in the detritus of downtown Los Angeles. Playing him as a sensitive, paranoid soul living precariously on the edge of sanity, Foxx is brilliant, letting the audience into his world little by little, in a guarded and suspicion fashion. His tormented inner self is on display often, since he is almost defenseless, but Foxx plays Ayers in a quiet, understated way, so that when he does muster his pride or rage, he is completely believable.

In this strange twist on a buddy film, based on a true story, Robert Downey Jr. is also believable as reporter Steve Lopez, but not nearly as likable. In fact,

for all the popularity of his columns, whose worldly morality is easily digestible, Lopez suffers from the common malady of idealistic journalists: He loves humanity in the abstract, but has trouble with individual people. He feels safer with cunning sentiments on paper than he does with the feelings beneath the words. He is glib and sharp in his writing, but clumsy in his relationships, as evidenced by his divorce from his wife (Catherine Keener), who also happens to be his managing editor and boss at work. As Foxx's Ayers struggles with sanity, Downey's Lopez is barely sane as well. To the eyes of the world he is a success, and that is the point of *The Soloist*—a point which becomes a bit too obvious.

Downey has played this sort of role before, a character adrift and searching for meaning. In fact, Lopez is not far from the enterprising, slightly askew reporter Downey played in *Zodiac*. In the hands of director Joe Wright (*Atonement* (2007)), this story becomes an existential encounter writ large. The central problem of the film is to explain how Nathaniel breaks through Downey's jaded perspective, how he becomes more than another good story, for Lopez is accustomed to using people and their heartbreaking tales opportunistically for his columns. Downey himself doesn't help much with this task. His Lopez seems to coexist on all planes simultaneously, detached from the shortcomings of his own life, distanced from his subjects and ultimately from himself by his habit of making every encounter into column material. Downey fails to convey what Nathaniel shows him that he has not been shown before.

Wright's answer is that Nathaniel's music is so sublime that it sends both the player and the listener into a transcendent, almost spiritual state. When Nathaniel plays the cello in a highway underpass, Wright's camera soars high above the concrete ditches of the city and soars with the birds—the music sets humanity free. When Nathaniel hears a symphony rehearsing, Joe fills the screen with pulsating colors that are supposed to represent Nathaniel's beyond-words experience of merging with the divine. Why Hollywood almost always feels that only classical music offers this pathway to Nirvana is a question best not asked.

Far from heavenly, Nathaniel's life has been hell. Obsessed with the music from an early age, he spends his time in solitude with his instrument. Attending Julliard, on his way to the top, he suddenly and inexplicably breaks down, hearing voices in his head that betray and frighten him. Foxx's haunted expressions are every bit as authentic as if he were witnessing an alien invasion—an invasion from the inside.

The Soloist raises tough questions about the tangled responsibilities of a storyteller who intervenes in the life of his subject to attempt to change it for the better.

Nathaniel is ultimately a meal ticket for Lopez, making the journalist's gifts not as selfless as they may seem. To the credit of screenwriter Susannah Grant, the question of journalistic exploitation is not dodged. But the same concerns apply to the movie itself. Wright used real homeless people in Los Angeles to lend his film a stunning realness and immediacy. The question of exploitation on a filmmaking must be asked because Wright's street scenes seem badly overwrought, filled with non-actors obviously acting out at their most outrageous.

In the end, Nathaniel's rage emerges, in a scene beautiful in his terror, and we are left unmoored. Everything after that in the film—the too-neat way in which the homeless man makes his own small progress in the world—pales after the scene in which the report gets his comeuppance. *The Soloist* is a cacophony of brilliant ambition, brutal missteps, and bizarre juxtapositions. Despite a storyline that, for all its originality, fits neatly with common Hollywood sentiments, it stretches for something more without quite reaching it.

Michael Betzold

CREDITS

Steve Lopez: Robert Downey Jr.
Nathaniel Ayers: Jamie Foxx
Curt: Stephen Root
Graham Claydon: Tom Holland
Jennifer Ayers: Lisa Gay Hamilton
Mary Weston: Catherine Keener
Flo Ayers: Lorraine Toussaint
Origin: USA
Language: English
Released: 2009
Production: Gary Foster, Russ Krasnoff; Dreamworks Pictures, StudioCanal, Working Title Films, Participant Media, Between Two Films; released by Paramount
Directed by: Joe Wright
Written by: Susannah Grant
Cinematography by: Seamus McGarvey
Music by: Dario Marianelli
Sound: Jose Antonio Garcia
Editing: Paul Tothill
Art Direction: Suzan Wexler
Costumes: Jacqueline Durran
Production Design: Sarah Greenwood
MPAA rating: PG-13
Running time: 105 minutes

REVIEWS

Dargis, Manohla. *New York Times.* April 24, 2009.
Denby, David. *New Yorker Magazine.* April 20, 2009.
Ebert, Roger. *Chicago Sun-Times.* April 23, 2009.
Edelstein, David. *New York Magazine.* April 20, 2009.
McCarthy, Todd. *Variety.* April 17, 2009.
Pais, Matt. *Metromix.com.* April 23, 2009.
Phillips, Michael. *Chicago Tribune.* April 24, 2009.
Puig, Claudia. *USA Today.* April 24, 2009.
Roeper, Richard. *RichardRoeper.com.* April 27, 2009.
Wilmington, Michael. *MovieCityNews.* April 24, 2009.

QUOTES

Steve Lopez: "I don't give a smooth fart whether or not we go."

TRIVIA

Many of the homeless people feature featured in the film are indeed homeless and not actors.

SORORITY ROW
(The House on Sorority Row)

Sisters for life...and death.
—Movie tagline
The sisters of Theta Pi are dying to keep a secret.
—Movie tagline

Box Office: $12 million

Horror films are cheap to cast, make and market, but they are also such consistently reliable moneymakers for Hollywood at least in part because their life-or-death stakes tap into the sense of heightened emotional investment that is a natural part of adolescence, where every friend's slight or romantically enigmatic text message matters so deeply. Teenage ticket buyers turn out to see on the big screen what are often idealized versions of themselves grappling with a more literalized form of death, feeling the metaphorical comparison, if not knowingly then at least on a subconscious level. And if their date squirms in their seat and gets a bit closer in the process, so be it.

It is no great surprise that genre do-overs of low-fi horror hits from the 1970s and 1980s have been a steady part of the recent Hollywood slate, from *My Bloody Valentine* (2009), *Prom Night* (2008), *The Hitcher* (2007) and *Black Christmas* (2006) to *When a Stranger Calls* (2006), *House of Wax* (2005), *The Texas Chainsaw Massacre* (2003) and of course Rob Zombie's two *Halloween* remakes (2007, 2009). Late to this game, and bringing nothing remotely of value or innovation to the trend, is the clamorous, desultory *Sorority Row*. An awful updating of Mark Rosman's *The House on Sorority Row* (1983), aka *Seven Sisters*, director Stewart Hendler's movie is a poorly scripted piece of claptrap that succeeds neither as an unnerving, gory suspense flick nor as a rib-nudging, "fun" horror romp.

The story centers around a quintet of college sorority friends—sensible Cassidy (Briana Evigan), drunkard "Chugs" (Margo Harshman), cautious Ellie (Rumer Willis), party-girl Claire (Jamie Chung) and bitchy queen bee Jessica (Leah Pipes). Believing that Chugs' brother Garrett (Matt O'Leary) has cheated on their friend and fellow housemate Megan (Audrina Patridge), the girls collude to play a prank and teach him a lesson by having Megan feign her death from a prescription pill overdose in the middle of making out with him. Positing that they have to cover up the "accident," the girls head to dump Megan's body in the obligatory nearby abandoned mineshaft, where, believing her to already be dead, Garrett plunges a tire iron into her. Their terrible mock scenario having now come true, the girls vote to cover up the death, and strong-arm Cassidy into taking part and remaining silent.

Flash forward a year. The most conflicted of her peers, Cassidy has tried to move on with her life, putting some distance between she and her sorority sisters, and settling into a seemingly stable relationship with new boyfriend Andy (Julian Morris). The other girls still live together in the house, with den mother Mrs. Crenshaw (Carrie Fisher), and to varying degrees still under the thumb of Jessica. Things take a turn, though, when the girls start receiving messages on their cell phones with incriminating video taken the night of Megan's death. Uncertain as to whether Megan somehow survived the incident and has returned to extract revenge, a guilt-stricken Garrett has snapped and is looking to kill off those he views as ultimately responsible, or someone else saw the event and is now attempting to blackmail them, the ladies are understandably freaked out. Nervousness turns to terror when they start getting picked off, one by one.

At the core of the problems with *Sorority Row* problems is its script, by Josh Stolberg and Pete Goldfinger. (Rosman also receives a writing credit, owing to his *Seven Sisters* screenplay.) There's a small bit of tension and surprise when the movie starts dispensing with some characters not involved in the scheme (a hapless young coed hiding in the sorority showers, not wanting to get on Jessica's bad side, meets her maker), but otherwise nothing about its conflict is particularly interesting or original. The skulking killer, clad in an oversized black rain slicker, so closely resembles the villain of *I Know What You Did Last Summer* (1997), except that he/she wields a tire iron instead of a hook, as to inspire derision. The manner in which the identity of

the killer is milked for attempted suspense additionally holds no intrigue.

Most damning, though, are the movie's wild shifts in tone. Much of the dialogue is delivered with angst-ridden panic or hardcore conviction, which makes lines like, "All I can see is my dad's face when he hears about this—it's going to kill him!" (delivered within moments of Megan's death) and "What happened to the tenets of sisterhood?" come across as unintentionally hilarious. Late-developing stabs at a more self-aware tone, placing the characters above the narrative fray, are starkly at odds with its attempts at eliciting scares.

Cinematographer Ken Seng delivers frenetic camerawork that Hendler and editor Elliot Greenberg then heavily process and chop up into dozens of intra-scene cuts. The stressed result is a clear attempt at manufacturing tension, but it does not work. Other attempts at air-quote modernization seem to include casual jokes at the expense of drug and alcohol abuse ("Roofie sex is the best—you get laid and get a good night's sleep!") and the inclusion of a character who sleeps with her psychiatrist for prescription pills.

Several of the performances are also especially embarrassing. Reality TV star Patridge displays the sort of mouth-agape inexperience one might expect, but her vacuity is mitigated by an early exit, and the fact that she's playing dead for much of her screen time. Other performers do not escape judgment so quickly. Willis is in over her head, conveying all jittery hysteria. Pipes' overly demonstrative cattiness is a weird non-match with the material, and at times makes her seem as if she is auditioning for a direct-to-video sequel to *Mean Girls* (2004).

A commercial washout almost immediately upon release in mid-September, *Sorority Row* opened to just over $5 million at 2,665 venues, en route to a paltry $11.7 million overall domestic gross—a rare instance of the marketplace rejecting a film well before it being poisoned by word-of-mouth. Even teenagers occasionally exercise good judgment, it seems.

Brent Simon

CREDITS

Cassidy: Briana Evigan
Ellie: Rumer Willis
Andy: Julian Morris
Jessica: Leah Pipes
Chugs: Margo Harshman
Claire: Jamie Chung
Megan: Audrina Patridge
Mrs. Crenshaw: Carrie Fisher

Origin: USA
Language: English
Released: 2009
Production: Mike Karz, Darrin Holender; Karz Entertainment; released by Summit Entertainment
Directed by: Stewart Hendler
Written by: Peter Goldfinger, Josh Stolberg, Mark Rosman
Cinematography by: Ken Seng
Music by: Lucian Piane
Sound: Anke Bakker
Music Supervisor: Julianne Jordan
Editing: Elliot Greenberg
Art Direction: Elise Viola
Costumes: Marian Toy
Production Design: Philip Toolin
MPAA rating: R
Running time: 101 minutes

REVIEWS

Edwards, Russell. *Variety.* September 9, 2009.
Holden, Stephen. *New York Times.* September 14, 2009.
Hunter, Allan. *Screen International.* September 9, 2009.
Hyden, Steven. *AV Club.* September 11, 2009.
Layne Wilson, Staci. *Horror.com.* September 11, 2009.
Moore, Roger. *Orlando Sentinel.* September 11, 2009.
Paras, Peter. *E! Online.* September 11, 2009.
Sobczynski, Peter. *EFilmCritic.* September 11, 2009.
Thomas, Kevin. *Los Angeles Times.* September 14, 2009.
Topel, Fred. *Can Magazine.* September 12, 2009.

QUOTES

Jessica: "You know Cassidy, your sarcasm makes you sound like a bitch. And nobody likes a bitch."

TRIVIA

The film was shipped to theaters using the name "Solidarity."

SOUL POWER

The greatest music festival that you have never seen.
—Movie tagline

An aurally engaging but somewhat intellectually halfhearted concert documentary that presupposes its audience agrees with the innate genius and watchability of its unvarnished footage, *Soul Power* is a gift to boomer-generation R&B fans, as well as a celebratory snapshot of an era in which artists and entertainers were if not radical agents of social change then at least more frequently and decidedly part of the outside world around them—a world experiencing and grappling with genuine upheavals in social justice and gender equality. Still, the fitful, fleeting nature of its emotional connection serves as a reminder that the choice of compelling subject matter alone does not necessarily make for a good nonfiction film offering.

In 1974, some of the most celebrated American R&B acts of the day came together with a collection of the most renowned musical groups in Africa for a three-day outdoor concert held in Kinshasa, Zaire. A longtime dream of South African bandleader Hugh Masekela and concert promoter and record producer Stewart Levine, the finally festival became a reality when they convinced boxing promoter Don King to try to combine the event with "The Rumble in the Jungle," the epic boxing match between Muhammad Ali and George Foreman, previously chronicled in the Academy Award®-winning documentary *When We Were Kings* (1997). It would eventually be cleaved from the fight itself, but the show, dubbed "Zaire '74," brought together musical luminaries such as James Brown, B.B. King, Bill Withers and Celia Cruz, among a host of others. At the peak of their talents and the height of their careers, these artists were inspired by a return to their African roots, as well as the enthusiasm of the Zairian audience, to give some of the best performances of their lives.

Soul Power is an experiential time capsule, depicting performances from the festival itself, but also all of the load-in and stage erection leading up to the event, which unfortunately means a decent clutch of material showcasing hippie construction workers in too-tight, rolled-up jean shorts. Still, this fact, as well as its collection of random moments—from The Spinners' Phillipé Wynne shadowboxing with Ali to writer George Plimpton briefly holding forth in drunken fashion at a party—lend the movie a sense of unfussy realism and authenticity. *Soul Power* is not a slick, overly polished promotional tract, in the vein of many modern-day concert films. And while there are big stars, equal spotlight is also given to some of the festival's lesser known acts, like Miriam Makeba, the Pembe Dance Troupe, The Crusaders and Cruz's colorfully-costumed backing band, the Fania All-Stars.

Despite all the intrigue attached to this glance back in time, however, there is the nagging feeling that the film is somehow less than the sum of its parts. It is not that *Soul Power* is without moments of amusement, power and exhilaration. There is a funny bit of loose-limbed material in which Ali swats at a nearby fly, and free associates about the differences between African flies and the fatter, complacent pests of his native America. And, naturally, several of the musical performances are stunning. Bill Withers' evocative, 2 a.m. performance of "Hope She'll Be Happier" is a thing of rare beauty, gripping in its stillness. Likewise, B.B. King's funky rendition of "The Thrill Is Gone," his fingers skipping wildly over his guitar's fretboard, is triumphantly illustrative of the manner in which music often effects and energizes its practitioners as much as an audience.

Still, the movie unfolds at a tremendous remove; it is like watching the rolling hills of a beautiful landscape through the window of a passing train. Debut director Jeffrey Levy-Hinte, who served as one of four editors on the aforementioned *When We Were Kings*, never finds a way to substantively connect the concert material to the outside world, nor the past to the present. Trading in great swatches of haphazardly framed compositions, he just presents a steady stream of what often feels like found footage.

Roughly the first half-hour of the movie deals with the concert's preparation, followed by an hour of performances seeded with backstage and off-day footage. Some of the sartorial sense on display—James Brown in a scoop-chested, bishop-sleeved unitard, for instance, with "GFOS" (for Godfather of Soul) emblazoned across the front—seems to delight native Zairians in the crowd, even as lines like "I don't know karate/But I know crazy!" fall flat. But apart from these cutaways to dancing audience members and one brief bit featuring a local reporter, there is no broader sense of how the festival is playing with native Africans. It would have been interesting for Levy-Hinte to return to Zaire, or just talk to some folks who were there.

Without imposing some sort of overarching voiceover narration or interwoven present-day reminiscences from either participating artists or concertgoers, though, *Soul Power* never achieves significant standalone form. Even for those familiar with the music of Brown, King and Withers, it feels like a couple standout music performances padded out with what would nowadays pass for deleted scenes included on a DVD.

Brent Simon

CREDITS

Himself: James Brown
Herself: Celia Cruz
Herself: Miriam Makeba
Himself: Don King
Himself: B.B. King
Himself: Muhammad Ali
Himself: George Plimpton
Origin: USA
Language: English
Released: 2008
Production: Jeff Levy-Hinte, Leon Gast, David Sonenberg; Antidote Film; released by Sony Pictures Classics

Directed by: Jeffrey Levy-Hinte
Cinematography by: Paul Goldsmith, Kevin Keating, Albert Maysles, Roderick Young
Sound: Tom Efinger
Editing: David Lewis Smith
MPAA rating: PG-13
Running time: 93 minutes

REVIEWS

Bradshaw, Peter. *Guardian.* July 10, 2009.
Gleiberman, Owen. *Entertainment Weekly.* July 9, 2009.
Hardy, Ernest. *Village Voice.* July 8, 2009.
Hornaday, Ann. *Washington Post.* August 14, 2009.
Morgenstern, Joe. *Wall Street Journal.* July 9, 2009.
Morris, Wesley. *Boston Globe.* July 16, 2009.
Phillips, Michael. *Chicago Tribune.* July 24, 2009.
Rabin, Nathan. *AV Club.* July 9, 2009.
Scott, A.O. *New York Times.* July 10, 2009.
Turan, Kenneth. *Los Angeles Times.* July 10, 2009.

SPREAD

It's a business doing pleasure.
—Movie tagline

The hooker with a heart of gold is more than just a cliché. It is a male fantasy. Guys can have all of the fun with little of the effort—perhaps no heavy relationship but also no heartbreak unless you are drinking yourself to death in Las Vegas. Naturally, this is a fantasy of the cinema. The cliché is the dogged assumption that men would be just as happy in their real lives to flip the script and make a living out of giving pleasure. As much as we can dream about the perfect situation, the key word that normally escapes us is "perfect." Perfect looks, perfect physique, the perfect rap and, of course, a willing partner looking for a little taste of perfect. The first rule is to move to Los Angeles. But, as movies have taught us, every rule states to never fall in love.

"I don't want to be arrogant here, but I'm a very attractive man." So says Nikki (Ashton Kutcher), a young hustler in the city of angels narrating pointers to his philosophy. It is a lifestyle by choice he claims he cannot help. It is also one that has left him homeless with just a cell phone and his charm to get him by. In need of a new temporary situation he spots a cougar attorney by the name of Samantha (Anne Heche). An introduction turns into a self-invitation, guarded flirtation turns to sex and, the next thing you know, Nikki has a spacious home to crash in while he makes an effort to fake all that boyfriend stuff—or "equity" as he calls it.

Once he has gathered enough points with cooking and orgasms, Nikki begins the quick fade into apathy.

Slickness turns to sloppiness as he gets caught throwing parties and enjoying football just a bit too much. His meal ticket would be in jeopardy if Samantha could just resist how this junior partner makes her feel. While out getting another meal, Nikki tries his charms on waitress Heather (Margarita Levieva) who is having none of it. Nothing if not persistent, the third time does turn out to be a charm and soon she is swimming fully-clothed in his pool—or Samantha's pool—and their relationship takes a turn. For someone so in tune with the ways of women, Nikki is not so quick on the uptake when he sees this supposed hash slinger in an $80,000 automobile. Do they have more in common than he knows?

Audiences quick to judge Nikki as a despicable human being preying on the intimate needs of women may choose to give up interest on whether he is capable of achieving happiness. This eventual turn of the plot from serial hustler to monogamist has worked in many films before, mostly in comedies where the light touch allows more forgiveness on our part. *Spread* is an immediately darker tale and for us to care about Nikki's redemption it has to be one of a becoming a better man rather than a search for a fairy tale ending. How does a man go from confident woman eater to a wounded puppy dog rushing to the airport with a ring in just a few beats? It is a question neither screenwriter Jason Dean Hall nor director David MacKenzie is able to answer.

MacKenzie is certainly interested in these types of anti-heroes. His filmography includes Ewan McGregor as a young drifter who allows sex to get him into trouble in *Young Adam* (2005) and Jamie Bell as a peeper with dead mommy issues in *Mister Foe* (2007). Those characters were true to their nature where Nikki seems to turn on a dime when he is tossed out of Samantha's luxury. Surely this is not the first time he has been dumped and the quick souring of his time with Heather hardly suggests a sensitivity lurking beneath the glossy persona he has created for himself. A sudden respect for how women are treated in strip clubs is a rather embarrassing reach for our empathy. The screenplay hints at Nikki and Heather being the pawns between the haves and the have-nots. Their marks, including hockey club owners and women who seek vaginal rejuvenation surgery, could have spun *Spread* into the class metaphor MacKenzie so desperately tries to pass off in the final image of a frog eating a mouse. Nikki maintaining the stomach for his chosen profession, despite his newfound reservations, would have been more honest than a lifetime of what Henry Hill would call, being "a shnook."

Spread is at its best during the first act, drawing us into the warped philosophy of its protagonist and chuckling at his success. The audience has a better shot at understanding Nikki if he does not change, allowing us to either be despised or fascinated by his constant con jobs. An opening moment of Nikki preparing for his night on the prowl as he glazes over in the mirror from a guy already disgusted with himself would have been beneficial into reexamining his search for ultimate stability. But that scene does not exist. A phone call to an absent mother does but it is just another "so what" moment in the second act of a life that is not interesting enough for the goose nor the gander.

Erik Childress

CREDITS

Nicki: Ashton Kutcher
Samantha: Anne Heche
Heather: Margarita Levieva
Harry: Sebastian Stan
Emily: Rachel Blanchard
Ingrid: Maria Conchita Alonso
Will: Hart Bochner
Origin: USA
Language: English
Released: 2009
Production: Jason Goldberg, Peter Morgan, Ashton Kutcher; Katalyst Films, Barbarian Films, Oceana Media Finance; released by Anchor Bay Films
Directed by: David Mackenzie
Written by: Jason Dean Hall
Cinematography by: Steven Poster
Music by: John Swihart
Sound: Coleman Metts
Music Supervisor: Elizabeth Miller
Editing: Nicholas Erasmus
Art Direction: Dins W.W. Danielsen
Costumes: Ruth E. Carter
Production Design: Cabot McMullen
MPAA rating: R
Running time: 97 minutes

REVIEWS

Anderson, Melissa. *Village Voice.* August 12, 2009.
Beardsworth, Liz. *Empire Magazine.* January 1, 2010.
Garrett, Stephen. *Time Out New York.* August 20, 2009.
Greenberg, James. *Hollywood Reporter.* August 13, 2009.
Gronvall, Andrea. *Chicago Reader.* August 20, 2009.
Holden, Stephen. *New York Times.* August 14, 2009.
Kelly, Christopher. *Dallas Morning News.* August 14, 2009.
Simon, Brent. *Shared Darkness.* August 22, 2009.
Travers, Peter. *Rolling Stone.* August 14, 2009.
Whipp, Glenn. *Los Angeles Times.* August 14, 2009.

STAR TREK

The future begins.
—Movie tagline

Box Office: $257.7 million

First of all, it needs to be stated that the writer is an unapologetic Trekkie (more of the original series, their film incarnations, and *Deep Space Nine* than the other offshoots). Any biased view of *Star Trek* is not intentional, but might be inevitable. However, as a devout fan of the original *Star Trek* crew and their cinematic adventures, I feel a bit like a traitor, but I have to come clean and admit that, after watching the new *Star Trek* (again and again and again and…), I'm finding it hard to convince myself that there was, in fact, any kind of *Star Trek* before the J.J. Abrams directed film. This reincarnation of *Star Trek* is so inventive, fun, and original that it is like experiencing the story and characters for the first time.

As the film begins in the year 2233, a Federation ship is attacked by a Romulan vessel commanded by Nero (Eric Bana) who is looking for Ambassador Spock (Leonard Nimoy). During the ensuing battle, the Federation ship is lost but not before a majority of the crew is evacuated; including a newborn named James Tiberius Kirk whose father, acting as captain, appropriately goes down with the doomed ship. From there, the film jumps forward a decade or so, providing glimpses of the young Kirk as a rebellious adolescent and then as an angry, directionless young man. Simultaneously, the story of a young half-human, half-Vulcan male named Spock is explored as he inappropriately shows emotion defending his human mother's honor and then choosing a life serving Starfleet over his Vulcan home world (again, due to a reluctance to allow an insult to his mother to go undefended).

When Spock and Kirk actually meet at Starfleet Academy, they do so under auspicious circumstances as Spock is bringing Kirk up on charges of academic misconduct. Kirk has cheated on a command test, the Kobayashi Maru (one of the many nods to the original series and films—fans will recall that the test was discussed at length in *Star Trek II: The Wrath of Khan* [1982]), designed by Spock. Of course the proceedings are put on hold when a distress call is received from Spock's home world of Vulcan.

It is soon revealed that Nero and his Romulan crew have attacked Vulcan and plan to destroy the planet. As it turns out, Ambassador Spock was attempting to save Romulus (the Romulans' home world) in the year 2387 when something went wrong and the planet was destroyed. The accident created a rift in time sending the elder Spock and the Romulans into the past. Nero plans on annihilating Vulcan and the Federation to exact revenge for the destruction of his planet and the death of his family. The classic Enterprise crew, now assembled through a series of fortunate events, must now stop Nero before he carries out his nefarious plans.

First and foremost, *Star Trek* is a flat-out excellent movie complete with crisp, sharp dialogue that propels a wonderfully written story that never muddles along just to get to the next action sequence. Director J.J. Abrams manages, as Owen Gleiberman puts it in *Entertainment Weekly*, to "rewire us back to the original *Star Trek*'s primal appeal." But, there's no way he could have managed this without the right actors assuming the roles of the crew of the Enterprise. The casting of the new crew may be the film's greatest achievement. The cast is superb. There's not one person who seems out of place or wrong for their part. While Chris Pine is wildly impressive assuming the iconic role of James T. Kirk and Zachary Quinto's Spock seems to be the role he was put on Earth to play, it is Karl Urban as Leonard McCoy who steals the show. Rounding out the familiar bridge crew (who are all given their own brief introductions) are Zoe Saldana as Uhura, John Cho as Sulu, Anton Yelchin as Chekov, and of course Simon Pegg as Scotty. All of these actors manage, as Liam Lacey correctly observes in the *Globe and Mail*, "to evoke the physical appearance and attitudes of familiar characters without suggesting impersonation" since they are allowed to "channel" the spirit and personality of each character instead of completely reinventing them. It's hard to imagine any Star Trek fan being upset with the cast unless they're just dead set on being opposed to the whole enterprise.

The central point of the film—the relationship between Spock and Kirk—is handled quite well from the very beginning. Abrams and his crew quickly establish (by following both of the characters' early lives) that the film is primarily about that relationship and how it affects (and is affected) by the universe around it. As Manohla Dargis observes in the *New York Times*, this friendship unfolds "in the tradition of many great romances [as] the two men take almost an instant dislike to each other, an antagonism that literalizes the Western divide between the mind (Spock) and body (Kirk) that gives the story emotional and dramatic force as well as some generous laughs." That dynamic is the core of *Star Trek*. The original series was always about the Spock/Kirk dynamic and not different locales, the Prime Directive, or any of that other nonsense (why else would they try to recreate it in every single incarnation, after all, weren't Data and Picard from the *Next Generation* playing at that same thing?).

The deceptively rich screenplay by writers Robert Orci and Alex Kurtzman succeeds in bringing to mind every iconic element from the Star Trek canon without completely halting the flow of the story to announce that they're giving a shout out. There's a minimal amount of reverence for the lore of Star Trek at work, but, there's no deconstruction of the Star Trek mythos either (something that could have been if the satire *Galaxy Quest* [1999] were produced as a *Star Trek* film). And that is something that deserves acknowledgement. After all, the original *Star Trek* spawned five television series (including an animated version) and ten feature films, and this film could have easily become as clichéd and stale as its predecessors. That being said, even the tried and true sci-fi constructs, such as time travel, are superbly utilized in *Star Trek*. As Ty Burr calls it in the *Boston Globe*, the aforementioned use of time travel in the film is "a genius move." Whereas in other films, such a plot device would turn into little more than a gimmick, in *Star Trek* it's a game changer that brilliantly launches a new era in Star Trek since, according to Burr, "it establishes the entire movie as an alternate, parallel 'Star Trek' universe in which [the filmmakers] can do as they wish."

Other technical aspects of *Star Trek* are similarly successful. The production design work by Scott Chambliss gives the Trek universe a new look and feel that, like the characters, is fresh yet at the same time very familiar. Daniel Mindel's cinematography does a splendid job of showcasing that design work (albeit with maybe a few more lens flares than were needed). Michael Giachhino's excellent score is effective throughout.

The film is less a prequel to the existing film series or a retooling of a somewhat dated concept than it is a full blown tear down and rebuild. And, believe it or not, that is a good thing. Everything about this film works and it may possibly be the best *Star Trek* film ever made (and yes, I realize to put any Star Trek film above *Wrath of Khan* could be considered blasphemy by many fans). But, let me say that *Wrath of Khan*, *The Voyage Home* [1986], *The Undiscovered Country* [1991], and even *First Contact* [1996] are the best offerings from the series, but the new film is far more of a cinematic experience than any of its predecessors. Not since *Wrath of Khan* has the property felt more cinematic and alive (especially during the fantastic space battles). Abrams's *Star Trek* is more than just a bigger, more elaborate television episode and does more than merely draw upon the formula the show perfected during its first two seasons. Abrams's film will appeal to everyone, regardless of their Trek heritage. The film succeeds because, as Ty Burr states, it trades "on af-fections sustained over 40 years of popular culture, *Star Trek* does what a franchise reboot rarely does. It reminds us why we loved these characters in the first place."

Some fans may complain that this isn't the *Star Trek* they remember (or are used to). They may also wonder where the "moral" lesson is. Or perhaps they will want to know why this movie isn't as jokey as the "whale" movie? Well, I would argue that that version of *Star Trek* was diluted and then run dry by one too many uninspired TV shows and movies to live long or prosper. Also, as Claudia Puig points out in *USA Today*: "There are no weighty scenarios or moral quandaries" here. *Star Trek* is, simply, a solid crowd-pleasing, action-adventure, sci-fi popcorn movie. That being said, as a reboot of a tired franchise, this film needed to quickly re-acquaint the audience with a significant number of characters and move the story along at an enjoyable, yet comprehensible pace, so perhaps, as Rober Ebert hopes in the *Chicago Sun-Times*, the next film "will engage these characters in a more challenging and devious story, one more about testing their personalities than re-establishing them." Ultimately, however, diehard fans may feel a bit of anger and a profound sense of loss when they realize that they can no longer claim proprietary rights to *Star Trek*. But, then again, that means a bold new world more tolerant of Trekkies (or Trekkers, depending on which camp you ultimately subscribe to) doesn't it? And that can't possibly be a bad thing.

Michael J. Tyrkus

CREDITS

James T. Kirk: Chris Pine
Spock: Zachary Quinto
Scotty: Simon Pegg
Leonard "Bones" McCoy: Karl Urban
Hikaru Sulu: John Cho
Uhuru: Zoe Saldana
Pavel Chekov: Anton Yelchin
Nero: Eric Bana
Amanda Grayson: Winona Ryder
Capt. Christopher Pike: Bruce Greenwood
Sarek: Ben Cross
Old Spock: Leonard Nimoy
Winona Kirk: Jennifer Morrison
Gaila: Rachel Nichols
Adm. Richard Barnett: Tyler Perry
Ayel: Clifton Collins Jr.
Capt. Robau: Faran Tahir
Keenser: Deep Roy
George Kirk: Chris Hemsworth
Stepdad: Greg Grunberg (Voice)

Starfleet computer: Majel Barrett (Voice)
Origin: USA
Language: English
Released: 2009
Production: J.J. Abrams, Damon Lindelof; Paramount Pictures, Spyglass Entertainment, Bad Robot, Mavrocine; released by Paramount Pictures
Directed by: J.J. Abrams
Written by: Roberto Orci, Alex Kurtzman
Cinematography by: Dan Mindel
Music by: Michael Giacchino
Editing: Maryann Brandon, Mary Jo Markey
Sound: Mark P. Stoeckinger
Costumes: Michael Kaplan
Production Design: Scott Chambliss
MPAA rating: PG-13
Running time: 127 minutes

REVIEWS

Bennett, Ray. *Hollywood Reporter.* April 20, 2009.
Burr, Ty. *Boston Globe.* May 5, 2009.
Dargis, Manohla. *New York Times.* May 8, 2009.
Ebert, Roger. *Chicago Sun-Times.* May 6, 2009.
Gleiberman, Owen. *Entertainment Weekly.* May 8, 2009.
Lacey, Liam. *Globe and Mail.* May 7, 2009.
Lane, Anthony. *New Yorker.* May 18, 2009.
McCarthy, Todd. *Variety.* April 22, 2009.
Puig, Claudia. *USA Today.* May 7, 2009.
Tallerico, Brian. *MovieRetriever.com.* May 7, 2009.

QUOTES

Scotty: ""I like this ship! You know, it's exciting!

TRIVIA

According to the audio commentary included with the DVD release of the film, J.J. Abrams had a meeting with George Lucas during which Abrams asked Lucas how he could make the film better, Lucas suggested adding lightsabers.

AWARDS

Oscars 2009: Makeup
Screen Actors Guild 2009: Stunt Ensemble
Nomination:
Oscars 2009: Sound, Sound FX Editing, Visual FX
British Acad. 2009: Sound, Visual FX
Writers Guild 2009: Adapt. Screenplay.

STATE OF PLAY

Find the truth.
—Movie tagline

Box Office: $37 million

Even though all that happens in the worthwhile, twisty thriller *State of Play* stems from the two sudden deaths in its opening scenes, the film is also about another, far slower demise that is both purposefully and rather wistfully acknowledged as the credits roll. The motion picture laments the gradual decline toward dissolution of daily print journalism, the time-honored, serious, careful, and in-depth relating of substantiated facts that has not quite passed as of yet but is considered by many to be passé. In recent years, more and more people have been getting their news with a mouse in their hand rather than with newsprint smudged upon their fingertips; instant (if oftentimes imperfect) gratification preferred over what is looked down upon as the journalistic equivalent of day-old, stale bread. A growing number of U.S. newspapers have folded when cutbacks did not quite cut it. That old, electrifying cry of "Stop the presses!" seems now to have a poignant ring of funereal finality to it.

State of Play is based upon the relentlessly-riveting 2003 BBC miniseries that had critics dropping any semblance of their British reserve in embracing it with accolades like "butt-clenchingly tense." The six-part television drama recalled the painstaking piecing-together of the dauntingly-complex, ever-expanding Watergate puzzle by the *Washington Post*'s Woodward and Bernstein in *All the President's Men* (1976). As in that film, smaller stories gradually coalesced into something much bigger as a newspaper's dogged, admirably-skilled reporters revealed conspiracy and corruption in the highest of places. As plans were formulated to ditch the English accents and ambience and transplant the basics of the acclaimed television production into American soil, the intimidating undertaking aimed to provide this feature film adaptation with its own identity and timely raison d'être.

In the wake of the disconcerting revelations concerning Blackwater mercenaries during the administration of George W. Bush, the story's all-too-surreptitiously-successful villain has been changed from the oil industry to a rapacious private security contractor hired by the U.S. Defense Department, accused of committing atrocities against Iraqi and Afghani civilians and poised to monopolize domestic security in a similar, frighteningly-unfettered manner. It is certainly a sobering, cautionary element for queasily-uneasy audiences to attempt to digest, and director Kevin Macdonald stressed in interviews that such ill-boding privatization is no Hollywood fabrication. The public—and the Republic itself—needs a Fourth Estate that is not only vigilant but highly proficient to keep tabs on such things, and this *State of Play* holds up the methodical, "fluff"-phobic, old-fashioned newspaperman to be revered and remembered as he is eclipsed, an endangered species being pushed into extinction by impetuously-blogging whippersnappers and an increasing taste for spicy tabloid fare. At what cost? "Give light and the people will find their own way," the E.W. Scripps newspaper motto has asserted for decades, and *State of Play* appears to want audiences to wonder what might befall the citizenry if things—or they themselves—become too dim.

Pondering the same thing is the film's venerable white knight of newspaperdom, who both figuratively and literally is actually more of an off-white knight. This version's Cal McAffrey (Russell Crowe) is the decidedly untidy ace reporter of the Washington Globe. He possesses lanky hair that looks long-unacquainted with shampoo, and a paunch below his untucked shirt that is added to with chili cheeseburgers, and snacks haphazardly, scarfing down food in his slovenly Saab. Cal works at a desk that can eventually be found under clutter rivaled only by what is contained in his majestically-messy apartment. Still, Cal's mind is incisive, his well-honed investigative skills deft. He is shown repeatedly knowing exactly who to contact in pressing an investigation forward, and seems to be on an affable, first-name basis with most.

One person with whom Cal has long been on a first name basis is his old college roommate and now U.S. Congressman Stephen Collins (Ben Affleck), but that did not stop *State of Play*'s flawed hero from at one point enjoying maximum familiarity with his longtime pal's wife, Anne (Robin Wright Penn). While Stephen, a lean, carefully-coiffed, formally-attired rising star, is in stark contrast to Cal, he is similarly presented as a noble but imperfect seeker of the truth. For while Stephen is valiantly uncovering the malignant and ominously-metastasizing power of PointCorp in public hearings, he has less admirably also been uncovering his lovely lead researcher, Sonia Baker, in private. When this mistress apparently commits suicide on the track of an onrushing subway car, Stephen's televised tears start tongues wagging unmercifully.

It may be hard for some viewers to accept Crowe and the decade-younger Affleck as men who were collegiate contemporaries. As the film progresses, one begins to theorize that perhaps Cal was simply still struggling to complete his journalism degree when Stephen matriculated due to an inability to grasp (or refusal to accept) the concept of conflict of interest. Once Cal's investigation into a seemingly-unrelated double shooting in a dark D.C. alleyway evidentially links up with the story colleague Della Frye (Rachel McAdams) is working on concerning the congressman's shameful canoodling causing Sonia's downfall, the seasoned reporter should have stepped aside. Cal's genuine sympathy for his grief-stricken friend, now under a character-assassinating,

tabloid-style attack (he endeavors to help Stephen draft a defense against the "bloodsuckers and the bloggers"), as well as concern for the man's welfare in light of what appears to be a case of outrageous and ruthless Point-Corp revenge ("They're gonna get you," Cal warns), certainly make this member of the press less than objective. Yet, Cal proceeds to the bitter end, and many will be incredulous that he never feels it necessary to ethically recuse himself so as to not pollute the Globe's investigation. Stephen also appears to find the situation puzzling, at one point asking, "Who am I talking to—my friend now, or am I talking to a reporter?"

While this problematic relationship between Cal and Stephen is what drove the BBC original (with Anne then also much more in the mix), the big-screen adaptation comes off as even more interested in its topical juxtaposition of Cal and Della. In focusing on how the old guard is being swept away by the new wave, Cal's formerly commensurate colleague has been updated into a bright-eyed, fleet-fingered young blogger who is initially assumed by both Cal and the audiences to be merely a lightweight gossipmonger. To heighten this contrast, the other reporters with whom they worked in the miniseries have almost completely been jettisoned from the proceedings. (Those who saw the television series will especially miss James McAvoy's Dan.) It is quite humorous to watch Cal look askance at Della as the film begins, the veteran slow crafter of hard news articles contemptuously and resentfully giving a cold shoulder to the neophyte who is gaining readers and garnering praise for, as he puts it, simply "upchucking online." However, after they are forced to work together in this ever-corkscrewing investigation, the two gradually find themselves complementing each other. It is interesting to note that it is Della who finally, exasperatedly, calls Cal out on his conflict of interest. Perhaps there is hope online, after all.

There are other elements here that are "ripped from today's headlines." (If hard-copy newspapers cease to exist, one wonders if that phrase will disappear along with it.) To save the Globe from going down the tubes, its new owners, like so many real ones, are purposefully veering toward sensationalism to make readership go up. As the paper's snappish, beleaguered editor Cameron Lynne (Helen Mirren) puts it, the paramount concern of the powers-that-be is "sales, not discretion." (Mirren is good, but the original's Bill Nighy was a truly fascinating creature, and, with his deadpan, droll delivery and monotone drone, a delightfully humorous one, as well.)

A telling shot in *State of Play* views Washington through crisscrossed power lines, a visual representation of the intriguing (but often troubling), intricate interconnectedness of Washington and how it operates, as well as the film's own web-like complexity. *State of Play* is thoughtful, intriguing, swiftly paced, and oh-so-densely plotted. It is also uniformly well-acted, including a particularly good turn by Jason Bateman as feeling-the-pinch PR man Dominic Foy. Especially suspenseful are the scenes of Sonia's murder and Cal's hallway and garage run-ins with Stephen's unhinged, murderous puppet, Robert Bingham (a thoroughly chilling, dead-eyed Michael Berresse). (The garage scene, along with Cal's late-night rendezvous with an insider informant, clearly pay homage to the Deep Throat of Alan J. Pakula's indelible classic.) Yet, despite many positive reviews, *State of Play* was only able to gross a less-than-hoped-for $37 million. Despite being crafted by three screenwriters with proven talent (Matthew Michael Carnahan, Tony Gilroy and Billy Ray), this condensed, less-textured adaptation does not play as well as it did in the wholly-absorbing British version. The final showdown here between Cal and Stephen, the latter revealed to have made choices that set murder in motion, is rat-a-tat-tat rushed. In the original, Cal and Stephen's climactic scene and its reverberations are potently powerful, not needing the arrival on-scene of a fully-fatigued and imposingly-armed batty Bingham.

At the very end of the BBC series, a weary Cal watches the culminating story being published, a profoundly trying experience finally ended. Considering the state of affairs taken heed of in this *State of Play*, the showing in its own coda of a newspaper's printing seems to speak of something else coming to an end, as well. The song chosen to accompany the sequence? Creedence Clearwater Revival's "Long as I Can See the Light."

David L. Boxerbaum

CREDITS

Cal McCaffrey: Russell Crowe
Stephen Collins: Ben Affleck
Della Frye: Rachel McAdams
Cameron Lynne: Helen Mirren
Dominic Foy: Jason Bateman
Anne Collins: Robin Wright Penn
Dr. Joy Jackson: Viola Davis
George Fergus: Jeff Daniels
Rhonda Silver: Katy Mixon
Origin: USA
Language: English
Released: 2009
Production: Tim Bevan, Eric Fellner, Andrew Hauptman; Andell Entertainment, Bevan-Fellner, Relativity Media, Studio Canal, Universal Pictures, Working Title Films; released by Universal Pictures
Directed by: Kevin MacDonald

Written by: Matthew Carnahan, Tony Gilroy, Billy Ray
Cinematography by: Rodrigo Prieto
Music by: Alex Heffes
Editing: Justine Wright
Sound: Skip Lievsay
Costumes: Jacqueline West
Production Design: Mark Friedberg
MPAA rating: PG-13
Running time: 127 minutes

REVIEWS

Childress, Erik. *EFilmCritic.com.* April 16, 2009.
Ebert, Roger. *Chicago Sun-Times.* April 16, 2009.
Edelstein, David. *New York Magazine.* April 13, 2009.
Hoberman, J. *Village Voice.* April 14, 2009.
McCarthy, Todd. *Variety.* April 14, 2009.
Pais, Matt. *Metromix.com.* April 16, 2009.
Rickey, Carrie. *Philadelphia Inquirer.* April 16, 2009.
Sarris, Andrew. *New York Observer.* April 15, 2009.
Sobczynski, Peter. *EFilmCritic.com.* April 16, 2009.
Tallerico, Brian. *MovieRetriever.com.* April 17, 2009.
Tobias, Scott. *AV Club.* April 16, 2009.

QUOTES

Detective Donald Bell: "Whatever you're sellin', I ain't buyin'."

TRIVIA

Brad Pitt and Edward Norton were originally to star in the film, which would have their first film together since *Fight Club.*

THE STEPFATHER

Daddy's home.
—Movie tagline

Box Office: $29 million

When the original *The Stepfather* came out in 1987, only the critics seemed to have noticed. At the time, domestic thrillers had not yet been as commonplace. Terry O'Quinn's performance in the titular role was appropriately heralded as uniquely scary and unsettling. Because of the lack of star power and the independent distributor's inability to promote the film beyond a short run at only a few select theaters, the movie had to find its audience on video where it eventually became a minor cult hit. Because of distribution rights, the movie had been on moratorium for over a decade, unable to surface on DVD until fall of 2009. So, what was the sense in a major studio producing a remake of what is largely a little-known niche film? Probably because nobody, save for a few true genre followers, would notice.

Over the past decade, horror fans have had to endure their most cherished films being turned into mostly sub-par and unnecessary remakes, so it may have only been a matter of time before the studios would get around to a relatively obscure film like *The Stepfather*. The original storyline certainly has all the making of a can't-miss concept that could work if mainstream audiences could better find it this time around. But would there be anything new to say with it?

The original film came at a time when 1950s nostalgia was commonplace and *The Cosby Show*, a series about what appeared to be a perfect family, was the #1 show in Reagan-era America. *The Stepfather* told the tale of a man who wanted that *Father Knows Best* type dynamic so much so that he would—and did—kill for it. When his image of the perfect nuclear family crumbles, he murders everyone in the house, changes his identity and moves onto the next single parent household. Even when the slightest crack in the otherwise perfect frame begins to appear, it sets him off on a psychotic rant, which he wisely keeps to himself in the basement of the house, his own private hell.

The remake serves no sociological purpose in 2009 America, except that the storyline cannot seem to exist without the aid of a cell phone, which is fast becoming the most over-used plot device in modern film. The storyline remains the same. When we first see David Harris (Dylan Walsh), it is Christmas morning and he has just finished murdering everyone in the house. He shaves off his beard while soft, angelic holiday music plays in the background. He leaves unassumingly and drives off to find his next perfect family in need of a father figure. Strangely enough, this re-telling makes the odd choice of introducing the audience to detectives on his trail, only to never allude to their existence ever again (the original spent a lot of time with a previous victim's brother hot on the lead's trail). Just as well, since this version of the movie feels long enough as it is without them adding to it.

Peter meets Susan Harding (Sela Ward) and two of her kids in a supermarket, where he pretends to be a widowed man whose wife and kids just died in a car accident. A title card reads "6 months later" and Peter has already moved in with the Hardings, much to the resentment of teenage son Michael (Penn Badgley), who has just returned home from military school.

Suspicions begin to pile up around Peter, mostly with Michael and the original father of the family, Jay (Jon Tenney), whose presence almost screams "Murder victim with a cell phone!" Michael and his dad's fractured relationship begins to mend when they share

their suspicions about Peter with one another. They form a bit of an alliance, but soon thereafter Peter murders the dad and takes his cell phone in order to keep up appearances that he is still alive and communicating with Michael via text message. Michael shares his suspicions with his girlfriend Kelly (Amber Heard), a character who probably feels the same way about wearing pants as she does senselessly murdering kittens. She serves no purpose to this film except to walk around scantily clad and denouncing all of her boyfriend's instincts.

Everything in *The Stepfather* remake seems to exist as a synergistic marketing scheme. The largely uninspired cast of TV actors works from a flimsily constructed screenplay with no personality whatsoever. Every face in this crowd is so perfectly chiseled and lifeless, it seems they could have been better put to use in a sequel to the remake of *The Stepford Wives*. The PG-13 rating—an all-too-common and reviled trend amongst horror enthusiasts—is meant to soften the violence so that younger viewers are allowed to pay admission and, perhaps afterwards, buy the soundtrack featuring overused music by all of their favorite third-rate "alternative" bands.

While the original *Stepfather* itself is cursed with a horrendously dated 1980s synth score, it manages to rise above its flaws even today. If the film had been a hit, its potent statement about repression and the façade of the perfectly all-American, Reagan-era family might have a slight cultural impact not unlike Adrian Lyne's far more popular 1987 domestic thriller, *Fatal Attraction*. The only impact the remake can seem to have is that maybe its poor box office numbers would signal an end to pointless remakes of horror films, an idea that should have been killed off long before it took hold of so many victims.

Collin Souter

CREDITS

David Harris: Dylan Walsh
Susan Harding: Sela Ward
Michael Harding: Penn Badgley
Kelly Porter: Amber Heard
Jay: Jon Tenney
Leah: Sherry Stringfield
Dylan Bennet: Jason Wiles
Origin: USA
Language: English
Released: 2009
Production: Greg Mooradian, Mark Morgan; Granada, Sony Pictures Entertainment; released by Screen Gems

Directed by: Nelson McCormick
Written by: J.S. Cardone
Cinematography by: Patrick Cady
Music by: Charlie Clouser
Sound: Steve Morrow
Music Supervisor: Michael Friedman
Editing: Eric L. Beason
Art Direction: Timothy Eckel
Costumes: Lyn Elizabeth Paolo
Production Design: Steven Jordan
MPAA rating: PG-13
Running time: 101 minutes

REVIEWS

Anderson, John. *Variety.* October 18, 2009.
Berkshire, Geoff. *Metromix.com.* October 16, 2009.
Burr, Ty. *Boston Globe.* October 18, 2009.
Doerksen, Cliff. *Chicago Reader.* October 18, 2009.
Holden, Stephen. *New York Times.* October 18, 2009.
Rocchi, James. *Redbox.* October 17, 2009.
Schager, Nick. *Slant Magazine.* October 16, 2009.
Sobczynski, Peter. *EFilmCritic.com.* October 16, 2009.
Thomas, Kevin. *Los Angeles Times.* October 18, 2009.
Weinberg, Scott. *FEARNet.* October 16, 2009.

QUOTES

David Harris: "Who am I here?"

TRIVIA

Terry O'Quinn, the star of the original film, was offered a role in the remake but turned it down.

THE STONING OF SORAYA M.

When a deadly conspiracy became a shameful cover-up.
—Movie tagline

Adapted from Freidoune Sahebjam's 1994 nonfiction bestseller of the same name, *The Stoning of Soraya M.* is an intellectually stimulating and generally well-acted—if also a bit slow, didactic and self-righteous—drama which shines a light on the disheartening gender inequity ingrained within Shariah law. In an era in which the gulf between Middle Eastern socio-cultural practices and Western understanding of said principled legal differences is frequently in the news, this Iranian set, internationally produced film has a certain informational benefit apart from its melodramatically-inflected art-house appeal.

When his car breaks down and leaves him stranded in the remote Iranian village of Kupayeh, journalist Freidoune (Jim Caviezel) happens upon Zahra (Oscar® nominee Shohreh Aghdashloo), an ostracized local woman who sees in him an opportunity to get out a remarkable story to the world at large. While he is waiting for his automobile to be repaired, Zahra tells Freidoune a harrowing and recent tale about her niece Soraya (Mozhan Marnò), a spirited but kindhearted mother of two whose abusive husband Ali (Navid Negahban) connived to condemn her to a terrible fate.

Wanting to rid himself of Soraya and wed a 14-year-old, Ali schemes with the village's mullah (Ali Pourtash), himself a former criminal and con man, to falsely accuse Soraya of infidelity. At first the lies seem to be designed to merely force Soraya's hand into granting him a divorce, but they eventually emerge as part of a broader, hard-line campaign of banishment and marginalization, which include a refusal to pay any child support, and turning Soraya's own children against her. The ultimate price for female infidelity is death by stoning, which Ali could waive, but instead pushes for; the only village figure of some repute standing in the way is Ebrahim (David Diaan), with whom Zahra tries to reason, and leverage a past friendship. The film flashes forward and back in time, interweaving Zahra's recounting of this story to Freidoune with Ali, the mullah and others trying to suppress the story from getting out of the village and into the world at large.

Director Cyrus Nowrasteh, a Colorado native whose past writing and directing credits include telepics *The Day Reagan Was Shot* (2001) and the controversial *The Path to 9/11* (2006), has an obvious interest in and talent for assaying the complex intersections of culture and politics. This fact, combined with his Iranian descent, generally helps give the film a rooted sense of place, of unfolding in a foreign land with its own legitimate, discrete set of customs and mores. The only hiccup in this regard comes when Ali, trying to incite public support for his claims of his wife's infidelity, stands in the village square and shouts, "I have no dignity left," which seems a perplexing and slightly dubious way to flog personal debasement and shame.

If the sociocultural backdrop is convincing—abetted by Joel Ransom's dusty, unfussy cinematography—it is too bad, then, that Nowrasteh paints in such broad theatrical strokes. One gets the impression that he mainly senses this story's drama is tied up in a simple, clanging juxtaposition of contrasting extremes. While not entirely untrue, this tack often just pits two-dimensional characters against one another in any given scene, with Soraya coming across as saintly and virtuous, Zahra as honorably crusading, and Ali almost cartoonishly vile. Ebrahim—not coincidentally the most interesting figure, trying to seek out compromise in a situation where there is no mutually beneficial middle ground—is essentially a stand-in for Western audiences. Adapting Sahebjam's bestseller with his wife Betsy Giffen, Nowrasteh also evinces overall a rather wooden ear for dialogue.

If they are thinly drawn, some of the performances still connect. Most memorable is Marnò, who exudes a plaintive soulfulness. Meanwhile, Negahban is effectively loathsome as Ali, though part of his unpleasantness surely lies in the physicality of his character—wiry, furrowed brows, offset by a meticulously groomed beard, that make him seem cultured, and thus slightly somehow more sinister.

At just under two hours, the film drags and dawdles considerably, with handfuls of scenes offering no greater character shading or nuance—just repetitions of the same basic arguments from each character. Part of this is somewhat effective at creating tension as to whether Ali's despicable schemes will work, but when one considers the film's actual title much of that tautness dissipates. Insofar as it pushes and pulls recognizable emotional levers, the film more or less works. A less fervent depiction of mob-mentality histrionics, though, and more of a personal embodiment of the collective public responsibility and right with respect to private business would give *The Stoning of Soraya M.* a lasting emotional impact that eludes it. As is, unfortunately, a deeper sense of how and/or why Ali's claims hold sociological sway just is not conveyed. These are perhaps sins of filmmaking omission more than commission—a matter of choice in focus, and screen time apportioned—but they represent a problem in relatability nonetheless.

Brent Simon

CREDITS

Zahra: Shohreh Aghdashloo
Freidoune Sahebjam: Jim Caviezel
Soraya M.: Mozhan Marno
Ali: Navid Negahban
Bita: Vida Ghahremani
Ebrahim: David Diaan
Mullah: Ali Pourtash
Hashem: Parviz Sayyad
Origin: USA
Language: English, Farsi
Released: 2008
Production: Stephen McEveety, John Shepherd; Mpower Pictures; released by Roadside Attractions
Directed by: Cyrus Nowrasteh
Written by: Cyrus Nowrasteh, Betsy Giffen Nowrasteh

Cinematography by: Joel Ransom
Music by: John Debney
Sound: Dennis L. Baxter
Editing: Geoffrey Rowland, David Handman
Costumes: Jane Anderson
Production Design: Judy Rhee
MPAA rating: R
Running time: 114 minutes

REVIEWS

Ebert, Roger. *Chicago Sun-Times.* June 25, 2009.
Holden, Stephen. *New York Times.* June 26, 2009.
Morris, Wesley. *Boston Globe.* June 25, 2009.
Rizov, Vadim. *Village Voice.* June 24, 2009.
Rodriguez, Rene. *Miami Herald.* July 10, 2009.
Schager, Nick. *Slant Magazine.* June 22, 2009.
Sobczynski, Peter. *eFilmCritic.com.* June 25, 2009.
Thomas, Kevin. *Los Angeles Times.* July 1, 2009.
Tobias, Scott. *AV Club.* June 25, 2009.
Uhlich, Keith. *Time Out New York.* June 25, 2009.

QUOTES

Ebrahim: "When a man accuses his wife, she must prove her innocence. That is the law. On the other hand, if a wife accuses her husband, she must prove his guilt. Do you understand?"
Zahra: "Yes, it's clear, all women are guilty, and all men are innocent. Correct."

STREET FIGHTER: THE LEGEND OF CHUN-LI

Some fight for power. Some fight for us.
—Movie tagline

Box Office: $8.7 million

Martial arts films can often get away with being thin on plot and short on brains. The driving force behind most films in the genre tends to be the main actor, whose incomparably fast moves can make even the most deadening screenplay come alive. If Jackie Chan had used some kind of Zen Buddhist tolerance exercise to ward off the hulking thugs in *Rumble in the Bronx* (1995), it never would have become a breakthrough crossover hit. The problem with this proven formula, though, comes when the marketplace gets flooded with so many cheap knock-offs and sequels to cheap knock-offs that it gets hard to tell one film from the other. The only question that remains is: will it be a male or female martial arts star?

In the case of the cheap knock-off sequel *Street Fighter: The Legend of Chun-Li*, the answer is female. In this case the actress in question, Kristin Kreuk, is not so much a martial arts star as she is a regular on the hit TV show *Smallville*. While she is certainly able to coast by on screen presence, she does not quite have the necessary background in the field to signal the next Michelle Yeoh or even Zhang Ziyi. Before the opening credits have rolled, *Street Fighter: The Legend of Chun Li* has two strikes against it: A stale storyline and a weak casting choice for an action star to carry it.

Street Fighter: The Legend of Chun Li is the semi-sequel to the completely forgettable 1995 Jean Claude Van Damme vehicle, *Street Fighter*, both of which are based on the once popular video game. This in-name-only sequel is its own movie, separate from the original, with only a few reoccurring names to stay consistent with the game in order to appease the fans. In spite of the ever increasing popularity of video games, their movie versions, by and large, have not enjoyed a successful track record at the box office over the past ten years or so. The very existence of a new *Street Fighter* movie remains all the more baffling.

The title indicates that we will be told the tale of a "legend." Unfortunately, Justin Marks' screenplay makes the mistake of having the character of Chun-Li narrate the story, thereby negating her "legendary" status. In the film, her father gets kidnapped by the sinister Bison (Neal McDonough, utilizing whichever accent he feels like using that day), leaving her to be raised only by her mother. When Chun-Li gets older and becomes a classically trained pianist, she starts receiving vague messages in the form of reoccurring spider web tattoos and a mysterious scroll.

These messages eventually lead her to the gritty streets of Bangkok, where Bison is setting up his latest real estate scheme via the ominous Shadaloo Corporation. Bison has kept Chun-Li's father alive throughout the years to help with these devious tasks and shows him pictures of the current Chun-Li as a way of keeping him alive to do his bidding. Bison typically has anyone who disagrees with him killed without giving it a second thought while traveling with his hulking henchman Balrog (Michael Clarke Duncan). While Bison busies himself with being evil, Chun-Li reluctantly gets schooled in the ways of Thailand style martial arts by Gen (Robert Shou), an all-seeing, all-knowing master of the arts who, of course, has been watching her for a long time and who mistakes fortune cookie truisms for complexity and depth.

Lurking on the sidelines of the storyline are Nash (Chris Klein) and Maya (Moon Bloodgood), two American homicide detectives who naturally have instant love/hate chemistry as they get paired up to track down Bison. Nash has made it his mission in life to take Bison

and the Shadaloo Corporation down, but as he laughably puts it, "Bison walks through raindrops." Eventually, Chun-Li begins her own search, which leads her through an array of incompetent henchmen and henchwomen, all of whom give her the information she needs before she cripples or beats them to death. In between these incidents, Gen teaches her the art of fireball making, a storytelling device that exists simply to appease the fans of the video game.

All of this would be completely forgettable were it not for the over-the-top performance by Chris Klein. As an arrogant and determined homicide detective, Klein adds as many exclamation points at the end of every line delivery as he possibly can. Whether he's staring off into space to deliver a soliloquy about the dangers of Bison or trying to put a lesser detective in his/her place by shouting down at them, Klein's hilariously spastic performance borders on parody, even though there is nothing in either his or director Andrzej Bartkowiak's career to suggest they have the instincts to willingly make that kind of artistic choice. The rest of the film is incredibly self-serious by comparison and Klein might be, too. Much like Nicolas Cage's hammy performance in 2006's *The Wicker Man*, Klein's Nash might turn this otherwise dreary exercise into a cult classic. Only time will tell.

Collin Souter

CREDITS

Chun Li: Kristin Kreuk
Balrog: Michael Clarke Duncan
Bison: Neal McDonough
Maya: Moon Bloodgood
Nash: Chris Klein
Gen: Robin Shou
Cantana: Josie Ho
Vega: Taboo
Origin: Canada, India, USA, Japan
Language: English
Released: 2009
Production: Ashok Amritraj, Patrick Aiello; Hyde Park Entertainment, Capcom; released by 20th Century Fox
Directed by: Andrzej Bartkowiak
Written by: Justin Marks
Cinematography by: Geoff Boyle
Music by: Stephen Endelman
Sound: Paul Clark
Music Supervisor: Michelle Silverman
Editing: Derek G. Brechin, Niven Howie
Costumes: Amanda Friedland
Production Design: Michael Z. Hanan

REVIEWS

Adams, Sam. *Los Angeles Times*. March 5, 2009.
Catsoulis, Jeanette. *New York Times*. March 2, 2009.

Hardy, Michael. *Boston Globe.* March 2, 2009.
Humanick, Rob. *Slant Magazine.* March 2, 2009.
McCarthy, Kevin. *CBS Radio.* February 27, 2009.
Nelson, Rob. *Variety.* March 2, 2009.
Pais, Matt. *Metromix.com.* February 27, 2009.
Rabin, Nathan. *AV Club.* March 2, 2009.
Scheck, Frank. *Hollywood Reporter.* March 2, 2009.
Sobczynski, Peter. *eFilmCritic.com.* February 27, 2009.

QUOTES

Charlie Nash: "This guy walks through the raindrops."

TRIVIA

Chun-Li translates to Spring-Beauty in Chinese.

SUGAR

Box Office: $1.1 million

Sugar, the new film from writer-directors Anna Boden and Ryan Fleck, who helmed the critically acclaimed *Half Nelson,* promises to be a standard sports story. There is the promising athlete from a poor family, Dominican pitcher Miguel "Sugar" Santos (Algenis Perez Soto), who has confidence, talent, and an ambitious dream of making it big in the major league. There is his meteoric rise from the island to spring training in Arizona to a big league farm team. Everything is in place for a cliché-ridden tale about the importance of believing in yourself and how sports is a metaphor for life. But *Sugar* rejects that road, taking its own brave path to something that may be less audience-pleasing, but more realistic.

In fact, *Sugar* is so observant that it could pass for a documentary. Boden and Fleck delve closely into the quiet conflicts in the character of Santos, showing how, in the real world, desire and confidence are not enough. This is one sports story that refuses to succumb to the standard clichéd plot line.

In the first segment, we meet Sugar as he toils in a baseball development camp for the fictionalized major league team the Kansas City Knights. With his fellow Dominicans, he labors to impress his bosses. There's a sense that the Dominicans are laboring on a sort of plantation, hoping to get free from the slavery of their impoverished lives.

On the weekends, Sugar returns to town, and we meet his mother, sister, girlfriend, and buddies. Little kids greet him and ask for baseballs. The film does not spare anything in depicting the poverty all around him. He longs for an escape, and with it a ticket to a modestly better life for his family.

In one of the film's many telling scenes, after Sugar gets an invitation to spring training, there's a celebration at which many of the townsfolk claim to be a relative or friend of his. They are all hoping to hitch a ride on the gravy train. He is taking the well-worn path, the only way out of the ghetto, that others have taken—but though the Dominican Republic has provided many baseball stars to the major leagues, still relatively few make it.

Sugar follows its protagonist to spring training in Arizona and then to a Kansas City minor league affiliate in Iowa (it is a thinly fictionalized version of the Davenport team). There he stays with an elderly farm couple who hosts their team's rookies every year and is not shy about sharing their sharp opinions about what each one of the players does wrong. Sugar suffers from language problems and cultural chasms and has trouble taking the lumps of misfortune on the diamond.

As a pitcher, Sugar is the center of attention, but he has trouble handling the pressure. Surrounded by unfamiliar people and difficult situations, he grapples with his immaturity and with the setbacks that come with playing baseball. His pride trips him up, and he feels rejected and increasingly alone.

Sugar is a movie filled with small moments. The customary overblown drama of sports sagas is here replaced by observant scenes. Even the dialogue is minimal and restrained. The baseball action is credible. But even more credible are the circumstances and situations that cause Sugar to gradually let go of his dream. Eschewing melodrama and big scenes, Boden and Fleck have made a movie so soft and sensitive that it may easily be overlooked. It's understated and beautifully crafted, though, and instead of sports being used as a metaphor for life, it's simply a vehicle to tell a coming-of-age story that goes in unexpected directions.

If anything, *Sugar* may err on the side of being two low-key. Certainly for most audiences who expect to be pummeled into submission, *Sugar* will be much too quiet and inconclusive. But Soto is an appealing young actor, and he's surrounded by a competent supporting cast. If the movie seems unsure about where it's going, it's because its protagonist is too. Life is not playing out for him according to a set script. It's full of unexpected twists. And when his dreams fail to exactly come true, they find new substance. Boden and Fleck do not provide the satisfaction of a neatly wrapped morality tale, and there may not be the vicarious pleasure of rooting for a larger-than-life sports star. What we discover, though, is that Sugar is a lot like the rest of us. And we are spurred to think a little more deeply about the other side of the coin of the athletic success story—those who don't make it big.

Michael Betzold

CREDITS

Miguel "Sugar" Santos: Algenis Perez Soto
Jorge Ramirez: Rayniel Rufino
Johnson: Andre Holland
Helen Higgins: Ann Whitney
Anne Higgins: Ellary Porterfield
Osvaldo: Jamie Tirelli
Stu Sutton: Michael Gaston
Earl Higgins: Richard Bull
Origin: USA
Language: English
Released: 2009
Production: Paul S. Mezey, Jamie Patricof, Jeremy Kipp
     Walker; Journeyman Pictures, Hunting Lane Films,
     Gowanus Projections, HBO Films, Single A Films; released
     by Sony Pictures Classics
Directed by: Anna Boden, Ryan Fleck
Written by: Anna Boden, Ryan Fleck
Cinematography by: Andrij Parekh
Music by: Michael Brook
Sound: Tom Efinger
Editing: Anna Boden
Costumes: Erin Benach
Production Design: Elizabeth Mickle
MPAA rating: R
Running time: 120 minutes

REVIEWS

Berkshire, Geoff. *Metromix,com.* April 2, 2009.
Ebert, Roger. *Chicago Sun-Times.* April 16, 2009.
Greenberg, James. *Hollywood Reporter.* January 25, 2008.
Hornaday, Ann. *Washington Post.* April 30, 2009.
McCarthy, Todd. *Variety.* January 24, 2008.
Scott, A.O. *New York Times.* April 2, 2009.
Sobczynski, Peter. *eFilmCritic.* April 16, 2009.
Sragow, Michael. *Baltimore Sun.* May 15, 2009.
Tallerico, Brian. *MovieRetriever.com.* April 17, 2009.
Turan, Kenneth. *Los Angeles Times.* April 2, 2009.

QUOTES

Earl Higgins: "No drinking. No cervezas in the casa. No chicas
     in the bedroom."

TRIVIA

After filming completed, the name of the Iowa team was
     changed from the Quad City Swing to the Quad City River
     Bandits (their original name).

SUMMER HOURS
(L'heure d'été)

Box Office: $1.7 million

Written and directed by Olivier Assayas, French import *Summer Hours* is a modest but perceptive cinematic treatise on mortality, and both the preceding anxiousness and ensuing swirl of conflicted emotions that any substantive discussion of death with a parent brings for adult children. An encapsulation of its plot-point particulars, either in aggregate or scene-to-scene, risks sounding like a dreadful bore, but *Summer Hours* locates the unlikely magic of the quotidian, and in doing so speaks quiet, universal truths about generational gaps in perception that have always existed and will exist forevermore.

The story centers on three far-flung siblings who come together with their respective families and significant others for a summer vacation back in France, and then must reconvene the following year to cope with the death of their mother Hélène (Edith Scob), who was herself the caretaker of a great batch of artwork and the broader legacy of her uncle Paul Berthier, a renowned painter. Singleton Adrienne (Juliette Binoche) lives in New York and works for a Japanese department store, designing various lines of accessories. Jérémie (Jérémie Renier) works for a large sneaker company, who has sent him to China and tapped him part of their important emerging market team. Economist/author Frédéric (Charles Berling) is the sole sibling who still lives in France.

It is largely for this reason that Hélène pulls Frédéric aside. In warm, clear-eyed fashion, and with a practical grasp of fissures that might develop which even her son cannot yet comprehend, she talks about her wishes for what should happen after her death. She wants to put on record her wishes concerning only a few select objects, but in a private moment after all her family has left, she confides to her housekeeper that she feels surrounded by "memories, secrets and stories that interest no one else." Cut to the following spring, after Hélène's peaceful passing. With her country house no longer required as a "home base" for gatherings, Hélène's children must decide whether the cost of upkeep is worthwhile. And are the various antiquities, some quite valuable, best served by auction, sustained ancestral holding or a donation to the Musée d'Orsay?

There is not a great deal of angsty teeth-gnashing or other actor-ly chewing of scenery in what could in lesser hands be easily reconfigured as a melodrama with much familial recrimination. Neither are there rapacious character motivations, rendered in broad strokes. Everything in *Summer Hours* is pitched at a fairly mild level of conflict and engagement. Jérémie needs money to finance the growth of his young family abroad, but presents his case for selling off the house and two valuable paintings tabbed as part of the collective inheritance simply and without acrimony, saying he will submit

SUNSHINE CLEANING

Life's a messy business.
—Movie tagline

Box Office: $12.1 million

Like the smash hit indie *Little Miss Sunshine* (2006), *Sunshine Cleaning* share a key word in the title, was produced by the same folks at Big Beach films, was set and shot in Albuquerque, features a dysfunctional family thrown together in difficult circumstances, has a large part for a precocious child, and includes in its cast a lovably gruff grandfather played by Alan Arkin. The moral lessons of both films are pretty much alike too, but then they are shared with many other movies: Believe in yourself, live your dream no matter what, and embrace the ones around you, even when they annoy you.

One other thing unites the two films: remarkable ensemble casts playing memorable, quirky, largely likable characters. Audiences can identify with the members of these families because they are familiar characters to anyone who has ever been in a family. In both films, there is no one miscast, and everyone, even the actor in the smallest part, gives an effective performance.

Sunshine Cleaning stands completely on its own though, with its own director (Christine Jeffs) and writer (Megan Holley), and above all its two stars, Amy Adams and Emily Blunt. Both these actresses are on similar points in their career paths, having accumulated many noteworthy roles in a few recent years. The strength of their performances here elevates the material into something special.

The plot is one of those serviceably simple ones, almost formulaic, but with enough quirkiness to appeal to a jaded generation of movie audiences. It's a story about two sisters—Rose (Adams), the older, responsible one, and Norah (Blunt), the younger, rebellious screwup. Rose was the most popular girl in high school, but now she's struggling to make it on her own while raising a son who is a brilliant misfit in school. Worse yet, she is in a forlorn love affair with a married police officer (Steve Zahn). From him she conceives the idea of opening a cleaning service that specializes in messy death scenes. She recruits her sister to join her, and wacky complications ensue.

One of the many appealing things about *Sunshine Cleaning* in a time of economic recession is that its characters are identifiably ordinary folks struggling to make ends meet. The obstacles they face are familiar, everyday ones—how to pay the bills and keep the kids in school. The plot simmers at a low heat of constant frustration. There are no Hollywood-style miracles, but simply a lot of complicated relationships.

The minor characters are intriguing too: the lesbian woman (Mary Lynn Rajskub) whom Norah pursues because she found a photo album of her mother at the mother's death scene, the cleaning supply store owner (Clifton Collins Jr.) who befriends Rose and her son and makes model planes despite having only one arm, and Arkin as Joe, the man with a thousand business schemes that always fall short of success. Even the little scenes are memorable and sometimes profound, as when Rose returns to a wedding shower with her high school friends and tries to defend the dignity of her life against the onslaught of her peers' more successful endeavors.

Gradually, the film circles into deeper, darker territory as we learn more about the tragedy that assaulted this family long ago, the loss that the sisters and their father share, and how their encounters with dying people reawaken painful memories and force a confrontation with the unspoken past. Even if the metaphors of the film are too painfully obvious—the "sunshine cleaning" being a way for the sisters to clean up the mess their mother left behind, Joe's inability to make anything work an obvious allusion to his marital failure—the movie wins with heart, guts, and authenticity. At the end, it veers dangerously close to the edge of mawkish sentimentality, with a cringing scene in which Rose "talks to God" over a CB radio, and yet, even that is saved by Adams' performance.

The two lead addresses redeem everything, making their characters throb with genuine emotion, transcending what could have been stereotypical family archetypes. Blunt is brilliant in her refusal to have Norah submerge completely into black sheep's clothing. Adams continues to show her tremendous range in both comedy and drama, bringing pathos to her complex role as the "other woman," the put-upon big sister, and the caring-if-frustrated mother. Even the predictable ending avoids feeling forced. Both Blunt and Adams are too good; they leave the edges of their characters ragged. Not everything is solved: the battle against ordinary life's troubles will continue. In another way that is much like *Little Miss Sunshine*, the triumph of this family feels like a heartening cry of independence—us against the world.

Michael Betzold

CREDITS

Rose Norkowski: Amy Adams
Norah Norkowski: Emily Blunt
Joe Norkowski: Alan Arkin
Oscar Norkowski: Jason Spevack
Mac: Steve Zahn
Lynn: Mary Lynn Rajskub
Winston: Clifton Collins Jr.

Randy: Eric Christian Olsen
Carl: Kevin Chapman
Origin: USA
Language: English
Released: 2009
Production: Peter Saraf, Marc Turtletaub, Glenn Williamson, Jeb Brody; Big Beach; released by Overture Films
Directed by: Christine Jeffs
Written by: Megan Holly
Cinematography by: John Toon
Music by: Michael Penn
Sound: Lori Dori
Music Supervisor: Sue Jacobs
Editing: Heather Person
Art Direction: Guy Barnes
Costumes: Alix Friedberg
Production Design: Joseph T. Garrity
MPAA rating: R
Running time: 102 minutes

REVIEWS

Ebert, Roger. *Chicago Sun-Times.* March 19, 2009.
Howell, Peter. *Toronto Star.* March 27, 2009.
Pais, Matt. *Metromix.com.* March 12, 2009.
Phillips, Michael. *Chicago Tribune.* March 19, 2009.
Puig, Claudia. *USA Today.* March 12, 2009.
Phillips, Michael. *Chicago Tribune.* March 19, 2009.
Rickey, Carrie. *Philadelphia Inquirer.* March 19, 2009.
Schwarzbaum, Lisa. *Entertainment Weekly.* March 11, 2009.
Scott, A.O. *New York Times.* March 13, 2009.
Tallerico, Brian. *HollywoodChicago.com.* March 20, 2009.

QUOTES

Rose Lorkowski: "There's not a lot that I am good at. But I'm good at getting guys to want me. Not date me, or marry me, but want me."

TRIVIA

During parts of the first and second seasons of *The Office* Amy Adams played Jim Halpert's (John Krasinski) girlfriend. In real life, Emily Blunt is Krasinski's girlfriend.

SURROGATES

How do you save humanity when the only thing that's real is you?
—Movie tagline

Box Office: $39 million

Movies featuring robots tend to focus on man's hubris and fear of the other or of technology in general.

Surrogates is different in that, while man's hubris is on definite display, the fear is of himself, not of his robotic counterpart. Part action film, part science fiction and part human drama, *Surrogates* never quite decides which it is and fails as a pastiche. Nonetheless, there are any number of arresting moments and images here which make it interesting viewing for fans of any of the above.

Tom Greer (Bruce Willis) is an FBI agent who lives in a future where the vast majority of people use surrogate others, robots made to their specifications, to experience life without risk. Hailed as a utilitarian boon, surrogates are smarter, stronger, better-looking, and allow the user to feel more intensely. The end result has drastically reduced real human contact and thus also reduced crime, prejudice, and other societal ills. But, ironically, as people become more and more dependent on the enhanced experiences surrogates provide they grow less able to deal with real life, staying hooked up to their unit virtually round the clock pausing only to perform absolutely necessary functions.

When Greer is called on to investigate a murder, an increasingly rare occurrence, he must contend with a growing number of opposing factions; the corporation which makes the surrogates, the religious cult which hates what they've done to society, the exiled corporation leader mourning the death of his son, and the renegade vandal whose own shadowy motives have him utilizing top secret technology to destroy surrogates around the city. When Greer's own surrogate is disabled he finds himself wandering an alien landscape, a human among shadows, wondering who he can trust.

If it all sounds a little messy, it is. *Surrogates* distills some wonderful images and top-notch action from the stellar graphic novel by author Robert Venditti and illustrator Brett Weldele. But somehow, as a whole, it falls flat, failing to convey the brokenness of the society it criticizes and failing to rise above the police procedural genre the source material riffs on so well. One has the sense this could make for dynamic television if only because viewers would have more time to experience the world through both sets of eyes, human and surrogate. But in the context of the feature film, director Jonathan Mostow (*Breakdown* [1997], *U-571* [2000], *Terminator 3: Rise of the Machines* [2003]) creates his most effective moments in the world of the surrogates, offering up the alienation and isolation of the real human race in a series of fairly pat and unimaginative moments. This is surprising given the generally strong sense of human drama his previous films have shown. Indeed there are elements in the screenplay by the writing team of Michael Ferris and John D. Brancato (*The Net* [1995], *Primeval* [2007], *Terminator: Salvation* [2009]) that give the performers room to move emotionally. But somehow the human dilemma here feels like an afterthought.

Credit is due for a neatly handled view of the future in which people can choose what they'll look like and even what gender they'll be. Greer's "surrie" (in the parlance of the film) is exactly the sort of smooth skinned, hilariously hair-doed hunkie version of himself one expects a man going through middle-aged crisis to come up with. A sly choice, this nonetheless belies *Surrogates* sprawling nature and is for the most part the only real improvement on the original graphic treatment.

Bruce Willis (*Sin City* [2005], *Grindhouse* [2007], *Live Free or Die Hard* [2007]) is solid as both Tom Greer and his surrogate but his presence here feels like casting leftovers; as if someone noting the need for a portrayal that would be both tough and sensitive thought it would be retro to get the man from *Die Hard* (1988).

Other standouts include Radha Mitchell (*Pitch Black* [2000], *Man on Fire* [2004], *Silent Hill* [2006]) as Agent Peters and James Cromwell (*The Green Mile* [1999], *I, Robot* [2004], *W.* [2008]) as exiled surrogate corporate executive Canter. But even here the film betrays a half-baked sensibility. Mitchell is virtually typecast as a second tier, albeit competent, performer at this point in her career and James Cromwell has likewise become heavily identified with this sort of troubled genius role.

In speaking of his good friend H.G. Wells, G.K. Chesterton once intimated that the great writers main fault was that he could imagine utopia but could never tell the reader quite how to get there. *Surrogates* imagines a dystopia and yet positively reverberates with our collective desire to have a surrogate anyway- cost be damned. We eagerly seek how to get there knowing the devil is in the details. The problem isn't *tech* or *mech*. The problem is that rather than fill our inner yearning with something real and pure we constantly want to build a better shell, or to use a metaphor Chesterton would have appreciated, clean the outside of the cup while leaving the inside caked with what weighs us down, takes off the shine that our new shell seems to promise. What *Surrogates* misses is the fact that while there is no surrogate for some things the problem isn't just that they get lost in our search for pleasure but that, like surrogates themselves, things like human contact and real love, become pointless. When we lose what makes us human, what can offer transcendence, we become the surrogates.

Dave Canfield

CREDITS

Tom Greer: Bruce Willis
Peters: Radha Mitchell
Maggie: Rosamund Pike

Stone: Boris Kodjoe
Canter: James Francis Ginty
Older Canter: James Cromwell
The Prophet: Ving Rhames
Strickland: Jack Noseworthy
Col. Brendon: Michael Cudlitz
Bobby: Devin Ratray
JJ the Blonde: Helena Mattsson
Armando: Jeffrey De Serrano
Origin: USA
Language: English
Released: 2009
Production: David Hoberman, Todd Lieberman, Max Handelman; Touchstone Pictures, Mandeville Films, Top Shelf Productions, Road Rebel, Wintergreen Productions; released by Walt Disney Studios
Directed by: Jonathan Mostow
Written by: Michael Ferris, John Brancato
Cinematography by: Oliver Wood
Music by: Richard Marvin
Editing: Kevin Stitt, Barry Zetlin
Art Direction: Tom Reta, Dan Webster
Sound: Jon Johnson
Costumes: April Ferry
Production Design: Jeff Mann
MPAA rating: PG-13
Running time: 88 minutes

REVIEWS

Abele, Robert. *Los Angeles Times.* September 25, 2009.
Berkshire, Geoff. *Metromix.com.* September 24, 2009.
Dargis, Manohla. *New York Times.* September 25, 2009.
Ebert, Roger. *Chicago Sun-Times.* September 27, 2009.
Hiltbrand, David. *Philadelphia Inquirer.* September 27, 2009.
Honeycutt, Kirk. *Hollywood Reporter.* September 24, 2009.
Howell, Peter. *Toronto Star.* September 25, 2009.
Jones, J.R. *Chicago Reader.* September 27, 2009.
McCarthy, Todd. *Variety.* September 24, 2009.
Tallerico, Brian. *MovieRetriever.com.* September 25, 2009.

QUOTES

Tom Greer: "Honey, I don't know what you are. I mean, for all I know, you could be some big, fat dude sitting in his stim chair with his dick hanging out."

TRIVIA

A close up shot of Strickland's FBI file shows his place of birth as Lynn, Massachusetts. Lynn is also the real life birth place of actor Jack Noseworthy, the actor who plays Strickland in the film.

SURVEILLANCE

Some suspense thrillers are interesting primarily because of the puzzle they present or the intense feelings they generate for the viewer. Some of Hitchcock's lesser films like *Rope* (1948) or *Dial M For Murder* (1954) could be described as utterly genre efforts, epitomizing a mythical universe where we feel safe even as we watch the most heinous acts being committed right before our eyes. Such universes make up a large bulk of what modern audiences think of as classic Hollywood suspense. One or two quick adrenaline rushes and the viewer exits the theater having been given a roller coaster ride that like almost all roller coaster rides glides safely back into the station so the next group can get on.

Of course, as Hitchcock entered the later stage of his career he also made nasty little suspense films like *Psycho* (1960), *Marnie* (1964) and *Frenzy* (1972) that were anything but safe. Those movies are not about harmless thrills and chills but about the horrid seamy nature of humanity that drenches the mundane just under the surface. That nice neighbor might not be nice at all. He might be a psychotic transvestite, a leering, baby-talking deviant, or, in the case of the characters in Jennifer Chambers Lynch's film *Surveillance*, chaos embodied.

Surveillance is, by turns, merely interesting, pandering, cliched, and breathtaking. It is not likely to be easily forgotten and this may be a far more useful piece of information for the potential viewer than whether or not it is in any conventional sense a "good" film. It is certainly a forceful one and will make itself felt most firmly and finally in the question it poses through the eyes of its young protagonist. "How do I survive this?"

FBI Agents are called in to investigate a series of murders in the Santa Fe desert which have left local law enforcement baffled. Three witnesses: Officer Jack Bennet (Kent Harper), a young drug addict named Bobbi Prescott (Pell James), and eight-year-old Stephanie (Ryan Simpkins) all have different stories to tell about the murder of Stephanie's family. It quickly becomes clear to their interrogators, Elizabeth Anderson (Julia Ormond) and Sam Hallaway (Bill Pullman), that everyone has an agenda other than merely getting at the truth. Through a series of flashbacks, prompted by the stories the witnesses tell, the truth about everyone begins to emerge but only those with eyes to see and ears to hear know what that truth is or what to do with it. And the biggest truth of all is that some things are just beyond knowing or controlling. Any further plot description would be largely synoptic and risk doing poorly what *Surveillance* does so well.

This is Jennifer Chambers Lynch's first film since the disastrous *Boxing Helena* (1993). That rocky start, in addition to a car accident and struggle with alcoholism and drug addiction, has prevented her from exploring a unique creative voice and she clearly missed being in the director's chair. This film has her deftly dissecting the suspense thriller by gradually revealing that sometimes the least interesting thing is who did it and how. To be sure the film indulges in caricature when a better narrative might have explored the same ideas through well-developed characters. The audience does not really learn much about any of these people. They are rather simply drawn types of characters from film and television. *Surveillance*, in this sense, is less resonant as a suspense thriller than it is as a series of observations of chaotic human pathology reflecting back to the viewer cultural ideas of serial killers, corrupt small town law enforcement, and the ultimate film cliché, the innocent victim.

Bill Pullman (*The Serpent and the Rainbow* [1988], *Zero Effect* [1998]) and Julia Ormond (*Legends of the Fall* [1994], *Smilla's Sense of Snow* [1997], *Inland Empire* [2006]) create an astonishing tension throughout. There is something clearly off in the relationship between the two FBI Agents. From their arrival, it is clear that, at the very least, they are lovers or merely closer than two FBI Agents should be. Pell James (*The King* [2005], *Zodiac* [2007]) also carries the part of female junkie forcefully, especially near the end of the film when she must navigate the psychotic emotional terrain of her captors.

Surveillance wears its own interest in cinema on its sleeve. But Lynch mines this material well, creating haunting POV, using the landscape as a both a symbol of freedom and entrapment, and showcasing that even cartoonishly rendered corrupt cops, drug addicts, innocent little girls, and over-the-top psychos can be shadows of a larger sense of good and evil in the real world. Within the contrast between the light and the darkness, the illusion of complete chaos and perfect order is a startling revelation about humanity caught in the midst of forces that it can neither control nor escape.

Dave Canfield

CREDITS

Elizabeth Anderson: Julia Ormond
Sam Hallaway: Bill Pullman
Bobbi Prescott: Pell James
Stephanie: Ryan Simpkins
Mom: Cheri Oteri
Dad: Hugh Dillon
Capt. Billings: Michael Ironside
Jim Conrad: French Stewart
Degrasso: Gill Gayle
Jack Bennett: Kent Harper
Origin: USA, Germany
Language: English

Released: 2008

Production: Kent Harper, Marco Mehiltz, David Michaels; Lago Film, See Film, Film Star Pictures; released by Magnet Releasing

Directed by: Jennifer Chambers Lynch

Written by: Kent Harper, Jennifer Chambers Lynch

Cinematography by: Peter Wunstorf

Music by: Todd Bryanton

Editing: Daryl k. Davis

Production Design: Sara McCudden

Sound: Rob Bryanton

Costumes: Sonja Clifton Remple

MPAA rating: R

Running time: 97 minutes

REVIEWS

Anderson, Melissa. *Village Voice.* May 12, 2009.

Berkshire, Geoff. *Metromix.com.* May 29, 2009.

Crook, Simon. *Empire Magazine.* March 6, 2009.

Dargis, Manohla. *New York Times.* June 26, 2009.

Felperin, Leslie. *Variety.* April 23, 2009.

Rea, Steven. *Philadelphia Inquirer.* April 2, 2009.

Robey, Tim. *Daily Telegraph.* March 6, 2009.

Simon, Brent. *Shared Darkness.* July 3, 2009.

Smith, Kyle. *New York Post.* June 26, 2009.

Tallerico, Brian. *MovieRetriever.com.* June 26, 2009.

QUOTES

Samm Hallaway: "You fired into your partner, and you opened him up like a can of soda! Pop! PING!"

TRIVIA

According to director Jennifer Chambers Lynch, the original subject matter of the film was witches.

T

TAKEN

They took his daughter. He'll take their lives.
—Movie tagline

His daughter was taken. He has 96 hours to get her back.
—Movie tagline

Box Office: $145 million

When *Taken*, the latest action film production from the seemingly inexhaustible Luc Besson (perhaps the only filmmaker who could make Roger Corman in his heyday seem lazy by comparison), made its debut in American cinemas last winter, most observers speculated that it would only last a week or two in theaters before disappearing without making much of an impact on the box office. After all, it had already played throughout the rest of the world (and could easily be found for downloading on the internet as a result), the only real name in the cast was Liam Neeson, an actor who hardly came across as the action hero type, and it was opening on Super Bowl weekend, a period when its largely male target audience would presumably be glued to the upcoming gridiron goings-on. And yet, to the astonishment of many, *Taken* had a huge opening weekend at the box office and then went on to become one of the surprise hits of the season. Once the shock wore off, people began to analyze its success in order to explain how it wound up doing so well. In retrospect, it is easy to see why it struck such a chord with audiences. Unlike most contemporary action blockbusters, which have become little more than extended product reels for the various CGI effects houses, this film actually delivers the goods and what it lacks in dramatic innovation, it more

than makes up for in energy, inspiration and sheer excitement.

Neeson stars as Bryan Mills, a seemingly ordinary guy who has just retired from his international job in order to reestablish ties with 17-year-old daughter Kim (Maggie Grace). At that moment, however, she is planning to go to Europe with a friend for the summer and while Bryan is initially against it, he finally relents agrees to give his permission provided that they follow his various safety rules to the letter. Of course, they do not and, within an hour of touching down in Paris, the two are kidnapped by Albanian gangsters as part of an international white slavery ring. Because Kim is on the phone with him when the snatch goes down, Bryan not only gets to hear the crime for himself but also gets to inform the lead kidnapper that it would be in his best interest to simply let her go right then and there, an offer that the guy sneeringly ignores. What he fails to realize, however, is that Bryan's old international job found him working for the C.I.A. as a "preventer"—the person who goes in and stops problems and problem causers, by any means necessary, before they can become problems. With the aid of a couple of former cohorts and the information gleaned from the phone call, he is able to figure out who is responsible and that he has about 96 hours to rescue Kim before she disappears forever. Naturally, he jumps on the first plane to Paris and the rest of the film shows him methodically working his way up the sleazy chain of command—low-level criminals, corrupt government officials, sleazy businessmen and the sleazier billionaires eager to purchase nubile flesh to satisfy their depravations—by employing throat punches, creative gunplay and outright torture to get the information he needs in order to save his daughter and the day.

Taken is not exactly the most blindingly original story ever filmed—even a cursory look at its narrative DNA will conjure up elements from *The Searchers* (1956), *Taxi Driver* (1976), *Hardcore* (1978), and at least half of the films that Charles Bronson made in the wake of *Death Wish* (1974)—and the dash of borderline xenophobia on display is a bit distracting, especially when you consider that the film was made by Europeans. In the hands of most action hacks, this could have resulted in a derivative and unpleasant piece of exploitation junk but Luc Besson and director Pierre Morel— who previously collaborated on the deliriously entertaining *Escape from New York* (1981) homage *District B-13* (2006)—have infused the material with enough style and energy to keep it from that sorry fate. Eschewing the wild comic-strip nuttiness, weirdo humor and gravity-defying stunts that defined their previous collaboration (possibly because the subject of white slavery does not as easily lend itself to oddball jokiness), Besson and Morel have instead taken a more serious and straightforward approach that is more suitable to the material. The action scenes are staged and executed in such a way that they seem almost plausible (even the climactic shipboard face-off is a little more low-key than expected) and while there are moments of humor on display throughout, it is of a decidedly darker nature than usual (such as when Bryan praises Paris's electric grid for its consistency before zapping a bad guy with thousands of volts to get him to talk) and is usually deployed to punctuate the action instead of subverting it, as is usually the case in a Besson film.

The other key asset that *Taken* has going for it is the central performance from Neeson, who has appeared in more than his share of action-oriented films over the years including *Excalibur* (1981), *Darkman* (1990), *Rob Roy* (1994), *Star Wars, Episode I: The Phantom Menace* (1999), *Gangs of New York* (2002), *Kingdom of Heaven* (2005), *Batman Begins* (2005) and the immortal *Krull* (1983). That said, he still does not have the looks of a traditional action star along the lines of The Rock or Jason Statham. In the case of this film, that is most definitely an asset. For one thing, the fact that he seems like an ordinary guy instead of a muscle-bound superhero helps give the story a little more plausibility. More importantly, he manages to pull off the same neat trick that Matt Damon does in the Jason Bourne films by shifting from schnook to killing machine with such precise skill and grace that we actually believe that it is him decimating the hordes of bad guys coming after him. And since he is a consummate actor, he is even able to take lines of dialogue that might have come across as silly in the hands of lesser actors and make

them work sensationally well—his brief speech over the phone to his daughter's kidnapper is destined to go down alongside Dirty Harry's "Do you feel lucky, punk?" as one of the great monologues in the history of the action genre.

Taken has a couple of minor flaws—the character of Bryan's ex-wife (Famke Janssen) is so crudely overdone as to strain credulity, though not as much as the sight of 25-year-old Maggie Grace trying unsuccessfully to pass herself off as 17, and the climactic fight may strike some as being almost too low-key after witnessing the spectacular set pieces that have preceded it. That said, the film has so much going for it, including the highest number of "you-gotta-see-this!" moments since *The Dark Knight* (2008) that most viewers will not even notice such things until much later, if at all. Simply put, *Taken* is a blast and even those who not disposed to the action genre are likely to find it to be one of the most ruthlessly efficient and purely entertaining films of its type to come along in a while.

Peter Sobczynski

CREDITS

Bryan: Liam Neeson
Kim: Maggie Grace
Lenore: Famke Janssen
Stuart: Xander Berkeley
Amanda: Katie Cassidy
Jean Claude: Olivier Rabourdin
Sam: Leland Orser
Casey: Jon Gries
Patrice St. Clair: Gerard Watkins
Marko: Arben Bajraktaraj
Origin: France
Language: English
Released: 2008
Production: Luc Besson, Pierre-Ange Le Pogam, India Osborne; Europacorp, M6 Films, Grive Prods.; released by 20th Century Fox
Directed by: Pierre Morel
Written by: Luc Besson, Robert Mark Kamen
Cinematography by: Michel Abramowicz
Music by: Nathaniel Mechaly
Sound: Alexandre Widmer, Thomas Bernard
Editing: Frederic Thoraval
Art Direction: Nanci B. Roberts
Costumes: Corinne Bruand
Production Design: Hugues Tissandier
MPAA rating: PG-13
Running time: 93 minutes

REVIEWS

Borrelli, Christopher. *Chicago Tribune*. January 30, 2009.
Corliss, Richard. *TIME Magazine*. January 30, 2009.
Dargis, Manohla. *New York Times*. January 30, 2009.

Elley, Derek. *Variety.* March 14, 2008.
Gleiberman, Owen. *Entertainment Weekly.* January 29, 2009.
Jolin, Dan. *Empire Magazine.* September 26, 2008.
Kennedy, Lisa. *Denver Post.* January 30, 2009.
Morris, Wesley. *Boston Globe.* January 29, 2009.
Pais, Matt. *Metromix.com.* January 29, 2009.
Tallerico, Brian. *HollywoodChicago.com.* January 30, 2009.

QUOTES

Bryan: "I don't know who you are. I don't know what you want. If you are looking for ransom, I can tell you I don't have money. But what I do have are a very particular set of skills; skills I have acquired over a very long career. Skills that make me a nightmare for people like you. If you let my daughter go now, that'll be the end of it. I will not look for you, I will not pursue you. But if you don't, I will look for you, I will find you, and I will kill you."

TRIVIA

Over the course of the film, Bryan kills 26 people.

THE TAKING OF PELHAM 123

Box Office: $65.5 million

Stepping on the subway's third rail will deliver quite a shock to one's system, but so can a Tony Scott film. Those who endured their first seizure or at least had to lie down with a very cold compress due to his *Domino* (2005) can attest to a visual style that was as unbridled as a feverishly-rabid runaway horse on acid. The film was bombastic, mind-taxing, ultra-frenetic, overcooked overkill, the excessiveness distracting and detracting from the storytelling rather than serving it. By comparison to what befell *Domino*, Scott thankfully shows signs of at least having located the reins while crafting his self-deemed superior "reinvention" of *The Taking of Pelham One Two Three* (1974), but the filmmaker is apparently still insufficiently interested in using them. Scott had initial reservations that a film largely composed of two men talking on the phone could be static, and so he characteristically endeavored to amp things up like that electrifying third rail.

Scott's *The Taking of Pelham 123* is set largely within the dark, dank subway tunnels beneath "The City That Never Sleeps," and the director's camera hardly ever pauses to do so either. It incessantly—and ultimately irritatingly—rotates vertiginously around characters in crisis to emphasize that things are dizzyingly and dangerously spinning out of control. Scott is a big fan of close-ups, and here his camera bores in insistently on people,

as if demanding to know what their next crucial move might be. It swoops downward from a Google Earth-type perspective into the congested maze of New York streets to highlight how daunting it will be to traverse all the way from Point A to Point B before the clock's final tick toward a literally lethal deadline. Speaking of which, Scott repeatedly zooms in on watches and stamps the screen with the number of minutes remaining, building tension with relentless reminders of how time is inexorably running out.

An atmosphere of anxiety is also elicited through the use of time-lapse footage that makes both the pedestrian and vehicular traffic positively gush through the city's various main arteries. He manipulates the image in multiple other ways, slowing things down or even slamming on the brakes to emphasize something or someone with a freeze-frame. To further enhance the edginess, Scott uses quick cutting, which gets purposefully more frenetic as the climax approaches. It is once again a semi-digestible force-feeding of Scott's smorgasbord of none-too-subtle tricks; some that succeed in making one nervous, but others that just get on one's nerves. In publicity for the film, the director often mentioned how New York is like a third lead in *Pelham* next to stars Denzel Washington and John Travolta, but his style throughout seems to be insisting on making it a quartet.

The original *Pelham*, which famously ends with a "Gesundheit," is not a timeless classic but nothing to sneeze at, a worthwhile caper film with an enjoyably-sardonic bristle about it. It is set amongst the hustling and bustling of a Big Apple that was at that point rapidly rotting at the core. The film features a tart and often-humorous turn by Walter Matthau as Zachary Garber, a veteran Manhattan Transit Authority cop who dutifully deals with the shockingly-brazen hijacking of the train that pulled out of the Pelham station at 1:23 p.m. The culprits are an identically-dressed and mustachioed group of more-or-less middle-aged men, none of whom would make one especially feel like fleeing to the other side of the street on sight. They refer to each other as Misters Blue, Green, Grey and Brown. Martin Balsam's Mr. Green, whose audible head cold eventually becomes his undoing, looks more like your average burnt-out nobody than a man likely to be a part of something noteworthily audacious. Revealing himself to be a steely and suave fiend is leader Mr. Blue (Robert Shaw, who would go after an even bigger catch the following year in Jaws), demanding that $1 million in ransom be delivered within exactly one hour or the subterranean commuters will never again see the light of day.

It was a chilling scenario in the 1970s, but this crime below Gotham may now have somewhat less ability to shock since the monumental monstrousness that befell the city from above on September 11, 2001. Recognizing this, Scott said that he wanted to make sure his take on the material would have the capacity to shake up audiences, enthusiastically stressing that his "Pelham on steroids" would indeed strike them as "dangerous" and "extreme." Thus, this time around, Shaw's chillingly-cold-blooded and precisely-calculating British mercenary has morphed into Travolta's canny but fiery Ryder, a volcanically-erupting and wickedly-humorous twisted terror who emerged from prison with a large tattoo on his neck and a seething desire for revenge against the city in his gut. Cohort Phil Ramos (Luis Guzman) is reminiscent of the original schemers (right down to the hat and mustache), but the rest of the team can now best be described as young, scarily-intense muscle. More bullets fly and blood spatters than in the original, some of the latter possibly emanating from audience members' ears during the film's most deafening moments.

In stark contrast to all the aforementioned aspects of exclamation point filmmaking is Washington's underplaying of Garber, as much a quiet, steady every-man as Travolta's Ryder is a flamboyant, maniacally-cackling mess. Scott's film has made changes to Washington's character in order to make the situation into which the man is thrust seem more intensely and complexly challenging. Garber is no longer an MTA detective with well-seasoned skills to draw upon but now merely an administrator temporarily demoted back to dispatcher while being investigated for possible acceptance of a bribe. He is thus like a thoroughly-rusty swimmer who finds himself suddenly catapulted into the deep end and required to swim and not sink—as others will go down with him.

One has to chuckle when New York's mayor (a quite enjoyable James Gandolfini) wonders in retrospect why they had not just speedily and more safely delivered the ransom money via helicopter. However, a simple, sane approach that would be preferable in the real world would neuter the drama of the reel one—and that is something that Scott of all people does not aim to do. Made on a budget of $100 million, *The Taking of Pelham 123* only grossed $65.2 million and received mixed reviews. A number of critics expressed their preference for the earlier version. In watching Scott's telling of the tale, one wishes the director would pull back from a style that has made him of late a story yeller more than a storyteller.

David L. Boxerbaum

CREDITS

Walter Garber: Denzel Washington
Ryder: John Travolta

Phil Ramos: Luis Guzman
Camonetti: John Turturro
Mayor: James Gandolfini
John Johnson: Michael Rispoli
Origin: USA
Language: English
Released: 2009
Production: Todd Black, Tony Scott, Jason Blumenthal, Steve Tisch; Relativity Media, Scott Free, Escape Artists; released by Columbia Pictures
Directed by: Tony Scott
Written by: Brian Helgeland
Cinematography by: Tobias Schliessler
Music by: Harry Gregson-Williams
Sound: Tom Nelson
Editing: Chris Lebenzon
Art Direction: David Swayze
Costumes: Renee Ehrlich Kalfus
Production Design: Chris Segers
MPAA rating: R
Running time: 106 minutes

REVIEWS

Burr, Ty. *Boston Globe.* June 11, 2009.
Ebert, Roger. *Chicago Sun-Times.* June 11, 2009.
Edelstein, David. *New York Magazine.* June 8, 2009.
Lemire, Christy. *Associated Press.* June 9, 2009.
Phillips, Michael. *Chicago Tribune.* June 11, 2009.
Ridley, Jim. *Village Voice.* June 10, 2009.
Scott, A.O. *New York Times.* June 12, 2009.
Simon, Brent. *Screen International.* June 8, 2009.
Tallerico, Brian. *HollywoodChicago.com.* June 12, 2009.
Travers, Peter. *Rolling Stone.* June 11, 2009.

QUOTES

Ryder: "Life is simple now. They just have to do what I say."

TRIVIA

The film was shipped to theaters using the code name "Watch Your Step."

TAKING WOODSTOCK

A generation began in his backyard.
—Movie tagline

Box Office: $7.5 million

The year 2009 marked the 40th Anniversary of the legendary Woodstock concert ("3 Days of Peace, Love and Music"). The anniversary of this event has been marked in the past by disastrous re-creations. Woodstock '94 was better known as a mud-soaked game of slip 'n' slide with background music than a cultural event, while Woodstock '99 was plagued with incidents of rape and bottles of water that cost more than an ounce of the drug of choice. Both events accepted corporate sponsorship, rendering both concerts irrelevant in rock and roll's history books long before the first note of music had been played. It became apparent that an event such as Woodstock could really only happen once, so why try again?

Still, it should come as no surprise that a movie on the making of the event—even if based loosely on the facts—would be released in theaters 40 years later almost to the day(s). Anniversaries of pivotal events have often inspired filmmakers to take a look back and re-examine what made them so important, but Ang Lee's *Taking Woodstock* seems to exist in its own universe. Instead of underscoring all the facts with the benefit of hindsight, it mostly downplays the whole event. Our main protagonist—a young man who just wants to save his town and his parents' fledgling hotel—appears to be unfazed by the endless sea of humanity that has descended onto his neighbor's precious farmland.

The movie exists entirely backstage of the event, never once focusing on the bands themselves. The first half of the film centers on Elliot Teichberg (Demetri Martin), a young interior designer who has moved back in with his parents (Imelda Staunton and Henry Goodman) at their fleabag hotel where they charge $1 just to use a towel. Times are hard for this town, but Elliott sees an opportunity to turn things around when the next town over rejects a promoter who wants to stage a 3-day concert in a field, free of charge. Elliot, who also happens to be the head of the Bethel Chamber of Commerce (such as it is), enlists the help of local dairy farmer Max Yasgur (Eugene Levy), who owns just enough land for the gig and is up for negotiating the use of it for a fair price, much to the chagrin of the other residents who do not want their town infested with hippies.

Elliot ignores their fear mongering, hateful looks and the anti-Semitic warning signs painted on the outside of his parents' house. The show must go on. Elliot's parents reluctantly rent out every room, yet seizing the opportunity to divide each room into three with bed sheets draped on clothesline, so as to squeeze in more customers and make more money. When their plan succeeds, they start warming up to the whole idea of the festival, even if the music and the people are not to their liking (one has to wonder how they got talked into housing a low-grade theater troupe in their barn for the past few months or years, but that may be another movie for another day).

The second half of the film is the event itself, but much like Elliot, we never get too close to the stage to know who is playing. We see glimpses of the full crowd and the seemingly small stage and its spotlights, but it comes across like a mirage more than a physical structure. Lee keeps the movie centered on the outskirts of the concert. In the movie's most triumphant shot, Elliot walks through the crowds and parked cars trying to get to the concert to see something—anything—and ends up hitching a ride on a police motorcycle. The more he walks among them, the more he becomes a part of the picture.

Naturally, Elliot undergoes a character arc typical of films that take place in this era. Up until now, he has lived a somewhat mundane existence, but the event of Woodstock finds him exploring homosexuality with one of the crew members, dropping acid and making friends with transvestite ex-Marine Vilma (Liev Schreiber). Of course, the war in Vietnam must also figure into the storyline somehow and it comes through via the drug-addled, wheelchair-bound resident Billy (Emile Hirsch), who seems to be one of the few people in the town Elliot can relate to.

If all of this sounds too familiar or unimaginative, it may be because there have already been so many movies on the subject of the 1960s that there does not seem to be anything new to say about it. Lee has always been a risk-taking director and one who steers clear of conventionalism, yet with the decadence of the 1960s as his focal point, he has somehow made his most conventional movie yet. As a surveyor of America's past, Lee has examined with perfection the sociological landscape of the so-called nuclear family with 1997's *The Ice Storm*, a movie that sums up the dreariness and narcissism of the 1970s better than any other movie on the subject.

It might seem like an unreasonable expectation to repeat that artistic success utilizing a decade that has been analyzed to death already, but Lee has consistently made an effort to try and reinvent whichever genre he takes on, with mostly positive results. Here, when he tries to emulate Michael Wadleigh's revolutionary 1970 documentary *Woodstock* by employing split-screen devices, the effect feels more like a step backwards for a forward-thinking director who has always been able to carve his own niche.

Still, while the second half of the film reveals little more than clichés and comes off as a bit of a mess, it remains a watchable mess and the first half of the film comes on quite strong. One of the movie's bigger laughs comes when the barn-dwelling amateur theater group prances naked in the field as a welcome wagon for the concert officials, which ends up not being any kind of deterrent in their decision making process. Imelda Staunton basically plays a caricature of an angry Jewish woman, but she does it with such conviction that it hardly matters how shallow her role really is. Eugene Levy surprisingly plays his role against his own type and ends up being the most satisfying aspect of the entire project. Unfortunately, his character completely disappears after the first half.

With *Taking Woodstock*, Lee has made his breeziest movie since 1993's *The Wedding Banquet*, a film that also explored the themes of homosexuality, a generational divide amongst family members and underlying dramas taking place beneath the surface of a major event. The leisurely pace typical of Lee's films is here, as well as an ending free of artifice and absolute closure. The film's coda—a reference to the tragic Rolling Stones 1969 Altamont Speedway Concert, often thought of as the symbolic end of the 1960s as we now know it—serves as a reminder of a generation that was too lost in a fog to realize their mistakes. Like the Woodstock concert itself, *Taking Woodstock* should not be really thought of as a mistake, but a misstep (by Lee) that hopefully will not be repeated anytime soon.

Collin Souter

CREDITS

Sonia Teichberg: Imelda Staunton
Vilma: Liev Schreiber
Max Yasgur: Eugene Levy
Billy: Emile Hirsch
VW Girl: Kelli Garner
VW Guy: Paul Franklin Dano
Dan: Jeffrey Dean Morgan
Elliot Tiber: Demetri Martin
Devon: Dan Fogler
Jake Teichberg: Henry Goodman
Tisha: Mamie Gummer
Michael Lang: Jonathan Groff
Origin: USA
Language: English
Released: 2009
Production: James Schamus, Ang Lee, Celia Costas; released by Focus Features
Directed by: Ang Lee
Written by: James Schamus
Cinematography by: Eric Gautier
Music by: Danny Elfman
Sound: Drew Kunin
Editing: Tim Squyres
Art Direction: Peter Rogness
Costumes: Joseph G. Aulisi

Production Design: David Gropman
MPAA rating: R

REVIEWS

Holden, Stephen. *New York Times.* August 25, 2009.
Honeycutt, Kirk. *Hollywood Reporter.* May 16, 2009.
Lane, Anthony. *New Yorker.* August 24, 2009.
McCarthy, Todd. *Variety.* May 16, 2009.
Phillips, Michael. *Chicago Tribune.* August 28, 2009.
Sharkey, Betsy. *Los Angeles Times.* August 25, 2009.
Sobcyznski, Peter. *eFilmCritic.* August 27, 2009.
Stevens, Dana. *Slate.* August 27, 2009.
Tallerico, Brian. *MovieRetriever.com.* August 28, 2009.
Zacharek, Stephanie. *Salon.com.* August 28, 2009.

QUOTES

Carol: "Everyone with their little perspective. Perspective shuts out the universe, it keeps the love out."

TRIVIA

No footage from the original Woodstock was used in this film. All concert footage was shot specifically for the film.

TERMINATOR SALVATION

We fight back.
    —Movie tagline
The end begins.
    —Movie tagline

Box Office: $125.3 million

McG, the self-preferred abbreviated alias of former music video director Joseph McGinty Nichols, always sounds like something that might come with a side order of fries, perhaps as part of a Happy Meal. However, there is certainly nothing happy about what is served up in his *Terminator Salvation,* the start of a planned trilogy which received mixed reviews and only earned back about two-thirds of its $200 million budget. McG's film is the third sequel to James Cameron's low-budget but highly-entertaining 1984 classic that featured an intimidating-looking and fiercely-determined robotic creature that was new on the scene playing the same onscreen. Arnold Schwarzenegger's potent portrayal of a hulking, hell-bent cyborg assassin from the future who created his own merciless L.A. crime wave ended up having audience appeal that, like the actor's prodigious pectorals, was surprisingly wide. In keeping with his character's now-famous utterance of "I'll be back," the actor returned for the colossal, exponentially bigger-budgeted *Terminator 2: Judgment Day* (1991) and the lesser, Cameron-less *Terminator 3: Rise of the Machines* (2003). These three engaging escapist films contained Mobius strip-relationships across time that were mind-bending and special effects that were mind-boggling, with some tension-relieving chuckle-inducing moments interspersed amongst those that chill and thrill. While Arnold makes a brief, CGI-inserted appearance towards the end of *Terminator Salvation,* the proceedings into which he once again struts his naked stuff are now stiflingly grim with no grins.

As the artificial intelligence-induced apocalypse ominously foretold in previous installments has here already come to pass, the Terminator series' tone has become oppressively bleak. (Worldwide nuclear destruction and near-extermination of humankind by rampaging machines will do that every time.) In depicting this unsettling grave new world from which life and hope have been almost completely expunged, McG desaturates his forbidding, war-ravaged visuals into near black and white, his predominant palette consisting of sooty, grimy grays and rusty, dusty, browns. There is also a great deal of darkness, regularly enlivened by a deadly explosion's glowing fireball. Even the film's credits, accompanied by music that signals dire straits ahead, are set against cold, metallic-looking murkiness that is accented in blood red.

Especially against such a decidedly-dreary backdrop, John Connor, the man prophesied to lead a resistance movement that would show extraordinary mettle against their metallic foe, should stand out in captivating contrast. Yet, as portrayed by able Christian Bale, this rescuer of the human race is also strikingly colorless, failing to exude that intangible, inspiring something that could draw mankind in general and viewers in particular to him. Granted his actions reveal him to be tenaciously gutsy and his words show him to be steadfastly good, but the character still manages to come off here as drably uninteresting and devoid of a palpable pull. It is impossible to warm up to him. That irritating, borrowed-from-Batman low raspiness that only varies into stern, eruptive (but still raspy) barks certainly does not help matters. Bale did, however, burst forth in truly remarkable fashion during his infamous YouTube-showcased tirade on the *Terminator Salvation* set.

Although nowhere near as spectacularly upstaged here as he was by Heath Ledger in *The Dark Knight* (2008), Bale's performance in *Terminator Salvation* recedes further into the background thanks to emerging Aussie Sam Worthington's magnetic portrayal of a half-man/half-metal hybrid. His Marcus Wright starts the film in 2003 as a soon-to-be-executed, self-loathing killer who is offered a chance for redemption, asked to nobly sign over his body for possible life-saving research after he himself no longer has any use for it. This request is made by cancer-ravaged Cyberdyne Systems' Dr. Serena Kogen (a profoundly peaked-looking Helena Bonham Carter), whose scientific advances will eventually be commandeered by evil conglomerate Skynet to snuff out lives rather than save them. As a result, when John Connor descends into the subterranean depths of a Skynet base in post-Judgment Day 2018 (notice how the messianic character lights a torch that illuminates the darkness), attentive audience members see Marcus lying amongst the disturbing last vestiges of the humankind—some horribly dead, and others horribly alive.

Marcus rises from the fiery remains of the subsequently-destroyed base a flummoxed phoenix, not recalling how he ended up where he is and confounded by his shockingly-decimated surroundings. He cannot understand why he is a dead man walking, unaware that he has been reborn as a terrible infiltration tool of Skynet that is replete with internal hardware and at least partially devoid of free will. He does retain his human brain and heart, as well as the guilt that gnaws at both. However, the drenching rainstorm and a later river immersion seem to symbolically represent a washing-away of sins on the way to some form of absolution before the credits roll.

One half-expects *Terminator Salvation*'s protagonists to join hands at some point and belt out a rendition of "Heart" from *Damn Yankees!* (1958), as the screenplay continually refers to that vital seat of passionate and compassionate emotion that sets man apart from machine. (How ironic, as the film itself often feels mechanical and deficient in feeling.) In a taped message, John Connor's mother (Linda Hamilton, seen only in a photograph) advises him to always "follow your heart" in deciding how to best and most conscientiously proceed against the enemy. Typical *Terminator* film formidable female Blair Williams (Moon Bloodgood) does not realize that that is who she is snuggling with as she rapturously compliments Marcus on the strongly beating heart in his chest. Or should one rightfully refer to him as "it," as understandably hyper-vigilant John Connor initially asserts? During the course of the film, Marcus rescues Blair after she ejected from her aircraft, and subsequently protects her from 100%-human inhumane goons. He seeks to extricate Kyle Reese (quite good Anton Yelchin), a tenacious teenaged resistance fighter and John Connor's future father (if he lives that long), and Star (Jadagrace Berry), the young man's companion, from Skynet's clutches. Marcus not only offers John Connor an indispensable hand in liberating key Kyle and friend, but also literally, selflessly, and heroically gives his heart as the film ends so that the mortally-injured leader of the resistance can fight on.

After chucking the chip he resentfully ripped from the back of his head, what remains of the person prevails over the programming, and Marcus autonomously chooses to atone. It is his second chance, and, at a crucial crossroads, this time Wright will do right. The character's identity crisis angst throughout *Terminator Salvation* is not only rather poignant but also thought-provoking. How interesting that a character who is not fully human is the one who comes off most compellingly and affectingly just that.

However, no one in *Terminator Salvation* charismatically seizes the audience and electrifies them into expectant excitement the way Schwarzenegger did as the exceptionally-solid core figure of the earlier films. A number of moviegoers reported eruptions of applause when fans suddenly laid eyes on that familiar face and formidable form late in McG's film, warmly embracing an old friend whose unexpected, sight-for-sore-eyes reappearance brought on an acute realization of just how profoundly he had been missed. That is probably not the sentiment the director hoped to elicit by including Arnold's image and more than one well-remembered line from the preceding *Terminator* films. Nevertheless, such winking references brought on a nostalgic reverence that made *Terminator Salvation* suffer by comparison. There are no new "Hasta la vista, baby!"-type lines or take-a-moment-to-catch-your-breath humorous interludes in which Arnold's fish-out-of-water time traveler sticks out like an immensely-swollen sore thumb or fails to quite grasp something. This time around, the mood is simply and pervasively dead serious.

No longer is there one robotic killer sent back from a nightmare of a future to nip a single savior in the bud: the nightmare itself has arrived, and killers are harrowingly everywhere and out to eradicate everyone. In McG's film, they appear loudly, frequently, and in a multitude of terrifying forms. Probably the most arresting is a skyscraper-tall Harvester that plucks poor Jane Alexander's Virginia out of the frame with alarming suddenness. There are subsequent, highly disconcerting scenes in which crowds of collected people are then horribly herded into Holocaust-like camps. With bombastic annihilation being attempted everywhere and seemingly every other second during the hellish proceedings, it is likely that many viewers would themselves have killed for even a little of that amusement from Arnold.

David L. Boxerbaum

CREDITS

John Connor: Christian Bale
Marcus Wright: Sam Worthington
Kyle Reese: Anton Yelchin
Kate Connor: Bryce Dallas Howard
Blair Williams: Moon Bloodgood
Barnes: Common
Dr. Serena Kogan: Helena Bonham Carter
Gen. Ashdown: Michael Ironside
Virginia: Jane Alexander
Star: Jadagrace
Origin: USA
Language: English
Released: 2009
Production: Moritz Borman, Jeffrey Silver, Victor Kubicek, Derek Anderson; Wonderland Sound and Vision, Halcyon Co.; released by Warner Bros.
Directed by: McG
Written by: Michael Ferris, John Brancato
Cinematography by: Shane Hurlbut
Music by: Danny Elfman
Sound: Mark Ulano
Editing: Conrad Buff
Art Direction: Troy Sizemore
Costumes: Michael Wilkinson
Production Design: Martin Laing
MPAA rating: PG-13
Running time: 115 minutes

REVIEWS

Anderson, John. *Variety.* May 18, 2009.
Covert, Colin. *Minneapolis Star-Tribune.* May 20, 2009.
Ebert, Roger. *Chicago Sun-Times.* May 20, 2009.
Edelstein, David. *New York Magazine.* May 18, 2009.
Lemire, Christy. *Associated Press.* May 18, 2009.
Murray, Rebecca. *About.com.* May 20, 2009.
Parker, Patrick. *Premiere Magazine.* May 20, 2009.
Pols, Mary F. *Time Magazine.* May 20, 2009.
Salem, Rob. *Toronto Star.* May 20, 2009.
Scott, A.O. *New York Times.* May 20, 2009.

QUOTES

John Connor: "I knew it. I knew it was coming. But this is not the future my mother warned me about. And in this future, I don't know if we can win this war. This is John Connor."

TRIVIA

Shortly before filming began, Helena Bonham Carter replaced Tilda Swinton who had originally been cast in the role of Dr. Serena Kogan.

TETRO

Every family has a secret.
—Movie tagline

When Francis Ford Coppola reemerged from a decade-long hiatus from moviemaking with *Youth Without Youth* (2007), a self-financed and decidedly surreal meditation on such weighty subjects as life, love, language and aging, it received a brutal dismissal from audiences and critics who seemed to take his desire to make a small, personal and extra-arty film—the kind of thing that many established filmmakers often talk about doing in interviews but which few ever quite get around to doing—instead of taking on a simpler and more commercially viable project almost as a personal insult. In the wake of such rejection, it might have been understandable if Coppola were to follow it up with something a little more commercially viable but it is clear that such things no longer hold much interest for him. As his latest effort, the audaciously arty and frequently dazzling family melodrama *Tetro* shows, it is doubtful that his position will be changing anytime soon and that is just fine as long as he continues to produce works as bold and brave and beautiful as this late-period masterpiece.

Written by Coppola (his first original solo screenplay since *The Conversation* [1974]), the film opens with Bennie (Alden Ehrenreich), a 17-year-old prep school runaway who is working as a waiter on a cruise ship that has just docked in Buenos Ares, Argentina for repairs. With a few days to kill, Bennie decides to look up his older brother Tetro (Vincent Gallo), whom he has not seen or heard from since his abrupt departure from home more than a decade earlier. During that separation, Bennie has built up an idealized version of Tetro in his head as a successful artistic type—the only possible reason that he can imagine why Tetro never came back for him in all that time—but when he arrives at his brother's doorstep for a long-awaited reunion, it does not go quite as planned. Tetro is instead a crank, hobbling around his apartment on a broken leg (the result of a recent encounter with a bus) and failing to live up to his alleged artistic potential (instead of supplying the plays for the local theater, he mans the spotlight) and displaying no burning desire to see his brother nor rehash any memories of their family history or the reasons why he left. A tentative truce is negotiated by Tetro's lovely and infinitely patient girlfriend, Miranda (Maribel Verdu), Bennie is allowed to stay, and the two brothers try to reestablish their fraternal bonds, although tensions begin to flare in Tetro any time the subject of their shared past is brought up.

Through hazy memories, inadvertent revelations and sordid details found in a cache of autobiographical scribblings that Bennie discovers in a hidden trunk, it eventually becomes apparent as to why Tetro is reticent to discuss their family history. Through a series of painful flashbacks, we discover that their father (Klaus Maria Brandauer), a world-famous orchestra conductor, was evidently a monster whenever he was off the stage—he willfully destroyed the career of his older brother in order to further his own, seduced Tetro's then-girlfriend out from under him for no other reason than to prove that he could and largely blamed him for the auto accident that killed his mother. Eventually, Bennie decides to utilize Tetro's writings as the basis of his own play, a move that does not exactly endear himself to his brother but which does capture the eye of the country's most powerful arts critic, the enigmatically-named Alone (Carmen Maura), who invites the play to compete as a finalist in Argentina's most revered arts festival. Bennie and the theatrical troupe go off to perform in the festival on a trip that signals his final journey into manhood, both literally, thanks to the offer from a sexy friend and her equally hot aunt to throw him "a pajama party without the pajamas," and metaphorically, thanks to the last-minute arrival of Tetro with a final revelation that forces Bennie to reevaluate his entire life and confront his family at last.

Telling stories about the familial ties that bind (and occasionally choke) and sibling relationships/rivalries is nothing new in the Coppola canon. What is different this time around is that while past films were either written or inspired by the works of others, *Tetro* is clearly a more personal exploration of these themes for Coppola, a man whose family is filled with several generations of artists. In interviews, Coppola has denied that the film is specifically autobiographical and while that may be true, the hurts and the conflicts that he depicts here are so raw and painful that it would be foolish to believe that they were invented completely out of whole cloth. Under normal circumstances, this is the kind of project that one might expect from a first-time writer or filmmaker and in such cases, the results are often on the dire side because they have not yet fully developed the artistic muscles required to transform life into art and because they lack the ability to recognize when something that may have been important to them from a personal standpoint does not work from a dramatic one. Coppola's screenplay is clearly the film's weakest weak point—the story starts off on the high end of the flamboyantly melodramatic scale and only pushes things further as it goes along and some of his narrative is so obliquely structured that it makes Tetro's own scribblings (which can only be deciphered using mirrors) look straightforward by comparison. The story is not bad, by any means, but at its heart, there is not much of anything on display here that one would not find in a Fifties-era weeper. It is the kind of thing that someone writes when they are young and hungry and desperate to show their feelings to the world and which they often find themselves cringing over when they encounter it again when they are older and presumably wiser.

While Coppola's screenplay may come across as the kind of thing written by a young man whose enthusiasm far outweighs his discipline, it has been directed by a veteran whose considerable powers have not ebbed at all and whose own enthusiasm at being able to tell a story in whatever way he sees fit, no matter how odd it may seem to some and regardless of its commercial prospects, grows more and more infectious as the story progresses. Yes, everything about *Tetro* is pitched at an operatic level right from the start, but, as it turns out, this is the correct approach for the material he is dealing with here. He could have easily told this story in a more restrained manner with a normal visual style and low-key performances and, who knows, he might have still gotten a good movie out of it. Instead, he frankly swings for the fences by taking this already wildly flamboyant tale and presenting it in such a way that everything seems almost ready to completely fly off the rails (which is exactly how both Tetro and Bennie perceive their lives to be) without ever quite losing control of the material, even when it veers into near-insanity in the last half-hour or so. The performances are equally stylized without going overboard as well—Gallo is the perfect embodiment of genius gone sour, newcomer Ehrenreich does a good job of representing the callow youth who gradually becomes a man (so good, in fact, that some have dismissed his performance as pretty-boy posturing), Verdu is the ideal version of the warm and nurturing woman who will do anything to keep the peace and Brandauer is never less-than-mesmerizing in his self-absorbed monstrousness. From a visual standpoint, *Tetro* is one of the most stunning visual experiences to come along since *The New World* (2005)—the satiny and seductive black-and-white cinematography (with occasional bits of striking color) from Mihai Malaimare Jr., is so gorgeous to behold that anyone who still holds onto the mistaken belief that this style photography is inferior to color should be forced to watch this film in order to realize for themselves just how wrong that particular assertion can be.

Funny, haunting, strange and striking in equal measure, *Tetro* is a triumph that reconfirms Francis Ford Coppola's position as one of the great American filmmakers. It is hard to think of another one working right now possessing both the audacity to come up with the idea of a film like this in the first place and the artistic skill to pull it off as well as he has done here. Inevitably, since it lacked the immediate appeal of his more commercial endeavors, it wound up suffering the same ignominious critical and commercial fate as *Youth Without Youth*. However, it is clear from those two films that Coppola is now more interested in making the kind of ambitious artistic statements that are designed to stand the test of time than in the anonymous blockbusters he could pull off in his sleep if he wanted. This type

of filmmaking seems to have reinvigorated Coppola's artistic spirit and while *Tetro* seems unlikely to replenish his coffers for a long time, the artistic dividends that it provides to viewers brave enough to seek it out more than make up for the financial ones.

Peter Sobczynski

CREDITS

Tetro: Vincent Gallo
Miranda: Maribel Verdu
Carlo/Alfie: Klaus Maria Brandauer
Alone: Carmen Maura
Bennie: Alden Ehrenreich
Origin: USA, Argentina, Italy, Spain
Language: English
Released: 2009
Production: Francis Ford Coppola; released by American Zoetrope
Directed by: Francis Ford Coppola
Written by: Francis Ford Coppola
Cinematography by: Mihai Malaimare Jr.
Music by: Osvaldo Golijov
Sound: Leandro de Loredo
Editing: Walter Murch
Costumes: Cecilia Monti
Production Design: Sebastian Orgambide
MPAA rating: Unrated
Running time: 127 minutes

REVIEWS

Dargis, Manohla. *New York Times.* June 11, 2009.
Ebert, Roger. *Chicago Sun-Times.* June 18, 2009.
Honeycutt, Kirk. *Hollywood Reporter.* May 14, 2009.
LaSalle, Mick. *San Francisco Chronicle.* June 19, 2009.
Lemire, Christy. *Associated Press.* June 10, 2009.
McCarthy, Todd. *Variety.* May 14, 2009.
Pais, Matt. *Metromix.com.* June 18, 2009.
Sarris, Andrew. *New York Observer.* June 10, 2009.
Sharkey, Betsy. *Los Angeles Times.* June 12, 2009.
Tobias, Scott. *AV Club.* June 11, 2009.

QUOTES

Carlo: "There's room for only one genius in this family."

TRIVIA

In September 2007, director Francis Ford Coppola's home in Buenos Aires was broken into and the burglars took all of his electronic equipment including his computer and the film's script.

THIRST
(Bakjwi)

Thirst, Park Chan-wook's daring twist on arguably the most overcooked genre of 2009, the vampire film, was one of the most mesmerizing genre pictures of 2009, further proof that Park is one of the most notable international filmmakers of his generation. Park's film is an inventive and sometimes shocking examination of faith, desire, sin, and sacrifice through the eyes of a man daringly unafraid to plumb the depths of the human soul for subjects that truly horrify most people. A man so interested in the concept of vengeance that he made three films about it (*Sympathy For Mr. Vengeance* [2002], *Oldboy* [2003], and *Lady Vengeance* [2005]), Park has made a career of blending striking visuals and resonant human drama. Not quite as moody as *Let the Right One In* (2008) but also nowhere near as audience-friendly as *Twilight* (2008), *Thirst* is truly a unique entry in the genre, one that uses vampire mythology as a starting point for a commentary on all desires (or thirsts) that are deemed forbidden. If Park were more condemning of the actions of his leads, *Thirst* could be described as a vampire morality tale. When man gives into his base instincts and crosses one line, it is notably easier to cross a second, third, and fourth one and there is arguably no more drastic a line for one to cross than drinking human blood.

Priest Sang-hyeon (Song Kang-Ho) is a good man. He is well aware of temptation for he has dealt with denying himself what his religion has deemed forbidden his entire life. The Priest volunteers for a medical experiment of which he is the only survivor. His survival comes with a serious cost: through a transfusion of bad blood he is transformed into someone who needs to drink blood for sustenance. (Of course, the parallel between drinking communal wine and pretending it is Christ's blood and a vampire Priest is not lost.) He started by drinking the blood of comatose victims to stay alive until he meets the fiery, sexy, and practically captive Tae-Ju (Kim Ok-vin), who awakens something much deeper inside of him. Soon, he is making passionate love to this young woman. The two form a twisted pair. She is fascinated by what this creature awakens inside of her and how it can save her from her miserable life. He is fed by his new passions and keeps going further and further to feed all of his thirsts—both of the blood and of the flesh.

The moral dilemma of a man of the cloth giving into his carnal need by what is essentially a disease given to him through no fault of his own naturally gives *Thirst* an amazing dramatic potential, one that Park exploits with over two hours of densely packed screenwriting. The moral gray areas of *Thirst*—drinking blood for sustenance and not enjoyment, the crimes that Sang-hyeon commits to save his new lover—make for riveting material. There are more interesting concepts well-executed in one reel of *Thirst* than the entirety of a dozen other vampire movies combined. And Park's visual

eye has arguably never been stronger. Some of the imagery in *Thirst,* particularly in the remarkable final act, is among the most creative and memorable of 2009.

All that holds *Thirst* back from *Oldboy* level perfection is a bit of a pacing problem. It is almost as if Park has more ideas than he know what to do with and crams them all into 133 minutes that needed a bit more tightening. The film takes a bit too long to build up steam and occasionally moves in frustrating fits and starts, as if it is building momentum only to lose it in a scene that goes on too long or one that merely rings a bit false. There is a truly incredible 110-minute movie buried in *Thirst* but the film as is repeats itself a few times before reaching its climax instead of building to it more organically. Even as the film begins to feel like its wrapping up, it has another two reels to go (although the borderline lunacy of the final act is truly something to behold including a sequence atop a cliff that stands among the most visually memorable of the year.)

No matter the minor flaws of its pacing, *Thirst* is a daring work from an innovative director. Even though it is arguably imperfect, there is so much to like about the film thematically, visually, and on a performance level, that it is easy to overlook small problems in the parts and merely be engrossed by the sum of them.

Brian Tallerico

CREDITS

Sang-hyeon: Kang-ho Song
Tae-ju: Ok-vin Kim
Kang-woo: Ha-Kyun Shin
Lady Ra: Hae-sook Kim
Origin: USA, South Korea
Language: Korean, Korean
Released: 2009
Production: Chan-wook Park, Su-hyeon Ahn; CJ Entertainment, Moho Film; released by Focus Features
Directed by: Chan-wook Park
Written by: Chan-wook Park, Seo-gyeong Jeong
Cinematography by: Jeong-hun Jeong
Music by: Yeong-wook Jo
Sound: Gun Jung
Editing: Sang-Beom Kim, Jae-beom Kim
Costumes: Sang-gyeong Jo
Production Design: Seong-hie Ryu
MPAA rating: R
Running time: 133 minutes

REVIEWS

Andrews, Nigel. *Financial Times.* October 16, 2009.
Ebert, Roger. *Chicago Sun-Times.* August 13, 2009.

Edelstein, David. *New York Magazine.* July 27, 2009.
Gonzalez, Ed. *Slant Magazine.* July 26, 2009.
Lee, Maggie. *Hollywood Reporter.* May 15, 2009.
Miska, Brad. *Bloody Disgusting.* July 10, 2009.
Phillips, Michael. *Chicago Tribune.* August 14, 2009.
Ridley, Jim. *Village Voice.* July 30, 2009.
Schwarzbaum, Lisa. *Entertainment Weekly.* July 29, 2009.
Sharkey, Betsy. *Los Angeles Times.* July 31, 2009.

QUOTES

Priest Sang-hyeon: "Grant me the following in the name of our Lord Jesus Christ. Like a leper rotting in flesh, let all avoid me. Like a cripple without limbs, let me not move freely. Remove my cheeks, that tears may not roll down them. Crush my lips and tongue, that I may not sin with them. Pull out my nails, that I may not grasp nothing. Let my shoulders and back be bent, that I may carry nothing. Like a man with tumor in the head let me lack judgment. Ravage my body sworn to chastity, leave me with no pride, and have me live in shame. Let no one pray for me. But only the grace of the Lord Jesus Christ have mercy on me."

THREE MONKEYS

In the hands of many other filmmakers, the action of Nuri Bilge Ceylan's *Three Monkeys* would likely play as a conventional noir that some critics would describe as "Hitchcockian." Ceylan is not like many other filmmakers. The internationally renowned director of the amazing *Distant* (2002) and highly-acclaimed *Climates* (2006) is much less concerned about traditional action that he is about the aftermath and the consequence. *Three Monkeys* may contain his most forceful and driven narrative to date, but the great Turkish director handles it with his own elegiac, mournful style. None of the driving action of the film—an accidental death, a murder, infidelity—actually happens on screen. Ceylan and his co-writers (Ebru Ceylan and Ercan Kesal) are much more interested in the ripple effect than in the actual throwing of the stone that creates it. It is the keeping of the secrets that tear unions apart more than the facts of the secrets themselves. *Three Monkeys* is ultimately a bit less effective than Ceylan's best work because of the relatively plot-centric and often monotonous screenplay not playing to the strengths of a filmmaker who is more of a visual poet than a precise storyteller, but it is still a work from an international talent who deserves much more attention stateside.

Three Monkeys focuses on four characters—a powerful man, his worker, the worker's wife, and their son. The powerful man, a politician named Servet (Ercan Kesal) is introduced in the opening scene of the film, half-asleep at the wheel. After a long opening take, it is revealed that Servet's drowsiness has led him to hit a pedestrian. The crime will surely destroy his political aspirations and tear his life apart. Servet calls his loyal servant, a driver named Eyup (Yavuz Bingol) and offers him a deal—if the man claims that he was behind the wheel at the time of the accident, Servet will pay him a tidy sum at the end of one year, the likely time of incarceration for the man. Go to jail; make enough money to change your life. The servant covers for the politician.

As with every morally questionable decision, the ones made by Servet and Eyup are not quite so cut and dry. The choice of Eyup ripples out to his family, a group that acts like the monkeys of the title—not seeing, hearing, or speaking of the true issues at play. Eyup's wife Hacer (the movie-stealing Hatice Aslan) and son Ismail (Ahmet Rifat Sungar) struggle for the year to make ends meet with no father figure, husband, or provider. A year can be a very long time for a family in emotional and practical crisis. Ismail refuses to get a job and Hacer is forced to go to Servet and ask for some of the payment in advance. Servet relents but it is later revealed to have come with an incredibly heavy cost, another gigantic secret for which no one will be able to cover.

Three Monkeys was shot by *Climates* lens specialist Gokhan Tiryaki and it reflects Ceylan's mournful, poetic style. The filmmaker works with a color palette that reflects the story's dark, depressing tone—browns, grays, and low-lit rooms. This is a world without color, as evidenced by several shots of storm clouds overhead. The dour tone of the material only occasionally allows for the visual beauty that Ceylan has found in other films and makes for an awfully draining experience. The film is oppressively bleak, resulting in an overall tone that could be described as monotonous. The dirge-like nature of the film makes it less emotionally satisfying then if Ceylan could have found a few more peaks and valleys in the lives of his characters. It is more rewarding to watch a fall from happiness than to watch characters who seem unable to find happiness regardless of the action of the film.

Having said that, *Three Monkeys* is still the work of one of the more interesting filmmakers of the recently-closed decade. Ceylan draws genuine, moving performances from a talented cast and it is clear why the man was chosen as the recipient of the Best Director prize at the Cannes Film Festival. The flaws of *Three Monkeys* are more a product of a bleak screenplay that what the director or cast did with it. Ceylan finds a few moments of stunning visual composition and his cast truly deliver the emotional punch he demands of them, resulting in a good-not-great work from an undeniably talented filmmaker.

Brian Tallerico

CREDITS

Eyup: Yavuz Bingol
Hacer: Hatice Aslan
Ismail: Ahmet Rifat Sungar
Servet: Ercan Kesal
Bayram: Cafer Kose
Origin: Turkey, France, Italy
Language: Turkish
Released: 2008
Production: Zeynep Özbatur; Zeynofilm, Pyramide Productions; released by Zeitgeist Films
Directed by: Nuri Bilge Ceylan
Written by: Ercan Kesal, Ebru Ceylan
Cinematography by: Gokhan Tiryaki
Sound: Umut Senyol
Editing: Nuri Bilge Ceylan
Art Direction: Harika Ceylan
MPAA rating: Unrated
Running time: 109 minutes

REVIEWS

Bradshaw, Peter. *Guardian.* February 13, 2009.
Calhoun, Dave. *Time Out.* February 12, 2009.
Chang, Justin. *Variety.* October 18, 2008.
Ebert, Roger. *Chicago Sun-Times.* July 16, 2009.
Howell, Peter. *Toronto Star.* April 24, 2009.
Kois, Dan. *Washington Post.* March 13, 2009.
Lacey, Liam. *Globe and Mail.* October 18, 2008.
Phillips, Michael. *Chicago Tribune.* July 17, 2009.
Scott, A.O. *New York Times.* May 1, 2009.
Thomas, Kevin. *Los Angeles Times.* March 27, 2009.

TRIVIA

The film was Turkey's official Academy Awards® submission for competition in the Foreign-Language Film category.

THE TIME TRAVELER'S WIFE

Box Office: $63.4 million

Many a wife has sighed with resignation as she must yet again gather up the clothes her husband has left in a heap upon the floor. Persisting quirks are unlikely to make a woman do anything alarming to Prince Charming, but they can certainly make her do a little pondering about her relationship. Clare (Rachel McAdams), the titular character of *The Time Traveler's Wife*, has far more to think about than most whenever she encounters her own mate's abandoned apparel, as the man has not merely ditched them there while changing to go out for

an evening with his buddies. Henry (Eric Bana) is not thoughtless but helpless, continually disappearing abruptly from within his duds to be jerked back and forth in time against his will due to a genetic anomaly. (As Henry always arrives at his destination completely nude a la Arnold Schwarzenegger's character in *The Terminator* (1984) and its sequels, he is forced to resourcefully appropriate clothes and whatever else it takes to temporarily get by.) Clare, like Henry himself, never knows when he will go, where he will be off to, or how long he will be away. Imagine trying to put down roots with a husband who keeps getting uprooted.

Only a grand, transcendent, ordained-by-fate attachment at the heart could keep a wife fundamentally certain about her feelings amid such chronic uncertainty, remaining constant to a spasmodically-there spouse. Luckily for Clare and Henry, it is just such an indelibly-etched-across-time ideal love that keeps them bound together through less-than- ideal circumstances. Those noting that Audrey Niffenegger's 2003 bestselling debut novel has been adapted for the screen by Bruce Joel Rubin, the man who garnered an Oscar® for dissolving audiences in tears over a couple's undying devotion in *Ghost* (1990), fully expected to once again be clutching Kleenex at the Cineplex. While tissues were likely less significantly saturated this time around, the admittedly—but not fatally—flawed *Time Traveler's Wife* is still a periodically moving, tenderly-rendered romantic fantasy that will make viewers contemplate such things as the preciousness and unsettlingly transitory nature of not only life itself but also the people with whom one desires to share it. Made on a budget of $39 million, the film struck enough of a chord to earn over $55 million despite more than a few dismissive reviews.

Numerous men have griped that films of this ilk make them ill. Still, even those who grudgingly agreed to attend likely felt rather recompensed upon observing McAdams' luminously lovely Clare. (Women, of course, enjoyed Bana in the buff.) With not only shining eyes but a general warm glow about her, the character could not be more of a comely, soothing-voiced sweetheart. Even if the alluring artist's appearance and personality were somehow not enough to bowl Henry over when she happens into the Chicago library where he works, this total stranger's talk of his being her lifelong best friend in itself does the trick. Clare fills Henry in on the first time he had appeared to her when she was just six years old (and well-played by Brooklynn Proulx) in a secluded meadow behind her family's home. (The twenty-something librarian does not know her because it is not until later on in his life that Henry will travel back in time and become acquainted with Clare earlier on in hers. Got that?) This first encounter is shown in an idyllic flashback that unfortunately has an unintentional but undeniable tinge of creepiness to it. While meant to let viewers witness the magical moment at which something oh-so-beautiful and pure is forever forged, a nude man suddenly striking up a conversation with an unattended little girl from behind (thankfully) dense shrubbery is hard to simply appreciate as the bonding of soul mates, no matter how gentlemanly he is. At least Henry waits until Clare is eighteen for their first kiss in that meadow, and the camera rejoices upward toward the heavens.

Unfortunately, getting hearts to similarly soar is impeded by a heaviness throughout, caused by the film's continual tilt toward the tragic. This dispiriting atmosphere manifests itself within the very first scene, which sets the audience up for a fall from the height of serenity. Henry is a carefree little boy at the time, cozily ensconced in the back seat of a car. It is driven by a mother so warm that no other heat source is likely needed within the vehicle as it travels through Christmastime snow. Suddenly, the car goes out of control, a visual metaphor for Henry's life itself. Horrified and helpless, the boy disappears in his inaugural instance of chronological yo-yoing, just seconds before a truck smashes into the automobile and kills his beloved mom. In contrast to those last lovely, loving moments, the discombobulated, naked tyke rematerializes at the scene of his devastating loss, both literally and figuratively out in the cold. How utterly depressing it is to hear Henry later relate that he has had to watch his mother die hundreds of times ever since, endlessly trying but failing to deter disaster. Never again wanting to have anything or anyone in his life that he cannot bear to lose, the obviously weary time traveler is shown to live a lonely, cursory, anchorless life.

Clare ardently accomplishes Henry's re-anchoring, yet she is also seen repeatedly, miserably, and increasingly resentfully alone during his absences once they are married. Eventually, in one of the film's most interesting scenes, she assertively vents her festering frustrations, understandably feeling like Destiny's (and, in a palpable sense, Henry's) powerless pawn, her right to a life of her own choosing having been abrogated at six. Claire longs for a normal life and a child. She gets the second after she and the audience endure two miscarriages, but only due to a calculated romp in the back seat with a younger, pre-vasectomied Henry who is blissfully unaware of how hazardous it can be to carry a prospective time traveler to term.

Once Alba (vibrant sisters Hailey and Tatum McCann) is born, there is a montage that nicely summarizes five years of familial contentment the audience fully expects to be summarily spoiled. No one was likely to have missed the film's obvious, ominous foreshadowing, including color desaturization of the image and the

seasonal decline toward winter. There is also the statement made to Henry by Clare's hunting enthusiast father about wanting someday to "take you out," followed later on by the most mature version of Henry briefly materializing with an agonizing bullet wound to the gut. Music is also often used rather heavy-handedly, pointing out meaning and underscoring emotion.

There are other problems, such as the way the film nearly grinds to a halt when the characters are looking into gene mutation minutia rather than each other's eyes. Yet, despite all this pain, ponderousness and head-scratching paradoxes, Bana and McAdams (the latter back in the mode of *The Notebook* [2004]) make one hope that their timeless twosome can somehow avoid running out of time. That Henry twice appears to his loved ones past his date of death—and apparently will again—dulls the impact of his demise, but it is nonetheless heartening. So are the scenes in which Henry is able to go back for an assuaging passing moment with his mother and go forward to chat with a happy, healthy Alba during Clare's latest iffy pregnancy. Those apt to gag on such bittersweet goo will prefer to steer clear, lest they find themselves yearning mightily for Henry's ability to disappear.

David L. Boxerbaum

CREDITS

Henry DeTamble: Eric Bana
Clare Abshire: Rachel McAdams
Gomez: Ron Livingston
Dr. David Kendrick: Stephen Tobolowsky
Richard DeTamble: Arliss Howard
Annette DeTamble: Michelle Nolden
Origin: USA
Language: English
Released: 2009
Production: Nick Wechsler, Dede Gardner; New Line Cinema, Plan B Entertainment; released by Warner Bros.
Directed by: Robert Schwentke
Written by: Bruce Joel Rubin
Cinematography by: Florian Ballhaus
Music by: Mychael Danna
Sound: Robert F. Scherer
Music Supervisor: Bob Bowen
Editing: Thom Noble
Art Direction: Peter Grundy
Costumes: Julie Weiss
Production Design: Jon Hutman
MPAA rating: PG-13
Running time: 107 minutes

REVIEWS

Anderson, John. *Washington Post.* August 14, 2009.
Burr, Ty. *Boston Globe.* August 13, 2009.

Chang, Justin. *Variety.* August 10, 2009.

Corliss, Richard. *Time Magazine.* August 14, 2009.

Dargis, Manohla. *New York Times.* August 14, 2009.

Ebert, Roger. *Chicago Sun-Times.* August 13, 2009.

Edelstein, David. *New York Magazine.* August 17, 2009.

Honeycutt, Kirk. *Hollywood Reporter.* August 10, 2009.

Sobczynski, Peter. *eFilmCritic.com.* August 13, 2009.

Tallerico, Brian. *MovieRetriever.com.* August 15, 2009.

QUOTES

Clare Abshire: "I wouldn't change one second of our life together."

TRIVIA

When reshoots for the film were required, production was put on hold so that Eric Bana's hair could grow out since he had shaved it for his role in *Star Trek.*

TRANSFORMERS: REVENGE OF THE FALLEN

Revenge is coming.
—Movie tagline

Box Office: $402.1 million

"I'm so excited And I just can't hide it I'm about to lose control And I think I like it!"

The above are lyrics from a Pointer Sisters hit that is heard early in *Transformers: Revenge of the Fallen,* but they may very well also be what director Michael Bay said on the verge of making this testosterone-fueled orgasmic explosion of a film. It is bewilderingly chaotic, roaringly-cacophonous, and awash with expository jargon that helped to make many feel as if they were drowning in a flood of incomprehensibility. Members of the audience who reacted that way will surely also have found themselves thinking that Bay's work is staggeringly overlong, gazing at the climactic scene's Pyramids of Giza and feeling like the film's start may have coincided with their construction. When these wearied viewers heard that the evil Decepticons aim to kill "slowly and painfully," it likely seemed as if the film itself was out to do them in in a similar fashion. By this sequel's end, returning protagonists Sam Witwicky (Shia LeBeouf) and Mikaela Banes (Megan Fox) say, "I love you" as feelings finally come to a head. Most reviewers, however, were left shaking theirs at the protracted mess, and what welled-up in them was just as passionate but nowhere near as tenderly idolatrous.

That said, Bay could not care a whit. Hearing such criticism might make him take a brief break from counting the many millions he has earned through such excess to give an unfazed shrug, but one doubts it would actually give him pause. He knows that there is a sizeable audience out there fervently anticipating such films, moviegoers who cannot get enough as opposed to those screaming "Enough!" The former group is likely made up of those in the vicinity of puberty's onset, or viewers who have grown up without growing more discriminating. They may or may not be personally acquainted with the 1980s Hasbro toys upon which the *Transformers* films are based, but all would think it would be way-cool to come into close contact with the unquestionably-hot Fox and the film's arsenal of equally smoking guns. To those decidedly-contrary critics, these steadfast fans would surely derisively echo one of the film's lines: "Who are you to judge what's best for us?" The other group of audience members, however, would likely choose words uttered by Jetfire (voiced by Mark Ryan), the most mature of the colossal creatures in this follow-up to Bay's equally-mammoth 2007 moneymaker: "I'm too old for this crap."

How appropriate that such an androgen-propelled film is absolutely studded with testicular humor. Sam's conspiracy-hound, techno-geek roommate, Leo (Ramon Rodriguez), gets tasered, and wincingly wonders how many times one can get zapped there and still have children. Later, Mikaela causes more trauma to his testes by crushingly landing upon them. Later, former Sect. 7 Agent Simmons (John Turturro), this time much more helpful and peculiar, pinpoints his location as "just below the enemy's scrotum," as a pair of massive metallic orbs swing between the Decepticon's legs like some sort of obscene wind chimes. Those viewers having a ball watching it all will also enjoy the repeated instances of dog's humping each other and a diminutive Decepticon enthusiastically doing the same to Mikaela's leg, as well as Simmons' ridiculous, gag-inducing sporting of a thong and brief, inadvertent snuggling with Leo while the two are simultaneously dozing. It is the kind of humor that has guys guffawing at peak levels while in junior high. However, judging by the deep-voiced chortles in the audience, it apparently does not get old even when one is no longer young.

A crowd-pleaser for males of any age is Fox, and Bay's camera drools over her throughout *Transformers: Revenge of the Fallen.* When she is introduced, the director aims to rev viewers up with a shot of her sexily straddling a motorcycle. It lingers on her long, bare legs before proceeding up to shorts sufficiently abbreviated to make them hardly worth having bothered to put any on at all. Fox has what appears to be a continual, post-coital sheen to her skin, sports even glossier lips that are always parted suggestively, and is always perfectly made up. What she does here is actually more like modeling:

she is posing as an actress. Lucky for Fox, the script calls for her to do little more than be arousing eye candy, suggestively whispering the word "camshafts" and often making far-fetched but fetching attempts to outrun fiery explosions. With that rather vacuous look in her eyes, one cannot help but always be a little surprised and relieved that she knows enough to run away and not towards them. As one perceptive Decepticon put it, "You're hot, but you're not too bright!"

Whoever it was who coined the phrase "less is more," it is safe to say that it was not Bay. In *Revenge of the Fallen,* he supersizes the moviegoing experience provided by the first film, with even more deafening, histrionic pandemonium. An early chase scene through Shanghai serves as sort of a scorchingly-hot adrenaline appetizer chock-full of crashing, crunching, and sparking. Such roaring, relentless, repetitive mayhem rules throughout the film as Optimus Prime (voiced by peter Cullen) and the other human-friendly Autobots once again battle hell-bent-on-destruction, devilish Decepticons (a Lucifer-like one here is aptly called The Fallen), and even fans will probably be hard-pressed to identify exactly who is bashing whom in any given shot. One suspects it probably does not matter to them, however, just as long as the commotion continues. The film's finale is interminable, let's-blow-everything-up-and-then-some rampaging rambunctiousness, but at least the world has been made safe once again—until the series' upcoming third installment. (Before then, one fervently hopes that Bay junks Autobots Mudflap and Skids, both offensive, Jar-Jar Binks-like embarrassments.)

There are lulls along the way that probably had many Transformer devotees twitching expectantly for the onset of yet more trouble. If they could have utilized a fast-forward button in the theater, such audience members would likely have bypassed the introductory scenes which have Sam going off to college as his empty-nester parents (Kevin Dunn and Julie White) head off to Paris for some consoling distraction. The lame campus interlude in which mom goes berserk on pot-laced brownies would have been skipped over in favor of the sequences in which the university's uniformly-gorgeous girls might perhaps go wild. One, a Decepticon disguised as a horny coed (Isabel Lucas), aggressively shoves Sam onto a bed and reveals what can be done with a five-foot, talented tongue.

Speaking of wagging tongues, there is a tiresome amount of expository bombast and bologna along with all the bomb blasts, crashes, Richter-scale-registering Transformer fisticuffs, and bullet-strafing military good times. (Josh Duhamel and Tyrese Gibson return to attractively engage in the latter.) Various characters speak often and at length while somehow maintaining a tone of grave seriousness about things that will fascinate some

and make others zone out as things drone on. Even before the title appears, as a voiceover narration intones that "our worlds have met before," the audience is shown a first encounter between prehistoric man and newly-arrived Transformers that appears to have gone far less smoothly than the Native American-Pilgrim First Thanksgiving. As the film hurtles forward, there are not only other narrated flashback sequences but also patience-trying tête-à-têtes, all featuring an increasingly rat-a-tat-tat and mind-taxing conveyance of minutely-detailed revelatory twaddle. There are residual Allspark shards, glyphs that map the way to energon sources, The Tomb of the Primes, Seekers, The Sun Harvester, The Dagger's Tip, and The Matrix of Leadership. While the characters end up in Egypt in the vicinity of the Sphinx and the aforementioned pyramids, a more appropriate setting might have been the Tower of Babel. "Do you know what it means?" asks a confounded Simmons at one point. "No," Sam replies, "What does it mean?" "I have no idea," Simmons admits, and few watching will absorb it all without difficulty, either. A Shakespeare quote seems monumentally out of place in connection with Bay's film, but "full of sound and fury, signifying nothing" sums things up awfully well.

Made on a whopping budget of $200 million, *Transformers: Revenge of the Fallen* had no problem grossing more than twice that before proceeding to rake even more in overseas. Critical reaction was mainly unfavorable and often scathing. *Rolling Stone*'s Peter Travers asserted that it had "a shot at the title 'Worst Movie of the Decade.'" When one reviewer stated that the film's box office take could make it "the biggest movie of all time," Roger Ebert snorted the following retort: "It's certainly the biggest something of all time," declaring it "a horrible experience of unbearable length." All that may need to be added is the tremendously-apt summing-up by the *Boston Globe*'s Ty Burr, who called Bay's *Transformers: Revenge of the Fallen* "2½ hours of tumescence disguised as a motion picture."

David L. Boxerbaum

CREDITS

Mikaela Banes: Megan Fox
Agent Simmons: John Turturro
Capt. Lennox: Josh Duhamel
Tech Sgt. Epps: Tyrese Gibson
Ron Witwicky: Kevin Dunn
Sam Witwicky: Shia LaBeouf
Starscream: Charles Adler (Voice)
Optimus Prime: Peter Cullen (Voice)
Origin: USA

Language: English

Released: 2009

Production: Dreamworks Pictures; released by Paramount Pictures

Directed by: Michael Bay

Written by: Ehren Kruger, Alex Kurtzman, Roberto Orci

Cinematography by: Ben Seresin

Music by: Steve Jablonsky

Editing: Roger Barton

Sound: Erik Aadahl, Ethan Van der Ryn

Art Direction: Jon Billington

Costumes: Deborah L. Scott

Production Design: Nigel Phelps

MPAA rating: PG-13

Running time: 147 minutes

REVIEWS

Bennett, Ray. *Hollywood Reporter.* June 16, 2009.

Dargis, Manohla. *New York Times.* June 23, 2009.

Douglas, Edward. *ComingSoon.net.* June 23, 2009.

Ebert, Roger. *Chicago Sun-Times.* June 23, 2009.

Franklin, Garth. *Dark Horizons.* June 23, 2009.

Hunter, Allan. *Daily Express.* June 19, 2009.

Lumenick, Lou. *New York Post.* June 23, 2009.

Phillips, Michael. *Chicago Tribune.* June 23, 2009.

Tallerico, Brian. *MovieRetriever.com.* June 24, 2009.

Wilonsky, Robert. *Village Voice.* June 24, 2009.

QUOTES

Optimus Prime: "Our races, united by a history long forgotten and a future we shall face together. I am Optimus Prime, and I send this message so that our past will always be remembered. For in those memories, we live on."

TRIVIA

Shooting on the sequel started the day after *Transformers* won the MTV Movie Award for Best Movie.

AWARDS

Golden Raspberries 2009: Worst Picture, Worst Director (Bay), Worst Screenplay

Nomination:

Oscars 2009: Sound

Golden Raspberries 2009: Worst Actress (Fox), Worst Support. Actress (White), Worst Remake, Rip-Off or Sequel

Screen Actors Guild 2009: Stunt Ensemble.

TRUCKER

Trucker looks like just another movie to pass over; another film festival entry grounded in the standard expectations of broken families and tough love. Four of every five movies from Sundance, where films like these are born and thrive, are interchangeable, save for the occasional performance that make us sit up, take notice and forgive all its remaining flaws. For some, *Trucker* could certainly fall into any of those lists of four. Thanks to the standout work by the actors though and familiarity that feels more like everyday life than conventions, *Trucker* becomes the fifth: the one to check out.

Michelle Monaghan plays Diane Ford, a long-haul trucker whose profession as a loner has translated into her personal life. Or is it the other way around? Opening on a one night stand built for her pleasure, Diane's only recurring human connection is that of her drinking buddy, Runner (Nathan Fillion). Unlike the usual type that pursues married men for the challenge, Diane likely takes comfort in his unavailability, even if he harbors a little crush on her. She had a husband once, but he's since remarried. One night the new wife (Joey Lauren Adams) shows up to Diane's house with bad news and worse news. Her ex, Leonard (Benjamin Bratt) is dying of cancer. Worse for her, he needs someone to watch his son, Peter (Jimmy Bennett); the son Diane left behind soon after he was born.

Neither of them are keen on this arrangement. By the next morning, the boy is already being watched by Runner, who has a gentler approach than the frustrated Diane. Peter doesn't make it easy for her either. He moves at his own pace, doesn't listen well and practically makes her beg for him to follow her. As the open road calls, the pair hit it together where her only parental instinct is to protect Peter from the casual everyday dangers she sees on the job. He knows Diane doesn't want him around and the harder she tries, the more painful it becomes for him. The boy admits to being afraid of her and doesn't know how to react when she puts on a nice face. But try they might as each faces the awareness they may be stuck with one another for longer than three weeks.

Films like *Trucker* don't depend on plotting to make the case for its characters. Thankfully it doesn't resort to the oldest device in the book—the road trip—to let the sun slowly rise on their relationship. Actors are frequently told to communicate through listening and writer/director James Mottern is asking us to do the same. Instead of looking ahead and waiting for the chink in the armor that's going to soften everyone up for a happy ending, if we just listen to the characters their emotions ring true.

"I guess you can tell by looking at me I'm not in the best shape of my life," Leonard says to Peter. The somewhat extra-pale makeup reflects that a bit too robustly, but Benjamin Bratt brings us back into this final quiet moment between father and son that is perhaps the strongest scene he's ever played. Nathan Fillion is best known to television audiences for his roles on *Firefly* and *Castle*, but just as he's proved in those shows as well as his work opposite Keri Russell in *Waitress* (2007), he continues to establish himself as one of the most effortlessly charming presences on any screen. The screenplay neglects Runner's relationship with his wife, seen in a single scene, while he's normally hanging out or doing favors for Diane. Yet we never look upon him as just another lout interested in a cheap affair. There's a good man in there who may have made a few wrong turns in his life and is now looking for someone whose frown he can turn around.

Bratt and Fillion are effective, but *Trucker* hinges on the turns from Monaghan and Bennett. At just the age of twelve, Bennett has had a film career that has bordered on child abuse —character-wise. He's had to survive two attempts at taking his family captive in *Hostage* (2005) and *Firewall* (2006), two deadly boat trips with *Poseidon* (2006) and *Evan Almighty* (2007), a possessed dad in *The Amityville Horror* (2005), the evil sister from *Orphan* (2009) and a mom played by Asia Argento in *The Heart Is Deceitful Above All Things* (2004) that would immediately put Diane in the running for mom of the year even if she tied him to the grill of her truck for a game of chicken. Prickly portrayals of youth caught in the middle of a dire situation can turn bad for audiences immediately interested in strangling the lad for making things so unnecessarily difficult. Mottern is careful in not turning Peter into an aggravator just for drama's sake. He's facing the death of his father, a mom that abandoned him and an uncertainty of where home will be and Bennett does a very good job at knowing when to pull back the stubbornness and become aware that the new people in his life are just trying to do their best by him.

Since her breakthrough role in a sexy Christmas outfit in Shane Black's *Kiss Kiss Bang Bang* (2005), Monaghan was settling into a long career of being the spunky girlfriend/female quota for casting directors. *Mission: Impossible III* (2006), *The Heartbreak Kid* (2007), *Made of Honor* (2008) and *Eagle Eye* (2008) kept her working but it was the few scenes in *Gone Baby Gone* (2007) where she was acting as more than just a loyal sidekick that there was a hint of range potential. In *Trucker* she finally gets the spotlight. More than just a stunt role in search of awards, Monaghan invests Diane with a confidence in her own solitude. She's in control of a life not dependent on big dreams or even some romanticized notion of the open road and she's not going to be quick to give it all up for a momentary lapse in believing she could be one of those everyday women. It's not a softening we're witnessing, but a gradual acceptance that there is someone in her life who needs her instead of wanting her.

Trucker is not hampered by its familiar story arc. There are no custody battles or metaphors about motherhood being the ultimate long haul. Like the films that have come before it, we anticipate a certain thawing in the heroine's resilience. Unlike *Frozen River* (2008) however, the ending feels far more natural when Diane is confronted with what the best is for her child. Will she give up and pawn him off on another or realize that she needs him too? The answer may be fairly obvious, but the way its handled by Mottern and his cast is moving and, most importantly, does not feel like just another movie.

Erik Childress

CREDITS

Diane Ford: Michelle Monaghan
Peter: Jimmy Bennett
Leonard Bonner: Benjamin Bratt
Runner: Nathan Fillion
Jenny Bell: Joey Lauren Adams
Rick: Bryce Johnson
Origin: USA
Language: English
Released: 2008
Production: Scott Hanson, Galt Niederhoffer, Celine Rattray, Daniela Taplin Lundberg; Plum Pictures, Hanson Allen Films, Hart-Lunsford Pictures; released by Monterey Media
Directed by: James Mottern
Written by: James Mottern
Cinematography by: Lawrence Sher
Music by: Mychael Danna
Editing: Deidre Slevin
Sound: Michael Suarez
Costumes: Johanna Argan
Production Design: Cabot McMullen
MPAA rating: R
Running time: 90 minutes

REVIEWS

Anderson, John. *Variety.* June 10, 2008.
Ebert, Roger. *Chicago Sun-Times.* October 8, 2009.
Farber, Stephen. *Hollywood Reporter.* October 9, 2009.
Gleiberman, Owen. *Entertainment Weekly.* October 14, 2009.
Holden, Stephen. *New York Times.* October 9, 2009.
Phillips, Michael. *At the Movies.* October 19, 2009.
Rodriguez, Rene. *Miami Herald.* October 29, 2009.
Scott, A.O. *At the Movies.* October 19, 2009.

Sharkey, Betsy. *Los Angeles Times.* October 16, 2009.
Tallerico, Brian. *MovieRetriever.com.* October 21, 2009.

TRIVIA

At one point, Demi Moore was considered for the lead in the film.

12 ROUNDS

Box Office: $12.2 million

Most action movies being made these days are admittedly pretty dumb—the question is, are they "Good Dumb" or "Bad Dumb"? "Good Dumb" action movies are the kind where all of the key elements—the characters, the stunts and the pacing, to name just a few—have been pushed to such outlandish extremes that it becomes obvious that everyone involved is in on the joke and the sheer outrageous goofiness of the proceedings turns out to be part of the charm. The *Transporter* series from producer Luc Besson is an excellent example of this kind of film—they are all hopelessly insane, to be sure, but they have been put forth with such heedless enthusiasm and energy that they can't help but appeal to the hyperactive 12-year-old boy inside all of us. Bad Dumb action films, on the other hand, are the ones that just tend to go through the motions and while they may be ludicrous, they just aren't ludicrous enough to make any impact at all. In the case of *12 Rounds*, the opening credits have barely finished when it becomes painfully obvious that this is going to be an extreme version of the Bad Dumb variety—a painfully derivative film whose sole burst of originality is that it primarily rips off *Die Hard with a Vengeance* (1995) instead of the original *Die Hard* (1988) and whose sole redeeming virtue is that it is about an hour shorter than *Transformers: Revenge of the Fallen* (2009).

As the film opens, amiably dopey New Orleans Police Detective Danny Fisher (World Wrestling Entertainment champion John Cena) stumbles upon a crime scene and inadvertently gets the drop on master criminal/terrorist/Irishman Miles Jackson (Aidan Glenn). In the process, Miles' girlfriend forgets to look both ways while running away and gets creamed by an oncoming van. Needless to say, Miles vows vengeance against Danny (who didn't actually do anything, if you stop to think about it) and one year later, he busts out of prison to make it happen by kidnapping Danny's wife (Ashley Scott) and forcing him to complete a series of twelve seemingly impossible tasks—mostly involving running around town while trying to prevent bombs from exploding or runaway streetcars from running over people too dense to get out of the way—if he ever wants

to see her alive again. From a plot standpoint, that is about it—Danny runs around from locale to locale saving the day while butting heads with a clueless FBI agent (Steve Harris), trying to figure out Miles' endgame and no doubt being repeatedly asked by people if his parents named him after the Elvis Presley character from *King Creole* (1958).

12 Rounds marks the second attempt by the WWE's filmmaking tentacle to transfer John Cena's ring stardom to the silver screen. Oddly enough, that previous attempt, *The Marine* (2006) was a pretty good example of a Good Dumb action movie—it was amusingly cheesy throughout, it was rarely boring and Robert Patrick was clearly having a blast playing the decidedly over-the-top villain. Although the two films have roughly the same premise (big chiseled galoot has his wife kidnapped by a master criminal and blows up a lot of stuff in his efforts to save her), *12 Rounds* never comes close to matching even that film—hardly a classic of the genre by anyone's estimate—in any aspect. Of course, one doesn't go to a movie like this for the performances or the screenplay but both categories are exceptionally poorly served here—Cena is such a muscle-bound blank here that he looks like he is auditioning for the long-awaited sequel to *Space Mutiny* (1988), Gillen is more obnoxious than mesmerizing and the screenplay is so bad that the only thing distracting viewers from the enormous plot holes is the clichéd dialogue in which people are described as being in the wrong place at the wrong time and asking questions above their pay grade. However, one *does* go to this kind of movie to see flashy action scenes delivered at a breakneck pace and in that regard, its failures are even more considerable—the sequences themselves are both derivative and ineptly constructed and the entire thing, despite essentially being one long chase scene, is astoundingly boring throughout.

Frankly, the only surprising thing about *12 Rounds* is that it was directed by none other than Renny Harlin, the Finnish-born filmmaker who was one of the top action directors of the early 1990s thanks to such blockbusters as *Die Hard 2* (1990) and *Cliffhanger* (1993). Unfortunately for him, his career began a steep descent shortly after hitting those heights and he has since had the ignominy of directing several enormously expensive failures (such as *Cutthroat Island* [1995], *The Long Kiss Goodnight* [1996] and *Driven* [2000]), a film that sat on the shelf for several years before finally getting released (*Mindhunters* [2005]), a film that went straight to video (*Cleaner* [2007]) and the kind of teeny-bopper horror schlock that one normally does at the beginning of one's career (*The Covenant* [2006]). Though I would hardly rank him as a great filmmaker by even the loosest definition of the term, he used to have a knack for producing impressive big-screen blockbusters back in the day but he just comes across here like some kind of anonymous hack who got the gig because no one else wanted it. For fans of the kind of cinematic spectacle that he used to specialize in, it is hard to know which aspect of *12 Rounds* is more depressing—the fact that he has been reduced to directing WWE vanity projects or the fact that, based on the evidence, he no longer seems to have the chops to even pull that off anymore.

Peter Sobczynski

CREDITS

Dr. Danny Fisher: John Cena
Miles Jackson: Aidan Gillen
Special Agent George Aiken: Steve Harris
Molly Porter: Ashley Scott
Det. Hank Carver: Brian White
Erica Kessen: Taylor Cole
Gonzalo Menendez: Ray Santiago
Origin: USA
Language: English
Released: 2009
Production: Mark Gordon, Josh McLaughlin, Michael Lake; WWE Studios; released by Fox Atomic
Directed by: Renny Harlin
Written by: Daniel Kunka
Cinematography by: David Boyd
Music by: Trevor Rabin
Sound: Paul Ledford
Editing: Brian Berdan
Production Design: Nicholas Lundy
Costumes: Jill Newell
MPAA rating: PG-13
Running time: 108 minutes

REVIEWS

Anderson, John. *Newsday.* March 30, 2009.
Berardinelli, James. *ReelViews.* March 30, 2009.
Berkshire, Geoff. *Metromix.com.* March 27, 2009.
Collis, Clark. *Entertainment Weekly.* March 30, 2009.
Cook, Linda. *Quad City Times.* April 2, 2009.
Goldstein, Gary. *Los Angeles Times.* March 30, 2009.
Lane, Jim. *Sacramento News & Review.* April 9, 2009.
Lee, Nathan. *New York Times.* March 30, 2009.
McDonagh, Maitland. *Hollywood Reporter.* March 30, 2009.
Rabin, Nathan. *AV Club.* March 30, 2009.

QUOTES

Detective Danny Fisher: "I'm training the world's most dominant pug. He's going through a bulking phase."

TRIVIA

Director Renny Harlin's son Lucas makes a brief appearance in the film as a boy wearing a hat on the street car.

2012

First, the Mayan calendar predicted it. Now, science has confirmed it. But we never imagined it could really happen.
—Movie tagline

Box Office: $166.1 million

If Roland Emmerich was not making movies he would likely be on a watch list somewhere. No one can get away with thinking so frequently about killing everyone in the world without being pulled out of every airport line and having a padded cell reserved for them. When Gene Wilder lamented that he "must have killed more men than Cecil B. DeMille" in *Blazing Saddles* (1974), how could he have known that another film-maker would soon displace both of them as the reigning king of cinematic genocide? Call this The Day After Independence Day Three Years From Now and then add any amount of vulgar adjectives to it. Somewhere in-between add the words dumb, illogical, disgusting, and xenophobic and it woukd be appropriate. Some may dismiss *2012* as just another harmless disaster extravaganza, but how many times do you keep stabbing yourself in the brain before you learn that it's a bad idea?

Like all disaster stories, or at least Emmerich's *Independence Day* (1996) and *The Day After Tomorrow* (2004), the film begins with the discovery of something ominous on the horizon. Or underneath the Earth. The crusts are shifting, water wells are boiling and solar flares are signaling the end is near. Geologist Adrian Helmsley (Chiwetel Ejiofor) is clued into the warning signs and tips off Chief of Staff Carl Anheuser (Oliver Platt) that it might be best to begin planning for the worst.

Three years later we begin meeting the potential fodder for the Earth's wrath. Jackson Curtis (John Cusack) is a failed writer and father now driving a limo for a living and doing his best to stay in the lives of his children, Noah (Liam James) and Lilly (Morgan Lily). Naturally, that baggage comes with an ex-wife, Kate (Amanda Peet), whom he still carries a flame for and a new plastic surgeon boyfriend, Gordon (Thomas McCarthy), who keeps reminding her of Jackson's failures as a man. With questionable parenting skills, Jackson takes the kids to Yellowstone, jumps a restricted fence and slowly inspects a dried-up lake complete with dead caribou lining it. Thankfully the military directs them elsewhere and Jackson comes face-to-face with Charlie

Frost (Woody Harrelson), the conspiracy-preaching voice of pirate radio who is also on to what the Mayan calendar apparently predicted as a cataclysmic event to scorch the Earth on December 21, 2012.

It turns out that the expert geologist is consistently off in predicting the exact timeline for the catastrophe. It's always sooner rather than later so that means it's happening NOW! Or forty-six minutes into the film. After a few road splits here and there and a complete separation of the Jewel from the Osco, the world begins falling apart. From the West Coast to the East Coast while the South Pole moves into Wisconsin, the Curtis family needs to get out of Dodge while dodging falling skyscrapers, rising water, volcanic fireballs and elderly drivers. In the midst of the chaos of the day, the Curtis family is almost killed by a pair of old ladies who can barely see over the steering wheel let alone that their doom is inevitable and having their car sprayed with sewage waste. Pilots laugh off close calls before either falling to their death or neglecting that all of Las Vegas and its guests are being swallowed up all around them. It does not seem a coincidence that the first person Emmerich kills in the film is be the head of the Louvre just doing his best to preserve high art. The fact that it is announced that his car crashed in the exact same tunnel as Princess Diana should be Exhibit A at how unbelievably tasteless *2012* is about to get.

In his one published book—a sci-fi tale about the survival of Atlantis—Jackson wrote about the selflessness of man being tested in the face of their own demise, a passage that bookworm Helmsley latches onto. Emmerich and co-writer/composer Harald Kloser are not big subscribers to this theory, despite presumably writing it. Those characters that do sacrifice themselves throughout the film, never quite do it for the good of the man or woman next to them but rather as some self-serving last gasp to witness the beautiful destruction first-hand or to go down with the sinking ship so as not to be judged by history. Another does manage to save a few members of their family but only after abandoning his wife out of spite and starting a riot charge that sends several others plummeting to their death.

Humanity is in shorter supply as the film progresses, but is booming compared to the frequent lapses in logic and credible screenwriting connections that gives coincidence a bad name. The next time you're on a delayed 747 flight because of a little sprinkle or windy conditions, you march right up to that cockpit and demand your money back for you have seen an amateur pilot maneuver a packed twin-engine plane through the turbulence of Armageddon while the runway falls away behind him. Twice! Jake and Elwood's Bluesmobile did not take on as much damage as the Curtis limo. You can't get a U.S. cell phone provider to save your life in Canada, but a guy walking through the Himalayas can get a signal into a secure location after half the world has been destroyed. How could Jackson be late for work if he's cut his weekend with the kids short? The plot inconsistencies fly faster than the next character who walks into a room saying "I think you need to see this."

Following the template for a disaster movie is never going to draw any extra criticism for all the wannabe Irwin Allen's out there. Introduce a variety of characters of various sex, class and race and then have them run away from the very pot that's melting. When done right it can be exciting as in *The Poseidon Adventure* (1972) or terrifying, especially if you're a kid, like *The Towering Inferno* (1974). A decade ago we were fortunate (or unfortunate) to get a direct compare-and-contrast in styles with Mimi Leder's *Deep Impact* (1998) and *Armageddon* (1998) in the same summer. Leder's film, while co-plotting the heroics of a space mission to stop the deadly comet, concentrated on the human elements and preparation for the disaster while Bay's film was all macho bravado and ridiculous destruction in a noisy, jingoistic package. When you hear words like "lottery" and the arguments over who will and won't be given a seat on the government's survival stimulus package, you have the makings of a film worth thinking about, even if it's just another parlor game. No one, especially humanist Helmsley, likes to hear that only the richest one percent are on the list. But someone had to donate the money to fund the big ships, right? Since the whole project is based upon the assertion that the Mayan calendar ends with this prediction, why not explore that a bit further? Use that as a jumping off point, let us meet the characters during the three years leading up to the event and then destroy the world as your big finale? Emmerich might have learned something from blowing his forty days and forty nights in the first forty minutes of *The Day After Tomorrow*; after which he was left with nothing but our heroes to outrun escaped wolves and an actual cold front that chased them around. No dice. It just made him realize he needed to find new landmarks to destroy for the final 100 minutes.

Science-blind, logic-blind and excitement-blind, Emmerich goes the extra mile to prove just how color-blind he is as well. As either a sign of the times or to continue the trend of global annihilation under the watch of a black President after Morgan Freeman in *Deep Impact*, Danny Glover is cast as our leader. Thandie Newton is his daughter. And with Ejiofor in a major role, African Americans content with the cliché of them being the first to go in films like this may take comfort that civilization is about to be repopulated again at the Cape of Good Hope in Africa. It's all part of that trademark Emmerich lack of subtlety who, in his ultimate can't-we-all-get-along moment, implicates the back-story of George Segal's Ebony-and-Ivory cruise boat entertainer as a guy who hasn't called his son in years because of his mixed-race marriage—only to do so "too late" before they all perish.

Sensitivity not being Emmerich's strong suit, if it's not enough to send thousands or millions of CGI humans flailing to their deaths, just kill them twice up close. At least two characters are presumably dispatched before our very eyes, once by a volcanic blast and another by a giant tsunami. The first could easily be misjudged as the final nail in their coffin, but the second one is actually cut back to later so he can be awakened from a pile of ashes and corpses and then killed once and for all. This is a film where Platt's advisor leaves his confused mother behind to "meet her maker on her own terms." For all the shots at religion being a baseless waste of hope, it's a bit disingenuous for the finale to be dependent on a trio of Arks that young Noah is desperately trying to board. Remember, this is the director who, after receiving negative reviews from Siskel & Ebert on *Independence Day*, crafted two lookalikes in *Godzilla* (1998), presented them as fools and had them give the trademark thumbs up and thumbs down. Is it any wonder he would name the thoughtless White House flunky, Anheuser? To the character's defense, at least he makes snap decisions in a crisis. If he was in the audience for *2012* he would have jumped out of his seat to leave and save himself as soon as possible.

Erik Childress

CREDITS

Jackson Curtis: John Cusack
Kate Curtis: Amanda Peet
President Wilson: Danny Glover
Adrian Helmsley: Chiwetel Ejiofor
Carl Anheuser: Oliver Platt
Laura Wilson: Thandie Newton
Charlie Frost: Woody Harrelson
Gordon Silberman: Thomas McCarthy
Origin: USA
Language: English
Released: 2009
Production: Roland Emmerich, Larry J. Franco, Harold Kloser; Centropolis Entertainment, Mark Gordon Company, Farewell Productions, Columbia Pictures; released by Sony Pictures Releasing
Directed by: Roland Emmerich
Written by: Roland Emmerich, Harald Kloser
Cinematography by: Dean Semler
Music by: Harald Kloser, Thomas Wanker
Sound: Paul N.J. Ottosson

Editing: David Brenner, Peter S. Elliot
Art Direction: Don MacAulay
Costumes: Shay Cunliffe
Production Design: Barry Chusid
MPAA rating: PG-13
Running time: 158 minutes

REVIEWS

Burr, Ty. *Boston Globe.* November 12, 2009.
Corliss, Richard. *Time Magazine.* November 12, 2009.
Coyle, Jake. *Associated Press.* November 11, 2009.
LaSalle, Mick. *San Francisco Chronicle.* November 12, 2009.
Rickey, Carrie. *Philadelphia Inquirer.* November 12, 2009.
Scott, A.O. *At the Movies.* November 16, 2009.
Tallerico, Brian. *MovieRetriever.com* November 13, 2009.
Travers, Peter. *Rolling Stone.* November 13, 2009.
Turan, Kenneth. *Los Angeles Times.* November 13, 2009.
Westhoff, Jeffrey. *Northwest Herald.* November 12, 2009.

QUOTES

Carl Anheuder: "Kind of galling when you realize that nutbags with cardboard signs had it right the whole time."

TRIVIA

Roland Emmerich has said that this will be his final disaster film: "I said to myself that I'll do one more disaster movie, but it has to end all disaster movies. So I packed everything in."

THE TWILIGHT SAGA: NEW MOON
(New Moon)

The next chapter begins.
—Movie tagline

Box Office: $296.3 million

In *The Twilight Saga: New Moon*, the second installment of the star-crossed romance featuring shy high schooler Bella Swan (Kristen Stewart) and the century-old drop-dead gorgeous vampire destined to love her, Edward Cullen (Robert Pattinson), Edward decides that the best thing he can do for Bella is stay out of her life, so for most of the film the shaggy haired vampire is not on-screen. To take her mind off her broken heart, Bella takes up with Jacob (Taylor Lautner), her younger, but still super hot friend from the Rez just outside her Forks, Washington town. Jacob wants to be more than just a way for Bella to forget about Edward for a few hours, but Bella just cannot shake her addiction to vampire-loving. The Bella-still-loving-Edward, Edward-appearing-in-Bella's-adrenaline-induced-hallucinations and Jacob-pining-over-Bella love triangle becomes more complicated when it is revealed that Jacob is not just the super cute boy next door, he is in fact a werewolf and therefore the sworn enemy of Edward's vampire coven. The *New Moon* story line pits Bella firmly in the middle, torn between the love of her life and her best friend and pits "Team Jacob" and "Team Edward" fans against one another as well.

But those are not the only tug-of-war elements associated with the movie. *The Twilight Saga: New Moon* also features a new director, Chris Weitz taking over from Catherine Hardwicke who helmed 2008's *Twilight*—when announced the change made headlines. Weitz brings a soundtrack-driven, teen romance movie vibe to *The Twilight Saga: New Moon* in place of Hardwicke's more ethereal approach to vampires in *Twilight*, so the real question nagging at all *Twilight Saga* fans is: Is *New Moon* a better movie than *Twilight*?

To properly answer this quandary, it is necessary to underline that, so far, each *Twilight Saga* movie has relied so heavily on audiences having had read Stephenie Meyer's books that it is difficult to talk about the movies as their own entities. Essentially, they are visual montage accompaniments to already well-known narratives, similar to the *Harry Potter* films. Therefore, it is easy to argue that any of the talent associated with the project (save maybe for the actors who have sky-rocketed to fame) starts out at a disadvantage. But, just as the *Harry Potter* films have evolved to become adaptations, with scripts taking liberties, filmic characters adding dimension to their book counterparts and directors enhancing atmosphere, so too does *The Twilight Saga: New Moon* seem to be moving into a more filmic direction, which is good. Unfortunately, the story and Weitz are still too limited by Meyer's novels to break out on their own, which makes for a poor film.

Still, despite the rather monotone theme of the film (*The Twilight Saga: New Moon* is all about Bella wanting to be a vampire so she can be with Edward forever) there are elements of Weitz's approach that are noteworthy. His take on *The Twilight Saga* is to make a more "fun and accessible teen movie" than "angsty, metaphoric paranormal drama" and it allows for a more inviting and engaging—although still predictable—experience. Knowing that audiences have come to gawk at, as well as compare and contrast, Edward and Jacob's physiques, Weitz provides calculated opportunities for them to do so. Edward makes his entrance in *The Twilight Saga: New Moon* in slow motion, hair and shirt fluttering in the wind, allowing tweens to analyze every detail of his pale skin, messy hair and amber eyes. Jacob on the other hand, appears (gratuitously) topless as much

as possible in order to emphasize actor Lautner's much publicized trips to the gym and also to provide eye candy while Edward is away. Weitz also deserves praise for making both male leads show what they are made of by stepping up the action on both the werewolf and vampire side. Jacob and his fellow wolves rip apart a vampire who crossed into forbidden wolf territory and Edward showcases his vampire strength against members of the Volturi, an elite Italian vampire clan who want to do him in. It is great to see both boys as more than just Bella-whipped mythical creatures, even for just a while. Weitz also revs up the soundtrack with age and action appropriate numbers, drawing audiences into the popular high-school film experience. The result is an engaging, action-packed and mainstream teen romance feel for the film, a welcome approach to an otherwise fluffy franchise that already survived an overly interpreted first film.

It is also interesting to note that Weitz succeeds in flexing his directorial muscle during *The Twilight Saga: New Moon*, proving that solid directors will always find opportunities to showcase their craft—even when the material is lacking. After Edward's departure, Bella sitting quasi-comatose in her room, watching the seasons spin outside her bedroom window, is a particularly well handled and effecting scene, destined to connect with every romantically-inclined eighth grader who has experienced an unrequited crush. Weitz also does well with the scenes set in Italy. Bella running toward Edward in a sea of red-cloaked townspeople is an intriguing and artsy image in a sea of otherwise predictable imagery. Even more noteworthy is the fact that Weitz manages to extract a more laid-back and approachable performance from Stewart. Though twinges of her pained, angsty, lines-delivered-through-gritted-teeth delivery remains, she actually comes off as more of an every day teen here, capable of smiling and joking in addition to pouting and longing.

It helps that the director was handed a solid-under-the-circumstances script by *Twilight* scribe Melissa Rosenberg, who works to provide filler and narrative development to link the scenes depicting the aforementioned pining, brooding and wanting to become a vampire. Rosenberg peppers the film with voiceovers featuring Bella's emails to Alice, Edward's sister. These explain what is going on in Bella's head (and sometimes in the film itself) making the story feel more structured and giving Bella a bit of depth. But unfortunately, both Weitz and Rosenberg are limited by what they can really do since the source material for the movies is packed with awkward, ill conceived action, is entirely devoid of characterization and seems to focus only on kissing. In the book, Bella's characteristics are chalked up to "shy" and "clumsy" with her one goal being to get Edward to turn her into a vampire. She gets paper cuts, she trips over bramble in the forest and she just does not see how Edward could be so into someone as plain as her. In fact, her linear focus on being with one guy forever, no matter how hot and muscled, starts to grate, so to does the "poor little me, what if he doesn't love me" storyline. To top it off, Meyer's concept of action is all about ways in which Edward and Bella can save each other and is not finely crafted as a unique story element. In that regard, both Weitz and Rosenberg are restrained when it comes to where they can take the story and the characters.

Audiences are going to expect pining, they are going to demand rescuing, and are not going to care about the particulars of said rescuing thanks to Meyer's lackluster set-ups, and the films need to deliver. The one good thing that Meyer does well is the kissing. The books have sold due to the sexual tension she creates between Bella and Edward and Weitz and Rosenberg play this up in *The Twilight Saga: New Moon*. Bella's need for Edward is obvious, Edward's pain at wanting to kiss her and simultaneously suck her blood jumps off screen. But, in the end, vampiric desire does not a good movie make. As fun as it can be to watch Bella and Edward flirt on screen, Jacob take off his shirt and morph into a werewolf, and as delightful as getting lost in this oddball world is, *The Twilight Saga: New Moon* does not possess any serious cinematic traits. Rather, it is an example of a capable director and screenwriter making the best of a bad situation.

Joanna Topor MacKenzie

CREDITS

Bella Swan: Kristen Stewart
Edward Cullen: Robert Pattinson
Jacob Black: Taylor Lautner
Alice Cullen: Ashley Greene
Dr. Carlisle Cullen: Peter Facinelli
Esme Cullen: Elizabeth Reaser
Emmett Cullen: Kellan Lutz
Rosalie Hale: Nikki Reed
Jasper Hale: Jackson Rathbone
Sam Uley: Chaske Spencer
Victoria: Rachelle Lefevre
Laurent: Edi Gathegi
Charlie Swan: Billy Burke
Jane: Dakota Fanning
Alec: Cameron Bright
Aro: Michael Sheen
Marcus: Chris Heyerdahl
Harry Clearwater: Graham Greene

Jessica: Anna Kendrick
Mike: Michael Welch
Eric: Justin Chon
Angela: Christian Serratos
Origin: USA
Language: English
Released: 2009
Production: Wyck Godfrey, Mark Morgan; released by Summit Entertainment
Directed by: Chris Weitz
Written by: Melissa Rosenberg
Cinematography by: Javier Aguirresarobe
Music by: Alexandre Desplat
Sound: Darren Brisker
Music Supervisor: Alexandra Patsavas
Editing: Peter Lambert
Art Direction: Catherine Ircha
Costumes: Tish Monaghan
Production Design: David Brisbin
MPAA rating: PG-13
Running time: 130 minutes

REVIEWS

Ebert, Roger. *Chicago Sun-Times.* November 19, 2009.
Franklin, Garth. *Dark Horizons.* November 19, 2009.
Germain, David. *Associated Press.* November 19, 2009.
Gilchrist, Todd. *Cinematical.* November 19, 2009.
Pais, Matt. *Metromix.com.* November 19, 2009.
Puig, Claudia. *USA Today.* November 19, 2009.
Rechtshaffen, Michael. *Hollywood Reporter.* November 18, 2009.
Tallerico, Brian. *MovieRetriever.com.* November 19, 2009.
Travers, Peter. *Rolling Stone.* November 19, 2009.
Turan, Kenneth. *Los Angeles Times.* November 18, 2009.

QUOTES

Edward Cullen: "I love you. You're my only reason to stay alive…if that's what I am."

TRIVIA

Robert Pattinson refused to wax his eyebrows as much as he did in the first movie, which resulted in a slightly bushier Edward Cullen.

AWARDS

Nomination:

Golden Raspberries 2009: Worst Support. Actor (Pattinson), Worst Screenplay, Worst Remake, Rip-Off or Sequel.

TWO LOVERS

Sometimes we leave everything to find ourselves.
—Movie tagline

Box Office: $3.1 million

If James Gray's *Two Lovers* cannot convince the viewer that love is a schizophrenic affair that is liable to drive one insane then nothing will. *Two Lovers* illustrates a triangle of codependency in a circle of indecision, second chances and second choices that should be the first. Gray is not interested in grand romantic gestures but the emotional force of believing you love somebody and the clash between belief and reality fuels a poignant thriller where the characters get both everything and nothing that they deserve.

When we first meet Leonard (Joaquin Phoenix), he's contemplating suicide and nearly succeeds before copping out at the last second. At home, mom and dad (Isabella Rossellini and Moni Moshonov) are understandably worried, this not being his first attempt, and they have guests on the way. Joining his father's business associate is his own family, including daughter Sandra (Vinessa Shaw). She has all the qualities of the girl next door—natural beauty, friendly and sporting a little crush on Leonard after seeing him dance with his mother at the family dry cleaning business. Leonard opens up to Sandra about his failed engagement—a break-up not of his wish due to some childbirth compatibility—as well as his dabbling in photography. The tracks are laid for a courtship of some promise. And then he meets the literal girl next door.

Her name is Michelle (Gwyneth Paltrow) whom he first sees in a shouting match with her father down the hall. He offers her some momentary solace in his parent's apartment and he immediately senses some attraction to her. Whether we (or he) know why does not matter. Michelle is going to be trouble for him regardless. The catch-and-release of their relationship starts as friendship for her and something more for Leonard. As Michelle continually knocks him back, either by ditching him at a club or asking him to play third wheel on a date with the married suitor (Elias Koteas) paying for her apartment, Leonard finds his own solace back with Sandra who offers him everything Michelle will not. The problem is that this new girl really needs a friend and Leonard cannot let go of the promise of something that was not just handed down to him.

Leonard's connection to Michelle is one that most would identify as doomed from the start. His feelings are more dominant and her self-centered pity leaves him feeling alone in more ways than one. Still, this is more than just "the lure of the shiksa" out of a *Seinfeld* episode. The rigidity of Leonard's Jewish background from the family meals to a business merger that potentially serves up Sandra as an incentive might be all the motivation he needs to pursue the party girl with the flowing blonde hair. As rational outside observers, the choice for Leonard is obvious and it's up to the screenplay by Gray and Ric Menello to convince us of

his rationale to not follow up on the proverbial bird in the hand. Perhaps the tragic compatibility of his last relationship steers him away from Sandra or maybe it is just as simple as Leonard not wanting a woman that reminds him of his mother. The consistent worrying and natural doting of mom—very well-played by Rossellini—only brings to the surface how 180 degrees wrong Michelle is for him.

Joaquin Phoenix walks a very difficult line with the audience here. There is almost a childlike awkwardness in his attempts at humor and to impress the two women; low-key and natural with Sandra and more bombastically showy with Michelle. Men and women alike should connect with Leonard's decisions in the same manner they do with a great horror show—especially during the implications of the quietly tense climax. We want to shout instructions to him and warn him of the impending danger in choosing the wrong path. At times it's easy to hate Leonard for not adhering to our wishes, but Phoenix also portrays him as a very sympathetic figure who keeps getting dragged into Michelle's personal dramas and it results in one of his very best performances. Paltrow and Shaw have the unenviable tasks of trying to create characters that aren't just competing archetypes for Leonard's affection. Shaw has less to work with as the almost virginal counterpoint to Michelle's emotional and physical exhibitionism. But she does a nice job, particularly in a moment where she recognizes her relationship with Leonard may be little more than just another parental setup of convenience than something true. On the flip side, Paltrow has to exist as a needy obstacle that's very easy for us to loathe. Yet, she makes us believe she has feelings and they exist solely towards Leonard as a friend. A friend she can use when she desperately needs one, but a friend nevertheless.

James Gray was well on his way to becoming the Guy Ritchie of melodramatic Brooklyn family crime dramas with *Little Odessa* (1994), *The Yards* (2000) and *We Own the Night* (2007)—the latter two also featuring Phoenix. With *Two Lovers* he is able to concentrate on the emotional traumas of the characters without the plot wranglings of gangsters and bullet-laden confrontations. His work here is so perfectly invested in these people that it is almost worth revisiting his previous works just to focus on the people. Frustrating as it can be to watch Sandra be the warm comfort amidst the cold dance between Leonard and Michelle, their behavior never rings false. Maybe in our own lives we have been one or all of these people and it's no accident when both Michelle and Leonard, at defining moments, take a second to look right at us either to get our approval or silently ask who we are to judge. Men and women can be equally naïve when it comes to wanting what they cannot have, especially at the expense of believing they can change the other to fit their perception of happiness. Some say it takes all kinds, when it reality it usually only takes two.

Erik Childress

CREDITS

Leonard Kraditor: Joaquin Rafael Phoenix
Michelle Rausch: Gwyneth Paltrow
Sandra Cohen: Vinessa Shaw
Ruth Kraditor: Isabella Rossellini
Ronald Blatt: Elias Koteas
Reuben Kraditor: Moni Moshonov
Origin: USA
Language: English
Released: 2009
Production: Donna Gigliotti, Anthony G. Katagas, James Gray; 2929 Productions, Tempesta Films, Wild Bunch; released by Magnolia Pictures
Directed by: James Gray
Written by: James Gray, Richard Menello
Cinematography by: Joaquin Baca-Asay
Sound: Tom Nelson
Music Supervisor: Dana Sano
Editing: John Axelrad
Art Direction: Pete Zumba
Costumes: Michael Clancy
Production Design: Happy Massee
MPAA rating: R
Running time: 110 minutes

REVIEWS

Bennett, Ray. *Hollywood Reporter.* February 9, 2009.
Ebert, Roger. *Chicago Sun-Times.* February 26, 2009.
Edelstein, David. *New York Magazine.* February 9, 2009.
Hoberman, J. *Village Voice.* February 10, 2009.
Lane, Anthony. *New Yorker.* February 17, 2009.
McCarthy, Todd. *Variety.* February 9, 2009.
Sarris, Andrew. *New York Observer.* February 11, 2009.
Scott, A.O. *New York Times.* February 13, 2009.
Stevens, Dana. *Slate.* February 13, 2009.
Tallerico, Brian. *HollywoodChicago.com.* February 27, 2009.

TRIVIA

The character of Michelle was created specifically with Gwyneth Paltrow in mind.

AWARDS

Nomination:

Ind. Spirit 2010: Actress (Paltrow), Director (Gray).

TYSON

The man. The legend. The truth.
—Movie tagline

Even though it has been quite a long time since he has stepped foot into the boxing ring and even longer since his astonishing dominance of the sport in the late eighties and early nineties, former heavyweight champion Mike Tyson is still such a polarizing figure that the mere existence of a documentary about his tumultuous life and career is anathema to them, especially one directed by a longtime friend who has chosen to approach the material entirely from Tyson's point-of-view instead of taking a more objective stance by interviewing other people to get the other side of the story. And yet, the resulting film, James Toback's *Tyson* is no mere hagiography or whitewash of Tyson's admittedly checkered past, the kind of thing that ESPN might commission as a puff-piece special. In fact, it is one of the most absorbing sports-related documentaries ever made and one sure to surprise and galvanize viewers of all persuasions.

Essentially, *Tyson* is a psychological travelogue that takes viewers on a guided tour of one of the more public lives of recent years to try to explain how a troubled kid could somehow emerge from a world of poverty and violence in the mean streets of Brooklyn to become one of the most famous people in the world thanks to his natural talents and a nurturing support system and then squander it all in a haze of ego, violence, stupidity and an inability to keep his inner demons at bay. The details of Tyson's life have, of course, been covered in minute detail over the years via books, magazine articles, television specials and Barbara Kopple's fascinating documentary *Fallen Champ: The Untold Story of Mike Tyson* (1993) but *Tyson* has one thing that those other things have largely lacked—the voice of Tyson himself guiding us through the material. Of course, the idea of listening to Mike Tyson speaking for ninety minutes about his life may strike some people as borderline unendurable, especially if they know him only as the brute whose only memorable quotes have involved his desire to eat the children of his opponents. This is not someone who is merely rehashing carefully polished accounts of his past with the cool distance of a talk show guest telling the same story for the umpteenth time—as he is recounting his stories, he does so in a way that is so disconcertingly direct and intimate that it feels as though he is still living through them after all these years (and in many ways, he is) and is just as surprised as anyone to see what has transpired in that time. Additionally, even though Tyson's side is the only one presented during the film, this is not a whitewash designed to paint him as some innocent who has been cruelly manipulated over the years. With the exception of the rape conviction that he still disputes, he pretty much accepts the blame for nearly everything that happened to him and there are moments, especially when Don King comes up, in which his anger rises to the surface and reminds us that even though he seems more or less at peace these days, the demons that have plagued him his entire life are still there.

Because he is known primarily for penning the Academy Award®-nominated screenplay for *Bugsy* (1991) and directing a string of fascinating, pungent and deeply personal films such as *Fingers* (1978), *Exposed* (1983) and *Two Girls and a Guy* (1997), some have expressed curiosity as to why James Toback would make a film like this in the first place. Well, the easy way to answer that question is to note that he and Tyson have been friends for many years—Toback even gave him small parts playing himself in *Black & White* (2000) and *When Will I Be Loved* (2004)—and presumably realized that if anyone was going to get Tyson talking about his life to the degree that he does here, it would be him. However, anyone familiar with Toback's previous films will instantly recognize that many of the elements that are touched on here are those that he has been long-obsessed with—race, sex, class, money violence, madness, self-destructive behavior, professional sports and people being torn between embracing and squandering their natural gifts in ways that no one, not even themselves, can begin to understand. Seen in that context, *Tyson* is a Toback film through and through and even though we never actually hear his voice, either literally or literarily, he still finds ways to subtly put his personal touch on the material, most obviously via a split-screen motif that helps accentuate the numerous forces pulling at Tyson even to this day.

At one point in *Tyson*, Tyson remarks that "No one that isn't an extremist can understand the mind of an extremist" and that is certainly the case here. In his own way, Toback is just as extreme a personality as Tyson. He has dealt with his share of overwhelming demons and therefore has a better understanding of what makes a guy like Tyson tick than most people. Because of this, he is able to get beyond the scandals and rumors and public meltdowns in order to get to the person beneath the headlines, a man whose life is still governed by the fear and anger that led him to unleash his wrath upon that bully long ago. This is an extraordinary portrait of a complicated and contradictory man and regardless of any previously held views towards him, it is complex

and thoughtful enough to force the viewer to reconsider and reshape them as a result.

Peter Sobczynski

CREDITS

Himself: Mike Tyson
Origin: USA
Language: English
Released: 2008
Production: James Toback, Damon Bingham; Fyodor Prods., Green Room Films; released by Sony Pictures Classics
Directed by: James Toback
Written by: James Toback
Cinematography by: Lawrence McConkey
Music by: Salaam Remi
Sound: David Geckler
Editing: Aaron Yanes
MPAA rating: R
Running time: 90 minutes

REVIEWS

Denby, David. *New Yorker.* May 4, 2009.
Ebert, Roger. *Chicago Sun-Times.* April 30, 2009.
LaSalle, Mick. *San Francisco Chronicle.* May 8, 2009.
Edelstein, David. *New York Magazine.* April 20, 2009.
Samuels, Alison. *Newsweek.* April 16, 2009.
Scott, A.O. *New York Times.* April 24, 2009.
Stevens, Dana. *Slate.* April 24, 2009.
Tallerico, Brian. *MovieRetriever.com.* May 1, 2009.
Turan, Kenneth. *Los Angeles Times.* April 23, 2009.
Wise, Damon. *Empire Magazine.* March 27, 2009.

QUOTES

Mike Tyson: "You feel like you're dead, because when you are in prison, that's the closest thing to death. You stay there so long, you become so used to being by yourself that, that you're used to talking to yourself, that you become your own best friend, and best company."

TRIVIA

Director James Toback has recalled Mike Tyson's reaction to first seeing the film as... Tyson sat in silence for several minutes, then remarked: "It's like a Greek tragedy, only I'm the subject."

U–V

THE UGLY TRUTH

Box Office: $88.9 million

With stars like Gerard Butler and Katherine Heigl, *The Ugly Truth* should at least look good and have some credible performances. It is an intriguing pairing of successful stars. But in the hands of director Robert Luketic (*Legally Blonde*), pretty faces are about all there is to see.

Heigl's Abby is a walking contradiction of personality traits. She is an impossibly competent and resourceful producer of a morning variety show on a Sacramento TV station who takes an inordinate amount of misplaced pride in how seriously she presents her local newsmagazine. In the opening scene, we see her breezing through the office, putting out fires left and right, like a high-level corporate executive. But soon it is revealed that in her private life she is a desperately clueless romantic, whose confident façade crumbles into that of a lovesick schoolgirl at the slightest provocation. In short, she's a post-feminist parody of a smart yet secretly idiotic career woman. Somebody like Maggie Gyllenhaal might have pulled this off in a campy sort of put-on, but Heigl is all wrong for the part. It is unbelievable for a second that Heigl would have any trouble in the romance department. She is a classically beautiful, near-perfect Hollywood specimen of feminine beauty who does not come off as in any way needy or incomplete, and she does not really know how to play vulnerable or ironic.

Yet needy Abby is. Her cat pushes a paw on the remote and accidentally switches to a local cable network airing an advice show hosted by a dinosaur of a pre-feminist male, Mike (Butler), who presents a craven view of what all men want and what all women need. Abby immediately calls up his listener line and gets flummoxed by him. It is obvious right from this moment exactly how the film is going to end up, and most of how it will get there. Abby and Mike will spend the movie fighting, superwoman versus caveman style, and eventually they will fall in love with each other.

The Ugly Truth unfolds predictably, from start to finish. Mike is hired by Abby's boss to become a regular on her show, instantly pumping up her ratings and infuriating her by dragging her high-minded TV mission down into the gutter of explicit sex talk, jello wrestling, and infuriating pronouncements against her notions of romantic love. He suddenly becomes her adviser in romance as she tries to corral her perfect man, a handsome doctor, Colin (Eric Winter), who just happens to be her next-door neighbor. (She meets him by chasing her cat up a tree and falling off when a branch breaks—a plot invention that dates back perhaps a century.)

Mike's counsel is a rather muddled mix: play hard to get, tease, manipulate his affections, and be tough, sweet, seductive, and distant by turns. Even on its own terms, the characters do not make sense: Mike criticizes Abby as a control freak, yet his recommended approach to her winning her man is to be constantly controlling and calculating. With a man she is attracted to, Abby melts into mush; she is a control freak who has absolutely no control.

The Ugly Truth lacks any irony or self-awareness that might have made its antics or its ridiculous dialogue at least occasionally tongue-in-cheek. Heigl does not have a solid notion of how to play her slippery character, who seems to embody a very stereotypically male and condescending view of womanhood —she is shrewish, distant, naïve, and easily flustered.

The Ugly Truth is an attempt at a 'women's movie' version of Judd Apatow's comedies, but not nearly as funny. For example, Abby spills her soft drink on Colin's pants at a baseball game, and the scoreboard "kiss cam" captures her furiously pawing at his crotch. Also, it is supposed to be funny that prudish Abby becomes comfortable with saying the common term for male genitalia. And that the remote control for a pair of vibrator panties falls out of her purse and into the hands of a young boy at the next table in a restaurant while Abby is explaining something to network execs. It is TV-typical 'wink-and-nod' stuff, but clumsily done.

Given the film's unwillingness to risk something original or meaningful from its set-up, it is no surprise that, in the end, Mike is revealed as the poor victim of romance gone awry, his heart repeatedly broken by fickle and betraying women, and that he is so sweet and kind that he will not take a job offer out of town because he is acting as a father substitute to his nephew. Of course, Mike is not the man he appeared to be, and has been waiting all his life for someone like Abby to rescue him from the misogyny he was forced to adopt to protect his battered soul. It is not genuine, even as a comic premise.

Butler grins and makes the best of this role, which never tests his talents, and Heigl keeps flashing her perfect smile, tossing her perfect hair, and being that impossibly beautiful and powerful Hollywood star playing a character who is pathetically weak and confused. Some things, alas, never change, and that is indeed an ugly truth.

Michael Betzold

CREDITS

Abby Richter: Katherine Heigl
Mike Chadway: Gerard Butler
Colin: Eric Winter
Elizabeth: Bonnie Sommerville
Joy: Bree Turner
Stuart: Nick Searcy
Georgia: Cheryl Hines
Larry: John Michael Higgins
Jim: Kevin Connolly
Dori: Yvette Nicole Brown
Josh: Nathan Corddry
Jonah: Noah Matthews
Origin: USA
Language: English

Released: 2009
Production: Steven Reuther, Kimberly di Bonaventura, Deborah Jelin Newmyer, Tom Rosenberg, Gary Lucchesi; Relativity Media, Lakeshore Entertainment; released by Columbia Pictures
Directed by: Robert Luketic
Written by: Kirsten Smith, Nicole Eastman, Karen McCullah
Cinematography by: Russell Carpenter
Music by: Aaron Zigman
Sound: Steve Morrow
Editing: Lisa Zeno Churgin
Art Direction: William Hawkins
Costumes: Betsy Heimann
Production Design: Missy Stewart
MPAA rating: R
Running time: 95 minutes

REVIEWS

Berkshire, Geoff. *Metromix.com.* July 24, 2009.
Corliss, Richard. *TIME Magazine.* July 23, 2009.
Dargis, Manohla. *New York Times.* July 24, 2009.
Ebert, Roger. *Chicago Sun-Times.* July 23, 2009.
Farber, Stephen. *Hollywood Reporter.* July 20, 2009.
McCarthy, Todd. *Variety.* July 20, 2009.
Puig, Claudia. *USA Today.* July 24, 2009.
Rickey, Carrie. *Philadelphia Inquirer.* July 23, 2009.
Sobczynski, Peter. *eFilmCritic.* July 23, 2009.
Tobias, Scott. *AV Club.* July 23, 2009.

QUOTES

Mike Chadway: "You have to be two people. The saint and the sinner. The librarian and the stripper."

TRIVIA

The film was shipped to theaters using the code name "Helpful Advice."

THE UNBORN

Evil will do anything to live.
—Movie tagline

Box Office: $42.7 million

Watching *The Unborn*, one gets the sense that writer-director David S. Goyer sat down and made a checklist of all the things that he felt he needed to include in a contemporary horror film to cater to the largest possible audience—a spunky heroine for female viewers, a spunky heroine with an incredible gluteus maximus for male viewers, the late-inning appearance of a respected actor with a fondness for scenery-chewing for the critics, plenty of cheap shocks involving bugs, blood and creepy-looking kids for those who can still find themselves shocked by such things, and a PG-13 rating that ensures a wider potential audience base for the studio heads. Unfortunately, it appears that instead of using these elements as the basis for a screenplay, Goyer simply decided to save time and effort by simply shooting the checklist instead and the result is a film so forgettable that it evaporates from the mind even as you are watching it.

Odette Yustman stars as Casey Beldon, a young college student who, as the film opens, is plagued by the usual supernatural nonsense that bedevils pretty young women in things like this—in this case, nightmares involving strange-looking dogs and a weirdo kid, visions of blood and bugs that no one else sees and the surprise revelation that she was a twin who inadvertently choked her brother to death in utero. Of course, Casey's friends and loved ones—lunkhead boyfriend Mark (Cam Gigandet), sassy best pal Romy (Meagan Goode) and her largely absent father (James Remar) all try to reassure her that nothing is wrong but she soon becomes convinced that she is being haunted by the spirit of her dead brother and that his soul has been possessed by a "dybbuk," a dark spirit from Hebrew mythology that will do anything to return to the world of the living. Oh yeah, it appears that the same dybbuk also haunted Casey's mom (a brief cameo from Carla Gugino) and a Holocaust survivor (Jane Alexander) whose twin brother was possessed by it as the result of a concentration camp experiment gone awry. To free herself once and for all, Casey calls upon the venerable Rabbi Sendak (Gary Oldman) to perform a kosher-style exorcism that offers up plenty of blowing wind, broken glass and flying bodies but results in little more than—Spoiler Alert!—a labored set-up for a sequel.

From its generic title to its equally generic scare attempts, there is nothing in *The Unborn* that even those who only briefly dabble in the horror genre have not seen a dozen times before and none of it works at all this time around. The closest thing to a fresh touch on display is how the movie eschews the usual Catholic trappings normally seen in this type of story in exchange for a more Hebrew-oriented slant on the material but Goyer winds up doing so little with this particular angle that most viewers will wonder why he bothered. His screenplay is a rehash of most of the big non-slasher horror clichés of the last few years and the only thing that stands out—the Holocaust angle—does so simply because it just seems spectacularly tacky to exploit a tragedy of that magnitude simply to goose up a cruddy an exceptionally unambitious horror movie. Goyer's direction is equally inept throughout. The first two-thirds of the film is paced so lethargically that it seems

twice as long as it actually is and the grand finale is rushed through so quickly that it is almost impossible to determine what happens to who, let alone how or why. As the heroine, Odette Yustlman (best known as the inspiration for the cross-town trek that formed the heart of *Cloverfield* [2008]) is undeniably beautiful but is so bland and colorless that she appears to have been cast solely because she serves as the support system for one of the most amazing hinders ever seen on screen. (Seriously, it gets so many close-ups here that it may well now have its own SAG card.) Not even Gary Oldman is able to help matters much when he finally turns up in the late innings; instead of the flamboyant scenery-chewing that might have been expected from the guy who went so cheerfully over-the-top in the likes of *Leon* (1994), *The Fifth Element* (1997) and *Hannibal* (2001), he glumly goes through his paces as though he is as embarrassed and mortified to be seen in something so lousy as this film as the audience is to see him in it.

The Unborn may not be the worst American horror film of recent years by a long shot but it is easily one of the most perfunctory. It is a complete drag from beginning to end and it is impossible to believe that anyone involved with its production could have possibly come away from it feeling as though they had succeeded in making something even moderately entertaining. Ultimately, *The Unborn* is too silly to work as horror, too dull to work as camp and too dumb for even the undiscriminating teen audience that it was clearly aimed at.

Peter Sobczynski

CREDITS

Casey Beldon: Odette Yustman
Rabbi Sendak: Gary Oldman
Mark Hardign: Cam Gigandet
Romy: Meagan Good
Sofi Kozma: Jane Alexander
Arthur Wyndham: Idris Elba
Janet Beldon: Carla Gugino
Gordon Beldon: James Remar
Origin: USA
Language: English
Released: 2009
Production: Michael Bay, Andrew Form, Brad Fuller; Platinum Dunes, Phantom Four; released by Rogue Pictures
Directed by: David S. Goyer
Written by: David S. Goyer
Cinematography by: James Hawkinson
Music by: Ramin Djawadi, Spring Aspers
Sound: Curt Frank

Editing: Jeff Betancourt
Art Direction: Gary Baugh
Costumes: Christine Wada
Production Design: Craig Jackson
MPAA rating: PG-13
Running time: 86 minutes

REVIEWS

Berkshire, Geoff. *Metromix.com.* January 8, 2009.
Dargis, Manohla. *New York Times.* January 9, 2009.
Debruge, Peter. *Variety.* January 9, 2009.
Honeycutt, Kirk. *Hollywood Reporter.* January 9, 2009.
Lemire, Christy. *Associated Press.* January 7, 2009.
Phillips, Michael. *Chicago Tribune.* January 9, 2009.
Pinkerton, Nick. *Village Voice.* January 6, 2009.
Puig, Claudia. *USA Today.* January 9, 2009.
Tallerico, Brian. *HollywoodChicago.com.* January 9, 2009.
Whipp, Glenn. *Los Angeles Times.* January 9, 2009.

QUOTES

Matty Newton: "Jumby wants to be born now."

TRIVIA

The character of Rabbi Sendak is named as an homage to Maurice Sendak, the writer of the classic children's book *Where the Wild Things Are.*

UNDERWORLD: RISE OF THE LYCANS

Every war has a beginning.
—Movie tagline

Box Office: $45.8 million

In a desperate attempt to cash in on a surprisingly eager fan-base, the *Underworld* franchise has resorted to producing a prequel, *Underworld: Rise of the Lycans.* This lackluster movie tells the story of the first vampire-werewolf couple, a pair of star-crossed lovers whose forbidden passion ignited a centuries-old war between vampires and werewolves (aka Lycans)—the very feud that made dating such a pain for Selene (Kate Beckinsale) and Michael (Scott Speedman) in the original *Underworld* (2003).

At the start of the movie, the vamps rule the roost. They hunt werewolves by night and enslave a fair number of them. But this precarious balance is thrown into a tailspin when Lucian (played as an adult by *Frost/Nixon*'s Michael Sheen) is born. Lucian is the first Lycan who possesses the ability to shift in and out of human form. He is therefore good at two things as far as the vampires are concerned: fighting and construction. Lucian also has a soft center. He yearns to control the beast within himself and can't stand to see how the Lycans allow themselves to be treated by the vampires. Trying to capitalize on Lucian's unique skill set and make an army out of his hybrid-kind, the vampire dark lord Viktor (Bill Nighy) procures a collar that keeps Lucian from shape-shifting while he's laboring (it's never really clear what all the building is about) and starves the otherwise good-at-heart Lucian until he has no choice but to snack on the men brought into his prison cell and inadvertently turn them into werewolves. The one thing that Viktor had not accounted for however is that Lucian is more than just a skilled laborer, he is also a skilled lover. He and the vampire's headstrong, wolf-hunting daughter Sonja (Rhona Mitra) are a secret item and meet frequently for x-game worthy trysts. They know that their love can never be as she is unwilling to run away with him (and regularly hunts Lycans for sport) and he is unwilling to be a pet to her father forever. One thing leads to another and the couple gets caught and blackmailed, Lucian rallies his werewolf allies and makes them yearn for freedom, all hell (and all wolves) breaks lose and a lifetimes-long battle begins.

Fans of the *Underworld* films might be willing to forgive the lack of chemistry between Lucian and Sonja (a tough sell as their affair is a key plot device) and even maybe overlook the predictable—and sometimes lagging—storyline, but it would be impossible not to notice that *Rise of the Lycans* simply does not look as sleek as the previous *Underworld* chapters.

Set in the Dark Ages, *Rise of the Lycans* mixes horse-drawn carriages with leather bustiers for an effect that is more laughable than intriguing. Sure, vampires are timeless and possess a flare for tight and revealing clothing, but seeing their 2009 dance club-ready selves interact with potato-sack wearing serfs just makes the film feel unsettled about its setting. The audience never gets a sense of exactly how many hundreds of years ago the story take places and it seems like no one on the production staff cared to ask either. Then there is the fact that the film is completely devoid of lore—no mention of vampire or werewolf mythology, no explanation as to how they came to be and how vampires were able to gain the upper hand and no mention at all about how the vampire hierarchy functions. Ultimately, *Rise of the Lycans* raises more questions than it answers about the species and the war between them. Not only for historical framework is this lore necessary, but also as a means to establish parameters for the storyline. Knowing and adhering to the "rules" of a place and a history could have focused this disorganized narrative.

Unhelpful is the fact that the film seems lit by candlelight, resulting in a low-budget feel. Unfortunately, the low-budget feel also transcends to the CGI visual effects. Combined with the poor lighting, it's often difficult to see—and therefore care about—who is killing whom. A lot of shape-shifting happens, but the transformation effects are not taken to a new level, in fact they seem more primitive than 2003's *Underworld*. Vamp vs. wolf action is also kept to a minimum, both in frequency and intensity. As for the performances, Mitra is great at ass-kicking, no doubt, but her ability to convey passion and heartbreak is non-existent, which is bad for a movie with a romance at its center. Nighy relies on his bright blue contact lenses to channel all emotion and the result leaves him looking perpetually surprised, not scary. The saving grace of the movie is Sheen who roars, loves and fights like he means it and brings intensity to an otherwise sloppy story.

Joanna Topor MacKenzie

CREDITS

Lucian: Michael Sheen
Sonja: Rhona Mitra
Viktor: Bill Nighy
Kraven: Shane Brolly
Andreas Tanis: Steven Mackintosh
Raze: Kevin Grevioux
Orsova: Elizabeth Hawthorne
Selene: Kate Beckinsale
Colomon: David Aston
Costa: Larry Rew
Origin: USA
Language: English
Released: 2009
Production: Tom Rosenberg, Gary Lucchesi, Richard Wright, Len Wiseman; Lakeshore Entertainment, Screen Gems, Sketch Films; released by Sony Pictures
Directed by: Patrick Tatopoulos
Written by: Danny McBride, Howard McCain, Dirk Blackman
Cinematography by: Ross Emery
Music by: Paul Haslinger
Sound: Richard Flynn
Editing: Peter Amundson
Art Direction: Gary Mackay
Costumes: Jane Holland
Production Design: Dan Hennah
MPAA rating: R
Running time: 93 minutes

REVIEWS

Corliss, Richard. *Time Magazine.* January 23, 2009.
Dargis, Manohla. *New York Times.* January 26, 2009.
Edwards, David. *Daily Mirror.* January 23, 2009.
Leydon, Joe. *Variety.* January 23, 2009.
Pais, Matt. *Metromix.com.* January 23, 2009.
Puig, Claudia. *USA Today.* January 26, 2009.
Rechtshaffen, Michael. *Hollywood Reporter.* January 26, 2009.
Sartin, Hank. *Time Out New York.* January 29, 2009.
Sobczynski, Peter. *eFilmCritic.com.* January 23, 2009.
Whipp, Glenn. *Los Angeles Times.* January 26, 2009.

QUOTES

Lucian: "I've lived by their rules my entire life. I've protected them, envied them, and for what? To be treated like an animal. We are not animals! Is this want you want? We can be slaves, or we can be...Lycans!"

TRIVIA

A 'Willhelm Scream' can be heard when the werewolves climb the wall and attack the various vampire guards.

THE UNINVITED

Can you believe what you see?
—Movie tagline

Box Office: $28.6 million

The Guard Brothers' *The Uninvited* is an American remake that offers little of the visceral impact and none of the style of its source, the far superior Korean film *A Tale of Two Sisters* by Ji-woon Kim. Ostensibly a psychological horror film, *The Uninvited* trips itself up by reducing the complex and deliberately ambiguous plotting of the original into a shock-driven, scare-fest, ending on a somewhat confused and transparent twist that is open to interpretation but hardly surprising and barely tinged with the tragic overtones of its emotionally evocative source material.

We open on Anna Rydell (Emily Browning), in session with her therapist, bemoaning her inability to remember what happened the night her mother died. After all-too-quick assurances that some things are best left forgotten, she is sent back home to, in the prescient words of her doctor, "get in some trouble." The good doctor's advice does not take long to come to horrific life. Her still grieving father, Steven (David Strathairn), has taken up with her mother's former nurse Rachel (Elizabeth Banks) a territorial wicked step mother type whose wickedness might not be limited to gold-digging. Anna's only comfort is her older sister, Alex (Arielle Kebbel). But even Alex, who is always just there when needed, may not be able to help when it comes to unraveling the truth about what happened the night their mother died. Soon, a series of ghostly visions and new tragedies seem to close in around the pair.

Sadly, screenwriters Craig Rosenberg , Doug Miro and Carlo Bernard, water down the tense series of terrifying ghostly visions, and ghastly violent events of the original not only by honing the material to fit the confines of a PG-13 rating but altering it to fit their chosen audience demographics rather than the allow the mature nature of the original story to drive home the horror of a character in psychological free-fall.

For instance, while Emily Browning is a very good actress one must question the decision to increase Anna's age to accommodate the casting. Anna as an older character is simply not as interesting. Menstruation used as such a potent symbol in the original is of course vetted completely; references to early childhood are also gone. Ultimately, Anna, and indeed all the characters in the film, are handled as cardboard cut-out characters in a standard mystery rather than as believable people in a complex thriller with elements of several genres.

If anything saves *The Uninvited* from being nothing more than a mere money-grab it is the uniformly excellent and distinguished cast who embody the archetypes laid out for them and do what they can to lift them off the page. David Strathairn (*Good Night, and Good Luck* (2005)) gives just the right touch of ennui to the widower father, making us pity him even as we despise his emotional retreat and Elizabeth Banks (*W.* (2008), *Zack and Miri Make a Porno* (2008)) is dynamic as the controlling and possibly murderous ice queen who plays at surrogate motherhood only to reveal a mantis like hunger for station.

While it can sometimes be a pleasure to see such talent on display, *The Uninvited* never rises above the level of middle-of-the-road TV fare either in the effect it is intended to produce or the overall quality of the production. The bottom line is a been-there-done-that sense that pervades the film from beginning to end.

One more positive attribute worth mentioning is that noted composer Christopher Young can add *The Uninvited* to his extensive resume of outstanding work that has been attached to lesser films. His orchestration here offers moments of poignancy, gripping tension and even surreal revelation, but there's nothing on the screen to match his mastery.

Finally, the direction in this film is only a little better than workman-like. The Guard Brothers seem to be at their best when they are not trying to figure out how to make thirteen-year-old girls jump and still get the MPAA rating they want. Even by that measure one cannot help but think of other recent, disappointing ghostly thrillers like *Gothika* (2003) or *1408* (2007), where big stars are staring out at us from the poster trying to convince us how scared they are but the film fails to deliver the fear. *The Uninvited* has no such face on its poster but the silhouette used in the marketing may well be the ghost of the original film crying out to remembered.

Dave Canfield

CREDITS

Anna Rydell: Emily Browning
Rachel: Elizabeth Banks
Alex: Arielle Kebbel
Dad: David Strathairn
Mom: Maya Massar
Matt: Jesse Moss
Dr. Silverstein: Dean Paul Gibson
Origin: USA
Language: English
Released: 2009
Production: Walter F. Parkes, Laurie MacDonald, Roy Lee; Cold Spring Pictures, Montecito Picture Co., Vertigo Entertainment; released by Dreamworks Pictures
Directed by: Charles Guard
Written by: Doug Miro, Carlo Bernard, Craig Rossenberg
Cinematography by: Dan Landin
Music by: Christopher Young
Sound: Rob Young
Editing: Jim Page, Christian Wagner
Art Direction: Margot Ready
Costumes: Trish Keating
Production Design: Andrew Menzies
MPAA rating: PG-13
Running time: 87 minutes

REVIEWS

Childress, Erik. *EFilmCritic.com.* January 29, 2009.
Ebert, Roger. *Chicago Sun-Times.* January 29, 2009.
Farber, Stephen. *Hollywood Reporter.* January 30, 2009.
Harvey, Dennis. *Variety.* January 29, 2009.
Morris, Wesley. *Boston Globe.* January 30, 2009.
Pais, Matt. *Metromix.com.* January 29, 2009.
Phillips, Michael. *Chicago Tribune.* January 30, 2009.
Scott, A.O. *New York Times.* January 30, 2009.
Tobias, Scott. *AV Club.* January 30, 2009.
Whipp, Glenn. *Los Angeles Times.* January 29, 2009.

QUOTES

Anna: "Geez when are they bringing in the stripper pole."
Alex: "I know, she's like a crack-whore without the dignity."

TRIVIA

Clever camera angles and forced perspective helped create the illusion that Elizabeth Banks was taller than Emily Browning when she is, in fact, two inches shorter.

(UNTITLED)

Everyone's got an opinion.
—Movie tagline

(Untitled) is a refreshing, smart comedy that does not set out to alienate any member of its audience when it so easily could have. It exists in the art world of New York. Its characters are artists, appreciators, buyers, sellers and people who know how to make a buck creating art for the masses with debatable value. A viewer not at all schooled in this world should not have a problem discerning the issues the movie raises. The movie assumes that most people have, at one time or another, seen a work of art and have asked themselves "Why is this art? Why should I care?" Sometimes the artists and the exhibitors themselves have no clue either. Things get trickier for these people when such questions impede on their personal lives.

At the center of the debate is Adrian Jacobs (Adam Goldberg), a musician who pays the bills by playing dull background piano music in a restaurant, but who chooses to express himself through his band, which consists of himself, another man and a woman (known only as The Clarinet). They play to audiences of no more than 20 people. Their music, such as it is, consists of little more than a chain being dropped in a bucket, inarticulate music on the piano, a scream and ripping paper, achieving little more than indecipherable cacophony. Rhythm is thrown right out the window from the outset. Adrian means to confront his audience with their preconceptions of what music should be, but to questionable extent.

His brother Josh (Eion Bailey), meanwhile, sells paintings by the truckloads to restaurants and hotels. "More people will see my work in those places that they would at the Museum of Modern Art," he declares. His paintings, as he says, blend in with everything. They will be seen by many, but hardly ever noticed. One night, Josh brings his art dealer and sort-of girlfriend Madeline (Marley Shelton) to one of Adrian's shows and she is immediately taken by him. While Josh urges Adrian to try, just once, to produce music that is accessible to the masses, Madeline shows signs of approval for the challenging work Adrian displays. He, in turn, likes her for the sounds her leather skirt makes when she moves and wants to sample it for his next recording. This proposal in his apartment escalates into a very funny love-making scene in which Adrian practically needs an instruction manual for how to remove the complex clothing off her body.

Through Madeline and her gallery, the audience meets many more artists and buyers. Ray Barko (Vinnie Jones) creates work using taxidermy and household items blended together to create something horrific and/or absurd. One buyer, Porter (Zak Orth), wants to add one of Ray's pieces to his collection, but Madeline sees his interest as superficial and will only deal to people who feel a true connection to an artist's work. She can afford

to do this, of course, because Josh's bland paintings help pay the bills. To give art away to the highest bidder, to her, would be nothing short of selling her soul.

Madeline's efforts appear to be noble, but her credibility comes into question by everyone around her when she decides to exhibit work by Monroe (Ptolemy Slocum), whose art consists of little more than a post-it note or a plain white wall, with a title that might read "Untitled plain white wall." She sees it as brave and full of meaning, while Adrian and Josh (separately) view it as pretentious, simplistic and stupid. When Madeline enlists Adrian and his band to play at her gallery for this particular exhibit, their performance perfectly suits the material and is, itself, a response to the age old question for all art: What do you think? He plays silence because, really, what else is there to say?

The relationship side of the story finds Adrian and Madeline developing a romantic bond, unbeknownst to Josh, who cannot figure out where his relationship—both working and professional—is going with Madeline. Josh tells Madeline that his goal is to eventually become an "artist." She corrects him by saying that to be an artist is "a gift, not a goal." She will not hold an exhibit for Josh, because she secretly hates his work. She prefers Adrian's work, but he hates just about everything she exhibits in her gallery. In the art world, taste matters when it comes to matters of the heart. Whatever art one appreciates becomes a big part of their identity.

Screenwriters Catherine di Napoli and Jonathan Parker (who also directs) have some fun at the expense of some of the pretentiousness of their characters, but they never treat them with disdain. Eventually, these people all become likable, in spite of their foibles. Their behavior does not cross over into caricature or parody. Although they may go to humorous extremes, their responses and mannerisms remain believable and interesting. When we see the artwork purchased by Porter displayed all over his apartment, it seems entirely plausible when he claims that he has never heard of Matisse. Likewise, the art depicted in the film does not let the audience off the hook by playing it simply for laughs. After the laugh, the audience must eventually think about the art in the same way the characters on screen are forced to think about it.

Goldberg plays his character with the right amount of insecurity, self-righteousness and contempt for all around him, but without coming across as overly arrogant. He has played this Woody Allen-type role before (*2 Days in Paris* [2007], for example), but not with this much disdain for all that surrounds him. He does not always have a witty retort to use as a defense mechanism. Often, the scowling look on his face says enough and the viewer feels for him. Shelton, as Madeline, speaks with great authority on the value of art and its appreciators. She plays her part with just the right amount of cool, but knowing full well that her character could stumble at any given moment.

If *(Untitled)* has a problem, it is that, like Adrian, it too often hides behind intellectualism and never truly gets under the skin of the viewer. There is plenty to think about, but little to feel. Perhaps that is the point. Should a movie about the art world be an artistic statement in itself? Not necessarily, but it should probably at least know its subject matter, as this film does. And how does one know if the art succeeds? Is it about thinking or feeling? Both? The main purpose for *(Untitled)* is to throw these (and many other) questions to the viewer without always providing the answers. At least one or two of these questions is bound to jumpstart a debate or two, and perhaps that is enough of a success.

Collin Souter

CREDITS

Adrian Jacobs: Adam Goldberg
Madeleine Gray: Marley Shelton
Josh Jacobs: Eion Bailey
Ray Barko: Vinnie Jones
The CLarinetist: Lucy Punch
Porter Canby: Zak Orth
Grant: Michael Panes
Helen Finkelstein: Janet Carroll
Morton Cabot: Ben Hammer
Monroe: Ptolemy Slocum
Origin: USA
Language: English
Released: 2009
Production: Jonathan Parker, Andreas Olavarria; Parker Film Co.; released by Samuel Goldwyn Films
Directed by: Jonathan Parker
Written by: Jonathan Parker, Catherine Di Napoli
Cinematography by: Svetlana Cvetko
Music by: David Lang
Sound: Bryan Dembinski
Editing: Keiko Deguchi
Costumes: Deidre Wegner
Production Design: David L. Snyder, Len X. Clayton
MPAA rating: R
Running time: 96 minutes

REVIEWS

Anderson, Melissa. *Village Voice.* October 20, 2009.
Ebert, Roger. *Chicago Sun-Times.* November 5, 2009.
Goldstein, Gary. *Los Angeles Times.* October 23, 2009.
Holden, Stephen. *New York Times.* October 23, 2009.
LaSalle, Mark. *San Francisco Chronicles.* November 5, 2009.
Pais, Matt. *Metromix.com.* October 22, 2009.
Phillips, Michael. *Chicago Tribune.* November 5, 2009.
Smith, Kyle. *New York Post.* October 23, 2009.
Sobczynski, Peter. *EFilmCritic.com.* November 6, 2009.
Tobias, Scott. *AV Club.* October 22, 2009.

UP

Box Office: $293 million

In the weeks prior to its release, Pixar's *Up* was greeted as a warning sign for Wall Street investors who had stock in the animation studio. It was the third Pixar movie in a row to defy convention after the lukewarm critical response of its otherwise successful *Cars* (2006). In the wake of this slight artistic drop-off, Pixar released the Brad Bird directed *Ratatouille* (2007), a film that, oddly enough, ended with a monologue about the value of criticism and what it means to be that critic. A year later, Pixar released *WALL*E* (2008), a film that told its story for 40 minutes without the use of dialogue. Now came the studio's tenth film, *Up*, a movie advertised with little more than a grumpy old man, a precocious boy scout and the image of a house with a thousand balloons attached to it floating in the clouds. Wall Street's cries of panic were not entirely unjustified.

Up is, at the very least, unconventional. It's not based on a children's book, is not a remake, is not a sequel, does not have any star power worth mentioning in the ads and does not mirror a storyline from a previous commercial success. It is purely the product of imagination from a studio that has always put its stories first. Even its 3-D effect feels like a reluctant compromise as a means of competing with every other animated film on the market. By 2009, it seemed that a studio couldn't release an animated film unless it was in 3-D. With *Up*, the viewer soon forgets that they're wearing a pair of glasses. It doesn't seem to matter either way, because the experience of *Up* isn't in the watching, but in the trying to guess where the story could possibly go next.

The audience presumably goes in knowing that at some point they will see a house with a thousand balloons attached to it. But it's the elements of the journey before and after that initial moment of reveal that no one can expect. Why is the old man in the trailer so grumpy? We find out that his beloved wife has died, his house is targeted for demolition and that he could soon end up in a nursing home. How did he come up with the idea of attaching balloons to his house? Because, among other things, he was a balloon vendor and still had canisters of helium in his basement. What else would he do with them?

The only element of the storyline that makes *Up* a commercially viable venture is the pairing of the cantankerous, elderly Cark Frederickson (voiced by Ed Asner) and the precocious 8-year-old boy scout, Russell (voiced by Jordan Nagai). With this dynamic, *Up* eventually becomes a Buddy Comedy, where mismatched archetypes get paired up, conflict with each other at first and eventually come to a mutual understanding of their similarities and differences. Because Russell was lurking near the bottom of the house when it took off, he and Carl are stuck with each other and Carl doesn't plan on landing the house until he gets to his destination in South America, where he and his wife had dreamed of going. But Carl never had a Grandson and Russell doesn't appear to have a father around. They each fill a void the other person's life.

For the most part, *Up* remains a completely original vision. Carl's travel plans do not work out, of course, but the journey encompasses the hunting for endangered species, dogs with electronic collars that give them real voices and a giant, colorful, ostrich-like bird who ends up joining Carl and Russell on their improbable quest. Miraculously, none of these elements come into the fray as non-sequitors.

The bird, whom Russell nicknames Kevin (in spite of the fact that it's a female), is being hunted by a somewhat crazed adventurer/explorer by the name of Charles Muntz (voiced by Christopher Plummer), who it just so happens Carl and his wife idolized in their youth. Charles now lives in a cave with the sinister plan of capturing the bird and living off the fame and glory of having discovered the species. Aiding him are his dogs, all of whom can talk via a voicechip in their collars. The sweetest of these dogs, Dug (voiced by Bob Peterson), is the first to meet Carl and Russell, but must also be a reluctant spy for Charles. The leader of the dogs has the appearance of a sinister Doberman, but whose Achilles Heel is too funny to mention to anyone who hasn't yet seen the film.

In true Pixar fashion, it all leads up to a big chase in the third act and it is to the writers' credit that they resisted underscoring the film's biggest visual pun (literally, a dogfight). It is also worth mentioning that the writers maintained the use of wordless storytelling that they mastered with their most previous outing, *WALL*E*. Here, as in that film, a love story has been told with visual eloquence. The film's opening, after the initial introduction of Carl and his wife Ellie (as kids meeting for the first time), the film follows their romantic progression from childhood to old age, setting the unknowing audience for the film's final, most poetic shot, an image that says so much without saying a word and bringing an unexpected and emotionally satisfying sense of closure.

It's hard to argue, however, that certain Pixar archetypes and conventions do exist within the storyline. As stated before, *Up* is, among other things, a Buddy Comedy, not unlike *Toy Story* (1995), *Finding Nemo* (2003) and *Monsters, Inc.* (2001) (also directed by Pete Docter). The character of Charles Muntz could be viewed as a re-imaging of the obsessive toy collector in *Toy Story 2* (1999). The absent-minded, but eager and well-meaning character of Dug seems to be borrowing from the similarly aloof character of Dory from *Finding Nemo*.

Yet, in spite of these similarities, *Up* never has the feel of a film that is on creative hold. The film moves at such a brisk pace and with surprises at nearly every turn that the viewer really doesn't have time to stop and think too much about what they're watching. The studio's writers continue to have a knack for taking the improbable and grounding it into something that seems somehow possible within the rules set up in whatever world they choose (the ocean, a child's closet, an empty planet, etc.). Of course, there's no way a thousand balloons could carry an entire house half way around the world. But what if they could?

As usual, the animators at Pixar have gone above and beyond the call of duty in regards to detail and eloquence. While *Up* bypasses the photorealistic animated quality that helped make *WALL*E* such a transcendent experience, the film manages to never feel too animated. It has a typically gorgeous palette of colors and background images that transport the viewer into the misty clouds, harsh jungles and deserts and Carl's rustic home that appears to be stuck in time. At one point, early in the film, we see sunlight reflecting harshly against one of the windows of the house while Carl has words with the evil real estate developers. It's a minor touch and not one that many people would notice, but it goes to show how much attention to detail the artists give to their sequences. Where would the sun be at this time of day? Why should anyone care? Yet, somehow, this detail matters.

With this, their tenth film, and with each new film defying the expectations of what an animated film should be (in most cases, snarky, shrill, pop culture-laden jokefests with forced sentiment), Pixar has solidified itself as an entity whose artistic merit joins the ranks of not only Walt Disney himself, but established and revered filmmakers such as Billy Wilder, Steven Spielberg and Martin Scorsese (to name a few), artists who have helped shape and re-shape what a movie could be. Directors' works and artistic choices have always been analyzed, criticized and the basis of intense discussion amongst film scholars and critics, but Pixar is one of the few studios to also warrant this kind of attention (with or without the Disney connection). As their films take more and more chances and the shareholders get more and more nervous, their future as a creative enterprise that exists to tell stories more than move merchandise remains a compelling and astonishing story in and of itself.

Collin Souter

CREDITS

Carl Fredricksen: Ed Asner (Voice)
Russell: Jordan Nagai (Voice)
Charles F. Muntz: Christopher Plummer (Voice)
Construction Foreman Tom: John Ratzenberger (Voice)
Beta: Delroy Lindo (Voice)
Dug/Alpha: Bob Peterson (Voice)
Gamma: Jerome Ranft (Voice)
Origin: USA
Language: English
Released: 2009
Production: Jonas Rivera; Pixar; released by Walt Disney Pictures
Directed by: Pete Docter, Bob Peterson
Written by: Bob Peterson
Cinematography by: Patick Lin
Music by: Michael Giacchino
Sound: Tom Myers
Editing: Kevin Nolting
Production Design: Ricky Nierva
MPAA rating: PG
Running time: 96 minutes

REVIEWS

Bradshaw, Peter. *Guardian.* May 13, 2009.
Childress, Erik. *EFilmCritic.* May 26, 2009.
Corliss, Richard. *Time Magazine.* May 8, 2009.
Ebert, Roger. *Chicago Sun-Times.* May 28, 2009.
Edelstein, David . *New York Magazine.* May 26, 2009.
McCarthy, Todd. *Variety.* April 23, 2009.
Pais, Matt. *Metromix.com.* May 27, 2009.
Puig, Claudia. *USA Today.* May 28, 2009.
Stevens, Dana. *Slate.* May 28, 2009.
Tallerico, Brian. *MovieRetriever.com.* May 27, 2009.

QUOTES

Dug: "Hey, I know a joke! A squirrel walks up to a tree and says, 'I forgot to store acorns for the winter and now I am dead.' Ha! It is funny because the squirrel gets dead."

TRIVIA

This is the first animated film, let alone 3D, to open the Cannes Film Festival.

AWARDS

Oscars 2009: Animated Film, Orig. Score
British Acad. 2009: Animated Film, Orig. Score

Golden Globes 2010: Animated Film, Orig. Score
Nomination:
Oscars 2009: Film, Orig. Screenplay, Sound FX Editing
British Acad. 2009: Orig. Screenplay, Sound.

UP IN THE AIR

The story of a man ready to make a connection.
—Movie tagline

Box Office: $83 million

Rarely has a film more deftly tapped into the national consciousness than Jason Reitman's *Up in the Air*, an incredibly accomplished dramedy that manages to bring three-dimensional characters to believable life but also finds a way to do so using the undercurrent of economic crisis and technological advancement flowing through American society in 2009. On one level, *Up in the Air* is a rather straightforward tale of a man without ties finally realizing that it is time to make a connection in his life. As a backdrop to his personally inspired story, Reitman uses the economic crisis of the late 2000s and the fact that technology is changing the way all of us interact to emphasize his story points without underlining them. *Up in the Air* continues a remarkable hot streak for this young filmmaker, artistically surpassing both of his acclaimed previous works, *Thank You For Smoking* (2005) and Best Picture nominee *Juno* (2007), to become one of the most beloved films of the year.

Very loosely based on a book by Walter Kim and adapted by Reitman and Sheldon Turner, *Up in the Air* tells the story of a man with very few physical belongings or personal connections to tether him to the ground. Ryan Bingham (George Clooney) spends so much of his life on the road that he has developed a value system that prizes the frequent flyer miles more than the people he meets while he racks them up. Through motivational speaking, Bingham exposes a lifestyle with no attachments or no contents in what he terms "your backpack." According to Bingham, everyone has a backpack filled with not only the physical belongings that tie them to the ground but the sometimes draining effect of family, friends, co-workers, etc. Bingham preaches a lightening of the backpack, a life philosophy that he has clearly taken to extremes. He enjoys nothing as much as his hotel perk programs and the VIP treatment he receives in airports around the world. He has flown more than the distance to the moon and happily spends two-thirds of the year on the road for his very unusual job. Ryan is hired to step in and do the dirty work of firing employees when a company needs to downsize. He is the grim reaper of the economic crisis and seems to be enjoying it. Like the lives he drastically changes with his arrival, Ryan's life will undergo a tumultuous upheaval.

As with most things, it starts with a girl. After returning from a trip, Bingham's boss (Jason Bateman) informs him that the company is cutting their travel budget, the very foundation of Ryan's existence. A new hire at the company, the confident young Natalie Keener (Anna Kendrick), has come with a webcam technology that will allow Ryan's job to be done from one location. Even the downsizing of American can now come via remote location. Ryan immediately discerns that not only is Natalie challenging his way of life but she is drastically underestimating the crucial human element of what they do. To give her a taste of that aspect of their profession, Bingham is forced to mentor the new hire around the country on a series of job executions, many of which Reitman stages by using non-actors who were recently fired to discuss their feelings about their treatment.

While on the road, Ryan develops sexual heat with a similar-minded, stunningly hot traveler named Alex Goran (Vera Farmiga). The two start with what seems like a mostly sexual arrangement—meeting in hotels while on geographically close job assignments—but it appears to be developing into something more. Through some prodding from the more idealistic Natalie, Ryan begins to reach out to Alex, even going as far as to take him to his sister's wedding, an event that it feels like he may not have even attended if not for the emotional thawing caused by his growing affection for Alex. In the final act, Ryan is thrown a curve that approximates the life-changing moments that he has turned into a career. Bingham is constantly telling the people that he fires that it could actually be a good thing, the fork in the path that takes them down a road that they should have been on all along. When Ryan's worldview is shattered, when his plans are derailed, he is put into a similar position although the ambiguous ending makes it clear to this viewer that he knows not where the next road will lead him.

Reitman took only the basic concept of Kim's book (which features neither the character of Natalie nor Alex) and turned it into a very personal piece about identity and connection. The screenplay for *Up in the Air* features clear thematic density but none of it is overwritten or as moralistically portrayed as even the plot description above might lead someone to believe. Like a lot of great films, *Up in the Air* can be an incredibly subjective experience. It can be merely a clever George Clooney comedy with some great performances and memorable lines. But for people at a crossroads not dissimilar to these characters, the film offers much more. Rarely has a film spoken more deftly to a crossroads that nearly everyone reaches at some point in their lives and a time-

less question—where am I going? And yet, Ryan never comes off as a plot device, as the overly self-award movie character that so many lesser directors would have turned him into. Reitman's greatest skill, one that earned him a Directors Guild of America nomination among other critical acclaim during awards season, is keeping his films about the characters; not merely about the themes. He lets the theme emerge from the character.

And he works with actors as well as anyone making this type of cinema today. George Clooney gives the most vulnerable performance that he has delivered in a decade, nearly playing off his reputation as a suave leading man to greater emotional impact. It is not difficult to see some of the life players that Clooney has portrayed before in films like *Ocean's Eleven* (2001) and *Michael Clayton* (2007) in Bingham, making his subtle emotional unraveling all the more effective. He is ably assisted by two of the best supporting actress performances of 2009 from Kendrick and Farmiga. The former, a relative newcomer after roles in *Rocket Science* (2007) and *Twilight* (2008), is simply fantastic in a crucial role that so many other actresses would have turned into a stereotype. Kendrick excels largely because of the traps she avoids, never turning Natalie into the cocky shrew that she could have easily become. Farmiga has been a remarkable, underrated actress for years, giving nomination-worthy work in films like *The Departed* (2006) and *Nothing But the Truth* (2008) and even elevating genre films like *Orphan* (2009). She imbues Alex with such sexy confidence that it is easy to see why Ryan wants to put her in his empty backpack. She is a woman worth breaking a life pattern to get closer to even if the cost of that choice is unclear. The entire supporting cast, including J.K. Simmons, Danny McBride, Melanie Lynskey, and Amy Morton, displays Reitman's skill with actors.

After just three films, Jason Reitman has become such an unbelievably confident director that seasoned veterans could learn a thing or two by watching his films. Great directors are like great storytellers, giving the audience the sense that they know exactly where they are going and that you can comfortably recline your seat and go along for the ride. That confident storytelling ability is apparent in every choice made during Reitman's production of *Up in the Air* from the casting to performances to even the music choices. And as Reitman's films get thematically richer and more subtle, they become even more effective. One can only marvel at where he will take audiences next.

Brian Tallerico

CREDITS

Ryan Bingham: George Clooney
Alex Goran: Vera Farmiga

Craig Gregory: Jason Bateman
Julie Bingham: Melanie Lynskey
Natalie Keener: Anna Kendrick
Jim Miller: Danny McBride
Kevin: Chris Lowell
Kara Bingham: Amy Morton
Maynard Finch: Sam Elliott
Steve: Zach Galifianakis
Bob: J.K. Simmons
Origin: USA
Language: English
Released: 2009
Production: Jeffrey Clifford, Ivan Reitman, Daniel Dubiecki, Jason Reitman; Cold Spring Pictures, DW Studios, Montecito Picture Co.; released by Paramount
Directed by: Jason Reitman
Written by: Jason Reitman, Sheldon Turner
Cinematography by: Eric Steelberg
Music by: Rolfe Kent
Sound: Steve Morrow
Editing: Dana E. Glauberman
Production Design: Steve Saklad
Art Direction: Andrew Max Cahn
Costumes: Danny Glicker
MPAA rating: R
Running time: 109 minutes

REVIEWS

Ansen, David. *Newsweek*. December 4, 2009.
Corliss, Richard. *Time Magazine*. September 14, 2009.
Dargis, Manohla. *New York Times*. December 4, 2009.
Ebert, Roger. *Chicago Sun-Times*. December 3, 2009.
Edelstein, David. *New York Magazine*. November 30, 2009.
Germain, David. *Associated Press*. December 2, 2009.
Lane, Anthony. *New Yorker*. November 30, 2009.
Morgenstern, Joe. *Wall Street Journal*. December 3, 2009.
Phillips, Michael. *Chicago Tribune* December 3, 2009.
Reed, Rex. *New York Observer*. September 16, 2009.

QUOTES

Ryan Bingham: "Anybody who ever built an empire, or changed the world, sat where you are now. And it's because they sat there that they were able to do it."

TRIVIA

Jason Reitman and Ivan Reitman are one of two father/son producing teams to be nominated for a Best Picture Oscar®. The other is Mario Cecchi Gori and Vittorio Cecchi Gori for *Il Postino: The Postman*.

AWARDS

British Acad. 2009: Adapt. Screenplay
Golden Globes 2010: Screenplay

Writers Guild 2009: Adapt. Screenplay
Nomination:
Oscars 2009: Actor (Clooney), Adapt. Screenplay, Director (Reitman), Film, Support. Actress (Farmiga, Kendrick)
British Acad. 2009: Actor (Clooney), Film, Film Editing, Support. Actress (Farmiga, Kendrick)
Directors Guild 2009: Director (Reitman)
Golden Globes 2010: Actor—Drama (Clooney), Director (Reitman), Film—Drama, Support. Actress (Farmiga, Kendrick)
Screen Actors Guild 2009: Actor (Clooney), Support. Actress (Farmiga, Kendrick).

VALENTINO: THE LAST EMPEROR

Box Office: $1.8 million

There are jobs whose functions, skill sets and regular duties can be readily grasped by almost everyone: teacher, police officer, athlete. Then there are the occupations whose everyday routines are defined largely by hyper-articulate, wildly over-the-top television shows: lawyer, politician, emergency room doctor. Finally, there are those jobs about which most Americans simply have no clue.

The long-running Discovery Channel show *Dirty Jobs* shines a light in revolving fashion on some of these occupations on the lower end of the socioeconomic spectrum, or at least the desirability index. Big-screen documentaries are mostly topical and issue-oriented, but because artistic impulse loves to see itself reflected, a few modestly budgeted nonfiction films—like *Crumb* (1995) or *Comedian* (2002)—center on creative, right-brained subjects who seem to have a cloud of ineffability that surrounds both their talents and the specifics of their daily schedules. Slotting loosely into this mold is *Valentino: The Last Emperor*.

A mostly fawning look into the life and times of iconic, Italian-born fashion designer Valentino Garavani, the movie is directed by first-time filmmaker Matt Tyrnauer, a special correspondent for *Vanity Fair* whose moving and shaking in the New York City literati scene no doubt helped him win entrée into the elite social circles which serve as a backdrop for the film. (Gwyneth Paltrow, Elton John and Elizabeth Hurley all pop up in party footage, chatting smilingly.) Following Garavani and his business partner and companion of 50 years, Giancarlo Giammetti, as they prepare for a big 45th anniversary celebration of haute couture, Tyrnauer rather listlessly documents the colorful closing act of the last true couturier's celebrated career.

Despite garnering mostly correspondingly positive reviews and beating fellow fashion documentary *The*

September Issue out of the gate by opening first, in March 2009, *Valentino: The Last Emperor* grossed only $1.7 million in American theaters, or about half of what the latter film pulled in. The chief reason may well be that while *The September Issue* spent some of its time tracking a relatable workplace rivalry that felt enriched and heightened in stakes by its tony surroundings, Tyrnauer scarcely discovers anything of note about any of the relationships that form the crux of his movie.

In fact, the director is so clearly infatuated with his subject that even when he does capture something approaching a moment infused with drama or intrigue—at one point Garavani has a tiff and insists that he stop being filmed, in another instance Giammetti asserts that his corporate boss' opinions "have no value" with respect to the actual direction of the company—Tyrnauer does not follow up on it. The general operating philosophy seems to be to simply point the camera to and fro, and see what it incidentally captures. This lack of intellectual rigor extends from everything from Garavani's personal life (he and Giammetti were apparently lovers for a dozen years, but the movie never even makes mention of this, let alone inquires as to how the dissolution of a romantic relationship might have impacted their business together) to unexplored, potentially interesting theses about the designer's professional development, since he confesses to being influenced mightily by the style of screen stars he glimpsed in films and magazines while growing up. Even a 2007 takeover of Valentino Fashion Group by British private equity firm Permira rates only cursory explanations via TV footage, information that scratches no deeper than a thumbnail. Owing to all this staggering incuriosity, there is no greater nut of meaning cracked within the movie, no matter all the rich style on display.

It is not offensively bad, it is just that *Valentino: The Last Emperor* is in essence a film with the pulse of an at-rest septuagenarian, which is exactly what its subject is; there is no thrill or revelation here, just a photo-capturing of lives of privilege that unfolds politely. The film has neither the pop vibrancy of *The Kid Stays in the Picture* (2002), nor the advantage of being a fascinating and unlikely reconstruction of an American pariah, like *The Eyes of Tammy Faye* (2000), to mention two other documentaries about leathery, overly tanned public figures. For all his industry celebrity, Valentino remains a relatively inscrutable figure to the average American, and Tyrnauer unfortunately seems to have no interest in popping that bubble.

There is no doubt—no matter how much or little one knows or cares about fashion—that there is an interesting movie to be made about Valentino, or one of the few other designers like him. Errol Morris looked at a quartet of unusual occupations in *Fast, Cheap & Out of Control* (1997), and located all sorts of fortifying sentiments and quirky life truths in their disparateness and unlikely similarities. In the rarefied air in which *Valentino: The Last Emperor* unfolds, Tyrnauer has the opportunity to peel back the emperor's curtain and show how this man has left a mark on the world, and even perhaps how the world has left a mark on the man. That he does not succeed is not the movie's worst failing. That he does not even try is far more disheartening.

Brent Simon

CREDITS

Himself: Valentino Garavani
Himself: Giancarlo Giammetti
Origin: USA
Language: English
Released: 2008
Production: Matt Kapp, Matt Tyrnauer; Acolyte Films; released by Vitagraph
Directed by: Matt Tyrnauer
Cinematography by: Tom Hurwitz
Music by: Joel Goodman
Editing: Bob Eisenhardt, Frédéric Tcheng
Sound: Peter Miller
MPAA rating: PG-13
Running time: 96 minutes

REVIEWS

Anderson, Jason. *Toronto Star.* July 10, 2009.
Anderson, Melissa. *Village Voice.* March 17, 2009.
Ebert, Roger. *Chicago Sun-Times.* March 26, 2009.
Gronvall, Andrea. *Chicago Reader.* March 27, 2009.
Holden, Stephen. *New York Times.* March 18, 2009.
Lacey, Liam. *Globe and Mail.* July 10, 2009.
Morris, Wesley. *Boston Globe.* April 16, 2009.
Phillips, Michael. *Chicago Tribune.* March 26, 2009.
Sobczynski, Peter. *eFilmCritic.com.* March 26, 2009.
Turan, Kenneth. *Los Angeles Times.* April 2, 2009.

TRIVIA

Both Giancarlo Giammetti and Valentino Garavani hated the film when they first saw it and it took director Matt Tyrnauer over five months of negotiations before he was able to show the film at the Venice film festival. There, the audience gave Valentino a standing ovation. He now loves the film.

WATCHMEN

*Justice is coming to all of us. No matter what we
do.*
—Movie tagline
Who watches the Watchmen?
—Movie tagline

Box Office: $107.5 million

Perhaps the best (and worst) thing one can say about
Zack Snyder's *Watchmen* is that it is a movie that is
almost impossible to assess solely on its own merits.
Virtually any discussion of the film has to include a
mention of its original source material—the monumental
1986 twelve-issue comic book series by Alan Moore and
Dave Gibbons—the life-cycle of the superhero film
genre, and the various benefits and pitfalls of the ever-
tricky book-to-film adaptation. Moore and Gibbons'
Watchmen has been described for more than two decades
as the "*Citizen Kane* of comic books," standing as
perhaps the most acclaimed graphic novel of all time. As
such, any *Watchmen* adaptation comes with significantly
higher expectations, from comic book fans and cultural
critics alike, than, say, *Punisher: War Journal.* And, while
the sheer ambition of the project might be enough to
cut the film some slack, it is hard not to see Snyder's
broad, flawed *Watchmen* as the perfect example of what
can go wrong when a film director tries to replicate the
experience of reading a graphic novel on the big screen.

To call Snyder's *Watchmen* a "literal" adaptation is a
massive understatement. The film is almost a slideshow
recreation of Dave Gibbons' illustrations, an exercise in
using the original panel-by-panel drawings as production storyboards, which, on a technical level, is a fairly

impressive achievement. (Alex McDowell's production
design is easily the highlight of the film.) The sheer
exactness on display in Snyder's replication of the iconic
images of Moore and Gibbons' *Watchmen* might, to
some, seem to be the ideal strategy for any comic book-
to-film adaptation. For decades, pundits have criticized
Hollywood adaptations of classic books for straying too
far from the source material, for inventing plotlines,
new characters, and new endings that seemingly work
against or deviate from the original text. Comic books,
however, are in a unique situation because they offer
readers both visuals and text. Fans occasionally gripe
about film adaptations of their favorite books when the
adapting filmmaker's vision contradicts the mental images they've created from reading the original text, but,
with graphic novels, the fans are beginning to feel more
and more entitled to see both the text and the visuals
reproduced verbatim on the big screen. Snyder's *Watchmen*, from its very inception, seems like a project
determined to prove that such a literal recasting of a
story from the page to the screen is the future of the
modern comic book movie.

Say what one will about *Watchmen*, but both its
supporters and detractors can agree that the film's first
few minutes are unquestionably the best part of the
movie. Set to Bob Dylan's "Times They Are A-Changin',"
the opening title sequence edits together an exquisite
slow-motion ode to Moore and Gibbons' original comic,
a montage right out of Gibbons' nine-panel layouts,
deftly setting up the world of *Watchmen* and the tone of
fading nostalgia and doom that permeates the film. In
this alternate timeline, the World War II era was
dominated by the rise of costumed heroes and villains,

street-bound superheroes straight out of the mundane world who donned masks to transform themselves into something special. As the 1960s began, the older generation of heroes receded and their descendents—in some cases, literally, their offspring—took up their mantle. However, the world of these new heroes and villains became infinitely more complicated by the emergence of Dr. Manhattan (Billy Crudup), the first "real" superhero, a blue-skinned, near-omniscient super-man, borne of a laboratory accident, who can rearrange matter with a wave of his hand and see backwards and forwards through time.

The introduction of Dr. Manhattan into the world grossly changes the direction of human history, perverting and altering the circumstances of such pivotal events as the assassination of John F. Kennedy and the Vietnam War. (Manhattan ends the Vietnam conflict in days.) Manhattan's limitless power and the growing violent tendencies of vigilantes eventually turns public opinion against superheroes until, in the 1980s, in a world where Richard Nixon is still the U.S. President, Congress outlaws all costumed heroes. Meanwhile, in this hostile environment, the Cold War between the U.S. and Russia has escalated to a fever pitch, moving the metaphorical "Doomsday Clock" to five minutes before midnight. i.e. the end is nigh. (The bulk of this history is conveyed during those impressive opening credits.)

The main story opens in 1985, with the murder of The Comedian (Jeffrey Dean Morgan), one of the few costumed heroes still sanctioned by the U.S. Government. During the late 1960s, the Comedian was a member of a superhero team known as "The Watchmen" with an interestingly dysfunctional group of other "heroes" such as Dr. Manhattan; the Batman-esque Nite Owl (Patrick Wilson); the second-generation she-hero, Laurie Jupiter, The Silk Spectre (Malin Akerman); the super-rich, super-intelligent Ozymandias (Matthew Goode); and the uncompromising, near-psychotic detective Rorschach (Jackie Earle Haley). Rorschach, one of the few vigilantes who still fights crime illegally, begins an investigation of the Comedian's death and tries to convince his old teammates that someone out there might be targeting former superheroes. Rorschach visits Dr. Manhattan—who has been working on alternate energy solutions with uber-rich Adrian Veidt, the former Ozymandias—and his girlfriend, Laurie Jupiter, and they are instantly skeptical of the off-kilter detective's theory. The only person even partially sympathetic to Rorschach is his former partner, Dan Dreiberg (Nite Owl), and, it has to be said, Wilson and Haley give the two most engaging, accessible performances in the film—which is even more impressive when you consider that both actors spend a large portion of their screen-time with their faces obscured by masks.

Following the Comedian's funeral, an unknown entity begins a smear campaign against Dr. Manhattan, hitting the obtuse, oblivious super-man with allegations that some of his closest friends and enemies have contracted cancer due to Manhattan's radioactive presence. The public relations nightmare causes Manhattan to unexpectedly teleport himself off-planet, which throws the world into turmoil, as one might expect when America's number one nuclear deterrent suddenly disappears. Soon, the other members of the Watchmen are targeted—Rorschach is jailed, someone tries to kill Ozymandias—inspiring the now-romantically entangled Nite Owl and the Silk Spectre to re-don their costumes, break Rorschach out of prison, and try to figure out who has been manipulating both the superhero community and the balance of world power behind the scenes.

Fans of Moore and Gibbons' *Watchmen* definitely won't be disappointed on a purely visual level with Snyder's adaptation. Alex McDowell's production design and Larry Fong's cinematography do a startling job of making Gibbon's illustrations come to life in a physical, textured way. And, aside from a few necessary edits—including a fairly major revision in the film's third act climax—David Hayter and Alex Tse's screenplay does find a way to condense twelve issues of unbelievably dense text into a two hours-plus motion picture. So, given all that, why does *Watchmen* as a film fail on such a profound level? Perhaps the reason is that Zack Snyder has reduced the original comic book into simply text and images, which he reproduces in a fashion that reminds one of cinematic tracing paper. What Snyder fails to grasp is that, like any other written work, comic books are more than the sum of their parts. No great novel is just text, just words on the page, and no great graphic novel is just text and image. Moore and Gibbons' *Watchmen* is filled with elements that Snyder, in his clinical attempts to capture the surface details of *Watchmen* so exactly, never grasps—elements like character, drama, tension, pacing, subtext, and emotion. Yes, every scene, every memorable line that fanboys have been drooling for decades to see on the big screen is in there, but none of the emotion driving those moments, none of the ephemera that made us care so much about Rorschach and Nite Owl, that made us dread for the on-set of nuclear war, have been captured at all.

As an adaptation, *Watchmen* is as soulless as they come, a film created in a fanboy vacuum where the dimensions of Silk Spectre's costume and the set dressing of Dan Dreiberg's apartment are more important than character motivation or the emotional honesty of any of the relationships in the film. (It does not help when the pivotal Silk Spectre-Manhattan coupling is played by the wooden Akerman and a giant blue CGI character.) Not a moment in *Watchmen* feels authentic, largely due to Snyder's blunt, inelegant direction. This is a film where everything is telegraphed to a ridiculous degree, where funerals unfold to the tunes of Simon and Garfunkel's "Sounds of Silence" and a character with plans for world domination is underscored by the ever-so-subtle lyrics of Tears for Fears' "Everybody Wants to Rule the World." If you want to know what Moore and Gibbons' *Watchmen* looks or sounds like, Snyder's film is passable, but if you want to know how the original *Watchmen* feels, avoid the movie at all costs.

As such, *Watchmen* the movie will probably stand as one of the most pivotal comic book adaptations in recent memory, if only because it will force the discussion of how future adaptations will be judged. Is a movie-version of a comic book great because it looks exactly like it did on the page? Or are there other criteria that adaptations need to meet, like existing, in and of itself, as an honest, well-crafted film? If that is the case, *Watchmen* definitely fails that litmus text and will stand as a testament of everything that's wrong with modern comic book movie adaptations.

Tom Burns

CREDITS

Rorschach/Walter Kovacs: Jackie Earle Haley
Dr. Manhattan/Jon Osterman: Billy Crudup
The Comedian/Edward Blake: Jeffrey Dean Morgan
Adrian Veidt/Ozymandias: Matthew Goode
Silk Spectre/Sally Justice: Carla Gugino
Silk Spectre II/Laurie Jupiter: Malin Akerman
Nite Owl/Hollis Mason: Stephen McHattie
Nite Owl II/Dan Dreiberg: Patrick Wilson
Moloch the Mystic/Edgar Jacobi: Matt Frewer
Origin: USA
Language: English
Released: 2009
Production: Lawrence Gordon, Lloyd Levin, Deborah Snyder; Legendary Pictures; released by Warner Bros.
Directed by: Zack Snyder
Written by: David Hayter, Alex Tse
Cinematography by: Larry Fong
Music by: Tyler Bates
Sound: Eric A. Norris
Editing: William Hoy
Art Direction: Francois Audouy
Costumes: Michael Wilkinson
Production Design: Alex McDowell
MPAA rating: R
Running time: 161 minutes

REVIEWS

Chang, Justin. *Variety.* February 26, 2009.
Simon, Brent. *Screen International.* February 27, 2009.

Gordon, Devin. *New York Magazine.* March 2, 2009.
Lane, Anthony. *New Yorker.* March 2, 2009.
Hoberman, J. *Village Voice.* March 3, 2009.
Ebert, Roger. *Chicago Sun-Times.* March 4, 2009.
Howell, Peter. *Toronto Star.* March 5, 2009.
Stevens, Dana. *Slate.* March 5, 2009.
Scott, A.O. *New York Times.* March 6, 2009.
Tallerico, Brian. *MovieRetriever.com.* March 6, 2009.

QUOTES

Rorschach: "I heard a joke once: Man goes to doctor. Says he's depressed. Says life is harsh and cruel. Says he feels all alone in a threatening world. Doctor says, 'Treatment is simple. The great clown Pagliacci is in town tonight. Go see him. That should pick you up.' Man bursts into tears. Says, 'But doctor I am Pagliacci.' Good joke. Everybody laughs. Roll on snare drum. Curtains."

TRIVIA

The first "official" image from director Zack Snyder's version of *Watchmen*—a test shot of Rorshach holding the Comedian's button—was hidden within the trailer for *300*.

WHATEVER WORKS

Box Office: $5.3 million

The pairing of Woody Allen and Larry David on the surface appears to be a perfect comedy match—two neurotic Jews from New York with their own way of looking at the world around him; Allen from the intellectual's perspective and David from the little things in daily social settings that annoy him to no end. Both have received their share of accolades in their respective fields. Allen has accumulated a staggering 14 nominations for writing screenplays—and a pair of wins for *Annie Hall* (1977) and *Hannah and Her Sisters* (1986)—while David has earned his share of nods for creating two of the best half-hour comedies ever on television—*Seinfeld* and *Curb Your Enthusiasm*. Yes, these are two personalities we would love to see share the screen and tear down the inconsistencies of the world around them. Alas, we are left to be satisfied with David channeling Allen in the manner that John Cusack and Kenneth Branagh have had to do before him. Only the satisfaction is limited to the acknowledgement that it is at least an improvement over Allen's recent sketchy resume that includes the likes of *Anything Else* (2003), *Scoop* (2006) and *Cassandra's Dream* (2007).

After four efforts overseas and away from his native New York, Woody returns to introduce us to Boris Yellnikoff (Larry David), a former physics professor—

and near-Nobel Prize nominee—who now teaches chess to kids in the park. Failed at marriage as well as at suicide, Boris now hangs with his male buddies complaining about all manners of social issues and, when they don't want to listen, he talks directly to us, aware that we're out here watching his every move. After returning home one evening he is stopped by the desperate Melodie St. Anne Celestine (Evan Rachel Wood), a homeless runaway from the South that just wants something to eat. Boris gives in, annoyed more by her dimbulb manner to recognize sarcasm than by his space being invaded, and soon a meal turns into a place to crash, which turns into a few days, then a mutual respect, developed crush and eventually marriage.

Neither appears bothered by the forty year age difference between them and Boris makes it clear their relationship is not bound by sexual attraction anyway. He doesn't even like sex. Someone who does notice the age difference is Melodie's mom, Marietta (Patricia Clarkson) who has tracked her down after having her own reasons to leave home. It seems that Melodie's dad, John (Ed Begley, Jr.), has left her for another woman and now she is intent to get her daughter away from this unpleasant, older individual. Melodie cannot help but see the lure of the handsome young actor (Henry Cavill) mom has found for her but fights the temptation she learned about back home to remain committed to her curmudgeonly savior. Meanwhile, mom is dropping her Southern upbringing by the hour and is too busy padding her own love life to be worried about Melodie's.

The Larry David we have come to love as himself on *Curb Your Enthusiasm* and through his doppleganger, George Costanza, on *Seinfeld* is in full swing in *Whatever Works*, only tweaked to 11 on the insult scale. David does not resort to turning Boris into the sort of stuttering characterization of Allen that other actors have gravitated towards when their director isn't putting in an appearance in front of the camera. Instead he brings the worst traits of his persona on *Curb* front and center at the risk of alienating those looking on beyond the fourth wall. Using any variation of Yiddish name-calling, Boris is unapologetic when he comes to confronting those that would challenge his insights or not live up to his superior intellect. Can his behavior be forgiven in our eyes since much of what he says is amusing? Because the supporting players do come off as dimwits in comparison? Or because he warns us up front that this is not "the feel-good movie of the year?"

The easy answer to all those questions is yes. Breaking the boundaries of everyday civility can carry the kind of shocking guffaw we might associate with Don Rickles. Boris is more like Tony Clifton trying to be Henry Higgins and the disparity between the characters' intellect and upbringing becomes more jarring as the

film sputters on. Since her breakthrough in the film, *Thirteen* (2003), Evan Rachel Wood has been playing the withdrawn young woman, occasionally rebellious, almost always angry about something. From her love affairs with an older Edward Norton in *Down in the Valley* (2005) to the daddy issues she's experienced in *Pretty Persuasion* (2005), *King of California* (2007) and *The Wrestler* (2008), the character of Melodie seems like another perfect transition, as if Allen wrote the role just for her in the same vein that Paul Thomas Anderson delved into Adam Sandler's on-screen persona for *Punch-Drunk Love* (2002). Melodie ultimately is just another of Woody's ditzy female caricatures who need a wiser elder to stimulate their appreciation of the Big Apple. Less Mariel Hemingway in *Manhattan* (1979) and more Mira Sorvino in *Mighty Aphrodite* (1995), an almost unrecognizable Wood turns in one of her best performances in what could be construed as one of the most condescending characters Allen has ever created.

The plotting of *Whatever Works*, which becomes more rambling when Melodie's parents begin going through their second half arcs, doesn't sneak its ultimate meaning towards a neutral purple state resolution. In Woody's world it's not just disillusioned, uneducated women who can be cured through a couple rounds with a nebbish scholar. Apparently a few weeks in New York is enough to turn red state religious nuts who believe they know how to define marriage into sexually loose provocateurs. We've seen the hypocrisy from religion to politics and thous protesting too much publicly while privately running the gamut of deadly sins. And it's always nice to see those types exposed either through journalism or fiction. Considering Woody has gone on record on saying that he wrote this story back in 1976 as a vehicle for Zero Mostel, that may be a way to suggest that he was ahead of the curve on the types of issues we face today. Though the way Allen folds in Melodie's casual three-way relationship and her new fondness for creating the kind of graphic naked photography that would turn Jesse Helms in his grave with John's inner discoveries, it's hard to fathom that the Boris Yellnikoff of 1976 or 2009 would cry rubbish if the shoe was on the other foot without the limp.

Then again, maybe Boris' experience with Melodie only accentuates his general motto of whatever works. "Any way you can filch a little joy in this pointless black chaos," he says we should seek it out and embrace it. Preferably another well-regarded American humorist, Steve Martin, said it better on the other coast when he remarked in *L.A. Story* (1991) that "there's someone out there for everyone—even if you need a pickaxe, a compass, and night goggles to find them." It's a lot easier to believe in the hopeless romantic rather than just the mere hopeless who would rather preach to you what's acceptable only to accept whatever comes along that doesn't make him angry. Those on our side of the screen manage to accept the give-and-take of the May-December relationship between Boris and Melodie and acknowledge the two performances that help make it work. By the time the scattershot laughs have died down and an entire party of people who would have dismissed each other on sight at the beginning are celebrating in unison in the end, it's enough to just make the viewer say "whatever."

Erik Childress

CREDITS

Boris Yellnikoff: Larry David
Melody St. Ann Celestine: Evan Rachel Wood
Marietta: Patricia Clarkson
John: Ed Begley Jr.
Randy James: Henry Cavill
Joe: Michael McKean
Origin: USA, France
Language: English
Released: 2009
Production: Letty Aronson, Stephen Tenenbaum; Wild Bunch, Gravier Productions, Perdido; released by Sony Pictures
Directed by: Woody Allen
Written by: Woody Allen
Cinematography by: Harris Savides
Sound: Gary Alper
Editing: Alisa Lepselter
Art Direction: Tom Warren
Costumes: Suzy Bensinger
Production Design: Santo Loquasto
MPAA rating: PG-13
Running time: 92 minutes

REVIEWS

Edelstein, David. *New York Magazine.* June 8, 2009.
Hoberman, J. *Village Voice.* June 16, 2009.
Lane, Anthony. *New Yorker.* June 15, 2009.
Scheck, Frank. *Hollywood Reporter.* April 24, 2009.
Scheib, Ronnie. *Variety.* April 24, 2009.
Scott, A.O. *New York Times.* June 19, 2009.
Stevens, Dana. *Slate.* June 19, 2009.
Tallerico, Brian. *MovieRetriever.com.* June 26, 2009.
Tobias, Scott. *AV Club.* June 18, 2009.
Turan, Kenneth. *Los Angeles Times.* June 19, 2009.

QUOTES

Boris Yellnikoff: "Why do all the religious psychotics wind up praying in my doorstep?"

TRIVIA

Zero Mostel was director Woody Allen's first choice to play Boris Yellnikoff, but Mostel's death in 1977 forced Allen to set the script aside until revisiting it in 2009.

WHERE THE WILD THINGS ARE

There's one in all of us.
—Movie tagline

Box Office: $77.2 million

Spike Jonze's wildly divisive *Where the Wild Things Are* may not have connected with as many audience members as fans of the film would have liked but even the debate over the film's overall quality never included disagreement regarding the fact that this is easily one of the most ambitious adaptations of a children's book in the history of cinema. Critics of the film felt that the ambition did not result in entertainment but many fans of the movie found themselves emotionally engrossed in the world created by Jonze and his wildly talented cast and crew. Like a lot of timeless fiction and film, *Where the Wild Things Are* may have divided audiences upon its release but history will recognize it as one of the best films of 2009; a remarkably daring and moving work from one of this era's most interesting filmmakers.

Based on Maurice Sendak's beloved book, Jonze and co-writer Dave Eggers' (*Away We Go*) screenplay (along with collaborator Catherine Keener) deviates from the book in that if it was a loyal adaptation it would run roughly six minutes long. Instead of sticking to plot, the team behind *Where the Wild Things Are* worked to recreate the feelings spurned by the book. They set out to make a piece driven by the confusing pool of emotions that results when a child realizes that he is no longer the king of the world. When big sisters get too old to play and when divorced mothers bring new men into the home, it can be a difficult time for a young boy and they often turn to fantasy to escape. Children use imagination and fictional worlds for a variety of reasons but Hollywood has almost always limited their usage to "escape." When a child creates a fantasy, escape is certainly a part of the emotional equation, but these are devices that are used to cope with reality as much as they are to flee it. *Where the Wild Things Are* is about a child using his imagination to come to terms with the swirl of emotional confusion that he sees in his own home, largely due to being a child of divorce.

Max (charming newcomer Max Records) is a lonely, frustrated, and bored boy right on the verge of becoming a man. His snow igloo has been destroyed by the too-cool friends of his older sister, his mom (Catherine

Keener) has brought a new man (Mark Ruffalo) into her life, and the awareness that he is no longer the center of the universe, as most loved children are for their first few years, is striking him with full force. After an emotional fight with his mother, Max flees his home and travels to an imaginary land where he is made king once again. But, even there, issues of loyalty, love, family, betrayal, and growing up thematically weave their way through the story. Daringly produced and beautifully conceived, *Where the Wild Things Are* has a lingering power common to only the most beloved family films in the history of the genre. It is beautiful, haunting, and unbelievably powerful; a daring cinematic swing for the fences that completely connects.

The bare bones plot of *Where the Wild Things Are* is still essentially as simple as Sendak's book: a kid named Max travels to a world with giant, furry creatures and comes home again. That is about it. In this version, the creatures are led by the lovable but moody Carol (voiced by James Gandolfini), who seems easily frustrated and is outwardly emotional and confused about a recent betrayal by KW (Lauren Ambrose). Carol is upset because KW has new friends that she has been going to visit, ignoring him and the rest of their gang, including Alexander (Paul Dano), Judith (Catherine O'Hara), Ira (Forest Whitaker), and Douglas (Chris Cooper). Shortly after his arrival, Max is named king of the wild things and fun is had building forts and dirt-clod-fighting, things any young boy would love to do in an imaginary world of lovable friends. As time goes on, however, insecurity and loneliness starts to manifest in the wild things, creatures that could be read as either parts of Max's own persona or just products of a vivid adolescent imagination.

Perhaps one of the elements of Jonze and Eggers' screenplay that turned off audiences was how open it is to multiple interpretations. The film meant something slightly different to nearly everyone who saw it and that is an incredibly rare thing in the world of the family film, a genre that almost always spoon feeds its audience with underlined moral messages and obvious drama. However, the greatest fables always have a subjectivity that not only allows them to be something different to each person that takes them in but allows them to play differently as time progresses. *The Wizard of Oz* (1939), for example, plays differently at age eight, twenty-eight, fifty-eight, and eighty-eight. *Where the Wild Things Are* has a similar power and will mean something different to each generation.

There is a scene late in the film in which Max is held safely inside of the body of a maternal wild thing while she argues with another. Children in the audience probably view the moment as nothing more than a gross but cool fantasy film moment. Older viewers may close their eyes and realize that the dialogue between the wild things could easily be that of a couple going through a divorce or at least what a child might hear while under the covers as his parents fight in the next room. Sometimes when children make up stories, they reveal things about their own insecurities and concerns about the real world more than when asked direct questions. Rarely has that element of storytelling and imagination been captured more distinctly and beautifully than here. For every child, reality eventually invades their imaginary worlds, as make-believe friends disappear and those who used to adore you are now too busy to play.

The young Max Records gives one of the most effective and genuine performances in the history of film. The stuttering, rambling style of Max grounds the world of the wild things in a realism that the film desperately needs to stay emotionally effective. The perfect design choices by Spike Jonze and his production team result in a world that does not feel like some ridiculous Wonderland. It is a nature-based world, the kind of fantasy a child might develop in the woods behind his house. It is a place like many children had in their backyard or neighborhood and played in when they were young, adding to the emotional effectiveness of the wild things by not making them too magical. The remarkable cinematography by Lance Acord perfectly balances the fantasy elements of the piece with the natural realism of this memorable world.

Even viewers who were thrown off by some elements of *Where the Wild Things Are* and dismissed the film on its initial release are likely to eventually find some meaning in this amazing film. Much like the book, greeted with confusion and raised eyebrows on its initial release by parents who deemed it too dark, the film version of *Where the Wild Things Are* will take time to become a beloved family classic. Viewers used to being spoon fed walked away feeling hungry but repeated viewing and word of mouth will be kind to the film, one that takes time to resonate in the heart and not just the head.

Brian Tallerico

CREDITS

Connie: Catherine Keener
Carol: James Gandolfini
Alexander: Paul Franklin Dano
Max: Max Records
Ira: Forest Whitaker (Voice)
Judith: Catherine O'Hara (Voice)
Douglas: Tom Noonan (Voice)
KW: Lauren Ambrose (Voice)

Origin: USA

Language: English

Released: 2009

Production: John B. Carls, Gary Goetzman, Tom Hanks, Vincent Landay, Maurice Sendak; Warner Bros. Pictures, Legendary Pictures, Village Roadshow Pictures, Playtone, Wild Things Productions; released by Warner Bros.

Directed by: Spike Jonze

Written by: Spike Jonze, Dave Eggers

Cinematography by: Lance Acord

Music by: Carter Burwell

Editing: James Haygood, Eric Zumbrunnen

Sound: Ren Klyce

Art Direction: Jeff Thorp

Costumes: Casey Storm

Production Design: K.K. Barrett

MPAA rating: PG

Running time: 101 minutes

REVIEWS

Berkshire, Geoff. *Metromix.com.* October 13, 2009.

Childress, Erik. *eFilmCritic.com.* October 15, 2009.

Ebert, Roger. *Chicago Sun-Times.* October 15, 2009.

Edelstein, David. *New York Magazine.* October 12, 2009.

Gilchrist, Todd. *Cinematical.* October 15, 2009.

Lemire, Christy. *Associated Press.* October 13, 2009.

Phillips, Michael. *Chicago Tribune.* October 15, 2009.

Pols, Mary F. *Time Magazine.* October 14, 2009.

Puig, Claudia. *USA Today.* October 15, 2009.

Travers, Peter. *Rolling Stone.* October 15, 2009.

QUOTES

Judith: "Happiness is not always the best way to be happy."

TRIVIA

If you look closely at the small pile of books that Max stands on in his room, you'll see that one in clearly *Where the Wild Things Are.*

AWARDS

Nomination:

Golden Globes 2010: Orig. Score.

WHIP IT

Be your own hero.
—Movie tagline

Box Office: $13 million

From the posters and movie trailers, it would be easy to pigeonhole *Whip It* as a run-of-the-mill, butch, girl-power anthem. And in a way it is: the girls on-screen are hot, tough, and capable, and it is impossible not to leave the movie without wanting to strap on a pair of skates and start your own derby league. But there's much more to Drew Barrymore's directorial debut than pretty girls on wheels. Beneath its tough, punk-rock, yes-we-can exterior full of tattooed broads who body check one another on roller skates lies a touching and spirited coming-of-age movie that's as heartfelt as it is badassed.

Bliss Cavendar (Ellen Page) is a small town Texas wallflower teen who is too smart for the pageants her mom has paraded her around in for most of her life. When she's not on stage answering questions about whom, dead or alive, she would most like to have dinner with, Bliss holds down a part-time job as a waitress in a BBQ joint where, together with her best friend, the fiesty Pash (Alia Shawkat), they plot ways to break free from their mundane small town USA existence. Opportunity knocks on a shopping day trip to Austin when Bliss learns about the retro-cool world of roller derby. Bliss and Pash venture out to a match and encounter an underground universe as far removed from their reality as they could imagine, full of loud, reckless women who don't give a damn and the emo boys who love them. Naturally, Bliss wants in. So she lies about her age, dusts off her pink roller skates, familiarizes herself with the Austin-bound bus schedule and joins "The Hurl Scouts," Austin roller derby's most-losing team. Along the way she falls in love, confronts her mom about the aforementioned pageants, and most importantly, gets comfortable in her own skin.

The nutshell rundown of the film's plot might sound tried-and-textbook, but thanks to director (and indie poster-child) Barrymore's managing of this unflinching and charismatic look at the teenaged experience, Page's inherent street smart cool, and Shauna Cross' hilarious script, *Whip It* is not only destined to become a much-quoted hipster favorite, it should be required viewing at slumber parties everywhere.

Cross adapted her novel *Derby Girl* for the screenplay and the result is a fun and fearless script full of sarcastic, poppy dialogue, and snappy one-liners, delivered by surprisingly layered characters that navigate the complicated world of high-school friendship, first love and team rivalry with both ease and familiarity. Everyone on screen has emotional baggage (kids waiting at home, boyfriends that don't call, quarter-life crises), but none of it weighs down the story. Instead, every character pops in their own way and adds color to an already vibrant palate. Though she sometimes ventures into "lesson learning" territory by having more experienced derby girls tell Bliss how it "really is," Cross redeems herself by not focusing on a takeaway message with her writing and by allowing her lead to mess up in the ways that all teenagers thinking they know better do and embracing the fall out when it happens.

Whip It also gets a boost from Page, who channels teen angst effortlessly. As with all fish-out-of-water flicks starring pretty actresses, it's a little hard aesthetically to buy Page as a confused, ugly duckling—she has the street cred to make oversized specs and frizzy locks look good—but she inhabits all levels of Bliss' tumultuous ride with such a fierce commitment it's impossible not to fall and cheer for her. Page imbues Bliss with both charming naïveté and misplaced frustration, not to mention awesome skating skills, giving her an every girl feel that's transfixing. But Page isn't the only one who shines on screen. Kristen Wiig (*Saturday Night Live*) gives an unsurprisingly funny, but surprisingly touching turn as Bliss' on and off the rink mentor. Marcia Gay Harden and Daniel Stern as Bliss' middle class and slightly out-of-touch parents strike the perfect balance of bewildered and loving, leading to a relatable, stirring and wonderfully acted family dynamic.

But the real strength of *Whip It* resides with first-time director Barrymore, whose keen take on teen angst and spirited approach to roller derby is lively and infectious. In the rink, Barrymore displays a natural savvy for action, bringing audiences into the moment, down in the rivalry skating with the Scouts. Outside of the rink, she focuses on relationships, extracting performances from her cast that are so true to life that they are almost painful to watch like bad karaoke and taking the film from just plain fun to fun and poignant. Barrymore's enthusiasm for roller derby is obvious, but her heart is with Bliss all the way. Consequently, so is ours.

Joanna Topor MacKenzie

CREDITS

Bliss Cavendar: Ellen Page
Maggie Mayhem: Kristen Wiig
Iron Maven: Juliette Lewis
Rosa Sparks: Eve
Bloody Holly: Zoe Bell
Pash: Alia Shawkat
Eva Destruction: Ari Graynor
Kami Kaze: Sydney Bennett
Brooke Cavendar: Marcia Gay Harden
Earl Cavendar: Daniel Stern
"Hot Tub" Johnny Rocket: Jimmy Fallon
Smashley Simpson: Drew Barrymore

Origin: USA
Language: English
Released: 2009
Production: Barry Mendel; Vincent Pictures, Barry Mendel Productions; released by Fox Searchlight Pictures
Directed by: Drew Barrymore
Written by: Shauna Cross
Cinematography by: Robert Yeoman
Music by: The Section Quartet
Sound: Christopher Scarabosio
Music Supervisor: Randall Poster
Editing: Dylan Tichenor
Sound: Christopher Scarabosio
Art Direction: Brent Kyle
Costumes: Catherine Thomas
Production Design: Kevin Kavanaugh
MPAA rating: PG-13
Running time: 111 minutes

REVIEWS

Ebert, Roger. *Chicago Sun-Times.* October 1, 2009.
Edelstein, David. *New York Magazine.* September 28, 2009.
Jones, J.R. *Chicago Reader.* October 2, 2009.
Nelson, Rob. *Variety.* September 14, 2009.
Pais, Matt. *Metromix.com.* October 1, 2009.
Pols, Mary F. *Time Magazine.* October 2, 2009.
Scott, A.O. *New York Times.* October 2, 2009.
Sharkey, Betsy. *Los Angeles Times.* October 2, 2009.
Sobczynski, Peter. *EFilmCritic.com.* October 1, 2009.
Tallerico, Brian. *MovieRetriever.com.* October 2, 2009.

QUOTES

Bliss Cavendar: "The last time I wore skates, they had Barbies on them."

TRIVIA

Ellen Page dropped out of *Drag Me to Hell* to take the roll in this film.

THE WHITE RIBBON
(Das weisse Band)

Box Office: $1.7 million

The masterful Michael Haneke saw his masterwork *Cache* (2005) appear on several lists of the best films of the 2000s at the end of 2009 and the beginning of 2010. It is not hard to think that if he had produced his latest work, the riveting and remarkable *The White Ribbon,* it too would have made many such lists with the benefit of a few years of re-watching and reconsidering. With arguably his most thematically daring and dense films, Haneke continues to cement his reputation as one of his era's most daring and intriguing filmmakers. This dark, insightful masterpiece about the human ability to deceive and the birth of the Nazi party could be used as a commentary on the rise of any kind of evil and the more personal realization that even the most close-knit communities hide their share of secrets. On one level, it is impossible to ignore that the children of *The White Ribbon* will be adults when the Nazis come to power in Europe, but Haneke has not made an overtly political film, choosing instead to focus on not just a group of character but an entire community. As ambitiously conceived and masterfully rendered as nearly any film released in 2009, this is easily one of the year's best.

On one level, Haneke, who wrote and directed, is playing with a very common theme—the hidden face of evil; the darkness behind the closed doors of an outwardly serene community. Like writers before him, he targets community leaders who preach and teach what they do not practice. It is the religious, medical, political, and educational leaders of one generation who will influence the next and they are sometimes the source of more pure darkness than one even wants to imagine. With lingering power, Haneke allows barely a single soul to escape judgment. This is not a story of good vs. evil or the haves vs. the have-nots, although both of those themes are at play. This is a story of the undercurrent of pure malevolence that can flow through a community so rapidly that it leads to the rise of the Nazi party.

The White Ribbon takes place in the village of Eichwald, Germany over roughly a year between 1913 and 1914. Like many small European towns at the time, and even now, Eichwald is a remarkably close-knit village where the practical and moral leaders hold sway like Kings in the days of old. The doctor, pastor, and baron do not just heal, guide, and employ—although those roles have bestowed importance upon them—they serve as cultural barometers for a community on the verge of a crisis.

The film opens with a man on a horse collapsing in a brutal fall. It turns out that a nearly invisible wire has been stretched between two trees near the man's house, who it is revealed is the town doctor. Why anyone would want to not only harm but potentially kill such an important figure sends a shockwave of suspicion through Eichwald. Shortly thereafter, a female worker of the baron's dies in a sawmill accident and the woman's son blames her employer. Class issues are clearly building prominence but they are far more cut and dry than the true dark secrets under the surface. As the film progresses, mysteries like the almost-deadly wire continue to pile up. The baron's son is abducted and tortured. A barn is

set on fire. And the children of the town are acting in a very peculiar manner.

Over time, it is revealed that perhaps the only "decent" man in town is the teacher, who narrates the story as a memory. Everyone else seems to have something to hide. In particular, the doctor has a cruel nature, displayed in a jaw-dropping scene with the midwife who he emotionally abuses, and an even darker secret with his own daughter. The pastor hides behind the power granted by his position. Haneke writes in a sweet love story for the doctor that nearly feels like a gift given the darkness that pervades the rest of his story. That the film ends with the beginning of World War I is not a spoiler but a recognition that Haneke clearly has lofty thematic aspirations, telling a large story with very small details.

As the mystery of *The White Ribbon,* one anyone who has seen a Haneke film will clearly know is not going to have a tidy resolution, deepens, Haneke peels back the layers of his fictional community to reveal what is underneath. He structures his screenplay so that the dramatic build of the film does not play like a traditional mystery, instead burrowing its way under the viewer's skin much in the way evil has burrowed its way into this small community. The film starts slow but the stunning imagery by master cinematographer Christian Berger goes from cold and distant to mesmerizing and hypnotic. The film is so methodically paced that it plays more like a death march than an expose or a thriller. Haneke and Berger, who deserved Oscar® consideration for Best Cinematography, frame several shots nearly like works of art but they never do so in a showy manner, always keeping the realism and the arc of the plot as the most essential ingredient. The complete lack of a musical score helps aid in the attempt at realism.

Very few films have as accurately recreated not just a time period but an entire community as a *The White Ribbon.* Eichwald feels not like a fictional village but a fully realized community with distinct, well-defined characters with clear roles within it. There is an authenticity to these characters and their execution that is rare in cinema. There are works of film that are accurately called visually sumptuous and many filmmakers work within a subgenre often granted the overused appellation of realism, but films that accomplish both are truly unique. There are images in *The White Ribbon* that stand among the most memorable of the last few years but it is the people that give the work its dramatic power. Michael Haneke's *Cache* has been deemed a masterpiece by many. Even his most ardent fans probably would not have guessed that he would make another one so shortly thereafter.

Brian Tallerico

CREDITS

The Baron: Ulrich Tukur
The Pastor: Burghart Klaussner
The Steward: Josef Bierbichler
The Schoolteacher: Christian Friedel
Eva: Leonie Benesch
Marie-Louise, the Baroness: Ursina Lardi
Anna, the Pastor's Wife: Steffi Kuhnert
The Doctor: Rainer Bock
Emma, the Steward's Wife: Gariela Maria Shcmeide
Ernst Jacobi (Narrated)
Origin: Germany, Austria, France, Italy
Language: German, Italian, Polish, Latin
Released: 2009
Production: Stefan Arndt, Veit Heiduschka, Margaret
Menegoz, Andrea Occhipinti; X-Films Creative Pool, Les
Films du Losange, Wega-Film, Lucky Red; released by Sony
Pictures Classics
Directed by: Michael Haneke
Written by: Michael Haneke
Cinematography by: Christian Berger
Sound: Guillaume Sciama, Jean-Pierre Laforce
Editing: Monika Willi
Art Direction: Anja Miller
Costumes: Moidele Bickel
Production Design: Christoph Kanter
MPAA rating: R
Running time: 150 minutes

REVIEWS

Ebert, Roger. *Chicago Sun-Times.* January 14, 2010.
Graham, Jamie. *Total Film.* November 13, 2009.
Pais, Matt. *Metromix.com.* December 29, 2009.
Lacey, Liam. *Globe and Mail.* September 11, 2009.
Levy, Emanuel. *EmanuelLevy.com.* May 24, 2009.
McCarthy, Todd. *Variety.* May 22, 2009.
Morgenstern, Joe. *Wall Street Journal.* January 7, 2010.
Neumaier, Joe. *New York Daily News.* December 30, 2009.
Phillips, Michael. *Chicago Tribune.* January 14, 2010.
Travers, Peter. *Rolling Stone.* December 22, 2009.

TRIVIA

The film was originally shot in color and then adjusted to
black-and-white during post-production.

AWARDS

Golden Globes 2010: Foreign Film
Nomination:
Oscars 2009: Cinematog., Foreign Film
British Acad. 2009: Foreign Film.

WHITEOUT

See your last breath.
—Movie tagline

Box Office: $10.3 million

When we think of graphic novels, our first thought may drift to "oh, another comic book trying to be taken seriously." That is the cynical approach to the medium that has translated into films as diverse as *Sin City* (2005), *Watchmen* (2009) and *Road To Perdition* (2002). Call it by whatever name you choose, your next thought may involve storylines that feature superheroes, fantastical storylines and visual representations that many filmmakers envy and would dream to copy some day. Knowing nothing about the history of Greg Rucka and Steve Lieber's contribution to the serialized literary world, all early signs pointed to *Whiteout* just being another cinematic murder mystery set under extreme conditions. Over two years in the can and a little more knowledge about its predecessor later, *Whiteout* is still pretty much just that. Although "extreme" and "cinematic" are two adjectives that should never be used to describe it.

It's the coldest, most isolated land mass on the planet. What better to heat up Antarctica than to bring in Kate Beckinsale, follow her into her room and watch her strip down to her underwear in preparation for a shower? This is how we are introduced to Carrie Stetko, the hardened U.S. Marshal during her last few days on this heavily populated research post. Why our tax dollars are being spent to send so many down to Antarctica is anyone's guess, but Stetko is about to finally earn her money when a dead body shows up. This one didn't expire due to the harsh weather or terminal boredom though. This was murder. It couldn't have anything to do with that plane crash from the prologue, could it?

Stetko's mentor, Dr. John Fury (Tom Skerritt), would hate for her to miss her window out of this snow-covered hell and offers to dismiss this as just another accident. Carrie is battling some professional demons, padded out in pointless evolving flashbacks. Constant light or constant dark in this area may be inevitable, but *Day for Night* (1973) this is certainly not. Stetko feels it's her duty though to work through the trust issues of her past and put the pieces together. Moving in on her turf though is U.N. investigator, Robert Pryce (Gabriel Macht), who shows up at about the same time that a guy in a mask is chasing down Stetko and knocking off more suspects. Not convinced? The first corpse fell from a chopper, so maybe base pilot, Delfy (Columbus Short) is involved. Or what about the cocky Australian, Russell Haden (Alex O'Loughlin), whose sole job appears to be either hitting on Stetko or partying it up with other anonymous "researchers"?

Despite hearing keywords like "meteor samples" and exploiting a setting most remembered for aliens found in the ice, *Whiteout* is completely devoid of any science-fiction or horror elements. That leaves director Dominic

Sena little wiggle room outside of manipulating snow-terror set-pieces to set the plotting apart from any standard hour-long television mystery. The only strides *Whiteout* makes is in proving that we have at least been able to move on far enough from 9/11 to be released eight years to the day and open with a plane hijacking. The secrets worth killing for on that Russian transport you would hope would be important enough considering its Cold War setting to create a specialized danger for our heroine later on. Government secrets, alien DNA, fuel for time traveling DeLoreans, Something! When all is finally revealed, it only becomes a final battle for what is lamest—what all the fuss is over or who is eventually responsible.

Unless the killer turned out to be Scrat from *Ice Age* (2002), there is no surprise in *Whiteout* that one would not be able to determine a full hour before they are unveiled. With less suspects to consider than your average game of Clue, spotting the bad guy should exert no effort on anyone who is still awake halfway through. Put it this way—when a certain character is introduced, either that person is going to be the next victim or the mystery villain. If he's still alive when you wake up, await for the unmasking and confession. With only so many avenues to milk suspense from the setting, Sena cannot help but go back to the same frozen well twice by reenacting the caught-in-the-blizzard/hold-on-to-the-rope chase for the climax that he already put Stetko through for her first big action sequence. Watching people you do not care about being chased through blinding snow is less exciting than seeing some dandruff-shedding Trekkie lean in real close to see which white dot is going to turn into the Enterprise during the opening credits.

Surely Sena had seen one version of *The Thing* (1951 or 1982) in his lifetime, but never picked up on the idea that it was the claustrophobic no-escape angle that helped make them so terrifying. For Heaven's sake, it's right there in the opening title cards— "it's the coldest, most isolated land mass on the planet." Apparently the director just stopped at the "coldest" part because cold hasn't been such an enemy since it seemingly hunted down characters in *The Day After Tomorrow* (2004). Researching the source material for this film, the only noticeable element mentioned in its transition to the big screen was the shifting of the second investigator's sex. So instead of having two gorgeous ladies being introduced in their underwear, we have to see the guy who played *The Spirit* (2008) waste lens space.

With two pairs of screenwriters on board—the Hoebers (Jon & Erich) and the Hayes' (Chad & Carey, responsible for other Joel Silver-produced Warner Bros. debacles, *House of Wax* [2005] and *The Reaping* [2007])—it would be interesting to know how they found so many people who felt there was something in the graphic novel worth adapting into anything but a CBS mystery movie of the week from the 1970s. The MacGuffin is standard issue. The motives are even more so. The suspense is non-existent and while you make think there's an alien replicating people who are supposed to be acting, it does not exist either. Considering the Hoebers are currently on tap to bring the board game Battleship to the big screen, they at least have a head start creating nothing out of something people once found enjoyable.

Erik Childress

CREDITS

Carrie Stetko: Kate Beckinsale
Robert Pryce: Gabriel Macht
Dr. John Fury: Tom Skerritt
Delfy: Columbus Short
Russell Haden: Alex O'Loughlin
Sam Murphy: Shawn Doyle
Origin: USA
Language: English
Released: 2009
Production: Susan Downey, Joel Silver, David Gambino; released by Warner Bros.
Directed by: Dominic Sena
Written by: Chad Hayes, Carey Hayes, Jon Hoeber, Erich Hoeber
Cinematography by: Christopher Soos
Music by: John Frizzell
Sound: Mark Larry
Editing: Martin Hunter
Art Direction: Gilles Aird, Martin Gendron, Jean Kazemirchuk
Costumes: Wendy Partridge
Production Design: Graham Walker
MPAA rating: R
Running time: 101 minutes

REVIEWS

Burr, Ty. *Boston Globe.* September 11, 2009.
Farber, Stephen. *Hollywood Reporter.* September 10, 2009.
Hoffman, Jordan. *UGO.* September 10, 2009.
Lowenstein, Lael. *Variety.* September 11, 2009.
Pais, Matt. *Metromix.com.* September 10, 2009.
Roeper, Richard. *Chicago Sun-Times.* September 11, 2009.
Scott, A.O. *New York Times.* September 11, 2009.
Sobczynski, Peter. *eFilmCritic.* September 10, 2009.
Tallerico, Brian. *MovieRetriever.com.* September 11, 2009.
Zacharek, Stephanie. *Salon.com.* September 11, 2009.

QUOTES

Carrie Stetko: "How bad is it?"
Delfy: "Bad enough that you don't want to see."

The film was shipped to theaters using the bogus name "Snowbound."

WOMEN IN TROUBLE

High hopes, high anxiety, high heels.
—Movie tagline

Sebastian Gutierrez made a small name for himself writing escapist fare like *Gothika* (2003), *Snakes on a Plane* (2006), and *The Eye* (2008) but his directorial effort on the star-studded *Women in Trouble* hints at a filmmaker much more interested in personal artists like Pedro Almodóvar and Robert Altman. Featuring several of the more underrated actresses working in Hollywood, Gutierrez's film is a near-miss from a writer/director who hopefully keeps making more of these interweaving passion pieces if just to iron out the kinks apparent in this one. Just because *Women in Trouble* does not quite click in the way its opening act makes one hope that it would, does not mean that there are not elements of the film that work. The entire project hints that the previously critically-reviled Gutierrez might have a great film in him if he continues to work to perfect this unusual formula. Sadly, that seems unlikely, as *Women in Trouble* proved to be an impossible film to market, and so its production company did not even bother to try, barely releasing the film and resulting a gross so minimal that IMDB.com does not even see the value in creating a page to list it (under $20,000 domestically).

With echoes of Robert Altman's narrative structure but clearly heavily influenced by the vibrant colors and passionate women of Pedro Almodóvar's work, *Women in Trouble* is certainly one of the more unique hybrids of 2009. The title characters include a porn star stuck in an elevator (Carla Gugino), a flight attendant (Marley Shelton) who watches her mile-high lover (Josh Brolin) die mid-coitus, a shrink (Sarah Clarke) who discovers that her husband (Simon Baker) is sleeping with one of his patients, a neurotic mother (Connie Britton), and two bickering call girls (Emmanuelle Chriqui & Adrianne Palicki) forced to run for their lives. Like Altman's work, Gutierrez weaves their stories in and out of each other's live but, smartly, does not rely on Quentin Tarantino-esque tricks of chronology. Cameron Richardson, Garcelle Beauvais-Nilon, and Joseph Gordon-Levitt also co-star.

From its raunchy set-up to the fact that Gugino and Britton spend a large portion of the film half-dressed in an overheated elevator, *Women in Trouble* walks a fine line between being borderline soft-core pornography and a tale of female empowerment (and the film's miniature gross means it will probably more often be classified as the former and appear on late-night cable television before the end of 2010). As its characters discuss sex and regularly strip to bra and panties, the audience is asked to both identify with their predicament and, clearly meant to notice how stunningly attractive they are. They may be in trouble, but they are still damn sexy. Gutierrez tries to balance camp and melodrama, as in when Chriqui and Palicki's call girls find time to discuss if they have ever thrown up while performing oral sex while on the run for their lives.

The delicate balancing act of comedy and drama becomes a little too unhinged for Gutierrez in the final act when his screenplay turns closer to the melodramatic side of the scale, looking for a climax. Most damagingly, not all of the lovely stars seem to think they are making the same film. TV veterans Clark and Britton ass dramatic tones to the film that feel surprisingly genuine but Chriqui and Palicki often seem as if they walked off the set of a wacky comedy. (Part of the problem is that the former two are wildly more talented actresses than the latter two.) Only Gugino, who has been romantically linked to Gutierrez, finds the perfect wavelength, straddling the line and often holding the film together as it threatens to come apart at the seams.

Reports are that Gutierrez shot *Women in Trouble* with a small crew in only twelve days time. It is remarkable how much sharper and more interesting a product he ended up with than the junk he wrote for the Hollywood machine that took more—budget, time, crew, etc. *Women in Trouble* is a fun, gorgeous film that nearly comes together as more than a mere pleasant diversion. It is only when the film is over and one considers the talented actresses involved and the potential of the concept (and the masters who clearly inspired it), that one wonders why it does not coalesce into something more honestly memorable. It is a film with undeniably gorgeous parts that never quite develops into a sum.

Brian Tallerico

CREDITS

Holly Rocket: Adrianne Palicki
Charlotte: Isabella Gutierrez
Elektra Luxx: Carla Gugino
Doris: Connie Britton
Bambi: Emmanuelle Chriqui
Maxine McPherson: Sarah Clarke
Cora: Marley Shelton
Rita: Rya Kihlstedt
Addy: Caitlin Keats
Darby: Cameron Richardson

Nick Chapel: Josh Brolin
Travis McPherson: Simon Baker
Bert Rodriguez: Joseph Gordon-Levitt
Origin: USA
Language: English
Released: 2009
Production: Sebastian Gutierrez; Gato Negro Films; released by Screen Media Films
Directed by: Sebastian Gutierrez
Written by: Sebastian Gutierrez
Cinematography by: Cale Finot
Music by: Robyn Hitchcock
Sound: Troy Dunn
Editing: Lisa Bromwell, Michelle Tesoro
Costumes: Denise Wingate
Production Design: Daniel Mailley
MPAA rating: R
Running time: 95 minutes

REVIEWS

Anderson, Melissa. *Village Voice.* November 10, 2009.
Childress, Erik. *eFilmCritic.com.* October 8, 2009.
Dargis, Manohla. *New York Times.* November 13, 2009.
DeFore, John. *Hollywood Reporter.* March 18, 2009.
Leydon, Joe. *Variety.* March 31, 2009.
Reed, Rex. *New York Observer.* December 10, 2009.
Smith, Kyle. *New York Post.* November 13, 2009.
Tobias, Scott. *AV Club.* November 12, 2009.
Whipp, Glenn. *Associated Press.* November 11, 2009.
Wilkinson, Ron. *Monsters and Critics.* November 16, 2009.

WORLD'S GREATEST DAD

Lance Clayton is about to get everything he deserves.
—Movie tagline

Bobcat Goldthwait is certainly a talent of many distinct flavors. Many remember him as living up to his name as the stand-up comic and *Police Academy* regular—his character arc from street punk to officer is documented in parts two to four—known for his signature bursts of screaming. He has worked steadily since then, mostly on TV, but then he embarked upon his first feature as a writer/director and delivered a little cult classic called *Shakes the Clown* (1991). While it took him a dozen years to make his next film—the hilarious *Windy City Heat* (2003)—he has since become a double invitee to the Sundance Film Festival with a pair of projects that have elevated his brand of audience-

squirming humor to heights that brushes off subject matter never thought of as taboo since most would not have the stones to tackle them in the first place. *Sleeping Dogs Lie* (2006) (aka *Stay*) concerned a lovely young woman whose brief experimentation with bestiality eventually forced her to confront the matter with her fiancé. *World's Greatest Dad* does not plunge into material easily dismissed as merely gross, but in many ways is more darkly uncomfortable because it is so successful in the way it tackles it.

Lance Clayton (Robin Williams) has a less-than-comfy job teaching high school poetry. He has few students, all disinterested and passing off rock lyrics as assignments. He is carrying on a clandestine relationship with Claire (Alexie Gilmore), another teacher who appears to be totally into him but is publicly flirty with Mike (Henry Simmons), the tall, handsome and younger creative writing professor. Lance's many attempts at writing novels have all been turned down and his class seems destined for downsizing. At least though, he has his son, Kyle (Daryl Sabara), who is first introduced performing asphyxiated masturbation to internet porn.

Kyle is the turbo-accelerated version of the problem teenager. He has all but one friend at school; a shy, complete opposite who watches as Kyle makes lewd remarks and gestures to the girls. As bad as he is in social situations (such as taking advantage of an opportunity to produce future bedroom material from his widowed father's new girlfriend), he is twice as awful to dad himself. Kyle is so stand-offish and insulting that the audience begins to think that Lance's coffee cup with the titular saying was an actual award rather than a novelty. Kyle would actually have to be imprisoned at Gitmo and "re-educated" in order to compete with Macaulay Culkin for title of *The Good Son* (1993). Nothing Lance can do will ever endear himself into being a part of Kyle's life. That is, until his son gets published.

Most films would delicately inch degrees towards drawing Lance and Kyle together. Not Goldthwait though. He is determined to show the viewer a virtually irredeemable little cuss undeserving of his father's love or the growing success that makes him a sudden sensation amongst a community that would just as easily ignored him or sent him away forever. Just as the hypocrisy amongst his peers grows unbearably phony, the audience is drawn even closer to Lance despite his behavior during this period which could be deemed unethical at best and tasteless at worst. But we root for him as he takes advantage of his colleagues' artificial exteriors and pretentious conformity to what society tells us is appropriate behavior once infamy becomes fame. Over the surface of Goldthwait's dissection of normality though is a lot of great, disturbing laughter; a true test of which comes with Williams' interview late in the film on an Oprah-like talk show. As he is asked questions, he begins to laugh uncontrollably. The audience understands why he is laughing, but knows the inappropriateness of it all. When they find themselves at this moment laughing even harder than he is, they will begin to understand what Goldthwait has accomplished here.

Williams finds absolutely the right tone for his performance as Lance, playing the role dead straight, almost dramatically (albeit without the thick beard that usually signals Williams in serious mode.) It is his best work since his psycho double-dip with *Insomnia* (2002) and *One Hour Photo* (2002) and that is paired with Goldthwait's finest outing as both a writer and director. *Windy City Heat* may have more big laughs, but the kind of subdued undercurrent of laughter through discomfort that never quite paid off with *Sleeping Dogs Lie* builds to great crescendos here and it may not strike people until it is all over how delicately he pulls it off. It is easy to just throw together a parental bonding film and encourage an audience to go home and hug their child. But it is far more difficult and brave to have a father admit his son is "a douchebag" and to make audiences not just laugh, but applaud.

Erik Childress

CREDITS

Lance Clayton: Robin Williams
Kyle Clayton: Daryl Sabara
Claire: Alexie Gilmore
Mike Lane: Henry Simmons
Andrew: Evan Martin
Jerry Klein: Tom Kenny
Bonnie: Mitzi McCall
Jason: Jermaine Williams
Bert Green: Toby Huss
Chris: Michael Thomas Moore
Heather: Lorraine Nicholson

Origin: USA
Language: English
Released: 2009
Production: Tim Perell, Sean McKittrick, Howard Gertler, Richard Kelly; Darko Entertainment, Jerkschool Prods.; released by Magnolia Pictures
Directed by: Bobcat Goldthwait
Written by: Bobcat Goldthwait
Cinematography by: Horacio Marquinez
Music by: Gerald Brunskill
Sound: Samuel Lehmer, Andrew Hay
Music Supervisor: Linda Cohen
Editing: Jason Stewart
Costumes: Sarah De Sa Rego
Production Design: John Paino
Running time: 99 minutes

REVIEWS

Ebert, Roger. *Chicago Sun-Times.* September 3, 2009.
Faraci, Devin. *CHUD.* April 10, 2009.
Gleiberman, Owen. *Entertainment Weekly.* August 26, 2009.
Hillis, Aaron. *Village Voice.* May 12, 2009.
Holden, Stephen. *New York Times.* August 21, 2009.
Jones, J. R. *Chicago Reader.* September 11, 2009.
Knopf, Scott. *Film Threat.* August 18, 2009.
Puig, Claudia. *USA Today.* August 28, 2009.
Rabin, Nathan. *AV Club.* August 20, 2009.
Weinberg, Scott. *Cinematical.* March 3, 2009.

QUOTES

Lance Clayton: "Come on now, Kyle, you must be passionate about something."
Kyle: "You wanna know what I like? I like looking at vaginas."

TRIVIA

Director Bobcat Goldthwait makes a brief cameo in the film as the driver who takes Lance Clayton (Robin Williams) to the talk show.

X–Z

X-MEN ORIGINS: WOLVERINE

Box Office: $179.9 million

A film is in dire straits indeed when its best scene consists of its opening credits. The title sequence of Gavin Hood's *X-Men Origins: Wolverine* is a dialogue free continuous single shot of mutant brothers Logan (Hugh Jackman) and Victor (Liev Shreiber) fighting as American soldiers in the Civil War, World War I, II and Vietnam. As each theater of war morphs into the next around the brothers, CGI changes their appearance, uniforms and opponents. This clever sequence is what the rest of *Wolverine* might have been: fresh, inventive, featuring innovative use of CGI and a storyline taking advantage of its characters' immortality and a canvas of over 150 years. Instead *Wolverine* dulls its blades with generic action, a lazy antagonism between its two main characters and a completely nonsensical plot necessitated by the film's unwise commitment to preserving the ludicrous continuity of the *X-Men* films that preceded it.

Following an exceptionally confusing opening sequence set in the Northwest Territory in 1845, the film picks up in Vietnam and establishes, in Logan and Victor, the tired dichotomy between using super powers for the good of humanity versus using them at the expense of humanity that was played out to exhaustion between Professor X and Magneto in the previous *X-Men* films. Victor is a bit too fond of indulging himself at the expense of innocents through the use of his mutant powers and, after killing a superior officer who was, along with Logan, trying to prevent him from raping a woman, he lands both himself and Logan on the firing squad. The moral implications of the exercise of power certainly is an appropriate theme for a super hero film, "with great power comes great responsibility" Uncle Ben told Peter Parker and audiences nearly a decade ago in *Spider-Man* (2002), however *Wolverine* isn't interested in putting in the hard narrative work of exploring that theme. The more ambitious *Spider-Man* was as interested in investigating the sacrifices involved in the responsible use of power as it was in depicting the good guys versus the bad guys. In *Wolverine*, the tacked on philosophical "tension" between Logan and Victor is just a lazy excuse to not have to bother developing either character or provide them with character specific motivations.

After Logan and Victor are "executed" (their regenerative powers do not allow them to be killed) by firing squad they are approached in the stockade by Colonel Stryker (a slumming Danny Houston) who wants to recruit them for a special team. What follows is the only vaguely original part of the film as Logan, Victor and the viewer are introduced to the rag tag gang of mutant misfits that the Colonel has recruited for his strike team. Among them are the overly talkative Deadpool (a scene stealing Ryan Reynolds, another sign that a film is in dire straits) and the teleporting John Wraith (will.i.am of The Black Eyed Peas). The squad trades amusing insults and is a PG-13 superhero version of Arnold Schwarzenegger's colorful crew in *Predator* (1987). The sequence which follows in which the team infiltrates an African warlord's base (and, of course, show off their individual superpowers in doing so) in pursuit of a mysterious metal Adamantium that the Colonel is obsessed with is playful and fun.

The rest of the film, however, is very much less so. Immediately following the base assault is an unconvincing sequence in which the suddenly sinister colonel orders his team to wipe out a group of villagers, My Lai style, for no particularly logical reason other than the plot requires a moral obstacle to be erected between Logan and his brother. Victor and the rest of the team are all on board but Logan has had enough and walks away (with the villagers presumably slaughtered...so much for great responsibility).

The film then jumps forward to the modern day. Logan has relocated to the wilds of Canada where he lives with his girlfriend, Kayla (Lynn Collins). As any viewer who has seen a Charles Bronson film can attest to, the idyllic situation is not destined to last. And, sure enough, Colonel Stryker (looking exactly the same as he did in Vietnam, perhaps he is distantly related to the immortal Logan and Victor) comes to warn Logan that Victor is picking off members of the disbanded and dispersed strike team. Stryker believes that Logan is the only one who can stop his brother but will only be strong enough to defeat him if he allows the colonel to inject Adamantium into his skeleton. Logan refuses but changes his mind after Kayla is killed by Victor. The remainder of the film, or so it seems, concerns his quest for vengeance.

After the injection procedure, Colonel Stryker again undergoes a plot-necessitated change of character and suddenly orders Logan's mind to be erased. However, the colonel has forgotten about Logan's mutant-enhanced hearing and his sinister plans are overheard by him. Logan flees and takes refuge in a local farmhouse owned by an elderly couple who might as well be a photo shopped Ma and Pa Kent from *Superman* (1978). Their plot function is to provide Logan with the means of getting to the next plot point and to then be slaughtered by Logan's pursuers and the narrative economy with which they fulfill this function is unintentionally hilarious. The generous Travis (Max Cullen) presents Logan with his dead son's leather jacket and motorcycle and is shot dead by a sniper round seconds after handing Logan the keys. His hospitable wife, Heather (Julia Blake), is killed seconds later by a sniper round through the chest as she brings out a tray of sandwiches. After dispatching the killers in a disappointingly conventional CGI sequence featuring a helicopter, Logan digs up the surviving members of the strike team and learns of mysterious happenings on Three Mile Island. Traveling along with Wraith to New Orleans (featuring a split second homage to *Easy Rider*) he links up with the only mutant to have escaped the island, Gambit (Taylor Kitsch), who reveals that Stryker has been capturing mutants and then harvesting their powers to create a Frankenstein monster.

At Three Mile Island there is ridiculous plot development after ridiculous plot development as the script tears itself apart trying to maintain the ludicrous continuity of the original films. Characters undergo plot-necessitated 360 degree changes of character. Characters who were thought dead reappear very much alive despite the fact that Logan's powers would have assuredly clued him in that the supposedly deceased person was playing possum. Amnesia plays a critical role (there are few surer signs of a lazy and desperate script than the use of amnesia as a plot device, with prophecies running a close second). In order for Logan to not remember his origins in the previous *X-Men* films which follow *Wolverine* chronologically, he has to be given amnesia which the film provides by having Stryker shoot Logan in the head at the end of the film (the bullet doesn't kill him, just conveniently erases his memory). However, while that explains why Logan does not later remember the young Cyclops (Tim Pocock), a prominent character in the *X-Men* films, who he has just rescued on Three Mile Island, it does not explain why Cyclops does not remember him. Consequently, the script goes through elaborate and silly contortions to explain this: Cyclops is conveniently blindfolded in all scenes where Logan is present and Logan never speaks to Cyclops directly or in his presence.

A reasonable question on the viewer's part is whether the absurdity of the plot even matters. After all, the source material for the film is a comic book about mutants with super powers. It's true that by the standards of the superhero genre ten years ago, when then recent developments in CGI allowed for super powers to be depicted in a convincing manner, *X-Men Origins: Wolverine* is a perfectly acceptable, serviceable superhero movie. It depicts the superhero's powers in a convincing manner and runs them through flawlessly executed and completely familiar CGI action sequences. The problem is that the genre has evolved since the inception of CGI enabled superhero films to depict superhero powers in a convincing way. Merely providing the audience with the novelty of seeing super heroes use their powers in a seemingly realistic way is no longer sufficient. Sophisticated superhero films like *Spider-Man* (2002), *Spider-Man 2* (2004), *Hellboy* (2004), *The Dark Knight* (2008) and *Iron Man* (2008) which take their stories and characters seriously, have raised the bar significantly since *X-Men* first appeared in 2000. *X-Men Origins: Wolverine* with its lack of ambition, one dimensional characters and thoroughly nonsensical story fares poorly in their company.

Star Trek (2009) showed how a creative script could address the continuity issue of a franchise as old and storied as *X-Men* while setting the franchise free. That film understood that the goal was to capture the essence of what made the original story appealing, not to abandon everything in an effort to preserve the continuity of that original story. *X-Men Origins: Wolverine* sadly lacks that wisdom and preserves the series' continuity at the expense of the story it is telling.

Nate Vercauteren

CREDITS

Wolverine/Logan/James Howlett: Hugh Jackman
Sabretooth/Victor Creed: Liev Schreiber
Deadpool/Wade Wilson: Ryan Reynolds
Beak/Barnell Bohusk: Dominic Monaghan
Gambit/Remy LeBeau: Taylor Kitsch
The Blob/Frederick J. Dukes: Kevin Durand
William Stryker: Danny Huston
John Wraith: will.i.am
Agent Zero/David North: Daniel Henney
Kayla Silverfox: Lynn Collins
Origin: USA
Language: English
Released: 2009
Production: Ralph Winter, Hugh Jackman, John Palermo, Lauren Shuler Donner; Dune Entertainment, Donners' Company, Seed Prods., Marvel Entertainment; released by 20th Century Fox
Directed by: Gavin Hood
Written by: David Benioff, Skip Woods
Cinematography by: Donald McAlpine
Music by: Harry Gregson-Williams
Sound: Guntis Sics
Editing: Nicolas De Toth, Megan Gill
Art Direction: Ian Gracie
Costumes: Louise Mingenbach
Production Design: Barry Robison
MPAA rating: PG-13
Running time: 107 minutes

REVIEWS

Chang, Justin. *Variety.* April 29, 2009.
Ebert, Roger. *Chicago Sun-Times.* April 30, 2009.
Honeycutt, Kirk. *Hollywood Reporter.* April 29, 2009.
Pais, Matt. *Metromix.com.* April 30, 2009.
Phillips, Michael. *Chicago Tribune.* April 30, 2009.
Phipps, Keith. *AV Club.* April 30, 2009.
Scott, A.O. *New York Times.* April 30, 2009.
Stevens, Dana. *Slate.* April 30, 2009.
Tallerico, Brian. *HollywoodChicago.com.* May 1, 2009.
Turan, Kenneth. *Los Angeles Times.* April 30, 2009.

QUOTES

William Stryker: "We're gonna make you indestructible. But first, we're gonna have to destroy you."

TRIVIA

With this movie, Hugh Jackman became the first actor since Christopher Reeve to play the same comic book hero in four consecutive films.

YEAR ONE

Meet your ancestors.
— Movie tagline

Box Office: $43.3 million

The Judd Apatow comedy factory enjoyed a consistent run of fairly inexpensive, vulgar, sweet, smart and sharp-edged comedies in the latter half of the decade, so much so that they seemed to be redefining and re-shaping what a comedy—particularly a romantic comedy—could be. Apatow's rotating stable of directors and actors, with their loose improvisational style, self-awareness, willingness to take a joke to the next raunchiest level without losing the brains, and insightful examinations of human behavior seemed well on their way to being the next James L. Brooks crossed with the next Harold Ramis.

The latter had been cast in a small role in Apatow's *Knocked Up* and also directed episodes of the hit TV show *The Office*, which also falls under the Apatow umbrella. It would only seem logical that Ramis step in and direct a feature for the Apatow clan, who had been modeling their own formulas after Ramis's own now-classic, sweet-smart-and-raunchy comedic accomplishments (*Animal House* [1978], *Caddyshack* [1980], *Stripes* [1981] and *Groundhog Day* [1993]). The match was a no-brainer for all involved.

Unfortunately, *Year One*, the end result of this collaboration, is that no-brainer. With obnoxious Jack Black and nimble Michael Cera as its protagonists, the thought going into the film must have been that the two actors will somehow make its wobbly premise stand up. But the movie's overall storyline—that of two gatherers in the year One being banished from their village and going off on a quest to find a new one, only to be sidetracked by run-ins with Cain and Abel, Isaac and Abraham and other such unlikely situations—is the least of its problems. The idea of the Apatow Company making a comedy where the only major change is that they are now all living in ancient times could work in theory, but they never actually sell it.

In it, Jack Black plays Zed, a rebellious and incorrigible hunter who gets demoted to gatherer status with his friend, Oh (Cera), who quite enjoys his menial job of looking for strawberries. After Zed takes a bite from the Forbidden Fruit off the golden apple tree out of undying curiosity, he is ordered to leave the village or face certain death. Oh reluctantly follows him and the two set off on a quest to start over in a newer, bigger village, maybe on the edge of the flat earth.

Along the way, they run into Cain and Abel (David Cross and Paul Rudd, respectively) where their conflict inevitably finds Cain killing Abel and then throughout the rest of the film, tries to frame Zed for the murder. Zed and Oh soon thereafter find themselves in the presence of Abraham (Hank Azaria) and his son Isaac (Christopher Mintz-Plasse) at around the time Abraham fancies the notion of employing male circumcision as a customary measure, much to the confusion and trepidation of Zed, Oh and Isaac ("No, trust me. This will catch on," Abraham says in one of the films funnier moments).

The latter half of the film finds Zed and Oh in Sodom, where they try mightily to fit in so as to take advantage of the loose morals and decadence on display. This being an Apatow product, the subplot about one or both male characters trying to get laid remains characteristically prominent. Oh loves Eema (Juno Temple), a village waif who all but ignores his advances. Zed has similar luck with Maya (June Diane Raphael), who was also banished from their village after Zed accidentally set the whole place ablaze.

The casting of Black and Cera is the first of the film's problems and it's a pretty good rule of thumb that if the two leads in a comedy are miscast, it's all but impossible to fix the rest. Both actors here are merely playing caricatures of their screen personas without so much as giving their characters any depth whatsoever. Black screams most of his lines with irony and sarcasm, while Cera does his usual self-deprecating, Woody Allen-like nervousness shtick that could end up defining his entire career from here on out. Both actors have talent and both have made attempts at straying from their acting formulas (Black more so than Cera), but the two of them together have no chemistry. It almost seems as though one is always trying to upstage the other.

The script, likewise, seems directionless, monotoned and philosophically confused. There's a subplot in which Zed thinks he might be the Chosen One, since he bit from the Forbidden Fruit and managed to suffer a lot while living to tell the tale. It's never quite clear if Zed actually believes in a higher power, because the movie itself doesn't appear to have a belief system, religious or otherwise. It's as if Ramis and company put all their effort into the poop-and-pee jokes and let the brains and humanity of the comedy (something Ramis usually excels at) fall by the wayside.

Since it's obvious that *Year One* was made strictly for laughs (nothing wrong with that, of course), it is futile to point out the flawed chronology of the events,

which would have taken place thousands of years apart, but here all happen at around the same time. Even when you forgive the movie for these kids of leaps in logic, the laughs, storyline and Ramis's usually spot-on direction should carry it. Shockingly, they do not. With an atypical premise that seems to want to take the Apatow Company into newer conceptual territory, it is by far the most complacent, pedestrian and comedically challenged of their efforts to date.

Collin Souter

CREDITS

Zed: Jack Black
Oh: Michael Cera
Princess Inanna: Olivia Wilde
Maya: June Raphael
Cain: David Cross
High Priest: Oliver Platt
Abraham: Hank Azaria
Isaac: Christopher Mintz-Plasse
Abel: Paul Rudd
Adam: Harold Ramis
Sargon: Vinnie Jones
Origin: USA
Language: English
Released: 2009
Production: Harold Ramis, Judd Apatow, Clayton Townsend; Ocean Pictures, Apatow Productions; released by Columbia Pictures
Directed by: Harold Ramis
Written by: Harold Ramis, Gene Stupnitsky, Lee Eisenberg
Cinematography by: Alar Kivilo
Music by: David Kitay, Theodore Shapiro
Sound: Steve Aaron
Editing: Craig P. Herring, Steven Welch
Art Direction: Richard Fojo
Costumes: Debra McGuire
Production Design: Jefferson Sage
MPAA rating: PG-13
Running time: 97 minutes

REVIEWS

Burr, Ty. *Boston Globe.* June 18, 2009.
Dargis, Manohla. *New York Times.* June 19, 2009.
Ebert, Roger. *Chicago Sun-Times.* June 18, 2009.
Howell, Peter. *Toronto Star.* June 19, 2009.
Pais, Matt. *Metromix.com.* June 18, 2009.
Phillips, Michael. *Chicago Tribune.* June 18, 2009.
Scheck, Frank. *Hollywood Reporter.* June 17, 2009.
Scheib, Ronnie. *Variety.* June 17, 2009.

Simon, Brent. *Screen International.* June 19, 2009.
Stevens, Dana. *Slate.* June 19, 2009.

QUOTES

Cain: "What transpires within the confines of the walls of
    Sodom, stays within the confines of the walls of Sodom."

TRIVIA

Stanley Tucci was originally going to play Noah in the film.
    However, after the box-office failure of *Evan Almighty* the
    character was cut from the film.

THE YOUNG VICTORIA

Love rules all.
    —Movie tagline
Her country. Her heart. Her majesty.
    —Movie tagline

Box Office: $10.4 million

One imagnes *The Young Victoria* being greenlit in
the wake of the tidal wave of critical acclaim and Oscar®
nominations that fell upon *The Queen* (2006) with the
simpleminded notion that what audiences responded to
most in that film was just a cheeky monarch—not any
multilayered sense of nuance, intelligence and humanity,
or the clash of intractable duty and tradition with more
modern concepts. A by-the-numbers slice of British
heritage cinema with a few grace notes of character
enlightenment through spunky dialogue, this is a film
nakedly made to court awards, yet so frustratingly
conventional and formulaic that if it could be retro-
engineered into a leather-bound text and sold as a history book, it would surely be more at home in that
format.

A much bigger deal abroad, where it grossed $8.1
million of its $12.7 million foreign theatrical haul in its
native United Kingdom, *The Young Victoria* failed to
connect with American costume drama fans, pulling in
only $2.8 million at the box office. It is a rare case of
arthouse audiences not taking the bait; *The Young Victoria* is not a terrible movie, just a completely inessential
one. It evinces no great reason for existing, other than to
provide paychecks to a couple familiar actors and give
rising star Emily Blunt the chance to get dolled up in
period garb and showcase some spitfire verve.

Blunt stars as Queen Victoria, who in June of 1837
became the youngest monarch in English history, suc-
ceeding her uncle, King William IV (Jim Broadbent), at
only 18 years of age. The film opens just prior to her
ascension, at a time when Victoria is still forbade from
walking down a flight of stairs without holding an adult's

hand, and chronicles the turbulent first years of her
reign. Like many a teenager leaving the nest, Victoria
chafes under the rules of her manipulative mother, the
Duchess of Kent (Miranda Richardson), and her advisor,
Sir John Conroy (Mark Strong), the latter of whom has
designs on trying to coerce Victoria into signing away
some of her powers and install him as regent.

Headstrong Victoria instead takes Lord Melbourne
(Paul Bettany), the charming Prime Minister, as her
political advisor, but quickly realizes there will always be
games afoot to curry favor, win influence and steal
power. Dispatched by King Leopold of Belgium
(Thomas Kretschmann) to win over Victoria and give
him updates as to her intentions, Prince Albert (Rupert
Friend) finds himself among several suitors. He and Victoria hit it off (despite a different taste in music), and an
apparently mutual and sincere love affair blossoms. After
the two wed, though, tensions start to emerge.

Writer Julian Fellowes has traded in this sort of
class-system/period piece political intrigue before, winning a Best Screenplay Academy Award® for *Gosford
Park* (2001) before receiving harsher critical notices for
the less justifiably less acclaimed *Vanity Fair* (2004). His
script for *The Young Victoria*, though, sags beneath the
weight of expository dialogue, and does not get much
mileage out of intrigue it attempts to till up with regards
to the manner in which selections are made for the
queen's court. There is a bit of unexpected liveliness—
King William's drunken denouncement of his sister-in-
law at dinner, for instance—and the movie's first hour
offers some wry, scheming pleasures, in that Victoria
and Albert each know others wish them to be their
pawns, and so they must factor that into how they chose
to react in every given situation. Once everyone's cards
are on the table, as it were, and the chief dramatic
conflicts laid more bare, *The Young Victoria* then
becomes a yawningly methodical recounting of events,
marching our leads inexorably toward the altar three
years hence, and beyond.

Working with cinematographer Hagen Bogdanski
and production designer Patrice Vermette, French-born
director Jean-Marc Vallée creates a nice-looking movie.
He also injects some sparkling flourishes atypical of such
genre fare, most notably in a sweeping, slow-motion assassination sequence that seems designed to be sent as a
video valentine to Michael Bay.

Blunt, who managed to slyly steal scenes opposite
Meryl Streep and Anne Hathaway in the box office
smash *The Devil Wears Prada* (2006), graduates smoothly
to lead roles here. She is fine in *The Young Victoria*,
honestly—beautiful, relatable and sympathetic, no small
feat when playing a queen. None of the movie's problems

are traceable to her. Most of the other performances are not so engaging, however. Friend is a bore as Albert (problematic, since the love story matters so deeply), and Richardson's haughtiness comes across as telegraphed, surface-level bitchery, not the result of generations of inbred royal entitlement.

After nearly an hour and forty-five minutes of insistently pitched recreations, Vallée and his cohorts are still not fully convinced that an audience realizes the importance of what they have just witnessed, so a series of increasingly desperate and unintentionally amusing codas hammer home the point before the closing credits: Victoria and Albert had nine children together, and among their descendants are the royal families of Spain, England and many other countries. Oh, and they *really* loved each other. From his death at typhoid at forty-two until her death four decades later at eighty-one years of age, Victoria had his clothes laid out every day. Potential viewers can skip the movie and just go read the encyclopedia entry.

Brent Simon

CREDITS

Queen Victoria: Emily Blunt
Prince Albert: Rupert Friend
Lord Melbourne: Paul Bettany
Duchess of Kent: Miranda Richardson
King William: Jim Broadbent
King Leopold: Thomas Kretschmann
Sir John Conroy: Mark Strong
Baron Stockmar: Jesper Christensen
Queen Adelaide: Harriet Walter
Duke of Wellington: Julian Glover
Sir Robert Peel: Michael Maloney
Victoria: Michaela Brooks
Origin: USA
Language: English
Released: 2009
Production: Sarah Ferguson, Tim Headington, Graham King, Martin Scorsese; GK Films; released by Apparition
Directed by: Jean-Marc Vallee
Written by: Julian Fellowes
Cinematography by: Hagen Bogdanski
Music by: Ilan Eshkeri
Sound: Jim Greenhorn
Music Supervisor: Maureen Crowe
Editing: Jill Bilcock, Matt Garner
Art Direction: Paul Inglis
Costumes: Sandy Powell
Production Design: Patrice Vermette

MPAA rating: PG
Running time: 104 minutes

REVIEWS

Elley, Derek. *Variety.* February 6, 2009.
Fear, David. *Time Out.* December 16, 2009.
Gleiberman, Owen. *Entertainment Weekly.* December 9, 2009.
Howell, Peter. *Toronto Star.* December 22, 2009.
Hunter, Allan. *Daily Express.* March 7, 2009.
Lane, Anthony. *New Yorker.* December 14, 2009.
Pais, Matt. *Metromix.com.* December 17, 2009.
Sharkey, Betsy. *Los Angeles Times.* December 17, 2009.
Taylor, Ella. *Village Voice.* December 15, 2009.
Zacharek, Stephanie. *Salon.com.* December 21, 2009.

QUOTES

Princess Victoria: "Do you ever feel like a chess piece yourself? In a game being played against your will."

TRIVIA

Producer Sarah Ferguson's daughter, Princess Beatrice of York (who is Queen Victoria's great-great-great-great-granddaughter), can be seen in a small role as one of Victoria's ladies in waiting.

AWARDS

Oscars 2009: Costume Des.
British Acad. 2009: Costume Des., Makeup
Nomination:
Oscars 2009: Art Dir./Set Dec., Makeup
Golden Globes 2010: Actress—Drama (Blunt).

ZOMBIELAND

This place is so dead.
—Movie tagline

Box Office: $75.6 million

At some point in the first decade of the 2000s, it was decided that zombies would be in vogue again. Starting with Danny Boyle's *28 Days Later* (2002) and continuing with the remake of *Dawn of the Dead* (2004) and the British comedy *Shaun of the Dead* (2004)—with countless film festival imitators and wannabes along the way—zombies became as much of the cinematic landscape in the last half of the decade as the montage and the blooper reel. Even George Romero, the pioneer of the genre, went back to his roots and used the living dead as a springboard for a satire on the Iraq War and the media with *Land of the Dead* (2005) and *Diary of* the Dead (2007), respectively. This new breed of zombie film even kick-started a debate that lives on to this day: Slow zombies or fast zombies? The aforementioned *28 Days Later* and *Dawn of the Dead* remake introduced us to zombies that can run. Romero has spoken out against fast zombies. Ask any purest and they will usually side with Romero.

Nevertheless, fast zombies rule the landscape in the 2009 zombie comedy *Zombieland*, and why not? In spite of the fact that fast zombies seem to break the rules of the genre, great movies have come out of the concept, regardless, and *Zombieland* is no exception. The movie does not concern itself with a code of ethics or standards and practices in appeasing a fan base. It simply wants to be fun and to hell with anyone who lets a silly argument get in the way of a good time. It is to the filmmakers credit that because of its tight script, fast pace and down-to-earth sense of humor, it is quite possible that purists will not even have time to ponder the issue (though, to be fair, the first movie to really introduce fast zombies was Dan O'Bannon's much-loved 1985 film, *The Return of the Living Dead*).

There are only about six characters total in *Zombieland*. The set-up is typical. The whole country has been over-taken by a disease that started with "patient zero" and now exists in a lawless state. Our main character and narrator is the humble, awkward and self-deprecating Columbus (Jesse Eisenberg), named after the city he comes from. All the characters (save for one, who plays himself) are named after the cities from which they hail as a way of not getting too personal or chummy with anyone they happen to meet. One day on a roadside cluttered with banged-up automobiles, Columbus meets Tallahassee (Woody Harrelson), perhaps the first human he has met in weeks. He is the opposite of Columbus: Tough, cocky and a pro when it comes to killing zombies.

They reluctantly pair up and *Zombieland* quickly becomes a road movie and buddy comedy. While scoping out a grocery store in hopes of finding a box of Twinkies (the object of obsession for Tallahassee), they come upon a young woman named Wichita (Emma Stone) and her little sister Little Rock (Abigail Breslin). Both are con artists who trust no one and it does not take long before the two girls have nabbed the guns and the truck from Columbus and Tallahassee. Eventually, the four meet up again and while they all have guns pointed at one another, they agree that such trust issues are meaningless when living in a world made up of nothing more than flesh eating demons. They head west with the plan of going to an amusement park where it is believed that zombies do not exist.

Like *Shaun of the Dead*, its obvious companion piece, *Zombieland* is as much about relationships (or, in this case, the pursuit of one) as it is about zombie killing, maybe even more so. Columbus dreams of one day brushing the hair away from a beautiful girl's face. Wichita, who might be too tough for Columbus and pretty much out of his league, is his only means in all of humanity for such a connection. Eventually, he lets himself get in touch with his bad-boy self, just as Tallahassee shows more endearing signs of vulnerability, particularly when he confesses that he cried during *Titanic* (1996). As is typical with road movies, everyone learns a little something about themselves from the other people around them—not always typical for a zombie movie.

First-time feature director Ruben Fleischer keeps the movie going at a brisk pace. At less than 90 minutes, *Zombieland* feels just right and never wears out its welcome. The tight screenplay by TV writers Rhett Reese and Paul Wernick is peppered with charming asides and love for its characters. It would have been easy to construct an apologetic, one-dimensional and ironic zombie comedy with this concept, but the creative team behind *Zombieland* knows how to get the audience to go along with the ride without feeling they have to dumb down the material. They never pander to the horror crowd. Instead, they arrange it so that girlfriends of horror fans will have a good time as well.

That is not to say that *Zombieland* is a strictly a zombie movie by way of Apatow-like feelings of angst and self-awareness. It has plenty of action, gore and quality kills that will certainly please genre fans. It becomes quite clear that everyone involved is having a great time and the feeling is infectious. Eisenberg has played this part before, but he remains a solid choice for these roles. With Harrelson (a perfect opposite), it almost seems as if his entire career has been building up to this moment It is a performance filled with surprises, especially since its set-up suggests a one-note caricature. Emma Stone exudes just the right amount of sexiness and toughness and Abigail Breslin, ubiquitous since her Oscar®-nominated performance in *Little Miss Sunshine* (2006), has all but assured her career as an actress who can probably do it all. The surprise cameo in the second act should remain just that.

But *Zombieland* is, in itself, a surprise. By 2009, the concept of a "zombie comedy" seemed incredibly passé. So many young independent filmmakers have tried their hand at mixing the genres that it becomes little wonder that most of them never make it beyond the festival circuit. The key to the successes of *Zombieland* and *Shaun of the Dead* is that they do not apologize or spend too much time winking at the audience. They have great respect for zombies (fast and slow), but even more respect for their characters and audiences.

Collin Souter

CREDITS

Tallahassee: Woody Harrelson
Columbus: Jesse Eisenberg
Wichita: Emma Stone
Little Rock: Abigail Breslin
406: Amber Heard
Himself: Bill Murray
Clown Zombie: Derek Graf
Origin: USA
Language: English
Released: 2009
Production: Gavin Polone; Relativity Media, Pariah Films; released by Columbia Pictures
Directed by: Ruben Fleischer
Written by: Rhett Reese, Paul Wernick
Cinematography by: Michael Bonvillain
Music by: David Sardy
Sound: Mary H. Ellis, Sean McCormack
Editing: Alan Baumgarten
Art Direction: Nicole LeBlanc
Costumes: Magali Guidasci
Production Design: Maher Ahmad
MPAA rating: R
Running time: 88 minutes

REVIEWS

Burr, Ty. *Boston Globe.* October 1, 2009.
Childress, Erik. *EFilmCritic.com.* October 1, 2009.
Corliss, Richard. *Time Magazine.* October 2, 2009.
Dargis, Manohla. *New York Times.* October 2, 2009.
Ebert, Roger. *Chicago Sun-Times.* October 1, 2009.
Harvey, Dennis. *Variety.* September 28, 2009.
Levin, Josh. *Slate.* October 2, 2009.
Phillips, Michael. *Chicago Tribune.* October 2, 2009.
Rabin, Nathan. *AV Club.* October 1, 2009.
Tallerico, Brian. *HollywoodChicago.com.* October 2, 2009.

QUOTES

Columbus: "The first rule of Zombieland: Cardio. When the zombie outbreak first hit, the first to go, for obvious reasons…were the fatties."

TRIVIA

The film was originally called "Another Day in Zombieland," but the studio feared people would think it was a sequel and stay away, so the title was simplified.

List of Awards

Academy Awards

Film: *The Hurt Locker*
Animated Film: *Up*
Director: Kathryn Bigelow (*The Hurt Locker*)
Actor: Jeff Bridges (*Crazy Heart*)
Actress: Sandra Bullock (*The Blind Side*)
Supporting Actor: Christoph Waltz (*Inglourious Basterds*)
Supporting Actress: Mo'Nique (*Precious: Based on the Novel 'Push' by Sapphire*)
Original Screenplay: Mark Boal (*The Hurt Locker*)
Adapted Screenplay: Geoffrey Fletcher (*Precious: Based on the Novel 'Push' by Sapphire*)
Cinematography: Mauro Fiore (*Avatar*)
Editing: Bob Murawski and Chris Innis (*The Hurt Locker*)
Art Direction: Rick Carter, Robert Stromberg, and Kim Sinclair (*Avatar*)
Visual Effects: Joe Letteri, Stephen Rosenbaum, Richard Baneham, and Andy Jones (*Avatar*)
Sound: Paul N.J. Ottosson and Ray Beckett (*The Hurt Locker*)
Sound Editing: Paul N.J. Ottosson (*The Hurt Locker*)
Makeup: Barney Burman, Mindy Hall, and Joel Harlow (*Star Trek*)
Costume Design: Sandy Powell (*The Young Victoria*)
Original Score: Michael Giacchino (*Up*)
Original Song: "The Weary Kind" (Ryan Bingham and T-Bone Burnett *Crazy Heart*)
Foreign Language Film: *El secreto de sus ojos*
Documentary, Feature: *The Cove*
Documentary, Short Subject: *Music by Prudence*
Short Film, Animated: *Logorama*
Short Film, Live Action: *The New Tenants*

British Academy of Film & Television Awards

Animated Film: *Up*
Film: *The Hurt Locker*
Director: Kathryn Bigelow (*The Hurt Locker*)
Original Screenplay: Mark Boal (*The Hurt Locker*)
Adapted Screenplay: Jason Reitman and Sheldon Turner (*Up in the Air*)
Actor: Colin Firth (*A Single Man*)
Actress: Carey Mulligan (*An Education*)
Supporting Actor: Christoph Waltz (*Inglourious Basterds*)
Supporting Actress: Mo'Nique (*Precious: Based on the Novel 'Push' by Sapphire*)
Editing: Bob Murawski and Chris Innis (*The Hurt Locker*)
Cinematography: Barry Ackroyd (*The Hurt Locker*)
Production Design: Rick Carter, Robert Stromberg, and Kim Sinclair (*Avatar*)
Costume Design: Sandy Powell (*The Young Victoria*)
Makeup: Jenny Shircore (*The Young Victoria*)
Sound: Ray Beckett, Paul N.J. Ottosson, and Craig Stauffer (*The Hurt Locker*)
Visual Effects: Joe Letteri, Stephen Rosenbaum, Richard Baneham, and Andy Jones (*Avatar*)
Music: Michael Giacchino (*Up*)
Outstanding Debut by a British Writer, Director, or Producer: Duncan Jones (*Moon*)
Outstanding British Film: *Fish Tank*
Foreign Film: *Un prophète*
Short Animation: *The Gruffalo* and *The Happy Duckling*
Short Film: *I Do Air*

Directors Guild of America Awards

Outstanding Directorial Achievement in Motion Pictures: Kathryn Bigelow (*The Hurt Locker*)
Outstanding Directorial Achievement in Documentary: Louie Psihoyos (*The Cove*)

Golden Globes

Film, Drama: *Avatar*
Film, Musical or Comedy: *The Hangover*

Animated Film: *Up*
Director: James Cameron (*Avatar*)
Actor, Drama: Jeff Bridges (*Crazy Heart*)
Actor, Musical or Comedy: Robert Downey Jr. (*Sherlock Holmes*)
Actress, Drama: Sandra Bullock (*The Blind Side*)
Actress, Musical or Comedy: Meryl Streep (*Julie & Julia*)
Supporting Actor: Christoph Waltz (*Inglourious Basterds*)
Supporting Actress: Mo'Nique (*Precious: Based on the Novel 'Push' by Sapphire*)
Screenplay: Jason Reitman and Sheldon Turner (*Up in the Air*)
Score: Michael Giacchino (*Up*)
Song: "The Weary Kind" (Ryan Bingham and T-Bone Burnett, *Crazy Heart*)
Foreign Language Film: *Das weisse Band—Eine deutsche Kindergeschichte*

Golden Raspberry Awards

Worst Picture: *Transformers: Revenge of the Fallen*
Worst Director: Michael Bay (*Transformers: Revenge of the Fallen*)
Worst Actor: All three Jonas Brothers (*Jonas Brothers: The 3-D Concert Experience*)

Worst Actress: Sandra Bullock (*All About Steve*)
Worst Supporting Actor: Billy Ray Cyrus (*Hannah Montana: The Movie*)
Worst Supporting Actress: Sienna Miller (*G.I. Joe: The Rise of Cobra*)
Worst Screenplay: Ehren Kruger, Roberto Orci, and Alex Kurtzman (*Transformers: Revenge of the Fallen*)
Worst Screen Couple: Sandra Bullock and Bradley Cooper (*All About Steve*)
Worst Remake, Rip-Off or Sequel: *Land of the Lost*

Independent Spirit Awards

Film: *Precious: Based on the Novel 'Push' by Sapphire*
First Film: Scott Cooper *Crazy Heart*
Director: Lee Daniels (*Precious: Based on the Novel 'Push' by Sapphire*)
Actor: Jeff Bridges (*Crazy Heart*)
Actress: Gabourey Sidibe (*Precious: Based on the Novel 'Push' by Sapphire*)
Supporting Actor: Woody Harrelson (*The Messenger*)
Supporting Actress: Mo'Nique (*Precious: Based on the Novel 'Push' by Sapphire*)

Screenplay: Scott Neustadter and Michael H. Weber (*(500) Days of Summer*)
First Screenplay: Geoffrey Fletcher (*Precious: Based on the Novel 'Push' by Sapphire*)
Cinematography: Roger Deakins (*A Serious Man*)
Foreign Film: *An Education*
Documentary: *Anvil! The Story of Anvil*

Screen Actors Guild Awards

Actor: Jeff Bridges (*Crazy Heart*)
Actress: Sandra Bullock (*The Blind Side*)
Supporting Actor: Christoph Waltz (*Inglourious Basterds*)
Supporting Actress: Mo'Nique (*Precious: Based on the Novel 'Push' by Sapphire*)
Ensemble Cast: *Inglourious Basterds*
Stunt Ensemble: *Star Trek*

Writers Guild of America Awards

Original Screenplay: Mark Boal (*The Hurt Locker*)
Adapted Screenplay: Jason Reitman and Sheldon Turner (*Up in Air*)
Documentary Screenplay Award: Mark Monroe (*The Cove*)

Obituaries

Mort Abrahams (March 26, 1916–May 28, 2009). American film and television producer Mort Abrahams worked on several major films of the 1970s and served as the producer-in-residence for the Center for Advanced Film and Television at the American Film Institute from 1989 to 1994. He got his start producing television like *General Electric Theater* (1954-1955), *The Third Man* (1959), and *The Man from U.N.C.L.E.* (1965-1966) and went on to associate produce only a few films but a few very notable ones including *Doctor Dolittle* (1967), *Planet of the Apes* (1968), *The Chairman* (1969), *Goodbye, Mr. Chips* (1969), and *Beneath the Planet of the Apes* (1970), for which he also recorded his only writing credit. Abrahams finished his career with executive producer credit on *To Find a Man* (1972), *The Homecoming* (1973), *Rhinoceros* (1974), *Luther* (1974), *The Man in the Glass Booth* (1975), *The Greek Tycoon* (1978), and *Seven Hours to Judgment* (1988), among others.

Frank Aletter (January 14, 1926–May 13, 2009). American actor Frank Aletter got his start on Broadway in the 1950s but will be most remembered for a consistent series of guest appearances on television from the mid-1950s through the 1980s. He would go on to television work, but his first non-stage credit is one of his most famous—the film *Mister Roberts* (1955). From there, Aletter scored a regular role as Buddy Flower on the show *Bringing Up Buddy* (1960-1961). The exposure from that led to regular work for the next three decades on hit programs including *The Twilight Zone* (1963), *My Favorite Martian* (1963), *Dr. Kildare* (1963), *The Fugitive* (1965), *The Mod Squad* (1970), *Maude* (1972), *Ironside* (1969-1973), *M*A*S*H* (1973), *The Six Million Dollar Man* (1975), *All in the Family* (1978), *Columbo* (1978), *Fantasy Island* (1978-1979), *The Love Boat* (1979), *Three's Company* (1981), *CHiPs* (1982), *Murder, She Wrote* (1985), *The Golden Girls* (1985), *Matlock* (1987), and many, many more. Aletter only appeared in a few films in that period but they were prominent works—*A Tiger Walks* (1964), *Tora! Tora! Tora!* (1970), *Run,*

Cougar, Run (1972), and *Private School* (1983). Aletter was elected Vice President of the Screen Actors Guild in 1987.

Terence Alexander (March 11, 1923–May 28, 2009). Born in Islington, London, England in 1923, Terence Joseph Alexander will be best remembered for his role in the British drama *Bergerac* (1981-1991), which ran for eighty-seven episodes on BBC1 for the majority of the 1980s. A young Alexander worked with John Gielgud on stage in *MacBeth* before joining the Army and serving in World War II, having half of his foot blown off by shrapnel in combat. He worked steadily for the next few decades, including roles in prominent films such as *The League of Gentlemen* (1960), *The Magic Christian* (1969), *Waterloo* (1970), and *The Day of the Jackal* (1973), but he claimed to be in the red when got the role he would play for a decade on *Bergerac*, one that would make him a star relatively late in life.

Wayne Allwine (February 7, 1947–May 18, 2009). Born in Glendale, California, Wayne Allwine was a legendary voice actor to millions who probably never knew the name of the man who voiced Mickey Mouse from 1977 until his death. In fact, Allwine was only the third Mickey Mouse, taking over from Jimmy MacDonald, who took over after Walt Disney stopped doing the role in 1946. (Bret Iwan is now the fourth vocal artist behind Mickey Mouse.) Allwine also worked as a sound editor on several major films including *The Black Hole* (1979), *Something Wicked This Way Comes* (1983), *Country* (1984), *Psycho III* (1986), *Innerspace* (1987), *Alien Nation* (1988), *Star Trek V: The Final Frontier* (1989), and more. Allwine's vocal skills, as Mickey and others, were on display in *Mickey's Christmas Carol* (1983), *The Black Cauldron* (1985), *The Great Mouse Detective* (1986), *Who Framed Roger Rabbit* (1988), *The Prince and the Pauper* (1990), *A Goofy Movie* (1995), *Fantasia 2000* (1999), along with dozens of other straight-to-DVD titles, TV specials, and even the *Kingdom Hearts* line of video games.

Obituaries

Ken Annakin (August 10, 1914–April 22, 2009). English film director Kenneth Cooper Annakin was born in Beverley, Yorkshire and began his career behind the camera as a documentary filmmaker, but will probably be most fondly remembered for work with Walt Disney Films on a series of adventure films in the 1950s and 1960s and for work with Darryl F. Zanuck in the 1960s. He worked consistently up until the 1980s. Notable credits as a director include *The Story of Robin Hood and His Merrie Men* (1952), *The Sword and the Rose* (1953), *Swiss Family Robinson* (1960), *The Fast Lady* (1962), *The Longest Day* (1962), *The Informers* (1963), *Those Magnificent Men in Their Flying Machines* (1965), *The Call of the Wild* (1972), *Paper Tiger* (1975), *The Pirate Movie* (1982), and *The New Adventures of Pippi Longstocking* (1988).

Army Archerd (January 13, 1922–September 8, 2009). The legendary film columnist and pundit was born in the Bronx, New York and graduated from UCLA in 1941. He began his incredible history with Hollywood in 1953 when he was hired to replace columnist Sheilah Graham at *Variety*. He quickly became a prominent part of the increasingly important Hollywood gossip scene, often breaking scoops before anyone else, most famously outing that Rock Hudson was undergoing treatment for AIDS in 1985. For half a century, Archerd remained one of the most read columnists of the Hollywood scene. In 1984, Archerd was given a star on Hollywood's Walk of Fame in front of Mann's Chinese Theater.

Bea Arthur (May 13, 1922–April 25, 2009). Actress-comedienne Bea Arthur was born in New York City. She rose to fame later in life, appearing in guest TV roles in the 1950s but not breaking through until she was in her forties and first on Broadway, appearing in the original production of *Fiddler on the Roof* in 1964. She would win a Tony Award two years later for her work in *Mame* and broke through as a TV star first as Archie Bunker's liberal neighbor on *All in the Family* (1971-1972) and later on her own spinoff *Maude* (1972-1978) and another massive hit *The Golden Girls* (1985-1992). Arthur will be best remembered for her television work, but she also appeared regularly in films, starring in *Lovers and Other Strangers* (1970), *Mame* (1974), *History of the World: Part I* (1981), and *For Better or Worse* (1995).

Val Avery (July 14, 1924–December 12, 2009). Prolific character actor Val Avery was born in Philadelphia, Pennsylvania as Sebouh Der Abrahamian and worked with the Armenian Youth Theater before serving as a flight instructor in World War II. He attended the Bessie V. Hicks School of Drama before moving to Manhattan and beginning a career in live television that landed him regular work both on the small and big screen. Notable film roles include parts (mostly tough guys) in *The Harder They Fall* (1956), *Edge of the City* (1957), *The Magnificent Seven* (1960), *Too Late Blues* (1961), *Hud* (1963), *Hombre* (1967), *Faces* (1968), *The Anderson tapes* (1971), *The Laughing Policeman* (1973), *The Killing of a Chinese Bookie* (1976), *Up in Smoke* (1978), *Gloria* (1980), *The Pope of Greenwich Village* (1984), and *Donnie Brasco* (1997).

Carl Ballantine (September 27, 1917–November 3, 2009). Born Meyer Kessler in Chicago, Illinois, Ballantine became a legend in the world of magic and vaudeville-style comedy,

sometimes billing himself as "The Great Ballantine," "The Amazing Ballantine," and "Ballantine: The World's Greatest Magician." He will be best remembered for the role of Lester Gruber on the popular sitcom *McHale's Navy* (1962-1966), but he had dozens of other film and television roles including *Speedway* (1968), *I Dream of Jeannie* (1968), *The Partridge Family* (1971), *Love, American Style* (1969-1972), *Revenge of the Cheerleaders,* (1976), *Laverne & Shirley* (1976), *CHiPs* (1978), *Fantasy Island* (1981), *Alice* (1982), *Trapper John, M.D.* (1981-1984), *Night Court* (1986), *Mr. Saturday Night* (1992), and *My Giant* (1998).

Gene Barry (June 14, 1919–December 9, 2009). Born Eugene Klass in New York City, Gene Barry got his start on Broadway in the 1940s, moved to television in the 1950s, and would appear in several major films, while also maintaining starring roles on three TV series—*Bat Masterson* (1958-1961), *The Name of the Game* (1968-1971), and *Burke's Law* (1963-1966), for which he won a Golden Globe. Notable film credits include *The Atomic City* (1952, his debut), *The War of the Worlds* (1953), *Back From Eternity* (1956), *Thunder Road* (1958), *Subterfuge* (1968), and Steven Spielberg's remake of *War of the Worlds* (2005). Barry is also well known for his Tony-nominated work as a gay nightclub owner in the first stage version of *La Cage Aux Folles* on Broadway. He also appeared in *Prescription: Murder* (1968), the first TV movie to feature a little character known as Lt. Columbo (Peter Falk).

Claude Berri (July 1, 1934–January 12, 2009). Born Claude Berel Langmann in Paris, France, Claude Berri would go on to act, write, produce, direct, and distribute film. Over the course of his career, Berri was nominated for twelve Cesar Awards, but never won, although he did take home the Oscar® for Best Short Film for *Le poulet* (1965) and was nominated in his role as producer when Roman Polanski's *Tess* (1979) was nominated for Best Picture. Notable credits include his direction of *Jean de Florette* (1986) and *Manon of the Spring* (1986), two of the most successful French films of the 1980s, *Germinal* (1993), and *Lucie Abrac* (1997). His first credit as an actor was in Claude Autant-Lara's *Le bon Dieu sans confession* (1953). He was working on his twentieth directorial credit (*Tresor*) when he passed away. In 2003, Berri was elected President of the Cinematheque Francaise.

Betsy Blair (December 11, 1923–March 13, 2009). Born in New Jersey as Elizabeth Winifred Boger before taking the stage name Betsy Blair, the actress was a child star who would eventually marry Gene Kelly. After a career as a child dancer, Blair joined the chorus at the International Casino in New York where Kelly was working as choreographer. The two were married in October 1941 and divorced sixteen years later. Blair's first credit was in *The Guilt of Janet Ames* (1947) and she went on to star in *A Double Life* (1947), *Another Part of the Forest* (1948), *Mystery Street* (1950), *Kind Lady* (1951), *Marty* (1955), *Calle Mayor* (1956), *The Halliday Brand* (1957), *Lies My Father Told Me* (1960), *All Night Long* (1962), *A Delicate Balance* (1973), and *Betrayed* (1988). She was nominated for an Academy Award® for Best Actress in a Supporting Role for *Marty*

Paul Burke (July 21, 1926–September 13, 2009). Television star Paul Burke was born in New Orleans, Louisiana in 1926 to a boxer and eventual restaurant owner. Burke got

436

MAGILL'S CINEMA ANNUAL

small film parts throughout his career but will be best remembered for his twice-Emmy-nominated turn on the hit *Naked City* (1960-1963). Burke made a number of guest appearances and took on another lead role later that decade on *12 O'Clock High* (1964-1967). He would give regular TV work one more shot in the short-lived *Hot Shots* (1986). Notable film roles included parts in *Fixed Bayonets!* (1951, his debut), *South Sea Woman* (1953), *Valley of the Dolls* (1967), and *The Thomas Crown Affair* (1968).

Kathleen Byron (January 11, 1921–January 18, 2009). British stage, screen, and television star Kathleen Byron was born Kathleen Elizabeth Fell in West Ham, London, England. The actress worked regularly in film from the 1940s through the 1990s but will be best remembered for her work with legendary director Michael Powell and the films he made with Emeric Pressburger in the 1940s after she made her debut in the Powell & Pressburger-produced *The Silver Fleet* (1943). During that era, Byron gave her most memorable performances in *A Matter of Life and Death* (1946), *Black Narcissus* (1947), and *The Small Back Room* (1949). Byron moved to Hollywood in the 1950s but would quickly return to England, where she did mostly television work in the 1960s and 1970s although she did become something of a genre icon appearing in *Night of the Eagle* (1962), *Twins of Evil* (1971), *Nothing But the Night* (1972), and *Craze* (1974). Other notable film roles throughout her career include *Prelude to Fame* (1950), *Tom Brown's Schooldays* (1951), *Young Bess* (1953), *Hammerhead* (1968), *The Legend of Robin Hood* (1969), *The Elephant Man* (1980), *Emma* (1996), *Saving Private Ryan* (1998), and *Les Miserables* (1998).

Jack Cardiff (September 18, 1914–April 22, 2009). British director and cinematographer Jack Cardiff was born in Great Yarmouth, Norfolk in 1914 and went on to such a prolific career behind the camera that he was awarded title of Officer of the British Empire in 2000 and an Honorary Oscar® in 2001. Cardiff started as an actor, appearing as a child in the silent films *My Son, My Son* (1918), *Billy's Rose* (1922), *The Loves of Mary, Queen of Scots* (1923), and *Tiptoes* (1927). Cardiff's life as a cinematographer began with a job as a second unit cameraman on Michael Powell & Eric Pressburger's *The Life and Death of Colonel Blimp* (1943). Powell & Pressburger promoted Cardiff to cinematographer on their next few films, including *A Matter of Life and Death* (1946), *Black Narcissus* (1947), for which Cardiff won an Oscar® and Golden Globe, and *The Red Shoes* (1948). Cinematography work followed on *Under Capricorn* (1949), *The Black Rose* (1950), *The Magic Box* (1951), *The African Queen* (1951), *The Barefoot Contessa* (1954), *War and Peace* (1956, Oscar®-nominated), *The Prince and the Showgirl* (1957), and others before Cardiff turned to directing himself. His debut directorial effort was *Web of Evidence* (1959), but he will be most remembered for *Sons and Lovers* (1960), which was nominated for seven Academy Awards® including Best Picture and Best Director. A series of relative directorial failures followed (and Oscar®-nominated cinematography for *Fanny*) and Cardiff ended his career as a cinematographer once again, shooting *Death on the Nile* (1978), *The Awakening* (1980), *Ghost Story* (1981), *Conan the Destroyer* (1984), and *Rambo: First Blood Part II* (1985).

David Carradine (December 8, 1936–June 3, 2009). The legendary character actor David Carradine seemed to have a comeback role waiting every time his star began to fade, appearing in over one hundred feature films (and over one hundred television appearances) and landing four Golden Globe nominations over his career. Born John Arthur Carradine in Hollywood, California, David Carradine is part of a family of actors that includes half-brother Keith, half-brother Robert, and nieces Ever Carradine and Martha Plimpton. Carradine's first credit was on the TV program *Armstrong Circle Theatre* (1963) but his first breakthrough would come a few years later in the series adaptation of *Shane* (1966). That role led to regular television and film work in the 1960s, but the early 1970s would be the most prolific time of Carradine's career, working on major films and becoming a cult icon due to his role on the TV series *Kung Fu* (1972-1975) (which he would reprise on *Kung Fu: The Legend Continues* decades later). Major films over his career included *Boxcar Bertha* (1972), *The Long Goodbye* (1973), *Mean Streets* (1973), *Death Race 2000* (1975), *Bound For Glory* (1976), *Q* (1982), *Lone Wolf McQuade* (1983), *North and South* (1985), *Bird on a Wire* (1990), and dozens of straight-to-video genre movies before returning to the spotlight after Quentin Tarantino gave him the title role in *Kill Bill: Vol. 1* (2003) and *Kill Bill: Vol. 2* (2004). Even after that comeback, Carradine went back to genre work that rarely saw a theatrical release, making several films a year until his death.

Mickey Carroll (July 8, 1919–May 7, 2009). Michael Finocchiaro was born in St. Louis, Missouri in 1919 and thirty years later he would be a part of an enduring classic, playing one of the munchkins in *The Wizard of Oz* (1939). He was one of the last surviving munchkins, memorable as the "Town Crier" with his purple cloak. He reportedly also marched as a munchkin soldier

Marilyn Chambers (April 22, 1952–April 12, 2009). Once the face of Ivory Soap, Marilyn Chambers would soon go on to become one of the most popular stars of the adult film movement of the 1970s and 1980s as pornography went from something under the popular radar to mainstream success and back again. Chambers broke through with one of the films that would forever change the modern depiction of sex, *Behind the Green Door* (1972). Chambers would attempt to find success in mainstream films including David Cronenberg's *Rabid* (1977) but mostly maintained notoriety through overtly sexual films like *Insatiable* (1980), *Up 'n' Coming* (1983), *The Marilyn Diaries* (1990), and *New York Nights (1994).*

Dennis Cole (July 19, 1940–November 15, 2009). Cole was born in Detroit, Michigan and modeled for men's physique magazines before breaking through in television drama in the 1960s. He was a TV regular in the 1970s and 1980s with a few film roles thrown in. His major TV work included regular roles on *The Young and the Restless* (1981-1982) and *Fantasy Island* (1978-1984) along with guest spots on *Charlie's Angels* (1977-1979), *Police Woman* (1978), *The Love Boat* (1977-1980), *Three's Company* (1983), *The Fall Guy* (1984), *The A-Team* (1985), and *Simon & Simon* (1986). His limited film career included roles in *Wheels of Fire* (1985), *Death House* (1987), and *Fatal Encounter* (1990).

Sadie Corre (May 31, 1918–August 26, 2009). English stage actress Corre may have only been 4' 1" but that height helped her to make a memorable impact in a number of highly beloved films including playing an Ewok in *Star Wars: Episode VI—Return of the Jedi* and a memorable dancer in *The Rocky Horror Picture Show* (1975). She also appeared in *The Dark Crystal* (1982), *Brazil* (1985), *Caravaggio* (1986), *Willow* (1988), *Who Framed Roger Rabbit* (1988), and *Funny Bones* (1995).

Ward Costello (July 5, 1919–June 4, 2009). Edward Costello, better known as "Ward," was a regular TV guest star, composer, lyricist, and film star who worked from the 1940s through the 1980s. Film credits include *Terror From the Year 5000* (1958), *The Gallant Hours* (1960), for which he also wrote the film's theme, *MacArthur* (1977), *Goldengirl* (1979), *Bloody Birthday* (1981), *Missing* (1982), *Firefox* (1982), and *Project X* (1987).

Michael Currie (July 24, 1928–December 22, 2009). Born Herman Christian Schwenk Jr., Michael Currie was a regular television guest star and film collaborator with Clint Eastwood, appearing in four films with the legendary icon. Film credits for the character actor include *Any Which Way You Can* (1980), *Dead & Buried* (1981), *Firefox* (1982), *Halloween III: Season of the Witch* (1982), *Airplane II: The Sequel* (1982), *Sudden Impact* (1983), *The Philadelphia Experiment* (1984), *The Dead Pool* (1988), *The Man Without a Face* (1993), and *G.I. Jane* (1997).

Dom DeLuise (August 1, 1933–May 4, 2009). Dominick DeLuise was born in Brooklyn, New York and would go on to become one of the most successful comic actors of his generation, also contributing behind the scenes in a role as director, producer, chef, and author. DeLuise graduated from the High School of Performing Arts in Manhattan. One of his first major credits was in a small dramatic role in *Fail-Safe* (1964), but he would become primarily known as a comedian on television and in film. Notable credits include Mel Brooks' *The Twelve Chairs* (1970), *Blazing Saddles* (1974), *Silent Movie* (1976), *The World's Greatest Lover* (1977), *The End* (1978), *The Muppet Movie* (1979), *History of the World: Part I* (1981), *The Cannonball Run* (1981), *Cannonball Run II* (1984), *Johnny Dangerously* (1984), *An American Tail* (1986), *Spaceballs* (1987), *Robin Hood: Men in Tights* (1993), and *Baby Geniuses* (1999).

Roy Disney (January 10, 1930–December 16, 2009). Walt Disney's nephew Roy Edward Disney was born to one of the most influential men in the history of Hollywood, Roy Oliver Disney, in 1930 and he would go on to run the company founded by his father and uncle for years after their deaths. He was the last living member of the Disney family actively involved with the company that bears his name. Roy Disney began working for the Walt Disney Company after graduating from Pomona College in 1951 and was elected to the Board of Directors in 1967. Perhaps the most important period of Disney's time at the company that bore his name was when he oversaw the comeback for Disney with *The Little Mermaid* (1989), *Beauty and the Beast* (1991), and *Aladdin* (1992). Roy Disney's career featured notable power struggles for the future of the company with Ron Miller in 1984 and with Michael Eisner nearly twenty years later. He was a notable philanthropist.

Jack Dunham (September 19, 1910–March 15, 2009). Walt Disney Animation Studios animator Jack Dunham was born in Bismarck, North Dakota in 1910. He would go on to play a major role in the development of American animation through his work at Disney and Walter Lantz Productions. In 1937, Dunham went to work for Walt Disney Animation Studio's and worked on *Snow White and the Seven Dwarfs* (1937). He served as an animation manager at the company and is also credited with work on *Fantasia* (1940), before his departure in 1947. He would later move to Canada, where he worked in live action and animated commercials. The *Montreal Gazette* reported in 2006 that Dunham had become homeless in his nineties, a sad end to a life that brought so much joy to so many.

Dick Durock (January 18, 1937–September 17, 2009). Durock was born in South Bend, Indiana and went on to appear in dozens of films as a stuntman and actor and is reportedly credited with work on over seven hundred television episodes, although he will be best remembered for playing the iconic Swamp Thing in *Swamp Thing* (1982), *The Return of Swamp Thing* (1989), and the TV series that ran from 1990 to 1993. Notable film credits include *The Enforcer* (1976), *Any Which Way You Can* (1980), *Silverado* (1985), *Raw Deal* (1986), *Stand by Me* (1986), *Blind Date* (1987), and *Delirious* (1991).

Farrah Fawcett (February 2, 1947–June 25, 2009). One of the most notorious poster subjects and television stars of all time was born Farrah Leni Fawcett in Corpus Christi, Texas in 1947. Fawcett dropped out of University of Texas at Austin during her junior year to try and make it in Hollywood and the rest was pop culture history. Fawcett appeared in a few films and made a number of guest appearances but it was a poster—a notorious one of the star in a red bathing suit—that would truly propel her to superstardom. Fawcett is widely known for playing Jill Munroe on *Charlie's Angels* (1976-77) but she only appeared on the show for one season. Notable film appearances include *Logan's Run* (1976), *The Cannonball Run* (1981), *Extremities* (1986), *The Apostle* (1997), and *Dr. T & the Women* (2000). She will also be remembered for a wildly successful series of television movies in the 1980s and 1990s including Emmy-nominated *The Burning Bed* (1984) and *Small Sacrifices* (1989).

Susanna Foster (December 6, 1924–January 17, 2009). Suzanne DeLee Flanders Larson was born in Chicago, Illinois in 1924. The American actress will be best remembered for playing the leading role in *The Phantom of the Opera* (1943). Foster signed with Paramount Pictures in the 1930s and would go on to appear in a number of hits for the studio in the 1940s. She retired from the film business in 1945 but would go on to make several notable stage appearances and attempts to comeback in television and film later in life. Film credits include *The Great Victor Herbert* (1939), *Top Man* (1943), *This Is the Life* (1944), *The Climax* (1944), *Bowery to Broadway* (1944), and *That Night with You* (1945).

Lorena Gale (May 9, 1958–June 21, 2009). Character actress Lorena Gale was born in Montreal, Quebec, Canada in 1958 and would go on to appear on television, in film, and to write award-winning plays. She is most remembered for a number of appearances in sci-fi and fantasy films and television programs. Gale's first credit was in the horror film *Visiting Hours* (1982) and she would go on to appear in *The Fly II* (1989), *Halloween: Resurrection* (2002), *The Butterfly Effect* (2004), *The Perfect Score* (2004), *The Chronicles of Riddick* (2004), *Fantastic Four* (2005), *Slither* (2006), *Things We Lost in the Fire* (2007), *The X Files: I Want to Believe* (2008), *Traitor* (2008), and *The Day the Earth Stood Still* (2008), along with dozens of television guest appearances.

Larry Gelbart (February 25, 1928–September 11, 2009). Comedy writer Larry Gelbart was one of the most popular and successful screenwriters of the 1970s and 1980s, landing two Oscar® nominations for his screenplays for *Oh, God!* (1977) and *Tootsie* (1982). Gelbart began his legendary comedy career working as a writer on *Your Show of Shows* (1950-1954) and graduated to film in the 1960s. Notable credits include *The Notorious Landlady* (1962), *Oh, God!* (1977), *Neighbors* (1981), *Tootsie* (1982), *Blame It on Rio* (1984), and *Bedazzled* (2000). He also earned high acclaim as developer and writer of the television program *M*A*S*H* (1972-1983) and as creator of *After MASH* (1983-1984). Gelbart also wrote the Broadway play *A Funny Thing Happened on the Way to the Forum,* for which he won a Tony Award.

Henry Gibson (September 21, 1935–September 14, 2009). American actor Henry Gibson may be best remembered for his role on the influential and beloved *Rowan and Martin's Laugh-In* (1968-1971) but he also amassed an impressive film career that lasted five decades and features work with many legendary directors. Born James Bateman in Philadelphia, Gibson served in the U.S. Air Force before stage and television work led him to his breakthrough role in *The Nutty Professor* (1963). He would go on to work consistently in television and appeared in *The Long Goodbye* (1973), *Nashville* (1975), *The Blues Brothers* (1980), *Innerspace* (1987), *The 'burbs* (1989), *Magnolia* (1999), and *Wedding Crashers* (2005). He ended his career as a regular on the ABC program *Boston Legal* (2004-2008).

Robert Ginty (November 14, 1948–September 21, 2009). Robert Winthrop Ginty was born in Brooklyn, New York and started his career in music before moving to Broadway, television, and film. He may be most remembered for producing, directing, writing, and starring in the action hit *The Exterminator* (1980). Ginty was a notable action star in the 1980s appearing in films like *Gold Raiders* (1983), *Warrior of the Lost World* (1983), *The Alchemist* (1984), *The Scarab* (1984), *The Exterminator 2* (1984), *Maniac Killer* (1987), *Programmed to Kill* (1987), *Code Name Vengeance* (1987), *Cop Target* (1990), and *Harley Davidson and the Marlboro Man* (1991). He also appeared in *Coming Home* (1978). He would end his career as a regular television director for a number of shows in the 1990s and early 2000s.

Maxine Cooper Gomberg (May 12, 1924–April 4, 2009). Best known for her role in the noir classic *Kiss Me Deadly* (1955), Maxine Cooper was born in Chicago, Illinois and first became interested in becoming an actress as a student at Bennington College. She entertained the troops during World War II, acted in England after the war, and returned to act in the United States in the 1950s. She made her film debut playing Velda in *Kiss Me Deadly* and went on to appear in *Autumn Leaves* (1956), *Zero Hour!* (1957), and *What Ever Happened to Baby Jane?* (1962), along with appearing on several television programs in the 1950s and 1960s.

Lucy Gordon (May 22, 1980–May 20, 2009). British actress and model Lucy Gordon was a Cover Girl model and appeared in small roles in big films before taking her life at the age of twenty-eight. Gordon made her debut in *Perfume* (2001) and went on to appear in *Serendipity* (2001), *The Four Feathers* (2002), *Spider-Man 3* (2007), and *Brief Interviews with Hideous Men* (2009).

John Hart (December 13, 1917–September 20, 2009). American actor John Hart became famous as a star of Western films and for playing *The Lone Ranger* (1952-1954) for two seasons on the legendary TV show. In an unusual Hollywood story, the producers of the program replaced star Clayton Moore with Hart for two seasons during salary negotiations, assuming that viewers would not care who was behind the mask, but were forced to bring Moore back after public outcry. Hart launched his career in the Cecil B. DeMille film *The Buccaneer* (1938) and played small roles in a number of films before he was drafted in 1941 and fought in World War II. After the war, he reignited his career by appearing in the movie serial *Jack Armstrong: The All-American Boy* (1947). After his stint on *The Lone Ranger,* Hart went on to appear in another serial *The Adventures of Captain Africa* (1955). He would find himself in the aura of the masked hero again when he appeared in the film *The Legend of Lone Ranger* (1981) and even played the Lone Ranger again on a few 1980s shows. In fact, his last credit was playing the hero in a guest spot on a 1982 episode of *Happy Days* (1982).

Clayton Hill (May 7, 1931–July 26, 2009). Born in Pennsylvania, Clayton Hill started his show business career singing on WTAE-Pittsburgh on Saturday mornings and returned to stage work there after being discharged from the U.S. Air Force. Clayton Hill broke into cinema after turning his role as weapons coordinator for George A. Romero's *Dawn of the Dead* (1978) into a zombie part in the film, famously being remembered as the "sweater zombie". Hill went on to appear on screen in *The Fish That Saved Pittsburgh* (1979), *Knightriders* (1981), *Maria's Lovers* (1984), *Rappin'* (1985), *Lady Beware* (1987), *Kenny* (1988), *Hellraiser III: Hell on Earth* (1992), and *River of Darkness* (2009).

Pat Hingle (July 19, 1924–January 3, 2009). Martin Patterson Hingle was born in Miami, Florida in 1924 and served in World War II before earning a degree from the University of Texas in radio broadcasting. The workhorse character actor appeared in nearly 200 films or television programs in his five decades in the business, most regularly playing authority figures. His breakthrough performance was in *Splendor in the Grass* (1961). Notable credits throughout his career include *Hang 'Em High* (1968), *Norma Rae* (1979), *Sudden Impact* (1983), *The Falcon and the Snowman* (1985), *Maximum Overdrive* (1986), *Batman* (1989), *The Grifters* (1990), *Batman Returns* (1992), *The Quick and the Dead* (1995), *Batman Forever* (1995), *Batman & Robin* (1997), *Shaft* (2000), and *Talladega Nights: The Ballad of Ricky Bobby* (2006).

John Hughes (February 18, 1950–August 6, 2009). Influential chronicler of the Midwestern adolescent experience in the 1980s, writer/director John Hughes only helmed eight films in his entire career but launched dozens of careers, imitators, and lifelong fans. Hughes started his career with National Lampoon, writing *Class Reunion* (1982) and *Vacation* (1983) for the comedy group before branching out on his own with a generation-defining directorial debut in *Sixteen Candles* (1984). Hughes introduced the world to a group of young stars commonly referred to as "the brat pack" in films like *The Breakfast Club* (1985), *Weird Science* (1985), and *Ferris Bueller's Day Off* (1986). Other directorial credits include *Planes, Trains & Automobiles* (1987), *She's Having a Baby* (1988), *Uncle Buck* (1989, and *Curly Sue* (1991). Writing credits include *European Vacation* (1985), *Pretty in Pink* (1986), *Some Kind of Wonderful* (1987), *The Great Outdoors* (1988), *Christmas Vacation* (1989), *Home Alone* (1990), *Career Opportunities* (1991), *Dutch* (1991), *Curly Sue* (1991), *Beethoven* (1992), *Home Alone 2: Lost in New York* (1992), *Dennis the Menace* (1993), *Baby's Day Out* (1994), *Miracle on 34th Street* (1994), *101 Dalmatians* (1996), *Flubber* (1997), and *Home Alone 3* (1997).

Michael Jackson (August 29, 1958–June 25, 2009). Michael Jackson may be forever remembered as "The King of Pop" but he also appeared in a few notable films including playing the Scarecrow in *The Wiz* (1978) and starring in the 3D extravaganza *Captain EO* (1986). He made a cameo appearance in *Men in Black II* (2002) and, of course, appeared as himself in the posthumously released concert film *Michael Jackson's This Is It* (2009). He also sang the Golden Globe-winning title theme song to *Ben* (1972).

Lou Jacobi (December 28, 1913–October 23, 2009). Canadian character actor Louis Harold Jacobovitch was born in Toronto, Ontario and began acting at a very young age working in theater. Jacobi appeared on stage in London and on Broadway and made his film debut in *Is Your Honeymoon Really Necessary* (1953). Notable career roles include Mr. Hans Van Daan—a part he originated on stage—in *The Diary of Anne Frank* (1959), Moustache in *Irma la Douce* (1963), Sam in *Every Thing You Always Wanted to Know About Sex * But Were Afraid to Ask* (1972), Uncle Morty in *My Favorite Year* (1982), and Gabriel Krichinsky in *Avalon* (1990).

Maurice Jarre (September 13, 1924–March 28, 2009). Three-time Oscar®-winning composer Maurice Jarre will be best remembered for scoring all of David Lean's films since *Lawrence of Aarabia* (1962). Jarre would win an Academy Award® for that score along with Lean's *Doctor Zhivago* (1965) and *A Passage to India* (1984). Maurice Jarre was born in Lyon, France, and studies at the Conservatoire de Paris, becoming director of the Theatre National Populaire before composing his first film score in 1951. Other notable scores include *The Year of Living Dangerously* (1982), *Witness* (1985), *Mad Max Beyond Thunderdome* (1985), *No Way Out* (1987), *Fatal Attraction* (1987), *Dead Poet Society* (1989), *Ghost* (1990), *Fearless* (1993), and *Sunshine* (1999).

Caro Jones (1923–September 3, 2009). Born in Canada, Jones moved to New York City when she was only eighteen years old, landing a job with the touring company of *Oklahoma* before becoming a major force as a casting director. Jones worked as a casting agent for stage and television, moving to casting film late in her career. In television, she worked as a casting director for such notables as Patty Duke, Sidney Pollack, Gene Hackman, William Shatner, Burgess Meredith, Johnny Carson, Martin Sheen, and George C. Scott. She went on to serve as casting director for Paramount Television. Notable film casting credits include *Rocky* (1976), *Cross Creek* (1983), *The Karate Kid* (1984), *Back to School* (1986), *The Karate Kid, Part II* (1986), *Can't Buy Me Love* (1987), *The Karate Kid, Part III* (1989), *Rocky V* (1990), *Toy Soldiers* (1991), *The Power of One* (1992), and *8 Seconds* (1994).

Jennifer Jones (March 2, 1919–December 17, 2009). Nominated five times for an Oscar® and winner for her first for *The Song of Bernadette* (1943), Jennifer Jones was one of the most beloved and acclaimed actresses of the 1940s and 1950s. Notable roles include *Since You Went Away* (1944—Oscar®-nominated), *Love Letters* (1945—Oscar®-nominated), *Duel in the Sun* (1946—Oscar®-nominated), *We Were Strangers* (1949), *Madame Bovary* (1949), *Carrie* (1952), *Love Is a Many-Splendored Thing* (1955—Oscar®-nominated), *The Barretts of Wimpole Street* (1957), *Tender Is the Night* (1962), and *The Towering Inferno* (1974).

Brenda Joyce (February 25, 1917–July 4, 2009). Born Betty Graftina Leabo in Excelsior Springs, Missouri, Brenda Joyce is most remembered as the second "Jane" in the notable series of Johnny Weissmuller *Tarzan* films. Joyce's first credit was in *The Rains Came* (1939) and she went on to star in *Here I Am a Stranger* (1939), *Private Nurse* (1941), *Right to the Heart* (1942), *Whispering Ghosts* (1942), *Little Tokyo, U.S.A.* (19442), *Strange Confession* (1945), *The Enchanted Forest* (1945), *Little Giant* (1946), *Danger Woman* (1946), and *Stepchild* (1947). Her films as Jane with Weissmuller include *Tarzan and the Amazons* (1945), *Tarzan and the Leopard Woman* (1946), *Tarzan and the Huntress* (1947), *Tarzan and the Mermaids* (1948), and *Tarzan's Magic Fountain* (1949).

Millard Kaufman (March 12, 1917–March 14, 2009). Baltimore native Millard Kaufman will be most remembered for two Oscar®-nominated scripts—*Take the High Ground!* (1953) and *Bad Day at Black Rock* (1955)—and for being credited with co-creating the character of Mr. Magoo in the short film *Ragtime Bear* (1949). Other screenwriting credits include *Unknown World* (1951), *Raintree County* (1957), *Never So Few* (1959), *Convicts 4* (1962), *The War Lord* (1965), *Living Free* (1972), and *The Klansman* (1974). Kaufman also fronted for blacklisted writer Dalton Trumbo on *Gun Crazy* (1950).

Troy Kennedy-Martin (February 15, 1932–September 15, 2009). Scottish film and television screenwriter Troy Kennedy-Martin will be most remembered for the influential BBC TV mini-series *Edge of Darkness* (1985) along with the screenplay for *The Italian Job* (1969). His career began writing for television in 1958 and created the popular series *Z-Cars* (1962-1978). He wrote the films *Kelly's Heroes* (1970), *The Jerusalem File* (1972), *Red Heat* (1988), and *Red Dust* (2004).

Shih Kien (January 1, 1913–June 3, 2009). Veteran Chinese actor Shih Kien, also credited as Shek Kin and Kien Shih, was a legendary villain in many Cantonese black and white Wuxia films but will be most remembered as Han in Bruce Lee's *Enter the Dragon* (1973). According to some reports, Kien appeared in more than 300 films before he retired in 1993 at the age of eighty. Kien was so well known for his villainous roles in his home country that his name became synonymous with bad behavior.

Allan King (February 6, 1930–June 15, 2009). Vancouver-born documentary film director Allan King was an influential filmmaker who attempted to shoot his subjects with as little interaction and influence as possible. King also directed episodic television and feature films, but was primarily a documentary filmmaker, working in the industry for fifty years from his debut film *Skid Row* (1956) to his final credit, *EMPz 4 Life* (2006). Notable works throughout his career include *Warrendale* (1967), *A Married Couple* (1969), *Silence of the North* (1981), *Termini Station* (1989), and *Dying at Grace* (2003). *Warrendale* won the Canadian Film Award for Best Feature Film of 1967.

Arnold Laven (February 3, 1922–September 13, 2009). With dozens of film and television credits as producer and director, Arnold Laven was a major part of the entertainment industry in the 1970s and 1980s. Born in Chicago, Illinois, Laven moved to Los Angeles with his family in the 1930s and got his start after getting a job as a mail room messenger at Warner Bros. After working with the U.S. Army's First Motion Picture Unit during World War II, Laven formed a third of the influential production company Levy-Gardner-Laven, which produced his first directorial effort, *Without Warning!* (1952). He went on to direct the films *Vice Squad* (1953), *Down Three Dark Streets* (1954), *Geronimo* (1962), and more. He ended his career as a major television director, helming episodes of *Gunsmoke* (1973), *Mannix* (1972-1973), *Ironside* (1972-1974), *Planet of the Apes* (1974), *Police Woman* (1974-1977), *The Six Million Dollar Man* (1975-1978), *The Rockford Files* (1978), *Fantasy Island* (1978-1979), *Eight is Enough* (1978-1979), *CHiPs* (1981), *Hill Street Blues* (1981-1982), *The Greatest American Hero* (1981-1983), and *The A-Team* (1983-1985).

Karl Malden (March 22, 1912–July 1, 2009). Born Mladen George Sekulovich in Chicago, Illinois, Karl Malden appeared in dozens of classic films during his seven decades in Hollywood. Sekulovich was born to a Czech seamstress and Serbian father and changed his name to Karl Malden in 1934, when he started to get serious about the theater career he had begun in high school. Malden first appeared on Broadway in 1937 but his acting career was interrupted by a stint in the Air Force during World War II. When he returned, he hooked up with Marlon Brando and Elia Kazan and won an Oscar® for Best Supporting Actor in *A Streetcar Named Desire* (1951). Other notable roles in the 1950s included roles in Alfred Hitchcock's *I Confess* (1953), *On the Waterfront* (1954), for which he was Oscar®-nominated, and *Baby Doll* (1956). Popular films throughout the rest of his career include *Birdman of Alcatraz* (1962), *How the West Was Won* (1962), *Gypsy* (1962), *The Cincinnati Kid* (1965), *Patton* (1970), and *Nuts* (1987).

Jack Manning (June 3, 1916–August 31, 2009). Born Jack Wilson Marks in Cincinnati, Ohio, Marks changed his name to Manning when he became serious about his acting

career. He began working on radio dramas in the 1940s and soon made his Broadway debut, appearing in over a dozen Broadway plays during his career, appearing with stars like Helen Hayes, Paul Robeson, Jose Ferrer, and Uta Hagen. The character actor moved to television and film later in his life, playing a lawyer in *Where's Poppa?* (1970), Mr. Weyderhaus in *The Owl and the Pussycat* (1970), a director in *The Great Waldo Pepper* (1975), and a photographer in *Frances* (1982). He was an acting teacher and director later in life.

Joe Maross (February 7, 1923–November 7, 2009). After serving in the Marines and graduating with a degree in theater arts from Yale, Joe Maross started his lengthy career in live television in the 1950s. He appeared in dozens of television shows and made several film appearances including *Run Silent Run Deep* (1958), *Elmer Gantry* (1960), *Zigzag* (1970), *Sometimes a Great Notion* (1970), *The Salzburg Connection* (1972), *Sixth and Main* (1977), and *Rich and Famous* (1981). Maross was a voting member of the Academy of Motion Picture Arts and Sciences.

Jean Martin (March 6, 1922–February 2, 2009). French stage and film actor Jean Martin will be most remembered in the world of theater, where he originated crucial roles in Samuel Beckett's *Waiting for Godot* and *Endgame*. In the 1960s and 1970s, Martin became popular with dozens of film and television roles including memorable turns in *The Battle of Algiers* (1966), *My Name is Nobody* (1973), and *Day of the Jackal* (1973). Martin faced trouble in 1960 when he was one of the signatories of the Manifesto of the 121, an act that demanded the government recognize the Algerian war as a struggle for independence, required the end of torture, and asked for respect for conscientious objectors. Martin's theater contract was revoked and he was banned from acting in radio and television. It was *The Battle of Algiers* that brought his career back to life. He worked in films by Jacques Rivette, Alain Resnais, Alain Robbe-Grillet, and Roberto Rossellini, for who he appeared in the director's final film, *The Messiah* (1975).

Al Martino (October 7, 1927–October 13, 2009). Born Alfred Cini in Philadelphia, Pennsylvania to Italian immigrants, Cini aspired to be a singer and began his career after serving in World War II as a U.S. Marine. The success of family friend Mario Lanza encouraged Cini to change his name to Al Martino and the singer found fame first with independent label BBS and later with Capitol Records. After several chart successes (including "Here In My Heart" and "I Love You Because"), Martino famously played the role of Johnny Fontane in *The Godfather* (1972). He also sang the film's theme "Speak Softly Love" and played the same role in *The Godfather, Part III* (1990).

Bob May (September 4, 1939–January 18, 2009). An American actor best known for playing the iconic robot on *Lost in Space* from 1965 to 1968, Bob May was born in New York City. The actor grandson of vaudeville comedian Chic Johnson, May first appeared in a comedy revue when he was only two years old. May worked on-screen in television and film but will be most remembered for thankless roles like the robot in *Lost in Space* and stunt work in films including *The Nutty Professor* (1963) and the remake of *Stagecoach* (1966).

Patrick McGoohan (March 19, 1928–January 13, 2009). Film and television star Patrick Joseph McGoohan will be most remembered for starring in the beloved series *Danger Man* (1964-1967) and *The Prisoner* (1967-1968) but he also had an extensive film career, working with David Cronenberg on *Scanners* and appearing in the Best Picture-winning *Braveheart* (1995). McGoohan was born in Astoria, Queens, New York City but his family moved back to Ireland shortly after he was born and Patrick moved again to England when he was still a child. After regular stage and television work, McGoogan appeared in films including *Hell Drivers* (1957), *Journey Into Darkness* (1968), *Ice Station Zebra* (1968), *Mary, Queen of Scots* (1971), *Silver Streak* (1976), *Escape From Alcatraz* (1979), *The Phantom* (1996), *A Time to Kill* (1996), and *Treasure Planet* (2002).

Ed McMahon (March 6, 1923–June 23, 2009). Detroit-born superstar Ed McMahon will be best remembered as the sidekick of Johnny Carson on *The Tonight Show* from 1962 to 1992 or for his roles as host of *Star Search* for twenty years or spokesman for Publisher's Clearing House, but he also had a small career on film with notable roles early in his career. Credits include *The Incident* (1967), *Fun With Dick and Jane* (1977), *The Last Remake of Beau Geste* (1977), *Full Moon High* (1981), *For Which He Stands* (1996), and *The Vegas Connection* (1999).

Daniel Melnick (April 21, 1932–October 13, 2009). Producer and former MGM chief Daniel Melnick oversaw several major films and TV series in his time behind the camera. Melnick is first credited with producing *Mr. Broadway* (1964) but his most notable credit would come with Sam Peckinpah's wildly influential *Straw Dogs* (1971). He would go on to produce or executive produce *That's Entertainment* (1974), *All That Jazz (1979), Altered States* (1980), *Unfaithfully Yours* (1984), *Footloose* (1984), *Quicksilver* (1986), *Roxanne* (1987), *Punchline* (1988), *Mountains of the Moon* (1990), *Air America* (1990), and *L.A. Story* (1991).

Marvin Minoff (June 26, 1931–November 11, 2009). American film and television producer Marvin Minoff will be most remembered for producing the infamous television interviews between journalist David Frost and former President Richard Nixon in 1977 that were turned into the Oscar®-nominated film *Frost/Nixon* (2008). Minoff began his career as an agent at the William Morris Agency and helped put together the casts for *Love Story* (1970) and *The French Connection* (1971). Minoff spent most of his career producing telefilms but he did produce two notable feature films—*Dominick and Eugene* (1988) and the Robin Williams vehicle *Patch Adams* (1998).

Vic Mizzy (January 9, 1916–October 17, 2009). American composer of themes for television and film, Vic Mizzy will be most remembered for the legendary tunes that accompanied the credits to *Green Acres* (1965-1971) and *The Addams Family* (1964-1966). Mizzy wrote numerous radio hits in the 1930s and 1940s before moving into film and television, penning Doris Day's "My Dreams Are Getting Better All the Time." Mizzy wrote the scores for five Don Knotts films including *The Ghost and Mr. Chicken* (1966) and *The Reluctant Astronaut* (1967). Other credits include *The Spirit is Willing* (1967), *The Perils of Pauline* (1967), *The Shakiest Gun in the West* (1968), *Did You Hear the One About the Traveling Saleslady?* (1968), and *The Love God?* (1969).

Zakes Mokae (August 5, 1934–September 11, 2009). Zakes Makgona Mokae was born in Johannesburg, South Africa but moved to Great Britain in 1961 and to the United States in 1969, where he became a notable character actor in stage, film and television, winning a Tony award in 1982. Mokae made his film debut in *Dilemma* (1962) and went on to appear in *The Comedians* (1967), *Fragment of Fear* (1970), *The Island* (1980), *Cry Freedom* (1987), *The Serpent and the Rainbow* (1988), *A Dry White Season* (1989), *Gross Anatomy* (1989), *A Rage in Harlem* (1991), *Vampire in Brooklyn* (1995), *Outbreak* (1995), and *Waterworld* (1995).

Ricardo Montalban (November 25, 1920–January 14, 2009). Mexican-born actor Montalban worked in film from the 1940s through the 2000s but would become most popular for playing the influential character of Mr. Roarke on the beloved TV series *Fantasy Island* (1978-1984). To a generation of Trekkies, he will always be remembered as the title character in *Star Trek II: The Wrath of Khan* (1982). He was born in Mexico City in 1920 and moved to Hollywood as a teenager, getting his big break by being cast in a small role in a play with Tallulah Bankhead in 1941. He appeared in several Spanish-language films in Mexico before making his English-language debut in *Fiesta* (1947). He worked with legend like Lana Turner, Esther Williams, and Clark Gable under the MGM banner for years. Montalban started to become a TV fixture in the 1960s and played the legendary Khan during the first season of *Star Trek* (1967), a role he reprised fifteen years later in the second feature film based on the show. Late-in-life roles included memorable turns in *The Naked Gun: From the Files of Police Squad!* (1988), *Spy Kids 2: Island of Lost Dreams* (2002), and *Spy Kids 3-D: Game Over* (2003).

Anna Karen Morrow (September 20, 1914–July 1, 2009). An American model turned film and television actress, Anna Karen Morrow is most noted for a regular role on the legendary soap opera *Peyton Place* (1965-1966) but also appeared in many other television series and films including *The Wrong Man* (1956), *Gunsmoke* (1966), *Star Trek* (1969), and *Marcus Welby, M.D.* (1972-1975). She married actor Jeff Morrow (*The Robe*) in 1947 and the two had a daughter named Lissa Morrow Christian.

Brittany Murphy (November 10, 1977–December 20, 2009). Brittany Anne Murphy was born in Atlanta, Georgia and quickly rose to fame as a young star before passing away from an as-yet-undetermined cause of death at the age of only thirty-two. Murphy scored her first credit on television with *Murphy Brown* (1991) when she was only fourteen years old, appearing in several series (including *Drexell's Class* , *Parker Lewis Can't Lose* , *Frasier* , *Party of Five* , and *Sister, Sister*) before breaking through as Alicia Silverstone's co-star in the hit film *Clueless* (1995). Subsequent film credits include *Freeway* (1996), *Drop Dead Gorgeous* (1999), *Girl, Interrupted* (1999), *Summer Catch* (2001), *Don't Say a Word* (2001), *Riding in Cars with Boys* (2001), *8 Mile* (2002), *Just Married* (2003), *Uptown Girls* (2003), *Little Black Book* (2004), *Sin City* (2005), *The Dead Girl* (2006), and *Happy Feet* (2006). Murphy also voiced Lu-anne Platter for 231 episodes of FOX's hit *King of the Hill* (1997-2009). When she passed away, Murphy had two more film roles to be released—*Something Wicked* (2010) and *Abandoned* (2010).

Peter Newbrook (June 29, 1920–June 19, 2009). British cinematographer, director, producer, and writer Peter Newbrook will be most remembered for second unit photography on *Lawrence of Arabia* (1962). Newbrook was camera operator on *Summertime* (1955), *The Bridge on the River Kwai* (1957), and *Follow That Man* (1961), along with being the President of the British Society of Cinematographers from 1984 to 1986. Newbrook directed *The Asphyx* (1973), wrote *She'll Follow You Anywhere* (1971), and shot and produced *Crucible of Terror* (1971)

Dan O'Bannon (September 30, 196–December 17, 2009). Born in St. Louis, Missouri, Dan O'Bannon would go on to become one of the most important and influential writers in the history science fiction and horror films. If he had only penned *Alien* (1979), he would have an important place in said history, but he was a part of over a dozen other important projects, working with directors like John Carpenter, John Badham, Tobe Hooper, and Paul Verhoeven. His first credit was with Carpenter on that director's breakthrough *Dark Star* (1974). He went on to write *Dead & Buried* (1981), a segment in *Heavy Metal* (1981), *Blue Thunder* (1983), *The Return of the Living Dead* (1985), which he also directed, *Lifeforce* (1985), *Invaders From Mars* (1986), *Total Recall* (1990), and *Screamers* (1995). O'Bannon also directed *The Resurrected* (1992) and worked in the miniature and optical effects unit for *Star Wars* (1977).

Collin Wilcox Paxton (February 4, 1935–October 14, 2009). Born in Cincinnati in 1935, Paxton is most remembered for the role of Mayella Violet Ewell in *To Kill a Mockingbird* (1962), but the actress has dozens of other film and television credits ranging four decades in the business. The first credit for Paxton (also credited as Colin Wilcox, Collin Wilcox, and Collin Wilcox-Horne over the course of her career) was in *Twice Upon a Time* (1953). She went on to appear on influential television programs including *Alfred Hitchcock Presents* (1959), *The Untouchables* (1962), *The Twilight Zone* (1964), *The Alfred Hitchcock Hour* (1964-1965), *The Fugitive* (1965-1966), *Ironside* (1972), *Gunsmoke* (1972), *Columbo* (1974), and *Little House on the Prairie* (1977). Notable film credits include *Catch-22* (1970), *The Baby Maker* (1970), *Jump* (1971), *Jaws 2* (1978), *Marie* (1985), and *Midnight in the Garden of Good and Evil* (1997).

Tullio Pinelli (June 24, 1908–March 7, 2009). Italian screenwriter Tullio Pinelli will be most remembered for the work he did with Federico Fellini on several of his classic films, including *I Vitelloni* (1953), *La strada* (1954), *Nights of Cabiria* (1957), *La Dolce Vita* (1960), and *8½* (1963), four of which earned him Oscar® nominations. He never won. Pinelli was born in Turin, Italy and spent the early part of his career as a lawyer while he dabbled as a playwright before meeting Fellini in 1947. Notable works throughout his career include the aforementioned Fellini films along with *Four Ways Out* (1951), *Alfredo, Alfredo* (1972), *Amici miei* (1975), *Il Marchese del Grillo* (1981), *Ginger & Fred* (1986), and Fellini's last film, *La voce della luna* (1990).

Harve Presnell (September 14, 1933–June 30, 2009). Born George Harvey Presnell, gruff character actor Harve Presnell starred in films from the 1960s through the 2000s but arguably found his most cinematic fame late in life after being memorably cast in the Best Picture-nominated *Fargo* (1995) from the Coen brothers. Presnell actually began his career in show business as a singer, performing with orchestras and operas before landing his first Broadway role in 1960. He would reprise the role and win a Golden Globe for the film *The Unsinkable Molly Brown* (1964). He would go on to appear in *Paint Your Wagon* (1969), but was largely unheard from until the mid-1990s when his career was resurrected in *Fargo*. Notable film appearances after that include *The Chamber* (1996), *Face/Off* (1997), *Saving Private Ryan* (1998), *Patch Adams* (1998), *The Legend of Bagger Vance* (2000), *The Family Man* (2000), *Mr. Deeds* (2002), *Old School* (2003), *Flags of Our Fathers* (2006), and *Evan Almighty* (2007).

John Quade (April 1, 1938–August 9, 2009). Born John William Saunders in Kansas City, Kansas, John Quade will be most remembered for playing Cholla, the leader of the motorcycle gang "The Black Widows," with Clint Eastwood in *Every Which Way But Loose* (1978) and *Any Which Way You Can* (1980). Quade made many guest appearances on television and also appeared in the films *High Plains Drifter* (1973), *Papillon* (1973), *The Sting* (1973), *The Outlaw Josey Wales* (1976), and *La Bamba* (1987). He also will be remembered for playing the Sheriff in the beloved mini-series *Roots* (1977).

Alaina Reed-Hall (November 10, 1946–December 17, 2009). Best known for the long-running role of Olivia on *Sesame Street* (1976-1988) and for playing a major role on *227* (1985-1990), Alaina Reed-Hall also had a stage and film career. Hall began her career on-stage as an original cast member of *Sgt. Pepper's Lonely Hearts Club Band on the Road* and productions of *Hair* and *Chicago*. Reed-Hall made her debut as Olivia, Gordon's younger sister, on *Sesame Street* in 1976 and appeared in the first *Sesame Street* film *Follow That Bird* (1985). She went on to other television appearances and several films including *Death Becomes Her* (1992), *Cruel Intentions* (1999), and *I'm Through with White Girls (The Inevitable Undoing of Jay Brooks) (2007)*.

Natasha Richardson (May 11, 1963–March 18, 2009). Natasha Jane Richardson was a part of Hollywood royalty, standing out in a family of actors and actresses that included mother Vanessa Redgrave, father Tony Richardson, grandparents Michael Redgrave and Rachel Kempson, sister of Joely Richardson, niece of actress Lynn Redgrave and actor Corin Redgrave, cousin of Jemma Redgrave, and wife to Liam Neeson. The death of the Tony Award-winning star from a tragic and unusual accident while she was still in the prime of her career was one of the most shocking of the year. Richardson's stage career began in England in the 1980s and she continued to actively work on the stage through the 2000s. Notable film roles include Mary Shelly in *Gothic* (1986), the title character in *Patty Hearst* (1988), the lead in *The Handmaid's Tale* (1990), Mary in *The Comfort of Strangers* (1990), Paula Olsen in *Nell* (1994), Elizabeth James in *The Parent Trap* (1998), Caroline Lane in *Maid in Manhattan* (2002), Countess

Sofia Belinskya in *The White Countess* (2005), and Constance Haverford in *Evening* (2007). Richardson passed away after injuries suffered from a fall during a ski trip.

Clint Richie (August 9, 1938–January 31, 2009). Ritchie was born in Grafton, North Dakota to J.C. and Charlotte Richie and moved to Washington when he was seven. The actor is best remembered for the role of Clint Buchanan on successful soap opera *One Life to Live,* playing the role from 1979 to 2004. Richie appeared on several major television shows along with many film roles including *The St. Valentine's Day Massacre* (1967), *Bandolero!* (1968), *Patton* (1970), *Joe Kidd* (1972), *Against a Crooked Sky* (1975), *Midway* (1976), and *A Force of One* (1979). He is reportedly credited with teaching Tom Selleck how to ride a horse.

Darrell Sandeen (July 13, 1930–January 26, 2009). Square-jawed character actor, Sandeen will best be remembered as cop Leland "Buzz" Meeks in the Academy Award®-winning *L.A. Confidential* (1997). After getting his start on Broadway, Sandeen eventually moves to Hollywood and appeared in television and films including *Bonanza* (1971), *Blazing Saddles* (1974), *They Call Me Bruce?* (1982), *Jumper* (2002), *Interview with the Assassin* (2002), *Pervert!* (2005), and HBO's *Big Love* (2007).

Budd Schulberg (March 17, 1914–August 5, 2009). Screenwriter Seymour Wilson Schulberg was born to B.P. Schulberg, the head of Paramount Pictures, and talent agent Adeline Jaffe Schulberg in New York City in 1914. Schulberg broke through with a collaboration on the screenplay for *Winter Carnival* (1939) with F. Scott Fitzgerald (an experience thinly fictionalized in the hit novel *The Disenchanted* in 1950), although, according to some reports, Schulberg was an uncredited contributing writer two years earlier on *A Star is Born* (1937). Writing credits include *Little Orphan Annie* (1938), *The Nazi Plan* (1945), *Nuremberg* (1946), and *Wind Across the Everglades* (1958), but Schulberg will most be remembered for his screenplay for the Marlon Brando and Elia Kazan classic *On the Waterfront* (1954), a work that won Schulberg the Academy Award® for Best Writing, Story and Screenplay.

Charles H. Schneer (May 5, 1920–January 21, 2009). A film producer most widely recognized for his influential work with special effects pioneer Ray Harryhausen, Charles H. Schneer was born in Norfolk, Virginia in 1920. Schneer studies at Columbia University and went to serve with the U.S. Army's Signal Corps Photographic Unit, joining Columbia Pictures after the war and being introduced to Harryhausen through a mutual friend. The two started with the wildly influential *It Came From Beneath the Sea* (1955). Schneer would go on to produce *20 Million Miles to Earth* (1957), *Hellcats of the Navy* (1957), *The 7th Voyage of Sinbad* (1958), *Mysterious Island* (1961), *Jason and the Argonauts* (1963), *First Men in the Moon* (1964), *The Golden Voyage of Sinbad* (1974), *Sinbad and the Eye of the Tiger* (1977), and *Clash of the Titans* (1981).

Ron Silver (July 2, 1946–March 15, 2009). Ronald Arthur Silver was born in New York City in 1946 and went on to become an accomplished actor, director, producer, radio personality, and political voice. After a few television appearances, Silver made his film debut in *Tunnel Vision*

(1976). Notable roles throughout the rest of his career included parts in *The Entity* (1981), *Best Friends* (1982), *Silkwood* (1983), *Romancing the Stone* (1984), *Blue Steel* (1989), *Enemies: A Love Story* (1989), *Reversal of Fortune* (1990), *Mr. Saturday Night* (1992), *Timecop* (1994), *Girl 6* (1996), *The Arrival* (1996), *Black and White* (1999), *Ali* (2001), *Find Me Guilty* (2006), and *The Ten* (2007), along with regular appearances on the hit show *The West Wing* from 2001 to 2006. Silver also made a name for himself on stage, working regularly with David Mamet, and caused a splash when his politics shifted dramatically from Democratic activist to a Republican one after the attacks of September 11th.

Arnold Stang (September 28, 1918–December 20, 2009). New York-born comic actor Arnold Stang got his start in radio children's programs before going on to film, television, and regular voice work for animation. Stang, who ended his career with over a hundred credits to his name, made his debut in a small role in *My Sister Eileen* (1942) before going on to dozens of voice credits in the 1940s and 1950s, most notably taking on the iconic role of Top Cat in the famous Hanna-Barbera cartoons. Stang appeared in numerous live-action films including *The Man With the Golden Arm* (1955), *It's a Mad Mad Mad Mad World* (1963), *Skidoo* (1968), *Hercules in New York* (1970), *Ghost Dad* (1990), and *Dennis the Menace* (1993).

Ray Dennis Steckler (January 25, 1938–January 7, 2009). Also known as Cash Flagg (and a half-dozen other pseudonyms), Ray Dennis Steckler made several names for himself as a screenwriter and actor in the world of low-budget cult films often played at drive-ins. His directorial debut was with *Wild Guitar* (1962) and other notable titles throughout his career as a director included *The Incredibly Strange Creatures Who Stopped Living and Became Mixed-Up Zombies!!?* (1964), *The Thrill Killers* (1964), *Rat Pfink a Boo Boo* (1966), *Sinthia, the Devil's Doll* (1970), *The Mad Love Life of a Hot Vampire* (1971), *Blood Shack* (1971), *Sexorcist Devil* (1974), *Perverted Passion* (1974), *Sex Rink* (1976), *The Hollywood Strangler Meets the Skid Row Slasher* (1979), *Debbie Does Las Vegas* (1981), and *Las Vegas Serial Killer* (1986).

Patrick Swayze (August 18, 1952–September 14, 2009). After a hard fight with cancer, action and drama star Patrick Swayze passed away at the far-too-young age of fifty-seven. Once voted "Sexiest Man Alive" by *People Magazine*, Swayze was most popular as a romantic leading man in the late 1980s and early 1990s. Swayze was born in Texas but moved to New York City in 1972 to finish his dance and ballet training. After graduation, he worked for Disney on Parade, making his film debut in *Skatetown, U.S.A.* (1979). He started to build a name and reputation with memorable performances in *The Outsiders* (1983), *Red Dawn* (1984), and the award-winning TV mini-series *North and South* (1985) and *North and South, Book II* (1986), before his breakthrough role in the mega-hit *Dirty Dancing* (1987). A string of major films would follow with *Road House* (1989), *Next of Kin* (1989), the Oscar®-winning *Ghost* (1990), *Point Break* (1991), *City of Joy* (1992), *Father Hood* (1993), and *To Wong Foo Thanks For Everything Julie Newmar* (1995). Swayze started taking smaller roles in the late 1990s and 2000s but still made an impact in films like *Donnie*

Darko (2001), *Waking Up in Reno* (2002), and *Powder Blue* (2009), before mounting a true comeback with his critically acclaimed work on A&E's cop show *The Beast* (2009). Filmed while he was undergoing treatment for cancer, *The Beast* will stand as Patrick Swayze's final work.

Clarence Swensen (December 29, 1917–February 25, 2009). One of the last surviving Munchkins from the timeless family film *The Wizard of Oz* (1939), Swensen was born in 1917 in Austin, Texas. Swensen was one of the twenty-five Munchkin soldiers who appeared alongside Judy Garland in the beloved classic. He is listed to have only one other film credit, an uncredited role in *The Terror of Tiny Town* (1938).

Harry Alan Towers (October 19, 1920–July 31, 2009). Born in London, England, Harry Alan Towers (who regularly used the pseudonym Peter Welbeck) would go on to produce over a hundred feature films along with amassing many screenwriting credits throughout a very long career. Towers was born into theater, as his father was a theatrical agent. He became a radio writer during World War II and worked in syndicated radio shows after the war including programs starring Orson Welles, Clive Brook, Michael Redgrave, John Gielgud, and Ralph Richardson. He moved into television in the 1950s and began writing and producing feature films in the 1960s. His first writing and producing credit was on *The Anatomist* (1962) but he would become better known for projects arguably of a lascivious nature like *Black Venus* (1983) and a string of other notable B-movies, including a number of Fu Manchu films in the 1960s and straight-to-video work in the 1980s and 1990s. He became associated with Cannon Films in the 1980s, producing a version of *Phantom of the Opera* (1989) starring Robert Englund and also notably produced three separate versions of Agatha Christie's *And Then There Were None* during his career. He was reportedly working on a script for *Moll Flanders* with director Ken Russell when he passed.

Mimi Weddell (February 15, 1915–September 24, 2009). Marion Rogers Weddell will be most remembered by modern audiences for playing Stanford's grandmother on *Sex and the City* (1998) and for being the subject of a documentary about her hats called *Hats Off* (2008). Interestingly, she did not even start her acting career until she was in her sixties with credits that include *Student Bodies* (1981), *The Purple Rose of Cairo* (1985), *The Thomas Crown Affair* (1999), and *Hitch* (2005).

Paul Wendkos (September 20, 1922–November 12, 2009). American television and film director, Paul Wendkos was born in Philadelphia, Pennsylvania and went on to a varied career featuring multiple genres but may be most remembered for directing several "Gidget" films. His first directorial credit came with Jayne Mansfield in *The Burglar* (1957) but he broke through with *Gidget* (1959). Later notable credits include *Because They're Young* (1960), *Gidget Goes Hawaiian* (1961), *Gidget Goes to Rome* (1963), *Guns of Magnificent Seven* (1969), and *The Mephisto Waltz* (1971), along with dozens of episodes of television. He ended his career filming made-for-television movies from the 1970s through to his retirement in 1999.

James Whitmore (October 1, 1921–February 6, 2009). Born James Allen Whitmore, Jr. in White Plains, New York,

Whitmore would go on to study at Yale and serve in World War II before beginning a long career in stage and film. Modern audiences will likely remember him most fondly as Brooks Hatlen in the beloved *The Shawshank Redemption* (1994) but he has a career that stretched back fifty years to his debut in *The Undercover Man* (1949) with Glenn Ford. With just his next film, *Battleground* (1949), Whitmore would land an Oscar® nomination for Best Supporting Actor and he would make an impact a year later in the very popular *The Asphalt Jungle* (1950). Notable credits over the next few decades included roles in *Kiss Me Kate* (1953), *Them!* (1954), *Oklahoma!* (1955), *Planet of the Apes* (1968), *Guns of the Magnificent Seven* (1969), *Tora! Tora! Tora!* (1970), and *Where the Red Fern Grows* (1974), before landing another Oscar® nomination for playing Harry S. Truman in *Give 'em Hell, Harry!* (1975). Just a few years later, Whitmore played a legendary U.S. President again in *Bully: An Adventure with Teddy Roosevelt* (1978). More recent credits includes roles in *The Relic* (1997) and *The Majestic* (2001). Whitmore also appeared in guest roles on dozens of television programs during his illustrious career.

Joseph Wiseman (May 15, 1918–October 19, 2009). Canadian actor Joseph Wiseman will be most remembered for playing the title character opposite Sean Connery in the James Bond film *Dr. No* (1962). Wiseman made his debut with Arlene Francis in *With These Hands* (1950) and went on to star in *Viva Zapata!* (1952), *Les miserables* (1952), *Three Brave Men* (1956), *The Unforgiven* (1960), *Bye Bye Braverman* (1968), *The Night They Raided Minsky's* (1968), and *The Valachi Papers* (1972). Wiseman also appeared on dozens of television programs, including playing Manny Weisbord on *Crime Story* (1986-1988).

Robin Wood (February 23, 1931–December 18, 2009). Robert Paul Wood was a Canadian-based film critic and professor who will be remembered as one of the most influential writers about the art of the movies. He wrote several books on stars and filmmakers as diverse as Arthur Penn, Alfred Hitchcock, Ingmar Bergman, and Arthur Penn during his career. Wood was born in London, England and taught there in the 1950s and 1960s. After being tapped to write for the journal *Movie* after they read an essay he wrote on *Psycho* (1960) for the legendary *Cahiers du Cinema*, Wood began a career as a film critic. He wrote his first book, *Hitchcock's Films* in 1965. Over the years, he taught at Queen's University in Kingston, University of Warwick, and York University. Film books published during Wood's career included *Ingmar Bergman, Arthur Penn, The Apu Trilogy, The American Nightmare: Essays on the Horror Film, Hollywood from Vietnam to Reagan, Sexual Politics and Narrative Film: Hollywood and Beyond, The Wings of the Dove: Henry James in the 1990s,* and *Rio Bravo,* named after the film that he reportedly called the best ever made on his death bed.

Edward Woodward (June 1, 1930–November 16, 2009). Edward Albert Arthur Woodward may be most remembered for his television work but he also appeared in several influential film roles including Police Sergeant Neil Howie in *The Wicker Man* (1973) and the title role in *Breaker Morant* (1980). Like a lot of actors of his generation, Woodward began his career in theater following World War II. He started in England and moved to New York, where he won three Tony Awards for his Broadway work. Woodward was so popular on stage that Laurence Olivier invited him to choose his own role at the Royal National Theatre in 1971 and the actor starred in *Cyrano de Bergerac*. He had only a few film roles but they were memorable ones including *The Wicker Man, Breaker Morant,* and *Hot Fuzz* (2007). He will likely be most remembered by modern audiences for his Golden Globe-winning lead role on the hit show *The Equalizer* (1985-1989).

Howard Zieff (October 21, 1927–February 22, 2009). American director Howard Zieff made an impact in the 1950s and 1960s as one of the most in-demand commercial photographers, spearheading inclufential campaigns for Alka Seltzer, Polaroid, and Volkswagen. Zieff's directorial debut came with James Caan in *Slither* (1973). Other films directed by Howard Zieff include *Hearts of the West* (1975), *House Calls* (1978), *The Main Event* (1979), *Private Benjamin* (1980), *Unfaithfully Yours* (1984), *The Dream Team* (1989), *My Girl* (1991), and *My Girl 2* (1994).

Selected Film Books of 2007

Amidi, Amid and John Lasseter. *The Art of Pixar Short Films.* Chronicle Books, 2009. An examination of the memorable vignettes created by Pixar including *Andre and Wally B, Tin Toy,* and *Mike's New Car.*

Anderson, Wes. *The Making of "Fantastic Mr. Fox": A Film by Wes Anderson Based on the Book by Roald Dahl.* Rizzoli, 2009. A companion piece to the film based on the book by Roald Dahl and featuring voice work by George Clooney, Meryl Streep, Jason Schwartzman, and Bill Murray.

Beaumont, Douglas M. *The Message Behind the Movie: How to Engage With a Film Without Disengaging Your Faith.* Moody Publishers, 2009. A teacher of Bible and Philosophy at Southern Evangelical Bible College advises people of faith how to interpret films, identify key ideas and plotlines, and not lose sight of their faith.

Bernardi, Daniel. *Filming Difference: Actors, Directors, Producers and Writers on Gender, Race and Sexuality in Film.* University of Texas Press, 2009. Creative voices discuss issues of difference in film, examining divides of gender, race, and sexuality through the critical eyes of the media makers themselves.

Bertellini, Giorgio. *Italy in Early American Cinema: Race, Landscape, and the Picturesque.* Indiana University Press, 2009. An examination of the origin of American cinema's fascination with Italy and Italian immigrants, tracing it from 19th century American painters to the filmmakers of the 20th century.

Bondanella, Peter. *A History of Italian Cinema.* Continuum, 2009. A comprehensive and up-to-date book on Italian cinema including coverage on films by Roberto Benigni, Bernardo Bertolucci, Franco Zeffirelli, Michael Radford, Gabriele Salvatores, Maurizio Nichetti, Giuseppe Tornatore, and more.

Boyle, Brenda M. *Masculinity in Vietnam War Narratives: A Critical Study of Fiction, Films and Nonfiction Writings.* McFarland, 2009. An examination of the cinematic movements that accompanied the Vietnam War and their impact on discourse all the way through the current wars in Iraq and Afghanistan.

Brizel, Scott. *Audrey Hepburn: International Cover Girl.* Chronicle Books, 2009. A collection of more than 600 international magazine covers featuring the iconic Audrey Hepburn that spans the course of her life and career with images that have not been available since they were first published. Includes biographical text.

Brody, Richard. *Everything Is Cinema: The Working Life of Jean-Luc Godard.* Holt Paperbacks, 2009. An analysis of the life and work of Jean-Luc Godard through hundreds of interviews tracing the arc of the director's early critical writing through his popular success to his later years.

Brook, Vincent. *Driven to Darkness: Jewish Émigré Directors and the Rise of Film Noir.* Rutgers University Press, 2009. An examination of the influence of Jewish Émigré directors including Fritz Lang, Billy Wilder, Otto Preminger, and Edward G. Robinson and how their Jewish culture was reflected in their work.

Buckland, Warren. *Film Theory and Contemporary Hollywood Movies.* Routledge, 2009. Senior Lecturer in Film Studies at Oxford Brookes University applies film theory, a study often used for classic film, on modern works including blockbusters such as *The Lord of the Rings* (2001-2003) and *Saw* (2004).

Buhler, James, David Neumeyer, and Rob Deemer. *Hearing the Movies: Music and Sound in Film History.* Oxford University Press, 2009. An exploration of film that examines music and sound in three parts—an analysis of a soundtrack in relation to the image track; the way music influences film form; a history of film music and sound.

Caron, Leslie. *Thank Heaven: A Memoir.* Viking Adult, 2009. A memoir of the Golden Era of MGM by the star of *An American in Paris* (1951), *Gigi* (1958), *Daddy Long Legs* (1955), and *Father Goose* (1964).

Casty, Alan. *Communism in Hollywood: The Moral Paradoxes of Testimony, Silence, and Betrayal.* The Scarecrow Press, Inc., 2009. An examination of the Hollywood Blacklist; its aftermath, influence and lasting impact on Hollywood.

Chandler, Charlotte *She Always Knew How: Mae West, a Personal Biography.* Simon & Schuster, 2009. A biography of Mae West from an author who interviewed one of the most famous actresses of all time before her death in 1980.

Chandler, Gael. *Film Editing: Great Cuts Every Filmmaker and Movie Lover Must Know.* Michael Wiese Productions, 2009. Employs 600 frames from recent blockbusters as a visual guide to the art of film editing and its importance to the success of a modern movie.

Ciment, Michel. *Film World: The Director's Interviews.* Berg Publishers, 2009. A collection of years of interviews by Ciment, film critic and editor of the French film review *Positif*, including Stanley Kubrick, Elia Kazan, Bernardo Bertolucci, Jane Campion, John Cassavetes, David Cronenberg, Atom Egoyan, Jean-Luc Godard, Peter Greenaway, Werner Herzog, Mike Leigh, Martin Scorsese, Lars von Trier, Andrei Tarkovsky, and John Boorman.

Cornell, Drucilla. *Clint Eastwood and Issues of American Masculinity.* Fordham University Press, 2009. A major feminist philosopher examines the work of an archetypically masculine director in Clint Eastwood and examines them from the perspective of social commentary and ethical philosophy.

Curtis, Tony and Mark A. Vieira. *The Making of "Some Like It Hot": My Memories of Marilyn Monroe and the Classic American Movies.* Wiley, 2009. A personal remembrance of the production of *Some Like It Hot* (1959) co-authored by one of its most notable stars.

Dawson, Nick. *Being Hal Ashby: Life of a Hollywood Rebel.* The University Press of Kentucky, 2009. A biography of influential filmmaker Hal Ashby, director of *Harold and Maude* (1971), *The Last Detail* (1973), *Shampoo* (1975), *Coming Home* (1978), *Being There* (1979), and more.

DeTora, Lisa M. *Heroes of Film, Comics and American Culture: Essays on Real and Fictional Defenders of Home.* McFarland, 2009. The Assistant Professor and Assistant Director in the English Department at Lafayette College covers a diverse array of subjects in terms of the modern hero in 20th and 21st century popular culture including film, comic books, and more.

DK Publishing. *Pixarpedia.* DK Adult, 2009. An encyclopedia of the films, shorts, characters, history, and information of Pixar Studios with thousands of photographs, illustrations, and pieces of behind-the-scenes information covering from *Toy Story* (1995) through *Up* (2009).

Doom, Ryan P. *The Brothers Coen: Unique Characters of Violence.* Praeger, 2009. With a structure that focuses on major characters of their films in each chapter, Doom spans the career of directors Joel and Ethan Coen from *Blood Simple* (1984) to *Burn After Reading* (2008), exploring the theme of violence in their work.

Downing, Lisa, and Libby Saxton. *Cinema and Ethics: Foreclosed Encounters.* Routledge, 2009. An application of ethical theories by Levinas, Derrida, Foucault, and Laca-nian psychoanalysts on modern films including works by Alfred Hitchcock, Ridley Scott, and more. Authored by the Professor of French Discourses of Sexuality at the University of Exeter and Lecturer in French and Film Studies at Queen Mary, University of London.

Eagen, Daniel. *America's Film Legacy: The Authoritative Guide to the Landmark Movies in the National Film Registry.* Continuum Pub Group, 2009. A survey of titles selected by the Library of Congress's National Film Registry chronologically catalogues 500 films from 1893 to 1995, including cast and credit information along with essays about each entry.

Ebert, Roger. *Roger Ebert's Movie Yearbook 2010.* Andrews McMeel Publishing, 2009. A collection of every film review written by Pulitzer Prize-winning film critic of the *Chicago Sun-Times* from January 2007 to July 2009 along with interviews, essays, tributes, and new questions and answers from Ebert's "Questions for the Movie Answer Man" columns.

Edwards, Gwynne. *Lorca, Bunuel, Dali: Forbidden Pleasures and Connected Lives.* I. B. Tauris, 2009. An expert on Spanish cultural history examines three of Spain's most influential creative voices connecting the commonalities and differences in their personal lives and how they impacted their work.

Eliot, Marc. *American Rebel: The Life of Clint Eastwood.* Harmony, 2009. Biographer to the stars Marc Eliot examines the life of filmmaker Clint Eastwood with a look at both his personal and professional successes and failures.

Englund, Robert and Alan Goldsher. *Hollywood Monster: A Walk Down Elm Street with the Man of Your Dreams.* Pocket, 2009. A memoir of the man who played Freddy Krueger, one of the most legendary villains in the history of horror cinema in *A Nightmare on Elm Street* (1984) and its many sequels.

Falsani, Cathleen. *The Dude Abides: The Gospel According to the Coen Brothers.* Zondervan, 2009. Award-winning author and columnist for the *Chicago Sun-Times* Falsani examines existential questions raised by one of Joel and Ethan Coen's most beloved films, *The Big Lebowski* (1998), and also looks at a few of the Academy Award®-winning filmmakers other works.

Farber, Manny and Robert Polito. *Farber on Film: The Complete Film Writings of Manny Farber.* Library of America, 2009. The work of legendary film critic Manny Farber (1917-2008) is collected in one volume from early weekly reviews for *The New Republic* and *The Nation* to later essays on Godard, Scorsese, Altman, and more.

Feder, Chris Welles. *In My Father's Shadow: A Daughter Remembers Orson Welles.* Algonquin Books, 2009. The daughter of Orson Welles and his first wife, Virginia, recounts life with a famous father and both her interactions with him throughout the years and escaping from his shadow later in life while also preserving the legacy of one of the most legendary film directors of all time.

Fisher, James Terence. *On the Irish Waterfront: The Crusader, the Movie, and the Soul of the Port of New York.* Cornell University Press, 2009. A detailed account of the true story that inspired Elia Kazan's *On the Waterfront* (1954) that investigates the Irish control over the New York ports in the 1940s.

Fitzpatrick, Lisa and James Cameron, Peter Jackson, and Jon Landau. *The Art of "Avatar": James Cameron's Epic Adventure* Abrams, 2009. A tie-in for the blockbuster film *Avatar* (2009) with over 100 exclusive full-color images that detail every element of production including not just film stills but early sketches, drawings, set designs, and more; accompanied by interviews with much of the creative team including animators, costume designers, and more.

Ford, Elizabeth A. and Deborah C. Mitchell. *Royal Portraits in Hollywood: Filming the Lives of Queens.* The University Press of Kentucky, 2009. An examination of the cinematic depiction of historical queens from the 1930s to present examining performances by Bette Davis, Judy Dench, Helen Mirren, Elizabeth Taylor, Greta Garbo, and more.

Frangioni, David. *Clint Eastwood Icon: The Essential Film Art Collection.* Insight Editions, 2009. A collection of over 400 pieces of film art that focuses on the iconic work and look of Clint Eastwood from his entire career and an examination of how thoroughly he has defined American cinema for the entire world from his Spaghetti Westerns through his work as Dirty Harry to his more recent, highly acclaimed directorial work.

Frost, Jacqueline B. *Cinematography for Directors: A Guide for Creative Collaboration.* Michael Wiese Productions, 2009. A handbook for aspiring filmmakers that focuses on the relationship between the director and the cinematographer and the importance of their collaboration.

Fumerton, Richard and Diane Jeske. *Introducing Philosophy Through Film: Key Texts, Discussion, and Film Selections.* Wiley-Blackwell, 2009. Pairs philosophical readings with popular films that reflect those readings to introduce readers to key areas of philosophy through works as diverse as *The Matrix* (1999), *Casablanca* (1942), and *A Clockwork Orange* (1971).

Gardner, Martin A. *The Marx Brothers as Social Critics: Satire and Comic Nihilism in Their Films.* McFarland, 2009. New York writer Gardner looks below the slapstick of the Marx Brothers to examine their work as a condemnation of American culture and asks why their films were relevant to both their era and today's society.

Gavin, James. *Stormy Weather: The Life of Lena Horne.* Atria, 2009. A biography of the famous singer and performer that examines her film work along with the segregation and racial attitudes that impacted her entire career.

Geraghty, Lincoln. *American Science Fiction Film and Television.* Berg Publishers, 2009. An examination of recent key works in the genre of science fiction both in film and television and the history that brought them to fruition.

Greven, David. *Gender and Sexuality in "Star Trek": Allegories of Desire in the Television Series and Films.* McFarland, 2009. Examines the *Star Trek* franchise from the original series through the J.J. Abrams 2009 reboot from the perspective of depictions of gender, race and sexuality. Written by an Associate Professor of English at Connecticut College.

Harlan, Jan, Jane M. Struthers, and Chris Baker. *"A.I. Artificial Intelligence": From Stanley Kubrick to Steven Spiel-* berg: The Vision Behind the Film. Thames & Hudson, 2009. Stanley Kubrick's regular Executive Producer, his storyboard/conceptual artist, and the Head of Publications at the University of Arts, London, where the Stanley Kubrick Archive is housed dissect the production of *A.I.: Artificial Intelligence* (2001) with hundreds of illustrations including photographs, stills, and extracts from Kubrick's notebooks.

Hauser, Tim and Pete Docter. *The Art of "Up."* Chronicle Books, 2009. The Best Picture-nominated Pixar film is chronicled with more than 250 examples of concept art that drove the production of *Up*, including storyboards, digital and pencil sketches, character studies, script samples, and full-color pastels. Pete Docter, the film's director, details the process with assistance from artists, animators, and other members of the production team.

Hayward, Philip. *Terror Tracks: Music, Sound and Horror Cinema.* Equinox Publishing, 2009. Australian film and popular music studies professor examines a number of scores from the horror genre and details the role they play in the creation of suspense, tension, and shock.

Herzog, Amy. *Dreams of Difference, Songs of the Same: The Musical Moment in Film.* Univ of Minnesota Press, 2009. Assistant Professor of Media Studies at Queens College examines an international selection of films that use music unexpectedly; in a more linear narrative than the typically fantastical musical genre.

Herzog, Werner. *Conquest of the Useless: Reflections from the Making of "Fitzcarraldo."* Ecco, 2009. Published in Herzog's native country of Germany in 2004 but not translated and published in the U.S. until 2009, the book is essentially a series of diary entries written from 1979 to 1981 during the production of *Fitzcarraldo* (1982).

Hess, Earl J. and Pratibha A. Dabholkar. *"Singin' in the Rain": The Making of an American Masterpiece.* University Press of Kansas, 2009. A detailed look at the production of *Singin' in the Rain* (1952) that uses multiple sources to piece together the history of one of the most beloved films of all time along with mini-biographies of stars Gene Kelly, Donald O'Connor, and Debbie Reynolds.

Hollyn, Norman. *The Lean Forward Moment: Create Compelling Stories for Film, TV, and the Web.* New Riders Press, 2009. Associate Professor at the School of Cinematic Arts at USC Norman Hollyn strives to teach readers how to apply his storytelling techniques to all aspects of filmmaking during all phases of the production process.

Housel, Rebecca, J. Jeremy Wisnewski, and William Irwin. *"Twilight" and Philosophy: Vampires, Vegetarians, and the Pursuit of Immortality.* Wiley, 2009. A companion for the *Twilight* (2008) film series that looks at the popular books and films from a philosophical viewpoint.

Irwin, Kenneth and Lloyd, Charles O. *Ruth Etting: America's Forgotten Sweetheart.* The Scarecrow Press, 2009. A biography of actress Ruth Etting (1896-1978), an American stage, radio, recording, and film star of the 1930s most widely known for her recording of "You Made Me Love You".

Irwin, William, Richard Brown, and Kevin S. Decker. *"Terminator" and Philosophy: I'll Be Back, Therefore I Am.* Wiley, 2009. An application of popular philosophies by writers including Descartes, Kant, and Karl Marx to *The Terminator* (1984) franchise by an assistant professor at LaGuardia Community College, an assistant professor of philosophy at Eastern Washington University, and the professor of philosophy at King's College.

Jonze, Spike, Dave Eggers, and the Editors of Mc-Sweeney's. *Heads On and We Shoot: The Making of "Where the Wild Things Are."* It Books, 2009. Including interviews with director Spike Jonze, writer Dave Eggers, and more members of the production team of *Where the Wild Things Are*, the book details all phases of the creation of the divisive film based on the beloved book by Maurice Sendak.

Jordan, Jessica Hope. *The Sex Goddess in American Film, 1930-1965: Jean Harlow, Mae West, Lana Turner, and Jayne Mansfield.* Cambria Press, 2009. A look at the development of the iconic sex goddess in film through the development of the medium focusing on the four title actresses and how they turned their feminine power into cultural currency.

Juuso, Jeremy.

Getting the Money: A Step-by-Step Guide for Writing Business Plans for Film. Michael Wiese Productions, 2009. With its pretty self-explanatory title, the founder of Jeremy Juuso Consulting, a firm that specializes in film financing, details a step-by-step approach to turning a film idea into actual celluloid.

Kaufman, David. *Doris Day: The Untold Story of the Girl Next Door.* Virgin Books, 2009. This massive (512 pp.) biography exhaustively details one of the biggest box office stars of all time from extensive research, interviews, and anecdotal stories about one of the film history's most enduring sweethearts.

Kaufman, J.B. *South of the Border With Disney: Walt Disney and the Good Neighbor Program, 1941-1948.* Disney Editions, 2009. The diplomatic efforts of Walt Disney have only recently come to light and they are detailed in this piece that explains how films like *Saludos Amigos* (1942) and *The Three Caballeros* (1944) were designed to counter Nazi propaganda and engender goodwill to the United States south of the border.

Keegan, Rebecca. *The Futurist: The Life and Films of James Cameron.* Crown, 2009. Crown, 2009. Timed to release with the theatrical takeover of *Avatar* (2009), Keegan's book examines the life and career of one of the current era's most influential filmmakers.

Kellner, Douglas. *Cinema Wars: Hollywood Film and Politics in the Bush-Cheney Era.* Wiley-Blackwell, 2009. An examination of the truths and perceptions about the battle between conservatives and liberals when it comes to Hollywood and the way modern films impacted the last Presidential regime through support or criticism.

King, Geoff. *Indiewood, USA: Where Hollywood Meets Independent Cinema.* I. B. Tauris, 2009. Professor of Film and TV Studies at Brunel University looks at the gray area between independent cinema and the Hollywood machine walked by auteurs like Quentin Tarantino, Charlie Kaufman, and Steven Soderbergh.

LaMarre, Thomas. *The Anime Machine: A Media Theory of Animation.* University of Minnesota Press, 2009. An edu-

cational analysis of the techniques, visual characteristics and unique storytelling style of anime.

Landau, Diana. *The Art of "A Christmas Carol."* Disney Editions, 2009. A companion piece to Robert Zemeckis' motion-capture telling of the Charles Dickens classic tale with stills and behind-the-scenes details about the making of the film.

LaVaughn, Sandra L. *How I Produced a Movie With Eight Thousand Dollars.* CreateSpace, 2009. A detailed account of the development of the author's first feature film, *The Blue Room* (2006), which she wrote, produced, directed, edited, and even booked in theaters herself.

Leachman, Cloris and George Englund. *Cloris: My Autobiography.* Kensington, 2009. An autobiography of the award-winning actress assisted by husband George Englund that tells the story of a life that led to a record-breaking nine Emmys and an Oscar® for her performance in *The Last Picture Show* (1971).

Levy, Shawn. *Paul Newman: A Life.* Harmony, 2009. A highly acclaimed look at the entire career of the recently deceased iconic star that examines both his career and his personal life as a father and husband.

Livingston, Paisley. *Cinema, Philosophy, Bergman: On Film as Philosophy.* Oxford University Press, 2009. Chair Professor of Philosophy and Dean of Humanities at Lingnan University looks closely at the influential work of director Ingmar Bergman and how it reflected his philosophies.

Lynch, Audry. *The Rebel Figure in American Literature and Film: The Interconnected Lives of John Steinbeck and James Dean.* Edwin Mellen Press, 2009. A study of the backgrounds of John Steinbeck and James Dean and how their commonalities impacted the success of *East of Eden* (1955).

Macnab, Geoffrey. *Ingmar Bergman: The Life and Films of the Last Great European Director.* University of California Press, 2009. A collection of essays by the author and interviews with filmmakers about the impact and influence of Ingmar Bergman.

Mallory, Michael and Stephen Sommers. *Universal Studio Monsters: A Legacy of Horror.* Universe, 2009. A chronicle of the prime of Universal Studios horror output from the 1920s to the 1950s featuring timeless characters such as Dracula, Frankenstein, and the Creature from the Black Lagoon.

Malloy, Tom. *Bankroll: A New Approach to Financing Feature Films.* Michael Wiese Productions, 2009. Another book that advises readers how to get the money they need to produce their first feature film.

Mank, Gregory William. *Bela Lugosi and Boris Karloff: The Expanded Story of a Haunting Collaboration, with a Complete Filmography of Their Films Together.* McFarland, 2009. What happened when Dracula met Frankenstein? Using dozens of interviews and extensive research, Mank's book summarizes not just the eight films in which Lugosi and Karloff co-starred but their entire career, includes hundreds of photographs.

Mann, William J. *How to Be a Movie Star: Elizabeth Taylor in Hollywood.* Mariner Books, 2009. One of our most written-about movie stars is featured in yet another tome about Elizabeth Taylor's luminescent star power and how it influenced the entire movie industry.

Maslon, Laurence. *"Some Like It Hot": The Official 50ᵗʰ Anniversary Companion.* Collins Design, 2009. A companion piece to one of the most beloved comedies of all time featuring unpublished images, posters, and documents from the MGM archive along with copious behind-the-scenes details on the making-of the film.

Matlin, Marlee. *I'll Scream Later.* Simon Spotlight Entertainment, 2009. An autobiography of the Academy Award®-winning star of *Children of a Lesser God* (1986) that candidly details her life as an actress, mother, activist, and role model for the deaf people of the world.

Meyer, Nicholas. *The View From the Bridge: Memories of "Star Trek" and a Life in Hollywood.* Viking Adult, 2009. The author, who directed *Star Trek II: The Wrath of Khan* (1982), wrote *Star Trek IV: The Voyage Home* (1986), and wrote and directed *Star Trek VI: The Undiscovered Country* (1991), three of the most acclaimed films in the franchise, looks back at their production and legacy.

Miller-Zarneke, Tracey and Judi Barrett. *The Art and Making of "Cloudy with a Chance of Meatballs."* Insight Editions, 2009. A companion piece to the Sony Animation film based on the beloved book by Judi and Ron Barret with numerous stills and behind-the-scenes details about its production.

Miyazaki, Hayao, Beth Cary, and Frederick L. Schodt. *Starting Point: 1979-1996.* VIZ Media LLC, 2009. With the help of translators Cary and Schodt, legendary animator Hayao Miyazaki tells the story of the bulk of his career with notes, sketches, and behind-the-scenes details.

Munroe, Roberta Marie. *How Not to Make a Short Film: Secrets of a Sundance Programmer.* Hyperion, 2009. The Sundance Film Festival has long been a springboard for directors looking to use their short film as a calling card to bigger and better things and Munroe screened submissions for the fest for five years along with being an award-winning short filmmaker herself.

Oeler, Karla. *A Grammar of Murder: Violent Scenes and Film Form.* University of Chicago Press, 2009. An examination of violence in film that focuses on the work of Jean Renoir, Alfred Hitchcock, Stanley Kubrick, Jim Jarmusch, and Sergei Eisenstein.

O'Steen, Bobbie. *The Invisible Cut: How Editors Make Movie Magic.* Michael Wiese Productions, 2009. Using hundreds of frame grabs from roughly a dozen famous scenes, the author details the importance and influence of the editor on a final film.

Pearson, Sidney. *Print the Legend: Politics, Culture, and Civic Virtue in the Films of John Ford.* Lexington Books, 2009. An exploration of the culture and virtues of regime building through the films of John Ford.

Pollard, Tom. *Sex and Violence: The Hollywood Censorship Wars.* Paradigm Publishers, 2009. A comprehensive look at the history of censorship in Hollywood, critically examining dozens of films by focusing on recurring issues of social and political attempts to censor the art of moviemaking.

Porter, Darwin. *Steve McQueen, King of Cool: Tales of a Lurid Life.* Blood Moon Productions, 2009. Controversial biography that attempts to bridge the gap between the legend of the always-cool Steve McQueen and the actuality of his life with sensational details about his childhood, work in pornography, and even his mysterious deaths.

Price, David A. *The Pixar Touch: The Making of a Company.* Vintage, 2009. The story of how Pixar became the most influential animation studio of the new century focusing on the founding CEO, Ed Catmull, along with the impact of Steve Jobs and John Lasseter on the company.

Reilly, Tom. *The Big Picture: Flimmaking Lessons From a Life on the Set.* Thomas Dunne, 2009. Using a life of experience that includes work on more than forty films, Reilly details the filmmaking process from a personal level that draws on work with Alfonso Cuaron, Sydney Pollack, Woody Allen, and many more.

Reiss, Jon. *Think Outside the Box Office: The Ultimate Guide to Film Distribution and Marketing for the Digital Era.* Hybrid Cinema, 2009. With the onslaught of new delivery methods for filmmaking outside of the traditional distribution model, Reiss advises the viewer on how to use advancements on the web and in the world of DIY programs to make their dreams come true.

Rippy, Marguerite H. *Orson Welles and the Unfinished RKO Projects: A Postmodern Perspective.* Southern Illinois University Press, 2009. An associate professor in the Department of Literature and Languages at Marymount University traces the impact of one of the most influential filmmakers of all time with a focus on his early film and radio projects shelved by RKO.

Rulli, Marti and Dennis Davern. *Goodbye Natalie, Goodbye Splendour.* Davern was the boat captain on the night of Natalie Word's fateful drowning and he tells his story of what happened that night to investigative journalist Marti Rulli.

Schickel, Richard and George Perry. *Bette Davis: Larger Than Life.* Running Press, 2009. The life and work of one of the most influential and acclaimed actresses in the history of film is examined in this lavish tribute piece.

Sellers, Robert. *Hellraisers: The Life and Inebriated Times of Richard Burton, Richard Harris, Peter O'Toole, and Oliver Reed.* Thomas Dunne Books, 2009. Regular biographer Sellers examines the life of four of the last century's most interesting actors with a focus on their alcoholic tendencies and bad boy behavior.

Shandley, Robert. *Runaway Romances: Hollywood's Postwar Tour of Europe.* Temple University Press, 2009. The author identifies and examines a new subgenre in the Hollywood 'European Travelogue' romance of the mid-1940s to mid-1960s.

Sorensen, Lars-Martin. *Censorship of Japanese Films During the U.S. Occupation of Japan: The Cases of Yasujiro Ozu and Akira Kurosawa.* Edwin Mellen Press, 2009. A book that focuses on the occupation period of Japan (1945-1952) and its effects on cinema, most notably through the wildly acclaimed work of Ozu and Kurosawa.

Spoto, Donald. *High Society: The Life of Grace Kelly.* Harmony, 2009. A biography of one of the most legendary stars of her era from childhood through her career to her life as the wife of Monaco's Prince Rainer and her early death.

Sutherland, Dr. Jean-Anne, and Kathryn M. Feltey. *Cinematic Sociology: Social Life in Film.* Pine Forge Press, 2009. A classroom text book designed to enhance understanding of sociological concepts through films as diverse as *The 40 Year Old Virgin* (2005) and *My Fair Lady* (1964).

Swayze, Patrick and Lisa Niemi. *The Time of My Life.* Atria, 2009. An autobiography by the recently deceased movie star that focuses on his battle against the pancreatic cancer that took his life.

Taraborrelli, J. Randy. *The Secret Life of Marilyn Monroe.* Grand Central Publishing, 2009. Using reportedly fresh research to examine the life of a well-documented film icon, Taraborrelli turns details released through the Freedom of Information Act to unveil the truth about the reported affair between Marilyn and Robert F. Kennedy.

Thomson, David. *The Moment of "Psycho": How Alfred Hitchcock Taught America to Love Murder.* Basic Books, 2009. Film critic David Thomson examines both the influence of *Psycho* (1960) and its place in the career of Alfred Hitchcock.

Ulin, Jeff. *The Business of Media Distribution: Monetizing Film, TV and Video Content in an Online World.* Focal Press, 2009. A business guide by the former head of sales for Lucasfilm about navigating new distribution models in use for taking film from concept to an audience.

Vieira, Mark A. *Irving Thalberg: Boy Wonder to Producer Prince.* University of California Press, 2009. A biography of Irving Thalberg, one of the most pioneering voices of the 1920s and 1930s as producer of dozens of epic films but

whose influence would not be recognized until decades after his tragic death at the age of thirty-seven.

Weber, Karl and Participant Media. *"Food Inc.": A Participant Guide: How Industrial Food is Making Us Sicker, Fatter, and Poorer—And What You Can Do About It.* PublicAffairs, 2009. A companion piece to the 2009 documentary about the food industry that expands on the arguments of the film and advises the reader on how to use the information gleaned from the movie to change the way they think about what they eat.

Wheatley, Catherine. *Michael Haneke's Cinema: The Ethic of the Image.* Berghahn Books, 2009. A critical examination of the work of award-winning filmmaker that focuses on what the author terms 'ethical cinema' and how Haneke uses it to impact his audience.

Young, Paul and Paul Duncan. *Art Cinema.* TASCHEN America, LLC, 2009. An argument of film's credibility as artistic medium and how actual artists like Michael Snow, Luis Bunuel, Jean-Luc Godard, Kenneth Anger, Stan Brakhage, and Matthew Barney have used the form to enhance the world of art.

Zeydabadi-Nejad, Saeed. *The Politics of Iranian Cinema: Film and Society in the Islamic Republic.* Routledge, 2009. A tool for studies of film and media studies along with examinations of Iranian cultural studies and the attempts at creating art in the Middle East by a teacher at the Institute of Ismaili Studies.

Zuckoff, Mitchell. *Robert Altman: The Oral Biography.* Knopf, 2009. An examination of the life and work of one of the most influential filmmakers of all time as told through the stories, reflections, and anecdotes of the people who arguably knew him best, including many of the stars of his decades of film work.

Director Index

Javier Abad
    Planet 51 *304*

J.J. Abrams (1966-)
    Star Trek *351*

Shane Acker
    9 *273*

Fatih Akin (1973-)
    New York, I Love You *268*

Thomas Alfredson
    Let the Right One In *225*

Woody Allen (1935-)
    Whatever Works *413*

Pedro Almódovar (1951-)
    Broken Embraces *45*

Christian Alvart
    Pandorum *293*

Wes Anderson (1969-)
    Fantastic Mr. Fox *118*

Peter Andrews
    See Steven Soderbergh

Nimrod Antal (1973-)
    Armored *19*

Judd Apatow (1967-)
    Funny People *133*

Guillermo Arriaga (1958-)
    The Burning Plain *54*

Olivier Assayas (1955-)
    Summer Hours *361*

Yvan Attal (1965-)
    New York, I Love You *268*

Ramin Bahrani
    Goodbye Solo *149*

Drew Barrymore (1975-)
    Whip It *417*

Sophie Barthes
    Cold Souls *70*

Andrzej Bartkowiak (1950-)
    Street Fighter: The Legend of
    Chun-Li *358*

Michael Bay (1965-)
    Transformers: Revenge of the
    Fallen *383*

Walt Becker (1968-)
    Old Dogs *286*

Stephen Belber
    Management *241*

Kristopher Belman
    More Than a Game *256*

Kathryn Bigelow (1952-)
    The Hurt Locker *171*

Peter Billingsley (1971-)
    Couples Retreat *77*

Jorge Blanco
    Planet 51 *304*

Neil Blomkamp
    District 9 *96*

Anna Boden
    Sugar *360*

Beeny Boom
    Next Day Air *270*

David Bowers
    Astro Boy *20*

Neal Brennan
    The Goods: Live Hard, Sell
    Hard *151*

James Cameron (1954-)
    Avatar *22*

Brandon Camp
    Love Happens *230*

Jane Campion (1954-)
    Bright Star *43*

Laurent Cantet (1961-)
    The Class *66*

Steve Carr
    Paul Blart: Mall Cop *298*

Nuri Bilge Ceylan
    Three Monkeys *380*

Larry Charles (1956-)
    Brüno *52*

Peter Chelsom (1956-)
    Hannah Montana: The
    Movie *159*

Ron Clements (1953-)
    The Princess and the Frog *312*

Ethan Coen (1957-)
    A Serious Man *334*

Joel Coen (1954-)
    A Serious Man *334*

Jaume Collet-Serra
    Orphan *289*

Chris Columbus (1958-)
    I Love You, Beth Cooper *178*

Scott Cooper
    Crazy Heart *81*

Francis Ford Coppola (1939-)
    Tetro *376*

Peter Cornwell
    The Haunting in Connecti-
    cut *163*

Zach Cregger
    Miss March *251*

John Crowley
    Is Anybody There? *200*

Bob Peterson
Up *404*

Donald Petrie (1954-)
My Life in Ruins *261*

Todd Phillips (1970-)
The Hangover *157*

Natalie Portman (1981-)
New York, I Love You *268*

Corneliu Porumboiu
Police, Adjective *306*

Alex Proyas (1965-)
Knowing *214*

Louie Psihoyos
The Cove *79*

Sam Raimi (1959-)
Drag Me to Hell *99*

Harold Ramis (1944-)
Year One *427*

Brett Ratner (1969-)
New York, I Love You *268*

Nicolas Winding Refn (1970-)
Bronson *47*

Jason Reitman
Up in the Air *406*

Guy Ritchie (1968-)
Sherlock Holmes *338*

Panna Rittikrai (1961-)
Ong Bak 2 *288*

Matt Robinson
The Invention of Lying *196*

Robert Rodriguez (1968-)
Shorts: The Adventures of the
Wishing Rock *340*

Carlos Saldanha
Ice Age: Dawn of the Dinosaurs *181*

Scott Sanders
Black Dynamite *34*

Lone Scherfig (1959-)
An Education *108*

John Schultz
Aliens in the Attic *5*

Robert Schwentke
The Time Traveler's Wife *381*

Tony Scott (1944-)
The Taking of Pelham 123
371

Henry Selick (1952-)
Coraline *75*

Dominic Sena (1949-)
Whiteout *420*

Lynn Shelton
Humpday *169*

Jim Sheridan (1949-)
Brothers *48*

Steve Shill
Obsessed *284*

Robert Siegel
Big Fan *33*

Brad Silberling (1962-)
Land of the Lost *217*

Sebastian Silva
The Maid *238*

Chris Smith (1970-)
Collapse *72*

Zack Snyder (1966-)
Watchmen *411*

Steven Soderbergh (1963-)
Che *59*
The Girlfriend Experience *145*
The Informant! *187*

Iain Softley (1958-)
Inkheart *193*

Stephen Sommers (1962-)
G.I. Joe: The Rise of Co-
bra *143*

Poalo Sorrentino
Il Divo *97*

Lodovico Sorret
See Tom Noonan

Burr Steers (1966-)
17 Again *336*

James D. Stern
Every Little Step *110*

Jeff Stilson
Good Hair *148*

Yojiro Takita
Departures *91*

Kevin Tancharoen
Fame *115*

Quentin Tarantino (1963-)
Inglourious Basterds *191*

Patrick Tatopoulos
Underworld: Rise of the Lycans *400*

Brian Taylor
Crank: High Voltage *80*
Gamer *137*

Betty Thomas (1949-)
Alvin and the Chipmunks: The
Squeakuel *8*

George Tillman, Jr. (1969-)
Notorious *280*

James Toback (1944-)
Tyson *394*

Phil Traill
All About Steve *6*

Aristomenis Tsirbas
Battle for Terra *31*

David N. Twohy (1955-)
A Perfect Getaway *300*

Tom Tykwer (1965-)
The International *195*

Jean-Marc Vallee
The Young Victoria *429*

Conrad Vernon (1968-)
Monsters vs. Aliens *253*

Lars von Trier (1956-)
Antichrist *16*

Matt Tyrnauer
Valentino: The Last Em-
peror *408*

Mark S. Waters (1964-)
Ghosts of Girlfriends Past *142*

Damien Dante Wayans
Dance Flick *88*

Marc Webb
(500) Days of Summer *126*

Chris Weitz (1969-)
The Twilight Saga: New
Moon *390*

Paul Weitz (1965-)
Cirque du Freak: The Vampire's
Assistant *64*

Ti West
The House of the Devil *168*

Gary Winick (1961-)
Bride Wars *42*

Tommy Wirkola (1979-)
Dead Snow *90*

James Wong (1940-2004)
Dragonball: Evolution *101*

John Woo (1948-)
Red Cliff *324*

Joe Wright
The Soloist *345*

David Yates (1963-)
Harry Potter and the Half-Blood
Prince *160*

Hoyt Yeatman
G-Force *140*

Robert Zemeckis (1952-)
A Christmas Carol *62*

Rob Zombie (1966-)
Halloween II *155*

Erick Zonca
Julia *210*

Harald Zwart (1965-)
The Pink Panther 2 *301*

Screenwriter Index

Shane Acker
9 *273*

Peter Ackerman
Ice Age: Dawn of the Dinosaurs *181*

Jonathan Aibel
Alvin and the Chipmunks: The
Squeakuel *8*
Monsters vs. Aliens *253*

Fatih Akin (1973-)
New York, I Love You *268*

Adam Alleca (1983-)
The Last House on the
Left *220*

Woody Allen (1935-)
Whatever Works *413*

Pedro Almodóvar (1951-)
Broken Embraces *45*

Kayla Alpert
Confessions of a Shopaholic *74*

Christian Alvart
Pandorum *293*

Hossein Amini (1966-)
Killshot *213*

Wes Anderson (1969-)
Fantastic Mr. Fox *118*

Judd Apatow (1967-)
Funny People *133*

Jesse Armstrong
In the Loop *186*

Guillermo Arriaga (1958-)
The Burning Plain *54*

Olivier Assayas (1955-)
Summer Hours *361*

Yvan Attal (1965-)
New York, I Love You *268*

Bahareh Azimi
Goodbye Solo *149*

Ramin Bahrani
Goodbye Solo *149*

Nicky Bakay
Paul Blart: Mall Cop *298*

Kim Barker
All About Steve *6*

Judi Barrett
Cloudy with a Chance of Meatballs *67*

Ron Barrett
Cloudy with a Chance of Meatballs *67*

Sophie Barthes
Cold Souls *70*

Ronald Bass (1942-)
Amelia *9*

Noah Baumbach (1969-)
Fantastic Mr. Fox *118*

Stuart Beattie
G.I. Joe: The Rise of Co-
bra *143*

Francois Begaudeau
The Class *66*

Stephen Belber
Management *241*

Kristopher Belman
More Than a Game *256*

David Benioff (1970-)
Brothers *48*
X-Men Origins: Wolverine *425*

Ronan Bennett
Public Enemies *317*

Daniel Berendsen (1964-)
Hannah Montana: The
Movie *159*

Michael Berg
Ice Age: Dawn of the Dinosaurs *181*

Glenn Berger
Alvin and the Chipmunks: The
Squeakuel *8*
Monsters vs. Aliens *253*

Carlo Bernard
The Uninvited *401*

Luc Besson (1959-)
Taken *369*

Ann Biderman
Public Enemies *317*

Brian Bird
Not Easily Broken *278*

Dirk Blackman
Underworld: Rise of the Lycans *400*

Simon Blackwell
In the Loop *186*

Neil Blomkamp
District 9 *96*

Mark Boal
The Hurt Locker *171*

Anna Boden
Sugar *360*

Mark Bomback
Race to Witch Mountain *323*

David Bourla
Push *320*

Maya Forbes
Monsters vs. Aliens *253*

Tom Ford
A Single Man *343*

Alastair Fothergill
Earth *105*

Dana Fox
Couples Retreat *77*

Scott Frank (1960-)
Night at the Museum: Battle of
the Smithsonian *271*

Kelly Fremon
Post Grad *309*

Cary Fukunaga (1977-)
Sin Nombre *341*

Robert Ben Garant (1970-)
Night at the Museum: Battle of
the Smithsonian *271*

Matteo Garrone
Gomorrah *147*

Massimo Gaudioso
Gomorrah *147*

Ricky Gervais (1961-)
The Invention of Lying *196*

Terry Gilliam (1940-)
The Imaginarium of Doctor Parnassus *182*

Tony Gilroy (1956-)
State of Play *353*

Adam F. Goldberg (1976-)
Aliens in the Attic *5*
Fanboys *117*

Peter Goldfinger
Sorority Row *346*

Akiva Goldsman (1963-)
Angels & Demons *12*

Bobcat Goldthwait (1962-)
World's Greatest Dad *423*

Tony Golroy
Duplicity *102*

Christopher Gore
Coco Before Chanel *69*
Fame *115*

David S. Goyer (1965-)
The Unborn *398*

Todd Graff (1959-)
Bandslam *30*

Susannah Grant (1963-)
The Soloist *345*

James Gray (1969-)
Two Lovers *392*

Sebastian Gutierrez
Women in Trouble *422*

Jason Dean Hall
Spread *349*

John Hamburg (1970-)
I Love You, Man *179*

Christopher Hampton (1946-)
Chéri *60*

John Lee Hancock (1957-)
The Blind Side *36*

Michael Haneke (1942-)
The White Ribbon *418*

Peter Harness
Is Anybody There? *200*

Kent Harper
Surveillance *365*

Timothy Harris (1946-)
Astro Boy *20*

Carey Hayes (1961-)
Whiteout *420*

Chad Hayes (1961-)
Whiteout *420*

David Hayter (1969-)
Watchmen *411*

Brian Helgeland (1961-)
Cirque du Freak: The Vampire's
Assistant *64*
The Taking of Pelham 123
371

Chris Henchy
Land of the Lost *217*

Jared Hess (1979-)
Gentlemen Broncos *139*

Jerusha Hess (1980-)
Gentlemen Broncos *139*

Guy Hibbert
Five Minutes of Heaven *127*

Scott Hicks (1953-)
The Boys Are Back *40*

Jody Hill
Observe and Report *283*

John Hindman
The Answer Man *14*

Erich Hoeber
Whiteout *420*

Jon Hoeber
Whiteout *420*

Michael Hoffman (1956-)
The Last Station *222*

Brad Hogan (1977-)
More Than a Game *256*

Megan Holly
Sunshine Cleaning *363*

Joel Hopkins
Last Chance Harvey *219*

Nick Hornby (1957-)
An Education *108*

Armando Iannucci
In the Loop *186*

Shunji Iwai (1963-)
New York, I Love You *268*

Peter Jackson (1961-)
The Lovely Bones *232*

Tracey Jackson
Confessions of a Shopaholic *74*

Kevin James (1965-)
Paul Blart: Mall Cop *298*

Nicholas Jarecki
The Informers *189*

Jim Jarmusch (1953-)
The Limits of Control *227*

Nicholas Jasenovec
Paper Heart *295*

Anna Jemison
See Anna Maria Monticelli

Seo-gyeong Jeong
Thirst *378*

Sheridan Jobbins
Easy Virtue *106*

David Leslie Johnson
Orphan *289*

Rian Johnson
The Brothers Bloom *50*

Freedom Jones
Fired Up! *125*

Kirk Jones (1963-)
Everybody's Fine *111*

Spike Jonze (1969-)
Where the Wild Things
Are *415*

Mike Judge (1962-)
Extract *112*

Robert Mark Kamen
Taken *369*

Richard Kelly (1975-)
The Box *39*

Robert Kenner
Food, Inc. *129*

Ercan Kesal
Three Monkeys *380*

Simon Kinberg (1973-)
Sherlock Holmes *338*

Harald Kloser (1956-)
2012 *388*

Steve Kloves (1960-)
Harry Potter and the Half-Blood
Prince *160*

David Koepp (1964-)
Angels & Demons *12*

Abby Kohn
He's Just Not That Into
You *164*

Olatunde Osunsanmi (1977-)
  The Fourth Kind *130*

Holly Gent Palmo
  Me and Orson Welles *245*

Vince Palmo
  Me and Orson Welles *245*

Chan-wook Park (1963-)
  Thirst *378*

Jonathan Parker
  (Untitled) *402*

Nathan Parker
  Moon *255*

Nils Parker
  I Hope They Serve Beer in
    Hell *176*

Elise Pearlstein
  Food, Inc. *129*

Ryne Pearson
  Knowing *214*

Anthony Peckham
  Invictus *198*
  Sherlock Holmes *338*

Pedro Peirano
  The Maid *238*

Oren Peli
  Paranormal Activity *296*

Joe Penhall
  The Road *326*

Tyler Perry (1969-)
  I Can Do Bad All By My-
    self *175*
  Madea Goes to Jail *237*

Charlie Peters
  My One and Only *262*

Bob Peterson
  Up *404*

Pamela Pettler
  9 *273*

Anna Hamilton Phelan
  Amelia *9*

Natalie Portman (1981-)
  New York, I Love You *268*

Corneliu Porumboiu
  Police, Adjective *306*

Aude Py
  Julia *210*

Michael R. Johnson
  Sherlock Holmes *338*

Ivan Raimi (1956-)
  Drag Me to Hell *99*

Sam Raimi (1959-)
  Drag Me to Hell *99*

Harold Ramis (1944-)
  Year One *427*

Kenneth Rance
  New in Town *267*

June Raphael
  Bride Wars *42*

Billy Ray
  State of Play *353*

Rhett Reese
  Zombieland *430*

Nicolas Winding Refn (1970-)
  Bronson *47*

Mike Reiss (1960-)
  Ice Age: Dawn of the Dino-
    saurs *181*
  My Life in Ruins *261*

Jason Reitman
  Up in the Air *406*

Guy Ritchie (1968-)
  Sherlock Holmes *338*

Panna Rittikrai (1961-)
  Ong Bak 2 *288*

Kim Roberts
  Food, Inc. *129*

Matt Robinson
  The Invention of Lying *196*

Tony Roche
  In the Loop *186*

Chris Rock (1966-)
  Good Hair *148*

Robert Rodriguez (1968-)
  Shorts: The Adventures of the
    Wishing Rock *340*

Melissa Rosenberg
  The Twilight Saga: New
    Moon *390*

Mark Rosman (1959-)
  Sorority Row *346*

Craig Rossenberg
  The Uninvited *401*

Bruce Joel Rubin (1943-)
  The Time Traveler's Wife *381*

Matthew Sand
  Ninja Assassin *277*

Scott Sanders
  Black Dynamite *34*

Roberto Saviano
  Gomorrah *147*

David Scearce
  A Single Man *343*

James Schamus (1959-)
  Taking Woodstock *372*

Robert Schooley
  Hotel for Dogs *166*

Henry Selick (1952-)
  Coraline *75*

Damian Shannon
  Friday the 13th *132*

Lynn Shelton
  Humpday *169*

Heyu Sheng
  Red Cliff *324*

Robert Siegel
  Big Fan *33*

Sebastian Silva
  The Maid *238*

Marc Silverstein
  He's Just Not That Into
    You *164*

Adam Simon (1962-)
  The Haunting in Connecti-
    cut *163*

James V. Simpson
  Armored *19*

Eric Singer
  The International *195*

Chuck Sklar
  Good Hair *148*

Kirsten Smith (1970-)
  The Ugly Truth *397*

Zane Smith
  My Bloody Valentine 3D *259*

Juliet Snowden
  Knowing *214*

Edward Solomon (1961-)
  Imagine That *184*

Poalo Sorrentino
  Il Divo *97*

Lodovico Sorret
  See Tom Noonan

Evan Spiliotopolos
  Battle for Terra *31*

Rick Stempson
  The Goods: Live Hard, Sell
    Hard *151*

Joe Stillman
  Planet 51 *304*

Jeff Stilson
  Good Hair *148*

Andy Stock
  The Goods: Live Hard, Sell
    Hard *151*

Josh Stolberg (1971-)
  Sorority Row *346*

J. Michael Straczynski
  Ninja Assassin *277*

Peter Straughan
  The Men Who Stare at
    Goats *247*

Gene Stupnitsky
  Year One *427*

Mark Swift
    Friday the 13th *132*

Quentin Tarantino (1963-)
    Inglourious Basterds *191*

Terri Tatchell
    District 9 *96*

Brian Taylor
    Crank: High Voltage *80*
    Gamer *137*

Chris M. Theson
    Imagine That *184*

Mike Thompson
    Love Happens *230*

James Toback (1944-)
    Tyson *394*

Michael Tolkin (1950-)
    Nine *275*

Alex Tse
    Watchmen *411*

Sheldon Turner
    Up in the Air *406*

David N. Twohy (1955-)
    A Perfect Getaway *300*

Vince Vaughn (1970-)
    Couples Retreat *77*

Vendela Vida
    Away We Go *24*

Chris Viscardi
    Alvin and the Chipmunks: The
       Squeakuel *8*

Jon Vitti
    Alvin and the Chipmunks: The
       Squeakuel *8*

Lars von Trier (1956-)
    Antichrist *16*

Fran Walsh (1959-)
    The Lovely Bones *232*

Craig Wayans
    Dance Flick *88*

Damien Dante Wayans
    Dance Flick *88*

Keenen Ivory Wayans (1958-)
    Dance Flick *88*

Marlon Wayans (1972-)
    Dance Flick *88*

Shawn Wayans (1971-)
    Dance Flick *88*

Michael H. Weber
    (500) Days of Summer *126*
    The Pink Panther 2 *301*

David Weissman
    Old Dogs *286*

Paul Weitz (1965-)
    Cirque du Freak: The Vampire's
       Assistant *64*

Paul Wernick
    Zombieland *430*

Ti West
    The House of the Devil *168*

Michael Jai White (1967-)
    Black Dynamite *34*

Mike White (1970-)
    Gentlemen Broncos *139*

Stiles White
    Knowing *214*

Cormac Wibberley (1959-)
    G-Force *140*

Marianne S. Wibberley (1965-)
    G-Force *140*

Tennessee Williams (1911-83)
    The Loss of a Teardrop Dia-
       mond *229*

Casey Wilson
    Bride Wars *42*

Kurt Wimmer (1964-)
    Law Abiding Citizen *224*

Tommy Wirkola (1979-)
    Dead Snow *90*

Wally Wolodarsky
    Monsters vs. Aliens *253*

James Wong (1940-2004)
    Dragonball: Evolution *101*

John Woo (1948-)
    Red Cliff *324*

Skip Woods
    G.I. Joe: The Rise of Co-
       bra *143*
    X-Men Origins: Wolverine *425*

Charlyne Yi (1986-)
    Paper Heart *295*

Robert Zemeckis (1952-)
    A Christmas Carol *62*

Rob Zombie (1966-)
    Halloween II *155*

Erick Zonca
    Julia *210*

Cinematographer Index

Barry Markowitz
Crazy Heart *81*

Horacio Marquinez
World's Greatest Dad *423*

Daniel Marracino
Capitalism: A Love Story *57*

Shawn Maurer
Black Dynamite *34*

Albert Maysles (1926-)
Soul Power *348*

Donald McAlpine (1934-)
X-Men Origins: Wolverine *425*

Lawrence McConkey
Tyson *394*

Seamus McGarvey (1967-)
The Soloist *345*

Robert McLachlan
Dragonball: Evolution *101*

Geary McLeod
Not Easily Broken *278*

Glen McPherson
See Glen MacPherson

Suki Medencevic (1963-)
I Hope They Serve Beer in
Hell *176*

Sharon Meir
The Last House on the
Left *220*

Pierre Milon
The Class *66*

Dan Mindel
Star Trek *351*

Charles Minsky
Post Grad *309*

Amir M. Mokri (1956-)
Fast & Furious *120*

M. David Mullen (1962-)
Jennifer's Body *207*

J. Michael Muro
Cirque du Freak: The Vampire's
Assistant *64*

Guillermo Navarro (1955-)
It Might Get Loud *202*

Giles Nuttgens (1960-)
The Loss of a Teardrop Diamond *229*

Ruairi O'Brien
Five Minutes of Heaven *127*

Daryn Okada (1960-)
Ghosts of Girlfriends Past *142*
The Goods: Live Hard, Sell
Hard *151*

Atsushi Okui
Ponyo *307*

Tristan Oliver
Fantastic Mr. Fox *118*

Marco Onorato
Gomorrah *147*

Trent Opaloch
District 9 *96*

Sandrine Orabona
Michael Jackson's This Is
It *250*

Tim Orr (1968-)
Observe and Report *283*

Marius Panduru
Police, Adjective *306*

Andrij Parekh (1971-)
Cold Souls *70*
Sugar *360*

Richard Pearce (1943-)
Food, Inc. *129*

Daniel Pearl (1951-)
Friday the 13th *132*

Brian Pearson (1967-)
My Bloody Valentine 3D *259*

Nicola Pecorini (1957-)
The Imaginarium of Doctor Parnassus *182*

Oren Peli
Paranormal Activity *296*

Mark Plummer
A Perfect Getaway *300*

Ekkehart Pollack
Gamer *137*

Marco Pontecorvo (1966-)
My One and Only *262*

Richard Pope
Me and Orson Welles *245*

Steven Poster (1944-)
The Box *39*
Spread *349*

Munn Powell
Gentlemen Broncos *139*

Roger Pratt (1947-)
Inkheart *193*

Robert Presley
A Christmas Carol *62*

Rodrigo Prieto (1965-)
Broken Embraces *45*
State of Play *353*

Catherine Pujol
The Class *66*

Declan Quinn (1957-)
New York, I Love You *268*
The Private Lives of Pippa
Lee *314*

Joel Ransom
The Stoning of Soraya M. *357*

Adam Ravetch
Earth *105*

Robert Richardson (1955-)
Inglourious Basterds *191*

Bob Richman
The September Issue *332*

Anthony B. Richmond (1942-)
Alvin and the Chipmunks: The
Squeakuel *8*
Miss March *251*

Eliot Rockett
The House of the Devil *168*

Robert Rodriguez (1968-)
Shorts: The Adventures of the
Wishing Rock *340*

Erich Roland
It Might Get Loud *202*

Philippe Rousselot (1945-)
Sherlock Holmes *338*

Jayme Roy
Capitalism: A Love Story *57*

Mauricio Rubinstein
New York, I Love You *268*

Paul Sarossy (1963-)
Adoration *2*

Harris Savides (1957-)
Whatever Works *413*

Tobias Schliessler
The Taking of Pelham
123 *371*

Nancy Schreiber (1949-)
Motherhood *258*

John Schwartzman (1960-)
Night at the Museum: Battle of
the Smithsonian *271*

Chris Seager
New in Town *267*

Andrzej Sekula (1954-)
Armored *19*

Jonathan Sela
Law Abiding Citizen *224*

Dean Semler (1943-)
2012 *388*

Lorenzo Senatore (1974-)
The Fourth Kind *130*

Ken Seng
Obsessed *284*
Sorority Row *346*

Ben Seresin
Transformers: Revenge of the
Fallen *383*

Gary Shaw
Moon *255*

Lawrence Sher (1970-)
The Hangover *157*
I Love You, Man *179*

Editor Index

Tracey Wadmore-Smith
    Fired Up! *125*
Christian Wagner
    The Uninvited *401*
Trevor Waite
    Is Anybody There? *200*
Martin Walsh
    Inkheart *193*
John W. Walter
    Capitalism: A Love Story *57*
Andrew Weisblum
    Fantastic Mr. Fox *118*
Steven Welch
    Year One *427*
Ti West
    The House of the Devil *168*
Dirk Westervelt
    Notorious *280*
Brent White
    Funny People *133*

Doobie White
    Gamer *137*
Monika Willi
    The White Ribbon *418*
Chris G. Willingham
    Dragonball: Evolution *101*
Julia Wong
    Extract *112*
    The Pink Panther 2 *301*
Craig Wood
    The Burning Plain *54*
Justine Wright
    State of Play *353*
Gabriel Wrye
    The Brothers Bloom *50*
Aaron Yanes
    Tyson *394*
Hongyu Yang
    Red Cliff *324*

Mark Yoshikawa
    Lymelife *234*
Adrian Younge
    Black Dynamite *34*
Barry Zetlin
    Surrogates *364*
Dan Zimmerman
    Night at the Museum: Battle of
    the Smithsonian *271*
Dean Zimmerman
    Night at the Museum: Battle of
    the Smithsonian *271*
Lucia Zucchetti
    Chéri *60*
Pablo Zumarraga
    Che *59*
Eric Zumbrunnen
    Where the Wild Things
    Are *415*

Art Director Index

Michael Ahern
    Cold Souls *70*

Gilles Aird
    Whiteout *420*

Scott Anderson
    The Messenger *248*

Hideki Arichi
    Moon *255*

Alan Au
    Paul Blart: Mall Cop *298*

Francois Audouy
    Watchmen *411*

Suzanne Austin
    Last Chance Harvey *219*

Ramsey Avery
    G-Force *140*

Maria Baker
    Ghosts of Girlfriends Past *142*

Laura Ballinger Gardner
    Notorious *280*

Patrick Banister
    Orphan *289*

Guy Barnes
    Brothers *48*
    My One and Only *262*
    Sunshine Cleaning *363*

Ben Barraud
    Julie & Julia *211*

Michael Barton
    The Collector *73*

Gary Baugh
    The Unborn *398*

Ann Marie Beauchamp
    Disgrace *94*

Curt Beech
    Couples Retreat *77*

Carlos Benassini
    Sin Nombre *341*

Mayne Berke
    I Can Do Bad All By My-
        self *175*

Jon Billington
    Transformers: Revenge of the
        Fallen *383*

Edward S. Bonutto
    The Haunting in Connecti-
        cut *163*
    New in Town *267*

Peter Borck
    Crossing Over *83*
    Gamer *137*
    The Men Who Stare at
        Goats *247*

Drew Boughton
    Everybody's Fine *111*

Tristan Paris Bourne
    The Great Buck Howard *152*

Thomas Brown
    Pirate Radio *302*

David Bryan
    The Hurt Locker *171*

Andrew Max Cahn
    The Hangover *157*
    He's Just Not That Into
        You *164*
    Up in the Air *406*

Stephen Carter
    Did You Hear About the Mor-
        gans? *93*
    Duplicity *102*

Harika Ceylan
    Three Monkeys *380*

Sue Chan
    Imagine That *184*

Nigel Churcher
    Amelia *9*

Erin Cochran
    Dance Flick *88*

Chris Cornwell
    Armored *19*
    Obsessed *284*

Bill Crutcher
    Me and Orson Welles *245*

Dins W.W. Danielsen
    Miss March *251*
    Spread *349*

Dennis Davenport
    The Boondock Saints II: All
        Saints Day *37*

Matteo De Cosmo
    Precious: Based on the Novel
        'Push' by Sapphire *310*

Katya Debear
    New York, I Love You *268*

Nick Dent
    In the Loop *186*

Gillian Devenney
    Five Minutes of Heaven *127*

John Dexter
    Land of the Lost *217*

Simon Dobbin
    Management *241*

James Donahue
    Bride Wars *42*

Jasna Dragovic
  The Brothers Bloom *50*

Henry Dunn
  Away We Go *24*

Timothy Eckel
  The Stepfather *355*

Priscilla Elliott
  The Box *39*
  The Invention of Lying *196*

Mark Erbaugh
  Madea Goes to Jail *237*

Nigel Evans
  Aliens in the Attic *5*

Craig Fison
  Mary and Max *244*

Richard Fojo
  Year One *427*

John Frick
  Bandslam *30*
  Friday the 13th *132*

Marc Gabbana (1966-)
  A Christmas Carol *62*

Halina Gebarowicz
  My One and Only *262*

Martin Gendron
  Whiteout *420*

Terry Gilliam (1940-)
  The Imaginarium of Doctor Parnassus *182*

Gershon Ginsburg
  The Road *326*

Elliott Glick
  Hannah Montana: The Movie *159*

Pablo González
  The Maid *238*

Ian Gooding
  The Princess and the Frog *312*

Brandt Gordon
  Killshot *213*

Austin Gorg
  All About Steve *6*
  Extract *112*

Ian Gracie
  X-Men Origins: Wolverine *425*

W. Steven Graham
  It's Complicated *203*

Peter Grundy
  The Time Traveler's Wife *381*

Roswell Hamrick
  Madea Goes to Jail *237*

Tom Hannam
  Invictus *198*

William Hawkins
  The Ugly Truth *397*

David Hindle
  Bright Star *43*

Shira Hockman
  The Last House on the Left *220*

Paul Inglis
  The Young Victoria *429*

Catherine Ircha
  The Twilight Saga: New Moon *390*

Michael Isaak
  Monsters vs. Aliens *253*

Barry Isenor
  Adoration *2*

Helen Jarvis
  Night at the Museum: Battle of the Smithsonian *271*

Deborah Jensen
  A Serious Man *334*

John R. Jensen
  Race to Witch Mountain *323*

Bo Johnson
  Alvin and the Chipmunks: The Squeakuel *8*
  Fired Up! *125*

Fernando Juarez
  Planet 51 *304*

Jean Kazemirchuk
  Whiteout *420*

Paul D. Kelly
  Confessions of a Shopaholic *74*

Paul Kirby
  The Brothers Bloom *50*

Timothy "TK" Kirkpatrick
  Halloween II *155*

Michael Knapp (1972-)
  Ice Age: Dawn of the Dinosaurs *181*

Kai Koch
  The International *195*

Sebastian Krawinkel
  Ninja Assassin *277*

Charles Kulsziski
  Motherhood *258*

Brent Kyle
  Whip It *417*

Francois-Renaud Labarthe
  Summer Hours *361*

Elis Lam
  Saw VI *331*

Neil Lamont
  Harry Potter and the Half-Blood Prince *160*

Simon Lamont
  Nine *275*

David Lazan
  Fast & Furious *120*

Nicole LeBlanc (1977-)
  Zombieland *430*

Tim Ledbury
  Fantastic Mr. Fox *118*

Janey Levick
  Bronson *47*

Mark Lowry
  Five Minutes of Heaven *127*

Patrick Lumb
  Public Enemies *317*

Don MacAulay
  2012 *388*

Gary Mackay
  Underworld: Rise of the Lycans *400*

Tamara Marini
  Duplicity *102*

Dawn Masi
  The Answer Man *14*

Masako Masuda
  Observe and Report *283*

Leon McCarthy
  The Damned United *87*

Jonathan McKinstry
  My Life in Ruins *261*

Rod McLean
  Inkheart *193*

Scott A. Meehan
  Fame *115*
  The Proposal *316*

Anja Miller
  The White Ribbon *418*

Melissa B. Miller
  The Private Lives of Pippa Lee *314*

Thomas Minton
  The Blind Side *36*

Carlos Moore
  The Girlfriend Experience *145*

Niall Moroney
  Sherlock Holmes *338*

Matt Munn
  Adventureland *3*
  Lymelife *234*

Andrew E. W. Murdock
  My Bloody Valentine 3D *259*

Axel Nicolet
  The Fourth Kind *130*

Clara Notari
  Che *59*

Ines Olmedo
  The Informers *189*

Music Director Index

Leo Abrahams
    Five Minutes of Heaven *127*

Mark Adler
    Food, Inc. *129*

Michael Andrews
    Funny People *133*

Spring Aspers
    The Unborn *398*

Tim Atack
    The Invention of Lying *196*

Klaus Badelt (1968-)
    Killshot *213*

Tyler Bates
    Halloween II *155*
    Watchmen *411*

Michael Bearden
    Michael Jackson's This Is
        It *250*

Christophe Beck (1972-)
    All About Steve *6*
    The Hangover *157*
    I Love You, Beth Cooper *178*
    The Marc Pease Experi-
        ence *243*
    The Pink Panther 2 *301*
    Post Grad *309*

Marco Beltrami (1966-)
    The Hurt Locker *171*
    Knowing *214*

Pollard Berrier
    Julia *210*

Boris
    The Limits of Control *227*

Mark Bradshaw
    Bright Star *43*

James Seymour Brett
    Planet 51 *304*

Michi Britsch
    Pandorum *293*

Michael Brook (1952-)
    Sugar *360*

Gerald Brunskill
    World's Greatest Dad *423*

Stephen Bruton
    Crazy Heart *81*

Todd Bryanton
    Surveillance *365*

Brian Bulman
    Alvin and the Chipmunks: The
        Squeakuel *8*

T-Bone Burnett (1948-)
    Crazy Heart *81*

Carter Burwell (1955-)
    The Blind Side *36*
    A Serious Man *334*
    Where the Wild Things
        Are *415*

Win Butler (1980-)
    The Box *39*

Jeff Cardoni
    Miss March *251*

Teddy Castellucci
    The Answer Man *14*

Nick Cave
    The Road *326*

Michael Cera (1988-)
    Paper Heart *295*

George C. Clinton
    Extract *112*

Charlie Clouser (1963-)
    Saw VI *331*
    The Stepfather *355*

Erran Baron Cohen
    Brüno *52*

Dale Cornelius
    Mary and Max *244*

Jane Cornish
    Every Little Step *110*

Bruno Coulais (1954-)
    Coraline *75*

Jeff Danna (1964-)
    The Boondock Saints II: All
        Saints Day *37*
    The Imaginarium of Doctor Par-
        nassus *182*

Mychael Danna (1958-)
    Adoration *2*
    (500) Days of Summer *126*
    The Imaginarium of Doctor Par-
        nassus *182*
    Management *241*
    The Time Traveler's Wife *381*
    Trucker *385*

Mirabela Dauer
    Police, Adjective *306*

Neil Davidge
    Gomorrah *147*
    Push *320*

Marius De Vries
    Easy Virtue *106*

John Debney (1956-)
    Aliens in the Attic *5*
    Hotel for Dogs *166*
    Old Dogs *286*
    The Stoning of Soraya M. *357*

Robert Kral
    The Haunting in Connecti-
        cut *163*

Jesper Kurlandsky
    Mammoth *240*

Rob Lane
    The Damned United *87*

David Lang
    (Untitled) *402*

Nathan Larson (1970-)
    The Messenger *248*

Christopher Lennertz (1972-)
    Adam *1*

Didier Leplae
    Collapse *72*

Hal Lindes (1953-)
    The Boys Are Back *40*

M. Lo
    Goodbye Solo *149*

Omar Rodrguez Lopez
    The Burning Plain *54*

Deborah Lurie
    9 *273*

Mark Mancina (1957-)
    Imagine That *184*

Clint Mansell (1963-)
    Moon *255*

Dario Marianelli
    Everybody's Fine *111*
    The Soloist *345*

Derick Martini
    Lymelife *234*

Steven Martini (1978-)
    Lymelife *234*

Richard Marvin
    Surrogates *364*

Harvey W. Mason (1947-)
    More Than a Game *256*

Michael J. McEvoy
    Me and Orson Welles *245*

Nathaniel Mechaly
    Taken *369*

Marcus Miller (1959-)
    Good Hair *148*

Mark Mothersbaugh (1950-)
    Cloudy with a Chance of Meat-
        balls *67*
    Fanboys *117*

Alex Murdoch
    Away We Go *24*

John Murphy (1965-)
    Armored *19*
    Crossing Over *83*
    The Last House on the
        Left *220*

Javier Navarrete (1956-)
    Inkheart *193*

Blake Neely (1969-)
    The Great Buck Howard *152*

David Newman (1954-)
    My Life in Ruins *261*

Randy Newman (1943-)
    The Princess and the Frog *312*

Thomas Newman (1955-)
    Brothers *48*

Tom Noonan (1951-)
    The House of the Devil *168*

George Oldziey
    Shorts: The Adventures of the
        Wishing Rock *340*

Mark Orton
    The Loss of a Teardrop Dia-
        mond *229*

Atli Orvarsson
    The Fourth Kind *130*

John Ottman (1964-)
    Astro Boy *20*
    Orphan *289*

Antony Partos
    Disgrace *94*

Michael Penn (1958-)
    Sunshine Cleaning *363*

Hector Pereira
    It's Complicated *203*

Lucian Piane
    Sorority Row *346*

John Powell (1963-)
    Ice Age: Dawn of the Dino-
        saurs *181*

Trevor Rabin (1954-)
    G-Force *140*
    Race to Witch Mountain *323*
    12 Rounds *387*

A.R. Rahman (1966-)
    Couples Retreat *77*

Yan Raiburg
    Police, Adjective *306*

J. Ralph
    The Cove *79*

Salaam Remi
    Tyson *394*

Craig Richey
    The September Issue *332*

Michael Rohatyn
    The Private Lives of Pippa
        Lee *314*

Kareem Roustom
    Amreeka *11*

Buck Sanders
    The Hurt Locker *171*

Felipe Perez Santiago
    Rudo y Cursi *328*

David Sardy
    Zombieland *430*

The Section Quartet
    Whip It *417*

Theodore Shapiro (1971-)
    I Love You, Man *179*
    Jennifer's Body *207*
    Year One *427*

Ed Shearmur (1966-)
    Bride Wars *42*

Clinton Shorter
    District 9 *96*

Alan Silvestri (1950-)
    A Christmas Carol *62*
    G.I. Joe: The Rise of Co-
        bra *143*
    Hannah Montana: The
        Movie *159*
    Night at the Museum: Battle of
        the Smithsonian *271*

Rob Simonsen
    (500) Days of Summer *126*
    Management *241*

Vinny Smith
    Humpday *169*

Johan Soderqvist (1966-)
    Let the Right One In *225*

Lodovico Sorret
    See Tom Noonan

Joey Stephens
    Observe and Report *283*

John Swihart
    New in Town *267*
    Spread *349*

Joby Talbot
    Is Anybody There? *200*

Teho Teardo
    Il Divo *97*

Florian Tesslof
    The Baader Meinhof Com-
        plex *27*

Carl Thiel
    Shorts: The Adventures of the
        Wishing Rock *340*

Stephen Trask
    Cirque du Freak: The Vampire's
        Assistant *64*

Tom Tykwer (1965-)
    The International *195*

Brian Tyler
    Dragonball: Evolution *101*
    Fast & Furious *120*
    The Final Destination *123*
    Law Abiding Citizen *224*

Performer Index

Quinton Aaron (1984-)
   The Blind Side *36*

Hiam Abbass (1960-)
   Amreeka *11*

Salvatore Abruzzese
   Gomorrah *147*

Yussef Abu-Warda
   Amreeka *11*

Jensen Ackles (1978-)
   My Bloody Valentine 3D *259*

Amy Adams (1974-)
   Julie & Julia *211*
   Night at the Museum: Battle of
      the Smithsonian *271*
   Sunshine Cleaning *363*

Joey Lauren Adams (1971-)
   Trucker *385*

Maria Adanez
   My Life in Ruins *261*

Chris Addison
   In the Loop *186*

Charles Adler
   Transformers: Revenge of the
      Fallen (V) *383*

Ben Affleck (1972-)
   Extract *112*
   He's Just Not That Into
      You *164*
   State of Play *353*

Shohreh Aghdashloo (1952-)
   The Stoning of Soraya M. *357*

Malin Akerman (1978-)
   Couples Retreat *77*
   The Proposal *316*
   Watchmen *411*

Raquel Alessi
   Miss March *251*

Jane Alexander (1939-)
   Terminator Salvation *374*
   The Unborn *398*

Sasha Alexander (1973-)
   Love Happens *230*

Muhammad Ali (1942-)
   Soul Power *348*

Debbie Allen (1950-)
   Fame *115*
   Next Day Air *270*

Krista Allen (1972-)
   The Final Destination *123*

Laura Allen (1974-)
   Old Dogs *286*

Laz Alonso
   Avatar *22*
   Fast & Furious *120*

Maria Conchita Alonso (1957-)
   Spread *349*

Bruce Altman (1955-)
   Bride Wars *42*

Lauren Ambrose (1978-)
   Cold Souls *70*
   Where the Wild Things Are
      (V) *415*

Joe Anderson
   Amelia *9*

Wes Anderson (1969-)
   Fantastic Mr. Fox (V) *118*

Michael Angarano (1987-)
   Gentlemen Broncos *139*

Jennifer Aniston (1969-)
   He's Just Not That Into
      You *164*
   Love Happens *230*
   Management *241*

Ann-Margret (1941-)
   The Loss of a Teardrop Dia-
      mond *229*
   Old Dogs *286*

Iris Apatow
   Funny People *133*

Maude Apatow
   Funny People *133*

Christina Applegate (1971-)
   Alvin and the Chipmunks: The
      Squeakuel (V) *8*

Anne Archer (1947-)
   Ghosts of Girlfriends Past *142*

Michael Arden
   Bride Wars *42*

Geoffrey Arend (1978-)
   (500) Days of Summer *126*

Moises Arias
   Hannah Montana: The
      Movie *159*

Adam Arkin (1956-)
   A Serious Man *334*

Alan Arkin (1934-)
   The Private Lives of Pippa
      Lee *314*
   Sunshine Cleaning *363*

Fred Armisen (1966-)
   Confessions of a Shopaholic *74*
   Post Grad *309*

Amber Armstrong
   Paranormal Activity *296*

Emily Browning (1988-)
The Uninvited *401*

Daniel Bruhl (1978-)
Inglourious Basterds *191*

Flavio Bucci (1947-)
Il Divo *97*

Carlo Bucciorosso
Il Divo *97*

Joan Juliet Buck
Julie & Julia *211*

Dragos Bucur
Police, Adjective *306*

Richard Bull (1924-)
Sugar *360*

Sandra Bullock (1964-)
All About Steve *6*
The Blind Side *36*
The Proposal *316*

Billy Burke (1966-)
The Twilight Saga: New
Moon *390*

Michael Reilly Burke (1969-)
The Collector *73*

Gedeon Burkhard
Inglourious Basterds *191*

Carol Burnett (1933-)
Post Grad *309*

Ellen Burstyn (1932-)
The Loss of a Teardrop Diamond *229*

Steve Buscemi (1957-)
G-Force *140*
The Messenger *248*

Shoshana Bush
Dance Flick *88*

Austin Butler (1991-)
Aliens in the Attic *5*

Gerard Butler (1969-)
Gamer *137*
Law Abiding Citizen *224*
The Ugly Truth *397*

Paul Butler
A Single Man *343*

Rose Byrne (1979-)
Adam *1*
Knowing *214*

James Caan (1939-)
Cloudy with a Chance of Meat-
balls (V) *67*
New York, I Love You *268*

Santiago Cabrera
Che *59*

Gino Cafarelli
Big Fan *33*

Nicolas Cage (1964-)
Astro Boy (V) *20*

Bad Lieutenant: Port of Call New
Orleans *28*
G-Force (V) *140*
Knowing *214*

Michael Caine (1933-)
Is Anybody There? *200*

Christian Camargo (1971-)
The Hurt Locker *171*

Bill Camp
Public Enemies *317*

Bruce Campbell (1958-)
Cloudy with a Chance of Meatballs (V) *67*

Antonia Campbell-Hughes (1982-)
Bright Star *43*

Bobby Campo
The Final Destination *123*

Bruno Campos (1974-)
The Princess and the Frog
(V) *312*

Bobby Cannavale (1971-)
Paul Blart: Mall Cop *298*

Salvatore Cantalupo
Gomorrah *147*

Chandler Canterbury
Knowing *214*

Peter Capaldi (1958-)
In the Loop *186*

Helen Carey
Julie & Julia *211*

Mariah Carey (1969-)
Precious: Based on the Novel
'Push' by Sapphire *310*

Peter Carlberg
Let the Right One In *225*

Jessica Carlson
Cirque du Freak: The Vampire's
Assistant *64*

Jack Carpenter (1984-)
I Love You, Beth Cooper *178*

Jim Carrey (1962-)
A Christmas Carol (V) *62*

Janet Carroll (1940-)
(Untitled) *402*

Crystal Cartwright
Paranormal Activity *296*

Nick Cassavetes (1959-)
My Sister's Keeper *264*

Katie Cassidy (1986-)
Taken *369*

Jessie Cave (1987-)
Harry Potter and the Half-Blood
Prince *160*

Jim Caviezel (1968-)
The Stoning of Soraya M. *357*

Henry Cavill (1983-)
Whatever Works *413*

Cladia Celedon
The Maid *238*

John Cena
12 Rounds *387*

Michael Cera (1988-)
Paper Heart *295*
Year One *427*

Michael Cerveris (1960-)
Cirque du Freak: The Vampire's
Assistant *64*

Alain Chabat (1958-)
Night at the Museum: Battle of
the Smithsonian *271*

Lacey Chabert (1982-)
Ghosts of Girlfriends Past *142*

Kathleen Chalfant (1945-)
Duplicity *102*

Robin Chalk
Moon *255*

Chen "Chang Chen" Chang (1976-)
Red Cliff *324*

Ben Chaplin (1970-)
Me and Orson Welles *245*

Kevin Chapman
Black Dynamite *34*
Sunshine Cleaning *363*

Sorapong Chatree
Ong Bak 2 *288*

Justin Chatwin (1982-)
Dragonball: Evolution *101*

Don Cheadle (1964-)
Hotel for Dogs *166*

Jake Cherry (1996-)
Night at the Museum: Battle of
the Smithsonian *271*

Morris Chestnut (1969-)
Not Easily Broken *278*

Maggie Cheung (1964-)
Inglourious Basterds *191*

Anna Chlumsky (1980-)
In the Loop *186*

John Cho (1972-)
Star Trek *351*

Justin Chon (1981-)
Crossing Over *83*
The Twilight Saga: New
Moon *390*

Katie Chonacas (1980-)
Bad Lieutenant: Port of Call New
Orleans *28*

Yun-Fat Chow
See Chow Yun-Fat

Margo Harshman (1986-)
Sorority Row *346*

Kevin Hart
Not Easily Broken *278*

Teri Hatcher (1964-)
Coraline (V) *75*

Anne Hathaway (1982-)
Bride Wars *42*

Shawn Hatosy (1975-)
Bad Lieutenant: Port of Call New Orleans *28*
Public Enemies *317*

Kali Hawk
Couples Retreat *77*

Ethan Hawke (1971-)
New York, I Love You *268*

Sally Hawkins (1976-)
An Education *108*

Elizabeth Hawthorne
Underworld: Rise of the Lycans *400*

Salma Hayek (1966-)
Cirque du Freak: The Vampire's Assistant *64*

Vanessa Haywood
District 9 *96*

Amber Heard (1986-)
The Informers *189*
The Stepfather *355*
Zombieland *430*

Anne Heche (1969-)
Spread *349*

Kare Hedebrant
Let the Right One In *225*

Hugh Hefner (1926-)
Miss March *251*

Katherine Heigl (1978-)
The Ugly Truth *397*

Ed Helms
The Goods: Live Hard, Sell Hard *151*
The Hangover *157*
Monsters vs. Aliens (V) *253*

Chris Hemsworth (1983-)
A Perfect Getaway *300*
Star Trek *351*

Zulay Henao
Fighting *122*

Jill Hennessy
Lymelife *234*

Daniel Henney
X-Men Origins: Wolverine *425*

Stig Frode Henriksen
Dead Snow *90*

Taraji P. Henson (1970-)
I Can Do Bad All By Myself *175*
Not Easily Broken *278*

Dolores Heredia (1966-)
Rudo y Cursi *328*

Howard Hesseman (1940-)
Halloween II *155*

Chris Heyerdahl
The Twilight Saga: New Moon *390*

John Michael Higgins (1963-)
Couples Retreat *77*
Fired Up! *125*
The Ugly Truth *397*

Paul Higgins
In the Loop *186*

Freddie Highmore (1992-)
Astro Boy (V) *20*

Amy Hill (1953-)
Couples Retreat *77*

Jonah Hill (1983-)
Funny People *133*
The Invention of Lying *196*
Night at the Museum: Battle of the Smithsonian *271*

Brennan Hillard (1990-)
Dance Flick *88*

Ciaran Hinds (1953-)
Race to Witch Mountain *323*

Cheryl Hines (1965-)
The Ugly Truth *397*

Ryoko Hirosue
Departures *91*

Emile Hirsch (1985-)
Taking Woodstock *372*

Gary Hirshberg
Food, Inc. *129*

Iben Hjejle (1971-)
Chéri *60*

Josie Ho
Street Fighter: The Legend of Chun-Li *358*

Robert Hobbs
Invictus *198*

John Hodgman
Coraline (V) *75*

Vegar Hoel (1973-)
Dead Snow *90*

Matt Hoey
The Great Buck Howard *152*

Dustin Hoffman (1937-)
Last Chance Harvey *219*

Philip Seymour Hoffman (1967-)
The Invention of Lying *196*
Mary and Max (V) *244*
Pirate Radio *302*

Robert Hoffman, III (1980-)
Aliens in the Attic *5*

Siobhan Fallon Hogan (1972-)
New in Town *267*

Hal Holbrook (1925-)
Killshot *213*

Andre Holland
Sugar *360*

Tom Holland (1943-)
The Soloist *345*

Tom Hollander (1969-)
In the Loop *186*

Lluís Homar (1957-)
Broken Embraces *45*

Bob Hoskins (1942-)
A Christmas Carol (V) *62*

Nicholas Hoult (1989-)
A Single Man *343*

Djimon Hounsou (1964-)
Push *320*

Arliss Howard (1955-)
The Time Traveler's Wife *381*

Bryce Dallas Howard (1981-)
The Loss of a Teardrop Diamond *229*
Terminator Salvation *374*

Leo Howard (1997-)
Shorts: The Adventures of the Wishing Rock *340*

Terrence Howard (1969-)
Fighting *122*
The Princess and the Frog (V) *312*

Steve Howey (1977-)
Bride Wars *42*

Jun Hu
Red Cliff *324*

Wei Huang
The Class *66*

Vanessa Anne Hudgens (1988-)
Bandslam *30*

Ernie Hudson (1945-)
Dragonball: Evolution *101*

Kate Hudson (1979-)
Bride Wars *42*
Nine *275*

Matthew Humphreys
Obsessed *284*

Barry Humphries (1934-)
Mary and Max (N) *244*

Sam Huntington (1982-)
Fanboys *117*

John Hurt (1940-)
The Limits of Control *227*
New York, I Love You *268*

Toby Huss (1966-)
World's Greatest Dad *423*

Danny Huston (1962-)
X-Men Origins: Wolverine *425*

Josh Hutcherson (1992-)
Cirque du Freak: The Vampire's
Assistant *64*

Timothy Hutton (1960-)
Lymelife *234*

Paul Iacono
Fame *115*

Jacky Ido (1977-)
Inglourious Basterds *191*

Rhys Ifans (1968-)
The Informers *189*
Pirate Radio *302*

Gianfelice Imparato
Gomorrah *147*

Michael Imperioli (1966-)
The Lovely Bones *232*

Michael Irby
Law Abiding Citizen *224*

Jeremy Irons (1948-)
The Pink Panther 2 *301*

Michael Ironside (1950-)
Terminator Salvation *374*
Surveillance *365*

Amy Irving (1953-)
Adam *1*

Chris Isaak (1956-)
The Informers *189*

Vlad Ivanov
Police, Adjective *306*

Tony Jaa
Ong Bak 2 *288*

Hugh Jackman (1968-)
X-Men Origins: Wolverine *425*

Michael Jackson (1958-2009)
Michael Jackson's This Is
It *250*

Neil Jackson
Push *320*

Samuel L. Jackson (1948-)
Astro Boy (V) *20*
Inglourious Basterds (N) *191*

Ernst Jacobi (1933-)
The White Ribbon (N) *418*

Gillian Jacobs
The Box *39*

Jadagrace
Terminator Salvation *374*

David James
District 9 *96*

Geraldine James (1950-)
Sherlock Holmes *338*

Kevin James (1965-)
Paul Blart: Mall Cop *298*

LeBron James (1984-)
More Than a Game *256*

Pell James (1977-)
Surveillance *365*

Thomas Jane (1969-)
Killshot *213*

Allison Janney (1960-)
Away We Go *24*
Jennifer's Body *207*

Famke Janssen (1964-)
Taken *369*

Cannon Jay
Not Easily Broken *278*

Ricky Jay (1948-)
The Brothers Bloom (N) *50*
The Great Buck Howard *152*

Marc John Jefferies
Notorious *280*

Eve Jihan Jeffers
See Eve

Carter Jenkins (1991-)
Aliens in the Attic *5*

Noam Jenkins
Adoration *2*

Ken Jeong (1969-)
All About Steve *6*
Couples Retreat *77*
The Goods: Live Hard, Sell
Hard *151*
The Hangover *157*

Héctor Jiménez (1973-)
Gentlemen Broncos *139*

Tim Jo
Fame *115*

Scarlett Johansson (1984-)
He's Just Not That Into
You *164*

Bryce Johnson
Trucker *385*

Corey Johnson (1961-)
The Fourth Kind *130*

Dwayne "The Rock" Johnson (1972-)
Planet 51 (V) *304*
Race to Witch Mountain *323*

Jake M. Johnson
Paper Heart *295*

Kirsten Johnson
Bride Wars *42*

Frankie Jonas (2000-)
Ponyo (V) *307*

Joe Jonas (1989-)
Jonas Brothers: The 3D Concert
Experience *208*

Kevin Jonas (1987-)
Jonas Brothers: The 3D Concert
Experience *208*

Nick Jonas (1992-)
Jonas Brothers: The 3D Concert
Experience *208*

Cherry Jones (1956-)
Amelia *9*

Felicity Jones (1984-)
Chéri *60*

James Earl Jones (1931-)
Earth (N) *105*

Orlando Jones (1968-)
Cirque du Freak: The Vampire's
Assistant *64*

Rashida Jones (1976-)
I Love You, Man *179*
New in Town *267*

Tyler Patrick Jones (1994-)
G-Force *140*

Vinnie Jones (1965-)
(Untitled) *402*
Year One *427*

Milla Jovovich (1975-)
The Fourth Kind *130*
A Perfect Getaway *300*

Malese Jow (1991-)
Aliens in the Attic *5*

Dru Joyce
More Than a Game *256*

Ashley Judd (1968-)
Crossing Over *83*

Adhir Kalyan
Fired Up! *125*

Takeshi Kaneshiro (1911-)
Red Cliff *324*

Sung Kang
Ninja Assassin *277*

Athena Karkanis
Saw VI *331*

Branka Katic (1970-)
Public Enemies *317*

Zoe Kazan (1983-)
It's Complicated *203*
Me and Orson Welles *245*
The Private Lives of Pippa
Lee *314*

James Keane (1952-)
Crazy Heart *81*

Michael Keaton (1951-)
Post Grad *309*

Caitlin Keats (1972-)
Women in Trouble *422*

Arielle Kebbel (1985-)
The Uninvited *401*

Elisabeth Moss (1982-)
   Did You Hear About the Morgans? *93*

Jesse Moss (1983-)
   The Uninvited *401*

Ebon Moss-Bachrach
   The Marc Pease Experience *243*

Donny Most (1953-)
   The Great Buck Howard *152*

Masahiro Motoki
   Departures *91*

Melkar Muallem
   Amreeka *11*

Armin Mueller-Stahl (1930-)
   Angels & Demons *12*
   The International *195*

Megan Mullally (1958-)
   Fame *115*

Carey Mulligan (1985-)
   Brothers *48*
   An Education *108*

Christina Murphy
   Dance Flick *88*

Eddie Murphy (1961-)
   Imagine That *184*

Bill Murray (1950-)
   Fantastic Mr. Fox (V) *118*
   The Limits of Control *227*
   Zombieland *430*

Mike Myers (1963-)
   Inglourious Basterds *191*

Jordan Nagai
   Up (V) *404*

Shido Nakamura (1972-)
   Red Cliff *324*

Leonardo Nam (1979-)
   He's Just Not That Into You *164*

Charles Napier (1936-)
   The Goods: Live Hard, Sell Hard *151*

Niecy Nash (1970-)
   Not Easily Broken *278*

Naturi Naughton
   Notorious *280*

Maria Nazionale
   Gomorrah *147*

Kevin Nealon (1953-)
   Aliens in the Attic *5*

Marife Necesito
   Mammoth *240*

Liam Neeson (1952-)
   Five Minutes of Heaven *127*
   Ponyo (V) *307*
   Taken *369*

Navid Negahban (1968-)
   The Stoning of Soraya M. *357*

Craig T. Nelson (1946-)
   The Proposal *316*

Judd Nelson (1959-)
   The Boondock Saints II: All Saints Day *37*

James Nesbitt (1966-)
   Five Minutes of Heaven *127*

Bebe Neuwirth (1958-)
   Fame *115*

George Newbern (1964-)
   Saw VI *331*

Thandie Newton (1972-)
   2012 *388*

Jan Nicdao
   Mammoth *240*

Austin Nichols (1980-)
   The Informers *189*

Lance E. Nichols (1955-)
   Bad Lieutenant: Port of Call New Orleans *28*

Rachel Nichols (1980-)
   G.I. Joe: The Rise of Cobra *143*
   Star Trek *351*

Lorraine Nicholson (1990-)
   World's Greatest Dad *423*

Bill Nighy (1949-)
   Astro Boy (V) *20*
   G-Force *140*
   Pirate Radio *302*
   Underworld: Rise of the Lycans *400*

Leonard Nimoy (1931-)
   Star Trek *351*

Alessandro Nivola (1972-)
   Coco Before Chanel *69*

Cynthia Nixon (1966-)
   Lymelife *234*

Kimberly Nixon
   Easy Virtue *106*

Amaury Nolasco (1970-)
   Armored *19*

Michelle Nolden
   The Time Traveler's Wife *381*

Tom Noonan (1951-)
   The House of the Devil *168*
   Where the Wild Things Are (V) *415*

Edward Norton (1969-)
   The Invention of Lying *196*

Jack Noseworthy (1969-)
   Surrogates *364*

Ralph Nossek
   My Life in Ruins *261*

Christopher Noth (1956-)
   My One and Only *262*

Michael Nouri (1945-)
   The Proposal *316*

B.J. Novak (1979-)
   Inglourious Basterds *191*

Tamar Novas
   Broken Embraces *45*

Osmar Nunez
   The Proposal *316*

Sophie Nyweide
   Mammoth *240*

Richard O'Barry
   The Cove *79*

Conan O'Brien (1963-)
   The Great Buck Howard *152*

Brian F. O'Byrne (1967-)
   The International *195*

Jerry O'Connell (1974-)
   Obsessed *284*

Keir O'Donnell
   Paul Blart: Mall Cop *298*

Chris O'Dowd
   Pirate Radio *302*

Esmeralda Oeurtaini
   The Class *66*

Catherine O'Hara (1954-)
   Away We Go *24*
   Where the Wild Things Are (V) *415*

Denis O'Hare (1962-)
   Duplicity *102*
   The Proposal *316*

Juliet Oldfield
   Bronson *47*

Gary Oldman (1958-)
   A Christmas Carol (V) *62*
   Planet 51 (V) *304*
   The Unborn *398*

Alex O'Loughlin (1977-)
   Whiteout *420*

Eric Christian Olsen (1977-)
   Fired Up! *125*
   Sunshine Cleaning *363*

Timothy Olyphant (1968-)
   A Perfect Getaway *300*

Kevin O'Neill
   Five Minutes of Heaven *127*

Julia Ormond (1965-)
   Che *59*
   Surveillance *365*

Leland Orser (1960-)
   Taken *369*

Aubrey Plaza
Funny People *133*

Jesse Plemons (1988-)
Observe and Report *283*

George Plimpton (1927-2003)
Soul Power *348*

Christopher Plummer (1927-)
The Imaginarium of Doctor Parnassus *182*
The Last Station *222*
9 (V) *273*
Up (V) *404*

Amy Poehler (1971-)
Alvin and the Chipmunks: The Squeakuel (V) *8*
Monsters vs. Aliens (V) *253*

Benoit Poelvoorde
Coco Before Chanel *69*

Michael Pollan
Food, Inc. *129*

Carlos Ponce (1972-)
Couples Retreat *77*

Scott Porter
Bandslam *30*

Ellary Porterfield
Sugar *360*

Blanca Portillo
Broken Embraces *45*

Natalie Portman (1981-)
Brothers *48*
New York, I Love You *268*

Franka Potente (1974-)
Che *59*

Monica Potter (1971-)
The Last House on the Left *220*

CCH Pounder (1952-)
Avatar *22*
Orphan *289*

Ali Pourtash
The Stoning of Soraya M. *357*

Chris Pratt
Bride Wars *42*
Jennifer's Body *207*

Keri Lynn Pratt (1978-)
I Hope They Serve Beer in Hell *176*

Kyla Pratt (1986-)
Hotel for Dogs *166*

Jaime Pressly (1977-)
I Love You, Man *179*

Carrie Preston (1967-)
Duplicity *102*

Kelly Preston (1962-)
Old Dogs *286*

Santisuk Promsiri
Ong Bak 2 *288*

Jonathan Pryce (1947-)
G.I. Joe: The Rise of Cobra *143*

Louie Psihoyos
The Cove *79*

Lou Taylor Pucci (1985-)
The Answer Man *14*
The Informers *189*

Keisha Knight Pulliam (1979-)
Madea Goes to Jail *237*

Bill Pullman (1953-)
Surveillance *365*

Lucy Punch
(Untitled) *402*

Maggie Q (1979-)
New York, I Love You *268*

Dennis Quaid (1954-)
Battle for Terra (V) *31*
G.I. Joe: The Rise of Cobra *143*
Pandorum *293*

DJ Qualls (1978-)
All About Steve *6*

Queen Latifah (1970-)
Ice Age: Dawn of the Dinosaurs (V) *181*

Maeve Quinlan (1964-)
Not Easily Broken *278*

Molly C. Quinn (1993-)
My One and Only *262*

Zachary Quinto (1977-)
Star Trek *351*

Olivier Rabourdin
Taken *369*

Daniel Radcliffe (1989-)
Harry Potter and the Half-Blood Prince *160*

Per Ragnar
Let the Right One In *225*

Aishwarya Rai (1973-)
The Pink Panther 2 *301*

Rain (1982-)
Ninja Assassin *277*

Mary Lynn Rajskub (1971-)
Julie & Julia *211*
Sunshine Cleaning *363*

Edgar Ramirez (1977-)
Che *59*

Efren Ramirez (1973-)
Crank: High Voltage *80*

Harold Ramis (1944-)
Year One *427*

Jerome Ranft
Up (V) *404*

Stephen Rannazzisi
Paul Blart: Mall Cop *298*

Dileep Rao
Drag Me to Hell *99*

Michael Rapaport (1970-)
Big Fan *33*

June Raphael
Year One *427*

David Rasche (1944-)
In the Loop *186*

Victor Rasuk (1984-)
Che *59*

Jackson Rathbone (1984-)
The Twilight Saga: New Moon *390*

Devin Ratray (1977-)
Surrogates *364*

John Ratzenberger (1947-)
Up (V) *404*

Lorna Raver
Drag Me to Hell *99*

Conner Rayburn (1999-)
The Invention of Lying *196*
Old Dogs *286*

Elizabeth Reaser (1975-)
The Twilight Saga: New Moon *390*

James Rebhorn (1948-)
The Box *39*
The International *195*

Max Records
Where the Wild Things Are *415*

Lynn Redgrave (1943-)
Confessions of a Shopaholic *74*

Nikki Reed (1988-)
The Twilight Saga: New Moon *390*

Norman Reedus (1969-)
The Boondock Saints II: All Saints Day *37*
Pandorum *293*

Keanu Reeves (1964-)
The Private Lives of Pippa Lee *314*

Rachel Regulier
The Class *66*

John C. Reilly (1965-)
Cirque du Freak: The Vampire's Assistant *64*
9 (V) *273*

Kelly Reilly (1977-)
Me and Orson Welles *245*
Sherlock Holmes *338*

Robb Reiner
Anvil! The Story of Anvil *18*

Catherine Reitman (1981-)
Post Grad *309*

James Remar (1953-)
The Unborn *398*

George Remes
Police, Adjective *306*

Mark Rendall (1988-)
My One and Only *262*

Jeremie Renier (1981-)
Summer Hours *361*

Jeremy Renner (1971-)
The Hurt Locker *171*

Jean Reno (1948-)
Armored *19*
Couples Retreat *77*
The Pink Panther 2 *301*

Larry Rew
Underworld: Rise of the Lycans *400*

Cisco Reyes
Next Day Air *270*

Dominique Reymond
Summer Hours *361*

Ryan Reynolds (1976-)
Adventureland *3*
The Proposal *316*
X-Men Origins: Wolverine *425*

Ving Rhames (1961-)
The Goods: Live Hard, Sell Hard *151*
Surrogates *364*

Giovanni Ribisi (1974-)
Avatar *22*
Public Enemies *317*

Christina Ricci (1980-)
New York, I Love You *268*

Cameron Richardson
Women in Trouble *422*

Miranda Richardson (1958-)
The Young Victoria *429*

Salli Richardson-Whitfield
Black Dynamite *34*

Andy Richter (1966-)
Aliens in the Attic *5*

Alan Rickman (1946-)
Harry Potter and the Half-Blood Prince *160*

Armando Riesco
Che *59*

Rob Riggle
The Goods: Live Hard, Sell Hard *151*

Amanda Righetti
Friday the 13th *132*

Charlotte Riley
Easy Virtue *106*

Sean Ringgold
Notorious *280*

Michael Rispoli (1960-)
The Taking of Pelham 123 *371*

Krysten Ritter
Confessions of a Shopaholic *74*

Elilio Rivera
Next Day Air *270*

AnnaSophia Robb (1993-)
Race to Witch Mountain *323*

Doris Roberts (1930-)
Aliens in the Attic *5*

Emma Roberts
Lymelife *234*

Emma Roberts (1991-)
Hotel for Dogs *166*

Grant Roberts
Invictus *198*

Julia Roberts (1967-)
Duplicity *102*

Shawn Roberts (1984-)
I Love You, Beth Cooper *178*

Craig Robinson (1971-)
Fanboys *117*
Miss March *251*
Post Grad *309*

Lara Robinson
Knowing *214*

Chris Rock (1966-)
Good Hair *148*

Rock, The
See Dwayne "The Rock" Johnson

Sam Rockwell (1968-)
Everybody's Fine *111*
G-Force (V) *140*
Gentlemen Broncos *139*
Moon *255*

Karel Roden (1962-)
Orphan *289*

Adam Rodriguez (1975-)
I Can Do Bad All By Myself *175*

Michelle Rodriguez (1978-)
Avatar *22*
Fast & Furious *120*

Raini Rodriguez
Paul Blart: Mall Cop *298*

Rebel Rodriguez (1999-)
Shorts: The Adventures of the Wishing Rock *340*

Sarah Roemer
Fired Up! *125*

Maurice Roeves (1937-)
The Damned United *87*

Seth Rogen (1982-)
Funny People *133*
Monsters vs. Aliens (V) *253*
Observe and Report *283*

Horacio Garcia Rojas
Julia *210*

Mark Rolston (1956-)
Saw VI *331*

Ray Romano (1957-)
Ice Age: Dawn of the Dinosaurs (V) *181*

Saoirse Ronan (1994-)
The Lovely Bones *232*

Stephen Root (1951-)
The Men Who Stare at Goats *247*
The Soloist *345*

Anika Noni Rose (1972-)
The Princess and the Frog (V) *312*

Chelcie Ross (1942-)
Drag Me to Hell *99*

Hugh Ross
Bronson *47*

Isabella Rossellini (1952-)
Two Lovers *392*

Emmy Rossum (1986-)
Dragonball: Evolution *101*

Evy Kasseth Rosten (1978-)
Dead Snow *90*

Andrea Roth (1967-)
The Collector *73*

Eli Roth (1972-)
Inglourious Basterds *191*

Mickey Rourke (1955-)
The Informers *189*
Killshot *213*

Eddie Rouse
Pandorum *293*

Troy Roush
Food, Inc. *129*

Deep Roy (1957-)
Star Trek *351*

Saul Rubinek (1949-)
Julia *210*

Alan Ruck (1960-)
I Love You, Beth Cooper *178*

Paul Rudd (1969-)
I Love You, Man *179*
Monsters vs. Aliens (V) *253*
Year One *427*

Maya Rudolph (1972-)
Away We Go *24*

Sherri Shepherd (1970-)
Precious: Based on the Novel
'Push' by Sapphire *310*

Ha-Kyun Shin (1974-)
Thirst *378*

Columbus Short (1982-)
Armored *19*
Whiteout *420*

Jake Short
Shorts: The Adventures of the
Wishing Rock *340*

Robin Shou (1960-)
Street Fighter: The Legend of
Chun-Li *358*

Gabourney "Gabby" Sidibe
Precious: Based on the Novel
'Push' by Sapphire *310*

Maggie Siff
Push *320*

Frederick Siglar
I Can Do Bad All By My-
self *175*

Augustin Silva
The Maid *238*

Gene Simmons (1949-)
Extract *112*

Henry Simmons (1970-)
World's Greatest Dad *423*

J.K. Simmons (1955-)
Aliens in the Attic (V) *5*
Extract *112*
I Love You, Man *179*
Jennifer's Body *207*
New in Town *267*
Up in the Air *406*

Johnny Simmons
Hotel for Dogs *166*
Jennifer's Body *207*

Ryan Simpkins
A Single Man *343*
Surveillance *365*

Molly Sims (1973-)
Fired Up! *125*

Nirut Sirichanya
Ong Bak 2 *288*

Stellan Skarsgard (1951-)
Angels & Demons *12*

Jenny Skavlan
Dead Snow *90*

Tom Skerritt (1933-)
Whiteout *420*

Micah Sloat
Paranormal Activity *296*

Ptolemy Slocum
(Untitled) *402*

Amy Smart (1976-)
Crank: High Voltage *80*

Kodi Smit-McPhee (1996-)
The Road *326*

Antonique Smith
Notorious *280*

Kerr Smith (1972-)
My Bloody Valentine 3D *259*

Maggie Smith (1934-)
Harry Potter and the Half-Blood
Prince *160*

Roger Guenveur Smith (1959-)
Fighting *122*

Shawnee Smith (1970-)
Saw VI *331*

Tasha Smith (1971-)
Couples Retreat *77*

Leelee Sobieski (1982-)
Public Enemies *317*

Bonnie Sommerville
The Ugly Truth *397*

Kang-ho Song (1967-)
Thirst *378*

Lodovico Sorret
See Tom Noonan

Algenis Perez Soto
Sugar *360*

Kevin Spacey (1959-)
The Men Who Stare at
Goats *247*
Moon (V) *255*

James Spader (1961-)
Shorts: The Adventures of the
Wishing Rock *340*

Timothy Spall (1957-)
The Damned United *87*
Harry Potter and the Half-Blood
Prince *160*

Scott Speedman (1975-)
Adoration *2*

Chaske Spencer
The Twilight Saga: New
Moon *390*

Jason Spevack
Sunshine Cleaning *363*

Jordana Spiro (1977-)
The Goods: Live Hard, Sell
Hard *151*

Elizabeth Spriggs (1929-)
Is Anybody There? *200*

Run Srinikornchot
Mammoth *240*

Nick Stahl (1979-)
My One and Only *262*

Sebastian Stan (1983-)
Spread *349*

Molly Stanton
Miss March *251*

Robert Stanton (1963-)
Confessions of a Shopaholic *74*

Martin Starr (1982-)
Adventureland *3*

Jason Statham (1972-)
Crank: High Voltage *80*

Imelda Staunton (1956-)
Taking Woodstock *372*

Mary Steenburgen (1953-)
Did You Hear About the Mor-
gans? *93*
The Proposal *316*

Oleg Stefan
Duplicity *102*

Bernice Stegers
My Life in Ruins *261*

Daniel Stern (1957-)
Whip It *417*

Frances Sternhagen (1930-)
Julie & Julia *211*

Jean-Francois Stevenin (1944-)
The Limits of Control *227*

Cynthia Stevenson (1963-)
I Love You, Beth Cooper *178*

Ray Stevenson (1964-)
Cirque du Freak: The Vampire's
Assistant *64*

French Stewart (1964-)
Surveillance *365*

Josh Stewart (1977-)
The Collector *73*
Law Abiding Citizen *224*

Kristen Stewart (1990-)
Adventureland *3*
The Twilight Saga: New
Moon *390*

Patrick Stewart (1940-)
The Invention of Lying
(N) *196*

Ben Stiller (1965-)
The Marc Pease Experi-
ence *243*
Night at the Museum: Battle of
the Smithsonian *271*

Ion Stoica
Police, Adjective *306*

Emma Stone (1988-)
Ghosts of Girlfriends Past *142*
Zombieland *430*

Sam Oz Stone
The Box *39*

Dirk Storm
  See Kevin Nealon

Lauren Storm (1987-)
  I Love You, Beth Cooper *178*

David Strathairn (1949-)
  The Uninvited *401*

David Strathrain
  Cold Souls *70*

Meryl Streep (1949-)
  Fantastic Mr. Fox *(V)* *118*
  It's Complicated *203*
  Julie & Julia *211*

Sherry Stringfield (1967-)
  The Stepfather *355*

Mark Strong (1963-)
  Sherlock Holmes *338*
  The Young Victoria *429*

Wes Studi (1947-)
  Avatar *22*

Michael Stuhlbarg
  A Serious Man *334*

Geoff Stults (1977-)
  I Hope They Serve Beer in
    Hell *176*

Jim Sturgess
  Crossing Over *83*

Thomas Sturridge (1986-)
  Pirate Radio *302*

Nicole Sullivan (1970-)
  Black Dynamite *34*

Bjorn Sundquist (1948-)
  Dead Snow *90*

Ahmet Rifat Sungar (1983-)
  Three Monkeys *380*

Daniel Sunjata (1971-)
  Ghosts of Girlfriends Past *142*

Donald Sutherland (1934-)
  Astro Boy *(V)* *20*

Kiefer Sutherland (1966-)
  Monsters vs. Aliens *(V)* *253*

Bo Svenson (1941-)
  Inglourious Basterds *191*

Hilary Swank (1974-)
  Amelia *9*

Tilda Swinton (1961-)
  Julia *210*
  The Limits of Control *227*

Souleymane Sy Savane
  Goodbye Solo *149*

Stephanie Szostak
  Motherhood *258*

Taboo
  Street Fighter: The Legend of
    Chun-Li *358*

Jorma Taccone (1977-)
  Land of the Lost *217*

Said Taghmaoui (1973-)
  G.I. Joe: The Rise of Co-
    bra *143*

Faran Tahir
  Star Trek *351*

George Takei (1940-)
  The Great Buck Howard *152*

Jeffrey Tambor (1944-)
  The Hangover *157*
  The Invention of Lying *196*
  Monsters vs. Aliens *(V)* *253*

Gerardo Taracena
  Sin Nombre *341*

Channing Tatum (1980-)
  Fighting *122*
  G.I. Joe: The Rise of Co-
    bra *143*
  Public Enemies *317*

Audrey Tautou (1978-)
  Coco Before Chanel *69*

Rod Taylor (1929-)
  Inglourious Basterds *191*

Scout Taylor-Compton (1989-)
  Halloween II *155*
  Obsessed *284*

Jon Tenney (1961-)
  The Stepfather *355*

Tessa la
  The Burning Plain *54*

Charlize Theron (1975-)
  Astro Boy *(N)* *20*
  The Burning Plain *54*
  The Road *326*

David Thewlis (1963-)
  Harry Potter and the Half-Blood
    Prince *160*

Alan Thicke (1947-)
  The Goods: Live Hard, Sell
    Hard *151*

Olivia Thirlby (1986-)
  The Answer Man *14*
  New York, I Love You *268*

Emma Thompson (1959-)
  An Education *108*
  Last Chance Harvey *219*
  Pirate Radio *302*

Ulrich Thomsen (1963-)
  The International *195*

Erik Thomson
  The Boys Are Back *40*

Billy Bob Thornton (1955-)
  The Informers *189*

Uma Thurman (1970-)
  Motherhood *258*

Rachel Ticotin (1959-)
  The Burning Plain *54*

Kevin Tighe (1944-)
  My Bloody Valentine 3D *259*

Lucas Till
  Hannah Montana: The
    Movie *159*

Jamie Tirelli (1945-)
  Sugar *360*

Ashley Tisdale (1985-)
  Aliens in the Attic *5*

Stephen Tobolowsky (1951-)
  The Time Traveler's Wife *381*

Frances Tomelty (1948-)
  Chéri *60*

Lily Tomlin (1939-)
  The Pink Panther 2 *301*
  Ponyo *(V)* *307*

Ane Dahl Torp (1975-)
  Dead Snow *90*

Pip Torrens (1960-)
  Easy Virtue *106*

Luis Tosar (1971-)
  The Limits of Control *227*

Lorraine Toussaint (1960-)
  The Soloist *345*

Nadia Townsend
  Knowing *214*

Michelle Trachtenberg (1985-)
  17 Again *336*

Antje Traue
  Pandorum *293*

Romeo Travis
  More Than a Game *256*

Stacey Travis
  The Great Buck Howard *152*

Ella Bleu Travolta (2000-)
  Old Dogs *286*

John Travolta (1954-)
  Old Dogs *286*
  The Taking of Pelham 123
    371

Verne Troyer (1969-)
  The Imaginarium of Doctor Par-
    nassus *182*

Stanley Tucci (1960-)
  Julie & Julia *211*
  The Lovely Bones *232*

Ulrich Tukur (1957-)
  The White Ribbon *418*

Robin Tunney (1972-)
  The Burning Plain *54*

James Tupper
  Me and Orson Welles *245*

Bree Turner (1977-)
The Ugly Truth *397*

John Turturro (1957-)
The Taking of Pelham 123
371
Transformers: Revenge of the
Fallen *383*

Tyrese
See Tyrese Gibson

Mike Tyson (1966-)
The Hangover *157*
Tyson *394*

Nadja Uhl (1972-)
The Baader Meinhof Complex *27*

Skeet Ulrich (1969-)
Armored *19*

Karl Urban (1972-)
Star Trek *351*

Lasse Valdal
Dead Snow *90*

Amber Valletta (1974-)
Gamer *137*

Dick Van Dyke (1925-)
Night at the Museum: Battle of
the Smithsonian *271*

Travis Van Winkle (1982-)
Friday the 13th *132*

Maggie VandenBerghe
Aliens in the Attic *5*

Jolie Vanier (1998-)
Shorts: The Adventures of the
Wishing Rock *340*

Shantel VanSanten (1985-)
The Final Destination *123*

Nia Vardalos (1962-)
My Life in Ruins *261*

Sofia Vassilieva (1992-)
My Sister's Keeper *264*

Peter Vaughan (1923-)
Is Anybody There? *200*

Vince Vaughn (1970-)
Couples Retreat *77*

Milo Ventimiglia (1977-)
Armored *19*
Gamer *137*

Maribel Verdu (1970-)
Tetro *376*

Nana Visitor
Friday the 13th *132*

Arnold Vosloo (1962-)
G.I. Joe: The Rise of Cobra *143*

Mark Wahlberg (1971-)
The Lovely Bones *232*

Kari Wahlgren
Aliens in the Attic *(V)* *5*

Tom Waits (1949-)
The Imaginarium of Doctor Parnassus *182*

Eamonn Walker (1959-)
The Messenger *248*

Paul Walker (1973-)
Fast & Furious *120*

Dee Wallace
The House of the Devil *168*

Eli Wallach (1915-)
New York, I Love You *268*

Dylan Walsh (1963-)
The Stepfather *355*

Harriet Walter (1950-)
Chéri *60*
The Young Victoria *429*

Julie Walters (1950-)
Harry Potter and the Half-Blood
Prince *160*

Rich Walters
My Bloody Valentine 3D *259*

David Walton
Fired Up! *125*

Christoph Waltz
Inglourious Basterds *191*

Ning Wang
Red Cliff *324*

Fred Ward (1943-)
Armored *19*
Management *241*

Sela Ward (1957-)
The Stepfather *355*

Wally Ward
See Wallace (Wally) Langham

Denzel Washington (1954-)
The Taking of Pelham 123
371

Mia Wasikowska (1989-)
Amelia *9*

Ken Watanabe (1959-)
Cirque du Freak: The Vampire's
Assistant *64*

Gerard Watkins
Taken *369*

Emily Watson (1967-)
Cold Souls *70*

Emma Watson (1990-)
Harry Potter and the Half-Blood
Prince *160*

Naomi Watts (1968-)
The International *195*

Craig Wayans
Dance Flick *88*

Damon Wayans, Jr. (1982-)
Dance Flick *88*

Keenen Ivory Wayans (1958-)
Dance Flick *88*

Marlon Wayans (1972-)
Dance Flick *88*
G.I. Joe: The Rise of Cobra *143*

Shawn Wayans (1971-)
Dance Flick *88*

Sigourney Weaver (1949-)
Avatar *22*

Haley Webb (1985-)
The Final Destination *123*

Steven Weber (1961-)
My One and Only *262*

Chris Wedge (1957-)
Ice Age: Dawn of the Dinosaurs
(V) *181*

Robin Weigert (1969-)
My One and Only *262*
The Private Lives of Pippa
Lee *314*

Rachel Weisz (1971-)
The Brothers Bloom *50*
The Lovely Bones *232*

Justin Welborn
The Final Destination *123*

Michael Welch (1987-)
The Twilight Saga: New
Moon *390*

Kenneth Welsh (1942-)
Adoration *2*

David Wenham (1965-)
Public Enemies *317*

Alexandra Wentworth (1965-)
It's Complicated *203*

Red West (1936-)
Goodbye Solo *149*

Shea Whigham (1969-)
Bad Lieutenant: Port of Call New
Orleans *28*

Ben Whishaw (1980-)
Bright Star *43*

Denzel Whitaker
Bad Lieutenant: Port of Call New
Orleans *28*

Forest Whitaker (1961-)
Where the Wild Things Are
(V) *415*

Betty White (1922-)
Ponyo *(V)* *307*
The Proposal *316*

Brian White (1973-)
Fighting *122*
I Can Do Bad All By Myself *175*
12 Rounds *387*

Jack White (1975-)
    It Might Get Loud *202*

Julie White
    Monsters vs. Aliens *(V)* *253*

Michael Jai White (1967-)
    Black Dynamite *34*

Mike White (1970-)
    Gentlemen Broncos *139*

Kym E. Whitley (1961-)
    Black Dynamite *34*

Ann Whitney
    Sugar *360*

Kristen Wiig (1973-)
    Adventureland *3*
    Extract *112*
    Whip It *417*

Olivia Wilde (1984-)
    Year One *427*

Jason Wiles (1970-)
    The Stepfather *355*

Tom Wilkinson (1948-)
    Duplicity *102*

Trina Willard
    Humpday *169*

will.i.am
    X-Men Origins: Wolverine *425*

Harland Williams (1967-)
    My Life in Ruins *261*

Jermaine Williams
    World's Greatest Dad *423*

Mark Williams (1959-)
    Harry Potter and the Half-Blood
        Prince *160*

Michael K. Williams
    The Road *326*

Michelle Williams (1980-)
    Mammoth *240*

Olivia Williams (1968-)
    An Education *108*

Robin Williams (1952-)
    Night at the Museum: Battle of
        the Smithsonian *271*
    Old Dogs *286*
    World's Greatest Dad *423*

Vanessa Williams (1963-)
    Imagine That *184*

Mykelti Williamson (1960-)
    Black Dynamite *34*
    The Final Destination *123*

Amanda Williford
    See Willa Ford

Bruce Willis (1955-)
    Surrogates *364*

Rumer Willis (1988-)
    Sorority Row *346*

Hope Olaide Wilson
    I Can Do Bad All By My-
        self *175*

Luke Wilson (1971-)
    Battle for Terra *(V)* *31*

Owen Wilson (1968-)
    Fantastic Mr. Fox *(V)* *118*
    Night at the Museum: Battle of
        the Smithsonian *271*

Patrick Wilson (1973-)
    Watchmen *411*

Rainn Wilson (1968-)
    Monsters vs. Aliens *(V)* *253*

Rita Wilson (1958-)
    It's Complicated *203*
    Old Dogs *286*

Marvin Winans
    I Can Do Bad All By My-
        self *175*

Oprah Winfrey (1954-)
    The Princess and the Frog
        (V) *312*

Katheryn Winnick (1978-)
    Cold Souls *70*

Mare Winningham (1959-)
    Brothers *48*

Eric Winter (1976-)
    The Ugly Truth *397*

Anna Wintour
    The September Issue *332*

Tommy Wirkola (1979-)
    Dead Snow *90*

Tom Wisdom (1973-)
    Pirate Radio *302*

Reese Witherspoon (1976-)
    Monsters vs. Aliens *(V)* *253*

Johanna Wokalek
    The Baader Meinhof Com-
        plex *27*

Aaron Wolff
    A Serious Man *334*

Benedict Wong (1970-)
    Moon *255*

Sarunyu Wongkrachang
    Ong Bak 2 *288*

Elijah Wood (1981-)
    9 *(V)* *273*

Evan Rachel Wood (1987-)
    Battle for Terra *(V)* *31*
    Whatever Works *413*

Ty Wood
    The Haunting in Connecti-
        cut *163*

Jamal Woodard
    Notorious *280*

Bokeem Woodbine (1973-)
    Black Dynamite *34*

Mary Woronov (1943-)
    The House of the Devil *168*

Sam Worthington (1976-)
    Avatar *22*
    Terminator Salvation *374*

Rick Worthy
    Duplicity *102*

Bonnie Wright (1991-)
    Harry Potter and the Half-Blood
        Prince *160*

Robin Wright Penn (1966-)
    New York, I Love You *268*

Martin Wuttke (1962-)
    Inglourious Basterds *191*

Xzibit (1974-)
    Bad Lieutenant: Port of Call New
        Orleans *28*

Tsutomu Yamazaki (1936-)
    Departures *91*

Cedric Yarbrough
    Black Dynamite *34*

Jose Maria Yazpik (1970-)
    The Burning Plain *54*

Anton Yelchin (1989-)
    New York, I Love You *268*
    Star Trek *351*
    Terminator Salvation *374*

Charlyne Yi (1986-)
    Paper Heart *295*

Dwight Yoakam (1956-)
    Crank: High Voltage *80*

You Yong
    Red Cliff *324*

Aaron Yoo
    Friday the 13th *132*

Henri Young
    Aliens in the Attic *5*

Regan Young
    Aliens in the Attic *5*

Chow Yun-Fat (1955-)
    Dragonball: Evolution *101*

Rick Yune (1971-)
    Ninja Assassin *277*

Odette Yustman
    The Unborn *398*

Steve Zahn (1968-)
    The Great Buck Howard *152*
    Management *241*
    A Perfect Getaway *300*
    Sunshine Cleaning *363*

Subject Index

Title Index

This cumulative index is an alphabetical list of all films covered in the volumes of the *Magill's Cinema Annual*. Film titles are indexed on a word-by-word basis, including articles and prepositions. English leading articles (A, An, The) are ignored, as are foreign leading articles (El, Il, La, Las, Le, Les, Los). Acronyms appear alphabetically as if regular words. Common abbreviations in titles file as if they are spelled out. Proper names in titles are alphabetized beginning with the individual's first name. Titles with numbers are alphabetized as if the numbers were spelled out. When numeric titles gather in close proximity to each other, the titles will be arranged in a low-to-high numeric sequence. Films reviewed in this volume are cited in bold with an Arabic number indicating the page number on which the review begins; films reviewed in past volumes are cited with the *Annual* year in which the review was published. Original and alternate titles are cross-referenced to the American release title. Titles of retrospective films are followed by the year, in brackets, of their original release.

A

A corps perdu. *See* Straight for the Heart.

A. I.: Artificial Intelligence 2002

A la Mode (Fausto) 1995

A Lot Like Love 2006

A Ma Soeur. *See* Fat Girl.

A nos amours 1984

Abandon 2003

ABCD 2002

Abgeschminkt! *See* Making Up!.

About a Boy 2003

About Adam 2002

About Last Night... 1986

About Schmidt 2003

Above the Law 1988

Above the Rim 1995

Abrazos rotos, Los. *See* Broken Embraces.

Abre Los Ojos. *See* Open Your Eyes.

Abril Despedacado. *See* Behind the Sun.

Absence of Malice 1981

Absolute Beginners 1986

Absolute Power 1997

Absolution 1988

Abyss, The 1989

Accepted 2007

Accidental Tourist, The 1988

Accompanist, The 1993

Accordeur de tremblements de terre, L'. *See* Piano Tuner of Earthquakes, The.

Accused, The 1988

Ace in the Hole [1951] 1986, 1991

Ace Ventura: Pet Detective 1995

Ace Ventura: When Nature Calls 1996

Aces: Iron Eagle III 1992

Acid House, The 2000

Acqua e sapone. *See* Water and Soap.

Across the Tracks 1991

Across the Universe 2008

Acting on Impulse 1995

Action Jackson 1988

Actress 1988

Adam pg. 1

Adam Sandler's 8 Crazy Nights 2003

Adam's Rib [1950] 1992

Adaptation 2003

Addams Family, The 1991

Addams Family Values 1993

Addicted to Love 1997

Addiction, The 1995

Addition, L'. *See* Patsy, The.

Adjo, Solidaritet. *See* Farewell Illusion.

Adjuster, The 1992

Adolescente, L' 1982

Adoration pg. 2

Adventureland pg. 3

Adventures in Babysitting 1987

Adventures of Baron Munchausen, The 1989

Bells Are Ringing [1960] 1983

Belly of an Architect 1987

Beloved 2003

Beloved Rogue [1927] 1983

Below 2004

Benchwarmers, The 2007

Bend It Like Beckham 2004

Benefit of the Doubt 1993

Bengali Night, The 1988

Benji: Off the Leash! 2005

Benji the Hunted 1987

Benny and Joon 1993

Bent 1997

Beowulf 2008

Beowulf & Grendel 2007

Berkeley in the Sixties 1990

Berlin Alexanderplatz 1983

Bernadette 1988

Berry Gordy's The Last Dragon 1985

Bert Rigby, You're a Fool 1989

Beshkempir: The Adopted Son 2000

Besieged 2000

Best Defense 1984

Best Friends 1982

Best in Show 2001

Best Intentions, The 1992

Best Laid Plans 2000

Best Little Whorehouse in Texas, The 1982

Best Man, The 1999

Best Man, The 2000

Best of the Best 1989

Best of the Best II 1993

Best of Times, The 1986

Best of Youth, The 2006

Best Revenge, The 1996

Best Seller 1987

Best Years of Our Lives, The [1946] 1981

Bestia nel cuore, La. *See* Don't Tell.

Betrayal 1983

Betrayed 1988

Betsy's Wedding 1990

Better Luck Tomorrow 2004

Better Off Dead 1985

Better Than Chocolate 2000

Better Than Sex 2002

Betty 1993

Betty Blue 1986

Between the Teeth 1995

Beverly Hillbillies, The 1993

Beverly Hills Brats 1989

Beverly Hills Chihuahua 2009

Beverly Hills Cop 1984

Beverly Hills Cop II 1987

Beverly Hills Cop III 1995

Beverly Hills Ninja 1997

Bewitched 2006

Beyond Borders 2004

Beyond Rangoon 1995

Beyond Reasonable Doubt 1983

Beyond Silence 1999

Beyond the Gates 2008

Beyond the Limit 1983

Beyond the Mat 2001

Beyond the Rocks 2006

Beyond the Sea 2005

Beyond Therapy 1987

Bhaji on the Beach 1995

Bian Lian. *See* The King of Masks.

Bicentennial Man 2000

Big 1988

Big Bad Mama II 1988

Big Bang, The 1990

Big Blue, The (Besson) 1988

Big Blue, The (Horn) 1988

Big Bounce, The 2005

Big Bully 1996

Big Business 1988

Big Chill, The 1983

Big Daddy 2000

Big Easy, The 1987

Big Fan pg. 33

Big Fat Liar 2003

Big Fish 2004

Big Girls Don't Cry, They Get Even 1992

Big Green, The 1995

Big Hit, The 1999

Big Kahuna, The 2001

Big Lebowski, The 1999

Big Man on Campus 1989

Big Momma's House 2001

Big Momma's House 2 2007

Big Night 1996

Big One, The 1999

Big Picture, The 1989

Big Shots 1987

Big Squeeze, The 1996

Big Tease, The 2001

Big Time 1988

Big Top Pee-Wee 1988

Big Town, The 1987

Big Trouble (Cassavetes) 1986

Big Trouble (Sonnenfeld) 2003

Big Trouble in Little China 1986

Biker Boyz 2004

Bikur Ha-Tizmoret. *See* Band's Visit, The.

Bill and Ted's Bogus Journey 1991

Bill and Ted's Excellent Adventure 1989

Billy Bathgate 1991

Billy Budd [1962] 1981

Billy Elliot 2001

Billy Madison 1995

Billy's Hollywood Screen Kiss 1999

Biloxi Blues 1988

Bin-jip. *See* 3-Iron.

Bingo 1991

BINGO 2000

Bio-Dome 1996

Bird 1988

Bird on a Wire 1990

Birdcage, The 1996

Birdy 1984

Birth 2005

Birth of a Nation, The [1915] 1982, 1992

Birthday Girl 2003

Bitter Moon 1995

Bittere Ernte. *See* Angry Harvest.

Bix (1990) 1995

Bix (1991) 1995

Bizet's Carmen 1984

Black and White 2001

Black Beauty 1995

Black Book 2008

Black Cat, The (Fulci) 1984

Black Cat (Shin) 1993

Black Cat, White Cat 2000

Black Cauldron, The 1985

Black Christmas 2007

Black Dahlia, The 2007

Black Dog 1999

Black Dynamite pg. 34

Black Harvest 1995

Black Hawk Down 2002

Black Joy 1986

Black Knight 2002

Black Lizard 1995

Black Mask 2000

Black Moon Rising 1986

Black Peter [1964] 1985

Black Rain (Imamura) 1990

Black Rain (Scott) 1989

Black Robe 1991

Black Sheep 1996

Black Snake Moan 2008

Black Stallion Returns, The 1983

Black Widow 1987

Blackboard Jungle [1955] 1986, 1992

Blackout 1988

Blackout. *See* I Like It Like That.

Blade 1999

Blade II 2003

Blade Runner 1982

Blade: Trinity 2005

Blades of Glory 2008

Blair Witch Project, The 2000

Blame It on Night 1984

Blame It on Rio 1984

Blame It on the Bellboy 1992

Blank Check 1995

Blankman 1995

Blassblaue Frauenschrift, Eine. *See* Woman's Pale Blue Handwriting, A.

Blast 'em 1995

Blast from the Past 2000

Blaze 1989

Bless the Child 2001

Bless Their Little Hearts 1991

Blessures Assassines, Les. *See* Murderous Maids.

Blind Date 1987

Blind Fairies *See* Ignorant Fairies

Blind Fury 1990

Blind Side, The pg. 36

Blind Swordsman: Zatoichi, The. *See* Zatoichi.

Blindness 2009

Blink 1995

Bliss 1986

Bliss 1997

Blob, The 1988

Blood and Chocolate 2008

Blood and Concrete 1991

Blood and Wine 1997

Blood Diamond 2007

Blood Diner 1987

Blood in Blood Out 1995

Blood, Guts, Bullets and Octane 2001

Blood Money 1988

Blood of Heroes, The 1990

Blood Salvage 1990

Blood Simple 1985

Blood Wedding 1982

Blood Work 2003

Bloodfist 1989

Bloodhounds of Broadway 1989

BloodRayne 2007

Bloodsport 1988

Bloody Sunday 2003

Blow 2002

Blow Dry 2002

Blow Out 1981

Blown Away 1995

Blue (Jarman) 1995

Blue (Kieslowski) 1993

Blue Car 2004

Blue Chips 1995

Blue City 1986

Blue Crush 2003

Blue Desert 1991

Blue Ice 1995

Blue Iguana, The 1988

Blue in the Face 1995

Blue Kite, The 1995

Blue Monkey 1987

Blue Skies Again 1983

Blue Sky 1995

Blue Steel 1990

Blue Streak 2000

Blue Thunder 1983

Blue Velvet 1986

Blue Villa, The 1995

Bluebeard's Eighth Wife [1938] 1986

Blues Brothers 2000 1999

Blues Lahofesh Hagadol. *See* Late Summer Blues.

Boat, The. *See* Boot, Das.

Boat is Full, The 1982

Boat That Rocked, The. *See* Pirate Radio.

Boat Trip 2004

Bob le Flambeur [1955] 1983

Bob Marley: Time Will Tell. *See* Time Will Tell.

Bob Roberts 1992

Bobby 2007

Bobby Jones: Stroke of Genius 2005

Bodies, Rest, and Motion 1993

Body, The 2002

Body and Soul 1982

Body Chemistry 1990

Body Double 1984

Body Heat 1981

Body Melt 1995

Body of Evidence 1993

Body of Lies 2009

Body Parts 1991

Body Rock 1984

Body Shots 2000

Body Slam 1987

Body Snatchers 1995

Bodyguard, The 1992

Bodyguards, The. *See* La Scorta.

Boesman & Lena 2001

Bogus 1996

Boheme, La [1926] 1982

Boiler Room 2001

C

Cabaret Balkan 2000

Cabeza de Vaca 1992

Cabin Boy 1988

Cabin Fever 2004

Cabinet of Dr. Ramirez, The 1995

Cable Guy, The 1996

Cache 2007

Cactus 1986

Caddie [1976] 1982

Caddyshack II 1988

Cadence 1991

Cadillac Man 1990

Cadillac Records 2009

Cafe Ole 2001

Cafe Society 1997

Cage 1989

Cage aux folles III, La 1986

Cage/Cunningham 1995

Caged Fury 1984

Cal 1984

Calendar 1995

Calendar Girl 1993

Calendar Girls 2004

Calhoun. *See* Nightstick.

Call Me 1988

Calle 54 2002

Caller, The 1987

Calling the Shots 1988

Came a Hot Friday 1985

Cameron's Closet 1989

Camilla 1995

Camille Claudel 1988, 1989

Camorra 1986

Camp 2004

Camp at Thiaroye, The 1990

Camp Nowhere 1995

Campanadas a medianoche. *See* Falstaff.

Campus Man 1987

Can She Bake a Cherry Pie? 1983

Canadian Bacon 1995

Can't Buy Me Love 1987

Can't Hardly Wait 1999

Candy Mountain 1988

Candyman 1992

Candyman II: Farewell to the Flesh 1995

Cannery Row 1982

Cannonball Run II 1984

Canone Inverso. *See* Making Love.

Cantante, El 2008

Cape Fear 1991

Capitalism: A Love Story pg. 57

Capitano, Il 1995

Capote 2006

Captain Corelli's Mandolin 2002

Captain Ron 1992

Captive Hearts 1987

Captive in the Land, A 1995

Captives 1996

Captivity 2008

Capturing the Friedmans 2004

Car 54, Where Are You? 1995

Caramel 2009

Carandiru 2005

Caravaggio 1986

Cardinal, The [1963] 1986

Care Bears Adventure in Wonderland, The 1987

Care Bears Movie, The 1985

Care Bears Movie II 1986

Career Girls 1997

Career Opportunities 1991

Careful He Might Hear You 1984

Carlito's Way 1993

Carmen 1983

Carnage 2004

Carne, La 1995

Caro Diario 1995

Carpenter, The 1988

Carpool 1996

Carried Away 1996

Carriers Are Waiting, The 2001

Carrington 1995

Cars 2007

Casa de los Babys 2004

Casa in bilico, Una. *See* Tottering Lives.

Casanova 2006

Casino 1995

Casino Royale 2007

Casper 1995

Cassandra's Dream 2009

Cast Away 2001

Castle, The 2000

Casual Sex? 1988

Casualties of War 1989

Cat on a Hot Tin Roof [1958] 1993

Cat People [1942] 1981, 1982

Catacombs 1988

Catch a Fire 2007

Catch and Release 2008

Catch Me If You Can 1989

Catch Me If You Can (Spielberg) 2003

Catch That Kid 2005

Catfish in Black Bean Sauce 2001

Cats & Dogs 2002

Cats Don't Dance 1997

Cat's Meow, The 2003

Cattle Annie and Little Britches 1981

Catwoman 2005

Caught 1996

Caught Up 1999

Cave, The 2006

Cave Girl 1985

Caveman's Valentine, The 2002

CB4 1993

Cease Fire 1985

Cecil B. Demented 2001

Celebrity 1999

Celeste 1982

Celestial Clockwork 1996

Cell, The 2001

Cellular 2005

Celluloid Closet, The 1996

Celtic Pride 1996

Cement Garden, The 1995

Cemetery Club, The 1993

Cemetery Man 1996

Center of the Web 1992

Center of the World, The 2002

Center Stage 2001

Central do Brasil. *See* Central Station.

Central Station 1999

Cours Toujours. *See* Dad On the Run.

Cousin Bette 1999

Cousin Bobby 1992

Cousins 1989

Cove, The pg. 79

Covenant, The 2007

Cover Girl 1985

Coverup 1988

Cowboy [1958] 1981

Cowboy Way, The 1995

Cowboys Don't Cry 1988

Coyote Ugly 2001

CQ 2003

Crabe Dans la Tete, Un. *See* Soft Shell Man.

Crack House 1989

Crack in the Mirror 1988

Crackdown. *See* To Die Standing.

Crackers 1984

Cradle 2 the Grave 2004

Cradle Will Rock 2000

Craft, The 1996

Crank 2007

Crank: High Voltage pg. 80

Crash (Cronenberg) 1997

Crash (Haggis) 2006

Crawlspace 1986

crazy/beautiful 2002

Crazy Family, The 1986

Crazy Heart pg. 81

Crazy in Alabama 2000

Crazy Love 2008

Crazy Moon 1988

Crazy People 1990

Creator 1985

Creature from the Black Lagoon, The [1954] 1981

Creepozoids 1987

Creepshow 1982

Creepshow II 1987

Crew, The 2001

Crime + Punishment in Suburbia 2001

Crime of Father Amaro, The 2003

Crimes and Misdemeanors 1989

Crimes of Passion 1984

Crimes of the Heart 1986

Criminal 2005

Criminal Law 1988, 1989

Criminal Lovers 2004

Crimson Tide 1995

Crisscross 1992

Critical Care 1997

Critical Condition 1987

Critters 1986

Critters II 1988

Crna macka, beli macor. *See* Black Cat, White Cat.

"Crocodile" Dundee 1986

"Crocodile" Dundee II 1988

"Crocodile" Dundee in Los Angeles 2002

Crocodile Hunter: Collision Course, The 2003

Cronos 1995

Crooked Hearts 1991

Crooklyn 1995

Cross Country 1983

Cross Creek 1983

Cross My Heart 1987

Crossed Tracks. *See* Roman de gare.

Crossing Delancey 1988

Crossing Guard, The 1995

Crossing Over pg. 83

Crossing the Bridge 1992

Crossover Dreams 1985

Crossroads 1986

Crossroads 2003

Crouching Tiger, Hidden Dragon 2001

Croupier [1997] 2001

Crow: City of Angels, The 1996

Crow, The 1995

Crucible, The 1996

Crude Oasis, The 1995

Cruel Intentions 2000

Cruel Story of Youth [1960] 1984

Crumb 1995

Crush (Maclean) 1993

Crush (McKay) 2003

Crush, The (Shapiro) 1993

Crusoe 1988

Cry Baby Killers, The [1957]

Cry Freedom 1987

Cry in the Dark, A 1988

Cry in the Wild, The 1990

Cry, the Beloved Country 1995

Cry Wolf [1947] 1986

Cry_Wolf 2006

Cry-Baby 1990

Crying Game, The 1992

Crystal Heart 1987

Crystalstone 1988

Cucaracha, La 2000

Cuckoo, The 2004

Cujo 1983

Cup, The 2001

Cup Final 1992

Curdled 1996

Cure, The 1995

Cure in Orange, The 1987

Curious Case of Benjamin Button, The 2009

Curious George 2007

Curly Sue 1991

Current Events 1990

Curse of the Golden Flower 2007

Curse of the Jade Scorpion, The 2002

Curse of the Pink Panther 1983

Cursed 2006

Curtains 1983

Cut and Run 1986

Cutthroat Island 1995

Cutting Edge, The 1992

Cyborg 1989

Cyclo 1996

Cyclone 1987

Cyrano de Bergerac 1990

Czlowiek z Marmuru. *See* Man of Marble.

Czlowiek z Zelaza. *See* Man of Iron.

D

Da 1988

Da Vinci Code, The 2007

Dad 1989

Dad On the Run 2002

Don't Cry, It's Only Thunder 1982

Don't Move 2006

Don't Say a Word 2002

Don't Tell 2007

Don't Tell Her It's Me 1990

Don't Tell Mom the Babysitter's Dead 1991

Don't Tempt Me! *See* No News from God.

Don't Touch the Axe. *See* Duchess of Langeais, The.

Doom 2006

Doom Generation, The 1995

Doomsday 2009

Door in the Floor, The 2005

Door to Door 1984

Doors, The 1991

Dopamine 2004

Dorm That Dripped Blood, The 1983

Dorothy and Alan at Norma Place 1981

Double Dragon 1995

Double Edge 1992

Double Happiness 1995

Double Impact 1991

Double Indemnity [1944] 1981, 1986, 1987

Double Jeopardy 2000

Double Life of Veronique, The 1991

Double Take 2002

Double Team 1997

Double Threat 1993

Double Trouble 1992

Double Vie de Veronique, La. *See* Double Life of Veronique, The.

Doublure, La. *See* Valet, The.

Doubt 2009

Doug's First Movie 2000

Down and Out in Beverly Hills 1986

Down by Law 1986

Down in the Delta 1999

Down in the Valley 2007

Down Periscope 1996

Down to Earth 2002

Down to You 2001

Down Twisted 1987

Down With Love 2004

Downfall 2006

Downtown 1990

Dracula. *See* Bram Stoker's Dracula.

Dracula: Dead and Loving It 1995

Dracula 2001. *See* Wes Craven Presents: Dracula 2001.

Drag Me to Hell pg. 99

Dragnet 1987

Dragon 1993

Dragon Chow 1988

Dragonball: Evolution pg. 101

Dragonfly 2003

Dragonheart 1996

Dragonslayer 1981

Draughtsman's Contract, The 1983

Dream a Little Dream 1989

Dream Demon 1988

Dream for an Insomniac 1999

Dream Lover (Kazan) 1986

Dream Lover (Pakula) 1995

Dream of Light 1995

Dream Team, The 1989

Dream With the Fishes 1997

Dreamcatcher 2004

Dreamchild 1985

Dreamer: Inspired by a True Story 2006

Dreamers, The 2005

Dreamgirls 2007

Dreamlife of Angels, The 2000

Dreams. *See* Akira Kurosawa's Dreams.

Dreams with Sharp Teeth 2009

Dreamscape 1984

Drei Sterne. *See* Mostly Martha.

Dresser, The 1983

Dressmaker, The 1988

Drifter, The 1988

Drifting 1984

Drillbit Taylor 2009

Drive 1992

Drive Me Crazy 2000

Driven 2002

Driving Miss Daisy 1989

Drole de Felix. *See* Adventures of Felix, The.

Drop Dead Fred 1991

Drop Dead Gorgeous 2000

DROP Squad 1995

Drop Zone 1995

Drowning by Numbers 1988

Drowning Mona 2001

Drugstore Cowboy 1989

Drumline 2003

Drunks 1997

Dry Cleaning 2000

Dry White Season, A 1989

D3: The Mighty Ducks 1996

Duchess, The 2009

Duchess of Langeais, The 2009

Duck Season 2007

Ducktales, the Movie 1990

Dude, Where's My Car? 2001

Dudes 1987

Dudley Do-Right 2000

Duel in the Sun [1946] 1982, 1989

Duet for One 1986

Duets 2001

D.U.I. 1987

Dukes of Hazzard, The 2006

Dulcy [1923] 1981

Duma 2006

Dumb and Dumber 1995

Dumb and Dumberer: When Harry Met Lloyd 2004

Dummy 2004

Dune 1984

Dungeons & Dragons 2001

Dunston Checks In 1996

Duolou Tianshi. *See* Fallen Angels.

Duplex 2004

Duplicity pg. 102

Dust Devil: The Final Cut 1995

Dutch 1991

Dying Gaul, The 2006

Dying Young 1991

E

E la nave va. *See* And the Ship Sails On.

Enfant, L'. *See* Child, The.

English Patient, The 1996

Englishman Who Went Up a Hill But Came Down a Mountain, The 1995

Enid Is Sleeping. *See* Over Her Dead Body.

Enigma (Szwarc) 1983

Enigma (Apted) 2003

Enough 2003

Enron: The Smartest Guys in the Room 2006

Enter the Ninja 1982

Entity, The 1983

Entrapment 2000

Entre les murs. *See* Class, The.

Entre nous 1984

Envy 2005

Epic Movie 2008

Equilibrium 2003

Equinox 1993

Eragon 2007

Eraser 1996

Erendira 1984

Erik the Viking 1989

Erin Brockovich 2001

Ermo 1995

Ernest Goes to Camp 1987

Ernest Goes to Jail 1990

Ernest Rides Again 1993

Ernest Saves Christmas 1988

Ernest Scared Stupid 1991

Eros 2006

Erotique 1995

Escanaba in da Moonlight 2002

Escape Artist, The 1982

Escape from Alcatraz [1979] 1982

Escape from L.A. 1996

Escape from New York 1981

Escape from Safehaven 1989

Escape 2000 1983

Escort, The. *See* Scorta, La.

Especially on Sunday 1993

Esperame en el cielo. *See* Wait for Me in Heaven.

Espinazo de Diablo, El. *See* Devil's Backbone, The.

Est-Ouest. *See* East-West.

Esther Kahn 2003

E.T.: The Extra-Terrestrial 1982

Etat sauvage, L' [1978] 1990

Ete prochain, L'. *See* Next Summer.

Eternal Sunshine of the Spotless Mind 2005

Eternity and a Day 2000

Ethan Frome 1993

Etoile du nord 1983

Eu Tu Eles. *See* Me You Them.

Eulogy 2005

Eulogy of Love. *See* In Praise of Love.

Eureka 1985

Eureka 2002

Europa 1995

Europa, Europa 1991

Eurotrip 2005

Evan Almighty 2008

Eve of Destruction 1991

Evelyn 2003

Even Cowgirls Get the Blues 1995

Evening 2008

Evening Star 1996

Event Horizon 1997

Events Leading Up to My Death, The 1995

Ever After: A Cinderella Story 1999

Everlasting Piece, An 2002

Everlasting Secret Family, The 1989

Every Breath 1995

Every Little Step pg. 110

Every Man for Himself [1979] 1981

Every Time We Say Goodbye 1986

Everybody Wins 1990

Everybody's All-American 1988

Everybody's Famous! 2002

Everybody's Fine 1991

Everybody's Fine pg. 111

Everyone Says I Love You 1996

Everyone's Hero 2007

Everything is Illuminated 2006

Eve's Bayou 1997

Evil Dead, The 1983

Evil Dead II 1987

Evil That Men Do, The 1984

Evil Under the Sun 1982

Evil Woman. *See* Saving Silverman.

Evita 1996

Evolution 2002

Excalibur 1981

Excess Baggage 1997

Exchange Lifeguards 1995

Execution Protocol, The 1995

Executive Decision 1996

Exiles, The 2009

eXistenZ 2000

Exit to Eden 1995

Exit Wounds 2002

Exorcism of Emily Rose, The 2006

Exorcist: The Beginning 2005

Exorcist III, The 1990

Exorcist, The [1973] 2001

Exotica 1995

Experience Preferred...but Not Essential 1983

Explorers 1985

Exposed 1983

Express, The 2009

Extract pg. 112

Extramuros 1995

Extreme Measures 1996

Extreme Ops 2003

Extreme Prejudice 1987

Extremities 1986

Eye for an Eye, An 1996

Eye of God 1997

Eye of the Beholder 2001

Eye of the Needle 1981

Eye of the Tiger, The 1986

Eye, The 2009

Eyes of Tammy Faye, The 2001

Eyes Wide Shut 2000

F

F/X 1986

F/X II 1991

Fabulous Baker Boys, The 1989

Fabulous Destiny of Amelie Poulain, The. *See* Amelie.

Face/Off 1997

Fierce Creatures 1997

15 Minutes 2002

Fifth Element, The 1997

50 First Dates 2005

51st State, The. *See* Formula 51.

54 1999

Fifty-Fifty 1993

Fifty-two Pick-up 1986

Fight Club 2000

Fighter 2002

Fighting pg. 122

Fighting Back 1982

Fighting Temptations, The 2004

Fille coupée en deux, La. *See* Girl Cut in Two, A.

Filles ne Savent pas Nager, Les. *See* Girls Can't Swim.

Fils, Le. *See* Son, The.

Filth and the Fury, The 2001

Fin aout debut septembre. *See* Late August, Early September.

Final Analysis 1992

Final Approach 1991

Final Cut 2005

Final Destination 2001

Final Destination, The pg. 123

Final Destination: Death Trip 3D. *See* Final Destination, The.

Final Destination 2 2004

Final Destination 3 2007

Final Destination 4. *See* Final Destination, The.

Final Fantasy: The Spirits Within 2002

Final Friday, The. *See* Jason Goes to Hell.

Final Option, The 1983

Final Sacrifice, The. *See* Children of the Corn II.

Final Season 1988

Final Season, The 2008

Find Me Guilty 2007

Finders Keepers 1984

Finding Forrester 2001

Finding Nemo 2004

Finding Neverland 2005

Fine Mess, A 1986

Fine Romance, A 1992

Finestra di Fronte, La. *See* Facing Windows.

Finzan 1995

Fiorile 1995

Fire and Ice (Bakshi) 1983

Fire and Ice (Bogner) 1987

Fire Birds 1990

Fire Down Below 1997

Fire from the Mountain 1987

Fire in Sky 1993

Fire This Time, The 1995

Fire Walk with Me. *See* Twin Peaks: Fire Walk with Me.

Fire with Fire 1986

Fired Up! pg. 125

Firefox 1982

Firehead 1991

Firelight 1999

Firemen's Bell, The [1967] 1985

Fireproof 2009

Firestorm 1999

Firewalker 1986

Firewall 2007

Fireworks 1999

Fires of Kuwait 1995

Firm, The 1993

First Blood 1982

First Daughter 2005

First Descent 2006

First Kid 1996

First Knight 1995

First Love, Last Rites 1999

First Monday in October 1981

First Name, Carmen 1984

First Power, The 1990

First Saturday in May, The 2009

First Sunday 2009

First Wives Club, The 1996

Firstborn 1984

Fish Called Wanda, A 1988

Fisher King, The 1991

Fistfighter 1989

Fitzcarraldo 1982

Five Corners 1987

Five Days One Summer 1982

Five Graves to Cairo [1943] 1986

Five Heartbeats, The 1991

(500) Days of Summer pg. 126

Five Minutes of Heaven pg. 127

Five Senses, The 2001

Flags of Our Fathers 2007

Flame in My Heart, A 1987

Flaming Star [1960] 1982

Flamingo Kid, The 1984

Flamme dans mon coeur, Une. *See* Flame in My Heart, A.

Flanagan 1985

Flash of Genius 2009

Flash of Green, A 1985

Flashback 1990

Flashdance 1983

Flashpoint 1984

Flatliners 1990

Flawless 2000

Flawless 2009

Flaxfield, The 1985

Fled 1996

Fleeing by Night 2004

Flesh and Blood 1985

Flesh and Bone 1993

Flesh Gordon Meets the Cosmic Cheerleaders 1995

Fleshburn 1984

Fletch 1985

Fletch Lives 1989

Flicka 2007

Flight of the Innocent 1993

Flight of the Intruder 1991

Flight of the Navigator 1986

Flight of the Phoenix 2005

Flight of the Phoenix, The [1966] 1984

Flight of the Red Balloon 2009

Flight to Fury [1966]

Flightplan 2006

Flintstones, The 1995

Flipper 1996

Flipping 1997

Flirt 1996

Flirting 1992

Harmonists, The 2000

Harold & Kumar Escape from Guantanamo Bay 2009

Harold & Kumar Go to White Castle 2005

Harriet Craig [1950] 1984

Harriet the Spy 1996

Harrison's Flowers 2003

Harry and Son 1984

Harry and the Hendersons 1987

Harry, He's Here to Help. *See* With a Friend Like Harry.

Harry Potter and the Chamber of Secrets 2003

Harry Potter and the Goblet of Fire 2006

Harry Potter and the Half-Blood Prince pg. 160

Harry Potter and the Order of the Phoenix 2008

Harry Potter and the Prisoner of Azkaban 2005

Harry Potter and the Sorcerer's Stone 2002

Harry, Un Ami Qui Vous Veut du Bien. *See* With a Friend Like Harry.

Hart's War 2003

Harvard Man 2003

Harvest, The 1995

Hasty Heart, The [1949] 1987

Hatchet Man, The [1932] 1982

Hatouna Mehuheret. *See* Late Marriage.

Haunted Honeymoon 1986

Haunted Mansion, The 2004

Haunted Summer 1988

Haunting, The 2000

Haunting in Connecticut, The pg. 163

Hauru no ugoku shiro. *See* Howl's Moving Castle.

Haute tension. *See* High Tension.

Hav Plenty 1999

Havana 1990

Hawk, The 1995

Hawks 1988

He Got Game 1999

He Liu. *See* River, The.

He Loves Me…He Loves Me Not 2004

He Said, She Said 1991

Head Above Water 1997

Head in the Clouds 2005

Head Office 1986

Head of State 2004

Head On 2000

Head-On 2006

Head Over Heels 2002

Heads or Tails 1983

Hear My Song 1991

Hear No Evil 1993

Hearing Voices 1991

Heart 1987

Heart and Souls 1993

Heart Condition 1990

Heart in Winter, A. *See* Coeur en hiver, Un.

Heart Like a Wheel 1983

Heart of a Stag 1984

Heart of Dixie 1989

Heart of Midnight 1989

Heart of the Game, The 2007

Heartaches 1982

Heartbreak Hotel 1988

Heartbreak Kid, The [1972] 1986

Heartbreak Kid, The (Farrelly/Farrelly) 2008

Heartbreak Ridge 1986

Heartbreaker 1983

Heartbreakers 2002

Heartburn 1986

Heartland 1981

Hearts in Atlantis 2002

Hearts of Darkness: A Filmmaker's Apocalypse 1992

Hearts of Fire 1987

Heat 1987

Heat (Mann) 1995

Heat and Dust 1984

Heat of Desire 1984

Heathcliff 1986

Heathers 1989

Heatwave 1983

Heaven (Keaton) 1987

Heaven (Tykwer) 2003

Heaven and Earth (Kadokawa) 1991

Heaven and Earth (Stone) 1993

Heaven Help Us 1985

Heaven's Gate 1981

Heaven's Prisoners 1996

Heavenly Bodies 1984

Heavenly Creatures 1995

Heavenly Kid, The 1985

Heavy 1996

Heavyweights 1995

Hecate 1984

Hedwig and the Angry Inch 2002

Heidi Fleiss: Hollywood Madame 1996

Heights 2006

Heist, The 2002

Helas Pour Moi 1995

Held Up 2001

Hell High 1989

Hell Ride 2009

Hellbent 1989

Hellbound 1988

Hellboy 2005

Hellboy II: The Golden Army 2009

Heller Wahn. *See* Sheer Madness.

Hello Again 1987

Hello, Dolly! [1969] 1986

Hello Mary Lou 1987

Hellraiser 1987

Hellraiser III: Hell on Earth 1992

Hellraiser IV: Bloodline 1996

Henna 1991

Henri Langlois: The Phantom of the Cinematheque 2006

Henry 1990

Henry and June 1990

Henry IV 1985

Henry V 1989

Henry Fool 1999

Henry Poole in Here 2009

Her Alibi 1989

Her Name Is Lisa 1987

Herbie: Fully Loaded 2006

Hercules 1983

Joe Somebody 2002

Joe the King 2000

Joe Versus the Volcano 1990

Joe's Apartment 1996

Joey 1985

Joey Takes a Cab 1991

John and the Missus 1987

John Carpenter's Ghosts of Mars 2002

John Carpenter's Vampires 1999

John Grisham's the Rainmaker 1998

John Huston 1988

John Huston and the Dubliners 1987

John Q 2003

John Tucker Must Die 2007

Johnny Be Good 1988

Johnny Dangerously 1984

Johnny English 2004

Johnny Handsome 1989

Johnny Mnemonic 1995

Johnny Stecchino 1992

Johnny Suede 1992

johns 1997

Johnson Family Vacation 2005

Joke of Destiny, A 1984

Jonas Brothers: The 3D Concert Experience pg. 208

Joseph Conrad's the Secret Agent 1996

Josh and S.A.M. 1993

Joshua 2008

Joshua Then and Now 1985

Josie and the Pussycats 2002

Journey into Fear [1943] 1985

Journey of August King 1995

Journey of Hope 1991

Journey of Love 1990

Journey of Natty Gann, The 1985

Journey to Spirit Island 1988

Journey to the Center of the Earth 2009

Joy Luck Club, The 1993

Joy of Sex 1984

Joy Ride 2002

Joyeux Noel 2007

Joysticks 1983

Ju Dou 1991

Juana la Loca. *See* Mad Love.

Judas Kiss 2000

Judas Project, The 1995

Jude 1996

Judge Dredd 1995

Judgement in Berlin 1988

Judgement Night 1993

Judy Berlin 2001

Juice 1992

Julia pg. 210

Julia Has Two Lovers 1991

Julian Po 1997

Julie & Julia pg. 211

Julien Donkey-Boy 2000

Jumanji 1995

Jument vapeur, La. *See* Dirty Dishes.

Jump Tomorrow 2002

Jumper 2009

Jumpin' at the Boneyard 1992

Jumpin' Jack Flash 1986

Jumpin' Night in the Garden of Eden, A 1988

Junebug 2006

Jungle Book, The 1995

Jungle Book 2, The 2004

Jungle Fever 1991

Jungle2Jungle 1997

Junior 1995

Juno 2008

Jurassic Park 1993

Jurassic Park III 2002

Juror, The 1996

Jury Duty 1995

Just a Kiss 2003

Just a Little Harmless Sex 2000

Just Another Girl on the I.R.T. 1993

Just Between Friends 1986

Just Cause 1995

Just Friends 2006

Just Like a Woman 1995

Just Like Heaven 2006

Just Looking 2002

Just Married 2004

Just My Luck 2007

Just One of the Guys 1985

Just One Time 2002

Just the Ticket 2000

Just the Way You Are 1984

Just Visiting 2002

Just Write 1999

Justice in the Coalfields 1996

Juwanna Mann 2003

K

K-9 1989

K-19: The Widowmaker 2003

K-PAX 2002

Kadisbellan. *See* Slingshot, The.

Kadosh 2001

Kaena: The Prophecy 2005

Kafka 1991

Kalifornia 1993

Kama Sutra: A Tale of Love 1997

Kamikaze Hearts 1995

Kamilla and the Thief 1988

Kandahar 2002

Kandyland 1988

Kangaroo 1987

Kangaroo Jack 2004

Kansas 1988

Kansas City 1996

Karakter. *See* Character.

Karate Kid, The 1984

Karate Kid: Part II, The 1986

Karate Kid: Part III, The 1989

Kate & Leopold 2002

Kazaam 1996

Kazoku. *See* Where Spring Comes Late.

Keep, The 1983

Keep the River On Your Right: A Modern Cannibal Tale 2002

Keeping Mum 2007

Keeping the Faith 2001

Keeping Up with the Steins 2007

Kerouac, the Movie 1985

Key Exchange 1985

Keys of the Kingdom, The [1944] 1989

Keys to Tulsa 1997

L.A. Story 1991

La Terre qui pleure. *See* Weeping Meadow.

Laberinto del Fauno, El. *See* Pan's Labyrinth.

Labyrinth 1986

Labyrinth of Passion 1990

Ladder 49 2005

Ladies Club, The 1986

Ladies' Man, The 2001

Ladri di saponette. *See* Icicle Thief, The.

Ladro Di Bambini, Il 1993

Lady and the Duke, The 2003

Lady Beware 1987

Lady Chatterley 2008

Lady Eve, The [1941] 1987

Lady in the Water 2007

Lady in White 1988

Lady Jane 1986

Lady Sings the Blues [1972] 1984

Ladybird, Ladybird 1995

Ladybugs 1992

Ladyhawke 1985

Ladykillers, The 2005

Lagaan: Once Upon a Time in India 2003

Lair of the White Worm, The 1988

Laissez-Passer. *See* Safe Conduct.

Lake House, The 2007

Lake Placid 2000

Lakeview Terrace 2009

Lambada 1990

L'america 1996

Lan Yu 2003

Land and Freedom 1995

Land Before Time, The 1988

Land Girls, The 1999

Land of Faraway 1988

Land of the Dead. *See* George A. Romero's Land of the Dead.

Land of the Lost pg. 217

Landlord Blues 1988

Landscape in the Mist 1989

L'Anglaise et le Duc. *See* Lady and the Duke, The.

Lantana 2002

Lara Croft: Tomb Raider 2002

Lara Croft Tomb Raider: The Cradle of Life 2004

Larger Than Life 1996

Larry the Cable Guy: Health Inspector 2007

Lars and the Real Girl 2008

Laserman, The 1988, 1990

Lassie 1995

Lassie 2007

Lassie Come Home [1943] 1993

Lassiter 1984

Last Act, The 1992

Last Action Hero 1993

Last American Virgin, The 1982

Last Boy Scout, The 1991

Last Call at Maud's 1993

Last Castle, The 2002

Last Chance Harvey pg. 219

Last Cigarette, The 2000

Last Dance, The 1996

Last Day of Winter, The 1987

Last Days 2006

Last Days of Disco, The 1999

Last Emperor, The 1987

Last Exit to Brooklyn 1990

Last Holiday 2007

Last House on the Left, The pg. 220

Last Hunter, The 1984

Last King of Scotland, The 2007

Last Kiss, The 2003

Last Kiss, The 2007

Last Legion, The 2008

Last Man Standing 1996

Last Mimzy, The 2008

Last Night 1999

Last of England, The 1988

Last of the Dogmen 1995

Last of the Finest, The 1990

Last of the Mohicans, The 1992

Last Orders 2003

Last Party, The 1993

Last Resort 1986

Last Resort 2002

Last Rites 1988

Last Samurai, The 2004

Last Seduction, The 1995

Last September, The 2001

Last Shot, The 2005

Last Starfighter, The 1984

Last Station, The pg. 222

Last Straw, The 1987

Last Supper 1996

Last Temptation of Christ, The 1988

Last Time I Committed Suicide, The 1997

Last Time I Saw Paris, The [1954] 1993

Last Summer in the Hamptons 1995

Last Wedding 2003

Lat den rätte komma in. *See* Let the Right One In.

Latcho Drom 1995

Late August, Early September 2000

Late Chrysanthemums [1954] 1985

Late for Dinner 1991

Late Marriage 2003

Late Summer Blues 1987

Latin Boys Go to Hell 1997

Latter Days 2005

L'Auberge Espagnole 2004

Laurel Canyon 2004

Law Abiding Citizen pg. 224

Law of Desire, The 1987

Law of Enclosures, The 2002

Lawn Dogs 1999

Lawless Heart 2004

Lawnmower Man, The 1992

Lawnmower Man 2: Beyond Cyberspace 1996

Lawrence of Arabia [1962] 1990

Laws of Attraction 2005

Laws of Gravity 1992

Layer Cake 2006

L' Ecole de la chair. *See* School of Flesh, The.

Leading Man, The 1999

League of Extraordinary Gentlemen, The 2004

League of Their Own, A 1992

Lean on Me 1989

Leap of Faith 1992

Leatherface 1990

Leatherheads 2009

Leave It to Beaver 1997

Leave to Remain 1988

Leaving Las Vegas 1995

Leaving Normal 1992

Lebedyne ozero. *See* Swan Lake.

Leben der Anderen, Das. *See* Lives of Others, The.

Lectrice, La. *See* Reader, The.

Leela 2003

Left Hand Side of the Fridge, The 2002

Legal Eagles 1986

Legally Blonde 2002

Legally Blonde 2: Red, White & Blonde 2004

Legend 1986

Legend of Bagger Vance, The 2001

Legend of Billie Jean, The 1985

Legend of 1900 2000

Legend of Rita, The 2002

Legend of Wolf Mountain, The 1995

Legend of Zorro, The 2006

Legends 1995

Legends of the Fall 1995

Leggenda del Pianista Sull'oceano, La. *See* Legend of 1900.

Lemon Sisters, The 1990

Lemon Sky 1987

Lemony Snicket's A Series of Unfortunate Events 2005

Leo Tolstoy's Anna Karenina 1997

Leolo 1993

Leon the Pig Farmer 1995

Leonard Part VI 1987

Leopard Son, The 1996

Leprechaun 1993

Leprechaun II 1995

Les Patterson Saves the World 1987

Less Than Zero 1987

Let Him Have It 1991

Let It Come Down: The Life of Paul Bowles 2000

Let It Ride 1989

Let the Right One In pg. 225

Let's Fall in Love. *See* New York in Short: The Shvitz and Let's Fall in Love.

Let's Get Lost 1988

Let's Make Friends. *See* I Love You, Man.

Let's Spend the Night Together 1983

Lethal Weapon 1987

Lethal Weapon 2 1989

Lethal Weapon 3 1992

Lethal Weapon 4 1999

Letter to Brezhnev 1986

Letters from Iwo Jima 2007

Leviathan 1989

Levity 2004

Levy and Goliath 1988

Ley del deseo, La. *See* Law of Desire, The.

L'heure d'été. *See* Summer Hours.

Liaison Pornographique, Une. *See* Affair of Love, An.

Liam 2002

Lianna 1983

Liar, Liar 1997

Liar's Moon 1982

Libertine, The 2007

Liberty Heights 2000

Licence to Kill 1989

License to Drive 1988

License to Wed 2008

Lie Down With Dogs 1995

Liebestraum 1991

Lies 1986

Life 2000

Life After Love 2002

Life and Nothing But 1989

Life and Times of Allen Ginsberg, The 1995

Life and Times of Judge Roy Bean, The [1972] 1983

Life Aquatic with Steve Zissou, The 2005

Life as a House 2002

Life Before Her Eyes, The 2009

Life Classes 1987

Life in the Food Chain. *See* Age Isn't Everything.

Life in the Theater, A 1995

Life Is a Long Quiet River 1990

Life Is Beautiful 1999

Life Is Cheap 1989

Life Is Sweet 1991

Life Less Ordinary, A 1997

Life Lessons. *See* New York Stories.

Life of David Gale, The 2004

Life on a String 1992

Life on the Edge 1995

Life or Something Like It 2003

Life Stinks 1991

Life with Father [1947] 1993

Life with Mikey 1993

Life Without Zoe. *See* New York Stories.

Lifeforce 1985

Lift 2002

Light Ahead, The [1939] 1982

Light It Up 2000

Light Keeps Me Company 2001

Light of Day 1987

Light Sleeper 1992

Lighthorsemen, The 1987

Lightning in a Bottle 2005

Lightning Jack 1995

Lightship, The 1986

Like Father Like Son 1987

Like Mike 2003

Like Water for Chocolate 1993

Lili Marleen 1981

Lilies 1997

Lilies of the Field [1963] 1992

Lillian 1995

Lilo & Stitch 2003

Lily in Love 1985

Limbo 2000

Limey, The 2000

Limits of Control, The pg. 227

Line One 1988

Lingua del Santo, La. *See* Holy Tongue, The.

Linguini Incident, The 1992

Linie Eins. *See* Line One.

Link 1986

Lion King, The 1995

Lionheart (Lettich) 1991

Lionheart (Shaffner) 1987

Lions for Lambs 2008

Liquid Dreams 1992

Liquid Sky 1983

Lisa 1990

Listen to Me 1989

Listen Up 1990

Little Big League 1995

Little Black Book 2005

Little Buddha 1995

Little Children 2007

Little Devil, the 1988

Little Dorrit 1988

Little Drummer Girl, The 1984

Little Giants 1995

Little Indian, Big City 1996

Little Jerk 1985

Little Man 2007

Little Man Tate 1991

Little Men 1999

Little Mermaid, The 1989

Little Miss Sunshine 2007

Little Monsters 1989

Little Nemo: Adventures in Slumberland 1992

Little Nicky 2001

Little Nikita 1988

Little Noises 1992

Little Odessa 1995

Little Princess, A 1995

Little Rascals, The 1995

Little Secrets 1995

Little Secrets (Treu) 2003

Little Sex, A 1982

Little Shop of Horrors [1960] 1986

Little Stiff, A 1995

Little Sweetheart 1988

Little Thief, The 1989

Little Vampire, The 2001

Little Vegas 1990

Little Vera 1989

Little Voice 1999

Little Women [1933] 1982

Little Women 1995

Live Flesh 1999

Live Free or Die Hard 2008

Live Nude Girls 1995

Live Virgin 2001

Lives of Others, The 2008

Livin' Large 1991

Living Daylights, The 1987

Living End, The 1992

Living in Oblivion 1995

Living on Tokyo Time 1987

Living Out Loud 1999

Living Proof: HIV and the Pursuit of Happiness 1995

L'ivresse du pouvoir. *See* Comedy of Power.

Lizzie McGuire Movie, The 2004

Ljuset Haller Mig Sallskap. *See* Light Keeps Me Company.

Loaded 1996

Local Hero 1983

Lock, Stock, and Two Smoking Barrels 2000

Lock Up 1989

Locusts, The 1997

Lodz Ghetto 1989

Lola 1982

Lola La Loca 1988

Lola Rennt. *See* Run, Lola, Run.

Lolita 1999

London Kills Me 1992

Lone Runner, The 1988

Lone Star 1996

Lone Wolf McQuade 1983

Lonely Guy, The 1984

Lonely Hearts (Cox) 1983

Lonely Hearts (Lane) 1995

Lonely in America 1991

Lonely Lady, The 1983

Lonely Passion of Judith Hearne, The 1987

Lonesome Jim 2007

Long Day Closes, The 1993

Long Dimanche de Fiancailles, Un. *See* Very Long Engagement, A.

Long Good Friday, The 1982

Long Gray Line, The [1955] 1981

Long Kiss Goodnight, The 1996

Long Live the Lady! 1988

Long, Long Trailer, The [1954] 1986

Long Lost Friend, The. *See* Apprentice to Murder.

Long Walk Home, The 1990

Long Way Home, The 1999

Long Weekend, The 1990

Longest Yard, The 2006

Longshot, The 1986

Longshots, The 2009

Longtime Companion 1990

Look at Me 2006

Look Who's Talking 1989

Look Who's Talking Now 1993

Look Who's Talking Too 1990

Lookin' to Get Out 1982

Looking for Comedy in the Muslim World 2007

Looking for Richard 1996

Lookout, The 2008

Looney Tunes: Back in Action 2004

Loophole 1986

Loose Cannons 1990

Loose Connections 1988

Loose Screws 1986

L'ora di religione: Il sorriso di mia madre. *See* My Mother's Smile.

Lord of Illusions 1995

Lord of the Flies 1990

Lord of the Rings: The Fellowship of the Rings 2002

Lord of the Rings: The Return of the King 2004

Lord of the Rings: The Two Towers 2003

Lord of War 2006

Lords of Discipline, The 1983

Lords of Dogtown 2006

Lords of the Deep 1989

Lorenzo's Oil 1992

Loser 2001

Losin' It 1983

Losing Isaiah 1995

Moon Over Broadway 1999

Moon over Parador 1988

Moon Shadow [1995] 2001

Moonlight and Valentino 1995

Moonlight Mile 2003

Moonlighting 1982

Moonstruck 1987

More Than A Game pg. 256

Morgan Stewart's Coming Home 1987

Moriarty. *See* Sherlock Holmes.

Morning After, The 1986

Morning Glory 1993

Morons from Outer Space 1985

Mort de Mario Ricci, La. *See* Death of Mario Ricci, The.

Mortal Kombat 1995

Mortal Kombat II: Annihilation 1997

Mortal Thoughts 1991

Mortuary Academy 1988

Morvern Callar 2003

Mosca addio. *See* Moscow Farewell.

Moscow Farewell 1987

Moscow on the Hudson 1984

Mosquito Coast, The 1986

Most Dangerous Game, The [1932] 1985

Most Fertile Man in Ireland, The 2002

Most Wanted 1997

Mostly Martha 2003

Mother 1996

Mother, The 2005

Mother Lode 1983

Mother Night 1996

Mother Teresa 1986

Motherhood pg. 258

Mothering Heart, The [1913] 1984

Mother's Boys 1995

Mothman Prophecies, The 2003

Motorama 1993

Motorcycle Diaries, The 2005

Moulin Rouge 2002

Mountain Gorillas 1995

Mountains of Moon 1990

Mountaintop Motel Massacre 1986

Mouse Hunt 1997

Mouth to Mouth 1997

Movers and Shakers 1985

Moving 1988

Moving the Mountain 1995

Moving Violations 1985

Much Ado About Nothing 1993

Mui du du Xanh. *See* Scent of Green Papaya, The.

Mujeres al borde de un ataque de nervios. *See* Women on the Verge of a Nervous Breakdown.

Mulan 1999

Mulholland Drive 2002

Mulholland Falls 1996

Multiplicity 1996

Mumford 2000

Mummy, The 2000

Mummy Returns, The 2002

Mummy: Tomb of the Dragon Emperor, The 2009

Munchie 1995

Munchies 1987

Munich 2006

Muppet Christmas Carol, The 1992

Muppets from Space 2000

Muppet Treasure Island 1996

Muppets Take Manhattan, The 1984

Mur, Le. *See* Wall, The.

Murder at 1600 1997

Murder by Numbers 2003

Murder in the First 1995

Murder One 1988

Murderball 2006

Murderous Maids 2003

Muriel's Wedding 1995

Murphy's Law 1986

Murphy's Romance 1985

Muse, The 2000

Muses Orphelines, Les. *See* Orphan Muses, The.

Music and Lyrics 2008

Music Box 1989

Music for the Movies: Bernard Herrmann 1995

Music From Another Room 1999

Music of Chance, The 1993

Music of the Heart 2000

Music Tells You, The 1995

Musime si Pomahat. *See* Divided We Fall.

Musketeer, The 2002

Must Love Dogs 2006

Mustang: The Hidden Kingdom 1995

Musuko. *See* My Sons.

Mutant on the Bounty 1989

Mute Witness 1995

Mutiny on the Bounty [1962] 1984

My African Adventure 1987

My American Cousin 1986

My Apprenticeship. *See* Among People.

My Architect 2005

My Baby's Daddy 2005

My Beautiful Laundrette 1986

My Best Fiend 2000

My Best Friend 2008

My Best Friend Is a Vampire 1988

My Best Friend's Girl 1984

My Best Friend's Girl 2009

My Best Friend's Wedding 1997

My Big Fat Greek Wedding 2003

My Bloody Valentine 3D pg. 259

My Blue Heaven 1990

My Blueberry Nights 2009

My Boss's Daughter 2004

My Boyfriend's Back 1993

My Chauffeur 1986

My Cousin Rachel [1952] 1981

My Cousin Vinny 1992

My Crazy Life. *See* Mi Vida Loca.

My Dark Lady 1987

My Demon Lover 1987

My Dinner with Andre 1981

My Family (Mi Familia) 1995

My Father Is Coming 1992

My Father, the Hero 1995

My Father's Angel 2002

My Father's Glory 1991

My Favorite Martian 2000

My Favorite Season 1996

Never Back Down 2009

Never Been Kissed 2000

Never Cry Wolf 1983

Never Die Alone 2005

Never Say Never Again 1983

Never Talk to Strangers 1995

Never too Young to Die 1986

Neverending Story, The 1984

Neverending Story II, The 1991

New Adventures of Pippi Longstocking, The 1988

New Age, The 1995

New Babylon, The [1929] 1983

New Eve, The 2001

New Guy, The 2003

New In Town pg. 267

New Jack City 1991

New Jersey Drive 1995

New Kids, The 1985

New Life, A 1988

New Moon. *See* Twilight Saga: New Moon, The.

New Nightmare. *See* Wes Craven's New Nightmare.

New Rose Hotel 2000

New World, The 2006

New Year's Day 1989

New York, I Love You pg. 268

New York in Short: The Shvitz and Let's Fall in Love 1995

New York Minute 2005

New York, New York [1977] 1983

New York Stories 1989

Newsies 1992

Newton Boys, The 1999

Next 2008

Next Best Thing, The 2001

Next Big Thing, The 2003

Next Day Air pg. 270

Next Friday 2001

Next Karate Kid, The 1995

Next of Kin 1989

Next Stop Greenwich Village [1976] 1984

Next Stop Wonderland 1999

Next Summer 1986

Next Year if All Goes Well 1983

Niagara Falls 1987

Niagara, Niagara 1999

Nice Girls Don't Explode 1987

Nicholas Nickleby 2003

Nick and Jane 1997

Nick & Norah's Infinite Playlist 2009

Nick of Time 1995

Nico and Dani 2002

Nico Icon 1996

Niezwykla podroz Balthazara Kobera. *See* Tribulations of Balthasar Kober, The.

Night and Day 1995

Night and the City 1992

Night at the Museum 2007

Night at the Museum: Battle of the Smithsonian pg. 271

Night at the Roxbury, A 1999

Night Crossing 1982

Night Falls on Manhattan 1997

Night Friend 1988

Night Game 1989

Night in Heaven, A 1983

Night in the Life of Jimmy Reardon, A 1988

Night Listener, The 2007

'night, Mother 1986

Night of the Comet 1984

Night of the Creeps 1986

Night of the Demons II 1995

Night of the Hunter, The [1955] 1982

Night of the Iguana, The [1964] 1983

Night of the Living Dead 1990

Night of the Pencils, The 1987

Night of the Shooting Stars, The 1983

Night on Earth 1992

Night Patrol 1985

Night Shift 1982

Night Song [1947] 1981

Night Visitor 1989

Night Watch 2007

Night We Never Met, The 1993

Nightbreed 1990

Nightcap. *See* Merci pour le Chocolat.

Nightfall 1988

Nightflyers 1987

Nighthawks 1981

Nighthawks II. *See* Strip Jack Naked.

Nightmare at Shadow Woods 1987

Nightmare Before Christmas, The 1993

Nightmare on Elm Street, A 1984

Nightmare on Elm Street: II, A 1985

Nightmare on Elm Street: III, A 1987

Nightmare on Elm Street: IV, A 1988

Nightmare on Elm Street: V, A 1989

Nightmares III 1984

Nights in Rodanthe 2009

Nightsongs 1991

Nightstick 1987

Nightwatch 1999

Nil by Mouth 1999

Nim's Island 2009

9 pg. 273

Nine pg. 275

9 1/2 Weeks 1986

9 Deaths of the Ninja 1985

Nine Months 1995

Nine Queens 2003

976-EVIL 1989

1918 1985

1969 1988

1990: The Bronx Warriors 1983

1991: The Year Punk Broke 1995

Ninety Days 1986

Ninja Assassin pg. 277

Ninja Turf 1986

Ninotchka [1939] 1986

Ninth Gate, The 2001

Nixon 1995

No 1999

No Country for Old Men 2008

No End in Sight 2008

No Escape 1995

No Fear, No Die 1995

No Holds Barred 1989

No Looking Back 1999

Russkies 1987

Russlands Wunderkinder. *See* Russia's Wonder Children.

Rustler's Rhapsody 1985

Rustling of Leaves, A 1990

Ruthless People 1986

RV 2007

Ryan's Daughter [1970] 1990

S

S.F.W. 1995

Sabrina [1954] 1986

Sabrina 1995

Sacrifice, The 1986

Saddest Music in the World, The 2005

Sade 2004

Safe 1995

Safe Conduct 2003

Safe Journey. *See* Latcho Drom.

Safe Passage 1995

Safety of Objects, The 2003

Sahara 2006

Sahara (McLaglen) 1984

St. Elmo's Fire 1985

Saint, The 1997

Saint Clara 1997

Saint of Fort Washington, The 1993

Saison des Hommes, La. *See* Season of Men, The.

Salaam Bombay! 1988

Salmer fra Kjokkenet. *See* Kitchen Stories.

Salmonberries 1995

Salome's Last Dance 1988

Salsa 1988

Salt of the Earth [1954] 1986

Salt on Our Skin. *See* Desire.

Salton Sea, The 2003

Saltwater 2002

Salvador 1986

Sam and Sarah 1991

Samantha 1995

Sam's Son 1984

Samba Traore 1995

Same Old Song 2000

Sammy and Rosie Get Laid 1987

Sandlot, The 1993

Sandwich Years, The 1988

Sang for Martin, En. *See* Song for Martin, A.

Sans toit ni loi. *See* Vagabond.

Santa Claus 1985

Santa Clause, The 1995

Santa Clause 2, The 2003

Santa Clause 3: The Escape Clause, The 2007

Santa Fe 1988

Santa Sangre 1990

Sara 1995

Saraband 2006

Sarafina! 1992

Satan 1995

Satisfaction 1988

Saturday Night at the Palace 1987

Saturday Night, Sunday Morning: The Travels of Gatemouth Moore 1995

Sauve qui peut (La Vie). *See* Every Man for Himself.

Savage Beach 1989

Savage Island 1985

Savage Nights 1995

Savages, The 2008

Savannah Smiles 1983

Save the Last Dance 2002

Save the Tiger [1973] 1988

Saved! 2005

Saving Grace (Young) 1986

Saving Grace (Cole) 2001

Saving Private Ryan 1999

Saving Silverman 2002

Savior 1999

Saw 2005

Saw V 2009

Saw IV 2008

Saw VI pg. 331

Saw III 2007

Saw II 2006

Say Anything 1989

Say It Isn't So 2002

Say Yes 1986

Scandal 1989

Scandalous 1984

Scanner Darkly, A 2007

Scanners III: The Takeover 1995

Scaphandre et le papillon, Le. *See* Diving Bell and the Butterfly, The.

Scarface 1983

Scarlet Letter, The [1926] 1982, 1984

Scarlet Letter, The 1995

Scarlet Street [1946] 1982

Scary Movie 2001

Scary Movie 2 2002

Scary Movie 3 2004

Scary Movie 4 2007

Scavengers 1988

Scenes from a Mall 1991

Scenes from the Class Struggle in Beverly Hills 1989

Scent of a Woman 1992

Scent of Green Papaya, The (Mui du du Xanh) 1995

Scherzo del destino agguato dietro l'angelo come un brigante di strada. *See* Joke of Destiny, A.

Schindler's List 1993

Schizo 2006

Schizopolis 1997

School Daze 1988

School for Scoundrels 2007

School of Flesh, 432

School of Rock 2004

School Spirit 1985

School Ties 1992

Schtonk 1995

Schultze Gets the Blues 2006

Science des reves, La. *See* Science of Sleep, The.

Science of Sleep, The 2007

Scissors 1991

Scooby-Doo 2003

Scooby-Doo 2: Monsters Unleashed 2005

Scoop 2007

Scorchers 1995

Score, The 2002

Scorpion 1986

Scorpion King, The 2003

Shall We Dance? 2005

Shallow Grave 1995

Shallow Hal 2002

Shame 1988

Shanghai Knights 2004

Shanghai Noon 2001

Shanghai Surprise 1986

Shanghai Triad 1995

Shaolin Soccer 2005

Shape of Things, The 2004

Shark Tale 2005

Sharky's Machine 1981

Sharma and Beyond 1986

Shatterbrain. *See* Resurrected, The.

Shattered 1991

Shattered Glass 2004

Shaun of the Dead 2005

Shaunglong Hui. *See* Twin Dragons.

Shawshank Redemption, The 1995

She Hate Me 2005

She Must Be Seeing Things 1987

Sherrybaby 2007

She-Devil 1989

Sheena 1984

Sheer Madness 1985

Shelf Life 1995

Sheltering Sky, The 1990

Sherlock Holmes [1922] 1982

Sherlock Holmes pg. 338

Sherman's March 1986

She's All That 2000

She's De Lovely. *See* De-Lovely.

She's Gotta Have It 1986

She's Having a Baby 1988

She's Out of Control 1989

She's So Lovely 1997

She's the Man 2007

She's the One 1996

Shiloh 2: Shiloh Season 2000

Shimian Maifu. *See* House of Flying Daggers.

Shine 1996

Shine a Light 2009

Shining, The [1980]

Shining Through 1992

Shipping News, The 2002

Shipwrecked 1991

Shiqisuide Danche. *See* Beijing Bicycle.

Shirley Valentine 1989

Shiza. *See* Shizo.

Shoah 1985

Shock to the System, A 1990

Shocker 1989

Shoot 'Em Up 2008

Shoot the Moon 1982

Shoot to Kill 1988

Shooter 2008

Shooting, The [1966] 1995

Shooting Dogs. *See* Beyond the Gates.

Shooting Fish 1999

Shooting Party, The 1985

Shootist, The [1976] 1982

Shopgirl 2006

Short Circuit 1986

Short Circuit II 1988

Short Cuts 1993

Short Film About Love, A 1995

Short Time 1990

Shorts: The Adventures of the Wishing Rock pg. 340

Shot, The 1996

Shout 1991

Show, The 1995

Show Me Love 2000

Show of Force, A 1990

Showdown in Little Tokyo 1991

Shower, The 2001

Showgirls 1995

Showtime 2003

Shrek 2002

Shrek the Third 2008

Shrek 2 2005

Shrimp on the Barbie, The 1990

Shutter 2009

Shvitz, The. *See* New York in Short: The Shvitz and Let's Fall in Love.

Shy People 1987

Siberiade 1982

Sibling Rivalry 1990

Sicilian, The 1987

Sick: The Life and Death of Bob Flanagan, Supermasochist 1997

Sicko 2008

Sid and Nancy 1986

Side Out 1990

Sidekicks 1993

Sidewalk Stories 1989

Sidewalks of New York, The 2002

Sideways 2005

Siege, The 1999

Siesta 1987

Sign o' the Times 1987

Sign of the Cross, The [1932] 1984

Signal Seven 1986

Signs 2003

Signs & Wonders 2002

Signs of Life 1989

Silence, The 2001

Silence After the Shot, The. *See* Legend of Rita, The.

Silence at Bethany, The 1988

Silence of the Lambs, The 1991

Silencer, The 1995

Silent Fall 1995

Silent Hill 2007

Silent Madness, The 1984

Silent Night 1988

Silent Night, Deadly Night 1984

Silent Night, Deadly Night II 1987

Silent Night, Deadly Night III 1989

Silent Rage 1982

Silent Tongue 1995

Silent Touch, The 1995

Silent Victim 1995

Silk Road, The 1992

Silkwood 1983

Silver City (Sayles) 2005

Silver City (Turkiewicz) 1985

Silverado 1985

Simon Birch 1999

Simon Magnus 2002

Simon the Magician 2001

Simone 2003

Simpatico 2000

Sticky Fingers 1988

Stigmata 2000

Still Crazy 1999

Still of the Night 1982

Stille Nach Dem Schuss, Die. *See* Legend of Rita, The.

Sting II, The 1983

Stir Crazy [1980] 1992

Stir of Echoes 2000

Stitches 1985

Stolen Life, A [1946] 1986

Stolen Summer 2003

Stomp the Yard 2008

Stone Boy, The 1984

Stone Cold 1991

Stone Reader 2004

Stonewall 1996

Stoning of Soraya M., The pg. 357

Stop Making Sense 1984

Stop! Or My Mom Will Shoot 1992

Stop-Loss 2009

Stories from the Kronen 1995

Stormy Monday 1988

Story of Qiu Ju, The 1993

Story of the Weeping Camel, The 2005

Story of Us, The 2000

Story of Women 1989

Story of Xinghau, The 1995

Storytelling 2003

Storyville 1992

Straight for the Heart 1990

Straight Out of Brooklyn 1991

Straight Story, The 2000

Straight Talk 1992

Straight to Hell 1987

Strange Brew 1983

Strange Days 1995

Strange Invaders 1983

Strange Love of Martha Ivers, The [1946] 1991

Strange Wilderness 2009

Stranger, The 1987

Stranger Among Us, A 1992

Stranger Is Watching, A 1982

Stranger Than Fiction 2007

Stranger than Paradise 1984, 1986

Strangers, The 2009

Stranger's Kiss 1984

Strangers in Good Company 1991

Strangers with Candy 2007

Strapless 1990

Strawberry and Chocolate 1995

Strayed 2005

Streamers 1983

Street Fighter 1995

Street Fighter: The Legend of Chun-Li pg. 358

Street Kings 2009

Street Smart 1987

Street Story 1989

Street Trash 1987

Street Wars 1995

Streets 1990

Streets of Fire 1984

Streets of Gold 1986

Streetwalkin' 1985

Streetwise 1985

Strictly Ballroom 1993

Strictly Business 1991

Strictly Propaganda 1995

Strike It Rich 1990

Striking Distance 1993

Strip Jack Naked (Nighthawks II) 1995

Stripes 1981

Stripped to Kill 1987

Stripped to Kill 2 1989

Stripper 1986

Striptease 1996

Stroker Ace 1983

Stryker 1983

Stuart Little 2000

Stuart Little 2 2003

Stuart Saves His Family 1995

Stuck On You 2004

Student Confidential 1987

Stuff, The 1985

Stupids, The 1996

Substance of Fire, The 1996

Substitute, The 1996

Suburbans, The 2000

Suburban Commando 1991

Suburbia 1984

subUrbia 1997

Subway 1985

Subway to the Stars 1988

Such a Long Journey 2001

Sudden Death 1985

Sudden Death 1995

Sudden Impact 1983

Sudden Manhattan 1997

Suddenly, Last Summer [1959] 1993

Suddenly Naked 2002

Sugar pg. 360

Sugar & Spice 2002

Sugar Cane Alley 1984

Sugar Hill 1995

Sugar Town 2000

Sugarbaby 1985

Suicide Kings 1999

Suitors, The 1989

Sukkar banat. *See* Caramel.

Sullivan's Pavilion 1987

Sum of All Fears, The 2003

Sum of Us, The 1995

Summer 1986

Summer Camp Nightmare 1987

Summer Catch 2002

Summer Heat 1987

Summer Hours pg. 361

Summer House, The 1993

Summer Lovers 1982

Summer Night with Greek Profile, Almond Eyes, and Scent of Basil 1987

Summer of Sam 2000

Summer Palace 2009

Summer Rental 1985

Summer School 1987

Summer Stock [1950] 1985

Summer Story, A 1988

Summertime [1955] 1990

Sunchaser 1996

Sunday 1997

Sunday in the Country, A 1984

They Drive by Night [1940] 1982

They Live 1988

They Live by Night [1949] 1981

They Might Be Giants [1971] 1982

They Still Call Me Bruce 1987

They Won't Believe Me [1947] 1987

They're Playing with Fire 1984

Thiassos, O. *See* Traveling Players, The.

Thief 1981

Thief, The 1999

Thief of Hearts 1984

Thieves 1996

Thin Blue Line, The 1988

Thin Line Between Love and Hate, A 1996

Thin Red Line, The 1999

Thing, The 1982

Thing Called Love, The 1995

Things Are Tough All Over 1982

Things Change 1988

Things to Do in Denver When You're Dead 1995

Things We Lost in the Fire 2008

Think Big 1990

Third World Cop 2001

Thirst pg. 378

Thirteen 2004

Thirteen Conversations About One Thing 2003

Thirteen Days 2001

Thirteen Ghosts 2003

13 Going On 30 2005

Thirtieth Floor, The 2000

Thirtieth Warrior, The 2000

30 Days of Night 2008

Thirty Two Short Films About Glenn Gould 1995

Thirty-five Up 1992

37, 2 le Matin. *See* Betty Blue.

Thirty-six Fillette 1988

This Boy's Life 1993

This Christmas 2008

This Is Elvis 1981

This is My Father 2000

This is My Life 1992

This Is Spinal Tap 1984

This Is It. *See* Michael Jackson's This Is It.

This Side of the Truth. *See* Invention of Lying, The.

This World, Then the Fireworks 1997

Thomas and the Magic Railroad 2001

Thomas Crown Affair, The 2000

Thomas in Love 2002

Those Who Love Me Can Take the Train 2000

Thou Shalt Not Kill 1988

Thousand Acres, A 1997

Thousand Pieces of Gold 1991

Thrashin' 1986

Three Amigos 1986

Three Brothers 1982

Three Burials of Melquiades Estrada, The 2007

Three...Extremes 2006

3:15 1986

Three for the Road 1987

Three Fugitives 1989

300 2008

3-Iron 2006

Three Kinds of Heat 1987

Three Kings 2000

Three Lives & Only One Death 1996

Three Madeleines, The 2001

Three Men and a Baby 1987

Three Men and a Cradle 1986

Three Men and a Little Lady 1990

Three Monkeys pg. 380

Three Musketeers, The 1993

Three Ninjas Kick Back 1995

Three Ninjas 1992

Three O'Clock High 1987

Three of Hearts 1993

Three Seasons 2000

Three Sisters 1988

3 Strikes 2001

3:10 to Yuma 2008

3000 Miles to Graceland 2002

Three to Get Ready 1988

Three to Tango 2000

Three Wishes 1995

Threesome 1995

Threshold 1983

Through the Eyes of the Children. *See* 112th and Central.

Through the Olive Trees 1995

Through the Wire 1990

Through the Window 2001

Throw Momma from the Train 1987

Thumbelina. *See* Hans Christian Andersen's Thumbelina.

Thumbsucker 2006

Thunder Alley 1986

Thunderbirds 2005

Thunderheart 1992

THX 1138 [1971] 1984

Thy Kingdom Come...Thy Will Be Done 1988

Tian di ying xiong. *See* Warriors of Heaven and Earth.

Tian Yu. *See* Xiu Xiu: The Sent Down Girl.

Ticket to Ride. *See* Post Grad.

Tideland 2007

Tie Me Up! Tie Me Down! 1990

Tie That Binds, The 1995

Tieta of Agreste 2000

Tiger Warsaw 1988

Tigerland 2002

Tiger's Tale, A 1987

Tigger Movie, The 2001

Tightrope 1984

Til' There Was You 1997

Till Human Voices Wake Us 2004

Tillsammans. *See* Together.

Tim Burton's Corpse Bride 2006

Time After Time 1983

Time and Tide 2002

Time Bandits 1981

Time Code 2001

Time for Drunken Horses, A 2001

Time Indefinite 1995

Time Machine, The (Pal) [1960] 1983

Time Machine, The (Wells) 2003

White Fang II: Myth of the White Wolf 1995

White Girl, The 1990

White Hunter, Black Heart 1990

White Man's Burden 1995

White Men Can't Jump 1992

White Mischief 1988

White Nights 1985

White Noise 2006

White of the Eye 1987, 1988

White Oleander 2003

White Palace 1990

White Ribbon, The pg. 418

White Rose, The 1983

White Sands 1992

White Sister, The [1923] 1982

White Squall 1996

White Trash 1992

White Winter Heat 1987

Whiteout pg. 420

Who Framed Roger Rabbit 1988

Who Killed the Electric Car? 2007

Who Killed Vincent Chin? 1988

Who Knows? *See* Va Savoir.

Who Shot Pat? 1992

Whole Nine Yards, The 2001

Whole Ten Yards, The 2005

Whole Wide World, The 1997

Whoopee Boys, The 1986

Whore 1991

Who's Afraid of Virginia Wolf? [1966] 1993

Who's Harry Crumb? 1989

Who's That Girl 1987

Who's the Man? 1993

Whose Life Is It Anyway? 1981

Why Did I Get Married? 2008

Why Do Fools Fall In Love 1999

Why Has Bodhi-Dharma Left for the East? 1995

Why Me? 1990

Why We Fight 2007

Wicked Lady, The 1983

Wicked Stepmother 1989

Wicker Man, The [1974] 1985

Wicker Man, The 2007

Wicker Park 2005

Wide Awake 1999

Wide Sargasso Sea 1993

Widow of Saint-Pierre, The 2002

Widows' Peak 1995

Wife, The 1996

Wigstock: the Movie 1995

Wilbur Wants to Kill Himself 2005

Wild, The 2007

Wild America 1997

Wild at Heart 1990

Wild Bill 1995

Wild Bunch, The [1969] 1995

Wild Duck, The 1985

Wild Geese II 1985

Wild Hearts Can't Be Broken 1991

Wild Hogs 2008

Wild Horses 1984

Wild Life, The 1984

Wild Man Blues 1999

Wild Orchid 1990

Wild Orchid II: Two Shades of Blue 1992

Wild Pair, The 1987

Wild Parrots of Telegraph Hill, The 2006

Wild Reeds 1995

Wild Thing 1987

Wild Things 1999

Wild Thornberrrys Movie, The 2003

Wild West 1993

Wild West Comedy Show. *See* Vince Vaughn's Wild West Comedy Show: 30 Days & 30 Nights—Hollywood to the Heartland.

Wild Wild West 2000

Wildcats 1986

Wilde 1999

Wilder Napalm 1993

Wildfire 1988

Willard 2004

William Shakespeare's A Midsummer's Night Dream 2000

William Shakespeare's Romeo & Juliet 1996

William Shakespeare's The Merchant of Venice. *See* Merchant of Venice, The.

Willow 1988

Wilt. *See* Misadventures of Mr. Wilt, The.

Wimbledon 2005

Win a Date with Tad Hamilton 2005

Wind 1992

Wind, The [1928] 1984

Wind in the Willows, The 1997

Wind the Shakes the Barley, The 2008

Wind Will Carry Us, The 2001

Window Shopping 1995

Window to Paris 1995

Windtalkers 2003

Windy City 1984

Wing Commanders 2000

Winged Migration 2004

Wings of Desire 1988

Wings of the Dove 1997

Winner, The 1997

Winners, The 2000

Winners Take All 1987

Winslow Boy, The 2000

Winter Guest, The 1997

Winter Meeting [1948] 1986

Winter of Our Dreams 1982

Winter Passing 2007

Winter People 1989

Winter Solstice 2006

Winter Tan, A 1988

Winter War, The. *See* Talvison.

Wiping the Tears of Seven Generations 1995

Wired 1989

Wired to Kill 1986

Wirey Spindell 2001

Wisdom 1986

Wise Guys 1986

Wisecracks 1992

Wish You Were Here 1987

Wishmaster 1997

Witchboard 1987

Witches, The 1990

Witches of Eastwick, The 1987

With a Friend Like Harry 2002

With Friends Like These... 2006

You Can Count on Me 2001

You Can't Hurry Love 1988

You Don't Mess with the Zohan 2009

You Got Served 2005

You Kill Me 2008

You So Crazy 1995

You Talkin' to Me? 1987

You Toscanini 1988

Young Adam 2005

YoungHeart 2009

Young Dr. Kildare [1938] 1985

Young Doctors in Love 1982

Young Einstein 1988

Young Guns 1988

Young Guns II 1990

Young Poisoner's Handbook, The 1996

Young Sherlock Holmes 1985

Young Soul Rebels 1991

Young Victoria, The pg. 429

Youngblood 1986

Your Friends & Neighbors 1999

Yours, Mine & Ours 2006

Youth Without Youth 2008

You've Got Mail 1999

Yu-Gi-Oh! The Movie 2005

Z

Zack and Miri Make a Porno 2009

Zappa 1984

Zapped! 1982

Zathura 2006

Zatoichi 2005

Zebdegi Edame Darad. *See* And Life Goes On.

Zebrahead 1992

Zegen. *See* Pimp, The.

Zelary 2005

Zelig 1983

Zelly and Me 1988

Zentropa 1992

Zero Degrees Kelvin 1996

Zero Effect 1999

Zero Patience 1995

Zeus and Roxanne 1997

Zhou Yu's Train 2005

Zir-e Poust-e Shahr. *See* Under the Skin of the City.

Zjoek 1987

Zodiac 2008

Zombie and the Ghost Train 1995

Zombie High 1987

Zombieland pg. 430

Zoolander 2002

Zoom 2007

Zoot Suit 1981

Zuotian. *See* Quitting.

Zus & Zo 2004

Zwartboek. *See* Black Book.